199

 St. Louis Community College

Forest Park
Florissant Valley
Meramec

Instructional Resources
St. Louis, Missouri

PLACING BLAME

PLACING BLAME

A General Theory of the Criminal Law

MICHAEL MOORE

CLARENDON PRESS · OXFORD
1997

Oxford University Press, Great Clarendon Street, Oxford OX2 6DP

Oxford New York

Athens Auckland Bangkok Bogota Bombay
Buenos Aires Calcutta Cape Town Dar es Salaam
Delhi Florence Hong Kong Istanbul Karachi
Kuala Lumpur Madras Madrid Melbourne
Mexico City Nairobi Paris Singapore
Taipei Tokyo Toronto Warsaw

and associated companies in
Berlin Ibadan

Oxford is a trade mark of Oxford University Press

Published in the United States
by Oxford University Press Inc., New York

British Library Cataloguing in Publication Data
Data available

Library of Congress Cataloging in Publication Data
Data available
ISBN 0–19–825417–2

1 3 5 7 9 10 8 6 4 2

Typeset by Hope Services (Abingdon) Ltd.
Printed in Great Britain
on acid-free paper by
Biddles Ltd.,
Guildford & King's Lynn

For my children, Samantha, Ellen, Aidan, and Gillian

PREFACE

This book has been written on the instalment plan over a number of years. Each of the chapters within it was conceived and executed as a self-contained paper on some isolatable aspect of criminal law theory. Nonetheless, with a little interstitial filling, mostly given by the long introductory chapter, the essays collectively address what I take to be the central questions of criminal law theory.

Because some of these essays were written some time ago, and because some of them were written as critiques of others' work, I have been tempted to rewrite them in a more positive vein while also taking into account my own later developed views. I have by and large resisted that temptation since I believe the essays can be welded together without such recasting. The major exception is the first chapter, where I have made some changes over the original. Some of these changes were necessitated by the addition of new chapters after the original introduction was written and published (chapter 6, for example, became a book of its own, now replaced with an essay giving an extended defence of that book against various criticisms). Other changes in the introductory chapter are due to alteration in my own thoughts about how criminal law theory is best organized. It seemed important that the 'glue' be as current as possible, even if the pieces glued together are of various vintages.

As the acknowledgements indicate, the chapters in this book have profited from numerous critical exchanges, both oral and written, at the workshops and symposia at which they were given. My thanks go to those numerous participants at those gatherings whose comments have made the essays better than they otherwise would have been. I doubtlessly have not satisfied much of the criticism which I received, as much as I may feel that I have benefited from it.

M.M.

Villa Serbelloni
Bellagio, Italy
July 1996

ACKNOWLEDGEMENTS

Chapter 1   Given to the Columbia/Tel Aviv Universities Conference on Substantive Legal Theory, Tel Aviv, Israel, 1989; to a Faculty Workshop, University of Pennsylvania Law School, 1990; first published in *Tel Aviv Studies in Legal Theory* (D. Friedmann, ed., Tel Aviv University Press, 1990).

Chapter 2   First published in *USC Cites* (1982), 9–15; included in M. Moore, *Law and Psychiatry: Rethinking the Relationship* (Cambridge University Press, 1984); largely reprinted in S. Kadish, S. Schulhofer, and M. Paulsen, *Cases and Materials on Criminal Law* (5th edition 1989).

Chapter 3   Given as a Mellon Lecture, University of South Carolina Philosophy Department, Columbia, 1984; to a faculty workshop, New York University Law School, 1984; to a colloquium, Program in Jurisprudence and Social Policy, University of California, Berkeley, 1984; to a faculty workshop, University of Southern California Law Center, 1985; to the Saturday Discussion Group of Southern California Legal and Political Philosophers, Los Angeles, 1985; as the keynote address, American Academy of Law and Psychiatry Annual Meeting, San Francisco, 1988; at a faculty workshop, University of Pennsylvania Law School, Philadelphia, 1988; first published in *Responsibility, Character, and the Emotions* (F. Shoeman, ed., Cambridge University Press, 1987), and reprinted in J. Feinberg and H. Gross, ed., *Philosophy of Law* (4th edition 1990, 5th edition 1994), and J. Murphy, ed., *Punishment and Rehabilitation* (Belmont, California: Wadsworth, 3rd edition, 1995).

Chapter 4   Given to the Fulbright Colloquium on Penal Theory, Philosophy Department, Stirling University, Stirling,

Scotland, 1992; first published in *Israel Law Review*, Vol. 27 (1993), 15–49.

Chapter 5   Given at the Conference on Culpability versus Harm as the Organizing Principle of the Criminal Law, University of San Diego, 1994; first published in the *Journal of Contemporary Legal Issues*, Vol. 5 (1994), 1–45.

Chapter 6   Originally given at the Symposium on Act and Crime, University of Pennsylvania Law School, 1994; first published in *University of Pennsylvania Law Review*, Vol. 142 (1994), 1749–840.

Chapter 7   Given to a faculty workshop, University of Southern California Law Center, 1986; first published in a symposium issue on causation, *Chicago-Kent Law Review*, Vol. 63 (1987), 497–521.

Chapter 8   Given to a colloquium, Program in Jurisprudence and Social Policy, University of California, Berkeley, 1980, to the Legal Studies Workshop, University of Pennsylvania Law School, 1993, and to the University of Southern California Law Center Faculty Workshop, 1993; first published in S. Shute, J. Gardner, and J. Horder, eds., *Action and Value in Criminal Law* (Oxford: Oxford University Press, 1993).

Chapter 9   Given to the Conference on the Intersection of Crime and Tort, Boston University, 31 March–2 April 1995; first published in *Boston University Law Review*, Vol. 75 (1995), 319–33.

Chapter 10   Given to the Conference on Psychoanalysis and the Philosophy of Mind, Department of Logic and Metaphysics, University of St. Andrews, Fife, Scotland, 1985; and (in expanded form), as the Charles Phelps Taft Lectures in Philosophy, to the 22nd annual symposium of the Philosophy Department, University of Cincinnati, 1986; first published in *Mind, Science, and Psychoanalysis* (P. Clark and C. Wright, eds., Oxford: Basil Blackwell, 1988).

Chapter 11   Given to the Van Leer-Jerusalem Foundation Conference in honour of H. L. A. Hart, Jerusalem,

Israel, 1984; to a faculty workshop, Stanford University Law School, 1980; to a faculty workshop, University of Southern California Law Center, 1984; first published in *Issues in Contemporary Legal Philosophy* (R. Gavison, ed., Oxford University Press, 1987).

Chapter 12   Given to the German-English-American Workshop on Basic Problems in Criminal Theory, Max Planck Institut fur Auslandisches und Internationales Strafrecht, Freiburg-im-Breisgau, West Germany, 1984; to a faculty workshop, University of Southern California Law Center, 1984; as a Mellon Lecture, University of South Carolina Law School and Philosophy Department, Columbia, 1984; to a Colloquium, Philosophy Department, Charlestown College, Charlestown, South Carolina, 1984; at a faculty workshop, Law School of Northwestern University, Chicago, 1985; at the Tuesday Night Circle, University of California at Los Angeles, 1985; and at the Philosophy Department and Law School, University of Wisconsin, Madison, 1985; first published in the *California Law Review*, Vol. 73 (1985), 1091–149, and reprinted in *Justification and Excuse: Comparative Criminal Law Theory*, Vol. II (A. Eser and G. Fletcher, eds., Max Planck Institute, Freiburg, 1987).

Chapter 13   Given to the Social Philosophy and Policy Center, Bowling Green State University, Conference on Crime, Culpability, and Remedy, San Diego, 1989; first published in *Social Policy and Philosophy*, Vol. 7 (1990), 29–58, reprinted in *Crime, Culpability, and Remedy* (E. F. Paul and G. Paul, eds., Basil Blackwell, 1990).

Chapter 14   Given to the Law and Psychiatry Workshop, School of Psychiatry, Menninger Foundation, Topeka, 1974; first published in the *Bulletin of the Menninger Clinic*, Vol. 39 (1975), 308–28.

Chapter 15   Given to the Annual Meeting of the American Society for Political and Legal Philosophy, Cincinnati, Ohio,

1983; and to a faculty workshop, University of Southern California Law Center, 1982; first published in *Nomos XXVII: Criminal Justice* (J. R. Pennock and J. W. Chapman, eds., New York University Press, 1985).

Chapter 16   Part of this chapter was given to the Conference on Community, Law and Morality, University of California, Berkeley, 1988, and first published in the *California Law Review*, Vol. 77 (1989), 539–51; the other part of this chapter was given to the faculty and graduate students, Seoul National University, Seoul, Korea, 1984, and to the Legislative Administration Agency, Republic of Korea, 1984, and first published in *USC Cites* (1984), 23–32.

Chapter 17   Given to a faculty workshop, School of Law, University of California, Berkeley, 1988; to a Psychology Department Colloquium, University of Nebraska, Lincoln, 1988; to a faculty workshop, University of Michigan Law School, 1989; to a faculty workshop, University of Southern California Law Center, 1989; to the Student Bar Lecture Series, University of Pennsylvania Law School, 1989; and to the Legal Theory Workshop of the Law School, McGill University, Montreal, 1989; first published in the *Israel Law Review*, Vol. 23 (1989), 280–344.

Chapter 18   Given to the Conference on Morality, Legality, and Drugs, at the State University of New York-Buffalo, 1995; and to the Second Annual Conference on Analytical Legal Philosophy, New York City, 1997; to be published in a conference volume by the Cornell University Press.

CONTENTS

LIST OF FIGURES

TABLE OF STATUTES

TABLE OF CASES

INTRODUCTION

1

A THEORY OF CRIMINAL LAW THEORIES

Admittedly, the title for this chapter sounds like a full employment act for legal theoreticians. Yet theorizing about an area of law is an activity, and like any activity we need a justification for it showing us why it is worth doing.[1] There is thus room and need for significant reflection on the nature and use of something called a 'theory of the criminal law'. The output of such reflection may appropriately be called a *theory* of criminal law theories, even if that conjures up images of a parade of theories without end.

So much by way of apology for the topic of this chapter. What I have to say about the topic comes in three large clumps. In the first clump I discuss legal theories generically, without particular reference to the criminal law. This portion of the chapter may be of interest to those who are not criminal lawyers, for here I discuss the sense in which one can have a theory of an area of law.

The second part of the chapter deals with theories of the criminal law. Here I describe the structure such theories must have, recognizing initially a distinction between the general and the special parts of the criminal law and then detailing the issues which a theory of each part must address. This part of the chapter may be seen as a charting of the logical space in which a theory of the criminal law must operate, since I seek to chart both the questions such a theory must answer, and the kinds of answers that are available, without myself yet answering these questions.

Thirdly and lastly, I finish with a brief description of my own theory of the criminal law. Here I describe but do not defend my own answers to the questions any criminal law theory must address. For the defence of these answers, one has to read the rest of the book.

In these three clumps I thus move from the more abstract questions to the more specific. My hope for the last two clumps (that

---

[1] On this much, at least, Stanley Fish and I can agree. See Fish, 'Dennis Martinez and the Uses of Theory', *Yale Law Journal*, Vol. 96 (1987), 1773–1800.

are specifically directed to criminal law theory) is that they illustrate the more general points made about theories of areas of law more generically. In addition, attention to criminal law theory may repay theorists of other areas of law by suggesting analogies to *certain* other areas of law even if not to all. For example, the fruitfulness of the distinction between the 'general' and the 'special' parts of the criminal law raises questions about superimposing such a distinction on tort law, contract law, and property law so that theories about them too are divided into theories of the special or the general parts.

There is no guarantee that criminal law theory is everywhere illustrative of what a theory of an area of law can and should be. In some respects criminal law is different and these differences result in some non-generalizable features unique to criminal law theory. It is commonly said, for example, that criminal law theory is parochial *vis-à-vis* the mainstream of legal theory in America, and to some extent this is true. Torts, contracts, and property theories, for example, share a common concern with the Coase Theorem and market alternatives to court-regulation that is not shared by criminal law theory. Attempts by economists to make criminal law theory 'non-parochial' in this regard only illustrate how different are the entitlements criminal law protects, and how different are the means and justifications for the protection it gives, from these other areas of law.

How generalizable the lessons of criminal law theory may be for theories of other areas of law is thus an open question. It is time we examine it by examining criminal law theory.

I. WHAT IS A THEORY OF AN AREA OF LAW?

A. The Nature of Theories

There are two clarificatory questions asked here: one, what sort of *theory* is one seeking when one seeks a theory of an area of law? And, two, what is the data for such a theory, i.e., what is an *area of law*? With regard to the first question, addressed in this section, we should distinguish at least initially three different kinds of theories: there are explanatory theories, descriptive theories, and evaluative theories.

I shall illustrate the differences with Richard Posner's initial foray into legal theory, his articulation of a 'theory of negligence' in tort law.[2] The database for Posner's theory was 1528 appellate cases decided by American state courts around the turn of the century. Each of these cases dealt with some aspect of negligence law. From these cases Posner extracted fourteen common law rules of negligence, which were:

1. The Learned Hand definition of negligence itself, as being behaviour whose risk of harm, discounted by the improbability of its occurrence, outweighs the utility the action promises to both actor and others.
2. The higher standard of care owed by common carriers to their passengers.
3. The lesser standard of care owed by landowners to those who trespass on their land.
4. The use of criminal statutes to set the standard of care owed to any member of the class of persons intended to be protected by the statute.
5. The use of industry-wide custom as a shield to negligence liability for those members of an industry whose behaviour conformed to such customs.
6. The bar to liability when the injured plaintiff was contributorily negligent.
7. The requirement that the defendant's action must be a cause-in-fact of the plaintiff's injury.
8. The requirement that the defendant's acts have been a proximate cause of the plaintiff's injury, in the sense that the injury the plaintiff suffered was an instance of the type of harms that were foreseeable to the defendant at the time he acted.
9. Employers' vicarious liability for the negligence of their employees when such negligence occurs during the course and scope of their employment.
10. The fellow-servant rule, according to which an employer was not liable to those of his employees who were injured by the carelessness of fellow employees.

---

[2] Posner, 'A Theory of Negligence', *Journal of Legal Studies*, Vol. 1 (1972), 29–96. I have chosen Posner's theory of tort law over his similar theory of criminal law (Posner, 'An Economic Theory of the Criminal Law', *Columbia Law Review*, Vol. 85 (1985), 1193–1231) because the former illustrates the questions to be raised about any such theory more clearly than the latter.

11. The bar to liability when the plaintiff voluntarily assumed a known risk and was injured thereby.
12. The recoverability for medical expenses, lost earnings, and pain and suffering when the plaintiff has made out a claim for negligence.
13. The non-compensability of death even when caused by negligence, except by way of compensating survivors for their pecuniary loss.
14. The 'take your victim as you find him' maxim, according to which a plaintiff may recover his full damages even if he has a pre-existing abnormal condition that greatly accentuated the extent of his injuries.

For purposes of developing a theory of negligence law, Posner regarded the 1528 decisions and the fourteen doctrines extracted therefrom as the *law* about which he was prepared to theorize. What are possible theories of such law? There are four major types of theories of tort law. There are retributive justice theories, according to which the purpose of tort law is the same as that of criminal law, which is to give those who deserve punishment what they deserve.[3] There are corrective justice theories, according to which the purpose of tort law is to correct an injustice between two parties; such injustice may be thought to occur: (1) when one party culpably causes harm to a non-culpable party;[4] or (2) when one party causes harm to another, however innocently;[5] or (3) when one party is unjustly enriched by his own behaviour *vis-à-vis* another, which unjust enrichment may take the form either of tangible benefits being possessed by the defendant[6] or of the less tangible benefit of asymmetrical risk imposition.[7] Thirdly, there are utilitarian theo-

---

[3] It is hard to find a modern theorist proposing such a theory of tort, given the centuries-old separation of tort and criminal law. One suspects that some jury awards in intentional tort cases are motivated by this theory.

[4] The traditional view, usually called the 'fault theory' of torts. E.g., O. W. Holmes, Jr., *The Common Law* (Boston: Little, Brown, 1881); John Finnis, *Natural Law and Natural Rights* (Oxford: Clarendon Press, 1980), 180–1, 184; Weinrib, 'Legal Formalism: On the Immanent Rationality of Law', *Yale Law Journal*, Vol. 97 (1988), 949–1016.

[5] Epstein, 'A Theory of Strict Liability', *Journal of Legal Studies*, Vol. 2 (1973), 151–204.

[6] As in *Vincent* v. *Lake Erie Transportation Co.*, 109 Minn. 456, 124 NW 221 (1910).

[7] Fletcher, 'Fairness and Utility in Tort Theory', *Harvard Law Review*, Vol. 85 (1972), 537–73.

ries, according to which the function of tort law is to enhance the community's welfare; this might be accomplished by requiring each industry or activity to 'internalize' its 'true' costs (via tort liability) and thus have the price of its goods reflect such costs, not leading to over or under production;[8] or such enhancement of welfare might be achieved by tort liability rules that clearly specify entitlements and obligations, allowing private parties to bargain to socially optimal positions about the allocation of resources;[9] alternatively, one might assume that transaction costs, free-rider problems, buy/sell asymmetries in preference patterns, and insufficiently equal distribution of assets prevent the market from efficient resource allocation, no matter how clear the tort liability rules, so tort law should mimic the outcomes a costless market would achieve in its allocation of liability;[10] finally, courts might achieve such community welfare by undertaking, on a case-by-case basis, to set rules that give parties incentives to minimize something nobody wants, viz., the sum of accident costs and the safety costs spent to prevent accidents.[11] Fourthly, there are distributive justice theories of tort law, according to which we should redistribute the whims of fate from those who happen to be first visited by them to some larger number who can better sustain them because the larger number can share the losses so each bears a manageable portion.[12]

Of these four possibilities, Posner argued for a version of the third. Posner's theory of negligence was statable as a principle of efficiency: 'the dominant function of the fault system [negligence law] is to generate rules of liability that if followed will bring about, at least approximately, the efficient—the cost justified—level of accidents and safety'.[13] The principle of efficiency holds that tort liability for negligence should be parcelled out so that each person is induced to spend that last dollar of safety costs that will prevent

[8] The view of 1950s welfare economics. For an expression, see Calabresi, 'Some Theories of Risk Distribution and the Law of Torts', *Yale Law Journal*, Vol. 76 (1961), 499–553.

[9] The implications of Ronald Coase's Theorem. Coase, 'The Problem of Social Cost', *Journal of Law and Economics*, Vol. 3 (1960), 1–44.

[10] The considered view of Guido Calabresi. *The Cost of Accidents* (New Haven: Yale University Press, 1970).

[11] Posner, 'A Theory of Negligence', *supra* n. 2.

[12] Arguably Roger Traynor's dominant theory. See *Escola* v. *Coca-Cola Bottling Co.*, 24 Cal. 2d 453, 150 P 2d 436 (1944) (Concurring opinion).

[13] Posner, 'A Theory of Negligence', *supra* n. 2 at 33.

more than a dollar's worth of accident costs, but no more than that (safety costs being as undesired as accident costs).

Now we are in a position to ask: what exactly could Posner be claiming about his theory of negligence law? What makes his *the* theory of negligence law, to the exclusion of justice or other utilitarian theories? In what sense could he claim that his theory was *better*?

One possibility is that Posner is making an evaluative claim: efficiency is what tort law *ought* to be about. In such a case Posner would be telling us that efficiency is not only good but that it is so good that it should guide our tort law doctrines to the exclusion of other goods like justice of various kinds. Yet Posner pretty explicitly eschews the mantle of moral philosopher. He sees himself as a scientist engaged in some value-neutral enterprise about the negligence law that existed 1875–1905, not the law that should have existed. This suggests a second reading of Posner, viewing him as a historian, not a moral theorist. As a historical theory, Posner's principle of efficiency becomes an explanatory principle, not an evaluative one. Judges decided the 1528 cases the way they did, announcing the fourteen doctrines that they announced, because they believed minimizing the sum of accident and safety costs was a good that ought to be realized through the tort law.

As a historical thesis Posner's theory is in no obvious way value-laden, for Posner as historian would not be asserting the desirability of efficiency. Rather, the historical fact that judges believed efficiency to be a desirable goal of tort law would be used to causally explain another historical fact, namely, the emergence of the fourteen doctrines and the making of the 1528 decisions. Using beliefs of historical persons to explain their behaviour is not a normative enterprise even if the beliefs doing the explaining are themselves normative beliefs.

Construing Posner to be a historian leads to a well recognized puzzle for his theory.[14] The puzzle stems from the fact that the judges Posner talks about did not *consciously* believe that they were using efficiency as their pole star in negligence law; so to make out a historical thesis, Posner would have to attribute *unconscious* beliefs to such judges. This latter move would make Posner the

---

[14] Cf. Michaelman, 'Political Markets and Community Self-Determination: Competing Judicial Models of Local Government Legitimacy', *Indiana Law Journal*, Vol. 63 (1979), 145–206.

competitor with Freud: our unconscious, Posner would have to say, is not a seething cauldron of libidinous and aggressive instincts; rather, we each, deep down, are caught in the grip of a rationality (in the economist's esoteric sense of that word) that we cannot control.

This is, of course, an implausible psychology in the extreme. So we should give Posner a third reading: his principle of efficiency is an abstract description of American negligence law in the relevant period. His theory, in other words, seeks neither to evaluate nor to explain the law; only to describe it in a highly general way. On this reading, Posner's principle of efficiency is itself part of American tort law, only it is an unobvious part because it is the unuttered and unseen principle that stands behind the obvious law (here, the fourteen doctrines).

Such a descriptive task is plainly distinct from the explanatory task of historical theories. Unlike historical explanations, a deep description does not deal with datable historical events (case decisions and emergence of doctrine, beliefs of judges) or with the causal relation that may exist between them. Rather, a descriptive theory deals with timeless propositions of law (the 1528 singular propositions of law that decided the relevant cases and the fourteen general propositions, and the proposition stated by the principle of efficiency) and the logical relations that may exist between them. True, if Posner's descriptive theory of tort law were accurate, that fact would itself cry out for some historical explanation; but this latter demand in no way makes Posner's descriptive claim into an explanatory one.

More questionable, as we shall see, is the line between descriptive and normative theories. Prima facie, the difference seems plain enough: normative theories evaluate the law we have by how well it measures up to some moral ideal for tort law, whereas descriptive theories take the law we have at face value and, without any reforming impulse, seek to give a short, abstract description of that law. The principles of a good normative theory need have no relation to the propositions of tort law, whereas the principles of a good descriptive theory must stand in some logical relationship to the (obvious) propositions of tort law.

The line is an important one for us to draw, because I take the most interesting theory of the criminal law to be one that is descriptive of what is known as criminal law's 'general part' and normative about what is known as criminal law's 'special part'. Thus, we shall need to examine with care the difference between a descriptive and a normative theory of an area of law if we are to understand criminal law theory. To begin with, we badly misdescribe descriptive theories like Posner's theory of negligence when we call them 'descriptive', if we mean by the label to exclude evaluations by the theoretician in their construction. For such theories cannot do what we want them to do and be value-free. We thus need to explore what such 'descriptive' theories are good for and then say more about their evaluative nature.

Why would anyone want a deep description of existing tort doctrine? What would such a theory be good for? Historical theories promise us the understanding that causal explanations always engender, and evaluative theories are necessary for intelligent reform of the law we have, but what good is a theory that merely redescribes the law we presently have?

One answer might be the aesthetic one: we find simple, highly general descriptions aesthetically satisfying because they speak to the architectonic need that motivates many of us to become theoreticians. Whatever the merits of this answer at the level of motivation, it surely is a poor justification for theory-building in law. 'Art for art's sake' works as a justification for true works of art, but legal theories—even the best of them—are pretty poor art. Such aesthetic 'justifications' are the first refuge for intellectual scoundrels. Developing descriptive legal theories must have a much more practical justification for it to be an activity worth doing.

One can see the justification for developing such theories by asking whether Posner the scholar intended Posner the judge to pay any attention to the principle of efficiency in his negligence decisions. Was the scholar's theory of negligence, in other words, proposed as part of the law such that it as well as the 1528 decisions and fourteen doctrines was binding on Posner *qua* judge? My own answer to this question is 'yes', that in giving a descriptive theory of an area of law I target my theories at judges. Such theories are not normative recommendations to judges about what tort or criminal law we ought ideally to have, else they would be purely evaluative theories; rather, such theories are recommended to judges because they purport to describe something that is already part of the law that binds judges. Such judicial targeting gives descriptive theorizing in law a point—if we can make sense of the idea that a theory is part of the law of which it is a theory.[15]

There are two problems that stand in our way of making sense of the idea that an unuttered, unused, and unknown theory like Posner's principle of efficiency could have nonetheless been part of American negligence law in the period 1875–1905. One is what I shall call the problem of authority: why would such a theory have any authority for a judge in that period? The second I shall call the problem of content: what is the relation (between doctrine and theory) that makes plausible any theorist's claim that his is the unique theory of an area of law?

With regard to the authority of a theory like Posner's, no judge ever uttered it, no case ever held it, no legislature ever passed it— so how can a purely descriptive principle like the principle of efficiency possess the authority of statutes, of precedent, or of any form of law? The answer is to be found in terms of the rule of law virtues: the very virtues that give point to having a legal system are served if descriptive principles like Posner's are regarded as part of the law. Two of these virtues merit particular attention.

The first is the enhanced predictability that deeply descriptive principles give to an area of law. The values served by the virtue of predictability are liberty (because more accurate planning is possible) and fairness (because surprise is reduced).[16] Deeply descriptive principles enhance predictability in two ways: first, they cover cases not covered by the less general doctrines and decisions, and thus make determinate (and thus predictable) what would be indeterminate without them; second, they serve a heuristic function even for situations already covered by the established doctrines (one principle being a lot easier to master and remember than 1528 decisions and fourteen doctrines). C. C. Langdell understood both of these points quite well in justifying *his* theory of contract law (a contract is a meeting of the minds).[17] With regard to the first point, Langdell famously argued that in the crossing acceptance/revocation of offer

---

[15] Cf. Raz, 'The Inner Logic of the Law', *Rechtstheorie*, Vol. 10 (1986), 101–17.

[16] For discussion, see Moore, 'A Natural Law Theory of Interpretation', *Southern California Law Review*, Vol. 58 (1985), 277–398, at 316–17.

[17] For a reconstruction of Langdell's insight here, see Morris Cohen, 'The Place of Logic in the Law', *Harvard Law Review*, Vol. 29 (1915), 622–39. As Cohen recognized: 'A legal system that works with general principles has powerful instruments . . . [A] generalized jurisprudence enlarges the law's control over the diversity of legal situations. It is like fishing with large nets instead of with single lines.'

problem there was an obvious answer: there was no contract because there was no point in time at which the minds of the parties met. Langdell's deep description of contract law—for there to be a contract there must be a meeting of the minds—yielded an answer to a situation that was otherwise unanswerable by recourse to any then existing rules of contract law.[18] Langdell stated the second point in his introduction to the 1879 edition of his contracts casebook, where he told his students that it was not difficult to master contract law because it was statable as a few general principles.[19]

The second rule of law virtue served by regarding general principles as part of the law is the virtue of treating like cases alike. The main value served by this virtue is equality—that if one person has been treated a certain way by the law, then another similarly situated has reason to complain if he is not treated similarly too.

Abstractly described principles may serve the virtue of formal justice by isolating the respects in which one case is truly like (or not-like) another. Posner's principle of efficiency, for example, may isolate for us a morally relevant difference between two otherwise hard to reconcile doctrines: the foreseeability criterion of proximate causation (rule 8 above), and the 'take your victim as you find him' maxim (rule 14 above). Litigants held not liable for unforeseeable types of harm under rule 8 are not treated unequally with litigants held liable for those unforeseeable types of harm that are due to the abnormal condition of the plaintiff under rule 14, Posner argues, because the defendants in each of the sets of cases are relevantly different (i.e., different from an efficiency point of view): economically rational actors must be able to calculate the accident costs of their activity, and only those that are foreseeable are calculable (thus rule 8),[20] but this rationale does not apply to pre-existing, abnormal conditions of plaintiffs, no matter how unforeseeable the extent of the harm to them (rule 14).[21]

Judges thus have some prima facie reason to regard deep, descriptive theories as part of the law that authoritatively binds them as judges, for doing so serves the values served by having law

---

[18] Langdell, *A Summary of the Law of Contracts* (Boston: Little, Brown, 1880), 1–2, 12–15.

[19] Langdell, *A Selection of Cases on the Law of Contracts* (Boston: Little, Brown, 2nd edn. 1879), viii–ix.

[20] Posner, 'A Theory of Negligence', *supra* n. 2, at 21.   [21] Id. at 48.

at all (the rule of law virtues). If this is right, then legal scholars have a very practical, non-aesthetic reason to propound descriptive theories of an area of law: it helps judges find those unobvious standards that bind them as judges.

Consider now the second problem for deeply descriptive theories of an area of law, the problem of content. What sort of logical relationship between theory and doctrine must exist to serve this virtue? In general, there would seem to be two possibilities: either the doctrines imply the theory ($R_1, R_2 \ldots R_{14}$ imply T), or the theory implies the doctrines (T implies $R_1, R_2 \ldots R_{14}$).[22]

Because one starts psychologically with the obvious law (the doctrines) and seeks to 'derive' the unobvious law (the theory) from it, it may seem tempting to think that $R_1, R_2, \ldots R_{14}$, imply T is the relationship.[23] Then the 'direction' of logical implication would follow the direction of psychological discovery. Suppose this were the relationship between doctrine and theory. Posner's fourteen doctrines of negligence law, for example, would imply the principle of efficiency, but not vice versa. Such a relationship trivializes Posner's theory in the sense that that theory could not determine the results in any hard case. To see this, symbolize how a theory determines a result in some case: Suppose R_{15} is the general proposition of law that decides the hard case but which has never been enunciated before. A theory T will decide that hard case if T implies R_{15}. If the relationship between the theory and the fourteen existing rules is that $R_1, R_2 \ldots R_{14}$ imply T, then, by the transitivity of 'imply' and the fact that T implies R_{15}, $R_1, R_2 \ldots R_{14}$ imply R_{15}. Yet if $R_1, R_2 \ldots R_{14}$ imply R_{15} then theory T decides no case not already decidable under the existing rules alone. T is only abbreviatory of the existing rules, but adds nothing to the scope of their coverage.[24] And if that is so, then T could do no enhancing of predictability by

---

[22] By use of the word 'imply', I intend to refer to the logical relation of material implication, not the pragmatic relation of presupposition.

[23] See, e.g., Rolf Sartorius, *Individual Conduct and Social Norms* (Encino, Calif.: Dickerson, 1975), 190–3, for suggestions in this direction.

[24] The point made in the text is exactly analogous to a standard objection to operationism and reductionism in the philosophy of science: if theoretical terms can be reduced to observational terms, then theoretical statements are implied by statements of experimental laws, and if this is so, then scientific theories are mere abbreviations of experimental laws and as such have no predictive power. See, e.g., Ernest Nagel, *The Structure of Science* (New York: Harcourt, Brace & World, 1961), 33–42.

making determinate those hard cases that were indeterminate under the existing rules of law.

Thus, the logical relationship sought by any theorist must be the converse of that which we have been examining, so that we now say that T implies R_1, R_2 . . . R_{14}. Now if T implies some new rule R_{15}, such new rule will not necessarily be the deductive implication of the old rule. For from T implies R_1, R_2 . . . R_{14} and T implies R_{15}, nothing can be inferred about the relationship between R_1, R_2 . . . R_{14}, on the one hand, and R_{15}, on the other. Put simply, R_{15} may well be a truly new rule that decides cases not decidable under the old rule.

Clarifying the relationship between theory and doctrine reveals what I have been calling the problem of content. The underdetermination thesis of Pierre Duhem, so revived by Quine,[25] holds that an infinite number of theories will stand in this relationship of implication to any finite set of rules like R_1, R_2 . . . R_{14}. A good heuristic[26] for seeing this Duhemian point is to imagine a new theory of torts, call it T_m (for Moore's tort theory). The content of T_m is simply this: 'R_1, R_2 . . . R_{14}, and where those rules do not apply, red-haired plaintiffs win and non-red-haired plaintiffs lose.' T_m implies R_1, R_2 . . . R_{14} because every proposition implies itself (R_1, R_2 . . . R_{14} implies R_1, R_2 . . . R_{14}) and the conjunction of any other proposition (for example red-haired plaintiffs win, non-red-haired plaintiffs lose) with the initial proposition implies that initial proposition. Since an infinite number of propositions can be conjoined to R_1, R_2 . . . R_{14}, an infinite number of theories will stand in the relation, T implies R_1, R_2 . . . R_{14}.

Underdetermination is also a problem for theory-construction in science, but there is an important difference between law and science in this regard. A particular scientific theory can be falsified by having its deductive implications for future events (i.e., predictions) turn out to be false. We can thus at least falsify a particular theory in science even if such falsification leaves an infinite number of theories with which to replace it. In law, however, we cannot do even

[25] W. V. Quine, 'Two Dogmas of Empiricism', in *From A Logical Point of View* (Cambridge, Mass.: Harvard University Press, 4th printing, 1980).

[26] But only a heuristic, for the obvious move to circumvent 'theories' like T_m is to refine the relationship between T and R_1, R_2 . . . R_{14} so that T must not only imply R_1, R_2 . . . R_{14} but do so via the inference rule of Universal Instantiation. See Nelson Goodman, *Fact, Fiction and Forecast* (Cambridge, Mass.: Harvard University Press, 4th edn. 1983), 67–70.

this. In law, the future events are new decisions, not natural events, and new case decisions can be made by the judge to come out one way or the other. A judge cannot test Posner's theory T or Moore's theory T_m, by waiting to see how he decides a case where they point in different directions (i.e., a case involving a situation not covered by Rules R_1, R_2 . . . R_{14} where the plaintiff does not have red hair (and thus should lose by T_m) but whose recovery would give the right incentives to efficient behaviour (and thus should win by T)). Even if a judge tries to predict his own decision in the test case supposed, he still has to make that decision, else he has nothing to predict; and in the making of the decision the judge, unlike the scientist, chooses which theory to falsify.

How, then, is the content of a descriptive theory determined from its doctrinal basis? Why, for example, is one likely to favour Posner's theory T to my theory T_m as the theory of negligence law? Only, I now wish to argue, by the evaluative choice that one of them is morally better. Rewarding red-hair and penalizing its absence is not a good thing, but decreasing the sum of accident and safety costs is a good thing, so Posner's T would be the theory of negligence law over my T_m (assuming for the moment that these are the only two alternatives).

Descriptive theories thus cannot be value-free theories. At the very least, a theorist such as Posner must evaluate efficiency to be a better good than the other goods achieved by all the other theories of tort law that fit the doctrines as well as the principle of efficiency. Values thus enter into descriptive theories at least as tie-breakers between equally well-fitting theories like T and T_m.

Values are part of descriptive theories of areas of law in two more important ways than this, however. The first of these additional avenues for evaluation to enter theoretical description can be seen by considering again the choice between the Moore theory of torts and Posner's theory. I previously assumed that the two theories equally well fit the data. Actually, the Moore theory of torts fits Posner's database better than does Posner's principle of efficiency. One can see this with R_6, the rule that contributory negligence by the plaintiff bars his recovery. T_m implies R_6, but Posner's efficiency theory T does not. As Posner admits, T implies R_6 only when the plaintiff can more cheaply avoid the cost of the accident than could the defendant; where both could have avoided the accident in a cost-effective way but the defendant could have avoided

it more cheaply than the plaintiff, T implies that contributory negligence should not be a bar to liability. Thus, on value-free grounds
of logic, T_m should be preferred to T as the deep description of tort
law. Yet no one should or will prefer T_m to T, because T_m is
morally silly whereas T states at least an intelligible value tort law
could seek.

Why is it so clear that T_m's better logical fit with rules R_1, R_2 . . .
R_{14} will lose out to T's superior morality in our selection of a
theory of negligence? To answer this question, recall why any
descriptive theory has authority for judges: T or T_m are authoritative for judges because they both serve the rule of law virtues of
predictability and formal justice. Such authority is only prima facia,
however, because the values of liberty, fairness, and equality are
not always going to be the most important values defining judicial
obligation. Sometimes other values will be more important, oblig-
ating a judge to sacrifice some of the rule of law virtues for other
goods. The moral arbitrariness of T_m versus the goodness of preventing unwanted accidents or inefficient preventative measures is
an instance where those other goods easily win.

Whether T or T_m is part of American negligence law is thus a
function of two variables: how well does each logically fit the decisions and doctrines of which it is a theory, and how good is the goal
it describes for tort law? The degree of logical fit is weighted by the
rule of law virtues that justify theories as having prima facie
authority, but that weighted fit is always balanced off against the
moral goodness of the content of the theory. Only the two together
determine the legal validity of theories like T and T_m.[27]

---

[27] This evaluative nature to descriptive theories of an area of law is strictly analogous to the evaluative nature of common law rules (like R_1, R_2 . . . R_{14}) themselves. To explain: there are a host of good reasons why precedent has authority for
our judges, including prominently the enhancement of predictability and the attainment of formal justice. These reasons, however, are not so good that judges should
never overrule precedents. Doctrines that are undesirable as a matter of policy
should be overruled in favour of other doctrines that have much less support in prior
case-law but much more to be said for them morally. Moreover, such overrulings
do not operate prospectively only; they declare the common law to have been what
it is now perceived to be. This means that what the common law is at any given
point in time is always a function of two items: what prior courts decided as a matter of historical fact, *and* how good is the content of the rules generated from those
prior decisions. Seeing this analogy to the criteria of validity for common law rules
should prevent one from thinking that descriptive legal theorists are partly reform-
ers of the law. See, e.g., Douglas Husak, *Philosophy of Criminal Law* (Totawa, NJ:
Rowman and Littlefield, 1987), 25: 'The theorist . . . must employ some criterion for

The third way in which values necessarily enter into descriptive theories is by the nature of the rule of law virtues themselves. More specifically, granting prima facie authority to descriptive theories on the ground that it serves *formal justice* itself dooms any attempt to state value-free descriptive theories.

The good of treating like cases alike is largely equality. True equality is achieved only when cases that are alike in all morally relevant respects are treated alike; equality is not achieved by treating as alike cases that are morally dissimilar even if they are similar by some announced criterion. Suppose, for example, I give a college education to my son on the explicit ground that he is male. My daughter has a strong claim to equal treatment even though she does not share the announced criterion of merit, because in all morally relevant respects—which do not include sex—she is like my son.

The upshot is that formal justice can only be achieved if the announced categories of likenesses (say rules R_1, R_2 . . . R_{14}) are *not* treated as fixing the demands of equality. Rather, formal justice demands that such announced categories be rejudged in terms of whether they capture the morally relevant features that justify like or different treatment. This is what allows Posner's principle of efficiency to penetrate announced rules like R_8 and R_{14} and show a difference (in efficiency) where the announced rules saw only a sameness (in terms of foreseeability).[28] Yet Posner's principle can achieve true equality in this way only if it captures the morally

deciding when a recalcitrant part of the substantive criminal law should be accommodated by a change in general principle, or when it should be condemned as unjust. In short, he needs to know when it is appropriate to describe and when to prescribe.' A descriptive legal theorist does not see the substantive criminal law as fixed in this way; rather, like common law rules, whether a 'recalcitrant' bit of doctrine *is* 'part of' Anglo-American criminal law depends in part on its fit with the best theory of that law. This is what it means to say that a theory is part of the law of which it is a theory.

[28] The demand for substantive evaluation (of morally relevant similarities and distinctions) made by equality is to be distinguished from any supposed 'contradictions' in an area of law. (See Husak, *supra* n. 27, at 24: 'No coherent theory of Anglo-American criminal law can be purely *descriptive* for the simple reason that the set of data (the substantive criminal law) it purports to describe is replete with contradictions.') In fact, rarely are there *contradictions* in announced criminal law doctrines, in any philosophically acceptable sense of that word; what there are are different treatments of classes of litigants that cannot easily be reconciled with the demands of formal justice (equality). Rules 8 and 14 mentioned in the text are of this character, inviting a theorist such as Posner to use his theory to show their hidden moral compatibility (not logical consistency).

relevant feature of torts cases that justify similar or different treatment. Only if Posner makes the value judgement that efficiency is good can efficiency function as the standard by which we judge whether one case is like another.

The evaluative demands of equality also explain why we so easily choose T over T_m as the theory of negligence. T at least uses a morally intelligible standard by which the likeness of past to future cases is judged. T_m does not pick a decision rule for future cases that is the same as the rules that decided past cases, for hair colour did not determine the results in cases covered by rules R_1, R2 . . . R_{14}. To that extent T_m treats litigants unequally, depending on whether their case falls within R_1, R_2 . . . R_{14} or not. Secondly, T_m states a morally arbitrary feature for deciding cases not covered by rules R_1, R_2 . . . R_{14}. Even if consistently applied, T_m does not further the value of equality because hair colour has no moral relevance to the right to win a tort suit.

In each of these ways descriptive theories of an area of law are also evaluative theories. This does not collapse descriptive theories into purely evaluative theories, however, because such theories take seriously the institutional history that makes up an area of law. Descriptive theories do not write on a clean slate to ask ideally, what law ought we to have? Rather descriptive theories describe the law we have. Such descriptions are evaluative in the three ways just indicated, but one of the ingredients in that evaluative process is an institutional history that may be far from ideal.

B. The Nature of Areas of law

Having clarified what we mean by theory, we now need to ask what we mean by an 'area of law'. What, in other words, is the *data* for a theory of criminal law. We have hitherto made do with some intuitive assumptions that Posner knew what he was talking about when he claimed that his 1528 decisions and fourteen doctrines were all part of something called 'negligence law'. Now we need to enquire more closely into what it is such an area of law can be and how we draw its boundaries.

Let me begin with John Austin's familiar distinction between general and particular jurisprudence.[29] Particular jurisprudence studies law as it exists within some particular legal system. It asks,

---

[29] John Austin, *The Province of Jurisprudence Determined* (Hart edn., London: Weidenfeld & Nicolson, 1954).

'What is law in America?', for example, and thus enquires into the standards that bind American judges. General jurisprudence, by contrast, is not a culture-specific study. It studies law as such, not law as it exists in a particular legal system.

If we apply this distinction to areas of law, we can see the two queries that will occupy us in this section. At the level of general jurisprudence, the main problem with thinking of areas of law is ontological: what kind of thing is an area of law when we are dealing with law in general and not the law of any particular legal system? At the level of particular jurisprudence we may be less puzzled about the ontological status of areas of law, but we should be curious about the problem of individuation: what makes tort law one area of law and criminal law another? Or is tort law several areas of law, of which negligence law is one?

These two problems—of ontology and of individuation—are most readily seen from the vantage points of general jurisprudence and particular jurisprudence, respectively. In fact, of course, both problems exist for areas of law in either kind of jurisprudence (since both problems exist for anything).[30] Since my interest in this paper is in a theory of criminal law as it exists in the Anglo-American legal culture, I shall confine myself to these two problems as they confront the task of constructing a theory of an area of law within particular jurisprudence.

With regard to the problem of ontology, we are helped in seeing what kind of thing an area of law might be by distinguishing three kinds of kinds. First, there are what philosophers call natural kinds. These are kinds like water or gold that not only exist 'naturally' (i.e., without human contrivance) but also have a nature to them that gives the essence of the kinds. Our best theories of gold and of water, for example, hold that their essential natures are given by atomic structure and molecular structure, respectively. Secondly, there are what are often called nominal kinds. A nominal kind is simply a set of individual things that shares no nature save a common name used to refer collectively to the class. Take the set of things called 'Figueroa Street'. There is no nature to 'Figueroa Streetness' that unifies each of the bits of asphalt making up the street; the only thing that unifies these otherwise diverse bits of pavement is that each is called, 'Figueroa Street'. Human convention wholly governs whether

---

[30] See Baruch Brody, *Identity and Essence* (Princeton: Princeton University Press, 1980).

a thing does or does not partake of Figueroa Streetness, namely, how Los Angeles maps and street signs name it.

Thirdly, there are functional kinds. A functional kind like a natural kind has a nature that each instance of the kind shares, but the nature is functional and not structural. Stomachs, for example, form a functional kind, for whether some thing is a stomach depends on the ability of that thing to perform the function constitutive of stomachs, viz., first-stage processing of food. Cubical, silicone-based stomachs would still be stomachs if they performed the function of stomachs, no matter how different structurally they might be.

If we play these distinctions out *vis-à-vis* areas of Anglo-American law, we see plausible instances of each kind of kind. Certain areas of law look to be functional kinds in the sense that they are more or less successful attempts to realize some underlying kind of justice. I shall shortly argue that Anglo-American criminal law is largely a formalized description of the requirements of retributive justice. American constitutional law looks like a loosely written description of that part of morality (political theory) that governs the structure of the framework within which ordinary politics may take place.[31] Anglo-American tort law might be seen as a halting and inconsistent attempt to describe corrective justice, as Ernie Weinrib has recently urged.[32] Whether contract law or property law can be seen in a similar way depends on what one thinks of the normative significance of promises and things, respectively. Are promises so important morally that when made they govern our obligations pretty much to the exclusion of other considerations? If so, then one might think contract law to be defined by its function of getting people to keep their promissory obligations, obligations that are distinct from the non-promissory obligations dealt with by criminal law and torts.[33] Analogously, are things so important to our self-constitution that there is a morality governing the relations between persons as they relate to things? If so, then one might think property law to be defined by its function of protecting those rights to self-constitution.[34]

[31] Cf. J. Waldron, 'A Constitution, The Constitution, Our Constitution', *British Journal of Political Science*, unpublished, 1995.   [32] Weinrib, *supra* n. 4.
[33] See Charles Fried, *Contract as Promise* (Cambridge, Mass.: Harvard University Press, 1982).
[34] See Radin, 'Property and Personhood', *Stanford Law Review*, Vol. 34 (1984), 957–1015.

Some areas of Anglo-American law are hard to think of as reflections of some underlying kind of morality. Take administrative law. My own teaching of that field left me wondering whether there was any there. There were assuredly decisions and doctrines of the National Labor Relations Board, of the Federal Communications Commission, the Federal Power Commission, etc., but did these share a nature other than the label, 'administrative law', that Felix Frankfurter happened to make stick to them? Some areas of law such as administrative law are surely arbitrary in the sense that they do not reflect any underlying moral distinctions. Such areas' constitution as areas of law can at best be justified by the heuristic needs of the legal profession. (Which is not to say that once such areas become entrenched in a particular legal system, reliance interests are not such that continued respect for the border of such nominal kinds is not warranted.)[35]

Consider lastly areas where a particular kind of legal remedy seems to mark the borders of the area in question. The Calabresi/Melamed view of property law is a good example, because Calabresi and Melamed took the protectability of entitlements by injunction to define what was and was not a property rule.[36] Analogously, some have thought that criminal law is marked by the punitive sanction, and have thus taken it upon themselves to distinguish punitive fines from civil damage awards in order to define the boundaries of criminal law.

To view an area of law in this way is to view it as something like a natural kind. Even though not found in nature, an area of law on this view has an essential nature that is given by its structural features. This is not to view an area of law as a functional kind because the essential nature is a structural feature, not a distinctive end that such an area of law serves. If we were to view law itself in this way, as is commonly done, we would see law's essence to be some structural feature, such as coercive sanctions. This is in marked contrast to thinking of law itself as a functional kind, a kind whose essence is given by the ends it seeks and not by the (structural) means used.[37]

[35] This seems to be Dworkin's way of regarding areas of law. See Dworkin, *Law's Empire* (Cambridge, Mass.: Harvard University Press, 1986), 250–4, 402–3.

[36] Calabresi and Melamed, 'Property Rules, Liability Rules, and Inalienability: One View of the Cathedral', *Harvard Law Review*, Vol. 85 (1972), 1089–128.

[37] See Moore, 'Law as a Functional Kind', in R. George, ed., *Natural Law Theory* (Oxford: Oxford University Press, 1992).

Whether any areas of law have such structural essences is an open question. There are kinds of human actions, and there thus are kinds of remedial acts that a judge can perform within a legal system. And it is certainly possible for a legal system to individuate its areas of law by differences in remedial judicial actions—witness the ancient 'areas' of law and of equity whose borders were marked in this way. Yet what we currently think of as areas of law hardly fit the kinds of judicial action. Take injunctive relief as a kind of judicial action. Many kinds of rights, governed by many areas of law other than property law, are protected by injunctive relief. What we at least currently include as property law in the Anglo-American system can thus hardly be equated with the obtaining of this kind of relief. When the fit is better, say between punitive sanctions and criminal law, this may turn out to be due to assumptions about the distinctive ends of criminal law, not its distinctive means of attaining them. What is the difference between a fine and a civil damage award, except that one serves a punitive purpose whereas the other serves a compensatory purpose?

Thus, as I am doubtful that law itself has any essential structural features,[38] so I am doubtful that areas of law have any such structural essences either. Most areas of law that come to mind are either functional kinds or nominal kinds. It is not clear that those who propose remedy-based definitions of areas of law would disagree, because usually such definitions are presented overtly as convenient stipulations, not discoveries of natures; usually those proposing such stipulations regard areas of law as nominal kinds whose borders can be moved at will.

When we have answered our ontological question of what kind of kind an area of law might be we will also have placed ourselves in a position to answer the individuation problem. If an area of law is a functional kind, then any law that serves the function essential to that area will be part of that area of law. If criminal law is a functional kind whose function is to achieve retributive justice, then punitive damages law 'in torts' is part of criminal law insofar as such damages truly serve a punishment purpose. If an area of law is a nominal kind, its borders will be wholly conventional. If administrative law is a nominal kind, then any law that is *called* administrative law (by the right people) is administrative law; if criminal

---

[38] See Moore, 'Law as a Functional Kind', *supra* n. 37.

law is a nominal kind, then any law that is administered by agencies (prosecutors, police, courts) that are *called* criminal law agencies, will be criminal law. If an area of law has a structural essence, then its borders are fixed by the use of the remedy marking the essence of the kind. If property law is the law regulating the use of injunctive relief, then any substantive law protecting entitlements with injunctive relief is property law.

My aim in what follows is to lay out the nature of a theory of the criminal law in terms of the questions it must raise and the possible answers it may adopt. In carrying out this aim I obviously must assume some boundaries to what is to be included as part of criminal law. We can justify what these boundaries are only if we can decide whether criminal law is in reality a functional kind, and, if so, whether its function is to seek retributive justice. It is to these questions that I shall now turn.

II. THE NATURE OF A THEORY OF THE CRIMINAL LAW

A. The Function of the Criminal Law

We cannot begin any taxonomizing of criminal law theories until we settle the questions of what kind of kind the criminal law is and what sort of good that it can achieve. These are distinct questions, but, as we shall see, the answer to one highly influences the answer to the other.

Few people believe that criminal law is only a nominal kind—that its doctrines are grouped together as an area of law only because of the accidents of history, that there is no nature such doctrines share that sets them apart from other areas of law other than the convention of our system to call them, or the agencies that administer them, 'criminal'. More typical is the use of the allegedly distinctive sanctions of the criminal law as the criterion of its identity and individuation. Such more typical view holds that what marks law as criminal law is the loss of life or liberty attendant upon criminal liability, a deprivation not attendant upon any other (i.e., civil) liability.

Such a view finds criminal law's essence in a feature of its structure—namely, in its remedy—and is what I earlier called something like a natural kind view of an area of law. Such a view need not be indifferent to criminal law's function(s). To be justified, such severe sanctions must serve some good, even if the good served is not the essence of criminal law. Typically, those viewing criminal law as identified by its distinctive sanctions hold a mixed view as to its functions. Such a view may hold that punitive sanctions are justified when they attain a sufficient level of incapacitation, deterrence, reform, and retribution (the traditional big four of punishment theory).[39] Since locking people up, scaring them, and changing them are not intelligible as intrinsic goods, such a mixed theory is better described first, in terms of a crime-prevention function (itself served by incapacitation, deterrence, and reform, and itself serving the utilitarian goal of making us all better off); second, in terms of the function of achieving retributive justice; and third, in terms of the function of achieving distributive justice by devoting extra social resources to those less advantaged members of the population (criminals) who need them.[40] There are other mixed theories of criminal law's function, of course, that do not mix all three of these types of intrinsic goods (retributive justice, utility, distributive justice), but mix only two, such as a mixed utilitarian/retributive theory or a mixed rehabilitative/utilitarian theory. One can also 'mix' the goals in different ways, lexically ordering the achievement of one goal over another as opposed to simultaneously maximizing both.[41]

In any case, such mixed punishment theories go hand in hand with the remedy-based view of criminal law because such a theorist has already fixed the essence of criminal law (by its remedy) and then asks, how should that remedy be used? A natural answer is, 'to maximize all the goods there are', leading to a mixed theory of punishment that mixes all the kinds of goods that the theorist happens to think there are.

What is wrong with this remedy-based view of the criminal law can be seen by enquiring into the intelligibility of asking, 'What is a punishment?', if one does not already have in mind an answer to

---

[39] See, e.g., Henry Hart, 'The Aims of the Criminal Law', *Law and Contemporary Problems*, Vol. 23 (1958), 401–41.

[40] I elaborate on these reductions in ch. 2, *infra*.

[41] The best known example of a mixed punishment theory is Herbert Hart's. See Hart, *Punishment and Responsibility* (Oxford: Oxford University Press, 1968), chs. 2 & 7. For other possibilities, see Andrew von Hirsch, *Doing Justice* (New York: Hill and Wang, 1976), ch. 6.

the question, 'Why do we punish?'[42] For if the structural feature that allegedly fixes criminal law's essence—punitive sanctions—is itself described only by the function served, then criminal law is a functional and not a natural kind.

Admittedly, we are not bereft of structural intuitions about what sanctions constitute punishments. Sanctions that are severely unpleasant to endure like death, confinement, the ducking stool, etc., seem easy examples. Yet would even these sanctions—let alone monetary fines—be punishments if they were not imposed for a punitive purpose? If a pound of flesh is the stipulated damages to be paid upon breach of some contract, the remedy, although very unpleasant to endure, is still for breach of contract, not a crime. Moreover, could not a gift of flowers be a punishment—as when we punish our friends' derelictions by being especially nice to them in order to heighten their feelings of guilt? If our purpose is punitive, the sanctions inflicted will be a punishment, no matter what their structural features might be. To explicate what a punishment is, then, one must explicate what a punitive purpose is.

The supposed structural essence of criminal law in terms of its distinctive remedy of punishment turns out to involve us in criminal law's function. This is not raised to argue for a retributive function for the criminal law based on what Herbert Hart once aptly called the 'definitional stop'.[43] No argument has yet been presented for any particular function of the criminal law. The only point so far is that one cannot get a handle on what sanctions constitute a punishment unless one has *some* function in mind as the goal of the criminal law. The result is that the criminal law is not to be identified with, nor can it be individuated by, any structural features of its allegedly distinctive remedies. Criminal law is *an* area of law only because it serves some distinctive good that we honour as its function.

We can satisfy ourselves that criminal law is a functional kind only if we can satisfy ourselves as to what its function is. To do this, we must first have some idea of how in general we find the function of anything, an area of law included.[44]

---

[42] See Hart, *supra* n. 41, at 4–5 for discussion of philosophical definitions of punishment.

[43] Id. at 5.

[44] On functional analysis generally, see Michael Moore, *Law and Psychiatry: Rethinking the Relationship* (Cambridge: Cambridge University Press, 1984), 26–32, 189–94, 285–9; Moore, 'Law as a Functional Kind', *supra* n. 37.

There are two components in our judgements of a thing's function. One is a judgement about its capacity: What can it cause? Such capacity judgements are heavily influenced by what sorts of thing the item has brought about in the past, which is why we often look for a thing's function in the actual consequences of its activities. The second component judgement is one of goodness: of all the states of affairs within the capacity of some thing to bring about, are any of them intrinsically good? If none of the effects a thing can cause are good, then it has no function (although like a poison it may of course have an evil *use*); if a thing can bring about some intrinsically good state of affairs, then that consequence is what the thing is 'good for', i.e. that is the thing's function.

Consider by way of example the current debate in psychology about the function of dreaming.[45] Does dreaming serve the function of keeping us asleep (Freud's hypothesis), some other function, or no function at all? We answer this question by first enquiring what dreaming has the capacity to cause. Does it cause the relaxation of that vigilant sentinel of our good opinions of ourselves, the Freudian 'censor', who while 'asleep at his post' lets by usually repressed wishes that find fantasized satisfaction in the dream and thus discharge their otherwise sleep-disturbing energy? Current research into that causal question suggests that the answer is 'no', that dreaming does not cause the prolongation of sleep through Freudian or any other mechanisms. But for illustration, suppose the evidence were the other way so that it did appear that dreaming tends to protect sleep from otherwise disturbing stimuli. We need a second kind of judgement to decide that the function of dreaming is to guard sleep. We need to judge that sleep is good. Sleep does not appear to be an intrinsic good—unless one's life is so bleak that death looks pretty inviting too—so sleep must bring about something else that is good. And this embroils us in another large debate in psychology: what is sleep good for?[46] There are lots of causal hypotheses here too (one of which is, incidentally, that we sleep in order to dream).

---

[45] See Moore, 'The Nature of Psychoanalytic Explanation', in L. Laudan, ed., *Mind and Medicine: Vol. VII of the Pittsburgh Series in the Philosophy of Science* (Berkeley: University of California Press, 1983), 5–78.

[46] See E. L. Hartmann, *The Functions of Sleep* (New Haven: Yale University Press, 1973).

What researchers are looking for as they search for, and then sift among, the effects of dreaming and of sleeping is some contribution these processes make to something that is intrinsically good, namely, health. Unless they find some causal linkage between these processes and health, they will not have found such processes' functions.

If we apply this process to the criminal law, the same two kinds of judgements are involved. First we ask, what consequences does the criminal law have the capacity to bring about? Remembering that this is an exercise in particular jurisprudence, I ask this question about the criminal law that I most intimately know, that of the Anglo-American system. Can Anglo-American criminal law bring about emphatic denunciation of wrongdoing? Can it bring about social cohesion? Can it predict violent propensities and incapacitate those with such propensities from hurting others? Can it educate people out of wanting to hurt others? Can it achieve retributive justice? Can it reinforce existing wealth disparities? Can it dampen movements for social change, and thereby entrench those in power?

Suppose for the moment that criminal law has the capacity to cause all of these effects to some significant degree. Which might be its function? Some of these effects are not only not intrinsically good, they do not even contribute to something else that is intrinsically good. Maintaining wealth disparities and dampening social change are in this category, so these cannot be the criminal law's function. If these were the only effects of the criminal law, then it would have no function. Others on this list are not intrinsic goods, but they may well have the capacity to contribute to something else that is intrinsically good which could then be criminal law's function. Denouncing wrongdoing, maintaining social cohesion, incapacitating or educating people are in this category. These are perhaps good depending on what else they cause. Typically, though not inevitably, the further good thing each of these things is thought to cause is the prevention of crime. Murder, rape, mayhem, etc., are bad, and their prevention is intrinsically good, so perhaps this is the function of criminal law. Yet the achieving of retributive justice is also good for its own sake—or so I shall argue.[47] So should we say that the criminal law has two functions of equal dignity, crime-prevention and retribution? Many people have said this,

---

[47] See chs. 2, 3, 4, infra.

and it is not an implausible thing to say. Yet there are two considerations that suggest that the only function of our criminal law is the achievement of retributive justice. One is the tension that exists between crime-prevention and retributive goals. This tension is due to retributivism's inability to share the stage with any other punishment goal. To achieve retributive justice, the punishment must be inflicted because the offender did the offence. To the extent that someone is punished for reasons other than that he deserves to be punished, retributive justice is not achieved.[48]

This is seen most easily in situations where the offence committed deserves a certain range of punishment, and then extra punishment is tacked on for crime-prevention reasons (such as to induce the criminal to talk and implicate others, or to strike a blow for general deterrence). That others cannot be convicted without an accused's testimony, or that his crime has become a popular one and his case a very public one, making him a useful object-lesson to others, are factors irrelevant to what the accused deserves. There is no retributive justice achieved in the imposition of such an increment of punishment.

Now suppose no identifiable increment of punishment is added for crime-prevention reasons. Rather, the accused is punished no more than he deserves. Yet part of the reason motivating those who punish him is that his punishment will serve as an example to others. Such a criminal may have no grounds for complaint, but we do: the criminal system is not achieving retributive justice. By seeking to achieve other goods through punishment, we necessarily lessen our ability to achieve the good of retribution.

The tension between retribution and any other goal of punishment such as crime-prevention prevents us from any comfortable 'mix' of goods for punishment. We cannot happily seek both goals and kill two birds with the proverbial one stone, for by aiming at one of the birds we will necessarily miss the other.

The second consideration militating against a mixed theory of criminal law's function stems from the structure of Anglo-American criminal law. The criminal law we have has a great deal more capacity to cause the achievement of retributive justice than

---

[48] This is not a 'definitional stop', substituting 'retributive justice' for 'punishment'. (See text at n. 43 *supra*.) Rather, if the analysis in the text is correct, it is because that is the nature of retributive justice. It is a theory, not a definition, doing the work here.

it does the prevention of crime. Partly this is due to factors extra-neous to the doctrines of the criminal law, such as the limited effi-cacy of deterrence. More important is the shape of our criminal law doctrines themselves. If one were seeking to maximize deterrence, or incapacitation, we would not have the doctrines we do. Consider but one example, the differential punishments for intentional homi-cide. Typically under American state law, intentional killing may be first degree murder if it was premeditated, voluntary manslaughter if it was done in a rage brought on by the victim's provoking act, or second degree murder if it was neither provoked nor premedi-tated. On crime-prevention grounds of deterrence or incapacitation, these are hard distinctions to justify. The more impulsive the killing, the more punishment there should be on deterrence grounds, for such draconian measures may be the only way to get the impulsive killer to stop and think. Analogously, second degree murders are typically intra-family killers who are highly non-recidivist, so on incapacitation grounds this class of criminals should be punished least. As we know, however, this is not how punishment is scaled by our homicide laws. Such laws make sense only if they are seen as attempting to grade culpability (by the degree of control exercised by the killer as he acted).

Examples of this sort abound in the criminal law. Such doctrines make utilitarianism look like so many bad reasons for what we believe on instinct anyway. It is thus difficult to make the utilitar-ian goal of crime prevention into even *a* goal of Anglo-American criminal law, given how often that goal's apparent implications are flouted by the doctrines supposedly serving it.

I thus assume in what follows that if retribution is an intrinsic good—as I have yet to show—then it is *the* intrinsic good that is the function of Anglo-American criminal law. I have of course only lightly sketched the argument for this conclusion. To make the second of my two points convincingly requires nothing less than a complete examination of all of the doctrines of Anglo-American criminal law, probing them for their ability to serve the goal of crime-prevention as well as the goal of retribution. My first point, about retributivism's intolerance for partners, could also no doubt be bolstered with further examples and analogies. Still, I assume that most of the weight of the argument must be borne by the pro-position defended in chapters 2, 3, and 4 namely, that punishing the morally culpable is intrinsically good. Those finding retributive justice intrinsically good probably have little trouble with the rest of the argument for retribution being criminal law's function; those thinking that 'two wrongs can't make a right' doubtlessly do not find the argument intelligible. So it is with the moral worth of retribution that issue is most crucially joined for most people.

The first question of a theory of the criminal law is the question of why we punish. My answer—to exact retribution—influences the possible shape of the rest of a criminal law theory. Alternative answers in terms of the utilitarian goal of crime prevention or the distributive justice goal of rehabilitation will similarly determine the shape of their respective criminal law theories. Thinking mine to be correct, I make no attempt in what follows to chart the structure a theory of the criminal law might have if it began with another goal (to say nothing of the 'theory' one could have if criminal law served no goal at all). Nonetheless, much of the structure below detailed will be shared by any criminal law theory that holds moral responsibility to be at least a necessary (if not sufficient) condition of criminal liability. I thus think that any plausibly just theory of the criminal law will share much of the structure of my retributivist theory of the criminal law.

B. The Two Parts of the Criminal Law

It has been traditional in Anglo-American criminal law scholarship to divide criminal law into two parts, a 'general part' and a 'special part'.[49] The usual way of describing this distinction is in terms of 'doctrines that apply to all crimes' (the general part) versus 'doctrines that define particular crimes' (the special part).[50] Doctrines of *actus reus*, *mens rea*, and causation apply to all crimes, so such doctrines are by this criterion assigned to the general part; doctrines defining the unique elements of the *actus reus* of rape, or the *mens rea* requirements peculiar to homicide, are assigned to the special part. Doctrines of conspiracy, attempt, solicitation, and complicity, while defining specific crimes, are usually assigned by this criterion to the general part because one can be guilty of attempting, soliciting, conspiring to commit, or aiding and abetting, almost any other crime whatsoever.

[49] Most famously, in Glanville Williams, *Criminal Law—The General Part* (London: Stevens & Sons, 2nd edn., 1961).

[50] See, e.g., George Fletcher, *Rethinking Criminal Law* (Boston: Little, Brown, 1978), 393. (The general part 'has as its object the study of issues that cut across all offenses . . .'.)

In teaching criminal law often the distinction between the general and the special parts is presented in this way in order to serve up a pedagogical justification for the exclusive focus of the basic criminal law course on the general part of the criminal law.[51] The argument is that students are better served by learning the doctrines that apply to all crimes than they would be by mastering the elements of specific crimes. Such doctrines of the general part vary less from jurisdiction to jurisdiction, and they have a greater longevity.

As much I have said myself to classes of criminal law students in explaining to them why they were not learning the elements of particular crimes. Yet there is a deeper way of drawing the distinction, serving a non-pedagogical purpose. To see this second way of drawing the distinction, think of two kinds of moral judgements we often make.[52] One is a judgement about what types of actions are right or wrong for persons to do. This answers an abstract or general question that does not ask after the responsibility of any particular person. Rather, such general judgements form what people usually think of as their moral code. The second judgement is about the responsibility of a particular person at a particular time. Such a judgement answers the questions of whether a person did such wrongs as are prohibited by one's moral code, and whether that person was culpable in the doing of such wrongs.

The first sort of judgement is about types of actions, while the second is about actors who have acted on some particular occasion. Such judgements call into play two quite different kinds of moral theories. The first requires that we apply a theory of substantive morality, the morality that tells us what types of actions are wrong to do (as opposed to the types of actions that are usually permissible or even morally virtuous to do). We invoke such a substantive morality to answer questions like, 'Is abortion wrong?', 'Is baby-selling wrong?', 'Is euthenasia permissible?', and 'Is suicide permissible?'

[51] Cf. Kadish, 'Why Substantive Criminal Law—A Dialogue', in *Blame and Punishment* (New York: Macmillan, 1987).

[52] This distinction is explored briefly in ch. 12. My thinking about this moral distinction has been influenced by George Fletcher's legal distinction between 'wrong-doing' and 'attribution' (Fletcher, *supra* n. 50), although I am unsure how closely the two distinctions match. Cf. Fletcher, 'Criminal Theory as an International Discipline: Reflections on the Freiburg Conference', *Criminal Justice Ethics*, Vol. 4 (1985), 60–72, summarizing the lively discussion of both distinctions at the 1984 Freiburg Conference on criminal theory.

The second kind of moral judgement requires that we apply what might be called the morality of fair fault ascription. Such a moral theory is a theory of responsibility, because it addresses the question of when a person is morally responsible in the doing of a wrongful action. Such a theory answers questions like, 'Is sleep walking an action?', 'Does the offender have to know of (and perhaps even accept) the substantive moral norms he is violating in order to be responsible for their violation?', and 'Is negligent inadvertence to the aspects of an action that make it wrongful enough to make one culpable for the doing of that action, or does one at least have to be aware of the risk that such aspects are present?'

The second way of drawing the distinction between the general and the special parts of the criminal law is to regard the general part as seeking to articulate a theory of responsibility, and the special part as seeking to articulate a theory of wrongful action. The special part lays down what actions are prohibited and the general part lays down the conditions under which an actor who does a wrongful action is liable to punishment.

By and large this second way of slicing the pie will be congruent with the first.[53] This is because of the content-neutrality of the theory of responsibility. Such a theory is content-neutral in the sense that it lays down the conditions under which one is responsible for the doing of a wrongful action, *no matter what the character of the wrongful action may be*. Mayhem and theft are two very different wrongful acts, but responsibility for doing them turns on the same conditions of wrongdoing and culpability. This feature of the theory of responsibility means that the criminal law doctrines that describe the content of such a theory will apply to all acts prohibited by the special part of the criminal law. Hence, the congruence in the two distinctions.

This second way of drawing the distinction between the two parts of the criminal law, like the first, allocates the inchoate crimes of attempt, conspiracy, solicitation, as well as the crime of complicity, to the general part. Now such allocation will be justified by seeing such doctrines as describing supplemental ways in which a person

---

[53] With the important exception of the defence of general justification (or 'balance of evils'). Doctrinally, general justification applies to all crimes and so would be assigned to the general part; morally, such justification, like all justifications, is part of morality's substantive norms and so the legal doctrines reflecting it would be assigned to criminal law's special part.

may be responsible (in addition to the primary way of culpably doing some wrong himself). Such doctrines will not be assigned to the general part simply because they define crimes parasitic on all other crimes.

Whether the second way of drawing the distinction is preferable to the first depends on what one takes the function of criminal law to be. My own theory is that criminal law is a functional kind whose function is to attain retributive justice. Retributive justice demands that those who deserve punishment get it. To deserve punishment, two things are necessary: one must have done a wrongful action, and one must have done so culpably. This requires two sorts of doctrines in the criminal law: those that specify which types of acts are wrong, and those that specify both the conditions under which one has done some wrongful act and the conditions under which one is culpable in the doing of that wrongful act. That is why we need both a special and a general part to the criminal law, and that is why the distinction between the two parts must map onto the distinction between a theory of substantive morality and a theory of responsibility. Criminal law's retributive function is best served in this way.

It is an interesting question whether other areas of law could make use of an analogous distinction between a general part and a special part. In property, for example, there are doctrines that apply to property in land, other doctrines that apply to property in ideas or in the form of their expression, other doctrines that apply to property in water, other doctrines that apply to property in wild animals, and yet other doctrines that apply to property in movable chattels. Such doctrines could constitute a 'special part' to property law. The general part would consist of those doctrines that apply to all types of property. Such doctrines of the general part might consist of acquisition rules, transfer rules, and use rules for all the things in which people can have a property interest.

Yet we have no general part to property law. This is because the doctrines of Anglo-American property law do not serve univocally *a* goal. They serve a triad of goals: utility (by allocating and regulating entitlements so as to maximize incentives to produce); fairness (by rewarding those who first mix their labour with a thing); and distributive justice (by reallocating entitlements so as to make the least well off better off). Moreover, if we leave particular jurisprudence for general jurisprudence for a moment, it is not at all clear that there is an intrinsic good that something called 'property law' could distinctively serve. The fairness of rewarding (with property rights) those who create or improve some thing does not swamp other goods in the way that retributive justice swamps its competitors. Property, as E. M. Forster once reminded us, just is not that important.[54]

The result of this lack of any distinctive goal to property law is the hodgepodge of doctrines we have, depending on whether we are dealing with real property, intellectual property, personal property, or property in water. For the lack of any distinctive goal to property law denies to that area of law any underlying moral distinction that could make sense of a general part. There is no theory analogous to the theory of responsibility for criminal law that could provide general rules for the acquisition, use and transfer of property of all kinds. Sometimes Lockean fairness wins out, as in the doctrines of accession (for personal property), first capture (for property in wild animals), copyright (for intellectual property), adverse possession (for real property), and prior appropriation (for water). As often, utility determines who may own what, and what such ownership entails, as in reasonable use doctrines (for water) and nuisance doctrines (for land). Occasionally distributive justice is the goal property law serves, as the developments in landlord-tenant law in the last thirty years in America illustrate.

Property law thus illustrates what an area of law must possess if it is to have a distinction between a general part and a special part. It must possess a content-neutral theory—analogous to the theory of responsibility—that governs all kinds of property, all kinds of contracts, all sorts of torts, etc. To have such a content-neutral theory, an area of law must have a contrasting, content-laden theory about what sorts of things should be the subject of property or of contract rights, what sorts of acts can constitute a tort, etc. And to have both of these theories as distinct theories, an area of law must have some distinctive goal that it serves that can make sense of why two such theories are needed. Criminal law has such a structure because it has such a goal; property law does not because it lacks such a goal. Contracts and torts may well have such

[54] E. M. Forster, 'My Woods', in his *Abinger Harvest* (London: Edward Arnold & Co., 1936). See Thomas Grey, 'The Disintegration of Property', in J. Chapman and R. Rennock, eds., *Nomos xxii: Property* (New York: New York University Press, 1980).

a structure, depending on how one assesses the intrinsic goodness—and the degree of that goodness' realization in Anglo-American law—of the morality of promise-keeping and of corrective justice, respectively.

C. The Nature of a Theory of the General Part of the Criminal Law

To serve retributive justice, criminal law must punish all and only those who are morally culpable in the doing of some morally wrongful action. It is the general part of the criminal law that lays down the conditions both of wrongful action and of culpability, and a theory of the general part is thus a theory of wrongdoing and culpability (or as I sometimes will call the union of these two, moral responsibility).

The theory of responsibility may usefully be divided into three parts. First, there is the theory of responsibility proper. Such a theory tells us what sorts of conditions must be present before someone is in the relevant sense morally responsible—for example, is intending to cause some harm sufficient, or must one try to cause, or even cause, the harm before one is morally responsible? Second, there are those subtheories that answer questions about the nature of the elements of responsibility—for instance, what is it to intend something, to try to cause it, or to cause it? Third, these elements of responsibility (action, intention, causation, absence of excuse) can have the nature that they do only if persons have a certain nature. The third theory needed is thus a theory of personhood.

In what follows I shall organize my discussion into these three subtheories. Such division may be helpful because it separates more plainly evaluative choices (between competing theories of responsibility proper) from intermediate-level metaphysical choices (between competing theories of action, intention, causation) from deepest-level metaphysical choices (between competing theories of personhood). Such divisions are heuristic only, however, because the phenomenon the theory of responsibility studies is one thing, moral responsibility. Because responsibility is a moral property that supervenes upon (and may even be type-identical with) the natural properties of voluntariness, intentionality, causation, lack of mistake or compulsion, and personhood,[55] a theory of responsibility *is*

---

[55] Supervenient relations between moral properties like culpability and natural properties like intentionality are explored by me in Moore, 'Moral Realism

a theory of act, intent, cause, excuse, and persons, however useful it may be to develop the theory in three stages.

1. The Nature of Responsibility   Herbert Hart fruitfully distinguished various senses of the word 'responsible' that are idiomatic within ordinary English usage.[56] (1) We sometimes use the word to ascribe a non-moral responsibility to a person or a thing, as when we say, 'The storm was responsible for the loss of the ship.' Here we mean only that the storm *caused* the loss of the ship. (2) Other times, we use the word to describe one's duties, as in, 'The captain was responsible for the safety of the ship and its crew.' (3) Sometimes we say that a person is a responsible individual, meaning that she generally meets her obligations. (4) Sometimes we say that a person has the capacity to be held responsible, as in, 'He was a responsible adult.' (5) Other times, we mean to ascribe legal liability to a person with the word, as in, 'The jury found the ship captain responsible for the loss of life.'

None of these usages capture the sense of 'responsibility' relevant to a theory of the criminal law. The sense of 'responsibility' needed here is the sense that names the conjunction of the moral properties of wrongdoing and of culpability. Some of the usages above name aspects of this sort of responsibility, such as that one caused a harm ((1) above) or that one is an accountable agent ((4) above); some mention a presupposition of this sort of responsibility, namely, that a moral obligation exists or existed ((2), (3) above); one usage names the legal consequence that follows from this sort of moral responsibility in a just legal system, namely, liability to legal sanctions ((5) above); but none of these usages names the relevant sort of responsibility itself, and it is this sort of responsibility itself that is the object of the needed theory.

What a theory of responsibility thus seeks is to elucidate the meaning of, 'X is responsible for Y', when 'responsible' is taken to mean, 'culpable wrongdoing'. We can usefully taxonomize theories about the nature of moral responsibility if we ask, first, who are the subjects ('X') of responsibility, second, what are the objects ('Y') of responsibility, and third, what kind of relation must exist between X and Y for X to be morally responsible for Y?

Revisited', *Michigan Law Review*, Vol. 90 (1992), 2424–533, at 2518–26; Moore, 'Moral Reality', *Wisconsin Law Review*, Vol. [1982], 1061–156.

[56] Hart, *supra* n. 41, 'Postscript on Responsibility'.

a. *The Subjects of Responsibility*

With regard to the subjects of responsibility, there is a large pool of things that might be such subjects. Individual human persons are the most obvious answer, but what about: 'little persons' (egos, ids, superegos, dream-censors, wills, personalities), 'big persons' (corporations, nations, platoons, armies), 'quasi-persons' (infants, mentally deranged), 'analogous persons' (computers, animals, Martians), former persons (corpses, human beings in irreversible comas), soon-to-be persons (foetuses, fertilized ova), or things that are not at all like persons (ships, stones, trees, rivers)? Theories of responsibility have been proposed that would allow in almost all of these items as moral agents capable of being the bearers of moral responsibility.[57]

Despite this embarrassment of riches, the division marking much contemporary controversy about responsibility is between individualist and communitarian theories of responsibility. The individualist thinks that responsibility is a property that only individual persons can possess (coupled usually with a theory of personhood that counts adult, sane, human beings as one person, and only counts such human beings as a person). Communitarian theories think that nations and communities of all kinds are the primary subjects of responsibility. Such a communitarian theory might hold, for example, that Ford Motor Co. was culpable as a company for its wrongful action of not recalling the dangerous Ford Pinto (and thus deserved to be punished on retributivist grounds) even though Ford does not possess the essential attributes of personhood.

b. *The Objects of Responsibility*

With regard to the objects of responsibility, there are two sorts of things one might be responsible for: datable events, such as wrongful actions or unjustified harms to others; or one's own character, a more-or-less enduring state, not a datable event. On a person-based view of responsibility, this comes to the question of whether we judge someone's responsibility with reference to the action she has done (or harm she has caused) at some isolatable point in time, or whether our judgements of a person's responsibility are directed

---

[57] See, e.g., Peter French, *Collective and Corporate Responsibility* (New York: Columbia University Press, 1984); Chris Stone, *Earth and Other Ethics* (New York: Harper & Row, 1987); Moore, *Law and Psychiatry*, *supra* n. 44, at 142–52.

to who she is in general, without reference to any particular act or harm caused.

If we individuate theories of responsibility along this dimension, there seem to be three possibilities: (1) an event-responsibility view that either denies the existence of character-responsibility or reduces it to event-responsibility (the latter reduction can be accomplished either by holding someone responsible for their character only insofar as that character was chosen by them—Aristotle's view—or by treating character as wholly constituted by bad acts—the behaviourist view of character); (2) a character-responsibility view that either denies the existence of event-responsibility or reduces it to character-responsibility (the latter reduction typically accomplished by treating persons as responsible only for acts that are 'in character' for them); (3) a dual view that admits the independent existence of two kinds of responsibility, one for what we do and another for who we are. On this last view, although bad character is evidence of bad acts, and although bad acts are evidence of bad character, responsibility for bad acts is not limited to those in character for the actor, and responsibility for bad character is not limited to only those aspects of character that are either chosen or are manifested in bad action.[58]

c. *The Responsibility Relation*

The third and most important dimension along which we should individuate theories of responsibility is by the nature of the relation asserted to exist between the subjects and the objects of responsibility. Let me illustrate the possibilities with a person-based view of responsibility that takes the object for which persons are responsible to be a datable event (act or harm) since this is obviously the view of responsibility overwhelmingly presupposed by the bulk of Anglo-American criminal law.

Very generally, two kinds of relations may be thought to exist between persons and the harms/acts for which they are responsible. I shall call these passive versus active relations. On a passive view of the matter, the subject of responsibility need not do anything to be responsible for some harm; the relation that makes him responsible for that harm is in this sense passive. The concept of original sin of Christian theology provides one example, for according to this doctrine we are each responsible for Adam's fall from grace

---

[58] Examples of each of these positions is discussed in ch. 13.

just by virtue of being persons who descended from Adam. Equally expansive was Jean Paul Sartre's briefly held view that we are each responsible for all the evil of the world just because we are a 'for-itself' (I would say, person).[59]

Less sweeping versions of passive responsibility theories are more plausible. Some think that members of nation states are responsible for what their governments do and perhaps even responsible for what 'their' government did before they were born. Those who hold present-day Germans responsible for Nazi atrocities apply such a passive responsibility theory.[60] Such theories are passive because it is one's status as a member of some group (some member(s) of which did some harm) that make one responsible for that harm.

A more plausible passive responsibility theory is that whereby we are as responsible for what we (passively) fail to prevent that we had the ability to prevent as we are for what we (actively) bring about. Indeed, on this theory actively causing some harm is just a special case of failing to prevent that harm from occurring (by failing to restrain ourselves). The relation between a person and a harm relied on by this theory is a capacity relation: could the person have prevented this harm? Such capacities can exist without any effort on our part and without knowledge that we have them.

Passive responsibility theories are not the same as group responsibility theories even when the passive relation making one responsible for some harm is membership in a group some member(s) of which caused that harm. Communitarian (or group) responsibility theories take groups to be the primitive or basic subjects of responsibility—*groups* are to be held responsible, not individuals within them necessarily. A passive responsibility theory, by contrast, takes individual persons to be the basic subjects of responsibility even while holding such individuals responsible because of membership in some group. To pursue the Ford Motor Co. example, an individualist, passive responsibility theory could hold members of the Ford family responsible because they owned the shares in the entity, Ford Motor Co.; on a group responsibility theory, Ford Motor Co. itself is the subject of responsibility and *it* is to be punished.

---

[59] Sartre, 'Existentialism is a Humanism', in Novak, ed., *Existentialism versus Marxism* (New York: Dell Publishing Co., 1966).

[60] See, e.g., Dworkin, *Law's Empire, supra* n. 35, at 167–75.

Active responsibility theories that relate a person to a harm via the properties of voluntariness, intentionality, causation, knowledge (absence of mistake), freedom (absence of compulsion), and rationality (absence of insanity, infancy) are by far the most familiar kind of responsibility theories there are, for these are the theories long enshrined in Anglo-American criminal law. Such theories are 'active' in the sense that they all require some kind of action by a person before that person may be held responsible.

If we hold constant the requirements that a subject be free, rational, and unmistaken at present, we may see four distinct views of responsibility here. The first I shall call the orthodox view. On this view someone ('X') is responsible for some state of affairs ('E') if and only if:

1. X voluntarily performed some action ('A'); and
2. A caused E to occur; and
3. Such causing of E by X was intentional.

Voluntariness, intentionality, and causation are on the orthodox view individually necessary and (remembering that the justifications and the excuses are being left out of the picture for now) jointly sufficient for responsibility.

A second view I shall call the 'moral strict responsibility' view.[61] On such a view, it is enough for responsibility that one cause a harm by one's voluntary action. It is not necessary that one has *intentionally* brought about the harm so long as one did bring about the harm.

A third view—let us call it the subjective view—relaxes the causation requirement of the orthodox view. It is enough for responsibility for some type of harm that one perform a voluntary act with the intention of bringing about that type of harm. On this view one need not in fact cause an instance of that type of harm to occur; one only need *try* to bring it about. The subjective view typically only relaxes the causation requirement. It does not eliminate any causal requirement, because typically defenders of this view require that the voluntary act *cause* some state of affairs even if it is not the state of affairs of the intended harm occurring; the state of affairs that must be caused on these typical version of this third view is that which we describe as a 'trying' or an 'attempting' to bring about the intended harm.

[61] Discussed briefly as a presupposition to the discussion of causation in ch. 7.

A fourth view relaxes both the intentionality and causation requirements of the orthodox view. If one person ('Z') causes some harm E to occur, then X may be responsible for E if X's voluntary act causes, not E, but an aiding of Z to cause E, so long as X intends to cause, not E itself, but again, an aiding of Z to cause E. There are still causation and intentionality requirements to this supplemental responsibility for aiding another, but they are not as stringent as they would be on the orthodox view of responsibility.

This fourth view of active responsibility can happily be combined with any of the preceding three views to produce a consistent theory of responsibility. For the fourth view restricts the domain of its relaxed intentionality and causation requirements to the situation where another person has brought about the morally bad state of affairs, and then asks, is the person under scrutiny also responsible for that state of affairs?

The first three views are not so happily combined, because they do not apply to neatly separated situations. There is thus some competition between such views, particularly between the orthodox view of responsibility and the subjective view. Despite this tension, Anglo-American criminal law adopts both the orthodox and the subjective views of responsibility. Causation matters somewhat to responsibility (the orthodox view), but its absence does not preclude a serious if lesser responsibility of those who try to cause harm (the subjective view). Such a combined theory has to regard responsibility as a scalar property—a more-or-less affair, not a black/white affair—with causation of harm grading responsibility. On this theory, there thus must be what many have called 'moral luck', i.e., one's responsibility is partly a matter of factors over which one had no control (such as succeeding in causing the harm one has tried to cause).[62]

We have been holding the excuses in abeyance while distinguishing four views of active responsibility and we now need to add them back in. Adding them in considerably complicates the varieties of possible active responsibility theories. To be clear about what the excuses are in morality, we need to distinguish three sorts of items that are *called* excuses in Anglo-American criminal law.[63] The first set consists of factors like unconsciousness, hypoglycaemic states, hypnosis, automatism, sleepwalking, ignorance of a morally

[62] Disussed in detail in ch. 5.
[63] This threefold division is developed in ch. 12.

relevant feature of one's action, intervening behaviour by a third actor who intentionally inflicts the harm the first actor was himself seeking to cause. In Anglo-American criminal law these are sometimes cast as excuse defences. In reality, these are not excuses at all but are simply ways of showing the absence of voluntary action (for unconsciousness, hypoglycaemic states, hypnosis, automatism, sleep-walking), intentionality (for ignorance), or causation (for intervening causes). The addition of these 'excuses' to our discussion obviously does not complicate our taxonomy because we have not in reality added anything.

A second set of what are called excuses in Anglo-American criminal law are what I call in chapter 12 the 'true excuses'. These are conditions of mistake (mistake of law, mistake of fact) or of compulsion (duress, natural necessity, provocation, addiction). These conditions are not merely the flip side of the act, intention, causation requirements—one acts intentionally in causing a harm, for example, when one acts under the threat of another (duress) or when one acts under the mistaken belief that the act in question is not illegal (mistake of law). Some room must thus be found for these conditions in a theory of responsibility proper.

The third set consists of what I call the status excuses—infancy, insanity, perhaps involuntary intoxication.[64] Although classified in law as excuse defences, these are not moral excuses. For these conditions threaten a much more fundamental presupposition of our responsibility ascriptions than do the true excuses. Infants, the insane, and the extremely intoxicated lack those basic capacities of rational thought that exclude them from being addressees of moral norms at all. The legal doctrines of these 'excuses' are in reality part of the law's attempt to answer the question, who (or what) are the proper subjects of moral responsibility and thus of legal liability? Thus, although a theory of responsibility proper must contain moral principles answering this question, such principles need not occupy us here.

I have not said anything thus far about that other category of defences in Anglo-American criminal law, the justification defences of self-defence, balance-of-evils, defence of others, defence of property, law enforcement privilege, and the like. This is because

[64] For use of the label 'status excuses', see ch. 12 *infra*. I explore insanity as the most notable of such excuses in ch. 14 *infra*, and in Moore, *Law and Psychiatry*, *supra* n. 44, ch. 6.

justifications are not part of the theory of responsibility. Rather, justifications are simply further spellings out of the substantive moral norms that constitute the subject matter for a theory of substantive morality. Self-defence, for example, is simply an exception to the moral norms, 'Don't kill another' and 'Don't batter another.' Self-defence does not answer the finger-pointing questions, who if anyone killed Jones, and who if anyone was responsible for the wrongful killing of Jones? Rather, it answers the prior question, are killings like that of Jones wrongful? A theory of responsibility accordingly need not contain any moral principles regarding the justifications.[65]

Having isolated what it is an active theory of responsibility must talk about in addition to act, intent and causation—viz., the true excuses—it is now time to talk about it. About the true excuses, there are, generally speaking, three positions a theory of responsibility might take. Two of these are extreme positions: no one is excused by compulsions or their own mistakes; or everyone is excused because everyone is compelled by the adverse circumstances of their own childhood, their genetic making, their unconscious, etc. The third position—actually a range of positions, of course—is that adopted by Anglo-American criminal law, which is that some people who cause harm by their voluntary and intentional actions are excused because of compulsion or mistake even though most are not.

d. *Anglo-American Criminal Law's Theory of Responsibility*
The number of variables on which any theory of responsibility must take a position are unfortunately too large to permit a summary of all possible theories. What can be done is to summarize the position taken on each of these variables by the theory of responsibility presupposed by Anglo-American criminal law. With regard to the subjects of responsibility, such theory is individualist, not

[65] Sometimes a defence that is generally classified as a 'justificatory defense' may operate as an excuse on certain types of occasions. 'Imperfect self-defence' (defendant mistakenly but sincerely believes that his victim was attacking him) and self-defence against innocent aggressors are two examples. Such examples do not change the statement in the text (that justifications are not conditions of culpability and thus belong to the special, not the general, part of the criminal law) because they are not examples of *moral* justifications, however they may be labelled in law. Moreover, as excuses, such examples do not even demand any new categories of excuse: mistake and compulsion, respectively, nicely accommodate such examples.

communitarian: the only fit subjects of responsibility are individual human persons. Not only does this exclude groups, animals, etc., but even some members of the human species (infants, insane) are not the fit subjects of responsibility. With regard to the objects of responsibility, such theory is ambiguous as to whether or not responsibility for character exists independently of responsibility for acts or harms; in any case, such theory asserts that only responsibility for acts or harms is the kind of responsibility relevant to legal liability. 'We judge the act, not the man' is the usual (if a bit misleading) slogan for this view. With regard to the relation between the subjects and objects of responsibility, the theory by and large adopts an active, not a passive, view of the matter (the qualification because of occasional responsibility for omissions). The active relation between a person and a harm that must exist in order for that person to be responsible for that harm is complex: first, disjunctively, either (the person's act caused that harm, and that harm was an instance of the types of harms intended or risked by that person), or (the person's act caused a close enough approximation of the harm to amount to a trying, and that harm was an instance of the types of harms intended by that person), or (the person's act caused aid to be given to another person who caused that harm, and aiding the other in causing that harm was the object of the first person's intention); and, second, the person was neither mistaken about any morally relevant aspect of his action nor was he compelled to do what he did.

I think this theory of responsibility accurately describes the kind of moral responsibility relevant to a proper criminal liability. I argue for one facet of this conclusion in chapter 5, where I attempt to show that the doing of a morally prohibited action like killing is as important to our overall moral responsibility as is the culpable mental states with which we do such an action. I argue for another facet of this conclusion in chapter 6, where I expand on my earlier argument in another book as to why we by and large have a lesser moral responsibility for our omissions than for our actions.[66] Finally, in chapter 13 I seek to justify why criminal law ought to be concerned with moral responsibility for our choices and actions, not with the moral responsibility we do bear for our character.

---

[66] Michael Moore, *Act and Crime: The Implications of the Philosophy of Action for the Criminal Law* (Oxford: Clarendon Press, 1993).

I also think that culpable wrongdoing as I have described it is the kind of responsibility presupposed by Anglo-American criminal law.[67] For both this and the preceding reason, the book is thus oriented around *this* sort of responsibility. Seeing that, the next task is to probe more deeply into its metaphysical presuppositions. This means we need next to examine the elements making up the relational part of such a theory—the elements of action, intention, causation, mistake, and compulsion. We also need to examine the non-relational elements of the theory—the subject and the object of the responsibility relation. The nature of the person presupposed by this theory of responsibility is most conveniently addressed separately (in the section after next); the fine-tuning needed to clarify the object of responsibility on this theory—I have intentionally waffled thus far between 'action', 'harm', and 'bad state of affairs'—is dealt with in that part of the theory of the special part dealing with the nature of wrongful action; which is chapter 17.

2. The Nature of the Elements of Responsibility

a. Wrongdoing

On the dominant theory of responsibility presupposed by Anglo-American criminal law responsibility is constituted by two properties: first, that an accused has done something wrongful and prohibited, and second, that the accused has been culpable in his wrongdoing. The first of these properties, wrongdoing, itself consists of two separable elements: first, that the accused has done some action, and second, that the accused has done an action of a type prohibited by the criminal law. I shall consider each aspect of wrongdoing separately.

i. Action

Perhaps the most basic element of the theory of responsibility examined here is that the subject of responsibility must have *acted*. Needed therefore is a theory about the nature of human action. There are three questions such a theory should answer: first, what is the essence of that type of event we call a human action? Second, what is the nature of those descriptions of types of human actions typically used in Anglo-American criminal law prohibitions? And

---

[67] See Moore, *Law and Psychiatry*, *supra* n. 44, ch. 2, for some defence of this descriptive claim.

third, how does one individuate both particular actions and types of actions?

As I argue in detail in the book that chapter 6 defends, what is usually called the '*actus reus*' requirement in Anglo-American criminal law is actually an amalgam of two quite separate requirements. One is what I shall call the act requirement proper: did the defendant perform any action at the relevant time(s)? The second is what I shall call the *actus reus* question proper: did the defendant's action possess those causal or other properties required to allow us to correctly describe his act as one of the wrongful and prohibited types, such as a killing, signalling, helping, etc.?

The act requirement is what criminal lawyers often refer to as the voluntary act requirement, or the requirement of voluntariness. It is the act requirement that raises the first of our three questions, that asking after the essence of human actions. About the essence of human actions, there are three sorts of theories. The first group of theories refuses the question in the sense that they deny that human actions have an essence. On this view, whether we characterize a bodily movement as an action or not depends on our choices as observers, not upon some fact of the matter about the bodily movement itself. One such theory proceeds from interpretivist assumptions about social science, assumptions about how human behaviour is a special kind of datum—a meaning-possessing datum—that requires creative interpretation by social scientists in order to be understood.[68] Another such theory proceeds from a speech-act semantics prevalent at Oxford in the 1950s and 1960s. On this view, what we observers are really doing when we purportedly *describe* a bodily movement as a human action is *ascribe* responsibility to a person for that movement; on such a view 'action' is a label we apply when we have decided that someone is responsible, not a criterion for deciding whether that person is responsible.[69] A third variation within this group of theories proceeds from the philosophy of the later Wittgenstein. On this view, a bodily movement will be characterized as a human action whenever that movement can be seen as an instance of rule-following (as

[68] On the *verstehen* tradition in social science, see Moore, 'The Interpretive Turn in Modern Theory: A Turn for the Worse?', *Stanford Law Review*, Vol. 41 (1989), 871–957, at 919–27.

[69] Hart, 'Ascription of Responsibility and Rights', *Proceedings of the Aristotelian Society*, Vol. 49 (1949), 171–94.

opposed to merely rule-governed) behaviour; a movement can be seen as an instance of rule-following, in turn, only if there is an agreement between observers that the behaviour should be so regarded, there being no private episodes determining that the behaviour *is* of that character.[70]

A second group of theories takes the question of action's essence more seriously, but gives a non-causal answer. That is, unlike the third group of theories which seek the essence of human action in some distinctive cause of human behaviour, this second group seeks action's essence in some non-causal feature of actions.[71] Prominently, the features fastened upon by this group of theories are the goal-directed, purposive, intelligent, non-observationally known, non-inferentially known, meaningful, intentional, intensional, or Intentional aspects of human actions, where all of these aspects are understood in non-causal terms.

The third group of theories share the common thesis that the essence of human action is to be found in the distinctive *cause* of actions, a cause not found in human behaviour that is not an action. I divide such causal theories of action into two subcategories: those that regard the causation by persons (involved in human actions) as a unique kind of causation, a kind often called 'agent-causation', and those that regard the causal relation needed for there to be an action as the ordinary, garden variety kind of causal relation found throughout science. Agent-causation theorists tend to propose very brief theories, because on their view the idea of agent as cause is 'primitive', i.e., it cannot be explicated in terms of some other notions.[72] Garden variety causal theorists tend to have more to say about the kind of event that is actions' distinctive cause. Some think that basic acts are caused by beliefs,[73] others, by

[70] Ludwig Wittgenstein, *Philosophical Investigations* (Oxford: Basil Blackwell, 3rd edn., 1958); Peter Winch, *The Idea of a Social Science* (London: Routledge and Kegan Paul, 1958).

[71] e.g., G. E. M. Anscombe, *Intention* (Ithaca, NY: Cornell University Press, 2nd edn., 1963); Richard Peters, *The Concept of Motivation* (London: Routledge and Kegan Paul, 1958); A. I. Melden, *Free Action* (London: Routledge and Kegan Paul, 1961).

[72] The two most notable exemplars of this view in recent philosophy have been Richard Taylor and Roderick Chisholm. See Taylor, *Action and Purpose* (Englewood Cliffs, NJ: Prentice-Hall, 1966); Chisholm, 'Human Freedom and the Self', in Gary Watson, ed., *Free Will* (Oxford: Oxford University Press, 1982). See generally Moore, *Law and Psychiatry*, supra n. 44, at 55–6, 71–2.

[73] Danto, *Analytical Philosophy of Action* (Cambridge: Cambridge University Press, 1973).

desires,[74] and yet others, by belief/desire sets whose contents form valid practical syllogisms.[75] Still others think that actions cannot be explicated by either beliefs or desires, but that what makes a bit of behaviour an action is some third kind of mental state, variously styled as a willing, a volition, a choice, or a simple intention.[76]

I have defended a causal theory of action of this last kind.[77] I do so on the grounds that willing (volition, choice, simple intention) is the best metaphysical account of human action and that, therefore, willing is the best moral account of one element of responsibility. If one takes this line, a further question arises as to the nature of this distinctive mental state. Are willings some phenomenological experiences that are not further analysable because based on non-observational, non-inferential knowledge? Or are willings (as a *type* of mental state) identical to some set of brain states? Or are willings a functional state—a state whose essence is given by the distinctive causal role it plays, but whose structural realization varies from brain to brain (or even time to time for a single brain)? These metaphysical views are known as dualist, physicalist, and functionalist views, respectively, in the contemporary philosophy of mind. As far removed as such questions may seem from criminal law, ultimately, as J. F. Stephen noted in his nineteenth-century treatise on criminal law,[78] a theory of criminal law will inevitably presuppose some position on them, and it may as well do so explicitly.

What I have called the *actus reus* requirement proper raises some general concerns on how action types are described, the second of my three earlier distinguished questions about actions. In particular, can anything general be said about the 7000 or so act-type descriptions typically used in a modern criminal code (such as that of the United Kingdom)? What properties are usefully grouped together for purposes of such criminal codes?

---

[74] John Austin, *supra* n. 29; Mackie, 'The Grounds of Responsibility', in Hacker and Raz, eds., *Law Morality and Society* (Oxford: Oxford University Press, 1977).

[75] Alvin Goldman, *A Theory of Human Action* (Englewood Cliffs, NJ: Prentice-Hall, 1970).

[76] Myles Brand, *Intending and Acting* (Cambridge, Mass.: MIT Press, 1984); Michael Bratman, *Intention, Plans, and Practical Reasoning* (Cambridge, Mass.: Harvard University Press, 1987); Alan Donagan, *Choice: The Essential Element in Human Action* (London: Routledge and Kegan Paul, 1987).

[77] See Moore, *Act and Crime, supra* n. 66.

[78] Sir James Stephen, *A History of the Criminal Law of England* (London: Macmillan, 1883), Vol. 2, 128–9. Each of these theories of mind are summarized in Moore, *Law and Psychiatry, supra* n. 44, at 183.

Philosophers have had many alternative ways of taxonomizing kinds of properties presupposed by different types of action descriptions. They have distinguished causally complex descriptions, conventionally complex descriptions, intentionally complex descriptions, and augmentationally complex descriptions, for example. My own view, defended in the book of which chapter 6 is a defence, argues that for criminal law purposes only two species of complexity in action description need be distinguished. These are causally complex descriptions, where a certain consequence must be caused by the bodily movement that is part of an action; and there are circumstantially complex descriptions, where a certain circumstance must exist at the time the relevant bodily movement occurs.

Where a theorist comes out in answering the first question about action (its essence) will heavily influence where he comes out regarding the third (its individuation). If, for example, human actions are bodily movements caused by beliefs, how one individuates beliefs will influence how one individuates the acts such beliefs cause. Analogously, if acts are willed bodily movements, how one individuates willings will influence how one individuates acts. Such influences are only partial, however, because acts are events that occur in the world, and a theory of act-individuation will also have to be compatible with some more general theory of event-individuation.[79]

These individuation questions, too, may seem far removed from the needs of criminal law theory. Yet on an active responsibility view of the criminal law, persons are responsible (and are to be held liable) only for those datable events we call their actions. Not only does this demand some account of what actions are, but it also demands that we say when someone is responsible for *an* action (as opposed to being responsible for several actions of similarly reprehensible character). A legal expression of this last concern is the Anglo-American prohibition against twice being put in jeopardy for the *same offence*, a question partly answered by one's theory of individuation of actions.[80] Additionally, unless one answers this

---

[79] On event-individuation generally, see Donald Davidson, *Actions and Events* (Oxford: Oxford University Press, 1981); and Lawrence Lombard, *Events: A Metaphysical Study* (London: Routledge and Kegan Paul, 1986). Judy Thomson argues that human acts are individuated no differently than any other events. Thomson, *Acts and Other Events* (Ithaca: Cornell University Press, 1977).

[80] Act individuation is partly determinative of the reach of the double jeopardy prohibition, but only partly so because the prohibition (the 'same offence')

and other[81] individuation questions about action, one cannot even begin to assess the adequacy of counterfactual analyses of causation. The truth value of the answer to the lawyer's familiar question—'but for the happening of the defendant's action, would the harm have occurred?'—for example, depends on how one individuates 'the defendant's action'.[82]

ii. *Causation*

If one believes as do I that all act-type descriptions used in Anglo-American criminal law prohibitions are at least causally complex, then a theory of criminal law must address what conditions must be present for a causally complex description to be correctly applied to some action. What is required by such descriptions, of course, is that the act in question possess the causal properties required by the action description contained in some criminal prohibition. The prohibition against killing, for example, requires that an act be the cause of a death. But what is meant by 'cause'?

Broadly speaking, there are two sorts of causal theories, those that analyse the causal relationship necessary to responsibility in terms of one relation and those that do so in terms of two. The two-relations theories are most familiar to Anglo-American criminal lawyers (because most entrenched in Anglo-American criminal law doctrine), so I shall begin with them.

Distinctive of all two-relations theories is the thesis that, in the context of responsibility assessment, 'caused' in the utterance, 'x caused y', names not one relation but two. The doctrinal expression of such kind of causal theories is of course the familiar distinction between 'cause-in-fact' and 'proximate (or legal) cause' in Anglo-

---

ultimately requires a theory of individuation of action types—is homicide different than battery, for example. Act individuation is nonetheless relevant because the same offence may be committed twice by someone (two different basic act tokens) and he may be doubly prosecuted and punished. See generally Moore, *Act and Crime, supra* n. 66, at chs. 12–14.

[81] One also needs to answer the question of complex act-individuation that has so occupied the philosophical literature: is moving my arm, thereby pumping the water, thereby poisoning another, one complex act-token or three? See, e.g., Anscombe, *supra* n. 71; Brody, *supra* n. 30, at 65–70; Moore, *Act and Crime, supra* n. 66, at ch. 11.

[82] On the relation between causation and event (versus fact) individuation, see John Mackie, *The Cement of the Universe* (Oxford: Oxford University Press, 1974); Jonathan Bennett, *Events and Their Names* (Indianapolis, Ind.: Hackett Pub. Co., 1988); Davidson, *supra* n. 79.

American criminal law. The most typical version of a two-relations theory goes something like this. The only truly scientific (or 'factual') aspect of causation is captured by the cause-in-fact requirement. This requirement may itself be analysed in various ways (see below), but in any case, this requirement by itself is far too promiscuous (in what it allows to count as a cause) for exclusive use in assessing responsibility. Accordingly, a second requirement must be added that is explicitly non-causal in any useful sense of that word. Such second, non-causal requirement may be the result of a moral calculation that it is unfair to punish people for harms they could not foresee; such requirement thus has the content that 'the harm must have been foreseeable'.[83] Or such requirement may take the form of a further mental state requirement: the harm (in fact) caused must have been 'within the risk' that made the actor's act negligent or reckless to do, or it must have been an instance of the type of harm he intended, in order to be a harm proximately caused by the act.[84] Or such requirement may take the form of an arbitrary space/time remoteness rule; for example: 'any victim who dies more than a year and a day from the date of the infliction of wounds did not die of those wounds',[85] or, 'railroads' failure to use adequate spark arrestors proximately cause houses to be destroyed only if the house in question is the one first ignited by the sparks, not if it is a house ignited by the burning of some other house that was itself ignited by sparks from the railroad'.[86] Or such requirement may take the form of *ad hoc* policy balances rendered on each occasion of responsibility assessment, as in: 'if, all things considered, it would be better that the defendant be held responsible for the harm he has in fact caused, then he has legally caused it'.[87]

[83] The familiar foreseeability criterion of proximate causation. For discussion of this criterion, ch. 8.

[84] The 'harm within the risk' analysis of Leon Green in torts. Leon Green, *Rationale of Proximate Cause* (Kansas City, Mo.: Vernon Law Book Co., 1927), 40–1. Adopted by the Model Penal Code, §2.03.

[85] The common law rule for homicide. See LaFave and Scott, *Criminal Law* (St Paul: West, 2nd edn., 1986), at 611.

[86] *Ryan* v. *New York Central*, 35 NY 210 (1866).

[87] The still influential views of Harry Edgerton. 'Legal Cause', *University of Pennsylvania Law Review*, Vol. 72 (1924), 211–22; see also Shavell, 'An Analysis of Causation and the Scope of Liability in the Law of Torts', *Journal of Legal Studies*, Vol. 9 (1980), 463–516; Calabresi, 'Concerning Cause and the Law of Torts', *University of Chicago Law Review*, Vol. 43 (1975), 69–108 (both relying explicitly on Edgerton's approach to proximate causation).

The last two of these familiar proposals for the tort and criminal law requirements of proximate or legal cause are poor candidates as theories of moral responsibility, for they rely on factors extraneous to responsibility to *place* legal liability on an agent who is without moral responsibility. In any case, none of these four proposals even attempt to capture anything about the causal relation. They are in effect proposals to add some third element to the conditions of wrongdoing (in addition to voluntariness and causation).

Such proposals have the force they admittedly possess only because of the non-discriminating view of cause in fact that they presuppose. The dominant theory of cause in fact is some kind of counterfactual theory: either that an act must be a *necessary* condition to the occurrence of a harm in order to be its cause,[88] or that the act be a *sufficient* condition,[89] or that the act be an insufficient but necessary condition of a set of conditions that is itself unnecessary but sufficient for the harm to occur.[90] The less dominant, sceptical theory is David Hume's: a particular act is said to cause a particular harm whenever there is a regular concurrence of events of these types. (Such a view is sceptical because it denies that there is such a thing as a causal relation between singular events; regular concurrence of types of events thus does not evidence some deeper relation, it constitutes it.)

Under either of these views of the causal relation, quite remote and unexpected events will be the consequences of some agent's action. Since morally as well as legally this seems counterintuitive, a theory of responsibility needs some limits beyond those provided by these theories of causation. The above four proposals for the meaning of 'proximate' causation are one way of describing such limits, although they require admitting some third, non-causal element into the theory of wrongdoing.

An alternative route to cabining wrongdoing to acceptable limits is to discover some different theory of the causal relation that is more discriminating than the counterfactual or regularity of concurrence views. Such more discriminating theories I call one-

---

[88] The law's familiar *sine qua non* test.

[89] See Judith Thomson, 'Causality and Rights: Some Preliminaries', *Chicago-Kent Law Review*, Vol. 63 (1987), 471–96, at 482–3, for examination of this view.

[90] The late J. L. Mackie's 'INUS' analysis of causation. Mackie, 'Causation and Conditionals', *American Philosophical Quarterly*, Vol. 2 (1965), 245–64, reprinted in E. Sosa, ed., *Causation and Conditionals* (Oxford: Oxford University Press, 1975).

relation theories because they do not divide the causation requirement into two different requirements. At least four such theories
are discernible in the philosophical/legal literature on causation.
One such view adopts some counterfactual theory of the causal
relation but changes the things that can be causes. That is, the usual
counterfactual theory asks whether some particular harm would
have occurred without the occurrence of some particular action.
The modified counterfactual theory asks whether this harm would
have occurred if the action in question had not possessed that
attribute that made it culpable to do. Suppose someone ('D')
intends to poison another ('V') and places unlabelled rat poison in
V's kitchen for the purpose.[91] The rat poison is not ingested by V,
but instead, it explodes from the heat of the stove, killing V. The
modified counterfactural theory would not ask, 'but for the act of
D in placing the poison in V's kitchen, would V have died?' Rather,
the modified theory would ask, 'but for the lack of labelling of the
rat poison placed in V's kitchen by D, would V have died?' This
second question may well be answered 'no', although the answer to
the first question is 'yes', making for a more discriminating notion
of causation.

A second more discriminating theory of causation is the elegant
theory explored by Herbert Hart and Tony Honoré.[92] Hart and
Honoré initially distinguish 'explanatory contexts' from 'attributive
contexts' as they examine causation, but ultimately seek a theory of
causation adequate to both contexts. They thus explicitly set aside
any attempt to construct a notion of causation limited in its applicability to situations where responsibility is being assessed. Theirs is
a theory of causation, not a theory of some non-causal element of
responsibility that must be added to causation. The Hart and
Honoré thesis is that in both explanatory and attributive contexts
we use the very same criteria to select, out of that large set of

[91] The example is that of Robert Keeton, *Legal Cause in the Law of Torts*
(Columbus: Ohio State University Press, 1963), 3. Keeton's view is expanded with
considerable sophistication by Wright, 'Causation in Tort Law', *California Law
Review*, Vol. 73 (1985), 1735–828; Wright, 'Causation, Responsibility, Risk,
Probability, Naked Statistics, and Proof: Pruning the Bramble Bush by Clarifying
the Concepts', *Iowa Law Review*, Vol. 73 (1988), 1001–77. Arguably John Mackie
came to share the view that properties of actions (not actions themselves) can be
causes. See his masterful, *The Cement of the Universe*, *supra* n. 82.

[92] H. L. A. Hart and A. M. Honoré, *Causation in the Law* (Oxford: Clarendon
Press, 1959) (2nd edn., 1985).

causally relevant conditions for any harm, those that were its causes. Abnormal natural events amounting to a coincidence, and free, informed, voluntary human actions are the kinds of conditions that are causes in both contexts. Not only are these two sorts of events selected as the causes out of a set of equally necessary conditions where (explanatory) historical narratives are constructed; these are also the kinds of events that break causal chains if they intervene between someone's action and some harm that would not have occurred but for that action.

A third view drops any connection to the counterfactual view of the causal relation, and sees causation paradigmatically as physical force. One might call this the Lockean view of causation, because Locke thought of causation as a power that inhered in objects.[93] The causal theories of Joseph Beale[94] and Richard Epstein[95] attempt to make more precise this physical force vision of causation through more particular paradigms of hitting, scaring, and compelling, or those conditions created by such hittings, scarings and compellings that store the force originated by these acts. Such force-based views of causation promise a much more discriminating notion of causation because of the spatial/temporal contiguity implicit in the idea of forces being unleashed and then spent.

A fourth view is probably also Lockean in its metaphysics about what causation at bottom is. But what is distinctive about this view is not its metaphysics but its scalar thesis: causation is a more-or-less affair, a scalar phenomenon; it is not a two-valued, yes/no affair.[96] A big fire is more of a cause of a house being destroyed than a little fire, even if both joined to form one fire before the house in question was burned. Such a view promises a more discriminating notion of causation because one holding this view might think that only big causes (or 'substantial factors') count when responsibility is being assessed. When a defendant's act is a big cause of some harm, defendant is responsible for that harm, but not otherwise.

[93] For a modern explication, see Richard Taylor, *Action and Purpose*, *supra* n. 72.

[94] Beale, 'Recovery for Consequences of an Act', *Harvard Law Review*, Vol. 9 (1895), 80–9; Beale, 'The Proximate Consequences of an Act', *Harvard Law Review*, Vol. 33 (1920), 633–66.

[95] Epstein, *supra* n. 5.

[96] The view of Jeremiah Smith, 'Legal Cause in Actions of Tort', *Harvard Law Review*, Vol. 25 (1911), 103–28, 223–52, 253–69, 303–21.

An active theory of responsibility of the type adopted by Anglo-American criminal law must defend some more discriminating notion of causation to be at all plausible. Since there are serious problems with each of these four views,[97] then either some other more discriminating theory of causation must be found or some non-causal, third element must be added to the theory of wrongdoing.

b. *Culpability*

The second property constituting the property of responsibility is culpability. Culpability itself consists of two properties: intentionality, and absence of excuse. I shall consider each in turn.

i. *Intention and Intentional Action*

Any theory of intention should ask and answer two questions. One concerns the nature of intentions—what sort of a thing are they, what is their essence? The other question asks the individuation question: when do we have an intention, as opposed to several intentions? It clarifies these questions considerably if we introduce a preliminary distinction before we taxonomize possible answers.

The distinction is between what Elizabeth Anscombe once called 'intention-with-which' and 'intentional action'.[98] The intention with which an action is done is the further intention with which it is done. I may intentionally hit someone in the face, but that fact does not answer the question of further intention: was the intention with which I hit that person to put out his eye or not? The intention involved in my intentionally hitting, by contrast, is not 'further' in the sense that it is enough that I intend the act I did (hitting) without intending some further consequence to be thereby brought about.

Anglo-American criminal law haltingly recognizes this distinction between those two kinds of intention in its doctrinal distinction between 'specific' versus 'general' intent. A specific intent crime is one requiring not only that one intend to do the prohibited act (for example, battery), but also requires that one do the act with some further intention (for example, to disfigure another by putting out his eye). A general intent crime, by contrast, has only the first *mens rea* requirement but not the second.[99]

[97] See *infra* ch. 7.   [98] Anscombe, *supra* n. 71.

[99] As every Anglo-American criminal law scholar knows, the specific versus general intent distinction is a mess. This is because a myriad of different legal consequences are made to turn on the distinction, including:

1. Specific intent crimes require purpose whereas general intent crimes allow either purpose or knowledge to suffice;   *cont./*

A theory of responsibility of the kind we are examining requires a theory of both intentional action and further intention. This is because such a theory of responsibility incorporates both the orthodox view of responsibility and the subjective view, and the most plausible versions of each view require intentional action, and further intention, respectively.

Consider intentional action first. The first issue to be addressed by any theory seeking its nature is to decide between two competing accounts. One, the 'purpose' account, holds that an action is intentional only when that action is among the actor's purposes (motives, reasons, further intentions) for acting. The other, the 'foresight' account, holds that an action is intentional whenever that action was among the actor's purposes *or* whenever an action of that type was foreseen by the actor to occur if he did what he wanted to do.[100] Suppose one places a bomb in an airplane after having insured the plane. One's reason to blow up the plane is to collect the insurance proceeds. Regrettably, the passengers will die when the plane is blown up in mid-air, and one knows this. When the passengers do die in this way, is their killing an *intentional* killing? The purpose account answers 'no', the foresight account answers 'yes'.

This choice between the purpose versus the foresight account of the nature of intentional action is greatly affected by the answer one gives to the other question about intentions, namely, how one

2. A presumption of intention follows from the fact that an accused did the prohibited action for general intent crimes, not for specific intent crimes;
3. Unreasonable mistake of fact negatives specific intent but not general intent;
4. Mistake of law negatives specific intent but not general intent;
5. Voluntary intoxication is capable of negating specific intent but not general intent;
6. Mental disease not amounting to legal insanity is capable of negating specific intent but not general intent.

There is no single conception of the distinction that can make sense of all these legal consequences. The first two, however, can be made sense of by the conception that specific intent is further intention, and general intent is intentional action. I take this to be the dominant conception of the distinction, as do some other commentators. See, e.g., W. LaFave and Scott, *Criminal Law* (St Paul: West Publishing Co., 2nd edn., 1986), 224.

[100] The foresight account is defended by H. L. A. Hart in 'Intention and Punishment', in *Punishment and Responsibility, supra* n. 41. The purpose account is defended in A. Kenny, 'Intention and Purpose', *Journal of Philosophy*, Vol. 63 (1966), 642–51. A more complete listing of the debaters here may be found in ch. 11; see also Moore, *Law and Psychiatry, supra* n. 44, at 78–9.

individuates them.[101] Suppose (as I argue in chapter 11) we individuate intentions not only by the person who holds them and the time at which they are held but also by their *objects*. Suppose further that one take the objects of intentions to be real-world events like human actions. Then if the act of blowing up the plane was identical to the act of killing the passengers, as I argue in chapter 6 that it is, to have intentionally done the first would be to have intentionally done the second; in such a case there could be no difference in result between the purpose and knowledge accounts, since both hold the bomber to be an intentional killer.

We thus need a theory of individuation of intention by their objects. This theory, in turn, will be heavily coloured by the ontological question of what we take intentional objects to be. As I explore in chapter 11,[102] there are three leading possibilities: those objects are real-world events, and are individuated accordingly by whatever theory of individuation one has for events; those objects are uninterpreted sentences, and are individuated syntactically in the way in which we individuate uninterpreted strings of symbols; those objects are propositions, and are individuated in whatever way we individuate propositions. What one takes objects of intentions to be determines how one individuates intentions, and this in turn determines what line, if any, can be drawn between the purpose and foresight accounts of intentional action.

Even when a theory of intentional action has answered the purpose versus foresight question, and the individuation (by intentional objects) question, deeper questions about the nature of intentional action remain. Baldly put, what is named by 'intentional' in the phrases, 'intentional killing', 'intentional wounding', etc.? One answer is the interpretivist answer we mentioned before in connection with acts: 'intentional' names nothing at all. Observers choose to characterize actions as intentional or unintentional, on this view, but there is no fact of the matter determining which they really are. Another answer treats 'intentional' as the name of a kind of mental state that causes actions. Such a view may collapse the intentional into the intended (the purposive account) or it may collapse the intentional into the foreseen (the knowledge account). In either case, the ultimate nature of intentional action will be given by the nature of purposes or of beliefs, about which

---

[101] This is the main point of the discussion in ch. 11.   [102] Id.

we mentioned three metaphysical theories (dualist, physicalist, functionalist). A third view regards 'intentional' as the name of a property some actions possess. Unlike the second view, this view does not treat the adjective, 'intentional', as if it were a noun ('intention') naming a mental state. Rather, this view treats 'intentional' like most adjectives, as the name of a property.[103] To be satisfied that 'intentional' names something and thus can do the work demanded of it by the orthodox view of responsibility, one has to figure out which of these accounts most accurately describes the intentional.

The theorist of further intention will confront much the same questions as those just canvassed by the theorist of intentional action. Interestingly, however, although the questions may be the same, many people's answers to them are different. Take the initial question, does the purpose or the foresight account more accurately describe a further intention? Suppose my earlier described greedy aeroplane-bomber did not succeed in blowing up the plane, although he did place the bomb with the intention that it blow up the plane mid-air. Now the question is not, did he intentionally kill the passengers? Rather, the question is, was the intention with which he placed the bomb, to kill the passengers? Common intuition, followed largely by Anglo-American criminal law, is that the answer to the second question is 'no' even though the answer to the first question would be 'yes' had the bomb exploded. This is to adopt the foresight account of intentional action but the purpose account of further intention.

As with intentional action, an answer to the question of individ-

---

[103] There are problems for this view stemming from the fact that actions may seemingly be intentional under some descriptions but not others. On Donald Davidson's (*Action and Events*, *supra* n. 79) highly plausible course-grained theory of complex action individuation, and on Leibniz's Law that a thing has all the same properties no matter how it is described, then 'intentional' cannot name a property of actions if it is to remain true that 'an action may be intentional under one description but not another'. I argue in ch. 6 that Davidson is right about complex act individuation—a particular hand moving *is* a pumping *is* a poisoning—these are one and the same particular acts. Leibniz of course was right about the indiscernibility of identicals—any property predicable of a thing under one description is predicable of it under any other description, for the same thing has all the same properties. And Davidson is therefore also correct in seeing that an individual act (token) cannot be intentional under one description, not intentional under another. Therefore, if we want to continue in our common practice of saying that an act of shooting may be intentional even though the killing that *was* the shooting was not, we must conclude with Davidson that 'intentional' cannot name a property.

uation is required if we are to make meaningful a choice between purpose versus foresight accounts of further intention. The same three theories of individuation are also here possible, depending on what kind of thing one takes the objects of further intentions to be (real world events, syntactic sentences, propositions).

With regard to the question of ultimate nature, three possibilities exist that parallel the possibilities for actions: intentions might be no things at all, but only the products of 'interpretive stances' taken by observers; intentions might be goals or purposes in some non-causal sense of those words; or intentions may be states that cause the behaviour for which they are further intentions. With regard to this last possibility, there are three variations that parallel those for simple intention (or willing): the intentions with which we act may be irreducibly phenomenological states (dualism), type-identical to brain states (physicalism), or functionally specified brain states of disparate physical realization (functionalism).

ii. *Excuse*
In addition to needing a theory of intention and intentional action a theory of culpability needs a theory of excuse. On the middle of the road theory of excuses adopted by Anglo-American criminal law, one more particularly needs a theory of excuses that explains why we are excused sometimes but not others. Even if we intentionally cause bad states of affairs to be brought about through our voluntary actions, sometimes we are not morally responsible for that harm anyway; we are 'excused'.

Since Aristotle it is traditional to regard the true excuses as being of two kinds, cognitive and volitional. The cognitive excuses are the mistake excuses: one falsely believed that some norm did not exist, or was not applicable, or that some aspect of one's action was not present or would not occur. The volitional excuses are the compulsion excuses: one could not resist the fear aroused by a human or natural threat, or one could not resist the emotions or cravings aroused by internal factors within one's self.

A theory of excuse of course need not be committed to these being the only excuses there are, nor to each of them being excuses. Whether conditions of mistake or compulsion excuse depends on the content of the theory. If we put aside utilitarian theories (because irrelevant to culpability),[104] there are three main competitors. One I

---

[104] I of course here assume that utilitarians cannot account for culpability. For

call the causal theory of excuse.[105] On this view, to be (strongly) caused to act is to be excused for the consequences of that action. A human threat, for example, excuses on this view only insofar as it operates as a (strong) cause of human behaviour.

A second theory is the character theory of excuse.[106] This theory presupposes an answer to the question, 'what are the proper objects of responsibility?', different than the answer I earlier gave. This theory of excuse assumes that we are ultimately responsible for our characters, not our actions. Our seeming ascription of responsibility for actions is misleading, because our acts are proxies for the bad characters such acts express. The excuses, on this view, serve a crucial filtering function: they sift out those of our actions not expressive of bad character and relieve us from responsibility for them. Character is thus ultimately the object of our responsibility since only actions expressive of such bad character are unexcused.

The third possibility is what I call the choice theory of excuse.[107] According to this theory, we are excused only when our capacities or our opportunities to choose to avoid evil are unduly diminished. A human threat, for example, sometimes so unhinges us that it may plausibly be supposed that our capacity to act contrary to the threat is diminished. More typically, a threat does not so unhinge us that we lack capacity; rather, if the consequences of not complying with the threat are serious, we lack the opportunity to avoid doing evil that most others have most of the time. On this theory, we care about diminished capacities and opportunities because choice (act and intent) can be the touchstone of culpability only when it is free and informed in this sense.

3. The Subject of Responsibility: The Nature of Persons Any theory of responsibility must have a theory of who or what are proper subjects of responsibility. To whom are moral norms addressed? I earlier mentioned a large range of possible subjects of responsibility, but to keep the discussion focused on the theory of responsibility presupposed by Anglo-American criminal law I shall

contrary views, see Brandt, 'A Utilitarian Theory of Excuses', *Philosophical Review*, Vol. 78 (1969), 337–61; Brandt, 'A Motivational Theory of Excuses in the Criminal Law', in R. Pennock and J. Chapman, eds., *Nomos xxvii: Criminal Justice* (New York: New York University Press, 1985).

[105] This theory is examined in detail in ch. 12.
[106] This theory is examined in detail in ch. 13.
[107] Examined in detail in ch. 13.

restrict my examination to individual persons as the subjects of responsibility. The theory then needed by the theory of responsibility is a theory of the nature of persons.

The most obvious doctrinal home of a theory of personhood in Anglo-American criminal law is in the defences of insanity and infancy. For these defences, unlike the defences reflecting the moral excuses, enquire directly into the *general* capacities of persons. They do not ask whether, at the particular time the defendant acted, there was a mistaken belief or a threat that was distorting judgement; they ask the more general question about whether the accused is enough of a person to be held responsible generally (including for this particular action).

About the infancy defence this classification is relatively uncontroversial. For centuries Anglo-American criminal law has used general capacity tests to separate the non-responsible infant from the responsible adult.[108] So classifying insanity is much more controversial. Ever since the M'Naghten decision in 1843,[109] Anglo-American criminal lawyers have attempted to force-fit insanity either into the true excuse category, or into the category of conditions that merely negate voluntary action or intention but do not operate as a true excuse. Those attempting the first of these two moves in the middle nineteenth century fastened onto the delusional character of some psychoses, making insanity a kind of mistake excuse; later attempts were made to liken insanity to a kind of compulsion excuse, the compulsion operating through either physical mechanisms (the nineteenth-century view) or the 'psychic mechanisms' posited to exist by twentieth-century dynamic psychiatry.[110] Criminal lawyers attempting the second of the two moves mentioned have typically been abolitionists about the insanity defence: for why would one use a separate defence for insanity if insanity is just one way of disproving intent or voluntariness?

Either of these force-fittings of insanity is disastrous for understanding the moral basis of the insanity defence. Insanity, like infancy, is part of the criminal law's recognition that not every member of the human species is a proper subject of responsibility

---

[108] This was the origin of the right and wrong test, as a test of general capacity for moral agency. See Platt and Diamond, 'The Origin of the Right and Wrong Test', *California Law Review*, Vol. 54 (1966), 1227–260.

[109] *R.* v. *M'Naghten*, 10 Clark and F200, 8 ENG REP 718 (1843).

[110] I describe this force-fitting in more detail in Moore, *Law and Psychiatry*, *supra* n. 44, at 218–32.

(i.e., a person). When properly located, the insanity defence is a theorist's royal road into the criminal law's presuppositions of what persons must be like.

If we do properly locate insanity *vis-à-vis* the other aspects of responsibility, we can then ask, what is the attribute the insane lack that persons possess? A most plausible answer is that the insane, like the very young, lack that general capacity we call rationality. They lack the ability to form and act on valid practical syllogisms that proceed from intelligible desires and from rational beliefs and which do not self-defeatingly conflict with other desires and beliefs held by the agent.

There are stronger senses of 'rationality', such as the transitively-ordered-preferences sense favoured by economists. There are also degrees of rationality, rationality being a scalar phenomenon. One question a theory of responsibility must address is the kind and degree of rationality a human being must possess in order to be a fit subject of responsibility.[111]

The insanity and infancy defences are the most accessible vantage points from which to see one attribute human beings must possess to be persons, namely, rationality. Yet such an attribute is much more fundamental to our responsibility assessments than merely providing the basis for one or two defences. If human beings were not rational in the sense I just described, we could not see them as acting for *intentions*. Intentions are mental states that can only be fully possessed by rational creatures—what Dan Dennett aptly calls 'intentional systems'.[112] Although infants, the insane, and animals can clearly have something like intentions on which they act, only adult, sane human beings are sufficiently possessed of rationality to fully act for reasons, the essence of intentionality. (This is the grain of truth to the otherwise wrong-headed view of the abolitionists that an insanity defence is unnecessary because the insane lack intentions.)

Once one sees that rationality is a presupposition of intentionality, it is tempting to think that it is also a presupposition of another element of responsibility, action. And it may well be true that only creatures who can act for reasons (intentions-with-which) can act

---

[111] *Law and Psychiatry, supra* n. 44, at 101–8.
[112] Dennett, 'Intentional Systems', in his *Brainstorms* (Putney, Vt: Bradford Books, 1978); see also Daniel Dennett, *The Intentional Stance* (Cambridge, Mass.: MIT Press, 1987).

at all. But whether possession of rationality is or is not required for a creature to be able to perform an action, it is not the only presupposition. Also needed is the attribute I have elsewhere called autonomy.[113] In addition to the capacity to form valid practical syllogisms consisting of beliefs and intentions-with-which, human beings must be able to initiate movement through choice (volition, will, simple intention) if they are to perform an action. Some form of this basic personal capacity must be added to rationality before there is a person eligible for responsibility, and a theory of responsibility must have a theory about the nature and extent of autonomy necessary for personhood.

There are of course other candidates for attributes persons must possess in order to be persons, besides rationality and autonomy. One such candidate is the attribute of emotionality—the capacity to feel those emotions on which most of us rely when we form moral judgements. To be person—the proper subject of responsibility—must one have the capacity to be outraged at injustice, compassionate for those less fortunate, resentful of transgressions, guilty at one's own moral mistakes, etc.? A theory of personhood has to take some position on this thorny question too.

Interestingly, even when we have answered questions like these about the essential *nature* of personhood, we will not fully have answered the question of *individuation*. What determines the boundaries that divide one person from another (or from something other than a person)? Sometimes this is a question of the 'size' of the person (or self) who is responsible: does my personal self include those emotions I experience as ego-alien? Those desires that are objectively 'out of character' for me, no matter how I experience them? Those intentions that are repressed from conscious experience of any kind? A theory of personhood must answer questions like these, for the answer it gives determines whether such states may operate as excuses or not. (For example, can I be compelled by one of 'my own' obsessive desires?)[114] Sometimes the problem of individuation presents itself as a 'how many' problem. Can there be several persons co-present in the body of a single human being? For example, a nervous bank clerk ('ego') presiding over the dispute between a sex-crazed monkey ('id') and a reproachful maiden aunt ('superego')? Or a personality that has its

---

[113] Moore, *Law and Psychiatry*, *supra* n. 44, at 108–10.
[114] On the 'size of person' question, see ch. 13 *infra*.

own character structure, memory, sense of itself, and another equally well-formed personality but with different character structure, memories, and sense of itself? In this case what may be excluded as beyond self-boundaries may itself be a person, only a different one. A theory of personhood must also have an answer to questions like these, for such answers make a great deal of difference to who is responsible (for example, in self-deception, is the (whole) human being responsible for the harm such self-deception can cause, given that he/she contains both an active deceiver and a passive deceived?)[115]

The theory about the essential attributes and individuation conditions of persons occupies the most abstract and most basic position within an overall theory of responsibility. The attributes of rationality and autonomy are not simply further elements of responsibility, to be added to the conditions of wrongdoing (voluntariness and causation) and of culpability (intentionality and excuse). Rationality and autonomy, together with some theory of the size of persons, are presuppositions needed to make sense of the requirements of these elements of responsibility. This hierarchical relationship is what makes it such a mistake to regard the few legal doctrines that approach these presuppositions directly—the defences of insanity and infancy—as just further instances of one of the elements of responsibility, the excuses.

D. The Nature of a Theory of the Special Part of the Criminal Law

1. Introduction: The Doctrines and Theories of the Special Part and their Audiences   Doctrinally, the special part of the criminal law consists of those legal standards that prohibit certain behaviour. One may think of it as the criminal law's Ten Commandments, with a bit of supplementation and elaboration. Killing is wrong, mayhem is wrong, etc., are the kinds of doctrines making up Anglo-American criminal law's special part.

By both of the criteria earlier mentioned for assigning doctrines to one part of the criminal law or another, the doctrines defining justificatory defences belong to the special part. The first criterion was whether a doctrine was applicable to all crimes. On this criterion, the doctrines of self-defence, defence of others, defence of

---

[115] See Moore, *Law and Psychiatry, supra* n. 44, chs. 3, 11.

property, and law enforcement privilege are not part of the general part because these are defences only to crimes of violence. The one justificatory defence of which this is not true is the general balance-of-evils defence,[116] for this is a defence applicable to all crimes. Nonetheless, if we advert to the second and preferred way of drawing the general/special parts distinction, the balance-of-evils defence too is part of the special part; for this defence too merely spells out what types of action are wrong in further detail than that given by the norms of prima facie obligation such as, 'Don't kill'.

The reason that this relatively obvious point is so often missed by criminal law theorists is because there are *excuses* connected to the justificatory defences. If you mistakenly believe that another is trying to kill you and you use deadly force in self-defence, you might in ordinary idiom be said to be 'justified' in what you did. But what you did was in fact wrong—it was a non-necessary killing—no matter how reasonable *you* may have been in believing and acting as you did. Your mistake is wholly irrelevant to the wrongness of your action, relevant as it may be to your culpability for doing that wrongful action.[117]

The other reason for the common miscategorization of the justificatory defences lies in the problem referred to as the 'problem of justificatory intent'.[118] Suppose D is a thoroughly malicious person who seeks out and kills V for the pure pleasure of it. Is D guilty of murder if, unbeknownst to him, V was about to kill D if D had not then and there killed V? It is common to suppose that the answer to this question is 'yes'. If this is so, then it is easy to think that since justifications involve a subjective element, intent, and since this element is part of culpability, then justification must be a culpability requirement.

The mistake in this chain of inferences lies in its premise, namely, that D is guilty of murder. D has done no wrong in killing the murderous V, although he tried to. D is analogous to the person who shoots at another, intending to kill him, but misses. In both cases, what we should hold the individuals responsible for is their trying to do a wrongful killing. On the subjective view of culpability, both

---

[116] In American law, most authoritatively expressed in Model Penal Code §3.02.

[117] Compare Greenawalt, 'The Perplexing Borders of Justification and Excuse', *Columbia Law Review*, Vol. 84 (1984), 1897–927.

[118] See, e.g., George Fletcher, *Rethinking Criminal Law* (Boston: Little, Brown, 1978), 557.

are seriously culpable—but not for a wrongful act that neither in fact did.

If all of this is seen clearly, then there should be no temptation to allocate justifications to culpability and thus to the general part. All we need see is the separability of the true question of justification—when are killings not wrongful—from the question of when killers are culpable in their killings, in order to avoid lumping the justifications with the excuses and thus to culpability, responsibility, and the general part.

The doctrines of justification are not only an unproblematic part of the special part, they form the royal road to understanding the core of a theory of the special part, namely, the theory of what types of action are wrongful. For if we understand the nature of justification, we will understand the nature of the moral norms that define wrongful action. This is because all of the hard issues about the content of moral norms like, 'don't kill' are reached only when the question of justification is raised, that is, only when some competing value is in the neighbourhood to make a killing seem much less obviously wrong, if it is wrong at all. It is for this reason that in this book the topic of wrongful action is approached only via the context of understanding the general justification defence of balance of evils.[119]

Aside from the issue of justification the doctrines of the special part have been the poor relation in criminal law theory. This is because most criminal law theory has been done from the vantage point of particular jurisprudence in a legal system already rich with numerous criminal prohibitions. What deeply descriptive theory can there be of the hodgepodge of acts prohibited in Anglo-American legal systems, except a trivial description that clumps prohibited acts into categories like, 'crimes against the person', 'crimes to property', 'crimes against the state', etc.? Moreover if the audience of deeply descriptive theories is principally judges seeking to find answers to hard cases not decidable on the basis of the existing rules, of what use is a descriptive theory of substantive prohibitions when only the legislature has the power to issue new prohibitions? A court is barred (by the doctrine that there are no longer common law crimes) from using such a theory to yield new prohibitions with which to decide novel cases.

---

[119] See ch. 17 *infra*.

If there is to be anything very interesting or very useful called a theory of the special part, it must be something other than a deep description of existing prohibitions in a particular legal system, which description is targeted at the judges of that system as its audience. An interesting and useful theory of the special part must be normative, not descriptive, urging what the law ought to be, not what it is; such a theory should be targeted, in the first instance, at least,[120] at legislators, not judges, telling legislators what sorts of things may legitimately be prohibited by them.

Even with these alterations a theory of the special part would not be interesting or useful if it did no more than specify ten or so prohibitions. Needed is something much more general: what are the principles that ought to guide the conscientious legislator in framing criminal prohibitions? Is the generally perceived immorality of an action—or its actual immorality—sufficient reason to prohibit it? Or may the legislator prohibit actions because they would be harmful to the actor's best interests, even though the actor may not think so? Or must there be harm to others from an action before the criminal law may prohibit that action? These are the sorts of questions that must be asked by a theory of the special part. We may see the answers to them as competing answers to one general question, what I shall call the question of proper legislative motivation: at what may (must) a legislature aim in framing criminal prohibitions?

The question of proper legislative motivation is only the first question to be asked by a theory of the special part. If, as I shall argue shortly, the exclusively retributive function of the criminal law demands that moral wrongs be legally prohibited, then the only legitimate legislative motivation is one seeking to prohibit morally wrongful action because it is morally wrongful. The next question *this* theory of legislation forces onto a theorist of the special part is a question of substantive moral theory: what makes an action wrongful? Is it its intrinsically wrongful nature, or the bad consequences to which it leads, or some combination of the two? This second question will force a third onto the theorist of the special

---

[120] The theory of the special part may also be of interest to judges when they either interpret or review the constitutionality of criminal legislation. This does not alter the point of the text that the primary audience of a theory of the special part are those legislators in our legal system who have the responsibility of deciding what should be criminally prohibited.

part: are there any limits to the use of the criminal law that should lead us to eschew prohibiting certain conduct even if it is morally wrongful? A number of different sorts of limits may suggest themselves: limits of fair notice mandated by the harshness of criminal sanctions; limits of liberty, based on the possibility that sometimes the goodness of allowing free choice will outweigh the badness of unpunished wrongful action; limits of convenience, based on the insight that allowing certain minor wrongs to go unpunished is a lesser evil than the costs necessarily attendant upon punishing such wrongs; and limits of epistemic modesty, given how fallible may be any legislator's grasp of moral truths about which actions are or are not morally wrongful.

The theory of proper legislative motivation, the theory of wrongful action, and the theory of the limits of criminal legislation, together make up the theory of the special part. I shall examine each of them in turn.

2. The Nature of a Theory of Proper Legislative Motivation A theory of proper legislative motivation is a theory about what states of affairs legislators may legitimately aim to achieve by their legislation. It is not a theory of how courts might justify legislation by its effects. It is thus no answer to liberal theories of legislation like Mill's to point out that 'no action is without its effect on others', for even if true such objection is irrelevant to Mill's point: that it is always illegitimate for legislators to *aim* at preventing anything other than harm to someone other than the actor whose behaviour is being regulated.

Since Mill, it is common to taxonomize possible theories of proper legislative aim around four kinds of aims.[121] A legislator might aim: (1) to prevent physical or economic harms to someone other than the actor; (2) to prevent psychic harms (or harms of moral offence) to someone other than the actor; (3) to prevent any kind of harm befalling the person whose behaviour is the subject of the prohibition; or (4) to prevent behaviour that harms no one but that is nonetheless morally wrong (such as breaking a secret promise to a dead friend).

---

[121] See, e.g., what might be called the 'Tucson Quartet': Joel Feinberg's four books, *Harm to Others, Offense to Others, Harm to Self, Harmless Wrongdoing* (Oxford: Oxford University Press, 1984, 1985, 1986, 1988).

A liberal theory of criminal legislation, such as Mill's, holds that only the first is a proper legislative aim. A majoritarian theory, such as J. F. Stephen's[122] or Lord Patrick Devlin's,[123] allows that (1) or (2) is proper. A paternalist theory will think that (3) is proper, probably in conjunction with one of the other aims.[124] The legal moralist theorist will think that (4) is proper together with whatever of (1), (2), and (3) that morality speaks to prohibit.

The problem with this way of distinguishing theories of legislation is that it hides the central issue facing any legislator: is it obligatory (or at least permissible) to aim at the prohibition of moral wrongdoing in one's criminal legislation, or should one restrain oneself in one way or another? The variables of types and sufferers of harm do not isolate this crucial moral issue because some types of harm-infliction are morally wrong and others may not be.

A better taxonomy is between what I below call 'exclusionary' versus non-exclusionary theories of legislative aim.[125] An exclusionary theory is a theory of restraint. It urges legislators to refrain from enacting their views of immorality into criminal prohibitions. Such restraint may be urged in the name of majoritarianism: popular morality should be reflected in the content of criminal legislation, on this view, not the legislator's best theory of the true morality.[126] Or such restraint may be urged in the name of ideal-excluding liberalism: no ideal of the good life should be sought to be promoted by criminal legislation.[127] Or such restraint might be urged in the name of a neutrality-based liberalism: although competing visions of the good life cannot help but motivate criminal legislation, care should be taken so that no vision is promoted more than another.[128]

In contrast to all such exclusionary theories is the non-exclusionary (or 'perfectionist') theory of legal moralism. On this

[122] J. F. Stephen, *Liberty, Equality, Fraternity* (London: 2nd edn. 1874).

[123] Patrick Devlin, *The Enforcement of Morality* (Oxford: Oxford University Press, 1965).

[124] Gerald Dworkin, 'Paternalism', in R. Wasserstrom, ed., *Morality and The Law* (Belmont, Cal.: Wadsworth, 1971).

[125] See ch. 16 *infra*.

[126] Sandel and Dworkin both consider majoritarian theories briefly in 'Moral Argument and Liberal Toleration', *California Law Review*, Vol. 77 (1989) 521–38; 'Liberal Community', *California Law Review*, Vol. 77 (1989), 479–504.

[127] See Joseph Raz, *The Morality of Freedom*, (Oxford: Oxford University Press, 1986), ch. 6, for a discussion of ideal-excluding liberalism.

[128] Id, at ch. 5.

theory, because an action is morally wrong is always a legitimate reason to prohibit it with criminal legislation. Put another way, a legislator should never restrain himself/herself from following his/her own best theories of what is morally wrong just because they are his/her own theories or just because they are theories of what it is morally wrong to do. Other goods may outweigh the good that is achieved by prohibiting behaviour that is immoral; but that the behaviour is immoral is always a valid reason counting in favour of prohibiting it.

My own theory is that the non-exclusionary view of legal moralism is the only correct theory of proper legislative aim. This theory follows from the point that criminal law is a functional kind whose function is to achieve justice in retribution. Retributive justice is not promoted by punishing those who have voluntarily, intentionally, and without excuse caused a legally prohibited state of affairs to obtain, *unless* that legally prohibited state of affairs is also a moral wrong. What is there to pay for if one has done no moral wrong? What is one morally responsible *for* if one has done no such wrong?[129]

These considerations become clearer perhaps if we remind ourselves what retributivism is. Retributivism is not the doctrine that it is unfair to punish those who could not help but violate the criminal law (because they did not act, they did not know what action they were doing, they were compelled or mistaken). A mixed theorist about punishment might well believe this and believe therefore that the conditions of responsibility make sense even when attached to criminal prohibitions of any content whatever.[130] A retributivist cares about the conditions of responsibility for an additional reason that is quite different than fairness, however. Such conditions form half the story of when someone deserves to be punished. In telling the retributivist story they make sense only when attached to substantive prohibitions that prohibit actions that are morally wrong. That a moral wrong was done is the second half of the story of when a person deserves to be punished, and there can be no deserved punishment (retributive justice) without this half too.

It may seem that there is still some slippage between a retributivist theory of punishment and a perfectionist (or legal moralist)

---

[129] I am indebted to the late Warren Quinn for convincing me of this.

[130] See, e.g., Hart, *Punishment and Responsibility*, *supra* n. 41, for the best-known expression of this view.

theory of criminal legislation. One reason for sensing such slippage we can quickly put aside. This is the view that a theory of punishment (such as retributivism) is a theory of judicial function whereas a theory of criminal legislation is a theory of legislative function, and, further, that one's theories might well urge different considerations as proper to these different offices. Some retributivists, for example, suggest that the proper reason to pass criminal legislation is to prevent harm whereas the proper reason to punish those who cause harm is to exact retribution.[131]

Such a narrow view of retributivism in particular, and of any theory of punishment more generally, will not do. Retributivism, like any theory of punishment, gives an answer to the question, 'what is the criminal law good for?' That answer, in terms of achieving retributive justice, is not a role-specific answer. Accordingly, legislators as well as judges have reason to aim in their respective actions to achieve retributive justice.

As argued above, retributive justice is achieved only when morally wrong actions are punished, not when morally permissible or morally obligatory actions are punished. Given the constraints on all legislators (retributivists included) set by the ideal of legality, moral wrongdoing can be punished only if it has been legally prohibited by statute. This means that retributivist legislators have some reason to prohibit each and every moral wrong, for otherwise such wrongs must go unpunished.

The argument thus far connecting a legal moralist theory of legislation to a retributivist theory of punishment can be put in terms of four principles:

1. The retributivist principle proper: that the function of the criminal law is to exact retribution in proportion to desert.
2. The meaning of desert: that the desert that triggers retributive punishment is itself a product of the moral wrong(s) done by an individual, and the moral culpability with which he did those wrongs.
3. The principle of justice in legislation: that the achieving of (distributive, corrective, or retributive) justice is always a valid reason counting in favour of legislation.

[131] To the extent that Herbert Hart was a retributivist at all—a 'retributivist in distribution', to follow his own self-labelling—he separated off the theory of legislation ('general justifying aim') from that retributive reason to punish. See Hart, *supra* n. 41.

4. The principle of legality: that criminal liability can only fairly be imposed for conduct that was clearly prohibited by statute at the time the accused acted.

From these four principles it follows that legislators have reason to pass statutes prohibiting all actions that are morally wrong. The moral wrongness of any sort of behaviour, in other words, is always some reason to legislate against it in the criminal law.

A legal moralist theory of legislation says more than this, however. Such a theory also says that the *only* actions that a legislator may prohibit are those that are morally wrong. Can this aspect of a legal moralist theory of legislation also be derived from a retributivist theory of punishment? The answer is yes, but it requires a fifth principle:

5. Citizens have no moral obligation to obey a law just because it is a law.

This fifth principle is necessary to the connection between retributivism and legal moralism because if it were not true, then every law violation—no matter what the law's content—would become a moral wrong. Under such circumstances, the legislator could prohibit anything; the violation of those prohibitions would nonetheless be morally wrong; and punishment would be deserved whenever the conditions of responsibility were met.

Contemporary political theory has not been kind to the view that citizens are obligated to obey the law just because it is the law, even when they live in relatively just regimes.[132] Accordingly, there is an uphill battle to be waged by anyone seeking to break the connection between retributivism and legal moralism by this route. My own view is that the passage of a law prohibiting certain conduct adds nothing to our antecedent moral obligations with respect to that conduct: if the conduct was morally wrong, our obligation not to do it is not strengthened by it becoming illegal, and if the conduct was morally permissible, we have no moral obligation not to

---

[132] See, e.g., M. B. E. Smith, 'Is There a Prima Facie Obligation to Obey The Law?', *Yale Law Journal*, Vol. 82 (1973), 950–76; Joseph Raz, *The Authority of Law* (Oxford: Oxford University Press, 1979), chs. 12–15; Hurd, 'Sovereignty in Silence', *Yale Law Journal*, Vol. 90 (1990), 945–1028; Hurd, 'Challenging, Authority', *Yale Law Journal*, Vol. 100 (1991), 1611–77; Regan, 'Law's Halo', *Social Philosophy and Policy*, Vol. 4 (1986), 15–30; Regan, 'Authority and Value', *Southern California Law Review*, Vol. 62 (1989), 995–1095; Alexander, 'Law and Exclusionary Reasons', *Philosophical Topics*, Vol. 18 (1990), 5–22.

do it just because the law prohibits it. Of course, when conduct is criminalized, citizens have new *prudential* reasons not to do the forbidden acts; loss of liberty or other punishments can provide excellent prudential reasons. But such change in our prudential reasons is irrelevant to our *moral* reasons for not doing some type of action, and the latter are unchanged for citizens (although not for judges) by the passage of criminal statutes.

It might seem that the limiting half of the legal moralist theory— that *only* moral wrongs may be prohibited by the criminal law— runs afoul of those numerous situations where *some* rule needs to be criminally enforced in order to achieve desirable social coordination, but *what* rule is adopted is not so important. Consider that old chestnut, the rules of the road. Suppose for purposes of argument (I actually do not believe this) that it does not matter which side of the road people drive on so long as they all drive on the same side. May a legislator enact legislation making it criminal to drive on the left, given that there is no antecedent moral wrong in driving on the left?

If legal moralism could not answer this question affirmatively, then it would be a bad theory of criminal legislation. Co-ordination problems do need to be solved, and criminal legislation may be one way to solve them.[133] The use of criminal law to solve co-ordination problems like getting people to drive on the same side of the road can be justified on legal moralist grounds because the passage of the law makes salient the solution to the problem. Everyone should now drive on the right. Those who drive on the left do a moral wrong because they violate antecedently existing moral norms against risking harm to others, and such moral wrong may legitimately be punished. The obligation to drive on the right comes from those existing moral norms together with the co-ordinate human activity made possible by the traffic law, not just from the passage of the traffic law. The moral wrong is thus not so much created by the legislation as it is a result of there being an antecedent moral obligation of all of us to solve co-ordination problems that if unsolved risk harm to all.

---

[133] On whether criminal sanctions are ever needed to solve purely co-ordination problems, compare Finnis, *Natural Law and Natural Rights*, *supra* n. 4; Green, 'Law, Co-ordination, and the Common Good', *Oxford Journal of Legal Studies*, Vol. 4 (1983), 299–324; Finnis, 'Law as Co-ordination', *Ratio Juris*, Vol. 2 (1989), 97–104.

3. The Nature of a Theory of Wrongful Action   If legal moralism is the correct theory of criminal legislation, then the next theory needed by a legislator is a theory of wrongful action. For on the legal moralist theory of proper legislative aim, what is morally wrong to do is what should be prohibited by the criminal law.

Hitherto I have made do with 'morally bad state of affairs', or 'morally bad action/harm', as place-holders to be filled in by a theory of wrongful action. Now it is time to present more clearly the ambiguities covered up by such place-holding phrases. There are two ambiguities we need to bring out to highlight the issues with which a theory of the special part must deal.

The first is an ambiguity in how morality regards some admittedly wrongful action like killing. Is the moral prohibition against killing an 'agent-relative' prohibition, that is, a norm telling each of us individually, 'Don't you kill anyone even if your doing so would prevent more killings by others?' Or is morality such that it enjoins each of us through our actions to minimize killings, our own and those of others? This latter injunction is termed an 'agent-neutral' injunction because it does not allow or require us to give any special status to our own killings *vis-à-vis* those by other people; we are to minimize killings by anyone.

The second ambiguity has to do with the exact target of moral norms. Is it complex action-types like killings that are intrinsically bad? Or is it states of affairs like deaths that are intrinsically bad and thus, a person-causing-of-death (that is, a killing) that is regarded as derivatively bad?

It is the justifications that bring out these latent ambiguities in the shape of morality, which is why I call them the royal road to insight about the nature of substantive moral norms. Suppose a terrorist is holding two hostages but what he wants is the death of a third person whom you are protecting. If he lines up the two and announces that he will kill them unless you kill the one in your protection, may (must) you kill the one? An agent-neutral morality enjoins you to minimize the number of killings that occur, giving no special weight to the fact that in the one case you must do the killing; therefore, you must kill the one. An agent-relative morality speaks to you directly: don't *you* kill, no matter that the consequence of you not killing is that two killings by someone else will take place.

Similarly, suppose that one person is drowning because pushed into a lake by a murderous enemy. Two other persons are also drowning through no fault of anyone's, including their own. If you have but one rope and time to save the one or the two, but not both, may (must) you throw the rope to the one? A morality aimed at killings should answer affirmatively, for a killing is so much worse than an accidental death; a morality finding deaths to be bad (and causing deaths by persons wrong only derivatively) should answer negatively: better to prevent two deaths than one.

A theory of wrongful action must thus choose between agent-neutral and agent-relative conceptions of morality, and between act-oriented and consequence-oriented conceptions of morality (or reach some accommodation between these seemingly opposed views), in order to specify *what* it is for which persons are responsible. Under each pole of these two oppositions, there are of course a wide variety of theories to choose between. With regard to agent-neutral views, there are act-consequentialist, rule-consequentialist, and trait-consequentialist views. Within the agent-relative conception of morality, there are simple absolutist views, holding morality to consist of exceptionless absolutes violation of which can never be justified 'though the Heavens may fall'; and much more complex agent-relative views, allowing exceptions to, and overrides of, morality's prohibitions. With regard to consequence-centered views, there are widely different consequences held to be bad: only pain is bad, pleasure good, or unhappiness bad, happiness good, or preference-frustration bad, preference-satisfaction good, are a few of the familiar (utilitarian) views.

Although a theory of the special part is in general directed to legislators in the Anglo-American criminal system, the theory of wrongful action has not in fact been dealt with as a legislative matter. Despite the Anglo-American doctrine that there are no common law crimes, legislatures everywhere have left the general nature of wrongful action to be worked out by the courts. One sees this in the open-ended balance-of-evils defence (and in the common law's 'defence' of necessity that preceded it), which leaves open entirely which sort of theory of wrongful action courts are to adopt. Because of this, I have discussed the theory of wrongful action in chapter 17 in terms of how one gives meaning to the general balance-of-evils defence.

4. The Nature of a Theory of the Limits of Criminal Law   On the legal moralist theory of proper legislative aim, morally wrong action ought to be prohibited by the doctrines of the special part of the criminal law. Saying this, and saying what morally wrongful action is, tells only half the story needed by a conscientious legislator. The other half is what else (besides the evil of moral wrongness going unpunished) counts in deciding what behaviour should be criminalized.

In chapter 18 I shall explore two such limiting considerations, one I call the presumption of liberty, and the other, the basic right to liberty.[134] These two limits are largely (although not exclusively) based on two separate ideals of autonomy.

The first of these ideals I call Kantian autonomy. Even if the function of criminal law is backward-looking—to punish those who deserve it—one of its predictable effects gives legislators a forward-looking reason to restrain their enacting every moral wrong into a criminal prohibition. Sanction-backed criminal norms coerce conforming behaviour out of those not otherwise inclined to so act. This coercive effect of criminal law (as opposed to its educative effect) necessarily impairs autonomy in a Kantian sense.[135] An old example is gift-giving. Assume we are all morally obligated to give a certain percentage of our income to those less fortunate. Criminal legislation coercing us to give that amount cuts into the ability of each of us to choose autonomously to give. Indeed, the moral worth of those 'givings' motivated solely by fear of sanctions seems very small when compared to true charity (autonomous giving).

To be sure, whether there is this kind of impairment of autonomy by all coercive sanctions depends on a Kantian view of morality, namely, the view that moral worth attaches to the reasons for which one acts as well as to the acts one does. Yet surely this is not very controversial. Those refrainings from hurting others motivated solely by fear of legal sanctions are of less value than those refrainings motivated by compassion and empathy for our fellows. Add to this moral fact the psychological fact that we cannot choose the reasons for which we act—we can only choose to act or not—and we can see that the sanctioning of any behaviour decreases the likelihood of *rightly motivated* right action.

---

[134] In ch. 18 I also revisit the issue of proper legislative aim insofar as each citizen's right (correlative of the legislature's duty) can be conceived as what I call the 'derived right to liberty'.

[135] See Raz, *The Morality of Freedom, supra* n. 127.

For a certain class of moral decisions by citizens there is an autonomy cost to use of the criminal sanction that can be prohibitively high. Interestingly enough, for these decisions the morally worthy 'right reason' does not involve compassion and empathy for others. On the contrary the right reason is much more selfish: it is almost any reason, so long as it is freely chosen. At issue here is concern about the formation of a sense of self that is a prerequisite for being a moral agent. Take decisions about sexual orientation, whether to become a parent, what job to pursue, what friends to have. What has the most moral worth about such decisions is not getting them right, but rather, allowing such decisions to speak for each individual making them. What I call in chapter 18 the Millian sense of autonomy. When legal coercion strongly interferes with such self-definition, the conscientious, legal moralist legislator must weigh the high autonomy cost of coercing right behaviour against the value of inducing more of that behaviour. Here allowing citizens to act for 'right reasons'—that is, their own fully chosen reasons—should swamp the increment of right action coercive criminal sanctions could achieve.

These two autonomy limits operate quite differently than one another. Coercion of any action offends Kantian autonomy, whereas only some decisions are protected by Millian autonomy. Yet what it protects, Millian autonomy protects much more strongly than Kantian autonomy. That is why in chapter 18 I call the latter protection a *presumption* of liberty, while the former has the requisite strength to be called a *right* to liberty.

The strength of the presumption in favour of liberty is increased by certain utilitarian considerations unrelated to the furtherance of autonomy (in either sense). In chapter 16 I explore some well-charted costs attendant upon use of the criminal sanction. Certain kinds of behaviours are costly to prohibit even if one is confident such behaviours are morally wrong. Behaviour that is usually done in private, that has limited impact upon others (except perhaps via their own imaginations of what the actors are doing), and that is so deeply motivated that if prohibited it will be done anyway, is very costly to criminalize. The costs include invasion of privacy (true privacy, not constitutional 'privacy', which is autonomy) through the enforcement techniques required to enforce such prohibitions; the creation of a 'crime tariff', making the activities much more profitable than they would otherwise be; the potential for discriminatory enforcement of laws that cannot be comprehensively enforced; and the disrespect for law in general engendered by having laws that cannot or will not be enforced.[136] A conscientious legislator has to balance the values disserved by criminalizing this class of behaviour against the goodness of punishing culpably done wrongful action. The result in those cases where the wrongdoing is not severe should be that such behaviour is not criminalized even though it is morally wrongful.

In addition to these limits imposed in the name of autonomy and utility, there is also what might be called the limit of epistemic caution. Anyone who believes that there are right answers to moral questions like, 'what actions are morally wrongful?', also should have some epistemic modesty about his own grasp of what those right answers are. After all, whatever one can be right about one can also be wrong about. The true implication, thus, of realism about morality is not some self-righteous attitude that leaps at every opportunity to cram one's own view of the good and the right down other people's throats. Rather, the attitudinal implication is one of humility in the face of hard moral questions, a humility accompanied by a curiosity about the differing answers to those hard moral questions discovered by others.

Some moral questions are not difficult to resolve. That murder is wrong, rape is wrong, deceiving one's friends is wrong, and homosexual sex is not wrong, are moral conclusions easy to reach. But some moral questions are neither easy, nor are answers to them uncontroversial. Euthanasia and torturing terrorists in order to extract life-saving information are in this category. About such questions a legislator might well hesitate to enact her own best theory of moral wrongdoing into law, for to do so shuts off that experiment in seeking the good that each intelligent life represents.

III. PREVIEW: MOORE'S CRIMINAL PHILOSOPHY

The theory of criminal law defended in this book can be summarily sketched. Of the possible functions for criminal law, only the

---

[136] See Packer, 'The Crime Tariff', *American Scholar*, Vol. 33 (1964), 551–7; Kadish, 'The Crisis of Overcriminalization', *Annals*, Vol. 374 (1967), 157–70; Norval Morris and Gordon Hawkings, *The Honest Politician's Guide to Crime Control* (Chicago: University of Chicago Press, 1970).

achievement of retributive justice is its actual function. Punishing those who deserve it is good and is the distinctive good that gives the essence, and defines the borders, of criminal law as an area of law. Such function demands that those subject to punishment: (1) have done something morally wrong, and (2) did so in a culpable way.

The responsibility a prerequisite of deserved punishment is the active responsibility of an individual person for his wrongful action. The relation of active responsibility that exists between a person and his wrong consists of the properties of wrongdoing and culpability, and these properties in turn consist of the properties of voluntariness and causation, and intentionality and lack of excuse, respectively. Voluntariness, in turn, consists in the willing of a bodily movement. A coarse-grained theory of individuating actions is presupposed; the essence of actions is given in terms of a causal theory whereby willings (or volitions) causing bodily movements are seen as the essence of human actions.

Causation is not identified with counterfactuals, nor is 'proximate' causation analysed on terms of foreseeability. Doubt is expressed about our presently having an analysis of causation that allows it to do the work demanded of it by the orthodox theory of responsibility. Intentionality is disjunctively analysed, 'intention-with-which' requiring purpose, and 'intentional action' allowing purpose or knowledge to suffice. A propositional theory of the objects of intentions is defended, itself then cashed out in terms of a metaphysical functionalism about minds, resulting in fine-grained theory of individuation for intentions. Excuse is analysed as given by the diminished capacities or opportunities to exercise free choice. The character and causal theories of excuse are put aside as both morally wrong and as lacking institutional support in Anglo-American criminal law doctrine.

The nature of persons who are culpability's subjects is given in terms of the attributes of autonomy and rationality. A theory of individuation is defended allocating just one person to possess these attributes per each adult, sane human being, with multiple personality and split-brain subjects presenting the only hard cases for this view.

The object of responsibility is given by the theory of wrongful action. I defend a complex agent-relative view of morality that views moral norms to speak to each agent individually. Such a moral theory is not an absolutist one, however, because it permits consequentialist calculations: (1) when a certain threshold of moral badness is reached; (2) when a moral norm does not apply to the situation, either because exceptions to a relevant moral norm are instantiated, or otherwise; or (3) when the conditions of *culpable* violation of such norms are not fully met.

My theories of proper legislative aim, and of the limits of criminal legislation, when combined, result in a liberal-in-content if illiberal-in-form theory of legislative restraint. On such a theory, legislatures prima facie should criminalize all immoral behaviour because it is immoral. This means enacting each of morality's agent-relative prohibitions into law, together with a set of justificatory defences that allows for the consequentialist justification such morality licenses. Such recommended criminalization is prima facie only, however, in light of the limits of legislation. Given those limits, legislatures have no business criminalizing abortion or deviant sexual practices, two recent examples of much current controversy. The values of Kantian autonomy, Millian autonomy, and the utilitarian costs of enforcement would outweigh any immorality such practices may possess going unpunished; as it happens, by my lights at least, such practices are not immoral anyway; or if they are, one might well have enough doubt about their immorality to stay the legislative hand.

PART I

THE THEORY OF CRIMINAL LAW'S FUNCTION

2

CLOSET RETRIBUTIVISM

Retributivism as a theory of punishment has enjoyed some resurgence among the legal theorists of the past thirty years—in marked contrast to the theory's earlier decline throughout most of this century, when it was often regarded as a remnant of our barbarous past.[1] This chapter is designed to persuade those who have not worked through any theoretical arguments in favour of retributivism how they themselves might be retributivists—closet retributivists, perhaps, but retributivists nonetheless. By 'retributivist' I refer to one who believes that the justification for punishing a criminal is simply that the criminal deserves to be punished. What I mean by 'closet' retributivism is a retributive theory held by those who have not thought through a theory of punishment, but who show themselves to be retributivists in the judgements they make and the reasons for which they make them. By and large I do not in this chapter attempt to show that such persons should be retributivists; only to show that they are.

In order to fulfil the limited ambition of this chapter, as well as the more ambitious undertaking of the next chapter, it is necessary to develop a classification scheme for theories of punishment. Having done this, I shall return to the kind of thought experiments that make retributivism the most plausible theory of what many in fact believe about punishment.

---

[1] See particularly Herbert Morris's splendid essays, 'Persons and Punishment', *The Monist*, Vol. 52 (1968), 475–501, reprinted in his *On Guilt and Innocence* (Los Angeles: University of California Press, 1976); and 'A Paternalistic Theory of Punishment', *American Philosophical Quarterly*, Vol. 18 (1981), 263–71. See also the very interesting essays by Herbert Fingarette, 'Punishment and Suffering', *Proceedings and Addresses of the American Philosophical Association*, Vol. 50 (1977), 499–525; by Jeffrie Murphy, *Retribution, Justice and Therapy* (Dordrecht: Reidel, 1979); and by Jean Hampton, 'The Retributive Idea', in Murphy and Hampton, *Forgiveness and Mercy* (Cambridge: Cambridge University Press, 1988). See also George Sher, 'Deserved Punishment', in his *Desert* (Princeton: Princeton University Press, 1987); Wojciech Sadurski, *Giving Desert Its Due* (Dordrecht: Reidel, 1985); Davis, 'Harm and Retribution', *Philosophy and Public Affairs*, Vol. 15 (1986), 236–66. See generally Galligan, 'The Return to Retribution in Penal Theory', in C. Tapper ed., *Crime, Proof and Punishment* (London: Butterworth, 1981).

I. THE PRIMA FACIE JUSTIFICATIONS OF PUNISHMENT

There is by now a familiar list of prima facie reasons given to justify the institution of punishment. Such a list usually includes: incapacitation, special deterrence, general deterrence, denunciation, rehabilitation, and retribution. A word about each of these reasons is in order. Incapacitation is the simplest of theories, because, as the name suggests, the good that punishment achieves is that it incapacitates an offender by doing something to him that prevents him from committing further crimes. Special deterrence has a similar aim in preventing crime, but a different means: punishing an offender deters him from committing further crimes upon his release. Likewise, general deterrence aims at the prevention of crime by punishing an offender, except that those who are deterred are others in the general population rather than the offender himself. All three of these traditional theories of punishment share a common goal thought to justify punishment, namely, the reduction of crime.

The ideas captured in the theory labelled 'denunciation', sometimes called the expressive theory of punishment,[2] are somewhat more complicated. One strand of this theory urges that punishment must express society's condemnation because doing so educates citizens in the wrongfulness of the conduct that the criminal law attempts to discourage. So stated, the denunciation theory is no more than a somewhat broader form of the general deterrence theory: both aim at the prevention of crime, one by scaring people out of it and the other by more subtle educational techniques.[3] Another strand of the denunciation theory asserts that the denouncing of crime via symbolic blaming coupled with harsh treatment, serves an end distinct from the prevention of future criminal conduct. Theorists of this stripe urge that crime must be denounced by pun-

[2] See, e.g., Joel Feinberg's 'The Expressive Function of Punishment', *The Monist*, Vol. 49 (1965), 397–423, reprinted in his *Doing and Deserving* (Princeton: Princeton University Press, 1970). H. L. A. Hart attributes this theory of punishment to Sir James Fitzjames Stephen and to Lord Denning in his *Punishment and Responsibility* (Oxford: Oxford University Press, 1968), 170–3.

[3] Indeed, some include such educational techniques as a form of general deterrence. See Johannes Andenaes, 'Does Punishment Deter Crime?', in G. Ezorsky, ed., *Philosophical Perspective on Punishment* (Albany, NY: State University of New York Press, 1972); J. Andenaes, *Punishment and Deterrence* (Ann Arbor, MI: University of Michigan Press, 1974).

ishment, because doing so maintains a sense of social cohesion. If punishments are inflicted, then citizens do not have the sense that the social contract has been broken with impunity by others. The good achieved on this branch of the theory is not the prevention of future crimes; rather, it is thought that a sense of community is itself a good thing that punishment helps to achieve.

Rehabilitation involves two quite different ideals of rehabilitation that are usually confused. These two rehabilitative ideals can best be separated by thinking about two different ways of rendering offenders non-dangerous. First, imagine that what is done is to place offenders in extraordinarily awful places of detention, with harsh treatment by inmates and guards. Here, non-dangerousness is achieved because such offenders either become 'penitent', or they are no longer willing to commit crimes because they are unwilling to risk again such awful treatment. For comparison, imagine that the same level of non-dangerousness can be achieved if prisoners are placed in much nicer facilities, with kinder personnel (all of them soft-spoken, in white coats, and manifesting sincere concern), a place in which extensive therapy programmes are undertaken. Imagine further that the second such programme, although much more expensive than the first, not only makes the offender non-dangerous but also makes him a flourishing, happy, and self-actualizing member of our society.

The first sort of rehabilitative ideal is one that is achieved when we make criminals safe to return to the streets. This sort of rehabilitative theory justifies punishment, not by appeal to how much better off the criminal will be at the end of the process, but rather by how much better off all of us will be if 'treatment' is completed because the streets will be that much safer. Such a theory seeks to rehabilitate the criminal only as a cost-effective means of shortening the expensive incarceration that would otherwise be necessary to protect everyone against crime. The second sort of rehabilitative ideal, by way of contrast, is a paternalistic theory. It seeks to rehabilitate the offender, not just so that he can be returned safe to the streets, but so that he can lead a flourishing and successful life. Such a theory justifies punishment, not in the name of all of us, but rather in the offender's own name; since it does so in his name, but contrary to his own expressed wishes (few offenders want to be punished), this kind of rehabilitative theory is paternalistic in character.

This paternalistic type of rehabilitative theory has no proper part to play in any theory of punishment, even in the minimal sense of constituting a prima facie justification of punishment.[4] There are three reasons why this is so. First, such a paternalistic reform theory allocates scarce societal resources away from other, more deserving groups that want them (such as retarded and autistic children or the poor) to a group that hardly can be said to deserve such favoured status, and, moreover, does not want such 'benefits'. As a simple matter of distributive justice it is difficult to argue that criminals should be favoured in the allocation of scarce social resources in these ways. To make such distributive justice arguments go, one has to claim that criminals suffer distinctive disadvantages entitling them to extra societal resources. One idea of this sort is that criminal behaviour is thought to constitute a disease, so that as diseased persons criminals deserve treatment. Yet the idea that 'crime is disease' rests on unjustifiably bloated notions of health and sickness, notions that conflate illness with badness.[5] An alternative idea having the same distributional implications is the thought that criminals do merit extra social resources being devoted to their welfare because they come predominantly from groups that have historically received less than their due from our society. Yet this idea, even if statistically true for general classes of people, ignores more precise individuation of who it is in our society that deserves extra social resources: those who are as disadvantaged economically and socially as the average criminal but who commit no crimes. Why allow criminal behaviour to serve as a proxy for social disadvantage, if one can use the latter criterion directly to guide remedial legislation?[6]

A second reason that should give one pause about rehabilitation as a prima facie reason for punishment stems from its paternalistic

---

[4] A conclusion also reached, on somewhat different grounds, by Herbert Hart. See Hart, *supra* n. 2, at 26–7.

[5] Arguing against this attempted 'psychiatrization of ethics' is one of the principal points of my book, *Law and Psychiatry: Rethinking the Relationship* (Cambridge: Cambridge University Press, 1984), chs. 4–6.

[6] A third idea, often confused with the two presented in the text, is that criminals, unlike the rest of us, are passive victims of their own backgrounds who 'can't help' but do what they do. This idea I call 'selective determinism' in ch. 12, and there reject it as an incomprehensible metaphysics (a kind of patchy, on-again, off-again free will metaphysics).

nature. As John Stuart Mill explored in detail,[7] paternalistic justifications of any piece of legislation should be regarded with suspicion. Criminals are not in the standard classes in society for which paternalistic state intervention is appropriate, such as the severely disordered, the young or others whose capacity for rational choice is diminished; such a paternalistic theory is suspect on this ground alone.

Third, such recasting of punishment in terms of 'treatment' for the good of the criminal makes possible a kind of moral blindness that is dangerous in itself. As C. S. Lewis pointed out years ago[8] adopting such a 'humanitarian' conceptualization of punishment makes it easy to inflict treatments and sentences that need bear no relation to the desert of the offender. We may do more to another 'for his own good' than we ever allow ourselves to do when we see that it is really for our good for which we act.[9]

Retributivism—the final theory used to justify punishment—is the view that punishment is justified by the desert of the offender. The good that is achieved by punishing, on this view, has nothing to do with future states of affairs, such as the prevention of crime or the maintenance of social cohesion. Rather, the good that punishment achieves is that someone who deserves it gets it. Punishment of the guilty is thus for the retributivist an *intrinsic*

---

[7] See below, ch. 16, where I distinguish paternalistic justifications (concerned with the good of the criminal) from legal moralist justifications (concerned with having the dictates of morality complied with, even though this may incidentally be good for the criminal). If we draw this distinction, I am uncertain whether Herbert Morris's revised retributive theory is truly paternalistic, as he himself labels it. See Morris, 'A Paternalist Theory of Punishment', *supra* n. 1.

[8] C. S. Lewis, 'The Humanitarian Theory of Punishment', *Res Judicatae*, Vol. 6 (1953), 224–30.

[9] Lewis's kind of argument against the rehabilitative ideal has limited efficacy because it may only yield the conclusion that 'involuntary rehabilitative treatment'— 'punishment', except for its purpose—is subject to certain non-treatment-justified side-constraints. Even a rehabilitationist might concede, for example, that, no matter how effective, behaviour-modification programmes using anectine therapy (which paralyses the involuntary muscle movements in breathing while oxygen is pumped into the patient, giving him the sensation of suffocating) are impermissible because violative of basic human rights. And such side-constraints need not commit the rehabilitationist to a mixed rehabilitationist/retributivist theory, because retributivist punishments are also arguably subject to the same side-constraints. On the latter possibility, see Jeffrie Murphy, 'Hatred: A Qualified Defense', in Murphy and Hampton, n. 1 *supra*, at 106–7. Still, to keep involuntary rehabilitative treatment *fully* within intuitively acceptable bounds, the rehabilitationist probably has to become a mixed theorist because he has to use moral desert as a check on reformative treatment.

good, not the merely *instrumental* good that it may be to the utilitarian or rehabilitative theorist.

Retributivism differs from a variety of views that are often paraded as retributivist, but that in fact are not. Such views are typically put forward by people who cannot understand how anyone could think that moral desert by itself could justify punishment. Such persons scramble about for other goods that punishment achieves and label these, quite misleadingly, 'retributivism'. The leading confusions seem to me to be seven in number.

1. First, retributivism is sometimes identified with a particular measure of punishment such as *lex talionis*, an eye for an eye,[10] or with a kind of punishment such as the death penalty. Yet retributivism answers a question prior to the questions to which these could be answers. True enough, retributivists at some point have to answer the 'how much' and 'what type' questions for punishments of specific offences, and they are committed to the principle that punishment should be graded in proportion to desert; but they are not committed to any particular penalty scheme nor to any particular penalty as being deserved. Separate argument is needed to answer these 'how much' and 'what type' questions, *after* one has described why one is punishing at all. It is quite possible to be a retributivist and to be against both the death penalty and *lex talionis*, the idea that crimes should be punished by like acts being done to the criminal.

2. Contrary to Anthony Quinton and others,[11] retributivism is *not* 'the view that only the guilty are to be punished'. A retributivist will subscribe to such a view, but that is not what is distinctive about retributivism. The distinctive aspect of retributivism is that the moral desert of an offender is a *sufficient* reason to punish him or her; the principle Quinton advocates makes such moral desert only a *necessary* condition of punishment. Other reasons—typically, crime prevention reasons—must be added to moral desert, in this view, for punishment to be justified. Retributivism has no room

[10] J. Wilson and R. Herrnstein, *Crime and Human Nature* (New York: Simon and Schuster, 1985), 496.

[11] Quinton, 'On Punishment', *Analysis*, Vol. 14 (1954), 1933–42. Herbert Hart calls this 'weak retributivism' (Hart, *supra* n. 2), and Jeff Murphy and J. L. Mackie call it 'negative retributivism' (Murphy, 'Retributivism and the State's Interest in Punishment', in J. R. Pennock and J. W. Chapman, eds., *Criminal Justice: Nomos XXVII* (New York: New York University Press, 1985), 159; Mackie, 'Morality and the Retributive Emotions', *Criminal Justice Ethics* (Winter/Spring, 1982), 3–10)).

for such additional reasons. That future crime might also be prevented by punishment is a happy surplus for a retributivist, but no part of the justification for punishing.

3. Retributivism is not the view that punishment of offenders satisfies the desires for vengeance of their victims. In this view the harm that is punishment is justified by the good it does psychologically to the victims of crime, whose suffering is thought to have a special claim on the structuring of the criminal justice system.[12] This is not retributivism. A retributivist can justify punishment as deserved even if the criminal's victims are indifferent (or even opposed) to punishing the one who hurt them. Indeed, a retributivist should urge punishment on all offenders who deserve it, even if *no* victims wanted it.

4. Relatedly, retributivism is not the view that the preferences of all citizens (not just crime victims) should be satisfied. A preference utilitarian might well believe, as did Sir James Fitzjames Stephen,[13] that punishment should be exacted 'for the sake of gratifying the feeling of hatred—call it revenge, resentment, or what you will—which the contemplation of such [criminal] conduct excites in healthily constituted minds . . .', or that 'the feeling of hatred and the desire of vengeance . . . are important elements of human nature which ought . . . to be satisfied in a regular public and legal manner'. Yet a retributivist need not believe such things, but only that morally culpable persons should be punished, irrespective of what other citizens feel, desire, or prefer.

5. Relatedly, retributivism is not the view that punishment is justified because without it vengeful citizens would take the law into their own hands. Usually it is those who are hostile to retributivism, such as Justice Marshall,[14] who link it to this indefensible idea.

[12] Ted Honderich, *Punishment: The Supposed Justifications* (London: Hutchinson, 1969), 30.

[13] James Fitzjames Stephen, *Liberty, Equality, Fraternity* (Cambridge: Cambridge University Press, 1967), 152. Jeffrie Murphy seems intent on running retributivism and this kind of preference-utilitarianism together in his recent essay, 'Getting Even: The Role of the Victim', *Social Philosophy and Policy*, Vol. 7 (1990), 209–25, at 212, 224–5. Murphy has come to blur this distinction because he has come to doubt that he can motivate retributivism as an 'abstract concern for justice' (as opposed to a concern for quelling the fires of vengeful emotions). Murphy's proper conclusion should be that retributivism is false, not that it is something that it is not.

[14] See Thurgood Marshall's opinion in *Gregg* v. *Georgia*, 428 US 153 (1976). Peggy Radin calls Marshall's kind of view 'revenge-utilitarianism'. Radin, 'Cruel Punishment and Respect for Persons: Super Due Process for Death', *Southern Californian Law Review*, Vol. 53 (1980), 1143–85 at 1169–73. The argument is that

Punishment for a retributivist is not justified by the need to prevent private violence, which is an essentially utilitarian justification. Even in the most well-mannered state, those criminals who deserve punishment should get it, according to retributivism.

6. Nor is retributivism to be confused with denunciatory theories of punishment.[15] In this latter view punishment is justified because punishment is the vehicle through which society can express its condemnation of the criminal's behaviour. This is a utilitarian theory, not a retributive one, for punishment is in this view to be justified by the good consequences it achieves—either the psychological satisfactions denunciation achieves, or the prevention of private violence, or the prevention of future crimes through the educational benefits of such denunciation. A retributivist justifies punishment by none of these supposed good consequences of punishing.

7. Finally, retributivism should not be confused with a theory of formal justice (the treating of like cases alike). Retributivism is not, as McCloskey has urged,[16] 'a particular application of a general principle of justice, namely, that equals should be treated equally and unequals unequally'. True, a retributivist who also subscribes to the principle of formal justice is committed to punishing equally those persons who are equally deserving. However, the principle of formal justice says nothing about punishing anybody for anything; such a principle only dictates that, *if* we punish anyone, we must do so equally. Why we should punish anyone is the question retributivism purports to answer, a question not answered by the distinct principle of formal justice. Moreover, notice that even if we have punished some persons in the past, so that the principle of formal justice demands that relevantly similar persons be punished in the future, that does not tell us the relevant similarities demanding similar treatment. Like cases should indeed be treated alike, but it takes some substantive theory of punishment to spell out when

the state must punish because otherwise private citizens will take the law into their own hands, and that such private vengeance leads to chaos and disorder. Punishment on such a view is justified by its ability to prevent these bad things. Retributivism has nothing to do with this essentially forward-looking justification. Moreover, this 'prevention of private vengeance' theory is to my mind not even a prima facie justifying reason for punishment. The obvious thing to do if citizens are going to violate the law by taking it into their own hands, is to deter those citizens by punishing *them*.

[15] See n. 2 *supra*.
[16] H. J. McCloskey, 'A Non-Utilitarian Approach to Punishment', *Inquiry*, Vol. 8 (1965), 249–63.

cases are truly alike. A utilitarian who also subscribes to the principle of formal justice should think that the dangerousness and deterrability of an offender (and of the class of potential offenders that she instantiates) are the relevant respects in which one case is relevantly like another.

Retributivism is a very straightforward theory of punishment: We are justified in punishing because and only because offenders deserve it. Moral responsibility ('desert') in such a view is not only necessary for justified punishment, it is also sufficient. Such sufficiency of justification gives society more than merely a *right* to punish culpable offenders. It does this, making it not unfair to punish them, but retributivism justifies more than this.[17] For a retributivist, the moral responsibility of an offender also gives society the *duty* to punish. Retributivism, in other words, is truly a theory of justice such that, if it is true, we have an obligation to set up institutions so that retribution is achieved.

II. THE TWO PURE THEORIES OF PUNISHMENT

It is common to reduce the survivors on this list of prima facie justifications of punishment to two general theories, the utilitarian theory and the retributive theory. To see how this is done, one need only consider the good state of affairs that is to be achieved by incapacitation, special deterrence, general deterrence, and rehabilitation (to the extent that it is of the first sort of rehabilitative theory, and not the second). For all four of these rationales for punishment share the prevention of crime as the good thing to be achieved that justifies punishment. In each case, the ultimate justification for inflicting the harm of punishment is that it is outweighed by the good to be achieved, namely, the prevention of future crimes by that offender or by others. This justification of an institution by the social welfare that it will enhance, makes all such theories instances of a utilitarian theory of punishment.

Thus, the denunciation theory of punishment is a second kind of utilitarian theory of punishment, insofar as the good that it seeks

[17] Compare K. G. Armstrong, 'The Retributivist Hits Back', in H. B. Acton, ed., *The Philosophy of Punishment* (London: Macmillan, St Martin's Press, 1969), at 155–7, who conceives of retributivism as only giving the state the *right* to punish but not the *duty* to do so. This is perhaps an eighth mischaracterization of retributivism.

to achieve is not simply the prevention of crime. To the extent one grants intrinsic value to social cohesion, and does not regard that as a value only because it contributes to the maintenance of public order, the denunciation theory can be distinguished from the other utilitarian theories just considered by the differing social good that it seeks to achieve. Nonetheless, it is still a utilitarian theory, since it outweighs the harm that is punishment by *some form* of net social gain that punishment achieves.

Both the prevention of crime and the maintenance of social cohesion are types of collective goods. The general utilitarian theory of punishment is one that combines these and any other form of collective goods that punishment might achieve, and calls them all a 'social gain'. Whenever the social gain outweighs the harm punishment causes to an offender or his family, such a theory would say that there is a 'net social gain'. Such a vocabulary allows us a succinct definition of any form of utilitarian theory: punishment is justified if and only if there is some net social gain achieved by it.

A retributivist theory is necessarily non-utilitarian in character, for it eschews justifying punishment by its tendency to achieve any form of net social gain. Rather, retributivism asserts that punishment is properly inflicted because, and only because, the person deserves it. That some people deserve punishment on such a theory, is both a necessary and a sufficient condition justifying criminal sanctions. A succinct definition of the retributivist theory of punishment, paralleling that given of the utilitarian theory, is that punishment is justified if and only if the person or persons receiving it deserve it.

III. THE MIXED THEORY OF PUNISHMENT

Once one grants that there are two sorts of prima facie justifications of punishment—effecting a net social gain (utilitarian), and giving just deserts (retributivist)—one can also see that in addition to the two pure theories of punishment there can also be mixed theories. There are two logically possible mixed theories,[18] although only

---

[18] If one abandons *criterial* theories of punishment (seeking necessary and sufficient conditions) for looser, *criteriological* theories (seeking only 'factors' that in some unspecified combination justify punishment), then there are more than two sorts of mixed theories. One might, for example, have a kind of sliding scale whereby

one of these merits any serious attention. There is first of all the popular form of mixed theory which asserts that punishment is justified if, and only if, there is both a net social gain achieved by punishment, *and* punishment is given to offenders who deserve it. Giving just deserts and achieving a net social gain, in such a case, are each individually necessary but only jointly sufficient conditions justifying punishment. The second logically possible mixed theory, would be one asserting that punishment is justified if, and only if, there is a net social gain achieved, *or* punishment is given to offenders who deserve it. Such a theory has no name, because there is no one, to my knowledge, who has ever adopted it. The reason such a theory is unnamed and unclaimed is because it shares the defects of each of the pure theories, utilitarianism and retributivism.[19] I shall accordingly put this 'mixed theory' aside from further consideration.

The first kind of mixed theory itself has two branches. By far the most usual and popular form of the theory asserts that we do not punish people *because* they deserve it.[20] Desert enters in, this theory further asserts, only as a limit on punishment: we punish offenders *because* some net social gain is achieved, such as the prevention of crime, but only if such offenders deserve it. It is, in other words, the achieving of a net social gain that justifies punishment, whereas the desert of offenders serves as a limiting condition on punishment but no part of its justification. The alternative branch of the mixed theory is just the converse of the branch just examined: one would urge that we punish *because* offenders deserve it, but *only if* there is some net social gain achieved by doing so.[21]

one will allow a big gain in utility to justify a punishment that is somewhat unjust. See C. L. Ten, *Crime, Guilt, and Punishment* (Oxford: Clarendon Press, 1987), 79–81, for an example.

[19] The main problem with the pure utilitarian theory of punishment is that it potentially sacrifices the innocent in order to achieve a collective good. The main problem with the pure retributivist theory of punishment is that it potentially requires punishment of the guilty even if no further good is achieved by doing so. The unnamed and unclaimed mixed theory would have *both* of these problems. C. L. Ten also notes this about what he also regards as a 'very strange' theory. Id. at 77.

[20] If one construes Hart's attempt to distinguish different *levels* of justification ('general aim', versus 'distribution', of punishment) to be no more than my distinction between justification and limitation, his is the best-known exemplar of this view. Hart, *supra* n. 2.

[21] See Andrew von Hirsch, *Doing Justice* (New York: Hill and Wang, 1976), ch. 6, who distinguishes these two forms of conjunctive mixed theories.

In such a case, the roles of net social gain and desert are simply reversed: giving offenders their just deserts serves as the justification of punishment, and the achieving of a net social gain as the limiting condition.

A cynic might view these two branches of the mixed theory as nothing more than an uncomfortable shuffle by mixed theorists: when accused of barbarism in punishing persons for retributivist reasons, they assert the first branch of the theory (they do not punish because some persons deserve it, but because of a collective good that is achieved). When accused of immorality in imposing harsh treatment on someone as a means of making everyone else better off, such theorists shift to the other foot, and claim they do not punish someone in order to achieve a net social gain, but only to give offenders their just deserts. The reason the cynic has a point here is that there is a sense in which the two branches of the theory are the same, namely, the sense that they justify exactly the same kinds of treatment for all cases. The only difference in theories is in the *motivations* of those who hold them. And while that may make a difference in our moral judgements of those who hold the different branches of the mixed theory of punishment, it does not make a difference in terms of the actual social institutions and judgements such theories will justify. For purposes of arguing against the mixed theory in this chapter it will suffice to lump both of these branches of the mixed theory together and call them 'the mixed theory of punishment'.

IV. THE ARGUMENT AGAINST THE PURE UTILITARIAN THEORY

In exploring one's thoughts leading to retributivism, it is perhaps easiest to start with some standard kinds of thought experiments directed against a pure utilitarian theory of punishment. A thought experiment is essentially a device allowing one to sort out one's true reasons for believing that certain propositions are true. To be successful, such a thought experiment need not involve any actual case or state of affairs, nor need the cases envisioned even be very likely; they only need be conceivable in order to test our own thoughts.

It is standard fare in the philosophy of punishment to assert, by way of several thought experiments, counter-examples to the utilitarian thesis that punishment is justified if and only if some net social gain is achieved. I shall here mention only two such counter-examples: scapegoating and preventive detention. With regard to the first, it might be recalled that D. B. Cooper successfully skyjacked an aircraft some years ago, and that this successful, unsolved crime apparently encouraged the mass of skyjackings that has cost American society a great deal in terms of dollars, lives, and convenience. Cooper wore large sunglasses in his escapade, and there was accordingly only a very limited description available of him. Imagine that shortly after his skyjacking we had the benefit of the knowledge that we now have by hindsight, and decided that it would better to punish someone who looked like Cooper (and who had no good alibi), in order to convince others that skyjacking did not pay. For a consistent utilitarian, there is a net social gain that would be achieved by punishing such an innocent person, and there is no a priori reason that the net social gain in such a case might not outweigh the harm that is achieved by punishing an innocent person.

The preventive detention kind of counter-example is very similar: imagine that a psychiatrist discovers that his patient has extremely dangerous propensities. His patient is also the accused in a criminal trial. It turns out, however, that the accused is not guilty of the crime for which he is charged, and in fact has committed no crime whatsoever. Should a judge who, we may suppose, is the only one who knows both that the man is dangerous and innocent, find the accused guilty? Doing so will prevent the predicted criminal behaviour of the defendant because the latter will be incarcerated. On a utilitarian theory, it is difficult to see why such a judgement would not be perfectly appropriate, as long as the prediction is reliable enough, and as long as the crimes predicted are sufficiently serious that the good of their prevention outweighs the harm of punishing that person, even though he has committed as yet no crime.

The general form of the argument arising from these kinds of thought experiments is that of a *reductio ad absurdum* argument. The argument has three premises:

1. Punishment should be inflicted if, and only if, doing so achieves a net social gain.
2. A net social gain would be achieved in this case by the infliction of punishment.
3. Punishment should not be inflicted in this case.

Each of these premises corresponds to steps in both of the thought experiments above. The first premise is simply a restatement of the utilitarian theory of punishment. The second premise presupposes that there are some cases where a net social gain can be achieved by punishing an innocent person, and asserts that this is such a case. The third premise asserts our intuition that such persons ought not to be punished.

All three premises together yield a contradiction:

4. Punishment should not be inflicted and punishment should be inflicted.

The first two premises have as their joint conclusion that the person should be punished; this conclusion, when conjoined with the third premise, produces the contradictory conclusion.

To avoid this contradictory conclusion, there are only three possibilities, corresponding to each of the three premises leading to it. One could give up the third premise and simply admit that in such cases the persons should be punished, despite their innocence. This move is a rather implausible one, inasmuch as it commits one to admitting that one will punish an entirely innocent person. The Australian philosopher, Jack Smart, is one of the few utilitarians willing to make this move.[22] This has earned Smart the following entry in Dan Dennett's humorous glossary of terms constructed out of philosopher's names:

Outsmart, v. To embrace the conclusion of one's opponent's *reductio ad absurdum* argument. (As in) 'They thought they had me, but I outsmarted them. I agreed that it was sometimes just to hang an innocent man.'[23]

The second possibility is to deny that there will be cases where there will be a net social gain from punishing an innocent person. This move is usually associated with the name of indirect utilitarianism and involves the idea that one cannot make a general practice of punishing the innocent, because then the harm of so doing (in terms of demoralization costs in society, character degradation costs, and the like) will outweigh any possible good to be achieved, even the

---

[22] J. J. C. Smart, 'Utilitarianism: For', in J. J. C. Smart and Bernard Williams, *Utilitarianism: For and Against* (Cambridge: Cambridge University Press, 1973), 67–73.

[23] Daniel Dennett and Karl Lambert, *The Philosophical Lexicon* (7th edn., privately printed, 1978), 8.

prevention of skyjacking.[24] The problem with this response, popular as it is, is that it fails to deal fairly with the nature of the thought experiment. That is, suppose that there are some risks of detection of punishment of innocent persons and thus, some risks of demoralization costs; such risk will only allow utilitarians to say that the number of cases in which punishment of the innocent will maximize utility is somewhat diminished. It does not foreclose as somehow impossible that there are such cases. Such cases are conceivable, and if in them one is still not willing to punish, one thereby shows oneself not to be a utilitarian about punishment.

This brings us to the third possibility: one can simply give up the first premise, that is, one can repudiate the utilitarian theory of punishment. Such thought experiments, I think, when clearly conceived and executed, show all persons who are not prepared to 'outsmart' their own firmest intuitions that they are not pure utilitarians about punishment.

V. ARGUMENTS AGAINST THE MIXED THEORY OF PUNISHMENT

The argument against the pure utilitarian theory of punishment does not by itself drive one into retributivism. For one can alleviate the injustice of the pure utilitarian theory of punishment by adopting the mixed theory earlier mentioned. Since under the mixed theory the desert of the offender is a necessary condition of punishment, it will follow from the mixed theory that in each of the kinds of counter-examples considered (where punishment is not deserved), punishment should not be given. There will be no contradictions generated, because the premises are consistent:

[24] The response classically associated with John Rawls's well-known article, 'Two Concepts of Rules', *The Philosophical Review*, Vol. 64 (1955), 3–32. The variations in formulation of indirect (or two-step) utilitarianisms since 1955 has been enormous. However, to the extent that any of such indirect utilitarianisms purport to give us the truth conditions of moral propositions such as, 'It is sometimes just to hang an innocent man'—and not merely the best decision-procedures justifying why we should *say*, or induce others to *believe*, such propositions (see Moore, 'Three Concepts of Rules', *Harvard Journal of Law and Public Policy*, Vol. 14 (1991), 771–95)—all such versions are subject to my objection in the text. For the most worries such as detection, etc., can do is justify us in setting up rule-utilitarian decision-procedures (institutions); it does not relieve the utilitarian decision-maker from confronting the blunt fact that his theory justifies the uncomfortable belief that some innocents should be punished.

1. Punishment should be inflicted if and only if doing so achieves both a net social gain and gives an offender his just deserts.
2. A net social gain would be achieved in this case by the infliction of punishment.
3. It is not the case that punishment would give an offender his just deserts in this case.
4. Punishment should not be inflicted.

From the first three of these premises, the conclusion is deducible that there should be no punishment. This is also what the fourth premise asserts, so that there is no contradiction when one substitutes the mixed theory for the utilitarian theory of punishment in the scapegoating and preventive detention thought experiments.

There is, nonetheless, another sort of thought experiment which tests whether one truly believes the mixed theory, or is in fact a pure retributivist. Such thought experiments are the kind that fill the editorial pages of our papers, when such opinions express outrage at the lightness of sentence in a particular case, or the lightness of sentencing generally in the courts of some communities. Consider some examples Mike Royko has used to get the blood to the eyes of readers of his newspaper column:

The small crowd that gathered outside the prison to protest the execution of Steven Judy softly sang 'We Shall Overcome'. . . .

But it didn't seem quite the same hearing it sung out of concern for someone who, on finding a woman with a flat tire, raped and murdered her and drowned her three small children, then said that he hadn't been 'losing any sleep' over his crimes. . . .

I remember the grocer's wife. She was a plump, happy woman who enjoyed the long workday she shared with her husband in their ma-and-pa store. One evening, two young men came in and showed guns, and the grocer gave them everything in the cash register.

For no reason, almost as an afterthought, one of the men shot the grocer in the face. The woman stood only a few feet from her husband when he was turned into a dead, bloody mess.

She was about 50 when it happened. In a few years her mind was almost gone, and she looked 80. They might as well have killed her too.

Then there was the woman I got to know after her daughter was killed by a wolfpack gang during a motoring trip. The mother called me occasionally, but nothing that I said could ease her torment. It ended when she took her own life.

A couple of years ago I spent a long evening with the husband, sister and parents of a fine young woman who had been forced into the trunk of a car in a hospital parking lot. The degenerate who kidnapped her kept her in the trunk, like an ant in a jar, until he got tired of the game. Then he killed her.[25]

Most people react to such atrocities with an intuitive judgement that punishment (at least of some kind and to some degree) is warranted. Many will quickly add, however, that what accounts for their intuitive judgement is the need for deterrence, or the need to incapacitate such a dangerous person, or the need to reform the person. My own view is that these addenda are just 'bad reasons for what we believe on instinct anyway', to paraphrase Bradley's general view of justification in ethics.

To see whether this is so, construct a thought experiment of the kind Kant[26] originated. Imagine that these same crimes were done in circumstances where there is no utilitarian reason to punish. The murderer has truly found Christ, for example, so that he or she is already reformed and thus is not dangerous; and the crime can go undetected so that general deterrence does not demand punishment (alternatively, we can pretend to punish and pay the person the money the punishment would have cost us to keep his or her mouth shut, which will also serve the ends of general deterrence). In such a situation, should the criminal still be punished?

Or consider the case that Sanford Kadish and Stephen Schulhofer include in their leading criminal law casebook, *State* v.

---

[25] Mike Royko, 'Nothing Gained by Killing a Killer? Oh Yes, There Is', *Los Angeles Times*, 13 Mar. 1981, Sec. II, 7. (Reprinted by permission of the Tribune Media Services.) Jeff Murphy also has his favourite Mike Royko quote: 'It's great to be back in Chicago where people still know how to hate.' Quoted in Jeffrie Murphy and Jean Hampton, *Forgiveness and Mercy* (Cambridge: Cambridge University Press, 1988), at 88.

[26] See Kant, *The Metaphysical Elements of Justice* (Indianapolis: Bobbs-Merrill, J. Ladd trans., 1965), 102: 'Even if a civil society were to dissolve itself by common agreement of all its members (for example, if the people inhabiting an island decided to separate and disperse themselves around the world), the last murderer remaining in prison must first be executed, so that everyone will duly receive what his actions are worth and so that the blood-guilt thereof will not be fixed on the people because they failed to insist on carrying out the punishment; for if they fail to do so, they may be regarded as accomplices in this public violation of legal justice.' Jean Hampton begins another such thought experiment from Dostoevsky's question of what to do with the Russian nobleman who unleashes his dogs to tear apart an eight-year-old child in the presence of the child's mother. Murphy and Hampton, *supra* n. 25, at 111. Dostoevsky in *The Brothers Karamazov* has Alyosha answer the question in terms that Royko and Kant would approve: ' "Shoot him!" Alyosha said softly.'

Chaney,[27] a case that also rouses our retributive juices. In *Chaney*, the defendant was tried and convicted of two counts of forcible rape, and one count of robbery. The defendant and a companion had picked up the prosecutrix at a downtown location in Anchorage. After driving the victim around in their car, the defendant and his companion beat her and forcibly raped her four times, also forcing her to perform an act of fellatio with the defendant's companion. During this same period of time, the victim's money was removed from her purse, and she only then was allowed to leave the vehicle after dire threats of reprisals if she attempted to report the incident to the police.

Despite this horrendous series of events, the trial judge imposed the minimum sentence on the defendant for each of the three counts, and went out of his way to remark that he (the trial judge) was 'sorry that the [military] regulations would not permit keeping [the defendant] in the service if he wanted to stay because it seems to me that is a better set up for everybody concerned than putting him in the penitentiary'. The trial judge also mentioned that as far as he was concerned, there would be no problem for the defendant to be paroled on the very first day of his sentence, if the parole board should so decide. The sentence was appealed by the state under a special Alaska procedure, and the attorney-general urged the Alaska Supreme Court to disapprove the sentence.

The thought experiment such a case begins to pose for us is as follows: Imagine in such a case that the defendant after the rape but before sentencing has got into an accident so his sexual and aggressive desires are dampened to such an extent that he presents no further danger of violence against women; if money was also one of his problems, suppose further that he has inherited a great deal of money, so that he no longer needs to rob. Suppose, because of both of these facts, we are reasonably certain that he does not present a danger of either forcible assault, rape, or robbery or related crimes in the future. Since Chaney is (by hypothesis) not dangerous, he does not need to be incapacitated, specially deterred, or reformed. Suppose further that we could successfully *pretend* to punish Chaney, instead of actually punishing him, and that no one

---

[27] *State* v. *Chaney*, 477 P 2d 441 (Alaska Sup. Ct. 1970). Kadish and Schulhofer presumably included *Chaney* for the same pedagogical purpose as those for which I use it here. S. Kadish and S. Schulhofer, *Cases and Materials on Criminal Law* (Boston: Little, Brown, 5th edn. 1989), 124–6.

is at all likely to find out. Our pretending to punish him will thus serve the needs of general deterrence and maintain social cohesion, and the cost to the state will be less than if it actually did punish him. Is there anything on the mixed theory of punishment which would urge that Chaney nonetheless should really be punished? I think not, so that if one's conclusion is that Chaney and people like him nonetheless should be punished, one will have to give up the mixed theory of punishment.

The argument structure is again that of a *reductio*, and is as follows:

1. Punishment should be inflicted if and only if doing so both achieves a net social gain and gives an offender his just deserts.
2. A net social gain would not be achieved in this case by the infliction of punishment.
3. Punishment should be inflicted.

Again these three premises generate a contradiction:

4. Punishment should not be inflicted and punishment should be inflicted.

From the first two premises, it follows that there should be no punishment; this contradicts the third premise that there nonetheless should be punishment.

One has, again, the choice of giving up one of the three premises of the argument. To give up the third premise is very unappealing to most people for it requires that people like Chaney should not be punished at all. Again, the tempting move is to assert that there will be no cases in which both utility would not be served by punishment and yet the offender deserves to be punished. One way to assert this is to deny that one will be sure enough that the danger is removed, or the ends of general deterrence served with only a pretended punishment of such deserving people. But as with the indirect utilitarian's defence of the pure utilitarian theory, this is simply to misunderstand the nature of the thought experiment. One only need think it conceivable that such dangers could be removed, or such ends of deterrence served, in order to test the truth of one's theory of punishment. And nothing in utilitarianism makes it even plausible to think that utility is always maximized by the punishment of the guilty.

If one is unwilling to give up the third premise (that punishment should be inflicted), even admitting that this is a case where no net social gain is achieved (thus accepting the second premise), then one has to give up the first premise. One has to give up, that is, the mixed theory of punishment.

C. L. Ten has recently urged that the mixed punishment theorist can avoid this result. Ten acknowledges the kind of thought experiment that gives trouble to the mixed theorist here,[28] but seeks to modify the mixed theory by adding in considerations of formal justice. Punishment in an individual case will be justified for Ten if and only if: either (there is a net social gain from this punishment *and* the offender deserves it) *or* (there is a net social gain from punishment of other offenders *and* equal justice demands that this offender be punished if those other offenders are punished).[29] It is this modification of the mixed theory that allows the mixed theorist to argue for 'punishment even though no overall utilitarian purpose is thereby served'.[30] Yet this surely will not do, for Ten has covertly smuggled a strong retributivist premise into his idea of equal justice. Equality demands that like cases be treated alike, but the crucial question is always, 'What are the relevant respects in which one case must be *like* another case in order to be deserving of like treatment?' Ten assumes that the only respect relevant here is moral desert, yet surely a mixed theorist is committed to saying that both moral desert *and* net social gain are relevant to punishability so that a person whose punishment does not serve both is not relevantly like a person whose punishment does serve both ends.[31]

---

[28] C. L. Ten, *supra* n. 18, at 47, considers a kind of Eichmann/Kant combination example: '[Consider] the example of a Nazi war criminal who escapes to an uninhabited island where 30 years later he is found leading "an idyllic existence". While he is still unrepentant for what he has done, he has no desire to cause further harm. (Let us also assume that his punishment would have no general deterrent effect on the behavior of others.)'

[29] See id. at 50–1, 79–80.   [30] Id. at 79.

[31] It is in addition unclear why only utility is needed in order to justify the earlier punishments Ten hypothesizes; a mixed theorist should think that earlier punishments serve both utility and retribution. Finally, Ten's modified mixed theory does not justify punishment of deserving persons *unless* there have been earlier punishments; the *first* offender in a society could thus not be punished if his own punishment did not represent a net social gain.

VI. AN ARGUMENT FOR RETRIBUTIVISM?

If one follows the predicted paths through these thought experiments, the end result is that one finds oneself, perhaps surprisingly, to be a retributivist. We might call this an argument from the back door for retributivism, because the argument does not assert in any positive way the correctness of retributivism. It only asserts that the two theories of punishment truly competitive with retributivism, namely, the pure utilitarian theory, and the mixed theory, are each unacceptable to us. That leaves retributivism as the only remaining theory of punishment that we can accept, assuming that we are not willing to give up the institution of punishment entirely. In some such way, one brings closet retributivists out of the closet to face whether, in the light of day, they are comfortable with their retributivist position. Whether they should be comfortable with their retributivism is the topic of the next chapter.

3

THE MORAL WORTH OF RETRIBUTION

I. ON JUSTIFYING RETRIBUTIVISM

In the last chapter I sought only to show that many of us have intuitive responses to particular thought experiments that reveal us to hold retributivist beliefs. In this chapter I seek to use this psychological fact as the basis for an inference to a moral fact, viz., that there is such a thing as retributive justice and that we should design our penal institutions so as to realize this kind of justice.

Retributivism, we should recall, is the view that it is a sufficient reason for us to have punishment institutions (i.e., the criminal law)—and for us to use those institutions to mete out a particular punishment to a particular person on a particular occasion—that the person deserve to be punished. Such sufficiency is construed as not merely giving our government the right to punish the guilty, but also and more importantly, as giving us the obligation to set up and support institutions to achieve such retributive justice.

Retributivism, so construed, joins corrective justice theories of torts, natural right theories of property, and promissory theories of contract as alternatives to utilitarian justifications;[1] in each case, the institutions and applications of punishment, tort compensation, property, and contract are justified by the rightness or fairness of

[1] I shall in this chapter make do with a somewhat imprecise distinction between utilitarian and retributivist theories. The imprecision arises because I leave aside for now (but see the beginning of the next chapter) the question of to what extent retributivism is an agent-relative (versus agent-neutral) moral theory, as those phrases are employed in chapter 17.

I allow 'retributivism' to label either sort of view, because they both raise the problem that is the focus of this chapter: how does one justify the rightness of punishing a guilty person just because he is guilty? Whether we are maximizing the punishment of the guilty (an agent-neutral view), or we are never letting an opportunity to punish the guilty go unheeded (an agent-relative view), the problem of intrinsic goodness requires a solution. I similarly allow 'corrective justice', 'Lockean', and 'promissory' theories to be either agent-relative or agent-neutral, since each of them possesses the same, unresolved ambiguity.

the institution/application in question, not by the good consequences each may generate. Further, for each of these theories,
moral desert plays the crucial justificatory role: tort sanctions are
justified whenever the plaintiff does not deserve to suffer the harm
uncompensated and the defendant by his or her conduct has created an unjust situation that merits corrective action; property
rights are justified whenever one party, by his labour, first possession, or intrinsic ownership of her own body, has come by such
actions or status morally to deserve such entitlements; and con-
tractual liability is justified by the fairness of imposing it on one
who deserves it (because of her voluntary undertaking and subsequent and unexcused breach).

Once the commitment of retributivism (to the intrinsic goodness
of punishing the guilty) is fully appreciated, it is often concluded
that such a view cannot be justified. You either believe punishment
to be inherently right, or you do not, and that is all there is to be
said about it. Hugo Bedau once expressed this attitude as a
dilemma for the retributivist:

Either he [the retributivist] appeals to something else—some good end—
that is accomplished by the practice of punishment, in which case he is
open to the criticism that he has a nonretributivist, consequentialist justification for the practice of punishment. Or his justification does not appeal
to something else, in which case it is open to the criticism that it is circular and futile.[2]

Such a restricted view of the justifications open to a retributivist
leads theorists in one of two directions: either they hang on to retributivism, urging that it is to be justified 'logically' (i.e., non-
morally) as inherent in the ideas of punishment[3] or of law;[4] or they
give up retributivism as an inherently unjustifiable view.[5] In either
case, retributivism is unfairly treated, since the first alternative trivializes it and the second eliminates it.

Bedau's dilemma is surely overstated. Retributivism is no
worse off in the modes of its possible justification than any other

    [2] Bedau, 'Retribution and the Theory of Punishment', *Journal of Philosophy*, Vol.
75 (1978), 601–20, at 616.

    [3] Quinton, 'On Punishment', *Analysis*, Vol. 14 (1954), 1933–42.

    [4] Fingarette, 'On Punishment and Suffering', *Proceedings of the American
Philosophical Association*, Vol. 50 (1977), 499–525.

    [5] S. I. Benn and R. S. Peters, *Social Principles and the Democratic State* (London:
Allan and Unwin, 1959).

non-utilitarian, justice-oriented theory. In the first place, one might become (like Bedau himself, apparently) a kind of 'reluctant retributivist'. A reluctant retributivist is someone who is somewhat repelled by retributivism but who nonetheless believes: (1) that there should be punishment; (2) that the only theories of punishment possible are utilitarian, rehabilitative, retributive, or some mixture of these; and (3) that there are decisive objections to utilitarian and rehabilitative theories of punishment, as well as to any mixed theory that uses either of these views in any combination. Such a person, as I argued in the last chapter, becomes, however reluctantly, a retributivist by default.

In the second place, positive arguments can be given for retributivism that do not appeal to some good consequences of punishing. It simply is not true that 'appeals to authority apart, we can justify rules and institutions only by showing that they yield advantages' or that 'to justify is to provide reasons in terms of something else accepted as valuable'.[6] Coherence, or 'non-foundationalist', theories of justification in ethics allow two non-consequentialist possibilities here:

1. We might justify a principle such as retributivism by showing how it follows from some yet more general principle of justice that we think to be true.
2. Alternatively, we can justify a moral principle by showing that it best accounts for those of our more particular judgements that we also believe to be true.

In a perfectly coherent system of our moral beliefs, the retributive principle would be justified in both these ways, by being part of the best theory of our moral sentiments, considered as a whole.

Neither of these non-foundationalist justificatory strategies is impaled on either horn of the supposed dilemma that Bedau articulates. Consider as an example of the first the plausible argument of Herbert Morris and others,[7] that the retributivist principle

---

[6] S. I. Benn and R. S. Peters, *Social Principles and the Democratic State,* at 175–6.

[7] Morris, 'Persons and Punishment', *The Monist,* Vol. 52 (1968), 475–501, reprinted in his *On Guilt and Innocence* (Los Angeles: University of California Press, 1976). Others defending a like theory include Jerrie Murphy, *Retribution, Justice and Therapy* (Dordrecht: Reidel, 1979); George Sher, *Desert* (Princeton: Princeton University Press, 1987); Michael Davis, 'Harm and Retribution', *Philosophy and Public Affairs,* Vol. 15 (1986), 236–66; Wojciech Sadurski, *Giving Desert Its Due* (Dordrecht: Reidel, 1985).

follows from a more general principle of fairness. Such a principle of fairness holds that it is unfair for anyone to keep advantages that all others have restrained themselves from seizing. Society, on this view is a scheme of mutual restraint and co-operation, and any free-rider on this scheme—i.e., one who enjoys the benefits of the scheme without paying the costs—should be made to 'pay' in the form of punishment. The principle of fair play that Morris references is not a 'good end', or a consequence, that punishment brings about. Rather, it is a more general principle that (together with suitable assumptions connecting punishment to payment, and criminal behaviour to free-riding) implies the retributivist principle that criminals should be punished because and only because of the wrongs they have culpably done. Nor is such a justification circular, since Morris builds his justification of retributivism with a logically distinct principle (fairness) that in no obvious way is itself justified by retributivism.[8] It is true that if Morris succeeds he will have shown the *intrinsic* goodness of retribution—that is, that retribution is good in-and-of itself, and not because it is *instrumental* to the attainment of something else that is good. But only if one confuses the status of the thing justified (intrinsic versus instrumental) with the status of the thing doing the justifying (circular versus non-circular) could one think that the intrinsic goodness claimed for retributivism makes the justification given for retributivism inherently circular.

The second non-foundationalist justificatory strategy is also immune to Bedau's dilemma. This is the strategy that begins with particular judgements about which one has some confidence, and asks, 'what general principle best fits these more particular judgements, so that the latter's truth is good evidence for the truth of the former?' This mode of justification is most familiarly associated with John Rawls,[9] so let us use the argument he gives for his general principles of distributive justice by way of illustration.[10] The

[8] Morris's kind of justification might be circular in the harmless sense that all coherence schemes are circular, if his justification of the principle of fairness is non-foundationalist in character. As I discuss in the text immediately below, such circularity is far from vicious and is what we should expect of the justification of *any* belief.

[9] See Rawls, 'Outline of a Decision Procedure for Ethics', *The Philosophical Review*, Vol. 60 (1951), 177–97.

[10] John Rawls, *A Theory of Justice* (Cambridge, Mass.: Harvard University Press, 1971).

particular judgements that together form the substantive[11] linchpin of Rawls's argument are the judgements that people do not have the right to gain whatever advantage they can from the social standing, wealth, or even natural talents with which they are born; these are morally arbitrary matters of contingent fact that no one has earned. Rawls's principles of justice are mostly an attempt to state the general principles that can best account for these 'considered judgments'. The principles of equal liberty, equality of opportunity, and the difference principle (inequalities allowed only if they make the least well off better off) are the general principles of equality that imply the more particular judgements that no one deserves their (unequal) place in the birth lottery.

There is no danger of this kind of justificatory argument being impaled on the first horn of Bedau's dilemma, for such justification does not at all attempt to ground itself in some further good achieved by acceptance of the principles to be justified. It may seem, however, that here there is a real danger of circularity and thus, triviality. 'For what', the critic might say to Rawls, 'have you done but state the general form of the particular judgements that you assumed to be true to start with? Surely those particular judgements themselves need first to be justified before they can be used to justify the general principles; and if the justification of those judgements is only that they follow from the two principles, then isn't the justification blatantly circular?'

The circularity charge to coherence theories of justification like Rawls's (and like that I shall be employing in this chapter) needs to be taken seriously. It is a deep question of moral epistemology to which I only intend here[12] to sketch an answer. That answer comes in three steps. The first step is to see that epistemic justification is by its nature non-foundationalist. In no field of knowledge—science as much as ethics—do we have the self-evident beliefs after which both rationalists like Descartes and empiricists like Carnap have long hankered. All we ever have with which to justify one

---

[11] 'Substantive', because I ignore the procedural judgements of fairness that form a large part of the justificatory apparatus of the book.

[12] I pursue this circularity worry further in the next chapter. A more complete sketch will be found in Moore, 'Moral Reality', *Wisconsin Law Review*, Vol. [1982], 1061–156; Moore, 'Moral Reality Revisited', *Michigan Law Review*, Vol. 90 (1992), 2424–533; Moore, 'Good Without God', in R. George and C. Wolfe, eds., *Natural Law and Liberalism* (Oxford: Oxford University Press, 1996).

belief, are other, *fallible* beliefs.[13] Second, this non-foundationalist nature to justification is radically holistic. That is, justification of any one belief—say in retributivism—is not simply a matter of showing that it best coheres with particular judgements of a retributive nature. It is partly that, but the coherence requirement is wider: the belief must also cohere with every other moral belief we have,[14] and, indeed, with everything else that we believe.[15] Belief in certain principles of justice are not 'sealed off' from beliefs about other subjects, but gain (or lose) credibility as they fit (or do not fit) those other beliefs too (for example, beliefs about the asymmetry of causation through time). Thirdly, and most crucially, coherence theories of justification are not simply matters of logical fit between general principles and particular judgements, however much John Rawls may have made it sound that way. Rather, we are justified in believing some principle like retributivism to be true when its truth does some explanatory work for us.[16] What work? In this instance, the work of explaining why it is that we have the strong emotional and cognitive responses we have to stories such as Royko's, Chaney's, Kant's, Dostoevsky's, or Ten's from the previous chapter. If the best explanation for why we have such responses is that we are caused to have them by the truth of retributivism—that is, by the existence of the entities and qualities to which the retributive principle refers—then we have good reason to believe the retributive principle. Such a justificatory schema might *look* circular, because the description of the items doing the explaining—here, a description of the retributive principle—may stand in some logical relation to the propositional contents of the beliefs

[13] Argued for in detail in Moore, 'Moral Reality', *supra* n. 12.
[14] See Daniels, 'Wide Reflective Equilibrium and Theory Acceptance in Ethics', *Journal of Philosophy*, Vol. 76 (1979), 256–82.
[15] See the works cited and discussed in Moore, 'Moral Reality', and 'Moral Reality Revisited', *supra* n. 12.
[16] For this 'best explanation' construal of coherence, see Gilbert Harman, *Thought* (Princeton: Princeton University Press, 1973). Although Harman himself, being a moral sceptic, does not think the best explanation strategy yields results in ethics, I and others have so taken coherence. See Moore, 'Moral Reality Revisited', *supra* n. 12; David Brink, *Moral Realism and the Foundations of Ethics* (Cambridge: Cambridge University Press, 1989); William Lycan, *Judgement and Justification* (Cambridge: Cambridge University Press, 1988); Nicholas Sturgeon, 'Moral Explanations', in D. Copp and D. Zimmerman, eds., *Morality, Reason, and Truth* (Totowa, N.J.: Rowman and Allenheld, 1984) and Richard Boyd, 'How To Be a Moral Realist', in G. Sayre-McCord, ed., *Essays on Moral Realism* (Ithaca: Cornell University Press, 1989).

being explained. Yet the circularity is no more vicious or problematic here than it is in the case where a general belief (for example, that all emeralds are green) is justified by the ability of the corresponding fact (that all emeralds are green) to best explain why it is that numerous people at numerous times have formed the perceptual belief that an item before them was both green and an emerald.

These remarks are doubtlessly too brief to be very convincing to any not already convinced of the meta-ethical views sketched. I shall take up more of these meta-ethical worries in the next chapter. For now, my hope is to clarify how I see the argument of this chapter proceeding.

As should be plain from the foregoing remarks, my justificatory strategy in this chapter will be the second of the two I distinguished. What I shall examine are particular judgements like, 'Steven Judy deserved to die for his murder of a mother and her three small children.' The thought experiments of the last chapter for me establish the prima facie superiority of retributive over utilitarian explanations of those judgements. What I shall next explore is why it is that many nonetheless reject the prima facie best explanation of their own judgements. Why is it that people often engage in a wild and (intellectually) unseemly scramble for any explanation *but* the retributivist one for their seemingly retributivist judgements?

II. THE CASE AGAINST RETRIBUTIVE JUDGEMENTS

The puzzle I put about particular retributive judgements is this: Why are these particular judgements so suspect—'primitive', 'barbarous', 'a throwback'—when other judgements in terms of moral desert are accorded places of honour in widely accepted moral arguments? Very generally, there seem to me to be five explanations (and supposed justifications) for this discriminatory treatment of retributive judgements about deserved punishment.

1. First and foremost there is the popularly accepted belief that punishment for its own sake does no good. 'By punishing the offender you cannot undo the crime', might be the slogan for this point of view. I mention this view only to put it aside, for it is but a reiteration of the instrumentalist idea that only further good con-

sequences achieved by punishment could possibly justify the practice. Unnoticed by those who hold this position is that they abandon such instrumentalism when it comes to other areas of morals. It is a sufficient justification not to scapegoat innocent individuals, that they do not deserve to be punished; the injustice of punishing those who do not deserve it seems to stand perfectly well by itself as a justification of our practices, without need for further good consequences we might achieve. Why do we not similarly say that the injustice of the guilty going unpunished can equally stand by itself as a justification for punishment, without need of a showing of further good consequences? It simply is not the case that justification always requires the showing of further good consequences.

Those who oppose retributivism often protest at this point that punishment is a clear harm to the one punished, and the intentional causing of this harm requires some good thereby achieved to justify it; whereas *not* punishing the innocent is not a harm and thus does not stand in need of justification by good consequences. Yet this response simply begs the question against retributivism. Retributivism purports to be a theory of justice, and as such claims that punishing the guilty achieves something good—namely, justice—and that therefore reference to any other good consequences is simply beside the point. One cannot defeat the central retributivist claim—that justice is achieved by punishing the guilty—simply by assuming that it is false.

The question-begging character of this response can be seen by imagining a like response in areas of tort, property, or contract law. Forcing another to pay tort or contract damages, or to forgo use and possession of some thing, is a clear harm that corrective justice theories of tort, promissory theories of contract, or natural right theories of property are willing to impose on defendants. Suppose no one gains anything of economic significance by certain classes of such impositions—as, for example, in cases where the plaintiff has died without heirs after his cause of action accrued. 'It does no good to force the defendant to pay', interposed as an objection to corrective justice theories of tort, promissory theories of contract, or natural right theories of property simply denies what these theories assert: that something good *is* achieved by imposing liability in such cases—namely, that justice is done.

This 'harm requires justification' objection thus leaves untouched the question of whether the rendering of justice cannot in all such cases be the good that justifies the harm all such theories impose on defendants. I accordingly put aside this initial objection to retributivism, relying as it does either upon an unjustifiable discrimination between retributivism and other justice-oriented theories, or upon a blunderbuss assault on theories of justice as such.

2. A second and very popular suspicion about retributive judgements is that they presuppose an indefensible omniscience about when the conditions of wrongdoing and (particularly) culpability are satisfied. Although this epistemological modesty could be based on our supposed inability to know what culpability *is*, more typically it is based on our supposed inability to know when the mental states required for culpability exist in the mind of another. As Beccaria put it centuries ago:

[W]hat insect will dare take the place of divine justice . . . ? The gravity of sin depends upon the inscrutable wickedness of the heart. No finite being can know it without revelation. How then can it furnish a standard for the punishment of crimes?[17]

We might call this the 'don't play God' objection.

One way to deal with this objection is to show that moral judgements generally (and judgements about culpability particularly) are knowable by persons. Showing this is a complicated business in epistemology, and since I have attempted such a showing elsewhere,[18] let me try a different tack. A striking feature of the 'don't play God' objection is how inconsistently it is applied. Let us revert to our use of desert as a limiting condition on punishment: we certainly seem confident both that we can know generally that we should not punish the morally innocent because they do not deserve it and that certain persons do not deserve punishment because they are innocent of any wrongdoing. Neither form of epistemological modesty gets in our way when we use lack of moral desert as a reason not to punish. Why should it be different when we use presence of desert as a reason to punish? If we can know when someone does *not* deserve punishment, is it not likely that we can know when

---

[17] Beccaria, *On Crimes and Punishments*, J. Grigson, trans., in A Manzoni, ed., *The Column of Infamy* (Oxford: Oxford University Press, 1964). Kant, too (rather inconsistently with his retributivism), thought that 'the real morality of actions, their merit or guilt . . . remains entirely hidden from us'. For a discussion of this and other anti-retributive passages in Kant, see Murphy, 'Does Kant Have a Theory of Punishment?', *Columbia Law Review*, Vol. 87 (1987), 509–32.

[18] See Moore, 'Moral Reality', 'Moral Reality Revisited', *supra* n. 12.

someone *does* deserve punishment? Consider the illogic in the following passages from Karl Menninger:

The very word *justice* irritates scientists. No surgeon expects to be asked if an operation for cancer is just or not. No doctor will be reproached on the grounds that the dose of penicillin he has prescribed is less or more than *justice* would stipulate.[19]

It does not advance a solution to use the word *justice*. It is a subjective emotional word. . . . The concept is so vague, so distorted in its applications, so hypocritical, and usually so irrelevant that it offers no help in the solution of the crime problem which it exists to combat but results in its exact opposite—injustice, injustice to everybody.[20]

Apparently the late Dr Karl knew injustice when he saw it, even if justice is a useless concept.

Analogously, consider our reliance on moral desert when we allocate initial property entitlements. We think that the person who works hard to produce a novel deserves the right to determine when and under what conditions the novel will be copied for others to read. The novelist's labour gives him or her the moral right. How can we know this—how can it be true—if desert can be judged only by those with godlike omniscience? Such epistemological modesty about just deserts would throw out a great deal that we will not throw out. To me, this shows that no one really believes that moral desert is unknowable. Something else makes us suspect our retributive judgements other than supposed epistemological modesty.

3. One particular form of moral scepticism merits separate attention in this context: this is the scepticism that asserts that no one is really responsible for anything because everything we do is caused by factors over which we have no control, and therefore none of us is really guilty or deserving of punishment. '*Tout comprendre c'est tout pardonner*', as the folk wisdom has it.

The main problem with this bit of folk wisdom is that it is false. To understand all (the causes of behaviour) is not to forgive all. To match proverb for proverb: 'Everybody has a story', as many convicts well know, realizing that such stories hardly excuse.[21]

To do more than match proverbs against this objection to

---

[19] Karl Menninger, *The Crime of Punishment* (New York: Viking Press, 1968), 17.
[20] Id. at 10–11.
[21] The matching proverb is from Stephen Morse. See Morse, 'Justice, Mercy, and Craziness', *Stanford Law Review*, Vol. 36 (1984), 1485–515, at 1499.

retributivism requires an extended excursion into compatibilist moral psychology. Since we shall take such an excursion in chapter 12, I will not here anticipate the argument defending the view that most people are responsible for what they do irrespective of the truth of determinism. In any case, if retributivism is to be rejected on hard determinist grounds, all justice theories in property, contract, and torts would have to be rejected as well, since no one could act in a way (viz., freely) so as to deserve anything.

4. A fourth popular suspicion about using moral desert as a justification to punish takes the opposite tack from the last objection. Here the thought is not that *none* of us are guilty, but rather that *all* of us are guilty—so that if we each got what we truly deserved, we would all be punished. How, then, can such a ubiquitous human condition be used to single out some but not all for punishment? Christ, of course, is the most famous purveyor of this argument when he dissuades the Pharisees from stoning an adulteress with an explicit appeal to their own guilt: 'He that is without sin among you, let him first cast a stone at her' (John 8:3–11).

If we take this literally (I will give it a more charitable interpretation later), this is pretty clumsy moral philosophy. It is true that all of us are guilty of some immoralities, probably on a daily basis. Yet for most people reading this chapter, the immoralities in question are things like manipulating others unfairly; not caring deeply enough about another's suffering; not being charitable for the limitations of others; convenient lies; and so forth.[22] Few of us have raped and murdered a woman, drowned her three small children, and felt no remorse about it afterwards, to revert to one of Royko's examples. It is simply false—and obviously so—to equate guilt at the subtle immoralities of personal relationships with the gross violations of persons that violent crime represents. We do not all deserve the punishment of a murderer for the simple and sufficient reason that we are not all murderers, or anything like murderers in responsibility.

One can of course quote more scripture here—'He that lusts after a woman has already committed adultery with her'—but that also is to miss some obvious and basic moral distinctions. Freud is surely to be preferred to scripture here, when he urged that we must give credit where credit is due: if our conscience is such that we do

---

[22] What the late Judith Shklar called the 'ordinary vices'. See her taxonomy in *Ordinary Vices* (Cambridge, Mass.: Harvard University Press, 1984).

not allow ourselves to act on our admittedly wicked fantasies, that makes us a better person than one who not only dreams of such atrocities, but brings them about.[23]

The short of it is that desert is not such a ubiquitous feature of human personality that it cannot be a marker of punishment. To think otherwise is to gloss over obvious moral distinctions, a glossing that to me is so obviously wrong that it can only be a cover for a judgement made on other grounds.

5. It is often said that retributive judgements are 'irrational'. They are irrational, it is said, because they are based on 'emotion rather than reason'. Such irrational emotion cannot be the basis for justifying a legal institution such as punishment. Legal institutions can be justified only by reason, not by yielding to irrational emotions, whether ours or others'. Henry Weihofen once stated this objection forthrightly:

It is not only criminals who are motivated by irrational and emotional impulsions. The same is true also of lawyers and judges, butchers and bakers. And it is especially true on such a subject as punishment of criminals. This is a matter on which we are all inclined to have deep feelings. When a reprehensible crime is committed, strong emotional reactions take place in all of us. Some people will be impelled to go out at once and work off their tensions in a lynching orgy. Even the calmest, most law-abiding of us is likely to be deeply stirred. . . . It is one of the marks of a civilized culture that it has devised legal procedures that minimize the impact of emotional reactions and strives for calm and rational disposition. But lawyers, judges and jurors are still human, and objective, rational inquiry is made difficult by the very irrationality of the human mind itself. . . . Consciously we want to be rational. We prefer to think of ourselves as governed by reason rather than as creatures swept by irrational emotions.[24]

This objection, as stated, proves far too much for its own good. Think for a moment about the intimate connection between our emotions and morality, a matter we explore later in this chapter. Although Kantian beings who could know morality without relying upon their emotions are perhaps conceivable—just barely—that surely is not us. We need our emotions to know about the injustice

---

[23] For quotations, citations, and argument, see Moore, 'Responsibility and the Unconscious', *Southern California Law Review*, Vol. 53 (1980), 1563–5, at 1629, n. 198. Compare Herbert Morris's discussion in his *On Guilt and Innocence*, *supra* n. 7, at 124–5.

[24] Henry Weihofen, *The Urge to Punish* (New York: Farrar, Straus, and Cudahy, 1956).

of racial discrimination, the unfairness of depriving another of a favourite possession, the immorality of punishing the innocent. Our emotions are our main heuristic guide to finding out what is morally right.

We do both them and morality a strong disservice when we accept the old shibboleth that emotions are opposed to rationality. There is, as I and others have argued,[25] a rationality of the emotions that can make them trustworthy guides to moral insight. Emotions are rational when they are intelligibly proportionate in their intensity to their objects, when they are not inherently conflicted, when they are coherently orderable, and instantiate over time an intelligible character. We also judge when emotions are appropriate to their objects; that is, when they are *correct.*

The upshot is that unless one severs any connection of our legal institutions to morals, one cannot condemn an institution because it is based on 'emotions'. Some emotions generate moral insights our legal system could hardly do without, such as the insight that it is outrageously unfair to punish an innocent person. Imagine condemning the legal ban on punishing the innocent because it is based on emotion and not on reason.

To be sure, there is also a sense of rationality opposed to emotionality.[26] This is the sense in which we view rationality as reason and will and see these faculties as 'unhinged' by powerful emotional storms. It is this sense of emotionality we use when we partially excuse a killer because the act was the product of extreme passion,

---

[25] Moore, 'Moral Reality', *supra* n. 12, at 1135–6; Michael Moore, *Law and Psychiatry: Rethinking the Relationship* (Cambridge: Cambridge University Press, 1984), at 107–8. See also the now considerable literature on the rationality of the emotions. Ronald de Sousa, 'The Rationality of the Emotions', in A. Rorty, ed., *Explaining Emotions* (Berkeley: University of California Press, 1980); de Sousa, *The Rationality of Emotion* (Cambridge, Mass.: MIT Press, 1987); R. Gordon, *The Structure of Emotions: Investigations in Cognitive Philosophy* (New York: Cambridge University Press, 1987); W. Lyons, *Emotion* (Cambridge: Cambridge University Press, 1980); Scruton, 'Emotion, Practical Knowledge, and Common Culture', in A. Rorty, *supra*; Calhoun, 'Cognitive Emotions?', in C. Calhoun and R. Soloman, eds., *What Is an Emotion?* (Oxford: Oxford University Press, 1984); Roberts, 'What an Emotion Is: A Sketch', *The Philosophical Review*, Vol. 97 (1988), 183–209. Those making use of the cognitive nature of the retributive emotions to argue for the propriety of allowing such emotions to guide our retributive judgements also include Jean Hampton and Jeff Murphy, *Forgiveness and Mercy* (Cambridge: Cambridge University Press, 1988), and Samuel Pillsbury, 'Emotional Justice: Moralizing the Passions of Criminal Punishment', *Cornell Law Review*, Vol. 74 (1989), 655–710.

[26] Moore, *Law and Psychiatry*, *supra* n. 25, at 86–90, 107–8; see also ch. 13, *infra*.

not cool rationality. It is also this sense of rationality versus emotionality that is sometimes played upon by those making this objection to retributivism. The picture is one in which the retributivist emotions unhinge our reason by their power.

Karen Horney's assumption that vindictiveness is always neurotic (and thus always undesirable) is based upon this kind of characterization:

Often there is no more holding back a person driven toward revenge than an alcoholic determined to go on a binge. Any reasoning meets with cold disdain. Logic no longer prevails. Whether or not the situation is appropriate does not matter. It overrides prudence. Consequences for himself and others are brushed aside. He is as inaccessible as anybody who is in the grip of a blind passion.[27]

There is more than a little truth to this conception of the emotional base of retributivism. Literature is rich in faithful depictions of otherwise rational and moral people being unhinged by an urge to punish another for a wrong. Susan Jacoby[28] recounts the tale of Michael Kohlhaas, written into a novel in the early nineteenth century by Heinrich von Kleist. Kohlhaas is depicted as a benevolent man, a horse dealer, friendly, kind, loyal to those around him, but one whose life is altered by the dominating passion of revenge. Kohlhaas's animals are maltreated by his neighbour—a man of higher social position—and Kohlhaas, in his unbending quest to make the offending squire pay, 'eventually destroys his business and his marriage [his wife is killed by the enemies he has made]; burns down the squire's house; murders innocent inhabitants of the castle; and incites a revolt that lays waste to much of the surrounding countryside'.[29]

This is pathological and is fairly described as reason being overcome by a domineering, obsessive emotion. Yet it is surely not the case that the retributive urge always operates like this. Pathological cases can be found for any emotions, including benevolent ones. We should not judge the moral worth of an emotion by cases where it dominates reason, unless we are willing to say that such an

---

[27] Horney, 'The Value of Vindictiveness', *American Journal of Psychoanalysis*, Vol. 8 (1948), 3–12, at 5.

[28] Susan Jacoby, *Wild Justice: The Evolution of Revenge* (New York: Harper and Row, 1984). For an update of von Kleist's tale, see the story of 'Coalhouse Walker' in E. L. Doctorow's *Ragtime* (New York: Random House, 1975).

[29] Jacoby, *supra* n. 28, at 51–2.

emotion typically leads to such pathology; and the retributive intuition described here does not. One can have the intuition that the guilty deserve punishment, and one can have emotional outrage when they do not get it, without having one's reason dominated by an emotional storm. We may feel morally outraged at some guilty criminal going unpunished, but that need be no more unhinging of our reason than our outrage at the innocent being punished. In both cases, intense emotions may generate firm moral convictions; in each case, the emotions can get out of hand and dominate reason—but that is no reason to discount the moral judgements such emotions support when they do *not* get out of hand.

Consider a third construal of this 'too emotional' charge against retributivism: some emotions are irrational in the sense that they can achieve no intelligible good for the individual who has them. John Rawls argued that the emotion of envy was irrational in this sense,[30] and more recently Jean Hampton has urged that what she calls malicious and spiteful hatreds are like this as well.[31] Hampton argues that the point of malicious or spiteful hatred is to shore up one's own sense of self-worth, a sense made shaky by the culpable violation of one's rights by the object of one's hatred. Such hatred is irrational for Hampton, not because such shoring up would not be a good thing for crime victims, but rather, because such hatred is incapable of achieving its point. Such hatred is necessarily self-defeating in achieving such point because it is incapable of causing the beliefs needed to shore up one's sense of self-worth.

Since Hampton distinguishes malicious and spiteful hatred from indignation, resentment, and moral hatred, it is not clear that she is convicting all retributive urges of this kind of irrationality. But if such a broadened charge were to be made, it surely could not be the complaint against all forms of the retributive emotions. For the retributivist has an easy answer to this kind of charge of irrationality: such emotions do have an intelligible and good object, that wrongdoers suffer and justice thus be done. One cannot urge that this is not good without begging the question about retributivism (whether requiting evil with pain is or is not just); and one cannot urge that the retributive emotions do not cause justice to be done without imposing a far too intellectualistic, means/end ratio-

[30] Rawls, *A Theory of Justice*, *supra* n. 10, at §§80–1.
[31] Hampton, 'Forgiveness, Resentment, and Hatred', in Murphy and Hampton, *supra* n. 25.

nality requirement on them. We have intelligible objects to our emotions even when our *feeling* such emotions does not cause the state of affairs that is their object, to come about. Feeling emotion is not always (or even often) a *strategy* whereby we cause some good to be realized, and the rationality of all of the retributive emotions cannot be judged on such a standard.

Despite the foregoing, I think that the most serious objection to retributivism as a theory of punishment lies in the emotional base of retributive judgements. As thus far construed, the objection is, as we have seen, ill-fated. If stated as an objection to there being an emotional base at all to judgements about deserved punishment, the objection is far too broad to be acceptable. All moral judgements would lose to such a charge if it were well-founded. If stated as an objection to the unhinging quality of retributive emotions, the objection is psychologically implausible. Any emotion in pathological cases can unhinge reason, and there is nothing about retributive emotions that make it at all plausible that they always unhinge our reason when we experience them. If construed as an objection to the lack of an intelligible good that the having of such an emotion can cause, the objection is both question-begging and too strategic in its conception of the rationality of emotions. The objection thus needs some other construal.

My own sense is that the true charge to be made against the rationality of the retributive emotions is this: the emotions that give rise to retributive judgements are always pathological—not in their intensity and consequent ability to unhinge our reason, and not in their lack of any point that they have or can serve, but in their moral nature. Some emotions, such as racial prejudice, have negative moral worth in the sense that to have them is to be a morally worse (less virtuous) person. The true worry that most people have about retributivism is that the retributive urge is one such emotion (or set of emotions).

In discussing this version of the objection to the emotional base of retributivism, I shall by and large rely on Nietzsche, who to my mind remains one of the most penetrating psychologists of the unsavoury side of our emotional life. He is also one of the few thinkers to have delved deeply into the psychology of revenge.[32]

---

[32] Although the appearance of the very interesting accounts of Murphy and Hampton (*supra*, n. 25) after this chapter was initially drafted gives reason to hope for a much richer literature.

There is surprisingly little written on revenge in modern psychiatry, in large part because psychiatrists regard revenge 'like sex before Freud . . ., condemned as immature and undesirable and thus unworthy of serious scientific investigation'.[33]

'Mistrust', Nietzsche's Zarathustra advises us, 'all in whom the impulse to punish is powerful.'[34] Nietzsche clearly believed that the retributive emotions can get in the way of that celebration of life that makes us better human beings. As he said in *The Gay Science*: 'I do not want to wage war against what is ugly. I do not want to accuse; I do not even want to accuse those who accuse. *Looking away* shall be my only negation.'[35] And as he repeated later: 'Let us not become darker ourselves on their [criminals'] account, like all those who punish others and feel dissatisfied. Let us sooner step aside. Let us look away.'[36]

What is the awful vision from which we should avert our gaze? If Nietzsche is right, truly a witches' brew: resentment, fear, anger, cowardice, hostility, aggression, cruelty, sadism, envy, jealousy, guilt, self-loathing, hypocrisy and self-deception—those 'reactive affects' that Nietzsche sometimes lumped under the French term *ressentiment*.[37] All this, Nietzsche believed, lies behind our judgements of retributive justice.

Consider first resentment. One of Nietzsche's deepest insights into moral genealogy is how much the retributive urge is based on resentment. As Max Scheler once explained Nietzsche's insight here: 'Revenge . . ., based as it is upon an experience of impotence, is always primarily a matter of those who are "weak" in some respect.'[38] If we feel physically, psychologically, or politically weak, we will feel threatened by those we perceive to be stronger, such as those willing and able to use physical violence. Moreover, if we are actually or vicariously injured by such stronger persons, our weakness may prevent us from venting in the most direct way the anger such violation generates. Rather than either venting such anger

---

[33] Harvey Lomas, quoted in Jacoby, *supra* n. 28, at 169.

[34] Friedrich Nietzsche, *Thus Spoke Zarathustra*, in W. Kaufmann ed., *The Portable Nietzsche* (New York: Viking, 1954), 212.

[35] Friedrich Nietzsche, *The Gay Science*, Kaufmann, trans. (New York: Vintage, 1974), 223.

[36] Id. at 254.

[37] Friedrich Nietzsche, *On the Genealogy of Morals*, Kaufmann, trans. (New York: Vintage, 1969), 74.

[38] Max Scheler, *Ressentiment* (Holdheim trans., New York: Free Press, 1961), 46.

directly through our own action (of retaliation), or at least feeling able to do so but choosing to refrain, our real or perceived helplessness transforms the anger into the brooding resentment of those who lack power. Such resentment, Nietzsche rightly thinks, can poison the soul, with its unstable equilibrium of repressed anger and repressing fear. A resentful person is burdened with an emotional conflict that is both ugly and harmful. It is better for us, because of this, to 'look away' rather than to brood about revenge.

Our weakness and its accompanying emotions of fear and resentment can also make our retributive inclination seem cowardly, herdlike, and weak. As Nietzsche observed at one point: ' "Punishment" . . . is simply a copy . . . of the normal attitude toward a hated, disarmed, prostrated enemy, who has lost not only every right and protection, but all hope of quarter as well . . .'[39] Yet unlike the victor in a fight who has won and who can afford to be merciful to a vanquished foe, those who wish to punish may feel that this is their first opportunity to get back, an opportunity they cannot afford to pass up. When Christ talks about throwing stones, it is not because we are all equally guilty that we should not throw the stones; rather, there is something cowardly in a group of persons throwing stones at one who is now helpless. Such cowardice can be exhibited by the need of such persons for group reinforcement (which is why avengers may refuse to throw the *first stone*— it would set one apart from the group). It is no accident that the retributive urge calls up images of mobs, groups who together finally find the strength to strike back at an only now helpless foe. Our fear and our resentment of criminals can make us look small and cowardly in our retaliation in a way that immediate retaliation by one without fear or resentment does not.

Our fear of criminals need not always be due to our sense of their power to hurt; sometimes we may feel such fears just because they are different. For some people, there is a link between fear of strangers and fear of criminals, a link partly reflected by the extraordinary group reinforcement they receive when their retributive urges are shared. Such a link is also reflected in the we-they attitude many adopt about criminals, an attitude suggesting that criminals are fundamentally different and outside the group about whom we need be concerned. This is the criminal as outlaw, an

[39] *Genealogy, supra* n. 37, at 72–3.

attitude that, although neither causing nor caused by prejudice and bigotries of various kinds, nonetheless invites such other fears of differences to get expressed in retributive judgements.

Even when we do not feel weak and threatened by criminals, we may find other emotions underlying our retributive judgements that are not very pretty. Surely one of the uglier spectacles of our times are the parties by fraternity boys outside the gates of prisons when an execution is taking place. What makes such spectacles so ugly is the cruelty and sadistic pleasure at the suffering of others that they express. Such people feel entitled to let go of the normal constraints on expressing such unsavoury emotions because the legitimacy of retribution licenses it. It is all right to enjoy the suffering of criminals, because it is deserved suffering. Deserved punishment, as Nietzsche perceived, can be 'a warrant for and title to cruelty'.[40] It can give us 'the pleasure of being allowed to vent [our] power freely upon one who is powerless, the voluptuous pleasure of doing evil for the pleasure of doing it, the enjoyment of violation'.[41] Our retributive judgements, in such a case, look like a rationalization of, and excuse for, venting emotions we would be better off without.

There are admittedly other avenues in this society for people to vent sadistic enjoyment of another's suffering. One that comes to mind are such films as *The Texas Chain Saw Massacre*. Reported audience reaction to a scene depicting a helpless female about to be dismembered by a chainsaw included cries of 'Cut the bitch'. The unrestrained sadism in such reactions is a deep sickness of the soul. To the extent that our inclinations to punish are based on a like emotion, it too, as Menninger says, lines us 'up with the Marquis de Sade, who believed in pleasure, especially the pleasure derived from making someone else feel displeasure'.[42]

There is also envy and jealousy sometimes to be found lying at the emotional base of our retributive inclinations.[43] We seem to have some admiration for criminals, an admiration reflected in the attention we give them in the media and the arts. We may admire their strength and courage; criminals, as Herbert Morris aptly describes it, may manifest 'what we too often do not, power and daring, a willingness to risk oneself for the satisfaction of strong

---

[40] *Genealogy, supra* n. 37, at 65.   [41] Id.
[42] Menninger, *supra* n. 19, at 201.
[43] Nietzsche, *Zarathustra, supra* n. 34, at 213.

desires'.[44] Thackery had the same insight, writing *Vanity Fair* in large part to show us how much more we admire strength (Becky) than we do the conventional moral virtues (Amelia). Moreover, within the breasts of most of us beat some criminal desires. Not only may we admire the strength of will criminals may exhibit, but we may also be excited by the desires they allow themselves to satisfy. We thus may suffer a double dose of envy, both of the desires acted on and the strength that is exhibited in acting on them. Such envy and jealousy fuels the retributive urge, because punishment will tear down the object of such feelings.

Guilt has an interesting relationship to envy here. If criminals sometimes do what we might like to do but restrain ourselves from doing by our guilt, crime may excite a particularly virulent kind of envy. We may be envious not only of the power and the satisfaction of desires represented by criminal behaviour, but even more of the freedom from guilt we may attribute to the criminal. Our own guilt in such a case may be challenged by apparent examples of such guiltless freedom to act on forbidden desires; if so, our defence is to transform the envy into the desire to destroy that which so challenges our own precarious balance between good and evil.

Guilt can give rise to our retributive judgements about others without the 'good offices' of the emotions of envy and jealousy. Such retributivist judgements may simply project our own guilt onto the criminal and by doing so, lessen our guilt feelings because we are better than he. Henry Weihofen aptly describes this Freudian insight about retribution:

No one is more ferocious in demanding that the murderer or the rapist 'pay' for his crime than the man who has felt strong impulses in the same direction. No one is more bitter in condemning the 'loose' woman than the 'good' women who have on occasion guiltily enjoyed some purple dreams themselves. It is never he who is without sin who casts the first stone.

Along with the stone, we cast our own sins onto the criminal. In this way we relieve our own sense of guilt without actually having to suffer the punishment—a convenient and even pleasant device for it not only relieves us of sin, but makes us feel actually virtuous.[45]

---

[44] Morris, *On Guilt and Innocence*, *supra* n. 7, at 132.

[45] Weihofen, *supra* n. 24, at 138. What I take to be non-virtuous about projected guilt is not the guilt (about which, more below) but the lessening of it by the self-deceptive mechanism of projection.

The retributive urge often seems to be accompanied by the additional non-virtues of self-deception and hypocrisy. Few people like to think of themselves as weak and resentful, fearful, cowardly, cruel and sadistic, envious, jealous, and guilt-ridden. Accordingly, if they possess such emotions and traits when they make retributive judgements, they have every reason to deceive themselves about it. Such self-deception Nietzsche thought to be 'the masterpiece of these black magicians, who make whiteness, milk, and innocence of every blackness . . .'[46] 'These cellar rodents full of vengefulness and hatred' have reconceived their black emotions into an abstract virtue:

We good men—*we are the just*—what they desire they call, not retaliation, but the triumph of *justice*; what they hate is not their enemy, no! They hate injustice, they hate godlessness; what they believe in and hope for is not the hope of revenge . . . but the victory of God, of the *just* God, over the godless.[47]

Self-deception and hypocrisy themselves are vices, and to the extent that our retributive judgements encourage them—because we cannot affirm the emotional base of such judgements—we would be better without them.

To this basically Nietzschean indictment of the emotions on which retributive judgements seem to be based, we may add the insight of some feminists that the urge to retaliate is an instance of a male and macho stereotype that is itself no virtue. As Susan Jacoby points out,[48] there are actually two not entirely consistent stereotypes that operate here. One is that revenge is a male prerogative because it is the manly thing to do. The other is that women are the greatest avengers because (harking back to Nietzsche) their physical and political weakness demands subtler, more repressed, and thus more intense modes of retaliation. Such views are compliments neither to men nor to women. Such stereotypes, like racial prejudice and other differences mentioned earlier, do not cause our retributive judgements so much as they find in such judgements a vehicle for their expression.

Finally, consider the kind of 'scoring mentality' that accompanies retributive judgements. As Scheler noted: 'It is of the essence of revenge that it always contains the *consciousness* of "tit for tat",

---

[46] Nietzsche, *Genealogy, supra* n. 37, at 47. See also Horney, *supra* n. 27, at 4.
[47] Nietzsche, *Genealogy, supra* n. 37, at 48.   [48] Jacoby, *supra* n. 28, ch. 6.

so that it is never a mere emotional reaction.'[49] Nietzsche too scorned the 'shopkeeper's scales and the desire to balance guilt and punishment' as a part of the retributive urge.[50] Retributivism requires a kind of keeping track of another's moral ledger that seems distasteful. Retributive judgements seem legalistic, a standing on one's rights or a satisfaction with 'doing one's duty' that psychologically crowds out more virtuous modes of relating to others. 'Bother justice', E. M. Forster has his protagonist exclaim in *Howard's End*. Margaret later goes on to say that she will have 'none of this absurd screaming about justice. . . . Nor am I concerned with duty. I'm concerned with the character of various people whom we know, and how, things being as they are, things may be made a little better'.[51] Aristotle understood the same point in his familiar thought that 'between friends there is no need of justice'. Relate to others in a way that does not concern itself with giving them their just deserts, positive or negative. Those who keep track of favours owed, debts due, or punishments deserved cut themselves off from modes of relating to others that can be both more virtuous (because supererogatory) and also more rewarding than demanding rights or acting on duties.

It may well be that insofar as the retributive urge is based on such emotions as these, or causes us to instantiate traits such as self-deception, the urge is bad for us.[52] It makes us less well formed, less virtuous human beings to experience such emotions—or, more accurately, to be the sort of person who has such emotions. This insight about what are and what are not virtuous emotions to have persuades many people that they ought not to make retributive judgements. For it is natural to feel that such judgements are contaminated by their dark emotional sources. Defence lawyers have long recognized our tendency to withdraw or soften our retributive demands once we see the emotional base for them. Consider Clarence Darrow's appeals to Judge Caverly's virtue in Darrow's famous closing argument in the Loeb and Leopold sentencing hearing:

---

[49] Scheler, *supra* n. 38, at 46.

[50] Friedrich Nietzsche, *The Dawn*, in W. Kaufmann, ed., *The Portable Nietzsche* (New York: Viking, 1954), at 86.

[51] Edward Morgan Forster, *Howard's End* (New York: Vintage Books, 1954), at 228.

[52] But see the careful limitation of this thesis *infra*, text at nn. 72–4.

I have heard in the last six weeks nothing but the cry for blood. I have heard from the office of the State's Attorney only ugly hate. I have heard precedents quoted which would be a disgrace to a savage race. . . .

[Y]our Honor stands between the future and past. I know the future is with me. . . . I am pleading for life, understanding, charity, kindness, and the infinite mercy that considers all. I am pleading that we overcome cruelty with kindness and hatred with love. . . . I am pleading for a time when hatred and cruelty will not control the hearts of men. When we can learn by reason and judgment and understanding and faith that . . . mercy is the highest attribute of man. . . . If I can succeed . . . I have done something to help human understanding, to temper justice with mercy, to overcome hate with love. I was reading last night of the aspiration of the old Persian poet, Omar Khayyam. It appealed to me as the highest that I can vision. I wish it was in my heart, and I wish it was in the hearts of all. 'So I be written in the Book of Love, I do not care that Book above, erase my name or write it as you will, so I be written in the Book of Love.'[53]

Persuasive words. For who does not want to be written in the Book of Love? Who wants to be written in the books of hate, cruelty, cowardice, envy, resentment, and the like? Judge Caverly certainly did not, and decided against a death sentence for Loeb or Leopold.

Yet the more one looks at this argument, the more questionable it becomes. What does the virtue of the holder of a judgement have to do with the truth (or lack of it) of that judgement? Why should we think that Judge Caverly's damaging his virtue by deciding against Loeb and Leopold—increasing his virtue if he decides the other way—has anything to do with the truth of the judgement 'Loeb and Leopold deserve to die'? How can a judge expect to reach sound moral conclusions about Loeb and Leopold by focusing on which decision will most enhance *his* (the judge's) virtue? This seems to be a form of *ad hominem* argument, and a rather selfish version to boot, given its narcissistic preoccupation with one's own virtue.

The most persuasive case against retributivism is thus in danger of complete collapse. The charge is this: even if it makes us morally worse to make retributive judgements—because of the emotions that give rise to such judgements—that lack of virtue on our part is simply irrelevant to the assessment of whether retributive judgements are true. To assess this issue requires that we look in greater

[53] G. E. Hicks, ed., *Famous American Jury Speeches* (St Paul, Minn.: West Pub. Co., 1925), 995, 1084.

detail at the connections between our emotions and our moral judgements, which I propose to do next.

III. MORALITY AND THE EMOTIONS

The charge laid at the end of the last section is a form of the 'genetic fallacy' objection. Such an objection urges that it is fallacious to infer the falsity of a proposition from some truths (no matter how unsavoury) about the genesis of people's belief in that proposition. A common example is to infer the falsity of our moral beliefs from facts like, they are caused by our second-Oedipal resolution, or, they are caused by our impotence in the face of others' power, etc.[54] The *ad hominem* argument presented in the last section is like this, because it infers the falsity of retributivism from the unnice emotional origins of people's belief in retributivism.

To respond adequately to this genetic fallacy objection, the anti-retributivist must establish that the emotional base of a moral judgement is relevant to that judgement's truth.[55] If we leave ethics for a moment, one can see that sometimes it is no fallacy to infer the falsity of a judgement from the truth of some explanation of why people come to such judgement. Suppose the proposition in question was: 'Sticks become bent when immersed in water, straight again when removed.' Suppose the common explanation for why people believe this proposition to be true is in terms of their perceptual experience with sticks partly immersed in water—namely,

---

[54] Moore, 'Moral Reality', *supra* n. 12, at 1097–101.

[55] It is important at this juncture to keep clearly in mind the argument structure to this point. We are engaged in the task of justifying belief in retributivism. We are prima facie justified in believing retributivism to be true because that theory seems to best explain the particular judgements that we make in particular cases (Section I). The opponent of retributivism responds that the unnice emotional origins of those particular judgements renders the truth of the latter suspect (Section II). The retributivist now replies, 'genetic fallacy—the causes for a belief are irrelevant to the truth of the proposition believed'. (This charge we shall explore in this Section III.) The enterprise we are *not* engaged in is trying to see whether retributive emotions are or are not virtuous for an individual to feel so that we might, if enough citizens feel them, design institutions so as to satisfy them. (See Murphy, *supra* n. 25 for an example of this different enterprise.) The latter may be a worthwhile enquiry in which to engage within a democratic or utilitarian political theory, but it is not relevant to the moral question I pursue, which is whether we are justified in believing that culpable persons who do wrong should be punished because and only because they deserve it.

they look bent to them. If we have grounds to believe that these perceptual experiences as a class are unreliable—an 'illusion'—then it is no fallacy to infer the falsity of the proposition from an explanation of people's beliefs showing such beliefs to be the product of an illusion. Knowing what we do about the unreliability of visual experience when light is refracted in mediums of different density, we are entitled to disbelieve those who rely on such experiences in coming to their beliefs about sticks in liquid.

The anti-retributivist would make a similar construction of the Nietzschean case against retributivism, likening Nietzsche's explanation of people's beliefs in retributivism (as due to the emotions of *ressentiment*) to an explanation of a perceptual belief in terms of a known illusion or hallucination. Whether there can be such a thing as a moral hallucination or illusion, and if so, whether the emotions of *ressentiment* should be seen as such hallucinating experiences, depends upon an affirmative answer to two questions:

1. Are any emotions epistemically relevant to the truth of moral judgements?
2. If so, is it the virtuous nature of an emotion that tells us whether it has epistemic import?

I shall consider these questions in order.

With respect to the first question, we should distinguish four different views on how the emotions are relevant either to the discovery or to the justification of moral judgements.

1. One is suggested by Kant's famous remarks in the *Groundwork*[56] to the effect that moral worth is found in actions motivated only by reverence for the moral law, not in actions motivated by the inclinations, no matter how benevolent or virtuous. Such a view would make the emotions that generate a moral belief irrelevant to the truth of that belief. Good emotions could as easily generate false beliefs as true ones, and bad emotions could as easily generate true beliefs as false ones. The truth of a moral proposition would be governed solely by reasoning from the categorical imperative or other supreme principle of morality itself discoverable by reason alone, not from any emotional experience.

---

[56] Kant, *Groundwork of the Metaphysics of Morals*, Paton, trans. (New York: Harper and Row, 1964), 65–7.

In this view there is no analogy between the relation of the emotions and moral truth, on the one hand, and the relation of perceptual experiences and scientific truth, on the other. Accordingly, a Kantian about this should find the genetic fallacy objection conclusive when applied to Nietzsche; the lack of virtue of the emotions that generate retributivism has nothing to do with the truth of retributivism because the emotions generally have no epistemic import for the truth of moral judgements. In this view the emotions are relevant neither to justifying a moral judgement as true nor to discovering it to be true.

2. An opposite conclusion about the force of the genetic fallacy objection in this context should be drawn by those who think that the emotions have everything to do with moral truth. This second view about the connection of the emotions to moral truth is the view of the conventionalist (or relativist) about morals. Lord Devlin's writings on the morality of homosexual behaviour provide a convenient example.[57] According to Devlin, homosexual behaviour is immoral (and may be legally prohibited) whenever enough people feel deeply enough that it is bad. 'It is not nearly enough', Devlin reminds us, 'to say that a majority dislike a practice, there must be a real feeling of reprobation. . . . No society can do without intolerance, indignation, and disgust; they are the forces behind the moral law . . .'[58]

In this view, the emotions of a people constitute moral truth. If most people feel deeply enough that a practice is immoral, then it is immoral, in this conventionalist view. This means that if the emotional base for some moral belief is undermined, then necessarily the belief cannot be true. If Nietzsche, for example, can show that the emotions that generate retributivist beliefs are contaminated, then necessarily retributivism is not morally right.

How could Devlin admit the possibility of this kind of undermining of the emotional base of retributivism, given the total absence of reason checking emotion in his conventionalist view of morals? For someone like Devlin, after all, morals just *are* feelings shared by a majority. Yet such majority feelings can be changed if that majority can be emotionally repelled by some of its own emotions. And if enough people are repelled enough by the Nietzschean

---

[57] Patrick Devlin, 'Morals and the Criminal Law', in R. Wasserstrom, ed., *Morality and the Law* (Belmont, Cal.: Wadsworth, 1971).

[58] Id. at 40.

case against *ressentiment*, then the retributive urge must be excluded from those conventions of shared feelings that constitute morality.

This conventionalist view about morality results in there being no genetic fallacy objection to be interposed against Nietzsche. To attack the emotional base of retributivism would be to attack retributivism itself.

Yet such a strong epistemic connection of the emotions to moral truth cannot be sustained. That a large percentage of Americans, perhaps a majority, have feelings of disgust, fear, and hatred of gays does not end a moral enquiry into the truth or falsity of the proposition that gays may be discriminated against, in housing, employment, or elsewhere. A person seeking to arrive at the truth about just treatment for minorities cannot accept his or her own emotional reactions as settling the issue (nor, more obviously, can the person accept the emotional reactions of others). Each must judge for himself or herself whether those emotions are harbingers of moral insight or whether they are the 'hallucinations' of the emotional life that must be discarded in our search for the truth. The same, of course, is true for our sense perceptions *vis-à-vis* scientific truths. Sticks may look bent when partly immersed in water, but that does not mean that they really are bent. Our sense perception is not veridical, and there is no reason to suppose that our emotions are any better guarantors of knowledge.[59]

3. This analogy of the emotions to sensory perception suggests a third way of thinking of the epistemic connection of the emotions to morality, a conception that is also, unfortunately, misleading. This is the route of intuitionism. An intuitionist, as I am here using the word, believes that the emotions stand to moral judgement in a relation exactly analogous to the relation between perceptual experience and scientific judgement. For an intuitionist, the analogy is only an analogy, however, for such a person sees morals and science as distinct realms of knowledge, each with their own distinct experiential base. Such an intuitionist will usually be a metaphysical dualist, believing that such distinct modes of knowing must imply that there are distinct modes of being. (An example of this is

---

[59] For a sustained attack on conventionalist meta-ethics, see Heidi Hurd's 'Relativistic Jurisprudence: Skepticism Founded on Confusion', *Southern California Law Review*, Vol. 61 (1988), 1417–509.

how introspectionism goes hand in hand with dualism in the philosophy of mind.)

In any case, the intuitionist will regard emotions as crucial to morals, for they are the data from which moral theory is constructed. Without the emotions generating intuitions, there could be no moral insight, for this kind of intuitionist. An intuitionist is not committed to the emotions being veridical; indeed, to maintain the parallel to sensory perception, the intuitionist should say that the felt justice of punishing for its own sake is *good evidence* that it is just to punish for its own sake, but allow that the inference could be mistaken.

4. I must confess there is much in the intuitionist's account that I find tempting. Still, the dead ends of dualistic metaphysics and the lumpy epistemology of discrete cognitive realms is sufficient reason to avoid intuitionism and non-naturalism in ethics, as it is to avoid introspectionism and dualism in psychology.[60] We can avoid this metaphysical and epistemological lumpiness by thinking of the emotions as heuristic guides to moral insight, but not as the experience out of which moral theory is constructed. In this view, moral knowledge does not rest on its own unique experiential base, the emotions. Such a view could even concede the empiricist idea that all knowledge (moral knowledge included) rests on sensory experience and the inferences drawable from it.

Consider a judgement that another is morally responsible for some harm. An intuitionist would view responsibility as a special kind of property not observable by the senses (a 'non-natural' property), and known only by that special faculty of intuition provided by our emotional life. I think, on the contrary, that responsibility is not a property in some special realm. True, we cannot see it but must infer its existence from other properties, such as voluntariness of action, accountability, intention, causation, lack of excuse or justification. But then we cannot see those properties either. We infer the existence of an intention in another from behavioural clues; we do not see causal relations, but infer their existence as well. Responsibility is no less a natural property of persons than is intentionality, voluntariness, and so on; none are visible properties, all must be inferred from other evidence. Yet these facts do not

---

[60] On the latter, see ch. 10 *infra*.

demand a special mode of existence, and a special mode of knowing, for any of such properties.[61]

If we think of (moral) properties such as responsibility in this way, then the emotions are not strictly necessary for there to be moral knowledge. We can imagine a being who could make correct inferences about responsibility, as about other things such as intentionality, even if he or she were devoid of any relevant emotional life. True, the being would not *feel* about, for example, justice as we feel about it; yet he or she could know injustice, in the sense of being able to pick it out, as well as we.

The emotions are thus heuristic guides for us, an extra source of insight into moral truths beyond the knowledge we can gain from sensory and inferential capacities alone. One might think of them as I would think of conscious experience *vis-à-vis* knowledge of mind: my conscious experience of deciding to get a haircut is one way I can come to know that I intend to get a haircut; yet I or others can come to know that I intend to get a haircut in a variety of other ways, including perhaps someday by physiological measurements. My introspective, 'privileged access' is only a heuristic guide to learning about my sensations, intentions, and so on that others do not possess. It is not essential to an intention that I be conscious of it, any more than it is essential to the injustice of an institution that I or others feel negatively toward it. The usual judgements I make about my intentions may be judgements reached by reflection on my conscious deliberative processes, just as my usual judgements about justice may be reached via some strong feelings; but the usual route to knowledge—of minds or morals— is not to be confused with what mental states or moral qualities *are*.

The upshot of this is that our emotions are important but not essential in our reaching moral truths. Contra Kant, there is an epistemic connection between our emotions and morality, but it is neither of the strong connections that conventionalism or intuitionism would posit. In the present context, the pay-off of seeing this latter point lies in seeing when we may find some emotions wanting as epistemic indicators of moral truth. It is possible, in this last view, for there to be emotions that are 'moral hallucinations',

---

[61] See my response to Mackie's well-known 'queerness objection' to moral qualities, in Moore, 'Moral Reality', *supra* n. 12, at 1086–8, 1117–36; 'Moral Reality Revisited', *supra* n. 12, at 2491–533.

and it is therefore open to a Nietzschean to claim that our retributive inclinations are of this kind.

We come, then, to the second question—is the virtue of possessing an emotion relevant to that emotion's epistemic import? We should begin by being clear about the two different ways in which the emotions may be connected to morality before we enquire into the relation between them. We have hitherto been discussing what I would call the epistemic connection of the emotions to morality, distinguishing strong views of this connection (like Devlin's) from weaker views, such as my own or Kant's. Yet there is another possible way in which morality is related to our emotional life. This is where the emotions are themselves the objects of moral judgement. I call this the substantive connection of morality to the emotions.

The substantive connection can be grasped by reflecting on the judgements we make when we are not concerned with ascribing legal liability. The part of morality that is incorporated into our criminal law is by and large the morality of will and reason, by virtue of which we make the crudest of responsibility ascriptions. Voluntariness of action, accountability, intentionality, causation, justification, and excuse are the primary categories in terms of which we judge someone as morally responsible and thus legally punishable. Compare the less legalistic moral judgements we make in daily life: we often think of ourselves or others as more or less virtuous, depending on what emotions we feel on what occasions. We make judgements, in other words, not just about the wrong actions a bad person wills, but also about the evil emotions a bad person feels. As Bernard Williams has noted, there is a morality:

about what a man ought or ought not to feel in certain circumstances, or, more broadly, about the ways in which various emotions may be considered as destructive, mean or hateful, while others appear as creative, generous, admirable, or—merely—such as one would hope for from a decent human being. Considerations like these certainly play a large part in moral thought, except perhaps in that of the most restricted and legalistic kind.[62]

Consider a person who feels little or no compassion for others less fortunate. This person's behaviour need not be that of a Scrooge— he may do all the morally acceptable things, such as donate to charities, help blind persons across the street, not inflict needless

[62] Williams, 'Morality and the Emotions', in his *Problems of Self* (Cambridge: Cambridge University Press, 1973), at 207.

suffering, and so on. Yet he does such things out of a priggish concern for propriety, including the propriety he attains by having a
good opinion of himself. He does not feel any compassion for the
objects of his charity; indeed, he regards them as inferior beings
who exist for him mainly to be the objects of his virtue. Such a person is morally inferior to—less virtuous than—another whose
actions may be no better but whose emotional life includes compassion.

Contrast this connection of the emotions and morality with the
epistemic connection. Staying with the example of compassion: we
may take our feelings of compassion for some disadvantaged persons to be the harbingers of a moral insight about what that group
deserves. Suppose you travel to India and find the poverty of many
Indians to be distressing. You might take that feeling of compassion to be the originator of a moral insight about the nature of distributive justice—namely, that the geographic limits you had
previously observed in applying some ideal of distributive justice
seem arbitrary, a matter of political expediency at best. In such a
case, the emotional experience of compassion may generate a firm
moral conviction that distributive justice knows no political boundaries or geographical limits, but extends to all persons.

The epistemic connection of the emotions to morality is quite different from the substantive connection. With the latter, we judge
the emotions as virtuous or not; the emotions in such a case are the
object of moral evaluation. With the former, we are not seeking to
judge the moral worth of an emotion as a virtue; rather, we seek to
learn from such emotions the correct moral judgements to make
about some other institution, practice, act, or agent.

Having distinguished the two connections of morality to the
emotions, it remains to enquire whether there is not some relation
between them. One wishing to use Nietzsche's kind of insights to
attack retributivism, and yet escape the genetic fallacy objection,
must assert that there is some such relation. The idea is that we use
our own virtue in possessing an emotion as the touchstone of
whether that emotion is 'hallucinatory' or not: if the possession of
an emotion makes us more virtuous, then that emotion is a good
heuristic for coming to moral judgements that are true; if the possession of an emotion makes us less virtuous, then that emotion is
a good heuristic for coming to moral judgements that are false. This
possibility, of course, would complete the anti-retributivist's answer

to the genetic fallacy charge. For then the vice of possessing the emotions of *ressentiment* gives us good reason to suppose that the moral judgements to which those emotions give rise—namely, retributive judgements—are false.

This is possible, but what reason do we have to think that such a connection—between the judge's virtue, and the truth of the judgement he or she is making—holds? Counter-examples certainly spring to mind; consider two of them.

1. As Herbert Morris has examined,[63] there is such a thing as non-moral guilt. Think, for example, of the guilt one might feel at having made a tragic choice: there were only two options, neither happy ones, and one chose to do the lesser evil. Using Philippa Foot's much-discussed example: A railroad switchman can only turn a moving trolley car onto one line or another, but he cannot stop it; he chooses to turn the car onto the line where only one trapped workman will be killed; on the other line, five workmen were trapped and would have been killed had the trolley car gone their way. The switchman did not do anything morally wrong, nor is he morally culpable in directing the trolley on the line where only one workman would be killed. The alternative being even worse, the switchman was justified in doing what he did. Still the switchman should feel regret, remorse, and even guilt at killing the one workman. The switchman who experiences such emotions is a more virtuous person than one who has a 'don't cry over what can't be helped' attitude toward the whole affair.

If both moral judgements are right—the switchman is not responsible (guilty), but his feeling guilty is virtuous—then we cannot say that the emotions that make us virtuous are necessarily the emotions that are good heuristic guides to moral truth. For if the latter were true, this switchman's (virtuous) feeling guilty should mean that the associated judgement, 'I am guilty', is true; but it is not.

2. Just as some emotions are virtuous even though their associated judgements are not true, so some emotions that are not virtuous to possess may nonetheless spawn judgements that are true. Think of the institution of private property and its Lockean justifications in terms of the exercised liberty of one who mixes her

[63] Morris, 'Nonmoral Guilt', in F. Schoeman, ed., *Responsibility, Character, and the Emotions* (Cambridge: Cambridge University Press, 1987).

labour with a thing. I think the Lockean judgement, 'she deserves the property right because she created the thing in the first place', to be true when applied to a novelist seeking copyright protections for a novel. Yet I also think that the emotions that are my heuristic guide to that judgement are suspect, at the least, in their enhancement of my virtue.

For are not the emotions that call to mind Lockean intuitions about deserved property entitlements essentially selfish emotions that make us worse for possessing them?[64] We are entitled, from what we have done, to exclude others from the enjoyment of the products of our labour. My intuition is that this is true, but I am not proud of the selfish emotions that generate this intuition. They seem to consist too much of pride and self-congratulation to be virtues. Yet the non-virtuous nature of the emotional base of Lockean property theories does not make me doubt their truth; it would be unfair to deprive another of the products of his or her labour, however much it would be better if we (and the other) did not beat our chests so much about our own accomplishments.

These examples are perhaps controversial, but I doubt that the point they illustrate is. The virtue (or lack of it) in the possession of our emotion is not an infallible guide to the epistemic import such as emotion may possess.

Is the first even a *fallible* guide to the second? A defender of retributivism might well think not. Such a person might compare the situation in science: What is the relevance, he or she might ask, of the virtue of a perceptual experience (say one induced by drugs) to the epistemic import of such an experience? What possible reason is there to think that the moral worth of a visual experience will correlate with its epistemic import? Tripping on LSD and looking at pornography may be equally lacking in virtue, but only one of them is likely to produce untrue beliefs about, for example, anatomical features of human beings.

Yet what if we substituted an example where the virtue in question is not so obviously removed from the truth of any scientific judgements? Suppose we focused on what might be called the 'virtues of a scientist', traits such as analytical capacity, creativity,

---

[64] Suggested in E. M. Forster's lovely essay, 'My Woods', in his *Abinger Harvest* (New York: Harcourt, Brace, and World, 1936). See also Lawrence Becker, *Property Rights* (London: Routledge and Kegan Paul, 1977), at 96.

curiosity, being careful, and ambition. It is not nearly so implausible to think that beliefs produced through the exercise of these traits are more likely true, and that those produced by the analytically dull, the plodding, the mechanical, the careless, or the lazy, are more likely false.

Similarly, in ethics we should recognize that the virtue of (or vice) of an emotion may often, but not always, be taken as an indication of the truth (or falsity) of the judgement to which it leads. Indeed, would it not be remarkable to think that one could arrive at the judgements about science or morals only through emotions or traits that made one morally odious? Although not contradictory, it would surely be an oddly cohering morality that valued, say, equal treatment and also extolled the virtue of those prejudiced attitudes that typically produce discriminating judgements. We value moral and scientific truth too highly to think that there could be any virtues so counter-productive to the attainment of truth.

In any case, what other criterion could there be for the epistemic reliability of the emotions? If such reliability had nothing to do with the virtue of such emotions, what would be our test? Rawls suggests that we look to those 'conditions favourable for deliberation and judgment in general'[65] when we seek to isolate those 'considered judgments' that in reflective equilibrium justify his two principles of justice. Which conditions are these?

[W]e can discard those judgments made with hesitation, or in which we have little confidence. Similarly, those given when we are upset or frightened, or when we stand to gain one way or the other can be left aside. All these judgments are likely to be erroneous or to be influenced by an excessive attention to our own interests.[66]

Yet this test is too dispassionate, too judicial. Rawls's test for *judgements* that have epistemic import cannot be turned into a test for *emotions* because Rawls, like Kant, pretty much ignores the emotional base of moral judgement.

If we look in this way for a purely cognitive test for when emotions are epistemically reliable, my suspicion is that we will always end up slighting the role of the emotions in generating moral insight. We will do this because a purely cognitive test will inevitably seek to derive a criterion of epistemic warrant that is independent of any theory generated from the emotions themselves.

[65] Rawls, *supra* n. 10, at 48.   [66] Id. at 47.

It is like attempting to set up a criterion of epistemic warrant for perceptual experiences without using any theory derived from such experiences. Yet surely in science we do not expect to have to come up with some prescientific test for the epistemic import of sensory experience *before* we meld those experiences into a scientific theory. Rather, we rely on the body of scientific theory itself to justify exclusions of experience from the data. It is because we know what we do about optics that leads us to discount the illusion that a stick partly immersed in water looks bent; it is because we know what we do about drugs, mental disease, sensory deprivation, and the like, that we discount hallucinatory perceptual experiences. In science we quite literally explain such experiences away by using the very theories of which such experiences are part of the data. We are entitled to make the parallel move in ethics, so that our substantive moral theories—not some pale, preliminary, judicial, non-moral litmus test—give us the criteria for weeding out emotions with misleading epistemic import. Those substantive theories of what justice is, for example, make it very unlikely that prejudice could be a virtue, or that compassion could not.

The upshot of all of this is that the genetic fallacy objection with which we began this section is inconclusive when interposed by the retributivist against the Nietzschean analysis of the retributive urge. If Nietzsche is right in asserting that our retributive beliefs are always motivated by the emotions of *ressentiment*, and right that the possession of those emotions makes us less virtuous, then we have grounds to reject retributivism as a theory of punishment. True, such a Nietzschean argument could not be a knock-down winner—from what has been said, it is possible that the non-virtuous emotions of *ressentiment* nonetheless generate true moral judgements about what wrongdoers deserve. Yet this would have to be established by justifying the retributive principle in some way other than by showing it to be the best expression of our more particular judgements about criminals. Without such independent justification of retributivism, Nietzsche gives us reason to believe the retributive principle to be false when he shows us how lacking in virtue are the emotions that generate retributive judgements. For without such an independent justification, here as elsewhere we are entitled to rely on the connection that generally (but not inevitably) holds between the virtue in possessing an emotion and the truth of the judgement that that emotion generates.

IV. MORAL OUTRAGE, GUILT AND THE TRUTH OF OUR PARTICULAR JUDGEMENTS

As previewed in the first part of this chapter, there are two justificatory routes a non-foundationalist might use in justifying retributivism. First, because of the Nietzschean attack on the retributive urge, a retributivist might abandon the justificatory route that begins with our particular judgements about punishment in individual cases, and instead focus on how retributivism is justified because of its coherence with other, more general moral beliefs we are prepared to accept. He or she might show how there is an odd lacuna in our moral judgements about desert if the retributive principle is not accepted. That is, when passing out rewards, the desert of those whose labour produced them is (for Lockeans) both a necessary and a sufficient condition for allocating a property entitlement in them. The presence of such desert justifies giving the reward to them; the absence of such desert justifies withholding it from them. Similarly, when passing out legal duties to pay for harms caused, the culpable wrongdoing of he or she who caused the harm and the lack of any culpable wrongdoing of he or she who suffers the harm, is (in standard corrective justice theories) both necessary and sufficient to justify tort liability. It is only with punishment that we have an asymmetry; namely (as even most non-retributivists will assert), that desert is a necessary condition of punishment, but not sufficient by itself to justify punishment.

Such an asymmetry does not by itself render a justice theorist's social theory incoherent if he or she rejects retributivism (although it might if one isolated a general principle of just deserts common to corrective justice, property allocations, and retributive justice). My only point here is that if there were such incoherence without retributivism, the latter would be justified even if the retributive urge is unworthy of us. Nothing in the Nietzschean case against retributivism could prevent this. Still, since my approach is to justify retributivism by using our more particular judgements about punishment, I need to take seriously the Nietzschean case against those judgements.

The problem with the Nietzschean case against retributivism does not lie, as we have seen, in its presupposition that generally there is a strong connection between virtuous emotions and true moral judgements, immoral emotions and false moral judgements. The real problem for the Nietzschean critic is to show that retributive judgements are *inevitably* motivated by the dark emotions of *ressentiment*. For if the critic cannot show this, then much of the contamination of those particular judgements is lifted. It is lifted because the retributive judgement would then not arise out of the kind of moral hallucination non-virtuous emotions typically represent; rather, the retributive judgement would be only the vehicle for the expression of the emotions of *ressentiment*—dangerous for that reason, but not lacking in epistemic import for that reason.

Consider an analogy in meta-ethics. The position I have defended elsewhere, moral realism, is an admittedly dangerous view about which to proselytize. It is dangerous because many people use moral realism as a vehicle to express intolerance and contempt for autonomy. Many people may even accept moral realism because it seems to them to have this potential for intolerant imperialism against the differing moral beliefs of others. Yet these psychological facts, to my mind, constitute little argument against the truth of moral realism. They do not because I am able to separate moral realism from intolerance: logically I see that a moral realist can defend tolerance, pluralism, and autonomy as much (more?) as anyone, and psychologically I do not see any inevitability in my moral realist views being motivated by intolerance. Making these separations, the fact that many people use moral realism to express their intolerance—or even are motivated to moral realist beliefs by their intolerance—loses any epistemic sting. It makes me cautious about holding forth about moral realism with intolerant audiences, but it does not give me reason to be cautious about the truth of moral realism.

As much seems to me to be true about retributivism. I shall make the argument in three steps: first, that the inevitability of linking *ressentiment* emotions to retributive judgements is weakened when one notes, as Nietzsche himself did, that *anti*-retributive judgements are also often motivated by some of those same non-virtuous emotions; second, that in our own individual cases we can imagine being motivated to make retributive judgements by the virtuous emotions of guilt and fellow-feeling; and third, that because punishment is a social institution, unlike private vengeance, it can help us to control the emotions retributive punishment expresses by controlling the aspects of punishment that all too easily allow it to express *ressentiment*.

1. A paraphrase of Zarathustra, of which Nietzsche no doubt would have approved, would be that we should beware all those in whom the urge to punish is either actually, or claimed to be, non-existent. As Nietzsche does tell us:

if you are cursed, I do not like it that you want to bless. Rather, join a little in the cursing. And if you have been done a great wrong, then quickly add five little ones: a gruesome sight is a person single-mindedly obsessed by a wrong. . . . A wrong shared is half right. . . . A little revenge is more human than no revenge.[67]

Everyone gets angry when their bodily integrity or other important interests are violated by another. If they care about other human beings, they are vicariously injured when someone close to them—or distant, depending on the reach of their empathy—is wronged. It is human to feel such anger at wrongful violation, and Nietzsche's thought is that not to express the anger in some retaliation is a recipe for *ressentiment* itself.

One might of course think that retaliation is a second best solution; better not to feel the anger at all so that the choice of expressing it in action, or of repressing it into the subtle revenge of pity, is not necessary.[68] Leaving aside whether such willing away of anger is possible, is it desirable? While it has a saintly ring to it to turn the other cheek so long as it is one's own cheek that has just been slapped, is it virtuous to feel nothing stronger than sympathy for the suffering of others at the hands of wrongdoers? Where is that compassionate concern for others that is outraged because another person has been so unnecessarily caused such suffering? Where is the concern for morality that is outraged because another person has so unjustifiably caused such a flouting of such obvious moral truths?

Karen Horney concluded that '[t]he vindictive person thus is egocentric . . . because he has more or less severed his emotional relations to other human beings'.[69] Yet is this not even more often true of one who feels anger only when he himself suffers at the hands of a wrongdoer, not when others suffer? An egocentric lack of compassion for others, coupled with a lack of any respect for moral

---

[67] Nietzsche, *Zarathustra, supra* n. 34, at 180.
[68] See Horney, *supra* n. 27, at 3, for thoughts in this direction.
[69] Id. at 12.

norms protecting others, may explain the anti-retributivist, forgiving attitude as easily as it may explain the desire for vengeance.

Sometimes the compassion for victims is not absent, but gets transferred to the person who is now about to suffer, namely, the wrongdoer. Such a transfer of compassion is not justified by the relative merits of the two classes of persons, unless we are to think that there is some reason to prefer wrongdoers to victims as the appropriate objects of compassion. 'Out of sight out of mind' is the reason that suggests itself, but this psychological tendency can hardly justify forgetting those who have suffered at the hands of others. My own view is that such a transfer of concern from victim to criminal occurs in large part because of our unwillingness to face our own revulsion at what was done. It allows us to look away from the horror that another person was willing to cause.

We almost cannot bear the sight. We invent for the wrongdoers a set of excusing conditions that we would not tolerate for a moment in ourselves. When they transgress, virtuous people know how ill it lies to 'excuse' themselves by pointing to their own childhood or past, their lack of parental love, their need for esteem, and other causes. Virtuous people do not use the childish 'something made me do it' because they know that that denies their essential freedom in bringing about some harm. They know that they did it, chose to do it, caused though that choice surely was by factors themselves unchosen. Yet we cannot stand to apply to criminals the same standard of responsibility that we apply to ourselves because we cannot stand to acknowledge that there is such a thing as evil in the world—and, worst of all, that it is not 'inhuman' but a part of creatures not so different from ourselves. Lack of anger at criminals, if it does not represent simple indifference to the sufferings of others, may represent our self-deception about the potential for evil in humanity.

Such lack of anger may also represent the same fear of criminals that can motivate retributive judgements. Nietzsche:

There is a point in the history of society when it becomes so pathologically soft and tender that among other things it sides even with those who harm it, criminals, and does this quite seriously and honestly. Punishing somehow seems unfair to it, and it is certain that imagining 'punishment' and 'being supposed to punish' hurts it, arouses fear in it. 'It is not enough to render him *undangerous*? Why still punish? Punishing itself is terrible.' With this question, herd morality, the morality of timidity, draws its ultimate consequence. . . . The imperative of herd timidity: 'We want that some day there should be *nothing anymore to be afraid of*!'[70]

By repressing anger at wrongful violation, we may be attempting to deny that we live in a society in which there really are fearful and awful people.

Yet again, our transfer of fellow-feeling from victim to criminal, and its accompanying elimination of anger, may represent something other than indifference or inability to face evil or our own fears. It may represent a narcissism that is itself no virtue. A criminal, after all, represents an opportunity to exercise (and display, a separate point) one's virtue. The virtue in question is compassion for someone now threatened with harm. Yet such egoistic compassion becomes something other than compassion. It becomes just what Nietzsche said it becomes, the elevation of self by pity. Remarkably, one can lose compassionate concern for another by the self-conscious egoistic caricature of compassion we distinguish as pity. In pity we do not care about the other any more for his own sake, but only insofar as he allows *us* to become, in our own and others' eyes, better. We should beware, to adopt yet another paraphrase of Nietzsche, all those who find others best when they find them most in need.[71] We should beware of them because such people lack precisely the ability to feel that compassion whose outward form they ape.

Resentment, indifference to others, self-deception, fear, cowardice, and pity are not virtues. They do not perhaps add up to the witches' brew of a full batch of the *ressentiment* emotions, but to the extent they motivate anti-retributive judgements, they make such judgements suspect. How can one accept, as Nietzsche did, that both retributive and anti-retributive judgements are often motivated by non-virtuous emotions? There are two possibilities. We could concede that neither the judgement that retributivism is true nor its negation are ever motivated by any but the *ressentiment* emotions, so that in this instance, we must abandon the epistemic connection between the virtue of an emotion and the truth of the judgement to which that emotion leads. Alternatively, we could deny that the *ressentiment* emotions exhaust the sort of emotions that can, and sometimes do,

---

[70] Friedrich Nietzsche, *Beyond Good and Evil*, Kaufmann, trans. (New York: Vintage, 1966), 114.
[71] Philippa Foot's paraphrase, in her 'Nietzsche: The Revaluation of Values', in R. Solomon, ed., *Nietzsche: A Collection of Critical Essays* (Garden City, NY: Doubleday Anchor Books, 1973), 168.

motivate retributive judgements. Although either tack defends retributivism, I think only the second to be true, so I shall pursue it.

2. There are two virtuous emotions that can, and sometimes do, motivate retributive judgements in particular cases. The first can be seen by returning to the lack of fellow-feeling that sometimes motivates anti-retributive judgements. If it is morally odious not to care about others—either directly about others' suffering or indirectly through a concern for morality—then must it not be virtuous to feel such concern? And if the answer to this question is 'yes', as I think it plainly is, then must it not also be virtuous to feel negatively *in some way* towards flagrant moral violations that hurt others, virtuous to allow such negative feelings to cause retributive judgements? If so, we need to distinguish this virtuous emotion of outrage from the non-virtuous emotions of *ressentiment* (for the very same emotion cannot both be virtuous and not-virtuous).

Fortunately, such an emotion has been nicely described in recent work by others. Jeff Murphy has described in detail the 'retributive hatred' that he finds it virtuous to feel in response to serious wrongdoing.[72] Jean Hampton extols the virtue of feeling 'moral hatred' (which she equates to Murphy's 'retributive hatred') at wrongdoing to oneself by others, and distinguishes this form of hatred from what she equates with Nietzsche's *ressentiment*, what she calls 'malicious' and 'spiteful' hatreds.[73] Likewise, Sam Pillsbury finds an emotion he labels 'moral outrage' to be perfectly appropriate as a response to wrongdoing, so long as it is distinguished from the non-virtuous 'passion for vengeance'.[74]

Common to all such accounts is the thought that we can and do feel morally repelled not only at bad actions, but also at the bad actors who do them; that we can and do have such feelings of revulsion without feeling weak, fearful or unable to vent our anger, without being cowardly or herd-like in our anger, without expressing either bigotry, prejudice, or fear of strangers without sadistic enjoyment or envy of any kind, without projecting our own guilt onto the wrongdoer, and without deceiving ourselves about any of the foregoing; and that it is virtuous to feel a moral outrage purified of *ressentiment* in response to serious wrongdoing. In my view, such revulsion is the only tolerable response of one who cares about other people and who cares about the morality that binds us together.

[72] Murphy, *supra* n. 25, at 88–110.   [73] Hampton, *supra* n. 25, at 61–83.
[74] Pillsbury, *supra* n. 25, at 689–90.

To the extent such outrage motivates the particular judgements that are our concern, its virtue evidences the truth of those judgements. An alternative motivation for such judgements is even more clearly distinct from the *ressentiment* emotions, and is, to my mind, even more clearly virtuous to feel. This is the emotion of guilt. As a thought experiment, imagine the guilt you would feel if you did the kinds of acts that fill the criminal appellate reports of any state. To take one such case, consider the well publicized murder of Bonnie Garland.

The psychiatrist Willard Gaylin interviewed a number of people closely connected to the brutal hammering death of Bonnie Garland by her jilted boyfriend, Richard Herrin. He asked a number of those in a Christian order that had been particularly forgiving of Richard whether they could imagine themselves performing such an act under any set of circumstances. Their answer was uniformly 'Yes'. All of us can at least find it conceivable that there might be circumstances under which we could perform an act like Herrin's—not exactly the same, perhaps, but something pretty horrible. All of us do share this much of our common nature with the worst of criminals. (For those with a greater we-they attitude toward criminals, the thought experiment that follows must be run with a somewhat less horrible act than Richard's.)

Then ask yourself: What would you feel like if it was you who had intentionally smashed open the skull of a 23-year-old woman with a claw hammer while she was asleep, a woman whose fatal defect was a desire to free herself from your too clinging embrace? My own response, I hope, would be that I would feel guilty unto death. I could not imagine any suffering that could be imposed upon me that would be unfair because it exceeded what I deserved.

Is that virtuous? Such deep feelings of guilt seem to me to be the only tolerable response of a moral being. 'Virtue' is perhaps an odd word in the context of extreme culpability, but such guilt seems, at the least, very appropriate. One ought to feel so guilty one wants to die. Such sickness unto death is to my mind more virtuous than the non-guilty state to which Richard Herrin brought himself, with some help from Christian counselling about the need for self-forgiveness. After three years in prison on an eight- to twenty-five-year sentence for 'heat of passion' manslaughter, Richard thought he had suffered quite enough for the killing of Bonnie:

HERRIN. I feel the sentence was excessive.

GAYLIN. Let's talk about that a little.

HERRIN. Well, I feel that way now and after the first years. The judge had gone overboard. . . .

Considering all the factors that I feel the judge should have considered: prior history of arrest, my personality background, my capacity for a productive life in society—you know, those kinds of things—I don't think he took those into consideration. He looked at the crime itself and responded to a lot of public pressure or maybe his own personal feelings, I don't know. I'm not going to accuse him of anything, but I was given the maximum sentence. This being my first arrest and considering the circumstances, I don't think I should have been given eight- to twenty-five years.

GAYLIN. What do you think would have been a fair sentence?

HERRIN. Well, after a year or two in prison, I felt that was enough. . . .

GAYLIN. How would you answer the kind of person who says, for Bonnie, it's her whole life; for you it's eight years. What's eight years compared to the more years she might have had?

HERRIN. I can't deny that it's grossly unfair to Bonnie but there's nothing I can do about it. . . .

She's gone—I can't bring her back. I would rather that she had survived as a complete person, but she didn't. I'm not, again . . . I'm not saying that I shouldn't have been punished, but the punishment I feel is excessive. I feel I have five more years to go, and I feel that's just too much. There's no . . . I don't see any purpose in it. It's sad what happened, but it's even sadder to waste another life. I feel I'm being wasted in here.

GAYLIN. But what about the people who say, look, if you got two years, then someone who robs should get only two days. You know, the idea of commensurate punishment. If it is a very serious crime it has to be a very serious punishment. Are you saying two years of prison is a very serious punishment considering what you did?

HERRIN. For me, yes.[75]

---

[75] Williard Gaylin, *The Killing of Bonnie Garland* (New York: Penguin Books, 1983), 325–7.

Compared to such shallow, easily obtained self-absolution for a horrible violation of another, a deep sense of guilt looks very virtuous indeed.

To be sure, there is an entire tradition that regards guilt as a useless passion.[76] For one thing, it is always backward-looking rather than allowing one to get on with life. For another, it betrays an indecision that Nietzsche among others found unattractive: 'The bite of conscience is indecent',[77] Nietzsche thought, because it betrays the earlier decision about which one feels guilty. Yet Nietzsche and his followers are wrong here. Guilt feelings are often a virtue precisely because they do look to the past. As Herbert Morris has argued, morality itself—including the morality of good character—has to take the past seriously.[78] The alternative, of not crying over spilt milk (or blood), is truly indecent. A moral being *feels* guilty when he or she *is* guilty of past wrongs.

The virtue of feeling guilty is not raised so that punishment can be justified by its capacity to induce guilt. That is a possible retributive theory of punishment—a kind of moral rehabilitative theory—but it is not mine.[79] Rather, the virtue of our own imagined guilt is relevant because of the general connection between the virtue of an emotion and its epistemic import. We should trust what our imagined guilt feelings tell us; for acts like those of Richard Herrin, that if we did them we would be so guilty that some extraordinarily severe punishment would be deserved. We should trust the judgements such imagined guilt feelings spawn because nonneurotic guilt, unlike *ressentiment*, comes with good epistemic credentials.

Next, we need to be clear just what judgements it is that our guilt feelings validate in this way. First and foremost, to *feel* guilty causes the judgement that we *are* guilty, in the sense that we are morally responsible. Second, such guilt feelings typically engender

[76] See, e.g., Walter Kaufman, *Without Guilt and Justice* (New York: Dell, 1973).

[77] Friedrich Nietzsche, *Twilight of the Idols*, in W. Kaufman, ed., The Portable Nietzsche (New York: Viking, 1954), 467.

[78] Morris, *On Guilt and Innocence*, supra n. 7, at 108.

[79] For examples of this kind of theory, which only some of its proponents think of as retributivist, see Morris, 'A Paternalistic Theory of Punishment', *American Philosophical Quarterly*, Vol. 18 (1981), 263–71; Hampton, 'The Moral Education Theory of Punishment', *Philosophy and Public Affairs*, Vol. 13 (1984), 208–38; Murphy, 'Retributivism, Moral Education, and the Liberal State', *Criminal Justice Ethics*, Vol. 4 (1985), 3–11.

the judgement that we deserve punishment. I mean this not only in the weak sense of desert—that it would not be unfair to be punished—but also and more important in the strong sense that *we ought* to be punished.

One might think that this second judgement of desert (in either its weak or its strong sense) is uncalled for by our feelings of guilt, that the judgement to which our guilt feelings lead is the judgement that we ought to repair as best we can the damage we have done. Such a view would justify corrective justice theories of punishment, but not retributive theories. Yet I think that this puts too nice a face on our guilt feelings. They do not generate only a judgement that we ought to make amends in this compensatory way. Rather— and this is what troubles many critics of guilt as an emotion—to feel guilty is to judge that we must suffer. We can see this plainly if we imagine ourselves having made provisions for Bonnie's family, comforting them in any way possible, and then feeling that our debt for killing her has been paid. It is so clear that such corrective actions do *not* satisfy guilt that to feel that they do is not to have felt guilty to begin with.

Our feelings of guilt thus generate a judgement that we deserve the suffering that is punishment. If the feelings of guilt are virtuous to possess, we have reason to believe that this last judgement is correct, generated as it is by emotions whose epistemic import is not in question.

Last, we should ask whether there is any reason not to make the same judgement about Richard Herrin's actual deserts as we are willing to make about our own hypothetical deserts. If we experience any reluctance to transfer the guilt and desert *we* would possess, had we done what Richard Herrin did, to Herrin himself, we should examine that reluctance carefully. Does it not come from feeling more of a person than Richard? We are probably not persons who grew up in the barrio of East Los Angeles, or who found Yale an alien and disorienting culture. In any case, we certainly have never been subject to the exact same stresses and motivations as Richard Herrin. Therefore, it may be tempting to withhold from Richard the benefit each of us gives himself or herself: the benefit of being the subjective seat of a will that, although caused, is nonetheless capable of both choice and responsibility.

Such discrimination is a temptation to be resisted, because it is no virtue. It is élitist and condescending toward others not to grant them the same responsibility and desert you grant to yourself. Admittedly, there are excuses the benefit of which others as well as you may avail themselves. Yet that is not the distinction invoked here. Herrin had no excuse the rest of us could not come up with in terms of various causes for our choices. To refuse to grant him the same responsibility and desert as you would grant yourself is thus an instance of what Sartre called bad faith, the treating of a free, subjective will as an object. It is a refusal to admit that the rest of humanity shares with us that which makes us most distinctively human, our capacity to will and reason—and thus to be and do evil. Far from evincing fellow-feeling and the allowing of others to participate in our moral life, it excludes them as less than persons.

Rather than succumbing to this élitism masquerading as egalitarianism, we should ask ourselves what Herrin deserves by asking what *we* would deserve had we done such an act. In answering this question we should listen to our guilt feelings, feelings whose epistemic import is not in question in the same way as are those of *ressentiment*. Such guilt feelings should tell us that to do an act like Herrin's is to forfeit forever any light-hearted idea of going on as before. One should feel so awful that the idea of again leading a life unchanged from before, with the same goals and hopes and happiness, should appear revoltingly incomprehensible.[80]

3. If we conclude, as I think we should, that there is such a thing as retributive justice, a kind of justice that is achieved by the punishment of the guilty because and only because they are guilty, then we have good reason to set up institutions that achieve such justice. It is certainly 'possible to argue', as Jeff Murphy has emphasized in his recent writings, 'that a goal is morally very important but

---

[80] One may have noticed that the thought experiment just concluded has six steps to it. It is perhaps helpful to separate them explicitly: (1) The psychological presupposition that it is possible to engage in the thought experiment at all—that we can imagine we could do an act like Richard Herrin's. (2) The psychological question of what we would feel if we did such an action—guilty and deserving of punishment. (3) The moral question of the virtue of that feeling—that guilt is a virtuous emotion to feel when we have culpably done such a wrongful act. (4) The psychological question of what judgements are typically caused by the emotions of guilt—the judgements that we are guilty and that we deserve to be punished. (5) The moral question of the correctness of the first person judgement that we deserve to be punished—as an inference drawn from the virtue of the emotion of guilt that spawns such a judgement. (6) The moral question of the correctness of the third person judgement that Richard Herrin deserves to be punished—as an inference drawn from the fact that we would deserve to be punished if we had done the act that Herrin did.

nevertheless to maintain that the pursuit of that goal is not a proper state role'.[81] Various liberal restraints on the proper sphere of legislation that we shall explore in chapters 16–18 should stay our hand when one moves from moral theory to the political theory needed to justify the setting up of institutions. Yet nothing in a properly conceived liberal political theory should stay our hand from setting up and supporting institutions to achieve retributive justice.

To begin with, justice is one of our dominant concerns, so that if the moral argument above presented convinces that justice requires that culpable wrongdoers be punished for their actions, we have strong reason to set up institutions to achieve such retributive justice. To think otherwise would be like conceding to Rawls the persuasiveness of his moral case for his vision of distributive justice while thinking that nonetheless that moral case gave us little reason to set up or support institutions that realize such form of justice.[82]

Moreover, none of the proper liberal worries that should on occasion stay our hand should lead us to eschew retributive justice when we set up institutions. The main such worry, the preservation of individual autonomy, argues in favour of retributive institutions, not against them. We respect someone's autonomy when we punish him only because he deserves it, not because his punishment is useful to others' welfare and not because his punishment is a therapy to cure his 'sickness'. Respecting the autonomy of criminals is

---

[81] Murphy, 'Does Kant Have a Theory of Punishment?', *supra* n. 17, at 511. See more generally Murphy, *supra* n. 79; and Jeffrie Murphy and Jules Coleman, *Philosophy of Law* (Boulder, Colo.: Westview Press, rev. edn., 1989), 123–4.

[82] Compare Murphy, *supra* n. 79, and Murphy, 'Getting Even: The Role of the Victim', *Social Philosophy and Policy*, Vol. 7 (1990), 209–25, at 224. Murphy uses the Rawlsian thought experiment of the hypothetical social contract to argue that while rational contractors would set up institutions 'to protect themselves against assault', they would not set up such institutions to secure retributive justice because that has a 'merely abstract worth', not much of a value given the 'rarity of an intense sense of abstract justice'. What Murphy has really done is to exhibit (once again) the inability of Rawls's form of thought experiment to capture our sense of justice. Why should we think that such sense of justice can be captured by self-interested calculation, even when done behind a veil of ignorance? The Rawls/Murphy thought experiment attempts what for me has always been an unnecessary and an impossible enterprise: to give a self-interested reason to a self-interested person why she should not be self-interested. The data in ethics from which we derive principles of justice need not and cannot be limited to what the *amoral* person can be brought to accept.

the grain of truth in the otherwise misleading slogan that 'criminals have a *right* to retributive punishment'.

Likewise, the liberal worry about legality is not a worry cutting against retributive punishment. True enough, the severe sanctions we attach as punishments heighten the concern for proper notice and the other attributes of legality. But that is a function of severe sanctions, not the retributive reason for imposing them; that heightened concern should be equally present for any punishment scheme, utilitarian and rehabilitative as well as retributive.

The third liberal limit we explore later, the costs to other values of attaining a certain form of justice, is always a relevant concern. It is always relevant to ask, 'at what cost do we attain some form of justice?' This should stay our hand from punishing certain forms of immoral behaviour. Trivial immoralities, and immoralities done in private, by consenting individuals, that are strongly motivated, are not worth the enforcement costs to criminalize and to punish. But one can hardly make the same argument about immoralities like murder, rape, robbery, and the like. The immorality of such acts is much greater, and thus the injustice of them going unpunished is also correspondingly greater. Moreover, in any accounting about setting up institutions to achieve justice, against enforcement and other costs we must balance any benefits. One obvious benefit punishment gives is crime prevention, through deterrence, education, and incapacitation. The *net* cost of achieving retributive justice may thus be quite small.

Finally, the liberal worry that stems from epistemic doubt does not argue against setting up institutions to achieve retributive justice. If the form of the argument that I have given in this chapter is correct, then the one item we should have doubt about is what emotions do lie behind our own retributive judgements. For it is admittedly not an easy task to separate the emotions one feels, and then in addition, discriminate which of them is the cause of one's retributive judgements. We can no more choose which emotion it will be that causes our judgements or actions than we can choose the reason for which we act.[83] We can choose whether to act or not and whether to judge one way or another, but we cannot make it be true that some particular reason or emotion caused our action

[83] On our inability to will the reasons on which we act, see Moore, 'Law, Authority, and Razian Reasons', *Southern California Law Review*, Vol. 62 (1989), 827–96, at 878–83.

or our judgement. We must look inward as best we can to detect, but not to will, which emotions bring about our judgements; and here there is plenty of room for error and self-deception.

When we move from our judgements about the justice of retribution in the abstract, however, to the justice of a social institution that exists to exact retribution, perhaps we can gain some greater clarity. For if we recognize the dangers retributive punishment presents for the expression of resentment, sadism, and so on, we have every reason to design our punishment institutions to minimize the opportunity for such feelings to be expressed. There is no contradiction in attempting to make a retributive punishment system humane; doing so allows penitentiaries to be faithful to their names—places for penance, not excuses for sadism, prejudice, hatred, and the like.

Even the old biblical injunction—'Vengeance is mine, saith the Lord'—has something of this insight behind it. Retributive punishment is dangerous for individual persons to carry out, dangerous to their virtue and, because of that, unclear in its justification. But implicit in the Biblical injunction is a promise that retribution will be exacted. For those like myself who are not theists, that cleansing function must be performed by the state, not God. If the state can perform such a function, it removes from retributive punishment, not the guilt, as Nietzsche[84] and Sartre[85] have it, but the *ressentiment* and its accompanying doubt about the correctness of such punishment.

---

[84] *Nietzsche, Genealogy of Morals*, supra n. 37, at 95.
[85] Jean-Paul Sartre, 'The Flies', in *No Exit and Three Other Plays* (New York: Vintage, 1955).

4

JUSTIFYING RETRIBUTIVISM

I shall address two concerns in this chapter: first, a further concern about what retributivism is, and second, how one justifies retributivism as the only proper theory of punishment. Both of these concerns stem from various criticisms that have been advanced against the argument for retributivism advanced in the previous chapters.

I. WHAT IS RETRIBUTIVISM?

As we have seen, retributivism is the view that we ought to punish offenders because and only because they deserve to be punished. Punishment is justified, for a retributivist, solely by the fact that those receiving it deserve it. Punishment of deserving offenders may produce beneficial consequences other than giving offenders their just deserts. Punishment may deter future crime, incapacitate dangerous persons, educate citizens in the behaviour required for a civilized society, reinforce social cohesion, prevent vigilante behaviour, make victims of crime feel better, or satisfy the vengeful desires of citizens who are not themselves crime victims. Yet for a retributivist these are a happy surplus that punishment produces and form no part of what makes punishment just; for a retributivist, deserving offenders should be punished even if the punishment produces none of these other, surplus good effects.

A number of ambiguities are present in retributivism that it may be helpful to readdress because they are so related to issues of retributivism's justification. One of these has to do with the connection of punishment to the desert of the offender. Retributivists assert that punishment is justified only if those who receive it deserve it, but that is not the connection between desert and punishment distinctive of retributivism.[1] Rather, the more distinctive assertion of the retributivist is that punishment is justified if it is

---

[1] The late John Mackie called this view 'negative retributivism'. J. L. Mackie, 'Morality and the Retributive Emotions', *Criminal Justice Ethics* (Winter/Spring,

given to those who deserve it. Desert, in other words, is a sufficient condition of a just punishment, not only a necessary condition.

The second ambiguity has to do with the moral demands that just punishment makes on state officials and citizens. The desert of offenders certainly gives such officials *permission* to punish offenders, and this permission to give just punishment is no mere Hohfeldian privilege but a (claim) right to punish. But retributivism goes further. As a theory of a kind of justice, it *obligates* us to seek retribution through the punishment of the guilty. This means that officials have a duty to punish deserving offenders and that citizens have a duty to set up and support institutions that achieve such punishments.[2]

The third ambiguity has to do with punishment itself: does retributivism purport to justify why we have punishment institutions generally, or only why we punish particular people on particular occasions? Some of the 'mixed theorists' we discussed in chapter 2 have wished to distinguish the general justifying aim of the criminal law from the justifications of particular decisions within an ongoing criminal law system.[3] While such a distinction certainly has its uses, it is of no use in wedding retributivist to, say, utilitarian concerns in justifying punishment. Even if one were to concede the existence of 'practice rules'—rules which require moral justification but whose application to particular cases is to be made with-

---

1982), 3–10; Mackie, 'Retribution: A Test Case for Ethical Objectivity', in Joel Feinberg and Hyman Gross, eds., *Philosophy of Law* (4th edn., Wadsworth, 1991), 677–84. Note that the negative retributivist, if he is truly a retributivist at all, must also be a positive retributivist. For the negative retributivist asserts that the justification for not punishing those who do not deserve it lies in the fact that there is no morally acceptable reason to punish in the absence of desert; this implicit appeal to the deserving of retributive justice is distinct from justifying the non-punishment of the innocent on grounds of fairness, liberty, or utility. (On the latter point, see Moore, *Act and Crime* (Oxford: Oxford University Press, 1993), ch. 3.)

  [2] David Dolinko has come to label this a 'bold' retributivism, to be contrasted with a 'weak' retributivism according to which it is only permissible to punish those who deserve it. Dolinko, 'Some Thoughts About Retributivism', *Ethics*, Vol. 101 (1991), 537–59, at 542. The late John Mackie called this pair 'positive' versus 'permissive' retributivism, respectively. Mackie, 'Retributvism: A Test Case for Ethical Objectivity', *supra* n. 1, at 678; Mackie, 'Morality and the Retributive Emotions', *supra* n. 1, at 4.

  [3] Most notably, H. L. A. Hart, *Punishment and Responsibility* (Oxford: Oxford University Press, 1968), and John Rawls, 'Two Concepts of Rules', *Philosophical Review*, Vol. 64 (1956), 3–32.

out resort to that moral justification[4]—such concession goes no distance towards introducing any alien concerns into either a retributive or a utilitarian punishment scheme. That is, if one is a
utilitarian in his justification of the practice of punishment, one will
remain purely a utilitarian even if one bars utility calculations in
applying criminal law rules; and *mutatis mutandis* for the retributivist. Retributivism is thus the view both that punishment institutions in general are justified by the giving of just deserts and that
the punishment of each offender is justified by the fact that he or
she deserves it.

The fourth ambiguity has to do with the 'consequentialist' versus
'deontological' nature of retributivism.[5] A consequentialist about
morality believes that the *rightness* of an action is exclusively a
function of the *goodness* of the consequences that that action produces; a deontologist about morality believes that the rightness of
an action is (sometimes at least) a function of the action's conformity with 'agent-relative' norms, norms that are addressed to each
person individually and that are not concerned with maximizing
conformity to such norms by oneself or others on other occasions.[6]

The distinction becomes clearer if we apply it to retributivism.
Take Kant's old example of the last murderer in an island society
that is about to disband and leave its island.[7] A retributivist
believes that the murderer should be punished because he deserves
it, even though no other good will thereby be achieved. The guilty,
in other words, must be punished. If one construes this retributivist
norm as an agent-relative norm, then the members of Kant's island
society are obligated to punish the last murderer even if by doing
so other guilty murderers elsewhere will go unpunished. (We might
imagine, for example, that if we punish this murderer, he will not
testify against other murderers who will thereby escape conviction
and punishment.) Alternatively, if one construes this retributivist

---

[4] This Rawls/Hart distinction has been carried into more recent discussions by
Joseph Raz. See his *Practical Reason and Norms* (Oxford: Oxford University Press,
1975). I argue against Raz's version of practice rules in Moore, 'Law, Authority, and
Razian Reasons', *Southern California Law Review*, Vol. 62 (1989), 827–96, and
Moore, 'Three Concepts of Rules', *Harvard Journal of Law and Public Policy*, Vol.
14 (1991), 771–95.

[5] See n. 1, ch. 3, *supra*.

[6] This distinction is explored in much greater detail in ch. 17.

[7] Kant, *The Metaphysical Elements of Justice* (Indianapolis: Bobbs-Merrill, J.
Ladd, trans., 1965), at 102.

norm as a norm describing a state of affairs that is to be maximized, then the members of Kant's island society should *not* punish the last murderer but should rather maximize the punishment of the guilty by their actions. The 'deontological' or 'agent-relative' retributivist regards the act of punishing the guilty as categorically demanded on each occasion, considered separately; the 'consequentialist' or 'agent-neutral' retributivist regards the state of the guilty receiving punishment as a good state to be maximized even when this means that some guilty persons are intentionally allowed to escape punishment.

It is usually assumed that retributivism must be of the agent-relative kind.[8] Often this assumption is made about retributivism, the better to criticize it. Thus, it might be argued that retributivism cannot justify any actual institution of punishment because any actual institution of punishment will make some mistakes in its findings of guilt, namely, some actually innocent persons will be found guilty.[9] How, then, could an agent-relative retributivist justify setting up retributivist punishment institutions? Not by weighing the evil of a guilty many not being punished (if there were no institutions of punishment) against the evil of a few innocents being punished (as will be the case if there are institutions of punishment)—for this mode of justification would be consequentialist, a mode not allowed to the (supposedly necessarily) agent-relative retributivist.

Alternatively, it might be thought that we rightly refuse to punish some guilty persons in order to be able to punish other, more seriously guilty persons—as when we give immunity, in order to extract testimony needed to convict the latter.[10] How can the retributivist accommodate these practices, given that the retributivist regards the punishment of the guilty to be categorically imperative whenever the opportunity to give such punishment presents itself?

Yet if a retributivist may be a consequentialist, these are obviously non-problems for his theory of punishment. With regard to

[8] See, e.g., Dolinko, 'Three Mistakes of Retributivism', *UCLA Law Review*, Vol. 39 (1992), 1623–57.

[9] See Dolinko, *supra* n. 8; Schedler, 'Can Retributivists Support Legal Punishment?', *Monist*, Vol. 63 (1980), 185–98. Compare Larry Alexander, 'Retributivism and the Inadvertent Punishment of the Innocent', *Law and Philosophy*, Vol. 2 (1983), 233–46.

[10] I owe this point to the oral comments of Dudley Knowles, my commentator at the Fulbright Colloquium at which this chapter was initially presented. Knowles's written commentary appears as 'Unjustified Retribution', *Israel Law Review*, Vol. 27 (1993), 50–8.

the first, a consequentialist-retributivist need not maximize the punishment of the guilty to the exclusion of maximizing other, equally valuable states of affairs, such as the non-punishment of the innocent. Such a retributivist may easily maximize *both* that those deserving punishment receive it *and* that those not deserving of punishment not receive it. Where in the actual design of punishment institutions the consequentialist-retributivist comes out on this balance need not here detain us;[11] the important point is that there is no incoherence, even prima facie, in such a retributivist setting up an institution that will punish some innocents in order to punish the guilty and forego punishing some guilty in order not to punish too many innocents.

Likewise with regard to the second problem, the consequentialist-retributivist will intentionally refuse to punish guilty persons whenever more guilty persons (or greater guilt) will be punished thereby. For the consequentialist-retributivist, no matter how intrinsically good it is that the guilty receive their deserts, more of that good is to be preferred to less of it.

Can the retributivist be a consequentialist? One can, of course, *define* retributivism so that a retributivist must be a deontologist. Yet I suspect that the temptation to so define retributivism stems from a simple confusion. The confusion is between the *intrinsic* goodness of retribution being exacted, on the one hand, and the categorical duty to punish the guilty on each occasion where that can be done, on the other. As I shall argue shortly in the next section, what *is* distinctively retributivist is the view that the guilty receiving their just deserts is an intrinsic good. It is, in other words, not an instrumental good—good because such punishment causes other states of affairs to exist that are good. Even if punishing the guilty were without any further effects, it would be a good state to seek to bring about, on this intrinsic goodness view of punishing the guilty. This distinction—between intrinsic versus instrumental goodness—is commonly confused with the distinction between

---

[11] The retributivist might adopt a principle of symmetry here—the guilty going unpunished is exactly the same magnitude of evil as the innocent being punished—and design his institutions accordingly. Or the retributivist might share the common view (that the second is a greater evil than the first) and design punishment institutions so that 'ten guilty persons go unpunished in order that one innocent not be punished'. See Jeffrey Reiman and Ernest van den Haag, 'On the Common Saying That it is Better that Ten Guilty Persons Escape than that One Innocent Suffer: Pro and Con', *Social Philosophy and Policy*, Vol. 7 (1990), 226–48.

deontological and consequentialist views of right action. The result is that something that is not distinctive of retributivism (that we each have an agent-relative obligation to see that the guilty are punished) is taken to be essential to retributivism.

Although I thus conclude that a retributivist may be a consequentialist, neither of the two problems above raised for deontological versions of retributivism should incline the retributivist towards the consequentialist version. The probable punishment of the innocent by any real-world punishment scheme is not much of a worry even for deontological versions of retributivism. We rightly set up many social institutions where we know that some percentage of individuals affected by them will be hurt or even killed, for example, coal mining, high-rise construction, and speed limits on freeways. That we know that some percentage of individuals will likely suffer these harms if we arrange these institutions as we do arrange them is not to be equated with either our intending that they be so harmed, or knowing that some identified individual will suffer that harm. Agent-relative moral norms bind us absolutely only with respect to evils we either intend or (on some versions) knowingly visit on specified individuals. One can thus arrange safeguards in coalmines, high rise construction, automobile travel, and punishment in ways that predictably will hurt some who do not deserve to be hurt, without for a moment ceasing to be an agent-relative theorist about morality.[12]

The same cannot be said about the intentional forgoing of any opportunity to punish a guilty offender in order to obtain the conviction and punishment of an even more guilty offender, which is why this common prosecutorial practice is more of a problem for the deontological version of retributivism. Yet the deontological retributivist might simply deny the propriety of the practice. More plausibly, if he is a 'threshold deontologist', as am I, he might more qualifiedly disavow the practice except when it is needed to punish some very deserving criminal(s).[13]

---

[12] I explore both the doctrine of double effect, and the analogous doctrine distinguishing knowing visitation of harms on specified people versus risking harm to some unidentified part of a class of persons, in ch. 17, *infra*. As I there show in detail, any deontological view of morality must incorporate some such limits as these in order to specify the domain over which morality's absolute prohibitions range.

[13] A 'threshold' deontologist refuses to violate a categorical norm of morality until not doing so produces sufficient bad consequences as to pass some threshold— then, he will override such categorical norms. See ch. 17, *infra*.

In any case, nothing in the present project requires that we decide between deontological versus consequentialist retributivism. Both are recognizable versions of retributivism. The most important point here is not to confuse the distinction between these two versions of retributivism with the quite different distinction between valuing the giving of just deserts as only instrumentally good, as opposed to valuing it as intrinsically good.

II. JUSTIFYING RETRIBUTIVISM

A. Morally Justifying the Retributive Principle by Particular Judgements

How is retributivism, so defined, to be justified? Very generally, there are three sorts of things which might be said to justify the retributivist principle of punishment. One is a conceptual claim: only when harsh treatment is imposed on offenders in order to give them their just deserts does such harsh treatment constitute *punishment*.[14] The conceptual claim is made about our concept of punishment, and the claim presupposes that that concept is captured by the purpose for which punishment is imposed as much as by any structural features that it may possess.

A second sort of justification of retributivism is a legal claim: within our legal system with its established doctrines and procedures, the implicit goal is the retributive one of seeking to give just deserts to offenders. The claim is an 'interpretive' (or as I prefer to say, a 'functional') one, in that it accepts established legal institutions at face value and asks, 'what goals makes the most sense of these?'[15] The claim is that the retributive goal fits our established doctrines well, whereas competing utilitarian goals like

---

[14] For this older form of argument, see, e.g., A. M. Quinton, 'On Punishment', *Analysis*, Vol. 14 (1954), 1933–42. For a related argument, seeking to tease retributivism out of our concept of law, see Herbert Fingarette, 'Punishment and Suffering', *Proceedings of the American Philosophical Association*, Vol. 50 (1977), 499–525.

[15] Ronald Dworkin regards such claims as interpretive, although I prefer the older if less fashionable label, 'functional'. For the difference, see Moore, 'Law as a Functional Kind', in Robert George, ed., *Natural Law Theories* (Oxford: Oxford University Press, 1992). The claim that Anglo-American criminal law is a functional kind whose implicit goal is the seeking of retributive justice—the claim advanced in ch. 1—is a functionalist claim.

crime-prevention fit so poorly that they seem like so many of F. H. Bradley's 'bad reasons for what we believe on instinct anyway'.

A third sort of justification of retributivism is a moral claim: our obligation to punish offenders so as to give them their just deserts is justified in this sense if the practice meets whatever epistemic standards we impose to justify any of our moral beliefs. If we are consequentialists about morality, and if our theory of intrinsically good consequences includes goods other than giving the guilty their due, then we may seek to justify this retributive value by its contribution to the maximizing of some other good(s) that we accept more readily than we accept the intrinsic goodness of retributive punishment. If we are not consequentialists about morality, or if our consequentialism admits of no goods that are more obviously intrinsically good than the good of achieving retributive justice, then our mode of moral justification cannot be in terms of some other value served by retributive punishment. Rather, we must justify retributivism in whatever way we justify actions and practices as being intrinsically right. However we justify the intrinsic rightness of not punishing the innocent, for example, is how we should justify the intrinsic rightness of punishing the guilty, on this general view of morality.

The kind of justification I have considered in this and the last two chapters is the third one, the moral justification of retributive punishment. Even though my ultimate claim for retributivism in this book is of the second kind, much of the work of defending such a descriptive theory is done by defending the purely moral claim that the obtaining of retribution is an intrinsic good. Thus I focus again on that moral claim alone.

In order to understand what we can rightfully ask for by way of moral justification we need to keep three distinctions in mind. One of these is the consequentialism/deontology distinction of the last section. The second of these we also adverted to earlier, that between the intrinsic versus the merely instrumental goodness of a state of affairs or of an act or institution. A state of affairs, act or practice is intrinsically good if its goodness does not depend on some further effect that the state of affairs, etc., produces. One might think that giving a novelist some reward for producing a novel is intrinsically good, it being no more than she deserves. Alternatively, if the goodness of such a practice of rewarding novelists with copyright monopolies inheres in the effects of the practice—by giving rewards one gives incentives to other novelists to produce novels, and novels are an intrinsic good—then the practice is only instrumentally good.

Notice that the notion of instrumental goodness is not to be identified as utilitarian. Utilitarianism is a kind of consequentialist moral theory with a particular theory about what is intrinsically good—pleasure, happiness, preference-satisfaction, or some other welfarist notion. For a utilitarian, all other goods are merely instrumental. There is nothing in the intrinsic/instrumental distinction that requires this kind of monism about what is intrinsically good. One might well be a pluralist in this regard, admitting that the welfare of persons is an intrinsic good while also thinking that not punishing the innocent, giving those who labour the fruits of that labour, not demanding the impossible from people, etc., are equally intrinsic and not merely instrumental goods.

As I mentioned in the last section, this intrinsic/instrumental distinction is often mistaken for the deontological/consequentialist distinction. Yet these are quite distinct oppositions. One might believe that giving those who labour the fruits of their labour is intrinsically good. This does not determine whether one is a consequentialist, so that the right institution (of copyright, say) is one that maximizes this intrinsic good by sacrificing its attainment in the short run for even more of it in the long run; or whether one is a deontologist, so that the practice of giving the novelist the fruits of her labours is the intrinsically right thing to do on any occasion on which one can do it.

The intrinsic/instrumental distinction is also often confused with the third distinction pertinent here, the distinction between first principles in ethics, and all other principles (let us call them 'secondary principles'). A first principle, as the name suggests, is the most general description of what it is intrinsically right to do or what states of affairs are intrinsically good to cause. Being first, such a principle cannot be deduced from some more general principle. This feature of first principles may suggest that such principles cannot be argued for at all and that they must therefore be defended as 'self-evident' or revealed by religious faith.

My own view of justification in ethics rejects these last connotations of the idea of first principles. On what is often termed a 'nonfoundationalist' or 'coherence' view of ethical justification, to say that a principle is the most general that can be formulated—and therefore that it cannot be argued for by showing it to be an instance of a yet more general principle—is not to say that the principle cannot be argued for at all. Rather, first principles are to be justified as abductive inferences from more particular principles and judgements.[16]

When John Stuart Mill argued for his first principle (of utility), for example, he saw that that principle could not be deduced from some yet more general principle—else the principle of utility would then not be a first principle.[17] Yet (on one interpretation of Mill) he did argue for the principle of utility on the grounds that it best described what was common to all more particular judgements about what states of affairs are desirable, namely, that they are desired. Similarly, when John Rawls argued for his two first principles of distributive justice, he did not seek to deduce them from some more general principle of justice as such. Rather, he sought to show how his two principles best described a range of particular judgements, both substantive (no one deserves his own talents) and procedural (hypothetical agreement in a fairly constructed setting for choice).[18]

It is a kind of category mistake to equate the first principle/second principle distinction with the distinction between intrinsic goodness/instrumental goodness. The latter is a metaphysical distinction between two sorts of value. The former is an epistemological distinction between two sorts of principles through the grasping of which values are known by us. Moreover, there is no tight linkage between the two distinctions. While a first principle presumably describes what is intrinsically good or intrinsically right, secondary principles may do so as well. I may, for example, believe that giving *this* novelist *this* sort of copyright protection is intrinsically right, believe that giving novelists copyright protection is intrinsically right, believe that giving property rights to anyone who creates a novel thing is intrinsically right, and believe that giving anyone what they deserve is intrinsically right, even though only the most general of these beliefs should be construed by me to have as its content a first principle.

[16] See Moore, 'Moral Reality', *Wisconsin Law Review*, Vol. [1982], 1061–156; Moore, 'Moral Reality Revisited', *Michigan Law Review*, Vol. 90 (1992), 2424–533. See also ch. 5, *infra*.

[17] John Stuart Mill, *Utilitarianism* (Indianapolis: Liberal Arts Press, 1957), 44.

[18] John Rawls, *A Theory of Justice* (Cambridge, Mass.: Harvard University Press, 1971).

This minor detour into some fundamental distinctions in ethics is essential if we are to keep proper perspective on various criticisms of my mode of justifying retributivism. For what if one were to hold that: (1) the retributive principle is a first principle; (2) the suffering punishment entails is an intrinsic good when inflicted on those who deserve it; and (3) we each have an agent-relative obligation to punish the guilty (even if other guilty persons would escape punishment) because the intrinsic goodness of such punishment is not to be maximized by our actions? If retributivism is taken to be a first principle describing an intrinsic value that we each categorically are enjoined to realize in our actions, then we must tailor our demands for its moral justification accordingly.

My own mode of justifying retributivism has tried to do this.[19] I take seriously the sorts of particular moral judgements that Kant-like thought experiments call forth in me and in most people I know: imagine an offender who does a serious wrong in a very culpable way—for example, Dostoevsky's Russian nobleman in *The Brothers Karamazov*, who turns loose his dogs to tear apart a young boy before the boy's mother's eyes; imagine further that circumstances are such (for example, Kant's island society about to disband) that no non-retributive purpose would be served by punishing this offender. Now imagine two variations: (1) you are that offender; (2) someone else is that offender. Question: should you or the other offender be punished, even though no other social good will thereby be achieved? The retributivist's 'yes' runs deep for most people.

As we explored in the last chapter, the main reason that thoughtful people often give for disavowing their own retributivist intuitions about such cases is that they think such impulses to be unworthy of them. More specifically, they understand that such judgements are the products of emotional responses by them to the brutal facts of such cases, and they disavow those emotions as unworthy of them. That is why I have found it important to separate the first and third person variations of the thought experiment. Such variations call forth quite different emotions, even if they lead to a common judgement of deserved punishment.

The third person variation of the thought experiment is admittedly quite troublesome in terms of the sort of emotions it calls

---

[19] See ch. 3, *supra*.

forth, as we have seen. Yet a number of legal philosophers have sought to rescue such kind of retributive judgements from this sort of disavowal. Jeffrie Murphy, Jean Hampton, and Samuel Pillsbury have each sought to distinguish a virtuous emotional response from responses of *ressentiment* to third person thought experiments.[20] In different ways they have each sought to distinguish a 'moral hatred' or a 'moral outrage' that is the only proper response of a moral being to the gross violations of morality by others that violent crime represents. To my mind, they have made their case: it evinces both a lack of empathetic identification with others who are victims, and a lack of attachment to morality, to be indifferent to culpable wrongdoing by another. The virtuous person may turn the other cheek when it is his cheek that has been slapped (although I doubt even this), but there is no virtue in turning someone else's cheek when they have been slapped. Violations of others' moral rights should make us angry at those who flout that morality, and that anger need not be tainted by cruel, sadistic, fearful, or resentful emotional accompaniments.

My own rescue of retributivism from the charge of base emotion was somewhat different in the last chapter. I there focused on the first person variation of the Kantian thought experiment, where we are to imagine that it is we who have culpably done some great wrong. Here there is a much lessened danger that our intuitions about desert will be tainted by the emotions of *ressentiment*. Rather, one emotion here predominates, and that is the emotion of guilt. A virtuous person would feel great guilt at violating another's rights by killing, raping, assaulting, etc. And when that emotion of guilt produces the judgement that one deserves to suffer because one has culpably done wrong, that judgement is not suspect because of its emotional origins in the way that the corresponding third person judgement might be.

It may be tempting to concede that in one's own case: (1) one would indeed feel very guilty if one culpably did such a wrong; (2) that such feelings of guilt would be virtuous to feel—indeed, the only tolerable response of a moral person; (3) that therefore the judgement which such emotion produces—that one *is* guilty and

---

[20] Jean Hampton and Jeffrie Murphy, *Forgiveness and Mercy* (Cambridge: Cambridge University Press, 1988); Samuel Pillsbury, 'Emotional Justice: Moralizing the Passions of Criminal Punishment', *Cornell Law Review*, Vol. 74 (1989), 655–710.

deserving of punishment—is true. Yet, one might refuse: (4) to generalize this judgement about one's own deserved punishment to others who do like wrongs. One might think that the standard that we apply to ourselves should not be applied to others.

This sounds like a generous way to think. It is important to see that it is not. To grant that you would be guilty and deserving of punishment, but that others who do the exact same wrong with the exact same culpability would not be, is to arrogate to yourself a godlike position. Only you have those attributes of moral agency making you alone a creature capable of being morally guilty; others are simply lesser beings, to be pitied perhaps, but not to be blamed as you would blame yourself. This is not moral generosity. Rather, it is an élitist arrogance that denies one's common humanity with those who do wrong. Such élitist condescension is no virtue, and provides no basis for refusing to endorse the last step in the first person version of the Kantian thought experiment, which step generalizes one's own potential for guilt and deserved punishment to other persons.

B. Critical Reconsideration of This Mode of Moral Justification

A variety of criticisms have been levelled at my justification of retributive punishment via particular thought experiments and the kind of particular judgements that they call forth. The leading criticisms seem to be five in number, which I shall deal with seriatim.

1. First is the charge of circularity. The charge is that the general judgement—that punishment should be imposed just because culpable wrongdoers deserve it—is being justified by nothing but itself. For what are the judgements in particular thought experiments but the judgements that punishment should be imposed (for example, on Kant's last murderer in the island society, on Dosteovsky's cruel nobleman, etc.) just because each of these culpable wrongdoers deserve to be punished? The worry here is one of question-begging: since the particular judgements with which we start are themselves retributive judgements, how can they justify the general retributive judgement without begging the question?

There are three ways of construing this question-begging (or circularity) worry. One is to construe it strictly: literally, the very same principle is being used to justify itself. So construed, the worry is groundless, for the particular judgements called forth by Kant-like thought experiments are not identical in content with the retributive principle itself. The retributive principle is the universalized judgement that all culpable wrongdoing ought to be punished; Kantian thought experiments give rise to particular judgements that particular persons in particular situations ought to be punished. The former judgement stands to the latter judgements as universally generalized to singular statements: aspects of the situations involved in the latter judgements are abstracted as relevant, and these are universalized into the general judgement that whenever these aspects are present punishment is obligatory. Strictly speaking, thus, the retributivist is not justifying the retributive norm by reference solely to itself. Rather, he is inferring a universally generalized statement from a set of singular statements.

A second, less-literal construal of the question-begging worry does not claim identity between the judgement to be justified, retributivism, and the particular judgements doing the justifying. Recognizing the distinction between universally generalized versus singular judgements, this form of the worry nonetheless insists that the particular judgements are themselves retributive. The worry is that the particular judgements are of the form 'the nobleman should be punished because and only because he deserves it'. The worry is that merely universalizing this singular judgement into the general judgement—that all those who deserve punishment should be given the punishment that they deserve—is trivial.[21]

---

[21] David Dolinko advances this form of the question-begging objection against my coherentist methodology with an example: 'Consider, as an analogy, a similar coherence justification for the view, say, that women are inferior to men, offered circa 1800 by one man to another. Someone has raised the question of whether it is really justifiable to treat women as inferior and is met with·the response that, "Well, of course, we all have the intuition that in *this* situation we should discriminate against women, and likewise in *this* and *this*; now, the best way of accounting for these particular judgements is to suppose women to be morally and intellectually inferior to men". Wouldn't one feel that the crucial question is being begged?' Dolinko, *supra* n. 2, at 557–8. Notice that Dolinko trivializes the inference in his analogy in the manner attacked in the text: the particular judgements are not that *this* person should be treated in some inferior way in this context; rather, the particular judgements already include most of the terms of the principle to be abstracted from them—that the inferior treatment is *discrimination*; that the only feature to be mentioned is that the persons discriminated against are *women*.

By his choice of analogy, Dolinko also of course hopes to suggest that a coherence mode of justification is no guarantee against moral error, for we are only cohering our own beliefs and attitudes. One can easily concede this possibility of error without for a moment conceding Dolinko's hoped-for conclusion (that this form of argument is question-begging). Our particular judgements of visual perception can

This form of the circularity worry would be a real worry if the presupposition on which it rests were true. What the worry presupposes is that the particular judgements from which justification proceeds are of the content just described. Yet such particular judgements are not that 'the nobleman should be punished because and only because he deserves it'. Rather, the particular judgements are that the nobleman should be punished, period. It is making such judgements about a wide range of particular cases, and abstracting from those cases what they have in common—the desert of the actors—that then allows the retributivist to infer the retributivist principle that offenders should be punished when but only when they deserve it. This is not a trivial inference, for the features of the situations in which we judge punishment to be appropriate could easily be otherwise. It could be the reformability, or the deterrability, either of the particular offender or of some class that he instantiates, that is the recurring feature present in the situations that call forth our judgements about the appropriateness of punishment in particular cases. As it happens, these are not the features of relevant situations that recur. The inference that it is the desert of the offenders that should be generalized from our particular judgements of punishment is thus not a trivial one. Such particular judgements thus possess a non-trivial justificatory force for sustaining the retributive principle.

The third and last form of the circularity worry focuses on desert itself. The worry here is that 'desert' simply means, 'a fit subject for retributive punishment', so that when one abstracts desert from particular cases (as the feature of them that caused judgements of punishment) one has done no more than start with particular retributive judgements in order to justify the general retributive judgement.[22] 'Desert', however, does not mean, 'a fit subject for retributive punishment', any more than 'death' means, 'a fit subject for concern by a mortician' or 'illness' means, 'a fit subject for

of course also be in error on occasion, but that does not eviscerate the power of those judgements to be good (if not conclusive) reasons for believing the principles abstractable from them.

[22] For an example of this form of the question-begging worry, see Mackie, 'Retributivism: A Test Case for Ethical Objectivity', *supra* n. 1, at 679 (' "Desert" is not such a further explanation, but is just the general, as yet unexplained, notion of . . . retributivism itself.') Dudley Knowles also adopts Mackie's view here, in advancing a like circularity worry. Knowles, *supra* n. 10, at 52.

concern by a medical doctor'.[23] Rather, 'desert' means culpable wrongdoing (at least with respect to blameworthy actions—a broader formulation is needed to encompass praiseworthy actions). When we abstract desert out as the recurring feature present in cases of prima facie justified punishment, we are thus not merely isolating 'punishability on retributive grounds'.

There are two aspects of desert that are worth drawing out a bit. The first is wrongdoing. A person does wrong whenever his voluntary act causes a state of affairs to exist that instantiates a moral norm that prima facie prohibits such acting and such causing, and there is no moral justification for this prima facie wrong. Wrongdoing is thus constructed out of the elements of action, causation, and (lack of) justification.[24]

Culpability is distinct from wrongdoing. A person may do wrong, say by killing a perfectly innocent victim, yet be nonculpable in the doing of that wrongful act. He may be insane, for example, or acting under extreme duress, or he may have mistakenly believed that his victim was trying to kill him. Likewise, a person may be very culpable and yet have done no wrong. He may have shot a stump, for example, while believing that he was shooting his old enemy. Culpability consists of the mental states with which an action may be done, and with the (lack of) excuse for the otherwise culpable doing of a wrongful action.

Desert is thus far from an empty concept, connoting no more than punishability on retributive grounds. To say that a person deserves punishment is to say that he has culpably done wrong (or, in some cases, that he is culpable even without wrongdoing). Inasmuch as wrongdoing and culpability are far from empty concepts, neither is desert.[25]

[23] These last examples are considered in Moore, *Law and Psychiatry: Rethinking the Relationship* (Cambridge: Cambridge University Press, 1984), 200–1.

[24] On wrongdoing, see Moore, *Act and Crime*, *supra* n. 1, ch. 7; also *infra*, ch. 5.

[25] Knowles disagrees with me that 'desert' means 'culpable wrongdoing'. His ear for idiomatic English tells Knowles that ' "culpable wrongdoing" is what the agent does. "Desert" is what he may or may not get in consequence'. Knowles, *supra* n. 10, at 52. Yet I use 'desert' as a synonym for the moral property, responsible. Such a moral property supervenes on the moral properties of culpability and of wrongdoing, which in turn supervene upon the properties of intentionality, freedom, voluntariness, and causation. There may well be an element of stipulative definition of 'desert' on my part, for I do not include liability to penal sanctions as part of the meaning of 'desert'. For those like Knowles unable to put aside the future-oriented connotations of 'desert', substitute the alternative word, 'responsible'. Nothing in

2. I suspect that some critics of my justificatory methods might well concede the above rebuttals of the three question-begging worries and yet still think that generalizing from particular judgements to the retributive principle cannot justify the latter principle.[26] To sustain this form of the objection, however, such a critic would have to believe two things: first, that there is no more general principle from which the retributive principle can be deduced; and second, that in the absence of such a more general principle, the retributive principle is in no sense morally justified.

The second of these beliefs we can quickly dispatch, for such a belief is no more than a return to a rationalist foundationalism in moral epistemology. Such rationalism leaves wholly unexplained how first principles are to be justified, since they cannot be deductively justified as following from some even more basic, 'more first' principles. Although some may find 'self-evidence', 'God's word', or 'transcendental deductions' to be acceptable starting points in justifying moral belief, I do not. First principles can be justified only by showing that they imply, but are not implied by, both secondary principles and particular judgements that we accept as true. To deny this as a form of justification would be to deny the possibility of justifying any first principle, and to deny that would be to deny the justifiability of any judgement that is itself justified by such first principles (which, on the rationalist view of justification here considered, are *all* moral judgements).

The history of rationalist justification schemes in ethics should not make one sanguine about finding indubitable first principles. The absence of such self-evident first principles is alone enough to dispatch the objection here considered to my mode of justifying the retributive principle. If retributivism is a first principle of morals, then it neither needs nor can have any other form of justification but the form I have offered. Still, the retributive principle seems to

my theory turns on what we call the moral property whose existence justifies liability for a retributivist.

Knowles also thinks that my usage of 'responsibility' and 'culpability' 'entails or implies a liability to some retributive response' (id. at 53–4), and thus there is still circularity. I do not think idiomatic English supports Knowles here; and in any case, again, stipulate such connotation away, if any indeed exists. Moral realists are entitled to have some name for the property I claim to exist, it not mattering much what that label may be.

[26] In his commentary upon this paper at Stirling my commentator, Dudley Knowles, appeared to take this view before eventually giving it up.

be part and parcel of yet more general principles, so it is worth pausing briefly to examine this alternative possibility.

The battleground of theory known as the philosophy of punishment is littered with the corpses of supposed general principles from which the retributive principle is supposed to follow. Giving an offender the punishment he deserves solely because he deserves it has been said to follow from a principle that: debts to society must be repaid (coupled with the further idea that crime creates a debt and punishment is a form of repayment); wrongs must be annulled (coupled with the further idea that punishment annuls them); God's anger must be placated (coupled with the further thoughts that God is a retributivist and that human punishment placates her); wrongdoing must be denounced (coupled with the further belief that punishment is the appropriate form of denunciation despite there being other, less draconian forms); etc.[27] David Dolinko correctly observes that in justifying retributivism I have taken the path of 'avoiding the common retributivist metaphors altogether rather than seeking to unpack and develop them'.[28] I have taken this path because I see very little that is correct (or in some cases even intelligible) in these views.[29]

One more general principle that does not seem clouded in metaphor is a general principle of desert.[30] Such a principle arises because of what might be called the 'secondary' moral rights and duties we all possess. I have a primary duty not to break (most of) my promises and another primary duty not to injure or kill (most of) my fellow persons; I have a primary right to keep (most of) the fruits of my own labours. I also have what I shall call secondary duties and rights—respectively, a duty either to perform my promise, even belatedly, or in some other way to put the promisee in as good a position as he would have been in had I kept my promise; a duty to correct the injustice that I have caused in injuring or killing another by making amends in whatever way I can, including compensation; and a right to have any who deprive me of the fruits of my own labours to give those things back (or pay

---

[27] For a more complete taxonomy, see J. G. Cottingham, 'Varieties of Retributivism', *Philosophical Quarterly*, Vol. 29 (1979), 238–46.

[28] Dolinko, *supra* n. 2, at 555.

[29] An exception may well be Herbert Morris's well-known principle of fairness, which may survive the by-now voluminous criticisms made of it. See Morris, 'Persons and Punishment', *The Monist*, Vol. 52 (1968), 475–501.

[30] This is to take up the suggestion I offered in the last chapter.

me their value where they cannot be given back). It is breach of these secondary duties that warrants the judgement that I ought to be made to keep my promise or pay its equivalent, or that I ought to be made to compensate the victims of my violence; it is violation of the duty correlative of my secondary rights that warrants the judgement that others ought to be made to give me back my property or its equivalent. We idiomatically make this ought judgement using the word 'desert': the promise-breaker deserves contract sanctions against him, the tortfeasor deserves tort law sanctions against him, and the labourer creating a thing deserves to have those incidents of ownership in that thing that are distinctive of property rights.

The unity of *a* principle of desert covering all of these situations does not lie in the species of legal coercion to be justified, although there is in fact some overlap in contract, tort, and property remedies. Nor does the unity of the principle lie in the intrinsic goodness of giving people what they deserve—for then the term 'desert' would mean no more than, 'intrinsically right'.[31] Rather, the unity of the principle of desert is to be found in the common conditions of culpability and of wrongdoing (or in their praiseworthy analogues, of 'meritability' and of 'right doing'). I refer to the elements of voluntariness, causation, and justification, and of intention and excuse, out of which wrongdoing and culpability respectively are constituted. There is a general principle of desert in that the conditions of wrongdoing and culpability are similar.[32]

The retributive principle—that offenders should be punished because and only because they have culpably done wrong—is an instance of this more general principle of desert. We all have primary duties not to do the sorts of acts that *malum in se* criminal statutes prohibit. We also have secondary duties to allow ourselves to be made to suffer if we have violated these primary duties. The

---

[31] I am doubtlessly regimenting the usage of 'desert' here a bit so as to give it this descriptive content. Some of the ordinary usages of 'desert' are such that it can mean no more than 'intrinsically right' or 'intrinsically ought to be done'. Such broad, purely evaluative usages of 'desert' account for the sense of Mackie and others that 'desert' is an empty concept. See nn. 22, 25, *supra*.

[32] For a comparison of some of the conditions of culpability in contract and criminal law, see H. L. A. Hart, 'Legal Responsibility and Excuses', in his *Punishment and Responsibility* (Oxford: Oxford University Press, 1968, 32). Leo Katz also explores the parallel between the conditions of praise and the conditions of blame in his *Ill-Gotten Gains* (Chicago: University of Chicago Press, 1996).

trigger for these secondary duties is again our culpability in violating the primary duties that define wrongdoing.

Although it takes considerably more detail than this to sketch the unitary principle of desert, my present interest is in a challenge presented to such a principle, however it may be filled out. I refer to the objection that desert does not give a sufficient reason to punish. As put by David Dolinko, who advances a form of this objection: 'In general, the sense of "fittingness" or "propriety" inherent in someone's *getting* what she deserves is a very poor guide to whether it is permissible to *give* her what she deserves.'[33]

Dolinko's main ground for reaching this conclusion (about the inconclusiveness of desert) lies in his ideas of rights. Dolinko correctly observes that each of us have rights generally not to be made to suffer. It is thus 'entirely possible for a person to deserve treatment which it would nevertheless violate his rights to be given', as Dolinko also observes.[34] One might, for example, believe that *lex talionis* is what each offender deserves, so that the torturer deserves to be tortured; yet one might well believe that the offender has a right not to be tortured anyway. Dolinko's hoped-for conclusion is that therefore, desert is in general a poor guide to answering the question of what we should do to offenders.[35]

Dolinko's general conclusion does not of course follow from his correct observation that we all have rights not to be deprived of our liberty, not to be tortured, not to be killed, etc. It would be a crude caricature of the retributivist to make him monomaniacally focused on the achievement of retributive justice. The retributivist like anyone else can admit that there are other intrinsic goods, such as the goods protected by the rights to life, liberty, and bodily integrity. The retributivist can also admit that sometimes some of these rights will trump the achieving of retributive justice (as in my *lex talionis* example above). Yet to assert that *all* such rights trump the achieving of retributive justice is simply to beg the question against the retributivist, whose essential thesis is that they do not. Particularly with regard to the rights to life and to liberty, culpably doing wrong forfeits such rights so as to achieve retributive justice, which one can accept without thinking that *all* rights of offenders are so forfeited.

---

[33] Dolinko, *supra* n. 2, at 543–4, 558; Dolinko, *supra* n. 8, at 1627–30.
[34] Dolinko, *supra* n. 8, at 1629.   [35] Id.

Dolinko's attempt to remedy this first defect of his analysis introduces a second. Dolinko correctly quotes me for the retributivist point that 'the moral desert of an offender is a *sufficient* reason to punish him or her'.[36] Because of the need of retributivists to show that giving an offender what she deserves does not violate any rights not forfeited by the offender's culpable wrongdoing, Dolinko would admonish me and other retributivists to 'acknowledge that "criminals deserve to suffer" is simply *not* a sufficient explanation of why we are morally permitted to inflict such suffering on them'.[37]

Here Dolinko fails to attend to the context-sensitivity of any talk about 'sufficient conditions', my own included. 'Sufficiency' is like 'qualitatively identical' in that we almost never use such words or phrases literally. What we always mean when we say of two distinct particulars that they are qualitatively identical, is that within some limited set of properties that the context invariably supplies, the two share 'all' of their properties. Similarly with 'sufficient': when we say that one condition was sufficient for another—as in the counterfactual statement that a particular fire was sufficient to burn down someone's house—we mean that within some limited set of conditions this one by itself was sufficient. Other conditions outside that set—such as the presence of oxygen in my fire example—are invariably *necessary* even while we idiomatically describe a condition within that set as 'sufficient'.

The retributivist's usage of 'sufficiency' is to be so construed. *Within the set of conditions constituting intelligible reasons to punish*, the retributivist asserts, desert is sufficient, i.e., no other *of these* conditions is necessary. Of course other conditions outside the set of conditions constituting intelligible reasons to punish may also be necessary to a just punishment, such as the condition that the punishment not violate any non-forfeited rights of an offender. That concession (implicit anyway in any intelligible usage of 'sufficient') in no way detracts from the distinctive claim of the retributivist: culpable wrongdoing (i.e., desert) is a sufficient reason to punish. More generally, such desert is a sufficient reason to attach the contract, tort, and criminal law sanctions to both promissory and non-promissory wrongs when culpably done, and to attach property law

---

[36] Id. at 1628 (quoting an earlier version of ch. 3).
[37] Id. at 1630.

protection to the meritable right-doing of one who creates a thing of value by her own labour.

By failing to recognize the context-sensitivity of any use of 'sufficiency', Dolinko also fails to recognize that he gives away his objection here when he admits that ' "a person's desert of X is always a reason for giving X to him, but not always a conclusive reason" because "considerations irrelevant to his desert can have overriding cogency in establishing how he ought to be treated on balance" '.[38] A retributivist can happily agree with this statement of Joel Feinberg's that Dolinko adopts, and not for a moment give up his claim that within the set of prima facie reasons to punish, desert alone is sufficient.

Even without the rights argument, I have the sense that for Dolinko there remains some 'gap' between the retributivist's judgement, 'X deserves punishment', and the retributivist's conclusion, 'therefore punishing X is morally justified'.[39] Yet Dolinko has made no showing that there is any gap here. As we have seen, the general principle of desert asserts that the culpable wrongdoing (desert) of X is a sufficient reason to visit various legal sanctions on X. As we have also seen, the context-sensitive use of 'sufficient' here allows for the possibility that there are overriding reasons (such as non-forfeited rights of X) not to visit these legal sanctions on X. But this last possibility presents a gap only when it becomes actualized. And what are the overriding reasons not to make the culpable promise-breaker restore the promisee to the *status quo ante*, to make the culpable tortfeasor compensate those whom he has hurt, and to make the criminal suffer his deserved punishment? Certainly the general rights of all of us not to suffer such sanctions provide us no such overriding reasons, since we forfeit such rights precisely by the culpable wrongdoing that constitutes desert.

It might seem that this difference between Dolinko and myself comes down to a burden of proof issue, Dolinko urging me to show that there are no such overriding reasons and I urging Dolinko to show that there are. If so, surely the burden of proof is on the critic of retributivism on this issue. After all, once it is admitted that desert constitutes a prima facie reason to punish, surely it is incum-

---

[38] Dolinko, *supra* n. 2, at 544 (quoting Joel Feinberg, 'Justice and Personal Desert', in *Doing and Deserving* (Princeton: Princeton University Press, 1970), at 60.)
[39] Id. at 545.

bent on those who urge we not punish to show us why we should stay our hand.

It might also seem that I have done little to justify the more general principle of desert, even if I have shown how the retributive principle follows from it. But of course, that objection can be raised *ad infinitum* for any answer that might be given. That is the problem with thinking that justification has to be a matter of deducing the principle to be justified from one that is yet more general. We must give up that picture of how justification must proceed. Once we do so, then whether we are justified in believing in retributivism cannot depend on our finding some yet more general principle with which to justify it.

3. A common objection to coherentist justification of moral principles goes like this: since the data being cohered into more general principles are our own judgements and feelings, the principles that result are only a coherent expression of our own sentiments. They can have no claim to ethical objectivity given the nature of the data out of which they are constructed. As Joel Feinberg puts it, in response to my retributive thought experiments: 'Is our reaction a reliable guide to moral judgement?'[40]

We should distinguish a naïve from a sophisticated version of this worry. In its naïve form, the thought is that it is necessarily the case that principles abstracted from our judgements and feelings in particular cases must be about our sentiments, not about some objective features of moral reality. This must be the case because the data from which the principles are abstracted are our own subjective feelings and judgements.

This form of the objection is naïve because it confuses the question of whether our judgements and feelings in moral thought experiments are subjective with the question of whether what those judgements and feelings are *about* is subjective. Of course, my judgements and feelings are mine, part of my mental states, and are in that sense subjective. But this goes no distance towards establishing that what my judgements and feelings are about are also subjective. My perceptual belief that I am now confronted by a bird on the branch beyond my window is a subjective mental state of

---

[40] Joel Feinberg and Hyman Gross, *Philosophy of Law*, 4th edn. (Belmont, Cal.: Wadsworth, 1991), at 630. For similar queries about my thought experiments, see Sanford Kadish and Stephen Schulhofer, *Cases and Materials on Criminal Law*, 5th edn. (Boston: Little, Brown, 1989), at 145.

mine; the bird and the branch, however, are not mental states of mine but have their own independent existence.

Some beliefs, of course, are about other subjective mental states. I can believe that I desire to go fishing, that I hate pretension, that I am in pain, that I am having the visual experience of seeing a bird, etc. In each case the object of my mental state of belief is some further mental state of mine. Yet in form our moral beliefs are not like this. When I believe that bullfighting is wrong, the object of my belief is not, prima facie, some further mental state of mine—it is about the institution of bullfighting and about a property that institution possesses, namely, its wrongness.[41]

One thus must sophisticate the objection to make it at all interesting. In its sophisticated form the objection concedes that principles abstracted from our judgements and feelings could be objectively true even though the data from which the principles are abstracted are (harmlessly) our own more particular subjective judgements and feelings. Indeed, the sophisticate here can also concede that both our particular judgements and the principles abstracted from them in form purport to be about independently existing moral qualities.[42] The sophisticate urges, however, that in fact such qualities do not exist because the best explanation for why we have the reactions we do (to Kant-like thought experiments) lies elsewhere.

The sophisticated form of this objection presupposes a certain view about moral epistemology and metaphysics—a view that I share and have called 'explanationism'[43]—so a brief description of this view may be helpful to understanding this form of the objection. The view is that we are justified in trusting our moral intuitions in particular cases to be evidence of objective moral facts if but only if the best explanation for why we have such intuitions includes those moral facts. The view anticipates that for any natural phenomenon (like our reactions to Kant-like thought experiments) there will be competing explanations. Each explanation will presuppose that a somewhat different set of features exist. If one

---

[41] For the classical argument concluding that our moral beliefs cannot be about our own moral beliefs, see G. E. Moore, *Ethics* (Cambridge: Cambridge University Press, 1912), and for an update, M. S. Moore, 'Moral Reality', *supra* n. 16, at 1075–9.

[42] A concession made by the late John Mackie in his *Ethics: Inventing Right and Wrong* (London: Penguin, 1977), ch. 1.

[43] Michael Moore, 'Moral Reality Revisited', *supra* n. 16, at 2491–501.

explanation is demonstrably superior to its competitors, then the natural phenomenon thus explained is good evidence for the features of the world that best explain it.

My mode of justifying retributivism supposes that the best explanation for why we have the reactions we do to Kant-like thought experiments is that those reactions are caused by the existing moral qualities of wrongness and of culpability, the combination of which I call *desert*. My sophisticated objector here flatly joins issue: the best explanation for the reactions we have to such thought experiments does not lie in the causal power of any objectively existing moral qualities of desert, but rather, in certain psychological facts about us and certain sociological facts about our society. If this latter explanation is best, then we should not take our reactions to evidence the objective truth of retributivism; only certain psychological and social truth about us and our society.

Although Nigel Walker has briefly adverted to this explanationist objection to my mode of justifying retributivism,[44] the detailed working out of the objection was done by the late John Mackie.[45] Conceding that 'it is plain that a considerable number of people have what would be called an intuition that a wrong action in itself calls for the infliction of suffering or deprivation on the agent',[46]

---

[44] Nigel Walker, *Why Punish?* (Oxford: Oxford University Press, 1991), ch. 9. Walker focuses on a fact he believes to be 'awkward' for the retributivist, which is 'the fact that by no means everyone perceives retribution as a duty', in response to my thought experiments. Walker anticipates that I might explain this fact by reference to a defective upbringing, but urges that I cannot avail myself of this explanation since it suggests that the perception which I posit 'is really a learned reaction to offending rather than an inborn intuition'.
To begin with, Walker gets the competing explanations a bit askew: 'inborn intuition' is not the explanation competing with Walker's social upbringing explanation; 'causation by the desert of offenders' is the competing explanation of our reactions offered by the retributivist. Secondly and more importantly, Walker is too Manichean in his competition between explanations. Surely *part* of why we believe anything (e.g., about physics) is due to our educational experiences; yet so long as another part of the overall explanation for why we believe (e.g., that protons exist) is that our perceptual beliefs about cloud chamber phenomena are caused by protons, then we have good reason to believe such truths of physics.

[45] See Mackie, 'Retributivism: A Test Case for Ethical Objectivity', *supra* n. 1, at 683; Mackie, 'Morality and the Retributive Emotions', *supra* n. 1. It is important to see that in these papers Mackie was not arguing against retributivism in substantive ethics; rather, he was arguing against moral realism in meta-ethics. Since my mode of justifying retributivism presupposes moral realism (in that the objective truth of retributivism causes us to have retributive attitudes), Mackie's attack on moral realism becomes an attack on my way of justifying retributivism.

[46] Mackie, 'Retributivism: A Test Case for Ethical Objectivity', *supra* n. 1, at 683.

Mackie nonetheless sought to explain such intuitions as the exclusive result of biological and sociological processes. Mackie's sort of explanation is a familiar one. It begins with an observation about the defensive function served by retributive attitudes: 'resentment of injuries is likely to discourage similar injuries, and so again will benefit the creature that feels and displays resentment . . .'.[47] Second, such defensive function will be favoured by its survival value in a process of natural selection.[48] Thirdly, such individualized feelings of resentment take their present, generalized form because co-operation in resentment defends each individual better than his own resentment against those that injure him could do.[49] Fourthly, the apparent objectification of these generalized feelings of resentment is due to the ever more superior preventive effects achievable if each regards his own resentments as being about an objectively existing desert.[50]

There is undoubtedly much truth in Mackie's explanation of our retributive reactions to culpable wrongdoing. Yet as thus far stated there is nothing in Mackie's explanation that excludes an explanatory role for an objective moral property of desert. After all, a good survival-related, evolutionary explanation can be given for our beliefs in the physical sciences, yet such explanation of those beliefs does not exclude a supplemental explanation in terms of the reality of physical objects and their properties.

So Mackie needs to disparage the retributivist's alternative explanation of our retributive attitudes (in terms of the moral property of desert causing us to have such attitudes), and not merely to propose his own psychosocial explanation of those attitudes. Mackie's argument here is twofold as he himself recognized.[51] Mackie's main argument was a very general one, arguing against objectivist explanations of any moral beliefs and not just against retributivist beliefs. The argument was that the 'queerness' of moral qualities—what they would have to be like if they existed, how they would be related to other qualities, how they would be known—was such that no good explanation could be proffered if it made use of such qualities.[52]

I shall here ignore this argument of Mackie's, since it does not distinctively attack objectivist explanations of *retributive* moral

---

[47] Mackie, 'Retributivism: A Test Case for Ethical Objectivity', *supra* n. 1, at 683.
[48] Id.   [49] Mackie, 'Morality and the Retributive Emotions', *supra* n. 1, at 8–9.
[50] Id. at 7.   [51] Id.   [52] Id. See also Mackie, *supra* n. 42, ch. 1.

beliefs and since I have dealt with it elsewhere in some detail.[53] Mackie's second argument is directed against retributive attitudes more specifically. Mackie's argument here was based on his conclusion that 'all attempts fail to make moral sense' of the retributive principle.[54] Yet Mackie's argument for accepting this conclusion was surprisingly weak. The argument consisted of running through the ten or so principles that have been invoked in the history of philosophy to justify the retributive principle, and finding all of them wanting. From this, Mackie inferred that there was no moral principle with which to justify ('make moral sense') of the retributive principle, and further, that therefore the retributive principle could not be objectively true (else it would fit better with other of our moral beliefs).

We should baulk at each of these steps of Mackie's. In the first place, the jury should still be out on Herbert Morris's fairness justification of retributivism, since each of Mackie's objections to that justification have spawned their own detailed literature in answer.[55] Secondly, Mackie passes over too quickly the possibility that a generalized principle of desert reveals that the retributive principle is not isolated from other moral beliefs that we hold, a possibility I explored earlier in this chapter. Thirdly, on a rather more tolerantly pluralistic view of morality's principles than that apparently held by Mackie, the retributive principle may itself be a first principle and thus cannot be made moral sense of, in Mackie's use of that phrase.

The oddest thing about Mackie's argument, however, lies in none of these particular queries. Rather, the argument as a whole goes no distance towards establishing what it was supposed to establish, which was the inferiority of the objectivist explanation of our retributive reactions in terms of a moral quality of desert. The ultimate irrelevancy of Mackie's argument to his intended conclusion stems from his failure to frame genuinely competing explanations for our attitudes of resentment. His sociological/psychological/biological explanation is a genuine candidate to explain these attitudes, but the ten or so principles he refutes are not. Such principles might

[53] Moore, 'Moral Reality', *supra* n. 16, at 1086–8, 1117–36; Moore, 'Moral Reality Revisited', *supra* n. 16, at 2501–6, 2513–26.

[54] Mackie, 'Morality and the Retributive Emotions', *supra* n. 1, at 4.

[55] See, e.g., Jeffrie Murphy, *Retribution, Justice and Therapy* (Dordrecht: Reidel, 1979); George Sher, *Desert* (Princeton: Princeton University Press, 1987).

justify the more particular retributive judgements and attitudes; however, they do not even purport to (causally) *explain* those judgements and attitudes. Indeed, it would be a kind of category-mistake to think that one timelessly true proposition of morality—say, that all debts to society should be paid—could *cause* another proposition (like that expressed by the retributivist principle) to be true.

The best face that one can put on Mackie's argument here is that a moral realist (i.e., one who believes that there are objective moral truths) must believe that morality is a seamless web of interlocking principles. With this belief, such a realist must then infer that retributivism is not an objectively true moral proposition, such inference being drawn from the supposed isolation of retributivism from other moral principles. So reconstrued, Mackie's argument is still hostage to my earlier objections: on a pluralist view of first moral principles, being 'isolated' (in the sense of not following from some yet more general principle) is no evidence of falsity; and the retributivism principle is not so isolated, joining natural right theories of property, corrective justice theories of tort, and promissory theories of contract to form a generalized principle of desert.

If we were to propose a better competitor to Mackie's psychological explanation of our retributive intuitions, such explanation would be along the following lines. There exists in the world a moral property of relevance to punishment, namely, desert. Desert is a property of an actor, consisting of the two moral properties of the wrongness of the act done and the culpability with which it was done (which properties themselves supervene on the properties of voluntariness, causation, and lack of justification, for wrongness, and on intentionality or negligence, and lack of excuse, for culpability).

The properties of wrongdoing and culpability cause most of us to believe that, when we have culpably done wrong, such acts are evil and that we are guilty. Given the duty to suffer brought into existence by our culpable wrongdoing, our belief that we are guilty includes a belief that we must suffer (i.e., be punished).

If this (moral realist) explanation of our retributive intuitions supplements (it need not supplant entirely) Mackie's explanation, then our punitive reaction to Kant-like thought experiments gives us good evidence for the truth of the retributive principle that culpable wrongdoers must be made to suffer.[56]

---

[56] For the superiority of moral realist explanations of our moral beliefs generally, see Moore, 'Moral Reality Revisited', *supra* n. 16, at 2491–533; Nicholas Sturgeon,

4. Distinct from any of the foregoing worries is the worry based on a distrust of the reliance upon emotions to justify retributivism. The worry is that the particular judgements Kant-like thought experiments call forth are suspect because they are both caused and accompanied by strong emotional responses. The worry is not the more precise, Nietzschean worry that the *sort* of emotions accompanying retributive judgements are bad for us;[57] rather, the concern here is the more general concern about *any* strong emotional reaction contaminating the rationality of the judgements it accompanies.

This worry has behind it two mistaken presuppositions. One is a presupposition about the strength of the connection between the having of certain emotional responses to a particular situation, on the one hand, and the truth of certain moral judgements about the situation, on the other. The second is a presupposition about the lack of cognitive content to the emotions themselves. If we correct both mistaken presuppositions—by weakening the connection claimed to exist between morality and the emotions, and by strengthening the case for there being cognitive content to the emotions—we will demotivate this fourth worry as well.

I suspect that those who worry about the rationality of emotion-laden moral judgements have one of two conceptions of how moral truth is connected to emotional response. One is the conception of emotivism (and of certain other forms of non-cognitivism, subjectivism, and conventionalism about morals): the 'truth' of a moral judgement is wholly constituted by the fact that a person (or group of persons) has a certain emotional response. A second conception is that of non-naturalist intuitionism: the emotions are the special sense-data of moral truth, so that the latter wholly depends on emotional responses in the way that scientific truth wholly depends on perceptual responses for an empiricist.

Both of these conceptions are too strong. The first makes morality too arational, and the second makes it too queer. Better is a third conception: our emotions are our main heuristic guide to discovering moral truths, but they are neither constitutive of such

'Moral Explanations', in David Copp and David Zimmerman, eds., *Morality, Reason and Truth* (Totowa, NJ: Rowman and Allanheld, 1984); David Brink, *Moral Realism and the Foundations of Ethics* (Cambridge: Cambridge University Press, 1989), ch. 7.

[57] Explored in the last chapter.

truth nor are they some special data base from which all moral truths necessarily are derived.[58] Emotional response stands to moral truth like experience of consciousness stands to truths about our minds: we happen to be so constituted that we learn a great deal about morality and mental states by our emotional and conscious experiences, respectively.[59] But in neither case should we identify morals or minds with these distinctive experiences, nor should we unduly privilege these experiences as being their own kind of special 'perception', each autonomous in its own sphere of knowledge.

How can it be that our emotions have even this weak, 'reliable heuristic' connection to moral truth? This question gets us to the second mistaken presupposition of the worry about emotions, for the question more generally asked is how can our emotional responses be reliable indicators of any truth? Are our emotions not indicators of our subjective states, but not of how the objective world is constituted?

One of the more interesting developments of the philosophical psychology of the last twenty years has been to suggest otherwise.[60] To begin with, the words we use to describe our emotions are like 'belief' (and unlike the words we use to describe sensations like pain) in that emotion-words take Intentional objects. We are not simply angry or fearful, but we are angry *at* something or fearful *of* something. This linguistic fact construes emotions, like beliefs, to be about the outside world, not about ourselves. Just as a belief that Jones is a thief is a belief about Jones, so an emotion of anger at Jones is an emotion about Jones.

Moreover, emotions as we understand them obey laws of proportionality. Most of us most of the time feel emotions of a certain kind and of a certain intensity with regard to certain sorts of situ-

---

[58] Explored in the last chapter.

[59] This heuristics view of consciousness is defended by me in ch. 10.

[60] A sampling of the now considerable literature on the rationality of the emotions: Ronald de Sousa, 'The Rationality of the Emotions', in A. Rorty, ed., *Explaining Emotions* (Berkeley: University of California Press, 1980); de Sousa, *The Rationality of the Emotions* (Cambridge, Mass.: MIT Press, 1987); R. Gordon, *The Structure of Emotions: Investigations in Cognitive Philosophy* (New York: Cambridge University Press, 1987); W. Lyons, *Emotion* (Cambridge: Cambridge University Press, 1980); Scruton, 'Emotion, Practical Knowledge, and Common Culture', in A. Rorty, *supra*; Calhoun, 'Cognitive Emotions?', in C. Calhoun and R. Soloman, eds., *What Is an Emotion?* (Oxford: Oxford University Press, 1984); Roberts, 'What an Emotion Is: A Sketch', *The Philosophical Review*, Vol. 97 (1988), 183–209.

ations. It is because of these laws of appropriate emotional response that psychiatrists can talk of 'displacing' emotions from their *real* (and appropriate) objects to the nominal objects towards which we sometimes think our emotions are directed.[61]

Finally, there is reason to think that these laws of appropriate and proportional emotional response are not simply products of cultural conditioning alone, but that the reason we *feel,* for example, guilty is often in part because we are in fact guilty of having culpably done some wrong. The moral fact of the matter often causes our moral beliefs through the intermediate causing of our emotional responses. Our emotions in such case become good evidence of the underlying moral landscape.

Consider by way of an example distinct from retributivism the way in which our emotional responses have been taken to evidence certain truths about moral dilemmas. A characteristic emotional response to a resolved moral dilemma is to feel guilty or in some other way regretful after one has decided to act in a way favouring one value over another.[62] No matter how certain one might be that one has done the right thing still one often feels this emotional 'tail' attached to the course of action chosen. Some would see this emotional experience as the harbinger of a deep truth about morality: that moral norms do not admit of large numbers of exceptions to accommodate cases of conflict with other moral norms, but that such norms are exceptionless and therefore irresolvably conflicting.[63]

Our emotions, thus, should not be seen as impediments to the rational justifiability of our moral judgements. Far from hampering our insights into the truth, our emotions are often our best route to discovering that truth. Think of how emotional many people get when the punishment of an innocent person takes place. Surely this anger and revulsion is not an impediment to the insight that it is unjust to punish the innocent; surely these emotions help

---

[61] On the implicit reliance on these laws of appropriate emotional response by Freud, see David Sachs, 'On Freud's Doctrine of the Emotions', in R. Wollheim, ed., *Freud* (New York: Anchor, 1975).

[62] Nicely described in Herbert Morris, 'Nonmoral Guilt', in F. Shoeman, *Character, Responsibility, and the Emotions* (Cambridge: Cambridge University Press, 1987).

[63] Joseph Raz, e.g., so takes this evidence. See the discussion in Moore, 'Law, Authority, and Razian Reasons', *Southern California Law Review*, Vol. 62 (1989), 827–96, at 860–1.

us to see this important moral truth. (Indeed, we find the emotions so helpful a heuristic to moral insight that we are tempted to excuse those who are emotionally blind, those who used to be called 'psychopaths' or 'sociopaths'.)

5. The fifth and last worry that has been raised about my mode of justifying the retributive principle from particular judgements has been a worry about the *reach* of the retributive principle when justified in this way. Joel Feinberg raises the query by asking, 'is the sort of case [Moore] treats as a paradigm sufficiently representative of crime in general for the purposes at hand?'[64] David Dolinko subdivides this worry into two concerns: (1) my 'strategy cannot establish a "duty" to punish more than a small subset of criminals'; and (2) my strategy 'would rationally justify their punishment even if their conduct were not criminal at all'.[65]

Consider the first of these two concerns. Dolinko elaborates the point as follows:

Moore . . . has stacked the deck by giving us a group of especially savage murders and inviting us to generate, from these examples, an intuition that 'criminals' as such ought to be punished . . .[66]

Less savage acts, or acts against *mala prohibita* statutes, or acts that are declared criminal by positively evil statutes, are crimes to which I supposedly cannot generalize my results.

A blanket response to Dolinko would proceed from the view that all criminal laws—whether prohibiting only slightly bad acts, morally neutral acts, or even morally good acts—obligate citizen obedience, at least in a reasonably just regime. Then all those who violate such laws do wrong, even if that same act would not have been wrong absent the criminalization of the act. Then those who culpably do such acts culpably do wrong, and deserve punishment just like my savage murderers.

I no longer accept the view that all criminal laws obligate citizen obedience in a reasonably just regime. The sustained assault of Barry Smith, Joseph Raz, Heidi Hurd, and others have convinced me otherwise.[67] Therefore my response to Dolinko must be more piecemeal.

---

[64] Joel Feinberg and Hyman Gross, *supra* n. 1, at 630.

[65] Dolinko, *supra* n. 2, at 555.   [66] Id. at 557.

[67] M. B. E. Smith, 'Is There a Prima Facie Obligation to Obey the Law?', *Yale Law Journal*, Vol. 82 (1973), 950–76; Joseph Raz, *The Authority of Law* (Oxford: Oxford University Press, 1979); Heidi Hurd, 'Challenging Authority', *Yale Law Journal*, Vol. 100 (1991), 1611–77.

Consider first acts that are less immoral than the brutal murders and rapes I have previously used to get the blood into the eyes of my readers. Examples from Dolinko: trading on inside information in the stock market; giving away ducklings to promote a store sale; or driving on the wrong side of the road.[68] Each of these is a moral wrong, even if not nearly as serious a wrong as taking another human life or violating a woman's bodily integrity. This is true of harming financial markets by insider trading; it is even true of giving ducklings to those who are not likely to care about them; it is certainly true of driving on the wrong side of the road once a statute has been put in place solving the co-ordination problem presented by crowded traffic conditions.

There should be no hesitation in generalizing the retributive intuition from more serious wrongs to these less serious wrongs. Of course, the amount of punishment should be less because the desert is less. It is also possible that the intuition of deserved punishment is less strong for many people in the cases of lesser moral wrongs. But surely, in testing our commitment to a principle, we should initially focus on those situations that work our intuition-pumps most vigorously. If the feature that generates our judgements and that is strongly present in such cases—say desert—is also present (even if less strongly so) in other cases, that is reason enough to generalize to those other cases. We do this all the time in teasing out the nature of different features of the world. We look at clear cases of causation, for example, in order to generate concepts and principles that we can then extend to resolve less clear cases of causation.[69]

Now consider acts that are morally neutral or morally good, even after they have been made criminal by statute. Dolinko's example: an ordinance forbidding giving food to homeless persons.[70] Dolinko defies me to find an intuition that these offenders should be punished because and only because they deserve it. Yet I decline the invitation. Such offenders should not be punished. They have done no wrong and thus, do not deserve punishment. Retributivism justifies punishment only when people deserve it, and desert requires both wrongdoing and culpability. In a legal regime whose criminal statutes criminalize morally neutral or even virtuous acts,

---

[68] Dolinko, *supra* n. 2, at 557.
[69] e.g., H. L. A. Hart and Tony Honoré, *Causation in the Law*, 2nd edn. (Oxford: Oxford University Press, 1985).
[70] Dolinko, *supra* n. 2, at 557.

retributivism cannot justify punishment (and neither can any other moral principle).[71] Retributivism presupposes a regime in which the legislature has followed what is variously called a 'legal moralist', 'perfectionist', or 'natural law' theory of criminal legislation.[72]

It is important to get some sense of how this presupposition of retributivism applies to real life regimes. As is well documented in the literature of the 1960s and 1970s in America,[73] we have admittedly overcriminalized behaviours. Even so, it is easy to overstate the point. Much of what is not obviously a moral wrong like mayhem, rape, and murder, is nonetheless a moral wrong.[74] It is wrong to deceive people into parting with their property, wrong to be cruel to animals, wrong to distress others for your own amusement. Even acts that are morally neutral become wrong when the criminal law prohibits them, if the law's prohibition solves either a co-ordination problem or a prisoners' dilemma that we each have an obligation to solve. Thus, many of what are called 'regulatory offences' may nonetheless prohibit actions that are morally wrong; if such statutes require at least negligence for culpability, then a retributive justification for punishment exists for those who violate such statutes.

This may seem to strengthen Dolinko's second point, which was that retributivism seemingly justifies punishing people when they culpably do something morally wrong even if that wrong is not prohibited by the criminal law. If there are as many moral wrongs as I have just indicated, that may seem to require the retributivist to punish many people whose behaviour is not criminal.

Yet here again we need to remind ourselves that retributivists are not monomaniacal about the achieving of retributive justice. Of course those who culpably do some (slight or great) moral wrong deserve some (slight or great) suffering, yet there are other intrinsic goods besides giving culpable wrongdoers their due and sometimes these other goods override the achievement of retributive justice. One such collection of goods we have called the principle of legality, which forbids punishment for acts not made criminal by

[71] I so stated in the predecessor of present ch. 1, Moore, 'A Theory of Criminal Law Theories', *Tel Aviv University Studies in Law*, Vol. 10 (1990), 115–85, at 177.
[72] Id.
[73] See, e.g., Sanford Kadish, 'The Crisis of Overcriminalization', *Annals of the American Academy of Political and Social Science*, Vol. 374 (1967), 157–70.
[74] See, e.g., Judith Shklar, *Ordinary Vices* (Cambridge, Mass.: Harvard University Press, 1984).

statute when done.[75] In most cases the values of liberty, fairness, equality, and utility that justify the principle of legality outweigh the achieving of retributive justice so that culpable actors who do moral wrongs that are not illegal should not be punished. But not always. As the Israeli trial of Eichmann and the Allied trials at Nuremberg illustrate, sometimes the wrong that would go unpunished if the principle of legality were observed is so enormous, and the evil of it not being punished thus so great, that the goods of legality are themselves overridden by the good of giving the guilty their due.

One might concede that legality stays the retributive punishment of moral (but not legal) wrongs by courts, yet think that legality can hardly stay the hand of legislatures in making all morally wrongful behaviour illegal. Given the broad reach of morality I have just suggested, it might then be thought that this implication of retributivism is unacceptable.

The problem with constructing a *reductio ad absurdum* argument against retributivism in this way, is that the conclusion is not at all absurd. Of course the immorality of conduct, no matter how slight, constitutes a prima facie reason to criminalize the behaviour. What is wrong ought to be punished, and since legality requires such wrongs first to be criminalized, a legislature has reason to make what is immoral also illegal. But again, this reason is subject to being overridden by other goods that outweigh the good of achieving retributive justice. In particular, the liberal goods of pluralism, tolerance, and autonomy (together with epistemic modesty in borderline cases of immorality) often outweigh the (minor) retributive good of punishing minor moral wrongs. It is simply a mistake to think that a perfectionist theory of legislation cannot be as liberal politically as one likes, depending on the weight to be given to these liberal goods.[76]

[75] On the principle of legality and the values for which it stands proxy, see Moore, *Act and Crime, supra* n. 1, ch. 9.

[76] See ch. 1 *supra*, chs. 16–18 *infra*. See also Joseph Raz, *The Morality of Freedom* (Oxford: Oxford University Press, 1987); Robert George, *Making Men Moral: Civil Liberties and Public Morality* (Oxford: Oxford University Press, 1993).

III. CONCLUSION

Once we put aside these five worries about my justificatory methods, we should return with renewed confidence to the particular judgements that Kantian thought experiments call forth in us. Of course Dostoevsky's nobleman should suffer for his gratuitous and unjustified perpetration of a terrible wrong to both his young serf and that youth's mother. As even the gentle Alyosha murmurs in Dostoevsky's novel, in answer to the question of what you do with the nobleman: you shoot him. You inflict such punishment even though no other good will be achieved thereby, but simply because the nobleman deserves it. The only general principle that makes sense of the mass of particular judgements like that of Alyosha is the retributive principle that culpable wrongdoers must be punished. This, by my lights, is enough to justify retributivism.

PART II

THE THEORY OF THE GENERAL PART: THE THEORY OF RESPONSIBILITY

SUBPART A
THE NATURE OF MORAL RESPONSIBILITY

5

THE INDEPENDENT MORAL SIGNIFICANCE OF WRONGDOING

I. INTRODUCTION

Any plausible theory of punishment gives some prominent role to the desert of offenders. Desert is the central property justifying punishment for retributivists, but it is also crucial to mixed theories of punishment as at least a limiting condition of when punishment is permissible. Seeing these connections of desert to a just punishment does not of itself answer the question of what responsibility consists in. That is the burden of this second part of this book.

As stated in the introductory chapter 1, there are a considerable number of possible conceptions of responsibility. Fortunately, our choice between them can be narrowed considerably if we restrict ourselves to those conceptions having some recognition within the doctrines of present Anglo-American criminal law. The concept of responsibility presupposed by Anglo-American criminal law is one whereby it is persons (not other entities such as groups) that are responsible for their choices (not their characters). Further, that responsibility is by and large an active one, that is, it is for actively chosen (rather than passively allowed) evil.

Left open by such a concept of responsibility is the competition between what I called in chapter 1 the orthodox versus the subjective conceptions of responsibility. On the orthodox view both culpability and wrongdoing matter to one's just deserts, whereas on the subjective view it is culpability alone that determines the extent of moral responsibility. On the orthodox view of responsibility, there are two independent desert-bases, wrongdoing and culpability. On this view of responsibility, to ask what punishment someone deserves is to ask how much wrong they did, and with what culpability they did that wrong.

To say that culpability and wrongdoing are two independent desert-bases—and the only two, at that—is not to say that each is sufficient for deserved punishment, nor is it even to claim that each is necessary to deserved punishment. It is to say that each is an independent determinant of how much punishment an offender deserves, given the presence of the other. That is, two offenders, each of whom unjustifiably kill an innocent victim, differ in their deserved punishments if they differ in the culpability with which they killed; likewise, two persons, each of whom execute the same voluntary act with the intention of killing an innocent victim and do so with equal lack of excuse, differ in their deserved punishments if they differ in the amount of wrong they each succeed in doing (viz., one kills, and the other does not).

It is this latter half of the asserted independence of both culpability and wrongdoing to desert that excites so much controversy and that is the topic of this chapter. Before coming to this claim, it may be helpful to say why I do not make any stronger claims for independence. One might say, for example, that culpability and wrongdoing are independently sufficient conditions of desert. This would be to say both: that those who culpably try or risk doing harm, but fail, should be punished; and that those who do cause harms to others by their voluntary acts should be punished even when those voluntary acts are unaccompanied by any culpable state of mind or culpable risk-taking. Yet the latter claim (what I called the 'moral strict responsibility' view in the first chapter) is much too strong a claim to make for the independence of wrongdoing as a desert-basis. Such a claim amounts to strict criminal liability, an anathema to most of us. We might well feel what Bernard Williams calls 'agent-regret' at our actions causing harm to others even when we are not in any way culpable in so acting, and we might on reflection even think that such a feeling is appropriate for a well-constituted person to feel about his own innocent harm-causing.[1] Yet it would be harsh to think that we deserve punishment in such 'to-be-regretted' situations. We may owe compensation or aid to those whom we innocently disadvantage by our actions, but we do not possess the desert required for a just punishment.

---

[1] B. Williams, 'Moral Luck', *Proceedings of the Aristotelian Society*, Supp. Vol. 50 (1976), 115–35, reprinted in B. Williams, *Moral Luck* (Cambridge: Cambridge University Press, 1981). (All page references are to the reprinted version.)

To say this is to say that culpability is a necessary condition of deserving any punishment. This suggests another claim about the independent moral significance of wrongdoing and culpability, namely, that each is independently necessary for anyone to deserve any punishment. Yet this claim too I reject. Culpability is necessary to desert, but wrongdoing is not.[2] Someone who shoots at another with the intent of killing him, but misses, or someone who passes on a blind curve but meets no oncoming traffic, deserves some punishment even though there is no wrongdoing. Culpability, in other words, is sufficient, meaning that wrongdoing is not necessary.

Between the two, wrongdoing and culpability, wrongdoing thus is something of the poor relation. For culpability is both independently necessary and independently sufficient as a basis for some punishment, whereas wrongdoing is neither. Yet wrongdoing is still an independent desert basis in the sense earlier explicated: when culpability is present, wrongdoing independently influences how much punishment is deserved. Indeed, here wrongdoing may not even be the poor relation, because the amount of wrong done may often swamp the degree of culpability with which it is done as the major determinant of how much punishment is deserved. A recklessly risked death (manslaughter) is punished much less severely than an intended death (murder), but then, an intent to cause death and a willingness to risk death are punished much less severely when no death ensues (attempted murder, reckless endangerment) than when it does (murder, manslaughter).

II. THE STANDARD EDUCATED VIEW DENYING WRONGDOING ANY INDEPENDENT MORAL SIGNIFICANCE

It is this independent moral significance of wrongdoing *vis-à-vis* culpability that I wish to examine here. Perhaps what fairly may be

---

[2] Those who make wrongdoing necessary to desert typically do so only by relaxing what wrongdoing is. See, e.g., George Fletcher, *Rethinking Criminal Law* (Boston: Little, Brown, 1978), 481, 489, where Fletcher both subjectivizes wrongdoing (so that it includes intent—that makes attempting a 'wrong') and substitutes 'risk of harm' for harm (so that wrongdoing includes negligence—that makes all crimes of risk imposition 'wrong'); see also Crocker, 'Justice in Criminal Liability: Decriminalizing Harmless Attempts', *Ohio State Law Journal*, Vol. 53 (1992), 1057–110, where Crocker follows Fletcher in the second of these moves so that he too can say that attempts and crimes of risk all require 'wrongdoing'.

called the standard educated view amongst criminal law theorists denies this independent moral significance to wrongdoing entirely. The late Herbert Hart, to take one notable example, held that any version of the retributive theory that accords such independent moral significance to the amount of wrong done 'has on occasion been stigmatized even by English judges as illogical'.[3] The 'illogicality' for Hart lay in the violation of formal justice, the maxim of equality demanding that like cases be treated alike:

Why should the accidental fact that an intended harmful outcome has not occurred be a ground for punishing less a criminal who may be equally dangerous and equally wicked?[4]

Hart intended his query to be rhetorical. It cannot matter to an offender's just deserts whether the wind, a bird, or a quantum shift moved the bullet that an offender sent on its way, intending to kill another, for these causal influences are wholly beyond the control of the offender. What he can control is whether he intends to kill and whether he executes that intention in a voluntary action of moving his finger on the trigger; all the rest is chance. The offender deserves to be punished only for factors he can control, not for those chance events he cannot control. Ergo, Hart's conclusion: whether an actor succeeds in doing the wrongful action he either tried to do, or risked doing, has no independent moral significance.

This conclusion has been concurred in by a majority of respectable criminal law theoreticians. In 1962 the drafters of the American Law Institute's Model Penal Code took this view, proposing that with one exception punishments for attempts should be equal to those for the completed crime attempted.[5] Since then many criminal law theoreticians who have addressed the issue have

---

[3] H. L. A. Hart, *Punishment and Responsibility* (Oxford: Oxford University Press, 1968), 129.

[4] Id. at 131.

[5] Model Penal Code §5.05(1) (Proposed Official Draft, 1962). Note that the Code does not have the strength of its own convictions when it comes to the most serious crimes, where punishment for attempts is less, nor when it comes to crimes of recklessness, where the punishment is either nothing or much less than for the completed crimes. See, e.g., MPC §211.2 (recklessly endangering death merely a misdemeanour, compared to recklessly caused death, which is made into a second degree felony by MPC §210.3).

concurred, including Joel Feinberg,[6] Stephen Schulhofer,[7] Richard Parker,[8] Michael Zimmerman,[9] Hyman Gross,[10] Andrew Ashworth,[11] Judith Thomson,[12] Steven Sverdlik,[13] Lawrence Becker,[14] James Gobert,[15] Nicholas Rescher,[16] and Sanford Kadish.[17] Kadish, for example, has recently concluded that allowing wrongdoing the status of an independent desert basis is, if not Hart's 'illogical', at least 'irrational'.

Behind all such criminal law theorists stands no less of a moral philosopher than Kant. In the famous opening lines of the *Groundwork*:

It is impossible to conceive anything at all . . . which can be good without qualification, except a *good will* . . . A good will is not good because of what it effects or accomplishes . . . it is good through its willing alone . . .[18]

Similarly, a person with a bad will is bad because of his culpable willing; no increment of badness attaches to a person because the wrongful act willed actually takes place. 'Nothing about what is

[6] Joel Feinberg, *Doing and Deserving* (Princeton: Princeton University Press, 1970), 33.

[7] Schulhofer, 'Harm and Punishment: A Critique of Emphasis on the Results of Conduct in the Criminal Law', *University of Pennsylvania Law Review*, Vol. 122 (1974), 1497–607.

[8] Parker, 'Blame, Punishment, and the Role of Result', *American Philosophical Quarterly*, Vol. 21 (1984), 269–76.

[9] Zimmerman, 'Luck and Moral Responsibility', *Ethics*, Vol. 97 (1987), 374–86.

[10] Gross, *A Theory of Criminal Justice* (New York: Oxford University Press, 1979), 423–36.

[11] Ashworth, 'Sharpening the Subjective Element in Criminal Liability', in R. A. Duff and N. E. Simmonds, eds., *Philosophy and the Criminal Law* (Wiesbaden, 1984); Ashworth, 'Belief, Intent, and Criminal Liability', in J. Eckelaar and J. Bell, eds., *Oxford Essays in Jurisprudence: Third Series* (Oxford: Oxford University Press, 1987); Ashworth, 'Criminal Attempts and the Role of Resulting Harm Under the Code, and in the Common Law', *Rutgers Law Journal*, Vol. 19 (1988), 725–72.

[12] Judith Thomson, 'Morality and Bad Luck', *Metaphilosophy* 20 (1989), 203–21.

[13] Steven Sverdlik, 'Crime and Moral Luck', *American Philosophical Quarterly* 25 (1988), 79–86.

[14] Lawrence C. Becker, 'Criminal Attempt and the Theory of the Law of Crimes', *Philosophy and Public Affairs* 3 (1974), 262–94.

[15] Gobert, 'The Fortuity of Consequence', *Criminal Law Forum*, Vol. 4 (1993), 1–46.

[16] Nicholas Rescher, 'Moral Luck', *Proceedings of American Philosophical Association*, Vol. 64 (1990), 5–20, reprinted in Daniel Statman, ed., *Moral Luck* (Albany, NY: State University of New York Press, 1993).

[17] Kadish, 'The Criminal Law and the Luck of the Draw', *Journal of Criminal Law and Criminology*, Vol. 84 (1994), 1501–23.

[18] Kant, *Groundwork of the Metaphysis of Morals*, H. J. Paton, trans. (New York: Harper, 1964), 61–2.

morally wrong with [such willing] can depend, for a Kantian, on its actual consequences.'[19]

The moral insight behind Kant's conclusions is easy enough to see. Our desert is determined by what we can control. On the Kantian principle that 'ought implies can', we cannot fairly be blamed for what we could not have done differently because we could not control it. We cannot control the wind that carries our bullet or the child who happens to dart before our speeding car. We can control whether we intend to kill someone with the bullet and whether we intend to drive fast despite the risk to children. Thus, our desert is wholly a function of such culpable intending, willing, and risking, our actual wrongdoing (or its absence) having no role to play.

Despite these impressive legal and moral credentials, I think the standard educated view to be mistaken. It does matter to our over-all desert *what* we do, as well as the culpability with which we do it, and a penal system should reflect this dependence of desert on the independent moral significance of wrongdoing in the amounts of punishment it metes out.

Despite their minority status within the academic legal community, these conclusions are hardly novel. What is surprising in my review of my predecessors here is the dearth of respectable argument for these conclusions.[20] Some of the arguments that have been advanced that may tempt one have been:

1. The argument from Christianity where moral luck pervades moral desert. According to Christian dogma, we are all morally unlucky in that someone else's sin, Adam's and Eve's—persons over whom we had no control—is something for which we are responsible; also, we are morally lucky because, through no virtuous willing of ours (except perhaps the willing of faith) we nonetheless can free-ride on God's supplementing our weakness of will with his stronger will, giving (lucky) us a moral credit we otherwise would not deserve.[21] In a moral system where our desert is so much a

[19] A. W. Moore, 'A Kantian View of Moral Luck', *Philosophy*, Vol. 65 (1990), 297–321, at 304.

[20] The one striking exception is Margaret Walker, 'Moral Luck and the Virtues of Impure Agency', *Metaphilosophy* 22 (1991), 14–27.

[21] As St Paul says, after his famous description of the weakness of his own will before the laws of sin that control his body: 'Miserable creature that I am, who is there to rescue me out of this body doomed to death? God alone . . .' Romans 7.

function of factors over which we have no control, why would one not measure deserved punishment by the amount of wrong done, even while recognizing that the accomplishment of such wrong also depends on some factors beyond our control?

2. The argument from retributivism, where retributivism is conceived of as the *lex talionis*. The *lex talionis* requires that an offender be punished equivalently to the punishment he imposed on someone else. This is fairly translated into 'a principle requiring punishment to be proportioned (in part at least) to harm done . . .'[22] The argument from retributivism is that it is causing harm (wrongdoing) that requires the offender to suffer a punishment, for he must pay for the harm which he inflicted. Without such wrongdoing, what is there to pay for?

3. The argument from the meaning of 'responsibility'. Herbert Hart once distinguished a variety of senses to the word 'responsible'.[23] One of these is task responsibility, where someone is responsible, say, for the safety of a ship. Another is accountability, where someone is said to be a responsible agent. Yet another is characterological, where we might say of someone, 'she is a responsible person', by which we mean, 'she regularly meets her task-responsibilities'. The sense of 'responsible' most relevant to deserved punishment is none of these, however; the proper sense is that of retrospective responsibility, where we say that someone is responsible *for* some bad state of affairs. The argument in favour of wrongdoing's moral significance begins with the linguistic observation that 'the offender must be responsible for something'.[24] The argument continues: without the wrongdoing (that is the causing of a bad state of affairs), 'there is nothing . . . for

[22] Michael Davis, 'Harm and Retribution', *Philosophy and Public Affairs*, Vol. 15 (1986), 236–66, at 239. Herbert Hart also mentions this argument from retributivism, *supra* n. 3, at 131, as does Andrew Ashworth (*supra* n. 11, at 735–6, 741–3). (Neither Davis nor Hart nor Ashworth subscribe to the argument.) See also Bayles, 'Punishment for Attempts', *Social Theory and Practice*, Vol. 8 (1982), 19–29, at 26.; Gobert, 'The Fortuity of Consequence', *supra* n. 15, at 7–11 ('the explanation for attaching legal significance to resulting harm rests . . . mostly on a theory of retribution . . .').

[23] Hart, 'Postscript on Responsibility', in *Punishment and Responsibility*, *supra* n. 3.

[24] Crocker, *supra* n. 2, at 1069.

which the defendant could be responsible. . . . An evil state of mind is not . . . something that one can be said to be responsible for, in the sense of criminal responsibility. . . . when we are focusing upon the defendant's state of mind we are not really making use of the concept of moral responsibility at all.'[25] On the correct assumption that desert is exclusively a matter of moral responsibility, this argument would conclude that wrongdoing is strictly necessary to any deserved punishment.

4. The argument from an expanded view of responsibility for character. Proceeding on the opposite tack from that of the linguistic argument just concluded, this argument concedes that we are responsible for who we are and not just for what we have done.[26] Yet this argument would include the causal property, being-a-person-who-has-done-some-wrong, to be one of the properties making us who we are. Bernard Williams suggests the beginnings of such an argument. Williams denies that:

> we might, if we conducted ourselves clear-headedly enough, entirely detach ourselves from the unintentional aspects of our actions . . . and yet still retain our identity and character as agents.[27]

Rather, Williams tells us:

> One's history as an agent is a web in which anything that is the product of the will is surrounded and held up and partly formed by things that are not . . . Responsible agency . . . cannot ultimately be purified—if one attaches importance to the sense of what one is in terms of what one has done and what in the world one is responsible for, one must accept much that makes its claim on that sense solely in virtue of its being actual. [28]

Thus Williams concludes that we have, and rightfully should have, an emotion of 'agent-regret about the involuntary'.[29] Someone else might conclude,[30] as Williams does not, that the fact that the wrongs we have done are as much a part of us as the mental states or states of character with which we

---

[25] Crocker, *supra* n. 2, at 1070–1.
[26] On the nature of responsibility for character, see ch. 13 *infra*.
[27] Williams, *supra* n. 1, at 29–30.   [28] Id. at 30.   [29] Id.
[30] See, e.g., Peter Winch, *Ethics and Action* (London: Routledge and Kegan Paul, 1972), 149–50 ('in doing something evil one becomes something evil').

did them betokens true moral responsibility and thus, deserved punishment.

5. The first person argument from agent-regret to the acceptability of punishment of those who will suffer it. A somewhat different argument than the one just constructed could be based on Williams's idea of agent-regret. If such regret at having caused harm is taken not to be mere shame, remorse, or generalized unhappiness with ourselves, but rather to be the felt emotion of guilt, and thus, of the justice of punishment for that guilt, then one might argue as follows:

> It is true that those who cause harm would be more inclined to regard a more severe punishment as appropriate and just; those who fail to cause harm would be outraged if they were punished as though they had. But what is the link between this observation about human nature and the theory of just punishment? What we need is an additional premise that would read: 'Punishment is just only if it is regarded as just by those who suffer it.' The way to make sense of this premise is . . . to ask ourselves whether if we were punished the same for culpably causing harm [as] for having a 'close call,' we would regard ourselves as justly treated. My assumption is that we would not; and if not, we can hardly defend treating others in a way that we would not regard as acceptable.[31]

The inference George Fletcher wishes to draw here builds on agent-regret at having caused harm by assuming such regret carries with it the acceptance of greater punishment as just; this acceptance by the offender then justifies the greater punishment, because if even he feels it is OK, it must be OK.

6. The third person argument from 'spectator regret' (or resentment). Another argument that begins with a psychological observation is what I shall call the argument from spectator-regret (or resentment). The psychological observation in this case is not in the first person, about what the agent who causes harm feels or should feel; rather, it is about what others feel when they learn of the agent having caused harm. Pride of place is usually reserved for Adam Smith in making this psychological observation:

> Our resentment against the person who only attempted to do a mischief, is seldom so strong as to bear us out in inflicting the same

---

[31] Fletcher, *supra* n. 2, at 483.

punishment upon him, which we should have thought due if he had actually done it. In the one case, the joy of our deliverance alleviates our sense of the atrocity of his conduct; in the other, the grief of our misfortune increases it.[32]

The normative conclusion that is drawn from this psychological premise is that we justly punish people more for harms caused than for harms attempted or risked. There are in general two routes from premise to conclusion here. The shortest route is through moral relativism, i.e., by thinking that what justice requires is what most people think or feel that it requires:

Differences in result must be taken into account as part of actus reus if classification and grading are to be rational. . . . These classifications are the result of a concern for grading offences so as to reflect societal notions of proportionality—of 'just deserts'—as a fundamental goal of the law of crimes.[33]

The second and longer route is to travel through intermediate value judgements of the form: it is democratic to follow the popular sense of justice; juries or other officials will nullify the application of the law if legal punishment diverges from the popular sense of justice; disrespect for law will be too great if legal punishment diverges from the popular sense of justice.[34] Increased punishment for results is *overall* just, on this view, because the injustice of flouting popular sentiment outweighs any injustice of unequal punishments.

7. The argument from the rehabilitative desirability of inducing agent-regret. Building on the desirability of agents who cause harm feeling greater regret than those who do not is a recently proposed 'solution to the problem of moral luck'.[35] This 'solution' concedes that we treat people unfairly if we

[32] Adam Smith, *Theory of the Moral Sentiments* (A. Macfie and D. Raphael, eds., 1976), 100.

[33] Crump and Crump, 'In Defense of the Felony Murder Doctrine', *Harvard Journal of Law and Public Policy*, Vol. 8 (1985), 359–98, at 362–3.

[34] See the litany of such intermediate value judgements collected in Burkhardt. 'Is There a Rational Justification for Punishing an Accomplished Crime more Severely Than an Attempted Crime?', *Brigham Young University Law Review*, Vol. [1986], 553–71, at 562–6. See also Ashworth, 'Criminal Attempts and the Role of Resulting Harm', *supra* n. 11, at 748–9; Schulhofer, *supra* n. 7, at 1524–33.

[35] Browne, 'A Solution to the Problem of Moral Luck', *Philosophical Quarterly*, Vol. 42 (1992), 345–56.

punish them for those actions in which chance plays a crucial role. The 'solution' also concedes that chance always plays a role in those actions that instantiate morally wrongful act-types like killing, maiming, etc. How then could moral luck be acceptable nonetheless? All that we need do is give up our hostile reactions and punitive practices with regard to culpable wrongdoing:

> [I]f our attitudes were different there would be no friction between our need to react to what the agent has done and our need to treat him fairly. Once we abandon certain attitudes and practices such as punishment, we are able to change our approach to responsibility. Without certain of our present attitudes and practices (punishment) there would be no *problem* of moral luck . . .[36]

Substituted for the retributive goal of punishment is the rehabilitative goal of getting wrongdoers to feel remorse (agent-regret) for the wrongs they have done. And while 'a person who feels remorse suffers, he suffers in the right kind of way, a way which involves no problem of unfair treatment and hence no problem of moral luck'.[37]

8. The argument connecting harm caused, not to desert, but to epistemically justified belief about desert. A recent proposal begins with the separation of 'what a person deserves for a particular deed . . . from the criticism we are actually entitled to level against him for doing it'.[38] Such a distinction is of course one that must be drawn because punishments are administered by us less-than-infallible creatures, and we are right to punish (or do anything else, for that matter) only in light of what we are epistemically justified in believing. The second step of the argument is less obvious; it is to connect harm caused by an agent with rational grounds to believe that that agent's culpability is greater:

> [L]uck in the consequences of one's actions . . . sometimes affects our grounds for seeing what a person deserves . . . Consider, for example, the reckless driver. Sometimes, if a driver harms no one,

---

[36] Id. at 354.   [37] Id. at 352.

[38] Richards, 'Luck and Desert', *Mind*, Vol. 95 (1986), 198–209, at 199. See also the late John Kaplan's endorsement of this epistemic version of moral luck in the 'Model Penal Code Conference' discussion of this topic, *Rutgers Law Journal*, Vol. 19 (1988), 801–3.

there is room for the belief that his speed and degree of attention are adequate: that he is sufficiently alert to avoid accidents if the need arises, that his speed is safe for a person of his skills, and so on. Even if these contentions are quite false, so that in fact his driving enacts a very dangerous level of unconcern and his behaviour deserves a very harsh response, the matter may be debatable so long as he does no actual harm.[39]

Harm caused on this view thus does not affect an actor's actual deserts—only culpability does that—but harm caused is one effective proxy for heightened states of culpability and may thus be taken as *good evidence* of greater desert.

9. The argument from substantive proportionality and economy of punishment. Suppose that one thought that the question here is not, 'why do we punish harm causers *more* than we punish harm riskers and harm attempters?', but rather, 'why do we punish harm attempters and riskers *less* than harm causers?' The assumption lying behind this shift of the question is that harm causers fully deserve the severe punishments they receive. This judgement is one of substantive proportionality, and on whatever scale we use, the assumption is, culpable harm causers by and large get what they deserve. Then the only question is why the equally culpable harm attempters and harm riskers do not get the same punishments. The answer is supposed to lie in the economy we should exercise in punishment when we can do so without injustice:

[W]e sometimes hold unequally responsible people who performed equally culpable acts . . . when they have unequally bad outcomes (we don't find the lucky drunken driver guilty of manslaughter). . . . Is there injustice here? . . . There is injustice when someone . . . is punished more than he deserves. That is not in question in [this] case: the driver is punished for the risk he took, and gets no more than he deserves. The lucky driver gets better than he deserves, but there is no injustice in this and it is supported by the principle of economy of punishment.[40]

[39] Richards, *supra,* n. 38, at 201.
[40] A. Kenny, 'Aristotle on Moral Luck', in J. Dancy, J. M. Moravcsik, and C. C. W. Taylor, eds., *Human Agency: Language, Duty, and Value* (Stanford: Stanford University Press, 1988), 118. On the economy of punishment part of this argument, see also Ashworth, 'Criminal Attempts and the Role of Resulting Harm', *supra* n. 11, at 746–8; Schulhofer, *supra* n. 7, at 1562–88.

10. The argument from corrective justice to retributive justice: that one deserves punishment whenever one is obligated to correct the injuries resultant upon one's acts. Many have seen that the kind of 'agent-regret' described by Bernard Williams is a plausible heuristic to a true theory of corrective justice. When we have acted culpably, but caused no harm to anyone else, we have done no one an injustice that we are duty-bound to correct. However, in such a corrective justice scheme 'we say that the unlucky driver [who causes harm] is morally worse than the lucky one [who causes no harm] in part because we hold people responsible for the results of their actions'.[41] Within corrective justice, 'to be responsible is to have an obligation to rectify bad consequences. If I break your vase, I must replace it.'[42] This plausible-enough reliance on responsibility for harms caused within corrective justice is then transferred over to retributive justice. Criminals are seen as having profited from their crimes whenever they succeed in their attempts, as opposed to when they only try but fail. As Michael Davis puts it, 'to attempt murder is . . . not worth as much as to succeed' because one who attempts but fails does not have 'the advantage of having done what he set out to do'.[43]

11. The argument that a chancy punishment fits a chancy crime. In the literature on how to remedy vagueness in the law there is the suggestion that one should fight fire with fire; instead of seeking to eliminate vagueness in legal predicates (by stipulative definitions, overlapping of predicates, and the like), we should attach remedies to such predicates that match them in their vagueness.[44] Instead of defining negligence more precisely, for example, we should allow the remedy in tort (liability for some percentage of damage) to vary directly with each party's degrees of negligence.

David Lewis recently introduced a like strategy into punishment for crimes. Conceding that punishment should be

[41] Andre, 'Nagel, Williams, and Moral Luck', *Analysis*, Vol. 43 (1983), 202–7, at 205.

[42] Id.

[43] Davis, 'Why Attempts Deserve Less Punishment than Complete Crimes', *Law and Philosophy*, Vol. 5 (1986), 1–32, at 28–9.

[44] See Moore, 'The Semantics of Judging', *Southern California Law Review*, Vol. 54 (1981), 151–294, at 199–200.

for culpability (harms risked or attempted), and not for the amount of wrong done, Lewis nonetheless suggests that the greater punishment for results can be justified as a means of matching the punishment deserved to the proper desert-basis for such punishment, culpability.[45] The essential insight is this: recognizing that the desert basis is seriousness of harm risked/attempted, discounted by the risk of its non-occurrence, the fitting punishment is a harm of equal seriousness being visited on the offender, discounted in the likelihood of its actually being inflicted on the offender by a like amount. In effect, the offender is punished for risking harm by a punishment that visits the same level of risk of the same level of harm on him. Such risked punishment might be realized by a penal lottery,[46] where the odds of actually receiving the punishment are adjusted to the odds the offender had of causing whatever harm he was seeking or risking. Alternative to such a penal lottery is using as a proxy the morally fortuitous fact about whether the harm risked was in fact caused. On any given class of offenders, all (when they act) suffer the risk of severe punishment; those who actually receive the greater punishment are picked out by the 'natural lottery' of causal happenstance. But nonetheless, each offender is subjected to the proper risk of punishment, since within a given class of offenders each offender's chance of severe punishment will equal exactly the chance of severe harm offences of this class risk. Actually receiving the severe punishment may not in some sense be deserved, but the *risk* of receiving it is fully deserved by each offender. If each offender knows before his act of this risk of punishment, and he nonetheless chooses to offend, how can he complain when the natural lottery put in play by his own act selects him as one of those on whom the risk of severe punishment materializes?

12. The argument that criminal law is and must be built upon 'social morality', not upon a 'private morality' that enquires closely into culpable mental states. Nils Jareborg has recently

---

[45] Lewis, 'The Punishment That Leaves Something to Chance', *Philosophy and Public Affairs*, Vol. 18 (1989), 53–67.

[46] For an early discussion of the fairness of the use of penal lotteries in connection with greater punishment for harms caused than harms risked, see Schulhofer, *supra* n. 7, at 1565–9.

defended this idea by first distinguishing 'conduct ethics' (where results matter) from 'mentality ethics' (where they do not), and then arguing:

Conduct ethics is the type of ethical metaphysics most suitable for dealing with large, anonymous moral communities and frequent types of acts. In assessing much of human behaviour there is simply no time for deep investigations and analyses. Normally we cannot count on loyal cooperation from the 'suspect.' A mentality ethics is simply impracticable for most of our everyday moral judgements. There must be something more tangible than a perhaps secret 'inner life.' A mentality ethics could function as a private morality (a morality where the idea of reciprocity within a moral community is absent), but hardly as a social morality.[47]

1. None of these arguments go any distance towards establishing the independent moral significance of wrongdoing. With regard to the first, even if one is a Christian, as I am not, one should eschew St Paul's blanket endorsement of the moral luck involved in there being a Christian God who supplements the weakness of will of the faithful. On this issue, one should be a more Kantian kind of Christian, one who refuses to recognize God's willings to be an adequate substitute for our own willing. As a Kantian scholar recently put it, 'That I should need *help* in this respect—that I should so much as be able to accept it—is precisely what Kant cannot accept.'[48] Besides, even if one allows that Christianity has moral luck running all through its view of morality, that would not commit one to the moral luck involved in thinking that success in wrongdoing independently matters to one's deserts. One might swallow the kinds of moral luck involved in both original sin and divine redemption without accepting the kind of moral luck involved in greater responsibility for bad consequences.

2. The argument from retributivism is too abbreviated to advance the discussion, for it assumes that the only form of retributivism is the one that adheres to the *lex talionis* (requiring one to pay back for harms caused). What is generically distinctive of retributive theories of punishment is the thesis that desert and desert alone justifies the infliction of punishment.[49] Left open is what exactly desert consists of. While the version of retributivism I

[47] Jareborg, 'Criminal Attempts and Moral Luck', *Israel Law Review*, Vol. 27 (1993), 213–26, at 225–6.
[48] A. W. Moore, *supra* n. 19, at 320.   [49] As I argued in chs. 2–4, *supra*.

adhere to is the one that regards wrongdoing and culpability both to be independent desert-bases, one has to argue for that version, which means one has to argue that desert attaches to consequences. Thus, that retributivism generically is the only just theory of punishment—a proposition that I too have defended—goes no distance toward making the more finely grained argument about what desert requires.

3. The linguistic argument about responsibility is of course correct that we cannot hold someone who attempts to kill, or who risks death, but who does not cause death, responsible *for* killing, for no killing took place. Yet nothing of moral relevance follows from this linguistic truth. The question is whether responsibility for a killing matters to one's just deserts, given that one intended or unreasonably risked the doing of such a wrong. If we must find something to be responsible for, it is easy to say that one who intends to kill is responsible for that intention, one who unreasonably risks death, for the choice to act in the face of such risk. The moral question is whether these latter responsibilities are the only ones that matter to one's just deserts, or whether a responsibility for actually killing independently matters to those deserts too. There is no advance on this moral question by paying attention to the obvious truism that failed attempters or riskers are not responsible for the harms intended or risked given that no such harms occurred.[50]

4. Bernard Williams's observations about emotions of 'agent-regret' similarly go no distance towards establishing the independent moral significance of wrongdoing. Williams urges that our 'identity and character' is altered by our acquiring the property, 'having caused unjustified harm to another'. Our histories have changed so *we* have changed. On any theory that says our just deserts are a function of who we are, this change in our character brings with it a change in our deserts. Yet surely this is to saddle a character theorist about responsibility with a quite alien notion of character. The 'who we are' question that is determinative of our responsibility for such a character theorist does not include all of our properties. Being six feet tall, for example, is a property some

---

[50] See Zimmerman, *supra* n. 9, at 383: 'The successful driver [who causes death to a pedestrian] is to blame for more events than the unsuccessful one . . . but this does not imply that he is to be evaluated negatively to a greater extent than is the unsuccessful driver.'

persons possess, but it has nothing to do with their morally relevant identity. Similarly, a character theorist about responsibility should deny that the historical properties acquired whenever we cause harm are essential to a person's character. What is essential are those more general inner dispositions of mind we call character traits—being greedy, being vain, etc. And these traits, he should say, are acquired and possessed by people without regard to whether they actually result in harm to others. Being greedy, vain, or quick-tempered may often lead to others being harmed, but whether they do or not is irrelevant to whether one is greedy, vain, or quick-tempered.

The character theorist of course has to argue for his version of character over Williams. But then, Williams has to argue for his version as well. The true psychological observation—that people who cause harm feel agent-regret—does not yield the moral conclusion needed, which is that the property of having caused harm makes them a morally worse person in fact (and not just in their view of themselves).

5. Fletcher's use of the notion of agent-regret is no more successful in establishing why wrongdoing is of independent moral significance. Fletcher makes the reasonable enough psychological assumption that those who feel greater guilt when they cause harm (than when they do not) also find acceptable and just a greater punishment. What is implausible is Fletcher's attempt to connect offender acceptance with justice. Surely punishments can be just in their severity no matter if some, most, or all offenders do not think so, and punishments can be unjust even if those receiving them accept them as just. One might respond: it is what offenders *ought* to think that matters, not what they do think, but what offenders (and all of us) ought to think is of course what needs to be shown by the argument.

6. The familiar argument that in the design of punishment institutions we ought to capitulate to the felt resentments of most citizens has been answered many times before.[51] If the popular judgement that results count is wrong, then we ought to educate citizens to the right view, not reinforce them in their error. Whatever one's meta-ethics, it is obviously false to equate the actual just deserts of offenders to what most people feel is their just deserts,

[51] See, e.g., Lewis, *supra* n. 45, at 54; Ashworth, 'Criminal Attempts and the Role of Resulting Harm', *supra* n. 11, at 748–9.

an equation made by the relativist version of this argument. The disrespect for law, jury nullification, and democracy arguments relied on by the non-relativist version of the argument also seem unlikely to justify a punishment scheme that we know to be unjust—and even if they did, that would not mean that we were giving offenders their just deserts when we punished them more severely for results, only that we overrode justice in the name of other values.

7. Next, the rehabilitative 'solution' of the problem of moral luck is of course no solution at all. The rehabilitationist who only wants to treat offenders so as to help them to come to the appropriate feelings of remorse for the wrongs they have done has so altered our question that it is no longer the same question at all. Such a rehabilitationist has a very different idea of justice: 'real justice requires that the wrongdoer feels remorse'.[52] This leads to a very different idea of just deserts: suffering may be deserved for wrong-doing, but it is only the self-inflicted suffering of feeling remorse. Justifying the independent moral significance of wrongdoing to this idea of just deserts goes no distance towards justly *punishing* wrong-doers more for the wrongs done than for wrongs attempted or risked.

8. The supposed epistemic 'solution' to the problem of moral luck is equally a non-starter here. To begin with, the argument makes a very implausible connection between causation of harm and evidence of culpability in having risked that harm. It simply is not true that the causation of harms is good evidence—let alone necessary evidence—of the degree of culpability of the actor who risked that harm. More importantly, on its own suppositions the epistemic argument already concedes the only point at issue about moral luck: how can our actual desert depend on factors over which we lack complete control? The answer given here—which is, 'it does not'—is no help, because it denies that there is such moral luck here at all. Our only luck, on this theory, lies in those who

---

[52] Brown, *supra* n. 35, at 352. Equally off the mark is Henning Jensen's 'solution' to the problem of moral luck. Jensen's rehabilitative ideal is to restore the moral integrity of an offender. Jensen's solution lies in the suggestion that more blame may be needed where harm results than where it does not because of the offender's greater felt need for being blamed. This only justifies *expressing* our judgements of blameworthiness, not the making of them. See Jensen, 'Morality and Luck', *Philosophy*, Vol. 59 (1984), 323–30.

would punish us not having enough information to prove our actual deserts.

9. The argument from substantive proportionality may well be correct about the deserved punishments for completed crimes within the Anglo-American system: by and large, it may be that most murderers get what they deserve, most rapists, etc. The argument is then further correct in its reframing of the question to why attempters and riskers get less than this punishment. But the answer this argument gives to its own reframed question is surely wrong. It *is* a matter of injustice if one who deserves a severe punishment gets less. Such undeserved, lesser punishment offends against both retributivist punishment theories—with their demand that the guilty not be underpunished symmetrical to their demand that the innocent not be overpunished—and against equality (usually here called comparative proportionality). But bypassing even these two objections, notice that this argument too concedes the only point in issue about moral luck; for the argument assumes that those who attempt or risk harm *deserve* as much punishment as those who cause that harm. It is only factors extraneous to desert that justify the lesser punishment.

10. Coming to the corrective justice/retributive justice argument, one should concede that corrective justice, rightly conceived, makes decisive whether harm was caused for the duties of compensation to arise. Culpability is not enough in torts because without wrongdoing there is nothing for which anyone has a right to be compensated. The sticky wicket here is the one that separates retributive justice from corrective. Retribution should not be confused with compensation, and just as the role of culpability *is* different in each, so could be the role of wrongdoing. The focus of retributive justice is moral responsibility, or desert, and the fact that there is another sort of moral responsibility does not help in the least in fleshing out the notion appropriate to retribution.

There are, of course, versions of retributivist theory that liken the duty to accept retributive punishment to the duty to make repayment and compensation. These are the familiar metaphors of the 'debt' to society an offender owes by offending, the need to restore the moral balance in the universe, the need to pay for the unfair advantage one has taken over the self-restraint exercised by more peaceful citizens. Yet unless one cashes out these metaphors literally to the actual profit or property made by successful (as compared with unsuccessful) offenders, these metaphors leave open what it is that triggers the offender's debt: is it the success of hurting others, or is it the free ride one has taken on their self-restraint by risking harm to them?

11. David Lewis's elaborate 'penal lottery' is only a clever distraction here. For the whole idea behind matching chance in punishment to chance in causing harm depends on the assumption that there is no such thing as moral luck with respect to consequences. Lewis tell us that this is not so: 'we have been asking all along how this sort of moral luck [for consequences] is possible'.[53] But he has not. For him, it is clearly impossible that our desert could be a function of consequences that themselves depend on factors over which we have limited control. That is why he matches punishments (harms varying in likelihood of imposition as well as in severity) to culpability—the degree of risk imposed—not to wrongdoing. We see yet again that this argument, if it were to establish the acceptability of punishing more for results than for risks, is incapable of establishing that we *deserve* more punishment for results than for risks. It too is thus irrelevant to the issue of moral luck.

Moreover, the whole idea of matching a risk of punishment to a risk of success in crime is incoherent. Admittedly, by using a random number generator or some such device we can adjust the risk of a selected punishment up or down. But to what risk are we matching the punishment risk? Any given action risks an indefinitely large number of types of harms, the degree of the risk imposed varying with the generality with which the typing of harms is done. In setting up one of Lewis's literal penal lotteries, how are we to select the type(s) of harms (and the consequent degree of their risks) that our punishment risk is to match? As I examine later in chapter 8, there is no non-arbitrary way to type the harms any action risks, and thus, no non-arbitrary way to fix the 'actual risk' (as opposed to defendant's perceived risk) imposed by any action.

12. Finally, Nils Jareborg's recent defence of what he calls a 'conduct ethics' has two problems with it. In the first place, there is no argument given to show us that there are or can be two kinds of morality—private morality and social morality—that comfortably coexist. The distinction is reminiscent of Patrick Devlin's like notion of 'public morality',[54] and is equally problematic. One might

---

[53] Lewis, *supra* n. 45, at 56.

say that there is a part or aspect of morality that is appropriate for adoption or use by public institutions, such as the socialized blaming practices both within and without the criminal law, and another part or aspect that is not—although even this is problematic on any legal moralist or perfectionist view of criminal legislation.[55] Secondly, the reason Jareborg gives to restrict 'social morality' to 'conduct ethics' is not much of a reason: lack of time in which to investigate, lack of an accused's co-operation, etc., are (as Jareborg himself recognizes) only practical considerations, not considerations going to morality's content. Moreover, if they were persuasive practically, they seem to go much further than Jareborg would take them, for they would suggest either strict liability (punishment without the impractical mental state enquiries) or no punishment for anyone (as Beccaria took this line of argument centuries ago[56]).

This litany of reasons justifying the moral luck presupposed by our current grading scheme for punishments are so far off the mark that one might conclude that there are no reasons capable of supporting the existence of moral luck. Perhaps this is another instance of F. H. Bradley's 'inventing bad reasons for what we believe on instinct anyway'.[57] Yet my thesis is that we can do better than Bradley's resignation to the irrational. That is what I at least try to do in what follows.

III. RECASTING THE PROBLEM OF 'MORAL LUCK'

Before we try to solve the problem of moral luck, perhaps we should first investigate whether we might dissolve it by showing that it is not a real problem at all. That there is a real problem here has been most influentially stated in contemporary philosophy by Tom Nagel:

[54] A. P. Devlin, *The Enforcement of Morals* (Oxford: Oxford University Press, 1959).

[55] Part III of this book defends a version of a perfectionist theory of criminal legislation.

[56] '[W]hat insect will dare take the place of divine justice . . .? The gravity of sin depends upon the inscrutable wickedness of the heart. No finite being can know it without revelation. How then can it furnish a standard for the punishment of crimes?' Beccaria, *On Crimes and Punishments*, J. Grigson, trans., in A. Manzoni, ed., *The Column of Infamy* (Oxford: Oxford University Press, 1964), at 17–18.

[57] Bradley, *Appearance and Reality* (2d edn., Oxford: Oxford University Press, 1897), xiv.

The problem develops out of the ordinary conditions of moral judgement. . . . It is intuitively plausible that people cannot be morally assessed
. . . for what is due to factors beyond their control. . . . Without being able
to explain exactly why, we feel that the appropriateness of moral assessment is easily undermined by the discovery that the act or attribute . . . is
not under the person's control. . . . [A] clear absence of control, produced
by involuntary movement, physical force, or ignorance of the circumstances, excuses what is done from moral judgement. But what we do
depends in many more ways than these on what is not under our control
. . . And external influences in this broader range are not usually thought
to excuse what is done from moral judgement . . .[58]

We do not control the normal wind pattern that carries our bullet
without deviation into the brain of our intended victim, we do not
control that a child did not stop at the last moment and so ran out
in front of our speeding car, so it seems that our lack of control
should vitiate any increased responsibility in such situations for the
deaths that result from our intention or our recklessness/negligence.
This is the problem of moral luck:

Where a significant aspect of what someone does depends on factors
beyond his control, yet we continue to treat him in that respect as an object
of moral judgement, it can be called moral luck. . . . And the problem
posed by this phenomenon . . . is that the broad range of external influences here identified seems on close examination to undermine moral
assessment as surely as does the narrower range of familiar excusing conditions.[59]

The problem of moral luck, as Nagel frames it, is how we can justify holding people more responsible for causing harm than for
merely intending or risking harm when they lack that *control* (over
whether the harm occurs or not) we generally require for responsibility.

Moral luck is good when an actor fails to cause the harm he has
intended or risked, for the actor gets moral credit for something
over which he lacked control; moral luck is bad when the actor
does cause the harm he intended or risked, because he gets moral
demerits for something over which he lacked control. Nagel's ques-

---

[58] Nagel, 'Moral Luck', *Proceedings of the Aristotelian Society*, Supp. Vol. 50
(1976), 137–51, reprinted in Nagel, *Mortal Questions* (Cambridge: Cambridge
University Press, 1979), at 25. (All subsequent references are to the reprinted edition.)
[59] Id. at 26.

tion is how such luck could be justified in the face of our control requirement for responsibility.

The question as Nagel poses it arises only if we think that there is such a thing as moral luck. By this, I do not mean to join Kant et al. in denying that wrongdoing has any independent moral significance. I mean that an anti-Kantian here might deny that there is any *luck* involved in being held more responsible for successful wrongdoing than for intended or risked wrongdoing that does not materialize. There undoubtedly is some luck involved in whether we cause the harms we intend or risk, but there will be *moral* luck only *vis-à-vis* some moral baseline of the normal that places all such luck on the side of the extraordinary.

We do have a criminal law doctrine that explicitly deals with the question of luck with regard to consequences. This is the doctrine of proximate causation. The proximate cause tests in criminal law have as their function the separation of harms in fact caused by a defendant's voluntary act into two camps: those freakishly so caused, in which event the actor is liable only for lesser crimes of attempt, specific intent, or risk-imposition; and those more normally so caused, in which event the actor is liable for the more serious punishments reserved for completed crimes. Sometimes these tests are explicit about their being tests of luck. The Model Penal Code, for example, provides that an act is the cause of a harm when the harm would not have happened but for the act, and [with complications here ignored] the 'actual result is not too remote or accidental in its occurrence to have a just bearing on the actor's liability or on the gravity of his offense'.[60] Even when the proximate cause tests are not explicitly directed to this freakishness or luck question, they implicitly aim at just this factor. The foreseeability test of proximate causation, for example, seems to be aimed at an actor's culpability: could he have foreseen that such a harm would result from his action? In reality, given the well-known conundrum about specifying the details of the harm about which to ask foreseeability questions,[61] what the test really asks is whether the 'freakishness of the facts refuses to be drowned' or not.[62]

[60] American Law Institute, Model Penal Code §2.03.
[61] On the conundrum, see ch. 8 *infra*.
[62] The quoted language is Clarence Morris, *Torts* (Brooklyn: Foundation Press, 1953), 174–7.

Consider some examples of Hart and Honoré's:[63] (1) A defendant culpably throws a lighted cigarette onto some bushes; the bushes catch fire, but would burn themselves out if it were not for a normal evening breeze that comes up, carrying the fire to the forest and burning it down. (2) Same as (1), except that the breeze that comes up is a gale force wind never before seen at this time of year, which wind uproots the burning bushes and carries them to a distant forest, which ignites and burns. (3) Same as (1), except no breeze, normal or abnormal, arises; rather, a would-be extinguisher of the fire in the bushes himself catches fire, and in his agony he runs to the forest, which burns. (4) Same as (1), except a second culpable defendant is the vehicle for transferring the fire from the bushes to the forest: he sees that the fire in the bushes is about to go out, so he pours a gasoline trail from the forest to the burning bushes, in order to burn down the forest, which then occurs.

On the direct cause notion of proximate causation that Hart and Honoré so elegantly explore the initial defendant in (1) and (3) is criminally liable for burning down the forest, whereas in variations (2) and (4) the causal routes from defendant's act to the ultimate harm are too accidental, too fortuitous, too much a matter of chance or luck, for the defendant to be liable for such harm; at most, he can be held only for attempted destruction of the forest, or for risking its destruction.

Notice that the normal breeze in (1), the gale in (2), the movements of the clumsy would-be fire extinguisher in (3), and the actions of the arsonist in (4), are all equally outside the control of the initial fire-starter. In Nagel's sense of 'luck', thus, all cases involve moral luck: bad moral luck in (1) and (3) where the fire-starter is held liable, and good moral luck in (2) and (4), where he is not. Nagel's sense of 'luck' is thus obviously not the same as that employed in the criminal law doctrines of proximate causation and the morality that underlies them, for those doctrines use a different notion of luck to distinguish some as matters of luck and others, not.

The notion of luck always involves some baseline of comparison. As the proximate cause tests of the criminal law use the notion, the baseline is the normal way things come about. When a defendant negligently operates a train too fast, so that he cannot stop it before

---

[63] H. L. A. Hart and A. M. Honoré, *Causation in the Law* (Oxford: Oxford University Press, 1959).

it hits another's railroad car, there is no luck involved in his injuring the second car because that is how such things normally happen. When, however, the same negligently speeding defendant causes the same damage to the same car, but does so because a first collision (which does no damage) throws the defendant against the reverse throttle of his engine, thereby knocking him unconscious, whereupon his engine goes in reverse around a circular track, colliding with the other's car and then causing it damage,[64] there is luck involved because of the abnormal conjunction of events taking place between defendant's act and the harm.

Moral luck, on this concept of luck, would exist whenever the consequence of moral blame or credit is brought on one in an abnormal, freakish, or chance way. If one were truly to blame for someone else's actions over whom one had no control, for example, that would be a case of (bad) moral luck. But if one's blameworthiness only comes about in the normal, non-freakish, not-by-chance way, there is no *moral* luck involved in such blameworthiness, wherever it exists, even if there is luck involved.

The crucial question, of course, is to spell out when blameworthiness attaches in a normal, as opposed to an abnormal, way. Nagel thinks that this notion of normalcy is to be fleshed out with his idea of control: blameworthiness for a harm would attach in a normal way only if the agent was in control of all factors causally contributing to that harm. Yet this is surely not the notion of normalcy presupposed by the criminal law's notion of luck. And this last observation is not the observation that Nagel requires *complete* control (of *all* factors) while the criminal law and the morality that underlies it only requires control of *some* factors; rather, the observation is that the notion of control is alien to the criminal law's idea of luck. The baseline is freakishness of causal route, not degree of control by the agent of the intervening factors. For notice again: the actors equally lack any control of the breezes or second agents whose interventions were necessary for the destruction of the forest in scenarios (1) to (4) above.[65] It is the normalcy of causal route

[64] Roughly the facts of *Bunting* v. *Hogsett*, 139 Pa. 363, 21 A 31 (1890).

[65] The lack of relevance of control to the law's notion of luck is further evidenced by the difference it makes legally whether the freakish facts (over which defendant has no control) come into being after the defendant's act or before. If a defendant cuts a bleeder, hits the proverbial thin-skulled man, or drops a wooden plank into a ship's hold already filled with flammable gas, he has caused the ensuing deaths or ship explosions even though these pre-existing conditions were extraordinary and

that decides the normalcy of moral blameworthiness in such cases, ideas of normalcy to which control is simply irrelevant.

Of course, one might respond: 'but the different notion of luck involved in the criminal law and in the morality that underlies it is just what Nagel is questioning'. Yet where is Nagel's beachhead within that system of criminal law and the morality that underlies it from which to launch this question? Nagel needs to show us that it is but a natural extension of our own moral notions to talk of cases (1)–(4) as equally matters of luck (and thus, equally matters of moral luck if we increase and reduce blame in the manner we do). For without such a showing of natural extendibility, Nagel is simply proposing a different notion of luck than the one we employ in our everyday moral and legal assessments, and we are entitled to ask for justification for this conceptual revision. By our ordinary moral and legal notions, the freakishness or chance of the causal route does make a moral difference, but there is no moral luck involved in being more to blame for the non-freakish result of one's acts. Luck, in Nagel's sense that is dependent upon partial lack of control, is simply alien to this analysis.

Another way to see the same thing is to focus on Nagel's notion of *control*. Here Nagel sees clearly that he needs a beachhead (within our ordinary moral notions) from which to extend his idea of control:

The condition of control does not suggest itself merely as a generalization from certain clear cases. It seems *correct* in the further cases to which it is extended beyond the original set. When we undermine moral assessment by considering new ways in which control is absent, we are not just discovering what *would* follow given the general hypothesis, but are actually being persuaded that in itself the absence of control is relevant in these cases too. The erosion of moral judgement emerges not as the obscure consequence of an over-simple theory, but as a natural consequence of the ordinary idea of moral assessment, when it is applied in view of a more complete and precise account of the facts.[66]

Yet Nagel is surely wrong about *his* idea of control being built into our ordinary idea of moral assessment. When we proximately cause

abnormal. The amount of control a defendant may have over these conditions can be as non-existent as his control over subsequently arising, but equally abnormal events, and thus it is plainly not the degree of the defendant's control that makes the difference for liability here.

[66] Nagel, *supra* n. 58, at 26–7.

just the harm we intended to cause by our action, we have not lacked *control* as we use that phrase in ordinary moral assessments.[67] The actor who lights the bushes in order to burn the forest, and whose act causes the burning of the forest without the intervention of any abnormal or freakish factors, is in *control* of that result, as we ordinarily use the word 'control'. Only would-be forest burners whose acts bring about the destruction of the forest in a chance or freakish way lack control in this sense, because their choices do not *cause* the harm. Nagel's stringent idea of control—where to control a result is to control all factors necessary to that result, even the normally occurring factors—finds no resonance in the ordinary notion of control, nor in the ordinary notion of moral assessment.

That, again, leaves Nagel having to argue for *his* notion of control as being morally correct, despite its *not* being an extension of our ordinary notion of responsibility. It is not obvious what such an argument would look like, since Nagel does not make it. My suspicion is that the only arguments available here are the same arguments as have been trotted out by incompatibilists on the free will issue for centuries. Incompatibilists have long sought to show that we must be in control over all factors that cause our choices in order for us to be responsible for both those choices and the wrongdoings such choices initiate. The question for incompatibilists has always been how they can support this demand for control, since it is not built into our ordinary notions of control. By our ordinary notions, we control our choices whenever such choices are not subject to threats or other coercion and when we have enough information to make them.[68] There are no beachheads within our ordinary moral criteria for the incompatibilists' alien idea of control.[69]

Nagel is in the same position as the more traditional incompatibilist about responsibility, except that in Nagel's case he wishes to import his alien notion of control into the causal chain that

---

[67] See, e.g., John Bishop, *Natural Agency* (Cambridge: Cambridge University Press, 1989), 23: 'What is necessary for an agent to be morally responsible for an outcome is just that the outcome should have been produced *through an exercise of the agent's control*, or in other words, through the agent's action. It is not necessary that the outcome shouldn't have been in any way subject to causal influences beyond the agent's control. One may exercise control without having total control over what happens.'

[68] The two true excuses to responsibility. See ch. 12 *infra*. [69] Id.

succeeds rather than precedes, choice. Despite this last difference, Nagel needs exactly what the traditional incompatibilist needs, which is some reason supporting the importation of this require- ment of control into the causal aetiology of wrongdoing. Neither Nagel nor the more traditional incompatibilist give us any such rea- son, because both of them think that this idea of control is already presupposed by our ordinary notions of moral assessment. Reject that claim, as I have in this section, and the 'problem of moral luck' disappears—at least, as a problem of luck (in its ordinary sense) determining our moral deserts.

IV. DOES WRONGDOING MATTER TO OUR OVERALL DESERTS?

It may surprise one that there is any question to ask, given the con- clusion of the preceding section. Yet we should not mistake what was there established. All I sought to show was that by our ordi- nary legal and moral notions of control and luck, there is no prob- lem of moral luck as such. This recasts our enquiry, but it does not end it. For the properly framed question still remains: does the cau- sation of bad results matter to our moral responsibility or not? This is not a question of whether 'moral luck' exists or not, for that way of putting it presupposes a baseline (of when we are lucky, of when we have control) that we do not accept, nor we need accept it, at least as a natural extension of our ordinary notions. Still, the ques- tion itself is an open one. Should we replace our ordinary notions of luck and control, supplant entirely the causal discriminations we make under the rubric of 'proximate cause', and say that desert is exclusively a function of culpability?

My own answer is 'no'. How one justifies that answer depends on how one conceives of justification of moral beliefs generally. Very generally, there are two schemes of justification: the tradi- tional view, according to which one justifies a moral belief by show- ing that it follows deductively from some most general belief that is self-evidently true; and the more contemporary view, according to which one justifies a moral belief by showing that it both implies, and is implied by, the moral beliefs that one provisionally (i.e., for purposes of justifying this belief) holds to be true. The first is usu- ally called a foundationalist view of justification, since the linear chain of ever more general moral beliefs must stop somewhere and that somewhere will be the foundation on which all else rests. The second is usually called a non-foundationalist view, inasmuch as no belief is taken to be the foundation on which all else depends; rather each belief naturally supports and is supported by the others, and is in that sense justified. Although my moral epistemology is non-foundationalist, I will start with the foundationalist alternative.

A. That Causation Matters Is a Foundational First Principle of Responsibility?

On the foundationalist view of moral justification some principles must be first in the sense that they are not themselves justified by further principles even though they justify all other moral beliefs. How one comes to accept such foundational first principles is a matter of some puzzlement and controversy. Often foundationalists take such first principles to be in some sense 'self-evident'.

It is long been fashionable to pooh-pooh any such claims of self-evidence in ethics.[70] Often such claims are dismissed on grounds that they involve a fallacious inference from facts to evaluative principles, or that there cannot be self-evident propositions since not everyone agrees with them, or that supposed self-evident first principles are at most the mere deliverances of unsupported intuitions. Consider Mill's hesitant defence of the utilitarian (or greatest happiness) principle as the first principle of morals.[71] Mill recognized that the principle of utility, being first, could not be deduced from some other moral principle. Nonetheless, Mill tells us, perhaps some grounds for adopting the principle could be adduced from the fact that most persons do in fact desire their own happiness. Perhaps, Mill cautiously inferred, that fact gives us some reason to believe that happiness is indeed desirable, i.e., good.

Such an attempt to infer a first principle of morals (happiness is good) from a fact (happiness is near universally desired) gave rise to the first of the above-referenced objections to self-evident first principles. Mill's inference was of course G. E. Moore's prime

---

[70] For contemporary examples, see Lloyd Weinreb, *Natural Law and Justice* (Cambridge, Mass.: Harvard University Press, 1987); Russell Hittinger, *A Critique of the New Natural Law Theory* (Notre Dame, Ind.: University of Notre Dame Press, 1987).

[71] J. S. Mill, *Utilitarianism* (Indianapolis: Liberal Arts Press, 1957), 44.

example of the 'naturalistic fallacy', the fallacy of inferring an evaluative conclusion from a non-evaluative premise.[72] Yet not only is there no such fallacy, but even if there were, Mill was not guilty of it on any fair construal of his inference. Mill was taking the judgements of most people—about what was desirable—to be evidence for the truth of his foundational first principle of ethics. Mill was not defining desirability or goodness in terms of what most people desire. That would be, not a 'fallacy' as G. E. Moore thought it was, but a lousy meta-ethics, namely, relativism. Rather, Mill was making the kind of evidential inference that we make all the time, using the beliefs of other well-informed persons as some evidence for the truth of the proposition believed.

Similarly, contemporary foundationalists rightly seek to avail themselves of the same sort of evidential inference, inferring the truth of their foundational first principles of morals from certain facts about human nature. Consider Robert George's example, the basic goodness of friendship, a good George and others take to be self-evident:

Dialectical arguments . . . may be employed affirmatively in support of a self-evident practical truth . . . the considerable anthropological evidence tending to show that various forms of friendship . . . are to be found in virtually all cultures . . . does show that a practical judgement of their intrinsic worth comports well with the data.[73]

Although George is rightly hesitant to say that there can be evidence for self-evidence,[74] he should not let the superficial verbal similarities mislead him here. The judgement that friendship is good could be self-evident in his sense, and the truth of that judgement could still be evidenced by the anthropological facts he references. Indeed, when George tells us that the truth of the judgement 'comports well with the data', what is he saying but that the best explanation for why almost everyone finds friendship to be good is that friendship *is* good, i.e., that the judgement is true?

The second complaint against self-evident truths of morality stems from the fact that not everyone finds them to be so self-evident, for if they did, people would not disagree about them so

[72] G. E. Moore, *Principia Ethica* (Cambridge: Cambridge University Press, 1903).
[73] Robert George, 'Recent Criticism of Natural Law Theory', *University of Chicago Law Review*, Vol. 55 (1988), 1371–429, at 1411–12.
[74] See id.

much. Yet sophisticated foundationalists have an easy answer to this objection, for the objection is far too lenient in the actors whose judgements are allowed to count when it comes to assessing the amount of disagreement there is about self-evident first principles. The objection does not count snakes, tigers, and polar bears amongst those whose judgements (about the goodness of friendship) are to be ascertained, but it is about as indiscriminating in its allowing virtually any member of the human species to count. Demonstrably, some members of the species, human being, lack much capacity for friendship, for example, what used to be called psychopaths. Others who may have had the native capacity nonetheless lack the experience of true friendship: no surprise, given their experience of it as disappointment and deception, that they do not judge it good. But why should the judgements of such emotional cripples deflect one who has had such experience, and who has a deep capacity for more from his self-evident certainty that friendship is good? As Aquinas noted long ago, while certain propositions 'are universally self-evident to all . . . [others] are self-evident only to the wise . . .'.[75] If any propositions of ethics are self-evident, surely they are in the latter category. As John Finnis notes in his own foundationalist defence of knowledge as self-evidently good:

The good of knowledge is self-evident, obvious. It cannot be demonstrated, but equally it needs no demonstration.

This is not to say that everyone actually does recognize the value of knowledge, or that there are no preconditions for recognizing that value. The principle that truth (and knowledge) is worth pursuing is not somehow innate, inscribed on the mind at birth. On the contrary, the value of truth becomes obvious only to one who has experienced the urge to question . . . [76]

Polling those who have had no experience with such things is like polling to see how the good of knowledge stands with them. We certainly do not do this with our factual judgements—asking, say,

---

[75] Aquinas, *Summa Theologica*, First Part of the Second Part, Q. 90, Ans. 2 (Anton Regis edn., *Basic Writings of Saint Thomas Aquinas* (New York: Random, 1945), Vol. 2, 774).

[76] John Finnis, *Natural Law and Natural Rights* (Oxford: Clarendon Press, 1980), 65.

the Flat Earth Society about astronomy—so we have no reason to be so democratic in matters of morality.[77]

Even so, there is still the third worry about self-evidence referenced earlier: are not such judgements—by the admission of their proponents—groundless, and thus, nothing more than their intuitions? In one sense, of course, what has already been said in answer to the first two objections to self-evidence also shows that self-evident first principles are not groundless. That is, if the best explanation for why so many people adjudge friendship to be good, is because the truth of the judgement causes people to make it, then the judgement itself is not ungrounded. The grounding would not in such a case be deductive, for the inference is rather abductive; still, to the extent that there is an inference from a fact to the truth of the self-evident first principle, that is a reason to believe the latter and thus is a sort of 'grounding'.

Moreover, the experience foundationalists claim to be necessary for the discovery of self-evident first principles might be taken to be a kind of grounding of those principles. If one includes in the experience necessary to judge friendship or knowledge good, things like the warmth of feeling friendship brings with it, the satisfactions and pleasure at having mastered a difficult proof or insight, etc., then such emotional experiences may also be thought of as a kind of (again, non-deductive) grounding.

Finally, some foundationalists allow themselves what Robert George calls 'dialectical arguments in defence of propositions claimed to be self-evident'.[78] As George construes such dialectical argumentation:

Dialectical argumentation focuses on the relationships between propositions (including putatively self-evident propositions) to be defended and other knowledge. The point of such argumentation is to highlight the unacceptable implications of denying the propositions to be defended . . .[79]

Such a dialectical argument in defence of the self-evident goodness of knowledge, for example, could be of the kind John Finnis constructs:

---

[77] For a more detailed discussion of our discriminatory treatment of moral beliefs *vis-à-vis* factual beliefs, see Moore, 'Moral Realty', *Wisconsin Law Review*, Vol. [1982], 1061–156, at 1095–6.

[78] George, *supra* n. 73, at 1410.   [79] Id.

The sceptical assertion that knowledge is not a good is operationally self-defeating. For one who makes such an assertion, intending it as a serious contribution to rational discussion, is implicitly committed to the proposition that he believes his assertion is worth making, and worth making *qua* true; he thus is committed to the proposition that he believes that truth is a good worth pursuing or knowing.[80]

How does all this bear on desert for the consequences of one's actions? A foundationalist defence of the principle that wrongdoing matters to one's deserts might well take that principle to be a foundational, first principle. So taken, it would be a mistake to seek to find some yet more general principle with which this principle could be deductively justified. Rather, the foundationalist's claim would be that this principle is self-evident.

There is much that is tempting about this claimed foundational status to the principle that causation matters to desert. It is a widely shared judgement that is the basis for much of the structure of both our legal and moral assessments and thus seems in that sense basic. It is also difficult to think of some more general, more basic principle with which to justify this one—'causation just matters' seems to be about the only argument one can give. We also seem to reach such judgement implicitly every time we experience resentment at the transgressions of others or guilt at our own transgressions. If there are any foundational first principles, the principle that causation matters to desert thus seems a good candidate for that status.

Beyond this prima facie self-evidence, one might also support the claims of self-evidence in the ways just discussed. That is, from the fact that almost everyone—including those ultimately holding the 'standard educated view' with which I began this chapter—has at least a strong tendency to judge wrongdoers who cause injury as more deserving than those equally culpable individuals who do not, one could infer the truth of the principle in question. For the best explanation for this nigh universal tendency may be that it is caused by the truth of the judgement. The moral fact that desert increases with wrongdoing causes the mental fact that people have a tendency to so believe.

Next, one might explain away the failure of this self-evident proposition to be evident to some, as due to their lacking in wisdom, the necessary experiences, or the capacity for either. Such

---

[80] Finnis, *supra* n. 76, at 74–5.

persons may lack, for example, the feelings of guilt in proportion
to wrongs done, an emotional experience that carries with it the
judgement that good intentions are not enough and that what one
does matters at least as much as what one intends to do to one's
deserts.

Finally, one might seek to show how denial of the principle in
question has unacceptable implications. For example, denial of
such a principle may well imply that no one is morally responsible
for anything, not for his intentions, killings, or character, if not for
the consequence of his actions. The apparent absurdity of that conclusion should lead one to deny the premise that generated it, and
to deny the denial of the principle that results matter is of course
just to assert that results matter.

I have sketched such arguments rather than made them, and I
have put even the sketches provisionally, because I myself am not
a foundationalist. Since these very same arguments will recur in the
non-foundationalist justification of the independent moral significance of wrongdoing,[81] I prefer to make them there, where my own
justificatory apparatus can be brought to bear. For foundationalists who share the defence of foundationalism of Finnis, George,
and others above discussed the translation from my idiom to theirs
should be easy enough.

B. Non-Foundationalist Reasons for Believing that Causation Matters

If we enlarge our notion of justification to include non-deductive
arguments as justifications, then the sorts of arguments foundationalists refer to as 'dialectical' or 'speculative' or 'rebutting', we
can refer to as justifications. We can do this because arguments that
infer general principles from more particular judgements are justifications for accepting those general principles just as much as
deductive arguments to those principles from some yet more general ones. And once we give up any linear, deductive picture of

---

[81] This similarity of argumentation between foundationalists and non-foundationalists suggests that the gap between them may be less than is commonly supposed. My own view is that once foundationalists like Finnis and George tech up
their notion of self-evidence in the ways indicated in the text, they become for all
intents and purposes non-foundationalists. All they need admit is that the arguments
and grounds with which they support their supposed 'foundational' first principles,
constitute justifications for belief as firm as any provided by deduction from some
yet more general principle.

what justification must be, there is no need to defend any principles as foundational or self-evident. Everything is disputable, even not disputable all at once.[82]

It is important to see that on this 'coherence' or non-foundationalist view of justification, there still will be first principles.[83] Such principles will be those principles of morality that are logically general and that are as semantically general as they can be while remaining true. No further principles, in other words, are available as deductive justifications for such first principles. The difference with the foundationalist lies in the epistemic status of such first principles. While the foundationalist believes that they must be self-evident, the non-foundationalist will demand justifying reasons for believing such principles to be true. Since such justifications cannot be deductive for such first principles, they must be a different kind of inference, what Peirce called abductive inference. The inference is to that most general truth of morality that best explains the more particular judgements that, for these purposes, are provisionally accepted as true. To argue for such non-foundational first principles will accordingly be to present a broad range of intuitively compelling particular judgements and argue that such judgements are best explained by the general moral truth to be justified. This is how I intend to proceed in what follows, starting with a narrow base of particular judgements and gradually expanding the base, the constant claim being that all such judgements are best explained by the fact that wrongdoing independently determines the extent of our just deserts.

1. Particular Judgements About Wrongdoing and the Amount of Deserved Punishment   The place to start is with those judgements about particular cases that many find to be intuitively compelling. I refer to the judgements that more punishment is deserved in cases where a risk materializes than in cases where it does not, and that more punishment is deserved when an attempt to hurt another succeeds than when it does not. Such judgements are common even to those holding the standard educated view, however much they think they should not think in this way. (If you are not one of

---

[82] I defend this general epistemological stance with respect to moral beliefs in Moore, 'Moral Reality', *supra* n. 77, at 1106–16; Moore, 'Moral Reality Revisited', *Michigan Law Review*, Vol. 90 (1992), 2424–533, at 2493–501.

[83] As I argued in ch. 4.

those, then we will have to start elsewhere—try the other starting-points later discussed.) The principle whose truth best explains this mass of judgements in particular cases is of course the principle that wrongdoing independently determines the extent of our just deserts, along with culpability.

Now the objections:[84] first, that this mode of justification is circular. The objection is that I have justified the principle—that wrongdoing matters to our deserts—by inferring it from judgements that are in reality no different than the principle itself. Yet there is no such circularity here. The principle being justified is logically general because it applies to *all* culpably acting persons, and says of them, that when their acts cause bad results, their deserved punishment increases. The particular judgements are not logically general. These are singular judgements that make reference to particular persons and particular actions and the particular punishments they deserve. The inference is from singular judgements of the form, 'if x is W (wrong), then x is HDP (higher in deserved punishment)', to universally generalized judgements of the form, 'for all things x, if x is W, then x is HDP'. Whatever the problems of inferring universally generalized statements from singular statements, circularity is not among them.

Second objection: that even if the inference is not circular explicitly, it is so implicitly because the presupposition needed to make the singular statements is nothing other than the general principle supposedly being justified. That is, the objection is that we think that Jones deserves more punishment for having killed Smith than he would if he had unsuccessfully tried to kill Smith only because we in general think that results matter. Yet even if this is true psychologically for most (or even for all) people, that does not affect the justificatory power of the singular judgements. For the singular judgements from which justification proceeds are not, 'Jones deserves more because results matter.' Rather, the judgements are simply, 'Jones deserves more.' What characteristics of Jones that make him deserve what he deserves are completely up for grabs in such singular judgements. It could be that Jones deserves more punishment than Brown because Jones is taller than Brown, because Jones is smarter, etc.—or, it could be because Jones killed

---

[84] These are culled from the literature critical of my way of justifying retributivism itself, discussed in the last chapter.

an innocent person whereas Brown only tried to. How we describe the features of Jones over which we universally generalize is not presupposed in singular judgements about Jones, once we properly formulate them. It is thus a genuinely inductive process by which we eliminate all the characteristics of Jones that could justify his greater punishment *vis-à-vis* Brown to arrive at the characteristic, Jones caused death whereas Brown did not.

Third objection: even if the inference is not explicitly or implicitly circular, it is no more than untutored intuition. Such cohering of a mass of intuitions about particular cases may tell us something about our moral sense, but it cannot tell us what is right. Such intuitional base for the inference is irretrievably subjective.

What this objection overlooks is what our particular judgements are *about*. My judgements are of course mine, and are in that harmless sense 'subjective'. But what these judgements are *about* is not me, but features of the world. When I judge, 'Jones deserves more punishment', my judgement is about a property of Jones's, his desert. On its face, the content of this judgement has nothing to do with me. Thus when I generalize such judgements into principles of the form, 'wrongdoing ups the desert of already culpable people', my generalized judgement is not about me either. It again is about features in the world.

What this objection thus has to be asserting is that there are no objective features of the world corresponding to moral terms like 'wrongdoing' or 'desert' so that the most our particular or general judgements can be about is our own mental states, however much they seem to be about something else. Yet this is just moral scepticism. It is a blunderbuss objection to *any* moral proposition being true or justified. As such, it carries no special weight against this form of justification for this moral principle. If one is more of a realist about morals, he will in general think that our particular judgements are caused by moral qualities like wrongdoing and desert and thus, that the seeming reference of such words is their real reference. Of course, such realism has to be argued for, but (fortunately) not here.[85] Assuming such realism generally to be true, then generally we have reason to believe that our particular moral judgements are causally responsive to real features of the world. Discovering the general principle that best fits these judgements is

[85] See Moore, 'Moral Reality', *supra* n. 77, 'Moral Reality Revisited', *supra* n. 82.

thus not to be dismissed as a kind of charting of our own internal, subjective state.

Fourth objection: even conceding the foregoing, this just cannot be right:

Consider as an analogy a similar coherence justification for the view, say, that women are inferior to men, offered circa 1800 by one man to another. Someone has raised the question of whether it is really justifiable to treat women as inferior and is met with the response that, 'Well, of course, we all have the intuition that in this situation we should discriminate against women, and likewise in this and this; now, the best way of accounting for these particular judgements is to suppose women to be morally and intellectually inferior to men.' Wouldn't one feel that the crucial question is being begged?[86]

Aside from trivializing the inference in his analogy (by making the particular judgements use or presuppose just the terms used in the general judgement), David Dolinko seems to be suggesting that even the most coherent of our judgements could be in error. But this should be conceded. A mode of justification—*any* mode of justification—has to concede the possibility that it may justify beliefs that are radically false. If it were not to concede this, then one slides into scepticism—for then, the truth of a proposition is constituted by the best grounds for believing it. To be a realist, one must have a potential gap between what we are justified in believing to be true, and what *is* true. On coherence models of justification, this means that anyone's perfectly cohered judgements could be radically false. This is particularly a possibility for those of limited experience (men of power circa 1800?) and some self-serving interest in systematically misjudging the moral status of those who serve them.

Despite my rebuttals of these objections, I think Dolinko accurately gauges many people's sense that justification that proceeds by generalizing over this narrow a range of judgements looks circular, question-begging, or in some other way trivial. Part of that sense is due to such people already knowing the answer to their generalizing efforts. Psychologically most adults have some developed, general moral views, and they do use these when they make and describe their particular judgements. To see the justifying force of our particular judgements, we must put aside such theory-

---

[86] Dolinko, 'Some Thoughts About Retributivism', *Ethics*, Vol. 101 (1991), 537–59, at 557–8.

dependent judgements as best we can and see with new eyes. Only then can we recapture the sense of discovery children and other moral novices experience: 'so this is what best accounts for this mass of particular judgements!' If we wish to recapture such sense of discovery about obvious truths about the physical world, we have to disengage in the same way from our developed theories. Otherwise, we tend to 'see' what in fact is a theoretical inference made from an earlier, less theory-dependent seeing.

The other way to lessen this sense of triviality is by broadening the class of judgements and experiences for which the principle in question is the best explanation. This I now propose to do.

2. Three Sorts of Experience Accompanying Our Particular Judgements About Wrongdoing and Desert

a. Greater Resentment at Successful Wrongdoing Than for Mere Attempting or Risking

There is no question that most of us much more deeply resent culpable actors who succeed in causing bad results than equally culpable actors who only risk or try for such bad results. The cruder uses of this psychological fact—the arguments from relativism, democracy, jury nullification, or disrespect for law—I earlier put aside as either irrelevant to desert or hopelessly wrong-headed. The use to which I now wish to put this psychological reaction is different. It is to say that for those (many) of us who feel such differential resentments, that is some evidence of the truth of the judgements to which such feelings lead, which are judgements of differential deserts.

To be sure, I here rely on what I hoped to have established in chapter 3. More specifically, I rely on two propositions: (1) our emotions, like our judgements, sometimes respond to objective moral features in the world; and (2) that the touchstone of our epistemically reliable emotion (as opposed to a kind of moral hallucination) is the virtue of feeling such an emotion. What I argued for in chapter 3 was: (1) we non-Kantian beings need our emotions in order to have moral insights; they are our main heuristics to discovering moral truths like the truth that it is unfair to punish innocent people; (2) it would be an extraordinary morality that considered an emotion like compassion to be virtuous to feel and at the same time considered the judgement of distributive justice to which such compassionate feelings lead to be false; a coherent morality should make its theory of virtuous emotion fit, at least roughly, its theory of just actions.

If this is right so far, then the next question is how virtuous we find the special resentment we feel on the successful wrongdoings of others. Granted, we resent culpable attempters and riskers, but we resent equally culpable wrongdoers even more, and the question is whether that feeling is virtuous. To be sure, the Nietzschean tradition we explored at length in chapter 3 regards all resentment as a sickness of small souls. Suppose we have overcome that worry by distinguishing a virtuous resentment, the kind felt by those with empathetic attachments to their fellow human beings and a love for the morality that binds us together. Such resentment is virtuous because it expresses outrage at the unnecessary suffering of victims of wrongdoing and because it expresses hatred of the flouting of morality such infliction of suffering involves.[87] More of such (virtuously felt) 'moral hatred' is some evidence for the truth of the judgement to which it leads—which is that those who succeed in doing wrong are morally worse than those who only try to do wrong, or risk it.

b. *Greater Guilt Feelings for One's Own Successful Wrongdoing Than for One's Attempting or Risking*

If we move from our third person feelings and judgements (about wrongs done by others) to the first person, we may see additional, relevant experience. I refer to the feeling of greater guilt experienced by many people when they succeed in causing (versus trying for or risking) bad results. If one does have such differential guilt feelings, the next question is whether it is virtuous to feel such guilt. Again, there is an entire tradition, again stemming from Nietzsche, that regards guilt as indecent, a useless crying over spilt milk (blood?). Again, assume as we did in chapter 3 that we reject that tradition, and affirm that guilt is a virtuous emotion.[88] When we feel more of it, as we do when we cause harm, that is some evidence for the truth of the judgement to which it leads, namely, that we are more guilty

---

[87] A task nicely undertaken in Jean Hampton and Jeffrie Murphy, *Forgiveness and Mercy* (Cambridge: Cambridge University Press, 1988); Pillsbury, 'Emotional Justice: Moralizing the Passions of Criminal Punishment', *Cornell Law Review*, Vol. 74 (1989), 655–710.

[88] See the lucid essays on guilt in Herbert Morris, *On Guilt and Innocence* (Los Angeles: University of California Press, 1973).

for having caused such harm than we would have been in the absence of doing so.[89]

This schematic presentation fails to capture the actual, devastating persuasiveness possessed by those strong guilt feelings aroused by having caused unnecessary suffering. Such guilt, when deeply felt, carries with it a conviction that one *is* guilty that is very difficult to deny. Such feelings, for relatively well-formed people, are their best indicator of responsibility.

Not only is there more guilt typically felt when bad results are caused than when they are not, but the guilt feelings have a different quality. While we feel guilt at our own culpable attemptings or riskings, that guilt has a kind of narcissistic preoccupation to it, a kind of keeping-our-own-moral-house-in-order flavour. Not so guilt at successful wrongdoing. What eats at us with such compelling power is that we were the cause of such dreadful results. We are not worried about our souls or about the state of our moral health. We are sick at what we have done. This guilt that reflects our concern for others is more virtuous than a guilt concerned only with our own moral health. This moral fact joins the psychological fact (that more guilt is experienced when harm is caused) in evidencing the truth of the judgement that results matter.

There is a related experience that also evidences the truth of the judgement that results matter. Commonly, when someone acts culpably but does not cause the harm attempted or risked, they experience, not just a lesser guilt, but also a sense of relief and a shudder at such a near miss. One who drives while seriously intoxicated and avoids hitting a child, for example, may realize that he culpably risked innocent life by his action. He may feel some guilt about having so acted, although much less guilt than if his act had become the wrong of killing. He may also feel very lucky that he escaped being a killer. He knows that such escape was not due to anything he did; the child just happened to be quick enough to get out of his way. Yet his sense of relief tells him that he has genuinely escaped something, namely, the moral guilt of being a killer, a particularly heinous form of wrongdoing. He has escaped such moral guilt even though he did nothing to engineer such an escape. In such cases we

---

[89] This use of guilt feelings to validate the judgement that results matter to desert parallels my use (in ch. 3) of guilt feelings to validate the retributivist judgement that desert by itself justifies punishment.

experience directly how extra bad it would have been to have been a wrongdoer as well as a culpable actor.

c. *Our Experience of Choice: That Wrongdoing Independently Matters*

There is another first person experience relevant to the present issue, and that is the forward-looking experience of choosing what to do. We have backward-looking feelings about choices already made that turned out well or ill. These are the experiences described in the preceding section. We also have experiences of choosing, when we do not yet know how our choices will turn out. These experiences also bear on whether results matter to our moral deserts.

Think of any moral decision between two or more alternatives where there is something to be said for each option. One might be deciding, for example, about how fast to drive through a residential neighbourhood on one's way to work, or about what level of safety precautions to put in one's mine, or about whether to give up one's normal career pursuits in order to see an ailing parent through his or her last days, or about whether one should physically abuse a terrorist suspect in order to obtain potentially life saving information. In thinking through any of such choices, we do not say to ourselves, 'It does not matter how my choice comes out, so long as I make a reasonable choice without any culpable intention.' Rather, what makes moral dilemmas so intractable is that it does matter how things come out from what we choose. Or so our experience of choosing tells us. Any attempt to tell oneself that it doesn't matter, that the only important thing is that we not be culpable in the way we make the choice, is far too smug and cheap a satisfaction with ourselves and our decision. We might call our more common, rather different experience the 'agony of moral choice', an agony that is not silenced by satisfying ourselves that we have made every reasonable inference from only reasonable beliefs and so that we cannot be blamed as culpable in our decision.

One might object that we can never be certain about our own culpability in making decisions, particularly *vis-à-vis* one's negligence, so that the continued agony of decision could reflect this continued uncertainty about our own culpability. Yet we make retrospective judgements about our own and others culpability all of the time, and there is no reason that we cannot make such judgements prospectively as well. For on the issue of culpability, all the data is in at the moment of decision. It is only the amount of our wrongdoing that is hostage to the future. What consequences our decisions bring about matters to whether the act we decide upon will become wrong or not, and we sense that independent moral significance of wrongdoing by our continued concern even after we have satisfied ourselves that we have done the best we can do as far as our decisional processes go.

One can see the same point from a slightly different vantage point if we focus on positive obligations. Suppose one faces the decision to help one's ailing parent through his last days, at some sacrifice to one's own professional goals. Suppose the kind of help the parent needs is help in accepting his own mortality, that is, help in accepting that some things are not going to be accomplished in this life and help in finding some acceptable beliefs about what happens after death. This is not help that is easy to give, and one's best efforts may easily result in failure. As one is engaged in this attempt to help, can one ever say to oneself that one's best efforts—the absence of any culpability on one's part—are all that matter, that it does not independently matter whether one actually succeeds in helping? What in such a case would deciding to help, or trying to help, look like? That one decided to do the best one could, that one decided to try to help? Or do we not choose *to help*, fulfilment of our choice being measured by helping and not by best efforts at trying to help?

In all such cases the experience of choosing seems to depend on there being significance to how our choices come out, that is, what consequences actually flow from them. To deny such significance would be to deny what makes such choices so agonizingly important to us. It would be to make our moral experience a lot more pleasant than in fact it is.

3. Other Judgements About Responsibility Affected by the Denial that Results Matter   If one were to adopt the standard educated view about the moral irrelevance of results, a large range of other judgements of responsibility would be affected. Indeed, as I shall argue in this section, the range of judgements affected would be so large that the notion of desert (or responsibility) would disappear entirely. One should thus view the argument that follows in two ways: first, as an incremental argument against the standard educated view, the increments being measured by the variety of other particular judgements about responsibility that both seem intuitive and yet would be overturned by the implications of the standard educated view; and, secondly, as a *reductio ad absurdum* argument, the absurd conclusion to which the standard educated view leads being that no one is responsible for anything.

The discussion which follows is organized in descending order of generality: as more and more of the judgements discussed have to be given up because of the standard educated view, we approach closer and closer to the demise of responsibility *in toto*. The discussion is also organized psychologically: as we move temporally backwards in the causal antecedents of those simplest bodily movements by virtue of which we do wrongs, judgements about the moral significance of volitions, of intentions, of motivations, of character, and of the factors (of environment and genetic endowment) that determine character, become challenged by the standard educated view. Again, ultimately the argument will be that none of these causal antecedents of action have moral significance if consequences do not, so that responsibility—even in its sense as culpability alone—disappears.

a. *Our Limited Capacities/Opportunities to Effectuate Choices, Intentions, and Plans*

Suppose one took the view that because one cannot control all factors influencing a bullet's flight into a vital organ of an intended victim, the death of that victim is not something that increases the deserts of the shooter. This same feature—lack of control of all factors—is present all the way up and down the chain of causes that precede and succeed one's choices. On my view of actions and the mental states that cause them,[90] the death of some intended victim should be causally explained by the factors represented on Figure 5.1.

More specifically, behind the event that was the death of the victim (7), there was:

(6) The movement of the defendant's finger on the trigger;
(5) The volition or willing to move the finger;
(4) The intention, plan, or choice (to kill the victim) that is executed by the more specific volition;

[90] See Moore, *Act and Crime: The Philosophy of Action and its Implications for Criminal Law* (Oxford: Clarendon Law Series, 1993), particularly at ch. 6.

(3) The set of beliefs and desires, the content of which form a valid practical syllogism, that are executed by one's intentions;

(2) The more general traits of character which cause one to have the beliefs and desires that motivate one on particular occasions;

(1) The kind of large, character-forming choices that Aristotelians and existentialists sometimes propose.

My hypothetical shooter may be the kind of greedy, heartless person (2) who desires to inherit his uncle's money, believes that if he kills his uncle, he will inherit his money (3), and because of this belief/desire set he decides to kill his uncle (4), which decision (or intention) is executed by willing the movement of his finger on the trigger of the gun pointed at the victim (5), which willing results in the finger moving (6), which finger-movement causes the death of the victim (7).

Just as a number of events could intervene between the movement of the trigger finger and the death of the victim that would rob the bullet of its normal capacity to kill, so a number of events could intervene between each of these mental states and their normal effects so as to rob them of their normal causal power. The absence of such intervening factors, and the presence of other contributing factors outside the actor's control, I have represented on Figure 5.2 by vertical arrows.

If, despite the presence of these uncontrollable, extraneous causal factors one is morally responsible for one's character, choices, or results, then one is equally 'lucky'. We should see such 'moral luck' as being of four kinds. First, there is result luck, which in my example is the luck involving the fortuities that could intervene between one's bodily movements (6) and real world results like the death of the intended victim (7). Second, there is what I shall call luck in execution, which is the luck involving the fortuities that could intervene between one's choices (4) and those bodily movements (6) that could execute those choices. Third, there is what I shall call planning luck, which is the luck involving the fortuities that could intervene between one's desires (3) and those choices or plans (4) that set one on the path to satisfying those desires. Lastly, there is what is usually called constitutive luck, which is the luck involving those fortuities causing one to have the character (2) that could lead to

FIGURE 5.1 The Causation of Bad States of Affairs by Desert-Related Factors

(1)	(2)	(3)	(4)	(5)	(6)	(7)
Character-forming choices →	Character →	Belief/Desire Sets →	Intentions (Choices) →	Volitions (Tryings) →	Bodily Movements →	Real World Effects

FIGURE 5.2 The More Complete Causal Story Behind Each of the Desert-Related Factors

(1)	(2)	(3)	(4)	(5)	(6)	(7)
Character-forming choices →	Character →	Belief/Desire Sets →	Intentions (Choices) →	Volitions (Tryings) →	Bodily Movements →	Real World Effects
Examples of non-controlled causal factors:	Genes & Environment of Defendant ↑	Uncle's writing of favourable Will ↑	Survival of victim from natural death ↑	End of distractions to defendant ↑	Adequate nerve signals ↑	Adequate gunpowder in bullets ↑

the specific belief/desire sets (3) that lead one to make culpable choices.

In the discussion that follows, I shall separately discuss the causal fortuities involved in executing luck, planning luck, and constitutive luck. My general argument will be that luck is luck, and to the extent that causal fortuitousness is morally irrelevant anywhere it is morally irrelevant everywhere.

One final organizational preliminary: it is common to distinguish two different ways in which something can lose its normal ability to bring about a certain result. We often distinguish defects in equipment from lack of any chance to use perfectly operating equipment. We call the first, diminished capacity, and the second, lack of opportunity.[91] Failures of our intentions to issue in the movements needed to execute them may occur because of either mental incapacities or lack of the opportunity to use perfectly adequate capacities.

Suppose I intend to kill Jones by shooting him and thus know that I at some point will need to will the movement of my finger on the trigger of a gun pointed at Jones. Having formed the intent, I may lack the opportunity to execute it. I may, for example, discover that Jones is never alone; or that he has removed himself from the jurisdiction; or that when I reach for my gun, finding Jones alone and vulnerable I discover that my pocket has just been picked by some thief; or that in a hundred different ways, none of which I have any control over, I never get the chance to shoot Jones.

Alternatively, I may have the opportunity to shoot and kill Jones—he is before me, alone, in the right circumstance, I have a loaded gun in my hand—but I suffer a sudden incapacitation. For example, as I raise the gun before I have willed my trigger finger to move someone who is a dead ringer for my long dead friend appears, the sight of which so startles and distracts me that I forget about my intention to kill Jones long enough for Jones to escape. Alternatively, such sudden loss of capacity can occur between my willing and my finger-movement: I get so excited at having the opportunity to kill Jones at last (recognizing how utterly fortuitous it is that I have such opportunity, see above) that my fingers tremble and shake so much that my willing fails to cause my trigger finger to move in the required way.[92]

---

[91] The capacity/opportunity distinction is explored in greater detail in ch. 13 *infra*.

[92] These particular examples are a variation of a philosophical favourite, called

I have no control whatsoever over these extraneous factors intervening between my intention and my bodily motion, no more than I have such control over wind speeds, bullet firing capacities, and the like that can intervene after I have moved my trigger finger. The possibility of there being such intervening factors—the necessity that there not be such intervening factors present for me to succeed—equally rule out any moral distinction between the one who intends to kill Jones, and does not, and the one who intends to kill Jones and succeeds, on the standard educated view. The focus of my responsibility, in other words, must on the standard view be on my intention to kill Jones, *all* that happens after that (including those mental states of volition) being morally irrelevant.

There are two possible responses for one holding the standard educated view: admit the *reductio* but deny that it is to an absurdity, or deny that there is any reduction. To adopt the first response is to say that intention alone is all that counts morally. That is easy enough to admit about the second sort of lack of capacity case, for there at least the agent does the last mental act (of willing) needed to kill Jones. In the other cases, we either have not got the opportunity to try (because we cannot find the victim, etc.) or we had the opportunity but were incapacitated from trying to execute our intention to kill Jones (because we were distracted at the wrong moment, etc.). Insofar as one finds *trying* to be of some moral salience, beyond simply *intending*, these cases should be troublesome.

That leaves the other response, which is to find some grounds to distinguish the cases. One possibility would be to draw the line between those factors that prevent success by occurring before bodily movement is initiated, and those that do so by occurring after bodily movement is initiated. Yet this line is surely arbitrary *vis-à-vis* the degree of control exercisable by an agent over the possible factors occurring on either side of this temporal line. Just because factors intervening before movement is initiated have to operate through my mind does not give me greater control over them. I need have no more control over whether I am distracted, startled, or excited, in the situation imagined, than I do over whether my finger, unbeknownst to me is not on the trigger I think it is on. I have

'deviant causal chain' examples. See Moore, *Act and Crime*, *supra* n. 90, at 159–61. Such examples, adjusted so that the actor succeeds in doing just what he intended to do, figure prominently in contemporary discussion of causal theories of action.

no more control over the brain and nerve events necessary for my intentions to cause the appropriate volitions, or for my volitions to cause the appropriate bodily movements, than I do over the wind on my bullets once I have sent them on their way.

A more plausible line would be built around the notion of mental trying: when I have the opportunity and the capacities to execute my intention to kill Jones down to the level of mental trying (volitions), that is sufficient morally, i.e., nothing that happens after that is relevant to my deserts. Yet how do I have any greater control over the factors that can prevent my having either the opportunity or the capacity to mentally try to kill Jones? Glitches can occur in my processes of inference (from intending to willing) as they can in the wind, and I equally control neither; the victim's movements that can prevent me from having any opportunity to try to kill him are no more under my control than are the movements of the wind that can deflect my bullet. How, then, can one distinguish—by degrees of control over possibly disrupting factors—these cases of failure of *internal* execution from the case of failure of *external* execution about which the standard educated view makes so much?

I conclude that there is no plausible line to be found that divides intervening factors (between the controlled and the uncontrolled) and that also saves the judgement that mental trying matters morally to one's deserts. Yet the latter is a strong intuition, in that it seems to matter whether one actually tried to execute one's intention to kill or not. One of the costs of the standard educated view about consequences is that one must give up this intuition.

b. *Our Limited Capacities/Opportunities to Make Choices*

One might not have been too disturbed at having to give up the notion that mental tryings have any relevance to desert, given the uncontrollable fortuities involved in making or executing such volitional tryings. After all, one could hold the line at intentions, plans, and choices. Those at least, can be of moral significance because those are fully under an actor's control. Yet this is not true either, as I propose to show in this section.

Again, we should distinguish failures to form a culpable intention due to lack of opportunity to do so, from those failures due to diminished capacity to do so. On the opportunity side, imagine that Smith is a vicious, violent individual who very much resents Jones for having taken his (Smith's) job. Smith's character in general, and his desires in particular, are thus very much pro the death of Jones. Given more time, Smith would have formed the firm intention to kill Jones, given Smith's character and his motivations. As it happens, Smith never got the chance to intend to kill Jones, because: Jones died of natural causes; Jones got fired from the job about which Smith was so envious; Smith became injured so that he could not accept the job about which he was so envious, even if it were offered to him on the death of Jones; etc. None of these are factors over which Smith has any control, yet whether Smith forms his culpable intention to kill Jones depends on whether such factors occur.

Likewise, Smith may get the opportunity to choose to kill Jones, but he may lack the capacity to make such a choice. To adopt an example of Joel Feinberg's, every time Smith begins to think of Jones having the job Smith wanted, specks of dust throw Smith into sneezing fits that prevent any envious rage from developing.[93] Alternatively, at the point when Smith is raging and is right on the verge of forming his intention to kill Jones, he is distracted by a loud noise which lasts long enough to dissipate the anger which otherwise would have lead Smith to intend to kill Jones.[94] Such extraneous dust motes and noises are not within the control of Smith, yet whether they occur determines whether Smith forms the culpable intention.

Feinberg's conclusion about these cases is the right one: 'in whatever sense legal responsibility for external states can be contingent on factors beyond one's control and therefore a matter of luck, in precisely the same sense can "moral" responsibility for inner states also be contingent and a matter of luck'.[95] As before, the standard educated view has two possible responses here: to accept Feinberg's conclusion, which is to admit that intention and choice are without any moral significance,[96] or to deny Feinberg's conclusion by denying that the lack of control over factors preventing choice from being made is the same as the lack of control over factors preventing choice from being realized in action.

---

[93] Feinberg, *supra* n. 6, at 35.   [94] Id.

[95] Id. For a similar conclusion, see also R. A. Duff, 'Acting, Trying, and Criminal Liability', in S. Shute, J. Gardner, and J. Horder, eds., *Action and Value in Criminal Law* (Oxford: Clarendon Press, 1993), at 102.

[96] For an example of this response, see Thomson, 'Morality and Bad Luck', *supra* n. 12.

The first sort of response is a much less palatable one here than it was in the previous section, for there, the fall back position was to the moral significance of intentions. The fall back position once one gives up on the moral significance of intentions has to be to character. This would be the view that our just deserts are determined exclusively by our character, that is, by what sort of a person we are in general. What we did, what we tried to do, and what we choose to do, would on this view have no more than evidentiary status *vis-à-vis* our deserts; only insofar as these items reflect good or bad character would they have any moral significance whatever.

This is not an attractive moral view. Its unattractiveness does not lie in the proposition that we are in some sense responsible for being the sort of person that we are, for we do have a responsibility for our characters (even if not a *punishable* responsibility).[97] Rather, the rub comes with saying that this is the only independent desert-basis there is. When we choose to do a wrongful act that is out of character for us, try to do it, and then do it, how can that have no bearing on our just deserts? The weakness of the character view lies precisely in its inability to deal with our momentary lapses from who, in general, we are. This would make immorality like the proverbial 'one-free-bite' rule in tort law (according to which a dog gets one bite without liability by its owner): a generally good person can do no evil, so long as he does it infrequently enough that such choosings are not in character for him.

This leaves the standard educated view with the other response, one that denies that the lack of control over factors producing intentions is the same as the lack of control over factors executing intentions into actions. Sanford Kadish adopts this line of defence:

[Y]ou may be lucky or not in whether circumstances present you with an occasion to make a moral choice that will reveal your moral shortcomings; for example, luck in whether you are ever presented with the need to choose to betray a friend or break a promise. But I don't believe that this threatens our sense of justice in blaming in the same way that luck in the outcome of an action (the harm doctrine) threatens it. The settled moral understanding is that what you deserve is a function of what you choose. It may be that you would not have had occasion to make a choice that revealed your badness if you had better luck. Nonetheless, you did make a choice—nobody made you—and it is that choice for which you are blamed. It is a different matter, however, to say that chance occurrences

---

[97] Argued for in ch. 12 *infra*.

that follow after you have made your choice determine what you deserve, for that is to rest desert upon factors other than what you chose to do. Fortuity prior to choice, therefore, may be accommodated to our notions of just desert; fortuity thereafter cannot.[98]

It is easy to understand (and agree with) the intuition that motivates Kadish here: choosing is central to our 'settled moral understanding' of desert, in the sense that choosing is central to at least one of the two bases for desert.[99] Thus it is very tempting to draw the line in the sand here, and to say that fortuities prior to choice do not matter even though the fortuities occurring after choice do. Yet a fortuity is a fortuity. Certain factors over which one had no control were determinative of whether or not the bullet found its target; yet certain other factors, over which one had no more control, were equally determinative of whether or not one chose to try to kill another with the bullet. With no more control by the actor, and no less determination of the relevant event, how are the second sort of factors to be distinguished from the first?

Of course, it is true that 'nobody made you' make the choice to shoot; the fortuitously occurring or not-occurring factors necessary for you to choose to shoot did not *make* you so choose. But it is equally true that no one made the bullet do exactly what you intended it to do when you put the gun against your victim's head; the absence of wind, of defective bullets, etc., did not *make* the bullet do what it did either. Nor did these factors make *you* do what you did, which was to kill. Nobody made you either choose to kill, try to kill, or kill, even though there had to be a number of factors present for any of these events to occur, and over none of those factors did you have any control.

The blunt fact is that we have no more control over all the factors necessary in order to choose to kill than we do over all the factors necessary for us to kill. Choice is thus not a line that can be used here. We have to go in one of two directions. Either we keep regressing, to motivations, to character, to factors that cause char-

---

[98] Kadish, *supra* n. 17, at 17–18. Also finding this line defensible is Kim Kessler, 'The Role of Luck in the Criminal Law', *University of Pennsylvania Law Review*, Vol. 142 (1994), 2183–237, at 2191.

[99] In ch. 13 I defend choosing over character as the touchstone of culpability (and thus, of excuse). Such a view in no way denies that choosing can involve wrongdoing, as much as culpability, and that consequences like death are an important aspect of such wrongdoing.

acter, in the search for something of which we are in full control; this as we shall see is a fruitless quest, so that ultimately no one can be responsible because no one can have such complete control over anything that can plausibly be identified with his moral agency. Or we give up this odd notion of control, as I urged in the earlier section, so that we can say that we are in control (in our new and better sense) of our choices because they are our choices—even though causally dependent on factors that are themselves unchosen.[100] And this starts us back from whence we have come, for in this sense of control we also control whether or not we execute our general choices with volitions, and in this sense of control we control our bodily movements when we will them with our volitions. Further, in this sense of control we control the gun in our hand, and we control the bullet, its impact on the victim, and his death; we chose each of these events as means and we tried to rule out the extraneous factors as best we could at all levels. It is, in this sense of control, ludicrous to deny that we controlled whether or not we killed when we put a gun at our intended victim's head and blew his brains out.

Thus, the standard educated view cannot stop the slide from choice to chosen results. If we control the first, we control the second—in any relevant sense of control. For those not yet persuaded to say this however, let us keep moving backwards up the causal chain that leads back from actions to their ultimate causal antecedents.

c. *Our Limited Capacities/Opportunities to Form Our Own Characters*

The strong demand for control by the standard educated view now leads that view back to character as the exclusive basis for desert. For as we have seen, if consequences are not within our control even when we intend them as means or ends, then (in that strong sense of control) simple bodily actions, the willings that cause them, and the intentions that cause those willings, are not within our control either. That leaves the standard educated view defending character as the one thing we can strongly control.

This last proposition is not, on its face, a very plausible one. While there is a nice debate within philosophy about the extent to

---

[100] The compatibilist view I defend in ch. 12 *infra*.

which we either form initially, or reshape later, our characters,[101] wherever one comes out in that debate it is pretty plain that we have less control over those enduring traits we call our character than we do over our choices, tryings, or actions at particular times. We simply have a limited capacity to make or remake ourselves. Genetic and environmental influences have a lot more to do with who we are than does any choice we might make about the sort of person we wish to be.

Even if this comparative fact were not so plainly true, it is still the case that we do not strongly control our characters. There are plainly many factors over which we have no control and that cause us to have the character we do. Our genetic endowment, and almost all of the crucial environmental influences when we are young, are not within our control. Character, thus, is among the least plausible candidates for something within our control, in this strong sense.

There are again two possible responses by those holding the standard educated view, either to admit the *reductio* but deny its absurdity or to deny the reduction. Neither of these responses has any plausibility here. The first would regress desert-bases past character to those factors that determine character. Yet those factors are genetic and environmental, and in no sense can we—our moral agency—be identified with items that are not part of us. This response in effect concedes that there is no such thing as moral responsibility, or desert. Rather, we are simply born into our deserts, and there is nothing we can do about it. While some might be attracted by this fatalistic, tragic notion of desert, it should be plain that there is no sense of personal responsibility to be found in it. In our ordinary sense of 'responsible', this view would in effect deny that anyone is responsible for anything.

Yet the alternative response is also a non-starter. For how could one deny that there is as much fortuity in the necessary factors that precede as succeed character? Surely, as we have seen, there is more uncontrolled fortuity in the factors that determine character than there is in the factors that intervene between character, choices, willings, movements, and consequences of movements. The only manoeuvre open here is for the holder of the standard educated view to claim for character what Sanford Kadish claimed for choice: who we are *is* our character, so that fortuities in determin-

---

[101] See the discussion and citations in ch. 13 *infra*.

ing who we are are irrelevant. True, we cannot control these factors, but that is because there is no *one* to do the controlling until those factors do their work.

I have called this elsewhere the 'character-stop' manoeuvre,[102] and I am in general in sympathy with it. For it is an essential move to make in defence of compatibilist moral psychology. Yet just as with a like manoeuvre by Kadish in defence of choice, if one says that character can be a desert-basis despite our lack of control over all or most of its causal antecedents, that slides one back down the causal chain to also say: that choice, willing, moving, and killing can also be desert-bases despite our lack of control over some of their causal antecedents. At least, there is nothing about our lack of control that disqualifies any of them as independent desert-bases, in addition to character.

Nicholas Rescher resists this parallelism (between lack of control over our character and lack of control over our intentions, willings, and their effects) by denying sense to the idea that we could control our character:

[W]hat . . . of one's inclinations, dispositions, and character. Are not these too issues outside our control? . . . these personality features are not merely things regarding which we happen to 'have no choice'—they are by their very nature things to which the idea of choice does not apply. [To say] that the agent 'has no control' over them involves a category mistake because the whole control issue is irrelevant here . . . these factors are not things that lie outside oneself but, on the contrary, are a crucial part of what constitute one's self as such.[103]

Rescher attempts to get too much mileage from the character-stop manoeuvre. It is not senseless to talk of control over our character—indeed, Aristotelians talk a good deal about this;[104] rather, it is empirically false that we have much control over those enduring

---

[102] Id.   [103] Rescher, 'Moral Luck', 156–7.

[104] Contrary to Rescher, there is a self or person who could be said to either be, or not be, in control of his character. Character is a poor third to two other criteria for unity of self, Lockean continuity of consciousness (or memory) and spatio-temporal continuity of the human body (on this, see Moore, *Law and Psychiatry: Rethinking the Relationship* (Cambridge: Cambridge University Press, 1984), ch. 11). On either of these two criteria of self, an agent can sensibly be said to control her character. Indeed, even on Rescher's view that persons are exclusively constituted by their characters *in toto*, we could sensibly speak of some character traits being or not being within an agent's control; the agent would in such a case be identified with those other traits of character that we would for these purposes be holding constant.

traits of ourselves that we call our character. Yet we are responsible for who we are nonetheless. And this compatibilist responsibility— a responsibility we each have despite our lack of control—begins the slide back up my *reductio* to responsibility for results over which we also have limited control.

It is this last slide back up my *reductio* that justified me in saying earlier that there is no problem of moral luck, by our ordinary notions of luck and of control. One has to overthrow those ordinary notions to have any problem of moral luck. Even when one does so, by substituting Nagel's strong sense of control, there is still no *separate* problem of moral luck. On such an incompatibilist sense of control, there is no room for responsibility at all, so the question of an added responsibility for consequences cannot arise.

V. CONCLUSION

The arguments from our particular judgements, from our accompanying emotional or other experience, and from this last *reductio*, constitutes my non-foundationalist case for the independent moral significance of wrongdoing. If I am right, when we intentionally kill, we deserve the extra punishment we typically receive over that we would have received had we only tried or intended to kill.

In closing, it is worth reiterating why this conclusion does not imply a very much less plausible one, namely, that we should be punished for wrongdoing even in the absence of culpability. If wrongdoing has independent moral significance to our just deserts, why does it not justify some punishment for crimes of either pure or impure strict liability?

Pure strict liability crimes are those crimes that do not require any culpable mental state (other than the willing necessary to action itself) for conviction. Impure strict liability crimes are those crimes that do require some culpable mental state but they do not attach such culpability requirements to all material elements of the offence or of the justificatory defences. Felony murder, intent to inflict grievous bodily harm murder, the common law legal wrong doctrine (where one does a more serious grade of the offence than one intends and is held for that more serious version of the crime), and the act-at-your-peril doctrine about the availability of the defence of others justification, are all examples of impure strict liability.

It has recently been argued that such doctrines of strict liability do no more than recognize the independent moral significance of wrongdoing that is also defended in this chapter.[105] Yet nothing that I have said commits me to defending these unfair doctrines. Results matter, but they do not matter that much or in that way. Culpability sets the outer limits of desert and thus, of proportionate punishment. (Proximately) causing the harm intended or risked brings one's deserts up to those limits but causing more harm than intended or risked does not increase one's deserts beyond those limits. (This is why I said that wrongdoing is something of the poor relation to culpability in the introduction.) Why culpability should have this dominant influence on deserts is itself an interesting question, but one that requires another chapter at least as lengthy as the present defence of wrongdoing's limited but independent moral significance.

[105] Crump and Crump, 'In Defense of the Felony Murder Doctrine', *Harvard Journal of Law and Public Policy*, Vol. 8 (1985), 359–98.

SUBPART B
THE ELEMENTS OF RESPONSIBILITY: WRONGDOING AND CULPABILITY

1. The Nature of Wrongdoing

a. The Nature of Human Action

6

MORE ON ACT AND CRIME

Central to any theory of wrongdoing is a theory of action. The predecessor of this chapter 6 defended a volitional theory of action according to which: (1) all human actions are event-particulars of a certain kind, not facts or proposition-like entities, and not concrete universals or abstract particulars; (2) those events that are human actions are themselves a compound of other events, consisting of a volition causing a bodily movement; (3) the effects of bodily movements are no proper part of actions, however much the having of such effects is presupposed by correct usage of various *descriptions* of actions, such as 'killing'; (4) omissions are not actions of some ghostly kind, but are rather the absence of there being any actions of a certain type; (5) such absent actions ('omissions') have no effects because they enter into no singular causal relations; (6) volitions that are parts of those events that are actions are a kind of intention, not belief or desire, even though such volitional intentions execute background motivational states of belief and desire; (7) all properties of actions can be classified as either causal properties or circumstantial properties; (8) the spatio-temporal location of actions lies where and when the volition-cum-bodily movement takes place, not where the effects of actions may occur. Further, the predecessor of this chapter defended a theory of criminal law, and of the morality that underlies it, according to which: (1) we are legally liable and morally responsible for our actions, not (very often) for failing to prevent harms, for being of a certain status, for having a certain mental state alone, or for mere bodily movements that are not actions; (2) all the actions that are moral wrongs and are prohibited by the criminal law have at least one causal property by virtue of which they are morally wrong and legally prohibited; (3) the amount of wrongdoing for which an offender deserves punishment is a function not only of the seriousness of the wrong(s) done, but also of: (a) how many distinct wrongs the offender did with any given act; and (b) how many times the defendant did each such different wrong.

Defence of these tenets required more than a chapter of this book. Accordingly, a book-length treatment of these theses was undertaken, published as *Act and Crime: The Philosophy of Action and its Implications for the Criminal Law*.[1] After that book's publication, the editors of the *University of Pennsylvania Law Review* organized and hosted a symposium on my book's defence of these theses. Eleven papers were invited and published. The chapter that follows is my response to some of the suggestions and criticisms made in those eleven papers. Since each paper contained many points, I do not attempt to respond to all of them. Nor shall I seek to respond to each author separately. Rather, I use this occasion to further my earlier discussion of seven topics in action theory: (1) the relevance of metaphysics and the philosophy of action to issues of legal and moral responsibility; (2) the proper way to conceive of omissions; (3) the moral and legal relevance of omissions so conceived; (4) whether the concurrence requirement—that act, mental state, and causation all concur for prima facie liability—is always true of our ascriptions of moral and legal responsibility; (5) the nature of the criminal law's voluntary act requirement and its application to troublesome cases such as sleepwalking and other dissociated states; (6) whether volitions are a kind of intention and how they contrast with other candidates for the immediate mental executors of those bodily movements that are actions; (7) whether actions and events are to be individuated by the properties they exemplify or in the manner I propose in *Act and Crime*. My hope for the chapter is that I describe both my original positions in *Act and Crime*, and my critics' suggestions, with enough depth that my replies are intelligible to readers unfamiliar with either the book or the symposium papers.

I. THE RELEVANCE OF THE 'HIGH METAPHYSICS' OF ACTION TO ISSUES OF LEGAL AND MORAL RESPONSIBILITY

In presentations of some of my more metaphysical papers over the years I have noticed a marked reluctance of political and legal philosophers to concede me a worthwhile topic. Indeed, even the

---

[1] Michael Moore, *Act and Crime: The Philosophy of Action and its Implications for Criminal Law* (Oxford: Oxford University Press, 1993).

use of the word 'metaphysics' often bothers my colleagues in legal/political philosophy. My suspicion is that many philosophers who specialize in legal or political philosophy choose to do so in part to get away from the abstractness and seeming irrelevance of metaphysical questions like, 'what is an action?' They also resist what they see as the cabining effect of the 'brute facts' of metaphysics dictating answers to the design of legal and political institutions when those answers to them seem better argued for on normative grounds.

Of the commentators on *Act and Crime*, Bernard Williams and, to a lesser extent, Sam Freeman, Stephen Morse, and Jennifer Hornsby seemed to have experienced a bit of this resistance to metaphysics. Williams, for example, urges that 'the criminal law, after all, has a set of special aims and purposes' and that it is these purposes that should guide 'the requirements that it imposes on describing people's actions', not a metaphysics of action that is 'motivated quite independently of those special purposes'.[2] Similarly, Freeman too finds the principles and norms relevant to criminal law to 'have their bases, not in metaphysical considerations, but in the practical necessities and interests of democratic citizens'.[3] Even were this not true, Freeman adds, we should 'avoid the metaphysics of action as much as possible' in criminal law because of the difficulties of obtaining agreement on the truth of any one version of such metaphysics.[4]

The structure of *Act and Crime* was designed to forestall such worries. For each of its three parts, the book begins with criminal law doctrine, probes that doctrine's moral point, and only then asks metaphysical questions about actions. This structure was adopted to justify a metaphysical analysis before any of it was done. Moreover, if the purposes behind the doctrines in question did not require a metaphysical answer, none was sought. For example, on the individuation of 'units of offence' required for double jeopardy, one might think that the metaphysics of event-tokens and of act-tokens should be used to give the legally appropriate answer. In chapter 14 I argue to the contrary, setting aside any metaphysics-

[2] Bernard Williams, 'The Actus Reus of Dr. Caligari', *University of Pennsylvania Law Review*, Vol. 142 (1994), 1661–73, at 1661.
[3] Samuel Freeman, 'Criminal Liability and the Duty to Aid the Distressed', *University of Pennsylvania Law Review*, Vol. 142 (1994), 1455–92, at 1456.
[4] Id. at 1455.

of-action-answer to the unit of offence question in favour of a 'wrong-relative' mode of individuation. I do this because the dominating purpose animating the double jeopardy requirement—to proportion punishment to desert—requires a count of the separate instances of wrongs done by an accused, not a count of the separate act-tokens he may have done in doing those wrongs.

Williams and Freeman applaud my eschewal of the metaphysics of action on such occasions.[5] They worry, however, that much of my book presupposes 'a more robust view of the role and possibilities of metaphysics' in criminal law theory.[6] They are right to worry, since I do have such more robust view. When the criminal law requires a voluntary act, I take that doctrine to require the doing of an action—as that natural kind of event is theorized about in the metaphysics of action. When the criminal law prohibits complex act types like killings, maimings, burnings, frightenings, etc., I take those doctrines to require the causing of certain states of affairs (deaths, disfigurements, etc.)—as the metaphysics of causation would analyse such causings. When the criminal law requires that a prohibited action take place *when* the actor also has a culpable mental state and *where* the state trying him has both jurisdiction to legislate and to adjudicate, I take those doctrines to require the finding of the temporal and spatial locations of actions—as the metaphysics of action would analyse such locations.

Each of these criminal law doctrines invites my metaphysical enquiries because of the moral points behind such doctrines. Such purposes are themselves subservient to the overarching purpose of criminal punishment, which is retributive: people should be punished because of (and only in proportion to) their moral deserts. This means that legal doctrines (such as that requiring a voluntary act or that requiring punishable acts to be instances of wrongful act-types like killings) are best interpreted so as to get at the moral deserts of offenders, and morality itself invites metaphysical answers to questions like, 'is sleepwalking really an action?'

There are five sets of concerns that appeared to motivate Williams, Freeman, Morse, and Hornsby to their sharing of a less optimistic view about the role of the metaphysics of action in criminal law theory (recognizing that not all of them share each of these concerns). This first concern comes from Williams's uniformly

[5] Id.; Williams, 'Caligari', *supra* n. 2, at 1662.
[6] Freeman, 'Duty to Aid', *supra* n. 3, at 1456.

practical view of the law, morality, and the metaphysics of action. Each of these areas of thought, Williams believes, is guided by its own unique purposes and concerns. And why should we think that a criminal law act requirement (guided, for example, by a concern not to punish the undeterrable) should track an act condition we might attach to our everyday ascriptions of moral responsibility (which are themselves guided, say, by the purpose of directing an appropriate response of shame)?

The probable difference in the purposes guiding the criminal law and those guiding our ordinary responsibility ascriptions exists for Williams only because of his own theories in political philosophy and in meta-ethics. More specifically, Williams is not a retributivist in his political philosophy about punishment. He thus thinks there are reasons other than giving guilty offenders their just deserts that justify and guide criminal sanctions. It is this more heterogeneous theory of punishment that allows him to think that the criminal law should be guided by a set of purposes that are unique to it. Then one might well think that such other purposes set aside the metaphysics of action because they set aside the morality (of desert) that requires such metaphysical analysis of action.

In addition, Williams is not a realist in his metaphysics of morality. He does not, in other words, believe that moral qualities like desert exist in the mind-and convention-independent way definitive of moral realism. Williams is thus free to think, as indeed he does, that the ascriptions of moral responsibility by one person to another are guided by 'the aim of directing some response' to the one about whom the ascription is made.[7] Moral responsibility ascriptions, in other words, are judgements made to achieve some purpose and not simply to describe the moral truth about someone. Such purpose of guiding responses of various kinds need have no correspondence with the purpose of getting the morality right, so Williams may also put the metaphysics of action aside just because he puts aside (as meaningless) any concern with the moral truths that require such metaphysical enquiries.

I cannot hope to bridge these first kinds of differences with Williams here, constituting as they do two large issues of political philosophy and meta-ethics. My only point here is to note that insofar as Williams's suspicions about the metaphysics of action

---

[7] Williams, 'Caligari', *supra* n. 2, at 1662.

stem from these sources, they presuppose a good deal against which I have explicitly argued in some of the essays collected in the present volume and elsewhere.[8] If one adopts the retributivist theory of punishment that I defend in Part I, then the guiding purpose of criminal law is to punish those who deserve it in proportion to their desert. If one adopts my own non-interest relative meta-ethics, then the finding of moral desert is not a matter of any purpose of ours, save the purpose of describing the moral facts of responsibility accurately. And if one adopts the view of the relevant moral facts about responsibility that I offer in chapter 3 of *Act and Crime*, one will find questions like, 'what is an action?', to be central in assessing moral desert.

A second set of concerns about the relevance of the metaphysics of action to the criminal law was openly avowed by none of my commentators. Yet I suspect it may have been present (and if not, it is certainly present in others). This concern stems from an anti-realist position about actions (and perhaps events more generally).[9] A good working hypothesis is that if you scratch a sceptic about the *utility* of a metaphysical analysis you will find a sceptic about the *truth* of that metaphysical analysis. This is certainly true in meta-ethics, where those who argue against the relevance of the moral realist/anti-realist debate are invariably sceptical anti-realists about morality. The same may be true here on the metaphysics of action. Thus, Williams wishes to substitute 'philosophical' for 'metaphysical' because I gather he is more comfortable discussing 'philosophical procedures' than he is discussing 'metaphysical truths'.[10] Also, Williams at one incautious point misreads my metaphysical analysis as if it were seeking a *conceptual* essence to actions, not a real essence[11]—but then, if one is an anti-realist about actions, such conceptual (or nominal) essences, are all the essences there are. Also, Williams seems to suggest that our ordinary ascriptions of action must be motivated by their own purposes (which need not be the same as the purposes of the criminal law),[12]

---

[8] On retributivism in the theory of punishment, see chs. 2–4 above. On moral realism in meta-ethics, see Moore, 'Moral Reality', *Wisconsin Law Review*, Vol. [1982], 1061–156; Moore, 'Moral Reality Revisited', *Michigan Law Reveiw*, Vol. 90 (1992), 2424–533.

[9] A variety of anti-realisms about actions are explored by me in Moore, *supra* n. 1, ch. 4.

[10] Williams, 'Caligari', *supra* n. 2, at 1661–2.   [11] Id. at 1669.

[12] Id. at 1661–2.

as if our ordinary ascriptions were not guided simply by a desire to get to the (moral and/or explanatory) truth of the matter. Also, Williams finds that 'there is something odd about discussing such cases [as somnambulism] and their relations to action in terms of *appearance and reality*'.[13] Yet if one were a realist about human actions constituting a natural kind, it would hardly be odd to think that there could be the 'fool's gold of actions' because the essence of natural kinds is often found in deeper, less knowable natures and not in easily known symptoms. Only someone who thinks that all there is to human action is what we see—such as an intelligent pattern of behaviour in sleepwalking—should find this potential divorce of appearance and reality 'odd'. Finally, and most tellingly, Williams finds significance in the fact that 'everyday users of action descriptions' do not ask or answer certain questions about actions that the criminal law must ask and answer.[14] More specifically, Williams thinks that this fact of ordinary usage of action verbs shows that 'there is no reason to suppose that philosophical procedures themselves [metaphysics of action?] can answer' such questions.[15] Williams's view must be that the metaphysics of action runs out of answers because the conventional discourse about actions has run out of questions. Only an anti-realist about actions could think this.

In chapter 4 of *Act and Crime* I deal with a variety of anti-realisms about human actions, or about events more generally. Since there is no explicitly argued for anti-realism amongst my commentators, there is no new argument to address. To the extent that doubts about the relevance of the metaphysics of action arise from this quarter, some new argument would have to be found.

A third set of concerns more plainly motivates the reservations about the role of metaphysics in criminal law theory of Morse, Hornsby, and Williams. This is the concern that the metaphysics of action, even conceding *arguendo* its relevance, yields no answers in problematic or borderline cases. Williams conceives of the concept of action as having an 'indeterminacy through vagueness'.[16] Such degree-vagueness in the concept of action creates a continuum between action and involuntary bodily movement, and on such a smooth and slippery slope, Williams tells us, 'it must be a scholastic illusion to suppose that somewhere on those slopes . . . real,

---

[13] Id. at 1667.   [14] Id. at 1662.   [15] Id. at 1663.   [16] Id.

full-blown action is suddenly to be found as opposed to mere bodily movement'.[17] On this point Stephen Morse finds common cause
with Williams, for about the sorts of problem cases Williams too
discusses Morse concludes that they cannot be 'decided by a natural kind theory of action' and must instead be reached by other,
more practical considerations.[18] Hornsby too suggests that 'perhaps it is not always determinate whether "is an action"
applies. . . .', stating that she would therefore be happy to concede
a vagueness in her own definition of action (since it would match
the vagueness of the concept of action).[19]

Under a non-metaphysical, epistemic interpretation of Morse,
Hornsby, and Williams, it would be easy to agree with them. The
epistemic interpretation is that we presently lack sufficient information to resolve questions like, 'are somnambulistic behaviours
really actions?' I myself regard the question as rather underdeter-
mined by the presently available evidence.[20] In default of such
information, we may indeed do better to repair to Morse's more
practical concerns.

Yet I understand Morse, Hornsby, and Williams not to be making an epistemic point. Rather, theirs seems to be the metaphysical
point that there are no metaphysical answers 'at the border', not
just that we at present lack sufficient information to justify belief in
one answer over another. Yet I am not sure that I see the backing
for their point when taken metaphysically. The vagueness of the
concept of action—or in our usage of the word, 'action'—is surely
no argument that the metaphysics of action is indeterminate in the
penumbral range of application of action terms. Vagueness and
open texture are conventional features of language use not reflective of what may or may not exist in the way of a hidden nature of
a natural kind.[21] If I am right in *Act and Crime* that human actions
are a natural kind of event, then it takes some argument besides
vagueness to suggest that there is no determinative answer in borderline cases.

---

[17] Williams, 'Caligari', *supra* n. 2, at 1672.

[18] Stephen Morse, 'Culpability and Control', *University of Pennsylvania Law
Review*, Vol. 142 (1994), 1587–660, at 1651.

[19] Jennifer Hornsby, 'Action and Aberration', *University of Pennsylvania Law
Review*, Vol. 142 (1994), 1719–47, at 1737, n. 59.

[20] M. Moore, *supra* n. 1, at 259.

[21] On vagueness as a conventional feature of language, see Moore, 'A Natural
Law Theory of Interpretation', *Southern California Law Review*, Vol. 58 (1985),
277–398, at 307–9.

So Morse, Williams, and Hornsby must be suggesting one of two things. They either disagree with me about human actions being a natural kind of event, or they must think that natural kinds may have fuzzy borders, that the kind, human actions, is one such fuzzy kind, and that somnambulism and hypnotic behaviours are in the fuzzy border of the kind.

Perhaps surprising to my commentators, I think either of these is genuinely possible. As I said in *Act and Crime*, 'what is and is not a natural kind is itself a matter of scientific discovery, not of conceptual necessity'.[22] I also think it possible for natural kinds to have fuzzy borders. If species, for example, are natural kinds—a much disputed point—their gradual evolution from one to another belies any bright line between them. The same could be true of the kind, human action. But one would like to see the argument and the evidence.

Whether there is a metaphysical answer about somnambulism, etc., is a question on which all the evidence is not in. The only point of the section of *Act and Crime* dealing with these problem cases[23] was to indicate what one should look for in the way of evidence in light of the volitional theory of action. It might indeed turn out that the volitional theory is falsified or that, under that theory, the evidence is indeterminate as to whether volitions cause the pertinent behaviour sequences in the way that would make them actions.

My disagreement with Morse, Hornsby, and Williams here is apparently a disagreement about the state of our evidence. They seem sure that there are no metaphysical answers about somnambulism and like cases whereas I think the evidence does not (yet) warrant that conclusion. Williams's label for my view, 'new scholasticism',[24] seems an odd one for what I would think of as a cautious empiricism.

A fourth set of concerns about the relevance of the metaphysics of action to criminal law theory is shared by at least Hornsby and Williams. They both think that moral responsibility is such that *action* does not play the decisive role I assign to it. Thus, even if the purposes of the criminal law mandated an exclusive focus on moral desert, and even if the metaphysics of action were such that it could generate determinate answers about what is and is not an

---

[22] Moore, *supra* n. 1, at 76.   [23] Id. at 257.
[24] Williams, 'Caligari', *supra* n. 2, at 1669, 1672.

action, moral desert itself is such that the metaphysical answers are idle.

Hornsby puts this cautiously as a question,[25] whereas Williams is more insistent. In his tale of the evil Caligari controlling the somnambulistic Cesare, what Williams 'wants to insist is that the conclusions about responsibility should not be based on supposing that the reason why Caligari and not Cesare is the murderer is simply that the killing of the town clerk was Caligari's action and not Cesare's'.[26] I want to insist on just the opposite, so I guess issue is joined here.

Williams is surely correct to assume that the somnambulistic Cesare is not morally responsible for the death of the town clerk caused by Cesare's sleep-stabbing. The question is why Cesare is not responsible. I think it is because he did not perform the action of *killing* the town clerk because he did not act at that time at all. Williams thinks that it is because Caligari controlled Cesare's objectives.[27] Williams's alternative explanation seems problematic. Having one's objectives controlled by another does not generally defeat responsibility. As I explore in *Act and Crime*,[28] when Patty Hearst had her objectives controlled by the Simbionese Liberation Army that did not relieve her of responsibility for bank robbery. What is relevant to her responsibility is whether she *executed* her newly implanted objectives, that is, whether she *acted*. The same is true of Cesare.

Williams himself seems to appreciate the nature of this execution perfectly well. He points out that the somnambulistic Cesare is so dissociated 'from considerations that essentially bear' on what he is doing that he 'cannot summon up . . . thoughts that would relate the killing to the rest of his life'.[29] This lack of integration of Cesare's implanted objective (to kill the town clerk) with many of his other objectives helps to explain why Cesare is not responsible for the death.[30] It even explains why Cesare could not have done any *acts* of agreeing to kill.[31] But for Williams, none of this lends support to the idea that Cesare does not perform the action of killing the town clerk.[32] Yet Williams has actually described why it is that Cesare did not perform the action of killing the town clerk.

[25] Hornsby, 'Abberation', *supra* n. 19, at 1740.
[26] Williams, 'Caligari', *supra* n. 2, at 1670–1.   [27] Id.
[28] Moore, *supra* n. 1, at 259–60.   [29] Williams, 'Caligari', *supra* n. 2, at 1671.
[30] Id.   [31] Id.   [32] Id.

Integration of conflicting objectives is one of the defining functions of volitions,[33] so that when that function is absent volition (and thus, action) is absent. The asleep Cesare did no actions of stabbing or killing. In fact, he slept through the whole thing.

The fifth and last set of concerns about reliance upon metaphysics in the criminal law is most directly voiced by Sam Freeman. Freeman's generally Rawlsian outlook inclines him to favour those legal principles that can be publicly understood and agreed upon by citizens in a democracy.[34] Insofar as criminal law principles take their content from the 'high metaphysics' of action, they will not be either understood or agreed on. Freeman therefore takes this to be a reason not to have criminal law doctrines and principles depend on such a metaphysics unless absolutely necessary 'as a last resort'.[35]

It is surely a desideratum of our criminal laws that they be knowable by those who must obey them, and this does require that such laws be understandable to that large majority of citizens not holding philosophy degrees in the metaphysics of action. Yet nothing in my view of the role of metaphysics in criminal law runs contrary to this ideal of legality. The difference between action and bodily movement, for example, is widely experienced and appreciated. Although metaphysicians may talk about it in unfamiliar ways, the difference they are talking about is not unfamiliar, even to the most unreflective among us.

Freeman of course worries that legal policy makers need greater understanding than the intuitive appreciation satisfactory for citizens. Such policy makers need to know, for example, whether Alvin Goldman's single instance trope metaphysics of actions is both correct and relevant to the tests for double jeopardy, or whether my 'wrong-relative' approach and 'coarse-grained' metaphysics is what is needed.[36] Freeman probably thinks that if Goldman and I show up in the Arizona or Pennsylvania legislatures with our different approaches to double jeopardy, we ourselves would be in some jeopardy of confinement.

Although the picture admittedly is amusing to contemplate, we should not allow difficulties in immediate translatability to be any

[33] Moore, *supra* n. 1, at 137–55, 258.
[34] Freeman, 'Duty to Aid', *supra* n. 3, at 1455–6.   [35] Id.
[36] Compare Moore, *supra* n. 1, Part III, with Alvin Goldman, 'Action and Crime: A Fine-Grained Approach', *University of Pennsylvania Law Review*, Vol. 142 (1994), 1563–86, at 1584–6.

more than practical limitations on where and when one argues metaphysics. We should not elevate them into principled limits on what is worth arguing about in the context of drafting a criminal code. We should rather agree with Bentham on this, who saw such enquiries, abstract as they are, as the indispensable first steps to a rational criminal law.[37]

II. OMISSIONS: CONCEPTUAL AND METAPHYSICAL ISSUES

We may now leave behind any general worry about my metaphysical programme for the criminal law and get to more particular objections. Legal liability for omissions does not fit comfortably with the theory of action developed in *Act and Crime*. Predictably, a number of commentators zeroed in on this fact in order to raise a number of problems for me. To keep some semblance of order here, it will be convenient to divide the problems into two groups. In this section I shall deal with conceptual and metaphysical worries about omissions, raising questions of what omissions are or how they may most fruitfully be conceptualized. In the following section I shall deal with moral and legal worries about what our responsibilities might be for omissions.

A. Omissions as Intentional Agency

A number of my commentators are tempted to conceive of omissions more narrowly than do I. My generic notion of an omission I introduced early in *Act and Crime*:

[O]missions are simply absent actions. An omission to save life is not some kind of ghostly act of saving life, and certainly not some ghostly kind of killing. It is literally nothing at all. An omission to save X at some time t is just the absence of any instantiation of the type of action, 'saving X'.[38]

This I recognized to be a broad conceptualization of omissions. Fletcher,[39] and Hornsby,[40] wish to narrow it to willed (intended,

---

[37] Jeremy Bentham, *Introduction To the Principles of Morals And Legislation* (Buffalo, NY, 1988 edn.), 72 n. 1. It is instructive that Bentham's favourite quotation from Helvetius was, 'If philosophers would be of use to the world, they should survey objects from the same point of view as the legislator.' Quoted in Gerald Postema, *Bentham and the Common Law Tradition* (Oxford: Clarendon Press, 1986), 263.

[38] Moore, *supra* n. 1, at 28.

[39] George Fletcher, 'On the Moral Irrelevance of Bodily Movements', *University of Pennsylvania Law Review*, Vol. 142 (1994); 1443–53, at 1444.

[40] Hornsby, 'Aberration', *supra* n. 19, at 1738–40.

chosen, etc.) refrainings, and perhaps, to willed refrainings when the actor could have prevented the harm and he knew that. They wish, that is, to conceptualize, for example, an omission by Y to save X at t as the choosing of the non-saving of X by Y at t where Y could have saved X at t and Y knew that.

There are three principal reasons offered for this narrower conceptualization of omissions. One is the unity possible within a theory of action if omissions too are conceived of in terms of willing. Then all acts, be they acts of commission or of omission, consist in an agent trying, choosing, intending, or willing that some state of affairs come into being or remain the same. Such a unified theory of action is of course the mental action theory favoured by Prichard,[41] Davis,[42] Hornsby,[43] and others.[44]

The second reason offered for the narrower conceptualization of omissions is the apparent absurdity of my broader conceptualization. To quote Fletcher: 'Dead men who do "literally nothing at all" do not omit.'[45]

Thirdly, it is claimed that the only interesting cases of omission are those where the 'actor' has directed her mind to some threatened state of affairs and to her capacity to prevent it, and where she chooses not to prevent it. As Fletcher puts it, 'the only kind of omitting that is interesting is the kind in which human agency is expressed'.[46] And again:

Agency is built into the standard example of the bystander who lets the child drown. The example would not even be interesting unless we assumed that the bystander chose to remain motionless and that she had an unrestrained option to intervene and rescue the child.[47]

None of these three reasons, as I now propose to show, go any distance towards justifying the narrower conceptualization of omissions over my broader notion. Consider the last point first, Fletcher's lack of interest in non-willed omissions. If Fletcher is like the rest of us, he probably has two sorts of interests relevant here, explanatory interests and moral interests. That is, he seeks a conceptualization of omissions that is explanatorily interesting—

---

[41] H. A. Prichard, *Moral Obligation* (Oxford: Oxford University Press, 1949).
[42] Lawrence Davis, *Theory of Action* (Englewood Cliffs, NJ: Prentice-Hall, 1979).
[43] Jennifer Hornsby, *Actions* (Oxford: Oxford University Press, 1980).
[44] See Moore, *supra* n. 1, at 95, n. 46.
[45] Fletcher, 'Moral Irrelevance', *supra* n. 39, at 1444.   [46] Id.   [47] Id.

because omissions (rightly conceived) explain things—and/or that is morally interesting—because omissions (rightly conceived) either capture a kind of moral responsibility, or they are the contrast case to something else that does capture a kind of moral responsibility.

Now consider two sets of omissions Fletcher finds interesting enough to mention them in his own paper: (1) 'failing to water the plant, when one reasonably expects the contrary, causes it to die';[48] (2) 'The failure to register for the draft, the failure to pay one's income tax, or the more common problem of government appointees: the failure to pay social security tax on household employees.'[49] Fletcher finds the first explanatorily interesting, yet notice, there is nothing in the example to suggest a willed non-watering of the plant. The person who watered the plant may simply have forgotten to water it. *We* expect that people who care enough for plants to own them will water them, and this expectation may make the omission to water explanatorily interesting to us—but *not* because there is any of Fletcher's 'human agency' or 'choosing' not to water the plant in the person whose omission Fletcher finds explanatorily interesting.

Fletcher finds the second set of examples morally and legally interesting because we can justly blame people for failing to pay their income or social security taxes and for failing to register for the draft. Yet we blame people for these omissions irrespective of any *choice* not to do so. 'I forgot' is no excuse here, because such forgetting would be negligent. Negligent omissions are surely interesting to Fletcher, but not because there is any of Fletcher's 'human agency' or 'choosing' not to pay or to register.

The problem of negligent omissions plagues the first reason as well. Granting that we hold persons responsible for such items, the unified view of actions—as trying, willing, intending, agency, etc.—draws a blank in accounting for them. If omissions must be intentional in order to *be* omissions, we shall need another name for negligent omissions. In which event the supposed unity of acts and omissions—in terms of some common element of intentional agency—is illusory.

I should have thought all of this was perfectly obvious since Bentham, who recognized that we cannot at the same time conceptualize omissions as willed and also capture the class of things that

---

[48] Fletcher, 'Moral Irrelevance', *supra* n. 39, at 1448.   [49] Id. at 1447.

holds our moral interest with this conceptualization.[50] As I said in *Act and Crime* in discussing Bentham's rejection of Fletcher's and Hornsby's conceptualization:

As Bentham himself recognized, many omissions are not willed yet they are punishable . . . Negligent omissions . . . are not willed omissions because one's mind was not directed to the situation calling for the action omitted.[51]

Coming to the second reason, the supposed absurdity of dead men omitting, there is indeed something odd in the kind of usages Fletcher's example illustrates. It is *not* odd to say that we all omit to feed a given beggar in India, even though we do not know who he is or what his needs might be. It *is* odd to say that Caesar omitted to prevent the ascension of Hitler to power in 1933, or that after our own deaths we omit to treat our friends well. The difference is that in the former case we could prevent the starvation of the beggar, whereas in the latter cases dead persons can do no preventing because they can do no things at all. They lack, that is, any ability to cause anything, being dead and all.

Such an oddity has nothing to do with the presence of 'human agency' or intention in the former cases and not in the latter, as Fletcher suggests. Willing, thinking, directing one's mind to it, etc., are all completely irrelevant to the oddity to which Fletcher directs our attention. There is not much point to saying that dead men omitted to do some particular type of act when we know, being dead, they have (and will continue) to omit to do *all* types of acts.

We could treat this usage oddity as semantic, in which event we restrict our concept of omissions to those non-instantiations of some type of action by those who could have performed an act of that type if they had chosen to do so. Or we could treat this usage oddity as I do in *Act and Crime*,[52] as only a pragmatic oddity. Saying that a dead person omitted to save some child on a given occasion is odd in the same way as it is odd to respond to the question, 'What caused the fire at the drugstore last night?', with the answer, 'the presence of oxygen in the air'. Telling people what we the speakers know they already know is pragmatically deviant even if semantically impeccable.

[50] Bentham, *supra* n. 37, at 72, n. 1.
[51] Moore, *supra* n. 1, at 24.   [52] Moore, *supra* n. 1, at 28, n. 31.

Conceptualizing omissions my way will indeed mean that there are 'trillions of omissions on the part of each person at any moment', as Hornsby notices.[53] I do not see why that is a problem, so long as one recognizes that almost all of these omissions lack the surprise that would make them explanatorily interesting and lack the features of negligence, knowledge, or intention that would make them morally interesting. And remember: one cannot restrict omissions to those that are willed, chosen, intended, etc., because that manner of conceptualization fails to include omissions we do find to be morally and explanatorily interesting—a fact Hornsby recognizes when she admits that she has no conceptualization of omissions to give that is narrower than my account and yet accommodates negligent and inadvertent omissions as omissions.[54] I still think my broader conceptualization is preferable: the generic notion of an omission is simply the absence of an action of a certain type, leaving more restrictive notions to be carved out as our interests require.

B. Supposed Motionless 'Actions'

A second set of concerns raised about my conceptualization of omissions focuses on omissions as absences of bodily motions. This is the objection of Corrado[55] and Fletcher[56] that motionless states of a person, when willed by them, are actions on their part, and that therefore my notion of omissions is too broad in this respect too.

Before dealing with this objection, we need to clarify a preliminary point on which Fletcher, but not Corrado, seems curiously confused. Fletcher says that I have different 'lines of thought' in my definition of omissions.[57] Fletcher thinks that my conceptualization of omissions as the absence of any willed bodily motions is different than my conceptualization of omissions as the absence of any act-token that instantiates the type of action omitted. The fact that I pointed out at the Symposium that this was a mistaken interpretation of me by Fletcher has resulted in his current, coy footnote, in which he declares: 'Alas, we must go by the printed page and not

---

[53] Hornsby, 'Abberation', *supra* n. 19, at 1739.   [54] Id.

[55] Michael Corrado, 'Is There an Act Requirement in the Criminal Law?', *University of Pennsylvania Law Review*, Vol. 142 (1994), 1529–61, at 1538–41.

[56] Fletcher, 'Moral Irrelevance', *supra* n. 39, at 1445, 1448.

[57] Id. at 1444.

by the preference of the author.'[58] By all means. The printed page to which I referred Fletcher during the Symposium was page 28 of *Act and Crime*:

An omission to save X at some time t is just the absence of any instantiation of the type of action, 'saving X'. On the metaphysical view of actions developed in chapters 4–6, actions are event-particulars of a certain kind, namely, willed bodily movements. An omission by A to save X from drowning at t is just the absence of any willed bodily movements by A at t, which bodily movements would have had the property of causing X to survive the peril be faced from drowning.

There is no distinct concept of omissions here; only the plugging in of my positive theory of action to my generic notion of an omission to say *what* it is that is absent when an action is absent.

Fletcher's confusion here is more serious than just confusing species and genus. It also leads him to misunderstand the specific notion of omissions as the absence of willed bodily movements. Fletcher thinks that if there are willed bodily movements by A at t, then there is no omission by A at t. For example: 'not voting is hardly the absence of bodily movement. One could be engaged in an infinite variety of activities in the time one should be voting.'[59] Yes, but unless those activities instantiate the type of action in question, *voting*, one is still *omitting to vote* by my criteria for an omission. What Fletcher fails to put together is that it is the absence of willed bodily movements *that instantiate some type of act V* that is an *omission to V*; mere presence of bodily motions at the time in question is irrelevant.

I thought that I had made this relatively clear in *Act and Crime*.[60] My example was the person, A, who omits to throw a rope to another, B, who is drowning. A dances a jig in celebration as B drowns. Is A now an actor? Yes, although plainly not a *killer* of B because A's dancing is not 'causally relevant to B's death'.[61] Does the fact that A is an actor at t preclude A being an omitter at t? Not in the least. A omitted to will any bodily motions that were relevant to preventing B's death. He did not, for example, throw a rope to B. A therefore *omitted* to save B while A did something else,

[58] Id. at 1445, n. 11.
[59] Id. at 1452. See also id. at 1448 ('whether the mother remains motionless as her baby dies is totally irrelevant' to whether she omits to save her baby).
[60] Moore, *supra* n. 1, at 29.   [61] Id.

namely, dance. (To be blunt I think I deserved a more careful reading here by Fletcher; and if he omitted to read this passage at all, then—despite my theory that makes omission liability rare—this is an omission for which I cheerfully hold Fletcher fully responsible.)

Let us now come to the 'motionless actor' objection proper. Consider first this proposed counter-example from Corrado:

> Suppose . . . that I was sitting in the car at the top of a hill, and that for reasons having nothing to do with my being in the car it began to roll down the hill. I have my hands on the wheel, but there is no occasion to turn, the road being straight. If I run down my enemy . . ., am I not liable for killing her?[62]

I think the correct answer to this is plainly a 'no'. Corrado has not done anything by sitting motionless in the car with his hands on the wheel. (He may have trouble *proving* that he did nothing to cause his enemy's death, but it is, as Corrado said at the Symposium, his hypothetical, and we can know with the certainty of an omniscient novelist that Corrado did not move.)

Corrado apparently thinks that the motion of the car and the working of its engine makes some difference here. Yet by hypothesis, the 'driver' did nothing to start the engine or the car's motion. The motion of the car is irrelevant, as is the corresponding motion of the 'driver' that is not willed or caused by him.[63] Corrado no more kills in his hypothetical than he would if he were thrown off a cliff by the wind, his body landing on his old enemy and thereby causing the latter's death.

Corrado presents a variation of his motionless driver hypothetical where our sense of responsibility and of action is stronger:

> I am driving down a long, straight highway; the car is on cruise control, and I am not moving the wheel . . . Suddenly and unexpectedly I see an old enemy standing in my lane about two hundred yards ahead of me. Her back is turned; she does not see me approaching . . . Thereafter I do not move, and the car runs over my old enemy, killing her.[64]

Surely, Corrado concludes, he killed the woman, yet he, Corrado, was motionless.

---

[62] Corrado, 'Act Requirement', *supra* n. 55, at 1540.

[63] As Aristotle observed long ago with his example of a man not acting when he is moved by the wind. *Nichomachean Ethics*, Bk. III, Ch. 1.

[64] Corrado, 'Act Requirement', *supra* n. 55, at 1538.

Corrado anticipates most of the five things I want to say about this case. The first is whether the driver does not indeed *kill* his old enemy because the driver's earlier willed bodily motions in starting and driving the car caused the death in question. Corrado puts aside this anticipated response by me because there is no culpable *mens rea* existing in the driver at those earlier times, quoting me to the effect that culpable *mens rea* must be simultaneous with the wrongful action.[65] This is true enough for the ultimate question of responsibility and liability, but it does not deal with the metaphysical question of action. For I do think that the earlier acts of driving are sufficiently proximate that they caused death, and therefore the driver did *kill* his old enemy. The intervening omission to turn does not alter that analysis.

But Corrado is right in his conclusion on liability: we cannot hold the driver liable for his earlier acts, because even though they were acts of *killing*, they were not caused or even accompanied by culpable *mens rea*. So consider, secondly, whether we fudge this question in the way invited by the Model Penal Code.[66] According to the Code, we only need find a larger 'course of conduct' included in which is some willed bodily motion. We are thus invited to say that the whole sequence of starting to drive, driving, and then remaining motionless is one 'course of conduct', that at some point during its happening a culpable *mens rea* arose, and that this larger whole both caused death and includes within it some willed bodily movements. This sloppy analysis, although common enough,[67] is unacceptable because of its unprincipled mode of aggregation of actions into one 'course of conduct'. This accordion-like concept invites the kind of scepticism I explore briefly in *Act and Crime*.[68]

Nor can one deal with Corrado's second kind of case with the third possibility here, the true doctrine of 'embedded omissions' that I explore in *Act and Crime*.[69] The Graham Hughes/Hyman Gross analysis would treat the absence of any movement turning the wheel as a circumstance in the presence of which the accused performs the (positive) action of driving. Yet Hughes and Gross cannot so analyse this case, because the acts of the driver are done

---

[65] Id. at 1538–9.   [66] American Law Institute, *Model Penal Code* § 2.01.
[67] Fletcher, e.g., seem to buy into this way of thinking, although he wrongly thinks that I join him in it. See Fletcher, 'Moral Irrelevance', *supra* n. 39, at 1445, n. 8.
[68] Moore, *supra* n. 1, at 35–7.   [69] Id. at 31–4.

before the relevant time during which the omission to turn occurs. One cannot thus treat the failure to turn as a circumstance in the presence of which positive actions are done. Only the *effects* of positive actions are continuing when the driver sees his old enemy in the road, and on my theory of action these effects (such as movement of the car) are no parts of the earlier acts of driving.[70]

Fourthly, in some of the cases Corrado imagines there may well be either the kind of displacement refrainings or resistings that I explore shortly herein. These are cases where an actor either moves one part of the body in order to keep another still, or he resists an outside force that would move his body unless he exerts himself. In Corrado's hypothetical, however, he stipulates that he is only 'lightly resting my hands on the wheel and failing to move them . . .'[71]

That leaves only the fifth and last possibility for holding his 'driver' for some form of homicide. This is the possibility I relied upon during the Symposium: the driver is liable, not because he intentionally killed his old enemy, but rather, because he innocently caused (by his earlier willed bodily motions of driving) a condition of peril for his old enemy that makes it his duty to rescue him. It is like lowering a safe over another that then breaks away: if I can prevent the safe from falling by no more than flipping a safety catch, I surely am duty-bound to flip it. If I omit to flip the switch with a culpable *mens rea,* then I am liable for my omission. As I discuss such cases in *Act and Crime,*[72] these are cases of true omission liability. They are not, however, counter-examples to my analysis of action.

Corrado objects that I cannot finesse his counter-example in this way. The creation-of-peril exception to omission liability, Corrado tells us:

does not fit the case at hand: *I* did not create the situation that put my victim at risk. She did, by standing in the road and not looking out for herself. My presence in the road is perfectly reasonable—I did not create the risk.[73]

But he did. His presence in the road is reasonable but that has no bearing on the *innocent* causation of the condition-of-peril excep-

---

[70] Id. ch. 11.   [71] Corrado, 'Act Requirement', *supra* n. 55, at 1538, n. 30.
[72] Moore, *supra* n. 1, at 34.
[73] Corrado, 'Act Requirement', *supra* n. 55, at 1539.

tion. His victim may be unreasonable, and she may have contributed causally to her own peril, but that does not take Corrado out of the exception. He put a force in motion that if he does not stop or redirect will kill. He thus has a duty not to omit to do these things, which duty he culpably fails to fulfil.[74]

Fletcher too seems enamoured of supposed motionless actions. His example:

Suppose that one of the guards at Buckingham Palace enters into a conspiracy with outsiders to kill the Queen. His signal to them about when they should bomb a certain portion of the palace is his remaining motionless an extra five seconds after the other guards begin to change their posture. . . . He contributes to her death by signalling that the bombing should proceed.[75]

But this is easy for my theory. The guard caused the co-conspirators to understand where the bomb should be placed by his earlier act of telling them where to place the bomb; his only caveat was that they were not to so place the bomb if he signalled them not to do so by moving with the other guards. The guard then omitted to so signal them by remaining motionless. The earlier act of speaking involved bodily motions, and thus was an action; when the speaking caused Austinian uptake with the co-conspirators, it then became an act of communicating. The act done was *not* an act of *signalling*, as Fletcher believes, for that is precisely the kind of act they omitted to do by standing still. The earlier act of communication the guard did do is enough aid to make the guard liable even under traditional complicity doctrines, let alone under the more lenient Model Penal Code or *Pinkerton* doctrines of complicity.[76]

Fletcher elsewhere considers a variation on the Buckingham Palace guard:

---

[74] Corrado makes two other worrisome points: (1) the punishment should be less if this is true omission liability than it would be for killing; and (2) true omission liability may not be as infrequent as I assume in *Act and Crime*. See Corrado, 'Act Requirement', *supra* n. 55, at 1539–40. Re (1), as I argue shortly in response to Freeman, some positive duties may be quite stringent, such as the duty to save one's own child. Stopping whatever we have put in motion from killing is surely also more stringent than our general moral duty to rescue strangers whom we have not imperilled. Re (2), I actually think that it takes considerable contrivance to manufacture counter-examples like Corrado's. Fortunately for my theory, the real world is not often so devious.

[75] Fletcher, 'Moral Irrelevance', *supra* n. 39, at 1447–8.

[76] *Model Penal Code* § 2.06; *Pinkerton* v. *United States*, 328 US 640 (1946).

Tourists regularly pause and stare in wonderment at the motionless guards standing in front of Buckingham Palace. Standing without moving for a few minutes is a feat worthy of praise at least as much as doing a back flip off the diving board. And standing motionless on one's head is an even greater feat.[77]

Shortly before he gives this example Fletcher complains that I have given a 'reckless summary of a complicated literature' on omissions.[78] Yet if Fletcher had paid more careful attention to the literature that I summarized, he would have seen that both I and that literature had dealt precisely with his kind of case. In *Act and Crime* I quote Myles Brand, for example:

The policeman who keeps his arm at his side and does not shoot the fleeing youth refrains from shooting him. . . . Idiomatically, we would simply say that he refrains from shooting the fleeing youth by keeping his hand by his side. Refraining, then, is one type of action.[79]

In *Act and Crime* I also quote the case posed by Julia Annas:

What about omissions and cases where acting involves precisely *not* moving the body? Suppose the boy stands on the burning deck, whence all but he had fled? It is his *standing* which is his action, and this involves no bodily movement, unlike his coming to stand there.[80]

Fletcher's hypothetical adds nothing to those of Brand and Annas, and so I shall simply repeat my reply to them, to Fletcher.

Briefly, I used in *Act and Crime* another portion of the literature Fletcher would like to see used in a non-reckless way, an article by Bruce Vermazen.[81] We should distinguish, Vermazen tells us, 'resistings' and 'displacement refrainings' from Brand's more generic 'refrainings'. 'A resisting occurs when an agent's body is about to be made to move by outside forces, but he keeps his body from moving by activating the appropriate muscles.'[82] Fletcher's example of standing on one's head is a good example of resisting,

---

[77] Fletcher, 'Moral Irrelevance', *supra* n. 39, at 1445.

[78] Id. at 1444, n. 6.

[79] Moore, *supra* n. 1, at 88, quoting Myles Brand, 'The Language of Not Doing', *American Philosophical Quarterly*, Vol. 8 (1971), 45–53.

[80] Moore, *supra* n. 1, at 88, n. 26, quoting Julia Annas, 'How Basic Are Basic Actions?', *Proceedings of the Aristotelian Society*, Vol. 78 (1978), 195–213.

[81] Moore, *supra* n. 1, at 88–9, relying on Bruce Vermazen, 'Negative Acts', in B. Vermazen and M. Hintikka, eds., *Essays on Davidson: Actions And Events* (Oxford: Oxford University Press, 1985).

[82] Moore, *supra* n. 1, at 87.

where Vermazen and I would conclude there is an action. For in such cases the actor constantly adjusts his muscles in order to keep gravity from moving his body. As long as we 'construe "bodily movements" to include muscle-flexings',[83] as we should in these cases where we use our muscles to resist an outside force, there is nothing inconsistent with my theory of action in concluding that such resistings are actions, not omissions.

A displacement refraining occurs when the actor keeps one part of his body from moving by moving another part of his body. Vermazen's example: Andy, who is tempted by food in front of him, keeps himself from eating it by twisting the buttons on his vest (which keeps his hands occupied so that they cannot reach for food). A more common variation: Alice lights up and smokes a cigarette in order not to eat. There is obviously no problem for my theory of action in concluding that actions occur in such cases even as one is omitting to do certain other actions.

About Brand's and Annas's examples of refrainings more generally, as about Fletcher's Buckingham Palace guard, my conclusion in *Act and Crime* still stands: 'such refrainings are not actions'.[84] Standing still may become so difficult physically that it is like standing on one's head, in which case it will become a resisting and thus, on my account, an action; yet as Annas's example of the boy 'frozen' to the deck illustrates, one more usually stands still and in standing still does nothing at all.

C. Omissions as Causes?

A third set of worries about my conceptualization of omissions stems from my denial that omissions *cause* anything. Recalling my view that 'omissions are literally nothing at all',[85] I defend Julie Andrews's view in *The Sound of Music*: 'Nothing comes from nothing, and nothing ever can.'[86]

Among the Symposiasts only George Fletcher challenged this aspect of my theory. Unfortunately Fletcher merely contented himself with denying what I had earlier asserted: 'But surely unexpected non-motion could be the cause of death.'[87] Fletcher recognizes that I think the opposite: 'Moore says that he has an argument against

---

[83] Id. at 88, n. 24.   [84] Id. at 88.   [85] Id. at 28.
[86] Julie Andrews and Christopher Plummer, 'Something Good', in Rogers and Hammerstein, *The Sound of Music*.
[87] Fletcher, 'Moral Irrelevance', *supra* n. 39, at 1448.

omissions as causes, but I find no case against the plausible position of Hart and Honoré that failing to water the plant, when one reasonably expects the contrary, causes it to die.'[88]

Fletcher did not look very hard. On pages 267–76 of *Act and Crime* I address six separate arguments against any notion of causation that would allow omissions to be causes. Since Fletcher did not find those arguments, or in any case did not address them, I shall not repeat them here. About examples like failing to water the plant, notice that Fletcher's use of 'causes' here need mean no more than the counterfactual: in the possible world where we do water plants, then, all else equal, they do not die. This is a true causal generalization connecting actions of watering with states of continued plant life. It is this generalization, and not some causal relation between omissions to water and plant deaths, that we invoke when we loosely talk of omissions causing things to happen.

Fletcher does better with his legal observation that when our criminal system does hold omitters liable, it sometimes does so under statutes prohibiting killings, maimings, etc.[89] Since on my own showing these verbs of action require a causing of death for their correct application, our law must presuppose that omissions can be causes. Fletcher is right about our law; our law is simply wrong about the metaphysics, as is Fletcher.[90] Anglo-American criminal law cannot make omissions be causes when they are not. It can only require those who apply it to come up with some substitute for causation in the case of omission liability; and this we easily do with the counterfactuals earlier mentioned.

D. Killing/Letting Die and Act/Omission

There were a host of interesting thoughts introduced by Frances Kamm's Symposium paper[91] that promise to supplement my act/omission distinction with other distinctions she finds to be morally salient. Kamm agrees with my conceptualization of the act/omission distinction: 'an act is a willed movement, an omission is a non-act of a particular sort, and . . . omissions do not cause events'.[92] Kamm focuses on the morally salient act-type, killing,

---

[88] Fletcher, 'Moral Irrelevance', *supra* n. 39, at 1448.   [89] Id. at 1450.
[90] Moore, *supra* n. 1, at 267–76.
[91] Kamm, 'Action, Omission, and the Stringency of Duties', *University of Pennsylvania Law Review*, Vol. 142 (1994), 1493–1512.
[92] Id. at 1495.

to supplement the act/omission distinction with two other distinctions.

The first is the distinction between killing and letting die. This
distinction is drawn with the aid of two background distinctions:
(1) where the act is the original cause of death versus where the act
only removes a defence against some force that will actually cause
death unless the defence remains in place; and (2) within the
removal-of-a-defence-against-death cases, where the actor removes
a defence he himself was providing versus where the actor removes
a defence independent of any that he was providing.[93] A killing is
an act that either is an original cause of death or is a removal of a
defence against death that was being enjoyed by the victim independently of any provided by the actor.[94] A letting die, by contrast,
occurs when the actor's act is not an original cause of death and is
only the removal of a defence against death that had been provided
by the actor herself.[95]

Kamm's second distinction is within the class of killings and,
indeed, within that subclass of killings that are killings because each
is an act that is an original cause of death. Within this subclass
Kamm wants to distinguish some killings that 'have practically the
same moral weight as the letting die by actively terminating aid'[96]
because such killings only cause the death of someone who was
dependent upon the actor for some defence against an otherwise
naturally occurring death. For example, the person providing
another with life support stabs him rather than terminating the life
support and letting nature take its course.

Kamm recognizes that these two distinctions have some affinities
with the 'relativized baseline test' I put aside as a test of act versus
omission.[97] For both the letting die and the lesser wrong killings
analogized to letting die, do no more than return the victim to the
status she would have been in, in the absence of the actor's initial
help. My refusal to use the relativized baseline test as the basis for
drawing the act/omission distinction does not mean I reject the
moral force of Kamm's distinctions. On the contrary, I agree with
Kamm on the moral force of the distinctions; the only question is
how to conceptualize that moral difference.

Kamm and I also agree that the act/omission line is not to be
conceptualized in this way. Where we disagree is whether the cases

[93] Id. at 1497–8.   [94] Id. at 1498.   [95] Id.   [96] Id.
[97] Moore, *supra* n. 1, at 27.

she calls letting die are not cases of killing. I think that they are killings, only killings of such lesser wrong that they (along with Kamm's original cause killings of dependants) are eligible to be justified much more easily than are ordinary killings.[98]

To see this alternative conceptualization of her cases, think first of a quite different sort of case, one like Bernard Williams's case of 'Jim'.[99] In my variation, the actor, 'Jim', is confronted with a macabre choice: if he selects one innocent villager out of fifteen assembled before a firing squad, that one will be shot but the rest will live; if Jim makes no selection, all fifteen will be shot. I am a deontologist about killings, so that one has an agent-relative moral duty not to kill.[100] Nonetheless I think Jim ought (or is at least permitted) to make his selection, for by doing so he is not *killing*. His act of selection is certainly an act; it enables another to kill; but the act is not a killing because it is not the proximate cause of death.[101] Between that act and the death that it enabled intervened the free, informed voluntary choice of the captain of the squad to kill.

Since killings are acts causing deaths, Jim does not kill. Therefore his act of enabling death does not violate the agent-relative prohibition against killing. But can we say the same of Kamm's cases of letting die? When we turn off the respirator of the patient who we ourselves are keeping alive with it, and the patient dies, there is no 'break' in the 'causal chain' between our act of flipping off the switch and the patient's death. We therefore *kill* the patient just as surely as does an intruder who does the exact same sort of action with the same sort of result.

We thus must locate the moral force of Kamm's letting die/killing distinction elsewhere. I would locate it as a partial exception to the moral norm against killing.[102] When all in a lifeboat will die anyway, it is permitted to *kill* one in order to save the rest. When a flood comes down a canyon, it is permitted to *kill* the occupants of a farm by removing a dyke that would have protected them, if that was the only way to save all in a village from death in the flood. These are the well-known 'already dead' and 'distribution' exemptions,[103] relieving us from the rigours of deontology so

[98] The idea of killings, torturings, and other wrongful acts being 'less wrong' when done in certain circumstances, and being thus more eligible for a consequentialist override of any agent-relative prohibition, is explored *infra*, ch. 17.

[99] J. J. C. Smart and B. Williams, *Utilitarianism: For And Against* (Cambridge: Cambridge University Press, 1973), 98–9.

[100] See ch. 17, *infra*.   [101] Id.   [102] Id.   [103] Id.

as to permit killings to be justified by sufficiently good consequences.

What such exemptions show us is not that these acts are not killings. Rather, they show us that such acts are sufficiently less wrong that good consequences—consequences which would not justify ordinary killings—may justify *these* kinds of killings. Such lessened wrongness also attaches to Kamm's cases of letting die and of killing of dependants. Given this lesser wrongness, such killings are much more easily *justified* by good consequences than are ordinary killings. This is why I said in *Act and Crime* that any relativized baseline conception of the act/omission distinction 'can be used to smuggle notions of justification in' as supposed differences in action.[104] I still think it preferable to keep this differential for potential justification out in the open, which requires that acts of letting die be recognized for the killings that they are.[105]

III. OMISSIONS: NORMATIVE ISSUES

A. The Variability of Wrongness and Liberty Limitations in Particular Cases

Sam Freeman and George Fletcher introduce a pair of difficulties that, while distinct, share a common solution. Freeman's point has to do with the lesser wrongfulness of violating our positive duties to act (i.e., not to omit) as compared to the greater wrongfulness of violating our negative duties not to act.[106] Freeman concedes (at least *arguendo*) that in any pair-wise comparison a negative duty might be more stringent than its positive counterpart—the duty not to kill is more stringent than the duty to prevent loss of life—yet he denies that *all* negative duties are stronger than *any* positive duty: 'Many failures to improve the world enormously outweigh in

---

[104] Moore, *supra* n. 1, at 27.

[105] I am unclear whether Kamm wishes to call duties not to do original cause killings of dependents and not to let die (where such duties exist), negative or positive. I suspect that it violates a positive duty to let die and that it violates a negative duty to kill dependents (in those situations where such duties exist). Whereas I think all killings—which include many of Kamm's letting die cases—violate a negative duty, if they violate a duty at all. We probably disagree about where the negative/positive line is most fruitfully drawn even though we may have no disagreement about the relative moral stringency of any of these moral duties.

[106] Freeman, 'Duty to Aid', *supra* n. 3, at 1462–4.

moral heinousness many acts that make it worse.'[107] Freeman's example: it is more wrongful to let a stranger's child drown when it could be saved at no risk and minimal effort, than it is to steal the child's purse.[108]

By this observation Freeman means to question one-half of my justification for not punishing most omissions on retributive grounds. I argue that while some failures to act are wrongful, they are not nearly as wrongful as their counterpart evil actions, so that the demand for punishment of retributive justice is less strong in the former cases than the latter.

Fletcher questions the other half of my account of why we by and large do not punish omissions, even when these violate a moral duty and are therefore wrongful.[109] The other half of my account is in terms of liberty: a law that (positively) coerces me to do some action takes away more of my liberty than does a law that (negatively) coerces me from doing some action. Fletcher accurately gauges the intuition behind this idea: on an opportunity-set conceptualization of liberty, a requirement that I do some act A effectively prohibits me from doing acts B, C, D, etc., whereas a requirement that I *not* do some act A only prohibits me from doing A.[110]

Fletcher raises two objections to this intuition: (1) 'whether a demand or a prohibition is more noxious depends on the content of that which is demanded or prohibited'.[111] Fletcher opines that prohibiting certain sexual practices (as 'sodomy') may be more liberty-limiting than requiring use of condoms.[112] (2) Whether liberty is taken depends on the actor's wants. Not being able to do acts he has no desire to do does not take away any liberty.[113]

Fletcher's second point rejects the opportunity-set notion of liberty, so I shall reserve my consideration of it until later. If we discard for now Fletcher's second point, then his and Freeman's can be combined into a single objection: some omissions may be sufficiently wrong, and the liberty diminished by a positive requirement that such actions not be omitted may be sufficiently small, that a

---

[107] Id. at 1463.   [108] Id.

[109] Fletcher, 'Moral Irrelevance', *supra* n. 39, at 1450–1.

[110] Id. at 1451.   [111] Id. at 1450.

[112] Id. Freeman raises a similar objection to my claims about liberty. Freeman, 'Duty to Aid', *supra* n. 3, at 1479.

[113] Fletcher, 'Moral Irrelevance', *supra* n. 39, at 1456.

retributivist ought to urge the punishment of such omissions. My *general* observations about differential wrongness and differential liberty may well be correct, in other words, and yet they will not together justify a blanket policy of not punishing omissions.

One might agree with Freeman's point that some violations of positive duties are morally worse than some violations of negative duties, and one might agree with Fletcher's point that some affirmative requirements impinge liberty less than some negative prohibitions; there would then be a theoretical possibility that we should criminalize more omissions than we do. Yet one would want to see the examples. Freeman's example—where the wrongness of omitting to save the child is greater than the wrongness of stealing the child's purse—will not do, because the liberty differential is still there. It diminishes liberty less to prohibit theft than it does to require life-saving activities. Fletcher's example—comparing the liberty diminished by a prohibition of sodomy versus a requirement of condom usage—will not do, because the wrongness differential is still there. On the view of morality (that I do not share) that regards deviant sexual practices as wrong, these acts will be much greater wrongs than the omission to wear a condom in non-deviant sex. On such a view of morality, those *acts* of sodomy should be punished, and the omission to use a condom not, because of this differential in wrongness—even conceding Fletcher his desired reversal of the normal liberty differential between the negative prohibition and the positive requirement.

Aside from waiting for better counter-examples—ones where the wrong of omission is serious and the diminishment of liberty by the positive requirement is small—there is something else that needs to be said here that was not said in *Act and Crime*. Francis Kamm gets at this with her observation that 'there are cases in which a negative duty is more stringent than a comparable positive duty even though failing to perform the negative duty would make the world better. For example, I must not euthanize someone against his will even though death would be in her interest.'[114]

Kamm is surely right to separate *stringency* of moral duty from the degree to which non-fulfilment of a duty will make the world better or worse. Good or bad consequences are not the measure of the stringency of an agent-relative duty. We should also separate,

---

[114] Kamm, 'Action, Omission', *supra* n. 91, 1495–6.

as Freeman does not, stringency of moral duty from the moral heinousness of the character of the person violating the duty. Beneficently motivated killing can violate a very stringent moral duty and yet evidence a not-so-heinous character in the killer.

Kamm thus rightly focuses on stringency of moral duty to the exclusion of these consequentialist and characterological considerations. Kamm's explanation for the differential stringency of negative over positive duties is in terms of rights-based (as opposed to only rights-correlated) duties.[115] Negative duties are grounded in the right of each person to 'a certain sort of inviolability of the person' whereas positive duties are not.[116] Positive duties may have correlative rights in the victims of their violation, but they are not rights-based duties.

Although I find Kamm's suggestion interesting and worth pursuing, my own explanation for the (across the board) differential in stringency between negative and positive duties is different. Consider three duties: (1) the (negative) duty not to kill; (2) the (positive) duty to prevent the death of one's own child; and (3) the (positive) duty to prevent the death of a stranger-child. Freeman is right that I am not enough of a libertarian to deny that we have any moral duties of the second or third sort. Yet I do deny that the third is an agent-relative obligation, whereas the first plainly is. We ought not to kill, in other words, even in situations where our doing so would prevent more killings by ourselves or others in the future; yet one cannot say the same of when we ought to prevent the deaths of strangers. If we confront one stranger-child in the water needing rescue, we are surely entitled not to save her if, by swimming to a larger group of drowning children, we can save them. Our duties not to omit are consequentialist (or 'agent-neutral') in their nature. Such duties are, for that reason alone, not among the stringent duties we call 'deontological' or 'agent-relative' duties, and the wrong of violating such duties is correspondingly less.

Some positive duties nonetheless may approach the stringency of negative duties in that such positive duties are plausibly thought to be agent-relative. The second duty above, the duty to save our own child, is such a duty. I take it that we at least have an agent-relative *permission* to favour our own child over another—or even over

---

[115] Kamm, 'Action, Omission', *supra* n. 91, 1495–6.   [116] Id.

several others—equally in need of rescue.[117] But we also have an agent-relative obligation to save our own child even if doing so means we cannot rescue some number of others. And this agent-relative obligation compares favourably (in terms of stringency) with the agent-relative obligation not to kill. Might I not be obligated to kill an innocent if doing so was the only way to save my child? (Even if this last question is to be answered negatively, the difficulty of answering it indicates the near parity in stringency of the two duties.)

In any case, the distinction between agent-relative and agent-neutral duties at least explains the across the board greater stringency of (almost) all negative duties versus (almost) all positive duties. It may in addition explain why some positive duties are nearly as stringent as their negative counterparts, a moral fact recognized by our criminalizing of omissions that violate such stringent positive duties.

B. Liberty as a General Freedom to Act

In addition to their questioning of the differential *amount* of liberty taken away by criminalizing positive duties as opposed to negative ones, Fletcher and Freeman also question the opportunity set notion of liberty that makes sense of such quantification. Fletcher's objection, as we have seen, depends on his thesis that liberty is want-relative in the sense that someone must want to do some action A before coercion against A limits that person's liberty.[118] This is surely wrong. Think of the old conundrum about false imprisonment: if the victim does not know of the confinement because he never desires to leave the room, has he been confined?[119] Surely the answer is 'yes', for the wrong of confining another and the loss of being confined are objective matters that do not depend on the subjective states of the victim. Happy slaves are still slaves. They may not want to do anything other than what they must do, but they are slaves because they are not free.

---

[117] Such agent-relative permissions are part of what Tom Nagel calls 'reasons of autonomy'. Thomas Nagel, *The View From Nowhere* (New York: Oxford University Press, 1985). On agent-relative permissions generally, see Samuel Scheffler, *The Rejection of Consequentialism* (Berkeley: University of California Press, 1982).

[118] Fletcher, 'Moral Irrelevance', *supra* n. 39, at 1451.

[119] Prosser's answer (even in torts, where there must be a compensable injury) was 'no'. William Prosser, 'False Imprisonment: Consciousness of Confinement', *Columbia Law Review*, Vol. 55 (1955), pp. 847–50.

Freeman has a more interesting basis for rejecting any opportunity-set notion of freedom.[120] Freeman shares with Ronald Dworkin (and many other non-libertarian, egalitarian liberals) the rejection of any value to natural liberty to do whatever one might wish:

[S]urely there is nothing intrinsically valuable about the natural liberty to do wrong . . . To assign intrinsic value to natural liberty as such, would imply that legal restrictions *per se* diminish this intrinsic value, and that there is ethical loss with the imposition of any legal restriction. But what could that loss be in the case of legal restrictions on clearly unjust or evil conduct?[121]

Freeman thus rejects my idea that there is value in our natural liberty even when we exercise it so as to 'make the wrong choice'.[122] Rather, Freeman thinks that there are only basic *liberties*, those more discrete rights such as the right to speak freely, to think and worship as we please, etc.

This is doubtlessly not the place to launch a defence of this well-worn question in political philosophy. Freeman is accurate in gauging what view of liberty underlies my brief references to liberty in *Act and Crime*.[123] For I do think that there is value in each of us having the natural liberty to do what we please, including the liberty to violate Freeman's 'perfect duties' (i.e., to make the wrong choice). Such liberty is the basis of the right of each citizen that legal coercion will be exercised only for legitimate reasons, the correlative duty of each legislator being to enact criminal laws only in pursuit of those reasons. Those legitimate reasons for criminal legislation do include punishing culpably done wrongs, but the good of punishing culpable wrongdoers must outweigh the bad of coercively interfering with choice.

It is a mistake to confuse this right to natural liberty with the much narrower, but much more powerful right to non-interference with certain sorts of decisions. What we think or say, what religious experiences we value, what sexual practices we admire, whether to have children, are part of what makes us who we are. They are aspects of a more powerful basic liberty that is easily confused with the broader but much weaker natural liberty. If one distinguishes these two different rights to liberty, then one can agree with

---

[120] Freeman, 'Duty to Aid', *supra* n. 3, at 1484–6.   [121] Id. at 1486.
[122] Moore, *supra* n. 1, at 57.
[123] Id. at 57–8; Freeman, 'Duty to Aid', *supra* n. 3, at 1485.

Freeman that 'however this list of basic liberties is drawn up in the end, it will not include a liberty to violate perfect moral duties'.[124] It will not, because the choices that can violate such duties are not the sort of self-defining choices protected by the more basic right to liberty. Freeman thus attributes a view to me that I do not hold insofar as I am said to think that 'inchoate "liberty" itself is an intrinsic good worth protecting whatever the costs'.[125] The basic liberty to define oneself may be so worth protecting, but a general, natural liberty certainly is not. But that is not to say that the general, natural liberty is not valuable at all.

Why is there *any* value in a natural liberty that includes a liberty to do wrong? Why should we be free of legal coercion when what we are coerced to do is our own perfect duty? By way of answer, consider Freeman's own example, Kant's imperfect, ethical duty of beneficence. Suppose that those of us who could easily afford it were under a duty to give a portion of our income to the poor. As Freeman notes, it was Kant's concern 'to make it a matter of an individual's discretion to choose when to fulfill this duty and whom one should choose to benefit as a result.'[126] After all, to be coerced into giving is hardly to *give* at all, and in any case a coerced 'giving' is not nearly so virtuous as a voluntary giving. Yet is this concern not perfectly general: whenever the law coerces, it cuts into the possibility of freely chosen good? The value of natural liberty lies in the possibility of autonomously chosen good, recognizing that the price a legal system pays for such a possibility is a matching possibility of a greater number of bad actions.

C. Legality Worries About Omission Liability

George Fletcher raises a little noticed problem about criminal liability for omissions that is not addressed in *Act and Crime*.[127] This is a problem stemming from the fact that Anglo-American penal codes do not always spell out what it is one must not *omit* to do. Homicide statutes prohibit acts of killing, for example, but there is no analogous statute criminalizing failures to save another when that other dies but could have been saved. Rather, our criminal codes rely on the simple statutory prohibition on killing, together

---

[124] Freeman, 'Duty to Aid', *supra* n. 3, at 1488.   [125] Id.
[126] Id. at 1476.   [127] Fletcher, 'Moral Irrelevance', *supra* n. 39, at 1450.

with the case-law on when there is a duty to prevent death, in order to criminalize omissions to save.

Fletcher finds there to be a 'wholesale breach of legality in the judicial development of duties that supplement the law of homicide'.[128] There are actually two legality worries here. The one apparently troubling to Fletcher is the non-statutory law that spells out when there are duties to prevent harms such as death that one is prohibited from actively causing (such duties exist for parents, for undertakers of rescue, for culpable or innocent causers of the condition of peril, and the like). There is also another legality worry about our present criminalization of certain omissions, and that stems from the metaphysical fact that an omission to save, even when a death ensues that the act omitted would have prevented, is not a killing.[129] Statutes prohibiting killings, thus, do not command acts of saving lives, any more than those prohibiting burnings, maimings, or kidnappings command acts of burn-prevention, disfigurement-prevention, or asportation-prevention. It is only because our courts analogize the failure to save a life that could have been saved, to killing, that allows them to punish omissions to save life under our homicide statutes. This smacks of 'crimes by analogy', one of the practices frowned upon by that branch of the principle of legality known as the doctrine that there are no common law crimes.[130]

Given the moral and metaphysical views presented in *Act and Crime*, the second of these legality worries would seem more serious than the first. Not only are omissions to save not killings, but acts that are killings are generally the more serious moral wrong, even when saving is obligatory and not merely supererogatory. The enactment of omission statutes would thus be desirable for two reasons: one, such statutes would command actions (i.e., prohibit omissions) that now are punished despite not being anywhere by statute required; and second, such statutes would attach lesser penalties to the omission to save than to active killing, a lesser punishment juries and judges now typically give anyway but without statutory guidance or authorization.

---

[128] Fletcher, 'Moral Irrelevance', *supra* n. 39, at 1450.
[129] Moore, *supra* n. 1, at 267–78.
[130] On legality, analogy, and common law crimes, see id. at 240.

D. Demonstrating the Comparative Strengths of Negative versus Positive Duties: Kamm's Post-Efforts Test

Francis Kamm agrees with me that negative duties are more stringent than positive duties, and she sees that I support this common conclusion with what she calls a defeasibility test.[131] Kamm helpfully seeks to supplement my use of a defeasibility test with what she terms her 'post-efforts' test.[132] What this test asks is what efforts would be morally appropriate to require of someone in order to prevent a harm he has either begun to cause by his action or begun to omit to prevent by his inaction.

Kamm actually relies on two different kinds of application of her test. In what I shall call her third-person application of the test, we ask what the actor or omitter should feel compelled to do in order to correct or prevent the harm. Kamm's example: the would-be killer who had almost drowned a baby should have to offer his life if doing so (for example, by giving his last breath underwater) would revive the submerged infant; yet the would-be omitter to save a drowning baby should not have to make this kind of sacrifice in order to save the life he previously had omitted to save.

In what I shall call Kamm's first-person application of the test, we ask what *we* could properly do *to* the actor/omitter after he has started to act or omit. To use again her example: we may kill a person who is drowning a baby in order to prevent the baby's death whereas we may not kill an omitter even if that will save the baby he is omitting to save (for example, by giving an incentive to the fellow standing next to him not to continue to omit to save the baby). From both of these sorts of applications of her test Kamm concludes that killings are worse than omissions to save.

I have two worries about the post-efforts test. My first worry corresponds with Kamm's third-person application of the test. There is a gap between both preventive and corrective justice, on the one hand, and retributive justice on the other. As the literature on moral luck that we canvassed in chapter 5 rather abundantly illustrates, we often have preventive and corrective duties that have a different character than the duties which give rise to retributive deserts. I may have reason to prevent, correct, and regret harms that I have caused or am innocently causing, but that does not

---

[131] Id. at 54–5.   [132] Kamm, 'Action, Omission', *supra* n. 91, at 1501.

mean that I should be punished for such innocently caused harms. I may have no retributive desert even though I have strong preventive and corrective duties.

My second worry corresponds to Kamm's first-person application of her test. Here, we *are* testing retributive desert, because we are asking what we may do to someone who is killing/omitting to save in order to get him to stop/start. Now my fear is that we are not testing anything but our straight retributive intuitions about comparative deserts: we may do more to prevent the would-be killer killing than we may to induce an omitter to save life because killing a killer is less wrong than killing an omitter;[133] but this last is only true because killers are morally worse than are omitters to save life. Yet this conclusion was the 'direct intuition' about just deserts that the post-efforts test was to supplant or at least supplement.

I say all of this rather provisionally because I welcome all the help I can get in arguing for the difference in moral stringency between positive and negative duties. Perhaps Kamm's post-efforts test can be reformulated so as to avoid these difficulties, or perhaps these are not real difficulties, in which case hers is a welcome addition to my more familiar defeasibility test.

IV. CONCURRENCE OF ACT, CAUSE, AND KATZ

Leo Katz in his contribution to the Symposium[134] restricted his focus to the relationship between the voluntary act requirement and the other elements of the prima facie case for criminal liability. In *Act and Crime* I defend the standard view of that relationship: the accused's voluntary act must simultaneously exist with, and in some cases be caused in the right way by, his culpable *mens rea*, and that same voluntary act must itself cause some legally prohibited result.[135] Leo Katz disagrees. He denies that the causal linkage of *mens rea*-voluntary act-prohibited result is sufficient for even prima facie criminal liability (prima facie liability is liability without con-

[133] This goes back to my earlier discussion (*supra*, n. 98) of how some killings, although wrongful, can be less wrongful on even an agent-relative view of morality.

[134] Leo Katz, 'Proximate Cause in Michael Moore's *Act and Crime*', *University of Pennsylvania Law Review*, Vol. 142 (1994), 1513–28.

[135] Moore, *supra* n. 1, at 35–6.

sidering excuses or justifications typically raised by the defences); and he denies that the extent of blameworthiness is governed by this relationship.

Katz presents fourteen alleged counter-examples to my concurrence principle. I am confident that not a one of Katz's cases is a true counter-example to my principle. I cannot go through them all in any great detail. I shall thus discuss the first of Katz's examples, show the various reasons making it not a true counter-example, and then show how these reasons equally well handle all of Katz's other examples.

Katz's first example is that of Alex and Bruce: Alex outruns his companion, Bruce, so that the bear eats Bruce rather than Alex.[136] Alex performs a number of voluntary acts in running. He does so knowing that the bear will kill Bruce so long as Alex runs faster than Bruce. His voluntary acts in some sense are causally related to Bruce's death at the paws of the bear (if Alex did not run, and Bruce did, Bruce would still be alive). Thus, Katz concludes, this is *'a pretty unequivocal illustration of an act that proximately causes harm but does not entail liability'*.[137]

Yet this is not a counter-example to my concurrence principle, for four reasons. First, in some of the 'ducking' cases the one who ducks (or runs) is not the proximate cause of the harm because the free, voluntary act of a third party intervenes. This might be true of the bear in the above hypothetical. It is certainly true of other of Katz's ducking cases, where Alison either switches briefcases or covers her official US government seal, with the desired result that another (Beatrice) is killed by terrorists. The terrorists intended to kill, meaning (on virtually anyone's notion of an intervening cause) that Alison did not proximately cause death, i.e., she did not do the legally prohibited action of killing.

Even if we thought that both Alex and Alison were prima facie liable, they are not *actually* liable because they were justified or excused by one defence or another. This means that their *ultimate* non-liability is not a counter-example to my concurrence principle, which only states a sufficient condition for prima facie liability. Each of the next three reasons raises one such possible defence.

---

[136] This is one of what Katz calls the 'ducking' cases. Katz, 'Proximate Cause', *supra* n. 134, at 1516–18.

[137] Id. at 1518 (emphasis in original).

Consider first the consequentialist version of the balance-of-evils defence. Alex's loss of life would be as great an evil as the loss of Bruce's life, and *mutatis mutandis* for Alison *vis-à-vis* Beatrice. As is well known, sometimes one can justify otherwise prohibited killings by balancing lives. This is permissible either: (a) when the killing is not your project but is someone else's; or (b) when the killing is done only by redirecting a force already in motion from its natural victim to another.[138] Bernard Williams's example of the first is where you are requested to decide who will be shot, but you do no shooting; and in default of a choice by you, all will be shot.[139] Judy Thomson's (and the Model Penal Code's) example of the second is where a flood will engulf an entire village, killing all of its inhabitants, but you may prevent that by redirecting the flood onto one farm, killing only its inhabitants.[140]

Katz's ducking cases fit both of these exemptions from the rigours of deontology, permitting consequentialist justifications to operate. Of course, Alex is trading one life for one, as is Alison. The evils thus are evenly balanced. One might well think, however, that such defence ought to be governed by a tipping principle: when the evils are even, the accused does no *net* evil by killing.

Katz anticipates the possibility of consequentialist justifications here. He therefore alters his example:

Suppose that Alison had known she would only be mishandled by the terrorists (perhaps because one of them knows her) but that Beatrice would be killed. She too would still have been entitled to duck (which in this case of course means covering her suitcase with an Air Libya sticker).[141]

This eliminates even a parity between evil caused and evil averted, and so no consequentialist justification is possible.

Yet this variation reveals the presence of two more defences lurking to relieve duckers from ultimate liability. One might have (as libertarians in particular often do) what is sometimes called a rights-based view of justification.[142] On this view we each have an agent-relative permission not to balance evils but to prefer our-

---

[138] See ch. 17 *infra* for further discussion of these permissions.
[139] J. J. C. Smart and B. Williams, *Utilitarianism*, *supra* n. 99, at 98–9.
[140] For citations and discussions, see ch. 17 *infra*.
[141] Katz, 'Proximate Cause', *supra* n. 134, at 1518.
[142] See Joshua Dressler, *Understanding Criminal Law* (Mathew-Bender, 1987), 182. Such rights-based conceptions of justifications are really agent-relative permissions to do acts that do not maximize good consequences.

selves to others. For example, a person otherwise unable to prevent a crotch grope except with the use of deadly force may use that deadly force against the would-be groper.[143] One might also think that we each are entitled to favour our own life (or the lives of those near and dear to us) over the lives of others, when someone must die. On such non-consequentialist versions of justifications, we are justified in ducking.

Alternatively, we often *excuse* people who do a greater evil in order to avoid a lesser one.[144] Such people are not justified on consequentialist grounds and they may not be justified on rights-based views of justification. Yet the instinct for survival or the fear of loss of one's own life or bodily integrity may be such that we find it understandable that one could not be a moral hero. Running from a bear as fast as one can is surely one such occasion.

These same four reasons recur to remove any sting in many of Katz's examples. Certainly the tale of the sailor and his daughter, who send the troopers to a neighbour's door (Katz's second example)[145] offers all four possibilities, being another sort of ducking case. Sometimes what saves the individual from ultimate liability is the agent-relative justification for his action (the third of the possibilities above). Thus, Daniel Drew (Katz's fourth example)[146] is entitled to leave a slip of paper that others can take 'advantage' of only if they are willing to trade on confidential information; Lincoln (Katz's fifth example)[147] is entitled to state the literal truth even though he knows it will mislead his audience, given his agent-relative permission to speak freely in the political arena. Given these justifications for conduct, these can hardly be counter-examples to my thesis about prima facie liability.[148]

[143] *State* v. *Philbrick*, 402 A 2d 59 (Me. 1979).

[144] On necessity as an excuse, not as a justification, see ch. 12 *infra*.

[145] Katz, 'Proximate Cause', *supra* n. 134, at 1518–19.   [146] Id. at 1519–20.

[147] Id. at 1520. (Alternatively, some may think that Lincoln did wrong, but if that is so he is still not a counter-example.)

[148] Notice that sometimes such justifications do not make their appearance as defences. Rather, at such times these justifications appear as either the absence of *mens rea* (for crimes of negligence and recklessness, which require *unjustified* risk-taking) or as the absence of *actus reus* (where we say that an act that literally violates some statute does not in law violate such statute because it was justified). On both points, see ch. 17 *infra*. When justifications operate in these latter two ways so as to defeat the prima facie case, they still present no counter-example to my concurrence principle. For remember, that principle requires concurrence of *mens rea* and *actus reus*, and where one or the other is absent, there is no *concurrence* of *mens rea* and *actus reus*.

In two of Katz's examples, the third and the sixth, it seems to me Katz is just wrong in denying that there is prima facie liability. Ethelbert, the would-be rescuer in Katz's third example who begins to rescue his old enemy, 'sloughs him off, as it were, and swims back by himself'.[149] If sloughing him off is an act, as Katz says it is, then Ethelbert is liable for homicide. That Ethelbert fits Kamm's category of a letting die (or perhaps of an original cause killing of a dependant)[150] does not matter. As I argued earlier,[151] these are killings, and all Kamm's categories do is make *killers* eligible for consequentialist justification. Ethelbert has no such justification, so he is not only prima facie liable, but is ultimately liable as well.

Likewise, Veronica, Katz's sixth example,[152] is liable for mayhem in taking the drug prior to conception in order to cause the child she (conditionally) intends to conceive to be born without an index finger. Surely we are past the conceptual problem that she need not have conceived the child at all, so she can conceive it in any shape she pleases—the old 'greater power includes the lesser' fallacy. Surely we are also past the old notion that she cannot owe a duty to the unborn or unconceived. Why then does Katz think that this is *'a strong example of an act . . . proximately causing harm but not constituting a crime'*?[153] Presumably because Katz thinks she is justified by an agent-relative permission here: she is justified because she will only take the drug if she will conceive, which she will only do if conceiving a finger-defective child is the moral thing to do (which Katz thinks it is because such a minor defect should not bar conception). Whereas I think she would be justified in conceiving at t_2, knowing of the defect, but that she is not justified at t_1 in taking the drug in order to cause the defect.

With this sixth example, Katz is really letting the cats out of the bag. For all of the examples in his paper from here on share a common form: the agent seeks to find a permissible route to an outcome that is legally prohibited unless justified. Such agents thus either try to find some agent-relative permission or excuse for their action, in which case they are not *ultimately* liable because they are either justified or excused; or they seek to remove their actions sufficiently that they are not the proximate cause of the legally

[149] Katz, 'Proximate Cause', *supra* n. 134, at 1519.
[150] See discussion *supra*, text at nn. 92–7.   [151] See *supra*, text at nn. 98–104.
[152] Katz, 'Proximate Cause', *supra* n. 134, at 1521.
[153] Id. (emphasis in original).

prohibited state of affairs, in which case they are not even prima facie liable. Sometimes they fail in their manipulative attempts, and therefore are ultimately liable, despite what Katz says. All of Katz's remaining examples fit into one of these three possibilities, none of which are problematic for my concurrence principle.

Septimus, the surgeon, curious about what it would be like to operate drunk, is not liable.[154] First, he was not the proximate cause at t_1, when he got himself intoxicated, because of the coincidence of a patient needing him; and, although his drunken acts at t_2 were the cause of the patient's injuries when Septimus operated, he was justified in operating (even drunk) because no one else was available. Obediah, the Charles ('Death Wish') Bronson of dog-haters,[155] is liable at t_1 for provoking the dog to attack him so that he could defensively kill it at t_2; the dog's provoked response is not an intervening cause, and Obediah's justification at t_2 for shooting the dog in self-defence is not a justification at t_1 for provoking the dog so as to kill him. (Nor is Obediah justified at t_1 by retrieving the toy, since the manner of retrieval—'sudden, startling, and aggressive'[156]—was not necessary to retrieve the toy and was only done to provoke the dog.) The Patty Hearst-like heiress[157] who releases her bodyguards so that she might be kidnapped and 'forced', into terrorism, is not liable, because her acts at t_1 of releasing her bodyguards do not proximately cause her bank robbery at t_2. If Katz succeeds in eradicating the intervening acts of the kidnappers or their agents in his more fanciful variations of this case,[158] then the heiress may have proximately caused her own 'duressed' bank robbery and is liable. Katz thinks not, I gather, because he thinks the heiress is legally privileged to release her bodyguards for any reason. If Katz were right about this, then she would be justified at t_1 and would not be ultimately liable (even though the concurrence of voluntary act, *mens rea*, and causation at t_1 would make her prima facie liable).

Mathilda, who refuses to learn cardio-pulmonary resuscitation (CPR) in order not to save her husband should he need her aid later,[159] did not cause anything, proximately or otherwise, by her omission. While she had a duty not to omit to save him if she could do so at t_2 (when he suffers a heart attack), she has no duty to learn CPR at t_1. Even though the act omitted at t_1 could have saved him,

---

[154] Id. at 1521–2. [155] Id. at 1527. [156] Id.
[157] Id. at 1522–3. [158] Id. at 1523, n. 36. [159] Id. at 1523.

let us suppose, in the absence of the duty there is no liability. She no more has to learn CPR than she has to become a doctor in order to jump on MacCauley's train to Meerut.[160]

Alaric, another Machiavellian dog-killer,[161] has engineered his justified killing of the dog at t_2 in a sufficiently roundabout way that I doubt that his walking around the neighbourhood is the proximate cause of the dog's death. He is not liable. (And if I am wrong about this, then he is liable, but he is still not a counter-example.) Ulysses, the last of Katz's curious drunkards,[162] is liable (as Katz admits) because his drunken acts of violence cause injury. His voluntary intoxication is no excuse under present law. Katz would change this, excusing him if he was: (1) cautious at t_1 about where and when he got drunk, and (2) so drunk at t_2 when he hit the visitor that he did something he would not have done sober. Even with law that Katz would prefer, why would this prima facie liable, but ultimately excused individual, present a counter-example?

Katz's regular trolley, regular surgeon, and twisted trolley scenarios in the last part of his comment all have to do with when consequential justification is permissible: it is when you redirect force (original trolley), not when you originate the force that kills (surgeon, twisted trolley), and it is again when you redirect force under the realization that this is the only way to kill one to some five since you cannot later kill him to save the five (original trolley *redux*). So what? In all variations there is prima facie liability because of the concurrence of voluntary act, causation of death, and *mens rea*, even if *ultimate* liability varies because of the various presence or absence of a balance-of-evils justification.

Katz has forgotten his hope of criticizing my concurrence principle; instead, he has focused on the development of an insight that motivates his forthcoming book.[163] Katz is interested in the path-dependence or formalism of agent-relative morality and of the criminal law that often mirrors that morality. He is thus fascinated by examples of manipulated justification and manipulated excuse. He has convinced me that these are fascinating examples and form the subject-matter for a marvellously interesting book. These examples, however, have very little to do with my concurrence principle.

---

[160] Moore, *supra* n. 1, at 55.
[161] Katz, 'Proximate Cause', *supra* n. 134, at 1523.   [162] Id. at 1523–4.
[163] Leo Katz, *Ill-Gotten Gains* (Chicago: University of Chicago Press, 1996).

The overlap of the two topics is to be found in their common focus on the question of the actor's liability for manipulating the situation at t_1, the earlier time. About this issue: I sometimes think that there is no prima facie liability because of the lack of proximate causal connection between the earlier manipulative act and the ultimate harm; I sometimes think that there is no *ultimate* liability because, while there is a proximate causal relationship, there is a justification for so acting at that earlier time; I sometimes think that there is a proximate causal relationship and that there is *no* justification for so acting, leading to ultimate liability. In the first set of cases, Katz often disagrees with me about proximate causation; in the third set of cases he often disagrees with me about the availability of some (unspecified) agent-relative permission to do the earlier manipulative act, even when done with the intent to kill, maim, etc. In neither of these classes of cases should our disagreement (about whether causation or justification is present) be mistaken for a disagreement about the concurrence principle. And even in the second set of cases, where we agree that there is no ultimate liability, our disagreement is about the meaning of the concurrence principle, not about its truth. I construe the principle such that it is not violated by cases where the defendant was justified whereas Katz construes the principle differently.

At the very end of his piece Katz hints at the system with which he would replace the concurrence principle. The idea seems to be that an actor should get credit if, after his initial act is done with culpable *mens rea*, he seeks to prevent those effects that will make that act wrongful and illegal. For example, the defendant starts a boulder rolling toward his old enemy in order to kill him but then has second thoughts and seeks, unsuccessfully, to stop the boulder. Katz is right about where 'the Moorean approach' goes in such cases: this is a murderer, and the early onset of remorse does not change that fact in the least. Katz might wish to reform the law here to provide for a partial defence of abandonment; but whether there were such a defence is of course irrelevant to the truth of the concurrence principle, which only deals with prima facie liability.

V. TESTING THE VOLITIONAL VERSION OF THE VOLUNTARY ACT REQUIREMENT: SOMNAMBULISM, HYPNOSIS, AND DISSOCIATED STATES AS ACTIONS?

Stephen Morse and Bernard Williams both examine my theory of action by seeing what implications it has for application of the criminal law's voluntary act requirement to certain problem cases. These cases are somnambulistic behaviour, behaviour under or due to hypnosis, and what Morse more generally characterizes as behaviour done when the 'actor' is dissociated in some way. Because the concerns of Morse and Williams are rather distinct, I shall consider each separately.

A. MacBeth, Caligari, and Williams

In applying my theory of action to these problem cases in chapter 10 of *Act and Crime*, I was not seeking to answer the question of whether these are actions so much as I was showing what questions we should ask in order to determine whether these are actions.[164] Although I incline to the view that most of these behaviours are not actions, and although Williams concludes that they are actions, our main disagreement is not about this conclusion but about what sorts of arguments are persuasive here.

Consider four sorts of arguments, the first being the argument from ordinary usage. In *Act and Crime* I urge that the idiomatic usage of the ordinary verbs of action to describe somnambulistic behaviours is not much of an argument for the conclusion that these behaviours are actions.[165] I attribute a contrary view about the persuasive power of ordinary usage to Herbert Hart, Douglas Husak, and Bernard Williams.[166] Williams now agrees that 'this would not have been much of an argument' and disclaims having made it.[167] This is fair enough, but Williams then goes on to attribute a kind of linguistic argument to me.[168] I am supposed to think that we can distinguish between literal versus metaphorical uses of action verbs (because we can distinguish 'actions' predicated of a human body from actions predicated of a person) and on this usage basis then tell whether some bit of behaviour is really an

---

[164] Moore, *supra* n. 1, at 256–7.
[165] Id. at 252–3.
[166] Id.
[167] Williams, 'Caligari', *supra* n. 2, at 1664.
[168] Id. at 1665–6.

action or only looks like an action but is not. Williams then points out that it is difficult if not impossible to separate English predicates into person-applicable predicates and body-applicable predicates; in addition, predications of somnambulistic behaviour 'seem to be paradigmatically the kind of predicate that is applied to a person'.[169] For these reasons, 'it is only if we have *already* decided that there is something peculiar about these predications that we would start to look in that direction'.[170]

I agree with this last thought of Williams: it is only because we have other grounds for thinking that somnambulistic behaviours are not actions that we have reason to explain away ordinary usage with something like my literal/metaphorical usage distinction. I did not think there was any positive argument to be made either way from these or any other facts of usage of action verbs.

So Williams and I apparently agree that ordinary usage cuts no ice one way or the other about how to classify these problematic kinds of behaviours. What then are better arguments here? Williams's discussion introduces three other sorts of arguments. The first certainly sounds like an argument from usage. It has to do with how we should describe what Caligari and Cesare do when Caligari directs the somnambulistic Cesare to stab the town clerk with a dagger, which has the result that the town clerk dies. Williams's description: Cesare 'kills (as we would naturally put it) the town clerk with a dagger.'[171]

Williams argues for this characterization thus: the town clerk was stabbed with a dagger; Caligari did not stab him with a dagger (although we might say that Caligari brought about the town clerk's death by a stabbing); therefore (there being only two possible stabbers on these facts) it must have been Cesare who stabbed the town clerk with a dagger. Since Cesare's stabbing of the town clerk with a dagger had the consequence that the town clerk died, Cesare killed the town clerk with a dagger.[172]

There are two ways to complete this argument here. One is the direction taken by Morse, who urges that the killing by Cesare was an action of his, albeit one for which he will most likely not be held responsible because excused.[173] The other is Williams's more agnostic direction:

---

[169] Id. at 1666.   [170] Id.   [171] Id. at 1670.   [172] Id. at 1670–1.
[173] Morse, 'Culpability and Control', *supra* n. 18, at 1650.

We should not have to struggle with these difficulties. Cesare . . . stabbed the town clerk. But he did it when he was asleep. . . . Whatever the best description, we can see how it is on these facts that Caligari is guilty of murder with respect to these deaths and Cesare is not, but that is not because no stabbing . . . was done by Cesare.[174]

Williams thus does not quite say that Ceasare's stabbing and killing of the town clerk was an action, for he recognizes that there are 'various dimensions in which what is done may fall short of the paradigm of fully voluntary action'[175] and somnambulism presumably shares some such dimensions.

In criminal law we cannot afford Williams's nonchalance about this question. Whether Cesare acts or not matters: (1) to whether Caligari can be charged with murder himself, or only as an accomplice to Cesare's murder; and (2) to whether the prima facie case for murder can be made out for Cesare or not. Williams doubtlessly thinks of these as criminal law-driven distinctions only, and the lawyers will just have to work it out in light of the criminal law's distinctive purposes.[176] I on the other hand take the criminal law's distinctions here to be one of the criminal law's attempts to cut nature at the joints, the *metaphysical* question of whether Cesare performed an action determining the *legal* question of which theory of liability is appropriate for Caligari and Cesare.

Morse's alternative completion of the argument, while tempted by Williams's kind of metaphysical agnosticism, nonetheless takes a position on somnambulism, viz., it is action and therefore if there is no liability for Cesare it's only because he is to be excused. Morse thus forces us to confront how Cesare's stabbing could not be an action. Notice that one should get off Williams's chain of inferences right at the start: just because the town clerk was stabbed with a dagger does not mean that someone stabbed him with a dagger. Imagine that a dagger is negligently left on a window sill, it falls and stabs the town clerk below—he was stabbed and killed with a dagger, but no person did any act of stabbing. Or imagine a variation on the scene depicted in a film of the never caught mass murderer in Texarkana: a trombone player is stabbed to death by a knife attached to a trombone, the trombone itself worked by an elaborately rigged up machine turned on by the killer. The victim

[174] Williams, 'Caligari', *supra* n. 2, at 1671–2.
[175] Id. at 1072.   [176] See discussion, text at nn. 2–8 *supra*.

was stabbed with a dagger but we may think that the killer did no stabbing.[177] Thus, to prosecute someone for killing of the town clerk by stabbing, we need not find a stabber, only a killer. And Caligari did kill the town clerk: his acts of directing Cesare caused the town clerk's death.[178] Cesare, on the other hand, did no killing and did no stabbing (even though Cesare's body was causally implicated in a stabbing and a killing)—indeed, Cesare, the person, slept through the whole nasty business! At the very least, there is nothing in this little story that argues against this last characterization. We are thus still looking for arguments one way or the other here.

A second additional argument might be based on a behavioural fact that is very striking about these cases. As I note in *Act and Crime*, somnambulistic and hypnotic patterns of behaviour are so responsive to the environment, so seemingly intelligent, that these cases do tempt one towards the conclusion that such behaviours are really actions persons perform.[179] Williams too is impressed by this behavioural fact and at times seems to think it sufficient for the conclusion that somnambulistic behaviours are actions:

There is no doubt that Lady MacBeth has picked up the light, found the door, undone its bolt, and carefully come down the stairs. Moreover, it is not a matter of mechanically determined routine which merely looks as though it were responsive to perceptual cues; some somnambulists . . . will walk around pieces of furniture that are not in their normal place. So why should we say these movements only *look like* actions?[180]

This sounds a lot like the Gilbert Ryle of 1949, who thought that all there was to mind and action was behaviour and dispositions to behaviour.[181] Against those who would attribute hidden, internal causes for such patterns and dispositions, Ryle was prone to parody: against the internal cause view of, say, mental disease, Ryle urged that we would not be able to tell on such a view whether 'the inner lives of persons who are classed as idiots or lunatics are as

---

[177] As Williams recognizes, id. at 1671, n. 23, I am probably more lenient than most in relieving ordinary English verbs of any very severe means-restrictions as part of their semantics. See Moore, *supra* n. 1, at 235–8. Even so, the window-sill and trombone- 'playing' killers of the text need do no acts of stabbing in order to cause both a stabbing and a death.

[178] Moore, *supra* n. 1, at 225–35.   [179] Id. at 249.

[180] Williams, 'Caligari', *supra* n. 2, at 1667.

[181] Gilbert Ryle, *The Concept of Mind* (London: Hutcheson, 1949). Ryle realized that this behaviourist interpretation of him was not strictly accurate, but that it was close enough to be a harmless misreading.

rational as those of anyone else. Perhaps only their overt behaviour is disappointing . . .'.[182]

Yet Ryle was wrong, and so is Williams to the extent he shares the argument. We have as good a reason to suppose that human actions form a natural kind of event as we do for mental diseases, physical diseases, intentions, species, elements, and other objects of scientific theorizing. Such natural kinds, including human action, may well have a hidden nature, so that surface indicators (such as behavioural patterns and dispositions) may well mislead about certain examples. My theory of action gives a theory about that hidden nature, one in terms of volitions. To argue that behaviour patterns and dispositions are sufficient for there to be human actions is just to assume that a natural kind theory of action such as mine is false. Assumptions are not arguments, however, and until my theory is falsified it is not much of an argument for somnambulistic behaviour being actions to say that they sure do look like actions.

Of course, perhaps Williams could be construed to be suggesting that such intelligent and environment-responsive patterns of behaviour are possible only if such behaviours are caused by volitions—in which case he would be using my theory to argue that somnambulistic and like behaviours are really actions. But so construed, Williams would then have to confront two points I make in *Act and Crime*. The first is that quite intelligent and responsive routines are guided by initiating and correcting states that are *subpersonal*, that is, no person ever has access or direct control over such states.[183] We know that this is true at some level of guidance for the most conscious and voluntary of actions; there is no reason that it might not be true at *all* levels of guidance for certain sorts of behaviours such as somnambulism. The second point is that when we are asleep we lack just that consciousness that marks the divide between the personal and the subpersonal.[184] Williams would have to argue that there is some other divide besides consciousness, but it is unclear what that would be.

Since this is more Morse's line of attack than Williams's, I shall defer discussion of it until the next subsection. Williams does tell us that somnambulistic behaviour is 'purposive', or 'explained by reasons', and that is the last argument of his that I shall consider.

---

[182] Gilbert Ryle, *The Concept of Mind* (London: Hutcheson, 1949), at 21.
[183] Moore, *supra* n. 1, at 152–3.   [184] Id.

Williams's main reason for his apparent conclusion (despite his occasional metaphysical agnosticism) that the somnambulistic behaviours of Lady MacBeth *are* actions, stems from his view that her behaviours are 'purposive', that they have an 'intentional contour', that 'they are explained by the kinds of reasons by which they would be explained if she were awake', that she did what she did because of her 'aims' while asleep.[185] As Williams concludes:

Her actions are purposively the same as actions that she might have performed when awake, and the same with respect to the reasons that we could ascribe to her. . . . actions of this kind have an intentional or purposive aspect.[186]

I would of course agree that, if Lady MacBeth acted purposely, or acted for a reason when she wandered about asleep, then she did act. Anything that is both F and G is certainly an F, no matter what the predicate represented by F might be. But that of course is not Williams's point. It must be that he sees for Lady MacBeth's behaviours while asleep an explanation by reasons, and from that he concludes that these must have been actions (because only actions are explained by reasons).

The question is thus whether her sleep behaviours are explained by reasons. This is not nearly so easy a question as Williams seems to think. First off we must distinguish justifying reasons from explanatory reasons. Lady MacBeth could have 'had a reason' for her opening of the door in the sense that she had *good* reason to do such a thing. Notice that in this justificatory sense of 'reason', she could also have 'had reason' to open the door even while lying in bed fast asleep. (For example, there was a fire and to survive it was necessary to open the door to ventilate the room.) Only explanatory reasons are of course relevant to assessing whether her opening of the door was an action.

Next, notice that not all desires that causally explain behaviours are explanatory reasons. For example: my desire to beat someone in chess causes my heart rate to go up; my desire to get out of prison causes me to rattle the bars in my cell window in frustration; my night-time desire to wake at a certain time the next morning causes me to wake at that time; etc.[187] Such 'mental cause'

---

[185] Williams, 'Caligari', *supra* n. 2, at 1664. [186] Id. at 1664–5.
[187] I mention these in Moore, *Act and Crime*, *supra* n. 1, at 256. They are explored at greater length in Moore, *Law and Psychiatry: Rethinking the Relationship* (Cambridge: Cambridge University Press, 1984), at 15–18, 291–301.

explanations do not give reasons for action. Typically lacking is both a means/end belief accompanying the desire, such as a belief that if I rattle the bars in my cell window I might escape; also lacking is any executory intention or volition whereby I exercise my agency in response to such desires. The desires simply cause the behaviours, and, as the above examples illustrate, such genesis in desire in no way guarantees that the behaviors are actions.

Behaviours can thus be desire-responsive without being actions. This is true even when the behaviours seem so cleverly to find their way to satisfying the object of the desire which produces them. Suppose, for example, that Freud's explanation of dreams were true: every dream represents the fulfilment of a desire, and dreams are caused by such desires.[188] When Freud famously dreamt that a real-life patient of his, Irma, was improperly injected by a fellow doctor, Otto (who in waking life had reproached Freud for the failure of Freud's cure of Irma), suppose that the dream indeed depicts the fulfilment of Freud's wishes for exoneration and for revenge, and suppose further the dream with that content was caused by these desires. Does this suggest that Freud's dreaming was an action of his, a sort of play put on for his own enjoyment while he was asleep, there not being much else to do? Not in the least. The desire for revenge and for exoneration may have caused the dream, and the dream cleverly respond to these desires by depicting their satisfaction, yet Freud did no action in dreaming.[189]

The same is true of somnambulistic behaviour. There may well be desires causing these behaviours, such behaviours often cleverly respond to such desires by delicate manoeuvring and adjustment, and yet such behaviours are not actions because they are not the *execution* of such desires by an agent forming the appropriate intentions or volitions. And if I am wrong about this, as I allow in *Act and Crime* I could be,[190] it will be because there are such executing intentions and volitions despite the agent's lack of consciousness. That, as I also say in the book,[191] would be to use my theory of action, not to argue against it.

---

[188] Explored by me in Moore, 'The Nature of Psychoanalytic Explanation', in Larry Laudan, ed., *Mind and Medicine: Explanation in Psychiatry and the Biomedical Sciences*, Vol. 8 of the *Pittsburgh Series in the Philosophy And History of Science* (Berkeley: University of California Press, 1983).

[189] Id. at 47–59.   [190] Moore, *Act and Crime, supra* n. 1, at 259.

[191] Id. at 262.

B. Morse on Dissociated 'Actions'

Although sharing some of Bernard Williams's doubts about the ability of any metaphysics to answer the question of whether somnambulistic behaviour is really an action, Stephen Morse is, like Williams, also prepared to go some distance down my road to see what there is to see. Morse begins his discussion 'undecided about the issue' whether somnambulism is an action,[192] and ends his discussion 'still undecided'.[193] Nonetheless, he helpfully probes my case for concluding that somnambulistic behaviours are not actions.

Morse begins by rejecting my challenge to the readers of *Act and Crime* to come up with a theory of action alternative to my volitional theory. He chooses to assess my theory as applied to sleepwalking and other dissociated behaviours.[194] Morse examines two sorts of evidence in assessing the application of my theory to somnambulism, 'the evidence from phenomenology and behaviour'.[195] Behaviourally, Morse thinks the evidence points to volitional causation of sleepwalking movements: 'the sleepwalker's behaviour strongly suggests that a true intention caused the goal-directed bodily movements'.[196] Morse is adverting to the same behavioural facts that impress Williams and, indeed, all of us about this class of behaviours: the responsiveness to the environment, the seeming pursuit of ends and goals. Everyone admits that at least some somnambulism behaviourally looks just like (volitionally guided) actions. Therefore Morse's inference: they are volitionally guided behaviours, that is (on my theory), actions.

Morse recognizes that I am not without a non-volitional explanation for these behavioural facts: 'It may well be that subpersonal agencies within us are achieving quite complex functions in these . . . kinds of case.'[197] Morse, however, raises two doubts about this non-actional explanation of the behavioural facts by me: (1) what further account can I give to 'suggest that subpersonal proto-actions are another natural kind' in addition to the natural kind I posit human actions to be?[198] And (2) what reason is there to think 'that nature has endowed us with functional subpersonal bare

---

[192] Morse, 'Culpability and Control', *supra* n. 18, at 1642. [193] Id. at 1651.
[194] Id. at 1644. [195] Id. at 1645–6. [196] Id. at 1646.
[197] Moore, *Act and Crime*, *supra* n. 1, at 257.
[198] Morse, 'Culpability and Control', *supra* n. 18, at 1645.

intentions to execute more general but still subpersonal intentions'?[199]

Take the second of Morse's points first. Let us first be clear about what needs explaining. I would not say that there are 'subpersonal bare intentions' or 'more general but still subpersonal intentions'. What I think is what I defend in *Act and Crime*: in somnambulism there are 'volition-like states [that] execute certain of our background states of desire, belief, and general intention'.[200] I eschew the idea of subpersonal mental states of intention, desire, or volition, because if they were only subpersonal they would not be mental states, of intention or of anything else. Mental states are states of whole persons.

This bit of precision matters because now what needs explaining can be easily explained. The reason we have to think that some truly subpersonal states guide sleepwalking behaviour is because such states do the micro-guiding of behaviour when we perform normal waking actions. In somnambulism what is missing are the personal executory states of volition that would make such behaviour action. What (at least sometimes) is *not* missing are the desires of the sleepwalker. These are not subpersonal desires or intentions, as Morse attributes to me, but the desire of the sleepwalker in the full sense of the word desire. Given the complexity of certain somnambulistic behaviour, its responsiveness and intelligence, it is reasonable to hypothesize that some of the sleepwalker's desires and general intentions are causing the movements, and that the movements are micro-managed by the same executory machinery (at the subpersonal level) that micro-manages our normal waking movements. That, at least, is my alternative hypothesis explaining the behavioural facts to which Morse adverts.

Seeing this answer to Morse's second point also goes a good way towards seeing the answer to his first. What Morse demands is that I come up with some hidden nature to somnambulistic behaviours that show them to be a natural kind in the same way that I point to volitions as the hidden nature of that natural kind we call human actions. Moreover, Morse's demand is that I come up with a *second* hidden nature for this *second* natural kind. This demand is part and parcel of Morse's and Williams's assumption that my natural

---

[199] Morse, 'Culpability and Control', *supra* n. 18, at 1645.
[200] Moore, *Act and Crime*, *supra* n. 1, at 257.

kind analysis of action cannot countenance fuzzy edges and scalar phenomena.[201]

Yet the account that I give here is intended to capture the close analogousness we all feel between sleepwalking and waking-walking (i.e., walking when that is an action). Sleepwalking shares some of the same goals and desires of the whole person of waking-walking; it also shares the same executory machinery at the sub-personal level. It thus looks a lot like action, much more so than reflex reactions, because it *is* a lot more like action than any reflex-reactions. Nonetheless, sleepwalking is not an action so long as it is not volitionally caused, which on the evidence it does not appear to be.

Morse also questions whether the evidence from phenomenology evidences a lack of volitions in somnambulism. At one point Morse analogizes sleepwalking to highway hypnosis and other forms of habitual behaviour that I concede to be actions. The phenomeno-logical evidence, Morse thinks, is equally lacking in both cases: 'the sleepwalker can't tell you about her phenomenology while she is dissociated, but neither can the admittedly volitional person per-forming habitual action on automatic'.[202] Yet surely there is still a difference between the two classes of cases. The driver 'on auto-matic' can quickly turn his attention to what he is doing if the need to do so arises, while the sleepwalker has no conscious attention to turn on to the details of his movements, being asleep and all. Also, the driver 'on automatic' often can remember what he was doing if asked soon afterwards, whereas the sleepwalker more typically has no remembered phenomenology to report on wakening.

At another point in his discussion of the phenomenological evi-dence for the lack of volitions in somnambulism, Morse focuses on memory. He posits that 'most dissociation cases, such as sleep-walking and fugue states generally, surely involve dynamically unconscious states . . .'.[203] The states Morse has in mind are not volitions, however, but only 'the agent's general intention to kill, assault or the like . . .'.[204] Since Morse also thinks that 'there is no reason to believe that unconscious agents might not recapture their general intentions if exposed to various forms of psychological

---

[201] See the discussion earlier, text at nn. 14–21 *supra*.
[202] Morse, 'Culpability and Control', *supra* n. 18, at 1646.
[203] Id. at 1650.   [204] Id.

methods . . .', he concludes that 'on Moore's own account, unconscious agents may act'.[205]

I would get off this train of inferences before it leaves the station,
for I do not think that most dissociated states involve dynamically
unconscious intentions. The *dynamically* unconscious is composed
of those repressed mental states that Freud told us could be recaptured in memory only by the extraordinary efforts of free association, transference, or some other extraordinary memory-jogging
technique. As I have argued elsewhere in detail,[206] I do not think
these sorts of unconscious mental states underlie much behaviour
(and certainly not *all* behaviour, as Freud thought).

Thus, if Morse were arguing that there are unconscious intentions of the kind I call volitions, I would simply disagree on the
evidence. Rarely if ever does psychoanalytic or any other memory-
jogging practice recover a memory of volitions and action (as
opposed to wish and desire). One of the examples I gave in *Act and
Crime* was the sort of phenomenal evidence Freud produced to
transform his accidental knocking of an ink-well into the action of
'executing' the ink-well: Freud remembered his desire for a new
one. Crucially, however, Freud did not remember executing that
desire into the movement that fulfilled it.[207]

This disagreement is somewhat idle, however, given what Morse
actually appears to be arguing. For Morse is not saying that there
are unconscious volitions, only unconscious general intentions.
These, he thinks, are sufficient to warrant the conclusion that an
unconscious agent acts. But they are not. Recall that on my
account of somnambulism, there are desires and general intentions
that are not dynamically unconscious—they are fully accessible to
the sleepwalker when he is awake. That these non-repressed desires
and intentions get fulfilled by somnambulistic behaviours does not
make those behaviours actions. *A fortiori*, that dynamically unconscious desires and general intentions get fulfilled by somnambulistic behaviours would not make such behaviours actions either.
Needed in either case are the volitions that execute such desires and
general intentions.

Despite these points and counterpoints, it remains true that the
behavioural and phenomenological evidence is far from conclusive

[205] Morse, 'Culpability and Control', *supra* n. 18, at 1651.
[206] Moore, *Law and Psychiatry*, *supra* n. 187, at 249–383; see also ch. 10 *infra*.
[207] Moore, *Act and Crime*, *supra* n. 1, at 251–2.

on the question of whether somnambulistic behaviours are actions.
Missing is a third sort of evidence that is crucial here, physiological evidence showing what brain structures are needed to perform
the functions that volitions perform. Despite the studies on the sup-
plementary motor area of the brain referred to in *Act and Crime*,[208]
our knowledge of the underlying structure is sufficiently scanty
that: (1) the basic question of 'whether volitions exist is very much
an open, scientific question',[209] and (2) 'we at present do not know
enough . . . about the mode of initiation of [somnambulistic behav-
iour] to resolve the issue definitively one way or the other'.[210]
This is why I said earlier that epistemically I am in agreement
with Morse and Williams about the lack of any *certain* answer
here.[211]

Despite the caution, I do go on in *Act and Crime* to give two reasons for placing our 'bets in the direction chosen by the American
Law Institute's Model Penal Code: bet that such movements are
not volitionally caused, and therefore are not actions'.[212] The first
of these reasons stems from the best theory we have about self-
boundaries, one in terms of consciousness: 'Consciousness seems
essential as part of our self-boundaries, so that if *we* (our conscious
selves) are asleep or are otherwise not active, then *we* don't will
anything . . .'[213]

Morse goes after this argument in three ways. First, I do not
'adequately defend why the ability to be aware of one's volitions
. . . is required for action or personhood . . . .'[214] Second, my
criterion is degree-vague because I do not 'indicate how much consciousness is necessary'.[215] Third, while to Morse too 'consciousness does *seem* part of our self-boundaries . . . this does not entail
that the unconscious agent's movements are not actions'.[216] Yet
one can assess the force of all three of these points only if presented
with an alternative theory of how we demarcate the line between
the personal and the subpersonal. In the absence of such an alternative theory, my defence of consciousness is like Churchill's for
democracy: not perfectly satisfactory, perhaps, but better than any
other that has been suggested. What else marks the boundary

---

[208] Id. at 163, n. 126, 165, n. 130.   [209] Id. at 165.
[210] Id. at 259.   [211] See text at nn. 19–20 *supra*.
[212] Moore, *Act and Crime, supra* n. 1, at 259.   [213] Id. at 257.
[214] Morse, 'Culpability and Control', *supra* n. 18, at 1644.   [215] Id.
[216] Id. at 1647.

between our selves and those somatic processes that we never control directly, if it is not consciousness?

Morse voices a fourth rejoinder to my self-boundaries argument and along the way has some fun using one of my well-known thought experiments against me. Morse performs a 'Moorean thought experiment about what emotional reactions a properly moral agent would and should have if, like Mrs Cogdon, she ever so effectively axe-bludgeoned her daughter to death while sleep-walking'.[217] Supposing that a properly constituted Mrs Cogdon would and should feel guilty, Morse infers that therefore she would *be* guilty of something. He further infers that the something she would be guilty of is something *she did*, namely, kill her daughter while asleep.

Mrs Cogdon does have something to feel guilty about, but it is not a supposed action she did while asleep. She should feel guilty for being the kind of person who so hates her daughter, or is so jealous of her, that she wishes her dead. We each have a responsibility for our character[218] and Mrs Cogdon has some lousy aspects to hers, about which she should feel guilty. Yet our responsibility for character is not to be confused with the kind of responsibility the criminal law cares about, which is responsibility for our *actions*.[219] Guilt and felt guilt for bad character is thus quite compatible with Mrs Cogdon not having performed an action when she axed her daughter to death.

It is also true that Mrs Cogdon may feel guilt beyond that guilt she feels for her jealous emotions and wishes. Something with which she was intimately related, namely, her own body, was causally responsible for the death of her daughter. She could feel bad about that. But then, many of us feel bad when things less intimately connected to us than our own bodies are the instrumentalities of others' misfortunes. When our children or our dogs hurt others, we often feel badly too, even when there was no active supervision of them on our part.

My second reason for betting that somnambulistic behaviours are not actions is that the lack of consciousness while asleep pre-

---

[217] Morse, 'Culpability and Control', *supra* n. 18, at 1646.
[218] See ch. 13 *infra* where I argue that morally we each have a responsibility for our character as well as for our actions, even if the latter responsibility is the only proper basis for liability to punishment.
[219] Id.

vents the resolution of conflicting desires and intentions and this resolving function is one of the crucial functions distinctive of volitions.[220] Perhaps because Morse finds this second reason to be 'even more promising',[221] he assembles a phalanx of arguments to defeat it. First off, Morse argues, resolution of conflict cannot be essential to the existence of volitions. This, for two reasons: (a) Even when there is conflict (as in cases of extreme emotional disturbance) and even when there is no resolution of that conflict because the agent's emotions seal off his restraining desires, still there is volitional action;[222] (b) Conflict of desires or of intentions is not ubiquitous,[223] yet even where conflict is lacking we often have volitions and actions. Therefore, for both these reasons, the conflict-resolving function cannot be essential to volitions. Second, there is no specification by me of how many such desires must be sealed off before the conflict-resolving function should be said to be absent.[224] Third, the unavailability of some desires/intentions sounds like an excuse—a kind of ignorance or lack of opportunity excuse—not negation of volition and action.[225] Fourth, there is some kind of conflict-resolving function going on even in somnambulism because 'the dissociated agent is not paralysed by conflict'[226]—he walks in his sleep, etc. Such non-paralysed responsiveness to *an* end at the very least implies a resolution of conflict about the various *means* that might be used to satisfy that end.[227] Moreover, such non-paralysed responsiveness does resolve the conflict of ends because 'the countervailing considerations are not obliterated, but simply out of occurrent awareness'.[228]

Morse's degree-vagueness point (the second above) is only moderately worrisome. Some *substantial amount* of one's desires and intentions must be accessible to an actor before he can be said to resolve the conflict between them with a volition, and when we are asleep only a few are.[229] Morse's third point (about how this looks like an excuse) is also not worrisome. Lack of volition in general

---

[220] Moore, *Act and Crime*, *supra* n. 1, at 258.

[221] Morse, 'Culpability and Control', *supra* n. 18, at 1647.   [222] Id. at 1649–50.

[223] Id. at 1648.   [224] Id.   [225] Id.   [226] Id.   [227] Id.

[228] Id.

[229] Morse puns my requirement that a 'fair sample' of such desires be accessible before the conflict-resolving function can be said to be performed, taking 'fair' to be normative (and thus fitting of his 'normative' theory of coercion). See id. at 1648. My use of the word 'fair' was not normative, referring only to a substantial sampling as in 'fair-to-middling'.

does look like an excuse,[230] so that its excuse-like appearance here should come as no surprise.

Morse's first and fourth points are more troublesome. They reveal that much more needs to be said to render plausible my conflict-resolving function for volitions. With regard to the ubiquitousness of conflict, I do think, unlike Morse, that conflict in our desires is always present because to satisfy any one desire is always at the cost of not then satisfying some other desire. As I put it in *Act and Crime*:

Unless I am an obsessional neurotic about keeping my hair trimmed (to a degree never observed even in mental wards), I desire not only a haircut; I desire many other things as well, the attainment of which can conflict with my getting a haircut on any given occasion.[231]

Our desires are for this reason always prima facie desires only, which is why we need those 'all-out' propositional attitudes of volition and intention.

With regard to the impassioned killer who acts despite not being able to access his restraining desires, I doubt that either Morse or I believe that such individuals lack access to a fair sample of their desires and intentions as they decide what to do.[232] For me this doubt springs from my sense that those 'carried away by their own emotions' typically allow themselves the luxury of 'letting go'. A bad temper for such people is like a well-known negotiating technique whereby one refuses to consider various things that should reasonably restrain one. Whereas sleepwalkers and other dissociated individuals do not have that control over the accessibility of the full range of their desires and intentions. They are thus more likely candidates for persons who lack the resolving functions served by volitions and intentions.

Morse's fourth point claims too much in the way of conflict resolution for such dissociated persons. That they do not suffer a paralysis of indecision is of course true, for their desires do issue in their somnambulistic behaviours. Yet a paralysis of indecision is only one way that conflicts of desires and intentions can fail to be

---

[230] See ch. 12 *infra*. [231] Moore, *Act and Crime*, *supra* n. 1, at 139.

[232] Such doubts are expressed by each of us in Stephen Morse, 'Psychology, Determinism, and Legal Responsibility', in G. B. Melton, ed., *Nebraska Symposium on Motivation 1985*, Vol. 33 (Lincoln: University of Nebraska Press, 1986), 35–85; and for me, in the paper now appearing as ch. 13 *infra*.

resolved. Another and more relevant way is for a desire or intention not to have any input into a decision, for a desire or intention so excluded is not resolved but 'lives on'. Morse's point that there is at least a resolution of conflicting *means* by somnambulists, even if not of *ends*, does not help. The selection of means always involves trade offs against other ends certain means will frustrate, and it is precisely conflict with those other ends that is not resolved by any 'decisions' made while asleep. Morse's point that conflict with these ends has been 'resolved, albeit on "thin" grounds' (because such ends are 'not obliterated'),[233] is not true. Ignoring certain desires or intentions is not the same as considering them and either rejecting them or integrating them into one's decision about what to do now. The conflict-resolving function of volition is not performed simply by behavioural output satisfying one pole of desires in conflict.

Each of these points deserves greater consideration than I have been able to give them here. I suspect that with such greater consideration Morse and I would be able to truly resolve any conflict that has remained, fusing our two sets of conflicting beliefs into one coherent set. But that is because we are not disassociated—that is, we communicate with each other regularly—allowing our conflict-resolution function to operate smoothly.

VI. VOLITIONS AS THE ESSENTIAL BEGINNINGS OF ACTIONS

A. Volitions in Analyses of Action

A number of my commentators have doubts about volitions as the unique instigators of actions. Some, such as Robert Audi,[234] see clearly that I have two different needs for volitions in *Act and Crime*: (1) to give an analysis of what actions are partly in terms of volitions; and (2) to complete the rational explanation of the changes we effect in the world by our actions. For the first need I use volitions to demonstrate the nature of the natural kind, human action; giving this theory about action's essential nature is as close as I come to analysing (or defining) the concept of human action. For the second need I use volitions to complete the causal chain

---

[233] Morse, 'Culpability and Control', *supra* n. 18, at 1648.
[234] Robert Audi, 'Volition, Intention, and Responsibility', *University of Pennsylvania Law Review*, Vol. 142 (1994), 1675–704, at 1675, 1685–7.

that begins with belief/desire sets, proceeds through more general intentions, and then proceeds through those less general intentions I call volitions, to the bodily movements and their effects in the world. Volitions for the second need are part of my explanation of human behaviour, a role independent of any they play in analysing action.

Separating these two needs for volitions in my theory is important because some worries about my volitional theory go only to my use of volitions in the analysis of action, not to my use of them in explaining behaviour. Jennifer Hornsby, for example, concludes that 'volitions must . . . be viewed as figments, filling an imagined lacuna'.[235] She finds volitions unnecessary, however, only because she sees my introduction of volitions as a substitute for another definition of action (namely, her own in terms of the things people do intentionally) that makes no mention of volitions.[236] Such satisfaction with alternative ways of defining the kind, action, do not of course touch upon the question of whether volitions have explanatory roles.

My main concern here is with the explanatory role of volitions, since that was the concern of most of my commentators. Still, it is worth pausing long enough to say why Hornsby's kind of definition does not obviate the need for volitions even if we restrict ourselves to an analysis of action. Hornsby's definition of action is: 'an *action* is a person's doing something intentionally', or, as she alternatively rephrases it, 'an action is a person's doing something in *attempting* to do something'.[237] These definitions are harmless enough, but they do not tell us very much. They are part and parcel of the older, ordinary language style philosophy that produced 'conceptual analyses' like, an action is intentional when 'a certain sense of the question, "Why?", is given application . . .'.[238]

This playing around between near synonyms does not tell us much, which is why it is relatively harmless. One of the harms that it cannot do is to rule out theories about the nature of the kind of thing to which words like 'action' refer. While ordinary language philosophy has historically enjoyed a curious kind of satisfaction with analyses like Anscombe's and Hornsby's, science has

---

[235] Hornsby, 'Aberration', *supra* n. 19, at 1732.   [236] Id. at 1731–2.

[237] Jennifer Hornsby, 'On What's Intentionally Done', in S. Shute, J. Gardner, and J. Horder, eds., *Action And Value In Criminal Law* (Oxford: Oxford University Press, 1993), 55, 60; see also Hornsby, 'Aberration', *supra* n. 19, at 1727.

[238] G. E. M. Anscombe, *Intention* (2d edn., Cornell University Press, 1963), at 9.

demanded more. We need to know what sort of things actions are, not just how native English speakers use 'action', 'intentionally', 'attempt', 'try', and 'Why?' Volitions may not be the right answer, but no amount of discovery of near synonyms for 'action' can show that the question to which volitions purport to be the answer is a question that need not be asked.

B. Volitions in Explanations of Behaviour

Most of what Bratman, Audi, Corrado, and Hornsby have to say about volitions goes to their explanatory role, so I shall devote the rest of this section to that. As Bratman notices,[239] my argument for volitions was in two steps: first, I argued for the distinctiveness of intention from both wants and beliefs;[240] second, I argued for the view that general intentions were not enough to explain actions but that much more concrete intentions—'volitions'—were also needed.[241] All of my commentators zeroed in on the second of these steps, either leaving the first for another occasion or explicitly agreeing with it.[242]

1. Audi's Alternative Action-Elicitors Of the rich array of considerations offered here, let me pick but a few for comment. Consider first Robert Audi's suggestion that volitions may not be explanatorily necessary.[243] Audi acknowledges that there must be some kind of 'action-elicitors' that are caused by more general intentions and which in turn cause bodily movements. And sometimes it is plausible, he thinks, that these action-elicitors are events matching my description of volitions. But most of the time Audi would substitute non-volitional items as the more likely candidates for the job of getting us moving: either perceptions, thoughts, decisions, a change in the balance of motivational forces, the overcoming of

---

[239] Michael Bratman, 'Moore on Intention and Volition', *University of Pennsylvania Law Review*, Vol. 142 (1994), 1705–18, at 1706.

[240] Moore, *Act and Crime*, *supra* n. 1, at 137–49.   [241] Id. at 149–55.

[242] See particularly Bratman, 'Intention and Volition', *supra* n. 239, at 1706. I am currently uncertain as to Audi's views on this. In writing *Act and Crime*, I assumed Audi was a reductionist about intention, reducing it to a combination of beliefs and desires. See Audi, 'Intending', *The Journal of Philosophy*, Vol. 70 (1973), 387–403, reprinted without change in Robert Audi, *Action, Intention, and Reason* (Ithaca, NY: Cornell University Press, 1993). Now, however, in both his present contribution and in ch. 3 of *Action, Intention, and Reason* Audi seems more sympathetic to the distinctiveness of intention.

[243] Audi, 'Volition, Intention', *supra* n. 234, at 1690–3.

inertia, or the striking-as-desirable-for-its-own-sake the doing of some action.[244] This seemingly more heterogeneous list of action-initiators is part of what Audi terms his 'guidance and control model' for explaining behaviour.[245] This model is said have two differences with my 'executive thrust model' of volitions: (1) Audi's model posits a release of energy, as from a compressed spring, whereas mine has the volition communicate its energy, as in the firing of a bullet;[246] and (2) Audi's eliciting events need have no Intentional content, 'given that the relevant intentions and other attitudes already have content sufficient to direct the action . . .'.[247]

Audi's general temptation is a very old one. It is the same temptation as gave rise to William James's ideo-motor theory of action, according to which action-initiators are 'images' of actions.[248] The temptation stems from a perceived greater respectability within psychology for cognitive than for conative mental states. The temptation is thus to replace thrusting things with seeing and releasing things. The temptation is succumbed to by some physiologists as well, who can imagine volitions as vetoers of actions even if they cannot imagine them as initiators of actions.[249] Yet the temptation is one to be resisted. As Myles Brand has noted, 'it is a deep insight of folk psychology that action is initiated only by events with non cognitive, motivational features.'[250] Our phenomenology at least since Plato has suggested to us that the states that move us to action are quite different than the states that represent the world to us as we wish or believe it to be. While our phenomenology could certainly be wrong about this, we have every reason to place our bets with it until science shows us that we should not.

Leaving Audi's general model for his more particular list of six substitutes for volitions, I find the list problematic first, because of its very heterogeneity. As Audi himself has recently noticed:

[O]ne powerful reason to adopt a volitional theory [is that] it supplies a causal factor which *genetically unifies* actions in terms of a common kind of origin, even if not necessarily its ultimate origin, in the psychology of the agent.[251]

---

[244] Audi, 'Volition, Intention', *supra* n. 234, at 1690–3.   [245] Id. at 1696–701.
[246] Id. at 1698.   [247] Id.
[248] See Moore, *Act and Crime*, *supra* n. 1, at 146–7, for citations and discussion.
[249] Benjamin Libet, 'Unconscious Cerebral Initiative and the Role of Conscious Will in Voluntary Action', *Behavioral And Brain Sciences*, Vol. 8 (1985), 529–66.
[250] Myles Brand, *Intending And Acting* (Cambridge, Mass.: MIT Press, 1984), 147.
[251] Audi, *Action, Intention, and Reason*, *supra* n. 242, at 79.

Audi's six different factors do not have this virtue, as he would no doubt acknowledge.

Audi's list also seems to take at face value the idiomatic things people often say when referring to action-elicitors. He is, that is, here unwilling to regiment these seemingly diverse sayings by a common referent. If we were to so respect idiomatic usage about the practical syllogism, it would, I suspect, usually be said to have only one premise. For rarely do we explain why we went downtown by saying *both*, 'because I desired to buy some groceries' *and* 'because I believed that, if I went downtown, I would buy some groceries'. More idiomatic is: 'because I wanted some groceries' or 'because I believed that groceries were easily available there'. More idiomatic still would be to report facts, not desires or beliefs, as in: 'because a new grocery store opened up down there'. The diversity of items cited as reasons in idiomatic, everyday discourse should not discourage us from unifying our motivational analysis in terms of our standard, two-premised practical syllogism. The same is true for what we casually say about immediate action elicitors.

2. Bratman's Rationality Constraints on What Can Be an Intention

Bratman's disagreement with me is a narrow one. He and I agree on what he accurately labels as the 'distinctiveness of intention' from desire and beliefs. We also agree that some action-initiators are necessary if the execution of our more general intentions into the appropriate bodily movements that execute them is not just magical. And I think we agree that these action-initiators are mental states—what Bratman calls 'executive representations',[252] or elsewhere 'endeavorings'[253]—and not merely subpersonal routines of our central nervous system. Where we disagree is on whether these action-initiators are a species of *intention* or not.

Bratman recognizes that I might argue for characterizing volitions as intentions on what he calls the 'simple view' that to intentionally do A is to intend to do A.[254] Such an argument would go like this: any bit of behaviour, to be an action at all, must be intentional under some basic description like 'moving one's fingers'; yet if I intentionally moved my fingers, then (on the simple view) I

[252] Bratman, 'Intention and Volition', *supra* n. 239, at 1717.
[253] Michael Bratman, *Intentions, Plans, and Practical Reason* (Cambridge, Mass.: Harvard University Press, 1987), at 130.
[254] Bratman, 'Intention and Volition', *supra* n. 239, at 1713.

intended to move my fingers; since such intent has the same object and function as what I call 'volitions', we have every reason to identify such intent with volitions. Bratman then seeks to undercut the simple view and thus, this easy route to justifying my categorization of volitions as intentions.

Yet I do not rely on the simple view to argue that volitions are a species of intention. For one thing, if one has decided, as Bratman and the criminal law have, to call actions done knowingly as having been done *intentionally*, then one certainly does not want the simple view. I may know that my act of freeing some prisoners will have the side consequence of killing some guards. But I do not intend to kill the guards. However, in such cases we may not be prepared to say we killed the guards, either intentionally or unintentionally, in which event this argument against the simple view will not work.

Bratman's real complaint against the simple view lies elsewhere. Bratman rejects the simple view mainly because it would require abandonment of one or both of two constraints on the rationality of intentions that Bratman finds his planning theory of intentions cannot do without. The first is that intentions must be consistent with beliefs: I cannot rationally intend A while believing A is impossible. The second is that intentions 'agglomerate': If I intend A, and if I intend B, then (if rational) I intend (A and B).

My own view of these rationality restraints on intention is that their plausibility varies with the level of generality of the intentions under view. Since Audi sees the same point, let me use his words. With regard to intention/belief consistency:

What Moore could say, then, is that while *long-range*, *future-directed intentions*, the kind most important in planning, must meet the relevant belief condition, *bare intentions*, the kind plausibly identified with volition, need not.[255]

And with regard to intention agglomerativity:

Conjunction [of intention] is to be expected above all when there is some occasion to get the two objects of the propositional attitude in question before the mind at once, and this is less likely with a momentary state than with a long-term one, such as an intention to pay a bill, or to educate one's children.[256]

---

[255] Audi, 'Volition, Intention', *supra* n. 234, at 1681.　　[256] Id. at 1683.

The point is that it is the planning function of intention that drives Bratman to his two restrictions, yet these restrictions are less and less necessary to successful planning as intentions become more and more specific. There is no reason anywhere up or down this scale to deny the honorific, 'intention', to those states that together execute belief/desire sets.

To some extent Bratman already must recognize this possibility of successful planning despite failures of agglomerativity and of intention/belief consistency *at some level*. For he concedes that executive representations, or what I call volitions, do execute more general intentions into the bodily movement programmes that satisfy them. And he concedes that agglomerativity and intention/belief consistency do not hold for these executory states. So planning obviously succeeds despite the failures of these least general executory states to conform to his two rationality constraints. All he need recognize now is that some degree of these failures could also be true of more general intentions, even if to a lesser degree as the intentions become more general (and thus, more central to planning).

3. Corrado on the Superfluity of Requiring Volitions for Liability

Corrado thinks that framing the voluntary act requirement of the criminal law in terms of volitions adds nothing to what is already required by the criminal law *mens rea* requirements. As he puts it, 'the requirement that what is done be volitional . . . is entailed by the *mens rea* requirement'.[257]

I am unsure what Corrado wishes to argue here. Does he want to say that the voluntary act and *mens rea* requirements are one and the same requirement? Or does he want to say that the requirement that there be a voluntary act is superfluous because all crimes require *mens rea*, and if the *mens rea* requirement is satisfied then the voluntary act requirement must be satisfied too? And under either of these readings, is it my volitional interpretation of the voluntary act requirement that causes it to be identical or redundant to the *mens rea* requirement, or are the two requirements so related

---

[257] Corrado, 'Act Requirement', *supra* n. 55, at 1544. Elsewhere Corrado says that the requirement that there be a volition 'is not independent' but 'follows from *mens rea* (id. at 1533), that 'there is no separate requirement of a volitional act' because it 'duplicates' the condition already secured by *mens rea* (id. at 1018), and that 'there is no independent volition requirement' (id. at 1546).

even under alternative interpretations of the voluntary act requirement? This latter point determines whether Corrado is criticizing my volitional account, or whether his observations are about criminal law doctrine more generally. I am more interested in the argument if it is directed against my volitional interpretation of the voluntary act requirement, so I shall so construe it.

I find very curious what Corrado means by 'the *mens rea* requirement'. He apparently thinks that crimes of general intent, specific intent, recklessness, negligence, and strict liability all have a common '*mens rea* requirement': 'the act must be intentional under some description or there cannot be a conviction. I take the need for that to be a *mens rea* requirement.'[258] Thus all crimes, in this sense, are crimes having as their *mens rea* the requirement of intention.

Corrado is insistent that his identity/redundancy point hinges on this sense of 'the *mens rea* requirement'. But if this is what Corrado means by *mens rea*, it is very easy to show an identity between his '*mens rea* requirement' and the voluntary act requirement, under any interpretation of the latter. For Corrado's supposed *mens rea* requirement is just another way of stating the voluntary act requirement. Intentionality in Corrado's sense is a criterion for action itself, as Donald Davidson[259] and, more recently, Jennifer Hornsby[260] have shown. As Davidson used to put it, 'to be an act at all is to be intentional under some description'.[261]

The voluntary act requirement is of course duplicative of the *mens rea* requirement when the latter is construed to be no more than the requirement that an *action* has been performed. But *mens rea* does not mean, 'that an action has been performed'. Like Humpty Dumpty, Corrado can of course mean what he pleases by '*mens rea*', but he cannot make the phrase mean what he pleases. The phrase means something quite different than what he means by it. '*Mens rea*' means some mental state of intention or belief having as its object a particular description of an action (not *any* description), or that substitute for true mental states we call negligence.

---

[258] Corrado, 'Act Requirement', *supra* n. 55, at 1017.

[259] Donald Davidson, *Essays on Actions and Events* (Oxford: Oxford University Press, 1980) at 46–50.

[260] Hornsby, 'On What's Intentionally Done', *supra* n. 237, at 55–60.

[261] Davidson, *Actions and Events*, *supra* n. 259, at 46.

Consider the *mens rea* requirements of intention or belief, where presumably Corrado's point is strongest. Suppose three crimes: assault with intent to kill, knowing importation of a controlled substance into the United States, and reckless (or 'depraved heart') murder. The voluntary act requirement requires that the accused intends that his body move at all; the *mens rea* requirements are, respectively, that the accused: intends his movements to cause death, believes that the goods he is transporting are controlled substance and that his movements will cause them to cross the border into the United States, or believes that his movements substantially risk death. Such intentions or beliefs required to satisfy the *mens rea* requirements of such statutes do not have at all the same objects as do the intentions (or volitions) to cause bodily movements (which is what the voluntary act requirement requires on my interpretation).

Since all of this was gone into in some detail in *Act and Crime*,[262] I am loath to interpret Corrado only to be making the point he seems to say he is making. Perhaps he should be interpreted to be saying that *mens rea* means the requirements of intention, belief and negligence just illustrated, but that if this (admittedly distinct) requirement is satisfied so too must be the voluntary act requirement. Yet this latter point does not go after my volitional interpretation of the voluntary act requirement specifically; it purports to apply to that requirement generically, however interpreted. Moreover, this point is pretty obviously false insofar as it applies to crimes of negligence and strict liability (where there is no *mens rea* requirement of intent or belief). The only way Corrado can hide the obvious falseness of this second interpretation of his thesis is by going back to the first interpretation, where he pretends that the *mens rea* requirement for crimes of negligence and strict liability require that the act be intentional under some description. Yet again: it is not the *mens rea* requirements of negligence or strict liability that require this; it is the voluntary act requirement.

Even with respect to crimes requiring intent or belief for their *mens rea*, the second interpretation of Corrado's thesis is false. As I argued in my discussion with Morse, it may sometimes be true that somnambulists have desires and general intentions and their sleep-behaviour is responsive to those mental states. Thus, some

---

[262] Moore, *Act and Crime*, *supra* n. 1, at 172–3.

somnambulists may satisfy a *mens rea* requirement of intent or belief. Yet what such somnambulists lack is what the act requirement requires: those volitions that execute their desires and intentions into actions.

4. Some Objections Not Here Reconsidered   These four objections to volitions of Hornsby, Audi, Bratman, and Corrado do not exhaust all the worries one might have about such items. Audi, for example, also worries whether volitions are as relevant to responsibility as I claim, proposing long-term intentions and wants as more relevant to responsibility because more constitutive of who we are.[263] Hornsby also voices her doubts that the subpersonal science will turn out in a way the verifies the existence of volitions.[264] Hornsby and Audi voice what Audi calls the 'phenomenological objection' to volitions, namely, there do not seem to be enough of them around in our experience to do the work I demand of them.[265] And Corrado raises his Chisholm-inspired incompatibilism to raise doubts about the need for a volitional account when a requirement that the choice be free would do the trick.[266] Since I have said pretty much what I had to say to each of these points in *Act and Crime*, or in other chapters of this book,[267] I shall say no more about them here.

VII. GOLDMAN, TROPES, AND FINE-GRAINED ACTION INDIVIDUATION

Alvin Goldman was the only one of my commentators to tackle the difficult problem of action-individuation, both as a metaphysical

---

[263] Audi, 'Volition, Intention', *supra* n. 234, at 1703.

[264] Hornsby, 'Aberration', *supra* n. 19, at 1735, n. 53.

[265] Id. at 1734–5; Audi, 'Volition, Intention', *supra* n. 234, at 1684–6.

[266] Corrado, 'Act Requirement', *supra* n. 55, at 1554.

[267] Namely: (1) that long-term intentions are no doubt more relevant to responsibility for one's *character*, but character-responsibility is not the relevant kind of responsibility for punishment (Moore, *Act and Crime*, *supra* n. 1, at 52–4; also *infra*, ch. 13; (2) that it is an open question how the science of the subpersonal will turn out, although I am probably more optimistic about that science matching the concepts of the folk psychology than is Hornsby (Moore, *Act and Crime*, *supra* n. 1, at 130–3, 163–5); (3) that the phenomenological evidence for volitions is better than Audi and Hornsby allow, if one takes preconscious mental states and mental states needed to learn routines into account (id. at 150–5); and (4) incompatibilist metaphysics cannot replace anything because it is false. Id. at 73–7; *infra* ch. 12.

matter and with regard to the law's need to deal with this issue.[268] Like me, Goldman finds the metaphysics of action to be of relevance to legal issues. More specifically, we both think that the metaphysics of action individuation has some bearing on the criminal law doctrines dealing with the spatio-temporal locations of criminal acts and on those doctrines dealing with double jeopardy. Since Goldman's metaphysics differs considerably from mine, his clear and succinct paper provides an instructive contrast to the approach taken in *Act and Crime*.

Goldman's is a single-instance trope metaphysics for all events, human actions included. Tropes are instances of properties.[269] Of some white dog, we should distinguish: (1) the object-particular, the dog, which *exemplifies* whiteness; from (2) the abstract universal, whiteness, which all white things share; from (3) the abstract particular or property-instance, or 'trope', which is the particular *instance* of whiteness that this dog possesses. An event-type such as killing is for Goldman an abstract universal, whereas an event-token such as Jones's act of killing Smith yesterday is an instance of the universal, killing. The 'fineness of grain' of Goldman's metaphysics comes from his insistence that an event is only a single property-instance, not a constellation of such instances.[270] Thus, what my 'coarse-grained' metaphysics would identify as one event, his would identify as being as many events as there are properties instantiated. The act-token, Jones killing of Smith yesterday, is different than the act-token, Jones moving his finger on the trigger, Jones firing the gun, Jones shooting Smith—even though Jones killed Smith by (what I would call) one single act having all of these properties.

In *Act and Crime* I recognized that I could not hope to deal adequately with all the arguments, pro and con, raised by the literature on the fine-grained versus the coarse-grained versus the moderately fine-grained views.[271] In the Symposium Goldman helpfully remedied this deficiency (at least as seen from his side of the street). I shall again eschew dealing with the full range of

[268] Goldman, 'Action and Crime', *supra* n. 36.

[269] Moore, *Act and Crime*, *supra* n. 1, at 68–9. See generally Keith Campbell, *Abstract Particulars* (Cambridge, Mass.: Blackwell, 1990).

[270] On single-instanced versus multiple-instanced trope accounts of events, see Goldman, 'Action and Crime', *supra* n. 36, at 1569; Moore, *Act and Crime*, *supra* n. 1, at 369–70.

[271] Moore, *Act and Crime*, *supra* n. 1, at 297.

arguments that Goldman addresses. In particular, I shall not respond to the 'by-relation' or the 'adverbial modifiers' arguments. This, not because these are not important arguments, but because they are sufficiently complicated issues that a great deal needs to be said, not all of which I at present know that I want to say. So I shall restrict myself to the issues Goldman raises in response to arguments of mine in *Act and Crime*. These are fruitfully grouped into three sets of issues, separately discussed below.

A. The Problem of Causes and Effects

Like most arguments on this issue, the arguments Goldman advances from causal relations involving events appeal to the Indiscernability of Identicals Principle, which states that identicals share all the same properties.[272] Goldman and I both explicitly assume that Leibniz's Law cannot be questioned for extensional contexts and that statements of causal relations are extensional.[273] Thus, the problem Goldman puts to me: an act that on my coarse view is but one act-token nonetheless seems to have different causal properties, depending on how it is described. Two of Goldman's examples:

1. Ned's playing the piano both puts Dolly to sleep and wakes Molly up. These being but three different ways of referring to a single act-token on my view, then if it is true that Ned's playing the piano caused Molly to wake up, then it must also be true that Ned's putting Dolly to sleep caused Molly to wake up. Yet, Goldman concludes, Ned's putting Dolly to sleep did not cause Molly's awakening, and therefore these are not merely different descriptions of one and the same act-token; since they have different *effects*, they must be different act-tokens.[274]

2. Dretske's car moving down the highway has a number of different aspects: it is moving, it is moving at 63 m.p.h., and it is moving in a certain direction. All just one event on my coarse view. Yet what aspect of this event we use to describe it makes a difference as to the truth of what caused it: Dretske's 'heavy foot is responsible for the speed, the dirty carburetor for the

---

[272] Moore, *Act and Crime*, *supra* n. 1, at 283, n. 9.
[273] Id.; Goldman, 'Action and Crime', *supra* n. 36, at 1573, n. 23.
[274] Goldman, 'Action and Crime', *supra* n. 36, at 1564–5.

intermittent pauses, and the potholes in the road for the teeth-jarring vertical component of the movement.'[275] Goldman thus concludes that these cannot be descriptions of one event, but must refer to separate events, for each has a different *cause*.

My general response in *Act and Crime* to this problem was to say that the events in such examples do have the same effects and causes, no matter how such events are described; but that some descriptions will sound odd because of redundancy: to say that Jones's killing of Smith caused Smith's death is pragmatically odd because we already know that Smith's death occurred by the way the act of Jones is described in the subject of the sentence (as a killing of Smith). To repeat in the predicate information already contained in the subject of a sentence always sounds odd.[276]

Goldman accurately points out that this explanation does not work for his piano example or for many other examples. So Goldman issues me a challenge:

[N]o appeal to repetition can explain the oddity in question. Of course, Moore may not restrict pragmatic oddity to repetition, but he does not identify any other source of pragmatic oddity that would cover the present case.[277]

Supplying such a source will be my present task.

Causal talk like saying, 'Ned's playing the piano *caused* Molly to wake up' or 'Dretske's heavy foot *caused* his car to move at 63 m.p.h.', is fraught with ambiguity. When we use 'cause', we may mean to describe singular causal relations between event-tokens or we may mean to describe causal generalizations relating to event-types.[278] Since on my coarse-grained view we individuate types very differently than tokens, things will sound very odd if we mean *token* but are taken to mean, *type*.

Take Dretske's car moving down the highway. There is only one event-token here, on my view. Therefore, anything that causes that event-token under one description of the latter also causes it (that same event-token) under any other. Dretske's heavy foot, his

---

[275] Id. at 1567, quoting Fred Dretske, *Explaining Behavior* (Cambridge, Mass.: MIT Press, 1988), 30.

[276] Moore, *Act and Crime, supra* n. 1, at 289, n. 19.

[277] Goldman, 'Action and Crime', *supra* n. 36, at 1565–6.

[278] See, e.g., Audi, 'Volition, Intention', *supra* n. 234, at 1694.

dirty carburettor, and the potholes all cause one event-token, the movement of his car at that time. What makes it *sound odd* to say things like, 'Dretske's lead-footing the accelerator caused the teeth-jarring motion', is the way we pick out the motion event. By picking it out with the description, 'teeth-jarring motion', we may easily be taken not to be referring to the event-token of movement; rather, we may seem to be (and in fact, usually are) referring to *properties* of one event-token as we explain with a causal generalization another *property* of another event-token. And it is just false that the *type* of event constituted by the property, depressed accelerator, causally explains the *type* of event constituted by the property, teeth-jarring vertical moving. There is no true generalization connecting these two types of events.

This explanation also fits Goldman's first kind of example. Ned's putting Dolly to sleep does cause Molly to wake up. We can remove any oddity by disambiguating the expression to make clear we are referring to act-tokens and the singular causal relations between them, not act-types and the causal generalizations that hold between them. 'The act which caused Dolly to go to sleep also caused Molly to wake up', does not sound odd at all because we have made clear that we are talking about an act-token doing some singular causing. The original way of putting it does not get rid of this ambiguity, so we could be taken to mean: 'it was a property of Ned's act, namely, that it put Dolly to sleep, that causally explains another property of Ned's act, namely, that it woke Molly up'. And this would be a peculiar thing to say since, on Goldman's stipulated facts, it is obviously false.

My account here of course relies on there being a distinction between statements describing singular causal relations between event-tokens and statements giving causal explanations in terms of true generalizations holding between event-types. Part of what determines whether such a distinction is viable is what one takes singular causal relations to be, if they exist at all. The analysis given in *Act and Crime* rejects the counterfactual interpretation of causation.[279] One reason to do so is precisely because such an analysis, which is very popular, elides the distinction between singular causal relations and causal generalizations. Counterfactuals are usually taken to deal with types of events, here asking, if an event of one

---

[279] Moore, *Act and Crime*, supra n. 1, at 268–75.

type did not occur, would an event of some other type also not have occurred?[280] Such an analysis of causation does not allow me my distinction, which is (another) good reason to reject it.

If we recognize the distinction and the latent ambiguity it infuses into many causal statements, then we have a ready explanation for Goldman's apparent counter-examples. Make clear that what is wanted in such examples are explanations[281] (and thus, generalizations about types), and we coarse folks would *not* say all the odd things Goldman attributes to us because they are obviously false. But make clear that what is wanted in such examples is not explanation but singular causal relations, then we coarse folks will say all the odd things Goldman wants us to say, but they will not sound odd any longer because everyone will be clear about what is meant.

Goldman has partially anticipated my response here, insofar as he foresees that 'the coarse-grained approach can say that there is but a single event which has many *aspects* or *facets*'.[282] Goldman urges that this will not help because the coarse-grained approach will still need some finely individuated 'facet-instances' to both cause and be caused by other 'facet-instances', or tropes. The facets themselves, which are abstract universals, will not do, 'for properties themselves do not participate in causal relations'.[283] Since we thus need property-instances to stand in these causal relations, we might as well call these finely individuated things, 'event-tokens'.

What Goldman overlooks (or perhaps rejects) is the difference between the causal generalizations used in giving causal explanations and statements of singular causal relations. Armed with that distinction, we have no need of any finely individuated things to stand in singular causal relations; rather, all we need are the properties themselves and the types they constitute to make true our causal generalizations. So armed, all we now need is to keep clear

---

[280] As I argue in ch. 8 *infra*, if counterfactuals are not taken to be about types, but are taken to be about tokens, then they would not be extensional. See also Davidson, *Actions and Events*, *supra* n. 259, at 157.

[281] Dretske is plain that it is explanation that interests him: '[W]hen the business at hand is explanation . . . there may be a variety of different things to explain about any given piece of behavior. Breathing is one thing; breathing deeply, in a person's ear, and when the person asked you to stop, are all different things and may, accordingly, all have different explanations.' Dretske, *Explaining Behavior*, *supra* n. 275, at 30. As long as we take 'things to explain' to be aspects or properties of act-tokens (or Hornsby's 'things done'), and not separate act-tokens, Dretske is surely correct about the possibility of separate explanations for separate 'things'.

[282] Goldman, 'Action and Crime', *supra* n. 36, at 1572.   [283] Id. at 1573.

what we are talking about when we talk about events, causes, and effects: are we talking about singular causal relations or causal generalizations? Where we are clear, we will not sound odd.[284]

B. The Spatio-Temporal Locations of Actions

Goldman remarks that I 'might be surprised to find a fine-grained theorist willing to yield ground on the spatio-temporal questions' of action location.[285] I am. Goldman is right that it never occurred to me that tropists about events would take what he calls the 'short view' of when and where such events occur.[286] Being surprised in this way does not leave me feeling as though I had gained some ground, however, as Goldman suggests. Rather, I feel a bit like the French in 1939, who having built a very nice wall of defences then saw the Germans disdain any frontal assault in favour of a flanking manoeuvre. It is only small comfort that Goldman thinks it was a 'reasonable'[287] wall to have built, given the deployment of enemy forces at the time it was built.

I am intrigued by Goldman's suggestion that a property-instance theory of events can adopt the short view of spatio-temporal location for events. This means that Goldman thinks that when Jones kills Smith by moving his (Jones's) finger at t_1, which causes an arrow to hit Smith at t_2, which causes Smith to die at t_3, the killing trope occurs only at t_1 and not over the interval, t_1–t_3, nor at t_3 alone.

It is not clear how we locate tropes. Goldman suggests that 'the temporal span or duration of an act-token [property-instance on his view] must be the period over which the agent exemplifies that act-type in question'.[288] For killings, we thus should ask when does the 'agent *exemplify* the act-type of killing'?[289] Yet my sense is that Jones becomes a killer of Smith only when Smith dies, for unless Smith dies, Jones is no killer. Jones by his act at t_1 can *become* a killer at t_3 if Smith dies then, but how can Jones *be* a killer at t_1 with no dead victim?

Another way to raise this query is by imagining that Jones moves his fingers at t_1 which causes the striking of Smith with the arrow at t_2, but that Smith does not die. If everything is the same in this

---

[284] At least to other metaphysicians. I think Sam Freeman thinks we all sound pretty odd. See text at nn. 36–7, *supra*.

[285] Goldman, 'Action and Crime', *supra* n. 36, at 1583.   [286] Id. at 1581.

[287] Id.   [288] Id. at 1582.   [289] Id.

revised scenario except for Smith's death at t_3, do we want to say that Jones exemplifies killing at t_1 but that it was a defeasible exemplification in the sense that, when it becomes clear that Smith will not die from the arrow, Jones will cease exemplifying the act-type of killing?

My own coarse-grained metaphysics of events allows me to adopt the short view here without difficulty. Jones's act of killing is done once he moves his fingers at t_1. Jones becomes a killer, and his act acquires the property of being a killing, only when Smith dies at t_3.[290] Goldman cannot say this, because for Goldman there is no one act of Jones that can later acquire the property of being a killing; the trope of being a killing is, on Goldman's fine-grained metaphysics, the act, and such a trope of killing cannot itself later acquire the property of being a killing.

Perhaps Goldman should retract his linkage between when an exemplifying of killing takes place with when an instantiation of killing takes place. Goldman like most tropists thinks that there is a 'subtle but important distinction . . . between *exemplifying* a property and *being an instance of* (or *case of*) a property'.[291] Objects like Jones exemplify properties like killing, whereas tropes are the instances of the act-type, killing. Goldman could then say that Jones exemplifies killing when he becomes a killer (which is at t_3 when Smith dies), but that Jones's act of killing (which is a trope) instantiates killing only at t_1. This would give Goldman the short view of actions, in other words, without having to say that actors are killers before anyone dies.

The problem with this move is that if one divorces the locations of property instances from the locations of objects exemplifying those properties, I do not know how one could locate tropes at all. Take the white dog of my earlier example. We cannot use whiteness to give location to this instance of whiteness, because whiteness is an abstract universal. If we give up the object exemplifying whiteness, the dog, as our locator, how could we assign the whiteness-instance possessed by the dog any location at all? If the whiteness trope does not come into existence only when the dog begins to exemplify the property of being white, I would not know how to locate the trope temporally. The same quandary would beset any

[290] Moore, *Act and Crime*, *supra* n. 1, at 285–6.
[291] Goldman, 'Action and Crime', *supra* n. 36, at 1568.

attempt to divorce the temporal location of killing instances from the exemplifying of killing done by people like Jones. But again, Jones exemplifies killing only when Smith dies.[292]

C. No Double Jeopardy for the Same Tropes?

Goldman is fascinated as am I about the intersection of action theory with the double jeopardy requirement of criminal law. He seeks to suggest how his different metaphysics of action yields a more comprehensible legal requirement than my coarse-grained view.

On my metaphysics of action there are two distinct questions that must be asked and answered in any double jeopardy case: (1) is the defendant who has performed one (coarse-grained) act-token nonetheless guilty of several offences (i.e., prohibited types of actions)? and (2) has the defendant who is guilty of but one offence (again prohibited type of action) nonetheless been guilty of having done that offence more than once?[293] In my schema, one must individuate types of actions (offences) to answer the first question, and one must individuate offence-tokens to answer the second question.

Goldman's fine-grained metaphysics may make it seem as if there is only one question to ask here, which is: how many offence-tokens did the accused do? Since an offence-token for Goldman is an instance of the conjunctive property described by each criminal statute, an accused who at t_1, t_2, and t_3 does some driving, and who does so on each occasion while drunk, unlicensed, and in an overweight vehicle, is guilty of nine offence-tokens (3 instances of 3 offences).

Yet the unitary nature of the question asked by Goldman's metaphysics is illusory. Notice that the individuation of tropes depends

---

[292] I have put aside Goldman's argument from a killing being a causing of death, and a causing of death taking place when the actor does the moving that causes the death. Id. at 1582–3. I do not think one gets much mileage out of 'causing' here, any more than Corrado does in his worries about whether 'causings can be events' and whether 'causings can cause other events'. (See Corrado, 'Act Requirement', *supra* n. 55, at 1533, n. 22.) This, because of a triple ambiguity about 'causing' in these contexts. In 'when did Jones's causing Smith's death take place?', we could be using 'causing' to refer to: (1) the act-token of Jones, which on my theory is when he moved his body at t_1; (2) the ending of the causal process, that is, at death at t_3; or (3) the entire process during which the causing did its work, $t_1–t_3$. See Moore, *Act and Crime*, *supra* n. 1, at 288. Given the nuanced meaning suggested by exactly how one phrases and emphasizes the question (a feature Goldman too notices, Goldman, 'Action and Crime', *supra* n. 36, at 1582–3) there is little meat for argument for anyone out of these usages.

[293] Moore, *Act and Crime*, *supra* n. 1, at 318–24.

partly on the individuation of the properties of which they are instances: different property, different trope. Therefore Goldman's trope individuation question has to ask and answer just the question I raised in chapter 13 of *Act and Crime*, which is how do we individuate universals for double jeopardy purposes? Goldman begins where I began in *Act and Crime*, thinking that each distinct statute describes a distinct property[294] (and thus, there will be a distinct instance of each property for Goldman). Yet this will not do, the most obvious reason being that this fine-grained an individuation of properties would allow multiple prosecution and punishment of lesser included offences.[295] Goldman seeks to accommodate this lesser-included-offence sense of 'same offence' with his notion of an act-tree.[296] (An act-tree for Goldman is that structured set of tropes that collectively is what we coarser types think is one act-token.)

This response by Goldman will not work. Goldman's act-tree notion answers a different question than the 'same offence' question asks, even when that latter question is restricted to lesser included offences.[297] When we ask in the abstract whether assault with a deadly weapon is or is not a lesser included offence of armed robbery, we are asking a question having nothing to do with Jones's or anyone else's particular actions. We are asking a question of property (or type) individuation: are these *types* of offences related in a way that for double jeopardy purposes they should be treated as one type. Whether a set of property-instances are all nodes on *one act-tree* cannot help with this double jeopardy question; for the structure of each act-tree is a question wholly dependent on the peculiarities of each particular (coarse-grained) act there is. An instance of armed robbery by Jones at t_1 will be part of one sort of act-tree, and an instance of armed robbery by Smith at t_2 will be part of another sort of act-tree. Nothing in either of these trees will help us to decide the abstract question about the types, armed robbery and assault with a deadly weapon.

So not only is there a disguised property individuation question contained within Goldman's approach to double jeopardy, his

---

[294] Id. at 328, 333–7; Goldman, 'Action and Crime', *supra* n. 36, at 1584–5.

[295] Moore, *Act and Crime*, *supra* n. 1, at 335–6.

[296] Goldman, 'Action and Crime', *supra* n. 36, at 1584–6.

[297] Offence types that are the same for double jeopardy purposes are not limited to lesser included offences. See the examples, Moore, *Act and Crime*, *supra* n. 1, at 346–9.

metaphysics gives him no better resources with which to answer it than are available to his coarser colleagues. We all have to individuate properties as best we can, even if some of us are doing so in order then to individuate tropes. My own approach to property individuation for double jeopardy purposes is what I call the individuation of morally salient act types.[298] It is a mode of individuation of properties no *less* available to Goldman's than to my own metaphysics, so I commend it to him.

Goldman's fine-grained metaphysics also does not obviate the need for asking my second sort of double jeopardy question. Indeed, Goldman's metaphysics and mine ask exactly the same sort of second question here: once we have individuated the relevant properties (offence types), how many instances of them did the defendant do? Moreover, Goldman's metaphysics give him no more resources than mine give me. This, for two reasons. First, because the 'unit of offence' question here is exactly the same for both Goldman and me. Over a fourteen-day drive, how many instances of 'joyriding' did the defendant do? Goldman's act-trees, and the tropes they are composed of, here can do no work for him, for what he needs is a principle of individuating whole act-trees, one from the other. How many acts of driving were begun by these basic acts?[299] How many tropes are within the tree of each of these basic acts, or whether we identify all such tropes with their generating basic act, are idle questions here, in the sense that the answers just do not matter to the individuation question asked.

It is easy to parody the difficulties of the trope theorist here. As one such theorist admits, 'continuous, gradual change gives anyone trying to count tropes a headache, but what is perhaps worse, plain stolid uniform unchangingness yields problems too'.[300] The parody would be unfair because the tropist is here no worse off than is the coarse-grained colleague. Their metaphysical differences make no difference here, for both must divide continuous swatches of behaviour like driving into one, several, or many instances.

---

[298] Moore, *Act and Crime*, *supra* n. 1, at 337–55.

[299] In Goldman's older terminology, the relevant individuation question here is one about *compound* actions, and being fine-grained or coarse-grained about *complex* actions is idle here. See Goldman, *A Theory of Human Action* (Englewood Cliffs, NJ: Prentice-Hall, 1970), 28, 34–7. See particularly id. at 37: 'there is no minimal (or maximal) temporal length for a unit of action. . . . [any] shortest unit . . . is quite arbitrary. Acts of this length could be subdivided into their temporal parts.'

[300] Campbell, *Abstract Particulars*, *supra* n. 269, at 140.

The second reason Goldman's metaphysics give him no leg up here is because the best interpretation of double jeopardy requires a principle of instance-individuation that is not purely metaphysical. As I argue in chapter 14 of *Act and Crime*, the principle wanted here is not one counting act-tokens as such, be they tropes or coarse act-tokens; wanted is a count of instances of distinct moral wrongs, because only this count determines desert and proportionate punishment. (I call this 'wrong-relative act-token individuation'.) And while an extremely fine-grained tropist might have some metaphysical differences with me even while sharing this approach, as I understand Goldman's current metaphysics I see no difference. If unconsented-to kissing is wrong, and John causes just one contact between his lips and Mary, both Goldman and I count there to be just one instance of such wrong despite different descriptions of that instance (such as, John kissing Mary, doing so tenderly, on the cheek, furtively, etc.).[301]

[301] Compare Moore, *Act and Crime*, *supra* n. 1, at 370–2, with Goldman, 'Action and Crime', *supra* n. 36, at 1570, n. 17.

b. The Nature of Causation

7

CAUSATION, RIGHTS-VIOLATIONS, AND WRONGDOING

To say of an actor that she is guilty of legal wrongdoing is to say more than that she performed *an* action. It is to say at least that much (which, on the analysis defended in the previous chapter, is to say that she willed some bodily movement and that that bodily movement was caused to occur by that willing). But neither morality nor the criminal law that is erected upon it concern themselves with such simple actions as moving one's finger. Rather, both morality and the criminal law prohibit actions such as killings, disfigurings, rapes, etc.[1]

The notion of causation is central to understanding what else must be true for actions of bodily movement to instantiate actions of the wrongful types, killings, maimings, rapings, etc.[2] Prima facie, a willed bodily movement will be a killing if and only if that bodily movement *caused* a death; analogously, a willed bodily movement will be a maiming if and only if it causes a disfigurement, and it will be a raping if and only if it causes a penetration. Only if one understands the causal relation between bodily movements and such further events can one understand either legal or moral wrongdoing.[3]

In the paper to which the original of this chapter was a response, Judith Thomson was centrally interested in the relation between

---

[1] For a detailed study of how criminal law prohibitions build up complex descriptions of act-types, see Michael Moore, *Act and Crime: The Implications of the Philosophy of Action for the Criminal Law* (Oxford: Oxford University Press, 1993), ch. 8.

[2] Besides causation, other items such as intentions, conventions, and various states of affairs we lump together as 'circumstances' must sometimes also be taken into account. See id.

[3] See id. for the argument that causation is always necessary to have an instance of an act-type prohibited by the criminal law, even if causation is not by itself always sufficient.

causing harm to another and doing (moral) wrong to another by violating that other's (moral) rights.[4] In her paper, Thomson doubts that anyone 'believes it follows from the fact that X did something, his doing of which caused Y to suffer a harm, that X infringed a right of Y's' and thus that X both violated his moral duty and thereby is guilty of moral wrongdoing.[5] Yet if carefully qualified, not only is this thesis not bereft of any adherents, but Thomson herself probably would subscribe to it.[6]

The qualifications are three. First, we need to take account of the possibility that a prima facie wrongful act is not actually wrongful because it is justified. As a type of action, killing is prima facie wrongful, but killings in self-defence or in defence of the lives of others are not. The thesis should thus be qualified, to the effect that if X does something, the doing of which caused Y to suffer a harm, then X did wrong in infringing a right of Y's, *unless* X's action was justified.

Second, notice that there is some slippage between rights-infringements and wrongdoings. Although a rights violation is sufficient for wrongdoing, it is not necessary, for there can be wrongdoing by X that violates no one's rights. For example: it is wrong of X to torture cats, but cats have no rights not to be tortured. Therefore, although causing some state of affairs to exist may well be essential to all wrongdoing, causing those states of affairs we call harms to persons is not.[7]

Third, we need to keep clear that culpability is irrelevant to the existence of wrongdoing. Causing harm to another without justifi-

---

[4] Judith Thomson, 'Causality and Rights: Some Preliminaries', *Chicago-Kent Law Review*, Vol. 63 (1987), 471–96.

[5] Id. at 471. Although Thomson only discusses rights-infringements in her article, I assume that she would recognize the correlativity between X's action being an infringement of Y's rights and X's action being wrongful *vis-à-vis* Y.

[6] See Judith Thomson, *The Realm of Rights* (Cambridge, Mass.: Harvard University Press, 1990), at 233.

[7] Compare Mark Kelman, 'The Necessary Myth of Objective Causation Judgements in Liberal Political Theory', *Chicago-Kent Law Review*, Vol. 63 (1987), 579–637, at 583. Mark Kelman, certainly no friend of Thomson's thesis, nonetheless finds a version of the thesis to pervade that strand of liberal thought he broadly labels 'libertarian'. Because libertarians are value sceptics, Kelman argues, they cannot find rights to be natural. Therefore, they 'must derive rights from a morally plausible general statement about what might constitute rights-violating behavior: *prima facie*, the obvious candidate is that one ought not to *cause harm* (at least without justification). We are all equally unentitled to cause harm . . .'. For Kelman's libertarian foe, wrongdoing is primary and rights-violation is secondary.

cation is sufficient for wrongdoing, but it is not sufficient for responsibility. Responsibility requires, in addition, that the wrongdoer be culpable. That X violated Y's rights with his action, and that X thereby did wrong, is one question; whether X is responsible because he did so culpably, is another and separate question which has nothing to do with causing Y harm.

So clarified, Thomson's thesis is a plausible one. The paper of Thomson's[8] to which this chapter was originally a response is not a frontal defence of, or assault on, that thesis, however, but some preliminary skirmishing.[9] The preliminaries to the thesis that Thomson examines all have to do with one problem for the thesis. This is the problem of whether causation is a sufficiently discriminating relation that it can limit causal candidates for any given harm only to those that are plausibly rights-violations (and thus, the most prominent kind of wrongdoing[10]). Thomson's story, 'BRICK', illustrates the problem.[11] In 'BRICK', B is hit by a brick thrown by A, who was trying to hit B but 'missed'; he hit C, whose body deflected the brick onto B, thereby causing B to lose his eye. If C's walking toward the bus stop, and B's sitting on the bench, are as much causes of B's loss of his eye as A's act of throwing the brick, then causation does not sufficiently discriminate; for no one (including Thomson), wants to say that C or B violated B's rights by their respective activities. To be plausible, Thomson's thesis must discriminate between those who are injurers and those who are either victims or innocent bystanders. Thomson's 'BRICK' example seems to suggest that causation is not so discriminating.[12]

In the body of her paper Thomson quickly discards three theses about causation that would allow it to do the discriminating work

[8] Thomson, 'Causality and Rights', *supra* n. 4.

[9] Thomson's article, id, was written as a preliminary to her later book, *The Realm of Rights*, *supra* n. 6.

[10] See n. 5 *supra*. [11] Thomson, 'Causality and Rights', *supra* n. 4, at 471–6.

[12] I ignore in the text a statement in Thomson's paper that puzzles me. She says: 'Unlike C, B is not an exception to the thesis that if X did something, his doing of which caused Y a harm, then X infringed a right of Y's. For even given that B's sitting down at the bus-stop caused the loss of an eye, the eye lost was B's own.' Id. at 485. That the eye lost was B's own seems to me to be a very good reason to deny that B violated B's rights. But then why does a friend of Thomson's thesis not need a notion of causation sufficiently discriminating that it excludes B's sitting as a cause? If B's sitting is a cause, B is as much a counter-example to Thomson's thesis as is C—unless one adds to Thomson's thesis the *ad hoc* stipulation that for all X and all Y to which the thesis applies, X cannot be identical to Y.

demanded of it by her thesis and then examines in greater depth a fourth thesis. The three quick discards are:

(1) The thesis that for any given harm there is only one cause;[13]
(2) The thesis that for any given harm there is only one *activity* that is the cause;[14]
(3) The thesis that for any given harm there is only one human action or natural event that we will say was 'the cause', namely, those acts that are fully voluntary or those natural events sufficiently abnormal that their occurrence with the harm amounts to a coincidence.[15]

Surely Thomson is right in rejecting (1) and (2). There is no remotely plausible concept of cause under which one could say either of these things. However, I tend to think that Thomson's explanation for why we use the locution, 'the cause',[16] is less successful. I think we mean what we say when we use 'the cause'; that the criteria that guide our selection for the application of this honorific phrase are not arbitrary or non-existent; but that such criteria are pragmatic constraints on utterance of the phrase in particular contexts, not semantic criteria having anything to do with what 'cause' means or with what the relation of causation is.

Thomson I suspect would agree with the very last of these comments. I infer this because she clearly rejects the relevance (to her thesis) of affirming or denying the third thesis. She explicitly puts aside the well-known thesis of Hart and Honoré[17] (which thesis had to do with causal selection being based on voluntary human actions or abnormal natural events amounting to a coincidence) as 'pragmatic' and not 'ontological'.[18] In this rejection of merely pragmatic theses about what we will say, Thomson reveals a metaphysical realism about causation that I share. Such realism distinguishes what people say when they use 'cause' and even the concept they implicitly employ when they talk of causation, from what the causal relation really is.[19]

---

[13] Thomson, 'Causality and Rights', *supra* n. 4, at 476–8, 487.
[14] Id. at 487–8.   [15] Id. at 477–8.   [16] Id.
[17] H. L. A. Hart & A. M. Honoré, *Causation in the Law*, 2nd edn. (Oxford: Oxford University Press, 1985).
[18] Thomson, 'Causality and Rights', *supra* n. 4, at 472–3.
[19] An example of clear-headed realism about causation is J. L. Mackie, *The Cement of the Universe* (Oxford: Oxford University Press, 1980), at ix.

Because such realism colours much of Thomson's argumentation throughout her essay, and because it is only implicit, it is worth making this presupposition explicit. Thomson at various points argues: (1) 'the question whether one event X causes another event Y can hardly be thought to turn on anyone's moral failings',[20] and, more broadly, 'What has morality to do with the question whether one thing caused another?';[21] (2) the question of motivation or intention of the actor 'surely cannot be thought to fix' the question of causation;[22] (3) the question of legal duty to act cannot be relevant to the question of whether a causal relation can exist from a mere omission to act;[23] (4) 'What have X's capacities to do with the question whether X's not doing something caused something else?';[24] and (5), most importantly, 'what is customary, and what is expected, do not affect the truth-values of causal claims. . . . [and therefore] it is hard to see how any counterfactual analysis of causality can be right.'[25] These points are as obvious as they are to Thomson only because 'cause' for her names a real relation that is not the same as things like morality, legal duty, or the intentions, capacities, or conventions of persons.

I do not bring Thomson's metaphysical presupposition into the foreground in order to criticize it. Quite the contrary. It is worth identifying in order to highlight the contrast between Thomson's realism and the anti-realism about causation of the Legal Realist tradition in American legal scholarship, and of the two sceptical traditions Legal Realism has spawned, the Law and Economics movement and Critical Legal Studies.[26] Consider Mark Kelman by

[20] Thomson, 'Causality and Rights', *supra* n. 4, at 471–2.   [21] Id. at 495.
[22] Id. at 485.   [23] Id. at 495.   [24] Id.   [25] Id. at 484.
[26] The scepticism about causation is most evident in Wex Malone, 'Ruminations on Cause-In-Fact', *Stanford Law Review*, Vol. 9 (1956), 60–99, although much of the early scepticism about the meaningfulness of the concept of proximate causation also infected causation itself. See Henry Edgerton, 'Legal Cause', *University of Pennsylvania Law Review*, Vol. 72 (1924), 211–44, 214–16, 241–3; Leon Green, 'Are There Dependable Rules of Causation?', *University of Pennsylvania Law Review*, Vol. 77 (1929), 601–28, at 604–6.

The influence of Malone, Edgerton, and Green is quite evident in the law and economics literature on causation. Thus, Guido Calabresi concludes to his satisfaction that 'in the law "cause in fact" . . . is in the end a functional concept designed to achieve human goals'. Calabresi, 'Concerning Cause and the Law of Torts: An Essay for Harry Kalven, Jr.', *University of Chicago Law Review*, Vol. 43 (1975), 69–108, at 107. There, he reached this conclusion on just the grounds Malone used in reaching a like conclusion. See id. at 105–6. Similarly sceptical of causation are Landes and Posner, 'Causation in Tort Law: An Economic Approach', *Journal of Legal Studies*, Vol. 12 (1983), 109–34. Landes and Posner, in their rush to replace

way of illustration of the latter tradition.[27] Kelman claims we must 'wake up' from the nightmare of liberal tort law because it is based on a notion of causation that is incoherent and unknowable.[28] Many of Kelman's more particular arguments for the incoherence of any concept of causation presuppose a very conventionalist view of the world. Specifically, Kelman presupposes (and at times asserts) that: (1) no one, including Thomson, can define causation;[29] (2) in any event, even if someone could define it, she could not get agreement by others that her definition is what 'cause' means;[30] and (3) her definition in any event would have an unprincipled and unjustified distinction built into its application to concrete cases, viz., that internal evidence overrules external evidence even when the latter, judged probabilistically, is the 'better evidence'.[31]

Thomson's metaphysical realism is surely secure against assumptions like these, even if they were to be argued for and not just assumed. For notice that they in turn presuppose, respectively: (1) that you must be able to define a word if that word is to have meaning;[32] (2) that most language users in the relevant linguistic com-

causation with probability theory, feel entitled to deride the philosophical attempt to define causation as 'fruitless', totally context-dependent in its meaning, and in any event irrelevant to the purposes for which tort law should use the concept. Id. at 109–11, 119. Steve Shavell explicitly adopts Edgerton's and Calabresi's 'instrumentalist' approach to causation, defining the concept so as to serve 'well-specified social goals'. Shavell, 'An Analysis of Causation and the Scope of Liability in the Law of Torts', *Journal of Legal Studies*, Vol. 9 (1980), 463–516, at 502. Shavell recognizes that there exists a common sense notion of cause that antedates the law, but in such a common-sense concept, 'questions about causation are to an important extent resolved by resort to intuitions about the justness of applying a rule of liability'. Id.

Calabresi, Landes and Posner, and Shavell are not fully aware of how truly sceptical they are about causation, because often they seek to rescue the concept by giving it a probabilistic definition. If they clearly saw the difference between *ex ante* probability theory, which deals with *types* of acts, and *ex post* causation theory, which deals with particular actions ('act-tokens'), they would see that they are not in any sense analysing causation but are replacing it with something else. On this, see Richard Wright, 'Actual Causation vs. Probabilistic Linkage: The Bane of Economic Analysis', *Journal of Legal Studies*, Vol. 14 (1985), 435–56.

[27] Kelman, 'Necessary Myth', *supra* n. 7.   [28] Id. at 637.
[29] Id. at 581.   [30] Id. at 587.   [31] Id. at 592–3.
[32] Think of all the words that we seem to use meaningfully that no one can define: the natural kind terms of ordinary speech, such as 'gold', 'lemon', or ' water'; nominal kind words such as 'game', for which only Wittgenstein's criteriological analysis can be given; dispositional terms such as 'greedy' or 'soluble'; theoretical terms such as 'kinetic energy' or 'force'; and terms typically used in evaluative speech acts, such as 'good' or 'right'. See Moore, 'The Semantics of Judging', *Southern California Law Review*, Vol. 54 (1981), 151–294, at 202–46. Kelman is as naïve as Socrates in

munity must agree on that definition if the word is to have meaning for that community;[33] and (3) that the evidence with which one verifies the application of a word to the world is determinative of that word's meaning.[34] Since anyone familiar with the developments in semantics of the last two decades will pretty much reject these presuppositions out of hand,[35] I think that we can pretty much put aside Kelman's anti-realism about causation. In addition, these conventionalist presuppositions to Kelman's more particular arguments assume a general anti-realist stance about the things (like causation) to which our words refer.

Not sharing this question-begging character are Kelman's specific arguments against any necessary condition analysis of causation.[36] I shall mention one of these three arguments, which leads to an intermediate conclusion (about the necessary condition analysis of causation, not causation itself) that Thomson, too, wishes to defend.

Consider the example of Hart and Honoré[37] on which Kelman

his insistence that we must be able to define whatever we claim to know. The insight garnered by a less psychological view of meaning is that we may mean a great deal more than we know when we say, 'X causes Y'.

[33] Why should we need agreement about what 'cause' means for it to have meaning? More plausibly, one should view linguistic communities as employing what Putnam calls a 'division of linguistic labour' (Hilary Putnam, 'The Meaning of Meaning', in *Mind, Language, and Reality* (Cambridge: Cambridge University Press, 1975), 215), such that most in a community can rely on others to fill in the theory that makes sense of the words they employ.

[34] Even if Kelman were right in his criticism of Thomson's earlier distinction between the two kinds of evidence with which we verify causal statements, only a verificationist about meaning would think that this irrationality in our methods of verification infects the meaning of those statements. For Thomson's distinction, see Thomson, 'Remarks on Causation and Liability', *Philosophy and Public Affairs*, Vol. 13 (1984), 101–33; see also Thomson, 'Liability and Individualized Evidence', *Law And Contemporary Problems*, Vol. 49 No. 3 (1986), 199–219. It is thus not Thomson who is 'confusing a reasonable practical rule of thumb [favouring one kind of evidence over another] with a principled definition'. Kelman, 'Necessary Myth', *supra* n. 7, at 593. Rather, it is Kelman who confuses practical rules of verification with meaning.

[35] See, e.g., the citations *supra* nn. 32–3.

[36] Kelman argues against the necessary condition analysis of causation, that: (1) no action has only a single description that correctly picks it out, yet the truth of the causal judgement, 'X caused Y', depends on how we describe X, and there is no principled way to pick one description of X over another. Kelman, 'Necessary Myth', *supra* n. 7, at 604–6; (2) there is a 'subset problem' in how we aggregate parts of events into whole events when we use events as causes, id. at 603–4; (3) there are some cases where we cannot know whether a causal relation exists but where we pretend to greater evidence than we possess, id. at 606–8.

[37] H. L. A. Hart & A. M. Honoré, *Causation in the Law* (1st edn., Oxford: Oxford University Press, 1959), 69.

builds:[38] A fire that burns down a house appears to have two necessary conditions, D_1 having started a fire near the house and D_2 pouring gasoline on that fire. (The second is necessary because D_1's fire was about to go out when D_2 threw on the gasoline.) According to Kelman, we might describe D_2's act either as 'pouring gas' or as 'doing whatever is needed to burn [down the house]'.[39] Because under the first description D_2's act was necessary, but under the second it is not (because D_2 would have done some other act causing the house to burn had he not done this act of gas-pouring),[40] and because we have no 'strong conventions' allowing us to prefer one description to the other,[41] we are left with no answer to the question of whether D_2's act was a necessary condition of the harm.

Notice that Kelman's example, if analysed his way, might force us to the view that causal contexts are not extensional. For if the substitutivity *salva veritate* of co-referring expressions holds true here,[42] then D_2's act should be a cause of a given event regardless of which descriptions of both that act and that event are chosen.

What Kelman overlooks is the move to preserve the extensionality of causal contexts made by the very literature he is attacking.

---

[38] Kelman, 'Necessary Myth', *supra* n. 7, at 605.   [39] Id.
[40] Id. at 606–7.   [41] Id.

[42] The doctrine of substitutivity *salva veritate* holds that if two expressions X and Y refer to the same thing, then anything that can be predicated of X can be predicated of Y without changing the truth values of the overall expressions in which they occur, and vice versa. For the classic treatment of the 'principle of substitutivity *salva veritate*' and extensionality versus intensionality generally, see W. V. Quine, *Word and Object* (Cambridge, Mass.: MIT Press, 1960); Quine, 'Reference and Modality', in *From a Logical Point of View* (2nd edn., Cambridge, Mass.: Harvard University Press, 1961), 139; and Quine, 'Quantifiers and Propositional Attitudes', in *The Ways of Paradox* (Cambridge, Mass.: MIT Press, 1966), 183. See also Leonard Linsky, ed., *Reference and Modality* (Oxford: Oxford University Press, 1971); and D. Davidson and J. Hintikka, eds., *Words and Objections, Essays on the Works of W. V. Quine* (Dordrecht, Holland: Reidel, 1969). The extensionality of causal contexts is more specifically discussed in G. E. M. Anscombe, 'Causality and Extensionality', *Journal of Philosophy*, Vol. 66 (1969), 152–9; Donald Davidson, 'Causal Relations', *Journal of Philosophy*, Vol. 64 (1967), 691–703; Follesdal, 'Quantification into Causal Contexts', in *Reference and Modality*, *supra*; Zeno Vendler, 'Causal Relations', *Journal of Philosophy*, Vol. 64 (1967), 704–13. See also Achinstein, 'The Causal Relation', Rosenberg and Martin, 'The Extensionality of Causal Contexts', and Lombard, 'The Extensionality of Causal Contexts: Comments on Rosenberg and Martin', all in *Midwest Studies in Philosophy*, Vol. 4 (1979), 369–86, 401–8, and 409–15. I myself conclude in the next chapter that any counterfactual analysis of causation, the necessary condition analysis included, cannot *both* preserve the extensionality of causal discourse *and* take the reference of descriptions like, 'D_2's pouring gas at t', to refer to whole act-tokens.

For Wright,[43] and behind him Mackie,[44] have anticipated Kelman's problem in the following way. If 'pouring gas' and 'doing whatever is needed to burn down the house' refer to the identical act-token, then there is a real problem for the extensionality of causation if different descriptions of that act-token yield different truth-values when plugged into the expression, 'x causes y'.[45] But, Wright and Mackie ask, why must the reference of these descriptions be taken to be to whole event-tokens? Consider four other construals of the reference of these descriptions. One is that these act descriptions refer to types of acts, abstract universals, not particular events. Such descriptions, so construed, do not refer to the same act-types, and, because of this, no violation of extensionality need take place in order to say, with Kelman, that how you describe such different types matters. To be sure, a problem with this construal is that causation for non-Humeans is a relation between act-tokens, not act-types. Wright and Mackie could take descriptions to refer only to act-types and not to particular actions only by presupposing a sceptical conclusion about causation, namely, that there is no such thing as singular causal relations.[46]

A second construal that Mackie explores at length is to take the descriptions 'pouring gas' and 'doing whatever is needed to burn down the house' to refer to those proposition-like entities we call facts.[47] Facts about events are much more finely individuated than are events themselves. For example, the fact that D_2 poured gasoline is a different fact than the fact that D_2 did whatever he had to do to burn down the house. Thus again, extensionality is preserved because these different descriptions do not refer to one and the same thing, so different truth values of 'x causes y' using these different x's are unproblematic.

A third construal of those descriptions' reference is explored at length by Richard Wright.[48] Wright countenances the possibility that such descriptions do not refer to acts at all, either types or

---

[43] Richard Wright, 'Causation in Tort Law', *California Law Review*, Vol. 73 (1985), 1735–828.

[44] Mackie, *Cement, supra* n. 19, at 258–69.   [45] See id. at 257.

[46] Cf. Saul Kripke, *Wittgenstein on Rules and Private Language* (Cambridge, Mass.: Harvard University Press, 1982), 66–8, wherein Kripke rightly labels any limitation of causal candidates to types of acts, not particular acts, as 'a sceptical solution to Hume's problem about causation'.

[47] Mackie, *Cement supra* n. 19, at 257–62.

[48] Wright, 'Causation', *supra* n. 43, at 1766–74.

tokens, nor to facts about act-types or act-tokens, but to properties or 'aspects' of act-tokens. So taken, these descriptions refer to different properties, one of which is causally relevant (pouring) and the other of which is not (doing the act with the motive of burning down the house). On this third construal of the reference of these descriptions, extensionality is preserved (at least in higher order logics), despite the fact that the differing descriptions matter, because they are descriptions of different properties; yet, contrary to Kelman, these not being descriptions of the same property, there is no arbitrariness in our causal ascriptions (because of a supposed arbitrariness in our description selection). Quite the contrary: there is a determinate (objective) answer to what properties are causally relevant to particular harms, as Wright concludes, so that what description one chooses is determined by what property is causally relevant. In Kelman's example, that the act-token possessed the property, being a pouring of gasoline, is causally relevant, and that it possessed the property of being motivated by a certain desire is not (there would have been that burning no matter what desire prompted the act of pouring the gasoline). Unless Kelman wishes to claim that properties cannot be causes, which he nowhere does, Wright is secure from his challenge based on alleged failures of extensionality in causal contexts.

Many non-Humeans about causation would object to Wright's construal of causes as properties by pointing out that universals (whether properties or types) cannot stand in singular causal relations, so that if there are such relations, properties cannot fit the bill. Yet someone with Wright's metaphysics can dodge this objection by a fourth construal of the reference of descriptions like 'D_2 pouring gasoline' and 'D_2 doing whatever is needed to burn down the house'. Wright might adopt the metaphysics of tropes (or property-instances) that we examined in our discussions of Alvin Goldman in the last chapter. Such property instances are individuated as finely as are the properties of which they are instances, so that with this reference there is no failure of extensionality in Kelman's example. And property-instances, if they exist, are a kind of particular and thus are eligible to stand in singular causal relations.

Thus, Kelman does not get his desired sceptical conclusion about the necessary condition analysis of causation without doing a great deal of metaphysical analysis of events and their properties that he does not even begin. We should turn, then, to Thomson's argument,[49] which leads to the conclusion sought by Kelman, viz., that the necessary condition analysis, even when sophisticated *à la* Mackie and Wright, cannot be an adequate analysis of causation.

Contrary to Kelman, Thomson assumes 'cause' names a real relation, and then finds the necessary condition analysis of it wanting for its inability to preserve this realism. More exactly, put in the form of a *reductio* Thomson's argument is:

(1) x is a cause of y if and only if x is a necessary condition of y (the necessary condition analysis of 'cause');

(2) x is a necessary condition of y if and only if, if x did not occur, y would not occur (the counterfactual analysis of necessity);

(3) if x did not occur, y would not occur if and only if, 'if x did not occur, y would not occur' has a truth value (a weak version of Tarski's disquotational device allowing semantic ascent);[50]

(4) 'if x did not occur, y would not occur' has a truth value if and only if some choice is made with respect to all features of the situation surrounding x, distinguishing those that are varied (along with the absence of x) from those that are held fixed as part of the background (the element of choice in imagining the possible world in which the counterfactual is to be tested);[51]

(5) if a choice is made with respect to all features of the situation, distinguishing those that are varied (along with the absence of x) from those that are held fixed as part of the background, then there is a convention or expectation guiding the choice of possible worlds in which the causal statement is tested.[52]

Therefore from (1), (2), (3), (4), and (5):

(6) x is the cause of y only if there is a convention or expectation that guides the choice of possible worlds in which the causal statement is tested.

[49] Thomson, 'Causality and Rights', *supra* n. 4, at 481–4.

[50] For a good, brief discussion of using Tarski-like truth sentences simply as 'disquotational' devices allowing semantic ascent, see Michael Devitt, *Realism and Truth* (Cambridge: Cambridge University Press, 1984), 28–31.

[51] Thomson, 'Causality and Rights', *supra* n. 4, at 483. [52] Id. at 483–4.

But (6) is inconsistent with Thomson's realism about causation:

(7) '[w]hat is customary, and what is expected, do not affect the truth-values of causal claims'.[53]

Therefore, since Thomson firmly holds to realism about causation (7), she must reject (6); yet since she accepts (2), (3), (4) and (5), to reject (6) she must reject (1), the necessary condition analysis of causation. Indeed, given her argument, Thomson must reject not only the necessary condition analysis of causation, but also *any* counterfactual conditional analyses of causation, Mackie's and Wright's included, an implication she explicitly recognizes.[54] Unlike Kelman, for Thomson this does not mean that we should give up on our concept of causation; only that we should abandon any counterfactual analyses of it.

Before assessing this argument of Thomson's, we should see where it fits in to the overall argument structure of her article. Recall that she seeks some discriminating notion of cause that will distinguish injurers from both sufferers and innocent bystanders; such a discriminating idea of cause allows one, in turn, to maintain that to cause harm to another is to violate that other's rights (which injurers do, but sufferers and bystanders do not).

Having summarily rejected three theses that would provide such a discriminating idea of cause, Thomson examines a fourth in the body of her article. This is a thesis about the domain over which the variable x can range in the two place predicate, 'x causes y'. The thesis is that the proper domain of x is event-tokens (including act-tokens), but not states. Such a thesis would allow one to exclude such states as C being at the bus-stop at the time A throws the brick in Thomson's 'BRICK' scenario, and arguably even excludes those events that cause harm only by causing states that cause harm, such as C's earlier walking toward the bus-stop as well.[55]

---

[53] Thomson, 'Causality and Rights', *supra* n. 4, at 484.   [54] Id.

[55] The 'arguably' is in the text because one would have to think that if the *state* of C being at the bus-stop at the relevant time cannot be a cause of B's harm, then neither can any *event* (such as C walking to the bus-stop) that caused that state be a cause of the harm. Thomson id. at 476, seeks to explain this view: 'since the causal role played by C's walking towards the bus-stop was exhausted by its having caused C's being at P at T . . . C's walking towards the bus-stop did not cause the loss of B's eye . . . but only caused a condition in which A's throwing the brick was able to, and did, cause the loss of B's eye'. For defences of just this sort of intuition (of the causal potency of *events* being exhausted by the creation of once-but-no-longer dangerous *states*), see Joseph Beale, 'The Proximate Consequences of an Act',

After knocking down various arguments in favour of the thesis,[56] Thomson searches for a positive argument for the opposite thesis that states can be causes. One such positive argument would be that 'x causes y' means 'x is a necessary condition for y'. For if 'cause' is analysed in terms of necessary conditions, states as well as events can be necessary conditions and thus causes.[57] Because of the *reductio* argument just sketched, however, Thomson rejects this (and every other) counterfactual analysis of causation.[58] We now need to examine this argument of Thomson's.

If I were a friend of the counterfactual analyses of causation, I would attack premises (4) and (5) in Thomson's argument. For I too endorse realism about causation (7), which leads me to reject the conventionalism explicit in (6). Further, since a counterfactual analysis of necessity seems right (2), and since one can hardly question (3), if one is not to reject the necessary condition analysis of causation (1), that leaves (4) and (5) as the suspect premises.

Before coming to the grounds on which one might suspect (4) and (5) to be false, we should see why these premises are at least plausible. I would describe their plausibility in the following way.[59]

Harvard Law Review, Vol. 33 (1920), 633– 58, at 651–2; Beale, 'Recovery for Consequences of an Act', *Harvard Law Review*, Vol. 9 (1895), 80–9, at 84–5; and Richard Epstein, 'A Theory of Strict Liability', *Journal of Legal Studies*, Vol. 2 (1973), 151–204, at 185. The Beale/ Epstein intuition is close to that dealt with by Thomson, for both think that causation is largely a matter of events, or 'active forces'. E.g., Beale, 'The Proximate Consequences of an Act', *supra*, at 641: 'nothing but an active force can bring about that change of conditions which we call a consequence'. They allow states to be causes only insofar as they are unstable, and even then they might say that it is the release of stored energy (an event) that is the cause, not the state of its storage. And for both Epstein and Beale, once a defendant's action (an event) has caused a state that is 'stable' (Beale) or 'not in danger of releasing or redirecting forces' (Epstein), the causation by the defendant's action has, as Beale put it, ' "exhausted itself" like a spent cartridge'. Beale, 'Recovery for Consequences of an Act', *supra*, at 85.

[56] Thomson, 'Causality and Rights', *supra* n. 4, at 476–80.

[57] Id. at 481.   [58] Id. at 481–4.

[59] See generally Nelson Goodman, *Fact, Fiction, and Forecast* (4th edn., Indianapolis: Bobbs-Merrill, 1983), 9–17; Roderick Chisholm, 'Law Statements and Counterfactual Inference', *Analysis*, Vol. 15 (1955), 97–105; Nicholas Rescher, 'Belief Contravening Suppositions', *The Philosophical Review*, Vol. 70 (1961), 176–96; Stalnaker, 'A Theory of Conditionals', in N. Rescher, ed., *Studies in Logical Theory* (Oxford: Blackwell, 1968), 165, for discussions of the problem of indeterminacy for counterfactual conditionals. The latter three essays are also collected in E. Sosa, ed., *Causation and Conditionals* (Oxford: Oxford University Press, 1975), at 147, 156, 165, which contains a discussion of the problem in its Introduction. *Causation and Conditionals*, supra, at 12–14.

When we say, contrary to fact, that 'but for x, y would not have occurred', there is a lot that we have left unsaid. Two items we have not mentioned are, first, what are we to imagine happened in place of x? If the statement in question is, 'if Smith had not set foot on the steps, the rotten beams under them would not have collapsed',[60] what replaces 'Smith setting foot on the steps' to test the truth of this counterfactual? If we replace it with 'Smith using a different stairway', the counterfactual may well be true; if we replace it with, 'Smith bounding up the steps at just the time he actually walked up the steps', it may seem to be false. Second, even once we choose, say, 'Smith using a different stairway' as the replacement, how many other things in the world are we to imagine having also changed along with Smith's change of entrance? For example, what had to change for Smith to have used a different entrance? Perhaps Jones, who is Smith's chauffeur and who is heavier than Smith, dropped Smith off at the safe entrance only to run Smith's forgotten briefcase up the rotten one. If this is what we vary, then the counterfactual may seem to be false; other events, neutral to weight equal to or greater than Smith's being on the stairs at the relevant time, would leave the counterfactual true.

On both of these bases one might find plausible the idea that the truth of a counterfactual depends on what we hold fixed and on what we vary; thus, (4). Further, one might think, with Thomson, that what we do fix or vary is a matter guided solely by convention and not by any limitations imposed by the nature of the causal relation. One convention we likely follow is: 'hold fixed normal features of the situation'. Following such a convention, we would thus hold fixed Smith's weight (which Thomson allows 'is not especially heavy') and thus not ask any counterfactual question where what replaces the real Smith stepping on the stairs is a lighter or a heavier Smith doing so.[61] Likewise, the variations on walking (jumping,

---

[60] See Thomson, 'Causality and Rights', *supra* n. 4, at 483.

[61] John Mackie, for example, finds that common sense views of causality employ an 'all-or-nothing' convention in considering what is to replace matters susceptible of continuous variation such as weight. In discussing whether a hammer-blow is necessary for the crushing of a chestnut, Mackie holds that 'we regard the hammer-blow as a unit, and simply do not consider parts or subdivisions of it or quantitative alterations to it. The alternatives considered are that I strike the chestnut in the way described and that I do not. In constructing possible worlds, in considering what might or would have happened, we either plug in the hammer-blow as a whole or leave it out as a whole.' Mackie, *Cement*, *supra* n. 19, at 44.

bounding, treading, etc.) would also be ruled out on similar grounds. Hence, the plausibility of (5).

Despite this plausibility, a friend of the necessity analysis of causation (which I am not) would reject (4) and (5). One ground for rejecting (4) would be that advanced by David Lewis, amongst others.[62] According to Lewis, when testing the counterfactual, 'if C had not occurred, E would not have occurred', we test it in that possible world that is *closest* to our actual world. That is, when we suppose, contrary to fact, that C did not occur, we further suppose changes from our actual world only to the minimum extent necessary to make it true (in this closest possible world) that C did not occur.[63]

Attractive as this view is, it would require (as Lewis recognizes) that we make sense of the idea of over-all similarity, i.e., similarity that is parasitic on no particular properties but only on all properties. As I have argued in the context of precedent and induction,[64] this is not a very plausible idea of similarity. Lewis sees the problem as one of vagueness (about similarity), but it is much deeper than that. Thinking that we can have a context-independent idea of similarity is like thinking that we can have a context-independent sense to 'attributive'[65] adjectives such as 'big'. How big something has to be to be 'big' depends on what kind of thing we are talking about. Similarly, 'similar' depends on its context of utterance to specify what property on which it is parasitic. And with this context-dependent notion of similarity, we are back where we started in seeking some basis for varying some properties, but not others, as we construct a possible world that is 'most similar' to our actual world.

Other doubts about (4) might be based on the following considerations. First, suppose that of the five possible ontologies for cause mentioned above (event-tokens, event-types, facts, properties, and

---

[62] See, e.g., David Lewis, 'Causation', *Journal of Philosophy*, Vol. 70 (1973), 556–67. See generally David Lewis, *Counterfactuals* (Cambridge, Mass.: Harvard University Press, 1973), and Michael Loux's introduction in M. Loux, ed., *The Possible and the Actual* (Ithaca, NY: Cornell University Press, 1979), 32–4.

[63] Lewis, 'Causation', *supra* n. 62, at 263.

[64] Moore, 'Precedent, Induction, and Ethical Generalization', in Laurence Goldstein, ed., *Precedent in Law* (Oxford: Oxford University Press, 1987). For somewhat similar doubts, see Hilary Putnam, *Realism and Reason* (Cambridge: Cambridge University Press, 1983), 218.

[65] For a discussion of attributive adjectives, see Peter Geach, 'Good and Evil', *Analysis*, Vol. 17 (1956), 33–42.

tropes) we restrict the singular causal relations to the first, whole event-tokens.[66]

Second, suppose we employ a very fine-grained mode of individuating event-tokens. Now, arguably, we do not get a dependence of the truth value of the counterfactual on how we complete the specification of the contrary-to-fact ('possible') world. If Smith walking up the steps did cause the collapse of the stairs, then it is true: no matter how else the possible world is specified,[67] if Smith had not walked just as he did, the stairs would not have collapsed just as they did. More specifically, returning to each of our two problems of incompleteness: first, it does not matter if Smith bounded (rather than walked) up the stairs, hitting just the same stair at the same time; although the stairs would still collapse (let us suppose), there would not be the same collapse that there actually was. In this example, the two collapses—the actual one, and the one that would have happened if Smith had bounded up the stairs—are not plausibly supposed to be qualitatively identical. For the heavier bounding would likely produce a slightly more rapid, deeper, or less time-consuming collapse.[68] Second, it does not matter if Smith's

[66] The importance of getting the 'ontology of causation' right has been emphasized by Davidson, 'Causal Relations', supra n. 42, Mackie, Cement, supra n. 19, at ch. 10; and, in a criticism of Mackie's earlier efforts, Jaegon Kim, 'Causes and Events: Mackie on Causation', Journal of Philosophy, Vol. 68 (1971), 426–41, reprinted in E. Sosa, ed., Causation and Conditionals (Oxford: Oxford University Press, 1975), 48.

[67] I assume that we do not allow variance of the laws that bear on Smith's walking up the steps being a cause of their collapse. If those laws were allowed to vary, then it might very well be the case that the very same collapse of the stairs would take place even in the absence of Smith stepping on them as he did. We might even think, following Popper, that we should exclude variance of any laws of science when we test the truth of a causation-generated counterfactual against all possible worlds. Karl Popper, The Logic of Scientific Discovery (3rd edn., London: Hutchison, 1968), 426–41. Then all that we may vary are the 'initial conditions' in which Smith's stepping took place, not any laws (including those governing that stepping). One of the benefits of excluding variance of any laws as we construct possible worlds is that it allows a crisp distinction between logical necessity (true through all possible worlds) and causal necessity (true through all possible worlds in which the laws of this world hold true). For development and criticism of this view, see Mackie, Cement, supra n. 19, at 209–30, and Lewis, 'Causation', supra n. 62, at 566–7.

[68] I assume that the two event-tokens are numerically distinct if they differ in properties other than certain relational properties (the relational properties excluded have to include the property, being-caused-by-Smith's walking, else the counterfactual analysis of causation becomes trivially true). That a difference in properties does not automatically betoken a non-identity between the entities possessing such properties, is due to the difficulties we have in making transworld identity claims, because

heavier chauffeur were to walk up the stairs just after Smith did—again, a different collapse of the stairs. The counterfactual, 'but for x, y would not have occurred' seems to remain true no matter how the possible world imagined is completed in its particulars. Thus (4) seems to be false in its assertion that counterfactual statements have truth values only when choices are made about fixed versus variable features of the actual world. And if (4) were false, then (5) could have no interest for us in this context.

Before coming to Thomson's defence and rebutting this friend of the counterfactual analyses of causation, let me turn to a second argument Thomson advances against counterfactual analyses of causation. For this argument too seems subject to the fine-grained sort of rejoinder just proposed, and it will be convenient to have both arguments before us before we consider the rejoinder on its merits. Although it is not clear that Thomson recognizes that she has made two distinct arguments against the counterfactual analyses of causation, she has. Her second argument for rejecting counterfactual analyses of causation is one she calls 'the counterfactual second agent objection'.[69] This objection builds on overdetermination examples of the pre-emptive kind: two fires, each sufficient to burn plaintiff's house, are headed in its direction; the first fire (F_1), as luck would have it, reaches the house first and burns it completely (if instantaneously) before the second fire (F_2) gets there. Thomson thinks that the counterfactual, 'but for F_1 occurring, the house's burning would not have occurred' is false even though F_1 is the cause of the house's burning. Ergo, the counterfactual is not an adequate analysis of causation.

The other examples Thomson uses in this argument are of the same pre-emptive sort: of the two events with equal capacity to cause some event, one gets there first and pre-empts the second from having the opportunity to cause the effect in question. Thus,

such difficulties force us to do something with Leibniz's otherwise true claim that identicals are indiscernible in their properties. See M. Loux, ed., *The Possible and The Actual*, *supra* n. 62, for a variety of approaches to this problem. I also leave aside the difficult question of whether, supposing the two collapses to be qualitatively identical in all respects, save being caused by Smith's walking, they may yet be numerically distinct. If one rejects Leibniz's other principle—the identity of indiscernibles—one might still believe that the actual collapse that occurred and the collapses that would have occurred in all possible worlds other than the actual one, are numerically distinct.

[69] Thomson, 'Causality and Rights', *supra* n. 4, at 482.

when a glass is shattered with a hammer, Thomson finds it plausible to say that the glass would have shattered anyway because another was waiting to smash it with a shoe if it was not smashed with a hammer;[70] likewise, when one person forgets to ring a bell, that forgetfulness could not be said to cause the absence of bell-ringing (on the counterfactual analysis) in that the bell's ringing would not have occurred anyway, because another stood ready to cut the wire to the bell.[71]

The rejoinder standardly offered to Thomson's counterfactual second agent objection is the same as was offered to her first objection. The idea is to individuate the event-tokens being caused so finely that the counterfactuals come out more in tune with our causal intuitions. Thus, one might say that the burning of the house that would have occurred had the second fire reached it would have been a different house burning than the house burning that actually occurred, qualitatively different in some of its non-relational properties and numerically different in any case. Likewise, one might suppose that the glass shattering that would have occurred had the shoe fallen would have been a different glass shattering than the one that actually occurred because of the hammer, and that the absence of a bell ringing because of a cut wire would be different from the absence of a bell-ringing because no one pushed it.

I doubt that this fine-grained rejoinder is adequate as a response to either of Thomson's arguments against counterfactual analyses of causation. To begin with, there seems no principled basis on which to draw the line as to how fine-grained to make the cross-world identity conditions for events. On a standard analysis of the matter, events' essences are given by three variables forming an ordered triple: an object, a property, and a time. A particular house-burning event, for example, has as its essence: the object, which is the house in question; the property exemplified, which is burning; and the duration of time over which the object exemplifies the property. The worry is how much variation to allow in the object (including its parts, such as the porch of the house), how much variation to allow in the property (crisping, singeing, etc.), and how much variation to allow in the temporal duration, *before* one refuses to identify an event in one possible world with its counterpart event in another.

---

[70] Id.   [71] Thomson, 'Causality and Rights', *supra* n. 4, at 484.

One cannot finesse this problem by demanding exact identity of objects, properties, and times, on pain of making every event the cause of every other event. Since possible worlds will differ in some respects other than the absence of the putative cause event being tested for, the effect events in those possible worlds will always differ somewhat from the effect event that actually occurred; so that if one demands exact identities, every event becomes necessary for every other event, and thus its cause on the counterfactual analyses of causation. Because this is absurd, the friend of the counterfactual analyses has to specify how much variation is to be allowed in making transworld event identity claims, and I see little prospect of any principled way to do this.

The second problem with this rejoinder lies in the difficulty in specifying which possible worlds we are to use when we test counterfactuals. If there were some objective fact of the matter as to which possible worlds were 'closer' to our actual world, as David Lewis has proposed, this would not be a problem. But Lewis's own use of 'closeness' of possible worlds to answer Thomson's pre-emption objection reveals how seemingly arbitrary this criterion is.

Lewis tells us that in pre-emptive concurrent cause cases like that of the two fires, the counterfactual analysis gives us (contra Thomson) the intuitively right answer: but for fire number one, the house would *not* have burned (despite the presence of fire number two waiting to burn the house). Lewis achieves this result by supposing that fire number one does its pre-empting work by causing some intermediate event d to occur, and it is d that prevents fire number 2 from burning down the house. Let d, for example, be the removal of fuel or oxygen from the immediate vicinity of the house. Now: the 'closest' possible world in which to test the counterfactual, 'the house would not have burned if there had been no fire number one', is a world in which d still occurs. Which gives one the desired answer.

The problem, of course, is that we have no reason to think *this* possible world is closer to our actual world than is a possible world in which d does not occur when the first fire does not occur. Until we can make 'close' look much less arbitrary than this, we have not defended the fine-grained rejoinder with any plausibility. And without such a rejoinder, the necessary condition analysis of causation is subject to the two objections Thomson advances against it.

One of the curiosities of Thomson's admittedly preliminary treatment of causation is that, although she tells us what causation is not (it is not analysed by counterfactuals), she never tells us what the causal relation is. No small task, to be sure, but in the absence of any analysis of 'causes' in the expression, 'x causes y', it is difficult to fix the domain over which the variables x and y may range. Thomson's handicap here is like the handicap we would face in specifying the domain of x and y in the expression 'x loves y' if we had no idea what the relation of love is.

Despite this handicap, Thomson concludes to her satisfaction that states as well as events can be causes. Her principal argument for this is by extension from a clear case. Thomson imagines a variation of 'BRICK' in which C walks toward the bus-stop 'precisely in order to deflect A's brick into B's eye'. Thomson argues:

(1) When C intends to deflect the brick into B's eye, 'it is surely correct . . . that C's walking towards the bus-stop caused the loss of B's eye'.[72]

(2) The intention with which C walked 'surely cannot be thought to fix whether the walking caused the loss of B's eye'.[73]

Therefore:

(3) It is [surely?] correct that C's walking toward the bus-stop caused the loss of B's eye even when C did not intend to deflect the brick into B's eye.

This is an odd argument, for what makes the clear case clear in (1) is the intention of C; yet (2) denies the relevance of the intention, allowing Thomson to decide the less clear case in (3). I do not see how such an argument can convince anyone. Anyone who finds (2) plausible (as do I) will not find (1) any more plausible than (3). And anyone who finds (1) more plausible than (3) will not find (2) plausible. I do not think, therefore, that there is an audience to which such an argument can appeal. It is like trying to convince someone (who is in doubt about whether a white, sweet object is a lemon) that it is a lemon, by arguing: 'this other object, because it is a yellow fruit tart of taste, is surely a lemon; yet surely the colour and taste are not essential to an item being a lemon; therefore, this first object, differing from the other object only in colour and taste, is also a lemon too'.

[72] Thomson, 'Causality and Rights', *supra* n. 4, at 484.   [73] Id.

Earlier in her article Thomson has the beginnings of another positive argument for why states as well as events can be causes. The argument as she states it proceeds from a single premise, namely:

(1) objects can be causes as well as events.

As Thomson puts it: 'We really do not use the verb "cause" that it can truly be said only of events that they cause things. People cause things. And so do bullets.'[74] From this premise about objects as causes, Thomson concludes that one of the arguments for why states *cannot* be causes,[75] is no good.[76]

As a friendly critic, let me see how Thomson might advance this as a positive argument for the thesis that states can be causes (and not merely a negative argument against the thesis that states cannot be causes). Add to Thomson's argument a second premise:

(2) The only distinction here worth defending is between events as causes versus all other things as causes; if items other than events can be causes, then so can states.

We might call this second premise the 'crossing of the Rubicon' premise, for it asserts that there is only one significant line to worry about here and that once that line is crossed, one might as well go on to sack Rome itself. Such mode of argument is reminiscent of Russell's argument for admitting qualities into our ontology as well as entities: since we have to let relations in anyway (to be able to talk of entities), we may as well let in other universals such as qualities.[77]

Thomson articulates a reason which might incline one to accept this kind of argument here. The line between events and all other things might have some significance because of the following considerations: causes explain changes in the world; if one believes that *only* change can bring about change,[78] and that only events are

---

[74] Id. at 479.

[75] The argument (against states being causes), against which Thomson is arguing, is set forth by her in id. at 474–6, 478.

[76] Id. at 479.

[77] See the excerpt entitled 'The World of Universals' from Bertrand Russell, *The Problems of Philosophy* (NY: H. Holt and Co., garden City, NY: 1912), reprinted in M. Loux, ed., *Universals and Particulars: Readings in Ontology* (Anchor Books, 1970), 16–23.

[78] Thomson, 'Causality and Rights', *supra* n. 4, at 475, 478.

changes, then one has reason to find the line between events and all other things significant when considering the question of what can be a cause.

Neither Thomson nor I believe that only changes are caused (as opposed to the persistence of stable states, for example), or that only changes can beget change, but a friend of the 'only events can be causes' thesis might very well believe both of these things. If so, then once Thomson establishes that objects (which are not changes) can be causes, she has crossed her adversary's Rubicon and he may as well surrender Rome. But has Thomson established that objects can be causes? She adverts to the facts of usage about 'causes', truthfully noting that we certainly say things like, 'Smith caused Jones's death' and '[t]hat bullet caused Jones's death'.[79] Yet as Thomson would plainly admit (given her realism about causation), the facts of ordinary usage are far from the last word on what causation is. As Quine has remarked, 'Many of our casual remarks . . . would want dusting up when our thoughts turn seriously ontological.'[80]

Why might we say the things Thomson imagines? One of our pragmatic rules for appropriate utterance is to say no more than is needed on particular occasions.[81] If someone wants to know only who by his actions caused Jones's death, or what instrumentality Smith used in killing Jones, to say, 'Smith caused Jones's death', or 'The bullet caused Jones's death' is all that needs to be said. We need take the apparent ontological commitments to persons or objects as causes no more seriously than we do when we say, 'there is something shared by both white dogs and white houses, namely, their whiteness'.[82] In each case, Quine admonishes us, we should paraphrase to find our true commitments.

The paraphrase that suggests itself here is just the one Thomson rather scornfully puts aside:[83] 'Smith caused Jones's death' is elliptical for, 'some act of Smith's (you do not need to know which one

[79] Thomson, 'Causality and Rights', *supra* n. 4, at 478.

[80] W. V. Quine, *Ontological Relativity and Other Essays* (New York: Columbia University Press, 1969), 100.

[81] H. P. Grice, 1967 William James Lectures, Harvard University, published as 'Logic and Conversation', P. Cole and J. Morgan, eds., 3 *Syntax and Semantics, Speech Acts* (New York: Academic Press, 1975), Vol. 3, 41, 45–6. As Grice puts his quantitative maxim for appropriate conversation: 'Do not make your contributions more informative than is required.' Id. at 45.

[82] Quine's example, in *From a Logical Point of View*, *supra* n. 42, at 13.

[83] Thomson, 'Causality and Rights', *supra* n. 4, at 479.

so I will not tell you) caused Jones's death', and 'the bullet caused Jones's death' is an ellipsis for, 'some event involving the bullet caused Jones's death'. Thomson rejects these paraphrases because she finds the notion of 'involving' hopelessly indeterminate:

[I]t is plainly unacceptable to say that 'Smith caused Jones' death' is elliptical for 'An event in one or another way involving Smith caused Jones' death', since every event in one or another way involves everybody. For example, Smith's shooting of Jones involves you in that it is an event which takes place on or before or after your fourth birthday; but you, after all, did not cause Jones' death. And I see no future in the effort to constrain the notion 'involvement' so as to make this idea work.[84]

This answer is much too short. Thomson's demand for any precision in spelling out the meaning of 'involvement' is misplaced. For if I am correct that we say such things in speech contexts where saying more would be inappropriate, then *saying more would be inappropriate*. 'Involve' is used here only as a place-holder for information that, given the context of the utterance, the listener does not need or want. In the absence of a context of utterance (i.e., in the null context),[85] we can only say the word does not mean, 'any relation to Smith', any more than it means 'no relation to Smith'. In this indeterminacy, this usage of 'involve' does not suffer at all in comparison with the way we ordinarily use 'similar': 'similar' never means, 'similar in all respects', any more than it means, 'similar in no respects'; it only means 'similar in relevant respects', the conditions of relevancy to be supplied when and if needed.[86]

All of this only blunts for me any facts of usage as constituting an argument one way or another about objects or persons as causes. Do people and bullets cause things, in some sense not reducible to events in which these objects are involved causing things? I am an educable agnostic on this question, but nothing in Thomson's article convinces me one way or the other.[87] Her reconstructed Rubicon argument, accordingly, lacks a plausible first

[84] Id.

[85] On the idea of a null context of utterance, see J. J. Katz and J. A. Fodor, 'The Structure of a Semantic Theory', *Language*, Vol. 39 (1963), 170–210, at 174.

[86] Cf. Nelson Goodman, 'Seven Strictures on Similarity', in his *Problems and Projects* (Indianapolis, Bobbs-Merrill, 1976).

[87] Nor do attempts at making 'agent-causation' primitive for persons convince me one way or the other. See Richard Taylor, *Action and Purpose* (Englewood Cliffs, NJ: Prentice-Hall, 1966).

premise. And in default of any other argument being advanced by Thomson, that leaves us with the old Scottish verdict on her attempt to show that states cannot be causes: 'not proven'.

My concluding comment is to question whether a restriction that allowed only events but not states as causes would give causation the kind of discriminating power demanded of it by her thesis connecting causing harm to rights-violations. I think not, for such a restriction seems both under- and over-inclusive. To begin with, the restriction is too restrictive in that it excludes factors that are plausibly rights-violations by defendants. Imagine a variation of Thomson's 'BRICK' scenario ('BANANA'?): A, a banana vendor, notices that a banana peel has dropped off his truck; knowing that B, whom A hates and wishes to see hurt, will be coming along shortly, A does not pick up the peel; B slips on the peel and falls, to his injury.

In 'BANANA', does not A violate B's rights? I think the answer might be 'yes', for two different reasons. Thomson herself mentions one of these:[88] A was both capable of preventing B's injury and, because it was his peel, A was under a duty to prevent the injury by removing the peel; A's duty is presumably the correlative of B's right, so that A's breach of duty is a violation of B's rights. Alternatively, it might be the case that there was some earlier act of A's (loading the truck with bananas, parking it where he did) that caused the state that caused B's fall and injury. In which case we would hold A liable for violating B's rights, not by omitting to pick up the peel, but rather by causing (through his positive actions) B's injury.

In either alternative it seems we need to conceive of states as causes. A's liability for omission seems to depend on the state of the peel being where it was causing B's fall—else how could A's failure to change *that state* have prevented B's injury? Similarly, for some earlier act of A's (such as parking his truck) to be the cause of B's injury, seemingly the state also must be a cause—for what the earlier act caused was a state which (with other events and states) caused B's injury.

This under-inclusiveness of the 'only-events-may-be-causes' thesis for Thomson's thesis was implicitly recognized by those who championed the former thesis. Beale, for example, thought that it

---

[88] Thomson, 'Causality and Rights', *supra* n. 4, at 494.

was only 'active forces'—which it seems fair to construe to be events but not states because the activity of a force for Beale was external change—that could be causes. Nonetheless, in order to maintain liability in cases like 'BANANA', Beale had to allow that the 'condition' (state) created by a defendant could be a cause:

If, then, this condition is unstable, if it is in appreciable danger of being acted upon by an oncoming force, the defendant who thus created a condition in the path of an oncoming force stands in a certain causal relation to the latter force, though the relation is worked out through the passive line.[89]

Epstein similarly saw that he could not restrict causation to his three paradigms involving acts by a defendant (force, fright, and compulsion); rather, to make plausible his thesis that causing another harm is to violate that other's rights Epstein allows that conditions, too, may be causes.[90] Like Beale before him, Epstein wants to hedge his metaphysical bets here: 'The creation of a dangerous condition, without more, does not cause harm in the narrow sense of the term. Some further act or event of the kinds already considered must be identified before the causal analysis is completed . . .'.[91] Still, Epstein too is driven to conclude that some states—the 'dangerous' or 'unstable' ones—can be causes, even if only in conjunction with events.

The *over*-inclusiveness of the 'events-only' thesis can be seen by varying Thomson's 'BRICK' slightly: let the victim, B, be walking as well as the bystander, C, and let the movement of each of them be necessary for the deflection of A's brick onto B's eye. The 'events-only' thesis may be discriminating, but it does not seem to be discriminating enough: neither B nor C violated B's rights by their walking, but their walking is equally a cause with A's throwing the brick under the 'events-only' thesis.

So even if the 'events-only' thesis were true, it seems a poor candidate to do the discriminating work demanded of it by Thomson's thesis connecting rights violations to causing harm. Are there any other restrictive analyses of causation that are themselves plausible enough to make Thomson's thesis plausible? In the legal literature on causation there are several possibilities, and I shall close by mentioning each briefly.

---

[89] Beale, 'Proximate Consequences', *supra* n. 55, at 643.
[90] Epstein, 'Strict Liability', *supra* n. 55, at 177–87.   [91] Id. at 177.

First, one might attempt to refine the Beale/Epstein paradigms so that the concept of causation that emerges better fits the demands of Thomson's thesis. Yet this is to work backwards, gerrymandering the concept of causation just so that it will fit the needs of the thesis (even though I would guess that that is pretty much the way Epstein arrived at his four 'paradigms' of causation). We need an independent analysis of what 'cause' means and what causation is that does not assume from the start that it has to fit some moral thesis. There is nothing in Epstein's method that would give us any reason to think his paradigms give either the meaning of 'cause' or describe the essence of the relation: such paradigms are partial descriptions of a few traditional legal causes of action (battery/trespass/assault/negligence/nuisance), not even an attempt at an analysis of the causal relation that exists quite independently of the law but on which the law is built.

Second, Hart and Honoré's justly celebrated theses about what is, and what is not, a direct cause, have more promise as an analysis of what causation is, but they too, as Thomson recognizes,[92] ultimately fail to focus on the metaphysical or the semantic questions about causation. As they themselves recognize in their recently reissued edition of their fine book,[93] their analysis is of the usage, in ordinary language, of 'cause'. They thus distinguish two different contexts of use, explanatory and attributive, and extract a concept (or concepts) of causation accordingly. This focus on the conditions in which the word 'cause' is appropriately uttered ensures that their analysis is, as Thomson puts it, 'pragmatic' and not 'ontological'.[94]

While I agree with Thomson's pragmatic interpretation of Hart and Honoré's causally discriminating principles, it would not be difficult to construct a metaphysical version.[95] In this version, there are two kinds of uncaused causes in the universe, free human actions and those natural events that are (given the circumstances in which they occur) 'just a coincidence'. On this gappy metaphys-

---

[92] Thomson, 'Causality and Rights', *supra* n. 4, at 472–3.

[93] H. L. A. Hart and A. M. Honoré, *Causation in the Law*, *supra* n. 17, at xxxiii–xxxiv.

[94] Thomson, 'Causality and Rights', *supra* n. 4, at 473.

[95] Sanford Kadish gives Hart and Honoré such a metaphysical reading with respect to one of their two criteria for intervening and ultimate causes, free human action. See Kadish, 'Complicity. Cause and Blame: A Study in the Interpretation of Doctrine', *California Law Review*, Vol. 73 (1985), 323–410.

ical view, we do not select one of these two events as 'the cause' of some other event because of pragmatic factors like explanatory relevance or the interests of the audience; rather, in this metaphysical version of their argument we rightly gravitate to these two features because they are the only features that are the ultimate causes of anything. Put another way, they are the beginnings of all causal chains, so they are rightly emphasized over any other subsequent links in the chain when we engage in attributive, explanatory or any other tasks involving 'cause'.

A third approach is to take causation to be an unanalysable primitive, and then to say that it is a relation that nonetheless admits of degrees. 'Cause' can be used to analyse other concepts, but no other concept can be used to analyse it; and the causal relation can be a more-or-less affair, so that one event can be 'more of a cause' of some harm than another event. Both of these views can fairly be attributed to Jeremiah Smith, whose highly influential series of articles in the 1911 *Harvard Law Review* concluded that all that may or need be said about causation to juries was whether or not the defendant's action was a 'substantial factor in producing the damage complained of'.[96]

Give Smith the two metaphysical assumptions above and his proposal is not nearly as vacuous as it has been thought to be by most subsequent scholars. If 'cause' is a primitive notion, then no test or definition need be attempted, as Smith himself argued.[97] If causation is a more-or-less affair, then one does need to specify how much of it is a prerequisite for liability, and Smith's answer was, 'a substantial amount'. Although 'substantial' is vague, its vagueness

[96] Jeremiah Smith, 'Legal Cause in Actions of Tort', *Harvard Law Review*, Vol. 25 (1911), 223, 253, 303. Both of Smith's metaphysical presuppositions find echoes in more contemporary literature. Thus, in philosophy Richard Boyd urges that we should take 'cause' as primitive and give up the fruitless quest for its analysis. Boyd, 'Materialism without Reductionism: What Physicalism Does Not Entail', in Ned Block, ed., *Readings in the Philosophy of Psychology* (Cambridge, Mass.: Harvard University Press, 1980). Richard Wright discusses a number of legal theorists similarly inclined. Wright, 'Causation', *supra* n. 43, at 1784–8. With regard to Smith's second presupposition, product liability torts have given rise to renewals of the idea that we should apportion liability, not with respect to fault, but with respect to degrees of causal contribution to an indivisible injury. This mode of joint liability/contribution presupposes, with Smith, that causation is a more-or-less affair that admits of degrees. See, e.g., Rizzo and Arnold, 'Causal Apportionment in the Law of Torts: An Economic Theory', *Columbia Law Review*, Vol. 80 (1980), 1399–429, at 1402–3.

[97] Smith, 'Legal Cause', *supra* n. 96, at 305–8.

may be a virtue if degrees of causation vary on a smooth continuum; precise stipulations are notoriously arbitrary when we seek to divide bald from not-bald, old from middle-aged. Moreover, notice how discriminating Smith's view could make causation: if there is a large size threshold for what counts as cause, then only a few of the many events or states necessary for the production of a harm are its causes. It might even turn out that all and only those acts that are 'large causes' are plausibly thought to be rights-violating acts—the discriminating notion of cause sought by the friends of Thomson's thesis.

As a fourth and last possibility, consider what I shall awkwardly call the Becht/Miller/Keeton/Wright view of causation.[98] Keeton's example[99] is helpful in elucidating this view. Suppose a defendant places unlabelled rat poison near a stove; because the stove was in the kitchen, the defendant's act also had the property of placing the rat poison near the food. The heat from the stove causes the rat poison to explode, injuring the plaintiff. If we ask whether the defendant's act of placing the rat poison where he did caused the plaintiff's injury, the answer is, 'yes'. But if we ask whether various properties of the defendant's action caused the plaintiff's injury, we can be more discriminating: that the rat poison was near the food was causally irrelevant, but that it was near to the stove was not.

To narrow the class of things that can be causes the Becht/Miller/Keeton/Wright view must defend two theses: first, a metaphysical thesis that only *properties* of event-tokens (or property-instances) may be causes and that the event-tokens themselves may not be causes; and second, a moral thesis that, in order to determine whether an actor is responsible for a harm, we ask the causal question only with respect to those properties of his act-tokens (or property-instances) that are relevant to his culpability. What this second thesis means with respect to the negligent actor who placed the rat poison in the kitchen, for example, is that we ask whether the property of his act that made it negligent (the placing near the food, assuming *arguendo* that was the only significant risk) caused the harm; and we get a determinate answer, namely, this property did

[98] Their views can be found, respectively, in: A. Becht and F. Miller, *The Test of Factual Causation in Negligence and Strict Liability Cases* (St Louis, Mo.: Washington University Press, 1961); Robert Keeton, *Legal Cause in the Law of Torts* (Columbus: Ohio State University, 1963); Wright, 'Causation', *supra* n. 43.

[99] Keeton, *Legal Cause, supra* n. 98, at 3.

not cause the harm and therefore this actor is not responsible for the harm (even though another property of his act did cause the harm).[100]

This view of the range of objects that can be causes in attributive contexts is highly discriminating in these contexts. In Thomson's 'BRICK' scenario, for example, only A's action has a property that is causally relevant to B's harm in attributive contexts, because only that property was relevant to someone's culpability. Much of the discriminating power of this view of cause, of course, stems from its moral thesis about how one picks properties about which to ask the causal question; it is thus difficult to characterize this view as a purely metaphysical view about causation answering to the needs of wrongdoing and rights.

Each of these four analyses of causation hold out some promise of providing the discriminating idea of causation needed by a friend of Thomson's thesis. Yet each also has serious, perhaps crippling, problems: Epstein's 'paradigms' are not the kind of paradigmatic examples that some ordinary language philosophers, at one time at least, thought could give the meaning of a word such as 'causes',[101] and even if they were, the 'paradigm case argument', as a mode of meaning analysis, is pretty much dead, and for good reason;[102] Hart and Honoré's analysis is either only pragmatic, or, if taken metaphysically, requires a gappy view of determinism that is anathema to those of us with more smoothly determinist world views; Smith's big-versus-little-cause discriminations not only require us to take causation to be primitive—always a problem in non-foundationalist theories of knowledge—but even worse, requires us to believe causation is a scalar phenomenon that admits of degrees;[103] and finally, the Becht/Miller/Keeton/Wright view relies

[100] For actors whose culpability is not negligence, but is intentionality or strict liability, this second thesis has to be worked out separately. See id. at 100–17; Wright, 'Causation', *supra* n. 43, at 1769–71.

[101] John Borgo has some fun with Epstein's misuse of the paradigm case argument in Borgo, 'Causal Paradigms in Tort Law', *Journal of Legal Studies*, Vol. 8 (1979), 419–55, at 427–32.

[102] See Moore, 'Semantics', *supra* n. 32, at 281–92, for a discussion of the paradigm case argument and its limitations.

[103] It is important that this metaphysical question not be made to appear to be easier than it is. Of course, different *types* of events have higher and lower probabilities for bringing about certain other *types* of events, so that if one confuses probability theory with the causal relation between event-tokens, as do Rizzo and Arnold, 'Causal Apportionment', *supra* n. 96, then there will appear to be nothing difficult about conceiving causation to be a scalar phenomenon. Rizzo and Arnold

on the controversial metaphysical view that a property (an instantiated property or 'trope'[104]) can be a cause in lieu of the act-token (that possesses such properties) being a cause.

My own prognosis is that the prospects for discovering the kind of discriminating view of causation required by Thomson's thesis are bleak. Causation may well be just too promiscuous a relation to play this large a role in our moral life. One point on which Thomson and I would fully agree, however, is the need for those interested in the question, lawyers included, to do the metaphysics without which it cannot be answered. The time is long past (if indeed ever it was appropriate) to say that 'the lawyer cannot afford to adventure himself with philosophers in the logical and metaphysical controversies that beset the idea of cause'.[105] Lawyers can ill afford not to so adventure themselves, and those who repeat these oft-quoted words usually do so to excuse an inexcusable ignorance.

---

attempt to justify their slide from probability to causation by observing that '[t]o identify causal relationships it is necessary to know something about the typical relations between events'. Id. at 1409, n. 54. Fair enough, but their conclusion does not follow. Epistemology (how we know something) is not metaphysics (what there is). My earlier scepticism about degrees of causation is expressed in ch. 12, *infra*.

[104] A trope is a concrete universal. That is, suppose some dog is white. The dog is a particular of a certain sort, an object. Whiteness is an abstract universal, and as such has no spatio-temporal location as do particulars. The particular property of whiteness that that dog possesses is a trope, or instantiated universal. Such concrete universals, if they exist, are not identical to either objects or their properties.

[105] Pollock, *Torts* (6th ed., New York: Banks Law Publishing Co., 1901), 36.

8

FORESEEING HARM OPAQUELY

I. THE CONCEPTUAL PROBLEM WITH FORESEEABILITY

Whether a harm was or was not foreseeable figures centrally in doctrines of proximate causation in both the law of torts and the law of crimes. The dominant test of proximate causation in torts makes a defendant liable when but only when the harm he in fact caused was, at the time he acted, foreseeable to him; and while foreseeability is not the dominant general test of proximate causation in Anglo-American criminal law, the concept figures prominently in the important notion of an intervening cause, where it is asked whether the event that is the intervening cause (of the ultimate harm) was itself foreseeable to the defendant at the time he acted.[1]

Apart from policy-based objections to the foreseeability test of proximate causation,[2] there have also been a number of conceptual objections urged against foreseeability. One of these stems from the ambiguity in what is meant by 'foreseeable'. On one understanding

[1] Much has been written either asserting or denying that the conceptions of proximate causation used in torts and criminal law are the same. Compare *State* v. *McFadden*, 320 NW 2d 608 (Iowa Sup. Ct. 1982) (denying that there is any difference and holding the foreseeability of the harm to be determinative in both fields) with *People* v. *Warner-Lambert Co.*, 51 NY 2d 295, 414 NE 2d 660 (1980) (asserting that the proximate cause test is more stringent in criminal law than in torts). The statement of the text is unproblematically true even in jurisdictions like New York, for foreseeability enters criminal law as a criterion of intervening causation (if not of proximate causation generally, as it is under the criminal law of jurisdictions like Iowa). See Rollin M. Perkins and Ronald Boyce, *Criminal Law*, 3rd edn. (Mineola, NY: Foundation Press, 1982), at 813, where the authors recognize the role of foreseeability in intervening cause cases in criminal law while denying that foreseeability is the general criterion of proximate causation in criminal law.

[2] Namely, that any proper theory of corrective justice or of punishment will make moral responsibility at least a necessary condition of legal liability; that moral responsibility for a harm requires causation of that harm, as causation is ordinarily understood; and that the ordinary understanding of causation is *not* in terms of foreseeability. On this last point, the still definitive treatment is H. L. A. Hart and A. M. Honoré, *Causation in the Law* (Oxford: Clarendon Press, 1959).

of this term, it is a normative notion: what is foreseeable is what the reasonable person—that is, the person of adequate ability to perceive danger and of adequate concern about that danger—would have foreseen. On an alternative understanding of the term, it is a strictly statistical notion: what is foreseeable is what the person of average capacities and concerns would have foreseen.

Another conceptual problem with the foreseeability test of proximate causation is the obvious vagueness of the term. Foreseeability is obviously a matter of degree that can vary along a smooth continuum, and the foreseeability test does not spell out *how* foreseeable a harm must be to be legally foreseeable.

Neither of these vagaries in the meaning of 'foreseeable' pose insurmountable difficulties for a test using the concept. With regard to the above-noted ambiguity, a legal decision-maker can simply stipulate either the normative or the statistical meaning, depending on which concept her normative theory best justified. With regard to the above-noted vagueness, a variety of remedies is possible. One would be to quantify degrees of foreseeability in terms of degrees of probability and to stipulate a certain level of probability as constituting foreseeability.[3] Alternatively, one might treat 'foreseeability' as akin to attributive adjectives, which lean on the nouns that they modify for their meaning;[4] this approach would create a sliding scale foreseeability test, less probability being required for more serious harms, more probability for less serious harms.[5] Or yet again, one could do neither of these things and still have a serviceable concept nonetheless. After all, many legal concepts are vague, yet that does not prevent them from having a core of easy applications (even if they also have a penumbra of not easy applications).[6]

More serious is a challenge to the coherence of the concept of foreseeability. I refer to what I shall call the multiple description problem. The problem arises because of two considerations. The

---

[3] On the difference between ambiguity and vagueness, and on the possibility of remedying the latter by precise, numerical definitions, see Michael Moore, 'The Semantics of Judging', *Southern California Law Review*, Vol. 54 (1981), 151–294, at 181–8, 193–200.

[4] On attributive (or sometimes, 'syncategorematic') adjectives, see ibid., 182, 243, 276.

[5] This of course would tend to collapse the foreseeability criterion of proximate causation toward the test for negligence.

[6] Glanville Williams, 'Language and the Law', *Law Quarterly Review*, Vol. 61 (1945), 71–86; H. L. A. Hart, 'Positivism and the Separation of Law and Morals', *Harvard Law Review*, Vol. 71 (1958), 593–629.

first is the well-known fact that there are many equally accurate ways to describe any particular thing. We often refer to particular persons by their proper name, but as often, by any number of definite descriptions: 'the teacher of Aristotle', 'the author of *Waverly*', 'the greatest running back in college football history'. Likewise, particular events are susceptible of alternative modes of reference that are equally accurate. A particular flood, for example, may have a name ('the Buffalo Creek Disaster'), and it will have many equally accurate definite descriptions: for example, 'the largest flood of the year', 'the most talked about event of the decade', 'the subject of a multimillion dollar lawsuit', etc. The reason that persons, objects, events, and other particulars may be so variously described in our language should be apparent: such particulars possess many properties, and an accurate description of such a particular may be formed simply by referring to one or more of these properties and prefixing the description with the definite article, 'the'.

The second consideration giving rise to the multiple description problem is the dependence of foreseeability on how a harm-event is described. Forty years ago Clarence Morris observed that how the harm was described makes a great deal of difference as to whether that harm was foreseeable.[7] One can describe any harm particularly enough to say of it (under that description) that it was *unforeseeable* or generally enough to say of it (under the second description) that it was *foreseeable*. Without some limits on permissible descriptions, the foreseeability rule of proximate causation is completely vacuous in the judicial decisions that it dictates.

Interestingly enough, Morris drew back from fully endorsing this sceptical conclusion about the foreseeability rule. He divided the proximate cause cases in torts into three classes:

Once misconduct causes damage, a specific accident has happened in a particular way and has resulted in a discrete harm. When, after the event, the question is asked, 'Was the particular accident and the resulting damages foreseeable?', the cases fall into the three classes: (1) In some cases damages resulting from misconduct are so typical that judge and jurors cannot possibly be convinced that they were unforeseeable. If Mr. Builder negligently drops a brick on Mr. Pedestrian who is passing an urban site of a

---

[7] Clarence Morris, 'Duty, Negligence and Causation', *University of Pennsylvania Law Review*, Vol. 101 (1952), 189–222, at 194–200; Clarence Morris, *Torts*, (Brooklyn, NY: Foundation Press, 1953), at 174–7.

house under construction, even though the dent in Pedestrian's skull is microscopically unique in pattern, Builder could not sensibly maintain that the injury was unforeseeable. (2) In some cases freakishness of the facts refuses to be drowned and any description that minimizes it is viewed as misdescription. For example, in a recent Louisiana case a trucker negligently left his truck on the highway at night without setting out flares. A car crashed into the truck and caught fire. A passerby came to the rescue of the car occupants—a man and wife. After the rescuer got them out of the car he returned to the car to get a floor mat to pillow the injured wife's head. A pistol lay on the mat rescuer wanted to use. He picked it up and handed it to the husband. The accident had unbeknownst to the rescuer, temporarily deranged the husband, and he shot rescuer in the leg. Such a consequence of negligently failing to guard the truck with flares is so unarguably unforeseeable that no judge or juror would be likely to hold otherwise. . . . (3) Between these extremes are cases in which consequences are neither typical nor wildly freakish. In these cases unusual details are arguably—but only arguably significant. If they are held significant, then the consequences are unforeseeable; if they are held unimportant then the consequences are foreseeable.[8]

Morris was certainly correct about there being varying degrees of predictability of the outcome of cases involving foreseeability. In some cases one does know with reasonable certainty that the harm will be held by juries or judges to be foreseeable; in others, that it will be held to be unforeseeable. There are also cases where such knowledge is not possible.

The tempting though mistaken account of this phenomenon (of partial predictability) is to return to the vagueness of the word 'foreseeable'. As we have seen, 'foreseeable' is a vague word, in the same way as 'bald', 'heap', and 'red' are vague words. There are degrees of foreseeability, of baldness, of 'heapedness', and of redness, and although there are clear instances (and clear non-instances) of each, there are also borderline cases where one does not know what to say.

Although 'foreseeability' is a vague word, its vagueness has nothing to do with Morris's taxonomy of proximate cause cases. One can see this by fixing more precisely on when the vagueness of 'foreseeable' does enter in. Once one has picked a description of the harm, then (and only then) does the vagueness of 'foreseeability' sometimes prevent one from knowing whether the harm was or was

    [8] Morris, *Torts, supra* n. 7, at 174–7.

not foreseeable to the defendant. Whether a harm (under a description) was sufficiently likely to occur so as to say that the reasonable, average person would have foreseen it, may have no answer; or it may be in the core of 'foreseeable' or in the core of 'unforeseeable'. Like any other vague word, 'foreseeable' will have cases in all three categories. Yet one can only intelligibly ask the question, 'was the harm foreseeable?', once one has picked a description of that harm. The taxonomy of Morris cannot thus be explained in terms of vagueness.

Unlike the vagueness problem, the multiple description problem threatens the foreseeability test with complete vacuousness. In Morris's Pedestrian-Builder case, for example, surely if we describe the harm-event in enough detail, that event was unforeseeable. For example: 'the indentation on Pedestrian's skull of such and such a depth, and such and such a pattern', due no doubt to the precise movement of Pedestrian when he was hit and to the angle and rotation of the brick at time of impact. These details, and the fortuity of the discrete physical forces that conjointly caused them, would be unforeseeable to all but an omniscient being. Likewise in the Louisiana case that Morris references, what if we redescribed the accident as follows:

Plaintiff was on the highway, using it in a lawful manner, and attempted to rescue two persons injured by defendant's negligence, and plaintiff was himself injured in undertaking the rescue.[9]

Given the law's predilection to hold the intervention of rescuers to be foreseeable, I take it that the harm so described was foreseeable.

If these cases that Morris took to be 'unarguably' foreseeable and unforeseeable, respectively, can be transformed in outcome by more specific or more general descriptions of the harm, no case seems immune to this outcome determinative redescription. Put another way, because of the multiple description problem the foreseeability test seems to decide no cases whatsoever.

[9] This redescription is a paraphrase of the equally general description given by the plaintiff in *Hines* v. *Morrow*, 236 SW 183 (Tex. Cir. App. 1922), which as Morris noted, was apparently accepted by the appellate court in upholding the jury verdict that the harm was foreseeable. Morris perhaps drew back from the more sceptical implications of his insight because he thought foreseeability to be essential to proximate cause. As he earlier had put it, 'attempts to escape from the significance of foresight in the field of legal remoteness are attempts to escape from our culture'. Clarence Morris, 'Proximate Cause in Minnesota', *Minnesota Law Review*, Vol. 34 (1950), 185–209, at 197.

It might seem that the foreseeability test just cannot be this vacuous in the face of the plain fact that each of us does have some capacity to predict the occurrence of future events. If each of us has some such predictive capacity, must there not be an average of such individual capacities, which average one might call the foresight of the reasonable person? Yet if we reflect on what our predictive capacities amount to, both individually and on average, we shall see how untouched is the multiple description problem by this plain fact. When we predict that an event will occur in the future, or when we judge retroactively that an event that has now occurred was predictable in the more remote past, we are given a description of that event. 'Can you predict that a fire will occur in that house?', and 'was the fire that occurred yesterday in that house predictable the day before yesterday?', are perfectly sensible questions to which we often know the answer. This is because the question asked feeds us a description of the event about which we are to make our predictions. We are never asked to predict an event described as, 'the event'; we are only asked to predict 'the fire', 'the automobile collision', 'the tree limb falling', or some other adequately described event. The problem with the foreseeability test is that it gives us no such descriptions of the harm. The test rather asks us to assess whether *the harm* that occurred was foreseeable. Unless we are to use the description, 'harm'—which our law makes plain we are not[10]—the test asks an unanswerable question. It is like being asked by another to predict the occurrence of x, where x is some event

---

[10] Such a very general description makes virtually all harms foreseeable. For if 'harm' is all that need be foreseeable, then so long as some sort of harm is foreseeable any sort of harm is proximately caused. If, for example, it is foreseeable that a dock will suffer slight oil slick damage from the defendant's negligently spilling virtually non-combustible oil into a harbour, then when the dock burns down (due to an extremely rare combination of conditions resulting in an unheard of temperature igniting the oil) that harm was foreseeable. Harm was foreseeable and harm occurred, and if we are not given any more determinate description of the harm than 'harm', the foreseeability rule is satisfied.

Criminal law here differs somewhat from the law of torts, for in criminal law the *actus reus* prohibited by the relevant criminal statute will give (or presuppose) some description of the harm. 'Death of a human being' is a good example in homicide prohibitions. Yet the main use of foreseeability in criminal law's proximate cause doctrine is with regard to intervening causation wherein it is asked, not whether the type of harm prohibited by statute was foreseeable, but rather, whether the intervening event that directly caused the prohibited harm was foreseeable (see n. 1 above). Criminal law no more gives authoritative descriptions of these intervening events than tort law does of the harm.

that may occur in the future but we are given no properties of x that would enable us to pick it out. Until x is given a description telling us some of its properties we have not yet been asked a complete enough question to be able to formulate an answer.

Consider by way of analogy a legal rule requiring us to judge whether two particular events are *similar*. No respects in which the events might be similar are specified, and the context of the rule does not give us any implicit criteria for isolating any property or properties with respect to which we are to judge the similarity of the events. Such a rule is completely vacuous because it has not asked us a complete question. For every event-particular is similar in some way(s) to every other event-particular, dissimilar in other ways. Until we know the relevant respects in which we are to judge two events to be similar, we can give no answer (because we can equally well give both answers). The foreseeability rule of proximate causation asks just such an incomplete question. Such incompleteness renders the rule completely vacuous, even though when we ask ourselves complete foreseeability questions (as we do in predictions in science and daily life) we often can give determinate and truthful answers.

II. EXTENSIONALITY, OPACITY, AND ANOTHER LOOK AT MORRIS'S PROBLEM

Such a sceptical conclusion about foreseeability may be welcome to those of a sceptical cast of mind generally, be they Legal Realists left over from a previous generation or one or other of that more contemporary variety of what Morris Cohen aptly called the 'stray dogs of the intellectual world',[11] those gadflies whose persistent scepticism keeps the rest of us honest. Yet in order to understand the present problem, one must forgo the headlong plunge into a broader scepticism about facts and factual descriptions that these sceptical intellectual fashions represent.

The multiple description problem is in no way dependent upon scepticism about reality. Nor is the thesis hostage to Jerome Frank's corrosive cynicism about judges' or juries' capacity for

[11] Morris R. Cohen, 'The Place of Logic in the Law', *Harvard Law Review*, Vol. 29 (1916), 622–39, at 625. I thus put aside the worries of some current stray dogs, that all law is sundered by what they call 'fundamental contradictions'.

finding (or sincerity in even looking for) the truth in particular cases.[12] On the contrary, one can assume some descriptions of the facts of a particular case are true, and others false, and that to enjoin legal fact-finders to find the truth in cases before them does not presuppose an unwarranted degree of optimism about human nature. Even so, the problem about the indeterminacy of foreseeability remains, for this problem is due to there being *too many true and accurate descriptions of reality*—not to there being no reality for any description to be accurate in representing.[13]

One way of understanding the discrete problem posed for foreseeability tests by the existence of many equally accurate descriptions of events, is to see why there is no analogous problem for most legal tests. Consider an old example I have used in other contexts, the former agricultural exemption to the Interstate Commerce Act. A federal statute generally required interstate motor carriers to obtain a certificate of convenience and necessity from the Interstate Commerce Commission. The agricultural exemption allowed those interstate carriers who transport 'agricultural commodities but not manufactured products thereof' to do so without obtaining the certificate. Suppose a carrier is apprehended carrying frozen, plucked, eviscerated, New York dressed poultry interstate without a certificate. In deciding whether the exemption applies, a court might describe the items carried as 'eviscerated chickens'. Yet there is nothing that singles out the use of the predicate, 'is an eviscerated chicken', to describe the things in the back of the carrier's truck. One could equally truthfully describe them as 'chickens', 'frozen, eviscerated chickens', 'formerly feathered bipeds', 'cargo', or in a hundred and one other ways. All are accu-

[12] Jerome Frank, *Law and the Modern Mind* (New York, 1930).

[13] Some Legal Realists perceived this point, although the use to which they put it was considerably different than that to which it is put herein. Walter Wheeler Gook, for example, in ' "Facts" and "Statements of Fact" ', *University of Chicago Law Review*, Vol. 4 (1937), 233–46, used the point to urge that the old pleading requirement that one state the facts constituting a cause of action provided no real guidance to a pleader given the many possibilities of different description. Similarly, Felix Cohen implicitly relied on the point in urging that there could be no value-free conception of precedent that enjoined a judge to discover the rule of a previous case from just the decision and the facts of the earlier case. Cohen, 'The Ethical Basis of Legal Criticism', *Yale Law Journal*, Vol. 41 (1931), 201–20; the point is more convincingly pressed home in Julius Stone, *Legal Systems and Lawyer's Reasonings*, (Stanford, Cal.: Stanford University Press, 1964), ch.7, § 12).

rate descriptions, and if truth is the only pedigree each potentially could be used in a truthful statement of the facts.

So far this multitude of equally true factual statements is not much of an embarrassment. A legal fact-finder should simply sift through all factual descriptions used by witnesses, decide which are true descriptions of what happened and which are relevant to the authoritative language it is his office to apply, and ignore the rest. The only difficulties of there being so many descriptions are practical ones—that, given limited time and limited evidence, it is more difficult to find the relevant descriptions, and mistakes will sometimes be made. There is no problem of different legal conclusions, depending on which description of the things carried is used.

To be sure, every legal standard, either by itself or in conjunction with others, must *potentially* license an inference to opposite conclusions. In the example just given, the Interstate Commerce Act not only provided that if an item is an agricultural commodity and not a manufactured product thereof it may be carried by a non-certificated carrier; the Act also provided that (with further exceptions here ignored) if an item is *not* an agricultural commodity, or *is* a manufactured product of an agricultural commodity, then it may be carried only on a certificated carrier. This means that the statute licensed an inference to either result: a certificate is not required for the interstate carriage of certain classes of items, required for all the rest. The same authoritative legal language potentially licenses contradictory inferences.

The assumption of course is that any one case will either fall on one side of the line or the other, that any particular item will either be classed as agricultural or non-agricultural, manufactured or not manufactured, in which event only one conclusion will be deducible *in any given case*. And this assumption is borne out by any plausible interpretation of the phrase, 'manufactured product'. Suppose an independently sufficient criterion of an agricultural commodity being transformed into a manufactured product, is that it is killed. Slaughtered cattle, frozen tomatoes, and eviscerated chickens, would thus all be manufactured products. Does it matter how the things in the carrier's truck are described in order to truthfully predicate 'killed' of them? Rather clearly it does not. However you describe those items, that they have been killed is true of them. (Under some descriptions, for example, 'cargo', one would get curious combinations; but one would not get a change of truth value of the sentence completed by the predicate, 'is killed'.) Thus, as 'chickens', as 'eviscerated chickens', as 'formerly feathered bipeds', we will be equally truthful in saying, they have been killed. Hence, under the suggested criterion of 'manufactured product'—killed— how the things in the truck are described does not matter.

There is a good reason for this. It is known as Leibniz's Law. Leibniz's Law holds that for any two things x and y, if x is identical with y, then anything truly predicable of x has to be truly predicable of y, and vice versa.[14] Put in other words, if two putatively distinct particulars are in reality one and the same thing, then they are indiscernible with respect to all of their properties at any one time. Thus, if x is an eviscerated chicken, and y is a formerly feathered biped, and x is the very same object as y, then anything that can be said of x can be said of y without change of truth value.

Leibniz's Law is generally thought to be a basic characteristic of any language adequate for science.[15] Scientific laws require that they be true of given objects in the world no matter how those objects are described. This is usually summarized by saying that the language of science is extensional. Insofar as the law employs an extensional language—a language in which one may substitute different descriptions of the same things without change of the truth values of the sentences in which such descriptions occur—the problem of arriving at contradictory decisions from the same legal standard will not arise.

'Foreseeability' does not seem like 'manufactured product' and other, more typical legal standards in this respect, for how the harm is described matters to the truth of expression of the form, 'that harm was (un)foreseeable'. Why this is so for words like 'foreseeability' has been the subject of considerable attention in twentieth-

---

[14] In the symbols of the predicate calculus with quantification and identity that I will use throughout these footnotes:

$$(x) (y) [(x = y) \supset (Fx \equiv Fy)]$$

I shall ignore interpretations of Leibniz's Law different than the indiscernability of identicals that make the truth of the Law more questionable. See, e.g., Mark Richard, *Propositional Attitudes* (Cambridge: Cambridge University Press, 1990), at 199–200.

[15] The most sustained contemporary argument to this conclusion is W. V. Quine's, most notably in his *Word and Object* (Cambridge, Mass.: MIT Press, 1960); see also his 'The Scope and Language of Science', in Quine, *The Ways of Paradox*, (Cambridge, Mass.: MIT Press, 1966).

century philosophy. From Frege[16] through the important work of W. V. Quine,[17] to Quine's collaborators and critics,[18] a good deal of effort has been devoted to working out an account of various contexts in which Leibniz's Law does not straightforwardly appear to hold. These contexts have been notably two: modal contexts, for example, where one might say, 'necessarily, nine is greater than five', and the contexts of what Russell called the propositional attitudes, for example, where one might say, 'Ralph believes the man in the brown hat is a spy'. Since the latter construction is the one of importance to law, I shall focus my attention on it exclusively. Even so limited, what follows is but a sketchy summary of some basics about propositional attitudes. Given the amount of work that has been done on oblique contexts since this chapter was written in the 1970s, spelling out these basics in any detail would be controversial.

It is commonly said that there are two problems about the propositional attitudes: failure of substitutivity, and failure of existential generalization. Both are closely related,[19] but I shall discuss each in order. To revert to Quine's now classic example:[20] suppose someone, call him Ralph, believes that a man he has seen in a brown hat is a spy. Suppose Ralph sees a grey-haired man on the beach, whom he knows to be a distinguished citizen; Ralph, thinking of spies, says to himself that that man, the man on the beach, is no spy. As it turns out, 'the man in the brown hat' and 'the man on the beach' are different descriptions of one and the same man,

---

[16] Gottlob Frege, 'On Sense and Reference', originally published as 'Sinn und Bedeutung', *Zeitschrift für Philosophie Und Philosophische Kritik*, Vol. 100 (1892), 25–50, translated and reprinted in P. T. Geach and M. Black, *Philosophical Writings of Gottlob Frege* (Oxford: Oxford University Press, 1960).

[17] In addition to *Word and Object, supra* n. 15, see particularly 'Reference and Modality', in Quine, *From a Logical Point of View* (Cambridge, Mass.: Harvard University Press, 1953), and 'Quantifiers and Propositional Attitudes', in Quine, *The Ways of Paradox, supra* n. 15.

[18] A series of essays on Quine's work on these topics is collected in Leonard Linsky (ed.), *Reference and Modality* (Oxford: Oxford University Press, 1971), in D. Davidson and J. Hintikka (eds.), *Words and Objections* (Dordrecht, Holland: Reidel, 1969), and in P. Hahn and P. Schlipp (eds.), *The Philosophy of W. V. Quine* (La Salle, Ill.: Open Court, 1986).

[19] For the argument that these two failures come to much the same thing, see Leonard Linsky, 'Reference, Essentialism, and Modality', in Linsky (ed.), *Reference and Modality, supra* n. 18. For a more complicated view, urging that there are cases where there can be one kind of failure without the other, see Brian Loar, 'Reference and Propositional Attitudes', *Philosophical Review*, Vol. 81 (1972), 43–62.

[20] In 'Quantifiers and Propositional Attitudes', *supra* n. 17.

whose name is Ortcutt, although Ralph did not know this. How should we describe Ralph's beliefs?

One thing that Ralph rather clearly believes is that the man in the brown hat is a spy. Let us represent this as follows:

(1) Ralph B (the man in the brown hat is a spy).

By hypothesis, it is also true that:

(2) The man in the brown hat = the man on the beach.

If Leibniz's Law held, (1) and (2) would yield:

(3) Ralph B (the man on the beach is a spy).

Yet (3) contradicts what Ralph himself would say about what he believes; Ralph would say that it is not the case that he believes that the man on the beach is a spy.[21] There is thus an apparent failure of substitutivity.

Turning to the second problem, failure of existential generalization: it is a rule of inference of modern logic that one may quantify open sentences with the existential quantifier. What this means in English is that if one predicates something about some one particular thing—for example, spyhood about the man in the brown hat—one is entitled to infer that 'there is someone such that he is a spy'.[22] This move is known as existential generalization both because one has generalized—one is no longer talking of some one particular person but of 'someone' —and because one is committed to the existence of some thing by saying, 'there is . . .'.

Existential generalization fails for sentences like (1). If we were to apply this rule of inference to (1) it would yield:

(4) There is someone such that Ralph B (he is a spy).[23]

Sentence (4) does not follow from (1) for the reason that (3) did not follow from (1): it does not take into account the fact that Ralph's beliefs about someone being a spy depend on a particular descrip-

---

[21] To be distinguished from something else Ralph would say, namely, that he believes that the man on the beach is not a spy. The non-belief in the text would be represented by: it is not the case that Ralph B (the man on the beach is a spy); the belief just distinguished would be: Ralph B (it is not the case that the man on the beach is a spy).

[22] From Sx (where 'S' is the predicate, 'is a spy') to $(\exists x)$ Sx.

[23] $(\exists x)$ [Ralph B (Sx)]. To be distinguished from the notional, Ralph B [$(\exists x)$ Sx]. See below.

tion of that person. Describe him as 'the man in the brown hat', and Ralph believes him to be a spy; describe him as 'the man on the beach', and Ralph has no such belief. (4) fails to take this dependence upon description into account, for it asserts that it is about an object in the world—Ortcutt—that Ralph has his beliefs about spyhood; and this is not true of Ralph, for he believes that the man in the brown hat is a spy but he does not believe that the man on the beach is a spy, even though these are seemingly two different descriptions of Ortcutt. (4), accordingly, does not follow from (1), even though the rule of inference known as existential generalization says that it should.

These two peculiarities of constructions using '. . . believes that . . .' extend throughout the propositional attitudes. Mental state descriptions using constructions such as '. . . intends that . . .', '. . . knows that . . .', '. . . is aware that . . .', '. . . wants that . . .', '. . . hopes that . . .', '. . . foresees that . . .', and the like, will share these failures of substitutivity and existential generalization. Many descriptions of actions will also utilize this kind of construction. If, for example, Ralph orders (selects, requests, seeks, asks for) the largest room in an inn, the true identity statement, 'the largest room in the inn = the dirtiest room in the inn', does not license one to conclude that Ralph ordered (selected, requested, sought, asked for) the dirtiest room in the inn.

Speaking very generally, there are only three strategies for dealing with this impasse between the demands of identity and our usage of contexts like that created by 'foreseeable', 'intend', and the like. The first strategy is to amend our notions of numerical identity and of modern logic to simply allow that there are exceptions to Leibniz's Law and existential generalization for these kinds of constructions. Such a strategy must distinguish expressions like:

(5) The man in the brown hat is a spy,

from expressions like (1). One would admit that Leibniz's Law, together with (5) and the identity statement given earlier as (2), would yield:

(6) The man at the beach is a spy.

But on this view the inference to (3) from (1) and (2) would be said to be barred because Leibniz's Law simply does not apply to the propositional attitudes.

This strategy is not only *ad hoc*, but it is wildly counterintuitive to our understanding of identity. If the phrase 'the man in the brown hat' as used in (1) truly refers to Ortcutt, so that (1) no less than (5) asserts something about Ortcutt (namely, in (1), a relation of believed-to-be-a-spy-by-Ralph), then that same thing should be assertable about Ortcutt no matter how he is described. Leibniz's Law, after all, only asserts the very plausible idea that qualitative identity follows numerical identity, that is, that anything has the same properties no matter how it is described. If identity does not mean this, it is hard to see what it does mean.[24]

Given that our notion of identity bars the postulating of some *ad hoc* exception to Leibniz's Law for constructions like '. . . is foreseeable', a second and more tempting strategy is to deny the insight of Morris with which we began. That is, it may be tempting to deny that how you describe the harm affects whether that harm is foreseeable. Then there would be no need to create exceptions to Leibniz's Law.

To see whether this is possible, let us return to our friend Ralph. On this view, we should take the phrase, 'the man in the brown hat', as used in (1) to refer to Ortcutt, but hold Leibniz's Law and existential generalization to be exceptionless. This view would then go on to say that Ralph does have the belief he is said to have in (3), despite his disclaimer that he does not; this view would also say that (4) logically follows from (1). Both of these last moves come to the same thing: what they presuppose is that the objects of Ralph's beliefs are not individuated by descriptions of real world objects, but by the underlying identities of the real world things (here, Ortcutt) themselves. What Ralph believes of Ortcutt under one description, he also believes under any other, on this view.

Such a view, rejecting the dependence of the propositional attitudes upon descriptions of their objects, was implicitly adopted by Edwin Keedy.[25] In Keedy's work the concept of intention was at issue, not belief or foresight, but the view was nonetheless the one

---

[24] See, e.g., Neil Wilson, *The Concept of Language*, (Toronto: University of Toronto Press, 1959), at 39 ('If identity does not mean universal interchangeability, then I do not really understand identity at all'); D. Follesdal, 'Quantification into Causal Contexts', in Linsky (ed.), *Reference and Modality*, *supra* n. 18, at 56 ('tampering with the substitutivity of identity may easily make the notion of identity unintelligible').

[25] Edwin Keedy, 'Criminal Attempts at Common Law', *University of Pennsylvania Law Review*, Vol. 102 (1954), 464–89.

here considered. Keedy was seeking to elucidate the common law test for when a criminal attempt was 'legally impossible' and therefore not punishable. The test centrally turns on the intention of the accused: if he had succeeded in doing all he intended to do and the result still would not have been criminal, then the attempt is legally impossible. Two of Keedy's applications of this test were:

If A takes an umbrella which he believes to belong to B, but which in fact is his own, he does not have the intent to steal, his intent being to take the umbrella he grasps in his hand, which is his own umbrella. . . . If a man mistakes a stump for his enemy and shoots at it, notwithstanding his desire and expectation to shoot his enemy, his intent is to shoot the object aimed at, which is the stump.[26]

Unpacked, the first hypothetical asserts that from:

(7) A intends (take that umbrella)

and the true identity

(8) that umbrella = A's own umbrella

it follows that:

(9) A intends (take A's own umbrella).

This, surely, is to abuse the concept of intention. To deny significance to differing descriptions of the intention's object is to alter radically our understanding of what an intention is. Moreover, the altered concept is not a serviceable one for making discriminations in culpability. Consider the legal impossibility test for criminal attempts. On Keedy's understanding of intention, all instances of attempts become cases of non-punishable legal impossibility. Take the pickpocket cases:

(10) The defendant intends (reach into this pocket).

Suppose the would-be pickpocket thought there was money in the pocket, but, as it turned out:

(11) This pocket = the empty pocket.

Therefore:

(12) The defendant intends (reach into the empty pocket)?

---

[26] Ibid., 466–7.

Surely not. The remedy to prevent this kind of wholesale exculpa-
tion of criminals who by happenstance are unsuccessful, is to give
'intent' its normal meaning.

The same holds true for 'belief', 'foresight', and 'foreseeability'.
Imagine a case involving a defendant who wielded a knife in such
a way that he cut off the plaintiff's left arm. Suppose that the defendant was engaged in some other activity but foresaw that the plaintiff would move in such a way that the plaintiff's left arm would be
cut. Analogously to sentence (1) above discussed we can say:

> (1a) The defendant foresaw (the cutting of plaintiff's left arm).

Suppose that the cutting of plaintiff's left arm was also the cutting
off of plaintiff's writing arm, the plaintiff being left-handed and the
cut being rather severe. The following identity statement is true:[27]

> (2a) The cutting of plaintiff's left arm = the cutting off of plain-
> tiff's writing arm.

If 'foresaw' were given Keedy's kind of reading, it would follow
both that:

> (3a) The defendant foresaw (the cutting off of plaintiff's writ-
> ing arm,

and

> (4a) There is some event of arm-cutting such that defendant
> foresaw that very event.

Just as before with respect to 'belief', (3a) and (4a) do not seem to
square with what we mean by 'foresee'. (3a) does not follow from
(1a) and (2a), for how the harm is described matters. If the defendant does not know that the plaintiff is left-handed, or that the cut
would amount to a cutting off, then (3a) is false. Similarly, the existentially generalized (4a) is false because it suggests that defendant
foresaw the harm under any description, which he did not.
'Foresee', like 'intent' and 'belief', depends on how the object of
foresight is described.

---

[27] Some 'fine-grained' modes of individuating particular events would not think
this identity to be true. See, e.g., Alvin Goldman, *A Theory of Human Action*
(Englewood Cliffs, NJ: Prentice-Hall, 1970), ch. 1. For a defence of the 'coarse-
grained' mode of individuating events, see Michael Moore, *Act and Crime* (Oxford:
Oxford University Press, 1993), ch. 11.

The construction, '. . . was foreseeable by . . .', will share this dependence upon description of 'foresee'. If we adopt the statistical notion of foreseeability, harms that are foreseeable are harms that the average, reasonable person in the defendant's situation would have foreseen. The average or reasonable person—the person of average foresight—foresees in the same way as do the rest of us: opaquely (that is, relative to some description of what is foreseen).

A more limited version of this second strategy (denying a dependence on description of the propositional attitudes) would be to regard the words naming such attitudes as having two senses, one of which allows substitutivity and existential generalization. Such a sense would be what Quine once called the 'transparent' (or *de re*) sense of 'belief' (to be opposed to the more usual 'opaque' or *de dicto*' sense of 'belief').[28] 'Belief' is called transparent when it allows substitution of identicals, opaque when it resists it. Suppose in lieu of (1) one said:

(13) Of Ortcutt Ralph B (he is a spy).

According to Quine what is meant by (13) is that Ralph believes of Ortcutt, under any description or name, that he is a spy. If so, 'belief' in (13) would be used transparently. So used, (14) and (15) would follow from (13) because of Leibniz's Law:

(14) Of man in the brown hat Ralph B (he is a spy).
(15) Of the man on the beach Ralph B (he is a spy).

Similarly, (4) would follow from (13) by existential generalization:

(4) There is someone such that Ralph B (he is a spy).

Notice that on such an account 'belief' (and all the words used in the propositional attitudes) is irreducibly ambiguous. With a definite singular term such as 'the man in the brown hat', we may mean either (1) or (14) in our use of 'belief'. Quine initially thought that the same ambiguity could be detected when one uses the *in*definite singular term,[29] as when we say that *a* person (i.e., someone) is a

---

[28] Quine, *Word and Object*, supra n. 15, at §30.

[29] Quine, 'Quantifiers and the Propositional Attitudes', *supra* n. 17; see also *Word and Object*, supra n. 15, § 31. A singular term is one that refers to a particular thing (as opposed to predicating some quality to it); an indefinite singular term is a singular term preceded by the indefinite article, 'a', which can usually be translated as the existential quantifier, 'some'.

spy. When we say that Ralph believes someone is a spy, we may mean (4) (there is some one particular person Ralph believes to be a spy); or we may mean:

(16) Ralph B (someone is a spy).

(16), unlike (4), only means that Ralph believes there are spies, while having no such belief about any particular person. Ralph's belief construed as (16) is not, as Quine mentions,[30] an occasion for calling the FBI, although construed as (4), it is. According to Quine's initial thought, (4) commits one to using 'belief' transparently, for no particular name or description is used in (4) with which to refer to the person believed to be a spy by Ralph.[31] (16), by way of contrast, does not commit one to using 'belief' transparently because Ralph does not have a belief about any particular person so that the question of the substitutability of different names or descriptions of that person does not arise.

The basic problem with this two senses account of the propositional attitudes lies in the continued oddity of the supposed transparent sense. Notice, first of all, that 'belief' taken transparently commits one to ascribing an indefinitely large number of beliefs to Ralph if we ascribe any belief to him. If we say, for example, that Ralph believes that Ortcutt is a spy, then we would be committed to saying that Ralph has a similar belief of spyhood about Ortcutt under any name or description which a native speaker of the language (but not necessarily Ralph!) might use to refer to Ortcutt. Similarly with taking, for example, 'intention' transparently: if one asserts that Ralph intended to cut off George's left arm, one would be committed to an indefinitely large number of intentions on Ralph's part. For example, Ralph intended to cut off George's writing arm, if George is left-handed; Ralph intended to cut off George's dirty arm, if George's left arm is dirty, etc.[32] Transparency seems to commit us to a mental life and a mastery of our language far greater than we in fact have.

Secondly, taking 'belief' to have a transparent sense leads one either to ignore what the believer himself would say about his beliefs or to ascribe numerous pairs of contradictory beliefs to him.

---

[30] *Word and Object, supra* n. 15, § 31.

[31] Ibid. Quine's intentionally paradoxical formulation: 'indefinite singular terms need referential position because they do not refer'.

[32] On a transparent reading of 'intention', see ch. 11 *infra*.

Take our friend Ralph again: if we take 'belief' in (1) as transparent, then we are committed to (3). Yet Ralph would say two things related to (3):

(17) It is not the case that Ralph B (the man on the beach is a spy).

And:

(18) Ralph B (it is not the case that the man on the beach is a spy).

(17) is the contradictory of (3);[33] to accept (3) is thus to ignore what Ralph himself would say about his beliefs. (18) is not the contradictory of (3); yet if we regard both (3) and (18) as true, we have ascribed beliefs to Ralph that have contradictory propositions as their contents.[34]

While recognizing some of these difficulties with postulating a transparent sense to 'belief', Quine nonetheless felt he was driven to such a sense in order to give an account of statements such as (4). More recent analyses, however, have shown that the very real distinction between the two uses of the indefinite article in (4) and (16) can be maintained *without* a transparent sense of 'belief'. One cannot both maintain that 'belief' has two senses, opaque and transparent (as above defined), and that there is the relation between such senses that Quine envisioned,[35] without leading to a collapse of the distinction (between (4) and (16)) that Quine was attempting to maintain.[36] The upshot of this and the preceding

[33] For a qualification of this, see David Kaplan, 'Quantifying In', in Davidson and Hintikka (eds.), *Words and Objections*, *supra* n. 18, at 274.

[34] Which is, as Quine himself points out, *almost* to say of Ralph that he believes a contradiction. If (3) and (18) imply: (19) Ralph B (the man on the beach is a spy, and it is not the case that the man on the beach is a spy) then Ralph does believe a contradiction. Only by denying the implication of (19) from (3) and (18) does Quine avoid ascribing belief in a contradiction to Ralph on a transparent reading of 'belief'. See Quine, 'Quantifiers and the Propositional Attitudes', *supra* n. 17.

[35] Ibid., 106.

[36] Quine originally thought that one could derive a transparent usage of 'belief' from any opaque usage. If Ralph believes (opaquely) that Ortcutt was a spy, and Ortcutt truly exists, then one could say that Ralph believes (transparently) of Ortcutt that he is a spy. The problem for this view of the relation between the two supposed senses of 'belief' was pointed out by Kaplan: Assume that Ralph believes (opaquely) that someone (but no particular person) is a spy. If Ralph is like most of us, he will believe (opaquely) that some one spy is the shortest spy. Thus, Ralph will believe (opaquely) that the shortest spy is a spy. Yet if there is someone who is the shortest spy, it follows from Quine's notion of the relation between the senses of 'belief'

considerations is that the idea of there being a transparent sense to 'belief' is a mistake.[37]

I conclude that we can tamper neither with the notion of identity nor with the description-dependence of the propositional attitudes in a way that alleviates the seeming conflict between the demands of each. Nor is Quine's purported halfway house a real option. One response to this dilemma would be to adopt the attitude of complete scepticism about terms like 'foreseeability': they are literally without any sense whatsoever. This was ultimately Quine's own attitude: if modal discourse and discourse about the propositional attitudes could not be regimented to fit within the extensional language of science, then they should be dispensed with in serious discussions.[38] Such an attitude, of course, is easier to state than to live with, particularly in a discipline such as the law whose doctrines are heavily laced with distinctions based on the propositional attitudes of belief, intention, and foresight.

The only other alternative is to adopt the third strategy available here: we should reconstrue the seemingly clear reference of the words appearing in the objects of the propositional attitudes. Perhaps 'the man in the brown hat' in (1) or 'the man on the beach' in (3) do not refer to Ortcutt, a particular; similarly, perhaps 'the harm done' does not refer to a particular event in the foreseeability test (making one liable if *the harm done* was foreseeable). If such phrases do not refer to a particular, then there would be no necessity to say that they refer to the same particular. If the phrases 'the man in the brown hat' in (1) and 'the man on the beach' in (3) do

---

that: Ralph believes (transparently) of the shortest spy, that he is a spy. Since we are now using 'belief' transparently, we may apply existential generalization to yield: there is someone such that Ralph believes him to be a spy. What we would have just accomplished is to merge what we wished to keep separate, namely the two senses of saying that Ralph believes that someone is a spy; for the argument just completed would show that the one sense of the expression implies the other. Kaplan, 'Quantifying In', *supra* n. 33, at 220. Quine came to agree with the form of this objection. See Quine 'Replies', in Davidson and Hintikka (eds.), *Words and Objections, supra* n. 18, at 337–8, 341–42.

[37] Although Kaplan would not perhaps so state his conclusion, his analysis of the transparent sense in terms of the opaque sense has the effect of eliminating the former as a distinct sense. Kaplan's limitations on the 'exportation' of an opaque usage of 'belief' into a transparent usage, become in effect limitations on the names or descriptions one can substitute (or existentially generalize over) in opaque contexts. In addition to the end of Kaplan's essay, *supra* n. 33, see Quine, 'Replies', *supra* n. 36, at 342.

[38] Quine, *Word and Object, supra* n. 15, at 221.

not refer to one and the same man, Ortcutt, Leibniz's Law need not be violated by denying an equivalence between (1) and (3). Put another way: there need be no substitutivity of descriptions because they are not descriptions of the same thing. Similarly, there is no reason to believe that one could generalize over people, as in (4), because no individual person is referred to by the phrase 'the man in the brown hat' in (1).

At this point one might appropriately ask, but if 'the man in the brown hat' in (1) does not refer to Ortcutt, the man, to what does the phrase refer? The difference between Quine and Frege lay in their answer to this question. A sceptical Quinean will say that the phrase is simply unclear in its reference—it is 'referentially opaque' in the manner of indirect discourse.[39] For Frege, by way of contrast, the phrase 'the man in the brown hat' refers to the *concept* (or sense or intension) of the man in the brown hat, but refers only 'indirectly' to the man in the brown hat himself.[40]

There are severe difficulties in working out either of these suggestions for statements like (1), where Ralph's belief seems plainly to be about a determinate particular, namely, a person he knows who is called Ortcutt. In some sense of aboutness, the phrase Ralph uses—'the man in the brown hat'—must be about Ortcutt, a particular. Any attempt to shift the referent of 'the man in the brown hat' from Ortcutt must accommodate this stubborn fact.

Things are more congenial for this reference-shifting strategy with regard to foreseeability. Foreseeability, like intentions and predictive beliefs but unlike present beliefs, by its nature deals with *future* events, events that have not occurred at the time the actor forms his predictive beliefs or intentions. Unlike objects or events like Ortcutt, which exist when the subject forms his mental state, it is thus less plausible to suppose that the mental states formed about future events take those particular events as their objects. Thus, the shift-in-reference strategy holds more promise for mental states involving future events, in that we may not have to accommodate the stubborn fact we face for present beliefs and other similar

[39] Indirect discourse is where we paraphrase what another said, as in: 'John said that logic is fun'. Unlike direct quotation (such as 'John said, "Logic is fun" ', where the reference of 'Logic is fun' is to the exact utterance of John's), the reference of 'logic is fun' is unclear in the paraphrased, indirect discourse.

[40] Gottob Frege, 'Thought', in P. F. Strawson (ed.), *Philosophical Logic* (Oxford: Oxford University Press, 1967).

mental states. I shall thus next explore what 'the harm' might refer to in the foreseeability test if it does not refer to the particular harm-event that in fact occurred.

III. THE ONTOLOGY OF FORESEEABILITY

We can see what sort of thing to which we might be referring when we say that *the harm* is or is not foreseeable, if we repair to another context in which the multiple description problem has loomed large. This is the context of causal statements proper, where we say things like, 'the spark caused the fire'. This shift of contexts is not only useful for illustration of the ontological possibilities for foreseeability statements; ultimately, in order to make sense of foreseeability we need to make sense of causal statements too, for we need to make sense of the idea that an actor is liable for just those foreseeable harms that he has in fact caused. We need, in other words, to link *what* it is that must be foreseeable to *what* it is that must be caused, since our liability rules in torts and criminal law assume some such linkage.

The answer that is most immediately suggested is that the *what* in both instances is the same and that it is a particular event. The actor who sends a spark into an inflammable environment in fact causes *the fire* that ensues, and *the fire* he caused was a foreseeable consequence of his spark-emitting activity—where 'the fire' refers to a particular event that occurred at a certain place during a certain interval of time. As we have seen, this most intuitive answer gives rise to insurmountable difficulties with regard to 'foreseeability'. Many have thought that this answer gives rise to equally trenchant problems for causal statements too.[41]

Whether the latter turns out to be true depends on how one analyses the causal relation. The dominant analysis in both law and

[41] Some of the literature on the extensionality of causal statements, is G. E. M. Anscombe, 'Causality and Extensionality', *Journal of Philosophy*, Vol. 66 (1969), 152–9; Adam Morton, 'Extensional and Non-Truth-Functional Contexts', *Journal of Philosophy*, Vol. 66 (1969), 159–64; Follesdal, 'Quantification into Causal Contexts', *supra* n. 24; J. L. Mackie, *The Cement of the Universe* (Oxford: Oxford University Press, 1980), at ch. 10; see also the differing views in P. Achinstein, 'The Causal Relation', A. Rosenberg and R. M. Martin, 'The Extensionality of Causal Contexts', and L. B. Lombard, 'The Extensionality of Causal Contexts: Comments on Rosenberg and Martin', all in French, Vehling, and Wettstein (eds.), *Midwest Studies in Philosophy*, Vol. IV (1979).

philosophy has been a counterfactual analysis: either the familiar necessary condition analysis of the law's *sine qua non* test, or John Stuart Mill's sufficient condition test, or Richard Wright's necessary element of a sufficient set test,[42] or John Mackie's insufficient but necessary element of an unnecessary but sufficient condition test,[43] or some other variation of David Hume's general theme that causation is to be analysed in terms of necessary and/or sufficient conditions. On any of these counterfactual analyses of causation, the multiple description problem will loom large so long as *what* is caused is taken to be a particular event. As Donald Davidson has noted, on these tests, 'the fuller we make the description of the effect, the better our chances of demonstrating that the cause (as described) was necessary, and the worse our chances of demonstrating that it was sufficient'.[44]

Davidson's point is illustrated by the attempt of some legal theorists to show that the necessary condition analysis of causation can handle the overdetermination cases (where there appear to be two or more events, each of which was sufficient to produce the harm).[45] Where two fires converge to burn down the plaintiff's house, each fire having been capable of burning down the house by itself, it appears that because each fire was sufficient for the burning neither was necessary, forcing the necessary condition analysis of causation to the unpalatable conclusion that neither fire caused the burning. Not so, say the defenders of the necessary condition analysis such as Herbert Wechsler and the other drafters of the American Law Institute's Model Penal Code;[46] for a more detailed description of the burning—such as, the burning of such-and-such an intensity, and of such-and-such a duration—will reveal that this (more fully described) burning would not have occurred without both fires converging as they did.

[42] Richard Wright, 'Causation in Tort Law', *California Law Review*, Vol. 73 (1985), 1735–828; Wright, 'Causation, Responsibility, Risk, Probability, Naked Statistics, and Proof: Pruning the Bramble Bush by Clarifying the Concepts', *Iowa Law Review*, Vol. 73 (1988), 1001–77.

[43] J. L. Mackie, 'Causes and Conditions', *American Philosophical Quarterly*, Vol. 2 (1965), 245–64.

[44] Donald Davidson, 'Causal Relations', *Journal of Philosophy*, Vol. 64 (1967), 691–703, reprinted in Davidson's *Essays on Actions and Events* (Oxford: Oxford University Press, 1980), at 157.

[45] These theorists are critically discussed in Wright, 'Causation in Tort Law', *supra* n. 42, at 1777–80.

[46] American Law Institute, *Model Penal Code and Commentaries* (Philadelphia, 1985), Comment to §2.03.

Far from rescuing the counterfactual analysis of causation, this defence reveals the incompatibility of that analysis with the idea that it is particular events that stand in causal relations. As we examined in the last chapter, no reason is given for why we should prefer a more detailed description of a harm-token to a less detailed one. And without some criterion for selecting the appropriate level of description, the causal relation (as analysed counterfactually) is completely indeterminate in all cases.

This dependence of all counterfactual analyses of causation upon how the harm is described leads theorists in one of two directions: either they reject the counterfactual analyses of causation in favour of a relational analysis;[47] or they reject the idea that the things eligible to be the effects of causes are particular events. It will serve our dual purposes here to briefly explore each option.

Donald Davidson's choice was to reject the counterfactual analyses of causation in favour of a relational analysis. Davidson urged that 'we must distinguish firmly between causes [and their effects] and the features we hit on for describing them . . .'.[48] Our descriptions of events like burnings properly make a great deal of difference when we are giving causal explanations, for such explanations relate facts (or propositions) about events, not events themselves, and facts, unlike events, are individuated by such descriptions. But such differing descriptions make no difference to the truth of causal statements like, 'the starting of the fire caused the burning of the plaintiff's house'. However we describe the two events, the first either caused the second, or it did not.

For the reasons that I urged in the last chapter and elsewhere,[49] Davidson is right: we should reject counterfactual analyses of the causal relation. That allows us to maintain the most intuitive ontology for the causal relation, namely, that the relation is between particular events. Since we cannot maintain this ontology for foreseeability, that raises the question of what relation might hold between the particular events that are caused, and the (*whatever*) that are foreseeable. Before we can settle that question, we need to

---

[47] For a summary of relational versus counterfactual analyses of causation, see Jonathan Bennett, *Events and Their Names* (Indianapolis: Bobbs-Merrill, 1988), chs. III, IV, and IX.

[48] Davidson, 'Causal Relations', *supra* n. 44, at 155. See generally Simon Eunine, *Donald Davidson* (Stanford, Cal.: Stanford University Press, 1991), at ch. 2.

[49] Moore, *Act and Crime*, *supra* n. 27.

settle what it is that is sensibly said to be either foreseeable or unforeseeable.

What the *what* might be that can be foreseeable can be glimpsed if we turn to those causal theorists who hang onto the counterfactual analyses of causation despite their recognition of the multiple description problem. They have only two moves available to them. The first is to move to what might be called feature, property, aspect, or type causation.[50] The idea is this. Every particular event has many aspects, features, or properties; such particular, accordingly, is an instance of various types of event, each type being constituted by one or more of these properties. We should thus distinguish particular events (henceforth, event-tokens) like the fire that burned down the plaintiff's house yesterday, from the type of event that this fire is (among others, a fire type of event). Causation, the argument goes, is a relation between event-types (or between properties, or between property-instances), not event-tokens. This allows one then to say that of course causal statements will seem to discriminate between different descriptions of the harm—such different descriptions in reality refer to different *types* of events, and the truth about whether there is a causal relation depends on what type(s) of events one is discussing. There might, for example, be a causal relation between the type, yellow fire and the type, presence of sodium, even if there is no causal relation between the presence of sodium and the more general type of event, fire. This would allow one to say what seems very intuitive to say—that the presence of sodium did not cause the fire as such but it did cause the yellowness of the fire—without violating Leibniz's Law.

The alternative move made by counterfactual analysts of causation is quite similar. It like the first move posits that the causal relation does not exist between event-tokens; rather, causes are proposition-like entities, not types or properties. Since one of the idiomatic usages of the word 'fact' is to refer to these proposition-like entities, such theories are usually called fact-causation theories.[51] The fact that the fire occurred is distinct from the occurrence

---

[50] For a lucid exposition along these lines, see Richard Wright, 'Causation in Tort Law', *supra* n. 42.

[51] e.g., see Mackie, *The Cement of the Universe, supra* n. 41; J. Bennett, *Events and Their Names, supra* n. 47.

of the fire; the second is an event-token, the first is a fact about that event-token.[52]

The move here considered urges that only facts are causally related to one another. The fact that there was a fire was because of the fact that a spark touched highly combustible materials, for example. This move too allows for one to account for the multiple description problem. For example, the fact that the fire burned yellow is distinct from the fact that the fire occurred at all (even though it was a yellow fire), so a fact-causation theorist could easily admit that the first but not the second fact was caused by the fact that sodium was present at the point of combustion. These are not different descriptions of the same thing, but different facts, so different causal relations can hold between them without violating the requirements of Leibniz's Law.

Similar as they are, these two moves do not amount to the same thing. Facts are not types of events. Facts are linguistic entities that can be either about event-types or event-tokens. Although the motivation for adopting these views is the same—to preserve extensionality for counterfactual analyses of causation in the face of the multiple description problem—the ontology presupposed by each view is different.[53]

Both of these moves are for me unmotivated with respect to causation, because I reject the counterfactual analyses of causation

---

[52] For a book-length treatment of this distinction, see Bennett, *Events and Their Names, supra* n. 47.

[53] In reality the move to types only lessens but does not eliminate the failures of extensionality for 'foreseeability' usages. Except for predicate nominalists—those who believe that properties and types have no existence save that given them by predicates in a language—the *same* property or type can be picked out by more than one description. (On why none of us should be predicate nominalists, see D. M. Armstrong, *A Theory of Universals* (Cambridge: Cambridge University Press, 1978), Part IV.) This means that one can still have different descriptions of the same universal that seem to yield differing truth values when plugged into the foreseeability formula. Suppose, for example, some instance of fire damage occurs and that it was foreseeable that some instance of fire damage would occur. Suppose further that, unbeknownst to anyone, a hermit named Jones lost his cabin to fire the day before; then another description of the same type would be, 'the type of harm that befell Jones' cabin yesterday'. Yet it was not foreseeable that there would today be an instance of the type of harm that befell Jones' cabin yesterday.

This lack of any complete elimination of the failures of substitutivity for 'foreseeable' makes the fact ontology preferable to the type ontology for constructions using 'foreseeability'. Still, in the text I shall continue to discuss both variants, since the type ontology has been the most favoured amongst legal and probability theorists.

anyway. Both such moves should be of interest in this context, however, for they are the two moves open to foreseeability theorists in order to preserve the coherence of that notion. The first would be to say that harm-tokens as such are neither foreseeable nor unforeseeable; only *types* of harms can be foreseen and thus only types of harms are or are not foreseeable. The proper legal test, on this view, would then ask: was the harm (-token) in fact caused by the defendant's action an instance of any type of harm, the occurrence of some instance of which was foreseeable to the defendant at the time that he acted? The second move would likewise deny that harm-tokens are either foreseeable or unforeseeable; but it would substitute facts for types, asking only whether the fact that the harm-token (that did occur) would occur was foreseeable to the defendant at the time that he acted.

Either of these moves rescues foreseeability from failures of extensionality by allowing one to deny that different descriptions like 'damage by fire' or 'damage by shock' refer to the same thing; for fire-damage is a distinct *type* of damage from shock-damage—as the fact that the fire damage occurred is a distinct fact from the fact that the shock damage occurred—even if some particular damage is an instance of both fire and shock types of damage. Yet neither of these reconstruals of the ontology of foreseeability by itself lessens the complete indeterminacy of the concept, for in neither case do we yet have a criterion for picking out what type of harm—or what fact about the harm that occurred—we should use as we ask, 'was *that* foreseeable?' And without such a criterion, both moves leave the foreseeability criterion completely indeterminate.

Herbert Hart and Tony Honoré early on noticed this about the foreseeability test for proximate causation:

It is usually agreed that 'it is not necessary to show that this particular accident and this particular damage were probable; it is sufficient if the accident is of a class that might well be anticipated as one of the reasonable and probable results of the wrongful act.' This view, although undoubtedly law, does not in itself provide any means of determining the class of harm or accident which must be foreseeable . . .[54]

An example makes this clearer: imagine a case in which it was foreseeable to the defendant that his act would damage property of the

---

[54] Hart and Honoré, *supra* n. 2, at 233. Hart and Honoré then go on to provide their own answers to this indeterminacy, answers that we shall examine below.

plaintiff. For example, the defendant's winding of the plaintiff's rare clock too tight would foreseeably damage the clock. Suppose, however, that the defendant's winding of the clock too tight does not, miraculously, damage it, but does cause a neighbour (who is driving down the street) to watch the defendant's excessive clock-winding so that the neighbour runs into and damages the plaintiff's car. If the type (or fact about) damage is fixed as generally as 'property damage', then the defendant proximately caused the harm; for it was foreseeable to the defendant that some property damage would occur, and some property damage did occur.[55] By contrast, if the types (or facts about) damage are focused more narrowly, say, as 'clock-spring breaking' and 'auto fender bending', then there is no proximate causation under the foreseeability test; for it was not foreseeable (by hypothesis again) that an instance of auto fender bending would occur, and while it was foreseeable that an instance of clock-spring breaking would occur, no such instance did occur. Very general types or facts make the harm almost always foreseeable (for example, the most general type, 'harm') and there will always be specific enough types or facts so as to make any harm unforeseeable.

The upshot is that although a shift to an ontology of types or facts gets the foreseeability theorist out of the literal incoherence of violating our Leibnizian ideas about identity, such shift does not render the foreseeability test a jot more determinate in its applications to particular cases. Needed to give the foreseeability test even the limited bite that Morris thought it had is some way of selecting certain types of harm, or facts about harm, as authoritative.

A natural thought would be that the law itself provides for such an authoritative typing of harms. Yet if one looks to the Anglo-American criminal or tort law for such details, he is bound to be disappointed. What one finds are suggestions like that of Justice Cardozo, who distinguished property type harms from personal injury type harms in dicta in his famous *Palsgraf* opinion:

There is room for argument that a distinction is to be drawn according to the diversity of interests invaded by the act, as where conduct negligent in

---

[55] Remember, once we eschew talking about the foreseeability of harm-tokens, we cannot refuse liability here on the ground that the harm that occurred was not the same as the harm that was foreseeable. Rather, the only question allowed us is whether the harm-token that occurred was an instance of the harm-type that was foreseeable, and with the broad type mentioned in the text, this is satisfied.

that it threatens an insignificant invasion of an interest in property results in an unforeseeable invasion of an interest of another order, as, for example, one of bodily security.[56]

Similarly, Viscount Simonds seems to regard *his* narrower typology of harms in *Wagonmound I* ('fire damage', 'shock damage') as established in law in the sense that the conventional heads of tort liability *generate* a legally natural typology.[57] The hornbook maxim in torts—that 'only the type of harm need be foreseeable, not the extent of the harm nor the precise means of its occurrence'[58]—also suggests that there is some such legally natural typology (as it gives but the slightest hints about what it might be).

The law has not developed these vague suggestions of Cardozo, Simonds, or Pollock. There is no distinctly legal typology of harms. If one were to summarize 'the law' on the topic, the summary by Harper and James is still about as much as one can get:

The inquiry . . . into the nature of the risks or hazards, the foreseeability of which makes conduct negligent, must be neither too refined nor too coarse. It is a matter of judgement in drawing the line . . . and this will vary from situation to situation.[59]

Juries are thus entirely on their own as they frame the types or facts about which they ask, was *that* foreseeable? Is there any reason to

---

[56] *Palsgraf* v. *Long Island RR*, 248 NY 339, 346–7, 162 NE 99, 101 (1928).

[57] [1961] AC 388 (PC Aust.) However, since damage by fire is *not* a recognized head of tort liability, what Simonds actually appears to have believed is that the harm for which one is liable determines the type of harm that must be foreseeable. Thus, 'the test for *liability for shock* is foreseeability of *injury by shock*'. The assumption seems to be that the extent of a defendant's liability can be used to set the type of harm about which we can ask, 'was an instance of this type foreseeable?' (I am indebted to Ken Kress for this interpretation of *Wagonmound I*.) The problem with the suggestion is that defendants are liable for particular harms; these harm-tokens have many properties; there is nothing in our practices in assigning liability in either torts or criminal law that picks out one of these properties for use in framing foreseeability questions. In *Wagonmound I*, for example, the defendant's liability was for the destruction of the plaintiff's dock; although that particular destruction was an instance of the type, fire-damage, it was also an instance of innumerable other types such as dock destruction, property damage, twenty-five minute yellow fire-destruction of a dock, etc.

[58] See, e.g., Pollock, 'Liability for Consequences', *Law Quarterly Review*, Vol. 38 (1922), 165–7, at 167 ('when it is found that a man ought to have foreseen in a general way consequences of a certain kind, it will not avail him to say that he could not foresee the precise course or the full extent of the consequences, being of that kind, which in fact have happened').

[59] Fowler V. Harper and Fleming James, jr., *The Law of Torts* (Boston: Little, Brown, 1956), Vol. II, §20.5(6).

believe that juries exercise any but a purely arbitrary judgement when they select, as they must, some types of harm about which to ask, was it foreseeable? In response to a very early version of this chapter it has been suggested that every society 'amalgamates accidents into a relatively small number of categories',[60] and that these form the types or facts relevant to foreseeability determinations.

There are three ways to take this suggestion. One is to think that in our normal descriptive, explanatory, and predictive activities in daily life we develop a typology of event-types that allows us to apply the foreseeability test.[61] Yet this is plainly an illusion. It is of course true that the causal laws by which we both explain and predict events are themselves formed over certain types or facts (called 'natural kinds') to the exclusion of all others.[62] To this extent those who know such causal laws do have a shared set of types of (or facts about) events. Yet this typology is far too rich to do the discriminating work demanded by the suggestion, for such a typology include the types or facts used by all known causal laws. There will be many such laws applicable to any particular event-token and, thus, many types such event-token instantiaties that satisfy this criterion. A particular fire, for example, will instantiate the causally relevant types: fire, yellow fire, fire of a temperature over 1000 degrees Fahrenheit, ash-producing fire, smokeless fire, oxidizing process, etc., etc. And if one seeks to make the typology more discriminating by allowing only those causal laws of the greatest precision, this will probably result in all harms being rendered unforeseeable.[63] For

[60] Steven Shavell, 'An Analysis of Causation and the Scope of Liability in the Law of Torts', *Journal of Legal Studies*, Vol. 9 (1980), 463–516, at 491.

[61] See, e.g., H. L. A. Hart and A. M. Honoré, *Causation in the Law*, *supra* n. 2, 234 (experience has taught us to anticipate rainstorm type events from dark cloud type events, not to anticipate storm, bad-weather, or rainstorm that lasts two hours types of events). For a recent summary of the varying hypotheses of cognitive psychologists about what are the optimal categories for prediction and information storage, see James E. Corter and Mark A. Gluck, 'Explaining Basic Categories: Feature Predictability and Information', *Psychological Bulletin*, Vol. 111 (1992), 291–303.

[62] On natural kinds, see Moore, 'The Semantics of Judging', *supra* n. 3, at 204–42. See also W. V. Quine, 'Natural Kinds', in his *Ontological Relativity and Other Essays* (New York: Columbia University Press, 1969); and Hilary Putnam, 'The Meaning of "Meaning"', in his *Mind, Language, and Reality* (Cambridge: Cambridge University Press, 1975). Nelson Goodman's 'projectible predicates' are what I and many others would call the names of natural kinds. Nelson Goodman, *Fact, Fiction, and Forecast*, 4th edn. (Indianapolis: Bobbs-Merrill, 1984).

[63] See D. L. Medin, 'Structural Principles of Categorization', in B. Shepp and T. Tighe, eds., *Interaction: Perception, Development and Cognition* (Hillsdale, NJ,

example, the most precise causal laws governing the motion of the workman's brick in Clarence Morris's earlier example are no doubt framed over very precise types of events—event-types like cuts of certain depths and configurations connected to event-types like rotations and velocities of a certain sort; and types of this precision are rarely if ever foreseeably instantiated on any given occasion.

The second way to take the suggestion is as a bit of the sociology of custom: without regard to the causal laws that make predictions possible, people just do clump individual events into certain types.[64] It is these familiar, ready-to-tongue types that are then used by juries as they ask and answer foreseeability questions. Yet there are two problems with this way of taking the suggestion. One is to question whether there is anything remotely approaching a typology of events with the necessary discriminating power to be found in customary categories. Take the case where the plaintiff's arm is cut off by the defendant's negligent action. Suppose it was foreseeable that the plaintiff's arm might be cut, but unforeseeable that it would be severed (by such a light blow with such a dull instrument). Surely arm-cuttings and arm-severings are equally entrenched types of events in our customary way of thinking, yet that an instance of one type would occur was foreseeable while the fact that the other would occur is not.

The second problem with this idea of using conventionally entrenched categories is a normative one. To the extent that there are such conventionally favoured ways of categorizing events, and to the extent that this is not simply in response to the natural categorization given by true causal laws, such conventional favouring is due to factors like the length of the word used in English to refer to the type, the frequency of the word's use, the average response time of native speakers to recognize a particular as being an instance of this

1983), 203–30. See also Corter and Gluck, *supra* n. 61, at 292, where it is argued that those categories maximizing the probability that any instance of the category will have some feature F (such as being the cause or the effect of a certain type of event) will be 'the most specific categories because they tend to have the least variability in features. For example, the probability that something can fly given that it is a robin is higher than the probability that something can fly given that it is a bird.'

[64] For suggestions about such conventional clumping of types for purposes of constructing the holding of a precedent, see Frederick Schauer, 'Precedent', *Stanford Law Review*, Vol. 39 (1987), 571–605. For a critique of the use of such conventional kinds in that context, see Michael Moore, 'Precedent, Induction, and Ethical Generalization', in Lawrence Goldstein (ed.), *Precedent in Law* (Oxford: Oxford University Press, 1987).

category rather than another, and the developmental sequence in which this category-name was learned *vis-à-vis* its competitors.[65] These factors seem irrelevant to the normative justifications given for the foreseeability criterion of proximate causation (either that it is *unfair* to hold a person liable for harms that he could not foresee, or that it is *inefficient* to do so because future actors cannot take such unforeseeable types of harms into account in planning their behaviour and so liability cannot achieve its deterrent function). Word length, developmental sequence, etc., are irrelevant to whether a category of events is a harm type category or not, yet the normative justifications for using foreseeability demand that the relevant category under which the events must be foreseeable must be a category of *harm*.

This last objection brings out a third way to take the suggestion, which is as an observation about morality and our moral beliefs. On this line, it is only because of a shared moral theory about the significant rights and interests possessed by persons that we are able to type harms sufficiently to enquire after their foreseeability. People might have some shared typologies of harms by virtue of the interest in bodily integrity, say, being distinct from the interests in reputation or in property, or the interest in the security of one's home might be distinct from the interest in other sorts of property. One would frame foreseeability questions, on this view, over those types of harms that correspond to such interests.[66]

The main problem with this view is that it yields outcomes quite at odds with those the foreseeability test is thought to give. Take the Louisiana case (of the rescuer shot in the leg by the deranged accident victim) that Morris took to be 'unarguably unforeseeable': the relevant interest seems to be that of bodily integrity, and the relevant type, the violation of that integrity i.e., an injury to the body. As instance of that type was surely foreseeable to the defendant who negligently failed to guard his stalled truck with flares, since

---

[65] See the extensive literature summarized in Corter and Gluck, *supra* n. 61, at 291.

[66] For suggestions on how harms might be related to rights and interests, see Joel Feinberg, *Harm to Others* (New York: Oxford University Press, 1984), 31–125; Michael Davis, 'Harm and Retribution', *Philosophy and Public Affairs*, Vol. 15 (1986), 236–66, at 239–47; Andrew von Hirsch, *Past or Future Crimes* (New Brunswick, NJ, 1985), 66–71; Andrew von Hirsch and Nils Jareborg, 'Gauging Criminal Harm: A Living-Standard Analysis' *Oxford Journal of Legal Studies*, Vol. 11 (1991), 1–38, at 21.

personal injuries in collisions are common; and an instance of that type in fact was caused to occur, namely the plaintiff was shot in the leg; therefore, contrary to Morris's observation, the harm *was* foreseeable.

There is I think a moral judgement guiding observations like Morris's here, but it has little to do with the rights and interests of persons, or, indeed, with foreseeability at all. When Morris held of such cases that 'the freakishness of the facts refuses to be drowned' and that any description that leaves out details about the use of the pistol by the deranged husband 'is viewed as misdescription', he was accurately describing the reactions of judges and juries to such cases. What explains such reactions, however, is not some implicit criterion of description that has thus far eluded us. Rather, Morris and the judges and juries he was describing are abandoning foreseeability entirely in favour of other conceptions of proximate causation. The power of the competing direct cause and remoteness conceptions of proximate causation lies precisely in the attention these conceptions pay to these details of intervening causation. To the extent the foreseeability theorist allows these sorts of moral insight to guide the typology of harms under which he asks, 'was this foreseeable?', he is abandoning his theory, not saving it.

I thus conclude that the criminal and tort law conceptions of proximate causation in terms of foreseeability are completely indeterminate in all cases. There is no legally established typology of harm that judges and juries are to use when they ask, 'was the occurrence of an instance of that type of harm foreseeable?' Nor do judges and juries have recourse to some unstated but shared (causal, conventional, or moral) typing of events that can fill in where law is silent.

To salvage the foreseeability criterion of proximate causation, one thus must urge that the law must change. The reform that most readily comes to mind, of course, is to supply an authoritative typology of harms. But how is such a typology to be framed? The most promising suggestions would be along the three lines we have already explored (with reference to the alleged implicit knowledge of judges and juries), and none of these, as we have seen, will fit the bill.

Alternatively, one might think that legal reform could adopt a 'harm within the risk' analysis of proximate causation. Under this approach, we should ask about the foreseeability of only those types of harms that are both: (1) types of which the harm-token that occurred was an instance, and (2) types of harms intended by the actor or foreseen by him, or types of harm the risk of which made his action negligent to perform.[67]

This would be a peculiar reform. Usually devotees of the harm within the risk analysis do not seek to salvage foreseeability but to eliminate it entirely. Under the harm within the risk approach, defendants are liable to criminal and tort sanctions whenever they in fact cause an instance of any type of harm that they intend, contemplate, or unreasonably risk. There is no room or need for an additional foreseeability question under this approach.

One could of course also reform the harm within the risk approach so that it does not supplant entirely the foreseeability question. This is easier said than done, however. Suppose we were simply to *add* the foreseeability question (restricted to the types of harms foreseen, risked, or intended) to the harm within the risk question. Will it not be the case that to answer the second question will also be to answer the first? Surely any type of harm that is actually foreseen, intended, or unreasonably risked by an action was also foreseeable to that actor, rendering the foreseeability question superfluous.

A more plausible reform of the harm within the risk formula would be to *substitute* the foreseeability question for the harm within the risk question, using the harm within the risk analysis only to frame the types of harm about which the foreseeability question is asked.[68] If the defendant intended (foresaw, unreasonably risked) *a fire*, then one asks whether it was foreseeable that an instance of the type, fire, would occur.

[67] In criminal law the most authoritative adoption of the harm within the risk analysis is in the Model Penal Code §2.03. (I use 'harm within the risk' as the generic label for 'harm within the intent, belief, or risk'.) The Code's drafters ultimately could not stomach the seeming implications of harm within the risk analysis, for they recognize liability even when 'the actual result is not within the purpose or contemplation of the actor' if 'the actual result involves the same kind of injury or harm as that designed or contemplated and is not too remote or accidental in its occurrence to have a just bearing on the actor's liability or on the quantity of his offense'. Notice that this provision frees the Model Penal Code's notion of proximate causation from the unduly restrictive grip of the harm within the risk analysis only to return courts and juries to individuate types with no guidance whatsoever.

[68] This seems to be Hart and Honoré's preferred solution to the description problem. See Hart and Honoré, *supra* n. 2, at 233 ('that class can be determined by reference to the generalizations which one would have recourse to in describing conduct as negligent').

One problem for this suggested reform is its seeming lack of motivation: what rationale for proximate causation would make normative sense of this ungainly marriage of foreseeability to harm within the risk? A second problem lies in the fact that the harm within the risk analysis does not isolate a type of harm (that could give determinacy to foreseeability) when that analysis is based on negligence. There is never one type of harm, the risk of which makes an actor negligent (except for the type, harm). Rather, negligence consists in acting in the face of all types of harm that the act may produce, discounted by the improbability of an instance of each type being caused to exist. Placing unlabelled rat poison near the stove in the kitchen is negligent in part because of some probability of a poisoning, but also because of some probability of an explosion, a falling, etc. Moreover, even if we leave aside all risks but the risk that the unlabelled rat poison would be eaten and the eater poisoned, that risk no more has a canonical description than does the corresponding harm. It might be a risk of ingesting 2.75 ounces of rat poison causing excessive vomiting, loss of memory, etc.; or it might be a risk of poisoning; or it might be a risk of bodily injury; etc. Which of these was *the* risk that made the actor negligent in placing unlabelled rat poison near the stove?

Even when the harm within the risk analysis produces unique types eligible to be plugged into the foreseeability formula—as it does for intended or foreseen harms, if not for negligently risked harms—the formula yields results unwanted even by friends of foreseeability. This is because the typing of harms (under which we are to ask, was *it* foreseeable) is now wholly dependent on the level of typing done by the actor as he framed his intentions or his beliefs. Return to the clock-winding example where the plaintiff's car was run into and damaged because of a third party's undue fascination with the defendant's excessive winding of the plaintiff's clock. If the defendant's belief was that 'he might very well break the plaintiff's clock', then we type the harm that must be foreseeable as 'clock-breakage', and the defendant is not liable because although it was foreseeable that an instance of that type would occur, it did not occur. If on the other hand the defendant's belief was that 'he might very well damage property of the plaintiff', then we type the harm that must be foreseeable as 'property-damage', and the defendant is liable (because an instance of that type of harm did occur and because it was foreseeable that it would). These results are not only counterintuitive but their dependence upon the breadth of the object of the defendant's belief or intent makes them seem arbitrary.

IV. CONCLUSION

Corrective justice theorists of tort and retributive justice theorists of the criminal law have good reason to reject the foreseeability criterion of proximate causation on normative grounds. For these theories demand that legal liability track moral responsibility, and moral responsibility for causing a harm requires causation of that harm in some ordinary sense, not in the artificial sense created by the foreseeability theory of proximate causation.

To this normative objection to foreseeability we should now add a conceptual objection: the multiple description problem shows the foreseeability conception of proximate causation to be incoherent. If we take *what* is (un)foreseeable to be particular events, then (so long as we refuse a transparent reading of what 'foreseeability' means) the multiple description problem reveals the concept to be nonsense in light of our firmly entrenched, Leibnizian ideas of identity. If, more plausibly, we take *what* is (un)foreseeable to be either types of events, or facts about events, no violation of the laws of identity need take place but the concept is still completely indeterminate in its implications for particular cases. That indeterminacy could be reduced by legal, conventional, or moral typologies of harms, but such typologies either do not exist or, if they do, do not decide proximate cause issues in a way that is at all intuitive, even to friends of foreseeability.

None of this makes the notion of foreseeability incoherent or indeterminate as that concept is used as part of what is meant by negligence, and in closing it is worth saying why this is so. The negligence standard obviously requires probability judgements by both actors and the juries that judge them. Yet the negligence standard does not require that some typology of harm be adopted that precludes contradictory judgements. Quite the contrary: the Learned Hand formula for negligence, properly construed, requires the actor to assess the likelihoods of his actions producing instances of *all* types of harm (balanced against the likelihoods of those same actions producing instances of all types of benefit). The non-negligent actor *sums* the discounted value of all such types of harms, sums the discounted value of all such types of benefits, and acts only if the number is positive. In that summing process he is not imposing a binary choice (foreseeable/unforeseeable), but only seeking a probability; moreover, he does not have to choose *one* such type, because he is adding *all* such probabilities, even the smallest ones. His only problems in such summing are (1) making sure that he does not double count (for types of harms that over-lap in their extensions); and (2) the amount of information required to make this enormously complicated calculation.[69] These are seri-ous enough practical problems in the application of the negligence standard, but they pale before the conceptual bankruptcy of the foreseeability conception of proximate causation.

[69] Mark Grady has undertaken to show how an adversary system can lessen the practical problem of information overload so as to ease the strain on fact-finders in making negligence determinations. Grady, 'Untaken Precautions', *Journal of Legal Studies*, Vol. 18 (1989), 139–56.

2. The Nature of Culpability

a. The Nature of Mental States

9

PRIMA FACIE MORAL CULPABILITY

I. INTRODUCTION

'Culpability' is often used to denote an actor's overall moral responsibility (or moral blameworthiness) with respect to some morally bad state of affairs. In this book I have used the word in a narrower sense, one in which culpability is only one of three ingredients in overall blameworthiness. Responsibility—or overall desert, or blameworthiness—as I conceived it in chapter 1 has two distinct dimensions and one presupposition attached to both. The presupposition is that any being who is held responsible must be sufficiently rational and autonomous to be a moral agent.[1] Only such beings are the addressees of the primary norms of morality that tell us what it is wrong to do, and only such beings are capable of being morally culpable. As set forth in chapter 1, the primary doctrinal locus of this moral presupposition within Anglo-American criminal law lies in the defence of insanity, which is where I explore it in chapters 14 and 15.

The two dimensions of responsibility are that, first, one has done something morally wrong, something that violates one's moral obligations. More specifically (except for breach of our positive obligations), this means that one's voluntary act must have in fact and proximately caused some morally bad state of affairs and there was no justification for having done so.[2] Secondly, in order to be blameworthy, one must have done such wrong *culpably*.

[1] Explored at some length by me in Michael S. Moore, *Law and Psychiatry: Rethinking the Relationship*, ch. 2 (Cambridge: Cambridge University Press, 1984).

[2] A view of wrongdoing defended in Michael S. Moore, *Act and Crime: The Philosophy of Action and its Implications for Criminal Law*, chs. 7–8 (Oxford: Oxford University Press, 1993). For related but distinct notions of wrongdoing, see George Fletcher, *Rethinking Criminal Law* (Boston: Little, Brown, 1978), 481, 489; Joachim Hruschka, 'Imputation', *BYUL Rev.*, Vol. [1986], 669–710; Lawrence Crocker, 'Justice in Criminal Liability: Decriminalizing Harmless Attempts', *Ohio St. LJ*, Vol. 53 (1992), 1057–110.

It is culpability in this three part scheme that interests me in this and the succeeding four chapters. Culpability in this narrower sense focuses on the actor, not the act (as in wrongdoing); further, culpability in this sense focuses on the mental states of the actor at the time of the wrongful act, not on the general capacities and opportunities possessed by the actor (as in moral agency). Roughly, one is culpable if he chose to do wrong in circumstances where that choice was freely made.[3]

There are two aspects to culpability in this sense. The first has to do with the mental states that allow one to say that one has *chosen* to do a wrongful act, and the second has to do with the conditions (of excuse) that must not exist else the choice is sufficiently unfree that no (or a lessened) blameworthiness attaches to it. The aspect of culpability that interests me in this and the succeeding two chapters is the first, what might be called prima facie culpability. I shall thus assume in what follows that the various conditions of excuse are not present, reserving for chapters 12 and 13 discussion of those conditions.

Two questions concerning prima facie culpability shall occupy me in this overview chapter: first, what mental states a wrongdoer must have in order to be prima facie culpable, and, second, what relation(s) there might be between moral culpability and the doctrines of legal liability in criminal law and torts. Such an essentially moral enquiry nonetheless looks both to psychology for the nature of moral culpability and to law for the legal consequences of it being found to be present.

II. TWO KINDS OF CULPABILITY AND THEIR PSYCHOLOGY

It is a fundamental feature of our psychology as rational agents that we act under representations of the world. We are, in other words, Intentional systems,[4] systems that *intend* to make the world be a certain way, *believe* that it is a certain way, *hope* that it might be a certain way, *wish* that it were a certain way, or *hate* the way we believe it is. Our mental states of emotion, desire, belief, and intention all operate on representational content. We never just

---

[3] 'Free' does not mean, 'not-caused'. See ch. 12, following.
[4] Dan Dennett's term in *Brainstorms*, ch. 2 (Putney, Vt.: Bradford Books, 1978).

believe or intend—we always believe that something is the case, intend that something become the case, etc. We represent the world to ourselves under the different modalities of belief, desire, intention, etc.

The key notion to understanding prima facie moral culpability is built on this fundamental feature of our psychology. The key notion is that we are prima facie culpable when we act under a representation of the world that would make our action morally wrongful if the representation were true. Between wrongdoing and culpability, the conceptually primary notion is thus wrongdoing, for it is the content of our primary norms of obligation (which norms define wrongdoing) that tell us what it is culpable to desire, believe, or intend.

The moral norms dealing with culpability are in one sense separate from the norms of wrongdoing. These norms of culpability are backward-looking norms for assessing responsibility for actions already done, and are distinct from the (partially) forward-looking norms of wrongdoing directing us to do or refrain from doing certain actions. The moral norms of culpability tell us when we may rightly hold a wrongdoer (which may include ourselves) responsible and when we may not. These secondary norms of culpability are as important in assessing an actor's responsibility as are the primary norms of wrongdoing. Both are crucial ingredients in determining moral desert.

Even so, the primary norms about wrongdoing are conceptually prior in the sense indicated, viz., it is acting under a representation of what we are doing that would be wrongful if true that makes us culpable. Culpability could thus be said to *be* wrongdoing in a sense, namely it is wrongdoing in the possible world created by our representational states. Wrongdoing itself, by contrast, is wrongdoing in the *actual* world, not in a *possible* world.

There may seem to be an apparent exception to this tight link between culpability and wrongdoing. Consider the moral opprobrium we undeniably attach to non-virtuous emotions.[5] We do blame people for not caring when they should, not feeling guilty when they should, feeling joyful when they should not, craving or wishing for things that are depraved. And the norms that tell us what emotions are virtuous do not seem to have their content deter-

[5] See Bernard Williams, *Problems of Self* (Cambridge: Cambridge University Press, 1973), 207–29.

mined by the norms of wrongdoing. There is a norm telling us that it is non-virtuous to feel delight at the sufferings of others, but that norm seems independent of any wrongdoing norm that enjoins us from acting in a way that causes others to suffer unnecessarily.

The reason why this exception is only apparent is because the moral norms about emotions do not have to do with culpability. Judging a person by what emotions she feels is part of our moral assessment of that person's character.[6] Such assessments are genuinely moral assessments, but they are not assessments of our culpability in doing some wrongful action. The content of those norms telling us which emotions are non-virtuous is independent of the norms of wrongdoing precisely because of this.

The kinds of representational states that are relevant to culpability are the mental states that take action-descriptions as their objects. These are the action-guiding states of desire, belief, and intention. To see how such states are action-guiding, consider a truncated version of the explanation I schematized in chapter 5 for why Smith killed his wealthy uncle, Jones, by shooting him with a gun:

(1) Smith desired to own Jones's wealth for its own sake.
(2) Smith believed that, if he killed Jones, then he would own Jones's wealth.
(3) Smith's desire in (1) and his belief in (2) jointly caused Smith to intend to kill Jones.
(4) Smith believed that, if he moved his finger on the trigger of his gun at t_1, then he would kill Jones at t_1 or shortly thereafter.
(5) Smith's intention in (3) and his belief in (4) jointly caused Smith to will the movement of his finger on the trigger of his gun.
(6) Smith's willing of the movement of his finger caused the movement of Smith's finger on the trigger of his gun.
(7) The movement of Smith's finger on the trigger of his gun in (6) caused Jones to die.

On my view of actions, the act of Smith killing Jones is the willing of the movement (5) causing the movement willed (6), which act becomes the wrongful act *of killing* by acquiring the causal property of causing Jones to die (7).[7] The mental states that explain that

[6] On our separate moral responsibility for character, see ch. 13, following.
[7] Argued for in M. Moore, *supra* n. 2, chs. 5 and 11.

action are of only three types: the desire in (1), the beliefs in (2) and (4), and the intention in (3).[8] There are thus only three sorts of representational states of relevance to prima facie moral culpability, those of desire, belief, and intention. We are culpable when we either: intrinsically want our actions to be of a sort that is wrongful; intend that they be of a sort that is wrongful as a means to something else that we intrinsically want; or believe that our actions are of a sort that is wrongful, even if we neither intrinsically want nor instrumentally intend for them to be of that sort.

This threefold division of all action-guiding representational states into motivational, conative, and cognitive types is as old as Plato's faculty psychology and as new as the defence of the folk psychology in contemporary cognitive science. Unfortunately the controversy as to whether there is such a threefold division is also both ancient and present today.

Consider first the distinction between motivational states of desire and conational states of intention. It is perfectly idiomatic in English to describe both Smith's desire in (1) and his intention in (3) as intentions with which his action was done, as Bentham, Anscombe, and many others have done; it is equally idiomatic to describe both states as desires, ultimate in (1) and mediate in (3). This linguistic fact leads many to refuse any distinction here. Yet the true psychology is not reflected in our ordinary usage of these terms. There is an important functional difference between those background states of desire that move us to action, and those executory states of intention that execute our desires: the first is only a component state in the inevitable conflict we experience between our desires, whereas the second is a resolution of that conflict in the form of a decision.[9] Smith desires a lot of things in competition with his desire to own Jones's wealth—including a desire not to go to jail—yet his intention to kill Jones represents a resolution of that conflict. We expect our desires to conflict (in the sense that all cannot be simultaneously realized at any given time) but to have conflicting resolutions of that conflict—to have conflicting intentions, in other words—would be criticizably irrational.

---

[8] The willing mentioned in (5) is a mental state, but: (1) willings are a kind of intention, as I argue in *Act and Crime*, *supra* n. 2, at ch. 6; and (2) willings are part of the action to be explained and are thus ineligible to be what causally explains that action.

[9] Id. ch. 6. See also Michael Bratman, *Intentions, Plans and Practical Reason* (Cambridge, Mass.: Harvard University Press, 1987).

Consider secondly the line between belief states, on the one hand, and both states of desire and intention, on the other. Many have thought that the distinction between knowing that one's action will be a killing, and either intending or desiring that it be such, is too fine to be drawn. Does the person who places a bomb on an aeroplane in order to collect the insurance on the plane not intend the death of the passengers, given that he knows for certain that they will die? If he knows that they will die with no less certainty than he knows the plane will be destroyed, can one distinguish the latter as an intended means from the former as an unintended but merely foreseen side-effect?

Despite the force of such queries, I think the answer to be in the affirmative.[10] Once one properly individuates the objects of intentions, we can and should distinguish believed side effects from both intended means and desired ends. On the view of individuation of representational states advanced in chapter 11, the hypothetical plane bomber only believed that his action of placing the bomb would be a killing; he neither desired it to be such, nor intended that it be such as a means to something else that be desired.

Suppose that we can distinguish these three kinds of states as a matter of psychology. That would not yet be to say that we should distinguish them for purposes of assessing moral culpability. If one took the view that all such states exhibit the kind of choice and control that lies at the heart of culpability, then for moral assessment purposes we would have no reason to distinguish such states even though they are psychologically distinct.

I doubt that this is true, however. Compare the murderer who forms his intention to kill only because of a desire that he kill for its own sake, with the more typical murderer who kills in order to achieve some other end, such as inheriting his victim's money. Although both are very culpable, to desire for its own sake that one do a wrongful action seems incrementally worse than intending to do such a wrongful action as a means to a generally permissible end. Killing or torturing, or disfiguring for the sheer joy of it seems rather paradigmatic of true evil.

Similarly, to know that one's actions will inevitably result in the death of an innocent is very culpable, but is it as culpable as intending the death of an innocent as a means to some other end?

---

[10] We shall explore this issue in ch. 11, following.

Compare the culpability of two bomber pilots both of whom do what they do in order to end a war sooner: the first pilot tries to hit only military targets with his bombs but he knows to a certainty that his bombs will kill non-combatants; the second pilot tries to kill non-combatants with his bombs because that will dispirit the enemy and end the war sooner. Assuming that the war is not so just that either pilot is justified in killing non-combatants, is not the first less culpable than the second even if both perform the identical wrongful action of killing innocent civilians?

It is true, as Herbert Hart once argued,[11] that an actor who kills possessed of any of these three mental states (of desire, intention, or belief) equally has *control* over whether he kills, and he chooses to go ahead. It is thus equally *fair* to apply legal sanctions to any of these three classes of killers, because each equally knew what they were doing and thus each equally had the opportunity not to do it. Yet to say that blaming would not be unfair is not to say that such blame is deserved. Fairness simply is not the same as culpability. Those who kill for the joy of killing, or who intend to kill as a means to other ends, aim themselves at evil, whereas those who know their acts will be wrongs are only willing to tolerate that fact without aiming for it. Aiming at evil on a given occasion makes one more culpable. This is not because it shows one to be possessed of an evil *character*; rather, the *choice* to do what one did at a given point in time has this differential (depending on how the wrongful action enters into the chain of one's reasons) culpability to it irrespective of whether such choice is 'in character' for the agent as not.

Why this should be so has long been a disputed matter within ethics. My own sense is that this differential culpability between intent and foresight has to do with the notion of authorship, or agency. We are the authors of evil when we aim to achieve it in a way we are not if we merely anticipate that evil coming about as a result of our actions. Indeed, such a general notion of authorship seems to be built out of three distinctions of which this is one. The most basic is that explored in chapter 6, between states of affairs that I actively bring about through my bodily movements and those that I passively fail to prevent. The second is the causal distinction (briefly touched on in chapter 17) between those states of affairs that my bodily motions cause and those states of affairs which

[11] H. L. A. Hart, *Punishment and Responsibility* (Oxford: Oxford University Press, 1968), 122.

others cause by their intervening actions but which my actions enable them to cause. The third component of authorship is the present idea, that aiming to cause some evil is to put that evil more squarely on one's moral ledger than when one merely tolerates such evil as a side effect of one's aims. All three distinctions together are needed to make out the full authorship of evil that makes us most blameworthy, and this last strand of such authorship should be no more problematic than the more commonly accepted strands of action and causation.

The cognitive state of belief (that one's act will be a morally wrongful one) is thus not sufficient for the most serious levels of culpability. Neither is it necessary.[12] It is true that either desires or intentions must be accompanied by some belief connecting one's act to the achievement of the object of one's desire or intention. This is the grain of truth to the idea that culpable states of belief are at least necessary to most serious culpability. Yet the beliefs in question need not be that one's actions will *certainly* achieve the objects of one's desires or intentions. Indeed, one can aim at an evil object while only believing that one's act has a slight chance of success. Although it is rare, one can even aim at the object of one's desire or intention while having no belief that one can attain it and even while having a belief that one cannot attain it. As a matter of psychology one can hope to achieve items that one knows one cannot achieve, although it may be criticizably irrational to do so.[13] In any of these cases, one cannot say that the most serious culpability of desire or intention needs a highly culpable belief. Most often there is such a belief, but not always, and not necessarily.

As suggested by these last remarks, the third most culpable mental state, that of belief, itself is capable of great variation in the culpability it betokens. There are two variables within the object of belief that determine the degree of culpability: (1) with what probability did the agent judge that his act would come to possess those attributes that would make it prima facie morally wrongful? and (2) with what probability did the agent judge that his act, although prima facie wrongful, would nonetheless come to possess other attributes that would make it all things considered not wrongful but justified? An actor who knows for certain that his act will be the

---

[12] Compare Antony Duff, *Intention, Agency, and Criminal Liability* (Oxford: Oxford University Press, 1990), 56–7, where Duff links intentions to beliefs.

[13] As I argue in M. Moore, *supra* n. 2, at 144.

killing of another and knows for certain that that other is trying to kill several innocents, is not culpable at all. One who knows for certain that his act will be the killing of an innocent and knows for certain none of the facts that could justify such an action exist, is highly culpable. We operate with a sliding scale here: the more likely the actor believes that his act will be a prima facie wrong, the more likely must he believe justifying circumstances to exist; otherwise, culpability is increased.

The differences in culpability between belief states at either end of this scale are quite large. Indeed, much of the temptation to regard culpability as exclusively a matter of belief (rather than desire or intention) stems from the amount of grading of culpability we do with belief by itself. The differences in culpability between belief states undoubtedly exceeds the difference in culpability between the most culpable belief (of certain wrongdoing) and the yet more culpable states of intention or desire.

Left out of this account of prima facie culpability is any mention of risk-taking in the absence of the actor possessing any of these mental states of belief, intention, or desire. It is undeniably true that we do blame people for risking that their actions might be of a wrongful sort even when they do not desire, intend, or believe that their actions will be of that sort. How should we characterize this form of culpability?

It has tempted some legal theoreticians to conceive of negligence as being radically different from the culpability of desire, intention, and belief. Such theorists conceive of negligence as a conduct requirement, not a mental state requirement.[14] Yet inadvertent and unjustified risk-taking is a culpability of mental state, not of conduct. For risk-taking and risk are epistemic notions. In a deterministic world, there is no such thing as a risk to an omniscient being because all future events have a probability of 1 or 0. It is only relative to the information base of a less than omniscient being that the idea of risk makes sense. '*Given what the actor believed*, was there a substantial risk that his action would be a certain kind of wrong?', is a question that makes sense. 'Was there a risk that his action would be a certain kind of wrong?', makes no sense unless the content supplies an implicit epistemic vantage point from which the risk is to be assessed.

[14] Kenneth W. Simons, 'Rethinking Mental States', *BUL Rev.*, Vol. 72 (1992), 463–554.

We could of course idealize an epistemic vantage point from which to assess risk, or we could take the average beliefs of some segment of humanity to supply some such conventional vantage point.[15] But risks judged from such idealized or conventional vantage points would have nothing to do with the culpability of the actor. It is the actor's epistemic vantage point—her 'information base', i.e., beliefs—that measures her culpability. Given what she believed, should she not have further believed that her actions unjustifiably risked harm or other wrongs to others?

Culpably inadvertent risk-taking thus involves a kind of epistemic failure. One who *acts* unreasonably is one who *believes* unreasonably in the sense that an inference about unjustified risk-taking is not drawn when it should be. However, what makes the actor culpable in such cases is not the failure to draw the inference—for if one had drawn the inference and performed the act in question, one would be more culpable, not less. What makes the actor culpable in these cases is the doing of some wrongful action while possessing those belief states from which the inference of wrongfulness was fairly drawable.

This admittedly is a distinct form of culpability, because the objects of a merely negligent actor's beliefs are not wrongdoings and yet he is culpable for those wrongdoings nonetheless. Such culpability that is not conceptually piggybacked onto wrongdoing is difficult to reconcile with the idea that it is the *choice* to do wrong that is the touchstone of culpability. For by hypothesis there is no choice—in the sense of desired end, intended means, or believed side-effect—that had wrongdoing as its object.[16]

This difference remains even after we refine what a 'choice to do wrong' means in certain ways that I have hitherto ignored. Notice that even in cases of strong culpability—desire, intention, and belief—the objects of the respective mental states need not be literally in terms of wrongdoing. One need not desire to do a moral wrong for its own sake in order to be most culpable; one need only desire to do a certain act A for its own sake, and it must also be the case that morality makes A wrong to do. One need not intend to do a morally wrong act as a means to be severely culpable; it is enough for this level of culpability that one intend a certain act A as a means, and that it be objectively true that morality forbids A.

[15] As does Crocker, e.g., in 'Justice in Criminal Liability', *supra* n. 2.
[16] A subject returned to at the close of ch. 13.

Similarly, one need not believe that his act is morally forbidden in order to attain the culpability of belief; it is enough that the actor believes he is doing act A, and it is objectively true that morality forbids A. One could encapsulate all of this by saying that 'ignorance of morality is no excuse'.[17]

Even with this qualification about the objects of the mental states, the difference between the most serious culpability and the culpability of negligence remains. Although the objects of desire, intention, and belief are descriptions of actions, not moral conclusions, still in cases of mere negligence there is no description of some action A (that morality makes wrong) that is the object of any of the actor's beliefs.

Another attempt to soften the difference between these two kinds of culpability might go this way. Suppose that for all the mental states of culpability there were what might be called 'forfeiture rules'. These would be rules allowing the substitution of the object of a mental state the actor did have, for one he did not have but which morality forbids as wrong. For example, A kills B, not intending to kill B, but intending to inflict grievous bodily harm on B. One might think that an intention whose object was 'grievous bodily harm' is close enough to an intention whose object was killing that the first can be substituted for the second. A's culpability then becomes that of one who intended to kill.

On this view negligence is just a substitution rule for belief states: when an actor believes that he is shooting at a target, believes he hears a shout of 'don't shoot', believes only humans make such sounds and usually only when in danger, yet does not believe that his shooting risks becoming a killing, he is culpable for believing (to the probability of reasonable inference) that he is killing.

The problem with this attempted accommodation of negligence to more serious culpability is that there are no such substitution rules in morality. The criminal law and the law of torts have admittedly adopted such rules in certain contexts,[18] yet the law is criticizable in precisely such contexts for departing from morality. One who intends to inflict grievous bodily harm has a level of culpability commensurate to that wrong, not a level of culpability commensurate to the wrong actually done but not intended.

---

[17] We do require a fair opportunity to learn morality, although not actual knowledge of morality.

[18] Some legal examples are explored in ch. 11, following.

Forfeiture rules fundamentally confuse wrongdoing and culpability.

I conclude that inadvertent risk creation cannot be accommodated within the choice model of culpability. Such inadvertent risk creation is rather a culpability of unexercised capacity, not of choice. I say this, without conceding to my critics[19] that choice should be abandoned or subsumed under unexercised capacity as the touchstone of culpability. Quite the contrary: choosing (desiring, intending, or believing) to do a wrongful act is the dominant form of culpability. This is the culpability that blames us for acting wrongfully in the world as we see it. Culpability as negligence blames us despite our acting rightly in the world as we see it. Although we can be somewhat culpable in not seeing the world more clearly, such culpability pales before that of wrongdoers who choose to do their wrongs in a world they see clearly.

Criminal law and the law of torts divide in their focus on one or the other of these two kinds of culpability. Criminal law—at least the core notions of common law crimes and *malum in se* crimes—focuses on the culpability of chosen wrongdoing. Tort law—at least the non-intentional, non-strict liability torts that are at its centre—focuses on the culpability of inadvertent (i.e., unchosen) wrongdoing. In the next section I wish to enquire why this might be so. If retributive justice is the goal of the criminal law, does such justice demand the culpability of choice? If corrective justice is the goal of tort law, does such justice demand (or can it at least be satisfied with) the culpability of inadvertence?

III. THE TWO KINDS OF CULPABILITY AND THE TWO KINDS OF JUSTICE

Why does the law of crimes focus on the culpability of choice whereas the law of torts focuses rather on the culpability of unused capacity? A simple answer might be proposed in terms of fairness of the notice variety: given the comparatively greater severity of the sanctions attached to criminal prohibitions, we require greater opportunity to know what is prohibited before criminal liability may be imposed. Negligence, it is further said, is inherently vague,

---

[19] e.g., Jeremy Horder, 'Criminal Culpability: The Possibility of a General Theory', *Law and Philosophy*, Vol. 12 (1993), 193–215.

so that such culpability should not be sufficient in criminal law. Yet this is a non-starter, for two reasons.

First, criminal law, unlike the law of torts, does not prohibit negligence *tout cour*. What Anglo-American criminal law typically prohibits are approximately 7,000 types of actions. Negligence is a kind of culpability with which those legally prohibited actions might be done. Citizens need to know what types of actions are generally prohibited, as well as which of those prima facie prohibited types are nonetheless permitted became of the existence of one or more justifying circumstances. Citizens do not need to know when they will be adjudged culpable because they should have believed they were likely to do an unjustified instance of a wrongful type of action. There is no notice worry about norms of culpability, negligence included.

Secondly, in terms of the trade-off invited between seriousness of wrong, degree of its risk, and justification for running the risk, there is no difference between negligence and the culpability of belief. Even if actors should have a fair opportunity to apply the norms of culpability to themselves before they act—which is what I dispute in my first answer—those norms involve the sliding scale trade-offs that make application difficult no less for belief-culpability than for negligence-culpability. In the case of culpability for belief, we must judge the seriousness of the wrong the actor believes herself to be doing, the likelihood with which she assessed she would be doing such a wrong, and the likelihood with which she assessed that circumstances would exist such that they would justify the wrong, i.e., make it permissible. It is no more (and no less) predictable how such judgements will come out than is it predictable how the similar judgements of negligence will come out.

We cannot thus locate the differential culpability requirements of the criminal law and torts in the former's greater concern with notice. Rather, we must locate the difference within the two kinds of justice that animate each of these areas of law. We must locate the difference, in other words, within the differential demands of retributive as opposed to corrective justice.

Corrective justice and retributive justice both are built upon the primary norms of morality that define wrongdoing. Both kinds of justice share this reliance on our primary norms of moral obligation, usually of a negative or prohibitory sort (like 'do not kill'). Such kinds of justice differ, however, in the secondary duties they impose on those who culpably violate these primary duties. Corrective justice obligates those who have culpably violated their primary duties to correct as best they can the wrong they have done someone. Retributive justice obligates those who have culpably violated their primary duties to suffer for the violation.

Punishing a wrongdoer by making him suffer can of course be seen as a way of 'making him pay' for his wrong. But such familiar indebtedness metaphors about retributive punishment should not be allowed to obscure a real difference in the secondary duties imposed by the two kinds of justice. A very wealthy person who compensates a victim right up to the latter's *ex post* indifference curve may well satisfy his duty to correct the situation left by his wrong. Such compensation need not, however, satisfy the wrongdoer's duty to undergo punishment for his wrong. The demands of retributive justice are not necessarily (and not even usually) satisfied by making the victim of the wrong whole again.

The duty to suffer, unlike the duty to correct, is not linked primarily to wrong done to some victims in the actual world. Such duty arises for victimless wrongs and even in the absence of wrongdoing entirely (as where one tries to kill, or risks killing, and fails). Although successful wrongdoing increases one's retributive deserts, such wrongdoing is not the trigger for retributive punishment as it is the trigger for corrective compensation. As I mentioned in chapter 5, wrongdoing is thus something of the 'poor relation' for retributive justice in a way that it is not for corrective justice.

Culpability correspondingly has a greater role to play in triggering retributive punishment than it does in triggering corrective justice duties. This greater role of culpability in retributive justice demands a stronger kind of culpability. Since it is doing most of the work in triggering the secondary duties of retributive justice, culpability in this context means the greater culpability of choice. Those who may not have done wrong in the actual world must have done wrong in their own minds before a duty to suffer retributive punishment arises.

By contrast, it is culpability that is the poor relation for corrective justice. On some views of corrective justice, no culpability at all is required to trigger the duty to compensate. (Those who innocently cause peril to another, for example, are often in tort law held to possess a kind of corrective justice duty to prevent the harm threatened if they can.) Although on my own view corrective justice is not *this* focused on wrongdoing to the exclusion of culpability, it remains true that culpability is not the main trigger for corrective justice duties, and that wrongdoing is. The culpability demanded by corrective justice is correspondingly less, so that the much lesser culpability of unused capacity can suffice. After all, if one of two relatively blameless parties must suffer a loss, why not have the one who is not quite blameless—because culpably negligent—bear it? The only instance in which such lessened culpability will not suffice is where the victim also is not blameless; in such circumstances, corrective justice should demand the more serious kind of culpability before an actor's wrongdoing triggers a duty to correct his wrong.

Anglo-American criminal and tort law by and large mirror these demands of retributive and corrective justice in their culpability requirements, although not in every detail. Criminal law centrally relies on what I have called the culpability of choice as its main trigger of liability. Negligence with respect to the most morally salient features of the *actus reus* remains an exceptional basis for liability; at least some level of culpability of the belief kind is generally required for the morally wrongful aspects of one's actions. Within the culpability of choice, our criminal law does not grade culpability precisely as I have described. Sometimes it distinguishes the culpability of belief from the culpabilities of desire and intention, as in the occasional common law requirements of a 'specific intent' or the Model Penal Code's requirement of 'purpose'. More often it elides all three kinds of most serious culpability into one category of 'general intent' or 'knowledge', grading instead within the culpability of belief by the degree of subjectively perceived risk of wrongdoing without justification. Nowhere to my knowledge do our liability doctrines distinguish the culpability of desired ends from that of intended means, although in sentencing such a distinction sometimes enters in.

With respect to the representational contents of the mental states required for the culpability of choice, our criminal law largely does what our morality does: whatever it would be morally wrong to do it is culpable to desire to do or intend to do, or believe one is doing. Notice that our criminal law does this even though its *actus reus* prohibitions often have more parts or elements to them than do the corresponding moral wrongs; in fixing the contents of the mental states of culpability our criminal law simply ignores those parts of its own *actus reus* prohibitions as are irrelevant to the moral wrongness of the act prohibited. The only difference between morality and the criminal law here is that the latter operates with only two classes of citizenship for those elements of the *actus reus* as are relevant to the moral wrongness of that action: all elements legally are classified as either results of voluntary acts or circumstances in which such acts take place. Results are presumed to be of major significance in measuring culpability; circumstances are presumed to be of minor significance in measuring culpability. These legal presumptions should be seen as rules of thumb for what sorts of elements of morally wrongful acts most importantly measure the culpability of the actor who chooses to do such an act.[20]

Tort law centrally relies on what I have called the culpability of unexercised capacity. The culpability of choice will also suffice for tort liability, but with the exception of those hold-overs from the ancient unity of crime and tort—the intentional torts, where punishment is still sought via punitive damages—such greater culpability is not necessary. The only real exception to this lies in those cases where the victim is not wholly without blame, where she too was contributionly negligent with respect to her own injury. There the tipping role of culpability within tort law requires the greater culpability of choice, recognized by the 'wilful and wanton' doctrine placing liability on such a seriously culpable defendant despite the (lesser) culpability of his victim.

Because tort law centrally focuses on the culpability of unexercised capacity, it has had to develop distinctions as to what sorts of incapacities excuse. Such excuses are quite distinct from the excuses for prima facie culpable choice: as I argue in chapters 12 and 13, the latter excuses all have to do with the difficulties the actor faced in not choosing to do wrong. Where no choice to do wrong is made because the prohibited wrongdoing is not perceived, although it should have been, the relevant form of excuse is different: the actor lacked just those capabilities of inference for whose non-exercise he is being blamed. To be blamed for non-use of a capacity, one must first have such a capacity.

Since the capacity in question is the capacity to see the risk that one's action will be wrong, the relevant incapacities will be cognitive. If one is too young, too crazy, too retarded, too stupid, too

---

[20] Explored by me in *Act and Crime*.

blinded by love, grief, or other passion, one may lack sufficient capacity of inference-drawing to be blamed for its non-use. Tort law of course does not quite make all the allowance that morality makes, mostly because of administrative worries. Still, it makes an attempt to mirror the culpability of unexercised capacity as does the criminal law to mirror its form of culpability, the more serious culpability of choice.

10

MIND, BRAIN, AND THE UNCONSCIOUS

I. INTRODUCTION

The present chapter no doubt will strike many readers as being something of a detour as we explore the psychology of culpability. This is because the chapter addresses issues of research programme and theory construction in psychology, and does so, moreover, for only one kind of psychology, the kind of dynamic psychiatry originating with Sigmund Freud. The chapter thus may seem far removed from the ethical topic of culpability.

The link to culpability is nonetheless there. The chapter is included to illuminate two areas pertinent to our enquiry into culpability. First, the chapter explores the ultimate metaphysical question of what those mental states (such as intentions, beliefs, and desires) that ground culpability, *are*. A version of metaphysical functionalism is articulated that may allay the fears of some lawyers, to the effect that mental states are no things at all. Second, the chapter explores what some have called my optimistic view about the survivability of the folk psychology (on which culpability is based) in the face of ever more challenging, technical psychologies.[1] For the research programme I outline in this chapter would, if well conceived, allow us to deepen the folk psychology on which the law rests, rather than jettisoning it in the face of more sophisticated psychological theories.

It may seem that neither of these tasks can be accomplished by looking to Freudian theory. After all, Freudian psychiatry has suffered a marked decline in the last half of this century, to the point that it is hardly even respectable within many circles. Yet despite this well-deserved decline, Freudian theory serves my two purposes exactly. One can articulate the kind of 'optimistic' research pro-

---

[1] See Jennifer Hornsby, 'Action and Aberration', *University of Pennsylvania Law Review*, Vol. 142 (1994), 1719–47, at 1735 n. 53.

gramme I here explore for much more contemporary theories in psychology, be they behaviourist, cognitive, physiological, ethological, or whatever. However much such decidedly non-Freudian theorists have ballyhooed that they were moving 'beyond freedom and dignity' (and the folk psychology on which such moral notions depend), in fact such theorists too are interpretable in light of the monistic, reductionist view of mind that follows. As I urge with respect to Freud in what follows, so would I urge with respect to such non-Freudian theories: the notions of self, intentionality, and personhood are secure against the insights of even those psychologies that explicitly eschew use of these concepts.

The specific topic of the chapter is the notion of the unconscious as it is and should be conceived in psychoanalytic theory. I use the unconscious as a convenient example with which to examine the status of the metapsychological theories of Freud. The concept of the unconscious, standing as it does with one foot in the clinical theory and the other foot solidly planted in the metapsychologies, should serve to illustrate some general points about Freud's metapsychological undertakings.

The argument will proceed in the following way. First, I shall distinguish what I call the pre-theoretical conception of the unconscious from what I shall call the theory-laden sense of the word. I shall also show how these two conceptions of the unconscious naturally track into a distinction, current amongst many psychoanalytic theorists, between two kinds of theory in psychoanalysis, the clinical and the metapsychological theories.

The rest of the chapter deals with two mistaken treatments of this distinction: the body of the chapter deals with the mistake of taking the distinction too seriously, so that one writes off the metapsychological theory as a kind of logically absurd attempt to bridge the supposedly unbridgeable gap between body and mind. In the conclusion I suggest that there is an opposite mistake, that of not taking the distinction seriously enough, so that the important boundaries of self and responsibility are ignored in the rush to integrate the concept of the unconscious into contemporary psychological theory.

II. THE TWO CONCEPTIONS OF THE UNCONSCIOUS

Although Freud often distinguished three senses of 'unconscious' as he used the word in his theory, these three senses of Freud's can be parsed into two conceptions.[2] The first is what I have called the pre-theoretical notion of the unconscious. The claims made with this conception are: (1) the existential claim that persons are possessed not only of mental states that are not the subject of present attention (preconscious), but also of states that are not subject to recall even if attention is directed toward them; (2) the relational claim that such mental states may influence behaviour as a cause or as a reason without awareness of their influence by the subject; (3) the epistemic claim that such states are accessible to the extended memory of the subject, who in principle can come to know that he had a mental state that was unconscious in the same way as he can come to know of any other contents of his mind, namely, by non-inferential recall; and (4) the content claim, according to which the objects of such mental states are (ultimately) sexual or aggressive in content. None of these claims are dependent upon Freud's metapsychology being true. The concept of the unconscious used in such claims is 'pre-theoretical' because of this independence; such claims are of course theoretical in the same sense as is common sense (or 'folk') psychology, of which such claims are an extension.

The second conception of the unconscious is Freud's theory-laden conception. Here one conceives of the unconscious as an aggregation of mental states that not only share the phenomenal property of being unconscious but also share a functional role (and perhaps some common structure) in the conflict-ridden and tension-reducing mechanisms that human beings are posited to be by the metapsychological theory. Mental states that are unconscious in this theory-laden sense could be aggregated into a 'System Ucs.', because of their systematic role within the mind, namely, as one pole of a set of basic conflicts all persons are supposed to possess. As Freud noted in his discussion of the concept in 1912, the 'index-value' of a state being unconscious was the important thing in his

---

[2] Michael S. Moore, *Law and Psychiatry: Rethinking the Relationship* (Cambridge: Cambridge University Press, 1984), 126–37.

metapsychological theory, not the phenomenal property of importance to the clinical theory.[3]

These two conceptions of the unconscious are matched by dual
conceptions of other concepts used in psychoanalytic theory. Thus,
for example, George Klein wrote of Freud having implicitly two
theories of sexuality. The clinical theory of sexuality, as Klein called
it, 'emphasizes the cognitive matrix—the meaning—of sexuality'.[4]
In studying the significance of sensual experience to persons, such
a clinical theory would focus initially on the mental experience of
infants regarding sensual pleasure, chart the 'conceptual affiliates'
that develop as the child develops patterns of sensual stimulation
and regulation, chart the pattern of conflict that can develop about
human sexuality, chart the ties between sensual activity and the
development of a self-conception and self-esteem. The 'drive-dis-
charge' theory of sexuality, by way of contrast, would talk not of
mental experience, meaning, conflict and self, but rather of energic
forces seeking discharge.

These kinds of attempts to distinguish two accounts among the
various of Freud's concepts should be seen as instances of a more
general divorce between clinical psychoanalysis and the metapsychological theories of psychoanalysis. What is in fact meant by this
general distinction is not always clear. My own reading of the
recent literature suggests several possibilities that the distinction is
not about. For one thing, it is not the distinction between theory
and therapy, for clinical psychoanalysis is itself a theory and not a
therapy. Modes of therapy, their success or lack of it, are part of
the data for a genuinely explanatory theory, whether clinical or
metapsychological. Secondly, the distinction is not that between
broader and narrower subject-matters for theory. That is, clinical
theory does not aim only at explaining the success/failure rate of
psychoanalytic therapy or the aetiology of the neuroses to which
such therapy is applied; rather, clinical theory at least purports to
be part of a general psychology that explains all human behaviour,
healthy as well as neurotic. Thirdly, the distinction is not one
between an object language and a metalanguage, because the

[3] Sigmund Freud, 'A Note on the Unconscious in Psychoanalysis', *Collected Papers*, Vol. 4 (London: Hogarth Press, 1959).
[4] George Klein, 'Freud's Two Theories of Sexuality', in M. Gill and P. Hoizman, eds., *Psychology versus Metapsychology, Psychological Issues Monograph 36* (New York: International Universities Press, 1976), 36.

metapsychology is not about statements in the clinical theory but, rather, is about the very same actions, states and entities as is the clinical theory.[5]

Perhaps the best way to get at the clinical theory/metapsychology distinction is that suggested by Morris Eagle:

An examination of the writings of advocates of the clinical-theory-only approach [Klein, Gill, Rycroft, Schafer] indicates that essentially what they mean by clinical formulations or clinical theory is an explanatory account in which a person's behaviour or symptoms are explained by reference to his conscious or unconscious aims, wishes and goals.[6]

The reason such writers focus on 'aims, wishes and goals' in order to draw their distinction is because of some general views about how such mental states differ from the events and states that figure in the explanations of natural science. The clinical theory is concerned with actions rather than with bodily motions, with reasons and not mere causes, with Intentionally characterized states rather than with the non-representational states of physical science, with 'experience-near' rather than 'experience-distant' concepts, with empathetic understanding rather than ordinary explanation. In all such ways, psychoanalysts have attempted to portray the clinical theory as conceived in the vocabulary of persons and the metapsychology as conceived in the vocabulary of mechanistic causation.

The pre-theoretical unconscious, being a phenomenal property of the mental states of persons, readily fits the clinical theory side of the distinction. The only reason one might think otherwise would be because one accepted various scepticisms about whether states can have the characteristics that make them mental states, and yet be unconscious. B. Rubinstein, for example, has argued that unconscious mental states cannot be a person's mental states, cannot be part of one's sense of self, because such states are not discovered through any first-person experience. This shows, both Rubinstein and Eagle conclude, that there can be no conception of the unconscious that is part of the clinical theory only; further, that unconscious wishes, emotions, etc., must be conceived in terms of brain states and thus must be part of the metapsychology.[7]

[5] Robert Holt, 'The Death and the Transfiguration of the Metapsychology', *International Review of Psychoanalysis*, Vol. 8 (1981), 129–43.

[6] Morris Eagle, *Recent Developments in Psychoanalysis* (New York: McGraw-Hill, 1984), 148.

[7] Id. at 150; B. Rubinstein, 'On the Possibility of a Strictly Clinical Theory: An

This view ignores Freud's extraordinary insight about extended memory. When a patient comes to see that he was unconsciously angry at some time in the past, he has done more than learn a bit of neurophysiology (indirectly he may have done that as well—see below). He has recovered the non-observational knowledge that he was angry, known that the anger was part of him, in the same way as he acknowledges his conscious anger as his. His unconscious anger is part of his self.[8]

One might think that such insight is a kind of performance by the patient whereby he makes the anger part of himself just by 'avowing it' to be his.[9] Yet this is not the way he sees it. He sees himself recapturing an experience that he was having even though he was unaware of it at the time. We should not restrict ourselves to a physiological conceptualization of unconscious wishes, beliefs, emotions, etc., on grounds of no privileged access when the clinical theory asserts that there is such access, only deferred.[10] Hence, there is no justification for denying a place to the pre-theoretical unconscious within the clinical theory just because of a temporary absence of privileged access.

The theory-laden unconscious is a conception belonging to the metapsychological theory. Freud's theoretical explanation for why some mental states are very hard to recapture (i.e., are unconscious) is cast in terms of the conflict between instinct and control that Freud meant to conceptualize with his topographical and structural metapsychologies. Hence, the 'System Ucs.' plainly belongs in the metapsychology. How much of what Freud called his dynamic unconscious goes into the metapsychological theory is a more

Essay on the Philosophy of Psychoanalysis', in M. Gill and P. Holzman, eds., *Psychology versus Metapsychology, Psychological Issues Monograph 36* (New York: International Universities Press, 1976), 245, 253–4.

[8] Michael S. Moore, 'The Nature of Psychoanalytic Explanation', *Psychoanalysis and Contemporary Thought*, Vol. 3 (1980), 459–543. Also in L. Laudan, ed., *Mind and Medicine: Problems of Explanation and Evaluation in Psychiatry and the Biomedical Sciences* (Berkeley: University of California Press, 1983); Stuart Hampshire, 'Disposition and Memory', *International Journal of Psycho-Analysis*, Vol. 42 (1963), 59–68. Repr. in S. Hampshire, *Freedom of Mind* (Princeton: Princeton University Press, 1971); David Wiggins, 'Locke, Butler and the Stream of Consciousness: and Men as Natural Kind', in A. Rorty, ed., *The Identities of Persons* (Berkeley: University of California Press, 1976).

[9] Morris Eagle, 'Anatomy of the Self in Psychoanalytic Theory', in M. Ruse, ed., *Nature Animated*, Vol. 2. (Dordrecht: Reidel, 1982).

[10] See Moore, *supra* n. 2, at 17, 135–6, 254–65.

difficult question. As I have argued elsewhere,[11] Freud made two claims with his dynamic sense of the word. His descriptive claim— about there being states that are not only latent (preconscious) but also very hard to recapture—is part of the clinical theory. Contrary to Grunbaum and others,[12] however, I think the explanatory claim in Freud's dynamic usage explaining why some mental states are so hard to recapture in terms of repression is properly part of the metapsychological theory, not the clinical theory.

Seeing how this issue is resolved clarifies the distinction between the two kinds of theories. If one thinks of repression in the way I would think of resistance, as an unconscious action a person engages in for various unconscious reasons, then one will classify repression as part of the clinical theory. For although unconscious, the repressing in such a case is an activity carried on by the self and recapturable by one's extended memory. Alternatively, however, one might think of repression as a kind of internal process that no person performs as an action, not even as an unconscious action, because the activity is beyond recapture by extended memory. The seeming intelligence of repression, the sense that repression makes in avoiding painful thoughts, is just the function it serves in keeping us healthy. Such a process should not be analogized to resistance, but rather to processes like those in the dream-work. The dream-work processes of secondary revision, displacement, and condensation are also not actions a person performs, even unconsciously; they are functionally defined processes that must take place if dreams are to have the form they have and yet be caused by the kind of unconscious wishes Freud envisioned.[13]

In a cogent recent paper Harvey Mullane[14] argues that repression should be construed in the latter way. Mullane distinguishes the material that is repressed from the repressing activity itself. The repressed material is part of the pre-theoretical unconscious and of the clinical theory, but the repressing activity itself, being beyond

---

[11] See Moore, *supra* n. 2, at 131–2.

[12] Adolf Grunbaum, *The Foundations of Psychoanalysis: A Philosophical Critique* (Berkeley: University of California Press, 1984); W. D. Hart, 'Models of Repression', in R. Wollheim and J. Hopkins, eds., *Philosophical Essays on Freud* (Cambridge: Cambridge University Press, 1982).

[13] Moore, *supra* n. 2, at 306–8.

[14] Harvey Mullane, 'Defence, Dreams and Rationality', *Synthese*, Vol. 57 (1983), 187–204.

the self-boundaries of extended memory, is part of the theory-laden unconscious of Freud's metapsychological story.

III. TAKING THE DISTINCTION TOO SERIOUSLY: THE ALLEGED CHASM BETWEEN BODY AND MIND

A presently popular way to take the distinction too seriously is to use it for the twofold purpose of insulating the clinical theory from scientific criticism; and writing off the metapsychology as an impossible enterprise. The general strategy of theorists like George Klein, Merton Gill, Roy Schafer, W. W. Meissner, Paul Ricoeur, Robert Steele, and H. J. Home, goes like this:[15] one takes the distinction between clinical theory and metapsychology to be a distinction between two different 'logical planes'[16] or two different 'types of discourse'.[17] The language of the clinical theory is the language of mind, meaning, and the humanities, whereas the language of the metapsychology is the language of physical events, mechanisms and natural science. Further, 'the logic and method of the humanities is radically different from that of science . . .'.[18] Accordingly, the two theories have nothing to do with each other but are descriptions (cum interpretations cum explanations) sufficient unto themselves in their respective realms of discourse.

This *Geisteswissenschaften* view is then used to say, first, that the clinical theory is exempt from the rigours of scientific validation because it is not science—it is hermeneutics. Second, this view renders illegitimate any attempt to create something like the metapsychology, which purports to explain the clinical theory. The entire metapsychology can be written off, on this view, not by a painstak-

---

[15] George Klein, 'Two Theories or One?', in *Psychoanalytic Theory*, (New York: International Universities Press, 1976); Merton Gill, 'Metapsychology Is not Psychology', in M. Gill and P. Holzman, eds., *Psychology versus Metapsychology, Psychological Issues Monograph 36* (New York: International Universities Press, 1976); Roy Schafer, *A New Language for Psychoanalysis* (New Haven, Conn.: Yale University Press, 1976); W. W. Meissner, 'Metapsychology—Who needs it?', *Journal of the American Psychoanalytic Association* Vol. 29 (1981), 921–38; Paul Ricoeur, *Freud and Philosophy* (New Haven, Conn.: Yale University Press, 1970); Robert Steele, 'Psychoanalysis and Hermeneutics', *International Review of Psycho-Analysis*, Vol. 6 (1979), 389–411; H. J. Home, 'The Concept of Mind', *International Journal of Psychoanalysis*, Vol. 47 (1966), 42–9.

[16] Klein, *supra* n. 4. [17] Gill, *supra* n. 15.
[18] Home, *supra* n. 15, at 43.

ing comparison of its tenets with adequate standards of scientific theory construction and validation, but by the discovery of one big, underlying mistake, the kind philosophers used to call a category mistake. Since the clinical theory and the metapsychology operate in different 'universes of discourse', it must be a mistake about the category in which such theories operate to conjoin the concepts of the clinical theory with those of the metapsychology into one over-arching theory. Psychoanalysis, on this view, can only be the clinical theory. The other stuff, the metapsychology, is just that—other stuff, the concern of some other discipline, presumably biology, but not of a true science of mind.

To understand how this sort of view is arrived at from more general views in the philosophy of mind and the philosophy of language, one can examine the work of Ilham Dilman[19] and Roy Schafer.[20] Dilman has concluded that the pre-theoretical unconscious cannot also be construed as a theoretical term in Freud's general metapsychological theories of human behaviour. Dilman's argument is based on the epistemic claim of deferred privileged access that is part of Freud's clinical theory. Freud's clinical ideal of 'making the unconscious conscious' is only attained by the recapture through memory (rather than by an inference from evidence) of what was previously unconscious. Dilman bases two arguments on this clinical ideal. The first is that it is a kind of category mistake to think that one could have such privileged access to a theoretical entity, as one would if the pre-theoretical unconscious were also the System Ucs. of Freud's topographical theory. As Dilman puts it:

One cannot talk of seeing an electron (not even as a possibility one might wish to speculate about) without sinning against logic; for if the concept of an electron is theoretical . . . then seeing cannot have a place in statements in which the concept of an electron has a place . . . While we can talk of observing the effects of electrons, the expression 'seeing an electron' is at best a misleading locution. The same would be the case of 'making the unconscious conscious' if the concept of the unconscious were a theoretical concept.[21]

---

[19] Ilham Dilman, 'The Unconscious', *Mind*, Vol. 68 (1959), 446–73; Ilham Dilman, 'Is the Unconscious a Theoretical Construct?', *The Monist*, Vol. 46 (1972), 313–42; Ilham Dilman, *Freud and Human Nature* (Oxford: Blackwell, 1983); Ilham Dilman, *Freud and the Mind* (Oxford: Blackwell, 1984).

[20] Schafer *supra* n. 15.   [21] 'The Unconscious', *supra* n. 19, at 455.

Dilman's second argument is also based on the privileged access we each have to the contents of our own pre-theoretical unconscious. Such privileged access gives rise to an asymmetry in the modes of verification of first- and third-person statements about our mental states, unconscious included. Dilman's argument is that treating the unconscious as a theoretical entity would do away with this asymmetry for unconscious mental states, because then even first-person statements would be verified only by inference from a theory, and not directly from awareness:

My main objection to the view that the unconscious is a theoretical construct has been that it does not recognize the difference between a person's recognition of his own unconscious feelings and desires and another person's recognition of them. It hinders a proper appreciation of what is involved in what is unconscious becoming conscious.[22]

This kind of argument can be constructed no matter what one takes to be the touchstone of mind. Roy Schafer fastens upon those aspects of language characteristic of our talk about personal agency as such a touchstone of mind. For Schafer too there can be no metapsychological theory about neurotic symptoms because these symptoms are accurately conceptualized as the actions persons perform for reasons. Because of this 'action language' conceptualization of neurotic symptoms, the metapsychology becomes an illegitimate enterprise for Schafer no matter how it is construed. If framed in terms of the non-action vocabulary of the economic metapsychology—forces, energies, and drives—then the theory is not a theory of mind because it has left the only vocabulary in terms of which mind can be discussed, what Schafer calls the 'action' vocabulary. If framed in terms of little people performing little actions for little reasons, Schafer's complaint is that such vocabulary is only appropriate for whole persons.

In short, for Schafer as for Dilman, Freud's metapsychology and its theoretical unconscious is caught in a dilemma: the mentalistic vocabulary of persons in terms of which clinicians prompt patients to recapture unconscious wishes and so on is not a vocabulary in which it makes sense to construct a deep theory such as the metapsychology purports to be. But it also is true that any theory constructed in a non-action vocabulary (or one without asymmetry in its modes of verification) cannot be a theory about the mind, for

[22] 'Is the Unconscious a Theoretical Construct?', *supra* n. 19, at 339.

these features—agency and privileged access—constitute what is mental.

It should be apparent that what we have encountered is the doctrine of category differences between the extensional, non-Intentional, observation-dependent, mechanistic, causal vocabulary appropriate to explain movements of bodies (including human bodies), on the one hand, and the intensional, Intentional, non-observational, purposive, reason-giving vocabulary appropriate to explain human actions, on the other. Which aspect of this apparent categorical divide is seized upon by sceptics about the theory-laden unconscious does vary. Dilman, as we have seen, seizes upon privileged access whereas Schafer picks semantic features of the action vocabulary. Other psychoanalytic theorists latch onto the fuzzier hermeneutic notion of meaning.[23] But the general dilemma for the metapsychology that each of them possess is wholly the same: no theory can be constructed 'on the mental side', and although theories are perfectly appropriate 'on the physical side', they cannot be theories of mind. The unconscious, on such a view, is something about which one can generalize in the clinical theory; it is not something one can develop a theory about in the metapsychology. Metapsychological concepts of the unconscious are simply the results of category mistakes, the mistaking of brain theory for a theory of mind.[24]

This cannot possibly be right. The philosophical doctrine of category mistakes has unfortunately got in the way of theory construction in psychiatry, truncating the idea of what the unconscious is and what a theory about it should be. To see this in any convincing detail would require that we re-examine the doctrine of categorical differences that dominated the philosophy of mind between Gilbert Ryle's *Concept of Mind* in 1949 and (roughly) 1965. Rather than engaging in what many philosophers would regard as an exercise of arguments now difficult to motivate, I shall only examine Roy Schafer's argument to exemplify the philosophical mistake common to all forms of the position.

Schafer essentially deploys two linguistic arguments in reaching his conclusion that a non-action language cannot be about mind. Firstly, he argues that the normal matrix of discourse in which we

[23] e.g., Home, Klein, Gill, Ricoeur, and Steele, *supra* n. 15.
[24] For the general form of this dilemma, see Daniel Dennett, *Content and Consciousness*, (London: Routledge and Kegan Paul, 1969), 90–6.

use words that truly refer to things is inappropriate to mental words. About 'anger', Schafer asks (in a close paraphrase of Ryle):

The vocabulary of anger . . . depends on the legitimacy of assuming or referring to an inside and an outside—but, I ask again, inside or outside of what? Where? Is anger anywhere? . . . The questions are unanswerable, of course, because they cannot be asked in a logical inquiry. Anger is not the kind of word about which such questions may be asked.[25]

From this feature of usage Schafer concludes that 'anger', and 'the unconscious' do not refer to anything, and that we must regard the unconscious not as a thing, but only as a property of actions. Second, Schafer argues that from usage it is possible to tell what the reference is of his preferred way of speaking (i.e., where actions are performed angrily or unconsciously). 'Angrily' or 'unconsciously' cannot refer to anything unknown to the speakers of these words; for what it is that guides the usage of these words from competent speakers is what the words mean. Schafer blatantly makes Ryle's ordinary language philosophy assumption that the rules of correct usage can fix the reference of the words used, so that, if speakers do not know the deep theory of the emotions or of the unconscious, then the things such theories postulate cannot be referred to by 'angrily' or 'unconsciously'.

Yet there is no reason to think that the patterns of usage to which Ryle or Schafer (or Dilman) advert can place any a priori limit on what it is that is referred to by mental words, 'unconscious' included. As Roderick Anscombe concluded in his generally perceptive review of Schafer's work, 'questions about how best to conceptualize the unconscious have more to do with fact than with language'.[26]

What Anscombe means can be got at through a Gedankenexperiment. Suppose we place ourselves back in ancient Babylon at just the time the Babylonian astronomers were discovering that the star that appeared in the morning (the 'Morning Star') and the star that appeared in the evening (the 'Evening Star') were one and the same thing, namely, the planet Venus. One can imagine a

[25] Schafer, *supra* n. 15, at 165.

[26] Roderick Anscombe, 'Referring to the Unconscious: A Philosophical Critique of Schafer's Action Language', *International Journal of Psychoanalysis*, Vol. 62 (1981), 225–41. See also A. Spiro, 'A Philosophical Appraisal of Roy Schafer's A New Language for Psychoanalysis', *Psychoanalysis and Contemporary Thought*, Vol. 2 (1979), 253–91.

Babylonian ordinary language philosopher 'disproving' the astronomer's claim in the following way: that he (the philosopher) has not been looking at stars, but at language use; that he has observed the phrases 'Evening Star' and 'Morning Star' in all of their ordinary uses, and that from such observation it is clear that the phrases appear in different categories of discourse (evening talk and morning talk); that, accordingly, the phrases cannot refer to the same thing, or else (by Leibniz's Law) the expressions would be equivalent, which their differing use shows that they manifestly are not; indeed, that it is absurd—the kind of absurdity ordinary language philosophers called a category mistake—to even speak of the Evening Star and the Morning Star existing in the same sense of 'exist'.[27]

The problem with this view of meaning, and with its accompanying doctrine of categorical differences, is that systematic connections in the ordinary usage of certain concepts are allowed to suspend questions of reference and identity in a way that is very counterintuitive. Why should the fact that ordinary people built up a set of systematic usages for the phrase 'Evening Star', and another set of usages for the phrase 'Morning Star', have anything to do with the questions of whether those phrases refer to something and whether the things to which they refer are in reality one and the same thing? To be sure, if there were something in the patterns of usage that showed us that the phrases did not refer, all well and good; yet none of the arguments ever deployed to show this have succeeded.[28]

The upshot is that we must reject the idea that there is some categorical divide that prevents one from asking about the things of which mental terms refer. The doctrines of categorical difference

[27] A close (if unsympathetic) paraphrase of Gilbert Ryle, *The Concept of Mind* (London: Hutcheson, 1949), ch. 1, 28.

[28] Typical arguments were those that confused speech-act pragmatic analyses with semantic analyses of meaning. Thus, action words were said not to refer because used to ascribe responsibility (H. L. A. Hart, 'The Ascription of Responsibility and Rights', *Proceedings of the Aristotelian Society*, Vol. 49 (1949), 171–94); words describing reasons for action were non-referential because they were used to give justificatory warrants rather than descriptions (A. R. Louch, *Explanation and Human Action* (Berkeley: University of California Press, 1966); words of sensation did not refer because used to express (but not describe) sensations (L. Wittgenstein, *Philosophical Investigations* (Oxford: Blackwell, 1958)). See also Dan Dennett, *Content and Consciousness*, *supra* n. 24, ch. 2, for an alternative kind of argument from usage (since abandoned) for the non-referential use of mental terms.

cannot justify the foreclosing of the question of whether the phrase 'pre-theoretical unconscious' ultimately refers, not only to the mental states recapturable by extended memory, but also to the primary process of Freud's metapsychological theory and ultimately, perhaps, to neurophysiology. No argument from ordinary usage can show it to be a category mistake to seek the answer to such a question by research and refinement of theory.

There are of course routes to showing the impossibility of the metapsychology that are alternative to the 'linguistic dualism'[29] of Rylean ordinary language philosophy. One such is metaphysical dualism. Yet such a metaphysical dualism is implausible for all the reasons Ryle so elegantly presented, as most psychoanalytic theorists seem to sense in their avoidance of it.[30] Metaphysical dualism leads to the blind alleys of mysterious relations, to *ad hoc* exceptions to laws like that of the conservation of mass and energy, and in general to dead endings of inquiry. It thus seems preferable to keep it as one's last-ditch position, a strategy to be adopted only when all else fails. Better to take seriously Intentionality, agency, and immediate, subjective experience as important attributes of mind yet try to integrate states with those characteristics into one's view of the natural world. The currently fashionable strategy for doing this is functionalism, usually conjoined with a kind of physical identity theory. Exploring such a strategy will allow us to see how Freud's metapsychological enterprise in particular, and any properly ambitious psychological theory in general, should be construed in light of a more contemporary philosophy of mind.

To understand functionalism we need to distinguish two kinds of it in the contemporary philosophy of mind. There is first of all the view which Ned Block has called metaphysical functionalism.[31] Metaphysical functionalism is the view that mental terms such as 'pain' refer to functional states of the human body (more specifically, brain and central nervous system). A functional state is a

---

[29] Carl Landesman's felicitous phrase, in C. Landesman, 'The New Dualism in the Philosophy of Mind', *Review of Metaphysics*, Vol. 19 (1965), 329–45.

[30] Benjamin Rubinstein notes this reluctance of his fellow psychoanalysts in B. Rubinstein, 'Psychoanalytic Theory and the Mind-Body problem', in N. Greenfield and W. Lewis, eds., *Psychoanalysis and Current Biological Thought* (Madison: University of Wisconsin Press, 1965).

[31] Ned Block, 'Introduction: What is Functionalism?', in N. Block ed., *Readings in Philosophy of Psychology*, Vol. 1 (Cambridge, Mass.: Harvard University Press, 1980).

state whose nature is given by its role (function) in explanations of behaviour. Pain, for example, is the state that plays the role of the cause of certain reflex reactions, as the cause of certain learning abilities, and plays the role of the effect of certain physical stimuli.[32]

Metaphysical functionalism by itself is not committed to there being any physical realization of the functional states so defined. Still, the motives for becoming a functionalist usually include the desire for there to be only one world, not the two posited by metaphysical dualism, so that most functionalists urge that those functional states that are states of persons' minds are physically realized. Instances of such states, in other words, are (identical with) certain physical states. Pain states, for example, may in human beings be certain stimulations in the cortex of the brain. That does not mean that pain as such is (identical with) such stimulations. On the functionalist theory pain is the state that plays certain causal roles; such functional states could be realized differently in different physical systems, and still be pain states.

A second kind of functionalism is what Block calls functional analysis.[33] This kind of functionalism is a research strategy, not a metaphysical position. This research strategy is part of the general research programme of relating mind to brain, psychology to neurophysiology. Within this general research programme there are two sub-strategies.[34] A 'bottom-up' strategy is to study the physical structures of the brain and try to discover how they function; eventually one hopes to work upwards from very particular functions of discrete physical structures to explain the molar behaviour and mental states of the whole person. A 'top-down' strategy, by way of contrast, starts with the behaviour and mental states experienced by the person and asks, 'What kind of subroutines might a system go through in order to arrive at such experience and such behaviour?' One might, for example, start with a person's perceptual beliefs about what he sees, and ask what steps he must have gone through in order to have begun with the visual stimulus with which he began and ended with the perceptual belief that he did.

---

[32] See id. See also Ned Block, 'Troubles with Functionalism', in C. W. Savage, ed., *Perception and Cognition, Minnesota Studies in the Philosophy of Science*, Vol. 9 (Minneapolis: University of Minnesota Press, 1978).

[33] Block, *supra* n. 31.

[34] M. Arbib, *The Metaphorical Brain* (New York: Wiley, 1972).

It is the second of these strategies that is called functional analysis. It is sometimes called 'homuncular functionalism' because its functionally defined subdivisions of a single person often are made to look like several smaller persons, or 'homunculi'. As described by William Lycan:

The homuncular functionalist sees a human being or other sentient creature as an integrated collection of component subsystems or agencies which communicate with each other and cooperate to produce their host creature's overall behavioral responses to stimuli. A psychologist who adopts the homuncular format and applies it to humans will describe a person by means of a flow-chart that portrays the person's immediately subpersonal agencies and their various routes of communicative access to each other. Each of these agencies, represented by a 'black box' on the original flow-chart, will in turn be described by a flow-chart which breaks it down into further, more specialized sub-subsystems which corporately produce its behaviour, and so on; and each of the subsystems,—subsystems and sub-
. . . subsystems will be characterized in terms of its job or function within the corporate hierarchy . . . at some point the psychologist would have to turn biologist, then chemist, and finally physicist in order to bring this explanatory process to completion.[35]

These two strategies are of course complementary, not antagonistic. One ultimately has to pursue both strategies, hoping in the end that workers pursuing each will meet. This means that the homuncular functionalist cannot claim any ultimate freedom from neurophysiology. If one is devising functional subroutines for subdividing mental operations in order to find connections of mind to brain, one would do well not to include subroutines that the physical equipment (the brain) just could not perform. There are many possible functional subdivisions of any mental operation. A homuncular functionalist is looking for that one organization that is in fact realized in the brain of his subject. Hence, the functionally defined states or processes this strategy posits should be thought of as hypotheses that more information about the structure of the brain may falsify; they should not be thought of as states or processes existing in their own 'realm of being', different from physical states; nor are the disciplines that define such states (linguistics, artificial intelligence, systems theory, or cognitive psychology)

---

[35] William Lycan, 'Psychological Laws', in J. Biro and R. Shahan, eds., *Mind, Brain and Function* (Norman, Okla.: University of Oklahoma Press, 1982), 16.

ultimately autonomous from the physical sciences. The top-down strategy is just a way of putting your trousers on one leg at a time.

Metaphysical functionalism can be thought of as a way of motivating the research programme of the homuncular functionalist, for it assures him that what he will find with his increasingly finely individuated functional states is the essence of the mind. By taking the position that it does on the reference of mental state terms, metaphysical functionalism tells the researcher that the best theory he can devise (for example, about the condensation, displacement, etc., of the dream-work) will be about dreaming.

Consider as a more familiar example the state of pain. Phenomenal descriptions of painful feelings will be about pain. Connecting such feelings of pain to their behavioural inputs (pain-causing stimuli) and outputs (pain-expressing behaviour) will be a theory about pain. So will a theory that connects various subpersonal routines that go on (reflex arcs, formation of pain-thresholds, and the like) together. So will a theory that correlates cortical stimulation with pain-experience, pain behaviour, and the subroutines of pain. All of these approaches will be progressively deeper theories about the nature of pain. Denied is any attempt to say that any of these scientific theories is not about pain, or that they use different concepts of pain. 'Pain' names a natural kind whose essential nature it is the business of science to reveal.[36]

The same is true for those mental states that make up the pretheoretical unconscious. The metapsychological story about them, in terms of repression, other mechanisms of defence, the dream-work, and the System Ucs., is a theory about those very same mental states and why they are unconscious. The 'System Ucs.' is not another sense of the word 'unconscious' just because it is part of a deeper story most ordinary users of the word 'unconscious' do not know; rather, the reference of both terms is to that same collection of states. In much the same way 'H_2O' is part of a deeper story about water that most ordinary users of 'water' at one time did not know; but that does not mean that 'water'and 'H_2O' referred to dif-

---

[36] Hilary Putnam, *Mind, Language and Reality* (Cambridge: Cambridge University Press, 1975); Mark Platts, *Ways of Meaning* (London: Routledge and Kegan Paul, 1979). Not all functionalists about mind subscribe to this kind of 'depth psychology'. See, e.g., Block, *supra* n. 31; Sidney Shoemaker, 'Some Varieties of Functionalism', in J. Biro and R. Shahan, eds., *Mind, Brain and Function* (Norman, Okla.: University of Oklahoma Press, 1982).

ferent things. Thus, on this Putnamesque version of metaphysical functionalism (compare the different versions of Block and Shoemaker), we have but one unconscious even if we have progressively deeper layers of theory about it.

It is fairly clear that Freud viewed his metapsychology as justified by its ability to relate mind to brain. From the unpublished 'Project' of 1895[37] to the *Outline* of 1940[38] he first and last saw his task as building a theory to relate brain to mind. As he put it in the *Outline*:

We know two things concerning what we call our psyche or mental life: firstly, its bodily organ and scene of action, the brain (or nervous system), and secondly, our acts of consciousness, which are immediate data and cannot be more fully explained by any kind of description. Everything that lies between these two terminal points is unknown to us.[39]

The metapsychology is Freud's attempt to make known to us what it is that lies 'in between' brain and mind.

Less clear is how much of Freud's metapsychology is fairly construed as an exercise in homuncular functionalism (the top-down strategy) and how much of it should be seen as pursuit of a bottom-up strategy. The 'Project', it seems to me, does represent Freud's attempt at a bottom-up strategy, but early in his career he was wise enough to see that he did not know enough about the structure of the brain to get very far. Abandoning the 'Project' was a significant shift for Freud. Although not giving up his hope of relating mind to brain, Freud did shift to the other strategy that was available to him, working from the top down.[40] The difference

---

[37] Sigmund Freud, 'Project for a Scientific Psychology', *The Standard Edition of the Complete Psychological Works of Sigmund Freud*, Vol. 1 (London: Hogarth Press, 1953), 281–93.

[38] Freud, *An Outline of Psychoanalysis*, Standard Edition, Vol. 23 (London: Hogarth Press, 1964).

[39] Id. at 144.

[40] There are important alternative interpretations of what Freud's abandonment of the 'Project' represents in terms of his underlying metaphysics:

1. He can be seen as never really giving up his physiological speculations, so that the later metapsychology is just as straightforward a physicalism as was the 'Project' of 1895.
2. He can be seen as returning to the dualism of Brentano, thinking that 'the mental' could be studied as a subject in its own right and by its own method, independently of any connection to physical science.
3. It was once fashionable to interpret Freud as adopting a behaviourist position about his depth psychology. There are two variants here: the 'shallow'

in the two strategies (again) is not that they ultimately aim at something different, but that they attack the same problem in different ways.

Unlike the 'Project' the metapsychology itself should be seen as an exercise in homuncular functionalism. Consider that aspect of the theory-laden unconscious Freud called 'primary process' thinking. The unconscious, Freud thought, has no idea of time; it replaces external with internal reality; terms and concepts have multiple reference, that is, ideas are 'condensed'; notions of identity are loosened because the affects attached to one object are 'displaced' onto another (which is to say that in the unconscious they are identified as one and the same object); contradiction is acceptable in the unconscious; and negation is unknown there.

These characteristics are not part of our pre-theoretical notions of the unconscious. They are not experienced, nor are they recapturable by any extended memory, as thoughts a person has. States with these relations and characteristics are subpersonal states hypothesized to exist as states underlying ordinary thinking in the same way that the subpersonal states of information preprocessing are hypothesized by cognitive psychologists to underlie conscious perception.

The homuncular functionalist should regard these six characteristics of primary process thinking as forming a system. A Chilean mathematician, Matte-Blanco, once attempted to weld these six characteristics together into a kind of logic, what he called a 'symmetrical' logic quite different from the 'asymmetrical' logic of Frege-Russell-Quine.[41] Such characteristics form a logic in the sense that they state the general principles of 'valid' inference in the unconscious. The thesis is that even irrationality may draw inferences systematically, that what is irrational need not be chaotic.

behaviourist interpretation of the metapsychology as a set of behavioural constructs. Albert Ellis, 'An Operational Reformulation of Some of the Basic Principles of Psychoanalysis', in H. Feigl and M. Scriven, eds., *The Foundations of Science and the Concepts of Psychology and Psychoanalysis, Minnesota Studies in the Philosophy of Science*, Vol. 1 (Minneapolis: University of Minnesota Press, 1956); T. R. Miles, *Eliminating the Unconscious* (Oxford: Pergamon Press, 1966). Alternatively, there is the 'deep' behaviourist interpretation that make the System Ucs. a theoretical entity in the neo-positivist sense of the later Carnap. David Rapaport, 'On the Psychoanalytic Theory of Motivation', in 1960 *Nebraska Symposium on Motivation* (Lincoln: University of Nebraska Press, 1960).

[41] I. Matte-Blanco, *The Unconscious as Infinite Sets* (London: Duckworth, 1975).

Such a systematization of unconscious inference drawing is a theory that seeks to explain ordinary thinking and the mental states that persons possess. Ordinary thinking is not perfectly rational; although we are all fairly good intuitive logicians—in the ordinary sense of 'logic'—we are not ideally rational inference drawers. One way of seeking to explain this fact is to see ordinary thinking (the 'secondary process') as an output of two subsystems. There is, Eric Rayner hypothesizes (in building upon Matte-Blanco), an 'interweaving of symmetrical and asymmetrical logics in the individual's emotional and intellectual life. In extreme emotions infinite experiences and symmetry probably hold sway. But mild, deep, or quiet emotionality is likely to contain thinking which compounds the two logics. In normal states the two logics seem to be in harmony while in pathology they are in discord.'[42]

There is no guarantee that this is a fruitful organization to give to the subroutines underlying ordinary thinking. There is no guarantee that there are two subsystems in conflict, or that, if there are, the opposition of ordinary to symmetrical logic is the way to define them. But some sort of states underlie ordinary thinking, and the primary process represents Freud's hypothesis about what sort of states they are. Such a hypothesis is not unverifiable. It must fit not only the (personal) characteristics of ordinary thought, but ultimately it must fit as well the physiology of the brain. There is thus no 'queer stuff' or 'unverifiability' objections to be lodged against this kind of theorizing.[43]

Consider as a second example the id/ego split posited by the structural metapsychology. If (contrary to Freud's express warnings) we take this to be directly about the brain, then we should look in the brain for corresponding subdivisions. Such subdivisions might be in gross anatomical terms—ego in the left hemisphere, id in the right, for example—or in more subtle electrochemical terms. In either case, since 'at present there is no indication that id, ego, and superego may one day be definable in strictly neuroanatomical terms',[44] one might well discard the structural metapsychology on

[42] Eric Rayner, 'Infinite Experiences, Affects and the Characteristics of the Unconscious', *International Journal of Psychoanalysis*, Vol. 62 (1981), 403–12, at 409.

[43] Contrary to Ernest Nagel's criticisms in this direction. Ernst Nagel, 'Methodological Issues in Psychoanalytic Theory', in S. Hook, ed., *Psychoanalysis, Scientific Method, and Philosophy* (New York: New York University Press, 1959).

[44] Rubinstein, *supra* n. 30, at 47.

the same ground as is often used to get rid of the economic metapsychology of psychic energy: such theories seem simply false if taken to provide straightforward, physiological descriptions.

Homuncular functionalism, in contrast to this bottom-up interpretation, is the strategy of restraint in looking right away for neurophysiological structures. As characterized by Dan Dennett,[45] it is only when the continued subdivision of functionally defined homunculi reaches the level 'where the homunculi are not more than adders and subtracters, by the time they need only the intelligence to pick the larger of two numbers when directed to, [will] they have been reduced to functionaries who can be replaced by a machine'. It is only at this point that 'a mechanistic view of the proceedings becomes workable and comprehensible'.

Ego, id, and superego are Freud's highest level of the subdivisions of self. The multiple functions assigned to each need to be separated and themselves broken down into subsystems of subsystems of . . . subsystems, before one should expect direct structural correlates. Ego, id, and superego may only be very high-level organizational principles; but once their role in a top-down strategy is understood, they may be no worse for that.

To construe the metapsychology as an exercise in homuncular functionalism provides a plausible enough insulation of the theory from any metaphysical embarrassment.[46] This is not of course to say that Freud succeeded in devising a fruitful functional subdivision of mind. In fact, there are three serious reservations to make about the metapsychology, even when viewed in this charitable light.

One is the lack of depth of many of the Freudian subdivisions. To have any chance of succeeding at connecting mind to brain, a top-down strategy must have great depth in the sense that there

---

[45] Daniel Dennett, *Brainstorms* (Montgomery, Vt.: Bradford Books, 1978), 80–1.

[46] At least, no embarrassments greater than those suffered by functionalism as a philosophy of mind generally. For problems in accommodating Intentionality and subjective qualia into a functionalist view of mind, see Block, *supra* n. 32; Paul Churchland and Patricia Churchland, 'Functionalism, Qualia, and Intentionality', in J. Biro and R. Shahan, eds., *Mind, Brain and Function* (Norman, Okla.: University of Oklahoma Press, 1982); Sidney Shoemaker 'Functionalism and Qualia', *Philosophical Studies*, Vol. 27 (1975), 291–315; R. C. Richardson 'Internal Representations: prologue to a Theory of Intentionality', in J. Biro and R. Shahan, eds., *Mind, Brain and Function* (Norman, Okla.: University of Oklahoma Press, 1982).

must be subdivisions of subdivisions of . . . subdivisions. One needs what Dennett calls an army of pretty stupid homunculi with which to replace the intelligent (whole) person; this, because to make structure/function correlations likely, one needs each homunculus to be so stupid that he need only flip a two-valued switch.[47]

The subdivisions of most of the metapsychology do not have depth in this sense. Consider the id/ego subdivision. Freud conceived of the id as 'instinctual cathexes seeking discharge—that . . . is all there is in the id'.[48] The ego, on the other hand, was assigned the functions of consciousness, sense perception, the perception and expression of affect, thought, control of motor action, memory, language, defence mechanisms, control of instinctual energy, the interpretive and harmonizing function, reality testing, and the capacity to suspend any of these ego functions and to regress to a primitive level of functioning.[49]

Without further subdivisions, the structural metapsychology takes us no further than Plato's like subdividing of the soul between rational reason and irrational appetite. Such subdivisions by Freud and Plato are much too large to be, by themselves, fruitful exercises in homuncular functionalism. The functions assigned to the ego in particular make it almost like a whole mind, with a full panoply of functions. This is no 'army of less clever homunculi', but one much too clever general. Needed are layers upon layers of further subdivisions if the structural metapsychology is to have a chance of succeeding as a top-down strategy.

A second problem with the metapsychology is that Freud could not bring himself to the kind of patience about seeking ties to physiology that marks a well-executed top-down strategy. Such impatience is particularly pronounced in the economic metapsychology. It has long been noticed that the psychological (functionalist) account of chapter VII B of *The Interpretation of Dreams* is patterned on the physiological speculation of Freud's unpublished 'Project' of 1895. Such functionally defined states, processes, and systems were not derived from a continued subdivision of the conflict Freud thought to exist between a person's mental states

---

[47] Dennett, *supra* n. 45.

[48] Sigmund Freud, *New Introductory Lectures on Psychoanalysis* (New York: Norton, 1965), 74.

[49] Jacob Arlow and Charles Brenner, *Psychoanalytic Concepts and the Structural Theory* (New York: International Universities Press, 1964), 39.

during dreaming. Freud did not arrive at these divisions by look-ing at the preconscious wish to sleep and an unconscious wish from childhood jointly producing through their conflict the manifest con-tent of a dream. Rather, Freud brought the economic metapsy-chology to his account of dreaming from his physiological speculations. This is not homuncular functionalism so much as bad bottom-up speculation about a physiology that Freud knew he did not know enough about. (Contrast this kind of illegitimate homuncular functionalism with the genuine article Freud also pro-duced in the dream theory, namely, the dream-work subdivisions.)

A subtler instance of Freud's impatience is to be found in the structural and topographical metapsychologies. Seen as part of Freud's concern with conflict, the System Csc./System Ucs. and ego/id splits are the beginning of a functional subdivision of self based on hints from the phenomenology of conflict. But these splits are also conceived by Freud in terms of 'distance' from physiology on the one hand and consciousness on the other. The id for Freud is tied to physiology and does all the moving of us to action and thought, whereas the ego consists of all the functions that mediate between the demands of the id (the instincts) and reality. One might label these two different id/ego splits as the horizontal split (of experienced conflict) and the vertical split (between physiology and consciousness).

Freud force-fits this vertical conception of the split onto his hor-izontal one because he thought he had to reach to physiology all at once. A pure top-down strategy would be more patient. One reward for such patience in this instance would have been much less con-fusion about what the split is. A second reward for patience here would also be less need to gerrymander the conflicts persons must experience (for example, about sex) in order for the id that is 'not-me' to match in content the id of the instincts.[50] Freed of the neces-sity to find such a match, Freud could have listened to his patients' conflicts without preconceptions about what must have been their conflicts. (This I take to be one of the central insights of Fairbairn and the object relations theorists,[51] rejecting as they do this verti-cal reading of the ego/id split and focusing instead on what I call

[50] See Moore, *supra* n. 2, at ch. 11; Eagle, *supra* n. 9; Eagle, *supra* n. 6.

[51] W. Ronald D. Fairbairn, *An Object-Relations Theory of the Personality* (New York: Basic Books, 1954). See the helpful discussion of the object relations theorists in Eagle, *supra* n. 6.

the horizontal reading. Although such object relations theorists see themselves as eschewing Freud's goal of relating mind to brain, they may unwittingly be furthering Freud's goal by forcing the theory into the patience about function/structure correlations that marks a top-down strategy.)

A third reward would be a set of subdivisions with a chance of succeeding as part of a programme connecting mind to brain. In a properly executed top-down strategy, the ego is as close to physiology as is the id. Even if we continue to conceive of the initial subdivision as one between the passions and that which controls them, the ultimate (and very finely) subdivided functions of control will correlate with physiological structure as much as will those subdivisions of the passions. One would not be 'closer' to physiology than the other, nor would one (ego) be correlated to physiology only through the other (id).

Actually, my own suspicion is that once one frees the structural and topographical metapsychologies from any need to reach immediately to physiology via one pole of their posited conflicts, we would not see ego and id as control and passions. Rather, if psychoanalysts were faithful to the phenomenology of conflict, we would see a rich variety of different conflicts being proposed as the initial subdivisions of self. A glance at the literature of the object relations theorists indeed shows this, for they have increasingly abandoned Freud's old subdivisions in their search for a more accurate description of the conflicts persons actually experience.[52]

The third problem for the metapsychologies as an exercise in homuncular functionalism is the most serious of all. Why should we think that the conflict experienced by neurotics is a way of beginning those functional subdivisions of self that will prove fruitful in developing the relations between mind and brain? How, in other words, could one expect to develop the general psychology that the metapsychology purports to be, from such narrow beginnings?

A Freudian, I should think, would seek to avoid this question by refusing its presupposition. He would deny that the 'data of conflict' are limited to the experiences of conflict-ridden neurotics. He should say, with Freud himself, that slips and dreams also are compromise formations arising out of the conflicts between mental

[52] Morris Eagle's suggestion as well, *supra* n. 6.

states in different systems; further, that normal adults as well as neurotics are conflict-ridden in all of their actions and experiences of everyday life, not just in their dreams, parapraxes, and occasional neurotic symptoms.

The main problem with this response is that it does not seem to be true. Reconsider the example of normal inference-drawing. What is the evidence for there being conflict between two subsystems, each with its own logic, the output of which is the good but not perfect inference-drawing capacities of normal adults? I do not think anyone has experiential clues that would suggest such a subdivision of normal inference-drawing. The conflict is rather a posited one by those already steeped in Freudian theory.

Consider a like claim that a Freudian could make about the acquisition of perceptual belief. All macro-seeing, he might say, is a compromise formation between conflicting subsystems; mistakes in perception would be seen as due to dominance of one subsystem by another, accurate vision being a blend of just the right proportions. This is a possible way to subdivide perception for a homuncular functionalist. But why would it ever occur to one to proceed with these kinds of subdivisions (rather than, say, ones that deal with co-operating subsystems with feedback loops to correct themselves)? Surely not any phenomenology of conflict about perceptual beliefs, no matter how lengthy or intense the psychoanalysis.

One can raise like charges even about some of the classic data of psychoanalysis, such as dreams. It looks very much as if Freud simply invented a wish to sleep that is supposed to be part of the double motivation of a dream in order to maintain a thesis that dreams, like symptoms, were compromise formations between the conflicting mental states belonging to different topographical systems.[53] Certainly Freud never recaptured—nor made any effort to recapture—the preconscious wish to sleep, as he did the unconscious wishes from childhood that also produce dreams. Conflict is not an obvious feature of dreaming as it arguably is for slips and symptoms.

If conflict is not the fundamental feature of our minds as we experience them, then it is unlikely that the functionally defined subdivisions of self that will prove fruitful in relating mind to brain

---

[53] See the discussion of the lack of phenomenal evidence for the wish to sleep in Moore, *supra* n. 2, at ch. 8.

will be found by beginning with the divisions experienced by conflict-ridden neurotics. That does not mean that there is no role for a metapsychology of some kind—even though in content it need resemble Freud's actual theory only slightly and even though it could not claim for itself the mantle of 'general psychology'.

Such a less ambitious metapsychology might proceed in the following way about the specific topic of this chapter, the pre-theoretical unconscious. Suppose that we began to attempt a top-down explanation of two claims of the clinical theory about the pre-theoretical unconscious: (1) that it exists, and (2) that it influences behaviour. We might explain the clinical fact that there are mental states that a person has a very hard time recapturing with the metapsychological theory that there is a process of repression that keeps such states from awareness. This process is beyond extended memory, and so must not be thought of as an action a person does (even unconsciously); rather, it is a process hypothesized to exist that has as its function the keeping of certain contents from consciousness. It might further be hypothesized that this keeping from awareness itself serves a function, namely the maintenance of some minimum level of coherence in a person's total set of his conscious/preconscious mental states such that he can have a sense of self-identity.

One might arrive at these hypotheses because of the content of the unconscious mental states that are either recaptured by patients in therapy, or for whose existence the analyst has good evidence despite the failure of the patient to avow them as his. If such mental states predominantly conflict with the patient's conscious/preconscious mental states, that is a reason to think that some process must be operating that sorts mental states in this systematic way.

Analogously, one might seek to explain why such unconscious mental states manifest themselves in behaviour in such peculiar ways. Why do symptoms, parapraxes, and dreams not directly express the unconscious wishes that cause them in the way conscious wishes are expressed in the actions they cause? Again, one might explain this clinical fact with a bit of metapsychological theory: certain processes occur that distort the wish in a way that makes it unrecognizable in the behaviour that it produces. The names for these functionally defined processes are the processes of the dream-work (for dreams) and the mechanisms of defence (for symptoms and parapraxes). If one were to explain why such processes of distortion occur, again one might hypothesize that the distortion that they cause has as its function the maintenance of a minimal level of coherence in the total set of a person's conscious/preconscious mental states, which in turn serves the function of allowing the person a sense of self-identity.

A homuncular functionalist might continue this line in the following way. First, he might seek to find a function for such a sense of self-identity, a function such a sense serves in enhancing the chances of survival. This would give him an evolutionary reason to expect there to be such a sense in persons and thus to expect them to have some such processes as repression for achieving and maintaining such a sense.[54] Second, the functionalist would subdivide the processes of distortion in the dream-work, for example, between those that distort by condensing multiple aspects of an unconscious mental state into one, and those that distort by displacing the affect normally felt towards one object onto another where such affect is normally inappropriate. He might then further subdivide each of these modes of distortion into submodes of condensation or of displacement. At some point, his hope would be to reach such simple operations that an on/off switch could perform them. For at that level a digital computer, or a brain, could be shown to realize the functionally defined subroutines.

In some such way psychoanalysts would seek to relate the mental phenomena with which they deal—neurotic symptoms, dreams, parapraxes—to brain processes via the metapsychological concepts of repression, condensation, displacement, and the like. As part of this task, they would here be explaining the existence (and influence on behaviour) of the pre-theoretical unconscious by reference to a metapsychological unconscious.

I think that this is just the sort of research programme in which psychoanalysis should be engaged. When conflict is a salient fact in an area of phenomenology or behaviour—as it arguably is for neurotic symptoms and parapraxes—then it makes sense to use the facets of experienced conflict as clues to underlying processes and structures. Even when conflict is not in the picture, if patients persistently experience dreams that, for example, have images in them that call to mind diverse references or inappropriate affect, a functionalist might well utilize these phenomenal facts in positing

---

[54] Eagle, *supra* n. 6.

subroutines of dream construction such as the processes of condensation and displacement.

IV. CONCLUSION

There is nothing impossible or absurd about explaining the existence and influence of (pre-theoretical) unconscious mental states in persons by the existence of subpersonal processes and states that have only functional definitions and that are beyond recapture by a person's consciousness (the theoretical unconscious). Second and more generally, there is nothing impossible or absurd about a metapsychological theory that explains all the facts (of conflict and otherwise) with which a clinical theory deals, even though the terms of such a metapsychology are not cast in the personal vocabulary of the clinical theory. Third, the particular metapsychological theories we have inherited from Freud—built as they are on a posited universal conflict and on a too hasty flight into physiology, shallow as they are in the degree of their subdivisions—are unlikely candidates for a true metapsychological theory.

To these three conclusions we need to add a fourth. This is a reminder that, no matter how successful the research programme outlined above might be in relating mind to brain via the subpersonal states of the metapsychology, we cannot afford to ignore the distinction between clinical theory and metapsychology (and thus, between the pre-theoretical unconscious and the theory-laden unconscious), as do some cognitive psychologists and systems theorists.[55] There is an important difference between my goals, conscious or unconscious, and the goals of repression, of the dream-work, and the like. My goals are part of me, my character structure. I am held responsible for them in law, morals and everyday life, and I take responsibility for deciding what they should be, both in therapy and out. None of these things is true about, for example, the goal of the dream-work, which is to distort the true meaning of the dream. That is not my goal, not even unconsciously. It is not accordingly, part of self.

[55] K. Bowers and P. Meichenbaum, eds., *The Unconscious Reconsidered* (New York: Wiley, 1984); Emanuel Peterfreund, *Information Systems and Psychoanalysis* (New York: International Universities Press, 1971); Jonathan Winson, *Brain and Psyche: The Biology of the Unconscious* (New York: Doubleday/Anchor, 1984).

As I briefly urged in chapter 6, this line between the mental states a person has and those subpersonal states posited by homuncular functionalism, should be drawn in terms of consciousness. That of which we are aware (conscious), can easily become aware (preconscious), or can potentially become aware through extensive procedures (unconscious), are all part of our selves.[56] The subpersonal states are not, and that is a fact worth marking in therapy, in the ethics of everyday life, and in the construction of adequate explanations in psychology.

[56] Even though the mechanisms of defence serve the function of maintaining self-cohesion by keeping certain states out of our sense of ourselves, such states are still part of our selves. Our *sense* of our self does not include such states when they are unconscious or experienced as ego-alien; but our true self does include such states. That is why *we* can be said to be conflicted when we have conflicting mental states even though one-half of the conflict is unconscious or otherwise rejected.

11

INTENTIONS AND
MENS REA

I. INTRODUCTION

A natural sequence of issues proceeding from the discussion of the preceding chapter would go something like this: if one accepts the functionalist view of mind laid out in chapter 10, then there should be a functionalist analysis of the concept that is of central importance to culpability, that of intention. Moreover, if the unconscious is both a concept of the folk psychology and is a concept of a depth psychology that underlies mental states such as intentions, then two implications for responsibility of an unconscious intentionality should be pursued: are we *more* responsible than we might suppose, because we are up to more mischief than we had thought? Or are we *less* responsible than we might suppose, because we (our conscious will) is merely the puppet dancing to a tune called by our unconscious?

I pursue none of these issues in this chapter, however. This, because I have directed a great deal of attention to these issues in previous books. I have urged that intentions are functional states whose roles are to mediate between background states of motivation and those (bodily) motion-guiding states of volition that are parts of actions. More specifically, such mediating role of intentions is performed by their having a distinctive 'all-things-considered' representational content not true of the desires whose conflict they resolve.[1] I have also urged that, while the concept of an unconscious intention is not an absurd concept,[2] nonetheless true unconscious intentions are much rarer than is supposed, with or without Freud;[3] further, that the insights of a properly conceived psychology of the

[1] Michael S. Moore, *Act and Crime: The Philosophy of Action and its Implications for Criminal Law* (Oxford: Oxford University Press, 1993), ch. 6.
[2] Michael S. Moore, *Law and Psychiatry: Rethinking the Relationship* (Cambridge: Cambridge University Press, 1984), ch. 7.
[3] Id. at ch. 8.

unconscious would rarely (although not never) alter our ordinary assessments of responsibility when made without reference to the unconscious.[4]

The topic of the present chapter thus pursues an issue about intentions quite distinct from any of these. I leave questions about the *nature* of that mental state we call 'intention', for questions about the representational *content* of intentions. This is sometimes put as the question of the Intentional object of intentions. This is also a metaphysical question about intentions, if a distinct one from any we have yet considered.

II. ONE ETHICAL CONTEXT FOR THE ISSUE OF CONTENT: THE DEBATE ABOUT DIRECT VERSUS OBLIQUE INTENTIONS

One way to see why we should care about the metaphysical question of content is to see how answers to that metaphysical question are presupposed by a familiar debate in ethics. The question debated is whether the most serious culpability with which a harm can be caused is marked by intention (in the sense of purpose), or whether some other mental state or set of mental states should be used as the marker of most serious culpability. Children commonly distinguish harm caused 'on purpose' from harm caused in other ways, and the question is whether such a focus on purpose is correct when serious culpability is being assessed.

One can get at this question—of the role of purpose in assessing culpability—only if one is clear about the concept of purpose, or what Bentham called direct intention.[5] As we saw in chapter 9, purpose is to be distinguished from mere belief or foresight that a harm is likely to occur (Bentham called such predictive beliefs 'oblique intentions'). The distinction between purpose and knowledge is a distinction based on the agent's reasons: there are those consequences that are part of one's chain of reasons for acting; whether intended as means or desired as ends, they are directly intended. On the other hand, there are those consequences that are believed by

[4] Michael S. Moore, *Law and Psychiatry: Rethinking the Relationship* (Cambridge: Cambridge University Press, 1984), at chs. 9–10.

[5] Jeremy Bentham, *An Introduction to the Principles of Morals and Legislation* (New York: Hafner, 1948), 200–21.

the actor to be substantially certain to occur that are not part of his chain of reasons for acting. These he knows will follow on states of affairs for which he acts, but he does not act in order to bring them about.

This distinction is sometimes put in terms of 'desire': an agent directly intends those consequences he desires to bring about and obliquely intends those consequences he expects to come about but does not desire to bring about. In fact, 'desire' is too imprecisely used in ordinary speech to mark the correct distinction here. One might directly intend some consequence yet not *desire* it (in a very popular sense of that word, at least); as where one intends to escape prison, and must kill the prison guard in order to do so. In such a case the death of the guard is one's chosen means and thus is directly intended, no matter how great may be the regret (and thus the lack of desire) with which the action is done. Alternatively, one might cause some harm, desire that it occur, and yet not directly intend that harm; as where one desires the death of the prison guard because one hates him, does an act knowing that it will kill him, but does the act for an entirely different reason, namely, to escape. In such a case a known consequence is desired, but the desire is not among the actor's chain of reasons for acting; the consequence is thus not directly intended.

The purpose/knowledge distinction is thus based, not on 'desire', but on the concept of reasons for acting. On a causal account of reasons,[6] the distinction will become a causal distinction: if a consequence is the object of either a belief/desire set or a belief/intention set that causes one's behaviour, then that consequence was the object of one's purpose; whereas if that consequence figures only in those beliefs, desires, or intentions that do not cause the act in question, then that consequence was only within the objects of one's predictive beliefs about what was probable or certain to occur.

To illustrate: imagine three persons, A, B, and C, each of whom has as his purpose the destruction of an aeroplane in mid-flight. A wants to blow up the plane because he has insured the life of the passengers and has as his ultimate purpose the collection of the money on their lives. B wants to blow up the plane because he hates certain of the passengers and wishes them dead for no further reason. C wants to blow up the plane because he has insured the plane

---

[6] I defend the causal account of reasons for action in Moore, *supra* n. 2, ch. 1.

and has as his ultimate purpose the collection of the money on the plane. Only A and B have as their purpose the death of the passengers. B has the death of the passengers as his motivating desire, or what I shall here call his ultimate purpose; A has the death of the passengers as his instrumental intention or what I shall here term his mediate purpose. C, while he knows that the passengers will surely die if he destroys the plane in mid-flight, does not have as his (ultimate or mediate) purpose that they die; their death is not necessary to achieve anything C wants to achieve. Accordingly, for C their death is a known side-effect to the achievement of C's purposes, whereas for A their death is a necessary means that forms part of the chain of reasons (purposes) for which A acts.

As I mentioned in chapter 9, H. L. A. Hart argued that the culpability of persons such as A and B on the one hand, and C on the other was the same; accordingly, Hart argued that no distinction should be drawn in the criminal law between knowing and purposeful killers: both were deserving of the most severe punishment reserved for the most serious category of homicide, murder.[7] Hart's argument here was quite straightforward and persuasive. Even the actor who only knows that some harm will come about as a result of his activities still has *control* over whether that harm will occur or not. Given his knowledge, he has as much control over causing the harm as the actor who has that harm as his purpose: both have *chosen* to bring it about. Accordingly, for either a utilitarian or a retributivist, Hart concluded, the criminal law should punish those who act knowingly equally with those who act with a prohibited harm as their purpose.

Others have disagreed. Anthony Kenny, for example, has urged that the criminal law should mark the difference between purpose and knowledge so that a directly intended death is murder but an obliquely intended death is only manslaughter.[8] Others, such as

[7] H. L. A. Hart, 'Intention and Punishment', *Oxford Review*, Vol. 14 (1967), 5–22, reprinted in Hart, *Punishment and Responsibility* (Oxford: Oxford University Press, 1968). Also finding the control issue determinative of culpability are Eric D'Arcy, *Human Acts,* (Oxford: Oxford University Press, 1963), 170–4, and Hans Oberdick, 'Intention and Foresight in Criminal Law', *Mind*, Vol. 81 (1972), 389–400.

[8] Anthony Kenny, 'Intention and Purpose', *Journal of Philosophy*, Vol. 63 (1966), 642ff., revised and reprinted as 'Intention and Purpose in Law', in R. Summers, ed., *Essays in Legal Philosophy* (Berkeley: University of California Press, 1968). Kenny's later views on the moral and legal importance of the distinction between purpose and knowledge are set forth in his *Will, Freedom and Power* (Oxford: Oxford University Press, 1976), and 'Intention and *Mens Rea* in Murder', in P. M. S. Hacker and J. Raz, eds., *Law, Morality, and Society* (Oxford: Oxford University Press, 1977).

G. E. M. Anscombe, have found more moral merit in the use of the distinction by the Catholic doctrine of 'double effect' than did Hart.[9] According to the latter doctrine, an evil knowingly brought about might be justified (depending on the circumstances) but an evil that it was the actor's purpose to bring about can never be justified. In the aeroplane case, for example, if A and C each have good reason for needing their respective insurance monies—to prevent an unjust war, for example—only C could raise the question of justification.

It is not my purpose in this chapter to take a position in this debate between Hart and his critics (although in chapter 9 I side with the critics). Rather, here I wish to examine what I would characterize as the metaphysical presuppositions of the debate itself. My target, in other words, is neither Hart nor his critics but rather the sceptic who would deny significance to the debate itself.

Both Hart and his critics presupposed that there is some correct way in which to fix the object of one's purposes. Without such an objective mode of saying *what* an actor's purposes might be, neither Hart nor his critics could meaningfully categorize cases as being instances of purpose or of knowledge. Take A and C, the earlier hypothesized plane-destroyers. Suppose we identified the blowing up of the plane with the passengers on it as the very same event as the killing of those passengers;[10] suppose further that we think that the identity of events implies the identity of the purposes that have those events as their objects. On both such suppositions we should classify C as well as A as someone who has the killing of the passengers as his purpose: for C by hypothesis had as his purpose the blowing up of the plane; because that event *was* the killing of the passengers, C's purpose also was to kill the passengers.

---

[9] G. E. M. Anscombe, 'Modern Moral Philosophy', *Philosophy*, Vol. 33 (1958), 1–10; also Anscombe, 'Reply to Bennett', in *Analysis*, Vol. 26 (1966), 208; also Anscombe, 'War and Murder', in R. A. Wasserstrom, ed., *War and Morality* (Belmont, California: Wadsworth, 1970). Anscombe's essential argument—that any deontological ethic requires that some moral distinction be drawn between results that are directly intended and those that are only obliquely intended on pain of incoherence in its 'absolute' moral prohibitions—has been seconded by a number of philosophers. See, e.g., J. L. Mackie, *Ethics* (New York: Penguin Books, 1977), 159–68; Charles Fried, 'Right and Wrong—Preliminary Considerations', *Journal of Legal Studies*, Vol. 5 (1975), 165–200. On this, compare Heidi M. Hurd, 'What in the World is Wrong?', *Journal of Contemporary Legal Issues*, Vol. 5 (1994), 157–216, at 165–93.

[10] The identity thesis here is defended by me in Moore, *supra* n. 1, at ch. 11.

To prevent this collapse of knowledge into purpose in every case, we need some theory that tells us how to individuate intentions by the objects on which they are directed, that is, that tells us when we have two different objects (and thus two different intentions) and when there is in reality only one. One can use the distinction between purpose and knowledge only if one has some such theory of individuation. Without such a theory, one would have no way to prevent the collapsing of every supposed case of knowledge into a case of purpose.

This problem has not gone unnoticed in the literature on intentions. Hart himself gave two examples as he briefly noted the difficulty: (1) G strikes a glass violently with a hammer because he wants the noise of the hammer making contact with the glass to attract the attention of someone else—did G necessarily intend to break the glass, given that he did intend to strike the glass hard enough to make some noise? Hart believed in such a case, that 'when a foreseen outcome is so immediately and invariably connected with the action done that the suggestion that the action might not have that outcome would by ordinary standards be regarded as absurd, or such as only a mentally abnormal person would seriously entertain: the connection between action and outcome seems therefore [in such cases] to be not merely contingent but rather to be conceptual'.[11] (2) Arguably different, Hart thought, was the case in which a doctor crushes the skull of a foetus in order to save the life of its mother. Here, Hart found it plausible to distinguish the crushing of the skull from the death of the foetus, so that an intention to do the former need not be identified as an intention to cause the latter as well.[12]

Other examples from the more recent literature include: (3) The eccentric surgeon, D, who 'wishes to remove P's heart completely from P's body in order to experiment upon it. D does not desire P's death (being perfectly content that P shall go on living if he can do

[11] Hart, 'Intention and Punishment', *supra* n. 7, at 120.
[12] Ibid., 123–4. This papal example is also discussed by Philippa Foot, 'The Problem of Abortion and the Doctrine of Double Effect', *Oxford Review*, Vol. 5 (1967), 5–15. Foot's intuitions here differed from Hart's: 'A certain event may be desired under one of its descriptions, unwanted under another, but we cannot treat these as two different events, one of which is aimed at and the other not. And even if it be argued that there are here two different events—the crushing of the child's skull and its death—the two are obviously much too close for an application of the doctrine of double effect.' Ibid., 6–7.

so without his heart), but recognized that in fact his death is inevitable from the operation to be performed.'[13] Anthony Kenny concludes of this case that because of the 'immediacy' of death upon removal of a heart, the directly intended heart removal is also a directly intended death. (4) If Espinoza intends to appoint Garcia, and Garcia is fifty years old, does Espinoza intend to appoint a fifty-year-old man? In his book on intention J. W. Meiland concludes that the answer is 'yes'; the second intention is 'inseparable' from the first, and so should be identified with it.[14] (5) Lord Hailsham recently posed the earlier given aeroplane hypothetical example for himself, concluding that an intention to blow up the plane would be conceptually 'inseparable' from an intention to kill the passengers, so that A, B, and C should be said to have directly intended the death of the passengers.[15]

Lastly, consider the following four examples of Tony Duff's:[16] (6) X intends to get drunk, does so, knowing full well that he will be hung over the next day; does X intend to be hung over? Duff thinks not: 'being drunk and being hung over are distinct, though causally related, states of affairs', and therefore X 'can intend the former without intending the latter'.[17] (7) I retain Brown's car, thereby depriving him of his own use of it; do I thereby intend to deprive Brown of the use of his car? Duff thinks so: 'my retaining Brown's car for my own use is not distinct from his being deprived of it, since these are aspects of the same state of affairs';[18] in such a case, if I intend the first state of affairs I intend the second as well. (8) Likewise, if I intend to decapitate Brown, wanting only his head to show to another, and not caring a fig about his living or dying, do I intend Brown's death? According to Duff, there is a 'logical

---

[13] Kenny, 'Intention and Purpose in Law', *supra* n. 8, at 149. The example is originally from Glanville Williams, *Criminal Law—The General Part*, 2nd edn. (London: Macmillan, 1961), at 39.

[14] J. W. Meiland, *The Nature of Intention* (London: Methuen 1970), at 13. This example is much like that of Robert Audi, 'Intending', *Journal of Philosophy*, Vol. 70 (1973), 387–403, at 396. 'Suppose that at a restaurant X intends to order lobster tails and believes that in ordering them he will be ordering the most expensive item on the menu, though he is not concerned with their price. Must X also intend to order the most expensive item on the menu?'

[15] *Hyam* v. *Director of Public Prosecutions*, [1975] AC 55, [1974] 2 All ER 41, 51–2.

[16] R. A. Duff, '*Mens Rea* and the Law Commission Report', *Criminal Law Review*, Vol. [1980], 147–60.

[17] Ibid., 153.   [18] Ibid.

connection' between decapitation and killing: ' "Brown is decapitated but survives" does not specify an intelligible possibility, since it is part of the logic of our concept of "human beings" that decapitation kills them: if we could imagine a being who was not killed by decapitation, that would not be a human being.'[19] Since decapitation logically entails death for Duff, to intend to decapitate *is* to intend to kill. (9) A, a man, intends to remain unmarried. According to Duff, because 'unmarried male' is synonymous with 'bachelor', A must also intend to remain a bachelor.[20] To intend the first *is* to intend the second.

Despite the attention to this problem in the literature, however, there is no agreement as to how we should individuate intentions by their objects.[21] Hart in one breath gave us two quite different tests—immediate and invariant causal connection, and conceptual connectedness. Kenny adopts the first of these, Lord Hailsham the second. Meiland would appear to think that the identity of intentions is governed by the identity of the events that are represented in the objects of such intentions. Duff in the first two of his examples would appear to agree with Meiland's event-identity test, but in Duff's last two examples he substitutes the stronger relations of entailment or synonymy for his earlier extensional test of identity. In brief, we face a variety of theories of individuation that are not the same nor is any argument given as to why we should prefer one to another.

Given this state of affairs it is not surprising to find metaphysical positions being gerrymandered so as to fit one's moral positions, and vice versa. Indeed, it is easy to see how one's metaphysics here may correlate naturally with certain moral or legal views about the relevance of purpose versus knowledge in marking most serious culpability. A fine-grained theory of individuation will refuse to classify many more states of affairs as directly intended than will a coarse-grained theory. A fine-grained theorist, accordingly, will have every incentive to consider knowledge no less than purpose as sufficient for most serious culpability. A coarse-grained theorist, on

---

[19] R. A. Duff, '*Mens Rea* and the Law Commission Report', *Criminal Law Review*, Vol. [1980], 153.

[20] Ibid.

[21] We have more agreement, perhaps, on the other two degrees of freedom by which we individuate intention-tokens, namely, the persons who hold them and the time at which such intentions are held.

the other hand, has a much lessened incentive to allow knowledge to be sufficient for serious culpability; for he can say that such states of affairs were directly intended without regard to the knowledge of the subject.

Consider as an example of this Glanville Williams's and Anthony Kenny's views on the case of the eccentric surgeon mentioned earlier.[22] Kenny's coarse-grained theory defines such a case as one of direct intention, so he has no need to allow knowledge to suffice in order to punish the doctor as a murderer. Kenny thus is free to argue, as indeed he does, that only direct intentions should be punishable as murder, for he can do so and yet capture cases like that of the eccentric surgeon anyway. Williams also finds it intuitive to punish the eccentric surgeon as a murderer, but Williams holds a more fine-grained theory of individuation, whereby one refuses to say that the intention to cut out the heart just is an intention to kill; Williams, accordingly, must argue (as he does) that knowledge should count equally with purpose when one gives legal meaning to the malice required for murder, for this is the only way Williams can punish severely cases such as the eccentric surgeon.

Scepticism about the meaningfulness of such a moral/legal debate arises the moment one becomes sceptical that there is any correct theory of individuation of intentions. Mark Kelman, for example, tells us that we use coarse- or fine-grained theories pretty much arbitrarily, whenever it suits us.[23] The result of such scepticism is to cast doubt on the existence of any distinction between harm directly intended and harm only foreseen as substantially certain to occur. For one can manipulate what is considered to be directly intended, and what only obliquely so, simply by shifting one's view of the metaphysics on which the distinction depends.

[22] Williams, *Criminal Law*, *supra* n. 13; Kenny, 'Intention and Purpose', *supra* n. 8. Hans Oberdick is quite explicit about this trade-off, rejecting Kenny's notion that any harm invariably connected with one's intentional act will itself be intended because Oberdick's moral position about knowledge does not require any coarse-grained metaphysics about intentions. See Oberdick, 'Intention and Foresight', *supra* n. 7, at 391.

[23] Kelman, 'Interpretive Construction in the Substantive Criminal Law', *Stanford Law Review*, Vol. 33 (1981), 591–673. See particularly 595–6, 620–33. Kelman does not see the issue as one of fine- or coarse-grained theories of individuation of intention, but talks instead of 'broad' and 'narrow' views of intentions. Despite the differing language, the problem Kelman is adverting to is how one individuates intentions by their objects.

One of my purposes in this chapter is to examine whether such scepticism is warranted. This I shall do by seeing what can be done about developing a consistent theory of how we individuate intentions by their objects. Although my focus is on the theory of individuation presupposed by the direct/oblique distinction, it is worth noting how pervasive is the legal need to have such a theory. In the law of criminal attempts, for example, one must have such a theory to render intelligible the question, 'If the accused did all he intended to do, would it have been criminal?'[24] Similarly, a theory of individuation of intentions is needed to give teeth to the constitutional prohibition against being twice put in jeopardy for 'the same offence', for sometimes that question will turn on whether the defendant had the same intention or two distinct intentions as he performed various acts.[25] Similarly, in the law of conspiracy one must decide that there is the 'common purpose to attain an objective' required for there to be a conspiracy. Finally, even if one rejects the moral and legal significance of the distinction between purpose and knowledge, one will still need a theory of individuation of mental states, in this case states of belief; one will need such a theory in order to distinguish those things one actually believes from those things an actor *should* believe if he were less negligent than in fact he is.

Despite the general need throughout criminal law for a theory of individuation of mental states by their objects, I shall focus on the context discussed above. Is there some principled basis to choose between Kenny's coarse-grained theory, or Williams's fine-grained theory? Or is it, as Kelman suggests, an essentially arbitrary deci-

---

[24] The dependence of this test on some theory of individuating intentions is discussed in H. L. A. Hart, 'The House of Lords on Attempting the Impossible', *Oxford Journal of Legal Studies*, Vol. I (1981), 149–66.

[25] See, e.g., *Irby* v. *United States*, 390 F 2d 432 (DC Cir. 1967), in which a defendant who broke into a house had an intention that may have been conditional and disjunctive: to take whatever property he found if the house were unoccupied (which constitutes housebreaking with intent to steal), or to take property by force from the owner of the house if the house were occupied (which if done, constitutes robbery). The defendant in *Irby* not only entered the house arguably with such an intention, but found the occupant therein and proceeded to rob him. Having pleaded guilty to one count of housebreaking and to one count of robbery, the issue as the court conceived it was whether the defendant had one intention or two. The majority of the court held that these were two distinct intentions, and therefore allowed consecutive sentencing for the two offences of housebreaking and robbery. See generally *People* v. *Neal*, 55 Cal. 2d 11, 9 Cal. Rptr. 607, 357 P 2d 839 (1960), for the California Supreme Court's 'single intent or objective' test for double jeopardy.

sion that reduces the debate (about the moral and legal relevance of the distinction between direct and oblique intentions) to so much ado about nothing?

III. THE METAPHYSICS OF INTENT INDIVIDUATION

Perhaps the place to start is by asking the ontological question, what are objects of intentions? Very generally, three possibilities suggest themselves: that they are sentences that do not refer to real objects in the world; that they are real objects in the world; and that they are propositions that are only 'indirectly' about real objects in the world. An example may help to make these possibilities intelligible. Suppose someone, Jones, intends to enter room no. 6. The object of his intention can in this case be divided into three parts: the subject, which is he, Jones; an action, his entering; and an (accusatory) object of the action verb, the room to be entered. The object of the intention is not any one of these, but all three together.

The three possibilities are: (1) that the object of Jones's intention is the *sentence*, 'He (Jones) enters room no. 6.' So construing intentional objects uses a special sense of 'sentence' here, namely, the words are said to lack reference and extension (and hence a truth value). The sentence is a sentence only in the limited sense that it is a string of symbols that is syntactically well formed, but devoid of the semantic interpretations that normally attach to these symbols in more ordinary contexts. This construing of intentional objects as sentence-like entities means that a mental state such as an intention should be viewed as a relation between a person X, and a (syntactic) sentence. There is no relation, on this view, between X and real world things, like actions or rooms, because these real world things are not (quite literally) talked about in such contexts.

On this view, one might analogize the words that appear in the objects of intentions to the word 'dint' as used in expressions 'by dint of'. Grammatically, 'dint' may look like a noun that has as its role the naming of something, but in reality there are no dints in the world. The expression 'by dint of' is what Quine called a fused idiom, one that contains parts (words) that *look* as if they refer to things, but which in reality play non-referential roles in language.[26]

---

[26] W. V. Quine, *Word and Object* (Cambridge, Mass.: Harvard University Press, 1960), at 244. Dan Dennett explicitly analogizes the objects of mental states to fused

Analogously, one might suggest, one should view the objects of intentions as fused idioms, which look syntactically as if they were meaningful sentences, some parts of which referred to things; in reality, however, objects of intentions are strings of symbols, and to say that Jones intends S, expresses only a relation between Jones and the sentence S.

This view gains some plausibility, perhaps, when one recalls Brentano's observation that many of the 'things' people want, wish for, hope for, or intend, do not exist in the real world. In such cases, one might say that they enjoy a special form of existence Brentano called 'Intentional inexistence'; or, if one wants to avoid that road to modern phenomenology, one can say with Quine that we need not bother about the existence of such 'things' because the words that seem to refer to them do not refer at all.

(2) The second possibility takes the opposite tack. It is committed to the view that words appearing in the sentence fragment, 'he enters room no. 6' have their normal reference and extension. 'He' refers to that person holding the intention; 'enters room no. 6' has as its extension those actions that constitute an entering of that room; and 'room no. 6' has its normal reference to that room.

Unlike the first view, this view of intentional objects as real world objects has the advantage of maintaining the ordinary semantics of the words that describe those objects. It does not suffer from the seeming implausibility of saying, as does the first view, that 'he' does not refer to the holder of the intention, or that 'room no. 6' does not refer to room no. 6. The second view, unfortunately, has some difficulty accommodating itself to Brentano's insight that the objects of intentions or other mental states may not exist as real world objects. What, one may ask, is the reference of the sailboat hoped for by Jones when that sailboat does not exist except as the object of a hope by Jones?

With intentions in particular, it will not do to think that the verbs of action, such as 'enter', refer to a particular action of entering; for that particular action has not yet occurred. Intentions, like beliefs about future occurrences (predictions), but unlike perceptual beliefs, inherently have to do with actions or states of affairs that have not yet occurred. Indeed, there is no guarantee that such intended or predicted actions will ever occur. Accordingly, the view

idioms in Dennett, *Content and Consciousness* (New York: Humanities Press, 1969), ch. 1.

being here considered must be modified so as to avoid saying that there is reference to such future actions or states of affairs that have not yet occurred and may not ever occur.[27]

Each of these two positions on the nature of intentional objects has a name in the philosophical literature, for each of them was distinguished by Quine. The first view is that mental state verbs create contexts that are *referentially opaque*; the second view is that such verbs create contexts that are *referentially transparent*.[28] Quine himself straddled the two views, urging that mental state verbs ('belief' was Quine's usual example) are inherently ambiguous, sometimes creating opaque contexts and sometimes transparent ones.

If one adopts an opaque view of the matter, so that objects of intentions are sentence-like entities, one adopts with it a very fine-grained mode of individuating intentions. For it matters, on the opaque view, exactly how the words are strung together as to whether two nominally distinct intentions are one and the same. Jones's intention to enter room no. 6 would, for example, be different from Jones's intention to go into room no. 6, and yet distinct from Jones's intention that room no. 6 be entered by him. This view

[27] Our ordinary way of talking about intentions can be very misleading in this respect, for we speak as if we formed intentions about *particular* actions or events (rather than about types of actions or events). E.g.: 'He intended the harm' where 'the harm' seems to refer to the particular event that occurred. I want to say that one never intends *the* harm; rather, one intends that there be *some* event-token that will instantiate some event-type. One forms intentions, in other words, over types of acts or states, not over particulars.

I am going against ordinary usage here because I can see no sense to the alternative. What would an intention be about if its object referred to a particular event, and yet that event never occurred? In such cases one has to say the reference is to a type and not to a particular. Yet surely nothing changes about what the intention was when the event *does* occur; surely one does not have an intention about a type that becomes an intention about a particular event, depending on subsequent events. Better to say: the intention is always about a type of event which, if the intent succeeds, will be instantiated by some event-token.

Probability theorists make this same move about predictive beliefs when they deny any sense to the question, 'what was the probability of a particular event occurring?' Predictive beliefs also only make sense when construed to be about *types* of events of which the actual events that occur may be instances. See ch. 8 above.

[28] My explication of the referentially opaque sense is something of a caricature of Quine's actual views. Quine never actually said what the reference or extension was for opaque contexts, other than that it was unclear ('opaque'). I have accordingly re-characterized the opaque sense in what is to me a clearer, if more far-fetched way: treat the objects of belief just like quoted sentences (rather than the *indirect* discourse favoured by Quine as the analogy to the propositional attitudes).

counts these as different intentions because the words used, or their syntax, are different, even if their (normal) meanings might be the same.

The transparent view, by way of contrast, implies a very coarse-grained theory of individuation. This view would imply that it does not matter how one describes or names room no. 6, nor how one refers to the action of entering; any intention whose object is the entering of that room is but one intention. An intention to enter room no. 6, for example, is (identical with) an intention to enter a room in which marijuana is being smoked, so long as room no. 6 is such a room.

Neither of these theories of individuation seems to conform to our intuitions about when intentions (or other mental states, for that matter) are the same. The opaque view is too fine-grained,[29] and the transparent view is too coarse-grained. An example showing the former is one where the only shift is a syntactic one (Jones intends that he enter room no. 6, versus Jones intends that room no. 6 be entered by him). Surely these are the same intentions, despite the differing syntax of the intentional objects. An example showing the latter is one we examined before in chapter 8. In discussing the impossibility doctrine in the law of criminal attempts, Edwin Keedy once thought: 'If A takes an umbrella which he believes to belong to B, but which in fact is his own, he does not have the intent to steal, his intent being to take the umbrella he grasps in his hand, which is his own umbrella . . .'.[30] Unpacked, the hypothetical asserts that from: (1) A intends (takes the umbrella in his hand), and the true identity, (2) the umbrella in A's hand = A's own umbrella, it follows that: (3) A intends (takes A's own umbrella). Surely this conclusion is to be resisted, denying as it does any importance to A's beliefs about *whose* umbrella he was taking.

In addition, neither of the ontological views that generate these theories of individuation are themselves very plausible (independently of their generating implausible theories of individuation). It

---

[29] On occasion the opaque view will not be fine-grained enough. Suppose two contracting parties utter identical sentences to one another about the shipping terms for goods sold by one to the other: 'Ex *Peerless*, Bombay'. Suppose further that each referred to a different ship by the word, '*Peerless*'. Their intentions differed (as the court held in this famous case) despite the identity of the symbols (syntactic sentences) uttered by each.

[30] E. Keedy, 'Criminal Attempts at Common Law', *University of Pennsylvania Law Review*, Vol. 102 (1954), 464–7.

is wildly counterintuitive to think that the 'he' and the 'room no. 6' in the earlier example in no way refer to the person who holds the intention or to room no. 6, as the opaque sense of 'intend' requires. On the other hand, it is strange to say that 'enters' in the example refers to some particular action that has not yet occurred and may never occur, as the transparent sense of 'intend' seemingly requires. And there are more technical objections to each of these views. Plainly needed is some third view.

(3) Enter, propositions. A view which construes the objects of intentions as being propositions has a number of virtues. To begin with, it implies a theory of individuation that need not be so fine-grained as the opaque view, nor as coarse-grained as the transparent view. One need not resist, for example, the identification of Jones's intention that he enter room no. 6, with Jones's intention that room no. 6 be entered by him; although the syntax of these sentences differs, the proposition expressed by them does not (or at least need not). On the other hand, one may resist identifications such as Keedy's: A's intention to take the umbrella in his hand (which A believes belongs to B) differs from an intention to take A's own umbrella—even if the umbrella taken *is* A's own umbrella—because the propositions are different for the two intentions. True, the proposition that is the object of the first intention is about A's umbrella, as is the proposition that is the object of the second intention hypothesized; yet (as Frege asserted) *how* one refers to that umbrella matters.[31] A, if he has the first intention, refers to that umbrella under the description, 'B's umbrella'; if A had the second intention, he would refer to that umbrella under the description, 'my own umbrella'. Since there are different *senses* to these singular terms (even though for A having the same *reference*), these are two different propositions; and with different propositions as their objects, these are two different intentions, contrary to Keedy's conclusion.

Viewing intentions as 'propositional attitudes' has additional virtues, independently of better conforming to our intuitions of when intentions are the same. With propositions one may thread

---

[31] G. Frege, 'The Thought: A Logical Inquiry', in P. F. Strawson, ed., *Philosophical Logic* (Oxford: Oxford University Press, 1967), 17–38; Frege, 'On Sense and Reference', in P. Geach and Max Black, eds., *Translations from the Philosophical Writings of Gottlob Frege* (Oxford: Oxford University Press, 1977), 56–78.

the narrow channel between the opaque view that words in Intentional objects have no reference or extension, and the transparent view that words in such contexts have (only) their normal reference and extension. A believer in propositions such as Frege will urge that words used in Intentional contexts refer ultimately to real world things, but do so 'indirectly'; the immediate reference of such words is to their sense. (Thus, to have the same proposition one must have not only the same ultimate reference, as in the Keedy example, but also the same sense.) With regard to Brentano's worry about non-existent things, this view would maintain that the *only* reference in such cases is to the sense (or properties) that would characterize such an object if it existed. To say that Jones intends that he enter room no. 6 would accordingly be construed so that: 'room no. 6' refers indirectly but ultimately to room no. 6, and directly to the sense of 'room no. 6', and 'enters' does not refer (even ultimately) to any particular action on Jones's part, even if pursuant to his intention he should enter room no. 6, 'enters' rather refers only to a *type* of action of which Jones's later action would be an instance.

Despite all of these virtues, this third view about Intentional objects runs into some thorny problems about propositions. One of these problems is perhaps not as bad as it appears. This is the 'queerness' objection, an objection that finds abstract entities such as propositions to be suspicious characters with which to populate the mind. That problem may be less serious than it appears if one can ultimately cash out propositions to functional states of mind and, ultimately, to physiology.[32] At least in their use as objects of mental states, there is nothing that demands that propositions be irreducibly abstract entities with no correlations in the functional organization of mind and in the structure of the brain.

More serious is the kind of post-Quinean scepticism about synonymy or sameness of sense. If one doubts that there is in natural languages any such relation, that seems to doom any Fregean theory of propositional identity, dependent as is the latter on a notion of sameness of sense. Such philosophical scepticism about synonymy and analytic relations leads some contemporary philosophers, such as Peter Geach, to 'doubt whether there is such a

---

[32] For one such attempt, see Brian Loar, *Mind and Meaning* (Cambridge: Cambridge University Press, 1982).

concept as propositional identity'.[33] Geach's conclusion is 'that nobody really has the faintest idea what he means when he says, the proposition that p is the same as the proposition that q'.[34]

Despite such deep and widespread philosophical scepticism about synonymy and analytic entailments generally, we each employ some common sense measure of when two words, phrases, or sentences 'mean the same thing'. Even Quine implicitly recognized as much, given his 'method of paraphrase' as one of the steps necessary to ascertain our true ontological commitments. However much the sophisticated philosophical arguments convince us that there can be no acceptable account of synonymy, we each employ some notion of sameness of meaning in everyday life.

This fact is not raised in order to elevate common sense over philosophical insight. Rather, it is to say that we each have beliefs about the correct ways to pick out and name an individual or a class of individuals. We each, that is, have some ideas about the sense (in the Fregean sense of the word) of our singular terms and of our predicates. Some ways of picking out particulars and universals are preferred by us and dubbed the 'meaning' of such words. These need not be (and often will not be) the actual senses of the words; rather, they will include all the images, names, and partial descriptions which each person employs to bring something before his own mind, what David Kaplan terms 'vivid' names.[35] Use of any of such vivid names or descriptions should, to the person involved, seem like the use of a synonym. He should say that 'bachelor' and 'unmarried male person', for example, are just different ways of picking out the same class of individuals and that both descriptions 'mean the same thing'.

These beliefs allow us to make sense of the idea of 'same sense' in a way that is not subject to Quinean objections. In the context of mental state individuation, we should say that two propositions are the same when the senses (meanings) of the words expressing them are believed to be the same by the holder of the mental states

[33] P. T. Geach, *Logic Matters* (Berkeley: University of California Press, 1980), at 176.

[34] Ibid., 170. For similar scepticism by Quine, see *Word and Object*, *supra* n. 26, at 200–21.

[35] David Kaplan, 'Quantifying In', in L. Linsky, ed., *Reference and Modality* (Oxford: Oxford University Press, 1971), 112–44.

in question.[36] This subjective test does not give a criterion of propositional identity generally; it only does so for the limited context of individuating propositions when they are the objects of mental states.

Not only does this subjectivist criterion of sameness of meaning avoid Quinean problems, but on reflection one should seek such a criterion here anyway. As Kaplan notes, 'the notion of a vivid name is intended to go to the purely internal aspects of individuation'.[37] Actual synonymy, if it existed, would be a relation within a language but about some particular person only insofar as that person's mental states made no mistakes about that language. In individuating mental states, however, what is wanted is some principle that is internal to the individual person whose mental states they are. The subjectivist criterion of 'same sense' satisfies this legitimate demand in a way that no purely language-based criterion could.

Assuming such a subjectivist move gets one around Quinean objections, the theory of individuation that results will have two requirements. Two nominally distinct intentions will be the same when the language used to describe their objects: (1) has the same reference and extension; and (2) where that language means the same to the holder of the intention(s) in question.

Application of each of these aspects of propositional identity reveals a fine-grained theory of individuating intentions quite at odds with Hart's and other legal philosophers' examples and assumptions. Take the first requirement, that there be reference to the same type of event or type of action. Hart was right to distinguish a crushing of the skull of an infant from a death of that infant, but wrong to identify the breaking of glasses with the striking of glasses. In each of these pairs of cases, there are distinct types

---

[36] It may seem that this subjectivist idea of synonymy is open to the kind of circularity objections that Butler advanced against Locke's memory criterion of personal identity: consciousness of personal identity cannot constitute a criterion of personal identity because 'the former presupposes the idea of personal identity'. Yet the circularity charge is warranted here no more than against Locke: I do not use our sense of the intersubstitutability of various ways of referring to the same thing as constituting a criterion of synonymy; whether there really is any relation in a natural language properly called synonymy I leave open. 'Believed synonymy' is for my purposes enough (just as 'believed self-identity' was enough for Locke). See, on the circularity problem, David Wiggins, *Sameness and Substance* (Cambridge, Mass.: Harvard University Press, 1980), ch. 6.

[37] Kaplan, 'Quantifying In', *supra* n. 35, at 135. See also Quine, *Word and Object*, *supra* n. 26, at 201–2.

of events (and thus, distinct types of intentions with regard to these types of events).

Although the identity conditions of particular events is quite tricky, and the identity conditions of types of events is trickier still,[38] one insight seems secure, and that is that nothing is the cause of itself. As David Hume noted, genuine logical relations (like identity) preclude the existence of causal relations, and vice versa. While the death of a foetus does not cause its skull to be crushed, a particular skull crushing may properly be said to cause the death of the foetus whose skull is crushed; while deaths do not have the power to cause skull crushings, skull crushings do have the power to cause deaths. Likewise, while the breaking of the glass does not cause the glass to be struck, striking a particular glass may cause it to be broken. And, while glass breakings do not have the power to cause glass strikings, glass strikings have the power to cause glass breakings. In short, the usual (asymmetrical) causal relations exist between each of these pairs of events, and between each of these pairs of types of events, that prevents identifying one as the other.

The same holds true for most of the examples quoted earlier in section II. Asymmetrical causal relations exist between: heart removals, and deaths; blowing up a plane in flight, and the deaths of any passengers on it; getting drunk, and being hung over; retaining another's car, and depriving him of his use of it; decapitation, and death. In each of such cases, there are distinct types of events, and an intent to bring about the first is *not*, accordingly, an intent to bring about the second. The test the courts and commentators have used here—about how 'invariant', 'immediate' or 'certain' are the causal sequences between the two types of events—is just the opposite of what one should be saying. That there is a causal connection at all between the pairs of event-types should lead courts exactly the other way, namely, to conclude that these are distinct types of events.

A few of the examples earlier examined are not of this sort. More plausibly one might identify the appointment of Garcia, and the appointment of a fifty-year-old man, as the same particular event, if Garcia is indeed fifty; likewise, one might identify remaining unmarried and remaining a bachelor as the same types of states of

---

[38] I explore the individuation of events, both tokens and types, in chs. 14 and 13, respectively, of *Act and Crime, supra* n. 1.

affairs. For such examples one must invoke the second aspect of propositional identity, that having to do with identity of meaning.

For most persons we know, 'bachelor' and 'unmarried male' are synonymous ways of picking out the same class of individuals. For such persons an intention to remain unmarried and an intention to remain a bachelor are one and the same intention. By contrast, an intention to appoint Garcia may be the same as an intention to appoint a fifty-year-old man, but only if the description, 'the fifty-year-old man', is the way in which the holder of the intention(s) calls Garcia to mind in this context. If Garcia's being fifty years old is not that important ('vivid') to the holder of the intention, then one cannot substitute, 'fifty-year-old man' for 'Garcia' in the object of the intention; for such intentions are distinct, and one is not necessarily the other.

The upshot of all this is that our metaphysics of intent individuation yield a theory quite at odds with that assumed by courts and commentators when they talk of 'the same intention'. It is not that we have no theory of intent individuation, as sceptics such as Kelman believe—one thus cannot argue that the distinction between direct and oblique intentions is manipulable at will. Still, the terms of the debate about direct and oblique intentions should change considerably when placed on its proper metaphysical foundations. Those such as Kenny who wish to argue for the primacy of purpose in explicating intention have much more of a job cut out for them than they acknowledge, as do those who would make moral sense of the doctrine of double effect.[39]

Those in Kenny's position (myself included) have but two options here. First, we can accept the fine-grained theory of individuation, and argue as I did in chapter 9 that nonetheless there is some difference in culpability between one who intends a harm and one who only knows that that harm will result from his activities. In such a case we must conclude that there *is* a moral difference between the killer who blows up a passenger-laden plane in order to collect insurance on the plane and the killer who blows up the plane in order to collect insurance on the passengers. Alternatively,

---

[39] Philippa Foot recognizes as much about the doctrine of double effect, when she acknowledges that a fine-grained theory of individuation would 'make nonsense of it from the beginning'. 'Abortion and Double Effect', *supra* n. 12, at 6. The 'non-sense' such a fine-grained theory threatens to make of the doctrine is that of a morally unjustifiable distinction, not some kind of literally nonsensical statements.

those favouring the moral significance of the purpose/knowledge distinction could attempt to work out some basis for a more coarse-grained theory of individuating intentions; given what has been said about the metaphysical correctness of a very fine-grained theory, the basis for their more coarse-grained theory must be some policy argument for equating two admittedly distinct intentions. In the context of criminal punishment, such policies should have to do with moral culpability. Needed to flesh out this alternative would be some moral theory that would justify saying that intentions that are really quite distinct should nonetheless be treated as the same for purposes of determining culpability.[40] It is to the possibility of there being such a moral theory of intent individuation that the next section is devoted.

IV. MORALLY EQUIVALENT INTENTIONS

In *Hyam* v. *Director of Public Prosecutions*[41] Lord Hailsham hinted at such an alternative moral basis for a coarse-grained theory of intent individuation. In *Hyam* the defendant had a relationship with a man who subsequently became engaged to be married to a Mrs Booth. In an effort to scare Mrs Booth into leaving town and breaking off the engagement, the defendant set fire to the front

[40] The discussion that follows in section IV is directed only at situations where there is no justification at issue, so that a doctrine of morally equivalent intentions deals only with the relative culpabilities of two quite culpable intentions. For (what I would take to be) a discussion of a moral theory of equivalent intention in the context of the doctrine of double effect, see Jonathan Bennett, 'Whatever the Consequences', *Analysis*, Vol. 26 (1966), 83–102, and John Finnis, 'The Rights and Wrongs of Abortion', *Philosophy and Public Affairs*, Vol. 2 (1973), 117–45. The jumble of factors that Bennett and Finnis identify as determining when an effect is intended as a means, or only known to be brought about as a side consequence, are each of them factors for which independent moral argument must be given. One should say of all of them, what Judith Thomson says of one of them, that 'it is hard to see how anyone could think that this question has any bearing at all on the question whether a given death is, on the one hand, an agent's ends or means, or on the other hand, a mere foreseen consequence of what he does to save his life'. Thomson, 'Rights and Deaths', *Philosophy and Public Affairs*, Vol. 2 (1973), 146–59, at 151. Put my way: what good is the distinction between direct and oblique intentions if to give the distinction any bite at all one must import into it a whole range of independent moral considerations that themselves require explication and defence? The direct/oblique distinction in such a case does no moral work and should be dropped from the discussion, letting the moral factors for which it is only a proxy do their moral work directly.

[41] [1974] 2 All ER 41.

entrance way of Mrs Booth's house, resulting in the deaths of Mrs Booth's two daughters. In affirming the defendant's conviction for murder, Lord Hailsham required that the defendant have a direct intention—mere knowledge, or oblique intention, could not suffice for murder. The question as Lord Hailsham therefore framed it was whether the defendant's mediate but direct intention to expose Mrs Booth to the serious risk of death was sufficiently like an intention actually to cause death or grievous bodily injury, that the one should be said to *be* the other so that the defendant could be punished as a murderer. Lord Hailsham assumed the intention that the defendant had—to expose Mrs Booth to risk in order to scare her— was 'logically' (i.e., metaphysically) distinct from an intention to cause either grievous bodily harm or death. Nonetheless:

[T]he moral truth [is] that if a man, in full knowledge of the danger involved, and without lawful excuse, deliberately does that which exposes a victim to the risk of probable grievous bodily harm . . . or death, and the victim dies the perpetrator of the crime is guilty of murder and not manslaughter to the same extent as if he had actually intended the consequence to follow. . . . This is because *the two types of intention are morally indistinguishable, although factually and logically distinct*, and because it is therefore just that they should bear the same consequences for the perpetrator . . .[42]

Like Kenny and myself, Lord Hailsham assumed that there is a significant difference in the culpability of those who directly intend a death and those who only obliquely do so. Nonetheless, he assumed there is some moral theory that justifies him in treating as an intention to kill or inflict grievous bodily harm, an intention that is admittedly not an intention to kill or inflict grievous bodily harm. Clearly this moral theory cannot be based on the *knowledge* of someone like Hyam that imposing a risk of death on Mrs Booth might well in fact kill her. If Lord Hailsham thought that, he would have had no business in distinguishing direct from oblique intentions; either, in such a case, should suffice for murder. What is needed by Lord Hailsham is a moral theory that does not depend on the knowledge of the acting subject as its basis for equating one intention with another.

A glimpse of such a theory may perhaps be found in the legal doctrine of transferred intent which holds that an intention to harm

---

[42] [1974] 2 All ER 55 (emphasis added).

A is equivalent in legal effect to an intention to harm B, where B is the person the defendant actually harms. The defendant did not intend to harm B, but if he did intend to harm A and in trying to do so harmed B, the intent to harm A will be sufficient *mens rea* for the completed offence of harming B intentionally.

One way to account for the doctrine of transferred intent is through a moral theory that says that the identity of a victim is a morally insignificant aspect of a defendant's intention; that, accordingly, the intention the defendant had (to harm A) will be treated as if it were the intention prohibited (to harm B), even though they are in reality different intentions. The harm intended is just as bad as the harm caused, so the intention is 'transferred' from one harm to the other.

Such a moral theory (of the substitutability of morally equivalent intentions) may also find expression in the legal doctrine of implied malice. Implied malice is said to exist when the defendant intends to kill someone but does not intend to kill any particular person; as where he shoots into a crowd indiscriminately. One might say in such cases that the intention the defendant had (to shoot anyone) is sufficiently bad that it will be 'transferred' to the harm the defendant actually caused, the death of some one particular person.

One might also glimpse outcroppings of such a moral theory in the legal doctrines surrounding felony-murder, grievous bodily harm murder, mayhem, and also in torts. For felony-murder, for example, one might think that although the harm intended (say, arson) is different from the harm caused (death), morally both are so bad that the intent to do the one should be identified as the intent to do the other. Likewise, for the doctrine of grievous bodily harm murder: even though the harm intended (grievous bodily harm) is different from the harm caused (death), the intent to do the former is so bad that it will be treated like the intent to do the latter as well. Similarly in mayhem: to be mayhem there must be disfigurement, yet American criminal law makes clear that an intent to hit will suffice as an intent to disfigure if disfigurement is caused by that hitting.[43] Tort law can be similarly construed: an intent to hit will suffice for the harm caused by hitting even if there was no intent to harm; an intent to hit may be thought culpable enough to

---

[43] *State* v. *Hatley*, 72 NM 377, 384 P 2d 252 (1963). See generally Wayne R. LaFave and Austin W. Scott, *Criminal Law* (St. Paul, Minn.: West, 1972), at 616.

classify the harm as intentionally accomplished rather than negligently so, giving rise to the more severe sanctions reserved for the intentional torts.[44]

There are two problems with the sort of moral theory just sketched. One is a query about the conceptual coherence of the theory, the other, about its moral correctness. The coherence point first: most of the cases where one is tempted to say the intention the defendant had is 'close enough' to the one prohibited to be identified as the same, are cases where the intended harm is not bad (or bad enough) by itself; it is only bad because it will probably cause a further harm, which is really bad. Consider the decapitation, heart-removal, and skull crushing examples. On the theory here considered, an intent to do any of these things is as bad as the intent to kill, and therefore these two admittedly different intentions will in law be said to be the same. The problem lies in how the culpability of the intent to decapitate, for example, is fixed. If the intent to decapitate is bad only because decapitations always cause deaths, and deaths are bad, then this alleged moral theory about morally equivalent intentions is in reality a back-door way to the objective theory of intention. What one is really saying in such a case is that this defendant, because he intended to decapitate (crush the skull, cut out the heart), should have known that what he was doing would cause a death, and this makes him as culpable as one who intends to cause a death.[45] If *this* is one's theory of individuating morally equivalent intentions, then the supposed moral theory here is no more and no different from the moral theory that says that negligence is as culpable as purpose when a harm is caused. Better to assert such a theory openly when it can be assessed for its (im)plausibility and not hide it by the language of morally equivalent intentions and the like.

These same remarks apply to *Hyam* itself. If one thought that risking harm to another, when that other knows of the risk and fears it, is an independently bad thing to do, then an intended risking of death can be equated to an intended killing without trivial-

---

[44] *Vosburg* v. *Putney*, 80 Wis. 523, 50 NW 403 (1891).

[45] The high degree of negligence here is undoubtedly what courts and commentators are getting at when they speak of the 'moral certainty' (Lord Hailsham) or the 'immediate and invariant connection' (Hart and Kenny) of the harm occurring if the defendant achieves what he is aiming at. One would indeed be very negligent not to have foreseen, e.g., death of passengers on a plane one plans to blow up in mid-air.

izing the theory of morally equivalent intentions. More plausibly, however, one might think that risking death to another is bad because you just might kill them. If this is so, then the intent to risk death is morally equivalent to an intent to cause death only in the trivial sense just mentioned (namely, where the badness of the intent to risk just is the negligence with respect to death that accompanies that intent).

Consider also Lord Hailsham's hypothetical example of the plane destroyed in mid-air with passengers aboard. Blowing up a plane without passengers in it is a bad thing to do. Yet I doubt that it is this badness that outrages us enough to be tempted to equate an intent to blow up the plane with the intent to kill the passengers. Rather, what outrages us enough to be tempted to equate the two is the *knowledge* of the defendant that his greedy act will kill many innocent people. It is his knowledge of the certainty of death, not his intent to destroy the plane, that inclines us so strongly to classify him as a murderer. In which case there is no moral theory that identifies the one intention as the other, save the very same moral theory that Lord Hailsham was trying to avoid by his requirement of a *direct* intention to kill for murder.

Not all instances of a supposedly independent moral theory will collapse in this way. Rape is bad independently of the risk of death to the victim; inflicting grievous bodily harm on another is bad independently of its risking death to the person so harmed; hitting is bad independently of the likelihood of disfiguring the person hit. In such cases, when one classifies, for example, an intent to rape or to inflict grievous bodily harm as enough for murder when death ensues, or when one classifies an intent to hit as enough for mayhem when disfigurement results, one is holding two intentions to be close enough in culpability to be treated as the same for punishment purposes. The problem in these cases, however, is that the moral theory that sanctions these identities seems wrong even though not incoherent. An intentional rapist may be very culpable, but he is not as culpable as an intentional killer. Someone who intentionally strikes another and puts out an eye because the other moved his head at the last second is culpable, but surely not as culpable as one who not only hits but intends to put out an eye with the blow.

Equating these cases is to operate with a kind of crude forfeiture theory, whereby once a defendant has crossed some threshold of culpability we should not care about making any further discriminations in the degree of culpability. Yet it is just this kind of forfeiture theory which was rejected by the courts of England over a century ago when they worked out the no substitution of *mens rea* rule in criminal law.[46] Even if the intent to do one thing is *more* culpable than the intent to do another,[47] if a defendant causes the second harm but not the first he should be liable only for the attempt to do the first; he should not be held liable for the second crime (unless knowledge or recklessness is enough—in which event he should be held for *those* mental states, not the other intention). The important moral principle that underlies these cases is one requiring the concurrence of act, intent, and causation before one is fully culpable. One needs a 'guilty mind' (here, direct intention) *with respect to the harm prohibited*, not with respect to some other type of harm, if one is fairly to be held responsible for causing that harm.

It may seem that the implied malice and the transferred intent cases are not subject to either of these objections. That is, in these cases, the harm intended may be thought to be bad independently of its risking the harm caused; and intuitively, it may seem more appealing to say that an intent to hit A or to hit anyone, where B is hit instead, will suffice for guilt at intentionally hitting B. The moral theory that would equate the two intentions may well seem neither incoherent nor incorrect.

Yet the implied malice and the transferred intent cases need not be accounted for by some moral theory as to when we may substitute intentions. An alternative way to account for such cases is to say that the intention some defendant actually had is an instance of just the type of intention the statute prohibits. We need not say of such cases that we are 'transferring' or implying intentions, nor need we seek moral grounds with which to justify treating as the same two in fact distinct intention-types.

---

[46] *R* v. *Pembliton*, 2 Cox Crim. Cas. 607 (1874) (intent to hit a person with a stone not substituted for the intent to damage property required for a conviction of malicious damage to property); *R* v. *Faulkner*, Cox Crim. Cas. 550 (1877) (intent to steal which, when acted upon, led to the firing of a ship, not substituted for the intent to fire the ship required for a conviction of arson).

[47] Consider in this regard the facts of *Pembliton* (*supra* n. 46): the defendant threw a stone, intending to hit another person. The stone instead broke a window. The defendant's conviction for malicious property damage was quashed because the intent to harm persons would not be substituted for the intent to damage property; this, despite the greater evil in what the defendant intended to do than what he in fact did.

The trick is to examine statutes that prohibit act-types such as intentional killings. For obvious reasons statutes are not formulated to prohibit the killing of particular, named persons. They rather prohibit the intentional killing of 'a human being'.[48] The indefinite article is ambiguous here:[49] the unlawful intent may be either an intent to kill someone, in the sense of some one particular person; or the prohibited intention may be an intention to kill someone in the sense of anyone. The ambiguity is in the scope of the existential quantifier. The first statement should be symbolized as:

$$1.\ \exists x[yI(Kyx)]$$

(there is some person x such that y intends that he kills x). The second statement, on the other hand, does not require quantification into the 'intend' operator:

$$2.\ yI[\exists x(Kyx)]$$

(y intends that there be someone he kills).

A reasonable construction of criminal statutes is to say that they make unlawful intentions of either type. If this is so then the transferred intent and implied malice cases quite literally instantiate one of the types of intentions prohibited by law. An intent to kill A, where B is killed instead, is an intent to kill someone in the sense of (1) above; an intent to kill anyone within a crowd is an intent to kill someone in the sense of (2) above. These being unproblematic instances of the types of intentions prohibited by law, there is no need for a moral theory of equivalent intentions in order to account for our intuitions that these cases merit the severe punishment reserved for *intentional* killers.[50]

---

[48] See, e.g., California Penal Code §188.

[49] Quine, *Word and Object*, supra n. 26, at 146–51.

[50] There are problems about the transferred intent cases but these are not problems connected with the insufficiency of the defendant's intention. Rather, they are proximate cause problems about the concurrence of the causation and *mens rea* elements. The concurrence principle holds that the defendant must have caused a particular harm that instantiates the type of harm intended. The question in such cases is whether we individuate types of harm by the person who suffers them or not. The transferred intent doctrine says that we do not take into account the identity of the victim; the problem is that we do take the identity of the victim into account in negligence cases (at least in jurisdictions following Cardozo's opinion in *Palsgraf* disallowing that there can be negligence 'in the air, so to speak'). However one comes

The upshot of all this is that there is no plausible moral theory that can urge us to identify two distinct intentions as the same. Whenever a legal theorist urges us to treat two distinct intentions as the same, one of two things is true: (a) either he is using knowledge or recklessness or negligence as the touchstone of culpability, despite his supposed concern with purpose; or (b) he is urging some crude forfeiture theory of culpability that is inconsistent with the basic moral requirement that there be proportionality between punishment and culpability. In the first case he does not have a theory of morally equivalent *intentions*; in the second case, while he has such a theory, it is not a very plausible one.[51]

out here will not affect the fact that the defendant's intention in these cases quite literally is an instance of the type of intention prohibited by statutes.

Imagine an analogous case, where the charge is mayhem: the defendant strikes the victim, intending to put out the victim's left eye; the victim turns his head at the last moment, and the right eye is put out instead. It does not require a doctrine of transferred intent to hold the defendant guilty of mayhem: he quite literally intended to put out 'an eye'. If there is a problem here, it is again one of proximate causation: do we individuate the types of harm so finely that we should say these are distinct types? I think not. The type of harm prohibited by the mayhem statute is disfigurement, so that if a defendant intended *a* disfigurement of someone and he caused a disfigurement of someone, then he satisfies the statute and the concurrence principle.

[51] This last point is implicitly recognized by those many courts that have sought to ameliorate the harshness of the felony-murder rule by requiring that the underlying felony be one 'inherently dangerous to human life'. By restricting in this way the kinds of intentions that can be substituted for an intention to kill, courts in effect have recognized that having a very bad intention by itself does not merit the sanctions attached to murder; rather, that bad intention (to do the underlying felony) must be one whereby the defendant manifests his recklessness (or extreme negligence) with regard to life. The felony-murder rule thus approaches a reckless/negligent homicide doctrine having nothing to do with substituting one bad intention the defendant had for the intention to kill, which he did not have. The next logical step is that taken by the Model Penal Code (Proposed Official Draft, 1962, s. 210.2), which reduces the felony-murder doctrine to no more than a presumption of recklessness manifesting extreme indifference to human life.

A similar development has taken place with the grievous bodily harm murder doctrine. Many states have reduced the harshness of the rule by defining 'grievous bodily harm' to be an injury 'likely to be attended with dangerous or fatal consequences'. *People* v. *Crenshaw*, 298 Ill. 412, 416, 131 NE 576, 577 (1921). By so limiting the intentions that can be substituted for an intention to kill, the courts have in effect required some recklessness with respect to death before they will substitute a grievous bodily harm intention for an intention to kill. Again, the Model Penal Code has taken the next logical step of eliminating the substituted intention entirely as a ground for murder, replacing it with an explicit question about the actor's recklessness in bringing about a death. See American Law Institute, *Model Penal Code and Commentaries, Part II*, Comment to section 210.2 at 28–9 (1980).

V. CONCLUSIONS

1. Contrary to the scepticism mentioned in the introduction, there is an answer to the question of what an individual directly intends and an answer to the question of whether his direct intention is the same as some type of intention prohibited by law and morality. The distinction between direct and oblique intentions, accordingly, is not an illusory one based on an arbitrary metaphysical posit. Those moral and legal philosophers who wish to debate the relative culpability of direct and oblique intentions have, accordingly, something to argue about.

2. The distinction is, however, a distinction that classifies cases quite differently from the way most legal theorists suppose. If one individuates intentions by their propositional objects, as I have here urged that we do in ordinary explanatory contexts, one will separate intentions that most theorists wish to hold the same. The result is to shift the debate about the moral relevance of the distinction considerably. Properly individuated, many of the mental states that are counted as direct intentions of a prohibited sort are in reality at best oblique intentions only. This makes the case for distinguishing direct intentions from belief in terms of their culpability more difficult, although not impossible.

3. There is no moral theory that is both coherent and correct and that allows one to identify admittedly distinct intentions as the same for criminal law purposes. Because legal theorists and judges have believed that there is such a theory, however, we have a criminal law that abuses the concept of intention and abuses the significant degree of culpability that concept marks. Crude forfeiture doctrines abound in criminal law, where an intention to do one thing (for example, inflict grievous bodily harm) is treated as an intention to do something else (that is, to kill). Disabused of the idea that there is some moral justification for equating such distinct intentions, we can see such doctrines for what they are: a dilution of purpose (and often even of knowledge) as the touchstones of most serious culpability and the substitution of negligence. Whether such substitution is a good idea is a matter that can be debated. One sees the right issue here, however, only by being clear about how one fixes the objects of intentions and other mental states. An intention to inflict grievous bodily harm is *not* an intention to kill, and there is no good reason to pretend otherwise.

b. The Nature of Excuse

12

CAUSATION AND THE EXCUSES

I. INTRODUCTION

In this and the succeeding chapter we leave prima facie culpability in the criminal law—as we have seen, a matter of desire, belief, or intention—and turn to the conditions that must be present if one of these mental states makes one actually, and not just prima facie, culpable. Those conditions can be phrased positively, as conditions of freedom in a certain sense; or negatively as conditions of excuse that must be absent if an intentional wrongdoer is to be actually culpable. Since the more usual phrasing is negative,[1] in these two chapters I shall pursue what I shall call a theory of excuse. The flip side of such excuses might be called freedom, so such a theory of excuse may alternatively be viewed as a theory about the sort of freedom presupposed by culpability.

Two preliminary enquires will occupy us in this introduction. The first is what the excuses are. The second is what a theory of such conditions should in general look like. I shall pursue each in the succeeding subsections.

A. What Are the Excuses?

Our first task is to determine exactly what a theory of excuses is a theory of. What, first of all, are the *legal* excuses? Think of the range of arguments a defendant might make in order to defeat a prima facie showing of legal responsibility. He might seek to show that he acted in ignorance of certain facts; that he was mistaken about the law; that the statute of limitations has run; that he acted in self-defence; that he was young, or crazy, or drunk; that he was threatened by others; that he was unconscious or asleep or acting

---

[1] The influence of H. L. A. Hart here is large. See Hart, 'The Ascription of Responsibility and Rights', *Proceedings of the Aristotelian Society*, Vol. 49 (1949), 171–94, at 180, 188–90, wherein Hart urges us not to pursue the 'will-o-the-wisp' of some one positive thing negated by the excuses.

under post-hypnotic suggestion; or that he did not cause the harm, but that some other intervening agent did. Our first need is to cull out of this seemingly heterogeneous set of defences those that raise excuses and then to impose some order on those that remain.

Two distinctions are helpful here. The first is between extrinsic policy defences and culpability defences. Many defences in criminal law are ways of showing that the actor was not morally blameworthy.[2] Some defences, however, are unconnected to the actor's blameworthiness. The statute of limitations is one example, and entrapment may be another.[3] Legal excuses are a subclass of those defences that show the lessened moral culpability of the offender.

Within the class of defences that do negate blameworthiness a second distinction is crucial: that between justifications and excuses. Criminal law theoreticians have formulated this distinction in various ways. Some describe the legal consequences of classifying a defence as a justification or an excuse. For example, a justification entitles others to do a like action, because they too will be justified, whereas an excuse is not generalizable in this way but is said to be a matter of individual justice to a particular actor. Alternatively, third parties may lawfully come to the aid of the actor whose action is justified, but they may not if his action is only excused. As a third example, the victim of a violent act may lawfully resist it if the act is excused but has no right to resist if the violent act is justified.[4] This formal approach is fine as far as it goes, but it does not go far enough. Showing the legal consequences of making the distinction does not tell us what the distinction is; such an analysis can only tell us what follows from the distinction once it is made. Needed is an analysis of the distinction itself.[5]

---

[2] In light of my theory of criminal law's exclusively retributive function, I here put aside any utilitarian theory of excuses. Therefore, in order to account for the excuse of insanity, for example, one must discuss not the insane's dangerousness or lack of deterrability, but rather one must seek some lack of moral responsibility. On the utilitarian theory of excuses and its problems, see H. L. A. Hart, 'Legal Responsibility and the Excuses', in *Punishment and Responsibility* (Oxford: Oxford University Press, 1968), 28–53; Richard Brandt, 'A Utilitarian Theory of Excuses', *Philosophical Review*, Vol. 78 (1969), 337–61.

[3] For a helpful discussion of the extrinsic policy defences and of the debate about the nature of entrapment, see Paul Robinson, 'Criminal Law Defenses: A Systematic Analysis', *Columbia Law Review*, Vol. 82 (1982), 199, 229–32, 236–9.

[4] George Fletcher, *Rethinking Criminal Law* (Boston: Little, Brown, 1978), 759–62.

[5] For a defence of the view that an analysis of legal concepts must include the criteria of their correct application, as well as the legal consequences attached to their

The difference lies in the fact that justifications answer a different moral question than do excuses. Justifications answer the general evaluative question of whether, all things considered, the sort of action under consideration was wrongful or permissible. Justifications answer this question in light of all the actual consequences and circumstances of the action being evaluated, not in light of the circumstances and consequences known to the actor.[6]In this sense justifications are said to answer an 'objective' moral question. Excuses answer a different question, the finger-pointing question of attribution: is there a culpable actor who is responsible for making the world worse than it was without the act? By focusing on the actor, excuses necessarily concern themselves with the subjective mental states of a particular actor. In this sense excuses are said to answer a subjective question.

Justifications and excuses both may ultimately relieve an actor of moral responsibility for some prima facie wrongful action, but they do so in markedly different ways. When an action is justified, any prima facie wrongfulness is eliminated by the other (and good) attributes of the action; when an action is excused, it is still wrongful but the actor cannot be held responsible for it because she is not culpable.

When we put aside the justificatory defences[7] and the extrinsic policy defences, we are left with the legal defences based on moral excuses. We can divide what are commonly thought of as excuse defences into three categories. There are, first of all, what I shall call the 'true excuses'. These are the mistake excuses (mistake of

authoritative use, see Michael Moore, *Law and Psychiatry: Rethinking the Relationship* (Cambridge: Cambridge University Press, 1984), 44–9.

[6] Compare Kent Greenawalt, 'The Perplexing Borders of Justification and Excuse', *Columbia Law Review*, Vol. 84 (1984), 1897–927. Greenawalt urges that actions the accused performed under mistaken beliefs about justifying circumstances (as in cases of imperfect self-defence, for example) should be treated as justified actions. Id. at 1907–11. To the contrary, these must be treated as excused actions, because this is the only way that the distinction can survive the elegant counter-examples to be found throughout Greenawalt's paper. (See Michael Corrado, 'Notes on the Structure of a Theory of Excuses', *Journal of Criminal Law and Criminology*, Vol. 82 (1992), 465–97, at 468.) If an actor mistakenly but reasonably believes he was shooting in self-defence, one might say that *he* was justified in doing what he did, but that his action was not justified. Because the action was wrongful, the actor's defence is one of excuse (mistaken belief), not of justification.

[7] Although there may be some dispute, I classify most invocations of the defences of others, self-defence, and the general balance-of-evils defence as justifications and not as excuses.

fact, mistake of law) and the compulsion excuses (duress, necessity, provocation, addiction). Such excuses are not merely means of disproving the prosecution's prima facie case, but are affirmative defences.[8] Nor do such excuses focus on the general status of the accused; instead they explain the defendant's particular actions in light of the events or states present at the time of the action. For both these reasons I shall classify mistake and compulsion as 'true' excuses.

Second, there are those issues an accused may raise to disprove the case in chief. Rightly conceived, these issues will not be raised as defences but only as means of rebutting items the prosecution must raise and prove. Consider three of them: (a) No voluntary action. An accused may show that he was asleep, unconscious, in shock, in a post-hypnotic trance, or reacting to the stings of bees. What he denies is that he *acted* or was the agent of the harm. (b) No *mens rea*. An accused may seek to show that he was ignorant of, or mistaken about, some circumstances surrounding his action, some consequence of his action, or some risk his actions created. He thus can deny that he knew of or was reckless with respect to some harm, or that he acted with that harm as his purpose.[9] (c) No proximate cause. An accused may show that his act, admittedly a but-for cause of the harm, nonetheless should not make him responsible because an intervening occurrence—an extraordinary natural event or a voluntary act by another party—was the real cause of the harm. These intervening causes are said to break the causal chain between a defendant's culpable act and the harm.

---

[8] A mistaken belief is not the same as ignorance. Mistake exists when the accused falsely believes that some proposition is true; in contrast, ignorance exists when the accused does not know that some true proposition is true. It is only ignorance, but not mistake, that necessarily negates intention or knowledge. If we supply the suppressed premise of rationality, namely, that a person's beliefs are consistent, then we may infer from mistake that there was ignorance, and thus mistake may negate that there was knowledge. Since usually we are confident in making this assumption of consistency in belief, we most often use mistake of fact to negate the *mens rea* requirement of crime. Sometimes, however (as in wilful blindness, where we do not assume consistency of belief), we use mistake of fact as a true excuse, exempting one from responsibility despite the presence of prima facie culpable *mens rea*.

[9] Ignorance and mistake of fact can be used to disprove purpose as well as knowledge because bringing about some harm is not often a defendant's purpose unless he believes that his action has some likelihood of bringing about that harm. If he is ignorant or mistaken as to that likelihood, bringing about the harm is unlikely to be his purpose because he lacks the means/end belief necessary to connect his action to the thing he wants to achieve.

A third category of conditions often lumped with the true excuses consists of the statuses of insanity, infancy, and intoxication. I call these conditions ones of *status* because they make a claim about the accused's general status, not about his state of mind at the time he acted. Duress, for example, is a true excuse because its exculpatory effect depends on a particular event (threat) that explains why the criminal performed the forbidden act. Infancy, in contrast, is not a true excuse because its exculpatory effect depends on the accused's general status. Juveniles as a class are considered incapable of committing crime because they are young and thus immature. They are not excused because they possessed some particular mental state or were confronted with some threat at the time of their crime. Similarly, involuntary intoxication negates responsibility because the accused was generally incapacitated, not because he was ignorant or in some other way lacked *mens rea*. As to insanity, there is admittedly some dispute about whether it operates as a true excuse or as a status defence. For now, let us include it as a status defence. I shall argue for this categorization later on in chapter 14.

In developing my own positive theory of excuse in the next chapter I shall confine my examples to the true excuses. In the present chapter, however, I allow myself greater leeway in what I shall consider as excuses. I do this so as to allow the theory against which I shall be arguing (the causal theory of excuses) what its proponents regard as their best examples. If the theory cannot account for these, *a fortiori* it cannot account for the data when properly narrowed to the true excuses.

B. What Is a Theory of Excuse?

Recalling the distinctions between explanatory, evaluative, and descriptive theories of law introduced in chapter 1, the theory sought in these two chapters is what I call a descriptive theory. By my earlier analysis, such a descriptive theory will have two aspects. The first is whether the theory stands in the proper logical relation to the doctrines of which it is a theory. The second is whether the theory reveals the doctrines to have a point that itself serves the ends of the criminal law. This functional part of the analysis in turn requires two evaluations, one as to the proper ends of the criminal law and the other as to the proper functions of more discrete doctrines (such as that of excuse) in serving those ends.

Recalling this about what I call descriptive legal theories will clarify the extent to which we are talking about legal excuses (defences of a certain kind to criminal liability) or moral excuses (exemptions of a certain kind from moral responsibility). Given the retributive end of the criminal law defended in Part I,[10] we are talking about both. More specifically: my ultimate interest lies in developing a (descriptive) theory of the legal excuses. However, since the function of the criminal law is to realize justice in retribution, the doctrines of legal excuse should be seen to serve that end. This means both that each legal excuse should correspond to some underlying moral excuse and that each moral excuse should find doctrinal expression in some legal excuse. Retributive justice is neither served by legally excusing those who are morally blameworthy nor by punishing those who are morally excused.

The fit between Anglo-American criminal law doctrines of excuse and the truths of morality is of course not perfect, even on my own theory of excuse developed in the next chapter. Still, not only is such a theory morally preferable to its competitors; but it also accounts for more of the legal doctrines we have than do those competitors. Or so I shall argue.

As one seeks to assess whether such argument succeeds, a final clarification may be helpful. This is with respect to those legal excuses that may seem to have no moral analogue. I refer to legal excuses such as mistake of law. Since such defences make no sense except with reference to a legal norm, it may seem that there can be no underlying moral excuse, as there is for duress, for example. Yet there is a moral excuse here, even if it is framed in terms having to do with the law. It is morality that demands that actors without a fair opportunity to acquaint themselves with the legal norms of a society be excused when they violate those norms, and legal doctrines of excuse can more or less approximate this aspect of morality.

II. THE CAUSAL THEORY OF EXCUSE

My target in this chapter is a theory of excuse that I call the causal theory. The causal theory is a descriptive theory in the sense devel-

___

[10] Even under a mixed theory of punishment, according to which moral desert is a necessary condition of punishment, moral excuses will figure in the account of some legal excuses (namely, the ones not justified on utilitarian grounds).

oped in chapter 1, so that it has two aspects to it. The purely descriptive aspect of the theory asserts that the established excuses of Anglo-American criminal law logically reflect a principle of causation. The principle is that when an agent is caused to act by a factor outside his control, he is excused; only those acts not caused by some factor external to his will are unexcused. The evaluative aspect of the causal theory of excuse asserts that the criminal law is morally right in excusing all those, and only those, whose actions are caused by factors outside their control. In a nutshell, the causal theory of excuse regards causation as the core of both legal and moral excuse.

My thesis in this chapter is that we must reject the causal theory of excuse. It neither describes accurately the accepted excuses of our criminal law nor provides a morally acceptable basis for deciding what conditions ought to qualify as excuses from criminal liability. I shall approach my thesis gradually, for some preliminary work must be done.

In section III, I attempt to show why the causal theory of excuse is so widely accepted. In examining the theory's plausibility, I undertake two tasks that correspond to the theory's purely descriptive and evaluative aspects. First, I examine some of the legal doctrines that have developed around each of the legal excuses. From these doctrines we might plausibly conclude that it is causation that underlies our established excuses. Second, I set out the moral argument one could make for this underlying causal principle.

The remainder of the chapter, sections IV and V, develop alternative arguments against the causal theory. Section IV assumes that human actions and choices, like all other events in the world, are caused. This assumption is standardly called 'determinism'. Taking determinism as an essential premise, I construct a *reductio* form of argument to show that the causal theory of excuse leads to the absurd conclusion that no one is responsible for anything. I then examine a number of dodges the causal theorist might make to avoid this absurdity and show that none is adequate. As a result, the causal theorist who accepts determinism at all must accept the kind of 'hard determinism' that makes moral responsibility an illusion.

Section V makes the alternative assumption that human actions and choices are not determined. For purposes of argument I grant that persons sometimes exercise free will, 'free' here meaning 'not caused'. I argue that even if we make this strong assumption, the causal theory is false. More specifically, I argue (1) that the causal theory describes the established legal excuses less well than other, non-causal theories of excuse, and (2) that moral responsibility for an action should be ascribed to an actor even when that action was caused by factors over which he had no control. Therefore both the purely descriptive and the evaluative aspects of the causal theory of excuse must be rejected.

Before launching into this discussion it may be well to use the remainder of this section to say why any of it matters. First and foremost, whether the causal theory of excuse is correct matters because so many people accept it. This is true not only of many theorists, some of whom I shall discuss in a moment, but also of the common sense beliefs of many educated laypersons. Common sense often adopts as folk wisdom the French proverb, '*tout comprendre c'est tout pardonner*'.[11] This common sense urges that we should excuse whenever we come to know the causes of behaviour[12] and that to do so is the mark of a civilized being.

Many distinguished judges, psychiatrists, and legal theorists, seeing themselves as civilized in this respect, have adopted the common sense view. This has had a number of ramifications. First, these persons propose adding new excuses to the criminal law or abolishing old ones by showing how certain conditions cause or do not cause criminal behaviour. For example, recent arguments for the abolition of the insanity defence have often been based on the assumption that insane criminals, who are excused, are no more strongly caused to act than are normal criminals, who are not excused. Such comparisons lead advocates of a causal theory of excuse to reject the insanity defence.[13] Likewise, proposals to add

[11] To understand all is to forgive all. The proverb is usually taken to assume that one understands another's behaviour when one knows the causes of that behaviour.

[12] About this kind of common sense, see Hyman Gross, *A Theory of Criminal Justice* (New York: Oxford University Press, 1979), 327–8; Stephen Morse, 'Crazy Behavior, Morals, and Science: An Analysis of Mental Health Law', *Southern California Law Review*, Vol. 51 (1978), 527–654, at 562; Morse, 'Failed Explanations and Criminal Responsibility: Experts and the Unconscious', *Virginia Law Review*, Vol. 68 (1982), 971–1084, at 1030.

[13] See Norval Morris, *Madness and The Criminal Law* (Chicago: University of Chicago Press, 1982), 53–76; see also Moore, 'The Determinist Theory of Excuses', *Ethics*, Vol. 95 (1985), 909–19 (reviewing Morris on this point). The American Medical Association has also accepted this line of argument in its Hinckley-inspired proposal to abolish the insanity defence. See Committee on Medicolegal Problems of the Am. Medical Ass'n., *Report of Conclusions and Recommendations Regarding the Insanity Defence* (Washington D.C., 1983).

new defences also are frequently based on the discovery of some new cause of criminal behaviour. Consider the late Chief Judge Bazelon's proposals to excuse those whose environment caused them to become criminals.[14] Or consider the debate about brainwashing that the Patty Hearst case occasioned. Brainwashing may be urged as a defence simply because brainwashing identifies a factor that causes criminal behaviour.[15] Proposals to create excuses for persons with an extra Y-chromosome[16] or for women suffering from premenstrual-tension syndrome[17] also are often based on causal grounds. One can intelligently assess these proposals to abolish or add excuses only if one has first answered the question common to all of them: Is causation the core of excuse?

Second, adoption of the causal theory of excuse leads many judges and theorists to slant their interpretations of the existing legal excuses. When the excuse of duress is applied in a particular case, for example, a judge must decide how serious and immediate a threat the accused must have experienced before he is excused. A causal theorist will pose the question in terms of whether the threat or the actor's will was the cause of the criminal act.[18] Or consider

[14] David Bazelon, 'The Morality of the Criminal Law', *Southern California Law Review*, Vol. 49 (1976), 385–405, at 388–98; see also *United States* v. *Alexander*, 471 F 2d 923, 957–65 (DC Cir. 1973) (as amended) (Bazelon, CJ, dissenting), *cert. denied*, 409 US 1044 (1972); Stephen Morse, 'The Twilight of Welfare Criminology: A Reply to Judge Bazelon', *Southern California Law Review*, Vol. 49 (1976), 1247–68.

[15] But see Comment, 'Brainwashing: Fact, Fiction and Criminal Defense', *University of Missouri-Kansas City Law Review*, Vol. 44 (1976), 438–79, at 460–1.

[16] See *People* v. *Yukl*, 83 Misc. 2d 364, 368–72 NYS 2d 313, 317–20 (Sup. Ct. 1975) (rejecting the XYY genetic evidence, but only because 'the genetic imbalance theory of crime causation has not been satisfactorily established and accepted'). As noted in the *Yukl* opinion, other courts in France, Australia, and New York have allowed evidence of XYY to go to the jury as a separate defence or as part of the insanity defence. Id. For discussions of the defence, see David Saxe, 'Psychiatry, Sociopathy and the XYY Chromosome Syndrome', *Tulsa Law Journal*, Vol. 6 (1970), 243–56; Lawrence Taylor, 'Genetically-Influenced Antisocial Conduct and the Criminal Justice System', *Cleveland State Law Review*, Vol. 31 (1982), 61–75; Note, 'The XYY Chromosome Defense', *Georgetown Law Journal*, Vol. 57 (1969), 892–922.

[17] No American court has yet considered the PMS defence. Sympathetic to the defence on purely causal grounds are Wallach and Rubin, 'The Premenstrual Syndrome and Criminal Responsibility', *University of California-Los Angeles Law Review*, Vol. 19 (1971) 210–312; see also Note, 'Premenstrual Syndrome: A Criminal Defense', *Notre Dame Law Review*, Vol. 59 (1983), 253–69 (discussing successful use of PMS as a mitigating factor in England).

[18] The question is so put in *R* v. *Hudson* [1971] 2 All ER 244.

the irresistible-impulse version of the insanity defence, which requires a judge to decide how compelled an accused must have been in order to be excused. A causal theorist again will interpret compulsion in terms of causation. Was the actor's conscious will the cause of his criminal act (in which case he was not 'irresistibly impelled')? Or was his unconscious motive the cause of his criminal act (in which case he was impelled to act by a factor he could not resist)?[19] If the causal theory of excuse is wrong, as I shall urge, some other interpretation of these defences is necessary.

Third, some of those accepting the causal theory will be psychiatrists called to testify as experts in criminal trials. It is no secret that many psychiatrists accept the causal theory as the best moral theory of excuse.[20] They may consciously or unconsciously frame their testimony about legal excuses accordingly.[21] Whether or not the causal theory of excuse is right will make a great difference in how we assess the weight and relevance of such testimony.

Fourth, as I show in Section IV, acceptance of the causal theory of excuse may lead to an unfortunate cynicism about the moral basis of the criminal law. If one accepts the determinist thesis that all events, including all human behaviour, are caused, and if one believes that causation excuses, then one must believe that moral responsibility is an illusion on which liability to criminal punishment cannot be built. For some cynics, this conclusion will lead to a purely utilitarian theory of punishment and of legal excuse.[22] For others, this conclusion will generate a deeper scepticism about the rationality of the substantive criminal law on any grounds, moral

[19] The question is so stated in *Pollard* v. *United States*, 171 F Supp. 474, 478 (ED Mich.), rev'd., 282 F 2d 450 (6th Cir. 1959), *mandate clarified*, 285 F 2d 81 (6th Cir. 1960).

[20] This was certainly true of the earlier psychiatrists who regarded responsibility as an illusion solely because they believed all behaviour was caused. See, e.g., Karl Menninger, *The Crime of Punishment* (New York: Viking Press, 1968). For a softer view, see Katz, 'Law, Psychiatry and Free Will', *International Review of Psycho-Analysis*, Vol. 5 (1978), 257. In 1945 the American Bar Association expressed concern over the determinist inclinations of psychoanalysis and the courts' inevitable problems with psychoanalytic testimony. 'Report of the Special Committee on the Rights of the Mentally Ill', *Annual Reports of the American Bar Association*, Vol. 70 (1945), 338–42, at 339.

[21] For a confession by my former colleague who manipulated testimony so as to fit his own causal theory of excuse, see Bernard Diamond, 'Criminal Responsibility of the Mentally Ill', *Stanford Law Review*, Vol. 14 (1961), 59–86, at 61–2.

[22] See Morris Eagle, 'Responsibility, Unconscious Motivation, and Social Order', *International Journal of Law and Psychiatry*, Vol. 6 (1983), 263–91.

or utilitarian.[23] In either case, such cynicism is pernicious and debilitating for those who suffer from it. Yet they can only be justified if the causal theory of excuse is right.

Even if the causal theory of excuse were not so widely accepted, we should examine it for the same reason we examine any other plausible theory about an area of law. Rejecting a theory often paves the way for formulation of better theories, theories that may capture the plausibility of the rejected theory while avoiding its mistakes. Building such general theories is part and parcel of the larger enterprise of seeking the best general expression of our criminal laws, a traditional task of academic criminal lawyers for at least a century.

III. THE SEDUCTIVE PLAUSIBILITY OF THE CAUSAL THEORY OF EXCUSE

Because the causal theory of excuse is my own reconstruction of a view to be found as an implicit (if crucial) premise in the thought of many criminal law theoreticians, I shall here draw out why such a theory seems plausible. Part of the motive for presenting in a sympathetic light a view with which I disagree and against which I later argue is to help causal theorists recognize themselves. Because a theory as above described has two dimensions, I shall hold up my 'mirror' to causal theorists from two angles, that of legal doctrine and that of moral correctness.

A. The Doctrinal Plausibility of the Purely Descriptive Part of the Theory

In the legal doctrines of excuse, one might find strong suggestions that the causal theory is *the* theory of excuse. From such suggestions one might conclude that the established doctrines fit with (that is, follow deductively from) the causal theory. In elaborating on these suggestions, I will follow the highly inclusionary, three-part taxonomy of the excuse defences developed in section I.[24]

---

[23] See Mark Kelman, 'Interpretive Construction in the Substantive Criminal Law', *Stanford Law Review*, Vol. 33 (1981), 591–673.

[24] Because we shall return to it later, it is helpful to summarize this three-part taxonomy of excuse defences as follows:

    I. The True Excuses

cont./

1. The True Excuses

a. Compulsion Excuses

The excuse of duress is made out when the accused has performed an otherwise criminal act under the threat of death or serious bodily injury. Causation is part of the test for duress because a defence exists only if the threat both 'causes the defendant reasonably to believe that the only way to avoid imminent death or serious bodily injury to himself or another is to engage in conduct which violates the literal terms of the criminal law, . . . and causes the defendant to engage in that conduct'.[25] In other words, the threat must cause the criminal act before it can operate as a legal excuse. Sometimes these causal requirements are stated in a way that makes causation by the threat rule out causation by the will of the actor. An English court of appeal, for example, recently ruled that duress excuses an accused 'if the will of the accused [was] overborne by threats of death or serious personal injury so the commission of the alleged offence was no longer the voluntary act of the accused'.[26] Such doctrines about the causal role of threats may seem to be specific instances of a general theory that causation by factors external to the actor's will excuses.

    A. Compulsion Excuses
        1. External Compulsions
           a. Duress
           b. Necessity
        2. Internal Compulsions
           a. Provocation
           b. Addiction
    B. Mistake
        1. (Some) Mistakes of Fact
        2. Mistake of Law
  II. Issues Negating the Case in Chief
    A. Unconsciousness, reflex, etc. (no action)
    B. Ignorance and Most Mistakes of Fact (No purpose, knowledge, or recklessness)
    C. Intervening Cause (No proximate causation)
  III. Status Defences
    A. Insanity
    B. Involuntary intoxication
    C. Infancy.

[25] W. LaFave and A. Scott, *Handbook on Criminal Law* (St Paul, Minn.: West, 1972), 374.
[26] *R* v. *Hudson* [1971] 2 All ER 244, 246.

The excuse of necessity can exculpate an accused when natural circumstance, rather than another's threats, has compelled his criminal act.[27] To the extent that it is recognized at all as an excuse, necessity is put in terms of 'irresistible force', 'overwhelming pressure', or 'teleological causation'.[28] These metaphors may be taken to suggest that like duress, necessity excuses because it has to some degree caused the accused's criminal act.

In American law, provocation is a means of mitigating the punishment for intentional homicides by reducing the crime from murder to voluntary manslaughter. Thus, it serves as an excuse, albeit a partial one. Often courts treat the provoking circumstance as a cause that competes with the defendant's own will. They excuse the defendant only when the external circumstances are the 'dominant cause' of the crime. As the Wisconsin Supreme Court once stated the rule, a defendant is legally provoked (and thus partially excused) when the provoking situation can be said 'to cause him, uncontrollably, to act from the impelling force of the disturbing cause, rather than from any real wickedness of heart'.[29]

Addiction—the constitutional defence of being addicted to drugs or alcohol—is distinct from any common law or statutory defence of intoxication. In *Robinson* v. *California*,[30] the US Supreme Court held it unconstitutional ('cruel and unusual punishment') to punish a drug addict for being a drug addict. A decade later, language in *Powell* v. *Texas*[31] indicated that the compelled nature of drug addiction had been crucial to the *Robinson* decision. In *Powell*, which suggested that alcoholics could not be punished for being alcoholics, five members of the Court were prepared to hold that an addict's non-public *use* of alcohol was compelled and therefore excused.[32] Further, they thought that the compulsive nature of drug addiction or alcoholism lies in the fact that these addictions are 'caused and maintained by something other than the moral fault of the alcoholic'.[33] Again, the doctrinal suggestion is that it is because

[27] Sometimes necessity is miscategorized as a justification, as in W. Lafave and A. Scott, *supra* n. 25, at 381; sometimes it is not recognized as a defence at all.
[28] George Fletcher, *supra* n. 4, at 819–20; Jerome Hall, *General Principles of Criminal Law*, 2nd ed. (Indianapolis: Bobbs-Merrill, 1960), 425.
[29] *Johnson* v. *State*, 129 Wis. 146, 160, 108 NW 55, 61 (1906).
[30] 370 US 660 (1962).
[31] 392 US 514 (1968).
[32] See id. at 548–9 (White, J, concurring); id. at 567–8 (Fortas, J, dissenting, joined by Douglas, Brennan and, Stewart, JJ).
[33] Id. at 561 (Fortas, J, dissenting).

alcoholism *causes* them to drink that alcoholics cannot be blamed for using alcohol.

b. *Mistake Excuses*

A causal theorist has a difficult time accommodating the excuse of mistake of fact within his theory. He has two routes open to him. First, he could treat beliefs as unchosen causes of behaviour. Beliefs, in other words, would be causal factors external to the will of the actor.[34] Therefore, according to the causal theory, they would excuse the actor from responsibility for any behaviour that they cause. Pursuing this route further, a causal theorist would say that mistaken beliefs cause behaviour and thus excuse, whereas true beliefs do not cause behaviour and do not excuse.

This route, whatever its plausibility or implausibility as a matter of psychological fact, does not fit legal doctrines about mistake of fact. What the causal theorist would like in the way of legal doctrine would be a requirement that the accused's mistaken belief must have caused his criminal act before he is excused. Yet legal doctrine does not impose such a causal requirement. Consider, for example, the concept of wilful blindness. Under the Model Penal Code's definition of this concept, a defendant who has a belief that would otherwise subject him to liability is excused if he also has a mistaken belief to the contrary. For example, a defendant who is aware of a high probability that his car is full of marijuana is excused from liability for transporting marijuana across the US border if he also believes (mistakenly) that there was no marijuana in his car.[35] The Model Penal Code does not require that the mistaken belief cause the defendant to drive the car (and the marijuana) across the border. His mistaken belief excuses him even though, had he known the marijuana was in the car, he still would have crossed the border.

---

[34] On the difficult question of whether beliefs are external to the will of the actor, see Barbara Winters, 'Acquiring Beliefs at Will', *Philosophy Research Archives*, Vol. 4 (1978), 433 and Winters, 'Believing at Will', *Journal of Philosophy*, Vol. 76 (1979), 243–56. In the text I allow the causal theorist alternative assumptions on this question.

[35] Model Penal Code §2.02(7) (Proposed Official Draft 1962): 'Requirement of Knowledge Satisfied by Knowledge of High Probability. When knowledge of the existence of a particular fact is an element of the offense, such knowledge is established if a person is aware of a high probability of its existence, unless he actually believes that it does not exist.'

The second route open to the causal theorist is to concede that all beliefs, both true and mistaken, operate as causes of behaviour, but to argue that beliefs are not causes external to the actor's will. The relevant causal connection thus would not be between beliefs and behaviour, but between beliefs and the factors producing those beliefs. When certain factors cause the accused to believe that he has no marijuana in his car, then he is excused. If, however, in the absence of these factors he chooses to believe that there is no marijuana in his car, then he is not excused. The causal theorist will classify chosen beliefs as uncaused and therefore restrict the excuse of mistake of fact to cases in which actor's beliefs are caused by factors external to his will.[36]

Mistake of law is not as troublesome to the causal theorist. To begin with, most mistakes of law do not excuse. 'Ignorance of the law is no excuse' is a time-honoured maxim of Anglo-American jurisprudence. Mistakes of law that do excuse can be divided into four classes: (1) mistakes about legal conclusions the accused must draw in order to have the *mens rea* required for the offence (for example, an alleged thief claims he did not know the property he took was 'owned by another'); (2) mistakes about whether an accused's act will aid an official in performing a public duty (for example, an accused charged with assault claims he thought he was helping a police officer make an arrest); (3) mistakes about the existence of a criminal prohibition when knowledge of the prohibition was not reasonably available to the public; and (4) mistakes of law induced by reliance upon official advice that proves to be erroneous.

The causal theorist can explain the first class of mistakes of law the same way he explains mistakes of fact. Such mistaken beliefs excuse only when they are caused by factors external to the will of the actor. If he chooses to believe, for example, that another's property is his own, then that (uncaused) belief will not excuse.

---

[36] Admittedly, even in the second route the causal theorist is bending doctrine a bit in order to make it fit his theory. For he is reading into the Model Penal Code's concept of wilful blindness a limitation transplanted from the English version of the doctrine (according to which the essence of wilful blindness is purposeful avoidance of knowledge). On the English doctrine, see Glanville Williams, *Criminal Law—The General Part*, 2nd ed. (London: Stevens & Sons, 1961), 157–9. Still, there is some plausibility in thinking that a chosen (mistaken) belief is not an excuse, even under the Model Penal Code.

The causal theorist need not account for the second and third exceptions to the rule that ignorance of the law is no excuse. These exceptions are not excuses at all, but are extrinsic policy defences. We eliminate responsibility for those who act in furtherance of what they believe to be an official's public duty in order to encourage aid to officials; we eliminate responsibility when laws are not reasonably available to citizens in order to maximize the liberty of all citizens. We 'excuse' particular criminals only as a means of achieving these extrinsic social goals, not because such criminals are not culpable.

To explain the fourth kind of excusing mistake of law, the causal theorist will say that the official who gives the wrong advice causes the defendant's criminal behaviour. The official is like the coercer who by his threats forces the accused to do what the coercer wants. The official gets his way by trickery or stupidity, not by threats, but the important causal element is the same: a third party, not the defendant, causes the harm. Therefore the defendant must be excused. According to this view, mistake of law is an excuse much like the subjective version of the entrapment defence, which excuses the accused if a government agent induced him to commit a crime he was not already predisposed to commit. In these cases, a causal theorist like Mark Kelman would assert the '[d]efendant's conduct is deemed determined by the [government] agent: The defendant would not have committed the crime had the agent never come along with the plan.'[37]

2. Excuses Negating the Case in Chief

a. No Action

There are many states or conditions an accused may assert to disprove that he performed a voluntary act. These include hypnotic suggestion, sleep, unconsciousness, hypoglycaemic episodes, reflex reactions, epilepsy, and the use of the defendant's body by another. The causal theorist wishes to show that all these conditions preclude voluntary action solely because they are causes of the defendant's behaviour.

Instances of human behaviour that are not actions fall into three categories.[38] First, there are motions of a person's body in which his own muscles are not involved. If one is carried into the street

[37] Kelman, *supra* n. 23, at 644.   [38] See Moore, *supra* n. 5, at 73.

by police officers, hurled through a window, or has one's arm moved by another person or by a falling rock, one has performed no action and cannot fairly be held responsible for the harm one's body may have caused. Second, there are motions of the body caused by the movement of one's muscles but over which the self— the acting, willing person—had no control. Reflex reactions to the doctor's hammer or to multiple bee stings are examples, as are an epileptic's movements during a seizure or a diabetic's movements during a hypoglycaemic episode. Third, there are motions of the body that we do not treat as the defendant's acts, even though they look identical to actions of an intelligent, goal-seeking agent. They pursue an intelligible goal by means of behavioural routines that may be both complicated and efficient. Yet despite appearances, these are not actions if the defendant was asleep, unconscious, or in a hypnotic trance. Because these motions have such a strong appearance of inner-directedness, they may tempt us to ascribe them to some second agent within the actor. Even if we do so fractionate the self, we do not attribute such behaviour to the agent who is the conscious will, the responsible self.[39]

A causal theorist will seize upon each of these three kinds of cases as instances of his theory. Each involves a kind of non-action, he will say, because an external cause precludes attributing the motion to the defendant as his act. In the first case, the external cause is a natural factor or the act of another person. In the second case, there is again an external cause, even though it operates through the muscles of the accused. In the third case, there may be an external cause, such as post-hypnotic suggestion or a shot to the stomach inducing unconsciousness. Or, as in the typical cases of somnambulism and unconsciousness, there may be no external cause. The causal theorist may attribute the defendant's movements to some internal stimulus or even to some second agent within the defendant. In either case, it is not the defendant who directs his movements, but his unconscious, his dream censor, or his bad digestion. His movements are non-actions because caused by some factor external to the actor's conscious will.

The causal theorist would take the way 'voluntary act' is typically defined as providing doctrinal support for his theory.

[39] Or so I argued in ch. 6 herein and in ch. 10 of Michael Moore, *Act and Crime: The Philosophy of Action and its Implications for Criminal Law* (Oxford: Oxford University Press, 1993).

According to the Model Penal Code, for example, an act is not voluntary if it was produced by a reflex or a convulsion, if it occurred during unconsciousness, sleep, or hypnosis or resulted from hypnotic suggestion, or if it otherwise 'was not a product of the effort or determination of the actor, either conscious or habitual'.[40] This enumeration of negating conditions suggests that we may discover what an action is only by identifying the conditions that preclude action,[41] and further, that these conditions exist whenever external causes for the behaviour in question can be found. In other words, such a doctrine may be taken to suggest that causation by factors external to the will of the actor precludes action and therefore negates responsibility.

b. *No* Mens Rea *(Ignorance)*

If one is ignorant of some circumstance affecting one's act, of the likelihood of some consequence of the act, or of the risk of either of these, then one does not have the belief states necessary for intention, purpose, knowledge, or recklessness as those terms are used in American criminal law. Ignorance, unlike mistake, should be regarded as simply the negation of these forms of *mens rea*.

A causal theorist will seek to explain the requirement of *mens rea* (and thus, why ignorance is an excuse) in the same way he explains the requirement of a voluntary act: both action and intention are possible only when no causes external to the actor's will produce the behaviour in question. Therefore, if causes beyond the actor's control produce his criminal behaviour, the actor cannot have any of the mental states required for *mens rea*. The legal doctrine requiring *mens rea*, accordingly, is simply an instance of a more general causal principle: there can be no responsibility for behaviour caused by factors beyond the actor's control.

Sometimes the criminal law specifies exactly what sort of causal factors may be sufficient to preclude intention or purpose. It is often said that a mentally ill or seriously intoxicated defendant cannot have the intention required for crime. The insanity defence is sometimes rationalized in this way.[42] More typically, the alleged

---

[40] Model Penal Code § 2.01(2) (Proposed Official Draft 1962).

[41] A number of theorists subscribe to this view, following Herbert Hart, *supra*, n. 1.

[42] See, e.g., Goldstein and Katz, 'Abolish the "Insanity Defense"—Why Not?', *Yale Law Journal*, Vol. 72 (1963), 853–76, at 863–4 (assuming that intention is negated by insanity).

inconsistency between mental illness/intoxication and intention only reduces the gravity of the offence by providing the defendant with the partial excuse of diminished capacity.[43] In either case, it is assumed that causation by some external factor precludes the intent required for culpability.

c. No Proximate Causation (Intervening Cause)

According to the direct cause conception of proximate cause, a defendant's action is the proximate cause of some harm if: (a) the act was a cause in fact of the harm; and (b) no other cause intervened between the time of the defendant's act and the occurrence of the harm to 'break the causal chain' and relieve the defendant of responsibility.

Again the causal theorist will claim that this legal doctrine exemplifies his general principle that external causes excuse. The external causes in this case are those called in law 'intervening causes'. According to Hart and Honoré, they are of two kinds: abnormal natural events amounting to a coincidence, and voluntary human action.[44] Whenever one of these external causes intervenes between act and harm, the first actor is excused.

Some causal theorists offer a further explanation of why intervening action by a second human agent breaks the causal chain between the first agent and the harm. According to Professor Kadish,[45] the legal doctrines defining causation and complicity presume that the second action is necessarily free; if it is an action at all, it cannot be caused. The second action, because it is uncaused, acts as a barrier through which causation by the first agent cannot be traced. According to this view, intervening acts by human agents become intervening causes precisely because causation of action is conceptually impossible. In some such way causal theorists like Kadish get double usage out of their conceptual claims that actions are necessarily uncaused: not only does this claim explain why we

---

[43] See Stephen Morse, 'Undiminished Confusion in Diminished Capacity', *Journal of Criminal Law and Criminology*, Vol. 75 (1984), 1–55, at 40–50 (rejecting the notion that mental disease or intoxication completely negates intention); see also Peter Arenella, 'The Diminished Capacity and Diminished Responsibility Defenses: Two Children of a Doomed Marriage', *Columbia Law Review*, Vol. 77 (1977), 827–65.

[44] H. L. A. Hart and A. M. Honoré, *Causation in the Law* (Oxford: Clarendon Press, 1959), 64–76, 292–312.

[45] Sanford Kadish, 'Complicity, Cause and Blame: A Study in the Interpretation of Doctrine', *California Law Review*, Vol. 73 (1985), 323–410, at 333.

treat some behaviour as an action and some not, but it also explains why we have the doctrines about proximate causation that we do. In each instance, the causal theory is buttressed by this conceptual claim, the merits of which we will address later.

3. Status Defences

a. Insanity

A causal theorist will not regard insanity as a defence of status; rather, he will regard it as an excuse on a par with the true excuses of compulsion or mistake. For him, insanity excuses because it causes criminal acts. Legal doctrine clearly has been influenced by this view of insanity. The New Hampshire test for insanity, which asks only whether the criminal act was the (causal) product of mental illness, directly expresses this causal theory.[46] The landmark opinion of Justice Doe, the principal architect of the New Hampshire test, makes his causal rationale quite clear:

For, if the alleged act of a defendant, was the act of his mental disease, it was not 'in law' his act, and he is no more responsible for it than he would be if it had been the act of his involuntary intoxication, or of another person using the defendant's hand against his utmost resistance . . . [W]hen disease is the propelling, uncontrollable power, the man is as innocent as the weapon . . .[47]

Former Chief Judge Bazelon's rationale for the more recent *Durham* insanity test also relied on the causal theory. The *Durham* test, like the New Hampshire test, exculpated from criminal responsibility those whose acts were the product of a mental disease. According to Judge Bazelon:

The legal and moral traditions of the western world require that those who, of their own free will . . . commit acts which violate the law, shall be criminally responsible for those acts. Our traditions also require that where such acts stem from and are the product of a mental disease . . . moral blame shall not attach, and hence there will not be criminal responsibility.[48]

Like Justice Doe, Judge Bazelon contrasted free and therefore culpable acts, with caused acts, which are excused because they are caused.

---

[46] See *State* v. *Pike*, 49 NH 399, 441–2 (1869) (Doe, J), overruled on other grounds, *Hardy* v. *Merrill*, 56 NH 227 (1875).

[47] Id. at 441.

[48] *Durham* v. *United States*, 214 F 2d 862, 876 (DC Cir. 1954) (footnote omitted), overruled, *United States* v. *Brawner*, 471 F 2d 969 (DC Cir. 1972).

The causal theory is equally evident in the 'irresistible impulse' test for insanity. The Alabama Supreme Court's leading formulation of that test in the nineteenth century described the 'duress of mental disease' as destroying the free agency of the insane. One prong of the Alabama test was whether 'the alleged crime was so connected with such mental disease, in the relation of cause and effect, as to have been the product of it *solely*'.[49]

More generally, all tests of legal insanity require that the defective mental condition be causally connected to the criminal act it purports to excuse. This is as true of the 'cognitive' versions of the test as of 'volitional' versions.[50] What this doctrinal fact may be taken to evidence is the general principle that any defendant who is caused to do something by events beyond his control must be excused. This principle conjures up a picture of insanity as 'an unseen ligament pressing on the mind, drawing it to consequences which it sees but cannot avoid'.[51]

b. *Involuntary Intoxication*

Unlike voluntary intoxication, involuntary intoxication is a defence in American law and not merely a means of disproving *mens rea*. The rationale for this defence may seem to be quite straightforward: if becoming intoxicated was not the actor's fault (because involuntary), and if he would not have committed the crime but for the intoxication, then he is not responsible for the crime. Whatever it was, human or natural, that caused him to become intoxicated is at fault; the actor is not responsible because his behaviour was caused by factors beyond his control. This is, of course, exactly what a causal theorist would say.

T. B. Macaulay seems to have adopted the causal rationale in drafting the Proposed Indian Penal Code, which included the following provision:

Nothing is an offense which a person does in consequence of being in state of intoxication, provided that either the substance which intoxicated him was administered to him without his knowledge, or against his will, or that he was ignorant that it possessed any intoxicating quality.[52]

[49] *Parsons* v. *State*, 81 Ala. 577, 597, 2 So. 854, 866–7 (1887).

[50] See Morse, 'Crazy Behavior', *supra* n. 12, at 531–2, 560–90, for a discussion of this.

[51] The language is that of Gibson, CJ, in *Commonwealth* v. *Mosler*, 4 Pa. 264, 267 (1846).

[52] T. B. Macaulay, *A Penal Code Prepared by the Indian Law Commissioners* (1837), 13–14, cited in S. Kadish, S. Schulhofer, and M. Paulsen, *Criminal*

This type of causal test has been accepted by only a few jurisdictions. One apparent example is Maine, whose Supreme Court recently held that 'there is no criminal responsibility for any acts otherwise criminal . . . if they are caused by defendant's intoxication which is not self-induced'.[53]

Legal doctrine is against the causal theorist in that most jurisdictions do not adopt Macaulay's straightforward causal test. In the vast majority of American jurisdictions, involuntary intoxication will excuse only when, in addition to causing behaviour, it also causes a severe diminishment of the actor's reasoning capacities.[54] The causal theorist cannot show that this extradoctrinal requirement follows from his theory. He should urge its elimination. Failing that, he should urge that this extra requirement be interpreted so that it becomes harmless surplusage: if the intoxication caused the criminal behaviour, it necessarily diminished the actor's reasoning capacity.

c. *Infancy*

A causal theorist attempting to explain why infancy excuses would liken it to his conception of insanity: the very young, like the insane, lack free will. According to this rationale, *everything* the infant does is excused because an infant is not yet free of the grip of a universal causation. Although 'infancy' does not name some entity as a cause of crimes in the way 'insanity' arguably does, still, the causal theorist will assert, causation is the core of this excuse too, because what excuses infants as a class is the fact that their behaviour is completely determined.[55]

Law and its Processes: Cases and Materials, 4th edn. (Boston: Little, Brown, 1983), 819.

[53] *State* v. *Rice*, 379 A 2d 140, 145 (Me. 1977) (footnote omitted).

[54] See W. LaFave and A. Scott, *supra* n. 25, at 347 n. 45.

[55] Since eventually infants do become responsible actors (when they become adults), the causal theorist is committed to the partial determinist view that there can be 'some' causation. (For an explanation of partial determinism, see *infra* Part IV, s. B). This implication makes the causal theorist's account of the infancy excuse very implausible. See Peter Strawson, 'Freedom and Resentment', in Gary Watson, ed., *Free Will*, G. Watson, ed., (Oxford: Oxford University Press, 1982), 75: 'Would it not be grotesque to think of the development of the child as a progressive or patchy emergence from an area in which its behavior is . . . determined into an area in which it isn't?' Yet the alternative implication possible here seems even more grotesque: that all of a sudden what was determined becomes free.

B. The Moral Plausibility of the Causal Theory of Excuses

The causal theorist will thus conclude that his general theory of excuse—that people are excused whenever their behaviour is caused by factors beyond their control—satisfies the descriptive requirement of a good legal theory: the existing legal doctrines of excuse follow from it as deductive consequences. As discussed earlier, he also must show that it is a good moral theory. What makes the causal theory morally correct, he will propose, is the principle that no one should be blamed for what he could not help doing. As H. L. A. Hart once observed:

[M]ost lawyers, laymen and moralists, considering the legal doctrine of mens rea and the excuses that the law admits, would conclude that what the law has done here is to reflect, albeit imperfectly, a fundamental principle of morality that a person is not to be blamed for what he has done if he could not help doing it. This is how Blackstone at the beginning of modern legal history looked at the various excuses which the law accepted. He said they were accepted because 'the concurrence of the will when it has its choice either to do or avoid the act in question' is the only thing that renders human actions praiseworthy or culpable.[56]

We can call this principle the principle of responsibility. The plausibility of such a moral principle should be readily apparent. What could be more unfair than punishing someone for something he could not help? Samuel Butler satirized the opposite view when, in *Erewhon*, he describes the 'justice' of a trial for the crime of pulmonary consumption. The trial judge, anticipating a charge of unfairness for meting out a severe sentence to the diseased defendant, responds:

It is all very well for you to say that you came of unhealthy parents, and had a severe accident in your childhood which permanently undermined your constitution; excuses such as these are the ordinary refuge of the criminal; but they cannot for one moment be listened to by the ear of justice. I am not here to enter upon curious metaphysical questions as to the origin of this or that. . . . There is no question of how you came to be wicked, but only this—namely, are you wicked or not?[57]

---

[56] H. L. A. Hart, 'Punishment and the Elimination of Responsibility', in *Punishment and Responsibility* (Oxford: Oxford University Press 1968), 174 (footnote omitted).

[57] Samuel Butler, *Erewhon* (London: Trubner, 1872), 107.

Our intuitions may well reject the moral premises of the Erewhonian legal system; it does matter to us how the crime originated. It may seem plausible that if the crime was caused by events over which the accused had no control, he could not help committing the crime and therefore should be excused.

IV. THE UNPALATABILITY OF THE CAUSAL THEORY OF EXCUSES: DETERMINISM, THE CAUSAL THEORY, AND RESPONSIBILITY

A. Determinism and the Causal Theory

Many people find determinism plausible, as do I. Determinism tells us that human choices and actions are caused and that those causes themselves have causes. One reason this idea is so plausible is that its opposite, indeterminism, is so implausible. After all, is it not extraordinary to think that part of our most basic metaphysical picture of what the universe is like—in terms of causal relations—should have no application to persons? Is it not extraordinary to think that agents who can clearly cause changes to occur in the world are themselves uncaused? We are all quite literally Aquinas's uncaused causers—that is, God—on such indeterminist views.

This part is written for those causal theorists who find determinism plausible. A serious problem for such causal theorists is how, according to their theory of excuse, anyone can be held morally responsible. If one accepts determinism—the doctrine that every event, including human actions and willings, has a cause— then it is hard to see why everyone is not excused for all actions. The formal structure of this argument is that of a *reductio ad absurdum*.

1. All human actions and choices are caused by factors beyond the actor's control (the determinist premise).
2. If an action or choice is caused by factors beyond the actor's control, then that action or choice is morally excused (the moral version of the causal theory of excuse).
3. If an action or choice is morally excused, then that action should not be legally punishable (the theory of punishment making moral culpability at least a necessary condition of legal liability).

Therefore:

4. No actions and choices should be legally punishable (the conclusion of universal legal excuse).

The most direct way to answer another person's *reductio* argument is to embrace the conclusion as not at all absurd. Yet the causal theorist can ill afford to do this by embracing the existence of universal legal excuse, for how then would his theory be a theory of legal excuse? His causal theory might contribute to an argument for radical reform of our criminal law by the elimination of any liability to punishment, but it is hard to see how it could serve as theory of the existing excuses of criminal law. Those excuses presuppose that some people are to be punished even if others are to be excused.

In addition, it surely is unpalatable to think that no one should be punished. As long as one does not allow oneself the easy out of saying that involuntary treatment does not constitute punishment, surely there are good reasons to want a legal system that punishes at least some offenders. If so, then for those reasons too the conclusion of the argument is a difficult one to swallow for the causal theorist, no less than for anyone else.

This leaves the causal theorist having to give up one of the three premises leading to the absurd conclusion that no one ought to be legally punishable. The first premise, that of determinism, he may find hard to relinquish. He may not share William James's professed ability to will to disbelieve determinism.[58] He may think, as I do, that determinism is simply true. The third premise is the theory of punishment according to which moral culpability is at least necessary for legal liability. The causal theorist should baulk at giving this up too. For to give up this premise would commit him to either a purely utilitarian or a purely rehabilitative theory of punishment, each of which is subject to deep and well-charted objections.[59]

If the causal theorist can give up neither of the other premises, he must give up his own theory in order to avoid the absurd conclusion that no one ought to be punished. It cannot be the case that moral culpability is eliminated just because an actor was caused to

---

[58] William James, 'The Dilemma of Determinism', in *The Will to Believe* (New York: Longmans, Green and Co., 1898), 147.

[59] See H. L. A. Hart, 'Changing Conceptions of Responsibility', in *Punishment and Responsibility* (Oxford: Oxford University Press, 1968), 186; H. L. A. Hart, *supra* n. 56, at 158, 209; M. Moore, *supra* n. 5, at 234–5, 238–40.

act by factors beyond his control. A determinist who believes in punishment but not in unjust punishment can come to no other conclusion.

Despite this *reductio* argument, many causal theorists who are determinists believe they need not abandon their causal theory. Very generally, they take one of two approaches: (1) they waffle on determinism in ways that seem to suggest some room for moral responsibility; or (2) they adopt an 'as if' strategy whereby we lawyers can pretend that people are free even though they really are not. I shall explore each of these approaches below.

B. The Partial Determinist Strategies

1. Degree Determinism   There are four waffling strategies open to causal theorists who are convinced that some form of determinism is correct and who yet reject the conclusion that no one is fairly punishable. The first and most popular is what I shall call determinism by degrees, or degree determinism. Degree determinism is a denial that all human actions are *fully* caused. The degree determinist believes in a continuum of freedom from causation: different actions can be more or less determined and thus more or less free. In his recent book on madness, Norval Morris assures us that there are 'degree[s] of freedom of choice on a continuum'.[60] Completely free actions and completely determined actions are ideal types, or as Morris calls them, 'polar conditions'.[61] All actions in the real world, Morris believes, will lie somewhere between the polar conditions. In order to salvage responsibility, the degree determinist needs an additional premise about where on the freedom/causation continuum responsibility ends and excuse begins. We might call this the 'baseline premise'. If we imagine free action to be at the low end of the continuum and determined action to be at the high end, we must draw a baseline above which actions are so determined that they must be excused and below which actions are so free that they cannot be excused. Morris appears to draw the baseline at the actions of those persons raised in conditions of gross social adversity. Morris believes they have just enough freedom to be fairly punished for their misdeeds.[62] Having established his baseline, Morris uses it to separate the responsible from the excused. Since Morris believes that the insane have as much freedom as

---

[60] Norval Morris, *supra* n. 13, at 61.   [61] Id.   [62] Id. at 62.

those raised in conditions of gross social adversity, he urges the abolition of the defence of insanity.

Degree determinism has many other adherents. Liberals like Bazelon also have seen the analogy between madness and social deprivation: both are at least somewhat 'criminogenic'.[63] Bazelon, however, draws the baseline lower on the continuum of degrees of causation than does Morris. Since the actions of *both* the mentally ill and the socially deprived are sufficiently determined, both should be excused.

Another haven for degree determinism is psychiatry. As indicated in the *Statement on the Insanity Defense* of the American Psychiatric Association, many psychiatrists are determinists who nonetheless believe that the moral issue raised by insanity is that of free will.[64] These psychiatrists also reconcile moral responsibility with their determinism by accepting Morris's continuum of freedom and causation. Stephen Morse recently has noted that in accepting the freedom/causation continuum, psychiatry aligns itself with certain common sense intuitions: 'Philosophically impure common sense consistently rejects the philosophically pure view [of the irrelevance of causation to responsibility] by assuming that the behaviour of all persons is subject to various causes and that these causes vary in their salience and strength.'[65]

Sheldon Glueck was another proponent of the degree-determinist continuum.[66] Glueck spelled out in more detail than have most causal theorists what it means to say that there is a continuum between free choice and determinism. Glueck found it helpful to 'imagine a simple chart which shows the freedom/determinism proportions of a feebleminded person, an extreme psychotic, an average "sociopathic" or psychopathic personality', and others. Then, Glueck told us, we might speculate that the feebleminded person's freedom/determinism mix 'will consist of, say, 10 percent . . . endowed intelligent free-choosing capacity, and 90

---

[63] See Bazelon, *supra* n. 14, at 394–7.

[64] See American Psychiatric Association, *Statement on the Insanity Defense* (Washington D.C., 1982), 8. For a further example of such thought in psychiatry, see Alan Stone, 'Psychiatry and Violence', in *Law, Psychiatry and Morality* (Washington, DC: US Government Printing Office, 1984), 53; Stone, 'Psychiatry and Morality: Three Criticisms', in *Law, Psychiatry and Morality*, 219–24.

[65] Morse, 'Failed Explanations', *supra* n. 12, at 1030.

[66] Sheldon Glueck, *Law and Psychiatry: Cold War or Entente Cordiale?* (Baltimore: Johns Hopkins University Press, 1962).

percent . . . predetermined blocking of freedom, of conscious, purposive choice and control'. By contrast, the 'chart of the psychopath or sociopath will consist of, say, 30 percent to 45 percent . . . amount of free-choice capacity, the balance to be rigidly controlled'. Glueck apparently set his baseline for responsibility at the 'free-choosing capacity of the "average, reasonable" or "prudent" abstract standard man of the law [which] will range, let us say, between 50 and 65 percent, leaving a 50 to 35 percent quantum of solid-line dominance'.[67]

I think very little sense can be made of any of this. It makes sense to say that we are determined or that we are free, but to speak of being partly determined or partly free makes as much sense as to speak of being partly pregnant.[68] To be sure, we can make comparative judgements that one cause is more important than another in producing behaviour. Indeed, there is quite a body of literature on the criteria we use in determining which conditions are more causally relevant than others in various contexts.[69] But none of this literature can make sense of the quite different comparative judgement about the relative importance of *all* causes on the one hand, and of freedom on the other. For the degree determinist, it has to be sensible to ask: how much causation was there? The problem is that such a question seems to make no sense at all.

Stephen Morse points out that one might attempt to work out the needed concept of 'degrees of causation' with the concept of

---

[67] Sheldon Glueck, *Law and Psychiatry: Cold War or Entente Cordiale?* (1962), at 12–13.

[68] Cf. Strawson, *supra* n. 55, at 75: 'Whatever sense of "determined" is required for stating the thesis of determinism, it can scarcely be such as to allow of compromise, borderline-style answers to the question, "Is this bit of behaviour determined or isn't it?" '

[69] Some of this literature deals with the question of why in historical analysis, ordinary speech, and the law, we will cite one necessary condition over others as 'the cause' of the harm. For examples, see Joel Feinberg, 'Action and Responsibility', in *Doing and Deserving: Essays in the Theory of Responsibility* (Princeton: Princeton University Press, 1970), 119; H. L. A. Hart and A. Honoré, *supra* n. 44, at 8–57; Morton White, *Foundations of Historical Knowledge* (Cambridge, Mass.: Harvard University Press, 1965), 105–81. Other literature deals with the sense to be made of one event being more important as a cause than another. See the discussions of causal apportionment in tort law in Kaye and Aickin, 'A Comment on Causal Apportionment', *Journal of Legal Studies*, Vol. 13 (1984), 191–208; Rizzo and Arnold, 'Causal Apportionment in the Law of Torts: An Economic Theory', *Columbia Law Review*, Vol. 80 (1980), 1399–429. Kaye and Aickin argue that one can make sense of causal apportionment only in terms of probabilities of *types* of events, not in terms of actual causal contributions to any particular event.

'predisposing causation', that is, causation that only predisposes, or makes more likely, bad behaviour but does not operate as either a necessary or a sufficient condition for that behaviour.[70] 'Strongly predisposing' would describe a factor that renders the bad behaviour highly likely, while 'weakly predisposing' would describe one that renders the behaviour only somewhat more likely. This is essentially a probabilistic notion. When certain factors make the probabilities of bad behaviour high enough (when a person is strongly predisposed to bad behaviour), responsibility is said to evaporate. Norval Morris seems to have exactly this probabilistic notion in mind when he talks about the comparative 'criminogenic effect' of various environmental or other factors.[71]

There is no doubt that predisposing causes exist. Explanations in terms of probabilistic laws—what Carl Hempel calls inductive-statistical explanations—are an unquestioned feature of both natural and social science.[72] It is also undoubtedly true that we will assign varying probabilities to the occurrence of bad behaviour depending upon which factors we use to explain or predict that behaviour. Yet the existence of these probabilistic explanations is not enough to resuscitate the idea of a causation/freedom continuum. These explanations correlate *types* of behaviour with *types* of causal factors. They do not purport to tell us to what degree a particular action is caused. They thus do not make intelligible and plausible a metaphysics of degrees of causation of *particular* actions.[73]

Only if one took the position that the only kind of explanation possible for human behaviour was of the probabilistic kind could one make plausible the metaphysics of degrees of causation for particular actions. If one could show that explanations of human behaviour are irreducibly probabilistic in the way explanations of the behaviour of electrons are irreducibly probabilistic, then perhaps the idea of predisposing causation could rescue the causation/freedom continuum.

Yet such a showing is to my mind very unlikely. It may well be that the factors social scientists cite as the causes of crime are not

---

[70] Morse, 'Failed Explanations', *supra* n. 12, at 1031. For further elucidation of the idea of a predisposing cause, see also Morse, 'Crazy Behavior', *supra* n. 12, at 564–6.

[71] Morris, *supra* n. 13, at 62.

[72] Carl Hempel, *Aspects of Scientific Explanation* (New York: Free Press, 1965).

[73] See Kaye and Aickin *supra* n. 69. See also Richard Wright, 'Actual Causation vs. Probabilistic Linkage: The Bane of Economic Analysis', *Journal of Legal Studies*, Vol. 14 (1985), 435–56.

sufficient conditions: they only make bad behaviour probable, not inevitable. Yet this lack of sufficient conditions may only reflect our ignorance of factors that inevitably produce the criminal behaviour. It is very controversial to assert that there is no set of sufficient conditions for human behaviour and that probabilistic explanations are the best we can give. Imagine a similar claim about explanations of the pattern of heads/tails landings of a coin that has been flipped repeatedly. Perhaps the only currently available explanation for a roughly fifty/fifty pattern of heads/tails is a probabilistic one. That does not rule out, however, the existence of a set of sufficient conditions that would explain each of the coin's landings and therefore also explain the overall pattern of landings. The physical laws governing matter in motion might explain the pattern of landings if only enough were known about the original force exerted on the coin each time it was flipped, the coin's physical features, the motion of the air, the features of the landing surface, and so forth.

To be sure, in subatomic physics a plausible case may be made for the claim that some events are *only* explainable in terms of probabilistic laws. But no similar case has yet been made about human behaviour.[74] Yet unless such a case is made, the thesis that there are strongly predisposing and weakly predisposing causes is not a metaphysical thesis that freedom and causation can exist in degrees; it can only be a thesis about the degree of our present ignorance. The degree determinist must therefore defend the dubious metaphysical position that human behaviour, like the behaviour of subatomic particles, *cannot* be explained by sets of sufficient conditions.[75]

---

[74] Adolf Grunbaum examines the issue and concludes that quantum physics is no help here. Grunbaum, 'Free Will and Laws of Human Behavior', in H. Feigl, W. Sellars, and K. Lehrer, eds., *New Readings in Philosophical Analysis* (New York: Century, Appleton, Crafts, 1972), 605, 620–2.

[75] Moreover, in defending this position the degree determinist cannot avail himself of some kind of Davidsonian non-reductionism. Donald Davidson has urged that the Intentional features of mental state and action individuation preclude the discovery of psychophysical laws about either of them. Donald Davidson, *Essays on Actions and Events* (New York: Oxford University Press, 1980), 245–59. Whether Davidson is right about this does not matter in the present context, for even if there can be no such laws connecting types of actions with *types* of physical events, it may well be the case that particular act-tokens are fully determined by some set of factors. (Indeed, Davidson seems to contemplate just such token/token identities and correlations even in the absence of any type/type identities and correlations.) The degree determinist does not need to show that types of actions cannot be explained by psychophysical laws, rather, he needs to show that *particular* actions cannot be

Not only must the degree determinist make plausible a metaphysics of degrees of causation, he also must show that the moral and legal excuses just reviewed apply only to actions that are highly probable because their occurrence is due to 'strongly predisposing' factors. No such showing has been made, nor, to my mind, is such a showing likely.[76] We would have to be convinced, for example, that there is a greater likelihood that an insane person, who is excused, will commit a crime than there is that a very greedy person, who is not excused, will steal money he finds lying in the street. No matter how certain we are that the greedy person will take the money, we will not be inclined in the least to excuse him. Yet, we can be totally unable to predict criminal tendencies in the very insane and still be quite willing to excuse them, in which case, excuse and responsibility do not correlate with strongly versus weakly predisposing factors.

2. Ignorance Determinism A strategy alternative to degree determinism is what might be called ignorance determinism. An ignorance determinist would admit that all human behaviour, like other events, is fully determined. Nonetheless, he might urge that what determines an actor's responsibility is not the degree to which the actor is caused to act, but rather the degree to which *we* have knowledge of the causes of his action. If studies showed us, for example, that eighty per cent of the children raised in a certain environment commit crimes, we would excuse them from responsibility. If there were no such studies and we were therefore ignorant of this probabilistic correlation, then those same children would be held fully responsible. Only those for whose actions social scientists could show strongly predisposing causes would be excused. In this way a partial determinist might seek to avoid the absurdity of degrees of causation and yet retain some notion that there is a continuum, in this case a continuum in the knowledge we possess about when behaviour is caused.

completely determined by physical factors in the way the position of an individual electron cannot be so determined. It is irrelevant whether laws about *types* of actions are or are not irreducibly probabilistic. After all, persons are held responsible for particular actions, not types of actions, and individual actions may be fully caused even if the only laws that can be cited to explain them are of a probabilistic kind.

[76] This argument has been made with respect to the specific defence of insanity. See Morse, 'Failed Explanations', *supra* n. 12, at 1031–2.

The problem with ignorance determinism is not that no continuum exists between our ignorance and our knowledge of the causes of various criminal acts. Rather, the problem lies in connecting that subjective probability continuum with responsibility. It is inconsistent with our basic moral beliefs to attribute responsibility according to our present, completely fortuitous, state of knowledge. If we truly believe that all behaviour is fully determined and that fully determined behaviour is not the actor's responsibility, it would be immoral to hold people responsible because *we* were ignorant of what caused them to act. To say otherwise would be tantamount to excusing those who have some particular excuse about which we have knowledge, but holding all others responsible because we are ignorant of what excuse they have—even though we believe that all of those others have some valid excuse. If causation by external factors excuses, it excuses everyone on determinist assumptions. Who is excused cannot be based on such a fortuity as how much of the causal story we happen to know at any particular time.

It may well be that what Stephen Morse calls 'philosophically impure common sense'[77] here joins Norval Morris and other theorists in urging some version of these first two strategies, whether based on degrees of causation, or on degrees of our own knowledge of causation. Undeniably, many people soften their judgements about responsibility when they know more of the causal story behind a person's bad behaviour. *Tout comprendre c'est tout pardonner* does indeed reflect such people's common sense beliefs about responsibility. Yet such philosophically impure common sense should not survive these insights into its philosophical impurity. If common sense believes that there can be a little bit of causation, then common sense is wrong—wrong because this belief is inconsistent with our basic metaphysical ideas about the kinds of causal relations that can exist. If common sense believes that the degree of an actor's responsibility can depend on the degree of our ignorance about a universally present, excusing condition, then common sense is wrong—wrong because this belief is inconsistent with our more basic moral belief that fortuitous factors unconnected to the actor can have nothing to do with his responsibility. Such inconsistencies cannot protect themselves under the mantle of common sense.

[77] See Morse, 'Failed Explanations', *supra* n. 12, at 1030.

3. Selective Determinism   A third kind of strategy that might occur to a causal theorist who is also a determinist might be called selective determinism.[78] A selective determinist will admit that all behaviour is fully caused, but he is selective about which causes excuse. If only some kinds of causes excuse, then determinism need not imply the elimination of responsibility because *excusing* kinds of causes need not be universally present. Yet to hold this view is to give up the causal theory of excuse, for now what excuses is not causation, but something else—whatever distinguishes excusing causes from non-excusing causes. One can be a determinist while exercising this selectivity, but one cannot advance a causal theory of excuses.

4. Dualistic Determinism   Fourth, and finally, the causal theorist might adopt what I shall call dualistic determinism. This is the view that although human actions and choices are caused, they are not always caused in the same way as natural events are caused. I call this dualistic determinism because it envisions two kinds of causation: causation that necessitates (for natural events) and causation that only inclines (for most human actions and choices). For a dualistic determinist, causal factors outside of the control of the actor usually only incline the actor towards a certain action but do not necessitate that he perform the action.[79]

The causal theorist would use dualistic determinism to salvage his theory of excuse in the following way. Most of the time actors are morally responsible because their actions are not caused in the sense of 'caused' that leads to excuse. Only when their actions are necessitated are they excused. In other words, the causal theorist avoids my general *reductio* argument by interpreting 'cause' in his causal theory of excuses differently from 'cause' in the determinist premise. This allows him to admit that determinism is true and yet avoid the conclusion that no one is morally responsible or legally punishable.

There are two problems with this strategy. The first is that one of the conceptions of causation does not seem very plausible. What

[78] See Paul Hollander, 'Sociology, Selective Determinism, and the Rise of Expectations', *American Sociologist*, Vol. 8 (1973), 147–53. Selective determinism is discussed at some length in Moore, *supra* n. 5, at 358–60.

[79] For a recent expression of dualistic determinism, see Antony Flew, 'Psychiatry, Law and Responsibility', *Philosophical Quarterly*, Vol. 35 (1985), 425–32.

is 'inclining causation' but another name for degrees of causation? The idea of an inclining but not necessitating cause presupposes the degrees of causation explored earlier, and is subject to the same objections. The second problem with dualistic determinism does not stem from the character of the kinds of causal relations posited. Rather, the problem lies in the idea that there can be *two* of them. While one might generally argue that all causes do not necessitate, to argue that only some do raises the general problem of metaphysical dualism discussed in the next section: how does one say anything intelligible about the relation between these two kinds of causes? How does one make sense of the idea that the very same kind of event—human behaviour—can be subject to both of these kinds of causal relations? Metaphysical dualisms threaten the coherence of our world view and should be seen as the harbingers of confusion rather than as acceptable solutions.

C. The Dualist Strategies to Show the Compatibility of Determinism and Responsibility

Since no partial determinist strategy makes much sense, many causal theorists attempt the alternative approach of reconciling determinism and responsibility. At first glance this approach seems to involve a logical contradiction. After all, the causal theorist is committed to the *in*compatibility of causation and responsibility. His slogan is: 'Causes excuse.' If the causal theorist does not tinker with the determinist premise of universal causation of behaviour in any of the ways just explored, he has his work cut out for him if he wants to avoid the implication of universal excuse.

Nonetheless, one finds a number of criminal law theorists pursuing just such a course. They accept the truth of determinism and yet adopt an 'as if' view of human freedom: we can design our institutions as if human action were not determined. This view recognizes that determinism may be the first postulate of science, but it takes free action as the first postulate of legal and moral thought. Franz Alexander and Hugo Staub articulated this view years ago:

[W]e may for practical purposes hold the individual responsible for his acts; that is to say, we assume an attitude as if the conscious Ego actually possessed the power to do what it wishes. Such an attitude has no theoretical foundation, but it has a practical, or still better, a tactical justification.[80]

[80] Franz Alexander and Hugo Staub, *The Criminal, the Judge, and the Public: A Psychological Analysis* (London: G. Allen and Unwin, 1931), 72–3.

Criminal lawyers have been very sympathetic to this 'as if' view. They are apt to be apologetic in the face of deterministic science, conceding that psychiatrists and others are correct when they say that humans beings are unable to do anything other than what their environment, unconscious, or heredity causes them to do. To justify our criminal laws, lawyers talk of *positing* free human actions, even though they admit that scientifically there is no such freedom.

An often-quoted statement of Jerome Hall illustrates this view:

Every science rests upon distinctive axioms or postulates that are accepted by the scientists as 'givens' . . . [Psychiatry] purports to be rigorously scientific and therefore takes a determinist position. Its view of human nature is expressed in terms of drives and dispositions which, like mechanical forces, operate in accordance with universal laws of causation.

On the other hand, criminal law, while it is also a science in a wide sense of the term, is not a theoretical science whose sole concern is to understand and describe what goes on. It is, instead, a practical, normative science which, while it draws upon the empirical sciences, is also concerned to pass judgement on human conduct . . . Its view of human nature asserts the reality of a 'significant' degree of free choice, and that is incompatible with the thesis that the conduct of normal adults is merely a manifestation of imperious psychological necessity. Given the scientific purpose to understand conduct, determinism is a . . . necessary postulate. Given the additional purpose to evaluate conduct, some degree of autonomy is a necessary postulate.[81]

A like view was expressed by Herbert Packer:

The idea of free will in relation to conduct is not, in the legal system, a statement of fact, but rather a value preference having very little to do with the metaphysics of determinism or free will . . . Very simply, the law treats man's conduct as autonomous and willed, not because it is, but because it is desirable to proceed as if it were.[82]

This kind of reconciliation by fiat cannot possibly work. The law demands more than that we *pretend* people are free and thus hold them responsible as *if* they were. A just legal system requires people to be truly responsible. If moral responsibility requires free action and if there is no such thing as free action, we cannot found our moral system on some supposed 'postulate' of free action that we

---

[81] J. Hall, *supra* n. 28, at 455 (footnote omitted).

[82] Herbert Packer, *The Limits of the Criminal Sanction* (Stanford: Stanford University Press, 1968), 74–5.

believe, as a matter of scientific fact, to be false. Our moral beliefs cannot be sealed off from our scientific beliefs in this way. If our moral beliefs require that we be free to be responsible and if determinism shows that we are not free, then we cannot be responsible for our actions.

My suspicion is that Alexander, Staub, Hall, and Packer could allow themselves this 'as if' position only because they did not believe that the moral quality of culpability existed in any convention-independent sense. This non-realist position about moral qualities then generated a kind of 'as if' attitude about morality itself—so why should they be concerned if one of the presuppositions of that morality had an admittedly fictional cast?

I assume to the contrary, that there is such a thing as moral responsibility[83] and that a just legal system will punish only morally responsible actors.[84] If our legal and moral system is based upon responsibility and if responsibility is based on human freedom, then we need to assert that human beings are really free. We cannot pretend that an essential presupposition of our legal and moral system is true when it is not.

If we accept determinism, however, we also are committed to asserting that human beings are not free; their behaviour is determined. Theorists like Packer and Hall thus need to assert what seems like a flat contradiction: that people are free and that they are not. The only conceivable way to do this, I think, is to adopt a once-popular kind of linguistic or metaphysical dualism. This dualism would allow the causal theorist to 'seal off' the legal/moral system from science. Determinism could then be true in one system of thought while its contradictory, free will, could be true in another. Kant attempted this approach in his metaphysical dualism about persons. He argued that we are 'noumenal' beings free of the laws of causation, and we are also 'phenomenal' empirical objects obeying the usual causal laws that all objects obey.[85] There is no contradiction in such a view because we are free only in one mode of being and determined only in the other.

---

[83] I argue for this assumption at length in Moore, 'Moral Reality', *Wisconsin Law Review*, Vol. [1982], 1061–156, and Moore, 'Moral Reality Revisited', *Michigan Law Review*, Vol 90 (1992), 2424–533.

[84] I argue for this assumption in Moore, *supra* n. 5, at 238–40.

[85] I. Kant, *Groundwork of the Metaphysics of Morals* (H. Paton trans., 1964), 118–21.

Like all metaphysical dualisms, whether they be between facts and values, minds and bodies, or propositions and sentences, Kant's dualism faces the very difficult task of describing the relations that exist between the two realms of being. There are two possibilities: either mental states interact with physical states ('interactionist dualism') or they do not ('parallelism'). Rejecting interaction is possible, but it denies what seems obviously true: that physical events in the real world cause mental events, and vice versa. How else could we even talk about, for example, perception and action?

Perception obviously begins with something physical—the stimulus in the environment and its impact on the retina, for example—and ends with something mental, namely, a belief. Analogously, action seems to begin with something mental—a willing, a desire, an intention—and ends with something physical, such as the physical movements of the actor's limbs. Saying that there is no interaction between the mental and the physical seems very much counter to our experience in these areas. Yet the interactionist alternative sounds even stranger. How can one describe the causal relations existing between objects that have mass and energy and exist in space/time co-ordinates, and objects that have no mass or energy and exist only in time, but not in space? If Gilbert Ryle[86] and the philosophy of mind he initiated have shown anything, it is that the relief metaphysical dualism gives from the tension between determinism and responsibility is purchased at much too high a price in coherence.

The more modern version of dualism follows the linguistic turn of twentieth-century philosophy, talking not about how things really are, but rather about how we conceptualize how things are. According to the linguistic dualism of the 1950s and 1960s, there are two different categories of concepts: (1) concepts of intention, choice, and action; and (2) concepts of motion and mechanistic cause.[87] According to this view, we have two quite different ways

---

[86] Gilbert Ryle, *The Concept of Mind* (London: Hutcheson, 1949).

[87] The philosophy of a generation ago was replete with different distinctions employed to develop the idea that mental-state words are in a different category from physical-state words. A sampling: (1) Gilbert Ryle's own view that one could detect an ambiguity in 'exists' such that one could no more conjoin 'mental' and 'physical' with 'existence' in one phrase than one could conjoin tides, hopes, and the average age of death in the sentence, 'they are all rising'. Id. at ch. 1; (2) the linguistic version of Franz Brentano's old view, that mental-state words are irreducibly

of conceptualizing ourselves: either as intelligent persons or as complicated bits of dumb clockwork. Conceptualized as clockwork, we are fully determined. But conceptualized as intelligent agents who make choices, we are free from determinism—free in the sense that it is a kind of 'category mistake' to say that our actions are caused. Again, there is no contradiction in saying both that our actions are free and that our bodily notions are determined, because the system of thought in which 'free' is true is different from the system of thought in which 'determined' is true. A causal theorist would complete this argument by saying that law and morality view persons as intelligent moral agents in one system of thought and that psychiatry and social science view persons as a kind of driven clockwork in a completely separate system of thought.

The problem with linguistic dualism's attempt to let us have both free will and determinism, and at the same time to save us from contradicting ourselves, is that no categorical barriers prevent us from conjoining mental words with physical words.[88] It makes per-

Intentional, whereas physical-state words are not (for a modern statement of Intentionality, see Roderick Chisholm, *Perceiving: a Philosophical Study* (Ithaca, NY: Cornell University Press, 1967); (3) a whole spate of views that developed from the work of Ludwig Wittgenstein in his *Philosophical Investigations*, (G. E. M. Anscombe trans., 3rd edn., Oxford: Basil Blackwell, 1968). These include: (a) the view that 'human action' is in a different category from (at least normal) causation, A. I. Melden, *Free Action* (London: Routledge and Kegan Paul, 1961); R. Taylor, *Action and Purpose* (Englewood Cliffs, NJ: Prentice Hall, 1966); Norman Malcolm, 'The Conceivability of Mechanism', *Philosophical Review, Vol.* 77 (1968), 45–72; (b) the view that the language of reasons (for actions) is different from the language of causes, A. I. Melden, *supra*; R. Taylor, *supra*; Malcolm, *supra*, nicely summarized and demolished in Donald Davidson, 'Actions, Reasons and Causes', *Journal of Philosophy*, Vol. 60 (1963), 685–700; (c) the view that reasons belong to normative discourse, not to the descriptive discourse of physical science, A. R. Louch, *Explanation and Human Action* (Berkeley: University of California Press, 1966); (d) the view that use of mental words, unlike the use of physical words, implies an early end to demands for evidence, G. E. M. Anscombe, *Intention*, 2nd edn. (Ithaca, NY: Cornell University Press, 1963); (e) the view that use of mental words, at least in the first person, is expressive only, not descriptive (L. Wittgenstein, *supra*); (f) the view that action and mental-state concepts are logically dependent on the concept of rules, whereas physical concepts are not, Peter Winch, *The Idea of a Social Science and Its Relation to Philosophy* (London: Routledge and Kegan Paul, 1958); Richard S. Peters, *The Concept of Motivation* (London: Routledge and Kegan Paul, 1958); (g) the view that action and mental-state concepts are built upon a concept of meaning that requires a special mode of empathetic awareness to gain understanding, George Henrik Von Wright, *Explanation and Understanding* (Ithaca, NY: Cornell University Press, 1971). In the text I have lumped all these different distinctions together into my very simple one.

[88] See ch. 10 *supra*. I earlier argued that such categorical barriers do not exist in Moore, *supra* n. 5, chs. 1, 4, and 7.

fectly good sense to speak of actions being 'caused' in the ordinary, physical science sense of 'caused'.[89] We can fully attribute causation of actions: to beliefs and desires, when we explain actions by reasons; to mental causes, such as emotions; to environmental stimuli, such as childhood experiences; and to physiological states or events, such as those balances of neurotransmitters in the brain that affect both our moods and our acts. The doctrine of category differences cannot eradicate the obvious fact that causal relations exist between our actions, on the one hand, and our mental states, environment, and physiology, on the other.

Although a thorough discussion would take us too far afield, it is worth pausing briefly to wonder at how a generation in philosophy could have been led to the counterintuitive results that a robust linguistic dualism demands.[90] The basic error was one of meaning theory. The ordinary-language philosophy that followed upon the work of Ryle and the later Wittgenstein took as its slogan that 'meaning is use'. In other words, one can find the meaning of words in natural languages simply by looking at how the words are used by native speakers of those languages. One discovers the 'logic' of each expression by doing 'conceptual analysis', without for a moment being concerned to enquire into the *reference* of the expressions and the identity conditions of the underlying entities.

For example, ordinary-language philosophers analysed the meaning of the concept of intention in terms of the concept's analytic or pragmatic relations with other mental-state concepts, like belief and desire. They were content to discover these relations of sense and pragmatic implication, building in such a way a matrix of systematically connected concepts. The largest of these matrices became a 'category', and to use a concept outside of its usual matrix became a 'category mistake'. They never asked, 'To what does the word "intention" refer? And does it (can it) refer to the same kind of thing that can be found in physiology?' They felt

[89] See David Hamlyn, 'Causality and Human Behavior', in N. Care and L. Landesman, eds. *Readings in the Theory of Action* (Bloomington, IN: Indiana University Press, 1968), 48; see also Davidson, *supra* n. 87.

[90] For a good description of the ordinary-language movement, see Richard Rorty, 'Introduction', in *The Linguistic Turn* (Chicago: University of Chicago Press, 1967). For a discussion of the development of the use of ordinary-language methods to discover a new dualism in language, see Richard Bernstein, *Praxis and Action* (Philadelphia: University of Pennsylvania Press, 1971), ch. 4; Landesman, 'The New Dualism in the Philosophy of Mind', *Review of Metaphysics*, Vol. 19 (1965), 329–45.

justified in ignoring these questions of reference and identity because, according to their meaning theory, meaning was use.

Such a view of meaning has had its day in the philosophy of language. Lawyers (any more than the clinical psychoanalysts we discussed in chapter 10) cannot insulate their talk from the insights of an advancing science. Otherwise, such lawyers become like my earlier imagined Babylonian ordinary-language philosopher who claims to disprove astronomers' identity claims with observations about the categories of discourse of the astronomically naïve.[91]

The problem for the ordinary-language view of meaning, and for its accompanying doctrine of categorical differences, lies in the fact that inferences from patterns of ordinary usage cannot replace scientific insight about the true nature of the things to which words refer. Science cannot be barred from making discoveries, whether about planets or about minds, in the way the doctrine of category differences claims it can. The more contemporary view of meaning that I explored in chapter 10 holds that the meaning of words like 'intention' is given by the best scientific theory that one can muster about the true nature of intentions, even though that theory may involve knowledge that most ordinary speakers do not have and that, accordingly, is not reflected in their ordinary usage. For example, most ordinary speakers do not know the functional role played by pain in regulating behaviour. They do not know the reflex arcs that generate immediate responses to pain. Nor do they know about differential pain thresholds or about cortical stimulation that takes place when a person is in pain. Most ordinary users of the word 'pain' know only the experience of pain and some of its behavioral expressions. Yet according to one highly influential, contemporary meaning theory,[92] the meaning of the word 'pain' cannot be limited to what ordinary users know but will also include whatever behavioural, functional and physiological facts that the best scientific theory tells us are part of pain.

As legal theorists, we should follow the contemporary philosophy of language in its rejection of linguistic dualism. If we do so, then we must face the question of reference from which that

---

[91] See ch. 10, *supra*.

[92] For such a view of meaning, see Hilary Putnam, 'The Meaning of Meaning', in *Mind, Language and Reality* (Cambridge: Cambridge University Press, 1975), 215; Moore, 'A Natural Law Theory of Interpretation', *Southern California Law Review*, Vol. 58 (1985), 277–398, at 322–38.

doctrine was to rescue us: do mental words like 'intention' refer to physical phenomena? If they do not, then we have to decide to what kind of phenomena they do refer. This path seems likely to take us back to metaphysical dualism. If they do refer to physical phenomena, then we cannot claim that we are both free (in one system of thought) and determined (in the other). We cannot assert without contradiction what Alexander, Staub, Hall, and Packer need to be able to assert, that persons are both free and that they are not.

Both metaphysical and linguistic dualism are drastic doctrines. Metaphysical dualism forces us to simply accept some inexplicable relations between mind and body. Linguistic dualism forces us to grant ordinary usage a priority over scientific theory that is very counterintuitive. The motive for adopting either of these drastic positions is the same: the desire to preserve our 'freedom and dignity' in the face of an advancing, mechanistic science. Unnoticed is that such drastic measures are unnecessary. To explain the mind in terms of the brain, or even to identify the mind with the brain, is not to explain the mind away. As I argue in the next section V, persons can be agents who act for reasons even in a world in which all mental states and all physical events are caused.

In any case, neither metaphysical dualism nor linguistic dualism could completely rescue the causal theory of excuse. It is true that either metaphysical or linguistic dualism would allow the causal theorist to avoid my general *reductio* argument; either would allow him to assert both that persons are free and that they are determined. Yet the causal theorist can do this only by erecting metaphysical or linguistic barriers between actions and causes. However, since some people are excused—and thus by his own theory, are excused by having their actions caused—the causal theorist must find a way to cross his own metaphysical or linguistic barriers. He must find a way of saying that some human actions are caused, for his causal theory of excuse asserts that some actions—the caused ones—are excused. This means that the causal theorist must place excused actions on the physical side of his metaphysical or linguistic divide, along with such obviously caused events as landslides, sunsets, or chemical reactions. In other words, he must take them out of the category of 'actions'. This is a plausible move when the behaviour in question is excused because it was not a voluntary action—for example, movements the defendant made while asleep. For behaviour covered by the other excuses, however, this tactic is not plausible at all. Consider duress. It seems wrong to say that because an action was caused by a threat (and is thus excused according to the causal theory of excuse), it is no longer an action. We still should conceptualize action in response to a threat as an action, and an intentional action at that. The result is that even if there existed metaphysical or linguistic divides that would help the causal theorist avoid my *reductio* argument, he could ill afford to adopt them because his own theory requires that he talk of caused choices and caused actions.

Furthermore, even if his theory allowed the causal theorist to cross these supposed divides, it is still incomplete until it tells him when he may do so. Why can he cross the supposed metaphysical or linguistic divide between caused behaviour and free action on some occasions but not on others? Why, in other words, should we adopt the 'driven clockwork' view of people when we excuse because of duress or provocation, if we do not adopt that view when we exclude environmental causes as excuses? To apply the causal theory of excuse in a non-arbitrary way, the causal theorist would need some principled way of choosing when to adopt one viewpoint and when to adopt the other.[93]

I conclude that the causal theorist cannot avail himself of the dualistic escape routes from the absurd conclusion that no one is morally responsible or legally punishable. If he wishes to retain the view that criminal punishment depends at least in part on moral culpability, then to avoid the absurdity of no one being punishable he must give up either determinism or his causal theory of excuse. My own view is that determinism is true. For me, therefore, the argument just concluded is sufficient to dispose of the causal theory of excuse. Other criminal law theorists, such as George Fletcher,[94] do not find determinism to be so plausible. For them, a different kind of argument against the causal theory must be made.

V. WHY THE CAUSAL THEORY IS WRONG IRRESPECTIVE OF THE TRUTH OF DETERMINISM

To make this argument, it is necessary to establish two propositions. First, despite the appearances, in fact the causal theory does

[93] This point is stressed in Kelman, *supra* n. 23, at 672.
[94] Fletcher, *supra* n. 4, at 801–2.

not account very well for the established legal excuses. Second, the moral principle that gives the causal theory what plausibility it has should be interpreted in a way that strips the causal theory of that plausibility. I pursue each of these tasks below.

A. The Causal Theory Inaccurately Describes the Legal Excuses

I shall not scrutinize the legal doctrines surrounding each of the excuses identified earlier. Here I wish to paint with a somewhat broader brush. I shall examine the case for the causal theory in the three areas where it seems most plausible: first, as an account of the compulsion excuses (duress, necessity, provocation, and addiction); second, as an account of unconsciousness, reflex, and the other conditions evidencing a lack of voluntary action; and third, as an account of the defence of legal insanity. This is a representative sample of the three kinds of defences I earlier identified. If the causal theory fails to account for these defences, it is fair to say that it fails generally.

1. Compulsion and Causation The philosophical distinction between causation and compulsion has been commonplace at least since the writings of Moritz Schlick[95] and A. J. Ayer.[96] Schlick at times was apt to misstate this distinction because of his Humean view that the causal laws of nature amount to no more than regularity of sequence between classes of events. '[T]he laws of nature must not be thought of as supernatural powers forcing nature into a certain behaviour . . . but simply as abbreviated expressions of the order in which events do follow each other.'[97] Left out of this description of causation is exactly the idea that causes all the problems here, namely the idea of causal *necessity*. Yet elsewhere Schlick stated the distinction between causation and compulsion in a way that is not hostage to the Humean regularity-of-sequence view of causation:

[95] Moritz Schlick, 'Causality in Everyday Life and in Recent Science', *University of California Publications in Philosophy*, Vol. 15 (1932), 99–125, reprinted in H. Morris, ed., *Freedom and Responsibility* (Stanford: Stanford University Press, 1961), 292; see also Moritz Schlick, *Problems of Ethics* (New York: Dover Publications, 1962).

[96] Alfred Jules Ayer, 'Freedom and Necessity', *Polemic* (Sept.–Oct. 1946), at 36.

[97] Schlick, 'Causality', *supra* n. 95, at 114, reprinted in H. Morris, ed., *Freedom and Responsibility* at 298–9.

[T]here can be in regard to [natural laws] no talk of 'compulsion.' The laws of celestial mechanics do not prescribe to the planets how they have to move, as though the planets would actually like to move quite otherwise, and are only forced by the burdensome laws of Kepler to move in orderly paths; no, these laws do not in any way 'compel' the planets . . .[98]

The difference between compulsion and causation comes to this: compulsion involves interference with practical reasoning. To be compelled is to have someone or something interfere with one's normal ability or opportunity to do what is morally or legally required. This interference may stem from one of two sources: (1) a person may be constrained to employ certain means by threats, orders or natural necessity, or (2) a person may be constrained to pursue certain objects by his own internal cravings for, or emotions about, those objects. In either case, compulsion requires an agent who reasons about what to do but whose opportunity or capacity to follow the normal dictates of that reason is interfered with either by external factors (threats, natural necessity) or internal factors (extreme emotion or cravings).[99] Schlick's example of the planets is apt because planets do not reason about how they should move. Since they have no practical reasoning, neither Kepler nor anyone else can interfere with it. To say that planetary motion is caused can hardly be to say that it is compelled.

Most causes of human behaviour do not operate as compulsions. Consider four kinds of causes we commonly use as explanations of human behaviour: beliefs and desires, character traits, physiological events, and environmental influences. When we explain an action by any of these kinds of causes, we do not mean that the actor was compelled. Simply because an actor is caused to act by his beliefs and desires, for example, it does not follow that his practical-reasoning processes have been constrained. I am caused, but not compelled, to go downtown by my desire to get a haircut. Going downtown is my uncompelled act, the product of my undisturbed practical reasoning. It is likewise with respect to character traits. If I am caused to engage in sharp practices by greedy character, this is not to say I am compelled. I am simply the type of person who characteristically and unconstrainedly deals with others in financial matters in a greedy way. Greed does not constrain my

[98] Schlick, *Problems of Ethics, supra* n. 95, at 147.
[99] I have developed this account of compulsion as an interference with practical reasoning in Moore, *supra* n. 5, at 86–90.

powers of practical reasoning; it merely describes how I decide when I am unconstrained.[100]

Similarly, physiological causes do not compel our acts. No doubt there are many physiological states and events necessary for each of us to engage in action. There even may be certain physiological conditions that underlie volitions or acts of will.[101] These physiological causes, however, do not disturb our practical reasoning. Rather, they are the conditions that make possible the execution of our desires and intentions in action.

Finally consider the environmental causes that behaviourists tell us can be conditions sufficient to explain adult behaviour. One might think that this type of causation is compulsion because it severely constrains our choices. John Hospers, for example, exercises this familiar argument to lay the groundwork for his assertion that the unconscious makes none of us responsible:

[E]veryone has been molded by influences which in large measure at least determine his present behavior; he is literally the product of these influences, stemming from periods prior to his 'years of discretion' giving him a host of character traits that he cannot change now even if he would . . . An act is free when it is determined by the man's character, say moralists; but what if the most decisive aspects of his character were already irrevocably acquired before he could do anything to mold them? . . . What are we to say of this kind of 'freedom?' Is it not rather like the freedom of the machine to stamp labels on cans when it has been devised for just that purpose?[102]

Hosper's last question is not as rhetorical as he seems to think. The freedom essential to responsibility is the freedom to reason practically without the kind of disturbances true compulsions represent. Machines have no such freedom because they have no practical reasoning capacities and so can hardly be disturbed in the exercise of those capacities. Persons, on the other hand, do have such capacities. The fact that what a person desires, believes, or intends is

---

[100] Character does not compel as long as 'character' means what Gary Watson has called the 'evaluational system', as distinguished from the 'motivational system'. The 'motivational system' represents those drives that we may experience as compulsions. See Watson, 'Free Agency', *Journal of Philosophy*, Vol. 72 (1975), 205, 215.

[101] For an attempt to revive the long-criticized concept of a volition and to hold the notion open to physiological instantiation, see Moore, *Act and Crime*, supra n. 39.

[102] John Hospers, 'Free Will and Psychoanalysis', in *Freedom and Responsibility*, Herbert Morris, ed., (Stanford: Stanford University Press, 1961), 463, 465.

caused by his environment in no way makes it difficult for him to reason practically.

Causation is not compulsion. If we want to show that some causally relevant factor constitutes a compulsion, we can do so only by showing that that factor interferes with practical reasoning. A threat, for example, can be a compulsion and thus an excuse for criminal conduct, but not because it is a cause of that conduct. A threat constrains an actor's choices in a way that other causes such as beliefs, desires, character traits, physiology, and the environment do not. The threat makes his choice a hard one in a way these other kinds of causes do not.

As an alternative example, consider addiction. Addiction is a cause of behaviour, but it is not because of this fact that addictions operate as compulsions and therefore provide an excuse. Rather, addictions can be compulsions because they make it difficult to do what the law demands. Unlike threats, the cravings characteristic of addiction do not constrain the actor's choices about how to achieve some legitimate end of his, such as survival. Still, addictions may make choices difficult in a way that beliefs, desires, character traits, physiology, and the environment do not. In this case, the constraint on choice is an internal one: the craving for an end that cannot be achieved without violating the law. Both the duress example and the addiction example show that what furnishes an excuse is the disturbance of practical reasoning, not the fact that the disturbance was caused.

Legal doctrines reflect this distinction. The law does not excuse actors whose behaviour is caused by just any threat, natural necessity, craving, or emotional disturbance. A threat, for example, must do more than cause an actor to do what his threatener wants. Even under the liberal Model Penal Code standard, the threat must be one that a 'person of reasonable firmness' would not have been able to resist.[103] This test does not merely ask whether the threat caused the act; rather, it asks whether the actor's choice was so difficult— his practical reasoning so constrained—that he should be excused.

The same is true for the excuses of inner compulsion, such as provocation and addiction. No jurisdiction's provocation formula is reducible to a simple causal test, for example: did the victim's provoking act cause the defendant's criminal act? Rather, the law

---

[103] *Model Penal Code* § 2.09(1) (Proposed Official Draft 1962).

asks whether the victim's provoking act aroused the defendant's emotions to such a degree that the choice to refrain from crime became difficult for the defendant. The legal doctrine reflects the philosophical distinction between emotions that only cause choice and emotions so intense that they distort the very process of choosing.

2. Action and Causation   There is also a sound philosophical distinction between saying that behaviour was caused by some external factor and saying that the same behaviour does not amount to an action by an agent. Behaviour might not be an action even if it were not caused; conversely, behaviour may be an action even though it is caused. The notions of action and causation are simply independent of one another.

We can see this by constructing a positive account of action—in other words, an account that does not simply exclude various kinds of non-action. As we do so we must ask whether that positive account contains any presuppositions about freedom from causation.

I have summarized my positive account of action at the beginning of chapter 6. Briefly, the essence of human action is the exercise of causal power by a person initially over his body and ultimately, through his body to more remote real world effects. This kind of causal power of persons is exercised through those mental acts of willing often called volitions.[104] Such causal power does not depend on freedom from causation.[105] It is perfectly compatible to think both that persons have causal power and that everything they do is caused by some set of factors external to their will. To see this, let us imagine a very simple example of action: some person X raises his right arm. Let us assume that we are correct in our belief that raising his arm up was indeed an action of his: X had good reason for wanting to raise his arm; he (to the best of his knowledge) raised his arm for that reason; he had the non-observational knowledge (characteristic of actions) that he willed the raising of his arm; and so forth. Now imagine the possible causal explanations for X's act. (1) His desire to get his jacket, together with his belief that if he raised his arm he could get his jacket, caused him to raise his arm. (2) His real (unconscious)

---

[104] See Moore, *supra* n. 39, at ch. 6.   [105] See id., ch. 4.

reason for raising his arm was that he wished to emulate the Nazi salute. (3) As a child, he habitually raised his arm when getting out of a chair because as an infant he had to raise his arm in order to get out of a high chair. (4) Certain chemical reactions in his brain caused a nerve impulse to be sent to the muscles of his right arm and those impulses caused his arm to go up. Any of these causal stories could be true or false; yet it still will be true that X raised his arm.

Some philosophers have thought that this cannot be true because action and causation are incompatible.[106] For them, giving causal explanations of behaviour is inconsistent with conceptualizing that behaviour as an action. For how can a person have causal power if each of the exercises of that power is caused? These philosophers find a metaphysical incompatibility between a person's causing (willing, choosing) some effect in the world and that person's causings (willings, choosings) themselves being caused. Such philosophers conclude that for any behaviour to be an act—an exercise of a person's causal power—it must be uncaused.

A causal theorist about excuses should welcome this conclusion. If it were true, it would show that the causal theory of excuses necessarily is true. For to say that wherever there is causation of behaviour there can be no action (and thus, no responsibility) is to say exactly what the causal theorist wants to say.

The problem is that the alleged metaphysical incompatibility between action and causation does not exist. The examples just given show that actions, choices, and willings do exist even though caused. Behaviour may be an action even if caused by mental states, physiological events, or environmental stimuli. To explain an act, a choice, or a willing, in terms of its causal antecedents, is not to explain it out of existence. Suppose we were to discover the physiological determinants of willing the motions of our bodies. That knowledge would not show us that we did not will motions; rather, it would show us more about what those willings were. To think otherwise would be like thinking that to explain the presence of Lake Michigan in terms of its causes (glaciation, etc.) is to show that there is no such thing as Lake Michigan.

It seems to me that the metaphysical incompatibilist is misled by his insight that in various ways the agency of persons is special. The

---

[106] See R. Taylor, *supra* n. 87, at 110–11, 116; Malcolm, *supra* n. 87, at 63–8.

agency of a person does seem different than the agency of a tree or of a stone. For one thing, it seems that we cannot give simple behavioural translations of talk about human actions, whereas we can give these translations for talk about the 'actions' of a tree, a stone, or an acid. Saying that a person raised his arm does not translate into the non-action language of bodily movement the same way that saying that a tree shed its leaves translates into a language not involving the agency of the tree. 'His arm went up' is not equivalent to 'he raised his arm', even though 'the leaves fell off the tree' is equivalent to 'the tree shed its leaves'.[107]

From this failure to find simple behavioural translations for the terms used to describe human actions, some metaphysical incompatibilists leap to the conclusion that no physical translation of human action language is possible at all. Such a leap is premature. The remedy to too simple a behaviourism is to complicate the account of human action in terms of inner causes. On my theory, human actions are not simply the movement of the human body; rather, human actions are compound events consisting of: (1) the willing of the particular bodily movement; (2) the happening of that bodily movement; and (3) a causal relationship between the willing and the movement willed.[108]

Incompatibilists usually have two sorts of reactions to causal theories of action such as my volitional theory. The first and least sophisticated is simply to assert that active agency can never be analysed in terms of passive mental states, that when a *state* of volition is proposed as the cause of bodily movements then a person's agency is necessarily excluded. This amounts to the view that a *person's* causing something—agency—is primitive in the sense that no causal explication of it is possible.

Incompatibilists who press this sort of point usually regard it as virtually self-evident. Yet far from having that elevated epistemic status, the point is actually such an extraordinary one that it demands strong justification. Most natural items in the world have features surprising to those who regularly use the names of such items. Why should human actions be any different? Incompatibilists tend to think that it is analytic of 'action', 'agency', and 'persons-causing', that no causes like volitions can be substituted in. Somehow the meaning of these terms is thought to

---

[107] See R. Taylor, *supra* n. 87, at 124.   [108] See Moore, *supra* n. 39.

preclude a theory of human action in terms of volitions-causing-bodily movements.

Yet how are such supposed analytic truths to be sustained? Certainly the facts of ordinary usage do not sustain such 'truths', for we talk of causing action all the time as my earlier four sorts of examples were meant to show. Of course, incompatibilists do not like my sort of examples. They claim that my examples are not really instances of true *causation* of action. The examples of caused behaviour the incompatibilist will propose will be more like: the wind blew the defendant's arm and thrust it upward; the defendant was thrown through a window; the defendant was stung by a bee and then engaged in a series of reflex movements. The incompatibilist will assert that his examples show the incompatibility of causation and action; they show that 'true' ('full', 'necessitating') causation of behaviour means that the behaviour in question cannot be an action. Yet the incompatibilist is gerrymandering his concept of causation in an *ad hoc* manner so as to include only his examples and to exclude counter-examples like those given earlier. To avoid the gerrymandering charge, he needs a general account of causation that is both independently plausible and that includes his examples of caused behaviour but excludes the earlier examples.

In any case, the real objection to this attempt to ground these supposed analytic truths in facts of ordinary usage is that raised in chapter 10: no amount of armchair language observation can cut off deeper and deeper scientific theories about the natures of natural kinds. Even if most native speakers of English used their language in a way making 'caused action' deviant—which they do not, but that was my first rejoinder—this linguistic fact would not rule out a theory of action that proposed states of willing to be part of the essence of this natural kind of thing.

Moreover, the very considerations that have led some philosophers to the view that exercises of causal power by a person—actions—are unique, are the ones that suggest that human action is a natural kind of event about which we should seek more and more knowledge. It is very probably a mistake to look for some essence of the willings of trees, because we do not really think that trees will or act. We do, however, think that persons will and act, and accordingly it makes sense to seek a theory of their willing. Such a theory may well be cast in terms of the functionally defined subroutines performed by certain brain structures, and surely these subroutines will themselves have causes. Rather than showing that actions and willings cannot be caused, the unique attributes of human action really suggest that there is a deeper nature to such events, one to be cashed out in terms of events that will themselves have underlying causes.

The more sophisticated response to causal theories of action such as my volitional theory also has as its conclusion that the uniqueness of human agency cannot be captured by volitional causings. The argument goes like this: between any volition, say, that one's toes move, and those toes moving, there can be what are called 'deviant causal chains'.[109] For example: I will that my toes move; that willing causes me to get very excited (because, for example, I have been paralysed for many years, have just been cured, and this toe movement will be my first after the cure); my excitement causes a purely reflex toe-jerking. The toe-jerking was not an action, the argument concludes, even though it is the object of my willing and it was caused by that willing; it just was not caused in the right way. Yet to spell out what the 'right way' is, is just to repair to some primitive notion of human agency, so we have not really analysed such agency in terms of volitional causings.

The answer to this more sophisticated incompatibilist argument is of the same general kind as was given to the less sophisticated argument. There are deviant causal chains, and when they exist as in the above example there is no human action. Therefore, causal theories of action like mine have to specify that the causal route from volition to bodily movement be non-deviant, and there is at present no way to do that except by reliance on our intuitions of agency. Yet this is not the problem the incompatibilist thinks it to be. What our intuitions of agency tell us is that there is a unique causal route from volition to movement when that movement is part of an action. It is up to our subpersonal science to tell us more about the nature of that route. About such causal route we are thus in no worse a position than we are about the nature of volitions themselves: in both cases we have strong phenomenal clues to the existence of things whose nature an advancing science of the subpersonal should reveal.

If incompatibilism (between causation and action) is as false as all this is meant to suggest, why do certain examples of caused

---

[109] See D. Davidson, *supra* n. 75, at 79–80.

actions *seem* to establish the incompatibility of causation and action? It is because these causal explanations tell us *more* than that the behaviour was caused. They also tell us that the person whose behaviour we are evaluating lacked the capacity or opportunity to act. We properly infer from this lack of capacity or opportunity to act that he did not act on this occasion.

Consider each of the three kinds of non-action identified earlier. The first occurs when a natural force or a human agent moves the defendant's body for him. Causal accounts like these properly lead us to infer that the defendant did not act. We do not make the inference of non-action on the basis of causation, however. Rather, we infer that there was no action because causal accounts of this kind show us that there was no opportunity or ability to perform an action. No human being has the ability to will his body to fly through the air the way it does, for example, when a group of other people or a gust of wind throws it through a window. The second type of non-action, such as reflex reaction, is similar. We know enough about the reflex arcs of the central nervous system to know that the will is inoperative when the knee is tapped and the leg moves. People simply have no opportunity to exercise their causal powers in such circumstances. The same is true of the third class of examples. When a person is unconscious or asleep, the self we regard as the responsible agent is absent in an important sense, even though the person's body moves. The responsible self has no capacity to will such movements because it is asleep or unconscious.

In some cases, we legitimately are in doubt as to a person's capacity to will the movements of his body, as, for example, when he is influenced by post-hypnotic suggestion. Note that we need not have any doubts as to the causal influence of the hypnotist's suggestion. We may be quite confident that the subject would not have raised his arm but for the suggestion, yet may easily conclude that the suggestion did not make the person incapable of willing the movement. It might have caused the arm to go up in the same way an ordinary suggestion does—by causing (calling to mind) an action the person wants to perform anyway but had not noticed the opportunity to perform until it was suggested to him. Alternatively, the suggestion might have caused him to have a desire on which he then acts by raising his arm. In either case, the suggestion causes the behaviour without at all changing its character from action to non-action.

The important point is that it is never causation *alone* that rules out action. Only those causal accounts that show that the accused lost the capacity or opportunity to will are incompatible with action.[110] Even then, it is the absence of the capacity or opportunity to will, not the cause of that absence, that is crucial. If one lacked the capacity or opportunity to act, one would not be responsible no matter what causal account explained one's incapacity or lack of opportunity. This would be true even if the only account was the mysterious assertion that there was no cause of the actor's incapacity.

Once it is recognized that a caused act is not necessarily an instance where the actor had no opportunity or capacity to act, it becomes apparent that the law recognizes as an excuse only lack of capacity or opportunity to act. Merely because behaviour is caused does not mean that the law will equate it with non-action and excuse it. Suppose, for example, I know that Z has a limited repertoire of jokes and that if reminded of one of them in a social setting, he will tell it. Suppose further that I trigger one of his known jokes with a paraphrase of its first line. The responsibility for telling the bad joke is still Z's (even if it is also mine), because his telling of it is still his action. I caused it, but it is his action nonetheless.[111] In contrast, the instances of behaviour that the law regards as involuntary and excusable are all instances of incapacity or lack of opportunity to act.

Consider the difficulties with the borderline defence of brainwashing that I discussed earlier in chapter 6. In the most famous recent example, the Patty Hearst case, we were certain of a causal connection between the conditioning Hearst received and her criminal behaviour. That certainty, however, was irrelevant to the issue of whether her behaviour was an action. She robbed the bank; it was her act, whether or not a situation that was not of her making implanted in her the beliefs that caused her to act. One might have allowed her some affirmative defence if she had not had adequate time between the conditioning and the criminal act in which to

---

[110] This point is made nicely in Jeffrie Murphy, 'Involuntary Acts and Criminal Liability', *Ethics*, Vol. 81 (1971), 332–42.

[111] The example is from Joel Feinberg, 'Causing Voluntary Actions', in *Doing and Deserving: Essays in the Theory of Responsibility* (Princeton: Princeton University Press, 1970), 152, 157–8.

reject or integrate her new beliefs into her character.[112] Such an affirmative defence is irrelevant to the issue of action. She plainly acted, whether or not her act was caused.

Causation is equally irrelevant to other proposed ways of negating voluntary action. Suppose high correlations are found between crime and certain environmental factors, or between crime and an extra Y-chromosome in some men, or between crime and premenstrual tension in some women. Suppose that it is further established that a defendant would not have committed a certain crime but for one of these 'criminogenic' factors. We can then say that the factor caused the crime. We still have said nothing relevant to the question of whether the defendant acted. If he had the capacity and the opportunity to will the movement of his body, he could act; if he exercised that capacity on a particular occasion, then on that occasion he acted. Nothing in the hypothesized causal stories is relevant to these questions. Only if it is shown that these factors caused a lack of capacity or opportunity to act will they be ways of showing that the defendant did not act. It is not enough to show that the factors caused the defendant's behaviour.

3. Insanity and Causation   The causal theory can explain the status defence no better than it does the other two types of excuse-like defences. To demonstrate this, we should examine the insanity defence, the status defence that most suggests the accuracy of the causal theory. (Infancy is a less likely candidate for causal excuse theorists because infancy involves no disease-entity or other thing to be identified as the cause of crime.) As I shall argue in greater detail in chapter 14, it is not because crazy people are caused to do what they do that they are excused; rather, crazy people are excused because they are crazy. Mental illness is directly relevant to responsibility in a way that other illnesses that may also cause crime, such as blindness, deafness, stomach cramps, and heart conditions, are not. Insanity betokens a difference so fundamental that we deny moral agency to those afflicted with it. The insane, like young infants, lack one of the essential attributes of personhood namely, rationality. For this reason, human beings who are insane are no more the proper subjects of moral evaluation than are young

---

[112] For a version of this argument, see Daniel Dennett, 'Mechanism and Responsibility', in Ted Honderich, ed., *Essays on Freedom of Action* (London: Routledge and Kegan Paul, 1973), 157, 178–9.

infants, animals, or even stones. Only beings who, like most of us, are fairly good practical reasoners can be the subjects of moral norms.

Nothing in this status conception of insanity implicitly refers us back to causation. It is not because their mental disease causes the insane to commit crimes that we excuse them, no more than it is because an infant's lack of rationality causes him to do bad that we excuse him. Rather, in both cases, we excuse because the actors lack the status of moral agents. Although we may colloquially attribute particular actions to their insanity, we do not mean that they are to be excused because of some supposed causal relation. We mean that they cannot fairly be blamed because *in general* they lack our rational capacities.

Doctrinal support for this view of legal insanity is admittedly scarcer than one might hope. The pre-*M'Naghten* test, for one, was consistent with this view. According to that test the accused was not legally insane if he could tell the difference between right and wrong.[113] This capacity was chosen as the mark of sufficient mental maturity that an offender could be held responsible. The test had been adopted from the test for responsibility for children, which as early as the fourteenth century drew the line of accountability at the ability to know of good and evil.[114] That language was drawn from the passage in the Book of Genesis in which God likens humans to God once they have come to know of good and evil.[115] Insofar as the law asked whether a person knew right from wrong, it was asking whether he was sufficiently like us to be a moral agent and thus responsible for his acts. When the *M'Naghten* test was adopted in 1843, however, this ancient wisdom was forgotten. The test measuring moral agency was supplanted by the language of mistake: only if the accused did not know the nature and quality of the particular act he did, or he did not know that it was wrong, was he to be excused.[116] *M'Naghten* transformed the insanity defence into a version of the mistake excuses.

[113] On the pre-*M'Naghten* tests for insanity, see Moore, *supra* n. 5, at 65–6.
[114] 5 YB *Eyre of Kent*, 6 & 7 Edw. 2 (1313), reprinted in 24 *Selden Society*, Vol. 24 (1909), 109.
[115] Gen. 3:22–3 (Revised Standard Version), quoted in A. Platt and B. Diamond, 'The Origins of "Right and Wrong" Test of Criminal Responsibility and Its Subsequent Development in the United States: An Historical Survey', *California Law Review*, Vol. 54 (1966), 1227–60, at 1227.
[116] *M'Naghten's Case*, 8 ENG REP 718, 722 (1843).

All the other tests for insanity repeated this tendency.[117] Rather than trying to determine when a being is enough like us to be considered a moral agent, courts have officially treated insanity as a true excuse rather than a status defence. The status conception of the defence, however, refuses to die. Jurors refuse to convict seriously deranged people even if these people are sane by the *M'Naghten* test or any other test, and jurors convict less seriously deranged individuals even if these people quite literally satisfy the terms of the applicable test. As the Royal Commission on Capital Punishment observed about English juries: 'However much you charge a jury as to the *M'Naghten Rules* or any other test, the question they would put to themselves when they retire is—"Is this man mad or not?" '[118]

Psychiatrists serving as expert witnesses often do the same thing. In New Hampshire, for example, where an accused was long excused only if his act was the 'product' of 'mental illness', psychiatrists at the state hospital gave their own meaning to the phrase 'mental illness' when they testified. This meaning is not the expansive one they used in clinical practice, but rather the more restrictive meaning captured by the popular labels 'mad' or 'crazy'.[119] More generally, psychiatrists testifying under any test typically assume that 'mental illness', 'disease of the mind', 'abnormality of mind', and like phrases appearing in the various insanity tests should be taken to mean, roughly, the extreme psychoses,[120] which is the nearest clinical equivalent to 'crazy'.

Thus, the 'law in action' rather than in the books—the test as actually applied by psychiatrists and jurors—restricts the excuse of legal insanity to those who are so lacking in rationality that they

[117] See generally Moore, *supra* n. 5, at 217–24.

[118] Royal Comm'n on Capital Punishment, *1949–53 Report* (1953), 322 (quoting Lord Cooper).

[119] See John Reid, 'The Working of the New Hampshire Doctrine of Criminal Insanity', *University of Miami Law Review*, Vol. 15 (1960), 14–58, at 19.

[120] See Arthur Goldstein, *The Insanity Defense* (New Haven: Yale University Press, 1967), 59–62; id. at 60–1 (reporting a 'quite widespread feeling among psychiatrists that all psychotics *should* be regarded as insane'); see also Robert Waelder, 'Psychiatry and the Problem of Criminal Responsibility', *University of Pennsylvania Law Review*, Vol. 101 (1952), 378–90, at 384. Waelder observes that a 'central core' of the concept of mental illness consists of 'conditions in which the sense of reality is crudely impaired, and inaccessible to the corrective influence of experience—for example, when people are confused or disoriented or suffer from hallucinations or delusions. That is the case in organic psychoses, in schizophrenia, in manic-depressive psychosis.'

are popularly considered crazy. This is because those psychiatrists and jurors have glimpsed a moral truth: the very status of being crazy precludes responsibility. Seeking some hidden cause of the accused's criminal behaviour is, accordingly, simply beside the point.

B. The Causal Theory Is Morally Incorrect

If the causal theory does not in fact fit very well with the established doctrines of excuse in the criminal law, then much of its plausibility as a theory of *legal* excuse evaporates. The theory then becomes a theory of *moral* excuse, a theory that does not reflect our criminal law so much as it urges us to change it. Specifically, the causal theorist at this stage must be seen as urging us to expand the categories of excuse so as to include conditions like brainwashing, possession of an extra Y-chromosome, premenstrual tension, adverse environmental background, and involuntary intoxication whenever they are known to cause crime.

Since there is no dearth of such proposals, let us look at the moral case for the causal theory. In order to appreciate this moral case, it is crucial that we keep clearly in mind what has been settled and what has been left open by the previous analysis. My overall argument against regarding causation as a moral excuse is made in three steps. Two of these steps have already been taken, but since they were taken in the context of describing our legal doctrines of excuse, they should be repeated here in the context of morally evaluating those doctrines.

First, action can be caused. The causal theorist bases his conclusion that causation is incompatible with moral responsibility partly on the thesis of metaphysical incompatibility that I discussed earlier, the thesis that actions cannot be caused. This conceptual claim about action leads to the following argument about moral excuse. If behaviour is caused, it is not an action; further, if a person's behaviour is not an action, then he cannot be morally responsible for it. It follows that a person is not morally responsible for any of his behaviour that is caused.

The earlier discussion of the compatibility of causation with the legal excuses based on lack of voluntary action was intended to accomplish more than a bit of legal exegesis. It showed that both inside and outside law, people can exercise their will even though their actions are caused. People do not need to stand outside the causal order—a truly extraordinary idea—in order to exercise those causal powers that are the essence of human actions. Eliminating this conceptual claim about actions eliminates one ground for thinking that where behaviour is caused, there can be no moral responsibility.

Second, moral excuses, like legal excuses, are not based on causation, but on interference with practical reasoning. My earlier arguments about the legal defences involving compulsion or insanity are equally applicable to the moral excuses that underlie the legal doctrines. The moral excuse of compulsion, for example, is available only when the actor's practical reasoning is constrained; it is not enough that the actions or the beliefs and desires guiding action were caused. The upshot is that at least the conventionally accepted versions of the moral excuses of compulsion and insanity are not based on the causal theory.

Third, does anything else have to be shown to answer the causal theorist's moral argument that causation and moral responsibility are incompatible? If human action can be caused, and if an action does not fit into one of the conventional categories of moral excuse simply because it is caused, then it may seem that nothing more need be said in order to show the compatibility of moral responsibility with causal accounts of action. Indeed, a strong tradition in philosophy takes just this position. When A. J. Ayer and Moritz Schlick, for example, pointed out the distinction between causation and compulsion,[121] they assumed they had answered the challenge of those who think that causation and moral responsibility are incompatible. They assumed this because they assumed that the challenge was motivated only by a conceptual confusion. Yet their response to the challenge does not do justice to the intuitive plausibility of the principle of responsibility mentioned earlier. Even after the conceptual confusions are cleared away, the causal theorist has a moral argument: if a person could not help doing what he did, he is not morally responsible for it. This is true even if his behaviour was an action, and an action not covered by the conventional moral excuses.

This argument merits a response, and therefore the compatibilist needs a third step to his argument, a step that meets the challenge to the adequacy of the standard moral excuses posed by the prin-

---

[121] Ayer, *supra* n. 96; Schlick, *supra* n. 95.

ciple of responsibility. One way to take on the causal theorist here is to reject the principle of responsibility outright. One might urge, as Harry Frankfurt has, that it is irrelevant to an actor's moral responsibility whether he could have done other than he did.[122] If he chose to do what he did, Frankfurt urges, then he is responsible, even if he could not have done otherwise.

In an attempt to establish this proposition, one can construct a thought experiment of the kind Frankfurt originated.[123] Suppose that neurophysiology has advanced to the point that with suitable equipment, one person can monitor the thoughts of another and even, if he wishes to, control those thoughts. Suppose further that one person (X) is debating whether or not he should assault a person against whom he has long had a grudge. Suppose further that for reasons of his own, another person (Y) wants the victim assaulted; Y is suitably equipped to monitor X's thoughts and does so. Now suppose that X decides to assault the person and does so. Y knew what X was thinking; he had the power to intervene and control X's choice and would have done so, if X had chosen not to assault the person. However, since X chose as he did, Y only monitored but did not interfere with X's thoughts. Frankfurt asks: Is not X still responsible for the assault, even though he could not have done other than he did? If he is responsible, the principle that one is responsible only if he could have done otherwise is false. X is responsible if he chose to act and acted, whether or not he could have done otherwise.

Unfortunately, such thought experiments only shift the locus of the argument. It is true that in the example, X could not have done otherwise, and yet we think it is morally correct to punish him. But, the causal theorist will respond, this is an easy case because we have not said anything about the factors that caused X's free choice. Since in our thought experiment X's choice apparently is uncaused, the intuition that X is responsible is not surprising. The causal theorist will propose to modify the example so that Y does have to interfere with X's thoughts in order to cause X to assault the person. Suppose, for example, that Y strengthens X's desire for revenge and weakens X's fear that he will be caught and punished.

---

[122] Harry Frankfurt, 'Alternate Possibilities and Moral Responsibility', *Journal of Philosophy*, Vol. 66 (1969), 829–39, at 835.
[123] Id.

Now we have a causal account of X's choice, and the intuition that X is responsible is considerably weaker.

A causal theorist would urge that all choices are ultimately like X's choice in the revised scenario. Substitute for Y the natural factors that cause choice, and you have the same problem one step removed: if an actor could not have *chosen* otherwise, it does not matter that his actions were the products of his choices. The principle of responsibility is recast into: an actor is responsible for his actions only if he could have chosen to do otherwise.[124]

Preferable to rejecting outright the principle of responsibility is reconstruing what it means. In some sense of the words, it is intuitively plausible that an actor can be held responsible only if he could have done other than he did. The causal theorist assumes that his is the only possible interpretation of this principle. He assumes that the word 'could' in the principle must mean 'could, no matter what'. Using this meaning of 'could', an actor could not have done otherwise if his actions were caused by factors not within his control. If an actor's unfortunate upbringing caused him to commit violent crimes, then he could not have done other than commit those crimes.

Ignored by the causal theorist is a famous alternative interpretation of the principle of responsibility that originated with G. E. Moore.[125] Moore argued that the 'could' in the above principle is not an unconditional 'could', but rather, a conditional one. In other words, when the principle says an actor 'could have acted other-

---

[124] See generally Richard Chisholm, 'Freedom and Action', in *Freedom and Action*, Keith Lehrer, ed., (1966); Chisholm, 'Human Freedom and the Self', in Gary Watson, ed., *Free Will* (Oxford: Oxford University Press, 1982), 26–7. Chisholm replaces the concern about determined actions with a concern about determined choices. Of course one can construct Frankfurt-like hypotheticals about choice as well as about action: suppose Y has the capacity to affect X's choice of the desires that will determine his choice of action. Y does not exercise his power because X chooses a set of desires that produces just the choice Y would like. This stratagem only moves the locus of the argument still further back, to the choices about desires that cause choice. No matter how far back up the causal chain we go, at some point there will be factors that cause choices—or choices of choices—and those factors will not themselves be chosen. The moral question that remains is whether we can fairly hold X responsible for his choices if they are the product of factors not within his control. If choice is the touchstone of culpability, how *can* X be culpable when he did not choose those factors? Frankfurt's kind of thought experiment only forces the causal theorist to reformulate his principle of responsibility.

[125] G. E. Moore, *Ethics* (Cambridge: Cambridge University Press, 1912), 84–95.

wise', it means that 'he could have *if* he had chosen (or willed) to do otherwise'.[126]

The consequence of Moore's conditional interpretation of the principle of responsibility is to make responsibility for an action compatible with causation of that action. For the only freedom the principle of responsibility now requires is the freedom (or power) to give effect to one's own desires. One's choices, or willings, in other words, must themselves be causes of actions for Moore's interpretation of the principle to be satisfied; it is not required that such choices be uncaused.

It can hardly be disputed that in ordinary speech there are senses of 'could' that express Moore's conception of ability. 'I could have run a mile in five minutes' is true if I had the physical capability to run that quickly; 'I could have fixed the clock yesterday' is true if I had the opportunity to do so.[127] In neither of these examples does 'I could' become incorrect or meaningless if there are causes for the action I could perform. The words 'I could' require only that my choices be capable of causing certain effects and that I have the opportunity to exercise my choice.

Once one sees these capability/opportunity senses of 'could', they are so perfectly ordinary that one might doubt whether ordinary speech has the sense of 'could' required by the causal theorist. Is there an unconditional sense of 'could' such that one could say in a conventional idiom: 'Even though he had both the capability and the opportunity to refrain from killing her had he chosen to do so, he could not have done otherwise than kill her because his choice and his action were caused'? Moore and his followers seemed to think that they could settle this question by linguistic analysis. P. H. Nowell-Smith, for example, once sought to sustain Moore's interpretation of the principle of responsibility by arguing that it would be 'logically odd' to use 'could' in any usage other than one in which it was implicitly conditional on opportunity or ability (in its

---

[126] Id. Moore seems to have preferred to analyse 'he could have done so' as 'he *should* or *would* have done so, if he had chosen to'. Id. at 90–3. To avoid J. L. Austin's objection—that we can say a person is able to do something when that person chooses to do it and yet *fails* to do it on that particular occasion—I prefer Moore's first formulation, which analyses 'could' as 'could if he had chosen'.

[127] For discussions of the various senses of 'can', see G. E. Moore, *supra* n. 125, at 84–95; Bruce Aune, 'Can', in Paul Edwards, ed., *The Encyclopedia of Philosophy*, Vol. 4 (New York: Macmillan, 1967), 18–20; and the readings collected in Myles Brand, ed., *The Nature of Human Action* (Glencoe, Ill.: Scott, Foresman, 1970).

usual sense).[128] Both Moore and Nowell-Smith were challenged by J. L. Austin on linguistic grounds,[129] and there has been a burgeoning literature since.[130]

Such a linguistic debate, however, cannot settle the meaning of the word 'could' as it is used in the principle of responsibility.[131] Suppose there were no ordinary sense of 'could' that is negated by the existence of sufficient causes. The causal theorist nonetheless could claim the freedom any speaker has to invent new meanings in order to make himself understood. Only if there were something in the meaning of 'could' that precluded its extension in this way would he be barred from his proposed new usage. And nothing in the linguistic analyses mentioned above can support this strong a claim. Nowell-Smith's 'logical oddness', for example, turns out to be no more than a pragmatic feature of language, if that; it is not a logical or even a semantic feature. It is wrong, therefore, to think that the causal theorist cannot make his interpretation of 'could' understandable to us, even if it sounds 'odd'. Novel moral insights often may involve the violation of pragmatic or even semantic conventions.

The upshot of this is that we need a moral argument to answer the question of which interpretation of the principle of responsibility is the morally compelling one. The moral argument that comes to mind appeals to the totality of our moral experience involving praise and blame. By 'moral experience', I mean to include both that range of emotions and attitudes partly described by P. F. Strawson [132] and Herbert Morris[133]—the attitudes of resentment, moral indignation, condemnation, approval, guilt, remorse, shame, pride, and the like—and that range of more cognitive judgements

[128] P. H. Nowell-Smith, *Ethics* (London: Penguin Books, 1954), 239–43.

[129] Austin, 'Ifs and Cans', in *The Nature of Human Action, supra* n. 127, at 161–78.

[130] See generally the articles collected in *The Nature of Human Action, supra* n. 127, and in *Free Will, supra* n. 124.

[131] Of course, if people see that what they meant by the principle of responsibility was always the conditional sense of 'can', then pointing out yet another conceptual confusion will produce moral agreement. The problem is that even after the distinction is pointed out, not everyone who subscribes to the principle of responsibility will admit that it is the conditional sense of 'can' that they meant. Rather, they will find that the unconditional sense is still the morally relevant sense to be given to the principle.

[132] Strawson, 'Freedom and Resentment', *supra* n. 55.

[133] Herbert Morris, *On Guilt and Innocence: Essays in Legal Philosophy and Moral Psychology* (Los Angeles: University of California Press, 1976).

about when an actor deserves moral praise or blame. We have such experience, not as armchair theoreticians, but repeatedly in our daily lives as we raise our children, deal with our fellows, and guide our own behaviour.

To justify any moral proposition is to show that it is a part of the most coherent account of our moral experience, considered as a whole.[134] That is exactly what I claim about the Moorean interpretation of the principle of responsibility. Our practices of assessing merit and responsibility are consistent with the proposition that persons are responsible for their (determined) choices, inconsistent with its negation. We therefore have very good grounds to believe that the principle of responsibility should not be interpreted as the causal theorist would like.

Part of the relevant moral experience we have described before. We undeniably parcel out both praise and blame for actions and choices we know to be caused by factors external to the actor's free will. Our moral life is built upon our praising or blaming people when they help a friend, tell a bad joke, create a work of art, or write a clear and truthful chapter about the excuses—even though we know at least some of the factors that caused these actions. It is hard to imagine how different our praising and blaming practices would be if we really tried to cabin them to situations in which we could think of no causal explanation for a person's behaviour. We would always be in doubt as to whether a person really deserved praise or blame.

Of course a causal theorist could simply adopt a tough-it-out attitude. He could claim that most of our moral experience is just false in light of the truth of his interpretation of responsibility. Yet no less than his opponent, the causal theorist needs an argument to explain why *his* interpretation of the principle is the right one. And how is the argument to proceed if he concedes that his interpretation of the principle would falsify much of our moral life? What are the aspects of our moral life on which he can rely to support his interpretation?

He cannot appeal to the supposed metaphysical incompatibility of action and causation, as we have seen. Responsible action is possible even when caused by factors over which the agent has no control. Nor can he appeal to the recognized moral excuses, such as

---

[134] See Moore, *supra* n. 83.

compulsion and insanity. These, as we have seen, do not have causation as their rationale. We can now appreciate the real bite of the first two steps of our three-step argument: by showing that actions are performable in an unbroken sea of causation, and by showing that the moral excuses are not partial and incomplete concessions to a more general causal principle, we have denied the causal theorist his most natural beachheads. He cannot claim that an actor is responsible only for his uncaused actions. Nor can he claim that our established moral excuses exculpate only uncaused actions. He is left with only a very isolated class of moral experience that speaks for his interpretation of the principle of responsibility.

That class of experience we have described before in our discussion of 'impure common sense'. It consists in the sympathy we may feel for wrongdoers whose wrongdoing was caused by factors such as social adversity or psychological abuse during childhood. There are three things to say about this range of moral experience. First, the moral judgement it seems to support does not fit with the much larger set of judgements about responsibility that we make in daily life. In seeking the most coherent expression of our moral judgements considered as a whole, these sympathetic judgements may simply have to be discarded. No area of human knowledge is perfectly coherent. Any systematic exposition of our sensory experience, for example, has to disregard certain visual experiences because they give us inaccurate information about the world. (Our perception of a 'bent' stick partially immersed in water is a good example.) The same can be said of our sympathetic responses to disadvantaged criminals.

Second, we should be suspicious of that class of moral or perceptual experiences whose existence we can explain in a way that does not presuppose their truth. That is, just as we discount our experience with sticks looking bent when immersed in water because we can explain the experience away, so we should discount any sympathy for disadvantaged criminals if we can explain why we feel that sympathy in terms of extraneous factors.[135] A feature of these moral experiences that should raise our suspicions is their asymmetry with regard to different kinds of causes: different causes of criminal behaviour will call forth in us widely varying intu-

---

[135] Any moral theory will have to reject some of the emotions that generate the theory in order to maintain overall coherence. See Moore, 'Moral Reality', *supra* n. 83, at 1136.

itions.[136] Psychological abuse during childhood or a ghetto upbringing may give rise to intuitions of excuse, but one rarely hears the same argument made to excuse criminals because of their happy childhood, their parents' wealth, or the advantages they may have enjoyed as a celebrity—even though such factors may well cause someone (for example, Loeb and Leopold, the Menendez brothers, O. J. Simpson) to become a criminal. This asymmetry could evidence a connection between our sympathy for the disadvantaged defendant and either (1) our own guilt at not having done enough to alleviate 'unhappy' causes of crime, or (2) our sense that those who became criminals because of adverse circumstances have 'already suffered enough'.[137] In either case, the experience of sympathy may betoken something other than a general judgement that causation of choice excuses.

Finally, we have reason to discount certain experiences and the intuitions they generate when, on examination, their appearance of moral goodness proves deceptive. We might, for example, find that our feelings of pity harbour a hidden resentment, that our feelings of guilt mask self-loathing, or that our feelings of vengeance hide our own desires to engage in the criminal violence we nominally abhor. In each case we turn our moral theory back onto the experiences that generate it to judge their moral worth in light of their true psychology. If we find them wanting, then we have reason to reject the moral judgements such experiences seems to support.

In the case of those feelings of sympathy on which the causal theorist relies, one aspect of their psychology should make us hesitate to honour them as sources of moral insight. There is an élitism and a condescension often (and perhaps invariably) connected with such feelings. To stand back and to refuse to judge because one understands the causes of criminal behaviour is to elevate one's self over the unhappy deviant. The elevation of self takes place because

[136] See Hollander, 'Selective Determinism', *supra* n. 78, at 148: '[T]he popular social determinism of our days is not consistent but selective. In general, it proposes (or implies) that only the behavior of "underdogs" is socially determined, . . . only the lower strata are cast into certain roles by more powerful social forces, groups or agencies, or are equally helpless victims of expectations or labeling.'

[137] For an example of this last idea, see the letter to the *New York Times* quoted in Hollander, *supra* n. 78, at 148: 'Listening to the stories behind each hijacker . . . points to a recurrent theme of frustration: to the hijacker the hijacking seems to represent a last, desperate effort for personal integrity in times that make this basic human feeling so hard to realize. It saddens me to hear these frightened, despondent men sentenced to more of the same despondency for 20 years.'

these causal theorists typically maintain high moral standards for themselves, yet refuse to judge others by those same standards. This discrimination betokens a refusal to acknowledge the equal moral dignity of others. It betokens a sense about one's self—as the seat of subjective will and responsibility—that one refuses to acknowledge in others. In Sartrean terms, it is to treat the disadvantaged criminal as an in-itself rather than as a for-itself.

By their nature, neither of these last two considerations can be conclusive. Experiences that are explicable for reasons unconnected to their truth and experiences that, when truly understood, demonstrate to us our own moral failings, may still lead us to make true judgements. One's hallucinations can result in true beliefs, and even moral lepers may stumble onto a moral truth or two. Still, considerations such as these give us strong reason to doubt that the sympathy we may well feel for disadvantaged criminals is evidence of a moral judgement about the incompatibility of causation and responsibility. And in any event, our first consideration, if correct, is conclusive: the causal theorist's interpretation of the principle of responsibility is inconsistent with the mass of our judgements about where it is just to praise and blame. Given the choice between discarding that interpretation and discarding the mass of moral experience with which it is inconsistent, it is easy to discard the contested interpretation. The result is to reject any requirement that, before we say an actor 'could have acted otherwise', we establish that his choice to act was uncaused. Put another way, the result is to affirm the proposition with which we began, that one is responsible for actions that result from one's choices, even though those choices are caused by factors themselves unchosen.

With the disappearance of the causal theorist's interpretation of the principle of responsibility, the last vestige of an argument for his moral position also disappears. For the third and last beachhead from which the causal theorist could launch his assault on the coherence of our moral system is denied him once his version of the principle is rejected. My case, accordingly, is complete once it is shown: (1) that behaviour can be an action even if it is caused; (2) that the moral excuses we have are not partial and inconsistent concessions to a general causal theory of excuse; and (3) that there are good reasons to reject the causal theorist's interpretation of the principle of responsibility and to reject the intuitions on which that interpretation is based.

There is thus no good reason to fear that in the realm of criminal law the legal excuses we presently recognize are arbitrary and isolated instances of a much more general moral excuse. There is no general moral excuse in terms of causation. Criminal law theoreticians who continue to argue that there is are either succumbing to the conceptual confusions we have exposed or giving undue weight to some isolated and inconsistent sympathies in the systematic articulation of our moral experience.

VI. CONCLUSION

The causal theory of excuses has too long exercised its influence over criminal law theory. Implicit adherence to it has clouded our confidence in the moral basis of punishment. It has produced some shaky metaphysics and even shakier moral theorizing by criminal lawyers. It has produced proposals to interpret or abolish the existing legal excuses, or to add new ones, that do not comport with the moral deserts of offenders. And it has blurred lines that should not be blurred, such as the line separating bodily movements that are actions from those that are not. For each of these reasons, we do well to be rid of it.

13

CHOICE, CHARACTER, AND EXCUSE

I. INTRODUCTION

Freud justified his extensive theorizing about dreams by the observation that they were 'the royal road' to something much more general: namely, our unconscious mental life. The current preoccupation with the theory of excuse in criminal law scholarship can be given a similar justification, for the excuses are the royal road to theories of responsibility generally. The thought is that if we understand why we excuse in certain situations but not others, we will have also gained a much more general insight into the nature of responsibility itself.

In this chapter I shall consider two additional theories of excuse, each of which instantiates its own distinctive theory of responsibility. One is what I shall call *the choice theory of excuse*, according to which one is excused for the doing of a wrongful action because and only because at the moment of such action's performance, one did not have sufficient capacity or opportunity to make the choice to do otherwise. Such a choice theory of excuse instantiates a more general theory of responsibility, according to which we are responsible for wrongs we freely choose to do, and not responsible for wrongs we lacked the freedom (capacity and opportunity) to avoid doing. The second I shall call *the character theory of excuse*, according to which one is excused for the doing of a wrongful action because and only because such action is not determined by (or in some other way expressive of) those enduring attributes of ourselves we call our characters. Such a character theory of excuse instantiates a more general theory of responsibility, according to which the primary object of our responsibility is our own character, and responsibility for wrongful action is derivative of this primary responsibility, our actions being proxies for the characters such actions express.

These abbreviated formulae require much clarification, some of which I undertake in the succeeding parts of this paper (sections II and III). I then compare the merits of the two theories in section IV, concluding that while two kinds of moral responsibility exist, based respectively on choice and on character, only the choice theory captures the kind of moral responsibility relevant to retributive punishment.

II. THE CHOICE THEORY OF EXCUSE

What I call the choice theory of excuse is also called the 'capacity conception of responsibility', the 'responsibility principle', the 'voluntarism principle', the 'Kantian theory of responsibility', the 'value of choice' theory of excuses, the 'voluntariness principle', the 'personhood principle', and my own earlier label, the 'disturbed practical reason' theory of excuse.[1] An early expression of the theory can be found in Blackstone[2] when he said that the legal excuses of his time could be 'reduced to this single consideration, the want or defect of *will*. An involuntary act, as it has no claim to merit, so neither can it induce any guilt: the concurrence of the will, when it has its choice either to do or avoid the act in question, being the only thing that renders human actions praiseworthy or culpable.'

Despite its long history and its many current adherents, the choice theory's classical modern expression is to be found in the writings of Herbert Hart.[3] In examining legal excusing conditions, Hart thought:

[1] See, respectively, to the labels used in the text: Nicola Lacey, *State Punishment* (London: Routledge, 1988), 62; Hyman Gross, *A Theory of Criminal Justice* (New York: Oxford University Press, 1979), 137; Sanford H. Kadish, 'Excusing Crime', in his *Blame and Punishment* (New York: Macmillan, 1987), 81–106, at 88; Michael D. Bayles, 'Character, Purpose, and Criminal Responsibility', *Law and Philosophy*, Vol. 1, no. 1 (Apr. 1982), 5–20, at 6; T. M. Scanlon, jr., 'Quality of Will and the Value of Choice' (unpublished manuscript, 1988), 42; George Fletcher, *Rethinking Criminal Law* (Boston: Little, Brown, 1978), 804; Joshua Dressler, *Understanding Criminal Law* (New York: Matthew Bender, 1987), at 185; Joshua Dressler, 'Reflections on Excusing Wrongdoers: Moral Theory, New Excuses, and the Model Penal Code', *Rutgers Law Journal*, Vol. 19, no. 3 (Spring 1988), 671–716, at 701; and Moore, *Law and Psychiatry: Rethinking the Relationship* (Cambridge: Cambridge University Press, 1984), 85–90.

[2] Sir William Blackstone, *Commentaries on the Laws of England*, Chitty, ed., Vol. IV (London, 1826), 20.

[3] See the essays collected in H. L. A. Hart, *Punishment and Responsibility* (Oxford: Oxford University Press, 1968).

What is crucial is that those whom we punish should have had, when they acted, the normal capacities, physical and mental, for abstaining from what it [the law] forbids, and a fair opportunity to exercise these capacities. Where these capacities and opportunities are absent, as they are in different ways in the varied cases of accident, mistake, paralysis, reflex action, coercion, insanity, etc., the moral protest is that it is morally wrong to punish because 'he could not have helped it' or 'he could not have done otherwise' or 'he had no real choice.'[4]

Such a theory of excuse is itself but an instance of a more general principle of moral responsibility: 'what the law has done here is to reflect, albeit imperfectly, a fundamental principle of morality that a person is not to be blamed for what he has done if he could not help doing it'.[5]

This theory of excuse, and its accompanying, more general theory of responsibility, was given two quite different justifications by Hart. Hart's early justification, found in his seminal 1957 paper, 'Legal Responsibility and Excuses',[6] arguably was a kind of rule-utilitarianism. The function or value of having duress, insanity, automatism, etc., be excuses to criminal liability was to maximize 'the efficacy of the individual's informed and considered choice . . .'[7] Hart more fully described the good that excuses achieved in the criminal law:

On this view excusing conditions are accepted as something that may conflict with the social utility of the law's threats; they are regarded as of moral importance because they provide for all individuals alike the satisfactions of a choosing system. Recognition of excusing conditions is therefore seen as a matter of protection of the individual against the claims of society from the highest measure of protection from crime that can be obtained from a system of threats. In this way the criminal law respects the claims of the individual as such, or at least as a *choosing being*, and distributes its coercive sanctions in a way that reflects this respect for the individual.[8]

Hart's idea here was that choice is a power that people prefer and whose exercise provides substantial satisfactions. It is therefore a

---

[4] See the essays collected in H. L. A. Hart, *Punishment and Responsibility*, *supra* n. 3, 152.

[5] Ibid., 174.

[6] H. L. A. Hart, 'Legal Responsibility and Excuses', Sidney S. Hook, ed., *Determinism and Freedom* (New York: New York University Press, 1958), and reprinted in Hart's *Punishment and Responsibility*, 28–53. (Subsequent references to this essay are to the reprinted version.)

[7] Ibid., 46.   [8] Ibid., 49 (emphasis in original).

good that competes with the good that is crime-prevention. The goodness of choice to people is largely due to the power we all want to predict the future.[9] As Scanlon puts Hart's point here: 'The most obvious reason why choice has value for me . . . is simply instrumental: I would like what happens (e.g., what appears on my plate) to conform to my preferences . . .'.[10] The way that the excuses of the criminal law further the good that is choice is by protecting unfree, unimpeded choice from criminal sanction; only my free choices will be sanctioned, and knowing that, I can maximally predict what will follow upon my decisions. As Scanlon puts it, if I can 'believe that if what happens depends on my subjective response under given conditions then the result is likely to coincide with what I want'.[11]

This rationale for having the excuses we do is arguably utilitarian, for it balances off the maximization of one good most people prefer, crime-prevention, against the maximization of another such good, the good that is free choice. It becomes a *rule*-utilitarian rationale once one says, as Hart did, that the attainment of the goodness of choice is not balanced against the attainment of the goodness of crime-prevention in one overall calculation of the good; rather, such calculations are assigned their own 'levels' of appropriate domain. The doctrines necessary to achieve a satisfactory level of free choice (once set by separate calculation) then operate as a constraint on the maximization of the good that is crime-prevention.

Hart's second and later justification for the choice theory of excuse—and the way he is usually read today—grounds it in considerations of fairness and justice that are not themselves products of utilitarian calculation. That is, the excuses and the 'could have done otherwise' principle they instantiate are seen as deontological, or non-consequentialist, side constraints that constrain the maximization of any utilitarian goals, crime-prevention and choice-maximization included. As Hart himself later recognized, there are constraints 'which civilized moral thought places on the pursuit of the utilitarian goal by the demand that punishment should not be applied to the innocent . . .'.[12] One of those constraints is 'that out of considerations of fairness or justice to individuals we should restrict even punishment designed as a "preventative" [i.e.,

---

[9] Ibid., 49.

[10] Scanlon, 'Quality of Will', *supra* n. 1, at 25.

[11] Ibid.

[12] Hart, *Punishment and Responsibility*, *supra* n. 3, at 80.

utilitarian punishment] to those who had a normal capacity and a fair opportunity to obey'.[13]

As important for our purposes as the justification of the choice theory of excuse is the meaning of the theory. What does it mean to say, 'one is responsible only for *free* choice', or that 'one is responsible if he *could* have done otherwise'? Although Hart made fruitful beginnings in the unpacking of these terms, more detail than he himself provided is needed if we are to understand the choice theory of excuse.

Take the word 'could' in the 'could have done otherwise' principle. There are three readings of 'could', only one of which is intended by the principle. The first is the weak, or behavioural, sense of 'could'. On this reading, our abilities (what we *can* do, or, counterfactually, what we *could* have done) are measured by what we actually do. If on some occasion we do run a mile in under four minutes, then on that occasion we *could* run a mile in under four minutes; if on some occasion we run a mile in over four minutes, then on that occasion we *could not* run a mile in under four minutes. This weak or behavioural sense of 'could' is obviously not what is wanted in the principle, because it trivializes our abilities into merely alternative descriptions of our behaviour. In this sense of 'could', a broken clock *could* tell the correct time twice every twenty-four hours (because it did so); a mechanically perfect clock that was set too fast *could not* tell the correct time (because it did not do so). These are not only not idiomatic usages of 'could'; they are nonsensical, because they eliminate the idea of general ability presupposed by 'can' and 'could'. Put simply: it has to be possible that I *can* do some things I do not in fact do.

The second reading of 'could' is the strong, or incompatibilist, sense of the word that we examined at the close of the last chapter. On this reading, we *can* do some action A only if A is not caused by factors external to the will of the actor. On this view, 'I could have run a mile in four minutes' means not only that there were no causes sufficient to prevent me from doing it, but also, had I done it, that there would have been no causes of that doing of it (other than my willing to do it, which itself must be uncaused).

I doubt that this is an ordinary or idiomatic sense of the word 'could', despite a defence of this sense of the word by no less an

---

[13] Hart, *Punishment and Responsibility, supra* n. 3, 201.

ordinary language philosopher than J. L. Austin.[14] Notice that to use this sense of the word in the statement about an accurately set, perfectly functioning clock, 'it can tell the correct time', attributes free will to the clock. In any case, the issue here is not a question of linguistic usage but of morals: is the incompatibilist sense the right sense to be plugged into the 'could have done otherwise' principle in order to make that principle true? I argued in the preceding chapter that it is not. Not wanting to duplicate that chapter's defence of compatibilist metaphysics, let me therefore only mention the incompatibilist sense of 'could' in order to put it aside. The choice theory of excuse as Hart and I have construed it does not require any libertarian metaphysics in order to make it true.[15]

What is required is a third, compatibilist, reading of the principle, which is this: 'he could have done otherwise' is elliptical for 'he could have done otherwise if he had chosen to'. His choice, in other words, was not made *impossible* by factors over which he had no control; his choice was a cause of his behaviour (even if it itself was caused). Moreover, his choice was not made *very difficult* by factors over which he had no control; his choice was what lawyers call an *intervening cause*, intervening between the factors that caused it and the action it caused.[16]

We arrive, then, at the crux of the interpretation of the choice theory of excuse. What makes choices impossible or very difficult? Notice the implausibility of the incompatibilist answer to this question (just to give my favourite dead horse a few more lashes): the incompitibilist thinks that the factors that *cause* choice, being themselves unchosen, *preclude* choice. Discover, for example, that will

[14] J. L. Austin, 'Ifs and Cans', H. Morris, ed., *Freedom and Responsibility* (Stanford: Stanford University Press, 1961).

[15] A libertarian in metaphysics (as opposed to political theory) believes that human actions are uncaused by any factors external to the will of the actor. A compatibilist, as I am here using the word, believes that choice and causation are compatible, so that the statements 'he chose to do that' and 'his choice was caused by factors themselves unchosen by him' can both be true of some actor and his action. Correspondingly, an incompatibilist believes that choice and causation are incompatible in the sense that the two statements just mentioned cannot both be true. (Notice that, on the choice theory of responsibility, a compatibilist about choice and causation will also be a compatibilist about responsibility and causation.)

[16] For an analysis of the notion of an intervening cause, see H. L. A. Hart and A. M. Honoré, *Causation in the Law* (Oxford: Oxford University Press, 2nd edn. 1985). As Hart and Honoré analyse it, for a human action to be an intervening cause it must be 'voluntary' in their extended sense of that word, which means not done in ignorance, not done in compulsion, not done while insane, etc.

(choice) is caused by certain complex sorts of brain states,[17] and, presto, you have really discovered that choice was impossible or very difficult: i.e., that either there is no choice (idiomatically, 'really no choice') or that all choices are hard choices (idiomatically, 'no real choice'). This seems about as plausible to me as saying that once you discover the causes for something like mental illness, that thing can no longer be said to exist.[18]

Be that as it may, I said we were putting aside incompatibilist views, for (when coupled with deterministic metaphysics) they make *all* choices impossible and thus all actions excused on the choice theory of excuse. Hart's answer was different. What makes choices impossible or very difficult is either an incapacity in the agent or the lack of fair opportunity to use a non-defective capacity. Hart thus subdivides the ability presupposed by his sense of 'could' into two components. One relates to the equipment of the actor: does he have sufficient choosing capacity to be responsible? The other relates to the situation in which the actor finds himself: does that situation present him with a fair chance to use his capacities for choice so as to give effect to his decision?

An example perhaps is helpful here. Imagine that someone who is accused of stealing in order to get money with which to purchase heroin proffers his addiction to heroin as an excuse. There are two versions of his excuse that are relevant on the choice theory as Hart construes it. One would be defective capacity: at the time of stealing, his faculty of reason was overcome by the compelling desire (construed as a reason-unhinging emotional storm) for heroin. The other would be lack of fair opportunity: at the time of stealing, he was not in the grip of any compelling desire or other emotion; rather, he coolly foresaw that if he did not get money for heroin, he would not get heroin, and that if he did not get heroin, he would eventually suffer the extremely unpleasant consequences of withdrawal symptoms. His opportunity to avoid stealing was thus less than for the rest of us, for (unlike the rest of us) not stealing had extremely unpleasant consequences for him.

---

[17] On the neurophysiology of willing, choice, and self-directed action, see Benjamin Libet, 'Unconscious Cerebral Initiative and the Role of Conscious Will in Voluntary Action', *The Behavioral and Brain Sciences*, Vol. 8, no. 4 (Fall 1985), 529–66. See also Myles Brand, *Intending and Acting* (Cambridge: MIT Press, 1984).

[18] One version of Tom Szasz's 'myth of mental illness' thesis. See Moore, *Law and Psychiatry*, *supra* n. 1, at ch. 4.

If addiction were an excuse for stealing, on the choice theory of excuse one or other of these variants would have to be true. That addiction is so implausible as an excuse for stealing is due to the implausibility of either of these claims being true. The defective capacity version depends on what many now regard as an implausible psychological story,[19] and the lack of fair opportunity version depends on a morally implausible view of how diminished our opportunities must be in order to excuse choices made in such circumstances. Thus, that addiction is a poor candidate for an excuse to stealing is something the choice theory of excuse can explain as well as it can explain why it is a candidate for an excuse at all.

Consider duress as a second example of excuse that allows us to delve more deeply into the nature of the choice theory of excuse. One is legally and morally excused for doing an illegal and wrongful act if the doing of it was caused by the threat of a third party to do something unpleasant to the the actor unless he complied with the threat. For example, D_1 is threatened with being shot in the knees unless he drives an IRA gunman to the location of a policeman who the gunman intends to kill.[20]

Put aside any justificatory readings of duress; assume that being shot in the knees is a lesser evil than is the evil of making possible the death of an innocent. D_1's claim can then only be excuse, not justification. There are two readings of D_1's excuse claim on the choice theory. He can tell a psychological story about how hard it was to even think about resisting the threat because his consciousness was flooded by a fear of being shot and a revulsion at the thought of seeing his own blood. Or he can tell a story of how unfair the gunman's threat made D_1's situation of choice, because the threat attached a consequence to D_1's choosing not to help the gunman that is not commonly attached to the choice of the rest of us not to aid terrorists. His first claim is defective capacity; his second, diminished opportunity.

A reason for favouring the opportunity version over the incapacity version of duress can be seen from the following example.[21]

---

[19] See, e.g., Herbert Fingarette, *Heavy Drinking: the Myth of Alcoholism as a Disease* (Berkeley: University of California Press, 1988), reviewed by me in *Ethics*, vol. 99, no. 3 (Apr. 1989), 660–1.

[20] Cf. *Lynch* v. *Director of Public Prosecutions* [1975] 1 All ER 913.

[21] Other reasons for favouring the opportunity versus the capacity version of the duress excuse as it is reflected in current criminal law doctrine are given by Dressler, 'Reflections', *supra* n. 1, at 708–12.

D_2 unjustifiably hates another, X, who is in fact an exemplary individual. Much to D_2's delight, X is dying. He can be saved, however, by a rare drug known to T. T threatens D_2 with T's giving the drug to X, and thereby saving X's life, unless D_2 robs a bank with T. D_2 is not otherwise inclined to rob the bank—he does not need the money—yet the thought of X being given the drug and not dying is more than he can stand. After days of not being able to keep the picture of X's happy, smiling, healthy face out of his mind, D2 reluctantly agrees to rob the bank with T.

Common intuition—at least if two decades' worth of criminal law students is any guide—tells us that D_2 is not excused for the bank robbery. Yet, on the capacity version of the duress defence, why not? D_2 was seemingly as incapacitated by his hatred of X as D_1 was by his fear of his own injury. D_2's faculty of reason apparently did not have the same capacity to make choices as does the reason of those not under such emotional distraction.

To reject D_2's proffered excuse is to reject the idea that this kind of (internal) incapacity can, by itself, excuse. The intuition that guides this rejection is the intuition that people like D_2 are responsible. This intuition of a larger responsibility has apparently motivated both Sandy Kadish's recent favouring of the opportunity version of excuses[22] and Stephen Morse's disfavouring of what he calls the 'internal compulsion' type of excuses.[23] Kadish and Morse, like Aristotle before them,[24] are worried that recognizing fears, cravings, instinctual desires, strong passions, or other internal states as excuses unduly reduces one's true responsibility. The child's 'something made me do it' is taken to be a bad imitation of an excuse, not the general form of an internally incapacitating excuse.

Freud had a similar insight about the proper extent of one's responsibility in the face of fears like those of my hypothetical D_1 and D_2. In discussing the responsibility of each of us for the content of one's dreams, Freud recognized the temptation to subdivide the self and to attribute the bad stuff to a 'not-me', an it or id within me but not identical to me. Freud rejected such a narrow

[22] Kadish, 'Excusing Crime', *supra* n. 1, at 101–2, 104–6.

[23] Stephen Morse, 'Psychology, Determinism, and Legal Responsibility', Gary Melton, ed., *Nebraska Symposium on Motivation 1985*, Vol. 33 (Lincoln: University of Nebraska Press, 1986), 35–85.

[24] Aristotle, *Nichomachean Ethics*, bk. III, ch. 1, in Richard McKeon, *Introduction to Aristotle* (Chicago: University of Chicago Press, 1973), 387–8.

notion of responsibility, disdainfully leaving 'it to the jurist to construct for social purposes a responsibility that is artificially limited
to the metapsychological ego'.[25]

Freud had his finger on what I take to be bothering Kadish,
Morse, and Aristotle: D_1's and D_2's responsibility are too circum-
scribed on the capacity version of the duress excuse because the *self*
who is being held responsible (or excused) is itself too narrow.
We—the persons or selves who are the subjects of responsibility—
are more than the faculty of reason that does battle with the faculty of emotion; we are our emotions as much as we are our reason.

Resolving this worry about internal factors operating as incapacitating excuses thus involves us in some deep questions that go
to the heart of the choice theory of excuse. One is the question
already mentioned: what self-boundaries does the theory presuppose? Does the responsible self who chooses include any emotions,
or is the responsible self who chooses only to be identified with the
conscious will, against which all emotions are alien and potentially
disturbing (incapacitating) factors? The example of D_2 should
incline the choice theorist strongly towards Freud's view: some
emotions, at least, have to be included within the self who chooses.
D_2's hatred of X is part of him; it cannot be seen as an alien factor that incapacitates *him* from deciding whether or not to rob the
bank.

Such an extended view of self may seen unavailable on the choice
theory of responsibility, for it may seem that to hold people like D_2
responsible for their actions requires a prior judgement holding
them responsible for being who they are (viz., people with these
kinds of emotions). This would mean that we are ultimately judging D_2 for his bad character, and—only in light of that judgement—then judging the culpability of his choice.

Whether this is so depends on a second fundamental question the
choice theorist about responsibility and excuse must answer: does
our choosing agency, the will, include those of our emotions that
are part of our self, or are such emotions not part of such agency
even though they are part of us? Such a question makes sense
because our subpersonal agencies (of perception, cognition, etc.)

---

[25] Sigmund Freud, 'Moral Responsibility for the Content of Dreams', in *Standard
Edition of the Works of Sigmund Freud*, ed. James Strachey (London: Hogarth Press,
1961), Vol. 19, 131–4. I discuss this passage from Freud and others on responsibility in Moore, *Law and Psychiatry, supra* n. 1, at 343–8.

are not coextensive with our personal selves;[26] it is thus possible that an emotion can be part of us and yet not part of our processes of choice. If this possibility is in fact realized in a case such as D_2, then when we hold D_2 responsible, it is not for his choice to do evil (for his choice was a hard one, given the emotion alien to it), but for the fact that he is evil in his emotional make-up.

If we think through what choosing to act (willing) is, we will find it difficult to keep emotions like D_2's hatred of X separate from D_2's choice to help T with the bank robbery. In its narrowest sense, willing is the initiation of motor responses like moving one's finger, raising one's arm, and the like. Such bodily movements are the simplest things one knows how to do, and it is through them that we cause more complex events in the real world. The choice that is the touchstone of responsibility for the choice theorist includes the willing of these movements, but much more besides. It includes the practical reasoning processes that lead up to the willing of bodily movements. It is here, antecedent to such willings, that intentions and plans are formed in light of the actor's desires and beliefs. It is here that the actor chooses his actions under more complex descriptions than simply 'moving my body': descriptions such as 'taking my revenge on X' or 'eliminating that hateful X'. Choice, to be morally interesting, must include not only the initiation of bodily movements but also the formation of the intentions and beliefs that guide and motivate the doing of such simple things. We choose our plans (complex actions), and not simply the simple movements that execute them.[27]

---

[26] I discuss Dan Dennett's distinction between personal versus subpersonal levels of explanation in *Law and Psychiatry, supra* n. 1, at 274–5. By 'subpersonal agency', I mean those centres of functioning posited to exist at the subpersonal level by the approach to mind we called in ch. 10 'homuncular functionalism'. A homuncular functionalist believes that the nature of a person's actions and thoughts are best approached by subdividing them into the 'actions' and 'thoughts' of subpersonal agencies each of who 'do' only a part of what the whole person does.

[27] This passage seems to have misled some of my critics (such as Jeremy Horder, 'Criminal Culpability: The Possibility of a General Theory', *Law and Philosophy*, Vol. 12 (1993), 193–215, at 201) into thinking that choice must involve consciously deliberative process whereby alternatives are formulated and reasons weighted. By choice I mean to designate nothing this phenomenologically rich. I mean nothing more than what I take to be usually meant by intention and belief, states that are often preconscious in the sense that we 'unthinkingly' form them. With Freud, I think of both our selves and our choosing agency as including that which allows us to perform many complex routines intentionally without having to direct our consciousness to them.

If this is what is meant by 'choice', then some emotions will necessarily have a place in this process. As Sabini and Silver observe: 'The emotions are connected to cognition, connected to desires and plans. . . .'.[28] On this view, the emotions are not invaders of our processes of reasoned deliberation, nor are they preemptors of such processes. Rather, our emotions are both products and causes of the judgements we make as we decide what to do. When we get angry, for example, our anger can itself be caused by judgement: for instance, that an innocent person has just suffered undeserved punishment. Such anger reflects our judgement that something immoral has just taken place.[29] Further, such anger at unjust treatment need not make reasoned choice more difficult. It may instead make choice easier by highlighting what we otherwise might have missed. Anger at injustice is at least as effective as reciting Kant when keeping the priority of justice before one's mind as one decides how to respond.

If all of this is true, then it may seem that Kadish and Morse are right: internal factors like emotions cannot be said to incapacitate our choices, except by an impermissibly narrow view either of who we are or of what our choosing agency consists.

As much as I agree with this in cases like D_2—where the emotion in question clearly seems both part of him and part of his choice to allow X to die—if all emotions are treated in this way, then there is no incapacitation of choice story to be told about D_1 either. True, D_1 may invoke the 'lack of fair opportunity' branch of excuse, whereby he is excused by his comparative lack of opportunity to avoid doing evil. Yet the diminished opportunity branch excuses D_1 without regard to how hard he found the choice; does not the D_1 who is 'overcome' by his fear of being shot and his revulsion at the thought of his own blood have some excuse in addition to diminished opportunity?

I am unsure how morality answers this question. It does not matter much in cases of duress, because the diminished opportunity

[28] John Sabini and Maury Silver, 'Emotions, Responsibility, and Character', F. Schoeman, ed., *Responsibility, Character, and the Emotions* (Cambridge: Cambridge University Press, 1987), 164–75, at 168.

[29] Being caused by judgement, such emotions obey laws of proportionality, keeping feeling proportional, both in type and intensity, to its object. (Grieve over a dead goose too long and it will not take a Freudian to surmise that the real object of your feeling is something else, something more appropriate to the nature and depth of your feelings.)

branch of the excuse is available in any event. The answer matters a lot to alleged excuses such as provocation, pathological gambling, or obsessional neurosis, where there is no plausible diminished opportunity story to be told. Common sense morality seems to reflect the idea that some emotions incapacitate choice, and thus excuse. Such an idea is based on a psychological view that holds that some emotions are not 'judgement-connected' in the two ways described before: (1) such emotions are not caused by judgements and so do not take Intentional objects (these emotions are described as 'blind rage' or 'free-floating anxiety'), and (2) such emotions cause behaviour in the way that anger or fear causes our heartbeats to increase: not by motivating a choice to act but by causing action directly without the mediation of choice and judgement.

My doubts about common sense morality here stem from my doubts about these psychological suppositions. Are any emotions truly free of corresponding judgements that justify them to the agent whose emotions they are? Is any rage truly blind, or any anxiety without its object? Do the emotions that allegedly cause action by 'short-circuiting' choice ever proceed except by a chosen letting go, a chosen self-indulgence?

A complete exposition of the incapacity branch of the choice theory of excuse would have to answer these questions. Since my purpose is merely to sketch the choice theory for purposes of contrasting it to the character theory, I fortunately can leave them open. We still need to clarify the diminished opportunity branch of the theory before we turn to the character theory of excuse. Think again of my example of the unjustifiably hateful bank robber (D_2). Why cannot such a bank robber make out the diminished opportunity version of the duress excuse? After all, his opportunity not to rob the bank was less than ours: if he did not rob it, this would have had the consequence that his old enemy X would have survived.

What this brings out is the sense of 'unfair opportunity' being used in the opportunity branch of the theory. Our opportunities to avoid wrongful action are not *unfairly* diminished simply because they are diminished. The 'cost' to D_2 of not robbing the bank should not have been regarded as a cost at all; in reality, it was a benefit that X not die. That D_2 did not so regard it made it psychologically harder for him (the narrow 'him') to refrain from robbing the bank. But D_2's *fair* opportunity is not measured by his psychological difficulties, but rather by the objective facts of the matter. Objectively D_2 had a fair opportunity not to rob the bank, even if subjectively he experienced it as a hard choice.[30]

This may raise a doubt about the opportunity branch of the choice theory of excuse: namely, how it differs from justification. For to lack a *fair* opportunity to avoid doing wrong, there must be some (objectively regarded) evil that one is avoiding, and that may seem to imply that one is justified in doing wrong. Yet the opportunity branch of excuse does not collapse into justification in this way. The fair opportunity idea could be called the 'failed justification' idea of excuse. Even though an actor does more bad than good in his action (and is thus not justified), he nonetheless may have lacked a fair opportunity to avoid doing wrong if he acted to prevent some substantial evil. Loss of one's bodily integrity by being shot in the knees is such a substantial evil; the survival of a good person is not such a substantial evil, explaining why D_1 but not D_2 may avail himself of the excuse of duress on the fair opportunity construal of it.

Antony Duff has recently rejected this defence of the diminished opportunity version of the duress excuse.[31] Duff apparently believes that diminished opportunity is an all or nothing affair: if the opportunities to avoid evil are so constricted that such evil can be avoided only by causing a greater evil, then the action that does not avoid the first evil is not wrongful because justified; but if the opportunities are less restricted than this, not only is the action unjustified but the actor can have no excuse of unfair opportunity. To revert to my example of D_1, if injury to his knees is a lesser evil than the enabling of the IRA execution of a policeman, then not only is D_2's action unjustified but his opportunity to avoid the greater evil cannot be sufficiently diminished to excuse him.

Duff comes to this conclusion because he thinks that neither morality nor a rational criminal law would be so redundant and inconsistent as to draw the same (diminished opportunity) line *twice* (once for justification and then again for excuse) and, moreover, draw it in different places. The answer to Duff lies in the

---

[30] Just as D_1 has a diminished opportunity sort of excuse, even if he experienced his choice as an easy one.

[31] R. A. Duff, 'Choice, Character, and Criminal Liability', *Law and Philosophy*, Vol. 12 (1993), 345–83, at 355.

insight that the questions of justification and diminished opportunity do not draw the same line twice. The insight stems from one of the basic distinctions organizing this book, the distinction between wrongdoing and culpability. As argued in chapter 1, justifications answer the question of whether an action is wrongful, that is, did it instantiate one of those agent-relative prohibitions of morality or did its bad consequences outweigh its good ones (often a violation of a background, agent-neutral obligation not to make the world worse)? This is not a question of the fair opportunity of an actor. 'Ought may imply can', as Kant famously proclaimed, yet that Kantian maxim should not be construed to collapse the question of whether a norm of morality has been violated with the question of whether an actor can fairly be blamed for the violation because he had a fair opportunity not to violate the norms.

Admittedly, justification questions and diminished opportunity questions are similar in that both are objective and both are straightforwardly moral questions. 'Opportunity' is relevantly defined for excuse purposes in a moral way, so that 'fair opportunity' takes into account the degree of evil an actor would have faced had he not done the evil he did. Yet there is no inconsistency in holding to what I take to be the common sense moral position here: morally acceptable alternatives to some wrongful action can be so diminished that the actor is excused and yet those alternatives are not *so* diminished that the actor was justified in what he did. To say anything else would be to eliminate entirely diminution of opportunity as a form of excuse.

III. THE CHARACTER THEORY OF EXCUSE

The choice theory just examined has come to be regarded as the traditional or orthodox view of excuse. There has recently arisen something of a chorus that is critical of the choice theory and instead puts forward a character theory of excuse.[32] This excuse

---

[32] The character theory of excuse is normally attributed to David Hume, who held that 'actions are objects of our moral sentiment, so far only as they are indications of the internal character.' David Hume, *An Enquiry Concerning Human Understanding* (LaSalle: Open Court, 1949), 108. Perhaps the foremost modern exponent of the character theory of excuse has been Richard Brandt. See Richard Brandt, *Ethical Theory* (Englewood Cliffs, NJ: Prentice-Hall, 1959), 465–74; Brandt, 'Blameworthiness and Obligation', A. Melden, ed., *Essays in Moral Philosophy*

theory is grounded in a general view of moral responsibility. On this general view, the ultimate object of our responsibility is our own character. Our responsibility for actions is derivative of our more fundamental responsibility for character.

On this view, the excuses, in both law and morality, serve a kind of filtering function. We are prima facie morally responsible and legally liable for wrongful and illegal acts, but we are only prima facie responsible and liable because we do not yet know whether such wrongful acts were truly expressive of our characters. If they are, we are actually responsible and liable; if they are not, we are neither. The excuses, in such a case, serve to filter out wrongful actions for which we are not responsible because they are not expressive of our character. In such a way the excuses reconcile the ultimate nature of moral responsibility—it is for character, not action—with the surface features of our moral and legal ascriptions: namely, that they are for actions and not character.

This theory of excuse, and the conception of responsibility that stands behind it, are both in considerable need of clarification. Let us begin with the more general conception of responsibility and work towards the filtering function of the excuses. First of all, what is it we are responsible for when we are said to be responsible for our characters?[33] The most initially tempting answer may be what

(Seattle: University of Washington, 1958), 1ff.; Brandt, 'The Utilitarian Theory of Excuse', *Philosophical Review*, Vol. 78, no. 3 (July 1969), 337–61; and Brandt, 'A Motivational Theory of Excuse in the Criminal Law', in S. Pennock and J. Chapman, eds., *Criminal Justice, Nomos 27* (New York: New York University Press, 1985). For other defences of the theory, see also Fletcher, *Rethinking Criminal Law*, *supra* n. 1, at 799–802; Robert Nozick, *Philosophical Explanations* (Cambridge: Harvard University Press, 1981), 387–84, 394–6; Bayles, 'Character, Purpose, and Criminal Responsibility', *supra* n. 1; George Vuoso, 'Background, Responsibility, and Excuse', *Yale Law Journal*, Vol. 96 (1987), 1661–86; Lacey, *State Punishment*, *supra* n. 1, at 67–78; Peter Arenella, 'Character, Choice, and Moral Agency: The Relevance of Character to Our Moral Culpability Judgments', *Social Philosophy and Policy*, Vol. 7 (1990) 59–83, and the as yet unpublished work of Tim Scanlon ('Quality of Will'). As Scanlon discusses ('Quality of Will', 13), the theory is implicit in Peter Strawson's general analysis of responsibility in terms of our reactive attitudes 'not simply at what happens to us or to others as a result of what is done, but at the attitudes of agents towards ourselves or others as revealed [in] their actions.' See P. F. Strawson, 'Freedom and Resentment', G. Watson, ed., *Free Will* (Oxford: Oxford University Press, 1982), 59–80. Gary Watson also explores this aspect of Strawson's thought in Watson, 'Responsibility and the Limits of Evil', F. Schoeman, ed., *Responsibility, Character, and the Emotions* (Cambridge: Cambridge University Press, 1987), 256–86, particularly at 265.

[33] For discussion of character, see particularly Brandt, *Ethical Theory*, 'Blameworthiness and Obligation', and 'The Utilitarian Theory of Excuse'. See also

I shall call the backward-looking behavioural answer. On this view, the character traits we ascribe to people are simply general descriptions of past actions. To be courageous is to have acted courageously in the past, to be honest is to have acted honestly in the past, etc.

One might also call this the verificationist idea of character, because it takes usual evidence of character—past behaviour—to be character itself, in the usual reductionist style of verificationism. What is wrong with this idea of character is what is wrong with verificationism generally: such reductions eliminate what they were supposed to explain. Take Michael Dummett's famous question about courage: can X have been a courageous man, when he is now dead and in his entire life no occasion ever arose that called for courageous behaviour?[34] Unlike Dummett, I think the answer to this question to be rather obviously 'yes',[35] showing that character is not *identical* to past behaviour (conceding that character is often *evidenced* by past behaviour).

This suggests a second sense of character; I shall call it the forward-looking behavioural sense. On this view, our traits of character name dispositions to future behaviour. Such traits thus can sensibly be attributed to persons whose behaviour never realizes them, because such persons can be *disposed* to act in certain ways even if they never do so act because the occasion never arises.

Gilbert Ryle held this dispositional view of character traits.[36] Ryle thought that persons as well as other objects possessed dispositions in his sense: namely, that certain predictions were true of them. A greedy person will (or would), in certain circumstances, act greedily; a soluble object will (or would), in certain circumstances, dissolve in water. But such dispositions are mere behavioural constructs, a part of an agent only in the sense that such predictive and counterfactual statements are true of that agent.

The problem with this view of character is that it is still too exclusively behavioural. Character, on this view, still does not say much about the person whose character it is. To remedy this, why not

Brandt, 'Traits of Character: A Conceptual Analysis', *American Philosophical Quarterly*, Vol. 7 (1970), 23–37.

[34] Michael Dummett, *Truth and Other Enigmas* (Cambridge: Harvard University Press, 1978), 14–16.

[35] See Brandt, 'Traits of Character', *supra* n. 33, at 26.

[36] Gilbert Ryle, *The Concept of Mind* (London: Hutcheson, 1949).

say, as Quine did against Ryle,[37] that every disposition like greediness requires there to be a dispositional *state* of greediness? Further, that the nature of this state may be physiological, so that certain brain states always underlie greedy behaviour; and/or the nature of this state may be reflected in our mental experiences, so that greediness involves certain characteristic emotional experiences and attitudes.[38] We do not adopt a purely behavioural view of solubility or brittleness (Ryle's example of dispositions in natural objects), seeking a physical nature to the *states* such dispositions require; so why be so parsimonious about the physical or phenomenological nature of the states that the character traits of persons require?

Character, on this enriched dispositional view, then becomes logically independent of both the past behaviour that typically evidences it and the future (or counterfactual) behaviour that will (or would) typically manifest it. Unlike the characters conceived of by Dummett and Ryle, character as I conceive it can *cause* the past behaviour that evidences it and will or could cause the future or hypothetical behaviour that manifests it—just because character so conceived is logically independent of such behaviours.

We now need to examine more carefully the nature of states of character like greediness, honesty, etc., in order to reveal an ambiguity on which the character theorist about responsibility needs to take a position. We know little of the physiology of character, so let us stick with its phenomenology. Freud and contemporary Freudians such as Morris Eagle[39] and Herbert Fingarette[40] have studied the ways in which we constitute our sense of ourselves through owning up to, or disowning, various emotions, desires, or behaviours. The phenomenological sense of the id is of the 'not-me', the ego-alien emotions, thoughts, etc., that (1) come unbidden by my will; (2) are experienced as not-me; and (3) cohere neither with the other emotions, etc., that we have nor with the picture we

---

[37] Willard Van Orman Quine, *Word and Object* (Cambridge, Mass.: MIT Press, 1960), 222–5. See also David Papineau, *Theory and Meaning* (Oxford: Clarendon Press, 1979), 182.

[38] To hark back to my general views on how phenomenology interacts with physiology and behaviour to get at the deep nature of mental states, discussed in ch. 10.

[39] Morris Eagle, 'Anatomy of the Self in Psychoanalytic Theory', in Michael Rulse, ed., *Nature Animated* (Dordrecht: Reidel, 1983), 133–61.

[40] Herbert Fingarette, *Self-Deception* (London: Routledge and Kegan Paul, 1969).

have of what we are like. Sometimes we repress such ego-alien entities into unconsciousness, and sometimes we defend our view of ourselves through other defence mechanisms like projection. In any case, 'we' select some subset of all the traits 'we' in some sense possess, and cohere that subset into a view of who 'we' are. (The scare quotes are there because one 'we' is arguably different from another.)

One of Freud's persistent theses about this kind of self-inflicted division of self was that the items typically experienced as ego-alien were instinctual desires and emotions such as sex and aggression. This same tendency can be seen in Gary Watson's discussion of character as well, dividing character into appetitive versus evaluational character.[41] Appetitive character is not what we identify as ourselves, but rather as what intrudes upon or potentially disturbs our selves; our self is to be found in that reflective, evaluative self that picks and chooses which of the desires, emotions, thoughts, etc., are worth being considered part of the self.

The choice faced by the character theorist is this: how broadly does he wish to identify character? Does the character of a person include only that which he reflectively identifies as 'me'? This would be a narrow and subjective view of character, for it excludes those actions, thoughts, and feelings that the person himself subjectively experiences as ego-alien. Or does the character of a person include not only those items *he* identifies as part of his sense of self, but also those he experiences as an *id*? This we shall call the broad and objective view of character, since it includes more items and does so on a non-subjective basis.

As we saw earlier, the choice theorist had to decide whether an emotion such as the hatred of D_2 for X was part of D_2's self, and if it was, whether such emotion was part of that part of D_2 that I called D_2's choosing agency. The character theorist faces a similar decision. If his intuition also is that people like D_2 are responsible, then the character theorist must argue that, no matter how ego-alien may be D_2's experience of his hatred for X, nonetheless (1) D_2's hatred is part of his self, and (2) the character trait that D_2's hatred instantiates is part of D_2's character (so that D_2's action can be expressive of D_2's character and thus not excused on the character theory of excuse). This would commit the character theorist

[41] Gary Watson, 'Free Agency', *Journal of Philosophy*, Vol. 72 (1975), 205–20.

to the broad, objective view of character whereby a person's character includes more than that with which he identifies. This allows the character theorist to say (quite plausibly, to my mind) that someone such as Bulstrode in George Eliot's *Middlemarch* has a character marred by greediness, even though Bulstrode's sense of who he is excludes greediness.

Aside from clarifying what character theorists should mean by 'character', one thing the discussion thus far reveals is that a commonly perceived difference between the character and the choice theories does not exist. It is commonly thought that the choice theorist cannot hold a person responsible for those of his actions that stem from strong emotions because such emotions impede choice (and should thus excuse on the choice theory of excuse), whereas the character theorist can easily hold such persons responsible for such actions because (on the character theory) responsibility for actions is only a proxy for responsibility for the emotional make-up such actions express. Yet, as we have seen, this difference can only exist if we make asymmetrical assumptions about the two theories: namely, we stick the choice theorist with a narrow view of choosing agency while we allow the character theorist the broad view of character. Whereas if we allow each theorist the most plausible assumptions about what choosing and character include, this difference disappears.[42]

One last nuance in our usage of 'character' needs attention here in order to keep clear the real differences that do exist between the two theories. Sometimes our talk of character is not about character *traits* or *attributes*; indeed, such talk does not use 'character' to name universals of any kind. Rather, we talk of characters doing things, and what we mean to designate is some particular agency. When we speak of characters in novels, we think in this way of character as a particular—in this case, the whole person in the novel. Sometimes we even speak of characters as particular agencies within the person. Bernard Williams notes this usage in his discussion of multiple-personalitied persons.[43] What we seem to mean

[42] Michael Corrado concludes from this concession of mine that the choice and character theories cannot be distinct. Corrado, 'Notes on the Structure of a Theory of Excuses', *Journal of Criminal Law and Criminology*, Vol. 82 (1992), 465, at 478–9, n. 22. Yet the lack of *this* difference between the two theories hardly means there can be *no* difference, as we shall see in the next section.

[43] Bernard Williams, *Problems of the Self* (Cambridge: Cambridge University Press, 1973), 15–18.

when we talk of different characters (personalities) operating within one person is that character names a particular, an agency within one person that itself chooses actions. Such a character (as a particular) can itself have a character (as a set of universals).

There is nothing wrong with this usage of 'character'. I come neither to praise nor to condemn such usage; only to bury it for purposes of this enquiry. For this cannot be what the character theorist on responsibility can mean by 'character', on pain of collapsing his theory into the choice theory. If 'character' simply names our choosing agency, then responsibility for character is simply responsibility for choice, and there is no debate to have about which is the correct theory of responsibility. For the two theories to be as different as they seem to be, there must be a metaphysical difference between that aspect of our selves we call our character and that part we call our agency of choice. One can heighten the difference between the two theories by claiming that either character or will *constitutes* the self exclusive of the other; to maintain any difference at all between the two theories, however, one must at least see some metaphysical difference between character and will.

If we are clear about what character is, we next need to enquire whether and in what sense we can be *responsible* for our characters. One debate a choice theorist could have with a character theorist about the excuses is whether there is a responsibility for character at all.[44] If there is not, if there is only responsibility for actions, then the excuses cannot have as their function the isolation of actions expressing bad character; if one is not responsible for one's character, then responsibility for action cannot be derivative of that responsibility.

This route to denying the character theory of excuse (by denying the character conception of responsibility that lies behind it) is not one I adopt. For I think it is obvious that, in some sense, we are responsible for being the kind of people that we are—i.e., for our characters. This includes responsibility for traits like greediness and honesty, emotions like love, gratitude, guilt, and envy, desires and ambitions, etc. There is a morality of virtue versus vice, not only for academic ethicists but also reflected in the common judgements

---

[44] This appears to be the point at which Nicola Lacey believes the two theories of excuse diverge. See Lacey, *State Punishment*, *supra* n. 1, at 68.

of daily life. We morally judge our own and others' general moral worthiness all the time.[45]

There is room for disagreement as to exactly how, and in what sense, we are each responsible for our characters. With regard to the 'how' question, there are two possibilities: (1) we are responsible for our characters because we *chose* to become persons with such character, or (2) we are responsible for our characters because we *are* (at least in part) our characters. The first possibility, of course, collapses the character conception of responsibility back into a choice conception of responsibility; on this view, the character theory of excuse becomes the idea that we hold persons responsible only for those choices (actions) expressive of their character, *and* we hold persons responsible only for those attributes of character that are themselves freely chosen. Choice ultimately is what matters on such a view, even if character mediately explains why we are responsible for some of our choices.

Despite the distinguished lineage of this first view in Aristotle,[46] there are two reasons for a character theorist to shy away from it. One is an empirical worry: do we really have much capacity to mould our characters? We do have some such capacity. We do form 'second-order desires'[47] or 'ego-ideals' about what kind of person we would like to become, and we have some causal power to effect changes in ourselves in conformity with such desires or ideals. Yet the social science on this issue gives little encouragement to thinking we have much of this power.[48]

Secondly, there is a conceptual worry: who is the 'he' who is

---

[45] Consider but one example: the moral judgement Morgan Forster invited us to make of Henry Wilcox in Forster's novel, *Howard's End*. Forster persuasively presents Henry as having a fatally flawed character because of his failure 'to connect', which defect was itself due to Henry's having a mind like 'an unweeded garden'. We rightly blame Henry for his flawed character, quite independently of the fact that that character leads him to do actions that are themselves clumsily hurtful to himself and others.

[46] Aristotle, *Nichomachean Ethics*, 395–9. For explications of the Aristotelian view, see Charles Taylor 'Responsibility for Self', Amelie Rorty, ed., *The Identities of Persons* (Berkeley: University of California Press, 1976), 281–99.

[47] Harry Frankfurt's description of our power to mould our own characters. Harry Frankfurt, 'Freedom of the Will and the Concept of a Person', *Journal of Philosophy*, Vol. 68 (1971), 5–20; Frankfurt, 'Identification and Wholeheartedness', Ferdinand Schoeman, ed., *Responsibility, Character, and the Emotions* (Cambridge: Cambridge University Press, 1987), 27–45.

[48] See Dressler, 'Some Reflections', *supra* n. 1, at 695–6 for doubts on these grounds.

choosing character? Does he himself have any character, and, if so, was it chosen too? To the character theorist who grounds responsibility for choice and action in responsibility for character, a characterless chooser is an odd legitimator of responsibility for the character he chooses; yet a chooser of character who already possesses character before he chooses invites an infinite regress.[49]

One might attempt to alleviate both these worries by what might be called the weak Aristotelian view.[50] This view concedes that our characters are formed initially by processes over which we have little choice or control; however, our responsibility for character comes from our later choices to *maintain* these already formed character traits. Patty Hearst, for example, may have had little choice in the processes that caused her to have the beliefs, desires, emotions, and dispositions that she had on emerging from the Symbionese Liberation Army's closet.[51] Responsibility for that character became hers, however, by the passage of time during which she maintained and/or failed to change those attributes of character. After some period of time, 'Tania' was the character for whom Patty was responsible.[52]

The weak Aristotelian view at least sounds empirically more plausible. Even so, the weak view cannot accommodate all the attributes of self that intuitively are the proper subject of moral judgement. Take the emotions, for example. There seems very little that we can do about willing our emotions into or out of being. (Thus, the oddness of questions like, 'why don't you love me?', as if not loving someone was a choice for which one was responsible.) Yet we do hold people responsible for their emotional make-up, including the presence or absence of particular emotions on partic-

[49] Seen clearly by Vuoso, 'Background, Responsibility, and Excuse', *supra* n. 32, at 1676; Susan Wolf, 'Sanity and the Metaphysics of Responsibility', Ferdinand Schoeman, ed., *Responsibility, Character, and the Emotions*, 46–62; and Gary Watson, 'Responsibility and the Limits of Evil', *supra* n. 32, at 281.

[50] See, e.g., Nozick, *Philosophical Explanations*, *supra* n. 32, at 396.

[51] For those too young to remember the Patty Hearst story, the 18-year-old Ms Hearst was kidnapped by a group of would-be revolutionaries who subjected her to physical abuse, isolation, and indoctrination. At some point it appeared that this heiress to the conservative Hearst family empire succumbed to this indoctrination and believed in the justice of the revolutionary cause. She renamed herself 'Tania' and appeared (complete with commando garb and assault rifle) in bank films as a voluntary participant in the revolutionary group's bank robbery.

[52] So argued by Dan Dennett, 'Mechanism and Responsibility', Theodore Honderich, ed., *Essays on Freedom of Action* (London: Routledge and Kegan Paul, 1973), 175–80.

ular occasions.[53] This inclines me to think that it is the second possibility that captures our responsibility for our character: we are responsible for our character because we are, in part, constituted by our characters.

Since we by and large do not choose to become or remain who we are, the sense in which we are *responsible* for our character no doubt differs from the sense in which we are responsible for our actions, which we do choose. 'Responsibility' may not even be the right word here, for it is a kind of aesthetic morality that governs our assessments of character. Someone who lacks good character is poorly made, a defective being for a being of his or her kind. Unlike most aesthetic judgements, however, our judgements of character have moral overtones. We shun those with bad characters, avoid their friendship, and disadvantage them in various ways. Moreover, we feel entitled to so treat them because they deserve no better. To the extent that such persons did not choose their character, they are to that extent morally unlucky in being the defective creatures they are. The morality of the virtues, like that governing actions and choices,[54] has a good deal of moral luck built into it.

All of this should be a welcome conclusion to a character theorist about excuse, for if he avoids the conclusion that we are responsible for our character only insofar as we choose our character, then he has conceded nothing to the priority of choice over character as the touchstone of responsibility. We should also be clear that such an answer also concedes nothing to the priority of character over choice, however. Thus far, all that has been established is that we have two different sorts of moral judgements that we appropriately make about persons: we hold them responsible for the actions they choose to do, and we hold them responsible for being the sort of people that they are. Although I have just rejected the claim that moral judgements about character are merely a disguised form of moral judgements about choice, that rejection says nothing in favour of the claim that moral judgements about choice are merely a disguised form of moral judgements about character. And it is this latter claim that the character theorist about excuse must establish.

---

[53] See the discussions of this in Moore, *Law and Psychiatry*, *supra* n. 1, at 343–7, in Bernard Williams, 'Morality and the Emotions', in his *Problems of the Self*, *supra* n. 43, at 207–29, and in Sabini and Silver, 'Emotions, Responsibility, and Character', *supra* n. 28.

[54] Recalling the discussion in ch. 5.

Before we assess this crucial claim of the character theorist on its moral merits, we have one last clarificatory question to explore about the claim itself. This is the question of the sort of relationship that the character theorist asserts to exist between character and action that makes an actor responsible for action. The character theory of excuse variously asserts that we are excused from responsibility for our actions when those actions do not *manifest*, *express*, *reveal*, or *indicate* bad character; when such actions are not the *result of*, not *determined by*, *explained by*, or are not *attributed to* bad characters; when such actions are not an *exercise* of a character defect; or when such actions are not *evidentiary* of bad character.[55] We need to be clearer about what is meant by these expressions.

Three different sorts of relations might be meant by them. The first would be a logical relation between character and actions that are 'in character'. On this view, the relation between someone's greedy action on a particular occasion and his greedy character is the logical relation between a particular and the universal that it instantiates. Such a view of the relation commits one to a behavioural view of what character is, and that is sufficient reason for the character theorist to avoid it.

Preferable on this ground is a second view of the relation, which is that it is a causal relation. A greedy action, on this view, is in character for a person only if that action was caused by that person's greedy character. This view of the relation presupposes a non-behavioural view of what character is, but that is a virtue—not a defect—of this relational view. There is a problem with this second view, however; it stems from the non-discriminating nature of the causal relation. Greedy character in a person can cause any number of behaviours besides greedy action. My greed can cause my heart rate to go up (for example, I get excited when I see large amounts of money). It can cause overtly generous behaviour (for example, Bulstrode in *Middlemarch*, who compensates for his greediness by overtly generous behaviour). Indeed, any given character trait can probably cause virtually any kind of behaviour on a

---

[55] All such expression may be found in: Nozick, *Philosophical Explanations*, *supra* n. 32, at 383; Bayles, 'Character, Purpose, and Criminal Responsibility', *supra* n. 1, at 7; Brandt, 'A Motivational Theory of Excuse', *supra* n. 32, at 165, 169, 170, 171; Lacey, *State Punishment*, *supra* n. 1, at 66; Fletcher, *Rethinking Criminal Law*, *supra* n. 32, at 799, 801.

given occasion. For example, suppose Van Gogh was greedy; his greed could have caused him to cut off his ear (for instance, by way of punishment of himself for not being paid enough for a picture).

George Vuoso, who sees the problem, attempts to contain the promiscuity of the causal relation by the pragmatics of explanatory utterance.[56] Vuoso attempts to limit the causal relation to those instances when it would be appropriate to say 'that character trait explains the action'. Yet we might well say that about any of the foregoing examples, and I doubt that a character theorist holds them to be examples of actions 'in character' for the greedy person.

If not, the character theorist has need of a more discriminating relation. The evidentiary relation is his best bet. Some act A will evidence some trait C if and only if not only C causes A, but also states of type C typically cause events of type A. Effects are evidence of their causes only when there is some general connection between the *class* of events that includes the effect and the *class* of events that includes the cause. Evidentiary inference is the more discriminating relation sought by the character theorist. Then acts of refusing to give to charities, forcing poor debtors to pay, paying employees as little as possible, etc., are acts 'in character' for the greedy person; lopping off one's ear, or giving away all of one's money, are not acts 'in character' for some greedy person even if they happen on some occasion to be caused by his greed.

This last clarification allows us to pinpoint what are and are not the differences between the two theories of excuse. The difference between the two theories has to lie in the kinds of causes of action they each find to be the touchstone of responsibility: character or choice. This is *not* the difference in the causal power of character versus that of choice. For example, one cannot contrast the character theory to the choice theory on the ground that the first is concerned only with the 'mesh' (or logical fit) of action with the actor's character and not with any historical enquiry into an action's causes.[57] The non-behaviourist account of character, and the evidentiary account of the relation between character and actions 'in

[56] Vuoso, 'Background, Responsibility, and Excuse', *supra* n. 32, at 1672–3.

[57] For the contrast between 'historical' versus 'mesh' theories of responsibility, see John Martin Fischer, 'Responsiveness and Moral Responsibility', Ferdinand Schoeman, ed., *Responsibility, Character, and the Emotions*, 81–100, at 103–5. Fischer is a choice theorist (his 'reasons-responsiveness' test being his way of measuring free choice) who criticizes certain character theorists (Frankfurt, Watson) for being ahistorical in the sense indicated in the text.

character' makes the character theory focus on an action's causal genesis too. Rather, the difference between the two theories boils down to the difference between a person's character and his choices. On the assumption that choices are possible only if a person has and exercises a choosing agency (will), the difference is between a person having a character and a person having a will. The evidentiary relation just discussed seems to isolate just such a difference: any action evidences the possession of a will, because a will can typically will anything and still be a will. But as we have seen, while a character *can* cause any action, to be possessed of a character precludes the possibility that one's character can *typically* cause any class of actions equally well. Characters, to be characters, can only typically cause some classes of actions, but not others. Character in this sense is inherently general, requiring typical causal connections to classes of actions; will and the choices that issue from it are in this sense particular, being equally capable of causing any particular act and not being tied to any general class of actions.

IV. CHARACTER VERSUS CHOICE AS THE TOUCHSTONE OF RESPONSIBILITY AND EXCUSE

Perhaps the place to start in assessing the moral merits of the two theories of excuse is with the main arguments put forward by the character theorists in favour of their theory. Unfortunately, of the four main arguments, three are irrelevant to the moral issue I wish to raise. Let me mention them, if only to put them aside.

One is the argument that proceeds from utilitarian (or, more broadly, consequentialist) theories of punishment. Richard Brandt[58] and Nicola Lacey[59] both make arguments of this type in favour of the character theory of excuse, Brandt from his rule-utilitarian theory of punishment and Lacey from her non-utilitarian but consequentialist theory of punishment. Briefly, the argument is that the preventive goals of punishment do not require its infliction on those whose actions have not manifested bad character, because such persons are not dangerous nor can their pun-

---

[58] See particularly Brandt, 'A Motivational Theory of Excuses', *supra* n. 32, at 184–94.

[59] Lacey, *State Punishment*, *supra* n. 1, at 65–72.

ishment have any significant deterrent effect. It is not clear to me that the character theory of excuse would better serve crime-prevention goals than would the choice theory. But in any case, the argument for me is a non-starter since it proceeds from an unacceptable theory of punishment. At the very least, moral innocence should operate as a side constraint on the pursuit of goals like crime prevention; what we need is a theory of excuse that tells us when someone is morally innocent. These utilitarian and consequentialist arguments do not tell us that, so we may put them aside.

A second argument in favour of the character theory is by far the major consideration which in fact motivates character theorists to adopt their theory.[60] This is the argument that proceeds from hard determinist premises. The assumption is that the choice conception of responsibility is in trouble because it is hostage to the questionable truth of libertarian (Strawson: 'panicky') metaphysics; if determinism turns out to be true, the choice conception is assumed to have the unhappy implication that no one is responsible for anything. Whereas, the character theorist thinks, responsibility can be preserved by his theory even in the face of determinism. So long as he rejects Aristotle's notion that we are responsible for our characters because we choose them, and sticks to the idea that we are responsible for our characters because we are our characters, he escapes any threat from determinism. For his idea of responsibility does not depend on an actor's choices being free. Rather, he can happily admit that responsible choices are caused by character, and that character in turn is caused by factors not themselves chosen by the actor. By *his* idea of responsibility, the actor is responsible for any actions in character just because he is his character. This is known in the trade as the 'character-stop' answer to determinism.[61]

---

[60] See Lacey, *State Punishment*, supra n. 1, at 65, 73; Vuoso, 'Background, Responsibility, and Excuse', *supra* n. 32; Strawson, 'Freedom and Resentment', *supra* n. 32; Scanlon, 'Quality of Will', *supra* n. 32; Watson, 'Responsibility and the Limits of Evil', *supra* n. 32; Fletcher, *Rethinking Criminal Law*, supra n. 32, at 801–2; Nozick, *Philosophical Explanations*, supra n. 32, at 393–6. Of the character theorists, only Richard Brandt and Peter Arenella see clearly that a characterological conception of responsibility has no advantage over a choice conception in answering the hard determinist. See Brandt, 'A Motivational Theory of Excuse', *supra* n. 32, at 172; Arenella, 'Character, Choice, and Moral Agency', *supra* n. 32.

[61] For a contemporary use of the character-stop argument, see Nozick, *Philosophical Explanations*, supra n. 32, at 395. The character-stop argument has not been without its critics. See e.g., John Hospers, 'Meaning and Free Will', *Philosophy and Phenomenological Research*, Vol. 10 (1950), 307–30.

There is nothing wrong with the character-stop strategy. This is why that part of morality known as the theory of the virtues is not hostage to the falsity of determinism. However, the character theorist overlooks the fact that the choice conception of responsibility has an answer just as good to the hard determinist: we are at least in part the agency that chooses whether to act or not; that agency's choices can themselves exist even if caused by factors external to the will; it would make choice a very peculiar event if it has to be uncaused in order to exist; there is no persuasive argument showing that choices have this peculiar feature; and the fact that some people find such arguments persuasive can be explained in ways having nothing to do with the truth of the arguments in question. I and others have sought to draw this argument out in detail, and the conclusion—that compatibilism between choice and causation is true—is so far from being problematic and worrisome within philosophy that it is now a kind of philosophical orthodoxy. As one not very sympathetic philosopher has recently observed, 'compatibilism, as a philosophical position, has become complacent'.[62]

Any argument for the character theory proceeding from that theory's supposed advantage in answering hard determinism had better first show why the philosophical orthodoxy about compatibilism is false. In addition, such character theorists must also address the *tu quoque* argument advanced against character as a desert basis in chapter 5. That argument was that character was just as much a matter of fortuity—a matter of moral luck—as is choice, so that any worries on that score about choice also need to be directed to character. Since neither of these showings have been made by character theorists, we should ignore arguments for the character theory built on this shaky metaphysical base.

A third argument for the character theory proceeds from a very general intellectual fashion prevalent today. This I have elsewhere called 'interpretivism'.[63] Briefly, the idea is that moral questions (if not the explanatory questions of social and even natural science) are interpretive questions, questions that seek the best interpretation of various social practices. To ask what responsibility is, or

---

[62] Ferdinand Schoeman, 'Introduction', *Responsibility, Character, and the Emotions*, 5. Schoeman appears to favour the character theory of excuse (see ibid., 2–3,) perhaps because he is not so convinced of the truth of compatibilism.

[63] Michael Moore, 'The Interpretive Turn in Modern Theory: A Turn for the Worse?', *Stanford Law Review*, Vol. 41 (1989), 871–957.

when a person is responsible, is to ask what the best interpretation of the 'blaming stories' prevalent in our society might be. The character theory of excuse appears to be favoured by interpretivists because such a theory requires 'more story' than does the choice theory. That is, to see whether an action expresses the agent's character requires a longer, more complete narration of what sort of person, in general, he is; whereas to see whether an action was freely chosen by an agent seemingly requires a more limited enquiry into his capacities and opportunities at the moment of acting.

It is hard to get a handle on just what this argument comes to. Even if one's meta-ethics commits one to viewing moral reasoning as storytelling and -retelling, why should one prefer 'more story'? Are not 'short stories' an appropriate genre? The interpretivists here sound like the psychiatrists of the 1950s who criticized the *M'Naghten* definition of insanity on the ground that it did not allow them to tell their psychiatric 'stories'.[64] In both cases, we should like to know why the stories someone wants to tell are *better*, and hopefully that betterness has something to do with their getting us closer to some relevant truth.

It is a fourth kind of argument in favour of the character theory of excuse that raises the relevant issues. Consider George Fletcher's non-utilitarian appreciation of the need for this kind of argument:

An inference from the wrongful act to the actor's character is essential to a retributive theory of punishment. A fuller statement of the argument would go like this: (1) punishing wrongful conduct is just only if punishment is measured by the desert of the offender, (2) the desert of the offender is gauged by his character—i.e., the kind of person he is, (3) and therefore, a judgement about character is essential to the just distribution of punishment.[65]

It is the second premise about moral desert, of course, that the character theorist must defend.

Despite her consequentialist leanings (and her resulting disavowals of any intent to answer the question of moral blameworthiness),

---

[64] See the discussion in Moore, *Law and Psychiatry*, 228. Because the *M'Naghten* test required that a defendant be unable to know either the nature and quality of his action or that it was wrong in order to be excused by reason of insanity, many psychiatrists were frustrated by the lack of fit of their 'stories' (psychiatric explanations) and the story the law required them to tell. In criticizing the *M'Naghten* test on this ground, what they overlooked was why the law should care that their story did not fit the law's concerns about responsibility and blame.

[65] Fletcher, *Rethinking Criminal Law, supra* n. 1, at 800.

Nicola Lacey presents some defence of this essential premise. She defends the moral view that 'it is unfair to hold people responsible for actions which are out of character . . . fair to hold them so for actions in which their settled dispositions are centrally expressed'.[66] In order to test the moral correctness of these conclusions, we should construct examples of two kinds: (1) an actor freely chooses to do wrong (i.e., he had the capacity and a fair opportunity not to so choose), and yet the action is 'out of character' for that actor; (2) an actor's behaviour is good evidence for a settled disposition (character) of a bad kind, and yet he has not (yet) chosen to act on that disposition. If the character theory were right, we ought to find it fair to punish the second but not the first, because the first but not the second has a moral excuse. However, I shall contend that we rightly find it fair to punish the first but not the second, because we rightly think the second but not the first to have a moral excuse.

As an example of the first kind, consider the killing of Bonnie Garland that formed the basis of my thought experiment about retributive punishment in chapter 3.[67] Bonnie was an undergraduate at Yale; Richard was a graduate student there. Richard had not had much experience with women, and he found Yale a lonely and alien place. He had grown up in the barrio of East Los Angeles, but had succeeded at getting good grades and was, by all accounts, a stunning success. He early and heavily committed himself emotionally to Bonnie once a romance had begun between them. Before too long, she found his neediness off-putting and sought to break off the relationship. Like many people whose kindness makes them weak and unintentionally cruel, she could not bring herself to break it off with Richard cleanly. He accordingly felt misled, hurt, and frustrated by her attempt to let him down gradually.

Staying over at her parents' house one night, Richard decided he could not stand it any more. He went down to the basement, looking around for something with which to kill her. He found a claw hammer and proceeded upstairs to her room with it. Finding her asleep, he beat her to death with the hammer. He had planned to commit suicide after the act, but found he could not bring himself to do it and instead sought out some Christian counselling.

Richard had the capacity to choose not to kill Bonnie, and he

---

[66] Lacey, *State Punishment*, *supra* n. 1, at 68.
[67] The facts again are taken from William Gaylin, *The Killing of Bonnie Garland* (New York: Pengiun Books, 1983).

had a fair opportunity to exercise that capacity. Nonetheless, he chose to kill her. For that, to my mind, he fully deserved the eight-to twenty-five-year sentence he received for Bonnie's killing. Yet a character theorist should find this conviction unfair, for the act was out of character for Richard. Richard himself felt that way about his sentence:

Considering all the factors that I feel the judge should have considered: prior history of arrest, my personality background, my capacity for a productive life in society—you know, those kinds of things—I don't think he took those into consideration. He looked at the crime itself . . . This being my first arrest and considering the circumstances, I don't think I should have been given eight to twenty-five years.[68]

Richard wanted credit for an otherwise good—even, in some ways, exemplary—life. He felt it was unfair to have eight years of his life taken from him because of a momentary choice that was at odds with who he really was and how he both had lived and would live his life. His choice to kill Bonnie in the middle of a sleepless night must have looked, in retrospect, like an unbelievable action for him.

Yet is there any doubt at all that Richard Herrin was seriously culpable for his choice? No matter how out of character this act was for him behaviourally, no matter how alien it seemed to him phenomenologically, *he* horribly violated another's rights at a single point in time. His generally good character puzzles us, because we do not understand very well how a generally kind, non-violent (if somewhat weak) individual could do what he did. But such explanatory puzzlement is not accompanied by a similar puzzlement about his responsibility: his clear choice to do evil is sufficient to make him very culpable.

Character theorists have two responses to such examples. They might deny that someone like Herrin is culpable. Or they could admit that someone like Herrin is culpable but deny that Herrin's action was really out of character. Consider each possible response in turn.

By 'bad character', Nicola Lacey means a settled hostility to, rejection of, or indifference to the values of the community that the criminal law exists to protect and foster.[69] Richard Herrin had no such settled hostility, indifference, or rejection, so presumably he

---

[68] Ibid., 325.   [69] Lacey, *State Punishment, supra* n. 1, at 189–90.

would be included by Lacey in the category of those excused: 'To punish those who have exhibited no such hostility [to the values protected by the criminal law] would be to fly directly in the face of those values themselves . . .'.[70]

Any theory of excuse that has an implication that people like Richard Herrin ought to be excused is a bad theory of excuse. Those character theorists opting for the first response above (denying that Herrin was culpable) obviously disagree. Their disagreement seems to me to be motivated by two intuitions, one metaphysical and the other moral. The metaphysical intuition is that it was not really Richard that did the killing, because who Richard is is guided by his character so that an act truly out of character like his killing of Bonnie was no act of Richard's. Lacey appears to adopt this idea when she holds that the criminal law should 'respond punitively only to actions which are in a real sense [the actor's] *own* . . .'.[71] She appears to equate this with actions centrally expressive of settled features of the actor's character. Elsewhere, Lacey elaborates that the criminal law should 'treat seriously the individuality and sense of identity of each citizen by responding punitively only to actions which are genuinely expressive of the actor's relevant disposition: with which the agent truly identifies, and can call her own'.[72] If this means what it seems to mean—what I have called the metaphysical intuition that actions we do are not *our* actions unless they are in character for us—then it is hostage to a very problematic theory of personal identity. This is the theory that holds character to swamp both spatio-temporal contiguity and unified consciousness as the touchstone of personal identity.[73] On this theory, we are only our character, a conclusion that has two startling implications. First, when 'we' radically change our character over time, we literally become someone else—not just another kind of person, but a different person. Second, multiple-personalitied persons are not single persons with multiple characters; they are rather many persons with one character each. This allowance of the possibility that many persons can inhabit one

---

[70] Lacey, *State Punishment*, *supra* n. 1, at 189.
[71] Ibid., 71.   [72] Ibid., 77.
[73] For a discussion of these three factors as determining personal identity, see Michael Moore, 'The Unity of the Self', in Michael Ruse, ed., *Nature Animated* (Dordrecht: Reidel, 1982), revised and reprinted as chs. 3 and 11 of Moore, *Law and Psychiatry*, *supra* n. 1.

body—either over time or even at one time—raises havoc with some basic metaphysical, moral, and legal ideas that are difficult to imagine giving up.[74] One of those ideas is just the sort of thing Lacey is apparently willing to abandon: namely, how we individuate and attribute actions to persons. Normally we do this by the body involved in the action: one movement by one body, one action. Yet multiple persons (characters) acting through one body could yield a variety of possibilities: several actions, if the movement was in character for several characters; one action, but by 'someone' other than the person at home at the time the action was performed; or no action, if the action was not in character for any of the characters sharing one human body. These implications are so unacceptable that we should not think of character as exclusively constituting the identity of persons—and if we do not think this, then we cannot think that an action out of character is no action of ours.[75]

The moral intuition that may motivate denials of culpability like Herrin's is a kind of 'there but for the grace of God go I' intuition, for isolated acts of violence like Herrin's may well seem possible for any of us in the right circumstances. Yet it would still be us, even if we slipped like Herrin slipped. . . . We are all basically good, we hope. Yet if we think about how we would view ourselves in this circumstance, would it in fact be excusing of ourselves, as Richard excused himself? Would it not rather be that we felt guilty unto death for our horrible violation of another? Far from leading to conclusions of excuse, for me this thought experiment yields a judgement of a very heavy culpability when someone like Herrin steps out of his otherwise good character to perform a wrongful act.

The second possible response to Herrin-like thought experiments by the character theorist is to admit Herrin's culpability but to deny that his action is out of character. Indeed, an extreme version of this response is to deny that *any* action that is freely chosen (in my sense of chosen by one with adequate capacities and fair opportunity to use them) can be out of character for an agent. Such an

---

[74] I explore some of these in *Law and Psychiatry, supra* n. 1, at 147–52.

[75] Perhaps Lacey intends a less metaphysical defence here. To speak of a 'sense of identity' is not necessarily to speak of personal identity, for as we discussed in the previous section of this chapter who we *think* we are need not coincide with who we are in fact. Yet then Lacey has no basis for saying that an action out of character is not *our* action. Rather, such a phenomenological observation can only generate the conclusion that we have disowned (not identified with) one of *our* own actions.

extreme version of this response of course renders the choice and character theories equivalent in the conditions which they would excuse (even though the rationale for such excuse could still differ).

What would tempt one to think that no freely chosen act could ever be out of character for the actor? Supposing we adopt the view of practical reasoning schematized in chapter 5, then what causes those bodily movements that are parts of actions are willings (volitions, tryings), and what causes willings are intentions (choices, plans), and what causes intentions are belief/desire sets in the form of a valid practical syllogism (motivations), and what causes those sets are general traits of character. One might think that the particular motivations of someone like Herrin are part of his character, no matter how idiosyncratic, short-lived, and inconsistent they might be with those more settled dispositions we call character traits; and that no action like Herrin's (where there is no incapacitating coercion) is ever unmotivated.[76]

Yet character simply cannot be defined so as to include idiosyncratic and instantaneous motivation inconsistent with one's long term traits. To have anything worth defending, character has to be identified with something 'lasting or stable' so that 'a purely momentary feeling or impulse is no part of the person's character . . .'.[77] It has to at least be possible, in other words, for there to be thoughts, feelings and actions that are out of character for a person, even if one wants to make the extreme response that no *freely chosen* actions are ever out of character for the person whose actions they are.

A move more acceptable than gerrymandering the concept of character is to try to show how freely chosen, bad actions that on the surface seem to be out of character, always have behind them either: (1) pre-existing, but *hidden*, character traits of a bad sort, or (2) *new* and changed character traits of a (now) bad sort. And of course, in any given case the possibility of such hidden or new defects of character is quite real even without relaxing the generality involved in calling something character. Someone may never have had the opportunity to show their jealous dispositions before, and yet act quite jealously when the occasion arises, even if only once; another may have so successfully repressed his jealous feel-

---

[76] Something like this is suggested in Corrado, 'Notes', *supra* n. 42, at 477–9; and in Horder, *supra* n. 27, at 206–8.

[77] Duff, 'Choice, Character, and Criminal Liability', *supra* n. 31, at 364.

ings and tendencies that he has looked to all the world (including himself) to be a very non-jealous fellow despite all the many opportunities he has had to exhibit such jealousy. Such a jealous trait in either case could exist despite it being quite hidden. Alternatively, someone may not in fact be of a jealous kind, but a single experience can transform him into a jealous person as he then acts in a jealous way. Although such a new trait of jealousy may be quite general, the possessor of it may even lack any other opportunity to exhibit his jealousy for the rest of his life.

The trick is to show why such hidden or novel defects of character *must* be present when there is freely chosen bad action, no matter how seemingly out of character the act in question. Clearly the motivation behind the alleged necessity here is the sense that behind every freely chosen action there is always some attitude or motivation that is general enough to be called character. Antony Duff has argued that whenever we choose in situations where we are uncoerced, in other words, we must be choosing in light of 'some intelligible conception of the good . . .' so that the only act that can be out of character is one that 'does not manifest "character" at all: it does not, that is, manifest the kind of valuational and motivational structure of attitudes and practical reasoning in which a person's "character", . . . consists'.[78]

Two points. First, my own reading of existential fiction like Gide's *The Vatican Swindle* and Camus's *The Stranger* is not that they depicted the psychologically impossible. Neither did it seem to me that Lafcadio or Mersault did not freely choose to push the old man out of the train, or shoot the Arab, respectively. They fully chose these wrongful acts, and did so as an *act gratui*, that is, for no further reason. Free and responsible choice does not require the acting 'under some intelligible conception of the good', even if most seriously wrongful acts in real life are of this kind. Rare as such intrinsically motivated killings, etc., may be, Duff's kind of necessity claim requires that they *cannot* occur, not that they hardly ever do occur.

Second, even when the actor has an intelligible conception of the good, cannot he freely choose to act against it? I refer to cases often called weakness of will, where the actor echoes St Paul in Romans 7: I know the good but find I do the bad. Duff seems to argue one

[78] Id. at 378.

of two things here: either that there is a set of attitudes of a sufficiently general sort that are opposed to the actor's main conception
of the good, so that the actor still acts 'in character' with this
weaker conception of the good even when he chooses to go against
his own (strongest) conception of the good; or that the failure to
act on his own conception of the good on this occasion must betoken a general tendency to abandon his own idea of the good, so
that his tendency to be weak of will is itself one of his character
traits!

One should see in either of these responses a kind of fixed determination to find bad character expressed in any freely chosen bad
action, no matter what. It is worth pausing to wonder what would
be accomplished if one could salvage a meaningful sense of character that was necessarily present with uncoerced choice. The character theory and the choice theory would in that event decide all
cases the same way, but that would not make them the same theory. Each would still assert the psychological and moral distinctiveness of its respective desert basis, even though some argument
other than my 'out of character' thought experiment would have to
be found to prefer one to the other.

I said that there were two kind of examples with which to test
the choice versus character theory of excuse on moral grounds. I
now turn to the second kind of example, where there is behaviour
revealing bad character, but no free choice to do wrong. Virtually
any preventive detention example will do—for example, Dallas
Williams, in whom psychiatrists detected violent character traits
even though Williams had not yet acted upon them.[79] May someone like Williams fairly be punished even though he has done nothing wrong?

The question is a hard one for the character theorist. After all,
he thinks that we are ultimately responsible for our characters and
that action-responsibility is only derivative of this more basic character-responsibility. If this is true, then why not punish people
directly for bad character, since that is the locus of their just
deserts? Why punish bad character indirectly, only through punishing actions expressive of it? George Fletcher seeks to answer this

---

[79] See Jay Katz, Joseph Goldstein, and Alan Dershowitz, *Psychoanalysis,
Psychiatry, and Law* (New York: Free Press, 1967), 526–35, for the history of the
real Dallas Williams.

question in terms of a value distinct from the justice of the guilty getting their just deserts, namely, privacy:

The limitation of the inquiry to a single wrongful act follows not from the theory of desert, but from the principle of legality. We accept the artificiality of inferring character from a single deed as the price of maintaining the suspect's privacy . . . Disciplining the inquiry in this way . . . secures the individual against a free-ranging enquiry of the state into his moral worth.[80]

I mention Fletcher's argument because it illustrates a kind of argument that cannot establish what the character theorist needs to establish here. Much of the literature on 'punishment for thoughts alone' is persuasive on why it would be undesirable for various reasons to dispense with the *actus reus* requirement of the criminal law.[81] But our moral question has only to do with moral desert. That punishment would be *deserved* because of bad character alone is something the character theorist seems committed to, however much other values prevent punishment of this class of deserving persons.

Nozick sees the need to escape this seeming implication of the character theory—namely, that people with bad character do deserve punishment directly for their character and not for actions, if any, expressing that character.[82] Yet Nozick's escape is only a statement of the conclusion needed by him: 'It is through actions that correct values are flouted; the actions constitute the flouting. . . . Since it is flouting that is to be punished, actions are required.'[83] Stated this tersely, Nozick's argument says little more than his conclusion. If flouting is a kind of action, then Nozick is by definition correct that only actions can constitute flouting: but why is the action of flouting required for a just punishment? Alternatively, if flouting is not necessarily a kind of action, why is not the possession of bad character a flouting of the values that show it to be bad?

If the character theory were correct, the answer given to Molière's Robespierre (when the latter asks why he is being condemned to death) should not be jarring: you are being condemned,

[80] Fletcher, *Rethinking, supra* n. 1, at 800–1.

[81] e.g., Lacey's argument in *State Punishment, supra* n. 1, at 199.

[82] Nozick sees the question clearly (*Philosophical Explanations, supra* n. 32, at 380–2) before giving his own answer (ibid., 383–4).

[83] Ibid., 384.

Robespierre is told, 'because you lack grace'. Yet the answer is jar-ring precisely because no one deserves to be punished for being a poor specimen of humanity. The aesthetic kind of responsibility that we admittedly do have for so much of our characters as are unchosen cannot fairly lead to punishment, because we could not have avoided possessing these aspects of ourselves. A choice theo-rist—even one such as myself who admits that there is such a thing as responsibility for unchosen character—can readily say this, because he conceives of the existence of two independent kinds of (and bases for) responsibility. I have yet to see how the character theorist can deny that character-responsibility alone makes it fair to punish, given his notion that character-responsibility is basic and act-responsibility only derivative.

Antony Duff attempts to circumvent the need for a moral argu-ment here by making a conceptual claim.[84] The claim is that one cannot be possessed of a character trait such as greediness without some action manifesting that trait. Accordingly, there is no possi-bility of unacted-upon character traits for which one would be held responsible, under the character theory. Yet this reply, surely, is both false and irrelevant.

The falseness first. Duff uses my example of courage but holds that:

A courageous person is not just someone who would respond courageously to danger, but someone who does respond thus . . . The point about some-one who has not yet faced a situation that calls for courage is not that we do not yet know whether he is courageous; rather, there is as yet no fact of the matter to be known.[85]

One might wonder on this account how anyone could act coura-geously for the first time. After all, surely *one* act of a courageous sort is insufficient to make one *generally* a courageous person; surely it takes a series of such acts before any general trait of courage emerges, if one follows Duff's verificationist line here. But then, the first act of a courageous sort could not be the act of a courageous person. And if this is so, how can Duff make out points earlier examined, about the explicability of acts seemingly out of character by hidden and novel traits of character? If Duff is right, then one cannot have a hidden, pre-existing trait of courageousness

---

[84] Duff, 'Choice, Character, and Criminal Liability', *supra* n. 31, at 372.
[85] Id.

because such traits do not exist until they are revealed by a series of actions. All hidden traits would have to be new traits for Duff, not pre-existing ones. Moreover, even new traits require more than one action to bring them into existence, thus ruling out truly novel acts still in character for an actor.

In any case, surely Duff's Dummett-like position here is false for the same reason such verificationism is always false, namely, what we are inferring is not to be confused with our evidence for inferring it. Duff's position depends on a return to Ryle's purely logical relationship between dispositions and the events some object is disposed to do. If we take the more scientific view—and surely the more ordinary view of common sense—dispositions like the trait of courage can exist without any courageous actions yet being exhibited; dispositions are thus states that have a nature in both phenomenology and physiology and are not pure 'behavioural constructs'; such states cause, but are not logically constituted by, the actions which are in character for them. On this view of the world, my moral thought experiment poses a very live question to which the character theory gives the wrong answer.

Now as to the irrelevance point: suppose that Duff were right, that there could be no character trait without some behaviour instantiating it. That would only require us to recast our thought experiment for the character theorist, for he is still committed to some counterintuitive punishments. Take Dallas Williams again, the violence-prone individual. Suppose Williams has committed a rape and a murder in the past, so that now his aggressive, hostile, uncaring character has been manifested. Suppose also that Williams has been fully punished for such past wrongs, which punishment in no way diminished Williams's dispositions to do more rapes and murders in the future. Now: is not the character theorist committed to punishment being deserved by Williams for his bad character, despite that character not yet having resulted in any more acts of violence? And is not such *double* punishment (for a character trait necessarily revealed by a past crime) as counterintuitive as my original single punishment for a trait not yet realized in behaviour?

Both of the sorts of examples we have been considering point to the choice theory of excuse, for only it excuses where there is no choice, no matter how much bad character may be exhibited (the second kind of example); it does not excuse where there is a free choice, however much out of character it may be (the first kind of example). I accordingly reject the character theory of excuse on these moral grounds.

V. CAPACITY, CHOICE, AND CHARACTER: THE TROUBLESOME CULPABILITY FOR NEGLIGENCE

In closing we need to take a brief detour from the theory of excuses proper into the underlying conceptions of culpability each such theory expresses. This allows us to return to a topic introduced in chapter 9, which is whether there is a kind of moral culpability for negligence. The question I pose here is whether either of the conceptions of culpability discussed in this chapter as underlying the two theories of excuse—the choice and the character conceptions— can accommodate culpability for negligence. Concluding, as I do, that criminal liability for negligence squares with neither of such conceptions, I shall then enquire how if at all to justify such liability.

Many character theorists think that people who negligently cause harm are morally responsible. Taking that judgement to be secure, they then may claim: (1) that such responsibility for negligent conduct cannot be squared with the choice theory, and (2) that such responsibility is just what one should expect on the character theory.[86] I shall address each of these two claims separately before returning to the underlying assumption that negligence generates responsibility.

Responsibility for negligence *is* difficult to square with the choice conception of responsibility for the obvious reason that a negligent actor does not choose to do the complex act (such as killing) that is forbidden. True, such an actor—just by virtue of being an actor—does choose to do *some* action, such as moving his finger on the trigger of his gun; and it also may be true that he chooses to do more complex acts (such as hitting a target) through his doing of the act of moving his finger. But in the sense of choice earlier

---

[86] Lacey makes both of these points: she concludes that 'negligence liability . . . sits unhappily with traditional conceptions of responsibility in the criminal law' (*State Punishment, supra* n. 1, at 105–6), and that 'the link with a possible rationale for negligence liability is obvious' (ibid., 66) on the character theory of responsibility.

described, he does not choose to do the kind of complex action forbidden by morality and law (such as killing the man standing behind the target) because his mind was not adverting to that aspect of his action.[87]

Herbert Hart's attempt to reconcile responsibility for negligence with the choice conception of responsibility results in a considerable alteration of the choice conception. Hart argued that although the negligent actor did not choose to do a wrongful act, he had the capacity and a fair opportunity to have chosen not to do it, and is therefore fairly blameable for his non-exercise of that capacity.[88] So long as we individualize the standard by which we judge an actor's behaviour so that we can say of him, 'he could have done otherwise, given his capacities',[89] then, Hart urges, we may blame negligent actors with as much confidence as we do intentional wrongdoers.[90]

In accommodating responsibility for negligence in this way, Hart, as he recognized, shifted the touchstone of responsibility from choice to capacity.[91] A choice to do a wrongful act then becomes only one way in which the actor's capacity to avoid evil goes unexercised; inadvertence is another. My objection to this shift is a moral one: it relegates choice to a subsidiary role in our responsibility assessments that our judgements will not and should not

[87] A choice theorist who rejects my notion of choice might deny that we ever do hold people responsible for unchosen actions. Negligence, he might say, is not a *mens rea* requirement like knowledge or recklessness; rather, it is a criterion of wrongful action. As such, the injunction 'don't kill negligently' is a shorthand for all the injunctions aimed at more particular actions, such as 'don't shoot at a target without first ascertaining whether someone is behind it or not'. And those latter acts, he might conclude, are chosen under every aspect that makes them wrongful. The lesser responsibility for a negligent (as opposed to intentional) killing is not due to the presence or absence of choice, but rather, to the differential wrongness of the acts chosen.

Tempting as this line may be, it slurs over the crucial fact that someone who only negligently kills (e.g., by shooting at a paper target without having a belief one way or another as to whether there are persons behind it) does not advert to just that feature of his action that makes it wrongful; in the example given, he does not make a choice one way or the other about death or injury to persons.

[88] H. L. A. Hart, 'Negligence, *Mens Rea*, and Criminal Responsibility', in *Punishment and Responsibility*, 136–57. I earlier adopted Hart's view in *Law and Psychiatry, supra*, n. 1, at 81–4.

[89] A point on which Hart's view of the moral idea of negligence diverges considerably from present law on the subject. See 'Negligence, *Mens Rea*, and Criminal Responsibility', *supra* n. 88, at 152–7.

[90] Ibid., 152.

[91] Ibid., 140.

support. What makes the intentional or reckless wrongdoer so culpable is not unexercised capacity—although that is necessary—but
the way such capacity to avoid evil goes unexercised; such wrongdoers are not even trying to get it right. Their capacity goes unexercised because that is what they choose. Choice is essential to their
culpability, not one way among others that they could have been
seriously culpable.

Does this mean that when we blame for negligence we blame for
character (the second of the character theorist's two claims here)?
Interestingly enough, although the choice theorist cannot easily
accommodate the culpability of negligence, neither can the character theorist. For the character theorist must bridge two gaps in
order to link her theory with responsibility for negligence. The first
is the gap between the failure of a negligent actor to advert to the
risk that made his action negligent *at the time of that action*, on the
one hand, and the *general tendency* of such an actor to be inadvertent about such risks, on the other. Thus, Lacey, for example, urges
that we may infer of the actor who makes an unreasonable mistake
of fact that 'this is a person who systematically, characteristically
makes unreasonable mistakes causing danger to the interests of
others . . .'.[92] This may indeed be an inference we may sometimes
draw, but ignored is the fact that we hold negligent actors responsible irrespective of whether one can draw such an inference or not.
Put simply, judgements of negligence do not depend on any general
traits of carelessness; an isolated act of negligence suffices for
responsibility for the harm that act causes.

The second gap is between the actor who does 'systematically,
characteristically make unreasonable mistakes' and the bad character of such an actor. Lacey thinks we can infer from the presence
of such mistake-proneness in a person that that person had a 'genuine practical indifference to the interests protected by the criminal
law', such as the interests of others in their bodily integrity.[93]
Again, this is indeed sometimes an inference we can draw about a
careless person, because a general attitude of indifference to others
does sometimes explain such carelessness. But one can be careless—
even characteristically so—without having a bad character in this
sense. Such carelessness can be due to awkwardness and stupidity

---

[92] Lacey, *State Punishment, supra* n. 1, at 66.   [93] Ibid.

as easily as indifference. And, again, we blame for carelessness irrespective of *why* one is careless.[94]

Thus responsibility for negligence fits poorly with either conception of responsibility. When we attribute moral responsibility to someone for a negligent act, we cannot base such attribution either on a judgement of culpable choice or of culpable character. Negligent actors may often have both, but to be negligent they need have neither. What this once suggested to me was that perhaps negligence by itself does not merit any moral blame, and that its presence in the law has to be explained on purely utilitarian grounds.[95]

Jeremy Horder has rightly criticized my choice conception of culpability on the descriptive ground that Anglo-American criminal law manifestly does punish sometimes for negligence.[96] Not only is this true, but morally also it seems wrong to say that we are not at least somewhat blameworthy for negligent conduct, certainly when we cause the harm risked but also when we do not. I thus returned in chapter 9 to the orthodoxy that there is a culpability of negligence. Since this is neither the culpability of choice nor of character, it must be a distinct form of culpability, what Hart aptly termed the culpability of unexercised capacity.[97]

Horder presses this concession into service as an argument against the choice theory. Because the conditions under which choice betokens actual, and not merely prima facie, culpability include adequate capacity and fair opportunity, why is not choice but one kind of unexercised capacity?[98] Horder in his rush to disagree with me here ignores something he knows as well as do I: that there is a 'fundamental difference' in the opportunity available to an actor who knows that he is doing the sort of action that is

---

[94] The extent to which this last statement is true depends upon the degree to which we individualize the standard of care by virtue of which we judge an actor negligent. If morality is like Anglo-American law here, ignoring the different degrees to which people are hasty, awkward, and stupid, then our judgements of carelessness are blind to these different explanations of carelessness.

[95] Moore, 'Choice, Character, and Excuse', *Social Philosophy and Policy*, Vol. 7 (1990), 28–58, at 58. Some character theorists have come to this conclusion too. See Bayles, 'Character, Purpose, and Criminal Responsibility', *supra* n. 32, at 10–11. Bayles sees that 'on the basis of one careless act, the inference to a careless attitude is less valid', sees that such carelessness 'does not indicate an attitude of indifference to standards of care', and concludes that, on the character theory, 'the basis for blame [for negligence] is much less sure'.

[96] Horder, 'Criminal Culpability', *supra* n. 27, at 199.

[97] Hart, *Punishment and Responsibility*, *supra* n. 88.

[98] Horder, 'Criminal Culpability', *supra* n. 27, at 200.

wrongful and chooses to do it anyway and the opportunity available to an actor to learn that an action he is doing is of a wrongful sort. As Horder rightly puts it, in the case of chosen wrongdoing it is 'the way that the opportunity to avoid wrongdoing was missed' that is crucial, not 'the fact that it was missed at all' true of merely negligent wrongdoing.[99] My way of marking this fundamental difference in the kinds of capacities and opportunities one needs in order to be culpable, is by distinguishing two kinds of culpability, one for choice and one for inadvertent risk-creation. If one wants to see both as underlain by some more general capacity/opportunity kind of culpability, that is harmless enough so long as one finds some other means of marking this fundamental difference.

[99] Horder, 'Criminal Culpability', *supra* n. 27, at 203.

SUBPART C
THE AGENTS WHO CAN BE RESPONSIBLE: THE NATURE OF PERSONHOOD

14

MENTAL ILLNESS AND RESPONSIBILITY

In this subpart we come to what I regard as the deepest and the most basic of the psychological suppositions on which the criminal law rests. These are the suppositions about the subjects of responsibility. Who or what can be morally responsible, what attributes a being must have to be held responsible, are the questions to which such suppositions give answer. The general form of that answer is in terms of persons, and so the suppositions in question amount to the criminal law's theory of personhood.

Since no statute, case, or other obvious source of criminal law doctrine even enacts a theory of personhood, one has to tease such a theory out of the doctrines that make up the general part of the criminal law. One does this by asking what persons must be like if the doctrines of the criminal law can fairly be applied to them. While all of the doctrines of the general part are relevant in ascertaining the law's theory of personhood, the doctrines surrounding the defence of legal insanity are the locus where the law's presuppositions about persons are closest to the surface. It is here (together with the legal defence of infancy) that the law most squarely addresses who it is that can be the fit subject of blame. I shall accordingly start in this chapter with an interpretation of legal insanity, saving until the chapter following some more general concerns about the criminal law's presupposed metaphysics of personhood.

I have elsewhere described the Anglo-American legal doctrines on insanity and their history.[1] The taxonomy of doctrines I found most useful was partly in terms of historical development, partly in terms of psychiatric paradigms about the salient features of mental illness, and partly in terms of the moral excuses lawyers had in

[1] Michael Moore, 'Legal Conceptions of Mental Illness', *Philosophy and Medicine*, Vol. V (1979), 25–69; revised and reprinted as ch. 6 of Michael Moore, *Law and Psychiatry: Rethinking the Relationship* (Cambridge: Cambridge University Press, 1984).

mind as they accommodated legal doctrines of insanity to the then prevailing psychiatric paradigms. Not intending to recapitulate that doctrinal exegesis here, suffice it say that Anglo-American criminal law has for centuries excused the seriously mentally ill, variously because: they have the understanding only of a wild beast, or of a child; they lack that mental maturity measured by their grasp of good and evil such that they are not moral agents; they are (delusionally) ignorant or mistaken about the nature and quality of their act, or that their act is morally or legally forbidden; their actions are the products of their disease, with 'disease' naming a brain lesion and the causal relationship between that brain lesion and their behaviour being one of physical causation; they are irresistibly impelled by their mental disease to perform their criminal acts; they lack substantial capacity either to appreciate the wrongfulness or criminality of their conduct, or to conform their conduct to the requirements of the law; their criminal acts were the products of their mental disease, 'disease' now naming a distinctively mental abnormality and the causal relationship between that abnormality and behaviour being any 'but for' (or counterfactual) relationship; they lack the intention or other *mens rea* element required for conviction, particularly if the crime is one requiring 'specific intent'.

The justification for this set of doctrines (all excusing the mentally ill from liability to punishment for their otherwise wrongful actions) depends on one's theory of punishment. For a utilitarian or a mixed theorist about punishment, to ask why we excuse a certain class of offenders from punishment is to ask what good (utilitarian) reasons exist to create an exception from punishment in favour of a particular class of offenders. Bentham for example, treated excuses in the criminal law from this perspective, justifying each exception from liability on utilitarian grounds.[2] It was, he thought, inefficacious to inflict pain on those who cause harm by accident, because such persons are not dangerous nor can others like them be deterred from future accidental behaviour. To run this line about the mentally ill is usually to enquire into their deterrability.

From the retributive perspective of this book, however, the justification of a defence like insanity has to be different. The relevant question for the retributivist has to involve the moral basis of such

---

[2] Jeremy Bentham, *An Introduction to the Principles of Morals and Legislation* (New York: Hafner edn., 1948), 170–1, n. 1.

legal defences. Why would it be morally wrong to punish a certain class of offenders? This form of the question asks not for a justification of such defence in terms of the good consequences achievable if we have it; rather, it ask for an articulation of the general principles of morality that would be violated by punishing those who are mentally ill.

Very often both types of analyses dictate that the criminal law excuse the same classes of offenders. Not only do we feel it would be morally unjust to punish those who cause harm by non-negligent accidents, but it would probably also be inefficient to punish such offenders. They are not dangerous, nor are others like them in need of deterrence. There is, however, no reason to expect that this happy coincidence of moral and utilitarian considerations will always exist. Indeed, in the case of the mentally ill we have just such a separation of the two. It has been a fundamental feature of our collective conscience for centuries that the mentally ill are not considered morally responsible for the harm they cause; yet, such individuals may be just as dangerous to society as sane criminals. Hence, we excuse mentally ill offenders from the moral blame associated with punishment in the criminal law, but we do not release them to society to cause further harm. In effect, we recognize that we cannot afford to let such dangerous individuals loose, but we are not morally justified in punishing them either.

Why do we believe it is morally wrong to punish the mentally ill? By virtue of what moral principles should such offenders be excused? Lawyers, philosophers, and others concerned with the question have suggested at least four answers.

The Negation of Free Will: Perhaps the most popular view is that the mentally ill are excused because the assumption of free will is not as appropriate for them as it is for normal individuals. That is, 'mental illness' is regarded as the name of a cause of behaviour. Admittedly we do not know much about the nature of such causes; but 'mental illness' is a promissory note in the sense that, while the referent of the phrase is partially unknown, it is hypothesized to exist. Another assumption is that the causation of the behaviour of the mentally ill excuses them from responsibility for any harm they may incur. Thus, according to this view, the mentally ill are excused because unlike the acts of normal individuals those of the mentally ill are not (contra-causally) free.

The Negation of Mens Rea: A second view is that mentally ill offenders are excused because they do not act with the kind of intention essential to both moral responsibility and legal liability. On this view, mental illness is an excuse in the criminal law because it negates *mens rea*—the guilty mind required for criminal liability.

Compulsion and Ignorance: Perhaps the prevailing view today among legal theorists has been that mental illness is not itself relevant to responsibility. On this view, the only reason mental illness seems to be morally relevant is because it is usually accompanied by mistake or ignorance on the part of the mentally ill offender, or compulsion, both of which are traditionally acceptable excuses throughout our moral and legal system. As I sketched in chapter 12, the 'true excuses' are reserved for those individuals who cause harm *in ignorance* of some relevant circumstances (for example, that there was poison in the tea) or who are acting under *compulsion* (for example, acting under threat or other external duress). Thus on this view the mentally ill are excused only because their symptoms include either delusive ignorance or some form of psychological compulsion. Since these features are thought to be present in all seriously ill offenders, we excuse them from moral responsibility.

Irrationality: Finally, the position I have long argued for is that we excuse the mentally ill because they are irrational.[3] In my view, we presuppose the rationality of another being when we describe and explain his actions in the same way that we describe and explain our own activities in daily life, namely, by use of the agent's desires, beliefs, and intentions. But if another being's rationality is in question, he cannot be understood in the same way and to the same extent as can normal individuals. This difference of intelligibility renders the mentally ill not responsible because, being to some degree incomprehensible, they are not regarded as moral agents. In this respect, they are like young children.

Which of these four positions one accepts has more than merely academic interest. If one believes, for example, that the mentally ill are excused only because 'mental illness' is the name of a partially known cause of behaviour, then once one becomes disenchanted with the possibility of finding such causes, one may easily conclude

---

[3] See reference, *supra* n. 1.

that the mentally ill should not be excused but should be punished like anyone else.[4] Or, if one believes that mental illness has no independent exculpatory force, that the mentally ill are 'excused' only because mental illness either negates intention (the second view mentioned above) or because it involves ignorance and compulsion (the third view), one again may conclude that the insanity plea should be abolished. The result, however, is not that the mentally ill should be punished, but that they should be excused by some other legal doctrines (absence of *mens rea*, mistake, duress).

None of these first three accounts is adequate, for none of them captures those general features of our shared moral values that lead us to excuse the mentally ill. Taking each in turn:

The Negation of Free Will: The first position, it will be recalled, attempts to account for our moral sense (that the mentally ill should be excused) in terms of a lack of free will. If taken seriously, this view would eliminate responsibility entirely as a viable concept. This view presupposes, first, that the criminal acts of the mentally ill are caused, and second, that any behaviour explicable by reference to causes is necessarily excused. As we saw in chapter 12, it is the second assumption that creates the trouble, for if one believes that causation necessarily excuses, and if one is a determinist (which is likely if one believes mental illness to be a kind of strong cause), then the general implication is that we are all 'excused' by an assumed but as yet unknown mechanistic factor determining human behaviour. In this view, no one would be responsible.

I realize that a large number of behavioural scientists may simply nod in agreement at this point, believing that the law and its moral underpinnings are simply naïve. Deterministic assumptions for many make the attribution of moral and legal responsibility an incoherent activity to be explained on purely historical grounds. Psychiatrists in particular are prone to accept without question the thesis that determinism is incompatible with responsibility. One of the burdens undertaken in the last half of chapter 12 was to relieve anybody of such confidence in incompatibilist metaphysics. If one reaches the conclusions there defended—that there is no inconsistency in thinking: (1) that fully voluntary human actions are caused by factors unwilled by the actor, (2) that actions caused by factors

---

[4] This is the line that Tom Szasz has been pushing for three and one-half decades. See, e.g., Szasz, *Law, Liberty, and Psychiatry* (New York: Macmillan, 1963).

outside the control of the actor are usually uncompelled actions, and (3) that actors caused by factors unwilled by them are nonetheless actors who 'could have done otherwise', in the relevant sense of those words—then there is no incompatibilism between determinism and responsibility.

If incompatibilism is rejected in general, then raising assumptions about the causation of behaviour by mental illness as the ground for excusing the mentally ill is a needless distraction. Questions of physical and psychological causation become as irrelevant to the issues of the moral and legal responsibility of the mentally ill as determinism in general is to the responsibility of normal individuals. Merely citing a cause of behaviour in no way precludes holding an actor fully responsible for that same behaviour. Hence, merely to assert the probable existence of such causes, either in general or with particular reference to the mentally ill, is not to say anything relevant about responsibility.

The Negation of Mens Rea: The second view was that mentally ill offenders are excused because those offenders who are mentally ill do not act with the required guilty mind. Since the *mens rea* requirement of the most serious crimes is intentionality, the argument usually is that the mentally ill who cause harm by their actions do not do so intentionally. Yet this statement is manifestly false. The criminal acts of the mentally ill are often intentional in every ordinary and legal sense of the word. As we have seen in chapter 11, the legal and moral debate about the meaning of the word 'intentional' has centred on the competing criteria of the knowledge and the purposes of the agent. The question is whether the consequence of an action was intended if the actor merely knew to a substantial certainty that it would follow from his acts, or whether the consequence must in addition have been in the chain of his reasons for acting. One might contrast, for example, the greedy manufacturer who knowingly sells poisoned food to the populace with the gravedigger who increases his business by the sale of such poisoned food. Is only the latter guilty of intent-to-kill murder?

The criminal acts of even the most severely mentally ill are often intentional under even the most restrictive of these criteria, that is, the criterion that one must act purposefully to act intentionally. M'Naghten not only knew to a substantial certainty that firing the bullet would cause grievous bodily harm to Drummond, but to inflict that harm was one of his purposes: it was the only way he saw to end the persecution to which he believed he was subject. While we would find the evidence for M'Naghten's belief in his persecution inadequate, his action of killing Drummond was intentional as one can see when one understands M'Naghten's peculiar beliefs. Despite this fact, we still feel the M'Naghtens of this world should be excused. Therefore, we must seek other grounds on which such feelings are to be explained.

Compulsion and Ignorance: According to the third view, we excuse the mentally ill because their actions are due either to excusable ignorance or are in some sense compelled. This is the official view of most lawyers and the basis of most legal tests of insanity. Under the *M'Naghten* test, one is excused only if he laboured under a mistake of fact (about the nature and quality of his act), or if he laboured under a mistake of morals or law (that the act was morally or legally wrong). Under the irresistible impulse test, one is excused if he was subject to an irresistible (that is, a compelling) impulse. The Model Penal Code simply combines the two and allows the defence if one 'lacks substantial capacity either to appreciate the criminality of his conduct or to conform his conduct to the requirements of law'.

If these legal formulations truly covered all those cases where we do not feel the accused to be morally blameworthy due to mental illness, then they would be good evidence for the correctness of the official view: we excuse the mentally ill only because they act in ignorance or are compelled to act as they do. But do these formulations capture all the cases where we hold individuals morally blameless because of mental illness? Or are such tests reflective of nothing more than lawyers' misgivings about the insanity defence, misgivings alleviated only by tacking onto mental illness (whose unique moral relevance they do not understand) more traditional excuses that lawyers do understand? One can only answer such questions by examining cases to see first of all whether we are willing to hold the individual morally blameworthy, and second whether and in what sense those individuals we do not wish to hold morally blameworthy were compelled to act as they did or were ignorant in some relevant respect. If we find cases where the actor seems blameless yet we cannot say the action was either compelled or done in excusable ignorance, then some other basis must be sought to account for our excusing the mentally ill.

I will not examine such cases here, for aside from giving a great deal of detail about particular cases one needs also to give an analysis of those overworked words *ignorance* and, particularly, *compulsion*.[5] One can get some idea of the issues involved by asking in what sense a mentally ill defendant was *compelled* to act as he did: he is not compelled simply because his behaviour was caused by his unhappy history. So did he feel compelled by some strong emotions as he acted? Or was he unconscious of such emotions, and if so what sense can be made of such unconscious emotions?[6] Should we identify *him* with the 'victim' of such emotions, or as much with the exciting emotion? Alternatively, by what criterion of 'knowledge' did he not know what he was doing, or not know that the law prohibited it? By the ordinary meaning of the word *know*, it would seem that many severely mentally ill defendants like M'Naghten know both of these things.[7] Such defendants may de delusional, but only rarely do such delusions relate to material elements of the *actus reus* or the elements of a justificatory defence.

I think the result of such an analysis would not show expressions such as 'beyond his control' or 'in ignorance of what he was doing' to be meaningless. Rather, once one makes their meaning more precise, it would turn out that some criminals we want to excuse would not be excused if the only grounds for excuse were mistake and compulsion. If this is so, then again we have failed to account for our moral sentiments with regard to the mentally ill.

Irrationality: In my view, only the fourth viewpoint—we excuse the mentally ill because they are irrational—adequately captures our moral sentiments. To see why this is so one must first understand the close connection between the concept of rationality and the

---

[5] On the general idea of compulsion, see Robert Audi, 'Moral Responsibility, Freedom, and Compulsion', *American Philosophical Quarterly*, Vol. 11 (1974), 1–14. Questioning whether mental illness is always or even often compelling are Joel Feinberg, 'What Is so Special About Mental Illness?', in *Doing and Deserving* (Princeton: Princeton University Press, 1971); Herbert Fingarette, *The Meaning of Criminal Insanity* (Berkeley: University of California Press, 1972); Moore, *Law and Psychiatry supra* n. 1, ch. 6.

[6] On the idea of unconscious emotions, see Moore, *Law and Psychiatry*, *supra* n. 1, at 377–8.

[7] On the abuse of the ordinary meaning of 'know' in cognitive versions of the insanity tests, see Fingarette, *Meaning*, *supra* n. 5.

idioms in which we understand ourselves and other persons in daily life. Here are two rather homely examples: suppose we ask Smith why he is carrying his umbrella to lunch. He replies that he believes it is going to rain. Suppose we ask Jones why he went across the street a moment ago, and he replies it was because he wanted some tobacco from the store across the street. Each, by his answer, has rendered his behaviour intelligible by giving us the practical reasoning that led him to do what he did. Each has supplied a part of the practical syllogism of his action, to use Aristotle's terminology.

For Aristotle, the full practical syllogism had two premises: (1) specifying what the agent desired, and (2) the beliefs that he had as to the means available to that desire's fulfilment. The conclusion of the syllogism was the action itself, for Aristotle. In ordinary speech we usually need only one part of the syllogism to make out the other. For example, Smith specified the belief while Jones specified the desire. The more complete practical syllogism for Smith would be: (1) I don't want to get wet on my walk to lunch; (2) I believe that it's going to rain and unless protected by an umbrella I will get wet on my walk to lunch; therefore, I will take my umbrella. Jones's practical syllogism, in terms of his (stated) desire and his (unstated) beliefs, is equally obvious.

These examples bring out a simple fact: we explain the actions of persons by reference to their beliefs and their desires (the latter includes motives, wants, wishes, pro-attitudes, ends, aims, goals, objects, purposes, etc.). By citing such beliefs and such desires, we see the action as a rational activity of an agent who is using the action to achieve something he wants. Such explanations rationalize an action in that they exhibit it as the rational thing to do given certain beliefs and certain desires. For example, if Smith were not rational, he could have a desire to stay dry, a belief that taking his umbrella was necessary for him to stay dry, and yet deliberately leave his umbrella in his office.[8]

One of the long-noticed oddities of Aristotle's account is his idea that an *action* like the taking of one's umbrella could be a 'conclusion' of practical reasoning. It seems preferable to think that some *description* of an action should be the conclusion.[9] Moreover, the

[8] On the idea of reasons for action, see Moore, *Law and Psychiatry*, *supra* n. 1, at ch. 1.

[9] Argued for in Michael Moore, *Act and Crime: The Philosophy of Action and its Implications for Criminal Law* (Oxford: Oxford University Press, 1993), at 138.

description of the action concluded upon should in some sense be the agent's own—after all, it is his decision. That means we should include the description as the content of some representational state of the actor, such as a desire or a belief. However, such a deciding state seems not to have the quality of a belief, for decisions are not mere predictions; likewise, such a deciding state does not have the quality of a new and merely instrumental desire, for decisions have an all-out quality that desires may plausibly be thought to lack.[10] Therefore, we should embrace a third kind of state possessed by the rational actor, one we may call a decision, choice, or more standardly, intention.

The last complication of Aristotle's account that we need stems from the observation that our intentions themselves are hierarchically ordered, from very general plans to very specific willings of the bodily movements that execute such plans. In chapter 6 I called the simplest intentions that execute the more general ones, volitions.[11]

We may schematize the explanation of human action in terms of the actor's practical syllogism so as to make explicit the presuppositions of rationality implicit in Aristotle's version. The full explanation in general form should have these premises: (1) Agent X wants result R to obtain. (2) X believes that action A will cause R to obtain. (3) If X believes that A will result in R, and if X desires R, then, *ceteris paribus*, X intends A. (4) *Ceteris paribus*. Therefore: (5) X intends A. In other words, to get to the intentions to do some action A, we need to know what the agent wanted, what he believed about the situation, and his ability to achieve through action what he wanted. In addition, we need to know that he is a rational creature in the fundamental sense, namely other things being equal, he will act so as to further his desires in light of his beliefs. And we held to know that other things are equal, namely, that the agent does not have desires and beliefs that conflict with the desires and beliefs on which he is about to act and that are stronger than the latter desires and beliefs.

To move from intentions to action involves the following premises: (6) X believes that if X wills bodily movement M, then that M will become A. (7) If X intends A, and if X believes M will

---

[10] Michael Moore, *Act and Crime: The Philosophy of Action and its Implications for Criminal Law* (Oxford: Oxford University Press, 1993), ch. 6.
[11] Id.

become A, then *ceteris paribus* X wills M. (8) *Ceteris paribus*. Therefore: (9) X wills M. If X's willing of M causes that bodily movement to occur, and if that bodily movement in turn causes M to acquire those causal or other properties that make it an action of type A, then we reach Aristotle's 'conclusion' of the practical syllogism: (10) X does action A.

We are now in a position to understand the sense of 'rationality' denied by mental illness. To say of someone that he is mentally ill is to say that he is irrational. The irrationality of agents is a function of the irrationality of their actions over time: the more often they act irrationally, the more irrational we judge them as agents to be. The crux of the matter is to understand in what sense(s) their actions are irrational. I think there are a number of senses, corresponding to each of the premises of the practical syllogism I just mentioned.

In extreme cases, we may be unable to make out any set of beliefs and desires by virtue of which we may view an action as rational. For example, the bodily motions of epileptics during a *grand mal* seizure, or the word salads of schizophrenics would seem to be non-rational activities in this sense. In such cases we are unable to assert the third premise I mentioned, that is, we are unable to see the action as the rational thing to do in light of any set of beliefs and desires that we can reasonably ascribe to the agent. This is not to say that we think the agent to be without beliefs or desires; rather, it is to say that the beliefs and desires they have do not have contents that stand in that relationship to the content of an intention demanded by *valid* practical inference. Given very much of this kind of irrational behaviour, an individual becomes, as Manfred Bleuler said of some of his schizophrenic patients, stranger to us than the birds in our gardens.

Almost as strange to us would be someone of whom the seventh premise could not be confidently and regularly asserted. This is the individual who decides firmly on a course of conduct A, believes if he performs some routine M then he will accomplish A, nothing prevents him from doing M, and yet refuses to do M. He is, as Aristotle might say, weak of will in that he cannot will himself to do that which he has decided to do. This is so irrational that when confronted with seeming instances of it, we tend to withdraw the judgement that the individual in question ever really did form the firm intention to A. We tend to say, 'he must have still been too conflicted in what he wanted to have really resolved the conflict by deciding to do A'.

There are also forms of irrationality corresponding to the having of each of the three kinds of mental states described in premise (1), (2) and (6), and (5) and (9). That is, it is sometimes irrational to desire, believe, or intend certain things. Take desire first. Some states of affairs are unintelligible for a person to want intrinsically, that is, for their own sakes. Wishing to expose one's green books to the sun, as it stands, is unintelligible for a person to want intrinsically, so if proffered as the reason for some action that action too becomes opaque to us.[12] Alternatively, our desires may be irrational in the economists' sense of the word, namely, intransitive in their ordering. I may desire A more than B, desire B more than C, and yet desire C more than A. Such intransitively ordered desires are irrational in that they lead to infinite cycling of the behaviours needed to satisfy such desires.

There is a third sense in which desires are irrational that needs to be put aside in this context. This is the sense of the rationalist tradition in ethics according to which an end can be irrational because it is morally or prudentially wrong to pursue. While my own meta-ethics commits me to the existence of this sense of 'irrational desire', this is not the kind of irrationality synonymous with mental illness. To think otherwise would be to collapse any distinction between the (mentally) sick and the bad.

Analogously to this last point about desires, one should not think that a merely *false* belief is for that reason alone an *irrational* belief to hold. Rationality of belief has to do with the epistemic situation of the actor and the degree to which that situation gives her warrant for believing what she does. A belief that one is made of glass, for example, is hard to square with the evidence available to one. This disproportion between the degree of confidence with which the belief is held, and the evidence supporting it, is what we usually mean by talking of *irrational* beliefs.[13]

As with desires, the irrationality of belief infects the rationality of action based upon it. The individual who avoids all contact with people because he believes he is made of glass and will shatter if touched behaves rationally enough in light of his desire not to be shat-

[12] See A. J. Watt, 'The Intelligibility of Wants', *Mind*, Vol. 81 (1972), 553–61.
[13] See Robert J. Ackermann, *Belief and Knowledge* (Garden City, NY: Doubleday, 1972).

tered and his belief that he is made of glass and will shatter if touched. But the belief itself is irrational, and actions predicated on irrational beliefs are themselves, in ordinary understanding, irrational actions.[14]

The rationality of intention that some mentally ill individuals lack is distinct from the rationalities of desire or belief. By saying that an intention is irrational, usually what we mean[15] is that the intention violates one of two relationships. The first relationship Michael Bratman calls intention-belief consistency.[16] Usually it is criticizably irrational to intend to cause some result R if I believe that this is impossible. It is not that such romantic quests, hopeless martyrdoms, etc., are psychologically impossible; only irrational in most circumstances. After all, if you know that you cannot attain the only object that moves you to action, why are you acting?

The second relationship is a relationship between intentions that Bratman calls intention-agglomerativity.[17] As discussed briefly in chapter 6, the principle of agglomerativity states that if X intends A and X intends B, then X intends (A and B). Bratman urges that this kind of intention agglomeration is necessary for us to build those even larger intentions we call plans. Most of the time, not to agglomerate is criticizably irrational because it is not to use plans to guide one's behaviour.[18]

The last senses of irrationality of relevance here have to do with the *ceteris paribus* clauses in premises (4) and (8). Since each is different, I shall consider each separately. The fourth premise asserts that the actor does not have other beliefs or desires that conflict with[19] the beliefs and desires on which she is acting and that are

[14] On the connection of the rationality of action with the irrationality of belief, see Theodore Mischel, 'Concerning Rational Behavior and Psychoanalytic Explanation', *Mind*, Vol. 74 (1965), 71–8.

[15] The hedging, because sometimes we call intentions irrational in that they do not follow from beliefs and desires as they should or in that they are inconsistent with one another. These irrationalities are better seen as relating to other premises, however (namely, premises (3) or (8)).

[16] Michael Bratman, *Intentions, Plans, and Practical Reasoning* (Cambridge, Mass.: Harvard University Press, 1983).

[17] Id.

[18] With the caveats mentioned in ch. 6 for certain rare kinds of general intentions, and for many less rare kinds of volitional intentions.

[19] Strict conflict between desires occurs when one desires both state of affairs q to come into existence and that q not exist. More common than this kind of necessary conflict in the object of one's desires is the conflict one experiences by desiring q, desiring p, and the world being such that we cannot have both p and q. E.g.: I desire dessert, and I desire not to break a diet.

held more strongly than the latter beliefs and desires. This premise is rarely satisfied for the mentally ill. Their desires are often inconsistent: by acting to fulfil one desire, they often frustrate another. While this circumstance is true for most of us some of the time, more of the mentally ill's desires conflict with things they more strongly want and yet they have not resolved their conflicting desires into a coherent, consistent set of wants. Acting on such unresolved conflicts of desire cannot be fully rational, because such actions necessarily frustrate some things one wants a great deal, although perhaps unconsciously.

Consider, lastly, the conflict in intention ruled out by premise (8). This premise asserts that there are no other intentions that conflict with the intention which explains the actor's action. Unlike desires, if intentions conflict in the sense that X intends to do A and intends not do A, such conflict is itself criticizably irrational without regard to which was the stronger intention.[20]

In these various senses, then, some of the actions of the mentally ill are non-rational or irrational. Since the rationality of agents is a function of the rationality of their actions over time, we think of the mentally ill as less rational than normal people.

Why should the irrationality of the mentally ill lead us to excuse them from moral responsibility? It is because our notions of who is eligible to be held morally responsible depend on our ability to make out rather regularly practical syllogisms for actions. One is a moral agent only if one is a rational agent, in the senses of 'rational' that I have mentioned. Only if we can see another being as one who acts to further her intentions, which intentions themselves achieve some intelligible end in light of some rational beliefs, will we understand her in the same fundamental way that we understand ourselves and others in everyday life. We regard as moral agents only those beings we can understand in this way.

Thus, societies that attribute moral responsibility to natural objects are regarded as primitive, because we are unwilling to accept the primitive animism subscribed to by such societies. If we did believe that natural objects possessed beliefs, desires, and intentions in light of which their movements are to be understood as

---

[20] This is because of the all-out nature of intentions as opposed to desires. We expect desires to conflict in the action they recommend on any given occasion, but intentions are formed when we have resolved such conflicts with a decision. Contradictory decisions are irrational in the way contradictory desires are not.

rational, our misgivings about attributing moral responsibility to such objects would evaporate. Moral responsibility and that mode of explanation I call 'practical reasoning' go hand in hand.[21]

Thus, it is easy to understand the historical tendency to analogize the mentally ill to infants and wild beasts.[22] For we do not think of these beings as engaging in practical reasoning to the same extent as do normal, adult human beings. Only when an infant begins to act in ways explicable by his practical syllogisms, do we begin to see him as a moral agent who can justly be held responsible. The same is true of the mentally ill.

The upshot of this analysis is simply this: mental illness (irrationality) is itself excusing. One who is mentally ill is not morally blameworthy for harm he incurs while he is ill. Not being morally blameworthy, he cannot be held liable to the sanctions of the criminal law. Some form of insanity defence is a proper reflection of our moral sentiments in this regard. Further, not only should the defence be retained, but it should be phrased so as to correspond to the moral issue being adjudicated by juries. The question put to juries should not be phrased in terms of the knowledge or compulsion of the accused, and certainly not in terms of speculative hypotheses about physical causation of the accused's behaviour. We can also dispense with the fiction that a mentally ill person's criminal action could not have been intentional. Rather, the question put to juries should be the moral question framed in terms of the actual criterion by which such moral judgements are made, that is, in terms of the irrationality of the accused: was the accused so irrational that he cannot justly be held responsible? It is not at all clear that juries do not ask just this question anyway, regardless of the wording of the insanity test in different jurisdictions.[23]

[21] Holmes traced this connection for some primitive European legal systems in Oliver W. Holmes, Jr., *The Common Law* (Boston: Little, Brown, 1881), Lecture I.

[22] A. M. Platt and B. L. Diamond, 'The Origins and Development of the "Wild Beast" Concept of Mental Illness and Its Relation to theories of Criminal Responsibility', *Journal of the History of the Behavior Sciences*, Vol. 1 (1965), 355–67.

[23] This position was taken by the Royal Commission on Capital Punishment: 'In many cases where a medical witness hazards the opinion that the accused at the time of his act was not conscious that it was wrong, it is difficult to suppose that the ordinary jury man regards this point as crucial; there can be little doubt that he often addresses his mind to the essential question whether the accused was so insane that it would be unreasonable to hold him responsible for his action.' (Royal Commission on Capital Punishment, *1949–53 Report*, London, 1953).

15

AN OVERVIEW OF THE CRIMINAL LAW'S THEORY OF THE PERSON

The last chapter illustrates a technique generally employable to attribute metaphysical views to the law: start with legal doctrine, isolate the values such doctrine serves, and then ask what features persons would have to have if those values are to be served effectively by those doctrines. If the doctrines making up the insanity defence serve the moral point that I think they do, then criminal law generally must suppose persons to be rational in the senses explicated—why else separate as non-responsible those who are irrational?

Rationality is one basic feature persons must generally possess for our criminal doctrines to have application to them. A second basic feature is what I shall call 'autonomy'. The concept of autonomy is a slippery one, in part because it lies so close to the values of liberty and privacy, and in part because so many people use it in so many different ways. With no attempt to accurately gauge these different usages, I shall employ the concept to label four relatively distinct things:[1] (1) One sense of autonomy is that explicated in chapter 6 in the analysis of human action. Here autonomy names a capacity that persons may plausibly be supposed to have, namely, the power to initiate actions. On the theory of action developed in chapter 6, this capacity involves the capacities to will bodily movements and to cause such movements to occur as a result of such willings. Autonomy in this first sense is thus a limited kind of causal power presupposed whenever we talk about a person causing or doing anything.

(2) A second sense of autonomy also names a causal power of persons, but one less limited than the power to initiate actions. Rather, the capacity is to cause further events to occur in the world

[1] Three of these senses I distinguished in Moore, *Law and Psychiatry: Rethinking the Relationship* (Cambridge: Cambridge University Press, 1984), ch. 2.

beyond movement of one's own body. This is the power to choose (or intend) such events to come about, and to cause such events to occur in response to one's choices. This is, as we saw in chapter 13, what makes choice so valuable to us: the more of such causal power we have, the more our choices can be the means to getting us what we want.

Freud tells us that we each start out with a grandly exaggerated idea of our own autonomy in this sense. The infant's supposed illusion of omnipotence would be the sense that one had as much autonomy in this second sense as one does in the first sense; that is, that one could will deaths, hurricanes, and breakfast like one can will the movement of one's finger. If that is the baseline, plainly we have less autonomy in this second sense than in the first, as all adults realize.

(3) A third sense of autonomy has a distinctively Kantian tinge: here, the central focus is on the reasons for which we act. One acts autonomously in this sense when one's actions are motivated by some reasons and not others. One does not have to subscribe to Kant's very austere view of what these reasons can be—for Kant, only a reverence for the moral law. One can think with Joseph Raz that morality provides us with a number of 'second-order reasons', that is, reasons either to act, or not to act, for certain reasons.[2] In any case, whatever the content of these reasons, morality is thought to make valuable not just right action but also and perhaps especially right reasons. It is this sense of autonomy that I argue in chapter 18 partially grounds our weak right to liberty against coercive legal sanctions.

Autonomy in this third sense is not a special case of autonomy in the second sense. That is, autonomy in this third sense does not name a capacity to *choose* to act for the right reasons. Although that is a possible sense of the word, it is not one I adopt; persons manifestly do not have the power to choose the reasons on which they act,[3] so I am loath to waste a sense of 'autonomy' on such a non-existent trait of persons. Of course, if people do act for the right reasons sometimes, then they must have a capacity to do so,

[2] Joseph Raz, *Practical Reasons and Norms* (Oxford: Oxford University Press, 1975); Raz, *The Morality of Freedom* (Oxford: Oxford University Press, 1986), chs. 2–4.
[3] Argued for in Moore, 'Authority, Law, and Razian Reasons', *Southern California Law Review*, Vol. 62 (1989), 827–96, at 878–83.

and autonomy is the name for that capacity. Only, capacity to act for right reasons does not involve any capacity to *choose* to act for those reasons. This unchosen, reason-conforming nature of this kind of autonomy faithfully reproduces the Kantian tinge here.

(4) The fourth sense of autonomy owes more to Aristotle and to John Stuart Mill than to Kant. Here autonomy names a special kind of the capacity named by the second sense of the word. The capacity is again a capacity to choose and to cause the realization of one's choice; the difference is that the objects of one's choices are the mental states of desire, belief, intention, and emotion that make up one's character. One forms 'second-order' desires[4] about one's own desires, for example, and one is autonomous in this sense if one's choice to execute such character-forming desires is causally efficacious.

In chapter 13 I expressed doubts about how much autonomy in this sense we each possess. Some, but not nearly as much as autonomy in the first three senses, was my answer. Nonetheless, in chapter 18 I argue that our strong right to liberty is grounded on this kind of autonomy.

The criminal law presupposes that persons are autonomous in these four senses of the word in the following way. Autonomy in the first and most basic sense of the word is of course presupposed by the voluntary act doctrine. When we exclude from our definition of criminally punishable human actions reflex movements, automatism of various kinds, and the other involuntary bodily movements mentioned in chapter 6, we are presupposing just this kind of autonomy. Such autonomy is a precondition of moral responsibility and thus of retributive punishment.

Autonomy in the second sense is presupposed by our increase in the punishment for successful execution of criminal intentions, as opposed to failed attempts. The legal and moral view defended in chapter 5 presupposes that persons do have a good deal of autonomy in this sense, viz., they can largely control what happens in the real world in a way that is responsive to their choices. If this were not true, so that whether a state of affairs intended by us actually came about was purely fortuitous, then neither our morality nor our criminal law could have the shape that they do, blaming more for success than for failure.

---

[4] Harry Frankfurt's well-known terminology. Frankfurt, 'Freedom of the Will and the Concept of a Person', *Journal of Philosophy*, Vol. 68 (1971), 5–20.

It is easy to go wrong about the third sense of autonomy, and thus, about how autonomy in this sense is or is not presupposed by our criminal law. One might think, for example, that there is something morally better about autonomous wrongful action than about non-autonomous wrongful action. This involves two mistakes. One, it supposes that autonomy in this third sense is a power to choose, so that one can speak of 'autonomous wrongful actions' and mean, 'wrongful action the reasons for which were fully chosen'. This, as we have seen, is not what autonomy here means. Second, the thought mistakenly attributes symmetry between right action and wrongful action as the locus for this kind of autonomy: if right action for certain reasons has independent moral worth, then wrongful action for certain reasons must too. Yet however this last idea is fleshed out—whether in terms of right reasons for wrongful action, or wrongful reasons for wrongful actions—it is a mistake to attribute autonomy in this sense to wrongful actions. There is no autonomy in this sense for wrongful actions; such autonomy only makes sense with regard to actions in conformity to the moral law.

Thus, we should not look for legal presuppositions of autonomy in this third sense in doctrines like those suggested in chapter 9, where I argued for increased culpability for ultimate (as opposed to mediate) purposes. That our criminal law in fact by and large does not increase punishment for such kinds of highly culpable mental states is just irrelevant in this context. Rather, the place to look for any presupposition of autonomy in this third sense is in any discernible limits in what is criminalized by the special part of the criminal law.

My own sense of what has been criminalized by the legal systems I lump under the label, 'Anglo-American criminal law', is that to the extent there is any pattern here at all, it is not one reflecting much respect for autonomy in this third sense. However, as I stated in chapter 1, the interesting kind of theory for the special part is an evaluative kind, not the descriptive kind more appropriate for the general part. My own beginnings in the direction of developing such a theory in Part III do make use of autonomy in this Kantian sense, partly grounding a presumption of liberty in just such autonomy.

Autonomy in its fourth sense, as the power to mould one's character by one's own design, I use in a similar way. That is, autonomy in this Millian sense grounds what I call the basic right to liberty, one of the limits on what should be criminalized by the prohibitions of the special part of the criminal law. At least in the United States, such autonomy of persons is also to some extent presupposed by the legal doctrines that we have, namely, the constitutional doctrines defining a sphere of 'decisional privacy'.

If I were wrong in certain of my arguments of chapters 5 and 13, then autonomy in this fourth sense would also be presupposed by the doctrines making up the general part of the criminal law. That is, if the desert basis for retributive punishment were character rather than choice, and if this could be so only if we choose our character, then a lot of autonomy in this fourth sense would have to be attributed to persons for our morality and law to be fairly applied to them. However, I argued against both of these propositions, and if I am right in either of such arguments, then little of autonomy in this fourth sense is presupposed by the doctrines of the general part of the criminal law.

Rationality and autonomy are the major presuppositions about persons made by the general part of the criminal law. Yet there is a third attribute of persons that should be added to these two, what I shall awkwardly call the emotionality of persons.[5] Emotions are distinct kinds of mental states from beliefs, desires, and intentions, as feeling is distinct from acting; thus, the capacity to experience such emotions is a distinct capacity from the capacities involved in rationality and autonomy.

The general part most obviously presupposes the emotionality of persons in its doctrines of excuse, and particularly in its doctrines of duress, necessity, provocation, and addiction. To the extent that these defences are based on diminished capacities (to choose the good in the face of incapacitating emotions aroused by threats, etc.), then the law supposes persons to have such (potentially incapacitating) emotions. Of course, in our law's grudging and limited acceptance of such compulsion excuse one should also see a reflection of another supposition about persons here: persons generally have a large capacity to resist the siren calls of their own emotions, which is why they can usually be held to be unexcused despite the presence of such emotions. Such presupposed self-mastery (a bit of

---

[5] See Moore, *Law and Psychiatry*, *supra* n. 1, at 107–8.

autonomy of the fourth kind), of course, presupposes something to be mastered, namely, the presence of emotions.

I argued in chapter 3 that we also need our emotions to discover and to justify moral insights, like the truths of retributive justice. Such argument only literally requires emotionality in those persons who are theorists about the criminal law, not in those persons who are subject to its doctrines. Yet if the argument of chapter 3 is correct in its epistemic suggestion for moral insight, it might incline one to the following about criminal law's subjects: such persons need those emotional capacities helpful to moral insight, else whatever their rationality and autonomy they would not be fully moral agents. Whether one adopts the suggestion is reflected in one's reaction to those who used to be called psychopaths. If the popular image of such individuals is taken at face value, psychopaths lack just those emotional capacities that allows them to care about morality as most people do. In this picture they are a kind of guiltless Glaucon: they see others bowing to the dictates of morality, but to the extent such bowings are not self-interested posturings, such persons just do not get why anyone does this.

My guess is that an empirical study of jury verdicts in insanity defence trials would reveal that such emotionally impaired individuals do not fare well. Thus, the 'law in action' that we have does not presuppose such emotional capacities in persons. The moral question, however, is more interesting, for it is plausible to suppose that moral agency presupposes the emotional capacities needed to 'get it' with respect to morality.[6]

Rationality, autonomy, and emotionality do not exhaust the criminal law's metaphysical presuppositions about persons. To these must be added two more attributes. One I shall call the attribute of unified character structure. That is, it is not enough for a being to have the mental states and causal powers described as the attributes of rationality, emotionality, and autonomy; in addition, those mental states and the actions they cause must have an intelligible pattern to them, both at any given time, and extended over time. Such intelligible general patterns are called character. Beings whose actions and mental states have no intelligible pattern

---

[6] See e.g., R. A. Duff, 'Psychopathy and Moral Understanding', *American Philosophical Quarterly*, Vol. 14 (1977), 189–200; Samuel Pillsbury, 'The Meaning of Deserved Punishment: An Essay on Choice, Character, and Responsibility', *Indiana Law Journal*, Vol. 67 (1992), 719–52, at 744–7.

we think of as less than persons, that is, as mentally ill (often diagnosed as 'borderline personality disorder'). Beings whose actions and mental states instantiate more than one intelligible pattern—that is, who over time instantiate several distinct such patterns—we also think of as mentally ill (often diagnosed as 'multiple personalities'). By excusing such beings from responsibility, our law reveals what it presupposes the rest of us to possess: some more-or-less coherent, and more-or-less enduring, character structure.[7]

The other presupposition about persons to be added is that they experience a unified consciousness, both at any one time, and over time. To be a responsible person, in other words, a being must not have the kind of divided consciousness attributed to co-conscious varieties of multiple personalities, separated left brain/right brain perceptual experiences, or fugue state automatisms. Neither can a being have the kind of division of memory allegedly experienced by multiple-personalized persons, nor the kind of shattered memory of a kind of constantly renewed amnesia, and still be a person.[8]

Rationality, autonomy, emotionality, unified character, and unified consciousness do exhaust the criminal law's metaphysical presupposition of what persons must be like, but only at what I shall now call one level of analysis. That is, possession of these attributes in turn may presuppose that a being has other attributes, calling for an even deeper metaphysical analysis. For example, it is commonly thought that for persons to be autonomous (in any of the four senses) they must be free, in the sense of uncaused in their choices. If this were true, then we should add contra-causal freedom as another attribute persons must have if they are morally blameworthy and liable to retributive punishment. Deeper yet, it is also commonly assumed that this kind of freedom from the grip of a seemingly universal causation in the natural world requires an even more striking feature persons must possess, namely, a kind of

---

[7] To say that a being will be a person only if it has an intelligible character structure to it is not to say that we only blame such beings for bad character. As I argue in ch. 13, we rightly punish persons for their culpable choices. That the idea of a person making such choices presupposes that that person *has* a character, does not commit one to blaming persons *for* their character, nor even to blaming them only for those actions *expressive* of that character. Chosen actions out of character are, in other words, possible, despite the fact that to be a person who can choose require that one *have* a character.

[8] For a summary of some of the data on multiple personalities and split brains, see Moore, *Law and Psychiatry, supra* n. 1, ch. 11.

mind-stuff that exists in its own realm of being and that this is exempt from the determination by natural causes. (This kind of metaphysical extravagance usually keeps going, so that the mind-stuff existing in time but not in space is given permanent duration, called 'soul', and then requires divine origins for its extraordinarily privileged existence.)

In chapters 12 and 10 I tried to show how our criminal law, and the morality that underlies it, are not committed to the strong metaphysical suppositions about persons usually called libertarianism, dualism, immortalism, and theism. One can say that persons must be free to be responsible, but what I hoped to show in chapter 12 was that such freedom is *not* an exemption from causation of the will. Rather, such freedom was simply the having of adequate capacities and opportunities to effectuate our choices. Further, persons must really have the mental states of belief, desire, and intention in order to be responsible, yet this ontological commitment does not bring with it any commitment to separate mind-stuffs or even worse, immortal souls and divine creators. Rather, the intent of chapter 10 was to show that with no more mysterious building blocks than behaviour, physical brain structure, and their functional organization, one can understand minds and mental states.

Another supposed deeper analysis of persons takes the opposite tack from the rather ghostly tack of the metaphysical incompatibilists and mind-body dualists just discussed. Here, the claim is that the only creatures who could possibly possess the mental states and causal powers making up the attributes of rationality, autonomy, and emotionality, are members of the species, human being. (In a slightly more generous mood, the mantle of personhood may be extended to other than human species, but only so long as they are the kind of soft-tissue, carbon-based intelligence systems that populate contemporary Hollywood fantasies.) On this view, persons thus must be embodied in a certain way, if not in a recognizable human body, then in a soft-tissue, carbon-based chemistry.

In these times of political correctness, such a presupposition about persons is a surprising bit of speciesism (or carbonism). What about our perhaps not so distant silicone-based brothers and sisters? Surely it is overly dogmatic to assert that such silicon realized 'artificial' intelligence *cannot* have beliefs, desires, and intentions with the content relations characteristic of rationality, that they *cannot* cause events to match the content of such states, that they *cannot* reprogram themselves, or (Hollywood's favourite) that they *cannot* feel emotion. All of this may turn out to be true, but if so it will only be by luck of the draw that these attributes of persons can only be possessed by carbon-based systems. It is thus too early to tell whether, to these five attributes of persons, we should add a sixth, embodiment in a human body.

There is at least one other attribute of persons that *is* presupposed by the possession of the attributes of rationality, autonomy, and emotionality. This is the attribute adverted to briefly in chapter 9, in terms of persons possessing representational states. All of the states making up rationality, autonomy, and emotionality are representational states in the sense that we represent the world to ourselves in one modality or another. That is, we want it to be a certain way, believe that it is a certain way, intend to make it a certain way, are angry that it is a certain way, etc. The technical name for all such representational states is that they are *Intentional* states. 'Intentional' is taken from Franz Brentano, who revived the word from the medieval scholastics to refer to states that are 'directed upon an object'.[9] Since such objects are not objects in the real world, they are called 'Intentional objects', or what I have been

---

[9] The word 'Intentional' is capitalized to distinguish this characteristic from the more familiar 'intention' or 'intentional' of ordinary speech. Brentano held that 'every mental phenomenon is characterized by what the scholastics of the Middle Ages called the Intentional Inexistence of an object and which we would call . . . the reference to a content, a direction upon an object'. Franz Brentano, *Psychologie vom Empirischen Standpunkt* (Leipzig, 1874). A selection of this work is translated in: R. Chisholm, ed., *Realism and the Background of Phenomenology* (Glencoe, Ill.: Free Press, 1960). A more modern characterization of Intentionality is in terms of three criteria: (1) A sentence is Intentional if it uses a name or description in such a way that neither the sentence nor its contradictory implies either that there is or there is not anything to which the name or expression truly applies. 'I hope for a 60-foot sailboat', e.g., does not imply that there is a 60-foot sailboat. (2) A sentence is Intentional if it contains a propositional clause whose truth or falsity is not implied by the sentence as a whole, or its contradictory. 'I hope that it will rain', e.g., does not imply that 'it will rain' is true or false. (3) A sentence is Intentional if codesignative names or descriptions cannot be substituted and preserve truth. I may, e.g., intend to order the largest room in some inn; even if the largest room is identical with the dirtiest room in the inn, one cannot substitute the second description for the first; I did not intend to order the dirtiest room in the inn. See Roderick Chisholm, *Perceiving: A Philosophical Study* (Ithaca: Cornell University Press, 1957), 170–1. On whether Intentionality is truly the 'mark of the mental', see William Lycan, 'On "Intentionality" and the Psychological', *American Philosophical Quarterly*, Vol. 6 (1969), 305–11; Dan Dennett, *Content and Consciousness* (London: Routledge and Kegan Paul, 1969), ch. II.

calling 'representations', or 'content' (or sometimes 'representational content').

It is currently a matter of great debate whether our ancient 'folk psychology' in terms of Intentional states can survive the insights of an advancing understanding of the brain.[10] In chapter 10 I advanced the optimistic view of the matter: the most likely discoveries of brain structures and their functional organization will not eliminate mental states like intentions; rather, the best explanations of human behaviour will remain at that high level of functional organization that commits one to the existence of things like intentions. But this is a contingent matter where science could point the other way, as current 'eliminative materialists' urge.

Some criminal law theorists have prematurely interred the Intentionalist metaphysics on which law and morality rest. They have not done so because of a special prescience about the outcome of the current scientific debate on the viability of research programmes like that outlined in chapter 10. Rather, they have come to this scepticism by three more questionable routes: (1) some criminal theorists, like other legal academicians, are descendants of the Legal Realist tradition according to which the use of a concept should be guided by the social consequences attached to that use, not by some underlying metaphysics; (2) some criminal theorists have imbibed of the anti-realism[11] about minds (and thus of persons) of the hermeneutic and Wittgensteinian traditions in philosophy; and (3) some criminal theorists have also imbibed of another version of anti-realism about minds, namely, that scepticism about the reality of mental states represented by behaviourism in philosophy and psychology. In the second half of this chapter I shall discuss each such purported basis for scepticism in turn.

I. LEGAL REALIST SCEPTICISM

Perhaps the easiest route to understanding the scepticism about Intentionalist or any other kind of metaphysics about persons

---

[10] John Greenwood, ed., *The Future of the Folk Psychology* (Cambridge: Cambridge University Press, 1991).

[11] A realist view about minds grants that there really are mental states, that in any taking of inventory of the furniture of the universe mental states must be included just as surely as tables and chairs. Such a philosophical realist about minds is to be distinguished from the ill-named legal realists, who were typically anti-realists in their metaphysics.

bequeathed to us by the legal realist tradition is to ask some more general questions about legal concepts and what it is to seek their meaning. Prima facie, one might advert to two quite distinct sorts of things in 'giving the meaning' of a legal concept such as 'criminal intent' or 'person': (1) one might seek to describe the set of *facts* under which the legal concept is correctly applied; or (2) one might seek to describe the set of *legal consequences* which attach to the authoritative use of that concept by a judge.

Consider the concept of ownership. If asked to give the meaning of the two-place predicate, 'x owns y', one might describe the facts under which a person x could correctly be said to own some thing y, facts such as that x received y as a gift from his uncle, that x purchased y, that x occupied y for a certain period, and the like. Alternatively, one might mention the kind of legal consequences that are supposed to flow from it being authoritatively pronounced of x, that he owns y. Such consequences include that fact that x may dispose of y by gift, sale, or devise; that x can be taxed on y; that x may enjoin interference by others in his use and enjoyment of y; and so forth.

The reason for this Janus-faced aspect of legal concepts lies in what Hohfeld called their 'dispositive' function.[12] Legal concepts such as ownership, malice, intention, or person, are used both to describe in legal terms the facts in particular situations and to 'dispose' of the issues in cases by prescribing what results a judge should bring about in his application of those concepts. Dispositive legal concepts form the 'conceptual cement' that connects a judge's factual findings to his legal remedies.

It is sometimes thought that this dual function of legal concepts renders them essentially ambiguous. George Fletcher, for example, finds criminal law theory seriously muddled because of the 'systematic ambiguity' he sees between the descriptive and the normative uses of concepts such as action or intention.[13] Yet ambiguity is

[12] Wesley Hohfeld, *Fundamental Legal Conceptions* (New Haven: Yale University Press, 1923), 27–31. See also Alf Ross, 'Tu-Tu', *Harvard Law Review*, Vol. 70 (1957), 812–25.

[13] George Fletcher, *Rethinking Criminal Law* (Boston: Little, Brown, 1978), 396–401. For a similar idea, see Daniel Dennett, 'The Conditions of Personhood', in Amelie Rorty, ed., *The Identities of Persons* (Berkeley: University of California Press, 1976), 175–96, wherein Dennett urges that we have two different concepts of a person, 'the moral notion and the metaphysical notion' (176). That different speech acts are being performed with 'person' is no argument that the word is ambiguous.

a semantic category having to do with two senses of a word.[14] 'Entertain', for example, is ambiguous in that it can mean thinking about or considering a question or it can mean hospitable and amusing behaviour. The two functions served by legal concepts is not a semantic distinction but rather a distinction of *use*. A judge performs two distinct speech acts when he uses a dispositive legal concept such as 'intention' or 'ownership' in a legal proceeding. His 'assertorial' speech act is to describe the facts before him, while his 'prescriptive' speech act is to prescribe that certain legal consequences should attach.

These same dual functions appear in our use of language to express moral judgements. To use a moral term, such as 'person' or 'intention', is often both to *describe* an entity or a state of affairs as being of a certain kind, and to *prescribe* that moral guilt or blame should attach to the entity or event so described. The difference between moral and legal usages is that the moral consequences prescribed are not fixed by conventional rules of such detail as are the legal consequences attached to dispositive legal concepts.

Scepticism about metaphysics is generated for many lawyers by their preoccupation with the consequences of using a concept such as person or intention. This preoccupation leads them to think that such concepts have no descriptive content, that we do and should guide our usage of them not by metaphysical truths about persons but by pragmatic policies having to do with what we want to achieve by use of these concepts in particular contexts. Consider in this regard the concept of an action. If one gives up on articulating the metaphysics of action, one will adopt something like H. L. A. Hart's once-held ascriptivist theory of action.[15] According to it, one first decides whether responsibility should be ascribed to some person for some harm, and only then whether the bodily motion causing the harm was his action. If one wishes to ascribe responsibility, his behaviour will be described in the Intentional idioms of action; if one wishes to say he is not responsible, the behaviour will not be so described.

Hart's kind of argument—because one is *ascribing* responsibility one cannot be *describing* some factual state of affairs with a

[14] For a discussion of genuine cases of ambiguity in legal uses of words, see Michael Moore, 'The Semantics of Judging', *Southern California Law Review*, Vol. 54 (1981), 151–294, especially 181–8.

[15] H. L. A. Hart, 'The Ascription of Responsibility and Rights', *Proc. Arist. Soc'y*, Vol. 49 (1949), 171–94. Hart later came to repudiate his ascriptivism.

concept such as 'action'—has been made for mental states as well as action. John Dewey, for example, argued that motives are characterizations of conduct that are merely 'a refinement of the ordinary reactions of praise and blame', so that 'motive words, such as "greed," simply [mean] the quality of [an] act as socially observed and disapproved'.[16] George Fletcher, analogously, analyses the concept of intention as having as one of its two meanings, 'an intent to act under circumstances (such as failing to enquire about the age of a sexual partner) that render an act properly subject to blame'.[17]

This kind of preoccupation with the consequences of saying that someone has performed an action, or done so with a certain intention, motive, or reason, is to be found with regard to each of the concepts in terms of which responsibility is ascribed in law and morals. Judge Andrews, in dissent in *Palsgraf* v. *Long Island Railroad Co.*,[18] speaking no doubt as an accurate representation of the thoughts of many contemporary lawyers, urged that the requirement of proximate cause 'is all a question of expediency' and of 'practical politics': 'What we do mean by the word "proximate" is that because of convenience, of public policy, of a rough sense of justice, the law arbitrarily declines to trace a series of events beyond a certain point.'[19] Stanley Ingber has analysed the excuse of duress as first consisting of the moral judgement that one is not responsible, and only then is the judgement made that the behaviour in question was 'involuntary'.[20] Thomas Szasz and his legal followers are constantly contending that phrases such as 'mental illness' have no descriptive meaning; such phrases are merely labels we apply to persons after deciding for one reason or another to degrade them as persons.[21]

The most general strain of this kind of legal thinking has been by the American Legal Realists. They held that in applying a legal term one must look to the legal *consequences* being prescribed by its authoritative use by a judge, and further, that it was an illusion to think that such legal terms had a *meaning* that determined their

---

[16] John Dewey, *Human Nature and Conduct* (New York: Holt, Rhinehart and Winston, 1922), 120–1.

[17] Fletcher, *Rethinking Criminal Law*, *supra* n. 13, at 397.

[18] 248 NY 339, 162 NE 99 (1928).   [19] Id. at 354, 162 NE at 104.

[20] Stanley Ingber, 'Book Review', *UCLA Law Review*, Vol. 27 (1980), 816–48, at 822–4.

[21] For discussion of this argument, and citation to the Szaszian literature, see Moore, *Law and Psychiatry*, *supra* n. 1, ch. 4.

correct use apart from such consequences. This general view came to be known as functionalism.[22]

Ethical philosophy has also had its share of theorists who urged that ethical utterances were used either to express the speaker's emotions or to prescribe what one ought or ought not to do.[23] These 'emotivist' and 'prescriptivist' theories in ethics urged that because such expressive or prescriptive function were served by moral uses of language, descriptive functions could not also be served.

If one adopted such a position about the legal or moral usages of the word 'person', one would urge that *anything* could be called a person—it would simply depend on whether one wished to attach the legal or moral consequences of being so labelled to that entity. Consider, for example the debate about whether corporations (as entities distinct from their shareholders, directors, and officers) are moral or legal persons. One adopting the functionalist analysis of legal concepts will collapse the question of whether corporations *are* moral persons into the question of whether they *should be called* moral persons in light of the consequences attached thereto. Christopher Stone, for example, argues that the question of whether 'it is *intelligible* to blame the corporation draws on considerations that it is *useful* to speak in that manner'.[24] Similarly in law, if one wishes to know whether a corporation is a legal person, one will enquire into 'the likely effect of holding the corporate body legally accountable. One wants to know how making the corporation the law's quarry will affect those both "outside" the corporation and those who labour "within," in terms of their perceptions (most importantly their self-perceptions) and their behaviour.'[25] Like any good functionalist, Stone relegates the descriptive

---

[22] Felix Cohen, 'Transcendental Nonsense and the Functional Approach', *Columbia Law Review*, Vol. 35 (1935), 809–49. For an exposition of the dependence of American legal realism upon a functionalist theory of meaning, see Robert Summers, *Instrumentalism and American Legal Theory* (Ithaca: Cornell University Press, 1982), 32.

[23] e.g., C. L. Stevenson, *Ethics and Language* (New Haven: Yale University Press, 1944); R. M. Hare, *The Language of Morals* (Oxford: Oxford University Press, 1952). For a helpful summary of the early forms of emotivism in ethics, see J. O. Urmson, *The Emotive Theory of Ethics* (Oxford: Oxford University Press, 1968).

[24] Christopher Stone, 'Corporate Accountability in Law and Morals', in J. Houck and O. Williams, eds., *The Judaeo-Christian Vision and the Modern Business Corporation* (Notre Dame: University of Notre Dame Press, 1982).

[25] Id. at 285.

question of whether corporations are legal persons and thus can intelligibly be held legally accountable as persons, to the scrap heap of intellectual history and (pejoratively) academic pursuits.[26]

My own view is that the legal and moral questions of whether some entity is or is not a person, whether that person performed an action, whether he did so intentionally or with a certain motive, whether that act proximately caused harm, whether the actor acted under threats of another amounting to duress, and whether the actor is mentally ill, are all factual questions. The concepts employed in discussing all such questions are not empty labels for a moral or legal conclusion reached on other grounds, or on no grounds at all; they are concepts having a descriptive and explanatory function, no matter what other expressive, prescriptive, or ascriptive functions they may serve in contexts such as those of responsibility assessment. It accordingly makes sense to seek the meaning of 'persons' and its related terms ('action', 'reasons') in terms of the facts that must be true if these concepts are to be correctly employed.

I have elsewhere addressed this kind of meaning-theory-generated scepticism about ethical discourse,[27] and will not recapitulate that branch of the argument. About legal utterances, it should be a simpler matter to see that preoccupation with the consequences of *saying*, for example, that a corporation is or is not a legal person, cannot be exclusive of some concern as to whether corporations *are* legal persons. If our legal concepts had as their only meanings that certain consequences could be achieved by their use, they would be completely vacuous. They could never be used in giving reasons to justify legal results, but only to summarize those results. At the least, therefore, any concepts actually doing any work in legal reasoning must have some descriptive content.[28] This is not to say that such content must always be given by an analysis into, for example, the metaphysics of what persons really are; it could come from legal conventions, like those that invest 'merger' in corporations law with meaning. In the case of such bor-

---

[26] *The Judaeo-Christian Vision and the Modern Business Corporation* (Notre Dame: University of Notre Dame Press, 1982) at 285.

[27] Michael Moore, 'Moral Reality', *Wisconsin Law Review*, Vol. [1982], 1061–156.

[28] Another way of putting the legal realist's point about meaning is to say that the meaning of legal concepts is wholly 'context-dependent', that is, that they depend on what (purpose) one wants to achieve in uttering them. For an attack on this Fullerian version, see Moore, 'The Semantics of Judging', *supra* n. 14, at 274–7.

rowed concepts as personhood, however, it is unlikely in the extreme to think that the meaning is to be found solely in legal conventions. In any case: to rebut the legal realist sceptic it is enough to show that the meaning of legal, ordinary, and moral concepts cannot be found solely in the consequences of authoritative utterance.

II. HERMENEUTIC SCEPTICISM

Another form of scepticism about the metaphysics of the person stems from a deep scepticism that anything 'in the world' is referred to when one talks about actions and mental states (and thus about persons). This doubt is a kind of anti-realism about minds and about anything that smacks of 'mentalism', including human action. There are different kinds of distrust of the mental. The behaviourist scepticism of private, non-physical, inferentially validated, internal but nonetheless causally efficacious states of mind, is considered below. Recently, more influential scepticism has stemmed from the Intentionality of mental concepts. The fear here has been that the *objects* of mental states cannot be specified objectively, that the only way such objects are fixed is by a certain interpretive stance adopted by the observer. Given the centrality of Intentional objects to saying what mental states *are*, the sceptical conclusion has been that they are not things at all.

Two criminal law theorists illustrate this kind of scepticism about the metaphysics of minds and persons. Hyman Gross oriented his *A Theory of Criminal Justice* around an explicit anti-realist position about mind. In considering specific intent, for example, Gross urges that 'the intent is part of the act not some state of mind that may have accompanied it'.[29] What Gross apparently has in mind here (to speak loosely) is G. E. M. Anscombe's point that many of our descriptions of action are formally descriptions of executed intentions.[30] One can, for example, redescribe a crouching as a hiding, if the purpose with which the crouching was done was to hide. 'In doing what he does,' Gross would say of such a croucher, 'the actor

[29] Hyman Gross, *A Theory of Criminal Justice* (New York: Oxford University Press, 1979), 103.
[30] See G. E. M. Anscombe, *Intention*, 2nd edn. (Ithaca, NY: Cornell University Press, 1963).

has a purpose that makes the act an act of that kind rather than of another kind . . . But having a purpose as one acts does not mean that one then has a purpose in mind.'[31] About purposes themselves, Gross argues that they 'are not accounts of mental occurrences or states at all, nor in fact are they accounts of any sort of personal occurrence or state'. The reason for this, we are told, 'is that an account of motives does not tell us what caused an act to be done, but tells us rather *in what cause* it was done. An account of the motives for an act is not an explanation telling why the act occurred, but rather an explanation of the role of the act in a larger story of the actor's pursuits.' Finally, about the crucial criminal law notion of acting *intentionally* (which Gross rightly distinguishes from acting with a further or 'specific' intention), Gross similarly urges that 'mentalism is objectionable because it purports to give an account of intentional and unintentional acts—and thus of culpability—in terms of the mental affairs of the actor'. Again, we are told that acting intentionally involves no reference to 'private inner workings' nor to 'what is going on in the mysterious region where acts originate'. Rather, when we say that an action is done *intentionally* we are merely rebutting someone else's claim that the act was non-standard ('unintentional') with respect to the actor's control. The actor's control, Gross further urges, is not a mental matter at all.[32]

George Fletcher's 'rethinking' of criminal law has also led him to an anti-realist position about minds (although of a somewhat less trenchant variety than that of Gross). Fletcher also explicitly rejects the 'mentalist bias in philosophical psychology',[33] and urges that we 'drop the notions of causation [by mental states] from the metaphysics of acting and willing'.[34] In place of the metaphysics defended earlier—of belief/desire sets causing intentions that then cause actions—Fletcher would emphasize the observer's role in interpreting behaviour as an action done for a certain aim or reason. We must stress 'the perception of human acting as a form of intersubjective understanding'[35] if we are to have an adequate theory of action or intention. Such intersubjective understanding is

---

[31] Gross, *Theory of Criminal Justice*, *supra* n. 29, at 100.

[32] All the quotations in this paragraph are from Gross, *Theory of Criminal Justice*, at 109, 98, 91, and 97. The last two sentences refer to 88 and 89.

[33] Fletcher, *Rethinking Criminal Law*, *supra* n. 13, at 437.

[34] Id., at 436.   [35] Id., at 436.

possible only if the observer and the actors share a 'form of life'. All of this is to deny that intending or acting are states or events that really exist in the world in the way that tables and chairs do; seeing an event as an action, or a state as an intention, on this view, depends entirely on there being a certain interpretive stance which the observer brings to these events in order to so view them.

These scepticisms about mind should be seen as part of a larger tradition that stems in part from the philosophy of the later Wittgenstein,[36] in part from certain work in the philosophy of history,[37] and in part from the influence of the hermeneutic tradition in Continental philosophy.[38] All of these traditions have in common their blurring of any distinction between the mental states that an actor really possesses, on the one hand, and the mental states his behaviour is interpreted as expressing because of the observor's interpretive stance, on the other. As G. H. Von Wright puts it, himself influenced by each of these traditions: 'Behavior gets its intentional character from being *seen* by the agent himself or by an outside observer in a wider perspective, from being *set* in a context of aims and cognitions.'[39]

Various reasons might convince one that such mental states as beliefs and desires do not exist except as some kind of fictional posits in the interpretive stance of an observer. Most pertinent to the scepticism considered here is that scepticism about mental states stemming from one of their long-noticed features, namely, their Intentionality. Because the objects of mental states are essentially linguistic, it might seem inevitable that the necessary linguistic characterization of those objects could come from nowhere else *but* the linguistic efforts of the interpreter. The only seeming alternative would be to think that the *actor* explicitly says to himself the sentence that forms the content of his beliefs, desires, intentions, and

[36] L. Wittgenstein, *Philosophical Investigations* (Oxford: Basil Blackwell, 1953).

[37] See Michael Oakshott, *Experience and its Modes* (Cambridge: Cambridge University Press, 1933); William Dray, *Laws and Explanation in History* (Oxford: Oxford University Press, 1957); R. G. Collingwood, *The Idea of History* (Oxford: Oxford University Press, 1946). For a sympathetic relating of Collingwood to the issues of contemporary action theory, see Rex Martin, *Historical Explanation: Reenactment and Practical Inference* (Ithaca: Cornell University Press, 1977).

[38] For a brief discussion of this tradition in German history and sociology, see G. H. Von Wright, *Explanation and Understanding* (Ithaca, NY: Cornell University Press, 1973), 4–7. See also Michael Moore, 'The Interpretive Turn in Modern Theory: A Turn for the Worse?', *Stanford Law Review*, Vol. 41 (1989), 871–957.

[39] Von Wright, *Explanation and Understanding*, supra n. 38, at 115.

emotions. Yet such silent soliloquies surely cannot be the source of such contents, because the observer often rewords the actor's own explicit formulation of his mental states into the observer's own language and his own idiom. We think this quite legitimate. Hence, the interpretivist sceptic concludes, the *only* way such objects or contents can be formulated is by the observer's 'empathetic understanding', his desire to fill out a story so that it makes sense, etc.

If I am right, the basic motivation for believing that ascribing 'real' beliefs or desires to an agent makes no sense lies in the difficulties one has in formulating the objects of mental states without observer interpretation.[40] That this is an insufficient motive for being an interpretivist can be seen by repairing to another 'essentially linguistic' context, that of reported speech. Suppose an observer reports: 'John said that Mary is a hard worker.' Such indirect speech, which does not quote the original speaker but paraphrases what he meant, is much like sentences of mental states in that both take propositional objects. In addition, in neither context is the connection between the dependent clause and the overall sentence truth functional. The truth of the overall sentence, 'John said that Mary is a hard worker', does not depend on the truth of the enclosed sentence, 'Mary is a hard worker.' John could have said it without Mary being a hard worker, just as John could have believed that Mary is a hard worker without Mary in fact being a hard worker. Moreover, just because John said that Mary is a hard worker, it is not true that John said that the laziest worker in the office is a hard worker—even if 'Mary' and 'the laziest worker in the office' both refer to one and the same person. From these three features one may conclude that the object of the 'saying that' is essentially linguistic, just as it is for belief, desire, and other Intentional mental states.

The truth of the overall sentence, 'John said that Mary is a hard worker', is a function of two items: (1) that there was some utterance U by John; and (2) that 'Mary is a hard worker' is an *accurate interpretation* of U. Thus an interpretive task *is* bound up in verifying the truth of the sentences of indirect speech. Yet that some interpretation is required for the truth of sentences reporting indi-

---

[40] Donald Davidson (despite his staunch adherence to a causal view of reasons) is led to what he calls 'the necessarily holistic character of interpretations of propositional attitudes' by this motivation. See Davidson, *Actions and Events* (Oxford: Oxford University Press, 1980), 238–9.

rect speech would tempt no one, I should think, to assert that there is no fact of the matter about what the utterance really was.[41] It is true, the observer must characterize (interpret) that utterance—itself a bit of language used by John—but surely the necessity of such interpretation is no argument at all that utterances do not exist except in the observer's 'story' or 'interpretive stance' or whatever. Utterances are real world speech acts by real world people who unproblematically exist.

An interpretivist might well respond that beliefs, desires and intentions are unlike utterances in a crucial way. While both beliefs and utterances take linguistic objects that require interpretation, utterances have an established text to be interpreted. For beliefs, he might ask, what is *the* authoritative formulation of their objects that can serve as the text against which all interpretations are to be judged for accuracy? One might urge that 'the text' forming the objects of beliefs is to be found in the actor's speech to himself about what he believes on certain occasions. But this idea—that we have beliefs only when we have engaged in some such silent soliloquy—is a very inaccurate view of mind. We unproblematically explain behaviour by reasons when the actor has engaged in no such explicit recitals of the premises of his practical reasoning.

The 'text' for beliefs, desires, or intentions is to be found in two sources: first, in the abilities of the actor to avow the objects of his mental states. These abilities do not depend on any silent sayings to oneself, nor need they be readily exercisable by an agent—they may be preconscious or even 'repressed'. Second, the text may be found in whatever physiological events turn out to be 'the language of thought' in the brain.[42] Hence, although finding the text is a more complicated affair for beliefs, desires, and intentions than for utterances, it is not the case that *no* text exists save that which an

[41] Davidson, who sees this analogy, believes that to say what the utterance *meant* is to infuse one's own (observer) concepts into the interpretation of the utterance. Yet Davidson would not dispute that a particular act of speech existed at a particular time, even if the act of speech requires interpretation to be understood.

[42] Whether there is anything that could be called a 'language of the brain' is a hotly contested matter. For an introductory, if sceptical, treatment of the issues involved, see Dan Dennett, 'Brain Writing and Mind Reading', in *Brainstorms* (Putney, Vt.: Bradford Books, 1978), 39–50. Compare Jerry Fodor, *The Language of Thought* (New York: Thomas Y. Crowell, 1975). Although one might doubt that the relation between language and brain physiology is as simple as the 'language of thought' school would suggest, surely some relation exists between language abilities and such physiology.

external observer brings with him when he seeks to explain the behaviour. Because a text exists, the need for interpreting that text—the object of beliefs, desires, and intentions—no more commits one to the interpretivist tradition than does a similar need commit one to interpretivism about utterances. Some interpretation is involved in formulating the objects of beliefs, of desires, and of utterances; in all cases, however, what was *really* believed, desired, intended, or uttered is a matter of fact.

III. BEHAVIOURIST SCEPTICISM

Another anti-realist form of scepticism about the metaphysics of persons that has had some influence with criminal law theorists stems from behaviourist psychology. Two kinds of behaviourism are relevant here, methodological behaviourism and logical behaviourism.[43]

Those philosophers and psychologists who are called 'methodological behaviourists' simply put mentalistic explanations to the side, urging that mental states are too 'private', 'internal', 'inferred', or in some other way unfit for a (methodologically) proper science of human behaviour. Although not classifying himself as a methodological behaviourist, B. F. Skinner is most consistently construed to be sceptical on methodological grounds about the utility of mental concepts.[44] For Skinner, concepts like belief, desire, or willing are to be shunned for a variety of reasons, the most important of which is that such explanations presuppose some kind of 'homunculi' who reside 'inside' the brain.

[43] For the separation of methodological from philosophical behaviourism, see Michael Martin, 'Interpreting Skinner', *Behaviorism*, Vol. 6 (1978), 129–38.

[44] Norman Malcolm (with a good deal of textual support) construes Skinner to be a reductionist about mental terms. See Norman Malcolm, 'Behaviorism as a Philosophy of Psychology', in T. W. Wann, ed., *Behaviorism and Phenomenology* (Chicago: University of Chicago Press, 1964), 141–54. In her attempt to construe Skinner in such a way as to immunize him from the defects of philosophical behaviourism, Brenda Mapel makes the case for Skinner as a non-reductionist. See Brenda Munsey Mapel, 'Philosophical Criticism of Behaviorism: An Analysis', *Behaviorism*, Vol. 5 (1977), 17–32. Dan Dennett nicely separates Skinner's various arguments against mentalist language, and rightly concludes that Skinner never even saw that he had to take a position on this issue: 'It is unfathomable how Skinner can be so sloppy on this score, for reflection should reveal to him, as it will to us, that this vacillation is over an absolutely central point in his argument.' Dennett, *Brainstorms*, *supra* n. 42, at 63.

Logical (often called 'philosophical', or 'analytical') behaviourism is not sceptical about the methodological adequacy of mental concepts; rather, this form of behaviourism is reductionist in character, for it asserts that mental words like 'belief' or 'desire' name either behaviour itself or *dispositions* to behave in certain ways—in any case, not inner states that cause behaviour. On such an account, to say that X believes that it is raining can be reduced to statements about what X is disposed *to do*, for example, carry his umbrella, not take long walks, say 'it is raining', etc. To explain an action by citing a belief or a desire, accordingly, will not be to name a set of states *causing* the action; rather, it will be to say that X was disposed to do an act of that type, much in the way that to explain the dissolving of a lump of sugar by citing the sugar's solubility will be to say that it was disposed to do that under certain conditions.

Such a reduction is mechanistic because the dispositions to which mental states are reduced are themselves mere theoretical stand-ins ('behavioural constructs') for the real causes of action, environmental stimuli. It is because of our past conditioning that we are disposed, for example, to avoid painful things; so that to explain that X avoided the fire because he did not want to get burned, is ultimately to say that events in his past caused him to engage in pain-avoidance behaviour.

Each of these forms of behaviorism has inclined some judges and theorists to a kind of scepticism about the mental states of belief, desire, and intending on which the metaphysics of persons is built. One who, for example, is convinced that mental states are too private, internal, or inferred to be the (methodologically) proper basis for psychology, will also believe that these same characteristics prevent mental states from being the touchstone of moral culpability and legal liability. Herbert Fingarette has nicely characterized this latter view:

In essence, the viewpoint in question consists in supposing that in saying these things we are trying to describe certain states as processes within the person's mind or 'inside another's skin.' Being internal, these states or processes are necessarily unobservable by others. Therefore, we ought not to try to judge what in the nature of the case we cannot know.[45]

---

[45] Herbert Fingarette, *The Meaning of Criminal Insanity* (Berkeley and Los Angeles: University of California Press, 1972), 82.

Such a view leads directly to the well-known 'objective' theory of mental states, according to which one puts aside any enquiry into whether a defendant actually believed his conduct would cause a certain result, in favour of an enquiry about whether a reasonable person would have foreseen such a result. The objective theory of mind in criminal law is often (but not inevitably) motivated by the same distrust of private, internal mental states that motivates some psychologists to become behaviourists.[46]

Similarly, if one is a logical behaviourist about mental states, one will believe that no one (criminal lawyers included) should be concerned about anything internal or private. Rather, the criminal law will be concerned with a mental concept such as an intention only because it names a *disposition* to engage in behaviour of a certain sort; when that behaviour is of a prohibited sort, the law cares about the intention only because it cares about dangerous propensities. As Justice Holmes put it, in discussing criminal attempts: 'The importance of the intent is not to show that the act was wicked, but to show that it was likely to be followed by hurtful consequences.'[47]

If one is either a methodological or a logical behaviourist one will be deeply sceptical about anything that could be called a metaphysics of personhood.[48] The inner states of personal causation (willing) and of causally efficacious beliefs, desires, and intentions either do not exist (logical behaviourism) or, if they do exist, are too private for use by law or science (methodological behaviourism). Yet the problem for a behaviourist sceptic is to make plausible either of these forms of behaviourism.

Sometimes methodological behaviourism is only a plea to pursue a particular strategy in building a theory with which to explain human behaviour. The strategy might be paraphrased as the injunc-

[46] As Jerome Hall points out, the objective theory of mental states need not rest on such anti-realist positions about minds: 'Holmes did not rest his theory upon that so-called "skeptical" position . . . He acknowledged that mental states can be discovered and, in the face of that, he maintained that this knowledge is irrelevant in modern penal law, and properly so! In sum, his theory challenges the ethics of penal law, not its epistemology.' Jerome Hall, *General Principles of Criminal Law*, 2nd edn. (Indianapolis: Bobbs-Merrill, 1960), 156.

[47] Oliver Wendell Holmes, *The Common Law* (Cambridge, Mass.: Harvard University Press, 1963), 56.

[48] Witness Richard Posner's behaviourist oriented scepticism about mental states in his 'The Jurisprudence of Skepticism', *Michigan Law Review*, Vol. 86 (1988), 827–91.

tion, 'see if you can explain behaviour using only environmental causes and eschewing mental states and neurophysiology'. Such an explanatory strategy need be sceptical about minds no more than it is about brains, since it eschews both in favour of causes of other kinds. The truly sceptical forms of methodological behaviourism must go further than this, and prefer behaviourist accounts because of suspicions about competing accounts in terms of mental states, on the ground for instance that mental states are private, internal, or inferred, and thus can only be known by their holder.[49] Yet we infer many things, such as forces, fields, electrons, kinetic energy; from the point of view of phenomenalism, we also infer the existence of physical objects from their appearances. The inference-laden nature of our knowledge about any of these things can hardly be a legitimate ground of scepticism.

Similarly, the privacy of mental states is easily overstated. It is true that we do have privileged access to our own states of mind, that is a privileged (because non-inferential) way of knowing what we desire or believe. It is not true, however, that *only* the holder of a state of mind can know its contents.[50] We make legitimate (warranted) inferences about others' states of mind every day, based on behaviour and what we know about a culture. Such explanatory inferences by others may supplement or supplant the agent's own beliefs about his mental states. We are not guessing at something that only the agent can know for certain when we make these inferences about others' mental states. Freud taught us as much, if indeed we needed the lesson.

The main thrust of Skinner's scepticism does not stem from these features of mental states, but from the fear earlier identified: mental states lead to the unacceptable positing of a homunculus in the brain, a little man in the machine, whose scientific status is about as high as that of a 'possessing demon' or goblin. Skinner's target here is just the metaphysical view of persons earlier described; what must be abolished, Skinner tells us, is 'the autonomous man—the inner man, the homunculus, the possessing demon, the man defended by the literature of freedom and dignity'.[51]

---

[49] Dennett, 'Skinner Skinned', in *Brainstorms*, *supra* n. 42, nicely separates these various methodological claims.

[50] For a separation of the claims of privileged access from those of incorrigibility, and an attack on the latter, see Moore, *Law and Psychiatry*, *supra* n. 1, ch. 7.

[51] B. F. Skinner, *Beyond Freedom and Dignity* (New York: Knopf, 1971), 200.

Skinner's fear is that persons conceived as autonomous agents present us with an unacceptable dilemma: either we conceive of them as 'uncaused causers', in which event no explanation is possible of why such agents do what they do; or, if we give an explanation, it will be in terms of another autonomous agent, and then another, leading to an infinite regress:

. . . the little man . . . was recently the hero of a television program called 'Gateways to the Mind' . . . The viewer learned, from animated cartoons, that when a man's finger is pricked, electrical impulses resembling flashes of lightning run up the afferent nerves and appear on a television screen in the brain. The little man wakes up, sees the flashing screen, reaches out, and pulls the lever . . . More flashes of lightning go down the nerves to the muscles, which then contract, as the finger is pulled away from the threatening stimulus. The behaviour of the homunculus was, of course, not explained. An explanation would presumably require another film. And it, in turn, another.[52]

Skinner's dilemma is a false one. Our metaphysics of rationality and autonomy does not presuppose an uncaused causer. Autonomy, as I have argued, should be conceived in terms of causal power, and yet the exercises of that power may be (and surely are) themselves caused. Secondly, the explanations possible are *not* limited to the autonomous acts of other little agents, leading to Skinner's feared infinite regress. We currently explain most such autonomous doings by the Intentional states of belief, desire, and intention, but there is no reason why those Intentional states may not themselves be explainable by non-Intentional states. That remains to be seen. Only an indefensibly strong (and very implausible) version of the doctrine of category differences we earlier encountered could sustain Skinner on this point.

Scepticism proceeding from logical behaviourism fares no better than does that proceeding from methodological behaviourism. Despite its famous proponents, logical behaviourism is virtually dead among philosophers, psychologists, artificial intelligence specialists, linguists, and others currently worrying about the nature of mental states such as 'belief' and 'desire'. This is in part due to a variety of philosophical attacks on philosophical behaviourism.[53]

---

[52] Skinner, 'Behaviorism at Fifty', in T. W. Wann, ed., *Behaviorism and Phenomenology* (Chicago: University of Chicago Press, 1964), 80.

[53] These included Norman Malcolm's epistemic arguments, based on the oddness of behavioural translations of first-person psychological reports ('I am in pain' is a

The death-knell for logical behaviourism has not come from any of these arguments, however (some of them, indeed, are not persuasive), but from other considerations. One is the erosion of the logical positivist theory of meaning underlying philosophical behaviourism. The main temptation to seek to reduce 'belief' or 'desire' to behaviour comes from a logical positivist view about meaning, according to which all non-analytic expressions must have presently verifiable conditions that can serve as the criteria for the correct use of those expressions. For mental terms such as 'belief', the only public evidence we have is the behaviour of the person whose belief it is—which leads directly to the reductionist analysis of logical behaviorism. Few persons today would subscribe to such a logical positivist theory of meaning, for reasons that I have detailed elsewhere.[54] Briefly, 'belief' can have meaning even if we have no criteria for its application. Beliefs, desires, and other mental states may be real physiological states of the brain, or they may be functional states of the brain that are not type-identical with brain states. This scientific question cannot be foreclosed by enshrining our present indicators of when mental states exist in others (behaviour of certain sorts) as if such indicators were analytically necessary or sufficient conditions. It is good evidence that someone is in pain, for example, when he engages in pain-expressing behaviour; such evidence however, cannot be said to be an analytically necessary or sufficient *criterion* for being in pain. An individual could learn the pain behaviour and not be in pain, or he

---

statement whose truth is not inferred by the actor from observing his own pain-behaviour). See Norman Malcolm, 'Behaviorism as a Philosophy of Psychology', in T. N. Wann, ed., *Behaviorism and Phenomenology*. Richard Peters and others also urged that behavioural reductions could not bridge the 'logical gulf' or 'categorical difference' between intelligent, rule-following, purposive action on the one hand, and colourless movements and other 'dumb' phenomena, on the other. See Peters, *The Concept of Motivation* (London: Routledge and Kegan Paul, 1958). More recently, Quine and others have urged that certain logical peculiarities of mentalistic language—having to do with 'belief' and other mental words taking *objects* or contents—preclude any kind of reduction, whether of a behavioural or a neuro-physiological kind. For Quine, as for Skinner, this means one should *avoid* 'belief', 'desire' and other Intentional idioms in formulating a truly scientific (and behaviourist) science of human behaviour; one should avoid such idioms precisely because one could *not* reduce them to scientifically respectable (i.e., non-Intentional) speech. See Willard Van Orman Quine, *Word and Object* (Cambridge, Mass.: MIT Press, 1960). Quine admits that 'there is no breaking out of the Intentional vocabulary by explaining its members in other terms' (220).

[54] Moore, 'The Semantics of Judging', *supra* n. 14, at 208–10.

could be in pain but not engage in the behaviour (curare, which paralyses but does not eliminate the painful feelings, is not an anaesthetic). Only in light of our best theory of what sort of state pain is can we answer whether someone is in pain. One cannot foreclose the development of such scientific theories by positing fixed connections (meaning connections) of 'pain' to certain kinds of behaviours.

Aside from this erosion of the meaning theory foundations of logical behaviourism, the position can be seen to be untenable simply by examining carefully attempted behaviourist reductions of mental terms like 'belief'. It is no accident that nowhere in *The Concept of Mind*[55] did Gilbert Ryle give more than a sketch of what a translation of mental terms into 'multi-track' dispositions would look like. The kind of translations Skinner casually throws off from time to time throughout his work are not persuasive even to his admirers, who regard them as loose paraphrases but not reductions.[56] Just as logical positivism's attempted reduction of object language to phenomenal language failed in large part because no adequate translations were ever proposed, so logical behaviourism has foundered in large part because of the reductionists' similar failure to deliver the promised translations.

Neither form of behaviourism can sustain the rejection of the subjective mental states of belief, desire, and willing. If one is going to argue either for the objective theory of mental states or for limiting the legal relevance of intentions to manifesting dangerous propensities, it will have to be on grounds other than those supplied by behaviourists.

More generally, none of the three forms of scepticism we have examined should shake the realist intuition that 'the state of a man's mind is as much a fact as the state of his digestion'.[57] Persons really possess the mental states of belief, desire, and intention, really will (cause) the movements of their bodies, and nothing from contemporary legal theory, philosophy, or psychology should convince us otherwise.

[55] Ryle, *The Concept of Mind* (London: Hutcheson, 1949).
[56] See Mapel, 'Philosophical Criticism of Behaviorism', *supra* n. 44.
[57] Bowen, J, in *Edington* v. *Fitzmaurice*, 29 Ch.D 459, 483 (1882).

PART III

THE THEORY OF THE SPECIAL PART: THEORIES OF LEGISLATION AND OF WRONGFUL ACTION

SUBPART A
THE THEORY OF PROPER LEGISLATIVE AIM

16

A NON-EXCLUSIONARY THEORY OF LEGISLATIVE AIM: TAKING AIM AT MORAL WRONGDOING

I. INTRODUCTION

As set forth in chapter 1, the most interesting sort of theory of the special part is an evaluative theory. Such a theory should answer the question, what ought to be made criminal? Since the job of creating criminal prohibitions in Anglo-American legal systems has for centuries been allocated to the legislature, the answer to the question here asked takes the form of a theory of legislation.

A theory of legislation as I conceive it will have the three parts I previewed in chapter 1: first, a theory of proper legislative aim; second, for those theories of legislative aim that make moral wrongdoing relevant, a theory of the general nature of those moral norms that make certain acts wrong to do; and third, a theory of the limits of legislation by virtue of which the attainment of proper legislative aim may be constrained.

In this chapter I shall pursue the theory of proper legislative aim. I shall do so in the following steps. First, I shall discuss very generally what a theory of legislative aim should look like: who is the audience of such a theory, why does such audience need such a theory, and should such a theory be substantive or merely procedural? Second, I shall present a taxonomy of possible substantive theories of proper legislative aim, a taxonomy that has been standard since John Stuart Mill. This taxonomy is developed in terms of who is harmed by the acts eligible for criminal prohibition. Third, I shall examine the views of Michael Sandel, who with others puts aside the Millian taxonomy in favour of a simpler one that focuses on the propriety of enacting morality into law. Fourth, I examine Sandel's arguments against the classic liberal's purported exclusion of substantive moral visions when enacting criminal laws. Fifth, since I agree with Sandel's conclusion but find his arguments for it wanting, I sketch how a retributivist legislator would justify the enactment of her own moral views into law. And sixth and lastly, I give an overview of how such a seemingly illiberal, retributivist legislator might nonetheless be quite liberal in the limits she imposes on what may be criminalized.

II. SUBSTANTIVE AND REPRESENTATIONAL THEORIES OF PROPER LEGISLATIVE AIM

A theory of legislation is a moral theory. A theory of proper legislative aim is a moral theory that defines the office of legislator. More specifically, it is that part of the theory of the legislative role that tells a legislator what sorts of considerations are proper considerations with which to motivate his legislation, and which ones are improper. On one view of the matter, there are no limits on the sorts of things a legislator might properly seek to achieve by legislation, short of the constitutional limitations of the form in which he enacts his laws. My own view, however, is that the legislative role ought not be conceived in such a limitless way. After all, the office of legislator is one of the institutions within our legal system that purports to have only limited powers. One needs a theory of this office that has some bite, no less than one needs a theory of the judicial role to act as a constraint upon the sorts of things that judges may consider as they decide cases. In each case, to conceive of the office as being a role of some kind, is presumably to constrain it in certain sorts of ways. This, because roles are by and large defined by their ability to limit the range of things persons who occupy such roles may consider as they exercise the powers given to them by their offices.

Very generally speaking, there are two kinds of theories of legislative aim that might be plausible in a democratic society. These I shall call representational theories and substantive theories. There are these two kinds of theories of the legislator's role, because there are also two models of the legislature prevalent in law and political science. There is the public choice model, in which a legislature is seen not as aiming at some public interest, but rather as simply being a body in which each of its members has his own individual interests to pursue; legislation on this model is simply seen as the summing (or some form of combination) of those individual interests. The second model of a legislature is called the social good model. According to this model, the legislature should be seen as passing legislation that aims at achieving some social good.

The two theories of legislation that correlate with the public choice and social good models of the legislature, are, respectively, the representational and the substantive theories of legislation. On the representational view, a legislator in a democratic society does his or her job whenever he is passive with respect to the wishes of his constituents. That is, a legislator on this view should be someone who seeks to determine his constituents' wishes on each particular issue, and then binds himself to vote the majority view of his constituents on those issues.

A substantive theory of legislation, contrastingly, would urge a more active and leadership role onto a legislator. That is, on this kind of a theory of legislation, a legislator acts best when he himself develops a theory about what would make the society for which he is a legislator better. The theory is substantive in the sense that the legislator must himself have some substantive theory about what would make the society for which he is a legislator better.

As a thought experiment testing which of these two kinds of theories of legislation is most desirable for a democratic society, imagine that the technological means were available so that on every issue that came before a legislative body the wishes of individual citizens could be known instantaneously. One might imagine, for example, that the TV sets of the nation were all rigged up so that by pressing a button on a weekly basis citizens could express their views on proposed legislation. Those favouring the representational theory of legislation should favour such a system. Yet I doubt that many of us would think that this very direct democracy would be a very good idea, for at least two reasons. One is the questionable value of what such a summing of individually expressed wishes would represent. Given the Nobel Prize-winning work of Kenneth Arrow, we know that the outcome of such a preference-expression system would depend upon how the questions were put, and what the alternatives to the proposals might have been.[1] There are severe problems of agenda influence here, which makes questionable the

---

[1] Kenneth Arrow, *Social Choice and Individual Values*, 2nd edn. (New Haven: Yale University Press, 1963).

idea that there can be anything that can claim the mantle of being 'the majority will' on some particular piece of proposed legislation. Second, even putting aside Arrow problems there is the fact that we expect more of our elected representatives than that they simply represent our views in the way in which a TV screen might be perfectly representational. Neither the TV screen nor a legislator trying to act like such a screen gives us the kind of moral leadership that we should expect from our elected representatives. Democracy works best when our elected representatives themselves do not respond to the wishes of their constituents in the way the representational theory proposes; we attribute to politicians who behave in this way motives of 'political expediency', a term of disapproval. By contrast, those legislators who vote on legislation in light of their own substantive theories we praise as 'acting on principle'. Such praise is appropriate because a legislator does better by providing us with his own views of what would make the society better. If ultimately we disagree with such principles despite the platform for persuasion which the office of legislator offers, we can vote them out.

III. THE MILLIAN TAXONOMY OF SUBSTANTIVE THEORIES OF PROPER LEGISLATIVE AIM

John Stuart Mill's famous essay, *On Liberty*, began a tradition that is highly influential, even today, in its conceptualization of possible theories of legislative aim.[2] According to this tradition, there are four such substantive theories that might command the attention of a legislator. The first is what I shall call unrestricted utilitarianism. Utilitarianism itself is the theory that legislation should aim at the maximizing of social welfare in some sense of social welfare (as pleasure, happiness, or preference satisfaction). There are essentially two ideas involved here: first, utilitarianism is committed to the view that happiness, or pleasure, or the satisfaction of wants, is the only intrinsically good thing with which any action, including

[2] John Stuart Mill, *On Liberty* (London: 1859). Joel Feinberg's magisterial four volume work continues and refines considerably Mill's taxonomy. Feinberg, *Harm to Others* (Oxford: Oxford University Press, 1984); Feinberg, *Offense to Others* (Oxford: Oxford University Press, 1986); Feinberg, *Harm to Self* (Oxford: Oxford University Press, 1985); Feinberg, *Harmless Wrongdoing* (Oxford: Oxford University Press, 1988).

the act of legislating, can ultimately be justified. Second, utilitarianism is a maximizing theory in that it asserts that more of such happiness, pleasure or want satisfaction is better than less of it. Implicit in this maximizing idea is an ideal of equality, in that when the maximizing is done, each person's interest counts for one but only for one, in Bentham's famous phrase.

Utilitarianism is 'unrestricted' in the sense that there are no kinds of side constraints or limitations placed upon the maximizing of social welfare that the utilitarian principle calls for. An exponent of this view, for example, will believe that society should legislate against certain behaviour whenever enough citizens are offended by the behaviour that their unhappiness outweighs the happiness of those who wish to engage in the behaviour. With regard to the issue of making adultery a crime, for example, if many citizens are offended by adulterous behaviour, then that will be a sufficient reason to prohibit the adulterous behaviour, so long as citizen offence is greater than the happiness adultery might bring to the participants. A contemporary exponent of this view has been Lord Devlin, who has urged the view that the moral offence of citizens is a sufficient basis for legislation, if the offence is sufficiently widespread and is of a sufficient intensity.[3]

A second type of substantive theory of legislative aim is what I shall call restricted utilitarianism. On this view the maximizing of the happiness of citizens is certainly a desirable aim of a legislator, but it is not the only aim; sometimes such happiness must be diminished in the name of the rights of individuals to their liberty or to other goods.

There are two ways in which such limits may be expressed in a utilitarian theory; in contemporary philosophy, it is common to express such limits as the side constraints imposed by the rights of others, which 'trump' utility.[4] This is in reality a mixed theory that gives up the essential utilitarian idea that the only intrinsic goods there are are welfare goods. The alternative mode of expressing such limits is by manipulating the domain of utilitarian calculation in just the way that prevents it ever from yielding a result contrary

---

[3] Patrick Devlin, *The Enforcement of Morals* (Oxford: Oxford University Press, 1965). Lord Devlin is alternatively interpretable as a relativist in his meta-ethics, rather than a preference-utilitarian in his ethics.

[4] The famous phrase of Ronald Dworkin, *Taking Rights Seriously* (Cambridge, Mass.: Harvard University Press, 1978).

to the rights of individuals. These are 'indirect utilitarianisms', according to which one distinguishes different items to be justified (rules versus acts, motives or traits versus acts, etc.) and then urges that the utilitarian calculation is proper only for the more general of these pairs.[5]

A classic example of the second of these kinds of limits is John Stuart Mill, who famously argued that the right to liberty could not be infringed by the maximizing of happiness of others. Mill's statement of this 'one very simple principle' is worth quoting:

that principle is, that the sole end for which mankind are warranted, individually or collectively, in interfering with the liberty of action of any of their number, is self-protection. That the only purpose for which power can be rightfully exercised over any member of a civilized community, against his will, is to prevent harm to others. He cannot rightly be compelled to do or forbear because it will be better for him to do so, because it will make him happier, because, in the opinion of others, to do so would be wise, or even right.[6]

Mill's version of restricted utilitarianism might be called harm-based utilitarianism, because the restriction Mill would place on a legislator is that 'hard harms' to others are the only things that can justify legislation that interferes with liberty. One can view this, as Mill himself did, as simply a restriction on when a utilitarian should seek to maximize; or one can, along with more modern writers, see Mill as in essence putting a side constraint on the calculation of utility, so that it cannot override the right to liberty (or some other goal of neutrality or equality) except on the showing of there being harm to others.

If a legislator were to utilize this theory of legislation in seeking to justify legislating against adultery, for example, he would have to find some harm that adultery causes to persons other than the participants in order to justify the legislation. He might, for example, think that adultery leads to divorce, and that divorce leads to badly developed children. If these consequences are indeed plausible, then he may have some basis of legislating against adultery, on the grounds that it will in fact cause a harm to non-consenting parties.

---

[5] See generally Lawrence Alexander, 'Indirect Utilitarianisms', *Ethics*, Vol. 95 (1985), 315–32.

[6] Mill, *On Liberty*, supra n. 2, at 8–9.

A third theory of legislation is the paternalistic theory. A legislator who acts paternalistically does not necessarily seek to maximize utility within a society. Rather, he adopts the welfare of a class of individuals as his target, seeking to legislate so as to make them better off, even if doing so makes others even worse off. The theory is fatherly ('paternalistic') in that it goes against the actors' own judgements about what makes them better off. A paternalist about adultery, for example, would not need to look to the harm caused children in order to justify legislation against that behaviour. Rather, he could argue that adulterous behaviour is bad for the participants, even if they disagree and wish to engage in such practices. Paternalism thus involves the judgement that the state knows better than the citizens what is good for them, either morally or otherwise.

The fourth and final theory of legislation is what has come to be known as 'legal moralism'. Legal moralism is a theory of legislation built on some version of a non-relativistic meta-ethics. That is, a legislator acting on this theory of legislation would believe that in some sense there are right answers to moral questions (about, for example, whether persons should be cruel to animals, or whether adultery is right or wrong) and that such right answers do not depend on what most people in his society happen to think about these matters. Further, a theorist of this type would believe that every legislator has the right and the duty to legislate his view of what the correct moral order is, into law.

If one applies such a theory of legislation to the example of adultery, the legal moralist legislator has a very short answer as to how such legislation is to be justified: adultery should be made illegal because it is immoral. The immorality of behaviour, on this theory of legislation, will be a sufficient condition with which to justify criminal legislation.

Each of these substantive theories has something to be said for it. Unrestricted utilitarianism can claim the plausibility of utilitarianism itself, which as a principle of legislation does better intuitively than it does as a theory of ethics generally. One might think, for instance, of laws that prohibit offensive sexual behaviour in public, as an example of where we will allow the offence of enough persons to outweigh the general preference of others to engage in any kind of sexual practice they might like. Mill's kind of restricted utilitarianism, of course, has the plausibility of a theory that heavily protects liberty against state interference. If one is a utilitarian to start with, Mill's theory will be plausible to the extent that one also has Mill's libertarian tendencies. Paternalism is perhaps the least plausible of the four substantive theories, given its antithetical nature to the libertarian, liberal tradition of the West. It becomes more plausible when one thinks of the state, not as the night-watchman performing the minimal function of keeping order amongst autonomous individuals, but more as the friend of each of its citizens. As eloquently expressed by John Donne:

No man is an island, entire of itself; every man is a piece of the continent, a part of the main; if a clod be washed away from the sea, Europe is the less . . . any man's death diminishes me, because I am involved in mankind; and therefore never send to know for whom the bell tolls, it tolls for thee.[7]

It is arguable that any society that cares for its citizens in the way that one individual cares for another, will not have the strong libertarian restrictions on legislation that Mill's antipaternalist theory espouses.

Legal moralism as a theory is not inherently either paternalistic or utilitarian. That is, one might think that the legal moralist must care about the moral welfare of offenders and thus is a moral paternalist or a long-range calculator of utility. Yet such paternalistic or utilitarian concerns are alien to the legal moralist. Criminal laws are justified because and only insofar as they prohibit moral wrongdoing. It is to make the world a morally better place that animates the legal moralist, not the welfare of citizens.

The plausibility of legal moralism can be seen when one considers whether there should be legislation against behaviour such as cruelty to animals, mutilation of dead bodies, or the survival of certain species. If one assumes that no large number of citizens would know of some of these kinds of acts, so that no one could be offended; if one further assumes that animals, dead bodies, and species are not the sort of actors whose interests can be harmed in a way that normally justifies legislation under Mill's harm principle; and if one assumes away for the moment any notion that it may be bad for the persons involved to mutilate bodies, extinguish species, or be cruel to animals, so as to take away any paternalistic justification; still, I suspect that most of us would feel that there

<hr>

[7] John Donne, 'Devotion XVII', *Devotions Upon Emergent Occasions: Together Death's Duel* (Ann Arbour: University of Michigan Press, 1959), 108.

ought to be laws against these kinds of behaviours anyway. If so, the basis must be because we think such behaviours are wrong, and we think society ought to legislate against such wrongs.

We may represent these four theories on the kind of chart presented as Figure 16.1. Classic liberalism restricts itself to row 1, or, in some versions like that of Joel Feinberg, to row 1 and some of row 2. The dominant question for all such liberal theories is how they justify the restriction of legislative aim to the elimination of harm to others. Utilitarian liberals like Mill have to make sense of some kind of indirect or two-level utilitarianism, no small feat in my view.[8] Contemporary rights-based liberals not only have to make sense of some general right to liberty, but also to show how such a right (or the discrete rights that make it up) can 'trump' or exclude other considerations of a seemingly relevant sort. Contemporary liberals who urge neutrality between competing conceptions of the morally good life for individuals, or who urge more extremely the complete exclusion of such moral considerations from the justification of legislation, have to show both that it is possible and that it is good to do either of these things.[9]

IV. RETAXONOMIZING POSSIBLE THEORIES OF LEGISLATIVE AIM

Before coming to the possibility or desirability of classically liberal theories of proper legislative ends, it is helpful to retaxonomize such theories away from the Millian taxonomy (by kinds of harms) and towards the simpler version suggested recently by Michael Sandel.[10]

One can motivate this shift in the following way. Most who discuss Mill's harm principle grapple with the question, why should the fact that an action harms others physically or economically be

[8] The general problem is how a utilitarian can justify *not* being a utilitarian at one of his levels of analysis. See David Lyons, *The Forms and Limits of Utilitarianism* (Oxford: Clarendon Press, 1965).

[9] A challenge explored in Joseph Raz, *The Morality of Freedom* (Oxford: Oxford University Press, 1987).

[10] Michael Sandel, 'Moral Argument and Liberal Toleration: Abortion and Homosexuality', *California Law Review*, Vol. 77 (1989), 521–38. See also Sandel, *Liberalism and the Limits of Justice* (Cambridge, Mass.: Harvard University Press, 1982); Sandel, 'The Procedural Republic and the Unencumbered Self', *Political Theory*, Vol. 12 (1984), 81–96; Sandel, 'Introduction' to *Liberalism and Its Critics*, (New York: New York University Press, 1984).

FIGURE 16.1 The Mill/Feinberg Taxonomy of Legislative Aim

TAXONOMY BY HARMS	LEGITIMATING PRINCIPLES	TYPICAL PROHIBITED BEHAVIOUR	PARTS OF MORALITY THAT MAY BE LEGISLATED	POLITICAL THEORY
PHYSICAL HARMS TO OTHERS	MILL'S HARM PRINCIPLE	MURDER	OBLIGATIONS NOT TO HARM OTHERS PHYSICALLY OR ECONOMICALLY	RESTRICTED UTILITARIANISM
PSYCHIC HARMS TO OTHERS	THE OFFENCE PRINCIPLE	INDECENT EXPOSURE	AND OBLIGATIONS NOT TO OFFEND OTHERS	UNRESTRICTED UTILITARIANISM
HARMS TO SELF	THE PATERNALISTIC PRINCIPLE	SUICIDE	AND OBLIGATIONS TO SELF (THE VIRTUES)	NON-UTILITARIAN
NO HARMS (BUT EVIL)	THE LEGAL MORALIST PRINCIPLE	CRUELTY TO ANIMALS	AND FREE-FLOATING OBLIGATIONS (ALL OF MORALS)	NON-UTILITARIAN

necessary for criminal prohibition? Yet suppose we ask after the other aspect of the harm principle: why should the fact that an action harms others physically or economically be *sufficient* for criminal prohibition? Granted, it is extremely intuitive to prohibit killings, maimings, etc., but is it the harm to others that is doing the work here? If so, why are not all such harms prohibited, such as competitive economic injury, killing in self-defence, etc.? Moreover, if our concern is harm-centred, why do we not prohibit omission to prevent such harms more than we do? And how do we distinguish omissions to prevent deaths that are punishable from those that are not, whenever we do draw that line?

My own answer is this: we care about harm to non-consenting victims because to cause such harms (and sometimes, to fail to prevent them) breaches our moral obligations. It is plausible to think that the world is a morally better place where moral obligations are kept than when they are not, so it is plausible to motivate criminal legislation with this end. If this is so, then plausibly *all* moral obligations should be legislated into law in this way. Yet a glance at the fourth column of Figure 16.1 shows that the Millian liberal only criminalizes the first sort of moral obligations, and the need to justify this limitation seems embarrassingly acute. We plausibly have obligations not to offend others unnecessarily, not to cause what Feinberg calls 'free-floating evils' even if they involve no harm to any person,[11] and we plausibly are enjoined by morality to virtue, no matter if such virtue is conceptualized as beyond obligation ('supererogatory') or as an obligation to one's self. Once the true basis for the sufficiency of harm to others as a justification is appreciated, why is not the Millian liberal committed to the legislation of *all* obligation?

The best move for the classic liberal is to refuse to get onto this slippery slope. The way to do this is by denying that it is ever proper to motivate criminal legislation with the notion of moral obligation. Yet this means giving up harm as a vehicle for taxonomizing liberal versus non-liberal theories of legislation.

One does not have to be a classical liberal to share in this desire for retaxonomizing theories of legislation. If the interesting debates about the theory of legislation are between liberals and conservatives on the one side, communitarians on the other, then we can

---

[11] Feinberg, *Harmless Wrongdoing*, *supra* n. 2, at 18.

display the issue on which such kinds of political theories diverge better with a simpler, non-harm-based taxonomy. Michael Sandel has focused on the crucial taxonomizing variable here: May a legislator aim in his legislation to further or retard (what he judges to be) the morality or immorality of practices like abortion and homosexuality? There are two answers to this question: 'yes' and 'no'. Sandel calls the 'yes' answer the 'naïve' view, the 'no' answer the 'sophisticated' view.[12] The naïve view holds that a legislator may and should use his own best judgement about the morality of homosexuality and abortion in framing laws regulating those practices. If such a legislator believes that homosexuality is immoral, but that abortion is moral, these beliefs count as proper reasons with which to motivate legislation banning homosexual behaviour but permitting abortions.

The naïve view is not hostage to any particular type of moral theory. A naïve legislator may be a consequentialist, holding that right action is always a function of maximizing good states of affairs. Such a naïve, consequentialist legislator may hold a welfare-based theory of the good, identifying good states of affairs with pleasure, happiness, or preference satisfactions, in which event he will be a utilitarian; or he may be a non-utilitarian, holding that what makes states of affairs good includes non-welfare-based items like virtues being realized, duties being done, equal distributions being achieved, and rights not being violated.

Alternatively, a naïve legislator may be a non-consequentialist in his moral theory, holding the rightness of actions to be independent of the goodness of the states of affairs those actions produce. On this view, morality consists of absolute norms that forbid actions violating them no matter how good the consequences.

Unfortunately, Michael Sandel unwarrantedly links the naïve view of legislative role to consequentialist morality of a certain type (what Sandel calls the 'teleological' view of morality). Sandel thinks that whenever a legislator 'grounds the right of privacy on the good of the practice it would protect'[13] (that is, whenever he is a consequentialist who views rights as only an instrumental means to the realization of other goods), that legislator has adopted the naïve view. By contrast, Sandel believes that whenever a legislator adopts the 'claim that the right is prior to the good'—meaning by this 'that

---

[12] Sandel, 'Moral Argument', *supra* n. 10, at 521.   [13] Id. at 535–6.

individual rights cannot be sacrificed for the sake of the general good' and 'that the principles of justice that specify these rights cannot be premised on any particular vision of the good life'—that legislator has adopted the sophisticated view.[14]

Neither of these connections holds at all. The morality that the naïve legislator may think proper to consult when he legislates may be of any type whatsoever. Sandel has simply confused a question of political theory—when may legislation seek to promote some moral view—with the most general question of substantive ethics that we will examine in the next chapter—what is the relation between the goodness of certain states of affairs and the rightness of behaviour tending to promote them? There is simply no relation between these questions, so that the naïve (or legal moralist) legislator could seek to incorporate libertarianism, egalitarianism, utilitarianism, or any other moral view in his legislation.

The sophisticated legislator, by contrast, does not have to face a choice of moral theories, for what makes him sophisticated is his refusal to embed his own moral view of practices like homosexuality and abortion in legislation regulating such practices. Sandel recognizes two kinds of sophisticated legislator: the majoritarian and the liberal. The majoritarian does not seek to pass judgement on the morality of abortion, homosexuality, etc., but rather legislates on such issues on the basis of what a majority in his society judge to be the morality of such practices. The liberal believes that 'the state should not impose a preferred way of life, but should leave its citizens as free as possible to choose their own values and ends, consistent with a similar liberty for others'.[15] Both the majoritarian and the liberal distance themselves from their own critical moral judgements when they legislate—that's what makes them 'sophisticated'—but they do so for different reasons. The majoritarian allows the majority's moral views to operate as a reason justifying legislation; the liberal allows each individual's moral views to govern his own behaviour and legislates so as to provide a fair framework for each individual to work out just what those moral views are.

Although Sandel does not explain it, the majoritarian might be led to his sophisticated view of legislative role by any of a number of routes: (1) democracy is good, and democracy works best when

---

[14] Sandel, 'Procedural Republic', *supra* n. 10, at 82. See also Sandel, *Liberalism*, *supra* n. 10, at 9.
[15] Sandel, 'Introduction', *supra* n. 10, at 1.

each lawmaker simply passes along the moral views of a majority of his constituents rather than basing legislation on his own moral view (the representative kind of theory earlier considered); (2) utility is good, and utility is enhanced when the preferences of a majority in society (that certain practices do or do not take place) are satisfied by legislation that regulates behaviour to conform to those preferences; (3) community is good, and community is enhanced when the divergent practices of the minority are stamped out (or at least kept out of sight) by law; or (4), the only thing that can sensibly be said to be good is what the majority prefers, for morality is nothing other than majority preference.

Sandel does mention four routes by which the liberal might be led to his sophisticated view of legislative role:[16] (1) the voluntarist view, which holds that it is intrinsically right that each choose her own plan of life to the greatest extent possible, given everyone else's similar opportunity for choice; (2) the minimalist or pragmatic view, which accords a right to choose life-plans an instrumental status, such right being a means to further social co-operation and harmony; (3) the utilitarian view, which in the hands of Mill and subsequent rule-utilitarians also accords the right to choose life-plans an instrumental value, such a right being a means to the greatest happiness in the long run; and (4) the relativist view, which grants each such a 'right' by default—that is, values being relative, no one can judge life-plans anyway, so one should not by legislation prefer one life-plan over another.

V. SANDEL'S REJECTION OF THE SOPHISTICATED VIEW OF LEGISLATIVE ROLE

Once we reframe the debate in this way, Sandel's conclusion in this debate is one with which I have considerable sympathy. It is that there is some 'truth in the naïve view . . . The justice (or injustice) of laws against abortion and homosexual sodomy depends, at least in part, on the morality (or immorality) of those practices.'[17] The proper legislator, in other words, cannot legislate about such practices without himself developing a moral view about such practices and treating that view as a reason for legislating one way or the other.

[16] Sandel, 'Moral Argument', *supra* n. 10, at 522.   [17] Id. at 521.

Sandel mostly defends this conclusion by attacking directly only two of the four kinds of liberal sophistication—voluntarist and minimalist liberalism—and ignores majoritarian sophistication altogether. Sandel does briefly dispatch the utilitarian basis for liberalism on the familiar (and correct) ground that utilitarianism is incapable of justifying the limited legislative role Mill described with his right to liberty because utilitarian calculations will not always coincide with what such a limited role demands.[18] Sandel also dismisses relativist liberalism in a similar manner; it is paradoxical, he rightly argues, to hold that all values are relative *and* to hold that liberty is good. As Sandel concludes, 'The relativist defence of liberalism is no defence at all.'[19] By process of elimination Sandel thus reaches his target, the kinds of liberalism he attributes to Kant and Dworkin (voluntarism) and to Rawls (minimalism).

Sandel's arguments against voluntarist and minimalist liberalism seem very thin, even to one such as myself who is sympathetic to their conclusion. Sandel presents two arguments, which he uses against both voluntarist and minimalist liberalism. The first is what I shall call the argument from non-neutral derivation. As Sandel puts it, 'the case for bracketing a particular moral or religious controversy may partly depend on an implicit answer to the controversy it purports to bracket'.[20] Put in my language: any lawmaker must justify why it is right for him not to base legislation about abortion on a moral view about abortion; such justification will itself involve the lawmaker in appealing to some moral view and that moral view will include some judgement about the morality of abortion.

This kind of argument is a familiar one in legal philosophy. Against purportedly value-free theories of adjudication, for example, it is often urged that any judge must justify why it is right for him not to base his decision on some moral view of the merits of the controversy before him. Such justification will itself involve the judge in appealing to some moral view, and that moral view will have to take into account the very values it purportedly justifies excluding.[21]

---

[18] Sandel, 'Introduction', *supra* n. 10, at 2–3.   [19] Id. at 1.
[20] Sandel, 'Moral Argument', *supra* n. 10, at 531.
[21] See, e.g., Dworkin, *Taking Rights Seriously*, *supra* n. 4, at 37–8, 48–58, 105–15.

I myself have used some such arguments to argue for the impossibility of value-free adjudication, either in common law or statutory reasoning.[22] But Sandel gives us no reason to think that such an argument can succeed in political theory. His fleshing out of the argument against minimalist liberalism consists of a single example: One who seeks to 'bracket' the controversy over the morality of abortion by letting the woman decide for herself cannot avoid a substantive position on the moral merits of that controversy, namely, a position on when life begins.[23] Yet without saying so, Sandel in this example assumes that minimalist liberalism is committed to something like Mill's harm principle, so that no harm *to another person* is a precondition of bracketing. I do not see liberalism so confined. A legislator might well justify the woman's right to choose for herself (and thus bracket the issue for himself) even though he concedes the foetus is a person harmed by her decision. Indeed, Judy Thomson famously constructed a view of this particular right having no 'no harm' justification for its existence.[24]

Sandel's fleshing out of the argument as it applies to voluntarist liberalism is no more successful. Sandel argues that 'the voluntarist justification of privacy rights is dependent—politically as well as philosophically—on some measure of agreement that the practices protected are morally permissible'.[25] What Sandel seems to mean here is that you get social co-operation and peace on issues like homosexuality only if people share a view on the moral merits of homosexuality—for example, the view that it is not immoral. Sharing only the view that each person has a right to do what she wants with her body is not enough for such co-operation and peace.

There are two things wrong with this argument: it is irrelevant and it is false. The irrelevance point first. This is supposed to be an argument against voluntarist liberalism. The voluntarist, as Sandel has defined him, attaches intrinsic importance to moral rights such as the right to do with one's body sexually what one will. So of what relevance is it to the *voluntarist* justification of bracketing the

---

[22] Michael Moore, 'A Natural Law Theory of Interpretation', *Southern California Law Review*, Vol. 58 (1985), 277–398; Moore, 'Precedent, Induction, and Ethical Generalization', in Laurence Goldstein, ed., *Precedent in Law* (Oxford: Oxford University Press, 1987).

[23] Sandel, 'Moral Argument', *supra* n. 10, at 531–2.

[24] Judith Jarvis Thomson, 'A Defense of Abortion', *Philosophy and Public Affairs*, Vol. 1 (1971), 47–66.

[25] Sandel, 'Moral Argument', *supra* n. 10, at 537.

moral issue of homosexuality that social co-operation will not be achieved? Social co-operation for the voluntarist is not the end that justifies granting each of us the legal right to choose; unlike the minimalist, the voluntarist justifies such legal rights by the moral rights to choose that we each possess.

Sandel's argument here also seems clearly false. In a society of devout voluntarist liberals, each deeply attached to the rights of others to make choices—even bad choices—for themselves, why would social co-operation and peace not be achieved? Is there some instinct of an extraordinarily imperialistic superego that forces even such committed, voluntarist liberals to cram their own values down other people's throats, despite a very conscious acceptance of the right to choose different lifestyles than our own?

Sandel's second argument is what I shall call the argument from non-neutral application. This argument asserts that even if there were some neutral justification (minimalist or voluntarist) for a right of each of us to decide whether to have an abortion or whether to engage in homosexual sex, this liberty-right would not be neutral in its application to particular decisions, however neutral it may be in its derivation. Some view of the moral merits about such practices must be smuggled in if such a right is to be given concrete application.

This argument too has its analogue in that part of legal philosophy known as the theory of adjudication. It is common to argue that general legal standards are indeterminate in their application to some, many, or perhaps all concrete cases. Such standards may be vague, ambiguous, or open-textured, and thus require a judge to make some value judgements in applying them. What cannot be accomplished is the exclusion of value judgements in adjudication, an exclusion that some theories of law require.

Sandel's use of this well-worn argument is puzzling. Against minimalist liberalism Sandel has the following to say:

Even given an agreement to bracket controversial moral and religious issues for the sake of social cooperation, it may be controversial what counts as bracketing; and this controversy may require for its solution either a substantive evaluation of the interests at stake, or the autonomous conception of agency that minimalist liberalism resolves to avoid.[26]

---

[26] Id. at 532.

Sandel's example of the ambiguity of 'bracketing' is provided by the differing views of Justices White and Stevens in *Thornburgh* v. *American College of Obstetricians and Gynecologists*.[27] Justice White urged the Court to bracket the moral issue of abortion by letting the state legislatures decide; Justice Stevens urged the Court to bracket the moral issue by letting each woman decide for herself. '[B]oth ways of bracketing are in principle consistent with minimalist liberalism', Sandel concludes;[28] so deciding between them involves the Court in either a view of the merits about the morality of abortion, or a view about persons and their intrinsic rights. And 'both solutions . . . would deny minimalist liberalism its minimalism . . .'.[29]

Sandel is here undone by his failure to separate constitutional law from political theory. His ambiguity in what bracketing comes to exists only because he has not decided whether the institution asking the question is a court or a legislature. If it is a court, of course there is an ambiguity, because considerations of court function intrude. Yet ours is a question of political theory, asked from the point of view of the legislator. From such a point of view there is no ambiguity of 'bracketing': To bracket the moral issue of abortion is, unambiguously, to let the woman decide for herself.

Sandel had a better point than his *Thornburgh* example allowed him to make. The point should have been that agreements run out in the details that they can govern. It is easy enough to agree that everyone has a right to free speech, harder to secure agreement that that means the Nazis can march in Skokie. Sandel's better point would have been to argue that no amount of purely liberal agreement about rights at a high level of abstraction will serve the minimalist ends of social co-operation and harmony. Needed is agreement in the details of how those rights are to be applied in concrete instances. Only agreement on the morality of practices like abortion allows agreement on concrete applications of an abstract right of liberty, the right that purports to bracket the moral controversy about abortion.

Sandel comes close to saying this when he applies the argument from non-neutral application to voluntarist liberalism. One of Sandel's voluntarist liberals, Ronald Dworkin, at one time thought that liberalism's political morality could be captured by the right of

---

[27] 476 US 747 (1986).   [28] Sandel, 'Moral Argument', *supra* n. 10, at 533.
[29] Id.

every citizen to equal concern and respect by her government.[30] Sandel points out an ambiguity in the quality of respect such a right guarantees: In the case of homosexuals, is it only the thin respect given those who act sinfully but within their rights? Or is it the richer respect possible if one likens homosexual sex to heterosexual sex, an analogy one can draw only if one thinks both are morally permissible?[31]

Sandel worries that if it is only the former respect, then this 'leaves wholly unchallenged the adverse views of homosexuality itself'.[32] Such unchallenged adverse views leave much potential for social disharmony, because voluntarist-based laws allowing homosexual behaviour are 'unlikely to win for homosexuals more than a thin and fragile toleration'.[33]

As an argument against voluntarist liberalism, this argument is misdirected. The voluntarist is a metaphysician about morality, holding that moral rights exist independent of whether they serve some conflict-minimizing function. How well or poorly such rights serve such a function is, for the voluntarist, irrelevant to their existence. Moreover, the most credible form of voluntarism holds that moral rights are not indeterminate in their content.[34] Our *knowledge* of the true nature of the right to equal concern and respect may be (and surely is) incomplete; but the *truth* about the nature of such a right need not be incomplete for someone with the voluntarist's metaphysical commitments.

Even when construed as an objection only to minimalist liberalism, the argument from non-neutral application is hostage to the unrealistic psychological assumption mentioned before. A society of sincere liberals could easily achieve harmony and co-operation without resolving their first-order differences about the morality of practices like abortion and homosexuality, as long as they strongly believed in the rightness of tolerance, pluralism, and autonomy. To think otherwise is to postulate some instinct of moral imperialism that I do not think is very plausibly an aspect of human nature.

---

[30] Dworkin, *Taking Rights Seriously*, *supra* n. 4, at 266–78.
[31] Sandel, 'Moral Argument', *supra* n. 10, at 537.   [32] Id.   [33] Id.
[34] See Dworkin's essay, 'No Right Answer?', in his *A Matter of Principle* (Cambridge, Mass.: Harvard University Press, 1985). For a more metaphysically robust interpretation of this right answer thesis, see Michael Moore, 'Metaphysics, Epistemology, and Legal Theory', *Southern California Law Review*, Vol. 60 (1987), 453–506.

Given the thinness with which Sandel has specified the arguments from non-neutral derivation and from non-neutral application, it has taken some reconstruction to attribute these arguments to him at all. Such arguments cry out for a more complete exposition, and one that makes such arguments generically, and not just as applied to the Supreme Court's treatment of abortion and homosexuality.

My suspicion is that a more complete, more generic exposition of these arguments would reveal their essentially question-begging character. Notice that both arguments assume that the morality of liberalism (misleadingly called the morality of right by Sandel) 'runs out' in two senses: first, in the sense that justification ultimately is impossible within the confines of such morality; and second, in the sense that application to concrete cases is also impossible within the confines of such morality. Both arguments further assume that the consequentialist morality that Sandel favours (misleadingly called by him the morality of the good) does not run out in either of these ways; that is why the morality of the good may supplement the liberal's morality of right. Such assumptions *support* Sandel's thesis (that the justice of laws against abortion and homosexual sodomy depend, at least in part, on the moral goodness of those practices) only in the Pickwickian sense that they *assume* it.

Any non-question-begging support for Sandel's thesis must come from arguments different than these. Sandel should give up possibility arguments and confront liberalism on the moral merits. Sandel accuses liberals and their fellow sophisticates, the majoritarians, of illegitimately trying to keep their conservative opponents off the playing field of first-order moral disputes. This, liberals do by saying that it is undesirable to incorporate any view of the moral merits of specific practices into political institutions, and that the only political debate to have is about the fair framework in which differing visions of the good life may compete.

Sandel's mode of argument against liberals is subject to the same objection: he is trying to keep liberals off the second-order playing field where differing visions of fair frameworks may compete. Rather than entering the tourney lists himself, making *normative* arguments why the liberal vision of fair frameworks is undesirable, Sandel disdains the tournament entirely as an *impossible* enterprise.[35]

[35] For a similar observation, directed against Critical Legal Studies, see Don Herzog, 'As Many As Six Impossible Things Before Breakfast', *California Law Review*, Vol. 75 (1987), 609–30.

VI. THE RETRIBUTIVISTS' CASE AGAINST CLASSICAL LIBERALISM

What is wrong with the modern liberalisms of John Rawls and Ronald Dworkin, against which Michael Sandel wishes to argue, is the same thing that is wrong with Mill's harm-based definition of liberalism. These are not conceptually impossible or incoherent political theories. Rather, they are morally undesirable theories, for all of them share a defect stemming from what I shall call their exclusionary nature. The liberal believes that one category of morality can exclude another category of morality from counting in judging the rightness of political institutions. Specifically, such a liberal believes that the goodness or badness of practices like abortion and homosexuality does not count at all in judging the rightness of political institutions dealing with such behaviour, because this kind of moral judgement is precluded by another kind of moral judgement (about fair political frameworks and the like). Such moral judgements on political structures operate not only as first-order reasons of morality, giving all rational agents a reason to set up the institutions such judgements justify, but also as second-order reasons of morality that exclude competing moral reasons from counting.[36] Morality, on this view, is a hierarchically organized set of reasons, some of which operate as exclusionary and protected reasons.[37]

Very generally speaking, the problem with this hierarchical view of morality is a moral problem: nothing that is morally good or bad can be excluded in judging the morality of a political institution without skewing one's judgements about the all-things-considered desirability of that institution.[38] One might think, as I argue in chapter 18, that the ideal of autonomy provides a very strong, first-order reason of morality not to regulate a woman's decision whether or not to have an abortion. Such an ideal does not provide a second-order reason that justifies excluding other first-order reasons of morality, such as the reason provided by the wrongness of

[36] For the difference between first-order and second-order moral reasons, see Joseph Raz, *Practical Reason and Norms* (Oxford: Oxford University Press, 1976).
[37] See Joseph Raz, *The Authority of Law* (Oxford: Oxford University Press, 1979), 16–18.
[38] Argued for in Moore, 'Law, Authority and Razian Reasons', *Southern California Law Review*, Vol. 62 (1989), 827–96.

killing a foetus. The woman's autonomy may *outweigh*, but does not *exclude*, the wrongness of killing a foetus. To hold otherwise, as does the classical liberal, is to invite systematic moral error.

This very general objection does not by itself justify the naïve (or legal moralist) theory of criminal legislation. For nothing in the rejection of hierarchically ordered morality speaks in favour of the relevance of moral wrongness to the question of what should be criminalized. Perhaps the moral status of potentially criminalized behaviour does not need to be *excluded* by some classically liberal argument; perhaps it is not relevant to the aims of the criminal law to start with.

Whether this is so depends of course on one's theory of punishment. If I am correct in the argument of Part I, the value served by the criminal law is the achieving of justice in retribution. If I am correct in the argument of Part II, the desert that triggers retributive punishment consists of the culpable wrongdoing of persons. If I am correct in the argument of chapter 9, both culpability and wrongdoing are based on the moral norms of obligation telling us what we are obligated to do or not to do: wrongdoing is the breach of such obligations in the actual world, and culpability is the breach of such obligations in the possible world created by the content of the actor's mental states.

Perhaps surprisingly, even accepting all this we will not quite yet have justified a legal moralist theory of criminal legislation. Needed is one more piece of the puzzle. This is the piece usually called the principle of legality. Justified by the rule of law values (which incidentally are quite separate from justice in retribution), the principle of legality requires that there be clear, public, consistent, prospective, general, legal rules prohibiting conduct before that conduct may be punished. When one adds the political ideals of many Anglo-American legal systems—about the separation of powers—the principle of legality demands rules with the above characteristics to issue from legislatures, not in increments from court decisions.[39]

Such demands of legality limit the achievability of retributive jus-

---

[39] The demands placed on the form of criminal law prohibition by the rule of law values, and by the political ideals of the separation of powers, are discussed by me in 'The Limits of Legislation', *USC Cites*, Vol. [Fall, 1984], 23–32, at 23–7, and in Michael Moore, *Act and Crime: The Philosophy of Action and its Implications for Criminal Law* (Oxford: Oxford University Press, 1993), ch. 9.

tice in any legal system. Depending on how one feels about crimes against humanity, such as the crime involved in the Israeli trial of Adolf Eichmann or in the Allied trials at Nuremberg, one may not *always* side constrain the achievement of retributive justice by the demands of legality. But most of the time, we rightly limit fully deserved punishment by the requirement that the moral wrongdoing has been statutorily prohibited at the time it was done.

This limitation on the achievement of retributive justice gives a legislature good reason to criminalize all immoral behaviour, for this is the only way the good of retributive justice can be achieved. In this way a retributivist about punishment becomes a legal moralist about criminal legislation.

VII. THE RETRIBUTIVIST-LEGAL MORALIST LIBERAL: A CONTRADICTION IN TERMS?

The preceding discussion paves the way to glimpsing the possibility of a naïve liberalism, one that is not subject to my or Sandel's objections to the sophisticated view. The naïve liberal admits that the (im)morality of practices like abortion and homosexuality counts in assessing political/legal institutions dealing with such practices. Such an admission is what makes him 'naïve' in Sandel's lexicon. What make him a liberal is how he comes out at the end of the day in assessing the rightness of laws dealing with homosexuality, abortion, and the like. For what I shall sketch here, and seek to show in greater detail in chapter 18, is how the retributivist who is also a legal moralist can and should agree with his more sophisticated allies that the criminal law has no business criminalizing behaviours such as 'deviant' sex, abortion, drug use, and the like.

There are four sorts of considerations that should make a properly retributivist legal moralism a quite liberal-in-outcome, if not liberal-in-form, theory of legislation. The first two sorts of limits stem from retributivism itself. The first of these begins with the thought mentioned in chapter 4, that no justice in retribution is achieved if what an actor has done (in the actual world or in his head) is not morally wrong. This seems to lead to an obvious limit to what may be legislated by a retributivist, confining criminal prohibitions to those acts that morality already obligates us not to do.

There is an intermediate step glossed over here, however, that needs to be mentioned. If one's political theory were such that law as such (that is, without regard to its content) at least prima facie obligated citizen obedience, then any citizen who violated the criminal law would have done something wrong and would merit punishment on retributive grounds. Since I do not believe that law as such obligates citizen obedience at all,[40] this worry is fortunately idle.

With this step taken, the legal moralist theory of legislation to which retributivism commits one then holds that all *and only* moral wrongs should be criminally prohibited. Depending on one's view of morality, this can by itself highly limit what should be criminalized. For those of us who think that morality is indifferent to sexual practices, and that avoidance of much else in the way of conventionally regarded 'vice' is only supererogatory but not obligatory, this by itself should stay legislatures from enacting much of what passes as 'morals offences' in our current criminal code.

Indeed, if one has this view of morality one probably will find John Stuart Mill's older formulation of liberalism intuitively appealing. It is because our most obvious and most stringent moral obligations are about causing serious harms to others that Mill's harm principle has the intuitive appeal it does. My legal moralist liberalism, coupled with my view of the limited scope of our moral obligations, would honour Mill's principle as a not always accurate but otherwise acceptable rule of thumb in this way.

The second set of considerations is closely related to the first. One may sometimes be in doubt whether some sorts of actions are morally obligatory or morally prohibited. Incest, for example. When in doubt, there is a good that may stay the legislative hand, namely, the potential resolution of that doubt by allowing different lifestyles the chance to flourish. As Mill famously argued, each life represents an experiment in alternative conceptualizations of the good, and if a given form has some real chance of not being morally odious that is some reason not to coerce it out of existence.

Usually the meta-ethical realism adopted by most legal moralists is thought to preclude the kind of doubt that gets this sort of argu-

---

[40] On this, see M. B. E. Smith, 'Is There a *Prima Facie* Obligation to Obey the Law?', *Yale Law Journal*, Vol. 82 (1973), 950–76; Joseph Raz, *The Morality of Freedom*, *supra* n. 9, chs. 2–4; Heidi Hurd, 'Sovereignty in Silence', *Yale Law Journal*, Vol. 99 (1990), 945–1028, at 1007–10; Hurd, 'Challenging Authority', *Yale Law Journal*, Vol. 100 (1991), 1611–77.

ment going. Mill himself thought he had to dredge logical space for the argument by holding that human nature was so diverse that on many questions there was no one, generally correct resolution.

Yet moral realists do not have to be epistemic simpletons.[41] They do not have to believe that they *know* answers to questions like that involving the morality of incest, just because they do believe there to *be* one, perhaps general, answer. Even when moral realists have reached a conclusion in which they have some confidence, they should realize that the very possibility that they are right strictly requires the possibility that they could be wrong in these views.

A third set of considerations that should incline a legal moralist theory of legislation to reach liberal outcomes stems from a familiar set of hidden costs that some kinds of laws pose more than others.[42] These costs should induce a legal moralist legislator to impose certain limits on the sorts of things that might be legislated, because such hidden costs are so heavy that the gains to be achieved (in retributive justice) simply cannot outweigh them. The kinds of costs I have in mind are these: first of all, there are of course the direct costs of enforcing any law. These are the costs of police time and court personnel and the like. For types of crimes that are relatively trivial in the degree of their wrongfulness, such as jaywalking, one might well think that public resources should be better spent on more important issues. Aside from the direct costs of enforcement, some crimes may be costly in terms of the problems they present to prove the elements of such crimes. Any crime, for example, that makes intention rather than behaviour its principal target, may impose as a cost a high risk to error amongst legal fact-finders. It is often argued, for example, that legislating against conspiracies gives rise to just this kind of problem. Third, some kinds of crimes that are typically done in a way such that they are unaccompanied

---

[41] My various attempts to be a non-simpleton have been: Moore, 'Moral Reality', *Wisconsin Law Review*, Vol. [1982], 1061–156, at 1155–6; Moore, 'Moral Reality Revisited', *Michigan Law Review*, Vol. 90 (1992), 2424–533, at 2460; Moore, 'Good Without God', in Robert George and Christopher Wolfe, eds., *Modernity, Liberalism, and Natural Law* (Oxford: Oxford University Press, 1996).

[42] A sampling of the literature here: Louis Schwartz, 'Moral Offenses and the Model Penal Code', *Columbia Law Review*, Vol. 63 (1963), 669–86 ; Herbert Packer, 'The Crime Tariff', *American Scholar*, Vol. 33 (1964), 551–7; Sanford Kadish, 'The Crisis of Overcriminalization', *Annals*, Vol. 374 (1967), 157–70; Packer, *The Limits of the Criminal Sanction* (Stanford: Stanford University Press, 1968); Gordon Hawkins and Norval Morris, *The Honest Politician's Guide to Crime Control* (Chicago: University of Chicago Press, 1973).

by non-participant eyewitnesses, may impose privacy costs in the gathering of the evidence needed to prove such crimes. An example might be legislation against homosexual behaviour, since the behaviour is typically done in private without non-participant witnesses. At one point in time, the federal park rangers in Yosemite National Park sought to enforce the legislation against homosexual behaviour by placing peep-holes over the stalls in the men's bathrooms, so that they could see into each of such stalls and check for illegal behaviour. This kind of evidence gathering is costly to a society, both in terms of the privacy of its citizens, and in terms of the dignity of all concerned.

Fourth, for behaviour that will be engaged in anyway even if legislated against, there will be a peculiar effect of prohibition, namely, the raising of the prices of the products or services necessary for such behaviour; this, in turn, may increase the profits of supplying such services or products, which in turn sustains organized criminal activities. This is typically known as the 'crime tariff'. Prostitution, for example, does not go away by being legislated against, as the experience of all societies has shown. By making it criminal, however, the supply is artificially restricted to those willing to engage in criminal behaviour, so that prices and profits are such as to draw in organized criminal activity.

Fifth, and finally, there are certain indirect costs for those kinds of laws that will predictably be under-enforced by law enforcement officials. The laws against prostitution may be an example here as well. The indirect costs appear to be four: first, there is the disrespect for law generated whenever one has laws that everyone knows will not be enforced, or enforced only sporadically; second, there is the potential for private extortion for laws that are typically unenforced, because one as a private citizen can always threaten to have the law enforced on this occasion even though without that citizen's going public with it, there would not be such enforcement; third, there is the potential for corruption of public officials because they are in effect free to enforce or not; and fourth, there is the potential for discriminatory enforcement by public officials, again, because they are free to enforce or not, and thus may do so arbitrarily.

One of the interesting features of this list of hidden costs is that it substantially overlaps in its recommended restrictions on legislation with the restrictions on legislation that a classical liberal theory of legislation would recommend. That is, wherever legislation will: (1) go against deep-seated beliefs and habits of a people, so that they will engage in the behaviour even if prohibited; (2) there are no victims of the crime other than the participants; and (3) where there are no witnesses of the crime other than the participants; then one has the sort of hidden costs articulated above. These three characteristics together argue against legislation in much the same areas that classically liberal theories of legislation would also argue against legislation, namely, against victimless and consensual crimes.

The fourth and last considerations militating towards a limited scope for criminal law are the most important and interesting of all. These considerations have to do with that elusive value, liberty, and its equally elusive companion, autonomy. I shall argue in chapter 18 that one can make sense of both notions, and that a right to liberty grounded in the value of autonomy significantly limits the permissible range of retributive punishment.

Critics of classical liberalism like Michael Sandel might think that this kind of restrained legal moralism is not liberalism, and of course it is not if liberals have to be 'sophisticates'. But the naïve liberal reaches virtually the same outcomes as the sophisticated liberal, even if his reasoning and supporting justifications are different. That the legislature has no business regulating either abortions or homosexual behaviour is an outcome my own view (naïve liberalism) easily reaches. Finding such a pattern of outcomes more useful as a classificatory device than the structure of reasons onto which the critics fasten, I call myself, and this view, liberal. While in these conservative times this may disqualify me from running for President, there is little else to be said against such labelling.

SUBPART B
THE THEORY OF MORAL WRONGFULNESS

17

TORTURE AND THE BALANCE OF EVILS

A legislator adopting the legal moralist theory of proper legislative aim makes *moral* wrongdoing central to *legal* wrongdoing. Prima facie for such a legislator all and only what is morally wrongful should be criminally prohibited. This places great weight on the idea of moral wrongfulness.

It is possible to think that morality consists of hundreds or thousands of specific injunctions of the Ten Commandments kind, and that that is all that can be said about moral wrongfulness. Yet few of the many philosophers who have spent much time in ethics have ever thought this. Rather, the assumption has been that morality has more structure to it than that and that a theory of substantive ethics is a description of that general structure.

At the most general level of ethics, that structure has been thought to be of one of two kinds. On one view morality consists in only one injunction to all of us all the time: maximize good consequences, and minimize evil ones. Of course, such a monistic theory of right action can (but need not) become very pluralistic in what are intrinsically good or intrinsically bad states of affairs. Nonetheless, the injunction to each of us is to maximize the one and minimize the other. On the alternative view, morality consists of many injunctions: we are enjoined not to kill, rob, pillage, etc. What keeps this view from collapsing into the first view merits careful scrutiny. For why could one not say that the adherence to each of these injunctions is intrinsically good, their breach, intrinsically bad, and then think that one is enjoined by morality to maximize the one and minimize the other?

What makes the second view distinct from the first is its refusal to make this last step. Rather, on the second view morality is personally addressed to each of us. Its injunctions say categorically to each individual: 'don't you violate this injunction now, even if your doing so now would minimize violations of this injunction by you or others in the future'.

The most general question of substantive ethics (as opposed to meta-ethics) is which of these two views about the shape of morality's injunctions is right. This is thus a kind of watershed issue for any theory of criminal law that would mirror its criminal prohibitions in the injunctions of morality.

In Part II I said that the royal road to the theory of moral culpability that underlay the general part of the criminal law lay in the excuses. Here there is an analogous truth; to see what general shape moral norms possess, the best heuristic is to look to the issues of justification. For it is here, where there is much to be said for doing something that is normally quite wrongful, that we can work our intuition pumps most vigorously in seeing the general shape of morality. Hard cases may make bad law, as Holmes warned us, but in ethics they are indispensable for sorting out what we think.

I will thus approach this most general question about wrongfulness through the issue of justification. Moreover, in this chapter I will pursue the issue of justification with respect to two actual cases on which I was asked to comment in the past. Since such cases involve deliberate torture by state security forces but where the potential for good consequences was high, the cases work our intuition pumps most vigorously.

In the first case, the No. 300 bus, a civilian bus operating within Israel, was hijacked by four Palestinian terrorists in 1984. Once the terrorists began killing passengers, the Israeli security forces stormed the bus. All four terrorists were reported killed in the retaking of the bus. As it happened, news footage subsequently revealed that two of the terrorists had been quite alive when they were lead away by the Israeli security forces. They were apparently beaten to death during interrogation, as one of their interrogators confessed to the newspapers upon his retirement recently.

The second case involved a junior officer in the Israeli Defence Force, a Lieutenant Nafsu. He had been accused of smuggling and hiding arms for the PLO. The interrogation which produced his admission in this regard had involved what was later called 'physical pressure'. Such 'pressure' consisted of slapping, pushing, hair pulling, sleep deprivation, cold showers, and misinformation and threats about his family.

These two cases brought to light the existence of a little known counter terrorist unit of Israel's General Security Service (GSS). This unit, the Investigation Unit, was set up in 1967 after acquisition of the occupied territories raised larger fears of terrorist activities within Israel. The unit was not a prosecutorial unit, and, indeed, during the early years of its existence was forbidden from testifying in criminal trials. The function of the unit was to prevent terrorism, not punish it.

The prevention methods of the unit included interrogative techniques involving physical abuse. Such techniques were not revealed even to prosecutorial agencies, and when agents of the unit were allowed to testify in criminal trials, as a matter of policy they would lie about the methods of interrogation.

The revelation of the existence of this unit and its practices in the two cases mentioned gave rise to the appointment of a Commission to study the situation. Appointed by the Israel Supreme Court, and headed by Moshe Landau, a retired Justice of that court, the Commission in 1987 issued its report in two parts, one of which was declassified and published.[1]

This chapter explores the questions raised by the issuance of the Landau Commission Report: what is the legal and moral status of torture of terrorist suspects and others, when that torture is engaged in by an agency of the State of Israel for the purpose of extracting information potentially saving many Israeli lives? More specifically, was the Commission right in its *retrospective* conclusion that 'the methods of interrogation . . . employed [in the past by the GSS] . . . are largely to be defended, both morally and legally . . .'?[2] Was the Commission right in its *prospective* conclusion that no new legislation is needed to deal with the methods of interrogation of the GSS because 'the GSS can turn a new leaf . . . within the framework of the existing law . . .'?[3]

The Commission's Report strongly condemns the long-standing practice of the GSS to have its investigators lie to prosecutors and courts about the interrogative techniques used to obtain confessions. The Commission 'utterly rejected' any notion that the GSS can hide its methods by perjury.[4] With this finding I shall not be concerned. More troubling is the Commission's approval of the

---

[1] Landau Commission, *Landau Commission Report* (Jerusalem: Government Printing Office, 1987).

[2] Id. at 4.   [3] Id. at 82.   [4] Id. at 77.

morality and legality of interrogations such as that of Lieutenant Nafsu. Such assaults during interrogation, the Commission concluded, are neither immoral nor illegal when they are, for example, conducted 'in order to induce him [the terrorist] to talk and reveal a cache of explosive materials meant for use in carrying out an act of mass terror against a civilian population . . .'.[5] The Commission found it 'self-evident',[6] 'according to the concepts of morality implanted in the heart of every decent and honest person',[7] that such interrogations are justified. From this moral conclusion two legal conclusions emerged: first, that there is no civil or criminal liability of GSS personnel for past interrogations under the defence of necessity;[8] second, that there is no immediate need for remedial legislation to govern future interrogations of terrorist suspects.[9] In what follows, I shall examine these two conclusions, and their moral premise as they relate to the general defence known in the criminal law as the 'balance-of-evils' defence, a defence to which the Commission attached 'central importance' in reaching its conclusions.[10]

II. THE RETROSPECTIVE QUESTION: WAS TORTURE EVER JUSTIFIED UNDER THE DEFENCE OF NECESSITY?

A. Necessity and the Balance of Evils

1. The Nature and Rationale of the Defence   In pursuing the question of the liability of GSS interrogators for past acts, I shall confine myself to criminal liability. I do this because both civil and criminal liability turn largely on the interpretation given to the defence of necessity, and, although there is a defence of necessity in tort law, the literature about it is not nearly so well developed as it is about the criminal law defence of necessity.[11]

---

[5] Landau Commission Report at 61.   [6] Id.   [7] Id. at 60.
[8] Id. at 91.   [9] Id. at 82.   [10] Id. at 83.
[11] On the defence of necessity generally, see Leo Katz, *Bad Acts and Guilty Minds* (Chicago: University of Chicago Press, 1987), at 8–81; George Fletcher, *Rethinking Criminal Law* (Boston: Little, Brown, 1978), 774–98; Glanville Williams, *Criminal Law—The General Part* (London, 2nd edn., 1961), at 722–46; Joshua Dressler, *Understanding Criminal Law* (Mathew Bender, 1987), at 249–57; Arnolds and Garland, 'The Defence of Necessity in Criminal Law: The Right to Choose the Lesser Evil', *Journal of Criminal Law and Criminology* Vol. 65 (1974), 289–301; Glazebrook, 'The Necessity Plea in English Criminal Law', *Cambridge Law Journal*, Vol. 30 (1972), 87–119; Tiffany and Anderson, 'Legislating the Necessity Defence in

Section 22 of Israel's Penal Law contains Israel's version of the criminal law defence of necessity. It provides:

A person may be exempted from criminal responsibility for an act or omission if he can show that it was done or made in order to avoid consequences which could not otherwise be avoided and which would have inflicted grievous harm or injury on his person, honour, or property or on the person or honour of others whom he was bound to protect or on property placed in his charge: provided that he did no more than was reasonably necessary for that purpose and that the harm caused by him was not disproportionate to the harm avoided.[12]

A number of preliminary remarks may help to locate this defence within the law of crimes. First, it is a *defence*. It is not part of the prosecution's prima facie case. The prima facie case against a GSS investigator employing *Nafsu*-like methods of interrogation against some suspect might be for assault, battery, or the more specific crime of using force or violence against a person for the purpose of extracting from him a confession or information.[13] The *actus reus* and *mens rea* requirements of such crimes should usually be satisfied in cases like Nafsu's, so that it is only by a defence like necessity that a GSS investigator may escape liability.[14]

Second, necessity provisions should be regarded as justification defences, not excuse defences. The precise borders of what is a justification and what is an excuse are a matter of some debate in current moral and criminal law theory.[15] As set forth in chapter 1, a

Criminal Law', *Denver Law Journal*, Vol. 52 (1975), 839–79; Comment, 'Necessity Defined: A New Role in the Criminal Defense System', *UCLA Law Review*, Vol. 29 (1981), 409–46.

[12] Penal Law, 1977 (LSI Special Volume), s. 22.   [13] Ibid., s. 277.

[14] That arguments of necessity enter a criminal trial only as matters of defence is not as obvious as it may seem. Both the *actus reus* and *mens rea* elements of the prosecution's prima facie case may have hidden necessity-like requirements in them. In construing what *acts* are prohibited by a criminal statute, courts will often go against the plain meaning of statutory language in order to exempt desirable violations of the statute. See, e.g., *Kirby* v. *United States*, 74 US (7 Wall.) 482 (1868) (literal obstructing of the federal mails held not to be an 'obstructing' within the meaning of the statute when done to effect the arrest of a federal mail carrier wanted for murder); see generally Moore, 'The Semantics of Judging', *Southern California Law Review*, Vol. 54 (1981), 151–294; Glanville Williams, *Criminal Law*, *supra* n. 11, at 724–8. Likewise, in considering what *mental states* suffice for the *mens rea* requirements of recklessness or negligence, courts consider only risk-takings that are *unjustified*. See, e.g., Model Penal Code, s. 2.02(2)(c) and (d).

[15] See Fletcher, *Rethinking, supra* n. 1, at 759, 762, 799–800–11; Dressler, *Understanding, supra* n. 11, at 179; Kent Greenawalt, 'The Perplexing Borders of Justification and Excuse', *Columbia Law Review*, Vol. 84 (1984), 1897–927.

justification shows that prima facie wrongful and unlawful conduct is not wrongful or unlawful at all. For example, killing another is prima facie both wrong and unlawful, but killing another in self-defence is neither because it is a justified act.[16] By contrast, an excuse does not take away our prima facie judgement that an act is wrongful and unlawful; rather, it shows that the *actor* was not culpable in his doing of an admittedly wrongful and unlawful act. For example, killing another is both wrongful and unlawful, and it remains so when done by an insane person; but such an actor is not liable for his admittedly wrongful act because he was not culpable in his doing of it.

In some penal codes it is clear that necessity is a justification defence. For example, the American Law Institute's Model Penal Code provides:

Conduct which the actor believes to be necessary to avoid a harm or evil to himself or to another is justifiable, provided that the harm or evil sought to be avoided by such conduct is greater than that sought to be prevented by the law defining the offence charged . . .[17]

This is not the language of excuse, for no mention is made of the actor's diminished capacities or impaired opportunities to make the right choices; rather, it is the language of justification, for the defence is only available when the actor did what was on balance the right thing to do (that is, he prevented more harm or evil than he caused by his action). The language of the Israeli Code is less clearly focused on justification exclusively, for it only requires that the harm caused by an actor not be 'disproportionate' to the harm he avoided by his action. While such language *might* allow for an excuse version of the defence, it certainly allows for some justification version.[18]

---

[16] Self-defence may sometimes be used as an excuse, not a justification. See *infra*, text at nn. 102–4.

[17] Model Penal Code, s. 3.02 (Proposed Official Draft, 1962).

[18] The failure of the Israeli Code to distinguish justification from excuse in its necessity provision could be due to the consensus of influential criminal law theorists in Israel that no legal consequences should attach to the distinction (that is, that a defendant and those who aid or resist him are equally liable or exempt from punishment no matter whether the defendant claims necessity as a justification or necessity as an excuse). See Gur-Arye, 'Should the Criminal Law Distinguish Between Necessity as a Justification and Necessity as an Excuse?', *Law Quarterly Review*, Vol. 102 (1986), 71–89; Kremnitzer, 'Proportionality and the Psychotic Aggressor: Another View', *Israel Law Review*, Vol. 18 (1983), 178–214, at 196–9. One can believe this and yet believe that it is crucial to recognize the distinction when one analyses provisions such as s. 22, for the criminal law mirrors morality here and in morality the distinction is basic.

Third, necessity provisions are usually catch-all justificatory provisions. That is, most penal codes make available specific defences for justifications such as self-defence, defence of others, defence of property, use of force in law enforcement, and the like. These more specific defences capture the most recurrent situations in which one person is justified in using force against the person or property of another. General necessity provisions stand behind these more specific provisions in the sense that they allow a defence in any of the infinitely various circumstances that may arise whereby violating the criminal code is the right thing to do (i.e., it is justified) because the alternatives were all worse. Violating the traffic laws to get an injured person to the hospital and burning several houses to create a fire-break needed to save a city from fire, are common examples.

The rationale behind such open-ended, justificatory defences as section 22 should by now be apparent. Any criminal code should allow punishment only where it can establish moral blameworthiness. Such moral blameworthiness, in turn, can only be established where an actor was neither justified nor excused in his actions. Yet the situations that may justify an actor in doing something otherwise criminal are so various that no set of specific justificatory defences can describe them all—'fact is richer than diction', as one ordinary language philosopher once put the point. Hence, the need for the open-ended, justification defence of section 22: to capture all those situations of justified behaviour not recurrent enough to warrant a specific defence for them.

2. The Fusion of the Legal and Moral Issues: The Moral Knowledge Needed to Apply the Defence   In light of the necessarily broad language used in provisions like section 22, the Commission's observation that 'this statutory provision has to be filled with interpretive content . . .'[19] is something of an understatement. When an actor such as a GSS investigator attempts to apply such a provision to his own contemplated behaviour, or when a court applies such a provision to behaviour already done, it should be clear that at least one kind of moral knowledge must be applied. The actor and the court that judges him must know what is good and bad, beneficial and harmful, and it must know comparatively what sorts of things are *worse* than others. Actors and courts need nothing less than the

[19] *Landau Report, supra* n. 1, at 53.

ability to rank-order quite different states of affairs from worst to best in order to judge whether some action produced more harm than good (and so was not justified) or produced more good than harm (and so was justified).

This kind of moral knowledge is required not only of *courts* seeking to apply the defence of necessity to situations like the *Nafsu* case. *Citizens* also must make the balance of evils required by this defence, and they must get the balance right if they are to avail themselves of the defence. One sees this last point in light of the differential treatment accorded mistakes of fact versus mistakes of value under the defence.[20] Citizens who believe they are justified because of certain erroneous factual beliefs may nonetheless use the defence; citizens who believe that they are justified because of certain erroneous value judgements may not use the defence.

The reliance on this kind of moral knowledge by the law is familiar in contexts other than the necessity defence.[21] In judging whether an action is negligent or reckless in either criminal law and torts, it is not enough to show that that action posed a significant risk of harm to others or that the actor was consciously aware of such a risk. In addition, the taking of the risk must be unjustified, that is, the consequence of not doing the action (and thus, not taking the risk) must be less bad than the harm risked.[22] One must, that is, 'balance the evils' to decide whether an act is negligent or reckless.

It should thus be obvious that the balance of evils or necessity defence calls for the application of moral knowledge of the familiar kind I have described. Less obvious is whether the defence does not also call for a second kind of moral knowledge in addition to the knowledge of what are better and worse states of affairs. Consider the following example, familiar in philosophy and legal

---

[20] See J. Dressler, *Understanding*, *supra* n. 11, at 251–3. It is this feature of the law of necessity that rules out any argument by terrorists that prevention of their future acts of terror is not a good consequence that may justify GSS torture. Terrorists may sincerely believe that their killing of innocent civilians is not wrong but right because it produces more good in the long run. They are just as incorrect in that belief as would be a GSS interrogator who believes that torturing an innocent child can be justified by the good consequences in the long run. The defence of necessity protects in neither case such moral error.

[21] See Michael Moore, *Law and Psychiatry: Rethinking the Relationship* (Cambridge: Cambridge University Press, 1984), at 83–4.

[22] See *supra* n. 14.

theory for the past twenty years.[23] S is a surgeon who, among other things, performs organ transplant operations. He has five patients, all on the verge of death for want of a vital organ. One needs a heart, two need one lung each, and two need a kidney apiece. V is a patient of S's who is perfectly healthy, visiting S only for an annual check-up. May S kill V in order to harvest V's organs, claiming as defence that he was justified by effecting a net saving of four lives?

Most people have a firm moral intuition that the answer to this question must be 'no', that it is not morally permissible in such a case to justify a prima facie wrongful action by the good consequences it produces. If this is true, and if there are other cases where good consequences cannot justify a prima facie wrongful action, then a second kind of moral knowledge is needed in order to be *morally* justified in doing some prima facie wrongful action. Needed is some moral knowledge of when good consequences may be used in justification, and when they may not. Needed is what I shall call knowledge of the proper domain for consequential calculation. When is the common saying that the 'end cannot justify the means' applicable, and when is it not?

One might think that this is only a moral problem, not a problem for applying the legal defence of necessity. After all, there is nothing in the language of either section 22 of Israel's Penal Law or of section 3.02 of the Model Penal Code that requires that this second kind of moral knowledge be utilized in applying this defence. Compare both provisions to that of Germany, whose penal code restricts the necessity defence by the requirement that the 'act be an appropriate means'.[24] As construed by George Fletcher, 'the principle of "appropriate means" signals absolute restraints on pursuing utility maximization'.[25] Put in my language,

[23] Philippa Foot, 'The Problem of Abortion and the Doctrine of Double Effect', *Oxford Review*, Vol. 5 (1967), 5–15, reprinted in Foot, *Virtues and Vices* (Oxford: Oxford University Press, 1981); Sanford Kadish, 'Respect for Life and Regard for Rights in the Criminal Law', *California Law Review*, Vol. 64 (1976), 871–901, reprinted in Kadish, *Blame and Punishment* (New York: Macmillan, 1987); Harris, 'The Survival Lottery', *Philosophy*, Vol. 50 (1975), 81–7; Thomson, 'Killing, Letting Die, and the Trolley Problem', *The Monist*, Vol. 59 (1976), 204–17, and Thomson, 'The Trolley Problem', *Yale Law Journal*, Vol. 94 (1985), 1395–415 (both trolley articles are reprinted in J. Thomson, *Rights, Restitution, and Risk* (Cambridge, Mass.: Harvard University Press, 1986); L. Katz, *Bad Acts*, *supra* n. 11, at 35 (subsequent references to these articles are to the reprinted versions).

[24] St GG, s. 34.   [25] Fletcher, *Rethinking*, *supra* n. 11, at 788.

under German law there are some acts so wrong that even very good consequences cannot justify them.

Yet I doubt that there is the contrast between German and American law on this point that Fletcher suggests. Even without the 'appropriate means' language of the German code, and despite the clearly utilitarian leanings of the drafters of Model Penal Code section 3.02,[26] American law does not justify acts like that of my hypothetical surgeon. As Sanford Kadish has observed, there are some acts:

fairly within the net-saving-of-lives, lesser evil doctrines that it is very doubtful courts would sanction—for example, killing a person to obtain his organs to save the lives of several other people, or even removing them for that purpose against his will without killing him. The unreadiness of the law to justify such aggression against non-threatening bystanders reflects a moral uneasiness with reliance on a utilitarian calculus for assessing the justification of intended killings, even when a net savings of lives is achieved.[27]

Kadish too notices that our moral knowledge about what makes actions right or wrong to do is not exhausted by calculating the good versus bad consequences of those actions. It is this second, non-consequentialist kind of moral knowledge that gives rise to the 'moral uneasiness' Kadish notices, a moral uneasiness as much a part of American law as is the consequentialist calculation itself.

Israel's section 22 should be read analogously. Although lacking any explicit language restricting the domain for consequential justification to actions that are 'appropriate means', section 22 cannot be read to justify the harvesting of organs from one to save two or more. This, because Israel too seeks a criminal law that reflects its fundamental moral beliefs. One of those beliefs is that the end, no matter how good, does not justify the use of any means to achieve it.

Another temptation to be resisted here is the following. It might be thought that there is no 'second kind of moral knowledge'

---

[26] The utilitarian and consequentialist flavour of the reasoning behind s. 3.02 of the Model Penal Code is accurately reflected in a student Note, 'Justification: The Impact of the Model Penal Code on Statutory Reform', Columbia Law Review, Vol. 75 (1975), 914–62, at 921–8. See also Kent Greenawalt, 'Violence—Legal Justification and Moral Appraisal', Emory Law Journal, Vol. 32 (1983), 437–97, at 465.

[27] S. Kadish, 'Respect for Life', supra n. 23, at 123. Compare the seemingly contrary assumption of G. Fletcher, Rethinking, supra n. 11, at 787–8, G. Williams, Criminal Law, supra n. 11, at 729, and Greenawalt, 'Violence', supra n. 26.

needed to apply the necessity defence. Rather, this view would continue, the only knowledge needed is consequentialist in nature; but the notion of what is a good or a bad consequence needs to be enriched. In my surgeon hypothetical, for example, the net savings of lives is a good consequence, but overlooked is a very bad consequence of killing V: V did not just lose his life (as he might, say, in an avalanche); he was *murdered*, and any full balance of the evils must take this very evil consequence into account. When that consequence is factored in, this line of thought concludes, it will show that the surgeon did not achieve 'the lesser evil' by his killing V, even though he did effect a net saving of four lives. Thus, the only moral knowledge needed here is knowledge of good and bad consequences—recognizing that what is good and bad is not simply a function of harms people suffer but also of the moral rights they have that are violated, the moral duties others have that are violated, etc.

Leo Katz in his fine first book on criminal law theory takes this line on the necessity defence.[28] Finding that the hypothetical surgeon clearly may not kill one to harvest the organs needed to save five, Katz concludes:

It would be wrong to say that a person is free to kill whenever he brings about a net savings of lives . . . Fortunately, the principle of necessity is more flexible than the argument of numbers out of which it grew: Applying that principle, we would probably conclude that in this case [the case of the surgeon] 'the harm or evil sought to be avoided' is not 'greater than that sought to be prevented by the law defining the offense charged'.[29]

Yet this interpretation of the defence of necessity is unacceptable. Consider the following variation of the surgeon hypothetical. Susan is a surgeon who performs transplant operations, harvesting organs from healthy victims whenever it is necessary to do so to effect a net saving of lives. Susan in the near future will harvest such organs from five healthy patients in order to save more than five dying patients. Sharon is another surgeon who knows this and knows that the only way to prevent this is to kill Susan's husband while he is on the operating table before Sharon. (Susan's husband has just been rushed in to Sharon for an emergency operation; Susan is so attached to her husband that she will not be able to carry on for

---

[28] L. Katz, *Bad Acts*, *supra* n. 11. Katz has subsequently surrendered the point.
[29] Ibid., at 35.

some time after his death.) Sharon also has several dying patients, and should Sharon kill Susan's husband Sharon would use the latter's organs to save as many patients as possible. If killing a patient to harvest his organs is such a great evil, may Sharon perpetrate that very evil in order to prevent even more of it from being done at the hands of someone else such as Susan?

Someone accepting Katz's interpretation of the necessity defence is committed to allowing Sharon to kill Susan's husband and to use that person's organs to save others. For notice that the very same moral view that makes Sharon's act so evil guarantees that the evil Sharon seeks to avoid—Susan's very same type of action, except done five times over—is much greater.[30] In other words, Sharon would be justified on Katz's view by having balanced the evils correctly. Yet I doubt that Katz or anyone else wishes to say that Sharon's act is justified. Sharon should be allowed the necessity defence no more than Susan, should Susan go ahead and harvest organs through murder. Both have violated a moral restriction on the means they may use, a restriction that is not reducible to some consequentialist calculation, no matter how sophisticated.

B. Various Moral Theories About When Good Consequences Justify Otherwise Evil Actions

My two surgeon hypotheticals are only designed to get one's intuitions in play, intuitions pointing to the need for a second kind of moral knowledge in applying the necessity defence to actual cases. We now need to examine the large moral issue actually involved to sort in a more systematic way the possible answers to my question of whether there are two kinds of moral knowledge needed here. Distinguishing between four sorts of moral theories frames the large moral issue I wish to examine. I shall discuss three in this section, paving the way for a detailed exposition of a fourth in the following section.

1. Act-Consequentialist Moral Theories
Someone who is an act-consequentialist in his moral theory will believe that there is no second kind of moral knowledge needed to apply the necessity defence, for an act-consequentialist judges the rightness (justifiabil-

---

[30] The general form of the argument in the text is pursued with great clarity by Samuel Scheffler, *The Rejection of Consequentialism* (Berkeley: University of California Press, 1982), 87–93, 98–101.

ity) of any action by one criterion only: does the act produce better consequences than any alternative action reasonably available to the agent?[31] *Any* act, be it torture, murder, rape, or whatever, may be done, on this view, if a net of good over bad results from it.

One problem with assessing this view is that by itself, it does not say very much. It only says: whatever is good, maximize it by your actions. Quite different versions of act-consequentialism can be produced by varying what it is that is thought to be good. One historically important variant here is act-utilitarianism. A utilitarian theory of the good holds that the only good state of affairs (to be maximized by the consequentialist principle) is the happiness, pleasure, preference satisfaction—or, more generally, welfare—of persons, each counting for one but only one (in Bentham's famous phrase). Specifically not included in the utilitarian theory of the good are states such as the state of moral rights not being violated, moral duties being done, moral virtues being realized. Only to the extent that people prefer these states does the utilitarian factor them into his calculus.

The problem with this utilitarian form of act-consequentialism has been stated many times. Consider Sam Scheffler's version of the objection:

[S]uppose that your country is waging a just war, and that an enemy agent you have captured tells you that he has planted a bomb in an area crowded with civilians and that, unless defused, it will soon go off, killing many people. Suppose that there is not enough time to conduct a general search for the bomb, and that all of your attempts to get the agent to reveal its location are unsuccessful. Suppose, however, that you have captured him with his family, and that by torturing his small child in front of him you could eventually destroy his resolve and get him to give you the information. Utilitarianism seems to imply not only that you may but that you *must* torture the child. These implications and others like them strike many people as entirely unacceptable.[32]

Whether one finds such implications unacceptable is one of the watershed questions the answer to which says a great deal about

---

[31] For this characterization of act-consequentialism, see Bernard Williams's contribution to J. J. C. Smart and Bernard Williams, *Utilitarianism: For and Against* (Berkeley: University of California Press, 1973), 86.

[32] Scheffler, 'Introduction', in Samuel Scheffler, ed., *Consequentialism and Its Critics* (Oxford: Oxford University Press, 1988), at 3.

the kind of morality to which one subscribes. For if the answer is no, that torture in these circumstances is morally right (and thus, legally justified), then one is probably a utilitarian as well as a consequentialist. For you would probably be saying that neither the rights of the innocent child, nor the virtue of his torturers, are of any weight in calculating the consequences of torturing the child. What does count as a bad consequence is the pain inflicted on the child, and, secondly, on his relatives and any others empathizing with him. Also counting as a bad consequence may be the preferences of many of your countrymen that what *they* see as the child's moral rights not be violated. But these are costs that can be outweighed by the good you are producing, the net welfare of saving many lives. A plausible application of the utilitarian version of act-consequentialism is thus to torture the innocent child.

I find this conclusion to be morally repugnant. No one should torture innocent children—even when done to produce a sizeable gain in aggregate welfare. Nor should a state allow such practices. As the Landau Commission observed:

the methods of police interrogation which are employed in any given regime are a faithful mirror of the character of the entire regime . . . All the more so with respect to the interrogation methods of a security service, which is always in danger of sliding towards methods practiced in regimes which we abhor.[33]

If I had been a Soviet citizen, to continue this example, I would have been deeply ashamed that the security force that acted in my name (the KGB) castrated and killed an innocent Arab who happened to be the brother of one of the terrorists who had kidnapped Soviet diplomats—even though that act brought about the release of the kidnapped diplomats and may well have prevented their deaths.

What this shows is that I am not a utilitarian in my theory of what are good and bad states of affairs. What it does not yet show is that I am not a consequentialist. For one might reject the utilitarian's exclusively welfarist notions of the good without abandoning the consequentialist principle that the right action is one that maximizes the good. One might, like Leo Katz discussed earlier,[34]

---

[33] *Landau Report, supra* n. 1, at 77.

[34] See the discussion about Katz earlier, text at nn. 28–9. For more general defences of non-utilitarian consequentialisms, see Tim Scanlon, 'Rights, Goals, and

enrich one's theory of the good to include non-welfarist notions like rights-violations as bad, duty-keepings as good. And one might use such a theory to say that the violation of an innocent child's right not to be tortured is so bad that it is not outweighed by the saving of many innocent lives.

One might. But no one on reflection should hold such a moral theory, for at least two reasons. One is the lack of any plausible account of why non-welfarist bads like killings and torturing, on the one hand, are so much worse than the corresponding welfarist bads such as naturally occurring deaths or pains, on the other.[35] Is it significantly a worse death if one is murdered than if one dies by accident (stipulating that in each case the death is painless and without forewarning)? So much worse that it would be impermissible for us to prevent an accidental death but not a murder, when we can only prevent one but not both? Answering both of these questions affirmatively is required by the non-utilitarian, consequentialist moral theory here considered; and such answers do not seem very plausible.

The second problem for this non-utilitarian consequentialism stems from the kind of example we considered before with the surgeon. Even if a murderous death is so much worse than an accidental death, murder on this theory is still the right thing to do if it is the only way to prevent two or more murders by someone else. Even if torturing an innocent person is so much worse than that person suffering identical pain by accident, torture of the innocent on this theory is still the right thing to do if it is the only way to prevent the torture of two or more innocents by someone else. On the non-utilitarian, consequentialist theory under consideration, in other words, the KGB might well have done the right thing in castrating and killing the brother of the Arab terrorist if they were right in their calculation that this act, bad as it was, was necessary to prevent more acts of the same kind being done to Soviet diplomats.

For both of these reasons one might well reject even this more moralistic form of act-consequentialism. For it is not moralistic

Fairness', in S. Hampshire, ed., *Public and Private Morality* (Cambridge: Cambridge University Press, 1978), reprinted in *Consequentialism and Its Critics, supra* n. 32, at 74–92, and Sen, 'Rights and Agency', *Philosophy and Public Affairs*, Vol. 11 (1982), 3–39, reprinted in *Consequentialism and Its Critics, supra* n. 32, at 187–223.

[35] See Scheffler, *supra* n. 30, at 109; Thomas Nagel, *The View from Nowhere* (New York: Oxford University Press, 1986), at 178.

enough in its implications for behaviour such as torturing the inno-cent.[36] If one agrees with this insight, the most natural move is to adopt some non-consequentialist moral theory. Before I consider such theories, however, a softened form of consequentialism needs brief mention.

2. Rule-Consequentialist Moral Theories   A traditional move[37] within consequentialist moral theory to avoid the unwanted conclusion that it is not only permissible but obligatory sometimes to torture an inno-cent child, is to adopt some version of rule-consequentialism. An acceptable definition of rule-consequentialism for our purposes is given by Gerald Barnes:

An act is right if and only if it conforms with an ideal set of rules; an ideal set of rules is any set of rules such that if everyone always did, from among the things he could do, what conformed with that set of rules, then at least as much good would be produced as by everyone's always conforming with any other set of rules.[38]

As Barnes's definition makes clear, the rule-consequentialist envi-sions a two-step procedure for any moral decision: first, you decide what the right rule is that you should adopt for your own and others' behaviour; second, when confronting a particular moral dilemma, you resolve it by simply applying the rule. Consequentialist calculation enters in only at the first of these two stages of decision. That is, you decide what is the *right rule* to adopt in light of the max-imally good consequences that would attend from universal obedi-ence to that rule; but you decide what is the *right act* to do simply by applying the right rule, not by re-engaging in consequentialist cal-culations.

As applied to Scheffler's example of torturing the innocent child of a terrorist in order to extract vital information from the terror-

---

[36] One might also reject act-consequentialism on the strictly consequentialist ground that if followed as a guide to moral decisions by individual agents it would not in fact produce the best consequences. See Donald Regan, *Utilitarianism and Cooperation* (Oxford: Oxford University Press, 1980), 12–53.

[37] See, e.g., J. Smart and B. Williams, *Utilitarianism, supra* n. 31, at 118–35.

[38] Barnes, 'Utilitarianisms', *Ethics*, Vol. 82 (1971), 57–64. On the different vari-eties of rule-consequentialism, and problems with each, see Richard Brandt, 'Toward a Credible Form of Utilitarianism', in Baruch Brody, ed., *Moral Rules and Particular Circumstances* (Englewood Cliffs, N.J.: Prentice-Hall, 1970); David Lyons, 'Utility and Rights', in Jeremy Waldron, ed., *Theories of Rights* (Oxford: Oxford University Press, 1984); Scanlon, 'Rights, Goals, and Fairness', *supra* n. 34, at 74.

ist, a rule-consequentialist might say that the right rule to adopt is, 'never torture an innocent', even though he recognizes that once in a great while sufficiently good consequences would follow from such torture that, if he were allowed to calculate the consequences, individual acts of torture could be justified on consequentialist grounds. He might say this for a variety of reasons: because individual consequential calculations are factually difficult, error possible, and systematic error in the direction of too much torture rather than too little probable; because individual consequential calculations are time-consuming, time is itself a cost, and the gains achievable by calculating on each occasion to find the exceptional cases when torture is desirable are outweighed by the costs of calculation; because torture harms the character of those who do it or know of it and do not prevent it, no matter that it is done only when necessary to extract vital information, and such damage to generally desirable dispositions is a cost that will always outweigh the good consequences achievable in the few cases where torture of the innocent could otherwise be justified. For any of these reasons, a rule-consequentialist would conclude, the right rule is, 'never torture the innocent', and the right behaviour of GSS interrogators is simply to apply this rule without themselves attempting to determine whether in the particular situation they would cause more good than harm by torturing the innocent.

In some such way the rule-consequentialist attempts to soften the apparently immoral implications of consequentialist moral theory. There are two problems, however, for this softened form of consequentialism. One is Kant's worry that even if consequential calculations justify the right rule they do not do so for the right reason.[39] Such calculations make contingent what we experience as categorical. 'Never torture the innocent' can be a rule justified on both consequentialist and non-consequentialist grounds; but only the latter mode of justification squares with how we feel about such absolutes, which is *not* that they are dependent on complicated calculations of consequences that easily could come out the other way (i.e., in favour of some torture of the innocent).

[39] I. Kant, *Groundwork of the Metaphysic of Morals*, J. H. Paton, trans. (New York: Harper, 1964). As Tom Nagel captures this Kantian insight: 'No doubt it is a good thing for people to have a deep inhibition against torturing children even for very strong reasons, and the same might be said of the other deontological constraints. But that does not explain why we find it almost impossible to regard it as a merely useful inhibition.' Nagel, *View*, *supra* n. 35, at 179.

The second problem with rule-consequentialism is that it seems irrational (in its own consequentialist terms) when applied as a decision procedure for individual acts of decision. If the rightness of action is ultimately a function of achieving the maximally good consequences available to the agent in that situation—which is what *any* consequentialist believes—then sometimes an agent ought to violate what he himself admits is the right rule. Suppose, for example, a GSS interrogator was certain about the immediately relevant facts in Scheffler's hypothetical—he knows there is a bomb, that it will kill innocents unless found and dismantled, that the only way to find it is to torture the child of the terrorist who planted it. Suppose further he is already in possession of this information, and the costs of calculating utility are thus already 'sunk'; suppose further that he himself is about to die and that he can keep his action secret, so that the long-term bad consequences stemming from his own or others' corruption of character will be minimal. In such a case, adhering to the best rule will not be best, on consequentialist grounds. Adhering to the rule in such circumstances would be mere 'rule-worship' as one well-known consequentialist has described it.[40]

For both of these reasons it is difficult to accept rule-consequentialist theories of morality. Try as they might, they cannot accommodate either the content or the categorical nature of moral norms like 'never torture an innocent child'. Logically, one is of course free to reject such moral norms instead of rejecting consequentialism. That, however, is an easier option to contemplate academically than it is to live with as one's morality.[41]

3. A Simple Absolutist View: Never Torture   If one gives up the attempt to sophisticate consequentialist theories so that they seem less immoral in what they would permit, then one's moral theory

---

[40] Smart, in J. Smart and B. Williams, *Utilitarianism, supra* n. 31, at 44. For the same criticism, see Peter Railton, 'Alienation, Consequentialism, and the Demands of Morality', *Philosophy and Public Affairs*, Vol. 13 (1984), 134–71, reprinted in *Consequentialism and Its Critics, supra* n. 32.

[41] Jack Smart's willingness to embrace consequentialism even at the cost of giving up common sense morality's constraints, like 'never hang an innocent man', has earned Smart the following entry in *The Philosophical Lexicon* (D. Dennett and K. Lambert, eds., 7th edn., 1978), at 8: 'Outsmart, verb; to embrace the conclusion of one's opponent's *reductio ad absurdum* argument. (As in) "They thought they had me, but I outsmarted them. I agreed that it was sometimes just to hang an innocent man." '

will be non-consequentialist in nature. The non-consequentialist about morality denies that an action is right just because, of the alternative actions available to an agent, it is productive of the best consequences. He severs, in other words, the connection between good consequences and right action that consequentialism asserts to exist. A non-consequentialist might well say about Scheffler's example, that it is always wrong to torture an innocent child, even when doing so produces better consequences (such as less torture of the innocent) than not doing so.

It is this feature of non-consequentialist theories that gives them the sobriquet, 'agent-relative views'. Such theories view morality as consisting of norms directed to each moral agent, norms whose content says, 'don't *you* torture an innocent child'. Such norms are 'agent-relative' in the sense that they do not direct each of us to minimize bad states of affairs, such as murders and tortures. For if that were the content of moral norms, we would be justified in torturing one person ourselves whenever it would prevent the torture of many persons by others. Rather, such norms direct us not to do the forbidden acts, leaving it to others to obey or disobey such norms, as they will.

It is often thought that this view of morality's nature can only be justified within a religious tradition.[42] For religion may give one an authoritative text that can be the source of absolute norms like, 'don't kill', 'don't torture', etc. Yet Kant is a prominent example who did not think this, divorcing his morality from any religious basis. In any case, I shall not deal with these large questions here, but I shall assume that agent-relative theories of morality are no worse off with respect to their justifiability and truth than consequentialist theories.

The simplest agent-relative view—and the one most popularly called to mind when one thinks of non-consequentialist theories—is what I shall call the absolutist view of morality. On this view, the moral norms that make up morality are: (1) short and exceptionless injunctions, such as 'thou shalt not kill'; (2) 'absolute' in the sense that they cannot be violated, whatever the consequences may be of not violating them on some occasion; and (3) applicable to

---

[42] Williams, in J. Smart and B. Williams, *Utilitarianism*, *supra* n. 31, at 90. I examine this question in Moore, 'Good Without God', in Robert George and Christopher Wolfe, eds., *Liberalism, Modernity, and Natural Law* (Oxford: Oxford University Press, 1996), concluding that God does not help here.

what we indirectly cause as well as what we directly do through our actions, applicable to what we allow to happen as well as to what we make happen.

It is perhaps this view of morality that underlies Amnesty International's advocacy of a flat ban on torture in any and all circumstances. Such an absolutist view of morality may also motivate Article 5 of the Universal Declaration of Human Rights and Article 3 of the European Convention on Human Rights, both of which provide flatly that 'no one shall be subjected to torture . . .'. Such a view of morality may also have influenced the Landau Commission, which found that 'the pressure must never reach the level of physical torture . . .'[43] and approved secret guidelines for coercive interrogative techniques for the GSS that 'will be far from the use of physical or mental torture . . .'.[44] If morality consists of such absolutes as 'thou shalt not kill', it plausibly contains the norm, 'thou shalt not torture' as well.

I do not think that morality includes such an absolute, however, because I do not think that morality contains any such absolutes (i.e., norms with these three absolutist characteristics). Why moral norms must be more complex in order to be plausible I explore in the succeeding section as I lay out the more complex agent-relative view of morality I shall defend.

C. A Complex Agent-Relative View of Morality

1. When Consequences May and May Not be Calculated on Agent-Relative Theories of Morality   No agent-relative view of morality can plausibly hold that we may never calculate the consequences of various courses of action and decide what to do based on such calculations. Where moral norms are not violated by any of the actions we are considering, we are not only free but often obligated to choose our course of action by considering those consequences. When a moral theory tells us what sorts of things its norms prohibit and permit, it thus necessarily also tells us when consequences may and must be calculated—namely, wherever the norms of morality are not applicable.

Finding this permissible/mandatory realm for consequential calculation is thus largely a matter of specifying in detail the content of all the moral norms there are. This of course I shall not under-

---

[43] *Landau Report, supra* n. 1, at 53.   [44] Id. at 80.

take, although in the subsequent subsection I shall undertake to describe the content of the moral norm most relevant here, the norm forbidding torture of another. Arguably, most agent-relative theories of morality also take some systematic view on 'the kind of thing to which absolutist prohibitions can apply'.[45] I shall first examine the considerable suggestions that have been made in this regard in recent moral philosophy, and then seek to reorder these suggestions in line with what I take to be their underlying insight about when we may (not) justify our acts by their good consequences. I undertake this philosophical task in order to display the general view of morality that I think to be correct in its full complexity so that some judgement can be made as to its overall rationality. Those impatient for concrete application of my complex agent-relative view of morality to torture may wish to skip this discussion, for the bottom line of the analysis for torture is that none of these complexities, no matter how construed, makes torture permissible.

a. *Suggested Limits on Consequential Calculation*

(i) *The allowing/acting distinction*

Thirty years ago Philippa Foot suggested that there was a morally important distinction 'between what one does or causes and what one merely allows'.[46] To use one of Foot's examples: if we rescue a group of five people from torture by another, rather than rescuing one person from such torture, where we cannot rescue all, we have only *allowed* the one to be tortured by someone else; whereas if we were to torture one person in our custody to prevent another from torturing five in his custody, that would be to *do* or *cause* torture ourselves. Foot's sense was that morality places *negative* duties on us not to do or cause things like torture, whereas morality places *positive* duties on us not to allow things like torture to be done where we can prevent it. Foot's further sense was that negative duties are much stricter than merely positive duties, so that

---

[45] Thomas Nagel, 'War and Massacre', *Philosophy and Public Affairs*, Vol. 2 (1972), 123–44, reprinted in *Consequentialism and Its Critics,* op. cit. *supra* n. 32, 51–73, at 57.

[46] Foot, 'Abortion', *supra* n. 23, at 26. George Fletcher has recently urged that the Talmudic example of keeping water for oneself when there is only enough for one presupposes adherence to an acting/allowing distinction, for self-love could hardly justify taking the water from another (which would be a killing, not an allowing to die). George Fletcher, 'Defensive Force as an Act of Rescue', *Social Philosophy and Policy*, Vol. 7 (1990), 170–9.

consequential calculation could be used to justify violations of the latter but less easily be used to justify violations of the former. In the first variation of Foot's torture example, where 'we are bringing aid (rescuing people about to be tortured by the tyrant), we must obviously rescue the larger rather than the smaller group'. In other words, since we will only be *allowing* one group or the other to be tortured whatever we do, we should guide our action by a calculation of the best consequences we can bring about. By contrast, in the second variation of Foot's torture example our only way to prevent the torture of five is to torture one ourselves, and here we may not be justified by the good consequences we seek: 'To refrain from inflicting injury ourselves is a stricter duty than to prevent other people from inflicting injury . . .'.[47]

Consider a second example, not involving torture, that may help to bring out the moral force of Foot's distinction. Suppose we are on a dock and there are two groups of persons drowning in the lake below us. One person is by himself, and the other group consists of five people. Since all are about to drown, we have time only to rescue one group with the one rope on the dock. May (must) we throw the rope to the group of five, even though that means we thereby *allow* one to drown? Even if the answer to this question is 'yes', as I believe it is, may (must) we also throw the rope to save the five when the one has already seized the rope to climb to safety, and we must dislodge him to free the rope to throw it to the five? If we shake the one off the rope to his death, we have caused his death, not merely allowed it. It is much less intuitive that we may justify this violation of a negative duty not to kill by the good consequences of saving five.

(ii) *The intending/foreseeing distinction*

A much more ancient distinction, going back at least to Aquinas, focuses on the intentions with which we act.[48] There is a distinction

---

[47] Foot, 'Abortion', *supra* n. 23, at 28–9, for both variations. Sometimes Foot believes we may justify the violation of a negative duty by good consequences. She construes her famous trolley example to be of that kind, where a trolley driver is justified in driving over and thereby killing one trapped workman if the consequence of his not doing so would have been to drive over and kill five.

[48] On the doctrine of double effect, see Foot, 'Abortion', *supra* n. 23; Nagel, *View*, *supra* n. 35, at 179–80; H. L. A. Hart, 'Intention and Punishment', in *Punishment and Responsibility* (Oxford: Oxford University Press, 1968); Jonathan Bennett, 'Whatever the Consequences', *Analysis*, Vol. 26 (1966), 83–102; G. E. M. Anscombe, 'Modern Moral Philosophy', *Philosophy*, Vol. 33 (1958), 1–19; John Finnis, *Natural*

between what we intend and what we *foresee*. Suppose, to use Foot's torture example, we foresee to a certainty that the one we have to leave when we rescue five will be tortured by another. There is no sense in which we *intend* that he be tortured. His being tortured by another is neither an end of ours, nor is it a means to that which is an end, the saving of five from torture. It is only a side-effect we know will come about by our rescuing the five and leaving the one. On the other hand, were we to yield to the threat of the tyrant—that we torture one else he will torture five—we would intend to torture the one. We would not have the torture of the one as an ultimate end—our ultimate end is to save five from torture—but we would have his torture as an intended means.

The 'doctrine of double effect' of Catholic theology has long used this distinction to draw the limits of consequential calculation. Where we intend the violation of a moral absolute like 'don't torture', whether as an end or as a means, we may not justify our action by the good consequences it will produce; where we only foresee (even to a certainty) that some act will take place that will violate a moral absolute, we may use good consequences to justify our action. In Foot's torture examples the doctrine of double effect thus yields the same result as Foot's doctrine that negative duties prevail over positive duties: we may justify our leaving one knowing he will be tortured, not justify our torturing one, *intending* to do so, even though in each case our actions will produce the good consequence of saving five from torture.

(iii) *The foreseeing/risking distinction*

As Sanford Kadish has observed with regard to moral absolutes like 'don't kill', the 'consequentialist standard is most firmly in evidence when unintended killing is involved. It is revealing that the judgements in this area [of risk creation] . . . permit life to be yielded when the costs of saving it, in terms of the comforts, conveniences and satisfactions of many, seem too high'.[49]

There are actually two distinctions at work here. One is between knowing to a practical certainty that someone will die or be tortured, and knowing only that there is a substantial risk that this will be the case. This is a distinction between perceived degrees of

Law and Natural Rights (Oxford: Oxford University Press, 1980), at 118–25; Charles Fried, *Right and Wrong* (Cambridge, Mass.: Harvard University Press, 1978), at 31–2.

[49] Kadish, 'Respect for Life', *supra* n. 23, at 29.

likelihood that some wrong action will take place. The second distinction is between knowing that somebody will be killed or tortured—somebody in the sense of no one in particular but someone—and knowing that some identified person will be killed or tortured.

The force of these distinctions may be appreciated with a familiar example.[50] Statistically we know that activities such as high speed freeway transportation, tall building construction, underground coal mining, etc. cost a certain number of lives each year. Yet we do not know on any given occasion that any particular person will be killed; we only know that there is a risk to someone on each occasion of driving, construction, mining, etc. In such circumstances we have no trouble at all in justifying the risk taken in terms of the undesirable consequences attendant upon lowering it—consequences such as higher transportation, construction, or mining costs. Consequential calculation, as Kadish observes, reigns supreme in such circumstances.

Our attitude changes considerably, however, when we deal with a trapped truck driver, construction worker, or miner. Now we know who is at risk, and we know the risk of death is a near certainty unless we act. Now consequential calculation seems much less acceptable. 'Save him whatever the cost' is much more descriptive of our attitude. One might thus think that one of the markers of the domain for consequential calculation is the distinction between risk to someone versus certain harm to some particular one: we may calculate the consequences to justify our action (or inaction) in the former case but not in the latter.

(iv) *The victim-in-peril/victim-not-in-peril distinction*
It is commonly thought that it matters (for purposes of permissible calculation of the consequences) whether the victim of our action was already in peril anyway. Abortion, for example, is often thought to be an easier decision when doing nothing will result in the death of both the foetus and the mother than when doing nothing will only result in the death of the mother. For in the former case but not the latter the victim of the abortive procedure—the foetus—will die anyway. It is here that the Catholic doctrine of

[50] See generally Charles Fried, *An Anatomy of Values*, Part III (Cambridge, Mass.: Harvard University Press, 1970).

double effect operates least intuitively for it prohibits killing the foetus equally in both cases.[51]

Some would thus substitute for the doctrine of double effect the following principle: when the victim of your proposed action is already in peril of suffering the harm you are contemplating inflicting, you may be justified in going ahead if the consequences (such as saving the mother) are sufficiently good; but where the victim is not in such peril, you are absolutely forbidden to inflict such injury upon him, no matter what the consequences.

Moral theory and criminal law commentary are both rich in examples that implicitly employ this principle. The official commentary to the Model Penal Code section 3.02 on the balance-of-evils defence explicitly approves application of that defence to the situation where a mountaineer must cut the rope holding him to his fallen companion else both, rather than one, will fall to their death.[52] Similarly, in situations of shipwreck two men who simultaneously come upon a plank sufficient to float only one of them may each with justification fend off the other; for whoever is the victim is already in peril of drowning.[53] Whereas where one has already seized the plank (and thus removed himself from the peril of drowning), others may not thrust him off the plank to save themselves.[54]

The most famous application of the defence of necessity in the criminal law, the nineteenth-century lifeboat cases, also belong in this category.[55] In *Holmes*, the lifeboat was too heavily laden to

[51] See Foot, 'Abortion', *supra* n. 23, at 30.

[52] Model Penal Code s. 3.02, Comments at 8 (Tent. Draft No. 8, 1958): 'So too a mountaineer, roped to a companion who has fallen over a precipice, who holds on as long as possible but eventually cuts the rope, must certainly be granted the defense that he accelerated one death slightly but avoided the only alternative, the certain death of both.' For a real life example of this situation, see Joe Simpson, *Touching the Void* (New York: Harper and Row, 1988).

[53] The example is an ancient one, to be found in both Bacon and Kant. Justice Holmes's version was: 'If a man is on a plank in the deep sea which will only float one, and a stranger lays hold of it, he will thrust him off if he can.' O. W. Holmes, *The Common Law* (Boston: Little, Brown, 1881), at 47. See the treatment of the plank hypothetical in I. Kant, *Metaphysical Elements of Justice*, J. Ladd, trans. (1965), at 41–2. See generally Williams, *Criminal Law*, *supra* n. 11, at 738.

[54] At least, they would not be *justified* in thrusting him off in these circumstances (see Fletcher, 'Defensive Force', *supra* n. 46); they might be excused, however. (See Bacon, *Maxims*, reg. 25.)

[55] *R* v. *Dudley and Stephens* (1884) 14 QBD 273; *United States* v. *Holmes*, 226 Fed. Cas. 360 (3d Cir. 1842). For commentary on these famous cases, see A. W. B. Simpson, *Cannibalism and the Common Law* (Oxford: Oxford University

stay afloat so the defendant lightened it by throwing some of the passengers overboard. In *Dudley and Stephens* the lifeboat was inadequately provisioned, so two of the crew killed another so that they could survive by eating his flesh and blood. Those critical of the courts' convictions in those cases often ground their criticism on the principle mentioned above. As Glanville Williams characterizes these cases, 'there is no choice as to who is to die; the only choice is how many are to die'.[56] The victim already being in peril makes these cases much easier to decide for the defendants than they would have been in the absence of this feature:

[T]he act of killing B may be of either of two kinds. B's death may be slightly accelerated, in the sense that, had A done nothing, B would still have died shortly afterwards. Or B may be deprived by the killing of what would probably have been a number of years of life; in other words, but for the killing he would have been safe. A killing of the former type can obviously be regarded much more leniently than the latter . . .[57]

(v) *The distinction between redirecting old threats and creating new threats*

Due to two influential articles by Judith Thomson many have come to accept what she calls a 'distribution exemption' from the absolutist prohibitions of morality.[58] As she herself describes this 'exemption': we can 'make be a threat to fewer what is already a threat to more'.[59] In other words, we can justify killing or torturing a few with the good consequences of preventing thereby the deaths or tortures of many when the manner in which we kill or torture is only to redirect a pre-existing threat not of our own making. We cannot justify such actions, even by the good consequences of saving many, when the manner in which we kill or torture is to create a new threat to our victims.

Examples speak with greater clarity than generalizations here. Consider three examples. The first is Thomson's own example where we stand at the switch of a railroad junction.[60] We see a run-

Press, 1984); Fuller, 'The Case of the Speluncean Explorers', *Harvard Law Review*, Vol. 62 (1949), 616–45; Katz, *Bad Acts, supra* n. 11, at 8–62.

[56] Williams, *Criminal Law, supra* n. 11, at 744. See also the Model Penal Code, Commentary, quoted *supra* n. 52.

[57] Williams, *Criminal Law, supra* n. 11, at 739.

[58] Thomson, 'Killing, Letting Die', and 'Trolley Problem', both in her *Rights, supra* n. 23.

[59] Ibid., at 108.

[60] Ibid., at 96.

away trolley car which we cannot stop; we can only direct it out to one of two tracks by pulling the switch beside us. If we do not pull the switch, the trolley will continue on the main track killing five trapped workmen; if we pull the switch, we will direct the trolley onto a spur track on which there is only one trapped workman. Thomson urges that we may (and perhaps even must) pull the switch, because in doing so we are only redirecting the pre-existing threat presented by the runaway trolley.

A second example comes from World War II, where British counter-intelligence had penetrated the German intelligence network in England that was responsible for calling in the accuracy of the German rockets aimed for London.[61] The British discussed whether they might not feed into the German intelligence system slightly inaccurate reports on rocket hits, thereby redirecting the German rockets from more populous central London to less populous outlying areas north of London. Had the British done this, Thomson's principle would have approved it, for their act would only have been one of redirecting a pre-existing threat, and thus allowed the consequential calculation about a net savings of British lives.

A third example is provided by the official commentary to Model Penal Code section 3.02.[62] Suppose, the Code drafters tell us, we were at the side of a dyke during the time of quickly rising flood waters. If we do nothing, the dike will hold, diverting the waters downstream where a city will be flooded with great loss of life. Alternatively, if we blow up the dyke, the flood waters will be averted onto a farm below us, killing all of its inhabitants. The drafters of the Code make clear that if we blow the dyke and kill the inhabitants of the farm, we will be justified (by the net savings of lives) because we have only averted a pre-existing threat that was going to kill someone.

In each case what seems to matter is that our actions only redirect a pre-existing threat. To confirm this, contrast these three examples with the following three variations: (1) we start a trolley to run over one, because unless we do so another will kill five; (2) we (like Truman in World War II) bomb two towns killing 150,000 inhabitants, in order to induce the surrender of Japan and to

---

[61] J. Glover, *Causing Death and Saving Lives* (London: Penguin, 1977), at 102. See also Katz, *Bad Acts, supra* n. 11, at 34.
[62] Model Penal Code s. 3.02, Comments at 8 (Tent. Draft No. 8, 1958).

prevent the loss of the millions of Japanese and American lives that would result from an invasion of the home islands;[63] (3) we start a flood by blowing up a dam in order to kill the inhabitants of a farm, because unless we do so a terrorist will blow up an entire city with a hidden nuclear device. In each of these last three examples, the same net savings of lives will be effected by our actions as in the three previous examples. Yet we may think this consequentialist consideration to be of less relevance or significance in the second set of examples than in the first. Such a difference, Thomson urges, is explained by her principle about creating new, versus redistributing old, threats: good consequences justify only when we redistribute a threat, not when we create a new one to some victim(s).

(vi) *The distinction between one's own and others' projects*

Bernard Williams has urged that there is an important 'distinction between my killing someone, and its coming about because of what I do that someone else kills them: a distinction based, not so much on the distinction between action and inaction, as on the distinction between my projects and someone else's projects'.[64] Williams's thought is that we are each peculiarly responsible for what we do through our actions; such actions form part of the *project* we each have that makes each of us the person that we are. We are not responsible for harms that someone else causes, for those are part of *their projects*; this, Williams thinks to be true even when we make possible the others' actions that produce harm.

Consider one of Kadish's examples: in 'the often-discussed hostage cases, in which a band threatens to kill two persons in their power in order to obtain the death of one person in the custody of another group . . . the group may desist from protecting the wanted person and permit the band to enter and kill him . . .'.[65] Although Kadish presents this as an example of an omission where we may use good consequences to justify it, Williams would treat it as an example of an action we do (sending out the one, or stepping out of the way) that allows another to kill him. When the terrorist band kills him, although our actions made it possible, it was not our doing—it was the terrorist band's doing. Therefore, we can justify our action by the good consequences we achieve, a net saving of

---

[63] This is Thomson's contrasting example. J. Thomson, *Rights, supra* n. 23, at 83.

[64] J. Smart and B. Williams, *Utilitarianism, supra* n. 31, at 117.

[65] Kadish, 'Respect for Life', *supra* n. 23, at 279, n. 32.

lives. By contrast, we may not ourselves kill the one the terrorist band wants killed, even though if we do not do so they will kill two hostages in their custody.[66] Williams would say that this is because that would force an action alien to us (killing an innocent) into the set of actions that define who we are and what projects speak for us. In other words, here we should not calculate consequences to decide what it is right to do.

Foot's earlier discussed torture example is also explainable on this ground. To alter it slightly (to excise its omission aspect), we may send one to be tortured by another if by so doing we will distract the torturer enough to allow five to escape torture; we may not torture one in our custody to prevent a terrorist from torturing five in his custody (he has threatened to do just that unless we torture one). The former act does not make torture our project so we may justify it by the good consequences we achieve; the latter act would make torture part of our project and, by Williams's distinction, cannot be justified by the equivalently good consequences of saving five from torture.

In a related context the criminal law of Great Britain, like that of many American states, declines to allow the defence of duress when the charge is murder. The thought behind this limitation is straight out of absolutist morality: the intentional killing of an innocent is so awful that no threatened consequences can justify or excuse anyone in doing it.[67] Yet for a time the English courts held that, despite the assimilation of accomplice liability to the liability of a principal, accomplices to murder may avail themselves of the duress defence.[68] For an accomplice only makes possible by his

---

[66] Ibid., at 280, n. 32.

[67] Although the defence of duress is best thought of as an excuse, not a justification, the English doctrine here discussed does not attend to that distinction. I accordingly feel some justification for treating the law of duress as an apt analogy illustrating the principle discussed in the text.

[68] *Lynch* v. *Director of Public Prosecutions* [1975] All ER 917. When an accomplice does more than make possible the principal's intervening act—where he actually participates in the killing—then duress is no longer available as a defence. (See *Abbott* v. *R* [1976] All ER 140; see also Katz, *Bad Acts*, supra n. 11, at 62–9.) This limitation also illustrates the principle in the text, because where the accomplice actually holds the victim while she is being skewered with a sabre wielded by the principal (the facts of *Abbott*), the principal's killing is not an act intervening between that of the accomplice and the harm; rather, both the sword thrust of the principal and the holding by the accomplice jointly kill. Failing to attend to this difference, the English courts have recently abolished the doctrine that accomplices may ever avail themselves of the defence of duress when the charge is murder.

action the killing by another; he does not himself kill. He may only drive the killer to the site of their crime, for example. In such a case, his act may be justified or excused by threats of death to himself and his family, even if an actual killing by him could not be.

(vii) *The causing/doing distinction*

Tom Nagel once argued that 'what absolutism forbids is *doing* certain things to people, rather than bringing about certain *results*'.[69] As Nagel elsewhere puts his distinction, it is 'between what one does to people and what merely happens to them as a result of what one *does*'.[70] Thus, to elaborate on one of Nagel's examples, if we ourselves bomb a village we do certain things to the villages which morality absolutely forbids, namely, we slaughter and maim innocent civilians;[71] such doings cannot be justified by the good consequences they may bring, such as shortening the war. On the other hand, those who manufacture the bomb casings eventually used by those who bomb civilians only bring about the result that they are slaughtered and maimed; presumably, because the death of the villagers is 'what merely happens to them as a result' of what the bomb casing manufacturer does, the manufacturer of such bomb casings can be justified by good consequences such as a shortening of the war and a lesser loss of life.[72]

b. *Reassessing These Limits on Consequential Calculation*

These seven distinctions, as thus far presented, may seem a heterogeneous lot. What, if anything, do they have in common? Why should they have anything to do with drawing the line between permissible and impermissible consequentialist justification? We may answer both questions by penetrating the surface features of these seven distinctions to get at their common core.

As I argued in chapter 9, there are three conditions for the full expression of our moral agency in a way that renders us morally responsible for some bad state of affairs. First, we must *act*. Only

---

[69] Nagel, 'War and Massacre', *supra* n. 45, at 58.   [70] Ibid., at 60.

[71] Ibid.

[72] Judy Thomson at one time came close to adopting Nagel's distinction. Needed, she thought, was some account of 'what it is to bring something about by doing something'. J. Thomson, *Rights*, *supra* n. 23, at 92. With such an account, she thought, perhaps we could make sense of the intuition 'that what matters in these cases in which a threat is to be distributed is whether the agent distributes it by doing something to it [which then causes harm to the victim], or whether he distributes it by doing something to a person'.

by our voluntary bodily motions do we even begin to put our stamp upon the world. Second, we must *desire* or *intend* (or perhaps even believe with certainty) that our actions will have those causal or other properties that will make them wrongful. And third, the bodily movements that we will must themselves *cause* the bad state of affairs necessary for there to be wrongdoing.[73]

If we re-examine the seven suggested limits on consequential calculation, we can see that they each instantiate one or another of these three conditions of responsibility. Take Foot's distinction of allowing (where good consequences count) versus doing (where they do not). Despite Foot's claim that 'there is no . . . general correlation between omission and allowing, commission and bringing about or doing',[74] the heart of Foot's distinction is the omission/commission distinction. Foot gives several reasons to think otherwise. The first is the 'ordinary language' observation that our use of the word 'allowing' is not always idiomatic if we align it with 'omitting'. This is true but irrelevant. It is true because it is a fact about the English language that verbs may be used in the active (rather than the passive) voice and yet describe omissions. It is irrelevant because it is the act/ omission distinction that marks an important moral difference, not the active/passive voice distinction.

This gets us to Foot's second reason, which is moral and not conceptual. Foot must think that the most stringent duties of morality enjoin us not only not to harm others but, sometimes, positively to help others. Thus, when we omit to give food to a starving beggar because we want his organs for medical research, 'we are inclined to see this as a violation of a negative rather than positive duty'.[75] That surely is not right.[76] Although we do wrong in refusing the food to Foot's beggar when we are motivated by the hope of harvesting his organs, surely we do much worse in poisoning him for his organs. Our more stringent negative duty is not to kill him; it does not include the positive injunction to save him.

---

[73] The Model Penal Code nicely duplicates these three conditions of responsibility in ss. 2.01 (voluntary action), 2.02 (culpable mental states), and 2.03 (causal responsibility).

[74] Foot, 'Abortion', *supra* n. 23, at 26.　　　　　　　　　　[75] Ibid., at 28.

[76] I am unclear as to Foot's ultimate views on her earlier starving beggar example. It may be she would now agree. See Foot, 'Immorality, Action and Outcome', in Ted Honderich, ed., *Morality and Objectivity* (London: Routledge, 1985), 23–38, at 37, n. 6 where she appears to reclassify the example as a violation of a merely positive duty but with a direct intention.

Foot's more recent reason for refusing to collapse the doing/allowing distinction into the action/inaction distinction is the ease with which the latter distinction can be manipulated by us to give us only the less stringent duty. Foot's example: 'it would be possible to change the moral character of certain trains of events by such simple expedients as building respirators which needed to be turned on each day'.[77] Yet the building of such 'omission machines' is itself an action done with culpable intent, so that if we now *fail* to turn on the respirator we will have earlier violated a negative duty not to kill (including not to kill indirectly by creating a machine that will kill for us unless we stop it). So Foot's allowing/doing distinction, properly construed, is nothing more than the familiar omission/action distinction, and thus is directed towards the first condition, that of voluntary action.[78]

It takes no similar reconstruction to see that the distinctions between purposeful and knowing action, and between knowing and risk-taking action, instantiate the second condition of fully expressing our moral agency. As I argued in chapter 9, we are more culpable when we seek to achieve some bad state of affairs than when we do not aim at it but nonetheless know it will come about as a result of our actions; and we are more culpable when we know our acts will produce such immoral results than when we only do an act aware that there is a risk of such results coming about because of what we do. We should see these two distinctions as competing attempts to locate the most significant break points in culpability, which competition need not be resolved to make our general point here: it is the culpability of the actor that here makes the difference whether consequential justification is permissible or not.

The remaining four distinctions each has to do with the third condition of responsible agency, causation. Take the victim in-peril/not-in-peril distinction. This I take to be proxy for a crude cause-in-fact judgement: when the victim is in peril, in the sense that he was going to die anyway, the temptation is strong to say we have not really (in fact) caused his death. His death in such cases

---

[77] Foot, 'Immorality', ibid., at 24. Leo Katz, in his delightful *Ill-Gotten Gains* (Chicago: University of Chicago Press, 1996), celebrates this possibility for deontological ethics. For additional criticism of Foot on this point, see Warren Quinn, 'Actions, Intentions, and Consequences: The Doctrine of Doing and Allowing', *Philosophy and Public Affairs*, Vol. 18 (1989), 334–51.

[78] With one qualification, this is also where Quinn comes out. See Quinn, 'Actions, Intentions, and Consequences', *supra* n. 77.

was overdetermined in the sense that the same kind of death would have occurred anyway, only at a somewhat later time. I say this is a *crude* cause-in-fact judgement because literally one does cause another's death even when the victim would have suffered the same kind of death had the actor not acted. Yet our intuition remains that one has not very much altered the world from the way it would have been in any event when the harm one causes was about to be visited on the victim anyway, without one's action. In such cases we may have the sense that our responsibility is diminished because our causal responsibility is more in question.[79]

The fifth distinction that Judith Thomson has emphasized, between redirecting a pre-existing threat and creating a new threat, also gains its plausibility from some causal intuitions. Thomson herself finds her proposed 'distribution exemption' puzzling: 'I do not find it clear why there should be an exemption for, and only for, making a burden which is descending upon five descend, instead, onto one. That there is seems to me very plausible, however.'[80] My suggestion is that the distribution exemption has as its rationale the idea that we only are a 'small cause' when we redirect a pre-existing threat not of our making; that, as such, our causal responsibility (and thus moral responsibility) is less than when we create a new threat and thus 'largely cause' the harm ourselves.[81]

The sixth distinction introduced by Bernard Williams, between our own and others' projects, is quite clearly built on causal notions. In their justly celebrated book, *Causation in the Law*,[82] Hart and Honoré go to some length to describe one dominant notion of proximate causation in both law and ordinary thought.

[79] Assuming that the argument of ch. 5 is correct, that we control the results of our actions sufficiently that how they turn out bears on our responsibility.

[80] Thomson, *Rights*, *supra* n. 23, at 108. Philippa Foot also seems to find this distinction intuitively appealing. See Foot, 'Immorality', *supra* n. 76, at 24–5, 37, n.3.

[81] This is not an unproblematic rationale, for it requires us to make sense of the idea that causation can be a more-or-less affair, a relation capable of being more strongly or less strongly present by matters of degree. In ch. 13 I questioned whether the causal relation is this kind of scalar phenomenon, more like the relation 'bigger than' than the relation 'brother of'. Nonetheless, the common moral intuition to which Thomson's distribution exemption points us does seem to be built on this scalar intuition about causal responsibility. The most obvious candidate for a suitably scalar conception of the singular causal relation would be a physicalistic conception where there can be varying magnitudes of force and the like. I discuss some of such conceptions in ch. 7, without resolving the question of their viability.

[82] H. L. A. Hart and A. M. Honoré, *Causation in the Law* (Oxford: Oxford University Press, 1959).

In the law we call this the 'direct cause' conception of proximate causation. A direct cause of some harm is any cause in fact where there is no intervening cause. An intervening cause either is that abnormal conjunction of natural events we think of as a coincidence, or it is a free, informed, deliberate, voluntary action of a third party that intervenes between the defendant's action and the harm.

The moral force of Williams's 'my project/someone else's project' distinction stems entirely from the causal intuition Hart and Honoré described. Specifically, Hart and Honoré tell us, our causal responsibility ends where some third party's voluntary action intervenes between our act and the harm our act *in fact* causes. This is why I may do an act that results in another being tortured by someone else, while I may not torture someone else myself to achieve the same good consequences. This is why I may step aside and thereby make possible the shooting of another by a terrorist band, while I may not shoot the one myself to achieve the same good consequences. Where I am causally responsible for the moral wrong— the second of each of these pairs of examples—I may not justify myself with good consequences, whereas where I am not causally responsible I may, for I am not nearly so responsible.

The seventh distinction Tom Nagel once emphasized, that between causing and doing, also derives whatever moral force it possesses from a distinction in our causal responsibility.[83] To begin with, there is a certain moral arbitrariness in the distinction as Nagel stated it, for it is an etymological accident whether the English language happens to have a 'causally-complex'[84] action verb to cover some situation we are judging. If it does ('killing', 'torturing', 'maiming', etc.), then we at least can classify the event as a doing; if it does not ('avalanching', 'house-collapsing', etc.), then what we did can only be classified as a causing because there is no *doing* to have been done. That causing death is a frequent enough occurrence that our language has a verb to cover it ('kill'), but that causing damage by avalanche is not, is a morally arbitrary difference.

---

[83] Nagel himself appears to have construed his own former distinction (between doing and causing) quite differently; now he aligns it with the intending/foreseeing distinction. Nagel, *View*, *supra* n. 35, at 179.

[84] On the idea of complex action verbs, see Michael Moore, *Act and Crime: The Philosophy of Action and its Implications for Criminal Law* (Oxford: Oxford University Press, 1993), ch. 8.

Nagel's linguistic distinction therefore has to stand proxy for some less morally arbitrary distinction. Although Nagel himself preferred to keep his distinction 'unanalyzed',[85] Jonathan Bennett[86] once put his finger on the relevant feature. We call a causing-death a *killing* only when there is a certain immediacy between what we do and another's death. We see this feature of our English usage best in the present-perfect tense, as in 'I am now killing him'. If we are shooting someone, this is an appropriate description; if we are loading the gun before we find our intended victim, this is not the appropriate description. In the latter situation we are only *preparing* to kill him. If later on we do find and shoot him, only the act of shooting but not the act of loading was an act of *killing*, even though both were acts causally necessary for the victim to die.

Immediacy of causation matters morally for the reasons lawyers have explored with their concept of proximate causation. Even without the existence of an intervening cause (in Hart and Honoré's sense), spatial/temporal remoteness between our act and a harm matters to our causal responsibility. Caesar's crossing the Rubicon may well be a necessary condition of some future nuclear accident, but Caesar's causal responsibility does not extend so far. Such diminished causal responsibility also betokens a lessened moral responsibility for the remote harms we in fact cause.

c. *Ruminations on the Rationality of Agent-Relative Views of Morality*

If these reductions are right, then our view of the domain of things to which moral norms apply is altered somewhat. Such norms categorically forbid intentionally done (or perhaps intended) complex actions like killing or torturing. Put in other words such norms prohibit our doing those voluntary acts that directly and proximately cause states of another's being killed or being tortured, when such acts are accompanied by an intent (or perhaps foresight) that such states will result.[87]

---

[85] Nagel, 'War and Massacre', *supra* n. 45, at 60.

[86] Bennett, 'Whatever the Consequences', *supra* n. 48, at 92.

[87] I think that such combination of intention and action as the object of morality's agent-relative prohibitions allows me to escape the difficulties for either alone so elegantly explored in Heidi Hurd, 'What in the World Is Wrong?', *Journal of Contemporary Legal Issues*, Vol. 5 (1994), 157–216. Nonetheless, serious difficulties no doubt remain in spelling out how moral norms can conjunctively prohibit both culpable intentions and wrongful actions.

By reducing a seemingly heterogeneous range of intuitive distinctions to the three distinctions that centrally matter to an agent's prima facie moral responsibility, what besides clarity have we accomplished? At a minimum, we have shown a kind of coherence to these intuitions, together with a consistency between them and the general idea of agent-relative theories of morality. The coherence point is probably obvious enough: if I am correct, the intuitions other philosophers have captured with their examples and distinctions are not *ad hoc*, isolated instances where consequential calculations are permissible even on agent-relative views. Rather, the general principle behind all of them is the principle that blameworthiness matters in determining when we may justify our acts by their good consequences: when a contemplated act would make us fully culpable were we to do it, we are forbidden to do it, irrespective of the good consequences we could achieve by doing it; when that act would not make us as fully blameworthy—because of the absence or diminishment of a voluntary act, culpable mental state, or causal responsibility—then we may do it, using those same good consequences as our justification.[88]

I sometimes think this to be a profound insight, sometimes a trivial one. In the former moments I am struck by the very systematic coherence of the distinctions above ordered around the three conditions of prima facie responsibility. In the latter moments I am struck by the thought, 'What else would you expect of agent-relative views of morality?' For such views interpret morality to say to each of us, 'Don't *you* intentionally do a morally prohibited action.' Such views are by their nature focused on the moral agency of each of us, so how could one be surprised that when the conditions of that agency are fully realized, one's intuitive sense that good consequences are irrelevant is strongest? (This latter insight is what I mean when I say that these intuitions are consistent with agent-relative views.)

---

[88] Notice that the other aspect of culpability, excuse, is absent in this articulation of the range of permissible consequential justification. Just because one may be somewhat coerced does not increase the permissibility of consequential justification. An excused, or partly excused wrongful action remains wrongful in the face of good consequences. This is true in the actual world (for wrongdoing) and in the possible world created by the actor's mental states (for culpability). One may still be excused or partly excused for such intentionally done wrongful actions; but the conditions of excuse do not insinuate themselves into the objects of agent-relative norms in the way that the act, intention, and causation conditions do. Put more simply, the excusability of an action or intention in no way affects the issue of their justification.

Seeing both the coherence and the consistency of our principles for ruling out consequential calculation raises a troubling question about the rationality of agent-relative theories of morality. Why should each of us act so as to preserve his or her moral innocence? Why is our own moral blameworthiness so important that it is morally forbidden to us to intentionally kill an innocent who was not in danger, if by so doing we can prevent the intentional killing of five others by someone else? I do not know a very good answer to this question, although there are quite a few stabs at it in moral philosophy.[89] I do know that I share Sam Scheffler's response to his own inability to find an intelligible answer to this question: 'I find myself in certain moods more impressed by the particular intuitions to which the [agent-relative] restrictions respond than by the general difficulties encountered in attempting to motivate them . . .'.[90] I thus shall leave for another day this very general problem in moral philosophy and assume that good consequences cannot justify our voluntarily acting in such a way that we intentionally cause certain states of affairs.

d. *The Limits on Consequential Calculation Applied to Torture*

Assuming the correctness of the complex agent-relative view just described, how do we judge the torture of innocents by GSS interrogators when such torture is conducted, for example, in order to locate a hidden bomb? The answer is surprisingly straightforward: there is nothing in any of the seven distinctions we have examined leaving any room for consequentialist justification in such a case. Torture is a voluntary act, not an omission to prevent pain; torture in the circumstances imagined is fully intentional—not just foreseen, but intended as a means to some further end; the victim of GSS torture is known, he is not a member of some larger class at

[89] See, e.g., Fried, *Right and Wrong*, *supra* n. 48; Nagel, *View*, *supra* n. 35, at 175–88. It does seem to me that any answer to this question will have to focus on the moral integrity or well-being of the agent to whom moral prohibitions apply and not on the unfairness or rights of the victim. (See Joseph Raz, *Morality of Freedom* (Oxford: Oxford University Press, 1987), at 284–7.) This suggests the need for a virtue-based account of deontological constraints, recognizing that we tend not to think of all duties as ultimately being duties we owe to ourselves (to be virtuous). For a sceptical discussion of this approach', see Samuel Scheffler, 'Agent-Centred Restrictions, Rationality, and the Virtues', *Mind*, Vol. 94 (1985), 409–19, reprinted in *Consequentialism and Its Critics*, *supra* n. 32, at 243, 254–5.

[90] Scheffler, *Rejection*, *supra* n. 30, at 114. Scheffler himself ultimately allows the difficulties to overcome the intuitions, at least for agent-relative prohibitions if not for agent-relative permissions.

risk for torturous treatment; such a victim is not already in peril of harms like torture, so that it is only the GSS that creates such a peril; there is usually no pre-existing threat of someone being tortured, with the only choice of the GSS being as to who will suffer it; there is no voluntary act by someone else that intervenes between the acts of the GSS interrogator and the pain of his victim, nor is there any spatial/temporal remoteness. In short, all of the conditions of prima facie blameworthiness are as fully met by the GSS interrogator as by the hypothetical surgeon about to harvest the organs of one to save five. The moral answer to both must be the same: you cannot torture or kill the innocent, even to achieve what are admittedly good consequences like saving five lives.

There is thus nothing in this first aspect of complex agent-relative moral views that licenses torture by the GSS. I now turn to the other two complexities that characterize this moral view to see if the same conclusion holds.

2. Complex Norms with Exceptions versus Exceptionless Absolutes

a. The General Need for Exceptions to Moral Norms

There are very few (if any) plausible candidates for the kind of short and snappy injunctions that can be fitted on one stone tablet. 'Thou shalt not kill' is a poor candidate for such a norm, because to be plausible it has to have exceptions built into it. Not telling lies, keeping our promises, or not committing adultery, are even less plausible candidates for exceptionless absolutes. What would we think of a person who could save his family from wrongful killing by another but refused to do so because the only means available involved: killing the aggressor, telling a lie to the aggressor, or not keeping a promise to the aggressor? Despite Kant's famous views to the contrary, I would think that such a person not only lacks virtue, but that he is derelict in his moral duties.

The point is that moral norms must have exceptions implicit in them to have any moral plausibility. To be morally plausible, 'thou shalt not kill' must be taken to be an elliptical reference to a much more complicated norm: 'Don't kill, unless in self-defence, to protect your family, to aid in a just war lawfully declared, to execute those deserving of the death penalty such as Adolf Eichmann . . .', etc. Outside of a text-based view found only in religious or conventionalist views of morality, there is no reason to suppose that moral truths are simple. Indeed, as science shows us about the world of non-moral fact, there is every reason to think that moral laws are quite complex—as complex as the scientific laws that govern the behaviour of physical objects.[91] No one expects all of science to be statable in ten rules of very short compass.

So the second complexity that must be introduced into any plausible agent-relative view is the possibility that norms like 'never torture' have implicit exceptions clauses to them. It may seem that such 'possibility of an indefinitely large number of exceptions' renders this into a consequentialist view of morality,[92] but this would be a mistake. We must distinguish *exceptions* to norms—exceptions which are simply a further filling out of the content of norms—from *overriding* norms on occasion even when we admit that they are by their terms applicable.[93] The distinction is as familiar as the common law lawyers distinction between *distinguishing* a precedent case's holding (by showing how an unstated exception to the holding exempts the present case from its true reach) and *overruling* a precedent case's holding (where we admit its applicability but refuse to follow it in the case at hand).

With this distinction in mind, we can see that consequentialism is the view that we should *override* moral norms like, 'don't torture', whenever the balance of good over bad consequences say we should. A non-consequentialist view of the complex kind here considered does not allow such overridings of moral norms; it does allow moral norms to be quite complex in their content because of its allowance of exceptions to norms like, 'don't torture'. The only way the complex agent-relative view would collapse into a consequentialist view of morality would be if one counted as 'exceptions' items like, 'unless good consequences dictate otherwise'. Such 'exceptions' would of course be nothing more than an invitation for a general consequentialist override of the norm in question.

[91] I argue for this in Moore, 'Moral Reality', *Wisconsin Law Review*, Vol. [1982], 1061–156; Moore, 'Moral Reality Revisited', *Michigan Law Review*, Vol. 90 (1992), 2424–533; Moore, 'Good Without God', *supra* n. 42.

[92] Of course, for social rules (unlike the laws of morality), an indefinitely large number of unknown exceptions defeats the purpose served by the existence of social rules. For the difference, see Moore, 'Three Concepts of Rules', *Harvard Journal of Law and Public Policy*, Vol. 14 (1991), 771–95.

[93] See John Rawls, 'Two Concepts of Rules', *Philosophical Review*, Vol. 64 (1955), 3–32, where Rawls distinguishes exceptions to the norm against breaking a promise from overriding that norm. See also Raz, *Morality of Freedom*, *supra* n. 89, at 361–2.

b. *Possible Exceptions to the Norm, 'Never Torture'*

(i) *Consent of the victim*

As an illustration of how exceptions to norms are not consequentialist overridings of norms, consider the situation in which the victim consents to what otherwise would be a violation of his rights. Often such consent operates to transform a prima facie wrong action into a rightful action.[94] For example, rape, where consent radically alters the nature of the action; or trespass, where consent creates a property interest (a 'licence') where otherwise there was a wrong. In such cases we do not reach the question of consequential justification overriding some moral norm because the norm itself—when fully spelled out so as to include an exception for consent—was not violated.

Consent is often not a defence to serious crimes such as homicide. This may, however, be for reasons unconnected to the moral rightness or wrongness of the defendant's action. Euthanasia, for example, is legally defined as murder just about everywhere, but not because the consent of the victim makes no moral difference; rather, there are utilitarian worries that if there were a defence of consent, many unconsented-to homicides might go unpunished because the only surviving witness—the defendant—can lie about the victim's consent with impunity.[95]

Even those who do not share my view that in certain circumstances euthanasia is not wrong *at all* may think that it is not as wrong as an unconsented-to homicide. Consider again the lifeboat cases. In *Holmes*, where some of the passengers had to be jettisoned if any were to live, would it be wrong to release someone (who is in some way restrained) in order that he might voluntarily jump overboard and save the boat? To push him in, if he is paralysed and requests such an action because he cannot do it himself? If either of these actions would be wrong at all, surely they are not *as* wrong as drowning one who does not volunteer.

What such situations show is the possibility that exceptions to moral norms need not make an all-or-nothing difference in the wrongness of an action to which they apply. Consent of the victim, for example, might lessen but not eliminate the wrongness of doing

[94] See Heidi Hurd, 'The Moral Magic of Consent', *Legal Theory*, Vol. 2 (1996), 121–46.

[95] See H. L. A. Hart, *Law, Liberty, and Morality* (Stanford: Stanford University Press, 1963), at 31.

the action to which consent was given. If this is so, then notice how plausible it is to say that consequential justifications may be given in those exceptional instances of killing, torturing, etc., that are not very wrong. Put in terms of the crowded lifeboat situation: even if it would be wrong to aid another to kill himself when in full possession of his faculties and for understandable reasons he wishes to do so (the general prohibition against euthanasia), it is not so wrong that it cannot be balanced against, and outweighed by, the saving of the lives of those remaining in the lifeboat.

Since terrorist suspects never consent to be tortured, the exception we are here examining needs to be broadened considerably if it is to be of any use to us here beyond a general illustration of how exceptions to moral norms operate in this complex agent-relative view of morality. One suggestion arising from the lifeboat cases is that if you consent to a fair procedure for determining who must suffer a harm, you cannot complain when that procedure determines that it will be you who suffer the harm.[96] This is based on an assumption of the risk intuition: one who voluntarily assumes a risk of which he is fully aware has less cause to complain when the risk materializes than someone who did not so assume it.

Such an intuition has no limitation to assumption of the risk of selection procedures in situations of common peril. Consider in this regard Judy Thomson's example:

Suppose an avalanche is descending toward a large city. It is possible to deflect it onto a small one. May we? Not if the following is the case. Large City is in avalanche country—the risk of an avalanche is very high there. The founders of Large City were warned of this risk when they built there, and all settlers in it were warned of it before settling there. But lots and lots of people did accept the risk and settle there, because of the beauty of the countryside and the money to be made there. Small City, however, is not in avalanche country—it's flat for miles around; and settlers in Small City settled for a less lovely city, and less money, precisely because they did not wish to run the risk of being overrun by an avalanche. Here it seems plain we may not deflect the avalanche onto Small City to save Large

---

[96] In *Holmes, supra* n. 55, the Court stated that if a fair procedure had been used to select who was to be thrown overboard, then the act would have been justified. In Lon Fuller's variation, it is not only the fairness of the selection procedure that makes a difference, but the victim's having consented to the procedure *ex ante* (i.e., before he knew he would draw the short straw). See Fuller, 'Speluncean Explorers', *supra* n. 55; Katz, *Bad Acts, supra* n. 11, at 51–6.

City: the Small Cityers have more claim against it than the Large Cityers do.[97]

What is doing the moral work in cases like Thomson's, as in the lifeboat-lottery cases, is not the bare fact of consent to run a certain type of risk.[98] Consent, unlike a promise, creates only very weak content-independent reasons for action in morality.[99] What makes it not wrong to prefer Small City to Large City is the unjust enrichment that would take place if such preference were not made. Where there is a benefit attached to running a certain risk, and where some opt for the benefit and the risk while others eschew both, it would unjustly enrich those who have benefited if the cost of their benefit (the risk) were transferred to someone else.

If we apply this discussion to torture, there is perhaps some weak argument that terrorists assume the risk of harsh treatment if caught. For if there is an established policy of so treating terrorists, and if it is publicized so that it is known, then those who seek (what they regard as) the benefits of terrorist activities cannot complain if the risks attendant upon obtaining those benefits materialize.

There are two things wrong with this argument. One stems from my doubts whether even explicit victim-consent could make torture permissible. The reason that victim-consent eliminates or lessens the wrongness of various actions harming the victim is because such consent shows there to have been no harm to this person (even if an identical state of affairs would be harmful to others). As Tom Nagel describes the moral force of victim-consent:

[T]here can be complications [to a deontological restraint]. One is the possibility of someone volunteering to be subjected to some kind of pain or damage, either for his own good or for some other end which is important to him. In that case the particular evil that you aim at is swallowed up in the larger aim for deontological purposes. So the evil at which we are constrained not to aim is *our victim's* evil, rather than just a particular bad

---

[97] Thomson, *Rights, supra* n. 23, at 87.

[98] Although on occasion such 'bare fact of consent' does do some moral work. What (of a non-utilitarian sort) can be said in favour of killing any fleeing felon (the old common law rule for policemen) was that he assumed the risk of being shot when he ran after the warning, 'stop or I'll shoot'.

[99] A 'content-independent reason' for action is a reason created by an act like a promise, or a vow, or a request of a friend. Such acts create new reasons to do what is promised, avowed, or requested, reasons whose force as reasons is independent of the goodness of the actions promised, etc. See generally Raz, *Morality of Freedom, supra* n. 89, chs. 2–4.

thing, and each individual has considerable authority in defining what will count as harming him for the purpose of this restriction.[100]

My doubt is whether torture would not be wrong even when consented to (presumably by a masochistic victim), for torture harms both torturer and victim no matter what the latter thinks about it.

The other thing wrong with the assumption of the risk argument is that it is far too sweeping in its implications to be acceptable. Such an argument could be made in support of any government policy, no matter how horrible, so long as it was well-publicized and regularly applied.[101] The reason this argument may seem persuasive is due, not to any assumption of the risk by terrorists, but to their blameworthiness as terrorists. It is thus to the possible exceptions relating to this aspect of the situation to which I now turn.

(ii) *Self-defence and defence of others analogies*

One thing the assumption of the risk discussion highlights is the difference it seems to make whether it is a terrorist or an innocent who is tortured. Other possible exceptions suggest themselves to account for this intuitive difference in terms of the differential responsibility of terrorists versus non-terrorists. The most obvious place to start is with the well-established exceptions to norms like 'don't kill' that exist for self-defence and defence of others situations. This right to resist aggression has often formed the basis for drawing distinctions between combatants and innocents in discussions of the morality of war,[102] and I shall use it for the same purpose.

We should deal at the outset with the possibility that resisting aggression is not an *exception* to norms against killing and torture, but is only an *excuse* for violating such norms. Such a possibility may occur to us because self-defence situations often happen quickly, bring our self-preservative instincts into action (instincts that we know are difficult to resist), and such situations are without criminal liability even if there are many culpable aggressors attacking us (so there is no net savings of lives to justify our actions) and/or the aggressors are themselves morally innocent

---

[100] T. Nagel, *View, supra* n. 35, at 182.

[101] On the problems with assumption of the risk arguments like that dealt with in the text, see Leo Katz, 'The Assumption of the Risk Argument', *Social Philosophy and Policy*, Vol. 7 (1990), 138–69.

[102] See Jeffrie Murphy, 'The Killing of the Innocent', *The Monist*, Vol. 57 (1973), 527–50; Nagel, 'War and Massacre', *supra* n. 45.

actors.[103] Yet, self-defence and defence of others are not excuses. We do no wrong when we kill or injure an aggressor, and we are not culpable when we intend to kill or injure an aggressor, and thus we need not *excuse* ourselves from anything.

Intuitively, we see this justificatory (rather than excusing) nature of self-defence with the following sort of example. Imagine someone ('D') with bad character who enjoys inflicting suffering on others. Through no fault of his own he is attacked in his home by a mugger ('V'), who demands his wallet. D refuses to give up his wallet, whereupon V tries to kill him. D defends himself by killing V. It was not a hard choice for D. He neither agonized nor was he at all fearful, being confident of his abilities to defend himself. Indeed, he welcomed the opportunity (as he put it later) to 'get in a free killing' of someone, enjoying every thrust of his knife into V's body. D is a pretty dreadful person and does not possess any of the diminished capacities or opportunities for choice we think of as prerequisite for excuse. Yet D is entitled to the defence of self-defence because he did no wrong in killing V.

How one fleshes out this intuition that self-defence is a justification has been the subject of some debate in criminal law theory and philosophy.[104] There are two sorts of accounts of the moral basis of self-defence as a justification, victim-based accounts and agent-based accounts.[105] The victim-based accounts focus on the culpability of the victim of the homicide (who is culpable because he begins as the aggressor even though he ends up as the victim). Such culpability is variously said to forfeit, override, or specify out of existence the aggressor's right to life[106] or to discount the value of

---

[103] On the excuse interpretation of self-defence, see Kadish, 'Respect for Life', *supra* n. 23, at 116.

[104] Compare Kadish, 'Respect for Life', *supra* n. 23; Thomson, 'Self-Defense and Rights', in Thomson, *Rights*, *supra* n. 23; Dressler, *Understanding*, *supra* n. 11, at 199–201; Montague, 'Self-Defense and Choosing Between Lives', *Philosophical Studies*, Vol. 40 (1981), 207–19; Wasserman, 'Justifying Self-Defense', *Philosophy and Public Affairs*, Vol. 16 (1987), 356–78; Montague, 'The Morality of Self-Defence: A Reply to Wasserman', *Philosophy and Public Affairs*, Vol. 18 (1989), 81–9.

[105] See Kadish, 'Respect for Life', *supra* n. 23. I put aside utilitarian accounts of the defence (e.g., in terms of deterring attacks by allowing victims to kill their attackers).

[106] These possibilities are discussed in Thomson, 'Self-Defense', *supra* n. 104. Rashi, a medieval commentator on the Talmud, appears to have adopted such a victim-based account of self-defence, for he treats the killing of a burglar as a trivial act: such a blameworthy person as a burglar 'has no blood' in the sense that he

his life, either entirely or in part. One problem with such victim-based accounts is that they do not seem to square very well with the 'innocent aggressor' cases,[107] for it is difficult to think that those who innocently pose a threat to us forfeit their right to life or have the value of their life discounted. Another problem with such accounts is that they leave unexplained why, when the aggression is ended, the aggressor's life regains its value or why his right to life is re-established. Such problems motivate the alternative, agent-based account, which speaks of a defendant's right to resist aggression.[108] Yet these latter accounts also are problematic in that they do not go very far—for an explanation of why it is not wrongful to kill an aggressor in terms of a right to kill an aggressor comes perilously close to tautology. Wanted is some more general account of why we each have such a right.

If we attend to our sense of fittingness when an aggressor trying to kill someone is instead killed himself, we may gain some insight into the moral basis for self-defence. Notice that the aggressor creates a situation in which someone must be killed, either he or his intended victim. He has wrongfully created a threat of harm that his intended victim can now only redirect but not eliminate. Since he is the one creating such a threat, he in all fairness is the one to be selected when someone has to bear the harm threatened.[109]

This account helps to explain the innocent aggressor cases. Aggressors may be innocent for a variety of reasons.[110] They may be trying to kill you or others, but are morally and legally excused (insane, very young, under duress of others, etc.); or they may not even be trying to kill you but are nonetheless physically part of a threat that is trying to kill you. Consider Sandy Kadish's illustration of the first of these two classes of cases:

Suppose a terrorist and her insane husband and 8-year-old son are operating a machine gun emplacement from a flat in an apartment building.

should be treated as one who is already dead. See Marilyn Finkelman, 'Self-Defense and Defense of Others in Jewish Law: The *Rodef* Defense', *Wayne Law Review*, Vol. 33 (1987), at 1257–87 at 1284–6; Fletcher, *Rethinking*, *supra* n. 11, at 256.

[107] These possibilities are discussed in Kadish, 'Respect for Life', *supra* n. 23.
[108] As in Id.
[109] For suggestions along this line, see Montague, 'Self-Defense and Choosing', *supra* n. 104.
[110] For a variety of examples, see George Fletcher, 'Proportionality and the Psychotic Aggressor: A Vignette in Comparative Criminal Theory', *Israel Law Review*, Vol. 8 (1973), 367–90; Robert Nozick, *Anarchy, State and Utopia*, (Cambridge, Mass.: Harvard University Press, 1974), at 34–5.

They are about to shoot down a member of the diplomatic corps, whose headquarters the terrorist band is attacking. His only chance is to throw a hand grenade (which he earlier picked up from a fallen terrorist) through his assailant's window. Probably under Anglo-American law he will be legally justified in doing so. His right to resist the aggressor's threat is determinative.[111]

The relatively innocent participants in this scenario—the insane husband and the 8-year-old child—are permissibly killed because they too are causers—non-culpable causers, but causers nonetheless—of the situation that demands someone die. They too are thus most fairly selected as the recipients of the harm whose threat they have set in motion.

One can perhaps extend this analysis to the second category of innocent aggressor cases. Consider the situation in which a terrorist ('T') takes on innocent bystander ('V') as a shield to use as T seeks to kill another ('D'). If D's only way to defend himself against T is to shoot through V, it is common to suppose, morally and legally, that he may do so.[112] The reason for this, I would think, lies in the 'ownership' of the risk (of T's violence) that V, through no fault of his own, has acquired. T's taking V as a shield was *V's* misfortune; V did nothing to deserve it but it's his nonetheless, like disease or a natural catastrophe. D is entitled to resist the shifting of that risk from V to himself, not because V caused the risk, but because it's his risk nonetheless.[113]

The application of this account of the moral basis of self-defence to GSS torture of terrorist suspects should by now be obvious enough. Terrorists who are captured do not now present a threat of using deadly force against their captors or others. Thus, the literal law of self-defence is not available to justify their torture. But the principle uncovered as the moral basis for the defence may be applicable. For if the terrorist knows the location of hidden bombs, or of buried hostages, or of caches of arms, or if he knows of future terrorist acts to be executed by others that he has aided, he has culpably caused the situation where someone must get hurt. If hurting

[111] S. Kadish, 'Respect for Life', *supra* n. 23, at 122.

[112] See Nozick, *Anarchy*, *supra* n. 110.

[113] Cf. Scanlon, 'Rights, Goals, and Fairness', *supra* n. 34, at 90, who suggests that judgements of a non-consequentialist sort may generally reflect a 'bias of the lucky against the unlucky'. The alternative account of the shield type of innocent aggressor cases is that the actor is excused, but not justified, in shooting through the shield to save himself.

him is the only means to prevent the death or injury of others put at risk by his actions, such torture should be permissible, and on the same basis that self-defence is permissible.

Torturing the terrorist in order to get him to reveal information that will prevent the very harm he has set in motion may be likened to the following scenario. Suppose another wishes to kill you. At an isolated location where no medical attention is available he puts poison in your food, which you eat; seeing you swallow the last bite, he then tells you what he has done so that you will know that you are dying; he also swallows the only supply of the antidote to the poison you have taken. If you can catch him, may you cut him open to extract the antidote in order to save yourself, even though you know such cutting will certainly kill him?

My own answer to this question is a rather clear 'yes'. True enough, his attack on you is over, if we construe 'attack' as an action and not as its continuing effects; so the literal law of self-defence may well not be available. Yet the poisoner has culpably caused the situation where someone must die. He is, to my mind, by far the best candidate to suffer the harm that someone must suffer.

Such an exception to the norm against torturing has of course no application to the torturing of the innocent, even when, as in Scheffler's earlier example,[114] such torture (of the terrorist's child) is the only way to induce the terrorist to reveal the location of a deadly bomb. For the child of the terrorist did not cause, nor is he himself part of, the threat created by the terrorist activity. As Robert Nozick observes, 'some uses of force on people to get at an aggressor do not act upon innocent shields of threats; for example an aggressor's innocent child who is tortured in order to get the aggressor to stop wasn't *shielding* the parent'.[115]

Less clearly within or without this exception are instances of torture of someone who had no hand in the terrorist activity that gave rise to the threat but who nonetheless possesses information that, if disclosed, would prevent the threatened harm from occurring. For example, the spouse of the terrorist who has planted a bomb had no hand in the activity that led to the bomb's planting, but she has been told by her husband where the bomb is located, and she refuses to disclose its location. May she be tortured for the information?

[114] See *supra* text at n. 32.   [115] See Nozick, *Anarchy, supra* n. 110, at 34.

One avenue that suggests that she might would be to consider her a part of the threat posed by her husband's activities because she fed, clothed, and supported him during the time of those activities. Yet, I would reject such a suggestion. It is like treating spouses of soldiers as combatants for purpose of drawing the line between morally permissible versus morally impermissible modes of warfare.[116] However that difficult line is drawn, surely there are *some* civilians (non-combatants) who may not be killed wherever and whenever they can be found, and for that to be the case spouses of combatants cannot themselves be considered combatants.

Nonetheless, my hypothetical spouse is unlike other civilians in that she could prevent the harm by no greater an act than speaking up. If we repair to our self-defence analogy, perhaps again this will focus our intuitions on this aspect of the hypothesized situation. Consider the following example of Jeffrie Murphy, what he calls 'the case of the homicidal diabetic':

He is chasing you through the woods of an enclosed game preserve, trying to kill you for sport with a pistol. However, because of his medical condition, he must return to a cabin in the middle of the preserve every hour in order that his aged mother can give him an insulin shot. Without it, he will take ill and die and will thus be forced to abandon his attempt to kill you. Even if blocking that insulin shot seems your only hope, killing the mother in order to do it would be a very doubtful case of self-defense.[117]

Yet is it so clear that we may not torture the mother in order to get her to reveal the insulin supply, or kill her, if she is told what her son is trying to do, told how she can prevent it, and she refuses? Does she not, by that refusal, become a part of her son's threat against which we are entitled to defend ourselves?

Consider a variation on Lon Fuller's famous trapped spelunkean explorers.[118] The explorers, it will be recalled, are trapped in a blocked cave without hope of rescue before they starve to death. They debate whether they may kill one of their number in order to save the rest by feeding on his body. The variation is: in the midst of this debate appears a cave dwelling hermit who knows another route of egress from the cavern; because he despises intruding

[116] For a discussion of who is innocent for purposes of the morality of war, see Murphy, 'Killing of the Innocent', *supra* n. 102; Nagel, 'War and Massacre', *supra* n. 45.

[117] Murphy, 'Killing of the Innocent', *supra* n. 102, at 538, n. 15.

[118] See Fuller, 'Speluncean Explorers', *supra* n. 55.

spelunkers, and to deter further intrusions, he refuses to reveal the route to safety. If someone has to be eaten to save the rest, would not such a Bad Samaritan be the best candidate? Short of eating him, would not torturing him to extract information he ought to reveal anyway be preferable? Troubling as they are, I think the answers to these questions to be 'yes'. The Bad Samaritan who could prevent *anyone* dying and who refuses to do so for no good reason[119] becomes part of the threat to be defended against, and should be treated accordingly.

(iii) *Prepaid punishment of the generally culpable*
I now wish to return to the victim-based accounts of self-defence. I do this not because they are good accounts of self-defence, for they are not. Rather, such accounts allow us to glimpse a third possible exception to norms like 'don't kill' in addition to the exception we have just examined that encompasses the right of self-defence.

There is a common moral intuition that culpable wrongdoing deserves punishment. This is the retributive urge that we examined in Part I. Retributivism asserts that it is not wrong to punish the guilty and, indeed, it is the state's duty to punish those who deserve it. Deserved punishment, in other words, is for a retributivist one of the exceptions to norms like 'don't restrain' or even, perhaps, 'don't kill'.

There are two obvious problems with extending this exception to torturing culpable terrorists on some theory that it is only a 'prepaid punishment plan': one, torture is not a morally permissible form of punishment; two, GSS interrogators are not courts and are not in a position to make the findings of guilt that only courts can make. Both these considerations combine to rule out any blanket exception in favour of torturing the quite blameworthy. (Otherwise, it would be morally permissible to torture terrorist suspects even when there is no life-saving information to be extracted from them.)

Yet remembering the possibility that not all exceptions to moral norms operate in an all-or-nothing fashion, perhaps it is *less* wrong

---

[119] That the Bad Samaritan has no good reason to refuse to prevent the harm is crucial here. Otherwise, we might think the healthy individual who refuses to give up his life so that five others may live with his organs is a Bad Samaritan deserving of sacrifice. Yet such an individual has a good reason not to give up his life and his organs: it is a very costly sacrifice to him. Similarly, if the spouse of a terrorist could show that she had good reason not to speak—a death threat by the terrorist organization, for example—then she too may not be the Bad Samaritan subject to harsh treatment. (I owe both of these points to Heidi Hurd.)

to torture the blameworthy than the innocent. Put crudely, their lives and rights are worth less precisely because they are morally odious individuals deserving of punishment, even if we are not their rightful punishers and even if death or torture is not their rightful punishment.

Consider the provocation defence to murder in Anglo-American criminal law to illustrate this possibility.[120] There is what I would call an unofficial version of the defence, unofficial in the sense that it is not the stated reason for the defence but it is, often enough, the reason that guides jurors in their application of the defence to the cases they must decide. This unofficial rationale comes out in the following kind of case: D is the husband of W. W was forcibly raped by her gynaecologist ('V') in V's office on one of W's regular visits to him. With no witnesses, W was unable to get the authorities to prosecute V for rape. Her deep distress over the incident leads to her suicide. D, in full possession of his faculties, and after giving the matter considerable thought over a period of several months after W's death, purchases a gun, walks into V's office, and shoots him dead with every bullet in the gun. D then waits for the police in V's office, as he intended to do all along.

Despite the lack of any 'passion overbearing reason'—the official, excuse rationale for the defence—the jury found for the defendant on his provocation defence, resulting only in a manslaughter, not a murder, conviction. It is not hard to reconstruct their reasoning: V was a very blameworthy human being who pretty much deserved what he got. True, there is no death penalty for rape—D's punishment was excessive. True, D was not the person to impose punishment of any kind. But D's action was much less wrong than it would have been had V not been the moral leper that he was.

If one agrees with the jury's reasoning in this actual case, as I do, then one glimpses the following possibility: while the killing or torture of another is wrong, where it is the killing or torture of someone deserving of serious punishment, it is significantly less wrong,

---

[120] Compare McAuley, 'Anticipating the Past: The Defense of Provocation in Irish Law', *Modern Law Review*, Vol. 50 (1987), 133–57, with Dressler, 'Provocation: Partial Justification or Partial Excuse?', *Modern Law Review*, Vol. 51 (1988), 467–80. An alternative legal example of where the degree of wrong done is affected by the blameworthiness of the victim to whom it is done, is provided by the felony-murder rule. If the person killed during the commission of a felony is a co-felon, it is common to refuse application of the felony-murder rule to the killer; this, presumably because taking the life of a co-felon is less wrong than taking the life of an innocent.

so much so that good consequences may justify the doing of it. Thus, in situations inviting a balance of evils, one may justifiably select those deserving of punishment anyway to bear the evil someone must bear. If you have only enough dialysis machines for ten, but twenty need them, you may exclude the morally odious first;[121] if the lifeboat is sinking, and some must go to save the rest, the known murderers amongst the passengers are good candidates for being the first to be tossed overboard.

Saying this is not to justify executing or torturing to death those who have culpably caused the death of innocents, as the GSS (apparently) did to those terrorists who took the No. 300 bus in 1984. But had those terrorists possessed information about the location of another bus full of civilians about to be destroyed by another terrorist band, and if the only way to prevent that loss of innocent life was to torture the captured, culpable terrorists, then such torture or death is morally permissible. The act is much less wrong because done to culpable terrorists, and the good consequences achieved may justify doing that lesser wrong.

3. Non-Absolute Moral Norms: Threshold Deontology   Apart from the exceptions that the content of moral norms must have for them to be plausible, a third modification of absolutism is the softening of the 'whatever the consequences' aspect mentioned earlier. This aspect of absolutism is often attributed to Kant, who held that though the heavens may fall, justice must be done. Despite my nonconsequentialist views on morality, I cannot accept the Kantian line. It just is not true that one should allow a nuclear war rather than killing or torturing an innocent person. It is not even true that one should allow the destruction of a sizable city by a terrorist nuclear device rather than kill or torture an innocent person. To prevent such extraordinary harms extreme actions seem to me to be justified.

There is a story in the Talmudic sources that may appear to appeal to a contrary intuition.[122] It is said that where the city is surrounded and threatened with destruction if it does not send out one of its inhabitants to be killed, it is better that the whole city should perish rather than become an accomplice to the killing of one of its

---

[121] See the discussion of the criteria used by the 'Seattle God Committee', which for a time decided who would live and who would die in Seattle, in Katz, *Bad Acts*, *supra* n. 11, at 53–6.

[122] *Tosefta*, *Trumot* 7, 23; Jerusalem Talmud, *Trumot* 8, 4(46b).

inhabitants. Benjamin Cardozo expressed the same intuition in rejecting the idea that those in a lifeboat about to sink and drown may jettison enough of their number to allow the remainder to stay afloat. As Cardozo put it:

Where two or more are overtaken by a common disaster, there is no right on the part of one to save the lives of some by the killing of another. There is no rule of human jettison. Men there will often be who, when told that their going will be the salvation of the remnant, will choose the nobler part and make the plunge into the waters. In that supreme moment the darkness for them will be illumined by the thought that those behind will ride to safety. If none of such mold are found aboard the boat, or too few to save the others, the human freight must be left to meet the chances of the waters.[123]

There is admittedly a nobility when those who are threatened with destruction choose on their own to suffer that destruction rather than participate in a prima facie immoral act. But what happens when we eliminate the choice of all concerned to sacrifice themselves? Alter the Talmudic example slightly by making it the ruler of the city who alone must decide whether to send one out in order to prevent destruction of the city. Or take the actual facts of the lifeboat case[124] to which Cardozo was adverting, where it was a seaman who took charge of the sinking lifeboat and jettisoned enough of its passengers to save the rest. Or consider Bernard Williams's example, where you come across a large group of villagers about to be shot by the army as an example to others, and you can save most of them if you will but shoot one; far from choosing to 'sink or swim' together, the villagers beg you to shoot one of their number so that the rest may be saved.[125] In all such cases it no longer seems virtuous to refuse to do an act that you abhor. On the contrary, it seems a narcissistic preoccupation with your own 'virtue'—that is, the 'virtue' you could have if the world were ideal and did not present you with such awful choices—if you choose to allow the greater number to perish. In such cases, I prefer Sartre's version of the Orestes legend to the Talmud: the ruler should take the guilt upon himself rather than allow his people to perish.[126] One should

---

[123] Cardozo, *Law and Literature and Other Essays and Addresses* (New York, 1931), at 113.

[124] *United States* v. *Holmes*, *supra* n. 55.

[125] Smart and Williams, *Utilitarianism*, *supra* n. 31, at 98–9.

[126] Jean-Paul Sartre, 'The Flies', in *No Exit and Three Other Plays* (New York, trans. L. Abel, 1955).

feel guilty in such cases, but it is nobler to undertake such guilt than to shut one's eyes to the horrendous consequences of not acting.

I thus have some sympathy for the Landau Commission's conclusion that 'actual torture . . . would perhaps be justified in order to uncover a bomb about to explode in a building full of people'.[127] If one does not know which building is going to explode, one does not have the consent of all concerned to 'sink or swim' together. On the contrary, one suspects that like Williams's villagers, the occupants of the building, if they knew of their danger, would choose that one of their number (to say nothing of one of the terrorist group) be tortured or die to prevent the loss of all. In any case, the GSS interrogator must choose for others who will pay the costs for his decision if he decides not to act, a cost he does not have to bear; this situation is thus more like my variation of the Talmudic example than the original.

Many think that the agent-relative view just sketched, allowing as it does consequences to override moral absolutes when those consequences are horrendous enough, collapses into a consequentialist morality after all. Glanville Williams, for example, in his discussion of the legal defence of necessity, recognizes the agent-relative view that 'certain actions are right or wrong irrespective of their consequences' and that 'a good end never justifies bad means'.[128] Williams nonetheless concludes that 'in the last resort moral decisions must be made with reference to results'.[129] Williams reaches this conclusion because, as Williams sees it, the agent-relative slogans just quoted reduce to the claim 'that we ought to do what is right regardless of the consequences, *as long as the consequences are not serious*'.[130]

Contrary to Williams, there is no collapse of agent-relative views into consequentialism just because morality's norms can be overridden by horrendous consequences.[131] A consequentialist is committed by her moral theory to saying that torture of one person is justified whenever it is necessary to prevent the torture of two or more. The agent-relative view, even as here modified, is not committed to this proposition. To justify torturing one innocent person requires that there be horrendous consequences attached to not torturing that person—the destruction of an entire city, or, perhaps,

---

[127] *Landau Report*, *supra* n. 1, at 60.
[128] Williams, *Criminal Law*, *supra* n. 11, at 729.   [129] Ibid.
[130] Ibid. (emphasis added).   [131] Nagel, 'War and Massacre', *supra* n. 45.

of a lifeboat or building full of people. On this view, in other words, there is a very high threshold of bad consequences that must be threatened before something as awful as torturing an innocent person can be justified. Almost all real-life decisions a GSS interrogator will face—and perhaps *all* decisions—will not reach that threshold of horrendous consequences justifying torture of the innocent. Short of such a threshold, the agent-relative view just sketched will operate as absolutely as absolutism in its ban on torturing the innocent.[132]

Despite this logical difference between agent-relative views of morality with a threshold, and consequentialist views of morality, there is of course a real danger that as a matter of psychological fact people will tend to confuse the two. As Bernard Williams has noted, it is very easy to slide from 'the idea that there was nothing that was right whatever the consequences'—the non-absolutist but agent-relative idea I have defended here—to 'the idea that everything depends on consequences'—the consequentialist view I reject.[133] For the threshold of exceptionally awful consequences is bound to appear as a somewhat arbitrary line wherever it is drawn. By the familiar process of adding just one more straw to the camel's back, people may thus push back the line further and further until the exceptional becomes the usual, and the balance of consequences always determines what it is right to do.[134]

---

[132] As Amartya Sen has observed, a threshold-deontology will *in some sense* be a consequentialist system: 'Such a threshold-based constraint system must rest ultimately on consequential analysis, comparing one set of consequences (badness resulting from obeying the constraint) with another (badness of violating the constraint itself, given by the threshold), and its distinguishing feature will be the particular *form* of the consequence-evaluation function.' Sen, 'Rights and Agency', *supra* n. 34, at 187–223, 190–1, n. 8. This will particularly be true of a threshold deontology that varies the threshold (where consequences begin to count) directly with the degree of wrongness of the act to be justified by its consequences. (That is, the greater the wrong to be done, the higher the threshold of bad consequences averted has to be to justify the action as right.)

Saying all of this still does not collapse threshold deontology into consequentialism. Even if the goodness of consequences is always relevant to the rightness of actions for a threshold deontologist, the goodness of consequences does not determine the rightness of actions as it does for a consequentialist. Contrary to Sen, the degree of (agent-relative) wrongness of an action does not translate into some degree of (agent-neutral) 'badness of violating the constraint'. The threshold deontologist does not think that the wrongness of *his* doing a certain act is just another bad consequence that can be outweighed by the better consequences of preventing like acts by others.

[133] Smart and Williams, *Utilitarianism*, *supra* n. 31, at 93.   [134] Ibid., at 91–2.

That this is a psychological danger is a reason not to tell people that there are thresholds of awfulness that justify prima facie immoral behaviour. It is not a reason to doubt that there are such moral thresholds for consequential calculation. It is the truth of this last proposition that governs the retrospective question with which I am here concerned. How one handles the psychological danger I pick up when I discuss the prospective question of new rules for GSS interrogations.

Even if threshold deontology does not collapse into consequentialism, many think such a view of morality to be arbitrary and irrational. Why should goodness of consequences not count at all and then, at some point, count enormously in the sense that it fully determines the rightness of action? What is overlooked by those convinced by this suggestion is that the threshold deontologist is not committed to denying that consequentialism is one moral principle among others. As Tom Nagel concedes, 'there is one important component of ethics that is consequentialist and impersonal'.[135] If our behaviour does not violate a moral norm like 'don't torture' (and is not excepted by a moral permission like 'you need not give away all of your money'), goodness of consequences does determine the rightness of actions.

Thus, for a threshold deontologist consequences always 'count'. For behaviour violating deontological restraints, however, until the threshold is reached the principle that makes such consequences count—the consequentialist principle itself—is outweighed by other moral principles. As the consequences get more and more severe, the consequentialist principle becomes of greater weight as applied to this situation, until at some point (the threshold) the consequentialist principle outweighs competing principles of morality. Even before such a threshold was reached, consequences counted but were of insufficient weight to determine the rightness of actions. An analogy may help here: imagine water slowly rising behind a dam until eventually it spills over. There is nothing arbitrary about thinking *both* that there is no spillover until the threshold of the dam's height is reached, and that each bit of water always counts in determining whether water will spill over the dam or not.[136]

If the rationality of a threshold-deontological view of morality is to be questioned, it will have to be on grounds other than these.

---

[135] Nagel, *View, supra* n. 35, at 164–5.   [136] I owe the analogy to Joseph Raz.

Perhaps the worry is not the apparent suddenness with which consequences seem to count for everything where before they counted for nothing; rather, the worry may be that any point we pick for a threshold beyond which consequences determine the rightness of action may seem arbitrary. Do we need there to be 500 people in a building about to be blown up by a bomb before we may torture an innocent to find the bomb's location, or will 450 do?

Although this worry can surely give rise to quite genuine perplexity and anxiety when we make practical decisions, it is not the basis of any very powerful objection to threshold deontology as a moral theory. For this is no more than the medieval worry of how many stones make a heap. Our uncertainty whether it takes three, or four, or five, etc., does not justify us in thinking that there are no such things as heaps. Similarly, preventing the torture of two innocents does not justify my torturing one, but destruction of an entire city does. And if an actual case arises where I have to say whether preventing the death of 450 people in a building is sufficiently good to justify the torture or killing of one innocent, I would want to know more details as to what was done to the innocent to extract the information—for where the threshold lies depends in part on the degree of wrong done.

4. Torture and the Balance of Evils   This has been a long and complicated discussion of a complex agent-relative view of morality. If one accepts the morality defended here, a brief statement of its implications for torture is as follows. First, one of morality's firmest norms is that torture is impermissible. We each have a moral duty not to torture another human being even when our doing so would prevent the torture (or other harm) to other human beings. Second, in the circumstances in which GSS interrogations took place, there is no construal of the limits of permissible consequential calculation that weakens or alters this absolutist conclusion. Whenever a state agency such as the GSS tortures, it does so through the intentional actions of its agents, to victims who are not in peril of torture anyway, and without the intervention of any third party or any complicated chain of natural causation. Third, the moral ban against torture applies less firmly to those who culpably cause the need for torture by planting the bomb that needs removal, etc.; such persons may be tortured when absolutely necessary to remove the threat that they have caused. Fourth, those who could remove the threatened harm at little cost to themselves are also less wronged if they are tortured to induce them to do what morally they ought to do anyway. When sufficiently good consequences can only be obtained by the torture of such persons, morality does not forbid it. Fifth, nothing in the preceding points justifies torturing the innocent, no matter how necessary such torture may be to prevent bad consequences. Only the most horrendous of consequences could justify the torture of those who neither caused a threat of serious harm nor become a part of such threat by refusing to remove it. The likelihood of such horrendous consequences ever actually following from not torturing an innocent are so remote that no GSS interrogator is likely to have faced such a situation.

If I am correct about these moral conclusions, then they should also form the basis for legal conclusions about the criminal liability of GSS interrogators for their past acts of torture. For Israel's balance-of-evils defence, like that of the Model Penal Code, is best construed to require just the kind of non-consequentialist moral reasoning that I have here attempted to display.

To actually apply these general moral conclusions to particular cases, much more would have to be said. First, there is the matter of 'justificatory intent'.[137] To avail himself of a balance-of-evils defence, a GSS interrogator must have tortured *in order* to prevent the harm whose threat justifies the torture. Use of torture as an investigative tool to aid in obtaining confessions for use in prosecuting terrorists does not meet this requirement, even if on some occasions such torture turns up life-saving information. Second, the GSS interrogator must have believed that the torture would in fact produce the kind of good consequences that alone can justify it. If life-saving information was being sought by torture, then there must have been some evidence on which the GSS interrogator based his beliefs: (1) that the terrorist had such information; (2) that the techniques adopted were likely to get him to divulge it; and (3) that the information would not have been rendered useless by the terrorist's organization having taken preventive measures on learning of the capture of one of its members.

[137] On justificatory intent, compare the differing views of Fletcher, *Rethinking*, *supra* n. 11, at 557, 559–60, with Moore, *Act and Crime*, *supra* n. 84, at ch. 7. Fletcher thinks (along with current law) that an actor whose act is justified objectively but who lacks justificatory intent is guilty of the completed crime; I think that such an actor does no wrong but because he did such a wrong in his own mind, his culpability merits punishment for attempt.

Third, the GSS interrogator must have adopted the 'least restrictive alternative' in his interrogative methods. I have deliberately refrained from defining 'torture' throughout my discussion so that euphemisms like 'pressure' or 'harsh treatment' do not make the moral dilemmas seem easier than they are. Still, it should be plain that there is a world of difference morally between the slight tortures of sleep deprivation and the severe tortures of physical mutilation. In order to satisfy the balance-of-evils requirement that the torture has been *necessary* to save lives, the GSS interrogator must have believed that no less draconian interrogative technique would have been as effective as the one he employed.

Lastly, and in an abundance of caution, let me reiterate the obvious. Nothing said herein implies that torturing terrorists in retaliation for their terrorist acts is justified. Torture is an evil, and is only eligible to be justified when a greater evil is prevented. Torture for its own sake or for retaliation is not a balance of evils. It is only evil.

III. THE PROSPECTIVE QUESTION: IS NEW LEGISLATION NEEDED?

A. What Behaviour of the General Security Service in Interrogating Terrorist Suspects Is Desirable?

Before deciding whether new legislation will better achieve some goal, one first must ask what the good is that such legislation should be trying to achieve. Specifically, what behaviour by its GSS interrogators should Israel desire for the future? To a large extent we have answered this prospective, legislative question by our answer to the retrospective, adjudicatory question. For open-ended provisions like Israel's Penal Law section 22 invite the kind of all-things-considered value judgements needed by a legislator no less than a judge. For the future Israel should want its GSS interrogators to get the moral balance described in this chapter right as much of the time as is humanly possible. Israelis should want this because they seek a state whose behaviour and whose morality they can openly affirm. As the Landau Commission observed, 'the methods of police interrogation which are employed in any given regime are a faithful mirror of the character of the entire regime . . .'.[138] It is

---

[138] *Landau Report, supra* n. 1, at 77.

difficult to be proud of a state whose police forces engage in 'inter-rogative methods like those practiced in regimes which we abhor'.[139] Thus, however one resolves the moral questions I explored in the preceding part of this chapter, one should employ that resolution here as well.

B. What Laws Will Produce That Behaviour?

The interesting question is how by law one may best achieve the morally right behaviour described before. The Landau Commission helpfully distinguished three general possibilities:[140] (1) to regard the interrogation of terrorist suspects by the GSS as in a 'twilight zone' that is 'outside the realm of law', so that what levels of 'pressure' the GSS uses, and when, would be up to it alone; (2) to promulgate laws to guide GSS behaviour while not intending to enforce those laws by their terms when they are violated by the GSS; (3) to promulgate rules that are designed both to guide GSS behaviour and to be enforced according to their terms. I shall explore each option briefly.

1. GSS Interrogations as 'Beyond the Law'   There are a number of reasons that might incline one to the view that the activities of a country's security forces are beyond the law. One stems from the ancient idea that situations of necessity are so extreme that the law can hope to have no influence on the motives that move citizens to act in such situations. As Francis Bacon put this point, in utilizing Cicero's well-known two men on one plank hypothetical: 'if either there lie an impossibility for a man to do otherwise, or so great a perturbation of judgement and reason as in presumption of law man's nature cannot overcome, such necessity carrieth a privilege in itself'.[141]

There are two ways to interpret this idea from Bacon. One is to say that acting in situations of necessity is done literally outside the reach of a nation's positive laws, so that normal proscriptions against murder and torture do not apply. Building perhaps on his well-known views that law has to serve an essential action-guiding function in order to be law at all,[142] Lon Fuller has his fictional

---

[139] Id.   [140] Id. at 77–9.

[141] Shedding, Ellis, and Heath, *The Works of Francis Bacon* (Philadelphia: Parry and McMillan, 1859), 343.

[142] Lon Fuller, *The Morality of Law* (2nd edn., Stanford: Stanford University Press, 1969).

'Justice Foster' take this interpretation of Bacon.[143] Alternatively and preferably, Bacon should be taken to mean that a nation's positive laws do reach behaviour in situations of necessity, but that one of the things those laws provide is that necessity is a defence.[144] The latter interpretation keeps necessitous behaviour governed by law and does not lead to the odd conceptual puzzles of how certain behaviour within a state's borders cannot be subject to that state's laws (even to the extent of having those laws grant a liberty to engage in that behaviour).[145]

In any case, however Bacon is construed, his 'psychological impossibility' of conforming to the law has no application to GSS interrogation of terrorist suspects. GSS interrogators, and those who make policy for them within the GSS, are not clinging desperately to a plank. It is not impossible for the law to have its educative and deterrent effect on GSS behaviour, so this cannot be a good reason for regarding that behaviour as 'beyond the law'.

A second reason sometimes suggested here is that it is unfair and unfitting for lawyers and judges after the fact to judge the behaviour of those acting *in extremis*. Leo Katz nicely catches this intuition:

Somehow what goes on in the spacious, soft-carpeted, high-ceilinged courtrooms of civilization seems to have little bearing on what men do to each other under circumstances as extraordinary as those in which the sailors and the spelunkers found themselves.[146]

What cannot fairly be judged in a courtroom, one might think, should be seen as 'beyond the law'.

Yet this too is an indefensible view to adopt for GSS behaviour, for both the reasons I advanced against Fuller's interpretation of

---

[143] As Justice Foster puts it: 'I take the view that the enacted or positive law of this Commonwealth, including all of its statutes and precedents, is inapplicable to this case, and that this case is governed instead by what ancient writers in Europe and America called "the law of nature".' Fuller, 'Speluncean Explorers', *supra* n. 55, at 620.

[144] The difference between these two interpretations of Bacon can be seen by attending to the distinction between what modal logicians call external versus internal negation: Foster's interpretation is that it is not the case that the law prohibits spelunkean homicide (external negation); the alternative interpretation is that it is the case that the law does not prohibit spelunkean homicide. The law covers the situation under the second interpretation; it does not under the first.

[145] For some of these puzzles, see Katz, *Bad Acts*, *supra* n. 11, at 31–2.

[146] Ibid., at 30.

Bacon: (1) one better alleviates any unfairness of after-the-fact judgement by having law that takes into account the psychological difficulties under which the behaviour judged was done, rather than saying such behaviour is beyond the reach of law at all; and (2) a state organization adopting deliberate policies does not act *in extremis*, but in fact engages in what looks like traditional law enforcement functions as a matter of deliberate state policy.

A third and deeper reason might be suggested for why behaviour like that of the GSS is beyond the law. That is the suggestion that the hard choices made in situations of necessity are beyond morality itself, and thus are beyond that reflection of morality we call the criminal law. Bernard Williams suggested such a view of morality as it applies to situations like that of torturing a terrorist's child in order to save a building full of innocent lives. A moral agent, Williams tells us, may in such situations:

find it unacceptable to consider what to do . . . Logically, or indeed empirically conceivable they [the situations] may be, but they are not to him morally conceivable, meaning by that that their occurrence as situations presenting him with a choice would represent not a special problem in his moral world, but something that lay beyond its limits. For him, there are certain situations so monstrous that the idea that the processes of moral rationality could yield an answer in them is insane: they are situations which so transcend in enormity the human business of moral deliberation that from a moral point of view it cannot matter any more what happens.[147]

Such a view does not depend on a psychological premise, as did the two earlier reasons we considered. Williams is not suggesting that reason is psychologically unhinged when we face the kinds of choice discussed in this article. Rather, it is morality itself that is left behind in such choice situations. Thus, Williams concludes, he would decide his hypothetical case of 'Jim'[148] in favour of Jim's killing one innocent native in order that nineteen other innocent natives not be killed by someone else.[149] But such a decision would not be dictated by morality:

Instead of thinking in a rational and systematic way either about utilities or about the value of human life, the relevance of the people at risk being

---

[147] Smart and Williams, *Utilitarianism*, *supra* n. 31, at 92.
[148] See text *supra* at n. 125.
[149] Smart and Williams, *Utilitarianism*, *supra* n. 31, at 117.

present, and so forth, the presence of the people at risk may just have its effect. The significance of the immediate should not be underestimated . . . we are not primarily janitors of any system of values, even our own: very often, we just act, as a possibly confused result of the situation in which we are engaged. That, I suspect, is very often an exceedingly good thing.[150]

I find this view of morality, and like views put forward by Elizabeth Anscombe[151] and Tom Nagel,[152] to be totally unacceptable. Such views treat morality and even practical rationality as 'running out' when the going gets tough. Morality and practical reason supposedly have nothing to say on what we ought to do; Sartre-like, we are told, we must just choose. Such views do not square with our experience with acute moral dilemmas. We never feel 'that from a moral point of view it cannot matter any more what happens'. What makes moral dilemmas such as those we have been exploring so acute is that it does matter what we choose to do. That is why we think as hard as we can about them and try to discover the best of an admittedly not very happy set of answers.

Williams's view makes morality only fit for a world that is better off than the world we actually inhabit. Morality is only applicable when things are 'nice'; moral theories are *ideal* theories in the pejorative sense of the word. Even Williams does not really believe this, for he can resolve hard moral dilemmas like the one he constructs about 'Jim'. GSS interrogative techniques in the face of terrorism might well be beyond the law if those techniques were beyond morality, but since the latter is not the case, neither is the former.

A fourth reason for thinking the GSS's war on terrorism is beyond the law lies in the unsavoury nature of torture. Intentionally inflicting pain on another human being for any reason is degrading and disgusting. One might think that even though such behaviour can be justified on occasion, its odious character prevents the law from giving it any recognition. Law, one might think—unless it is going to ban flatly such unsavoury behaviour— cannot otherwise regulate it.

An example of what detailed legal regulation of torture would look like is provided by the T'ang (AD 618–907) and Ch'ing (AD 1655–1911) Codes of China, which allowed torture of witnesses as well as suspects to obtain information and confessions.[153] Both

---

[150] Smart and Williams, *Utilitarianism*, *supra* n. 31, at 118.
[151] Anscombe, 'Modern Moral Philosophy', *supra* n. 48, at 17.
[152] Nagel, 'War and Massacre', *supra* n. 45, at 72–3.

Codes define with precision permissible instruments of torture, which instruments had to be governmentally inspected and stamped; bamboo for beating, for example, is divided between light and heavy, with precise measurements of each. The amount of torture is specified: for beatings, for example, the T'ang Code allowed a suspect to be beaten a maximum of three times during a sixty-day period, with a total limit of 200 blows during this period; the Ch'ing Code allowed thirty blows per day, with the heavy bamboo. The circumstances of use was specified: for the very painful ankle-squeeze, only homicide or robbery justified its use, and even then, it was never to be used on a woman.

There is surely something grotesque and ugly about detailed regulations of this kind. (Surely part of the reason why Israel has kept secret its classified regulations on GSS 'pressure' on terrorists is a similar distaste.) Yet part of what makes such regulations so distasteful is that they only tell half the story, which is the evil that may be done by torture; they do not tell of the evil being prevented whenever torture is justified. If I am right in the moral conclusions reached earlier, those are conclusions of which no one should be ashamed. The law, like the morality that underlies it, can speak openly about them. One can say what the Parker Commission in England said of British interrogative techniques when used against Irish Republican Army suspects in order to save life:

[T]he answer to the moral question is dependent on the intensity with which these techniques are applied and on the provision of effective safeguards against excessive use ... Subject to these safeguards, we have come to the conclusion that there is no reason to rule out these techniques on moral grounds and that it is permissible to operate them in a manner consistent with the highest standards of our society.[154]

I conclude that there is no good reason to think that the subject of permissible torture must remain outside the reach of law. On the other hand, there are quite good reasons why such behaviour should remain subject to court-enforced law. The main reason is obvious: without such legal restraint, the potential for abuse is

[153] See Ch'u T'ung-Tsu, *Local Government in China* (Cambridge Mass.: Harvard University Press, 1962), 125; D. Bodde and C. Morris, *Law in Imperial China* (Philadelphia: University of Pennsylvania Press, 1973), 97–8. (I am indebted to Hugh Scogin for this information.) For other examples of legalized torture, see E. Peters, *Torture* (New York: Basil Blackwell, 1985).

[154] Quoted in *Landau Report*, *supra* n. 1, at 73.

enormous. The American experience with a like claim made by the Nixon Administration—that national security placed government agents outside the laws against burglary and the Fourth Amendment—underlines the obvious dangers of telling any governmental agency they are 'beyond the law'. It took Sir Thomas More, Lord Coke, and their common law brethren several centuries to convince the English kings that they too were subject to the law. It took a unanimous US Supreme Court and much American travail to convince Richard Nixon that the same applied to him. It is not a lesson that should need repeating in Israel.

2. Acoustic Separation: One Law for the GSS, Another for the Executive?   Sometimes the best way to hit a target is not to aim at it. When shooting an arrow in a steady crosswind, one does best by aiming to the side of the target by that amount one estimates the wind will carry the arrow during its flight. Similarly in law, sometimes a legislator best achieves her targeted behaviour by *not* describing that behaviour in the content of her laws. This will be the case whenever those who must obey such laws have a 'steady crosswind' in their motivation, viz., whenever they are systematically prone to erring one way rather than another.

It is often said that this condition is met in necessity cases where the life being saved includes the actor's own. Self-preservation being the instinct that it is, the argument goes, actors systematically err in their own favour as they calculate when life must be taken to save even more life. *Dudley and Stephens*[155] was rightly decided, on this view, because it gave the right incentive structure to those in lifeboats: since the court held that any homicide will be murder, those *in extremis* will wait until death is almost upon them before they kill another. That is optimal because it results in life being taken only when it is truly necessary to preserve more life. Whereas, it might be thought, a rule that did not flatly ban homicide but allowed it when necessary to save more life would encourage too much killing, given everyone's self-preservative instincts.

There is of course the nagging problem of fairness to actors like Dudley and Stephens who did not overly favour themselves and who did kill only when it was necessary to save more life. This the court took care of by inviting executive clemency, which was eventually and quietly granted to Dudley and Stephens.

---

[155] *Dudley and Stephens, supra* n. 55.

This divorce between the stated law that citizens (including GSS interrogators) are to apply to their behaviour, and an unstated targeted behaviour that the lawmaker wishes to achieve with the stated law, Meir Dan-Cohen has called 'acoustic separation'.[156] The acoustic separation is between what the GSS interrogator hears (the stated law, for example, 'never torture') and what some other official hears (the unstated, targeted behaviour, for example, 'torture only when justified in Moore's long and complicated chapter'). If the other official is the Executive, then a pardon or other form of executive clemency would be appropriate for those GSS interrogators whose behaviour was 'on target' even though violative of the stated law—only, of course, when such pardon or clemency could be given without public attention.

The psychological premise that would motivate this view has some accuracy when applied to GSS interrogators. Such interrogators, if allowed to calculate at all, will probably err in favour of too much torture too often. This may be because: they have just witnessed the death or injury of innocents at the hands of the terrorists they are about to interrogate, so that their fellow-feeling for such suspects is at low ebb; their patriotism inclines them to favour Israeli lives being saved over non-Israeli lives being lost; the accepted criteria for success in their job is in terms of arms discovered, lives saved, etc., not in terms of rights and dignities preserved; and, last but not least, brutal treatment brutalizes the inflicter of it.

For this reason, were I writing Israel's laws, I would make no provision for the 'threshold deontology' I described in my complex agent-relative view of morality. I assume that a patriotic GSS interrogator will torture an innocent person when the consequences of not doing so are so horrendous that the consequential override of the threshold deontologist is morally required. I further assume that he will do so no matter that the stated law forbids it. Whereas were the stated law to include a provision saying that a GSS interrogator may do anything to anyone if the consequences of not doing so are horrendous enough, probably more torture would take place than could be morally justified. I thus think Israeli law should contain a flat ban on torture of innocents.

---

[156] Meir Dan-Cohen, 'Decision Rules and Conduct Rules: On Acoustic Separation in Criminal Law', *Harvard Law Review*, Vol. 97 (1984), 625–77.

Whether such a flat ban should encompass those who possess information whose transfer would save lives and injury, but who refuse without justification to divulge such information, is a difficult question. Certainly the same danger of GSS interrogators systematically erring in favour of too much torture is present. On the other hand, the moral error is less serious, and the likelihood of error is less (because the area of morally permissible torture is greater), *if* the person interrogated does possess life-saving information. I conclude, with some misgiving, that torture of those possessed of life-saving information, even though not themselves terrorists, should not flatly be banned. Nor, of course, should torture of terrorist suspects themselves.

Even the flat ban on torture of the innocents has some unfairness built into it. Those GSS interrogators who torture the innocent on those very rare occasions when it is justified—the horrendous consequences threshold—have cause for complaint that they will be punished although they did the right thing. Their behaviour was the targeted behaviour even though violative of the stated law. Of course, like Dudley and Stephens and the GSS personnel pardoned in the No. 300 bus affair, such interrogators may hope for executive clemency, the granting of which alleviates the unfairness. Still, a legislator sharing the complex agent-relative moral views I described earlier has to be willing to impose some unfairness as a cost of flatly banning even torture of the innocent.

3. A Law of Torture That Means What It Says   Other than the flat ban on torture of the innocents above described, Israel should have a law on torture that means exactly what it says. Open to question, however, is exactly how much the law should say on this subject. How much detail should be written into law, and how much should be left to individual decision under more general standards?

There are two kinds of details that could be written into law, corresponding to the two kinds of moral knowledge required to apply the balance-of-evils defence. First, one could specify both sides of the consequentialist balance. One could spell out the evils being done, like the Chinese torture schedule adverted to earlier; and one could spell out the evils being averted, such as numbers of lives, etc. Presumably, one would create a kind of sliding scale, more evil tortures requiring greater evils averted. Second, one could specify the limits on consequential calculation I described in my complex, agent-relative view of morality.

I think there are good reasons not to do either of these things. I do not think such reasons have to do with it being dishonourable to spell out the limits of legal torture. What is morally right cannot be dishonourable (although it certainly can be painful and guilt-producing). Rather, such reasons have to do with J. L. Austin's earlier quoted aphorism that 'fact is richer than diction'.[157] The circumstances making torture of terrorists and others justifiable are too various to be captured by 'per se' rules of justified torture. This is the reason that section 22 of the Israeli Penal Law, and like provisions of American and German law, are formulated as broadly as they are. Any greater precision will be at the cost of accuracy.

Consider the American experience in trying to define the like concept of negligence. Oliver Wendell Holmes thought that negligence could eventually be reduced to much more determinate rules, such as his rule that a motor car must 'stop, look, and listen' when coming to a railroad crossing. Anyone knows that such a rule is both over- and under-inclusive of cases with respect to negligence. It is over-inclusive because it includes cases where not stopping is not negligent because one can see clearly in both directions; it is under-inclusive because stopping, looking, and listening may not be enough precautions to be reasonable, as where there is a lot of noise and vision is blocked so that the motorist who only stops, looks, and listens cannot tell whether a train is coming. The lesson is that fact *is* richer than diction for concepts like negligence or necessity. Sir William Scott thus had it right when he wrote in 1801:

The law of cases of necessity is not likely to be well furnished with precise rules . . . whatever is reasonable and just in such cases, is likewise legal. It is not to be considered a matter of surprise, therefore, if much instituted rule is not to be found on such subjects.[158]

Other than the flat ban on torturing the innocent, section 22 is all the law on torture Israel should want or need.

What is needed is something that *by law* is very hard to achieve, namely, a shared set of attitudes within the GSS that abhors torture as inherently evil while at the same time allowing that, on

[157] J. L. Austin, 'A Plea for Excuses', *Proceedings of the Aristotelian Society*, Vol. 57 (1956), 1–30, at 21.
[158] *The Gratitudine*, (1801) 165 ENG REP 450, at 459.

occasion, some evils are greater. The procedural reforms within the GSS suggested by the Landau Commission are helpful in fostering such attitudes. Having higher level officials sign off on extraordinary interrogative techniques, and steering those techniques away from the kinds of physical abuse that breeds sadism in those who use them, are steps in the right direction.

SUBPART C
THE THEORY OF THE LIMITS OF CRIMINAL LEGISLATION

18

LIBERTY'S LIMITS ON LEGISLATION

I. INTRODUCTION

As previewed at the end of chapter 16, a properly retributivist-legal moralist legislator may nonetheless be quite liberal in the restrictions he places on what should be made criminal. Whether this is so in part depends on two substantive moral judgements: (1) How extensive are our moral obligations? And (2), is there some value extraneous to those behind our obligations such that some of those actions that we are plainly obligated not to do should nonetheless not be criminalized? This chapter approaches both questions under the guise of a right to liberty.

I shall approach the topic of liberty in part through application of the analysis to one perennial question facing a legislator, namely, the question of whether to criminalize the recreational use of drugs. Although a good deal of the chapter works through the analysis in the abstract, it is hoped that the last part dealing with drugs also illuminates the general points made during the more abstract analysis.

Anything that could be called a general right to liberty has proved quite elusive to the considerable number of philosophers who have pursued it. The nature of such a general right is elusive for two sorts of reasons. The first is conceptual: it is not clear that there is one coherent conception of liberty. It seems to many that the word, 'liberty', is both ambiguous and vague. It is ambiguous insofar as it refers to quite different sorts of things, such as political liberty versus the metaphysical liberty of free will, and such as in the old conundrum between negative liberty as absence of restraint versus positive liberty as the power to achieve something. It is vague insofar as the kinds and degrees of restraint that deny liberty are underspecified. For example, do private threats, internal cravings, criminal sanctions, and tempting offers, all equally erode the recipient's liberty?

The second reason for the elusiveness of any general right to liberty is normative: even if some one thing is specified by 'liberty' with enough precision to be worth talking about, it is not clear that there is anything intelligibly good about liberty as such. The liberty to be a murderer seems of little or no value, and thus liberty as such—without specifying the acts one is at liberty to do—seems to have little or no value. The liberty of speaking freely may have great value, for example, but that might be because of the existence of a particular right of free speech, not because there is a general right of liberty.

Attempting to make the general right to liberty less elusive will be one of the tasks undertaken in this chapter. Such an undertaking is perhaps particularly useful in the context of the particular question of drug policy, for even amongst those theorists sympathetic to a rights-based approach to drugs the analysis tends to be long on application, but short on explication, of the concept of liberty.[1]

Like most philosophy, political philosophy maximizes its chances of arriving at better answers if its questions are better framed. Accordingly, I shall spend a moment framing the questions I wish to pursue. In the first place, the right to liberty whose nature interests me is a moral right, not a legal (or more specifically, an American Constitutional) right. Although the badly misnamed 'privacy' decisions of the US Supreme Court for the last thirty years are the best known locus for any general right to liberty, such a legal right is not my concern. True enough, those who share my theory of constitutional interpretation[2] will take the constitutional right to follow closely the underlying moral right. But it is the nature of the latter that is my concern, leaving it to another day to argue for the constitutional enforcement of such a moral right. This means that it will be out of place to argue from US Supreme Court precedents as if they gave an authoritative exposition of liberty. In

---

[1] Three of the leading books on the topic of drug policy devote but little attention to the general idea of limited state power or of citizen liberty. See Douglas N. Husak, *Drugs and Rights* (Cambridge: Cambridge University Press, 1992), at 61–8; David A. J. Richards, *Sex, Drugs, Death, and the Law* (Totowa, NJ: Rowman and Littlefield, 1982), 1–25; John Kaplan, *The Hardest Drug* (Chicago: University of Chicago Press, 1983), 102–9.

[2] See Michael Moore, 'Do We Have an Unwritten Constitution?', *Southern California Law Review*, Vol. 63 (1989), 107–39; Moore, 'A Natural Law Theory of Interpretation', *Southern California Law Review*, Vol. 58 (1985), 277–398.

this ethical enquiry such decisions have only the weight of the persuasiveness of the reasons offered within them, nothing more.

I thus continue in this chapter the focus of this Part III on a theory of legislation. Such a theory has as its audience legislators and those who would advise legislators, not courts. Part of the legislative role such a theory defines includes the protection of the moral rights of those citizens who are subject to such legislation, even if one's theory of adjudication is one (like my own) that also assigns to courts this duty to respect moral rights.

Second, I shall not argue that people have moral rights. Rather, I shall assume that there are such moral entities as rights and frame my enquiry by asking whether a general right to liberty is among them. Since the very idea of a right (which the right-holder may waive or choose to exercise) already involves the idea of liberty,[3] this may seem like assuming an answer to my question before I start. Yet one could easily assume that people have rights but still deny that any general right to liberty exists. On this view, there are only *liberties*, each of which has to be argued for individually because not part of some general right of liberty.[4]

This latter issue is worth pausing over because it is an important one. If there are only distinct liberties, each protecting distinct interests or goals, then in the sense I care about liberty does not exist. For on the latter view, 'liberty' would be strictly abbreviatory of the rights persons possess, but those rights themselves would have nothing in common save that they are rights. For liberty to be a distinct right, it has to be more than the freedom involved whenever we have a right.

Third, I shall not engage in any lengthy conceptual analysis as to the 'primary' or 'focal' concept of liberty. Rather, I shall cut through this Gordian knot with a simple stipulative definition that adopts the traditional, negative definition of liberty: liberty is the absence of constraint, and political liberty is the absence of coercive legal sanctions. Unlike lexical definitions, stipulative definitions

---

[3] An idea of Locke's that the 'choice theory' of rights embraces and elaborates. The choice theory of rights is so named because it emphasizes that the holder of a right has the choice as to whether to waive it or exercise it. For discussion and citations, see Michael Moore, *Law and Psychiatry: Rethinking the Relationship* (Cambridge: Cambridge University Press, 1984), 92–3.

[4] The view of John Rawls, *A Theory of Justice* (Cambridge, Mass.: Harvard University Press, 1971), and of Ronald Dworkin, *Taking Rights Seriously* (Cambridge, Mass.: Harvard University Press, 1978), 270–1.

are not hostage to others' usage of the term being defined. To judge a stipulative definition is, thus, not to judge its accuracy as a report of any linguistic fact. Rather, my stipulation must be judged by how well it captures some salient moral facts. If liberty in the traditional sense I intend captures a value or values usefully clustered together, that will justify my stipulation in the only way it can be justified.

Such 'Alexandrian' solutions may seem a bit short with knotty problems like that of negative versus positive liberty. Yet stipulations like mine do not really solve such problems; rather, they begin an approach to such problems. My hypothesis is that absence of legal coercion may have unitary value. If so, my stipulation serves its purposes in forcing us to focus on that value. The enquiries temporarily put aside are then very much left open: is there a relationship between such value(s) as are protected by negative political liberty, and some larger value (such as the overall ability to choose) captured by the notion of positive liberty? And is such power to choose dependent on absence of private threats, presence of economic opportunities, as much as it is dependent upon absence of legal coercion? And does such power to choose ultimately involve some kind of 'libertarian' metaphysics of the kind we explored in chapter 12? I have not resolved any of these questions with my stipulative definition; only deferred them on the hypothesis (yet to be vindicated) that we are dealing with a pair of trousers that requires us to put one leg on at a time.

The fourth and last clarification of my enterprise in this chapter is to see that there is an alternative way of framing my enquiry that is revealing. Often the enquiry about a general *right* to liberty of citizens is framed as an enquiry about the general *duty* of legislators to respect certain principled limits in the use of state coercion. When the enquiry is put in the latter way, it is often put as a matter of finding the 'limits of state action', the 'limits of the criminal sanction', or the 'limits of legislation'.[5] These two questions—of citizen right and legislative duty—are highly related but not quite the same. They are related because here (although not generally[6]) it is

[5] As in, e.g., Wilhelm von Humboldt, *The Limits of State Action*, originally published in 1854, J. W. Burrow, trans. (Cambridge: Cambridge University Press, 1969); Herbert Packer, *The Limits of the Criminal Sanction* (Stanford: Stanford University Press, 1968); Michael Moore, 'The Limits of Legislation', Asia Foundation Lectures on Legislation, Seoul, Korea, 1984, published in *USC Cites* [Fall, 1984], 23–32.

[6] See Moore, *Law and Psychiatry, supra* n. 3 at 91.

plausible to suppose the correlativity thesis to be true: for any citizen right to liberty there is a correlative legislative duty, and vice versa. Even so, there is a difference between a right to liberty that is basic (from which the legislative duty is the mere correlative) and a right to liberty that is derived from the more basic legislative duty. Despite this difference, I intend a 'right to liberty' to encompass both such sorts of rights, if they exist.

II. SOME PROBLEMS WITH ANY GENERAL RIGHT TO LIBERTY

If political liberty is conceived of in the traditional way as the absence of governmental coercion, then a general right to such liberty would be a right generally to be free of coercive laws. It would approximate Louis Brandeis's famous definition of the general right of 'privacy': it is 'the most comprehensive of rights and the right most valued by civilized men, the right to be let alone'.[7]

Save for perhaps some extreme anarchists, everyone recognizes immediately the problem with such a right: it would abrogate those restraints at the heart of morality and civil society. As Robert Bork puts it: 'A general right of freedom . . . is a manifest impossibility. Such a right would posit a state of nature, and its law would be that of the jungle.'[8] Any theory that implies that we each have a right to murder, steal, etc., at will, is a non-starter.

There are only two strategies open to the defender of a general right to liberty (when that right is conceived as the right to be free of governmental coercion): one is to circumscribe the kinds of actions protected by the right so that acts of violence, etc., are outside the circle of liberty; the other is to weaken the right so that it can be overridden by other legitimate interests such as the interest of citizens in their bodily integrity.

The time-honoured maxim for libertarians pursuing the first strategy is that the circle of liberty includes only those actions as are compatible with a like liberty for others.[9] The idea here is that

[7] *Olmstead* v. *United States*, 277 US 438, 478 (1928).
[8] Robert Bork, *The Tempting of America* (New York: Macmillan, 1990).
[9] See, e.g., Rawls, *A Theory of Justice*, *supra* n. 4, at 244; John Hospers, 'What Libertarianism Is', in Tibor Machan, ed., *The Libertarian Alternative* (Chicago: Nelson-Hall, 1974).

liberty (of others) limits liberty (for each), so that no other value is needed to trump liberty—for if there were some such other value, then the right to liberty applies to *all* actions but is overridden as to some, which is the second strategy. To pursue this first strategy is thus to hold that 'only liberty can limit liberty', another time-honoured maxim of libertarian philosophy.

Despite its distinguished lineage, the only reason that these maxims (and the strategy they instantiate) are not plainly false is that they lack the coherence to have any truth value. Ask yourself this question: why is not a Hobbesian society of war of all against all compatible with these maxims? Is not the liberty of one person to rob, murder, and pillage compatible with a like liberty for everyone else? The libertarian has to say no, that to harm others in these ways takes away their liberty and therefore such actions are not compatible with a like liberty for all.

This libertarian rejoinder makes very little sense, because there is a shift in the meaning of liberty when one equates being killed or being robbed with a loss of *liberty*. These are not losses of negative liberty, for the dead and the poor are just as free of governmental restraint after they are killed or robbed as they were before. The 'like *liberty* of all' must therefore mean positive liberty, the power or opportunity to choose to do a variety of things, a power that death and poverty do diminish. Yet with this play on the meaning of 'liberty', what sense are we to make of the maxim? In what sense are the powers or opportunities of others *like* the freedom from governmental restraint that we are to test under the maxim?

Perhaps we are to compare the amount of opportunity a given absence of governmental coercion will engender for one person, with the amount of opportunity it will engender for everyone else. Since the amount of opportunities each of us has depends on many things besides the absence of legal coercion, this comparison cannot be between the total opportunity sets of all of us without failing completely as a test of negative liberty. Yet if we ask only what *increment* of opportunity absence of legal coercion makes to each of us, the increment is the same—laws forbidding sleeping under the bridges of Paris equally affect the *incremental* opportunities of the rich and the poor to find shelter, so long as we ignore the obvious differences in the *total* opportunities of each of them with respect to housing.

The upshot is that no clear sense is to be given to the idea that harming others diminishes their liberty. Moreover, even if one could give some sense to the equation, isn't the equation in any event disingenuous? After all, the equation suggests that what is wrong with murder is that it deprives the victim of his liberty. If we take this in the positive sense of liberty, what is wrong with causing another to die is that death ends our choosing opportunities. And is this not a bit of over-intellectualization, the giving of one reason too many?[10] What is wrong with murder is that you end someone's life. Their life surely has a value beyond simply the opportunity to *choose* that is present only when they are alive. Yet if life has value independent of its opportunities for choice, so that murder is wrong independently of its effect on positive liberty, then it is not liberty that is limiting liberty when we justify laws forbidding murder. Rather, it is another value, the value of life, that is trumping liberty, and to say this is to abandon the first strategy for the second.

The second strategy concedes that the circle of liberty extends to all actions, murderous ones as much as any others. Yet this second kind of defence of a general right to liberty argues that the right is justifiably overridden in cases of violence to others. This concession too leads to its own problems.

There are a variety of problems with any such fully general but easily overridable right. One is that which concerns Samuel Freeman: 'surely there is nothing intrinsically valuable about the natural liberty to do wrong . . . To assign intrinsic value to natural liberty as such would imply that legal restrictions per se diminish this intrinsic value and that there is ethical loss with the imposition of any legal restriction. But what could that loss be in the case of legal restrictions on clearly unjust or evil conduct?'[11] A slightly different concern is Ronald Dworkin's: 'we can maintain that idea only by so watering down the idea of a right that the right to liberty is something hardly worth having at all . . . I can have a political right to liberty . . . only in such a weak sense of right that the so called right to liberty is not competitive with strong rights . . . In any strong sense of right . . . there exists no general right to

---

[10] Compare Martin Heidigger's analysis of death: 'Death is the possibility of the absolute Impossibility of Dasein.' *Being and Time*, J. Macquarrie and E. Robinson, trans. (New York: Harper and Row, 1962).
[11] Samuel Freeman, 'Criminal Liability and Duty to Aid the Distressed', *University of Pennsylvania Law Review*, Vol. 142 (1994), 1455–92, at 1486.

liberty at all.'[12] Another is Joseph Raz's worry: 'We feel intuitively that some liberties are more important than others. The restriction of the more important liberties is a greater restriction of liberty than that of the less important ones.'[13]

This chorus of criticisms concedes conceptually that we can isolate a common element to the freedoms to murder, to drive on a certain street, to choose with whom we will be sexually intimate—namely, the absence of state coercion about any of these actions. Still, the worries are, what could intelligibly be thought to be good to this common element? Moreover, how could the possession of this goodness explain why we override the liberty to do some actions so much more easily than others? What common measure of liberty would find there to be little of it in the freedom to murder, and lots of it in the freedom to choose sexual intimates? One needs a good common to all unfettered actions, no matter what their moral quality, and yet that good must be elastic enough to yield to other goods served when we legally prohibit morally bad actions and not yield when the state purports to regulate morally good actions. Moreover, even if we find such a marvellously elastic, yet intelligible and common intrinsic good, how do we base a *right* on such a good when it loses so often and so easily to other goods?

III. THE PRESUMPTION OF LIBERTY

Despite these worries, there is an intelligible set of values served by negative liberty as such, values which apply equally to all actions no matter what their moral quality. One of these values we can get at by retracing our steps a bit. As we saw in Part II of this book, the touchstone of our culpability assessments of persons lies in the choices they make. Although such choices need not be contra-causally free (chapter 12), and although such choices need not proceed from their character (chapter 13), choice whose object is a moral wrong makes us blameable (chapter 9). Moreover, the conditions of excuse reveal that it is only when we have a fair opportunity to avoid choosing to do wrong that our choices make us fully

---

[12] Dworkin, *Taking Rights Seriously*, *supra* n. 4, at 268–9.
[13] Joseph Raz, *The Morality of Freedom* (Oxford: Clarendon Press, 1986), at 13.

and actually culpable. A threshold of fair opportunity, in other words, is a precondition of moral culpability.

None of this strictly requires that we find opportunities (above the baseline required for responsibility) to be intrinsically good. Nonetheless, such does seem to me to be the case. Having more opportunities is good because it allow us to have a large and more diverse set of projects with some realistic hope of success. As Rawls once put it in describing such liberty as a 'primary good', the having of more opportunities is good because it allows you to get what you want, whatever it may be that you want.[14] If this is so, then positive liberty, conceived of in terms of size of opportunity set, is one of the intrinsic goods to which freedom from legal coercion is a means.

This of course reduces negative liberty to an instrumental good, not an intrinsic good, but as an interest that applies to all actions that is the most that can be said for negative liberty. Three other sets of values exist, however, to which negative liberty is the means, and these add somewhat to its strength.

One of these is what I introduced in chapter 15 as Kantian autonomy. According to Kant, morality cares at least as much about the reasons for which people act as the actions they do.[15] Specifically, the highest moral value attaches to good actions chosen by the agent because they are good, not to good actions alone. Accordingly, legal coercion always diminishes the possibility of attaining morality's highest value, because the law's coercive sanctions induce many to act for those merely prudential reasons (fear of punishment) that have no moral worth.

Kantian autonomy operates rather differently than does positive liberty in giving weight to the instrumental value of negative liberty. Unlike the case of positive liberty, there is no value to be found in autonomous wrongful action as there is value in increased opportunities even when such opportunities are used to choose badly. Indeed, in Kant's sense the idea of autonomous *wrongful* action makes no sense. Autonomous action in this sense is doing right actions for the right reasons. Such autonomous decision—in

---

[14] Rawls, *A Theory of Justice, supra* n. 4, at 396. See also the discussion of H. L. A. Hart and Tim Scanlon in ch. 13 above.

[15] For an explication of Kant's evaluation of good motives, see Barbara Herman, 'On the Value of Acting from the Motive of Duty', ch. 1 of her *The Practice of Moral Judgement* (Cambridge, Mass.: Harvard University Press, 1993).

the sense of acting out of a concern for morality and not merely out of prudence—is an important moral desideratum, and state coercion always renders such decision-making less likely. Therefore, against the goods of punishing and preventing any given wrongful behaviour by criminal prohibition must be balanced the bad of preventing some autonomously chosen *rightful* behaviour. It is the lost possibility of autonomously chosen rightful behaviour that is the autonomy-related cost of criminal prohibition. Negative liberty is thus always good in that it serves to preserve this possibility of autonomously chosen rightful behaviour.

The last two goods to which negative liberty is instrumental are utilitarian in character. One stems from a nearly universal preference of persons to make their own decisions, free of the interference of others, including the state. One might even think that at some formative periods of their lives, persons must be free of such coercive influences in order to have preferences worth summing in a utilitarian calculus.

Another set of utilitarian considerations are those addressed in chapter 16. Criminal prohibitions spend scarce social resources: if they are enforced, that taps those resources directly; if they are not enforced, that has its less direct costs in terms of loss of respect for law and the like.

These four sets of values all combine to justify caution in the use of the criminal sanction. They thus all respond to Samuel Freeman's earlier expressed worry that nothing intelligibly good can be found in freedom from state coercion about morally odious actions. Negative liberty is a common means to these four items, each of which is good, even when the act one is free to do is morally odious. Moreover, this list of goods served by negative liberty also answers Joseph Raz's worry. Each of these four goods is generally served, across the board, by negative liberty attaching to *all* actions. A general liberty interest that was common to all actions, but elastic enough to gain great strength for some actions and very little strength for others, would be a puzzle. The negative liberty justified by its service of these four values is not elastic in this way; it uniformly applies to all actions.[16] Loss of such negative liberty is a constant cost to criminal prohibitions, of murder as well as jaywalking.

---

[16] The exception is to be found with some of the costs of enforcing criminal laws; as set forth in ch. 16, some of these costs are concentrated in the passage of laws aimed at certain kinds of behaviours.

With respect to Ronald Dworkin's criticism, it *is* a misnomer to speak of there being a general *right* to be free of legal coercion, for a right that loses so often is best not thought of as a right at all. It is better to conceptualize the instrumental goodness of negative liberty as a 'presumption of liberty'.[17] Contrary to what the critics of this way of conceptualizing it have thought,[18] 'presumption' accurately captures the fact that there is always some reason not to legally coerce behaviour, namely, that to do so diminishes the opportunities of those coerced, diminishes the likelihood of autonomously chosen rightful behaviour, etc. It is the constancy and the relative weakness of this liberty interest that the phrase 'presumption of liberty', is designed to capture.

The presumption of liberty should not be confused with two other demands that we might reasonably impose on criminal legislation. One of these is the demand of rationality in legislation. One might well think that simple rationality demands that legislation be reasoned. Actions done without reasons are done without reason, that is, are arational if not irrational. Yet rationality does not generate the strength of restriction on coercive legislation that is generated by the presumption of liberty. Rationality requires that legislators not enact legislation as they might write poetry in their spare time, for no reason save its own pleasure. But rationality (in the sense of having *some* reason) does not generate any kind of requirement that the reasons produced in favour of a piece of legislation have any amount of weight or force to them. Rather, legislation is reasoned (and rational in this sense) whenever some intelligibly good end is plausibly served by the legislation in question, irrespective of the compellingness, or the lack of it, of that end.

Another distinct demand is that placed by the conservative principle which holds that, other things equal, the status quo is to be preserved. Such a principle is backed by the ideas that change always involves effort, that institutional change always disrupts expectations, and that the past has a presumption of wisdom in its favour; accordingly, the principle further holds, unless there is some

---

[17] The terminology of Joel Feinberg, for example. Joel Feinberg, *Harm to Others* (Oxford: Oxford University Press, 1984), at 9, 207.

[18] Douglas Husak, 'The Presumption of Freedom', *Nous*, Vol. 17 (1983), 345–62; Raz, *The Morality of Freedom, supra* n. 13, at 8–12.

offsetting benefit, change in law is to be avoided.[19] Yet what this principle demands is that legislation *changing the status quo* have some moderately compelling reason behind it. There is no demand from this source that *coercive* legislation be justified by some good reason. After all, repealing legislation that removes coercive sanctions for some behaviour would also have to have good reasons to justify it, by this Burkean kind of conservative principle.[20]

The presumption of liberty is not only distinct from the principles of rationality and Burkean conservatism, it is also stronger in the demands it places on a legislator to justify any use of coercive legal sanctions. The strong preference of most for liberty, the need of it to have preferences worth caring about, the desirability of maximal opportunities for choice, the goodness of rightly motivated choice, and the direct and indirect social costs of legal coercion, all combine to demand of legislators some quite good reason to criminalize behaviour.

With seriously immoral behaviour that demand is easily satisfied. But for minor immoralities like breaking most promises, breaking confidentialities, infidelities of various kinds, the presumption of liberty should stay the legislative hand. Punishing such immoralities is a good, but it is not so good that it outweighs the instrumental good of the liberty to be sacrificed for it.

Despite this not insignificant bite to the presumption of liberty, it remains true that it does not satisfy most libertarians' ambitions for a right to liberty. In the first place, it is sufficiently undemanding that it should not be thought of as a *right* at all. In the second place, it does not conceive of negative liberty as an intrinsic good, and this merely instrumental status does not match the hopes of a more ambitious libertarianism. I accordingly turn to two stronger rights to liberty, what I distinguish as a derived versus a basic right to liberty.

IV. THE DERIVED RIGHT TO LIBERTY

The derived right attaches to all actions, no matter what their moral status. This is not a right to do any action, nor is it a right

---

[19] For an encapsulated critique of this kind of Burkean conservatism, see Moore, 'The Dead Hand of Constitutional Tradition', *Harvard Journal of Law and Public Policy*, Vol. 19 (1995), 263–73.

[20] See Raz, *supra* n. 13, at 12.

to have any action unfettered by governmental restraint. Rather, the right is that of every citizen not to have his or her behaviour regulated *for the wrong reasons* by the government. One does not, for example, have a right to murder, nor does one have the right that the government not prohibit and punish murder. Rather, one has a right that the government not prohibit murder because, say, of a view that murder is bad for the murderer's chances of salvation.

The right against improperly motivated legislation owes its content to the fact that the right is not basic but is the correlative of a more basic *duty* on the part of legislators to enact legislation for certain reasons but not others. Every legislator requires a theory of the legislative role, just as every judge requires a theory of the judicial role. As I explored in chapter 16, a crucial part of such a theory for a legislator is a theory of the permissible aims of coercive legislation. The derived right to liberty is no more than a right that legislators conform to their duties in this respect.

Such a right does nothing to further the libertarian ambition that there be a sphere of action immune to governmental regulation. This ambition I will explore further in the next section. Nor does the derived right have anything to do with the presumption of liberty. In thinking of the derived right to liberty we need to put aside any general liberty weakly protecting all actions in favour of a more absolute right of a different content. This is the right to properly motivated use of state coercion, the right I call the derived right to liberty.

The content of the derived right to liberty is given in terms of the reasons that are improper to motivate coercive legislation. The most famous description of those improper reasons has been that given by John Stuart Mill: that the behaviour being prohibited would cause harm to someone other than the actor (and any consensual partners) sufficiently justifies legal prohibition, and no other reason is permissible.[21] On the latter part of Mill's thought specifically: neither the immorality of the targeted conduct, nor harm to the actor from such behaviour, nor the offence such

[21] John Stuart Mill, *On Liberty*, originally published in 1859; all subsequent page references are to *J. S. Mill's On Liberty in Focus*, John Gray and G. W. Smith, eds. (London: Routledge, 1991).

behaviour might offer others, constitute reasons permissibly motivating coercive legislation.[22]

The most famous objection to Mill's scheme has been J. F. Stephen's conceptual one, to the effect that Mill could not separate actions affecting only the actor (which are not the state's business) from those affecting others (which can be the state's business). As Stephen put it:

The truth is that the principle about self-protection and self-regarding acts . . . is radically vicious. It assumes that some acts regard the agent only, and that some regard other people. In fact, by far the most important part of our conduct regards both ourselves and others . . .'[23]

Insofar as 'self-regarding acts' are defined by Mill as acts that affect no one but the actor, Stephen observed that 'every act that we do either does or may affect both ourselves and others' and that therefore Mill's 'distinction . . . is altogether fallacious and unfounded.'[24]

For example, riding a motor cycle without wearing a helmet may most obviously affect the rider, yet his injury also affects others because: they see his bloody mishap and are made sick; he is insufficiently insured and requires public medical assistance; his injury causes suffering to his loved ones; etc.

We shall have occasion in the next section to examine this familiar objection of Stephen's in light of Mill's anticipatory responses to it. For now, however, it is sufficient to see that Stephen's objection is wide of the mark insofar as Mill is talking about proper legislative *ends*. As such, Mill faces no need to isolate a sphere of action that is immune to state regulation and thus Mill has no need to isolate actions that affect no one save the actor. As a theory of proper legislative aims, Mill's injunction is to legislators not to aim at the good of the actor himself, the offence his behaviour causes to others, etc. Motor cycle riders have no derived right to be free of coercive requirements of helmets; they only have the derived right that the state not coerce them into wearing helmets for their

---

[22] Joel Feinberg has been the most careful taxonomist of Mill's excluded legislative aims. See his magisterial *Harm to Others*, supra n. 17; *Harm to Self, Offense to Others*, and *Harmless Wrongdoing*, all Oxford: Oxford University Press, 1985, 1986, 1988.

[23] James Fitzjames Stephens, *Liberty, Equality, Fraternity*, originally published, 1873, Liberty Fund edn., Stuart Warner, ed. (Indianapolis: 1993), at 17.

[24] Id. at 231.

own protection, because it offends others to see helmetless motor cycle accidents, or for some other illegitimate reason. Even if no action is without its harmful effects on others, those effects are not an inevitable part of the reasons for which the legislature prohibits the action. Thus a legislator can meaningfully be enjoined by Mill not to aim at preventing certain effects of certain kinds of actions.

The real worry about Mill's fleshing out of the legislature's duty, and of the correlative, derived right to liberty, is a normative worry, not a conceptual one. The normative worry is often encountered by Millian liberals when conservatives press the kinds of questions I introduced in chapter 16: (1) What makes harm to others a good reason to prohibit actions? Is it not the fact that causing most forms of harm to others is *morally wrong* that licenses state coercion? Indeed, is not any morally useful concept of *harm* tied to the notion of a state of affairs that it is morally wrong to bring about?[25] So are not the limits of moral obligation (and thus of wrongness) the only true boundary to our liberty of action to which limits the harm principle is but an imperfect proxy? (2) Further, how can we punish any omissions (which cause no harms although they may constitute failures to prevent such harms) except on the ground that in some cases we are morally obligated not to omit to help? Indeed, does not Mill himself distinguish punishable omissions from the bulk of omissions precisely on the grounds of moral obligation and thus moral wrongness?[26] (3) Further, if there are harmless wrongdoings—to use Joel Feinberg's well-chosen phrase to name moral wrongs which harm no one—do not we properly punish some of them, such as cruelty to animals, defamation of the dead, distortion of history, extinction of beauty, etc.?[27] If one admits that these are proper prohibitions, and one admits that they should apply across the board even when no person would be harmed by the prohibited behaviour, must one not admit that the aim is to prohibit simply because these behaviours are morally odious? (4) Finally, if there are harm-causings that are not morally wrong such as knowingly bankrupting an economic competitor, do we not properly refuse to prohibit them? And does this not show again that the proper concern of a legislator is moral wrongdoing, not harmful effects on others?

[25] See Michael Davis, 'Harm and Retribution', *Philosophy and Public Affairs*, Vol. 15 (1986), 236–66.
[26] Mill, *On Liberty*, supra n. 21, at 32.
[27] Some of Feinberg's examples in *Harmless Wrongdoing*, supra n. 22.

I find this fourfold conservative fusillade difficult to duck. Indeed, most of it I have come to accept, distant as it is from the Millian liberalism with which I began political philosophy. The theory of proper legislative aim to which these suggestions point is that legislators should prohibit morally wrong actions, and they should do so precisely because those actions are morally wrongful. This is often called the legal moralist theory of legislation, since it aims to legislate morality into law.

Perhaps Mill's most basic mistake here was to attempt to derive a theory of proper legislative aim from a defective theory of punishment based in utilitarianism. I refer not to Mill's well-known difficulty in moving logically from the utilitarian principle—with its well-known tendency to produce uncertain calculations of utility—to the resolute and crisp injunctions of his harm principle.[28] Rather, I refer to utilitarianism's inevitable dealing in harms rather than wrongs.

A properly retributive theory of punishment does not make this mistake. As we saw at the end of chapter 16, retributivism, when combined both with the principle of legality and the insight that law as law does not even prima facie obligate citizen obedience, yields the legal moralist theory of proper legislative aim: all and only moral wrongs should be prohibited by the criminal law, for the reason that such actions (or mental states) are wrongful (or culpable) and deserve punishment.

Liberal political theory has often been tempted to think that one can justify principled limits to the reach of criminal legislation without taking a position on the proper theory of punishment. While this is true for the presumption of liberty and the basic right to liberty, both of which operate externally to constrain the attainment of the ends of punishment, it is not true here, for the derived right to liberty. Some theory of punishment has to be relied upon here because it is only in light of criminal law's general aims that one can derive what is permissible legislative motivation, and then also, what is *impermissible* legislative motivation. For the derived right of liberty, there can be no short cut that truncates this chain of inference.

If the legal moralist theory of proper legislative aim is correct, then we quickly reach the sort of question of substantive ethics that

---

[28] A criticism of Mill voiced, e.g., by Gerry Dworkin in his 'Paternalism', in Richard Wasserstrom, ed., *Law and Morality* (Belmont, Cal.: Wadsworth, 1971).

we confronted in the last chapter: what are our moral obligations? On the legal moralist theory of proper legislative aim (to which the derived right to liberty is the correlative) this central question of ethics is also determinative of the content of our derived right to liberty.

If one disagreed with me in the last chapter, and one holds to a purely consequentialist theory about morality, then the content of any derived right to liberty contracts to the vanishing point. For one of the unsettling complications of a purely consequentialist ethics is that we are *never* free of the demands of moral obligation in our actions. Put another way, unbridled consequentialism always obligates us to maximize good consequences, minimize bad ones, in everything we do. This is, as is commonly objected, only a morality for saints.

At the very least, such a morality has to be tempered with agent-relative permissions to do actions that predictably will not be optimal in their consequences.[29] Moreover, I argued that the consequentialist principle is (up to a certain threshold of horrendous consequences) pre-empted by agent-relative obligations, obligations that are imposed by morality on each of us not to do certain actions even when such actions would be productive of quite good consequences.

If this is correct so far, then all actions can be divided into three classes: (1) There are actions that we are not obligated to do or not to do. Such actions are not the subject of any agent-relative prohibition, and they are the subject of an agent-relative permission allowing us not to optimize consequences. Much of our daily routine surely falls into this class of morally indifferent actions. (2) There are actions we are obligated to do, or to refrain from doing, but such obligation is only based on the consequentialist principle. These actions are not, that is, the subject of any agent-relative prohibition. I argued briefly in chapter 6 with respect to Francis Kamm that such obligations are characteristically less stringent than are the obligations created by agent-relative prohibitions. (3) There are actions like that examined in the last chapter, the torturing of innocents, about which we have quite stringent obligations because such obligations are derived from an agent-relative prohibition.

[29] Samuel Scheffler, *The Rejection of Consequentialism* (Berkeley: University of California Press, 1982).

The implications of this view of morality for the legal moralist legislator should be obvious. Citizens have a (derived) right to liberty protecting them against the criminalization of actions in the first category. On my view of sex, for example, morality by and large does not concern itself with much of what passes for social mores in our society on the topic of sex. I think that it trivilizes morality to think that it obligates us about what organ we insert into what orifice of what gender of what species. Accordingly, retributivist/legal moralist legislatures have no reason to criminalize the wide variety of sexual practices currently prohibited in many Anglo-American jurisdictions, and citizens have the moral right that they do not do so.

Only behaviours in the second two categories can be within the purview of a properly motivated legislator. Even here, however, it is worth noting that much of the behaviour in the second category is not subject to moral obligations of sufficient stringency that the good of their punishment outweighs the goods protected by the presumption of liberty discussed in the last section. In my disagreement with Fletcher and Freeman in chapter 6, for example, I argued that our consequentially-derived, positive obligations to render aid to strangers in distress are usually too weak to be used as the basis of justifying overriding the presumption of liberty. Our criminal law thus rightly draws back from criminalizing much of such positive obligations in the name of liberty.

If morality has the shape I suppose it to have in these ways, then a legal moralist theory of legislation will be quite liberal in its content even if not in its form. Such a theory would not prohibit anything that is not immoral, and it would not prohibit much that is not so seriously immoral that the badness of not punishing it outweighed the good protected by the presumption of liberty.[30]

If morality has the shape that I think it to have, then the differences with Millian liberalism are less than first meets the eye. Although promoting morality is not excluded as an improper motive, as it is for classical liberals, nonetheless the limited view of what constitutes serious immoralities keeps much of our behaviour unregulatable by the criminal law.

[30] For other examples of what is sometimes called 'perfectionist' liberalism, see Raz, *Morality of Freedom*, *supra* n. 13; Robert George, *Making Men Moral* (Oxford: Oxford University Press, 1993). Given the discussion to be had shortly, 'perfectionist' is not the right label of my brand of moralistic liberalism.

The difference between the legal moralist liberal and the classical liberal thus lies not so much in the content of recommended restrictions on legislation, but in the form of the argument for those restrictions. Classical liberals refuse to challenge conservatives on first order moral issues like the (im)morality of homosexuality, abortion, or drug usage; they rather prefer second order arguments showing why the first order arguments are inappropriate aims of legislation in a secular democracy. By contrast, legal moralist liberals concede the appropriateness of legislating morality but have quite limited views in what they see that morality requiring.

Legal moralist liberals thus do not exclude the aim of promoting morality through state coercion, as do classical liberals. What about paternalisticly motivated legislation, the chief thing excluded by Mill's harm principle? Is the moral or other good of the actor whose behaviour is being regulated permissible motivation for the regulation? Consider the moral good of the actor first, and notice that there are two cases where the moral good of the actor seemingly could be enhanced by state coercion. One is where the action coerced is morally obligatory, and the other is where the action coerced is supererogatory or otherwise virtuous but is not obligatory.

With respect to the prohibition and punishment of actions that are morally obligatory, some retributivists would not distinguish between the legislative motivation of punishing culpable wrongdoers through enacted law and the legislative motivation of promoting the moral good of offenders. Failing one's obligations is never good for an individual's moral ledger, and some retributivists have argued that only punishment can balance that individual's accounts. This is the familiar 'restoration of the balance' metaphor of such retributivists. Such retributivists find the paternalistic concern with the moral welfare of offenders to be a part of the retributivist concern that moral wrong be punished so that to aim for the one is to aim for the other.[31] For such retributivists there is no reason to deny this kind of moral paternalism a place amongst the permissible ends of criminal legislation.

[31] Herbert Morris, 'A Paternalistic Theory of Punishment', *American Philosophical Quarterly*, Vol. 18 (1981), 263–71; Jean Hampton, 'The Moral Education Theory of Punishment', *Philosophy and Public Affairs*, Vol. 13 (1984), 208–38.

It seems to me that such paternalistic versions of retributivism are motivated by a desire to put a nicer face on retributivism than it can in fact bear. We rightly punish culpable wrongdoers because they deserve it, but I doubt that they deserve it because receipt of such punishment will make them better. At least, I doubt this if 'better' means anything other than, 'have received their just deserts'. If 'better' means, they come to feel guilty, they see the error of their ways, they accept morality's binding force, they are no longer disposed to violate others' rights, etc., then I doubt that punishment often achieves this and I doubt that we really believe it does as we justify retributivism to ourselves. And if making the offender 'better' through punishment only means, 'he no longer deserves punishment because he has received his just deserts', then I would consign such paternalism to the scrap heap of discarded metaphors about retributivism catalogued in chapter 4.

The upshot is that legislators should not aim at the moral welfare of offenders in their framing of criminal prohibitions, even when that moral welfare involves an offender's breach of moral obligations. Still less should the legal moralist legislator aim to promote the moral welfare of citizens when what is involved is in fact a moral virtue, not dereliction of moral duty.

Supererogatory but not obligatory actions are those actions which we have no moral duty to do but which would make us more virtuous if we were to do them. Camus's famous example in *The Fall* is of this kind, for the protagonist in the novel fails to jump in to save a woman drowning in the Seine.[32] Given the risks involved in any rescue attempt, it is plausible to suppose that there is no duty to rescue in these circumstances; still, attempting a rescue would be very much to the man's credit, morally speaking.

One might well think that the world would be a morally better place if people were more virtuous than they are, and that the promotion of that moral good could justify state coercion. One problem with coercing virtue lies in the difficulty of doing so, at least in the first instance. This is due to the fact that virtuous action depends heavily on the motivation of the actor. Gift-giving is an extreme example, for to coerce the otherwise virtuous action of charitable giving is to make the action something else, something like paying a tax rather than giving a gift. It is perhaps true that

[32] Albert Camus, *The Fall*, Justin O'Brien, trans. (New York: Vintage, 1956).

long application of coercive sanctions to induce virtuous behaviour might change the habits of the people coerced for the better, so that they eventually come to give gifts for their own sake and not for fear of punishment. Yet such educative by-products of punishment are rather incidental, difficult to effect, and haphazard.

In any event, suppose, at least *arguendo*, that some gain in virtue could be achieved in the long term by coercing virtuous behaviour. Even so, it would be wrong for the state to punish people for failures of virtue. Fundamentally, such people do no wrong. Failing none of their moral obligations, such people do not deserve to be punished, and the right to be free of undeserved punishment trumps whatever gains of virtue could be induced by prohibiting less than virtuous, but non-obligatory, behaviour.

Now suppose, alternatively, that virtue cannot be coercively induced, even in the long run. One might yet think that the world is better if virtuous actions are done (even if no virtue is achieved because such acts are done for the wrong reasons). It is somewhat better, for example, if people in peril are rescued by those who risk life or limb to rescue them, even if the rescuers exhibit no virtue in their actions because they did them only out of fear of legal sanctions. This would not be a more virtuous world, but only a better one because more innocent lives would be preserved than would be lost in failed rescue attempts. Yet notice how heavy would be the price of this somewhat better world. First, there is the cost *in virtue* because of the cost in autonomy attendant upon legal coercion: some who would have rescued for morally worthy reasons of beneficence now rescue for non-virtuous, prudential reasons. Second, not all will be induced by the law to undertake risky rescues, and those persons will be punished even though they do not deserve to be punished because they have not failed in any of their moral obligations. As before, each person's right to be free of undeserved punishment trumps whatever gains there might be in attempting to coerce virtuous behaviour and thereby bringing about at least a better (if not a more virtuous) state of affairs.

Now let us consider non-moral paternalism, where the state aims to enhance the welfare of a class of citizens even against that class's judgement of what that welfare is. Even if it is neither obligatory nor supererogatory to refrain from smoking, may the state aim at the happiness of smokers by banning it? Mill's answer was of course no, but for reasons that are hard to sustain in a post-Freudian world. Few today would unqualifiedly subscribe to Mill's view that each person is the best judge of what makes him happy or satisfied.[33] The fallibility of judgement of each of us on even fundamental matters like choice of marriage partners is too painfully obvious to reassert Mill's confident proclamation that we are each the supreme epistemic authority on what we truly desire.

The most that can be said for the epistemic argument is that the officials who make up the state too are fallible in their judgements of welfare, and that the relevant question is that of comparative epistemic positions. Certainly on many questions, such as selection of marriage partners, some individuals are better situated epistemically to judge the conditions of their own happiness than is the state. Yet this is a topic-by-topic and individual-by-individual comparison that need not favour each individual's judgement. One might well think that cigarette smokers would be happier over the course of their lifetime if they did not smoke even if that goes against their own judgements on that question.

Despite this epistemic judgement, my own sense is that it would be wrong to criminalize smoking in private (where there is no secondary smoke harm to others, so that the aim of the prohibition would be the health of the smoker). It would be wrong because smoking in private is not morally wrong, nor is it even lacking in virtue. There is then no retributive justice to be achieved by punishing such behaviour.[34]

As we saw in chapter 4, it is easy to misapprehend the limits placed on the use of the criminal sanction by the retributive end of punishment. Critics of retributivism often charge that as an exclusive end of punishment retributivism would not allow prohibitions against traffic offences or against a variety of other acts that solve co-ordination problems but are not moral wrongs. Yet the charge is groundless, because we each have a moral obligation to solve co-ordination problems to achieve important goods such as personal safety, so that the use of a criminal statute to set the salient con-

---

[33] As Herbert Hart observed in his qualified defence of Mill, *Law, Liberty, and Morality* (Stanford: Stanford University Press, 1963).

[34] Notice that this retributivist argument for a derived right to liberty does not go beyond restrictions in the use of the criminal sanction. Sin taxes and other forms of non-punitive discouragements to smoking are not ruled out. Compare Mill, *supra* n. 21, at 114: 'To tax stimulants for the sole purpose of making them more difficult to be obtained, is a measure differing only in degree from their entire prohibition; and would be justifiable only if that were justifiable.'

ventions solving such problems may be appropriate on retributivist grounds.

Smoking in private, however, is not an act that requires that kind of co-ordination with the acts of others such that some public good is achieved that we all have an obligation to maintain. The only good in such a case is the welfare of the individual, and his failure to achieve that good is not morally wrong and therefore not punishable.

From the point of view of a thoroughgoing perfectionist/retributivist, any form of paternalistic motivation is thus out of bounds. What about the last of the Mill/Feinberg categories of possible legislative motivation, that of offence to others? May a legislature prohibit certain actions on the ground that such actions offend some number of citizens, either morally or otherwise? In one sense this question is easy to answer for a legal moralist liberal, and in that sense of the question the answer is a resounding 'no'. If the view in question is that a majority's offence at certain behaviour makes that behaviour morally wrong[35]—because morality just is what the majority in society take offence at—then such a view must be rejected. What society believes is wrong is one thing, but what *is* wrong is something else entirely. Any meta-ethics that denies this basic distinction between mores versus morality, conventional versus critical morality, what is believed to be right and what is right, is hopelessly relativistic and is to be rejected out of hand.[36] The retributive theory of punishment, and its accompanying legal moralist theory of legislation, enjoins legislators to prohibit actions that *are* morally wrong, no matter if such actions offend few citizens because few citizens believe them to be wrong; conversely, these theories enjoin legislators not to prohibit actions that are not morally wrong, no matter how many citizens erroneously believe such actions to be morally wrong and take offence accordingly at such actions.

[35] The apparent view of Lord Devlin in his *The Enforcement of Morality* (Oxford: Oxford University Press, 1965).

[36] As Simon Blackburn points out, one does not have to be a moral realist to regard this distinction as fundamental to everyone's moral experience. Noncognitivists like Blackburn also find it so. See Blackburn, 'Rule-Following and Moral Realism', in S. Holtzman and C. Leich, eds., *Wittgenstein: To Follow a Rule* (London: Routledge and Kegan Paul, 1981), at 171. See also Michael Moore, 'Moral Reality Revisited', *Michigan Law Review*, Vol. 90 (1992), 2424–533, at 2467–8.

A second and more interesting view of offence as a reason for legislation emerges if we put aside relativistic ethics. It is plausible to suppose that the unnecessary causing of some forms of offence to other people is morally wrong, really wrong and not just believed to be wrong by the society in question. Shocking the sensibilities or the senses of others for no good reason in some instances is wrong because so unnecessary. The public changing of sanitary towels on Feinberg's famous bus of offence is one example, as are some cases of overloud music, public oral sex, and the like.[37] That the offence taken no doubt depends on cultural sensibilities that vary somewhat from place to place makes such impositions no less wrong, and there is no meta-ethical relativism in such judgements. The wrong is harming others' sensibilities unnecessarily. The relevance of culture is to the question of whether there are such sensibilities to be harmed, not to the question of whether it is right or wrong to harm them.

Despite this, a legal moralist liberal should be suspicious of offence as a justification of criminal legislation. For while it may be morally wrong to offend the sensibilities of others unnecessarily, it is not usually deeply immoral to do so. Usually, therefore, except for the grossest of behaviours, the good of punishing such minor immoralities is insufficient to overcome the presumption of liberty and the values it represents.

I conclude that the derived right to liberty is not as weak as it may have seemed when we began. True, it does not immunize any sphere of action from state coercion; it equally protects all potential actions from badly motivated state coercion. And it is true, the crisp limits on permissible legislative motivation that Mill defined with his harm principle cannot be defended. Yet for retributivists about punishment such as myself, the derived right of liberty has a good deal of life. By limiting the permissible aim of state coercion to the punishment of moral wrongs, paternalistically motivated prohibitions are impermissible, as are most prohibitions enacted to prevent moral offence to the majority in a society. By accepting the view that morality regards much of our conduct as beyond the bounds of obligation, much of the criminalization of sexual practices is also illegitimate even when those criminal prohibitions are aimed to prevent and punish these supposed immoralities.

[37] Feinberg is very persuasive on this point. See his *Offence to Others, supra* n. 22, at 10–22.

V. THE BASIC RIGHT TO LIBERTY

Despite the robustness of both the presumption of liberty and the derived right to liberty, there remains the sense that there is a stronger right to liberty, one that does immunize a sphere of action from all state regulation save for regulation justified by the most compelling of reasons. This stronger right to liberty is what the United States Supreme Court has been struggling to define since its *Griswold* decision in 1965, albeit often under the unhelpful rubric of 'decisional privacy'.[38]

Consider first the woman's right to have an abortion at issue in *Roe* v. *Wade*.[39] Concede for purposes of argument that a foetus is a full-blown person from the date of its conception. Such concession makes the killing of the foetus a quite serious wrong, not at all outweighed by the inconveniences of carrying the foetus to term if it is not aborted. Even so, at least in some cases such as rape many share Judy Thomson's intuition that the woman has the right to be free of state coercion forcing her not to do this great wrong.[40] Such a right trumps an admittedly legitimate reason for the use of state coercion, namely, the punishment of what (on the *arguendo* concession here assumed) would be morally wrong. Such a right thus cannot be a part of the presumption of liberty, for it is no minor immorality that is outweighed by the instrumental goodness of liberty. Nor is such a right derivative of some failure of legislative duty, because the legislature could be seeking to prohibit abortion because and only because it is morally wrong.

Notice that much the same can be said about suicide, mistakes in parenting, and certain seriously harmful speech. Suicide is often deeply hurtful to persons other than the actor, persons to whom the actor is bound by many ties and to whom the actor owes an obligation to stay alive. At the very least, we owe such duties to our children. We do a serious wrong to such people when we suicide, yet my firm sense is that no one (including the state) has the right to prevent someone from killing themselves.

Similarly, there are some people who clearly should never be parents because they are so lousy at it that they raise extraordinarily

---

[38] *Griswold* v. *Connecticut*, 381 US 479 (1965).

[39] *Roe* v. *Wade*, 410 US 113 (1973).

[40] Judith Thomson, 'A Defense of Abortion', *Philosophy and Public Affairs*, Vol. 1 (1971), 47–66.

damaged and defective human beings. There are many kinds of parental abuse apart from physical and sexual abuse. Some parents make their favouritism between siblings apparent on a daily basis, making the less favoured develop feelings of worthlessness and despair. Some parents when they divorce poison their children against the other parent. Some parents make servants out of their children, others spoil them rotten. Some parents dominate their children's ambition, telling them exactly what they will be in all aspects of life. Some imbue them with religious beliefs that can only be described as deranged; and some simply ignore their children emotionally, leaving them to find what warmth they can in this life. Given the dependence and blind trust of children on their parents, these are deeply immoral behaviours. Yet we tend to think that the state should not use the criminal law to punish such wrongs.

Lastly, consider free speech. As the early critics of Mill noted, often speech causes injuries to others. Revealing a damaging truth from the distant past of a now well-respected and virtuous citizen, so that the life he has so painstakingly reconstructed is destroyed, is an example of such harmful speech.[41] Imposing this harm on someone purely for motives of private gain is a plausible candidate for a serious moral wrong, and thus the punishment of such wrong is a legitimate state concern. Despite this, the right to be free of state coercion on the content of speech trumps this otherwise legitimate state concern.

It may seem that these examples need not betoken the existence of some right to liberty stronger than the presumption of liberty earlier delineated. After all, the goods that justify the presumption of liberty can also outweigh legitimate reasons prima facie justifying state coercion, and perhaps this explains why the state ought not to coerce citizens out of abortion, suicide, parental abuse or harmful speech.

Yet there are two reasons to doubt that the presumption of liberty can explain our intuitions about such cases. One is the absoluteness we may feel about the liberty right that does not match the contingency of the balance of values being suggested to explain it. That balance is between the evil of wrongful actions going unpunished (if the acts are not prohibited) versus the evil of frustrating the goods behind the presumption of liberty (if the acts

---

[41] Suggested by the facts of *Briscoe* v. *Readers Digest*, 4 Cal. 3d 529, 93 Cal. Rptr. 866, 483 P 2d 34 (1971).

are prohibited). The delicacy and contingency of this balance does not match the certitude and absoluteness many feel about the liberty rights in question.

The second reason lies in the degree of moral wrongness that attaches to these actions, at least on the suppositions imagined. If foetuses are persons, then abortion is a form of active killing; if it is morally wrong, it is quite seriously so. Indeed, if such a wrong is performed by anyone other than the mother, the wrong done is so serious one may liken it to deliberate murder.[42] Likewise, to destroy the happiness of loved ones forever by suicide, to ruin a child forever, and to destroy someone's life by speaking about their distant past for profit or even mere pleasure, are serious moral wrongs. The goods to which negative liberty is instrumental and which give rise to the presumption of liberty seem too light a counterweight to outweigh the desirability of punishing moral wrongs of this degree of seriousness. Such goods plausibly outweigh the good of punishing the (usually) minor moral wrongs of lies, broken promises, breaches of confidence, most offensive behaviours, and even breach of our comparatively weak, positive obligations to help strangers in peril.[43] But the goods behind the presumption of liberty lose hands down to the good of punishing murder, rape, theft, and other serious moral wrongs. If abortion and the like are more like the latter than the former, it takes something stronger than the presumption of liberty to trump the state's justification for use of coercion.

It may seem puzzling to think that morality could contain within it *both* the obligation on one person not to do some action *and* a liberty right of that person with respect to that very same action. It may even seem as though there is a formal contradiction in such examples. If these purported to be examples where: (1) it would be morally wrong of an actor to do some action A, yet (2) the actor was morally permitted (had the right) to do A, then there would be a formal contradiction. Yet notice this is not what is being claimed about abortion rights, suicide rights, parental rights, or the right of free speech. If it was morally wrong of the actor to A, then the actor was obligated not to A, and if the actor was obligated not to A, then it cannot be the case that the actor was permitted to A. All this can be true, and yet it is consistent to think that it would be

---

[42] Cf. *Keeler* v. *Superior Court*, 2 Cal. 3d 619, 470 P 2d 617 (1970).

[43] The late Judith Skhlar catalogues our many daily and minor immoralities in *Ordinary Vices* (Cambridge, Mass.: Harvard University Press, 1984).

wrong of the state to coerce the actor to fulfil her obligation not to A. The liberty right in question is no more than that the state not coerce her to fulfil her obligation, and there is nothing formally contradictory about these two moral injunctions.

Still, even if there is no formal contradiction, one may think that it is a peculiar morality that makes wrong both some action A and another action, B, that would prevent A. If A is wrong, must not B be at least permissible, and perhaps even obligatory? Despite the apparent force of this query, any liberty worth having has to give us the right not to be interfered with as we do wrong. Notice that this is true of the presumption of liberty as much as it is of the basic right discussed in this section. If our liberty ends where our obligations begin, in an important sense we have no liberty.[44]

The apparent oddness is perhaps due to confusion of the liberty right not to be interfered with in the doing of some wrong, with two other situations, both of which Heidi Hurd helpfully labels as violations of her 'correspondence thesis'.[45] Hurd rightly finds odd any morality that make us 'moral gladiators' against one another, so that one person's moral success can be attained only through some other person's moral failure. Such morality would be odd, not in the sense that it formally contradicted itself, but rather, in the sense that it would look like a cruel joke played on the human race by an unkindly god. Thus, if morality: (1) obligated one person to do some action A, and also obligated another to prevent A; or (2) permitted one person to do action A, and also permitted or obligated another to prevent A, then Hurd's correspondence thesis would be violated.

Notice that the liberty right here in question is not odd in this way, for there is no gladiatorial aspect to such a right. One actor by hypothesis is obligated not to do some wrongful act A, but no other actor is obligated or permitted to force the first actor to do A. That would be gladiatorial and thus odd in this sense. On the contrary, if there is the liberty right I hypothesize, the second actor is obligated not to interfere with the first actor's choice, whether that is to do right or wrong. The second actor's moral success (in

[44] In some sense, there would be some liberty, namely, the liberty to act where morality is silent and liberty to act in a non-virtuous way, where the lack of virtue was a failure of supererogation and not a failure of obligation.

[45] Heidi M. Hurd, 'Justifiably Punishing the Justified', *Michigan Law Review*, Vol. 90 (1992), 2203–324, at 2205–12.

not interfering) is compatible with the first actor's moral success (in not doing A), for it is up to the latter whether she will succeed or fail. This is not a gladiatorial combat, but rather, the kind of restraint in allowing another to find her way that is distinctive of liberty.

If such a basic right to liberty is both intuitive and not self-refuting, the next question is how we are to generalize from examples such as abortion so as to describe some *general* sphere of liberty of action that is immune from otherwise quite legitimate state coercion. Such a general sphere of liberty will be normatively plausible only if we can also find some value other than those behind the presumption of liberty to back up such a strong immunity from state coercion.

In seeking such a sphere and the value behind it, we should again start with John Stuart Mill. The motivational reading I earlier gave Mill's *On Liberty* is only one plausible reading. An equally plausible, alternative interpretation is that Mill did intend to mark out a basic right to liberty with his harm principle, so that actions that harmfully affect no one other than the actor and his consensual partners cannot be prohibited by the state for any reason.

So construed, now J. F. Stephen's old objection comes into its own. The objection, it will be recalled, was that no action done in a society of persons is without its effects on others, and further, that no action that has a *harmful* effect on the actor will be without harmful effects on others.

There have been two lines of defence of Mill against this familiar charge, both of which are suggested in Mill's essay *On Liberty*. One I shall call the mechanical line of defence. Mill said that 'there is a sphere of action in which society . . . has, if any, only an indirect interest; comprehending all that portion of a person's life and conduct which affects only himself . . .', and qualified the latter phrase thusly: 'When I say only himself, I mean directly, and in the first instance: for whatever affects himself, may affect others *through* himself . . .'.[46] Mill's suggestion is that we limit ourselves to those proximate or direct effects when we ask whether an action *affects* only the actor. Those acts which injure those who care about the actor because such acts injure the actor are self-regarding acts, on this criterion, and may not be prohibited by the state. This

---

[46] Mill, *On Liberty, supra* n. 21, at 32–3.

limitation allows Mill to 'fully admit that the mischief which a person does to himself, may seriously affect, both through their sympathies and their interests, those nearly connected with him' [47] without conceding that such acts are anything but self-regarding.

Mill also suggests a mechanical limitation distinct from the limitation to proximate effects. Some actions 'primarily' concern the actor only, others 'chiefly' concern society.[48] Mill's suggestion seems to be that we can sum all the effects of any action, and divide actions by whether their chief, primary, or major effects are on the actor himself or on others.

There are obvious difficulties with drawing a workable line with either of these suggestions, but the main difficulty with them lies elsewhere. However patched up, they seem unlikely to draw the line of permissible state coercion in an intuitive place. Surely the first and most direct effect of the draft dodger or the insurance defrauder, each of whom for their different reasons cause serious physical injury to themselves by self-mutilation, is the injury to self; yet equally surely, those actions affect others enough (however indirectly) to justify state coercion against those actions. Conversely, the most direct effect of an abortion is to kill the foetus, yet the basic right to liberty may well immunize the woman's decision from state coercion despite this direct effect on another.

The second line of defence abandons a mechanical line for a moral one. On this interpretation of Mill's distinction, it is not any effect on others that matters. Rather, there must be an effect injurious to a distinct *interest* of someone other than the actor. This was John Ree's well-known interpretation of Mill's harm principle,[49] and it has been adopted by Joel Feinberg's qualified defence of Mill insofar as Feinberg defines *harms* to others as set-backs to their *interests*.[50] Mill's actual language is important. Our liberty ends, he said when we injure 'the interests of one another; or rather, certain interests, which either by express legal provision or by tacit understanding, ought to be considered as rights . . .'.[51] We leave our sphere of liberty, in other words, when our conduct causes that kind of harm to another's interests that such other ought to have a legal right against suffering.

---

[47] Mill, *On Liberty*, supra n. 21, at 96.   [48] Id. at 73, 90.
[49] John C. Rees, *John Stuart Mill's On Liberty* (Oxford: Clarendon Press, 1985), at 137–55.
[50] Feinberg, *Harm to Others*, supra n. 17.   [51] Mill, *supra* n. 21, at 90.

It should be apparent that this cannot serve as a way to define a basic right to liberty. If others ought to have a legal right to protection of a certain interest, then the actor ought to have a legal obligation not to do the action that unjustifiably injures that interest, that is, the actor is outside his protected sphere of liberty. Yet what are the criteria for when injuries to the interests of others are of such kind or magnitude that they ought to have a legal right to protection? Without telling us this, Mill's criterion tells us nothing. Mill cannot mean that others ought to have a legal right to protection whenever the actor has a *moral* obligation not to so act, for then our liberty begins only where our obligations end, and we have no basic right to liberty. In cases such as abortion, suicide, free speech, or even the good Samaritanism to strangers discussed under the presumption of liberty, our freedom from state coercion does not end where our obligations begin, for we ought to be free of state interference even when we are doing the wrong thing. It is the wrongness of such actions that gives the state good reason to legislate against them, which is why it takes liberty to trump this otherwise legitimate state interest.

Perhaps we should leave Mill's rights qualification out. Then the sphere of strongly protected liberty would be defined by actions that injure the interests of others (without regard to the unhelpful, further requirement that it is only such injury to such interests as warrant legal protection that is meant). Yet this moral criterion will not work either. Surely both foetuses, potential suicides, and those in peril have interests in continuing to live, as do children have an interest in a flourishing life, and those with long past secrets, an interest in continued secrecy. It is just the injuring of such interests that grounds our moral obligation not to act in the requisite ways. If the basic right to liberty protects us in such cases anyway, it cannot be defined as a right that ends where others' interests begin.

We need thus some line other than Mill's harm principle, however construed, to demarcate the sphere of action in which we have the right to be free of state coercion even if we act wrongfully. One possibility is to revert to some kind of indirect utilitarianism so revived in our own time by Louis Schwartz, Sandy Kadish, Norval Morris, and Herbert Packer.[52] As we saw in chapter 16, we can

---

[52] Louis Schwartz, 'Moral Offenses and the Model Penal Code', *Columbia Law Review*, Vol. 63 (1963), 669–86; Sanford Kadish, 'The Crisis of Overcriminalization', *Annals*, Vol. 374 (1967), 157–70; Gordon Hawkins and Norval Morris, *The Honest*

isolate a class of morally wrongful behaviours that nonetheless should be immune to state prohibition because the costs of prohibition will usually outweigh any gains in punishing immoral behaviour. Actions that (1) are typically performed in private so that there are no non-participant witnesses, (2) have little direct effect on others besides the participants, so that they are 'victimless crimes', and (3) are strongly motivated to the point that much of such behaviour will continue to take place even if legally prohibited, are said to have the litany of enforcement costs earlier described, which costs are typically higher for behaviours with these attributes than for behaviours without them. The conclusion is that the state should not enforce such strongly motivated, private, consensual behaviours as prostitution, deviant sex, alcohol, tobacco, and (arguably) drugs, and citizens ought to have the correlative legal right that the state do not do so.

As a rule of thumb, this seems roughly right. Two points however. One, it is only a rule of thumb about how the calculation of costs and benefits *usually* comes out. As such, it cannot match the certitude about liberty we may feel in cases like abortion or free speech. Two, even as a rule of thumb it is even roughly right only in those instances when the behaviour in question is not seriously immoral. If one took the view that smoking, drinking, deviant sex, prostitution, or recreational drug use, for example, were all deeply immoral activities, then it is far from obvious that the enforcement costs would outweigh the punishment of such behaviour made possible by legal prohibition.

The most that can be made of this utilitarian line is thus of a somewhat stronger presumption of liberty for behaviours with these four characteristics: where the immorality of a given behaviour is small, yet the enforcement costs are high because of the private, strongly motivated, and consensual nature of the conduct, legislators ought to eschew prohibition, and citizens have the correlative right that they do so. Like the presumption of liberty generally, however, this utility-based 'right' is not capable of having the bite demanded by a strong right to be free of state coercion even when doing seriously immoral actions.

A third tradition attempting to draw a line demarcating a sphere of strongly protected liberty uses the line between acts and omis-

Politician's Guide to Crime Control (Chicago: University of Chicago Press, 1970), 1–28; Herbert Packer, 'The Crime Tariff', *American Scholar*, Vol. 33 (1964), 551–5.

sions. Some libertarians would argue that at least part of the domain immune to state coercion is the domain of omissions.[53] The state can prohibit us from doing certain actions, but may not require us to do certain actions (through prohibiting the corresponding omissions).

There is plainly some appeal to this libertarian idea, but it overstates it to define a basic right of liberty around it. To begin with, this could not be a complete definition of such a right because it would seriously *understate* the extent of our liberty. It is far too expansive of state power to say that the state may prohibit any action. Abortion, suicide, many forms of parental abuse, and harmful speech are actions, yet any basic right to liberty should encompass them. Secondly, a complete freedom from positive legal requirements *overstates* the extent of our liberty. By my lights, we should not be free of state coercion with respect to rescuing our own child, for such rescue is neither a merely supererogatory act on our part nor is it only weakly obligatory. It is a strong moral obligation on the part of each of us, and I see no intuitively plausible restriction on the state's power to coerce us to conform to such strong obligations. Of course, often our positive moral obligations are weak enough that the costs of prohibition outweigh the good achieved by prohibition. But this much the presumption of liberty already protects, and in just these terms.

I come thus to the fourth and last way of defining the sphere of action protected by a basic right to liberty. The United States Supreme Court has been the most convenient expositor of this fourth way of defining the content of a basic right to liberty. This, even though of course the Court has been ultimately concerned to define an American constitutional right, not in the first instance a moral right. Yet the Court has sought to define a constitutional right 'that a certain sphere of individual liberty will be kept largely beyond the reach of government',[54] and the Court has recognized that such a constitutional right is based on an identical moral right that is 'older than the Bill of Rights' in our Constitution.[55] Thus the Court has been for thirty years engaged in precisely the kind of political philosophy that is our concern here.

[53] e.g., Richard Epstein, 'A Theory of Strict Liability', *Journal of Legal Studies*, Vol. 2 (1973), pp.151–204.

[54] *Thornburgh* v. *American College of Obstetricians and Gynecologists*, 476 US 747, 772 (1986) (Stevens J concurring).

[55] *Griswold* v. *Connecticut*, 381 US 479, 486 (1965).

The Court has given various expression to the 'sphere of individual liberty' largely immune to governmental regulation. In *Roe* and *Griswold* themselves, the Court rather sparely noted that only those rights to make choices that are 'fundamental' or 'basic' are included in this protected sphere. In *Eisenstadt* this was fleshed out slightly: the sphere includes 'matters so fundamentally affecting a person as the decision whether to bear or beget a child'.[56] Only in the dissenting opinions of Justices Blackmun and Stevens in *Bowers* v. *Hardwick* do we get any real attempt to articulate the boundaries of the sphere of protected liberty.

Justice Stevens continued to flesh out the idea of basic or fundamental decisions immune to state regulation in terms of the effect on the decision-maker's own life of such decisions: the individual has the 'right to make certain unusually important decisions that will affect his own, or his family's, destiny'.[57] Thus, because the decisions whether to conceive a child (*Griswold*), whether to carry it to term (*Roe*), and with whom and in what way one will be sexually intimate (*Bowers*), all have large effects on one's life, they are strongly protected decisions.

Perhaps Justice Blackmun had such a purely causal analysis in mind when he too described the sphere of strongly protected liberty in terms of decisions that 'form so central a part of an individual's life'[58] and when he partially defined centrality in terms of a decision that 'contributes so powerfully to the happiness of individuals'.[59] Yet more likely centrality to one's life is to be given a rather different reading. A decision is central, or important (or fundamental, or basic), not because it has major consequences for one's life, but because it determines the very sort of person one will become. In Blackmun's language, these are decisions that alter 'dramatically an individual's self-definition';[60] protection of such decisions protects one's 'ability independently to define one's identity';[61] these are decisions that are 'central to . . . the development of human personality . . .'.[62]

What Blackmun was driving at was the idea that some decisions make us who we are and are in that sense self-defining. John Stuart

---

[56] *Eisenstadt* v. *Baird*, 405 US 438, 953 (1972).

[57] *Bowers* v. *Hardwick*, 478 US 186, 217 (1986) (Stevens J dissenting), quoting *Fitzgerald* v. *Porter Mem. Hosp.*, 523 F 2d 716, 719 (7th Cir. 1975) (Stevens J).

[58] *Bowers*, 478 US at 204 .   [59] Id. at 205.   [60] Id.

[61] Id. (quoting *Roberts* v. *United States Jaycees*, 468 US 609, 619 (1984)).

[62] Id. (quoting *Paris Adult Theatre I* v. *Slaton*, 413 US 49, 63 (1973)).

Mill had the same idea insofar as he defended liberty on the grounds that we have to be allowed to make those choices about what we shall desire, feel, and believe, on pain of our having no character at all: 'A person whose desires and impulses are his own . . . is said to have a character. One whose desires and impulses are not his own, has no character, no more than a steam-engine has a character.'[63] Our desires, feelings, and beliefs are not our own, according to Mill, if they are merely the product of social coercion or mere conforming imitation of social convention: 'He who lets the world . . . choose his plan of life for him has no need of any other faculty than the ape-like one of imitation. . . . But what will be his comparative worth as a human being?'[64]

Both Blackmun and Mill are articulating a version of one of Aristotle's ideals. This is the ideal of the self-made individual, in a distinctly non-economic sense of the phrase. It is the ideal of each of us choosing our characters without undue influence of others (including the heavy-handed influence of state coercion). It is the ideal of the autonomous individual freely choosing the kind of person she will be, in a sense of autonomy that is considerably richer than the spare, Kantian notion (of acting for right reasons) that I employed as one of the goods justifying the presumption of (negative) liberty.

Aristotle thought that we choose our character as we choose all the many particular actions that cause us to be who we are. This is not the kind of choice I have in mind here, however. Being free of state coercion in making all the choices we make in daily life is a good, the good I explored in terms of positive liberty and its justification of the presumption of liberty. What is needed to make out a sphere of choices strongly immunized against state coercion is some line separating some choices meriting this extra protection from all the others. If we were to follow the suggestions of some members of the United States Supreme Court, we should draw this line in terms of choices so fundamental that they affect our identity, what are called our 'self-defining' choices.

There are two ways of conceptualizing the idea of self-defining choices. One is objective and harks back to the causal notions of Justice Stevens: some choices have more impact on our lives and, in that sense, such choices are more determinative of our character

---

[63] Mill, *supra* n. 21, at 76.   [64] Id. at 75.

than others. Decisions about who we marry, whether to become a parent, what schools and courses of study to pursue, how to raise our children, what careers to pursue, when and how to die, have a lot more impact on our lives than decisions about where to take a vacation, or which route we take to work. The other conceptualization is subjective in that character is the object of our choice and not simply the product of it. That is, on this view self-defining choices involve mental states (of desire, belief, and intention) whose objects are not actions but are further mental states or general traits of character.[65] On this view, our choices to become more considerate, to count material things less, to be more caring towards others, to believe the best about people, or to become more trustworthy, are self-defining choices. Correspondingly, choices to do some particular kind action, to visit our parents tonight, to ignore evidence of a disreputable sort about a friend, and not to disclose a friend's secret to another, are not self-defining choices because the objects of such choices are particular actions.

There are problems with either of these views. A minor problem with the objective or purely causal conceptualization is its degree vagueness. Except for those existentialists who believed that a few large choices determine the rest of our lives, most of us rightly sense that the degree of causal impact choices may have on a life varies along a smooth continuum. Still, this is a minor problem in the sense that all line-drawing problems are minor. A whole great big bunch of stones plainly make up a heap even if one cannot precisely say how many stones it takes to make a heap.

More serious is the seeming fortuity lurking in the fact that some choices have very large impacts upon our lives. Watching a particular movie, reading a particular book, deciding to switch airlines at the last moment from a plane that, as it turns out, crashes, deciding to pick up your Social Security cheque on a day when the Social Security office is bombed, all can change one's life forever. The fortuity of the degree of causal impact any choice may have does not match our intuitive sense that some choices are more worthy of protection than others.

One might think that this problem can be eliminated by saying that any particular choice that instantiates a *type* of choice that is

---

[65] This roughly corresponds to Harry Frankfurt's notion of 'second-order' mental states. See Frankfurt, 'Freedom of the Will and the Concept of the Person', *Journal of Philosophy*, Vol. 78 (1971), 5–20.

typically large in its impact on persons' lives is a character-forming choice and therefore subject to the protections of the strong right to liberty. Yet without some restrictions on *types* of choices beyond simple causal judgements, any particular choice that does have a large impact on the subject's life is an instance of *some* type of choice that typically has a large impact. Take the choice of route to work where the route chosen produces an accident and confinement to a wheelchair for life. Such a particular choice is not only an instance of the type, choosing one's route to work, which is not typically a choice having a large impact; such a particular choice is also an instance of the type, choosing a route in the circumstance that one or more possible routes will result in disaster if chosen, which type of choice does typically have a large impact.

Of course, one might say, but the actor did not *choose* to court disaster by her selection of route. Yet this is to leave the causal question—what effects does a choice produce—for the subjective question, what was the object of the choice? This takes us to the second and subjective conceptualization of a self-defining choice. It is only choices where the choosing subject knows of the relevant circumstances and of their power to alter his life, and chooses in light of that knowledge, that we have a self-defining choice protected by the basic right to liberty. One who chooses his route to work in ignorance of the life-changing potential of his choice does not make a self-defining choice, despite it being a choice that alters his life forever.

Unfortunately, the subjective conceptualization of self-defining choices seems to protect large numbers of trivial choices too. If I choose to believe a friend on a given occasion, resolve not to think of some obsessionally recurring melody, or choose to still my rage at a sudden remark, these are pretty trivial choices even though their objects are mental states and not actions. Needed is some restriction in the objects of the choices beyond simply the restriction to mental states or character traits. Needed is a restriction to those choices that the choosing subject knows will have a broad impact over a long term on her life, or at least she intends that they have such an impact (recognizing the possibility of a weakness of will known to the subject herself).

If self-defining choices is the line we are to draw, then two interrelated questions spring to mind. One is whether such choices are really possible for us, as a matter of psychology. The other is why unfettered ability to make such kinds of choices should have such value that they define a moral *right* to liberty, and not just the normal presumption in favour of liberty.

Turning to the first of these two questions, in chapters 12 and 13 I sought to put away one sense in which one might say that we *cannot* choose our character. This was the incompatibilist's contra-causal sense of 'can', where we *can* do something only if there are no causes of our doing it (other than our own choices, desires, or intentions to do it, in which event such mental states must themselves be uncaused). The relevant question is not whether our choices are caused by factors themselves unchosen; as a determinist, I assume that they are. Rather, the question is whether our own characters are among the effects in the world that we can intentionally cause.

Our abilities here are plainly fragile. We have limited capacities to will individual mental states of belief, desire, or emotion into existence, although there are sometimes some indirect causal routes that we can employ to this end.[66] Our capacities to bring about long-term changes in our mental make-up, and in the actions that make-up will cause, are surely at least as limited. That the best examples of weakness of will reside here evidence how often we fail at our various resolutions to change our character.

Our causal power over our characters is thus plainly limited. As I concluded in chapter 13, we have no meaningful power to cause ourselves to have a certain character initially, and we have limited power to change an already formed character that we do not like. Yet the value of being unfettered in the making of self-defining choices may not be wholly dependent on our causal powers in this regard.

To see whether this is so, let us interrupt this psychological investigation with the moral investigation I mentioned earlier: why would the power to choose one's character have value, assuming we have some of such power? One answer is in terms of the value of having a character of integrity and coherence. As I argued in chapter 15, having one's actions, emotions traits, and mental states together possess some minimal threshold of coherence is necessary for a being to have any character and to being a person. Possessing such minimal coherence and integrity is of great value because

[66] See Moore, 'Authority, Law, and Razian Reasons', *Southern California Law Review*, Vol. 62 (1989), 827–96, at 878–82.

being a person is of such great value. Yet above such minimal threshold of coherence, marked by our concept of mental illness, ever greater coherence of character is of ever greater value.

If this is so, then to the extent our sense of who we are and wish to be itself has coherence, and to the extent we have the causal power to change our character with choice made in light of such ego-ideal, then that power to choose will also have value. It has value because it is the means by which we bring greater integrity and coherence into our character, that is, into who we are (and not just who we think we are).

There is a second way in which our unfettered power to make self-defining choices has value, other than the production of a character of integrity that has value. This can be seen if we advert to a well-known thought experiment raised by Aldous Huxley. Suppose, Huxley said, we could have a virtuous character programmed into our hardware though no effort of our own. Should we not 'instantly close with the offer', as Huxley thought?[67] What we would lose, of course, was the pride of authorship, that we were the authors of our own virtues.

Such pride of authorship reveals who we think we are. The 'we' who would be the author of our own character is the we of self-consciousness. Given the general importance of consciousness to our sense of self, it is not surprising that our strongest identifications are with the experiences of reflexive consciousness, where the objects of our musings are (the rest of) ourselves.

Given this locus of identification in self-consciousness, it becomes of great value to achieve congruence between our actual character and the sense possessed by self-awareness of who we are and wish to be. Yet the process of achieving such congruence is very much a two-way interaction. Sometimes, we change our character in response to what we choose; perhaps more often, we change what we choose in light of the character we come to see ourselves as having. In either case, whether we 'change for the better' or 'come to like ourselves better', we merge who we are with who we want to be. Such congruence is not only of great value, but in this way it demands less of the causal power to remake ourselves in our own image.[68]

[67] T. H. Huxley, 'On Descartes' *Discourse on Method*', in *Methods and Results* (New York: Macmillan, 1893), ch. 4 .

[68] For other explications of the value of self-definition, see Stanley I. Benn, *A Theory of Freedom* (Cambridge: Cambridge University Press, 1988), 155–6, 170–83;

VI. THE LIBERTY TO TAKE DRUGS

If we apply the foregoing analysis to the criminalization of recreational drug use, we should ask, first, whether the presumption of liberty is overcome by the desirability of punishing such drug use, second, whether such drug use is protected by the derived right to liberty because there is no immorality in such use to be aimed at by penal legislation, and third, whether such drug use is protected by the basic right to liberty because using drugs recreationally is a self-defining choice for such users. With regard to the presumption of liberty, we need in turn to ask two basic questions: (1) Is it morally wrong to take drugs for recreational purposes? We need to ask this question in order to assess what retributive interest the state can have for prohibiting such drug usage. Even if it is morally wrong for anyone to use drugs recreationally, and even if the state were to prohibit such usage because of its moral wrongness, that only gives the state the possibility of justifying the prohibition. To actually justify the prohibition, we must answer a second question affirmatively: (2) Is recreational drug use so wrong that the good of the punishment of such wrongs outweighs the costs in positive liberty, Kantian autonomy, preference satisfaction, and other indices of social welfare?

With regard to the derived right to liberty, the question of the immorality of drug use is also central. For if recreational drug use is not immoral in the sense of breaking our obligations, then there can be no moral wrongdoing to be aimed at in penal legislation, and each citizen has the right that such prohibitions not be enacted.

With regard to the basic right to liberty, two subquestions are implicated. The first is whether a choice to lead a life of regular drug use, with all the effects of intoxication and perhaps addiction, can qualify as a self-defining choice, or is it a choice to have no character, and is such choice precluded from being a kind of self-definition? Second, if it is a possible mode of self-definition to choose the life of intoxication, does the state nonetheless have sufficient reason to override this right because of the great harms caused by drug use?

John Gray, 'Mill's Conception of Happiness and the Theory of Individuality', in Gray and G. W. Smith, eds., *J. S. Mill On Liberty In Focus* (London: Routledge, 1991); Thomas E. Hill, Jr., *Autonomy and Self-Respect* (Cambridge: Cambridge University Press, 1991), 29–37, 43–51.

a. The Morality of Recreational Drug Use

Central to all three interests in liberty is the question, is there anything morally wrong with taking drugs for non-medicinal reasons? Let me put aside momentarily the more fine-grained questions of whether it is morally obligatory on each of us not to use drugs for fun, or whether it would at least be more virtuous of us not to use drugs although we are not obligated to refrain. My initial, coarse-grained question is this: ought we to refrain from recreational drug use (where 'ought' contains both the ought of obligation and the ought of supererogation and virtue)? I ask the coarse-grained question first, because if the answer to it were negative, one would not need to resolve the difficult issues lurking in the fine-grained questions.[69]

Some would deny that the coarse-grained question has any general answer, applicable to all persons at all times. I am not primarily referring to those sceptics in meta-ethics who deny that any ethical questions—be they about the good life or the good society—have answers. Rather, I refer to value pluralists like Joseph Raz[70] who think that often two or more values conflict in their recommended action on a given occasion and that often (but not always) such values are incommensurable in the sense that there can be no correct weighing of one against the other. One might think, for example, that recreational drug use gives pleasurable sensation and heightens certain forms of creative endeavours while at the same time lessening one's resolve not to harm others physically, and that there is no way to balance these values to arrive at an overall judgement on whether one ought to refrain from such drug use.

Mill was not a believer in the incommensurability of values. (Indeed, as a monistic utilitarian, how could he be?) Yet Mill too denied that there was likely to be a *general* answer to questions like that about recreational drug use. For Mill, there may well be an answer for each individual as to whether they ought to refrain; but what Mill denied was that there was any general answer, good for all persons. People's natures differ, and since for Mill the answer depends on those natures, so must those answers for each individual.

---

[69] I come back to the finer-grained analysis in the succeeding subsection where the surviving candidates can be assessed.

[70] Joseph Raz, *The Morality of Freedom, supra* n. 13, ch. 13.

I call these the three easy routes to liberalism, for notice how easy each of them can make belief in the restraint of state power. If one is muddle-headed enough to accept the sceptical proposition that no ethical questions have right answers and that therefore one right answer is that the state should not seek to enforce any purported right answers, then liberal toleration can 'follow' from ethical scepticism. If one accepts the Razian theses that some values are incommensurable and that there are some cases where incommensurability prevents determinate answers, then in the latter cases the state must stay its hand because it has no moral ought to enforce with its legislation. If one accepts the Millian thesis that what we ought to do on issues like drugs varies from individual to individual, then the state may not prohibit generally such behaviour, and if the carving out of individual cases is too difficult because of the near infinite variation of individual natures, then the state must not prohibit for anyone.

We should eschew all three of these easy routes to liberalism. The first, while common enough, is literally incoherent. The second I believe to be false, although that is no easy matter to show.[71] Our experience with hard moral choices tells us that there is no indeterminacy even in such cases, for we continue to agonize over what is the right choice long after we recognize the apparent difficulty of weighing different values. The third could be true, depending on what sort of moral norm makes drug use immoral. If, for example, the potential immorality of drug use lay in the intoxicated drug user's propensity to do physical injury to others, and if such propensity varied enormously between persons, then Mill's thesis could be plausible. But as I explore below, I do not think that the immorality of drug use lies in such variables.

So—there is an answer here, and it is now legitimate to ask what that answer is. My own belief is that almost all people ought to refrain from sustained long-term recreational use of at least certain mind-altering drugs. I can think of five possible bases for reaching this judgement, and, since it matters to the legal enforceability of this ought which is correct, I shall mention all five.

---

[71] It is not enough to show that morality is objective, even in the strong sense of the moral realist. One must also connect realism in ethics to bivalence, the thesis that every meaningful proposition about morals is either true or false. I do argue that the first meta-ethical position makes the second more plausible. Moore, 'Moral Reality Revisited', *Michigan Law Review*, Vol. 90 (1992), 2424–533, at 2437–8.

The first proceeds from an asceticism that is difficult to make even plausible today. Drug taking, like sex, can be quite pleasurable. To some temperaments, such pleasure, unjustified as it often is by loftier goals such as creativity or procreation, is sinful. I mention this basis mostly to put it aside, since asceticism is rarely avowed openly as an ideal by anyone these days, even outside of California.[72]

Still, it is important to raise this first consideration because I suspect that it explains why the liberty to take drugs has been so largely neglected, at least when compared to libertarian crusades on behalf of sexual orientation, abortion, free expression, and the like. Recreational drug use, like oral sex, is not typically motivated by some loftier goal that commands much respect. Its typically hedonic character thus tends to demotivate any impassioned crusades in its defence. This in no way is said to justify the laws we have prohibiting such drug use; only to explain the unconscious grip our own asceticism may have upon us, a grip that explains our ignoring what I shall ultimately argue is a rather clear violation of liberty by the widespread criminalization of drugs.

A second and more serious possibility of why drug use is morally wrong is to be found in the kind of wrongs to which drug taking may contribute. On this view, drug taking becomes morally wrong derivatively because it causes other things to occur, and these are clearly moral wrongs. The best variant of this form of argument is to point to the relaxed inhibitions, fuzzy judgement, or greater indifference produced by even moderate intoxication.[73] One might think that one ought to avoid recreational drug use because such use unnecessarily risks that the drug user will: fail to support his children; fail to prevent the conception of drug-damaged foetuses and babies; engage in violent behaviour; batter one's spouse; drive her automobile into persons or property; etc.

---

[72] Although Nietzsche may well be right, that asceticism is one way to develop that kind of self-control and transformative power we value as Millian autonomy.

[73] As David Richards points out (*Sex, Drugs, supra* n. 1, at 165–6), many of the bad things drug use is said to cause can plausibly be laid at the doorstep of criminalizing drug use. Stealing to get money to buy drugs, for example, is a function of the high price of drugs, itself a function of the artificial restriction of supply caused by criminalization. Likewise, the violence of drug dealers is due to criminalization. Unlike Richards, (id. at 166), I assume that use of some drugs 'releases inhibitions or criminal tendencies' and thus does result in other crimes, even without the effects of criminalization of drug use.

Such risk taking can be morally culpable and thus properly punishable on retributive grounds. Even though one may succeed in doing no wrong, if such a wrong was the object of a desire, an intention, or a predictive belief—or if it should have been the object of a predictive belief, given what else we did believe about the world—we are morally culpable and deserve to be punished for such culpability.[74]

Notice, however, that this is not to say that drug use as such is generally wrong or culpable. What is wrong are the further states of affairs that drug use is said to cause, and what is culpable is the having of the requisite mental state with those future wrongs as its object. That means that the person who is aware of a substantial and unjustifiable risk that his ingestion of a drug on a given occasion will cause him to drive so as to hurt others, may be punished, as may the drug user who knows she is pregnant and should know the effect on foetal development of the drugs she is taking. But this is worlds removed from punishing drug use as such.

The deserved punishability of various forms of risk taking through the use of drugs goes no distance towards establishing the ought statement with which we began. We ought to support our children, we ought not run over people with our automobiles, etc., and we are morally culpable whenever we knowingly risk doing those wrongs for insufficient reason. It is simply false to think that such culpability always, most of the time, or even typically accompanies drug usage.

Notice that one can say all of this and not deny that Anglo-American criminal law is correct in its punishment of most intoxicated defendants. The theory that makes such punishments correct, however, is not that drug taking is itself wrong or even that it is derivatively wrong because it risks other wrongs. Rather, what makes such punishments correct is that the drug-intoxicated driver, parent, etc., culpably do wrong when they kill with their car, fail to support their children, etc. If intoxication does not negate the mental states required for culpability (however much liberal 'diminished capacity' theorists have thought so),[75] likewise our classifying drug taking as not wrong does not immunize such culpable individuals from punishment. But we should be clear what we rightly punish

[74] Chapter 9, *supra*.
[75] See Stephen Morse, 'Undiminished Confusion About Diminished Capacity', *Journal of Criminal Law and Criminology*, Vol. 75 (1984), 1–55.

such people for: it is the wrongs culpably done under the influence of drugs, not for the taking of drugs with those influences.

Those who think that if we cannot punish intoxicated wrong-doers for becoming intoxicated we cannot punish them at all, usually make the following mistake. They think that because the act of drug taking at t_1 causes (in a but-for sense) the actor to do the wrong at t_2 that actor cannot be blameworthy for the act at t_2 because that act was not free. Suppose it is true that but for the ingestion of a certain drug one would not have had one's inhibitions lowered enough to punch someone on the nose. This causal judgement in no way diminishes the blameworthiness of the batterer.[76] I can cause myself by one act to do a later act without in anyway diminishing my responsibility for the later act. For example: having accidentally dropped a five dollar bill in an outhouse, I throw a fifty dollar bill after it. Now I 'have to' go in and retrieve the fiver. I have caused myself to do the later act, but it was still my freely chosen action.

We thus can punish the intoxicated driver, the intoxicated wife beater, etc., because of the culpable mental state with which they do such wrongs. We can even punish the intoxicated individual who knows that his act of intoxication substantially and unjustifiably risks the doing of such wrongs. When we punish in either case we need not and should not be punishing someone simply because he is intoxicated, for that by itself is not the wrong.

It is true that in the criminal law we sometimes use one morally innocuous act as a proxy for another, morally wrongful act or mental state. Thus, many states criminalize the possession of certain sorts of tools useful exclusively for burglaries. The state can prove knowing possession of burglary tools more easily than it can prove an intent to burgle, or attempted burglary, so such laws are argued for on this evidentiary ground. One might then argue that the prohibition of drug taking could serve this kind of proxy function. Which indeed it could, but the problem with the argument is its premise. Such 'proxy crimes' are generally illegitimate.[77] For what is this 'proxying function' but an evasion of our normal requirements of

---

[76] Argued for in ch. 12.

[77] The illegitimacy of 'proxy crimes' is argued in Michael Moore, *Act and Crime: The Philosophy of Action and its Implications for Criminal Law* (Oxford: Oxford University Press, 1993), 21–2. Compare Husak, *Drugs and Rights, supra* n. 1, 178–95, who does not disapprove of such crimes *per se* but limits their use so as to make drug prohibitions unjustifiable on any analogy to such crimes.

proof beyond a reasonable doubt? If when we punish drug taking we are really punishing culpable risk-taking, then the 'proxying function' allows us to prove the latter only in the Pickwickian sense that we are conclusively presuming it. If we think we should relax the burden of proof in criminal cases somewhat, why do we not be up front about it rather than hiding such relaxation of proof under the creation of proxy crimes?

Of course, some defenders of proxy crimes say: 'but possession of burglar's tools is *always* accompanied by the culpable intent to use them to burgle'. Yet if this is so, then such possession will be very good evidence of such culpable intent, but the state should at least be put to the test about such alleged inevitable connection. *Mutatis mutandis* for prohibiting drug use as a proxy for wife beating, reckless driving, etc.

Sometimes proxy crimes are defended on grounds other than short-circuiting proof problems for the prosecution. Rather, such crimes are defended on the preventive ground that they isolate a convenient point in time from which it is predictable that some moral wrongs will occur, and such wrongs can thus be efficiently prevented by preventing the earlier, non-wrongful act. It may be easier for the police to prevent burglaries by allowing them to arrest people for possession of burglary tools, for example, than it is to do so by waiting for the possessor to actually attempt a break-in with such tools. Likewise, it may be easier to prevent spousal abuse, child abuse, other non-stranger violence of various kinds, if the police can arrest intoxicated individuals rather than having to wait for such individuals to attempt these wrongs.

The problem with this defence of 'wrongs by proxy' is that it gives liberty a strong kick in the teeth right at the start. Such an argument does not even pretend that there is any culpability or wrongdoing for which it would urge punishment; rather, punishment of a non-wrongful, non-culpable action is used for purely preventive ends. We rightfully eschew such preventive incapacitation generally in our punishment theories, and we should not allow such practices to enter unwittingly because disguised as supposedly independent crimes.

A third possible moral question about use of drugs stems from the observation that drug users 'drop out' of socially useful occupations, at least during the period of their intoxication but more likely over the longer period when they are not intoxicated but are so enamoured of this one form of pleasure that they give up the attitudes of ambition and self-discipline inconsistent with a hedonistic outlook. The argument is that our talents are not ours to squander in this way, that we each hold our talents in trust for the betterment of society, that to abuse this trust is morally wrong. Although Benjamin Rush is a well-known expositor of this argument,[78] a clear example of such motivation at work is the mandatory closing hours for English pubs, justified on the grounds that abusers should not be allowed to squander their time and talents during working hours.[79]

One answer to Rush's argument is that given to the previous argument: when and if a person abuses drugs to the point that he is not contributing his share of the social product, then he should be punished. Prior to such breach of social obligation, punishment is premature and unjustified. A second and distinct answer should equally bar resort to this argument: morality does not obligate us to be good workers or more generally, effective contributors to the social good. Whether and how we use our talents is up to us. There are clearly better and worse ways of using such talents, and one good way is surely for social betterment in all its dimensions. It is not, however, the only good use of such talents. It is a peculiar blindness of those who have dedicated their talents to social reform to think this, but the sometimes magnificent (if ultimately selfish) achievement of artists and scientists belies any such narrow vision. Moreover, whether we use our talents in *any* good way is, as I shall argue shortly, not a matter of moral obligation. I certainly have many discrete obligations not to make the world worse; but my positive obligations to make it better are fewer and weaker, and do not include some obligation to be the most effective assembly line worker my (unintoxicated) talents might allow me to be.

One way in which drug usage may make people less willing to contribute their talents to the betterment of society is that they do not vote or otherwise participate in the political life of a democracy. And here, it might be said, we each have a *duty* to support just institutions, at least to the minimal extent of voting in public

---

[78] Benjamin Rush, *An Enquiry Into the Effects of Ardent Spirits on the Human Body and Morals* (Brookfield, Mass.: E. Merrian and Co., 1814), quoted and discussed in Richards, *Sex, Drugs, supra* n. 1, at 171–2.

[79] John Kaplan, *Hardest Drug, supra* n. 1, at 132, gives another example in the prohibition of bowling during the time of Edward III on the ground that it distracted men from archery practice.

elections.[footnote] If drug use leads people not to fulfil this obligation, then on that ground it may be prohibited.

Yet again, if not voting is obligatory and not merely supererogatory, and if not voting may be criminalized on just this ground, why should we not generally criminalize not voting, for any reason? We do not criminalize non-voting because we realize the value of Kantian autonomy: the reason for which one votes matters. One whose voting is compelled, even if the content of his vote is not compelled, is one whose voice is not fully his own; the collective voice of a bunch of such people thus has less legitimating force. If this prevents us from criminalizing non-voting itself, how could one possibly criminalize some other action, like taking drugs, on the ground that that action makes not-voting more likely?[80] That would be like criminalizing dancing on the grounds that it lead to heterosexual intercourse while not criminalizing such sex itself.

I come to the fourth sort of moral doubt one may have about recreational drug use. This stems from the belief that the haze of intoxication is not itself a form of human attainment and that in fact such intoxication inhibits genuine forms of human flourishing. Drug use may prevent students from doing well in school, artists from painting, composing, writing, sculpting, etc., scientists from creative endeavours, as well as social engineers from investing their energy and creativity in finding better forms of social arrangements. Drugs in such a case undercut our perfectionist ambition to be the best we can be in any field of potential human excellence.

With these factual beliefs I am in agreement. I say this despite my exposure to the counter-culture of the 1960s in America. Aldous Huxley told me when I was an undergraduate about the wonders of the Mexican mushroom, and Timothy Leary, that my generation should 'tune in, turn on, and drop out' by tripping on LSD. David Richards, also of my vintage, echoes some of that overly optimistic attitude towards the 'mind-expanding' potential of hallucinogenic drugs.[81] All such echoes from the past are like the echoes one still

[80] I follow Doug Husak here, regarding what he calls an 'inchoate principle' according to which no act should be prohibited on the ground that it causes another act unless the latter act is itself criminal. Husak, *Drugs and Rights*, *supra* n. 1, at 184.

[81] See Richards, *Sex, Drugs, supra* n. 1, at 170, where Richards finds some use of drugs 'to express self-respect by regulating the quality and versatility of [some persons'] experiences in life', to 'promote the rational self-control of those ingredients fundamental to the design of a fulfilled life', and to be 'one means by which the already existing interests of the person may be explored or realized'.

hears occasionally from radical psychiatry on the topic of mental illness. R. D. Laing told us that schizophrenia was an existential voyage of discovery for the few with the courage to take it.[82] Such grandiose descriptions of what in fact is a pretty pathetic condition are so false that it borders on cruelty to use them. That same is true for 1960s euphoric descriptions of drugs. One has to be pretty high on them already to judge the states induced to be any kind of path to profundity or 'authenticity'. Worthwhile human achievement is not so easily purchased.

Moreover, use of drugs can easily interfere with those creative endeavours of the best and the brightest of us. Here, one needs to keep a balanced view, for in some forms of artistic expression drugs may enhance rather than retard one's abilities. In any case, suppose the effect of drugs for most forms of excellence is negative. That still leaves the moral conclusion to be drawn by the argument. Who has the right that any of us achieve our highest potential? To whom are we obligated to be the best we can be? Was Mozart obligated to be Mozart, given the relative poverty, unhappiness, and ill health pursuit of his talents as a composer cost him? Was it our right to demand this of him?

There is surely something noble in the extremes of human achievement and we rightly are stirred when we witness it or appreciate its fruits. But equally surely, no one owes us this. They do no wrong if they eschew the high and perilous road for the low and comfortable one. Criminalizing such failure of virtue, but not of obligation, seems out of the question.

So, too, must be the criminalizing of behaviours that impede such creative quests. Not just Edward III's bowling, but bridge, television, action movies, excessive vacations, and all else that makes up the dulling narcotic of daily life, should be criminalized on the same basis. Except in the amounts needed (like sleep) to keep questing, they all get in the way of our becoming more like a character in Ayn Rand's novels: immensely creative, heroically energetic, sucking in great draughts of life's essences with every breath. Nobody can be obligated to be this way, any more than they are obligated to be a moral saint in their dealings with others.

The fifth and last possible basis for regarding recreational use of drugs to be immoral stems as much from the allegedly addictive

---

[82] R. D. Laing, *The Divided Self* (London: Tavistock Publications, 1960); Laing, *The Politics of Experience* (New York: Ballantine Books, 1967).

nature of regular drug use, as from the intoxicating effect of each such use. Both extreme intoxication and addiction are likened to a kind of suicide, a deadening of the capacities that make us moral agents. Unlike the last suspicion which we examined, where drug use was condemned for its disabling of us from our highest forms of flourishing, here the charge is that drug use drops us below the threshold of what makes us a person and a moral agent. It is likened to a voluntary bringing on of mental illness, a kind of mental illness where the capacities of rationality and autonomy are so eroded that we cease to count as a person. Thus, the charge of a kind of suicide.

As before, we need to separate the factual claims here from the moral conclusions. The factual claims have to do with the degree to which our own capacities for rational and autonomous action are eroded. Since these claims are different for intoxication than for addiction, let us consider each separately. Intoxication certainly erodes those cognitive capacities that constitute our practical rationality. I refer to the capacities to resolve conflicts between our desires so as to form a stable preference order; to form rational beliefs in the sense of holding them only with that certainty proportionate to the probative force of the evidence available to us; to form intentions and plans that execute appropriately the background motivations formed by those preferences and beliefs; to execute those plans and intentions with the appropriate physical movements; to keep our intentions consistent with our beliefs so that we do not attempt what we know to be impossible or even highly unlikely of success; and to restrain those impulses and emotions whose satisfactions usually are not, on reflection, what we most want.[83] The difficult but highly relevant factual question is how much these capacities are degraded by intoxication.

The criminal law's armchair social science on this issue has long been something of a mess. Our law has assumed that intoxication can often be so severe that the intoxicated actor is unable to form the intentions (or sometimes beliefs) required for conviction of various crimes. Yet intoxication, whether by alcohol or by other drugs, is almost never this severe. The intentions required for conviction of rape or murder, for example, are so simple that if an actor has

---

[83] I explore the concepts of rationality as it relates to mental illness in Moore, *Law and Psychiatry*, *supra* n. 3, at ch. 2; I explore autonomy and the rationality of intention in Moore, *Act and Crime*, *supra* n. 77, at ch. 6.

not become so intoxicated that he has lost consciousness he almost certainly possesses the intention required for conviction.[84]

The erosion of our capacities of practical rationality are less severe, and subtler, than the law of diminished capacity often assumes. Nonetheless, such erosion does exist, and I assume that extreme states of intoxication approach the loss of reality testing often taken to be the mark of mental illness severe enough to be called legal insanity. When Kant likened such extremely intoxicated individuals to being 'simply like a beast, not to be treated as a human being',[85] he was echoing what his contemporaries thought of severe mental disease.[86]

About addiction, whether to alcohol or to other drugs, the evidence is also conflicted.[87] Despite this conflict, perhaps we can at least pinpoint what factual issues are of most relevance in asking whether addiction is a kind of suicide of personhood (an insanity), as can be extreme intoxication. Addiction, like intoxication, is not plausibly thought of as an across-the-board reduction in our capacities for practical rationality. Addiction is more like what Freud used to call his 'obsessional neurotic' patients.[88] There is in addiction a kind of fixation of desire somewhat analogous to the frozen beliefs of the paranoid schizophrenic. This is the 'craving' conception of addiction, where the desire for drugs of the unintoxicated addict is: (1) experienced phenomenologically as a hunger, that is, as a datable sensation of need; (2) experienced as 'ego-alien', that is, as an urge alien to one's sense of self and an intruder on that self's sense of control; (3) unamenable to correction, restraint, or even delay by other desires the actor in other, quieter moments might say he values more; (4) accompanied by the belief that, if the

[84] See Morse, 'Undiminished Confusion', *supra* n. 75.

[85] Kant, *The Metaphysical Principles of Virtue*, J. Ellington trans. (Indianopolis, Indiana: Bobbs-Merrill, 1964), at 88.

[86] For discussion of the 'wild beast' test of legal insanity, see A. Platt and B. Diamond, 'The Origins and Development of the "Wild Beast" Concept of Mental Illness and its Relation to Theories of Criminal Responsibility', *Journal of the History of the Behavior Sciences*, Vol. 1 (1965), 355–67.

[87] On alcoholism as an addiction, e.g., compare Herbert Fingarette's conclusions with the literature he critically discusses, in his *Heavy Drinking* (Berkeley: University of California Press, 1987).

[88] Two famous examples are the lady who rang for her maid constantly in order to show her a spot on a table cloth (*Introductory Lectures on Psycho-analysis*, Lecture XVII) and the young officer who found himself on trains to repay a debt he did not owe ('Notes Upon a Case of Obsessional Neurosis', in P. Rieff, ed., *Three Case Histories* (New York: Macmillan, 1963)).

desire is not satisfied, the threat of the unpleasant consequences of withdrawal will ensue; (5) becoming ever increasing in its needs for amounts of drugs to satisfy it.

Jon Elster quite properly urges that we should look for (and expect to find) the physiological correlates of these psychological states.[89] For present purposes it will not matter whether there are such physical states nor what their contours might be,[90] for we can make out the issue of 'moral suicide' with the psychological variables alone. The claim would be that addiction is a kind of possession, not by demons, witches, spirits, or agents of any kind, but rather, by the imperious necessity of ego-alien desire. There is a drivenness, and a lack of freedom, in both addiction and obsessional neurosis when pictured in this way.

The factual question is to what extent this picture is true. How urgent are the experienced cravings of the addict or the obsessional neurotic? How divided is the consciousness of the addict and of the obsessional neurotic, so that such cravings are repressed into unconsciousness, projected, or otherwise defended against to the point that when experienced they are experienced as impulses alien to one's self, as a kind of unwelcome intruder? How dominant are such desires behaviourally, so that in any contest with other (non-alien) desires, the craving always wins?[91] How often do addicts predict that they will suffer withdrawal symptoms if they cease taking drugs, how severe do they foresee such symptoms as being, and how much do such predictive beliefs of addicts figure in the reasons that motivate their continued drug taking? Finally, to what extent do addicts actually develop a tolerance for their drugs (in the sense that it takes ever increasing amounts to generate the same psychological effects), and to what extent do their drug-taking behaviours reflect this?

Since I have no more than armchair hunches about the answers to these questions, I shall concede the drug prohibitionist her best

[89] Jon Elster, 'Rationality and Addiction', in P. de Greiff, ed., *Morality, Legality, and Drugs* (Ithaca, NY: Cornell Univ. Press, 1997).

[90] For the reasons outlined in ch. 10, *supra*. When we correlate brain structure with mental functioning we are likely discovering more about what the mental states in question actually are, not showing that such states are really just fictions.

[91] See Marshall's wry observation that Leroy Powell, an alcoholic said to be unable to control his drinking, managed to stay sober on the day of his trial because he wanted to stay out of jail. *Powell* v. *Texas*, 392 US 514, 525 (1968) (plurality opinion).

factual case here. Assume there is a large degree of all five of these things, sufficiently so that when we assess the moral responsibility of addicts for their drug-seeking behaviours, we excuse them to the same extent that we excuse obsessional neurotics, 'kleptomaniacs', and those who kill under the influence of a strong emotion aroused by the provoking acts of their victim. Such conditions do not amount to anything like insanity, but they might amount (under the generous factual assumptions here indulged) to a partial excuse of inner compulsion.[92]

We are now freed to ask the moral question about both intoxication and addiction: is there anything morally troubling about voluntarily placing one's self in these states of intoxication and addiction? Surely, on these factual assumptions, the answer is yes. We are each of value as persons, and we plainly diminish what is valuable about us as persons when we erode our rationality and our autonomy in these ways. Addiction of course is mild in the degree of its erosion of personality compared to extreme intoxication; but because the obsessive desire (symptomatic of addiction) is to do actions producing such intoxication, addiction will be morally troublesome for precisely the same sort of degradation of personality as is intoxication.

Moreover, it is here, at last, that we reach a moral obligation not to take drugs. Just as we sometimes have a moral obligation not to commit literal suicide, so we sometimes have a moral obligation not to commit the kind of metaphorical suicide that (on the factual assumptions here made) addiction represents. Certainly when we are responsible for young children, but also when there are others who love us or depend on us, we are obligated to stick around.

This moral obligation does not readily translate into a general obligation not to take drugs recreationally, which is what the legal moralist legislator needs in order to justify a blanket prohibition on recreational drug use. In the first place, just as some kinds of actual suicides are not wrongful, so some kinds of mental/moral suicides are also not wrongful. One's health may be so deteriorated, one's grief or other pain may be so intense, or in any number of other circumstances the balance of life's prospects against its burdens may be so unfavourable, that one is justified in actually killing himself. One would in like circumstances also be justified in the deadening of the pain by the deadening of one's capacities that

---

[92] Explored in Moore, *Law and Psychiatry, supra* n. 3, ch. 10.

addiction and continuous intoxication can cause. So there can be no across-the-board condemnation of suicide of either kind by the legislator whose criminal law would track moral obligation.[93]

Secondly, to say that addiction can be a kind of moral suicide is not to say anything about what sort of act it takes to become an addict. Only on the very strong assumption that addiction is caused by taking just one drink, just one puff, or just one shot, could one liken acts of drug use to acts like putting a gun to one's head. If becoming an addict is very much more a chosen way of life, as Herbert Fingarette urges that alcohol addiction is,[94] then individual acts of drug taking are moral suicide only in the extended sense that individual acts of smoking or of overeating are a killing of oneself.

b. Liberty With Respect to Drug Use

If the foregoing argument is correct, then with one possible exception every citizen has a derived right to liberty against criminalization of recreational drug use. For on a legal moralist theory of proper legislative motivation, a legislator may criminalize only that which he may condemn as morally wrong, and there is by and large no breach of moral obligation in taking drugs.

Theorists who wish to dispute this rather obvious conclusion, who are tempted to criminalize drug taking even if it is not morally wrong so long as it is lacking in virtue, forget a basic fact about criminalizaiton: we have to punish people who violate criminal laws. Such theorists tend to think of criminal laws as pure preventives, so that if some act is morally undesirable—whether wrong or not, no matter—that is sufficient reason to criminalize it. Yet crime demands punishment, and on any morally respectable theory of punishment those who do no wrong cannot be punished. One cannot simply pass a law criminalizing drug taking and have that undesirable practice stop; one will have violators of such a law, and one has to be willing to punish them if one is willing to prohibit their behaviour (on pain, among other things, of there being *no* prevention achieved by such prohibition).

The one exception to this otherwise crisp conclusion is the obligation we have not to commit moral suicide sometimes, which may

---

[93] A legislator might handle this problem by qualifying a blanket prohibition on drug use with a general balance-of-evils justificatory section like Model Penal Code §3.02.

[94] Fingarette, *Heavy Drinking*, *supra* n. 87.

translate into an obligation not to take drugs regularly enough that we regularly lose our moral personality. Since there is such an obligation, when it is violated there is a moral wrong that could be the basis of justified legislation. To see whether this is so, we must examine the presumption of liberty and the basic right to liberty, which I now propose to do.[95]

About the basic right to liberty I can be relatively brief. For the very arguments that convince prohibitionists of the immorality of drug taking should also convince them that a chosen life of such drug taking is the kind of self-defining choice protected by the basic right to liberty. That is, grant the case outlined above—that addicted drug taking is a kind of suicide, and that that is what obligates us not to do it. By my lights, that same analogy also generates the conclusion that it would be wrong of the state to prohibit this form of suicide, as any other. How we end our life is a 'defining moment' for us. It is our final way of saying to the future who we were. It is our final signature. The same is true for the 'little death' the loss of ourselves in drugs is said to be. We found so little of value in the normal life of persons in our society that we 'dropped out' of it, not just economically but mentally and morally.

One does not have to be a Timothy Leary to think this. Indeed, as I said before, I am not. Such dropping out, like suicide itself, is usually an unjustified, wrongful, and even pathetic choice. Yet it is a self-defining choice, in the morally neutral sense of that phrase I used earlier. I do not like the self-definitions of many people, and in some of those cases such styles of life seem morally wrong. Yet it is their right to so constitute themselves, up to some threshold, at least, of moral awfulness.[96]

In truth, of course, the analogy of addiction-caused drug taking (whatever that might be) to suicide is only an analogy, not an exact

[95] We should also look at such a right because some no doubt disagree with my characterizations of most of the moral failings of drug takers to be failures of virtue, not failures of obligation. Nothing, incidentally, that was said in that regard deals with the interesting question whether those who aid drug users to use drugs are not wrongdoers and not simply lacking in virtue. Even if we think that we should not criminalize lack of virtue, it may be that those who enable or aid another to lack such virtue do wrong and deserve punishment. We might criminalize the aiding of suicide, for example, on this ground, even if we were convinced that suicide was not wrong but only lacking in virtue by the one doing it.

[96] I have glossed over—and will continue to do so—the difficult question of when the reasons to do so are compelling enough for a state to violate its citizens' rights, including the basic right to liberty. For some suggestions, see ch. 17.

replication. For in fact addiction only degrades aspects of our moral personhood, it does not end them. Some might therefore urge that the more proper analogy is to Mill's famous contract of slavery. In slavery, after all, the person is fully around, in full possession of her faculties, after the choice to be a slave. But since her liberty is gone, even Mill conceded that such a choice should not be enforced in the courts.

The enforceability of contracts of slavery has some features extraneous to our present concerns, making it not a very useful analogy. For when a court enforces a contract, it lends its power to seeing that the act contracted for is done, against the present wishes of one of the contracting parties. That is a kind of state sanctioning of slavery one could well eschew. Yet that eschewal is irrelevant to the question of whether the state should punish an individual for becoming a slave. In order to get the intuition pumps working, suppose that there exists a part of the world that practises slavery and that any foreigner who goes there is automatically and inevitably made into a slave for life. Should a rightly conceived criminal code prohibit travel to such a place, punishing those who attempt such travel with full awareness that they will become a slave. (Like suicide, it would be impossible to punish the completed crime here.)

Does it at all matter to this question that the person who decides to sacrifice his liberty will be fully in possession of his faculties after his decision? My own sense is that it does not, but if it does, then try this variation: the place travelled to does not enslave you, it only keeps you in a state of constant intoxication by drugs until you are fully addicted to them, and you fully know that when you go. May the state punish you for attempting to go? This, of course, is just our actual case.

A better way to test our sense of whether drug taking is a self-defining choice that should be protected by the basic right to liberty is to ask ourselves whether the state should criminalize and punish private citizens who prevent others from degrading their moral personalities. Suppose someone has chosen to become an addict, or has chosen to join a brain-washing cult. Suppose further such choices are made in circumstances that make them morally wrong, and not just lacking in virtue. If such choices are protected by the basic right to liberty, then it would be wrong for *anyone* to prevent them, not just wrong for the state to do so. So surely the state is justified in punishing such wrongful interference with liberty? Yet, the thought might go, surely one should be able to prevent their children, their spouse, or their friends from degrading themselves in these ways. They may kidnap their grandchildren out of Moonie cults, confine their friends to places where no drugs or alcohol are available, to free them from the blight of these degradations.

My own sense is that we are not free to do these things, that we do wrong when we do them, and that such wrong is sometimes strong enough reason to overcome the presumption of liberty to justify punishment. We may of course seek to persuade, cajole, manipulate, give financial incentives, etc., to our grown children, spouses, and friends not to make unwise choices in these directions, but then, so may the state. But neither we nor the state can coercively prevent them from such self-destructive choices. Only when their choices are made by those not fully possessed of their faculties—because too young, too crazy, etc.—may we prevent the exercise of their choices. But once our children are grown up, and our friends sane, we must respect such life-forming choices, even if we know they are wrong.

If we turn to the presumption of liberty, even this weakest of liberty interests raises hurdles higher than can be leapt by the would-be prohibitionist of drugs. The welfare branch of this argument has been made before, and very tellingly. In straight welfare terms the 'war on drugs' has not had enough success to be worth the enormous costs of attempting to enforce it, including the indirect costs of violence between dealers, financing of organized crime, and property crimes by addicts in search of artificially high-priced drugs. The limited good obtained by punishing the limited wrongs done by taking drugs simply has not been worth the enormous cost.[97]

This is probably the ground on which the political change required to repeal the present criminalization of drugs will be found. Losing a war is a good reason to stop fighting it. In this chapter, however, I have focused on more principled arguments of liberty outlining why this was never a war we were entitled to fight to start with.

---

[97] I also think Kantian autonomy weighs heavily here, for refraining from temptations like those offered by drugs on one's own (i.e., without legal coercion) has much higher value than just coerced sobriety.

REFERENCES

Achinstein, P., 'The Causal Relation', *Midwest Studies in Philosophy*, Vol. 4 (1979), 369–86.

Ackermann, Robert J., *Belief and Knowledge* (Garden City, NY: Doubleday, 1972).

Alexander, Franz and Staub, Hugo, *The Criminal, The Judge, and The Public: A Psychological Analysis* (London: G. Allen and Unwin, 1931).

Alexander, Lawrence, 'Law and Exclusionary Reasons', *Philosophical Topics*, Vol. 18 (1990), 5–22.

Alexander, Lawrence, 'Pursuing the Good—Indirectly', *Ethics*, Vol. 95 (1985), 315–32.

Alexander, Lawrence, 'Retributivism and the Inadvertent Punishment of the Innocent', *Law and Philosophy*, Vol. 2 (1983), 233–46.

American Bar Association, 'Report of the Special Committee on the Rights of the Mentally Ill', *Annual Reports of the American Bar Association*, Vol. 70 (1945), 338–42.

American Law Institute, *Model Penal Code and Commentaries* (Philadelphia, 1985).

American Medical Association, *Report of Conclusions and Recommendations Regarding the Insanity Defense* (Washington, DC, 1983).

American Psychiatric Association, *Statement on the Insanity Defense* (Washington, DC, 1982).

Andenaes, Johannes, 'Does Punishment Deter Crime?', in G. Ezorsky, ed., *Philosophical Perspectives on Punishment* (Albany, NY: State Univ. of NY Press, 1972).

Andenaes, Johannes, *Punishment and Deterrence* (Ann Arbor: U Mich. Press, 1974).

Andre, Judith, 'Nagel, Williams, and Moral Luck', *Analysis*, Vol. 43 (1983), 202–7.

Annas, Julia, 'How Basic Are Basic Actions?', *Proceedings of the Aristotelian Society*, Vol. 78 (1978), 195–213.

Anscombe, G. E. M., 'Causality and Extensionality', *Journal of Philosophy*, Vol. 66 (1969), 152–9.

Anscombe, G. E. M., *Intention*, 2nd edn. (Ithaca, NY: Cornell University Press, 1963).

Anscombe, G. E. M., 'Modern Moral Philosophy', *Philosophy*, Vol. 33 (1958), 1–19.

Anscombe, G. E. M., 'Reply to Bennett', *Analysis*, Vol. 26 (1966), 208.

Anscombe, G. E. M., 'War and Murder', in R. A. Wasserstrom, ed., *War and Morality* (Belmont, California: Wadsworth, 1970).

Anscombe, Roderick, 'Referring to the Unconscious: A Philosophical Critique of Schafer's Action Language', *International Journal of Psycho-Analysis*, Vol. 62 (1981), 225–41.

Aquinas, Thomas, *Summa Theologica*, Anton Regis edn., *Basic Writings of Saint Thomas Aquinas* (New York: Random, 1945), 2 vols.

Arbib, Michael, *The Metaphorical Brain* (New York: Wiley, 1972).

Arenella, Peter, 'Character, Choice, and Moral Agency: The Relevance of Character to Our Moral Culpability Judgments', *Social Philosophy and Policy*, Vol. 7 (1990), 59–83.

Arenella, Peter, 'The Diminished Capacity and Diminished Responsibility Defenses: Two Children of a Doomed Marriage', *Columbia Law Review*, Vol. 77 (1977), 827–65.

Aristotle, *Nichomachean Ethics*, in Richard McKeon, *Introduction to Aristotle* (Chicago: University of Chicago Press, 1973).

Arlow, Jacob and Brenner, Charles, *Psychoanalytic Concepts and the Structural Theory* (New York: International Universities Press, 1964).

Armstrong, D. M., *A Theory of Universals* (Cambridge: Cambridge University Press, 1978).

Armstrong, K. G., 'The Retributivist Hits Back', in H. B. Acton, ed., *The Philosophy of Punishment* (London: Macmillan, St. Martin's Press, 1969).

Arnolds and Garland, 'The Defense of Necessity in Criminal Law: The Right to Choose the Lesser Evil', *Journal of Criminal Law and Criminology*, Vol. 65 (1974), 289–301.

Arrow, Kenneth, *Social Choice and Individual Values*, 2nd edn., (New Haven: Yale University Press, 1963).

Ashworth, Andrew, 'Belief, Intent, and Criminal Liability', in J. Eckelaar and J. Bell, eds., *Oxford Essays in Jurisprudence: Third Series* (Oxford: Oxford University Press, 1987).

Ashworth, Andrew, 'Criminal Attempts and the Role of Resulting Harm Under the Code, and in the Common Law', *Rutgers Law Journal*, Vol. 19 (1988), 725–72.

Ashworth, Andrew, 'Sharpening the Subjective Element in Criminal Liability', in R. A. Duff and N. E. Simmonds, eds., *Philosophy and the Criminal Law* (Wiesbaden: Steiner, 1984).

Audi, Robert, *Action, Intention, and Reason* (Ithaca, NY: Cornell University Press, 1993).

Audi, Robert, 'Intending', *Journal of Philosophy*, Vol. 70 (1973), 387–403.

Audi, Robert, 'Moral Responsibility, Freedom, and Compulsion', *American Philosophical Quarterly*, Vol. 11 (1974), 1–14.

Audi, Robert, 'Volition, Intention, and Responsibility', *University of Pennsylvania Law Review*, Vol. 142 (1994), 1675–704.

Aune, Bruce, 'Can', in Paul Edwards, ed., *The Encyclopedia of Philosophy*, Vol. 4 (New York: Macmillan, 1967), 18–20.

Austin, J. L., 'Ifs and Cans', in H. Morris, ed., *Freedom and Responsibility* (Stanford: Stanford University Press, 1961).

Austin, J. L., 'A Plea for Excuses', *Proceedings of the Aristotelian Society*, Vol. 57 (1956), 1–30.

Austin, John, *The Province of Jurisprudence Determined* (Hart edn., London: Weidenfeld and Nicolson, 1954).

Ayer, Alfred Jules, 'Freedom and Necessity', *Polemic* (Sept.–Oct. 1946), 36–.

Barnes, 'Utilitarianisms', *Ethics*, Vol. 82 (1971), 57–64.

Bayles, Michael, 'Character, Purpose, and Criminal Responsibility', *Law and Philosophy*, Vol. 1 (1982), 5–20.

Bayles, Michael, 'Punishment for Attempts', *Social Theory and Practice*, Vol. 8 (1982), 19–29.

Bazelon, David, 'The Morality of the Criminal Law', *Southern California Law Review*, Vol. 49 (1976), 385–405.

Beale, Joseph, 'The Proximate Consequences of an Act', *Harvard Law Review*, Vol. 33 (1920), 633–58.

Beale, Joseph, 'Recovery for Consequences of an Act', *Harvard Law Review*, Vol. 9 (1895), 80–9.

Beccaria, *On Crimes and Punishments*, J. Grigson, trans., in A. Manzoni, ed., *The Column of Infamy* (Oxford: Oxford University Press, 1964).

Becht, A. and Miller, F., *The Test of Factual Causation in Negligence and Strict Liability Cases* (St Louis, Mo.: Washington University Press, 1961).

Becker, Lawrence C., 'Criminal Attempts and the Theory of the Law of Crimes', *Philosophy and Public Affairs*, Vol. 3 (1974), 262–94.

Bedau, Hugo, 'Retribution and the Theory of Punishment', *Journal of Philosophy*, Vol. 75 (1978), 601–20.

Benn, Stanley I., *A Theory of Freedom* (Cambridge: Cambridge University Press, 1988).

Benn, S. I. and Peters, R. S., *Social Principles and the Democratic State* (London: Allan and Unwin, 1959).

Bennett, Jonathan, *Events and Their Names* (Indianapolis: Bobbs-Merrill, 1988).

Bennett, Jonathan, 'Whatever the Consequences', *Analysis*, Vol. 26 (1966), 83–102.

Bentham, Jeremy, *An Introduction to the Principles of Morals and Legislation* (New York: Hafner edn., 1948).

Bernstein, Richard, *Praxis and Action* (Philadelphia: University of Pennsylvania Press, 1971).

Biro, J. and Shahan, R., eds., *Mind, Brain and Function* (Norman, Okla.: University of Oklahoma Press, 1982).

Bishop, John, *Natural Agency* (Cambridge: Cambridge University Press, 1989).

Blackburn, Simon, 'Rule-Following and Moral Realism', in S. Holtzman and C. Leich, eds., *Wittgenstein: To Follow a Rule* (London: Routledge and Kegan Paul, 1981).

Blackstone, William, *Commentaries on the Laws of England*, Chitty, ed., Vol. IV (London, 1826).

Block, Ned, 'Introduction: What is Functionalism?', in N. Block, ed., *Readings in Philosophy of Psychology*, Vol. 1 (Cambridge, Mass.: Harvard University Press, 1980).

Block, Ned, 'Troubles with Functionalism', in C. W. Savage, ed., *Perception and Cognition, Minnesota Studies in the Philosophy of Science*, Vol. 9 (Minneapolis: University of Minnesota Press, 1978).

Bodde, D. and Morris, C., *Law in Imperial China* (Philadelphia: University of Pennsylvania Press, 1973).

Borgo, John, 'Causal Paradigms in Tort Law', *Journal of Legal Studies*, Vol. 8 (1979), 419–55.

Bork, Robert, *The Tempting of America* (New York: Macmillan, 1990).

Bowers K. and Meichenbaum, P., eds., *The Unconscious Reconsidered* (New York: Wiley, 1984).

Boyd, Richard, 'Materialism without Reductionism: What Physicalism Does Not Entail', in Ned Block, ed., *Readings in the Philosophy of Psychology* (Cambridge, Mass.: Harvard University Press, 1980).

Bradley, F. H., *Appearance and Reality* (2nd edn., Oxford: Oxford University Press, 1897).

Brand, Myles, *Intending and Acting* (Cambridge, Mass.: MIT Press, 1984).

Brand, Myles, 'The Language of Not Doing', *American Philosophical Quarterly*, Vol. 8 (1971), 45–53.

Brand, Myles, ed., *The Nature of Human Action* (Glencoe, Ill.: Scott, Foresman, 1970).

Brandt, Richard, 'Blameworthiness and Obligation', A. Melden, ed., *Essays in Moral Philosophy* (Seattle: University of Washington, 1958).

Brandt, Richard, *Ethical Theory* (Englewood Cliffs, NJ: Prentice-Hall, 1959).

Brandt, Richard, 'A Motivational Theory of Excuse in the Criminal Law', in S. Pennock and J. Chapman, eds., *Criminal Justice, Nomos 27* (New York: New York University Press, 1985).

Brandt, Richard, 'Toward a Credible Form of Utilitarianism', in Baruch Brody, ed., *Moral Rules and Particular Circumstances* (Englewood Cliffs, NJ: Prentice-Hall, 1970).

Brandt, Richard, 'Traits of Character: A Conceptual Analysis', *American Philosophical Quarterly*, Vol. 7 (1970), 23–37.

Brandt, Richard, 'A Utilitarian Theory of Excuses', *The Philosophical Review*, Vol. 78 (1969), 337–61.

Bratman, Michael, *Intentions, Plans, and Practical Reasoning* (Cambridge, Mass.: Harvard University Press, 1983).

Bratman, Michael, 'Michael Moore on Intention and Volition', *University of Pennsylvania Law Review*, Vol. 142 (1994), 1705–18.

Brentano, Franz, *Psychologie vom Empirischen Standpunkt* (Leipzig, 1874).

Brink, David, *Moral Realism and the Foundations of Ethics* (Cambridge: Cambridge University Press, 1989).

Brody, Baruch, *Identity and Essence* (Princeton: Princeton University Press, 1980).

Brown, 'A Solution to the Problem of Moral Luck', *Philosophical Quarterly*, Vol. 42 (1992), 345–56.

Burkhardt, 'Is There a Rational Justification for Punishing an Accomplished Crime More Severely Than an Attempted Crime?', *Brigham Young University Law Review*, Vol. [1986], 553–71.

Butler, Samuel, *Erewhon* (London: Trubner, 1872).

Calabresi, Guido, 'Concerning Cause and the Law of Torts: An Essay for Harry Kalven, Jr.', *University of Chicago Law Review*, Vol. 43 (1975), 69–108.

Calabresi, Guido, *The Cost of Accidents* (New Haven: Yale University Press, 1970).

Calabresi, Guido, 'Some Theories of Risk Distribution and the Law of Torts', *Yale Law Journal*, Vol. 76 (1961), 499–553.

Calabresi and Melamed, 'Property Rules, Liability Rules, and Inalienability: One View of the Cathedral', *Harvard Law Review*, Vol. 85 (1972), 1089–128.

Calhoun, C., 'Cognitive Emotions?', in C. Calhoun and R. Soloman, eds., *What Is an Emotion?* (Oxford: Oxford University Press, 1984).

Campbell, Keith, *Abstract Particulars* (Cambridge, Mass.: Blackwell, 1990).

Camus, Albert, *The Fall*, Justin O'Brien, trans. (New York: Vintage, 1956).

Cardozo, Benjamin, *Law and Literature and Other Essays and Addresses* (New York: Harcourt, Brace, 1931).

Chisholm, Roderick, 'Freedom and Action', in *Freedom and Determinism*, Keith Lehrer, ed. (New York: Random House, 1966).

Chisholm, Roderick, 'Human Freedom and the Self', in Gary Watson, ed., *Free Will* (Oxford: Oxford University Press, 1982).

Chisholm, Roderick, 'Law Statements and Counterfactual Inference', *Analysis*, Vol. 15 (1955), 97–105.

Chisholm, Roderick, *Perceiving: A Philosophical Study* (Ithaca: Cornell University Press, 1957).

Chisholm, R., ed., *Realism and the Background of Phenomenology* (Glencoe, Ill.: Free Press, 1960).

Churchland, Paul and Churchland, Patricia, 'Functionalism, Qualia, and Intentionality', in J. Biro and R. Shahan, eds., *Mind, Brain, and Function* (Norman, Okla.: University of Oklahoma Press, 1982).

Ch'u T'ung-Tsu, *Local Government in China* (Cambridge, Mass.: Harvard University Press, 1962).

Coase, Ronald, 'The Problem of Social Cost', *Journal of Law and Economics*, Vol. 3 (1960), 1–44.

Cohen, Felix, 'The Ethical Basis of Legal Criticism', *Yale Law Journal*, Vol. 41 (1931), 201–220.

Cohen, Felix, 'Transcendental Nonsense and the Functional Approach', *Columbia Law Review*, Vol. 35 (1935), 809–49.

Cohen, Morris, 'The Place of Logic in the Law', *Harvard Law Review*, Vol. 29 (1916), 622–39.

Collingwood, R. G., *The Idea of History* (Oxford: Oxford University Press, 1946).

Comment, 'Brainwashing: Fact, Fiction and Criminal Defense', *University of Missouri-Kansas City Law Review*, Vol. 44 (1976), 438–79.

Comment, 'Necessity Defined: A New Role in the Criminal Defense System', *UCLA Law Review*, Vol. 29 (1981), 409–46.

Cook, Walter Wheeler, ' "Facts" and "Statements of Fact" ', *University of Chicago Law Review*, Vol. 4 (1937), 233–46.

Corrado, Michael, 'Is There an Act Requirement in the Criminal Law?', *University of Pennsylvania Law Review*, Vol. 142 (1994), 1529–61.

Corrado, Michael, 'Notes on the Structure of a Theory of Excuses', *Journal of Criminal Law and Criminology*, Vol. 82 (1992), 465–97.

Corter, James E. and Gluck, Mark E., 'Explaining Basic Categories: Feature Predictability and Information', *Psychological Bulletin*, Vol. 111 (1992), 291–303.

Cottingham, J. G., 'Varieties of Retributivism', *Philosophical Quarterly*, Vol. 29 (1979), 238–46.

Crocker, Lawrence, 'Justice in Criminal Liability: Decriminalizing Harmless Attempts', *Ohio St. LJ,* Vol. 53 (1992), 1057–110.

Crump and Crump, 'In Defense of the Felony Murder Doctrine', *Harvard Journal of Law and Public Policy*, Vol. 8 (1985), 359–98.

Dan-Cohen, Meir, 'Decision Rules and Conduct Rules: On Acoustic Separation in Criminal Law', *Harvard Law Review*, Vol. 97 (1984), 625–77.

Daniels, Norman, 'Wide Reflective Equilibrium and Theory Acceptance in Ethics', *Journal of Philosophy*, Vol. 76 (1979), 256–82.

Danto, Arthur, *Analytical Philosophy of Action* (Cambridge: Cambridge University Press, 1973).

D'Arcy, Eric, *Human Acts* (Oxford: Oxford University Press, 1963).

Davidson, Donald, 'Actions, Reasons and Causes', *Journal of Philosophy*, Vol. 60 (1962), 685–700.

Davidson, Donald, 'Causal Relations', *Journal of Philosophy*, Vol. 64 (1967), 691–703, reprinted in Davidson's *Essays on Actions and Events* (Oxford: Oxford University Press, 1980).

Davidson, Donald, *Essays on Actions and Events* (New York: Oxford University Press, 1980).

Davidson, D. and Hintikka, J. eds., *Words and Objections* (Dordrecht, Holland: Reidel, 1969).

Davis, Lawrence, *Theory of Action* (Englewood Cliffs, NJ: Prentice-Hall, 1979).

Davis, Michael, 'Harm and Retribution', *Philosophy and Public Affairs*, Vol. 15 (1986), 236–66.

Davis, Michael, 'Why Attempts Deserve Less Punishment than Complete Crimes', *Law and Philosophy*, Vol. 5 (1986), 1–32.

Dennett, Dan, *Brainstorms* (Montgomery, Vt.: Bradford Books, 1978).

Dennett, Dan, 'Brain Writing and Mind Reading', in *Brainstorms* (Putney, Vt.: Bradford Books, 1978).

Dennett, Daniel, 'The Conditions of Personhood', in Amelie Rorty, ed., *The Identities of Persons* (Berkeley: University of California Press, 1976), 175–96.

Dennett, Daniel, *Content and Consciousness* (New York: Humanities Press, 1969).

Dennett, Daniel, 'Intentional Systems', in his *Brainstorms* (Putney, Vt.: Bradford Books, 1978).

Dennett, Daniel, *The Intentional Stance* (Cambridge, Mass.: MIT Press, 1987).

Dennett, Daniel, 'Mechanism and Responsibility', in Theodore Honderich, ed., *Essays on Freedom of Action* (London: Routledge and Kegan Paul, 1973).

Dennett, Daniel and Lambert, Karl, *The Philosophical Lexicon* (7th edn., privately printed, 1978).

de Sousa, Ronald, 'The Rationality of the Emotions', in A. Rorty, ed., *Explaining Emotions* (Berkeley: University of California Press, 1980).

de Sousa, Ronald, *The Rationality of the Emotions* (Cambridge, Mass.: MIT Press, 1987).

Devitt, Michael, *Realism and Truth* (Cambridge: Cambridge University Press, 1984).

Devlin, Patrick, *The Enforcement of Morality* (Oxford: Oxford University Press, 1965).

Devlin, Patrick, 'Morals and the Criminal Law', in R. Wasserstrom, ed., *Morality and the Law* (Belmont, Cal.: Wadsworth, 1971).

Dewey, John, *Human Nature and Conduct* (New York: Holt, Rhinehart and Winston, 1922).

Diamond, Bernard, 'Criminal Responsibility of the Mentally Ill', *Stanford Law Review*, Vol. 14 (1961), 59–86.

Dilman, Ilham, *Freud and Human Nature* (Oxford: Blackwell, 1983).

Dilman, Ilham, *Freud and the Mind* (Oxford: Blackwell, 1984).

Dilman, Ilham, 'Is the Unconscious a Theoretical Construct?', *The Monist*, Vol. 46 (1972), 313–42.

Dilman, Ilham, 'The Unconscious', *Mind*, Vol. 68 (1959), 446–73.

Doctorow, E. L., *Ragtime* (New York: Random House, 1975).

Dolinko, David, 'Some Thoughts About Retributivism', *Ethics*, Vol. 101 (1991), 537–59.

Dolinko, David, 'Three Mistakes of Retributivism', *UCLA Law Review*, Vol. 39 (1992), 1623–57.

Donagon, Alan, *Choice: The Essential Element in Human Action* (London: Routledge and Kegan Paul, 1987).

Donne, John, *Devotions Upon Emergent Occasions: Together Death's Duel* (Ann Arbor: University of Michigan Press, 1959).

Dray, William, *Laws and Explanation in History* (Oxford: Oxford University Press, 1957).

Dressler, Joshua, 'Provocation: Partial Justification or Partial Excuse?', *Modern Law Review*, Vol. 51 (1988), 467–80.

Dressler, Joshua, 'Reflections on Excusing Wrongdoers: Moral Theory, New Excuses, and The Model Penal Code', *Rutgers Law Journal*, Vol. 19 (1988), 671–716.

Dressler, Joshua, *Understanding Criminal Law* (New York: Matthew Bender, 1987).

Dretske, Fred, *Explaining Behavior* (Cambridge, Mass.: MIT Press, 1988).

Duff, R. A., 'Acting, Trying, and Criminal Liability', in S. Shute, J. Gardner, and J. Horder, eds., *Action and Value in Criminal Law* (Oxford: Clarendon Press, 1993).

Duff, R. A., 'Choice, Character, and Criminal Liability', *Law and Philosophy*, Vol. 12 (1993), 345–83.

Duff, R. A., *Intention, Agency, and Criminal Liability* (Oxford: Oxford University Press, 1990).

Duff, R. A., '*Mens Rea* and the Law Commission Report', *Criminal Law Review*, Vol. [1980], 147–60.

Duff, R. A., 'Psychopathy and Moral Understanding', *American Philosophical Quarterly*, Vol. 14 (1977), 189–200.

Duff, R. A. and Simmonds, N. E., eds., *Philosophy and the Criminal Law* (Wiesbaden: Steiner, 1984).

Dummett, Michael, *Truth and Other Enigmas* (Cambridge: Harvard University Press, 1978).

Dworkin, Gerald, 'Paternalism', in R. Wasserstrom, ed., *Morality and the Law* (Belmont, Cal.: Wadsworth, 1971).

Dworkin, Ronald, *Law's Empire* (Cambridge, Mass.: Harvard University Press, 1986).

Dworkin, Ronald, 'Liberal Community', *California Law Review*, Vol. 77 (1989), 479–504.

Dworkin, Ronald, 'No Right Answer?', in his *A Matter of Principle* (Cambridge, Mass.: Harvard University Press, 1985).

Dworkin, Ronald, *Taking Rights Seriously* (Cambridge, Mass.: Harvard University Press, 1978).

Eagle, Morris, 'Anatomy of the Self in Psychoanalytic Theory', in M. Ruse, ed., *Nature Animated* (Dordrecht: Reidel, 1983).

Eagle, Morris, *Recent Developments in Psychoanalysis* (New York: McGraw-Hill, 1984).

Eagle, Morris, 'Responsibility, Unconscious Motivation, and Social Order', *International Journal of Law and Psychiatry*, Vol. 6 (1983), 263–91.

Eckelaar, J. and Bell, J., eds., *Oxford Essays in Jurisprudence: Third Series* (Oxford: Oxford University Press, 1987).

Edgarton, Henry, 'Legal Cause', *University of Pennsylvania Law Review*, Vol. 72 (1924), 211–44.

Ellis, Albert, 'An Operational Reformulation of Some of the Basic Principles of Psychoanalysis', in H. Feigl and M. Scriven, eds., *The Foundations of Science and the Concepts of Psychology and Psychoanalysis*, *Minnesota Studies in the Philosophy of Science*, Vol. 1 (Minneapolis: University of Minnesota Press, 1956).

Elster, Jon, 'Rationality and Addiction', in P. de Greiff, ed., *Morality, Legality, and Drugs* (Ithaca, NY: Cornell Univ. Press, 1997).

Epstein, Richard, 'A Theory of Strict Liability', *Journal of Legal Studies*, Vol. 2 (1973), 151–204.

Eunine, Simon, *Donald Davidson* (Stanford, Cal.: Stanford University Press 1991).

Fairbairn, W. Ronald D., *An Object-Relations Theory of the Personality* (New York: Basic Books, 1954).

Feinberg, Joel, 'Action and Responsibility', in *Doing and Deserving* (Princeton: Princeton University Press, 1970).

Feinberg, Joel, 'Causing Voluntary Actions', in *Doing and Deserving* (Princeton: Princeton University Press, 1970).

Feinberg, Joel, *Doing and Deserving* (Princeton: Princeton University Press, 1970).

Feinberg, Joel, 'The Expressive Function of Punishment', *The Monist*, Vol. 49 (1965), 397–423, reprinted in his *Doing and Deserving* (Princeton: Princeton University Press, 1970).

Feinberg, Joel, *Harm to Others* (New York: Oxford University Press, 1984).

Feinberg, Joel, *Harm to Self* (Oxford: Oxford University Press, 1985).

Feinberg, Joel, *Harmless Wrongdoing* (Oxford: Oxford University Press, 1988).

Feinberg, Joel, 'Justice and Personal Desert', in *Doing and Deserving* (Princeton: Princeton University Press, 1970).

Feinberg, Joel, *Offense to Others* (Oxford: Oxford University Press, 1986).

Feinberg, Joel, 'What Is So Special About Mental Illness?', in *Doing and Deserving* (Princeton: Princeton University Press, 1971).

Fingarette, Herbert, *Heavy Drinking: The Myth of Alcoholism as a Disease* (Berkeley: University of California Press, 1988).

Fingarette, Herbert, *The Meaning of Criminal Insanity* (Berkeley and Los Angeles: University of California Press, 1972).

Fingarette, Herbert, 'On Punishment and Suffering', *Proceedings and Addresses of the American Philosophical Association*, Vol. 50 (1977), 499–525.

Fingarette Herbert, *Self-Deception* (London: Routledge and Kegan Paul, 1969).

Finkelman, Marilyn, 'Self-Defense and Defense of Others in Jewish Law: The Rodef Defense', *Wayne Law Review*, Vol. 33 (1987), 1257–87.

Finnis, John, 'Law as Co-ordination', *Ratio Juris*, Vol. 2 (1989), 97–104.

Finnis, John, *Natural Law and Natural Rights* (Oxford: Clarendon Press, 1980).

Finnis, John, 'The Rights and Wrongs of Abortion', *Philosophy and Public Affairs*, Vol. 2 (1973), 117–45.

Fischer, John Martin, 'Responsiveness and Moral Responsibility', in Ferdinand Schoeman, ed., *Responsibility, Character, and the Emotions* (Cambridge: Cambridge University Press, 1987).

Fish, Stanley, 'Dennis Martinez and the Uses of Theory', *Yale Law Journal*, Vol. 96 (1987), 1773–800.

Fletcher, George, 'Criminal Theory as an International Discipline: Reflections on the Freiburg Conference', *Criminal Justice Ethics*, Vol. 4 (1985), 60–72.

Fletcher, George, 'Defensive Force as an Act of Rescue', *Social Philosophy and Policy*, Vol. 7 (1990), 170–9.

Fletcher, George, 'Fairness and Utility in Tort Theory', *Harvard Law Review*, Vol. 85 (1972), 537–73.

Fletcher, George, 'On the Moral Irrelevance of Bodily Movements', *University of Pennsylvania Law Review*, Vol. 142, (1994), 1443–53.

Fletcher, George, 'Proportionality and the Psychotic Aggressor: A Vignette in Comparative Criminal Theory', *Israel Law Review*, Vol. 8 (1973), 367–90.

Fletcher, George, *Rethinking Criminal Law* (Boston: Little, Brown, 1978).

Flew, Antony, 'Psychiatry, Law and Responsibility', *Philosophical Quarterly*, Vol. 35 (1985), 425–32.

Fodor, Jerry, *The Language of Thought* (New York: Thomas Y. Crowell, 1975).

Follesdal, D., 'Quantification into Causal Contexts', in Linsky, ed., *Reference and Modality* (Oxford: Oxford University Press, 1971).

Foot, Philippa, 'Immorality, Action and Outcome', in Ted Honderich, ed., *Morality and Objectivity* (London: Routledge, 1985), 23–38.

Foot, Philippa, 'Nietzsche: The Revaluation of Values', in R. Solomon, ed., *Nietzsche: A Collection of Critical Essays* (Garden City, NY: Doubleday Anchor Books, 1973).

Foot, Philippa, 'The Problem of Abortion and the Doctrine of Double Effect', *Oxford Review*, Vol. 5 (1967), 5–15, reprinted in Foot, *Virtues and Vices* (Oxford: Oxford University Press, 1981).

Forster, Edward Morgan, *Howard's End* (New York: Vintage Books, 1954).

Forster, E. M., 'My Woods', in his *Abinger Harvest* (London: Edward Arnold and Co., 1936).

Frank, Jerome, *Law and the Modern Mind* (New York, 1930).

Frankfurt, Harry, 'Alternate Possibilities and Moral Responsibility', *Journal of Philosophy*, Vol. 66 (1969), 829–39.

Frankfurt, Harry, 'Identification and Wholeheartedness', in Ferdinand Schoeman, ed., *Responsibility, Character, and the Emotions* (Cambridge: Cambridge University Press, 1987), 27–45.

Freeman, Samuel, 'Criminal Liability and Duty to Aid the Distressed', *University of Pennsylvania Law Review*, Vol. 142 (1994), 1455–92.

Frege, Gottlob, 'On Sense and Reference', originally published as 'Sinn und Bedeutung', *Zeitschrift für Philosophie Und Philosophische Kritik*, Vol. 100 (1892), 25–50, translated and reprinted in P. T. Geach and M. Black, eds., *Philosophical Writings of Gottlob Frege* (Oxford: Oxford University Press, 1960).

Frege, G., 'The Thought: A Logical Inquiry', in P. F. Strawson, ed., *Philosophical Logic* (Oxford: Oxford University Press, 1967).

French, Peter, *Collective and Corporate Responsibility* (New York: Columbia University Press, 1984).

Freud, Sigmund, 'Moral Responsibility for the Content of Dreams', in *The Standard English Edition of the Complete Psychological Works of Sigmund Freud*, ed. James Strachey (London: Hogarth Press, 1961), Vol. 19, 131–4.

Freud, Sigmund, *New Introductory Lectures on Psychoanalysis* (New York: Norton, 1965).

Freud, Sigmund, 'A Note on the Unconscious in Psychoanalysis', *Collected Papers*, Vol. 4 (London: Hogarth Press, 1959).

Freud, Sigmund, 'Notes Upon a Case of Obsessional Neurosis', in P. Rieff, ed., *Three Case Histories* (New York: Macmillan, 1963).

Freud, *An Outline of Psychoanalysis, Standard Edition*, Vol. 23 (London: Hogarth Press, 1964).

Freud, Sigmund, 'Project for a Scientific Psychology', *The Standard English Edition of the Complete Psychological Works of Sigmund Freud*, Vol. 1 (London: Hogarth Press, 1953), 281–93.

Fried, Charles, *An Anatomy of Values* (Cambridge, Mass.: Harvard University Press, 1970).

Fried, Charles, *Contract as Promise* (Cambridge, Mass.: Harvard University Press, 1982).

Fried, Charles, *Right and Wrong* (Cambridge, Mass.: Harvard University Press, 1978).

Fried, Charles, 'Right and Wrong—Preliminary Considerations', *Journal of Legal Studies*, Vol. 5 (1975), 165–200.

Fuller, Lon, 'The Case of the Speluncean Explorers', *Harvard Law Review*, Vol. 62 (1949), 616–45.

Fuller, Lon, *The Morality of Law* (2nd edn., Stanford: Stanford University Press, 1969).

Galligan, 'The Return to Retribution in Penal Theory', in C. Tapper ed., *Crime, Proof and Punishment* (London: Butterworth, 1981).

Gaylin, Walter Willard, *The Killing of Bonnie Garland* (New York: Penguin Books, 1983).

Geach, Peter, 'Good and Evil', *Analysis*, Vol. 17 (1956), 33–42.

Geach, P. T., *Logic Matters* (Berkeley: University of California Press, 1980).

George, Robert, *Making Men Moral: Civil Liberties and Public Morality* (Oxford: Oxford University Press, 1993).

George, Robert, 'Recent Criticism of Natural Law Theory', *University of Chicago Law Review*, Vol. 55 (1988), 1371–429.

Gill, Merton, 'Metapsychology Is not Psychology', in M. Gill and P. Holzman, eds., *Psychology versus Metapsychology, Psychological Issues Monograph 36* (New York: International Universities Press, 1976).

Glazebrook, 'The Necessity Plea in English Criminal Law', *Cambridge Law Journal*, Vol. 30 (1972), 87–119.

Glover, Jonathon, *Causing Death and Saving Lives* (London: Penguin, 1977).

Glueck, Sheldon, *Law and Psychiatry: Cold War or Entente Cordiale?* (Baltimore: Johns Hopkins University Press, 1962).

Gobert, James, 'The Fortuity of Consequence', *Criminal Law Forum*, Vol. 4 (1993), 1–46.

Goldman, Alvin, 'Action and Crime: A Fine-Grained Approach', *University of Pennsylvania Law Review*, Vol. 142 (1994), 1563–86.

Goldman, Alvin, *A Theory of Human Action* (Englewood Cliffs, NJ: Prentice-Hall, 1970).

Goldstein, Abraham, *The Insanity Defense* (New Haven: Yale University Press, 1967).

Goldstein and Katz, 'Abolish the "Insanity Defense"—Why Not?', *Yale Law Journal*, Vol. 72 (1963), 853–76.

Goodman, Nelson, *Fact, Fiction, and Forecast*, 4th edn. (Indianapolis: Bobbs-Merrill, 1984).

Goodman, Nelson, 'Seven Strictures on Similarity', in his *Problems and Projects* (Indianapolis: Bobbs-Merrill, 1976).

Gordon, R., *The Structure of Emotions: Investigations in Cognitive Philosophy* (New York: Cambridge University Press, 1987).

Grady, Mark, 'Untaken Precautions', *Journal of Legal Studies*, Vol. 18 (1989), 139–56.

Gray, John, 'Mill's Conception of Happiness and the Theory of Individuality', in Gray and G. W. Smith, eds., *J. S. Mill On Liberty In Focus* (London: Routledge, 1991).

Green, Leon, 'Are There Dependable Rules of Causation?', *University of Pennsylvania Law Review*, Vol. 77 (1929), 601–28.

Green, Leon, *Rationale of Proximate Cause* (Kansas City, Mo.: Vernon Law Book Co., 1927).

Green, Leslie, 'Law, Co-ordination, and the Common Good', *Oxford Journal of Legal Studies*, Vol. 4 (1983), 299–324.

Greenawalt, Kent, 'The Perplexing Borders of Justification and Excuse', *Columbia Law Review*, Vol. 84 (1984), 1897–927.

Greenawalt, Kent, 'Violence—Legal Justification and Moral Appraisal', *Emory Law Journal*, Vol. 32 (1983), 437–97.

Greenwood, John, ed., *The Future of Folk Psychology* (Cambridge: Cambridge University Press, 1991).

Grey, Thomas, 'The Disintegration of Property', in J. Chapman and R. Pennock, eds., *Nomos xxii: Property* (New York: New York University Press, 1980).

Grice, H. P., 'Logic and Conversation', in P. Cole and J. Morgan, eds., *Syntax and Semantics, Speech Acts* (New York: Academic Press, 1975), 3.

Gross, Hyman, *A Theory of Criminal Justice* (New York: Oxford University Press, 1979).

Grunbaum, Adolf, 'Free Will and Laws of Human Behavior', in H. Feigl, W. Sellars and K. Lehrer, eds., *New Readings in Philosophical Analysis* (New York: Century, Appleton, Crofts, 1972).

Grunbaum, Adolf, *The Foundations of Psychoanalysis: A Philosophical Critique* (Berkeley: University of California Press, 1984).

Gur-Arye, Miri, 'Should the Criminal Law Distinguish Between Necessity as a Justification and Necessity as an Excuse?', *Law Quarterly Review*, Vol. 102 (1986), 71–89.

Hacker, P. and Raz, J., eds., *Law, Morality, and Society* (Oxford: Oxford University Press, 1977).

Hahn, P. and Schlipp, P., eds., *The Philosophy of W. V. Quine* (La Salle, Ill.: Open Court, 1986).

Hall, Jerome, *General Principles of Criminal Law,* 2nd edn. (Indianapolis: Bobbs-Merrill, 1960).

Hamlyn, David, 'Causality and Human Behavior', in N. Care and L. Landesman, eds., *Readings in the Theory of Action* (Bloomington, Ind.: Indiana Univ. Press, 1968).

Hampshire, Stuart, 'Disposition and Memory', *International Journal of Psycho-Analysis*, Vol. 42 (1963), 59–68.

Hampshire, S., *Freedom of Mind* (Princeton: Princeton University Press, 1971).

Hampton, Jean, 'The Moral Education Theory of Punishment', *Philosophy and Public Affairs*, Vol. 13 (1984), 208–38.

Hampton, Jean, 'The Retributive Idea', in Murphy and Hampton, *Forgiveness and Mercy* (Cambridge: Cambridge University Press, 1988).

Hampton, Jean and Murphy, Jeffrie, *Forgiveness and Mercy* (Cambridge: Cambridge University Press, 1988).

Hare, R. M., *The Language of Morals* (Oxford: Oxford University Press, 1952).

Harper, Fowler V. and James, Fleming, Jr., *The Law of Torts* (Boston: Little, Brown, 1956), 2 vols.

Harris, 'The Survival Lottery', *Philosophy*, Vol. 50 (1975), 81–7.

Hart, Henry, 'The Aims of the Criminal Law', *Law and Contemporary Problems*, Vol. 23 (1958), 401–41.

Hart, H. L. A., 'The Ascription of Responsibility and Rights', *Proceedings of the Aristotelian Society*, Vol. 49 (1949), 171–94.

Hart, H. L. A., 'Changing Conceptions of Responsibility', in *Punishment and Responsibility* (Oxford: Oxford University Press, 1968).

Hart, H. L. A., 'The House of Lords on Attempting the Impossible', *Oxford Journal of Legal Studies*, Vol. I (1981), 149–66.

Hart, H. L. A., 'Intention and Punishment', *Oxford Review*, Vol. 14 (1967), 5–22.

Hart, H. L. A., *Law, Liberty, and Morality* (Stanford: Stanford University Press, 1963).

Hart, H. L. A., 'Legal Responsibility and Excuses', in his *Punishment and Responsibility* (Oxford: Oxford University Press, 1968).

Hart, H. L. A., 'Negligence, *Mens Rea*, and Criminal Responsibility', in *Punishment and Responsibility* (Oxford: Oxford University Press, 1968), 136–57.

Hart, H. L. A., 'Positivism and the Separation of Law and Morals', *Harvard Law Review*, Vol. 71 (1958), 593–629.

Hart, H. L. A., 'Punishment and the Elimination of Responsibility', in *Punishment and Responsibility* (Oxford: Oxford University Press, 1968).

Hart, H. L. A., *Punishment and Responsibility* (Oxford: Oxford University Press, 1968).

Hart, H. L. A., and Honoré, A. M., *Causation in the Law* (Oxford: Clarendon Press, 1959).

Hart, H. L. A., and Honoré, A. M., *Causation in the Law*, 2nd edn. (Oxford: Oxford University Press, 1985).

Hart, W. D., 'Models of Repression', in R. Wollheim and J. Hopkins, eds., *Philosophical Essays on Freud* (Cambridge: Cambridge University Press, 1982).

Hartmann, E. L., *The Functions of Sleep* (New Haven: Yale University Press, 1973).

Hawkins, Gordon and Morris, Norval, *The Honest Politician's Guide to Crime Control* (Chicago: University of Chicago Press, 1973).

Heidegger, Martin, *Being and Time*, J. Macquarrie and E. Robinson, trans. (New York: Harper and Row, 1962).

Hempel, Carl, *Aspects of Scientific Explanation* (New York: Free Press, 1965).

Herman, Barbara, 'On the Value of Acting from the Motive of Duty', ch. 1 of her *The Practice of Moral Judgment* (Cambridge, Mass.: Harvard University Press, 1993).

Herzog, Don, 'As Many As Six Impossible Things Before Breakfast', *California Law Review*, Vol. 75 (1987), 609–30.

Hicks, G. E., ed., *Famous American Jury Speeches*, (St Paul, Minn.: West Pub. Co., 1925).

Hill, Thomas E., Jr., *Autonomy and Self-Respect* (Cambridge: Cambridge University Press, 1991).

Hittinger, Russell, *A Critique of the New Natural Law Theory* (Notre Dame, Ind.: Univ. of Notre Dame Press, 1987).

Hohfeld, Wesley, *Fundamental Legal Conceptions* (New Haven: Yale University Press, 1923).

Hollander, Paul, 'Sociology, Selective Determinism, and the Rise of Expectations', *American Sociologist*, Vol. 8 (1973), 147–53.

Holmes, Oliver Wendell, *The Common Law* (Cambridge, Mass.: Harvard University Press, 1963).

Holt, Robert, 'The Death and the Transfiguration of the Metapsychology', *International Review of Psychoanalysis*, Vol. 8 (1981), 129–43.

Home, H. J., 'The Concept of Mind', *International Journal of Psychoanalysis*, Vol. 47 (1966), 42–9.

Honderich, Ted, *Punishment: The Supposed Justifications* (London: Hutchinson, 1969).

Horder, Jeremy, 'Criminal Culpability: The Possibility of a General Theory', *Law and Philosophy*, Vol. 12 (1993), 193–215.

Horney, Karen, 'The Value of Vindictiveness', *American Journal of Psychoanalysis*, Vol. 8 (1948), 3–12.

Hornsby, Jennifer, 'Action and Aberration', *University of Pennsylvania Law Review*, Vol. 142 (1994), 1719–47.

Hornsby, Jennifer, 'On What's Intentionally Done', in S. Shute, J. Gardner, and J. Horder, eds., *Action and Value In Criminal Law* (Oxford: Oxford University Press, 1993).

Hospers, John, 'Free Will and Psychoanalysis', in *Freedom and Responsibility*, Herbert Morris, ed. (Stanford: Stanford University Press, 1961).

Hospers, John, 'Meaning and Free Will', *Philosophy and Phenomenological Research*, Vol. 10 (1950), 307–30.

Hospers, John, 'What Libertarianism Is', in Tibor Machan, ed., *The Libertarian Alternative* (Chicago: Nelson-Hall, 1974).

Hruschka, Joachim, 'Imputation', *BYUL Rev.*, Vol. [1986], 669–710.

Hume, David, *An Enquiry Concerning Human Understanding* (LaSalle: Open Court, 1949).

Hurd, Heidi, 'Challenging Authority', *Yale Law Journal*, Vol. 100 (1991), 1611–77.

Hurd, Heidi, 'Justifiably Punishing the Justified', *Michigan Law Review*, Vol. 90 (1992), 2203–24.

Hurd, Heidi, 'The Moral Magic of Consent', *Legal Theory*, Vol. 2 (1996), 121–46.

Hurd, Heidi, 'Sovereignty in Silence', *Yale Law Journal*, Vol. 99 (1990), 945–1028.

Hurd, Heidi, 'What in the World is Wrong?', *Journal of Contemporary Legal Issues*, Vol. 5 (1994), 157–216.

Husak, Douglas, *Drugs and Rights* (Cambridge: Cambridge University Press, 1992).

Husak, Douglas, 'The Presumption of Freedom', *Nous*, Vol. 17 (1983), 345–62.

Huxley, T. H., 'On Descartes' *Discourse on Method*', in *Methods and Results*, ch. 4 (New York: Macmillan, 1893).

Ingber, Stanley, 'Book Review', *UCLA Law Review*, Vol. 27 (1980), 816–48.

James, William, 'The Dilemma of Determinism', in *The Will to Believe* (New York: Longmans, Green and Co., 1898), 147.

Jareborg, Nils, 'Criminal Attempts and Moral Luck', *Israel Law Review*, Vol. 27 (1993), 213–26.

Jensen, 'Morality and Luck', *Philosophy*, Vol. 59 (1984), 323–30.

Kadish, Sanford, 'Complicity, Cause, and Blame: A Study in the Interpretation of Doctrine', *California Law Review*, Vol. 73 (1985), 323–410.

Kadish, Sanford, 'The Criminal Law and the Luck of the Draw', *Journal of Criminal Law and Criminology*, Vol. 84 (1994), 1501–23.

Kadish, Sanford, 'The Crisis of Overcriminalization', *Annals of the American Academy of Political and Social Science*, Vol. 374 (1967), 157–70.

Kadish, Sanford H., 'Excusing Crime', in his *Blame and Punishment* (New York: Macmillan, 1987), 81–106.

Kadish, Sanford, 'Respect for Life and Regard for Rights in the Criminal Law', *California Law Review*, Vol. 64 (1976), 871–901, reprinted in Kadish, *Blame and Punishment* (New York: Macmillan, 1987).

Kadish, Sanford, 'Why Substantive Criminal Law—A Dialogue', in *Blame and Punishment* (New York: Macmillan, 1987).

Kadish, Sanford and Schulhofer, Stephen, eds., *Cases and Materials on Criminal Law*, 5th edn. (Boston: Little, Brown, 1989).

Kamm, Frances, 'Action, Omission, and the Stringency of Duties', *University of Pennsylvania Law Review*, Vol. 142 (1994), 1493–1512.

Kant, *Groundwork of the Metaphysis of Morals*, H. J. Paton, trans. (New York: Harper, 1964).

Kant, *The Metaphysical Elements of Justice*, J. Ladd, trans. (Indianapolis: Bobbs-Merrill, 1965).

Kant, *The Metaphysical Principles of Virtue*, J. Ellington, trans. (Indianapolis: Bobbs-Merrill, 1964).

Kaplan, David, 'Quantifying In', in Davidson and Hintikka eds., *Words and Objections* (Dordrecht: Reidel, 1969), reprinted in L. Linsky, ed., *Reference and Modality* (Oxford: Oxford University Press, 1971).

Kaplan, John, *The Hardest Drug* (Chicago: University of Chicago Press, 1983).

Kaplan, John, 'Model Penal Code Conference', discussion *Rutgers Law Journal*, Vol. 19 (1988), 801–3.

Katz, J. J. and Fodor, J. A., 'The Structure of a Semantic Theory', *Language*, Vol. 39 (1963), 170–210.

Katz, Jay, Goldstein, Joseph, and Dershowitz, Alan, *Psychoanalysis, Psychiatry, and Law* (New York: Free Press, 1967).

Katz, Leo, 'The Assumption of the Risk Argument', *Social Philosophy and Policy*, Vol. 7 (1990), 138–69.

Katz, Leo, *Bad Acts and Guilty Minds* (Chicago: University of Chicago Press, 1987).

Katz, Leo, *Ill-Gotten Gains* (Chicago: University of Chicago Press, 1996).

Katz, Leo, 'Proximate Cause in Michael Moore's Act and Crime', *University of Pennsylvania Law Review*, Vol. 142 (1994), 1513–28.

Katz, 'Law, Psychiatry and Free Will', *International Review of Psycho-Analysis*, Vol. 5 (1978), 257.

Kaufmann, Walter, *Without Guilt and Justice* (New York: Dell, 1973).

Kaye and Aickin, 'A Comment on Causal Apportionment', *Journal of Legal Studies*, Vol. 13 (1984), 191–208.

Keedy, E., 'Criminal Attempts at Common Law', *University of Pennsylvania Law Review*, Vol. 102 (1954), 464–89.

Keeton, Robert, *Legal Cause in the Law of Torts* (Columbus: Ohio State University Press, 1963).

Kelman, Mark, 'Interpretive Construction in the Substantive Criminal Law', *Stanford Law Review*, Vol. 33 (1981), 591–673.

Kelman, Mark, 'The Necessary Myth of Objective Causation Judgments in Liberal Political Theory', *Chicago-Kent Law Review*, Vol. 63 (1987), 579–637.

Kenny, Anthony, 'Aristotle on Moral Luck', in J. Dancy, J. M. Moravcsik, and C. C. W. Taylor, eds., *Human Agency: Language, Duty, and Value* (Stanford: Stanford University Press, 1988).

Kenny, Anthony, 'Intention and *Mens Rea* in Murder', in P. M. S. Hacker and J. Raz, eds., *Law, Morality, and Society* (Oxford: Oxford University Press, 1977).

Kenny, Anthony, 'Intention and Purpose', *Journal of Philosophy*, Vol. 63 (1966), 642–51, revised and reprinted as 'Intention and Purpose in Law', in R. Summers, ed., *Essays in Legal Philosophy* (Berkeley: University of California Press, 1968).

Kenny, Anthony, *Will, Freedom and Power* (Oxford: Oxford University Press, 1976).

Kessler, Kim, 'The Role of Luck in The Criminal Law', *University of Pennsylvania Law Review*, Vol. 142 (1994), 2183–237.

Kim, Jaegon, 'Causes and Events: Mackie on Causation', *Journal of Philosophy*, Vol. 68 (1971), 426–41, reprinted in E. Sosa, ed., *Causation and Conditionals* (Oxford: Oxford University Press, 1975).

Klein, George, 'Freud's Two Theories of Sexuality', in M. Gill and P. Holzman, eds., *Psychology versus Metapsychology, Psychological Issues Monograph 36* (New York: International Universities Press, 1976).

Klein, George, 'Two Theories or One?', in his *Psychoanalytic Theory* (New York: International Universities Press, 1976).

Knowles, Dudley, 'Unjustified Retribution', *Israel Law Review*, Vol. 27 (1993), 50–8.

Kremnitzer, Mordehai, 'Proportionality and the Psychotic Aggressor: Another View', *Israel Law Review*, Vol. 18 (1983), 178–214.

Kripke, Saul, *Wittgenstein on Rules and Private Language* (Cambridge, Mass.: Harvard University Press, 1982).

Lacey, Nicola, *State Punishment* (London: Routledge, 1988).

LaFave and Scott, *Criminal Law* (St Paul: West, 2nd edn., 1986).

Laing, R. D., *The Divided Self* (London: Tavistock Publications, 1960).

Laing, R. D., *The Politics of Experience* (New York: Ballantine Books, 1967).

Landau Commission, *Landau Commission Report* (Jerusalem: Government Printing Office, 1987).

Landes and Posner, 'Causation in Tort Law: An Economic Approach', *Journal of Legal Studies*, Vol. 12 (1983), 109–34.

Landesman, C., 'The New Dualism in the Philosophy of Mind', *Review of Metaphysics*, Vol. 19 (1965), 329–45.

Langdell, C. C., *A Selection of Cases on Contracts* (Boston: Little, Brown, 2nd edn., 1879).

Langdell, C. C., *A Summary of the Law of Contracts* (Boston: Little, Brown, 1880).

Laudan, L., ed., *Mind and Medicine: Problems of Explanation and Evaluation in Psychiatry and the Biomedical Sciences* (Berkeley: University of California Press, 1983).

Lewis, C. S., 'The Humanitarian Theory of Punishment', *Res Judicatae*, Vol. 6 (1953), 224–30.

Lewis, David, 'Causation', *Journal of Philosophy*, Vol. 70 (1973), 556–67.

Lewis, David, *Counterfactuals* (Cambridge, Mass.: Harvard University Press, 1973).

Lewis, David, 'The Punishment That Leaves Something to Chance', *Philosophy and Public Affairs*, Vol. 18 (1989), 53–67.

Libet, Benjamin, 'Unconscious Cerebral Initiative and the Role of Conscious Will in Voluntary Action', *Behavioral and Brain Sciences*, Vol. 8 (1985), 529–66.

Linsky, Leonard, 'Reference, Essentialism, and Modality', in Linsky, ed., *Reference and Modality* (Oxford: Oxford University Press, 1971).

Linsky, Leonard, ed., *Reference and Modality* (Oxford: Oxford University Press, 1971).

Loar, Brian, *Mind and Meaning* (Cambridge: Cambridge University Press, 1982).

Loar, Brian, 'Reference and Propositional Attitudes', *The Philosophical Review*, Vol. 81 (1972), 43–62.

Lombard, L. B., 'The Extensionality of Causal Contexts: Comments on Rosenberg and Martin', in French, Vehling, and Wettstein, eds., *Midwest Studies in Philosophy*, Vol. IV (1979), 409–15.

Lombard, Lawrence, *Events: A Metaphysical Study* (London: Routledge and Kegan Paul, 1986).

Louch, A. R., *Explanation and Human Action* (Berkeley: University of California Press, 1966).

Loux, Michael, ed., *The Possible and the Actual* (Ithaca, NY: Cornell University Press, 1979).

Loux, Michael, ed., *Universals and Particulars: Readings in Ontology* (garden City, NY: Anchor, 1970).

Lycan, William, 'On "Intentionality" and the Psychological', *American Philosophical Quarterly*, Vol. 6 (1969), 305–11.

Lycan, William, 'Psychological Laws', in J. Biro and R. Shahan, eds., *Mind, Brain and Function* (Norman, Okla.: University of Oklahoma Press, 1982).

Lyons, David, *The Forms and Limits of Utilitarianism* (Oxford: Clarendon Press, 1965).

Lyons, David, 'Utility and Rights', in Jeremy Waldron, ed., *Theories of Rights* (Oxford: Oxford University Press, 1984).

Lyons, W., *Emotion* (Cambridge: Cambridge University Press, 1980).

McAuley, 'Anticipating the Past: The Defense of Provocation in Irish Law', *Modern Law Review*, Vol. 50 (1987), 133–57.

Macaulay, T. B., *A Penal Code Prepared by the Indian Law Commissioners* (1837), cited in S. Kadish, S. Schulhofer and M. Paulsen, *Criminal Law and its Processes: Cases and Materials*, 4th edn. (Boston: Little, Brown, 1983), 819.

McCloskey, H. J., 'A Non-Utilitarian Approach to Punishment', *Inquiry*, Vol. 8 (1965), 249–63.

Mackie, John, 'Causation and Conditionals', *American Philosophical Quarterly*, Vol. 2 (1965), 245–64, reprinted in E. Sosa, ed., *Causation and Conditionals* (Oxford: Oxford University Press, 1975).

Mackie, John, *The Cement of the Universe* (Oxford: Oxford University Press, 1980).

Mackie, John, *Ethics: Inventing Right and Wrong* (New York: Penguin Books, 1977).

Mackie, John, 'The Grounds of Responsibility', in Hacker and Raz, eds., *Law Morality and Society* (Oxford: Oxford University Press, 1977).

Mackie, John, 'Morality and the Retributive Emotions', *Criminal Justice Ethics* (Winter/Spring, 1982), 3–10.

Mackie, John, 'Retribution: A Test Case for Ethical Objectivity', in Joel Feinberg and Hyman Gross, eds., *Philosophy of Law*, 4th edn. (Belmont, Cal.: Wadsworth, 1991).

Malcolm, Norman, 'Behaviorism as a Philosophy of Psychology', in T. W. Wann, ed., *Behaviorism and Phenomenology* (Chicago: University of Chicago Press, 1964), 141–54.

Malcolm, Norman, 'The Conceivability of Mechanism', *The Philosophical Review*, Vol. 77 (1968), 45–72.

Malone, Wex, 'Ruminations on Cause-In-Fact', *Stanford Law Review*, Vol. 9 (1956), 60–99.

Mapel, Brenda Munsey, 'Philosophical Criticism of Behaviorism: An Analysis', *Behaviorism*, Vol. 5 (1977), 17–32.

Martin, Michael, 'Interpreting Skinner', *Behaviorism*, Vol. 6 (1978), 129–38.

Martin, Rex, *Historical Explanation: Re-enactment and Practical Inference* (Ithaca: Cornell University Press, 1977).

Matte-Blanco, I., *The Unconscious as Infinite Sets* (London: Duckworth, 1975).

Medin, D. L., 'Structural Principles of Categorization', in B. Shepp. and T. Tighe, eds., *Interaction: Perception, Development and Cognition* (Hillsdale, NJ, 1983), 203–30.

Meiland, J. W., *The Nature of Intention* (London: Methuen, 1970).

Meissner, W. W., 'Metapsychology—Who needs it?', *Journal of the American Psychoanalytic Association*, Vol. 29 (1981), 921–38.

Melden, A. I., *Free Action* (London: Routledge and Kegan Paul, 1961).

Menninger, Karl, *The Crime of Punishment* (New York: Viking Press, 1968).

Michelman, Frank, 'Political Markets and Community Self-Determination: Competing Judicial Models of Local Government Legitimacy', *Indiana Law Journal*, Vol. 63 (1979), 145–206.

Miles, T. R., *Eliminating the Unconscious* (Oxford: Pergamon Press, 1966).

Mill, John Stuart, *On Liberty*, originally published in 1859, reprinted in *J. S. Mill's On Liberty in Focus*, John Gray and G. W. Smith, eds. (London: Routledge, 1991).

Mill, John Stuart, *Utilitarianism* (Indianapolis: Liberal Arts Press, 1957).

Mischel, Theodore, 'Concerning Rational Behavior and Psychoanalytic Explanation', *Mind*, Vol. 74 (1965), 71–8.

Montague, Philip, 'The Morality of Self-Defense: A Reply to Wasserman', *Philosophy and Public Affairs*, Vol. 18 (1989), 81–9.

Montague, Philip, 'Self-Defense and Choosing Between Lives', *Philosophical Studies*, Vol. 40 (1981), 207–19.

Moore, A. W., 'A Kantian View of Moral Luck', *Philosophy*, Vol. 65 (1990), 297–321.

Moore, G. E., *Ethics* (Cambridge: Cambridge University Press, 1912).

Moore, G. E., *Principia Ethica* (Cambridge: Cambridge University Press, 1903).

Moore, Michael, *Act and Crime: The Philosophy of Action and its Implications for the Criminal Law* (Oxford: Clarendon Press, 1993).

Moore, Michael, 'Choice, Character, and Excuse', *Social Philosophy and Policy*, Vol. 7 (1990), 28–58.

Moore, Michael, 'The Dead Hand of Constitutional Tradition', *Harvard Journal of Law and Public Policy*, Vol. 19 (1995), 263–73.

Moore, Michael, 'The Determinist Theory of Excuses', *Ethics*, Vol. 95 (1985), 909–19.

Moore, Michael, 'Good Without God', in Robert George and Christopher Wolfe, eds., *Liberalism, Modernity, and Natural Law* (Oxford: Oxford University Press, 1996).

Moore, Michael, 'The Interpretive Turn in Modern Theory: A Turn for the Worse?', *Stanford Law Review*, Vol. 41 (1989), 871–957.

Moore, Michael, 'Law, Authority, and Razian Reasons', *Southern California Law Review*, Vol. 62 (1989), 827–96.

Moore, Michael, 'Law as a Functional Kind', in R. George, ed., *Natural Law Theory* (Oxford: Oxford University Press, 1992).

Moore, Michael, *Law and Psychiatry: Rethinking the Relationship* (Cambridge: Cambridge University Press, 1984).

Moore, Michael, 'Legal Conceptions of Mental Illness', *Philosophy and Medicine*, Vol. V (1979), 25–69.

Moore, Michael, 'The Limits of Legislation', Asia Foundation Lectures on Legislation, Seoul, Korea, 1984, published in *USC Cites* [Fall, 1984], 23–32.

Moore, Michael, 'Metaphysics, Epistemology, and Legal Theory', *Southern California Law Review*, Vol. 60 (1987), 453–506.

Moore, Michael, 'Moral Realism Revisited', *Michigan Law Review*, Vol. 90 (1992), 2424–533.

Moore, Michael, 'Moral Reality', *Wisconsin Law Review*, Vol. [1982], 1061–156.

Moore, Michael, 'A Natural Law Theory of Interpretation', *Southern California Law Review*, Vol. 58 (1985), 277–398.

Moore, Michael S., 'The Nature of Psychoanalytic Explanation', *Psychoanalysis and Contemporary Thought*, Vol. 3 (1980), 459–543, revised and reprinted in Larry Laudan, ed., *Mind and Medicine: Explanation in Psychiatry and the Biomedical Sciences*, Vol. 8 of the *Pittsburgh Series in the Philosophy and History of Science* (Berkeley: University of California Press, 1983).

Moore, Michael, 'Precedent, Induction, and Ethical Generalization', in Laurence Goldstein, ed., *Precedent in Law* (Oxford: Oxford University Press, 1987).

Moore, Michael, 'Responsibility and the Unconscious', *Southern California Law Review*, Vol. 53 (1980), 1563–5.

Moore, Michael, 'The Semantics of Judging', *Southern California Law Review*, Vol. 54 (1981), 151–294.

Moore, Michael, 'A Theory of Criminal Law Theories', *Tel Aviv University Studies in Law*, Vol. 10 (1990), 115–85.

Moore, Michael, 'Three Concepts of Rules', *Harvard Journal of Law and Public Policy*, Vol. 14 (1991), 771–95.

Moore, Michael, 'The Unity of the Self', in Michael Ruse, ed., *Nature Animated* (Dordrecht: Reidel, 1982).

Morris, Clarence, 'Duty, Negligence, and Causation', *University of Pennsylvania Law Review*, Vol. 101 (1952), 189–222.

Morris, Clarence, 'Proximate Cause in Minnesota', *Minnesota Law Review*, Vol. 34 (1950), 185–209.

Morris, Clarence, *Torts* (Brooklyn: Foundation Press, 1953).

Morris, Herbert, *On Guilt and Innocence: Essays in Legal Philosophy and Moral Psychology* (Los Angeles: University of California Press, 1976).

Morris, Herbert, 'Nonmoral Guilt', in F. Schoeman, ed., *Responsibility, Character, and the Emotions* (Cambridge: Cambridge University Press, 1987).

Morris, Herbert, 'A Paternalistic Theory of Punishment', *American Philosophical Quarterly*, Vol. 18 (1981), 263–71.

Morris, Herbert, 'Persons and Punishment', *The Monist*, Vol. 52 (1968), 475–501, reprinted in his *On Guilt and Innocence* (Los Angeles: University of California Press, 1976).

Morris, Norval, *Madness and the Criminal Law* (Chicago: University of Chicago Press, 1982).

Morris, Norval and Hawkings, Gordon, *The Honest Politician's Guide to Crime Control* (Chicago: University of Chicago Press, 1970).

Morse, Stephen, 'Crazy Behavior, Morals, and Science: An Analysis of Mental Health Law', *Southern California Law Review*, Vol. 51 (1978), 527–654.

Morse, Stephen, 'Culpability and Control', *University of Pennsylvania Law Review*, Vol. 142 (1994), 1587–660.

Morse, Stephen, 'Failed Explanations and Criminal Responsibility: Experts and the Unconscious', *Virginia Law Review*, Vol. 68 (1982), 971–1084.

Morse, Stephen, 'Justice, Mercy, and Craziness', *Stanford Law Review*, Vol. 36 (1984), 1485–515.

Morse, Stephen, 'Psychology, Determinism, and Legal Responsibility', in Gary Melton, ed., *Nebraska Symposium on Motivation 1985*, Vol. 33 (Lincoln: University of Nebraska Press, 1986), 35–85.

Morse, Stephen, 'The Twilight of Welfare Criminology: A Reply to Judge Bazelon', *Southern California Law Review*, Vol. 49 (1976), 1247–68.

Morse, Stephen, 'Undiminished Confusion in Diminished Capacity', *Journal of Criminal Law and Criminology*, Vol. 75 (1984), 1–55.

Morton, Adam, 'Extensional and Non-Truth-Functional Contexts', *Journal of Philosophy*, Vol. 66 (1969), 159–64.

Mullane, Harvey, 'Defense, Dreams and Rationality', *Synthese*, Vol. 57 (1983), 187–204.

Murphy, Jeffrie, 'Does Kant Have a Theory of Punishment?', *Columbia Law Review*, Vol. 87 (1987), 509–32.

Murphy, Jeffrie, 'Getting Even: The Role of the Victim', *Social Philosophy and Policy*, Vol. 7 (1990), 209–25.

Murphy, Jeffrie, 'Involuntary Acts and Criminal Liability', *Ethics*, Vol. 81 (1971), 332–42.

Murphy, Jeffrie, 'The Killing of the Innocent', *The Monist*, Vol. 57 (1973), 527–50.

Murphy, Jeffrie, *Retribution, Justice and Therapy* (Dordrecht: Reidel, 1979).

Murphy, Jeffrie, 'Retributivism and the State's Interest in Punishment', in J. R. Pennock and J. W. Chapman, eds., *Criminal Justice: Nomos XXVII* (New York: New York University Press, 1985).

Murphy, Jeffrie and Jean Hampton, *Forgiveness and Mercy* (Cambridge: Cambridge University Press, 1988).

Nagel, Ernest, 'Methodological Issues in Psychoanalytic Theory', in S. Hook, ed., *Psychoanalysis, Scientific Method, and Philosophy* (New York: New York University Press, 1959).

Nagel, Ernest, *The Structure of Science* (New York: Harcourt, Brace, and World, 1961).

Nagel, Thomas, 'Moral Luck', *Proceedings of the Aristotelian Society*, Supp. Vol. 50 (1976), 137–51.

Nagel, Thomas, *Mortal Questions* (Cambridge: Cambridge University Press, 1979).

Nagel, Thomas, *The View From Nowhere* (New York: Oxford University Press, 1985).

Nagel, Thomas, 'War and Massacre', *Philosophy and Public Affairs*, Vol. 2 (1972), 123–44, reprinted in S. Scheffler, ed., *Consequentialism and Its Critics* (Oxford: Oxford University Press, 1988), 51–73.

Nietzsche, Friedrich, *Beyond Good and Evil*, Kaufmann, trans. (New York: Vintage, 1966).

Nietzsche, Friedrich, *The Dawn*, in W. Kaufmann, ed., *The Portable Nietzsche* (New York: Viking, 1954).

Nietzsche, Friedrich, *The Gay Science*, Kaufmann, trans. (New York: Vintage, 1974).

Nietzsche, Friedrich, *On the Genealogy of Morals*, Kaufmann, trans. (New York: Vintage, 1969).

Nietzsche, Friedrich, *Thus Spoke Zarathustra*, in W. Kaufmann, ed., *The Portable Nietzsche* (New York: Viking, 1954).

Nietzsche, Friedrich, *Twilight of the Idols*, in W. Kaufmann, ed., *The Portable Nietzsche* (New York: Viking, 1954).

Note, 'Justification: The Impact of the Model Penal Code on Statutory Reform', *Columbia Law Review*, Vol. 75 (1975), 914–62.

Note, 'Premenstrual Syndrome: A Criminal Defense', *Notre Dame Law Review*, Vol. 59 (1983), 253–69.

Note, 'The XYY Chromosome Defense', *Georgetown Law Journal*, Vol. 57 (1969), 892–922.

Nowell-Smith, P. H., *Ethics* (London: Penguin Books, 1954).

Nozick, Robert, *Anarchy, State and Utopia* (Cambridge, Mass.: Harvard University Press, 1974).

Nozick, Robert, *Philosophical Explanations* (Cambridge: Harvard University Press, 1981).

Oakshott, Michael, *Experience and its Modes* (Cambridge: Cambridge University Press, 1933).

Oberdick, Hans, 'Intention and Foresight in Criminal Law', *Mind*, Vol. 81 (1972), 389–400.

Packer, Herbert, 'The Crime Tariff', *American Scholar*, Vol. 33 (1964), 551–7.

Packer, Herbert, *The Limits of the Criminal Sanction* (Stanford: Stanford University Press, 1968).

Papineau, David, *Theory and Meaning* (Oxford: Clarendon Press, 1979).

Parker, Richard, 'Blame, Punishment, and the Role of Results', *American Philosophical Quarterly*, Vol. 21 (1984), 269–76.

Perkins, Rollin M. and Boyce, Ronald, *Criminal Law*, 3rd edn. (Mineola, NY: Foundation Press, 1982).

Peterfreund, Emanuel, *Information Systems and Psychoanalysis* (New York: International Universities Press, 1971).

Peters, E., *Torture* (New York: Basil Blackwell, 1985).

Peters, Richard, *The Concept of Motivation* (London: Routledge and Kegan Paul, 1958).

Pillsbury, Samuel, 'Emotional Justice: Moralizing the Passions of Criminal Punishment', *Cornell Law Review*, Vol. 74 (1989), 655–710.

Pillsbury, Samuel, 'The Meaning of Deserved Punishment: An Essay on Choice, Character, and Responsibility', *Indiana Law Journal*, Vol. 67 (1992), 719–52.

Platt, A. and Diamond, B., 'The Origins and Development of the "Wild Beast" Concept of Mental Illness and Its Relation to Theories of Criminal Responsibility', *Journal of the History of the Behavior Sciences*, Vol. 1 (1965), 355–67.

Platt, A. and Diamond, B., 'The Origins of the "Right and Wrong" Test of Criminal Responsibility and Its Subsequent Development in the United States: An Historical Survey', *California Law Review*, Vol. 54 (1966), 1227–60.

Platts, Mark, *Ways of Meaning* (London: Routledge and Kegan Paul, 1979).

Pollock, 'Liability for Consequences', *Law Quarterly Review*, Vol. 38 (1922), 165–7.

Pollock, *Torts* (6th edn., New York: Banks Law Pub. Co., 1901).

Popper, Karl, *The Logic of Scientific Discovery* (3rd edn., London: Hutchison, 1968).

Posner, Richard, 'An Economic Theory of the Criminal Law', *Columbia Law Review*, Vol. 85 (1985), 1193–231.

Posner, Richard, 'The Jurisprudence of Skepticism', *Michigan Law Review*, Vol. 86 (1988), 827–91.

Posner, Richard, 'A Theory of Negligence', *Journal of Legal Studies*, Vol. 1 (1972), 29–96.

Postema, Gerald, *Bentham and the Common Law Tradition* (Oxford: Clarendon Press, 1986).

Prichard, H. A., *Moral Obligation* (Oxford: Oxford University Press, 1949).

Prosser, William, 'False Imprisonment: Consciousness of Confinement', *Columbia Law Review*, Vol. 55 (1955), 847–50.

Putnam, Hilary, 'The Meaning of "Meaning" ', in his *Mind, Language, and Reality* (Cambridge: Cambridge University Press, 1975).

Putnam, Hilary, *Mind, Language and Reality* (Cambridge: Cambridge University Press, 1975).

Putnam, Hilary, *Realism and Reason* (Cambridge: Cambridge University Press, 1983).

Quine, W. V., 'Natural Kinds', in his *Ontological Relativity and Other Essays* (New York: Columbia University Press, 1969).

Quine, W. V., *Ontological Relativity and Other Essays* (New York: Columbia University Press, 1969).

Quine, W. V., 'Quantifiers and Propositional Attitudes', in his *The Ways of Paradox* (Cambridge, Mass.: MIT Press, 1966).

Quine, W. V., 'Reference and Modality', in his *From a Logical Point of View* (Cambridge, Mass.: Harvard University Press, 1953).

Quine, W. V., 'Reference and Modality', in his *From a Logical Point of View* (2nd edn., Cambridge, Mass.: Harvard University Press, 1961).

Quine, W. V., 'Replies', in Davidson and Hintikka, eds., *Words and Objections* (Dordrecht: Reidel, 1969).

Quine, W. V., 'The Scope and Language of Science', in his *The Ways of Paradox* (Cambridge, Mass.: MIT Press, 1966).

Quine, W. V., 'Two Dogmas of Empiricism', in his *From a Logical Point of View* (Cambridge, Mass.: Harvard University Press, 4th printing, 1980).

Quine, W. V., *The Ways of Paradox* (Cambridge, Mass.: MIT Press, 1966).

Quine, W. V., *Word and Object* (Cambridge, Mass.: MIT Press, 1960).

Quinn, Warren, 'Actions, Intentions, and Consequences: The Doctrine of Double Effect', *Philosophy and Public Affairs*, Vol. 18 (1989), 334–51.

Quinton, Anthony, 'On Punishment', *Analysis*, Vol. 14 (1954), 1933–42.

Radin, Margaret, 'Cruel Punishment and Respect for Persons: Super Due Process for Death', *Southern California Law Review*, Vol. 53 (1980), 1143–85.

Radin, Margaret, 'Property and Personhood', *Stanford Law Review*, Vol. 34 (1984), 957–1015.

Railton, Peter, 'Alienation, Consequentialism, and the Demands of Morality', *Philosophy and Public Affairs*, Vol. 13 (1984), 134–71.

Rapaport, David, 'On the Psychoanalytic Theory of Motivation', in 1960 *Nebraska Symposium on Motivation* (Lincoln: University of Nebraska Press, 1960).

Rawls, John, 'Outline of a Decision Procedure for Ethics', *The Philosophical Review*, Vol. 60 (1951), 177–97.

Rawls, John, *A Theory of Justice* (Cambridge, Mass.: Harvard University Press, 1971).

Rawls, John, 'Two Concepts of Rules', *Philosophical Review*, Vol. 64 (1955), 3–32.

Rayner, Eric, 'Infinite Experiences, Affects and the Characteristics of the Unconscious', *International Journal of Psycho-Analysis*, Vol. 62 (1981), 403–12.

Raz, Joseph, *The Authority of Law* (Oxford: Oxford University Press, 1979).

Raz, Joseph, 'The Inner Logic of the Law', *Rechtstheorie*, Vol. 10 (1986), 101–17.

Raz, Joseph, *The Morality of Freedom* (Oxford: Oxford University Press, 1987).

Raz, Joseph, *Practical Reasons and Norms* (Oxford: Oxford University Press, 1975).

Rees, John, *John Stuart Mill's On Liberty* (Oxford: Clarendon Press, 1985).

Regan, Donald, 'Authority and Value', *Southern California Law Review*, Vol. 62 (1989), 995–1095.

Regan, Donald, 'Law's Halo', *Social Philosophy and Policy*, Vol. 4 (1986), 15–30.

Regan, Donald, *Utilitarianism and Cooperation* (Oxford: Oxford University Press, 1980).

Reid, John, 'The Working of the New Hampshire Doctrine of Criminal Insanity', *University of Miami Law Review*, Vol. 15 (1960), 14–58.

Reiman, Jeffrey and van den Haag, Ernest, 'On the Common Saying That it is Better that Ten Guilty Persons Escape than that One Innocent Suffer: Pro and Con', *Social Philosophy and Policy*, Vol. 7 (1990), 226–48.

Rescher, Nicholas, 'Belief Contravening Suppositions', *The Philosophical Review*, Vol. 60 (1961), 176–96.

Rescher, Nicholas, 'Moral Luck', *Proceedings of American Philosophical Association*, Vol. 64 (1990), 5–20.

Richard, Mark, *Propositional Attitudes* (Cambridge: Cambridge University Press, 1990).

Richards, David A. J., *Sex, Drugs, Death, and the Law* (Totowa, NJ: Rowman and Littlefield, 1982).

Richards, N., 'Luck and Desert', *Mind*, Vol. 95 (1986), 198–209.

Richardson, R. C., 'Internal Representations: Prologue to a Theory of Intentionality', in J. Biro and R. Shahan, eds., *Mind, Brain and Function* (Norman, Okla.: University of Oklahoma Press, 1982).

Ricoeur, Paul, *Freud and Philosophy* (New Haven, Conn.: Yale University Press, 1970).

Rizzo and Arnold, 'Causal Apportionment in the Law of Torts: An Economic Theory', *Columbia Law Review*, Vol. 80 (1980), 1399–429.

Roberts, 'What an Emotion Is: A Sketch', *Philosophical Review*, Vol. 97 (1988), 183–209.

Robinson, Paul, 'Criminal Law Defenses: A Systematic Analysis', *Columbia Law Review*, Vol. 82 (1982), 199–291.

Rorty, Richard, 'Introduction', in *The Linguistic Turn* (Chicago: University of Chicago Press, 1967).

Rosenberg, A. and Martin, R. M., 'The Extensionality of Causal Contexts', *Midwest Studies in Philosophy*, Vol. 4 (1973), 401–8.

Ross, Alf, 'Tu-Tu', *Harvard Law Review*, Vol. 70 (1957), 812–25.

Royal Commission on Capital Punishment, *1949–53 Report* (London, 1953).

Royko, Mike, 'Nothing Gained by Killing a Killer? Oh Yes, There Is', *Los Angeles Times*, 13 March 1981, Sec. II, 7.

Rubinstein, B., 'On the Possibility of a Strictly Clinical Theory: An Essay on the Philosophy of Psychoanalysis', in M. Gill and P. Holzman, eds., *Psychology versus Metapsychology, Psychological Issues Monograph 36* (New York: International Universities Press, 1976).

Rubinstein, B., 'Psychoanalytic Theory and the Mind-Body problem', in N. Greenfield and W. Lewis, eds., *Psychoanalysis and Current Biological Thought* (Madison: University of Wisconsin Press, 1965).

Rush, Benjamin, *An Enquiry Into the Effects of Ardent Spirits on the Human Body and Moral* (Brookfield, Mass.: E. Merriam and Co., 1814).

Russell, Bertrand, 'The World of Universals' from his *The Problems of Philosophy* (New York: H. Holt and Co., 1912), reprinted in M. Loux, ed., *Universals and Particulars: Readings in Ontology* (Garden City, NY: Anchor Books, 1970), 16–23.

Ryle, Gilbert, *The Concept of Mind* (London: Hutcheson, 1949).

Sabini, John and Maury Silver, 'Emotions, Responsibility, and Character', in F. Schoeman, ed., *Responsibility, Character, and the Emotions* (Cambridge: Cambridge University Press, 1987), 164–75.

Sachs, David, 'On Freud's Doctrine of the Emotions', in R. Wollheim, ed., *Freud* (New York: Anchor, 1975).

Sadurski, Wojciech, *Giving Desert Its Due* (Dordrecht: Reidel, 1985).

Sandel, Michael, 'Introduction' to *Liberalism and Its Critics* (New York: New York University, 1984).

Sandel, Michael, *Liberalism and the Limits of Justice* (Cambridge, Mass.: Harvard University Press, 1982).

Sandel, Michael, 'Moral Argument and Liberal Toleration: Abortion and Homosexuality' *California Law Review*, Vol. 77 (1989), 521–38.

Sandel, Michael, 'The Procedural Republic and the Unencumbered Self', *Political Theory*, Vol. 12 (1984), 81–96.

Sartorius, Rolf, *Individual Conduct and Social Norms* (Encino, Calif.: Dickerson, 1975).

Sartre, Jean-Paul, 'Existentialism is a Humanism', in Novak, ed., *Existentialism versus Marxism* (New York: Dell Publishing Co., 1966).

Sartre, Jean-Paul, 'The Flies', in *No Exit and Three Other Plays* (New York: Vintage, 1955).

Saxe, David, 'Psychiatry, Sociopathy and the XYY Chromosome Syndrome', *Tulsa Law Journal*, Vol. 6 (1970), 243–56.

Scanlon, T. M. Jr., 'Quality of Will and the Value of Choice' (unpublished manuscript, 1988).

Schafer, Roy, *A New Language for Psychoanalysis* (New Haven, Conn.: Yale University Press, 1976).

Schauer, Frederick, 'Precedent', *Stanford Law Review*, Vol. 39 (1987), 571–605.

Schedler, 'Can Retributivists Support Legal Punishment?', *The Monist*, Vol. 63 (1980), 185–98.

Scheffler, Samuel, 'Agent-Centred Restrictions, Rationality, and the Virtues', *Mind*, Vol. 94 (1985), 409–19.

Scheffler, Samuel, ed., *Consequentialism and Its Critics* (Oxford: Oxford University Press, 1988).

Scheffler, Samuel, 'Introduction', in Samuel Scheffler, ed., *Consequentialism and Its Critics* (Oxford: Oxford University Press, 1988).

Scheffler, Samuel, *The Rejection of Consequentialism* (Berkeley: University of California Press, 1982).

Scheler, Max, *Ressentiment*, Holdheim, trans. (New York: Free Press, 1961).

Schlick, Moritz, 'Causality in Everyday Life and in Recent Science', *University of California Publications in Philosophy*, Vol. 15 (1932), 99–125, reprinted in H. Morris, ed., *Freedom and Responsibility* (Stanford: Stanford University Press, 1961), 292.

Schlick, Moritz, *Problems of Ethics* (New York: Dover Publications, 1962).

Schoeman, Ferdinand, 'Introduction', *Responsibility, Character, and the Emotions* (Cambridge: Cambridge University Press, 1987).

Schulhofer, Stephen, 'Harm and Punishment: A Critique of Emphasis on the Results of Conduct in the Criminal Law', *University of Pennsylvania Law Review*, Vol. 122 (1974), 1497–607.

Schwartz, Louis, 'Morals Offenses and the Model Penal Code', *Columbia Law Review*, Vol. 63 (1963), 669–86.

Shavell, Steven, 'An Analysis of Causation and the Scope of Liability in the Law of Torts', *Journal of Legal Studies*, Vol. 9 (1980), 463–516.

Shedding, Ellis and Heath, *The Works of Francis Bacon* (Philadelphia: Parry and McMillan, 1859).

Sher, George, *Desert* (Princeton: Princeton University Press, 1987).

Shklar, Judith, *Ordinary Vices* (Cambridge, Mass.: Harvard University Press, 1984).

Shoemaker, Sidney, 'Functionalism and Qualia', *Philosophical Studies*, Vol. 27 (1975), 291–315.

Shoemaker, Sidney, 'Some Varieties of Functionalism', in J. Biro and R. Shahan, eds., *Mind, Brain and Function* (Norman, Okla.: University of Oklahoma Press, 1982).

Simons, Kenneth W., 'Rethinking Mental States', *BUL Rev.*, Vol. 72 (1992), 463–554.

Simpson, A. W. B., *Cannibalism and the Common Law* (Oxford: Oxford University Press, 1984).

Simpson, Joe, *Touching the Void* (New York: Harper and Row, 1988).

Skinner, 'Behaviorism at Fifty', in T. W. Wann, ed., *Behaviorism and Phenomenology* (Chicago: University of Chicago Press, 1964).

Skinner, B. F., *Beyond Freedom and Dignity* (New York: Knopf, 1971).

Smart, J. J. C., 'Utilitarianism: For', in J. J. C. Smart and Bernard Williams, *Utilitarianism: For and Against* (Cambridge: Cambridge University Press, 1973).

Smith, Adam, *Theory of the Moral Sentiments* (A. Macfie and D. Raphael, eds., 1976).

Smith, Jeremiah, 'Legal Cause in Actions of Tort', *Harvard Law Review*, Vol. 25 (1911), 103–28, 223–52, 253–69, 303–21.

Smith, M. B. E., 'Is There a Prima Facie Obligation to Obey the Law?', *Yale Law Journal*, Vol. 82 (1973), 950–76.

Sosa, E., ed., *Causation and Conditionals* (Oxford: Oxford University Press, 1975).

Spiro, A., 'A Philosophical Appraisal of Roy Schafer's A New Language for Psychoanalysis', *Psychoanalysis and Contemporary Thought*, Vol. 2 (1979), 253–91.

Stalnaker, 'A Theory of Conditionals', in N. Rescher, ed., *Studies in Logical Theory* (Oxford: Blackwell, 1968).

Statman, Daniel, ed., *Moral Luck* (Albany, NY: State University of New York Press, 1993).

Steele, Robert, 'Psychoanalysis and Hermeneutics', *International Review of Psycho-Analysis*, Vol. 6 (1979), 389–411.

Stephen, Sir James, *A History of the Criminal Law of England* (London: Macmillan, 1883), 2 vols.

Stephens, James Fitzjames, *Liberty, Equality, Fraternity*, originally published, 1873 (Indianapolis: Liberty Fund edn., Stuart Warner, ed., 1993).

Stevenson, C. L., *Ethics and Language* (New Haven: Yale University Press, 1944).

Stone, Alan, 'Psychiatry and Morality: Three Criticisms', in *Law, Psychiatry and Morality* (Washington, DC: US Government Printing Office, 1984), 219–24.

Stone, Alan, 'Psychiatry and Violence', in *Law, Psychiatry and Morality* (Washington, DC: US Government Printing Office, 1984), 53.

Stone, Christopher, 'Corporate Accountability in Law and Morals', in J. Houck and O. Williams, eds., *The Judaeo-Christian Vision and the Modern Business Corporation* (Notre Dame: University of Notre Dame Press, 1982).

Stone, Christopher, *Earth and Other Ethics* (New York: Harper and Row, 1987).

Stone, Julius, *Legal Systems and Lawyer's Reasonings* (Stanford, Cal.: Stanford University Press, 1964).

Strawson, Peter, 'Freedom and Resentment', in Gary Watson, ed., *Free Will* (Oxford: Oxford University Press, 1982).

Sturgeon, Nicholas, 'Moral Explanations', in David Copp and David Zimmerman, eds., *Morality, Reason and Truth* (Totowa, NJ: Rowman and Allanheld, 1984).

Summers, Robert, ed., *Essays in Legal Philosophy* (Berkeley: University of California Press, 1968).

Summers, Robert, *Instrumentalism and American Legal Theory* (Ithaca: Cornell University Press, 1982).

Sverdlik, Steven, 'Crime and Moral Luck', *American Philosophical Quarterly,* Vol. 25 (1988), 79–86.

Szasz, Thomas, *Law, Liberty, and Psychiatry* (New York: Macmillan, 1963).

Taylor, Charles, 'Responsibility for Self', in Amelie Rorty, ed., *The Identities of Persons* (Berkeley: University of California Press, 1976), 281–99.

Taylor, Lawrence, 'Genetically-Influenced Antisocial Conduct and the Criminal Justice System', *Cleveland State Law Review*, Vol. 31 (1982), 61–75.

Taylor, Richard, *Action and Purpose* (Englewood Cliffs, NJ: Prentice-Hall, 1966).

Ten, C. L., *Crime, Guilt, and Punishment* (Oxford: Clarendon Press, 1987).

Thomson, Judith, *Acts and Other Events* (Ithaca: Cornell University Press, 1977).

Thomson, Judith, 'Causality and Rights: Some Preliminaries', *Chicago-Kent Law Review*, Vol. 63 (1987), 471–96.

Thomson, Judith Jarvis, 'A Defense of Abortion', *Philosophy and Public Affairs*, Vol. 1 (1971), 47–66.

Thomson, Judith, 'Killing, Letting Die, and the Trolley Problem', *The Monist*, Vol. 59 (1976), 204–17.

Thomson, Judith, 'Liability and Individualized Evidence', *Law and Contemporary Problems*, Vol. 49 (1986), 199–219.

Thomson, Judith, 'Morality and Bad Luck', *Metaphilosophy*, Vol. 20 (1989), 203–21.

Thomson, Judith, *The Realm of Rights* (Cambridge, Mass.: Harvard University Press, 1990).

Thomson, Judith, 'Remarks on Causation and Liability', *Philosophy and Public Affairs*, Vol. 13 (1984), 101–33.

Thomson, Judith, 'Rights and Deaths', *Philosophy and Public Affairs,* Vol. 2 (1973), 146–59.

Thomson, Judith, 'The Trolley Problem', *Yale Law Journal*, Vol. 94 (1985), 1395–415.

Tiffany and Anderson, 'Legislating the Necessity Defense in Criminal Law', *Denver Law Journal*, Vol. 52 (1975), 839–79.

Urmson, J. O., *The Emotive Theory of Ethics* (Oxford: Oxford University Press, 1968).

Vendler, Zeno, 'Causal Relations', *Journal of Philosophy*, Vol. 64 (1967), 704–13.

Vermazen, Bruce, 'Negative Acts', in B. Vermazen and M. Hintikka, eds., *Essays on Davidson: Actions and Events* (Oxford: Oxford University Press, 1985).

von Hirsch, Andrew, *Doing Justice* (New York: Hill and Wang, 1976).

von Hirsch, Andrew, *Past or Future Crimes* (New Brunswick, NJ: Rutgers University Press, 1985).

von Hirsch, Andrew, and Jareborg, Nils, 'Gauging Criminal Harm: A Living Standard Analysis', *Oxford Journal of Legal Studies*, Vol. 11 (1991), 1–38.

von Humboldt, Wilhelm, *The Limits of State Action*, originally published in 1854, J. W. Burrow, trans. (Cambridge: Cambridge University Press, 1969).

von Wright, George Henrik, *Explanation and Understanding* (Ithaca, NY: Cornell University Press, 1971).

Vuoso, George, 'Background, Responsibility, and Excuse', *Yale Law Journal*, Vol. 96, (1987), 1661–86.

Waelder, Robert, 'Psychiatry and the Problem of Criminal Responsibility', *University of Pennsylvania Law Review*, Vol. 101 (1952), 378–90.

Waldron, Jeremy, 'A Constitution, The Constitution, Our Constitution', *British Journal of Political Science*, unpublished, 1995.

Walker, Margaret, 'Moral Luck and the Virtues of Impure Agency', *Metaphilosophy* Vol. 22 (1991), 14–27.

Walker, Nigel, *Why Punish?* (Oxford: Oxford University Press, 1991).

Wallach and Rubin, 'The Premenstrual Syndrome and Criminal Responsibility', *University of California-Los Angeles Law Review*, Vol. 19 (1971), 210–312.

Wasserman, 'Justifying Self- Defense', *Philosophy and Public Affairs*, Vol. 16 (1987), 356–78.

Watson, Gary, 'Free Agency', *Journal of Philosophy*, Vol. 72 (1975), 205–20.

Watson, Gary, 'Responsibility and the Limits of Evil', in F. Schoeman, ed., *Responsibility, Character, and the Emotions* (Cambridge: Cambridge University Press, 1987), 256–86.

Watt, A. J., 'The Intelligibility of Wants', *Mind*, Vol. 81 (1972), 553–61.

Weihofen, Henry, *The Urge to Punish* (New York: Farrar, Straus, and Cudahy, 1956).

Weinreb, Lloyd, *Natural Law and Justice* (Cambridge, Mass.: Harvard University Press, 1987).

Weinrib, Ernie, 'Legal Formalism: On the Immanent Rationality of Law', *Yale Law Journal*, Vol. 97 (1988), 949–1016.

White, Morton, *Foundations of Historical Knowledge* (Cambridge, Mass.: Harvard University Press, 1965).

Wiggins, David, 'Locke, Butler and the Stream of Consciousness: and Men as a Natural Kind', in A. Rorty, ed., *The Identities of Persons* (Berkeley: University of California Press, 1976).

Wiggins, David, *Sameness and Substance* (Cambridge, Mass.: Harvard University Press, 1980).

Williams, Bernard, 'The Actus Reus of Dr. Caligari', *University of Pennsylvania Law Review*, Vol. 142 (1994), 1661–73.

Williams, Bernard, *Moral Luck* (Cambridge: Cambridge University Press, 1981).

Williams, Bernard, 'Moral Luck', *Proceedings of the Aristotelian Society*, Supp. Vol. 50 (1976), 115–35, reprinted in his *Moral Luck* (Cambridge: Cambridge University Press, 1981).

Williams, Bernard, 'Morality and the Emotions', in his *Problems of Self* (Cambridge: Cambridge University Press, 1973).

Williams, Bernard, *Problems of Self* (Cambridge: Cambridge University Press, 1973).

Williams, Bernard, 'Utilitarianism: For And Against', in J. J. C. Smart and B. Williams, *Utilitarianism: For And Against* (Cambridge: Cambridge University Press, 1973).

Williams, Glanville, *Criminal Law—The General Part* (London: Stevens & Sons, 2nd edn., 1961).

Williams, Glanville, 'Language and the Law', *Law Quarterly Review*, Vol. 61 (1945), 71–86.

Wilson, J. and Herrnstein, R., *Crime and Human Nature* (New York: Simon and Schuster, 1985).

Wilson, Neil, *The Concept of Language*, (Toronto: University of Toronto Press, 1959).

Winch, Peter, *Ethics and Action* (London: Routledge and Kegan Paul, 1972).

Winch, Peter, *The Idea of a Social Science and Its Relation to Philosophy* (London: Routledge and Kegan Paul, 1958).

Winson, Jonathon, *Brain and Psyche: The Biology of the Unconscious* (New York: Doubleday/Anchor, 1984).

Winters, Barbara, 'Acquiring Beliefs at Will', *Philosophy Research Archives*, Vol. 4 (1978), 433.

Winters, Barbara, 'Believing at Will', *Journal of Philosophy*, Vol. 76 (1979), 243–56.

Wittgenstein, Ludwig, *Philosophical Investigations*, G. E. M. Anscombe, trans., 3rd edn. (Oxford: Basil Blackwell, 1968).

Wolf, Susan, 'Sanity and the Metaphysics of Responsibility', in Ferdinand Schoeman, ed., *Responsibility, Character, and the Emotions* (Cambridge: Cambridge University Press, 1987), 46–62.

Wright, Richard, 'Actual Causation vs. Probabilistic Linkage: The Bane of Economic Analysis', *Journal of Legal Studies*, Vol. 14 (1985), 435–56.

Wright, Richard, 'Causation in Tort Law', *California Law Review*, Vol. 73 (1985), 1735–828.

Wright, Richard, 'Causation, Responsibility, Risk, Probability, Naked Statistics, and Proof: Pruning the Bramble Bush by Clarifying the Concepts', *Iowa Law Review*, Vol. 73 (1988), 1001–77.

Zimmerman, 'Luck and Moral Responsibility', *Ethics*, Vol. 97 (1987), 374–86.

INDEX